Handbook *for* Biblical Interpretation

Handbook *for* Biblical Interpretation

AN ESSENTIAL GUIDE
TO METHODS, TERMS, AND CONCEPTS

SECOND EDITION

W. Randolph Tate

Baker Academic
a division of Baker Publishing Group
Grand Rapids, Michigan

© 2006, 2012 by W. Randolph Tate

Published by Baker Academic
a division of Baker Publishing Group
P.O. Box 6287, Grand Rapids, MI 49516-6287
www.bakeracademic.com

The first edition was published in 2006 by Hendrickson Publishers under the title *Interpreting the Bible: A Handbook of Terms and Methods.*

Printed in the United States of America

Library of Congress Cataloging-in-Publication Data
Tate, W. Randolph.
    Handbook for biblical interpretation : an essential guide to methods, terms, and
concepts / W. Randolph Tate. — 2nd ed.
        p. cm.
    Rev. ed. of: Interpreting the Bible.
    Includes bibliographical references (p.   ) and indexes.
    ISBN 978-0-8010-4862-3 (pbk.)
    1. Bible—Criticism, interpretation, etc. I. Tate, W. Randolph. Interpreting the Bible.
II. Title.
BS511.3.T38 2012
220.601—dc23   2012019345

Except as otherwise indicated, all Scripture quotations are from the New Revised Standard Version of the Bible, copyright © 1989 by the Division of Christian Education of the National Council of the Churches of Christ in the U.S.A., and used by permission.

Quotations marked NETS are taken from *A New English Translation of the Septuagint* © 2007 by the International Organization for Septuagint and Cognate Studies, Inc. Used by permission of Oxford University Press. All rights reserved.

The internet addresses, email addresses, and phone numbers in this book are accurate at the time of publication. They are provided as a resource. Baker Publishing Group does not endorse them or vouch for their content or permanence.

12   13   14   15   16   17   18   7   6   5   4   3   2   1

Contents

Preface to the Second Edition

My original purpose has not changed for the second edition: to make critical approaches for interpreting the Bible accessible not only to scholars but also to students and nonspecialists. Although there are some excellent works similar to this one,[1] I still feel that the combination of critical interpretive methods and their related literary terminology makes this work unique.

However, I have made the following changes to this edition:

1. I have deleted theological terms that lacked clear relevance to literary concerns.
2. I have removed appendixes A and B, since the handbook is designed not to be a commentary on biblical texts but to be a guide to the methods employed in interpreting the biblical text.
3. I have added a handful of entries on some current interpretive approaches along with the appropriate terms associated with them.
4. The author and Scripture indexes and the bibliography have been updated to reflect the changes to this edition.
5. The title of the work has been changed to make its primary purpose clearer to readers and to distinguish it more clearly from my hermeneutics textbook, *Biblical Interpretation: An Integrated Approach*.

---

1. E.g., David Aune, *The Westminster Dictionary of New Testament and Early Christian Literature and Rhetoric* (Louisville: Westminster John Knox, 2003); Stanley E. Porter, ed., *Dictionary of Biblical Criticism and Interpretation* (London: Routledge, 2007); John Hayes, ed., *Dictionary of Biblical Interpretation* (2 vols.; Nashville: Abingdon, 1999); Richard N. Soulen and R. Kendall Soulen, *Handbook of Biblical Criticism*, 3rd ed. (Louisville: Westminster John Know, 2001); Michael D. Coogan, ed., *The Oxford Encyclopedia of the Books of the Bible* (2 vols.; New York: Oxford University Press, 2011).

Preface to the First Edition

This work is patterned after an extremely useful book, *A Handbook to Literature*, published by Prentice-Hall and now in its eighth edition. It is essentially an extended glossary of the terminology currently used in interpreting the Bible. More specifically, it focuses on the vocabularies of the various interpretive methods that biblical scholars use in speaking about the biblical texts. Covered herein are approximately fifty methods, both old and new, ranging from source criticism to social-scientific criticism to deconstruction.

There are two primary reasons for writing a book of this sort. First, there presently is nothing available that is as comprehensive or as accessible as this work. The few handbooks on the market are limited in scope to the New Testament (NT), to the Old Testament (OT), or to other particular areas of interest. It is therefore often the case that if a student, pastor, scholar, or any interested person wants to know something about a particular method, he or she must sift through literally hundreds of pages in a variety of scholarly works. Most of these books are written by scholars with other scholars as the target audience, which means that the language is more often than not inaccessible to the nonspecialist. With this work, I have attempted to do the sifting and then to condense the materials into manageable synopses that employ scholarly but accessible terminology. The book also provides in a single volume an extensive but certainly not exhaustive list of terms associated with biblical studies. Of course, one of the primary problems with a work such as this is determining what to include and what to omit. In the course of compiling this book, questions arose about the distinction between theological and literary terms, between critical and literary terms, and between critical and technical terms. For the sake of focus, I have included only those terms that relate in some way to interpreting the biblical texts as literary documents. Theological terms are included whenever theological and literary concerns converge.

Second, by presenting the various methods together in one place, this book highlights the role that methods play in the interpretive process. Most people outside the professional fields related to biblical studies are unaware of the constitutive role of interpretive methods. Methods are doors of access to the biblical texts because they actually determine what kinds of questions interpreters put to the texts. Literary source criticism, for example, asks questions about the genesis of a text, while reader-response criticism asks questions about the role that a reader's response plays in determining meaning. Redaction criticism relates meaning to authorial intention, while social-scientific criticism asks questions about the relation between authorial intention and the defining structures of the author's social location. This book should assist readers in recognizing that, while these methods do not ask the same questions or have the same focus, each one can contribute to our understanding of the biblical texts. Furthermore, in order to make the book as relevant as possible, I have attempted to give adequate, albeit abbreviated, illustrations of biblical usage.

The articles range from a few words to several pages. The longer articles cover the major structural aspects of literature (e.g., plot, characterization, setting, point of view) and the critical methods. Despite their length, such articles are still only synopses rather than exhaustive essays. This truncation is necessary due to the nature of the book. However, I have attempted to give some background, development, key figures, and key ideas of each method, along with an illustration of how it has been, is presently, or may be applied to the reading of the Bible.

The bibliography at the end of the book is not exhaustive. The risk of including such a bibliography is that some works that should be included are not and some that probably should not be included are. I have attempted, however, to include a variety of scholarly works that I think represent a range of opinions in six areas: general critical theory, biblical critical theory, hermeneutics, the Bible as literature, general biblical studies: Hebrew Bible, and general biblical studies: New Testament. The reader will find concordances, commentaries, lexicons, and other study aids cited in connection with relevant entries in the handbook itself.

Cross-references to other entries within the handbook are indicated in small capitals.

Acknowledgments

Special appreciation is due to Evangel University for providing three summer research grants and a sabbatical for work on this project. These grants provided both the time and finances that made the work possible. I also want to acknowledge a group of my students who provided valuable research into the critical methods that make up such an important part of this book. These students included both English and biblical studies majors in two demanding courses—a senior seminar for English majors on critical theory and a postmodern philosophy/humanities course for both English majors and biblical studies majors. The following students were instrumental in this work: Ruth Hain (postcolonial criticism), Jesse Gonzalez (cultural materialism), Tyler Nelson (deconstruction), Timothy Schoonover (Marxist criticism), Bret Badders (cultural criticism), Erin Kuhns (postmodern criticism), Glenn Perkins (social-scientific criticism), Jeremy Hahn (reception theory), Todd Schoenberger (ideological criticism), Joel Lang (queer theory), Derek Chirch (phenomenological criticism), Bobbi Frith (postcolonial feminist criticism), Kara Beary (intertextual criticism and psychoanalytic criticism), and Heather Rooney (*mujerista* criticism).

I am also indebted to Jessica Frank, my student worker for four years, for entering the bibliography. She contributed an enormous amount of her own time checking and double-checking the entries for uniformity.

Abbreviations

GENERAL AND BIBLIOGRAPHIC

ASV	American Standard Version
AV	Authorized Version (= KJV)
b.	born
BCE	before the Common Era
ca.	circa
CE	in the Common Era
cf.	*confer*, compare
chap/s.	chapter/s
D	Deuteronomistic source
d.	died
E	Elohist source
e.g.	*exempli gratia*, for example
esp.	especially
i.e.	*id est*, that is
J	Jahwist (Yahwist) source
JB	Jerusalem Bible
JBL	*Journal of Biblical Literature*
JSOTSup	Journal for the Study of the Old Testament: Supplement Series
KJV	King James Version (= AV)
L	Lukan source
lit.	literally
LXX	Septuagint
M	Matthean source
MT	Masoretic Text
NAB	New American Bible
NASB	New American Standard Bible
NEB	New English Bible
NETS	*A New English Translation of the Septuagint* (2007)
NJB	New Jerusalem Bible
NIV	New International Version
NKJV	New King James Version
NRSV	New Revised Standard Version
NT	New Testament
OT	Old Testament
P	Priestly source
PMLA	*Publications of the Modern Language Association of America*
Q	Gospel sayings source (perhaps from the German *Quelle*, "source")
REB	Revised English Bible
RSV	Revised Standard Version
RV	Revised Version = English Revised Version
s.v.	*sub verbo*, under the word
TEV	Today's English Version = Good News Bible
TLB	The Living Bible
TNIV	Today's New International Version
v/vv.	verse/s
Wis.	Wisdom of Solomon

HEBREW BIBLE / OLD TESTAMENT

Gen.	Genesis	Josh.	Joshua
Exod.	Exodus	Judg.	Judges
Lev.	Leviticus	Ruth	Ruth
Num.	Numbers	1–2 Sam.	1–2 Samuel
Deut.	Deuteronomy	1–2 Kings	1–2 Kings

1–2 Chron.	1–2 Chronicles		Dan.	Daniel
Ezra	Ezra		Hosea	Hosea
Neh.	Nehemiah		Joel	Joel
Esther	Esther		Amos	Amos
Job	Job		Obad.	Obadiah
Ps./Pss.	Psalm/Psalms		Jon.	Jonah
Prov.	Proverbs		Mic.	Micah
Eccles.	Ecclesiastes		Nah.	Nahum
Song	Song of Songs		Hab.	Habakkuk
Isa.	Isaiah		Zeph.	Zephaniah
Jer.	Jeremiah		Hag.	Haggai
Lam.	Lamentations		Zech.	Zechariah
Ezek.	Ezekiel		Mal.	Malachi

NEW TESTAMENT

Matt.	Matthew		1–2 Thess.	1–2 Thessalonians
Mark	Mark		1–2 Tim.	1–2 Timothy
Luke	Luke		Titus	Titus
John	John		Philem.	Philemon
Acts	Acts		Heb.	Hebrews
Rom.	Romans		James	James
1–2 Cor.	1–2 Corinthians		1–2 Pet.	1–2 Peter
Gal.	Galatians		1–3 John	1–3 John
Eph.	Ephesians		Jude	Jude
Phil.	Philippians		Rev.	Revelation
Col.	Colossians			

A

ABECEDARIUS

Although the word in English (abecediary) refers to a book containing the alphabet for the purpose of learning it, in literary studies, it is a type of acrostic (also referred to as an alphabetical acrostic) in which the first letters form the alphabet. According to J. A. Cuddon, "in the Old Testament most of the acrostics belong to the alphabetical or abecedarian type" (6). A biblical example is Ps. 119, in which the 176 lines are divided so that there is a group of 8 lines for each of the 22 letters of the Hebrew alphabet.

Bibliography. J. A. Cuddon, *The Penguin Dictionary of Literary Terms and Literary Theory* (4th ed.; London: Penguin, 1998); William Harmon and C. Hugh Holman, *A Handbook to Literature* (8th ed.; Upper Saddle River, NJ: Prentice Hall, 1999); Ross Murfin and Supryia M. Ray, *The Bedford Glossary of Critical and Literary Terms* (2nd ed.; Boston: St. Martin's Press, 2003); Leland Ryken, *Words of Delight: A Literary Introduction to the Bible* (Grand Rapids: Baker, 1987).

ABSENCE

A key theme in the writings of Jacques Derrida that refers to his rejection of the notion that MEANING is present in objects (*see* SUBJECT/OBJECT), especially in written TEXTS. Derrida refers to two absences guaranteed by writing: "absence of signatory" and "absence of the referent" (*Of Grammatology*, 40–41; *see* REFERENTIAL [QUALITY OF] LANGUAGE). By the former, he suggests that any claims of meaning made about a TEXT are independent of the AUTHOR, who has not determined the meaning of the text. Hence, to speak of meaning in terms of an author's INTENTION is itself meaningless: the author is absent. By the latter, he claims that a text has no external or extra-textual reference. A text is "no longer a finished corpus of writing, some context enclosed in a book or its margins, but a differential network, a fabric of traces referring endlessly to something other than itself, to other differential traces" ("Living On / Border Lines," 84). A text has no single recoverable meaning but is a network of differences that may generate an endless chain of meanings, always DEFERRING any finality. Therefore, meaning is not present in the text, as water can be present in a bottle, but is absent. Derrida makes these claims based on a radicalization of key concepts in the work of Ferdinand de Saussure, especially Saussure's insistence on the arbitrary nature of the SIGN and his idea that meaning is a result of the relations of difference between signs. Based on the latter notion, Derrida insists that signs do not point to external referents, but to other signs (*see* REFERENTIAL [QUALITY OF] LANGUAGE). Consequently, a text becomes a differential network in which signifieds become signifiers in an endless chain of SIGNIFICATION. In addition, most postmodern critics (*see* POSTMODERN CRITICISM) reject the notion that there exists a one-to-one correspondence between language and external reality, that the structures of language parallel the structures of reality so that language is capable of accurate representation of reality. If signs refer in a differential manner to other signs, then meaning is not always already present in reality, but is always absent. Thus, reality becomes a construct of language, a linguistic entity.

Bibliography. Jacques Derrida, "Living On / Border Lines," in *Deconstruction and Criticism* (ed. Harold Bloom et al.; New York: Seabury, 1979), 75–176; idem, *Of Grammatology* (trans. Gayatri Chakravorty Spivak; Baltimore: Johns Hopkins University Press, 1977).

ACCLAMATION. *See* LITURGICAL FRAGMENTS

ACCOMMODATION

The belief that divine revelation of the biblical TEXTS is written primarily to ordinary people, and that the texts were written in such a way as to be comprehensible to such readers. According to Anthony Thiselton (531–35), some contemporary biblical CRITICS (e.g., Mark Labberton; Andrew Kirk) and literary critics (e.g., David Bleich) have insisted on making room for the ordinary, nonprofessional reader. They recognize that the MEANINGS proposed by professional interpreters are offered within professional CONTEXTS and are no more legitimate or natural than those INTERPRETATIONS proposed within nonprofessional contexts. In other words, LITERARY theories that focus on the role of the reader in creating meaning should accommodate nonprofessional reading communities.

Bibliography. Anthony Thiselton, *New Horizons in Hermeneutics* (Grand Rapids: Zondervan, 1992).

ACROSTIC

A composition, typically in VERSE, arranged so that when certain letters are selected according to a pattern, they spell words, phrases, or sentences. Where the initial letters form a word, phrase, or sentence, the acrostic is called a true acrostic. When the final letters work in this fashion, the acrostic is a telestich. Acrostics are also formed when the middle letters are so used (a mesostich) and when the first letter of the first line, the second of the second line, the third of the third line, and so forth (a cross acrostic) are used. An acrostic in which the first letters form the alphabet is called an abecedarius (Harmon and Holman, 4). A biblical example of the latter is Ps. 119, in which the 176 lines are divided so that there is a group of 8 lines for each of the 22 letters of the Hebrew alphabet. Other acrostics occur in Pss. 9–10; 25; 34; 37; 111; 112; 145; Prov. 31:10–31; and Nah. 1:2–10. However, most acrostics are lost in TRANSLATION (Soulen and Soulen, 1).

Bibliography. William Harmon and C. Hugh Holman, *A Handbook to Literature* (8th ed.; Upper Saddle River, NJ: Prentice Hall, 2000); Richard N. Soulen and R. Kendall Soulen, *Handbook of Biblical Criticism* (3rd ed.; Louisville: Westminster John Knox, 2001).

ACTANT

In SEMIOTICS, the function or role occupied by a character in a NARRATIVE, thus a basic structural unit in all narratives. As originally defined by A. J. Greimas in 1966, the term refers to three basic BINARY OPPOSITIONS in a sentence, each opposition epitomizing a fundamental element in narrative: SUBJECT/OBJECT for desire; sender/receiver for communication, and helper/opponent for assistance and opposition. According to Greimas, since a narrative is essentially an extended sentence, these binary oppositions form the basic STRUCTURE for all narrative. Consequently, the actantual structure or the actants constitute a GENRE. All narratives can be read according to this actantual model: a sender sends an object to a receiver, the object is carried to the receiver by the SUBJECT, and finally the subject may receive assistance from helpers and be frustrated by opponents. The actantual structure is the skeleton for, or basic structure for, any narrative.

Later, Greimas modified the theory by limiting the actants to four along the axes of subject/object and sender/receiver. From these two axes, others may be derived. The actantual model has been effective in analyzing not only literary texts, but philosophical, religious, and scientific ones as well. The model has allowed scholars to retrain their focus away from the psychological makeup of characters to the underlying forces governing actions, thus uncovering the political and polemical structure of narratives. *See* STRUCTURALISM.

Bibliography. Christian Vandendorpe, "Actant," in *Encyclopedia of Contemporary Literary Theory* (ed. Irena R. Makaryk; Toronto: University of Toronto Press, 1993), 505–6.

ACTION

The series of events that constitute the PLOT in a work of FICTION. Action includes what characters do, say, and think. Action in literature is understood as orderly, arranged in such a way as to suggest a SUBJECT and THEME. This type of arranged action is customarily structured with a beginning, middle, and end. The action of a SHORT STORY, PLAY, novel, NOVELLA, or NARRATIVE POEM does not answer the question "What is the story about?" but rather "What happens in the story?" For example, a person who writes a PRÉCIS of a STORY simply recounts what happens in the action rather than offering an EXPOSITION of the story. The plot of such accounts as Jonah, Ruth, Matthew, or Song of Songs is constituted by the action of each and is concerned with what the text says, not what it means, although the latter concern develops out of the former.

ACTUALIZATION

In HERMENEUTICS, the process by which MEANINGS of TEXTS are derived. The articulation of meaning is founded on ASSUMPTIONS about this process and the location of meaning. In contemporary hermeneutics, there are four complementary but distinct processes, each based on a different basic assumption. The first process is author as context and is based on the assumption that a text contains a message that must be discovered or actualized by the reader. In other words, meaning is a quality of the text. In biblical texts, that meaning is the revelation given through the texts, and as such, this meaning can be actualized by successive generations of readers. The second process, history as context, assumes that the meaning of a text is bound to the text's CONTEXT, that the text's anchorage to its life setting and history not only shapes its meaning but also limits the interpretive options available to interpreters. Simply put, a text's meaning is inseparable from the world within which it was given birth, and readers must actualize meaning in conversation with this world (Thiselton, 11–13). The third process is community as context and assumes that reality is always a contextually constructed one and that all objects obtain their SIGNIFICANCE or are understood within that context-relative reality. Consequently, meanings of texts are created (actualized) within communities using certain methods (*see* CRITICAL

METHODOLOGY). Since both the community and method determine the questions put to the text, meaning is contingent on the way various communities define reality and on the methods these communities deem acceptable. Meaning in this SENSE is always a function of the interests, community LITERARY CONVENTIONS, methods employed, and the HORIZON OF EXPECTATION of the readers (Thiselton, 63–66). The fourth process, reader as context, assumes that meaning is not a function of the community and method on the one hand or the text on the other, but is somewhere between the two. The meaning of a text is only virtual or potential and is realized or actualized through a dialogue between the structures of the text and the creative activities of the reader. In this last process, the reader assembles meaning that is only potential in the text in terms of TEXTUAL STRATEGIES that initiate certain interpretive activities by the reader.

Bibliography. Anthony Thiselton, *New Horizons in Hermeneutics* (Grand Rapids: Zondervan, 1992).

ADIAPHORA

From the Greek meaning "indifferent things." The Stoics (*see* HELLENISTIC PHILOSOPHIES) considered some things as natural and necessary (e.g., food), natural but unnecessary (e.g., sex), and unnatural and unnecessary (e.g., sadism). Beyond these, however, were things indifferent: things neither to be desired nor shunned. So in the NT, adiaphora are matters of faith that are morally neutral. Since they are "neither commanded nor forbidden in SCRIPTURE" (McKim, 4), a person may exercise "liberty of conscience" (cf. Rom. 14:17; 1 Cor. 6:12; 8:8; Gal. 5:6).

Bibliography. Donald K. McKim, *Westminster Dictionary of Theological Terms* (Louisville: Westminster John Knox, 1996).

ADMIRATION STORY

A narrative genre classification that Leland Ryken applies to the GOSPELS. According to Ryken, the controlling agenda of the Gospels is the SELECTION AND ARRANGEMENT of materials in order to exalt the hero of the STORY. They are designed to provide the basis (both biographical and etiological [*see* ETIOLOGY]) for promoting the hero of the story. Other scholars (Bultmann, Dibelius, Taylor) focus on the role of the Gospels as "self-contained stories" that reflect the needs and interests of the very early church. Hence, if biographical or etiological interests are not primary among the Gospel writers, then the stories should be read within the ideological CONTEXT (*see* IDEOLOGICAL CRITICISM; IDEOLOGY) of the early church.

Bibliography. Rudolf Bultmann, *The History of the Synoptic Tradition* (trans. John Marsh; Oxford: Blackwell, 1963); Martin Dibelius, *From Tradition to Gospel* (2nd ed.; Cambridge: James Clarke, 1971); Leland Ryken, *Words of Life: A Literary Introduction to the New Testament* (Grand Rapids: Baker, 1987); Vincent Taylor, *The Formation of the Gospel Tradition* (2nd ed.; London: Macmillan, 1935).

ADONAI

From the Hebrew word *'ădōnāy*, "Lord," used as an oral substitute for the TETRAGRAMMATON (*YHWH:* YAHWEH, or Jehovah) in the Jewish liturgical reading of the HEBREW BIBLE because the Hebrews considered the name *Yahweh* (the actual name for God) too holy to be uttered.

AEON

From the Greek word meaning "age" or "epoch." In the NT (e.g., Mark 10:30; Gal. 1:4; Heb. 6:5) the present evil age will give way to the age to come, a period marked by the reign of God.

Bibliography. Donald K. McKim, *Westminster Dictionary of Theological Terms* (Louisville: Westminster John Knox, 1996).

AETIOLOGY. *See* ETIOLOGY

AFFECTIVE CRITICISM. *See* READER-RESPONSE CRITICISM

AFFECTIVE FALLACY

A central concept in NEW CRITICISM introduced by W. K. Wimsatt Jr. and Monroe C. Beardsley in 1949. The fallacy is committed when attention is given to the effect of the TEXT rather than to the text itself, "a confusion between what a text is and what it does" (Harmon and Holman, 7). To judge a work of art in terms of its results is to commit the affective fallacy. In New Criticism, attention is directed exclusively on the text itself as the source of any effect.

Bibliography. William Harmon and C. Hugh Holman, *A Handbook to Literature* (8th ed.; Upper Saddle River, NJ: Prentice Hall, 1999).

AFRICAN AMERICAN CRITICISM

A brand of race CRITICISM (*see* RACE, CLASS, AND GENDER CRITICISM) having fundamental ASSUMPTIONS that race is an essential element of LITERARY analysis and that the American LITERARY CANON has been irreversibly informed and shaped by Africans and African Americans.

Background. African American literary criticism has a rather youthful place in the American literary tradition, beginning primarily with the philosophical assertions of W. E. B. Du Bois, and continuing through the 1920s with the Harlem Renaissance, up until the 1960s, when it was gradually integrated into modern American society through channels of black power and the black aesthetic (Bertens, 108). Essentially, African American literary theory has "taken a variety of forms, often grounding itself in other approaches but always revising them according to its own concerns and agendas" (Geollnicht, 8). Specifically, as African Americans have gained strength and power in society, their ideals and values have altered, thus initiating changes in how they perceive their "blackness" as an important attribute of their culture, particularly in regard to literature and aesthetics. African American theorist Barbara Christian argues that contrary to traditional ways of theorizing, African Americans do not portray what they perceive to be theory in a traditional critical form; rather African American theory is "often in narrative forms, in the stories we [African Americans] create, in riddles and proverbs, in the play with language" (quoted in Geollnicht, 6). It is somewhat difficult to pinpoint the exact form and IDEOLOGY of African American critics simply because as social and political issues change within society, so do the perspectives of African Americans. Yet, the list of African Americans with significant roles in LITERARY CRITICISM is far-reaching. However, influential African Americans such as W. E. B. Du Bois, Richard Wright, Amiri Baraka, Ralph Ellison, James Baldwin, Langston Hughes, and Zora Neale Hurston are, in addition to being key thinkers in their movement, also influential writers who have been instrumental in bringing credibility to African American literature through integration into the mainstream canon. Likewise, contemporary critics such as Toni Morrison, Alice Walker, and, more important, Houston A. Baker Jr. and Henry Louis Gates Jr. attempt to defend African American ideology under the premise of deconstructive postmodern thought (*see* DECONSTRUCTION; POSTMODERNISM/POST-MODERNITY). Even if they are writing fiction, African Americans often write with a sociological or ideological purpose in mind; their writing attempts to bring about change and a restructuring of cultural values and norms.

Primary concerns. First, African American literary critics establish their values on the premise that their writing must exploit or at least reveal the traditionally dismal and repressive plight of black persons; through revealing their plight, these authors hope to foster change in both the attitude and behavior of the oppressive majority. Thus the African American's establishment of literature as an art is "no mere idle acceptance of 'art for art's sake,' . . . but rather a deep realization of the fundamental purpose of art and of its function as a taproot of vigorous, flourishing living" (Locke, 50). However, this attempt to portray the passionate living of African Americans in order to foster change is done under the guise of slave NARRATIVES, SERMONS, FOLKLORE, ORAL TRADITION, and language. Thus African American authors use their fictional writings to accurately depict the deeply rooted social problems common to their people. Specifically, "the African-American person, critic, theorist, or writer operates in a context of opposition to oppressive situations" (Blackshire-Belay, 5). W. E. B. Du Bois furthers the notion that African American literature serves as a way to bring change, although

he does so in a more negatively connotative way: "All art is propaganda and ever must be . . . propaganda for gaining the right of black folk to love and enjoy" (42). Clearly, African Americans most often write, either consciously or unconsciously, with a social or political agenda that will celebrate their blackness.

Second, in addition to their desire to bring out change, African American critics focus on works in which black persons and their role in society are primary. According to African writer Asante, "Literature by African or African-American writers must reflect and treat African peoples as subject, not objects; and African ideals, values, culture, history, traditions and worldviews must inform any such creation, analysis, or presentation" (quoted in Abarry, 133). Thus there remains no other subject more important in African American writing than the individual—a notion often referred to as Afrocentric aesthetics. Essentially, this perspective's basic premise asserts that "meaning, ethos, motifs, technique, and form all emanate from the worldview of African peoples and reflect their own sense of beauty, goodness, and . . . truth" (Abarry, 134). Based on this notion, then, African American critics focus on the ways in which writers of color incorporate spirituals, work songs, blues, jazz, tales, and Ebonics—all aesthetic elements unique to the African tradition—into many of their works. All of these criteria, according to Langston Hughes, "intend to express our individual dark-skinned selves without fear or shame" (48).

Of the aforementioned aesthetic elements, folklore, jazz, and language are perhaps the most essential elements on which African American literary critics focus. Folklore itself derives from the oral tradition common to African American literature, and critics maintain that it has been a key component in both understanding and interpreting black texts. Though the notion of folklore as a credible form of literature has been questioned, some writers assert that folklore "infuses all levels of society" and that it is "born out of political rhetoric, a testimony to the historical struggle for civil liberties, equality, and dignity" (Prahlad, 565).

In addition to folklore, musical influence from both jazz and blues has influenced the content (*see* FORM/CONTENT) and STYLE of black texts. The impact of such musical traditions, then, is far-reaching since "the blues lie at the boundary of African culture, where residual African elements pass over into American [culture]: . . . the song becomes a poem which is no longer sung, but written and printed" (Prahlad, 565). Thus, the blues/jazz music TRADITION serves as the pivotal point between the African American oral tradition and the traditional white literary aesthetic (Williams, 179). Clearly, as many African American critics have come to believe, it is difficult to separate the various forms of black aesthetics, both oral and written, as they are so closely interwoven.

Apart from folklore and music, language is a determining factor in what composes the basis for African American literary theory. Here Houston Baker argues that "no analyst can understand the black literary text who is not conscious of the semantic levels of black culture" (197). Basically, language is such an integral part of the African American literary tradition that it cannot be separated from origin and cultural identity. "The linguistic exercise among African-Americans . . . and other 'colonized' people can be seen as one modest attempt among many to repossess their histories" (Mazrui, 79). African American writers must use language that reflects the culture lest they cease to be part of the culture's traditions at all. Seemingly, then, African American critics look at the oral tradition of folklore, musical influence, and black linguistic (*see* LINGUISTICS) patterns to identify ways in which African American writers have preserved African origin and culture.

However, certain African American critics focus on texts in which the authors try to "shed their race" and thus adopt the mainstream ideologies of the white majority. Specifically, when African American criticism began to fully establish itself in the 1960s, there were many critics who desired to establish their own literary canon separate from the white majority; this notion, however, proved futile as many writers strove for integration of black

and white cultures. Similarly, contemporary critics assert the notion of poststructuralists (*see* POST-MODERNISM/POSTMODERNITY) that "whatever African-American texts have in common, there is no such thing as an essential, innate 'Blackness' in their authors" (Bertens, 109). Essentially, many contemporary critics, such as Henry Gates, note that African Americans are not different from other American writers; rather, they develop their work under different cultural and historical origins.

And third, African American critics recognize and tolerate different schools of thought within their ranks. While African American literary critics differ in some of their basic principles, it is not the critics themselves but the time periods in which these critics live that dictate the primary ideological differences between the various influential critics of African American literature. This idea is what influential contemporary critic Houston A. Baker refers to as "generational shifts" (Goellnicht, 6). Subsequently, Baker's primary assertion is that African American writings must be understood within African American culture of specific time periods.

Accordingly, beginning in the 1950s, generational shifts, as Baker defines them, can be divided into philosophies based on integrationist ideals of social equality, black power, black arts and aesthetics, and finally integration into mainstream literature. Similar, but differing slightly from the philosophy of Baker, is the division of the black literature movement into five main schools of thought, beginning with the Harlem Renaissance in the 1920s: primitivist school, naturalistic protest school, existentialist school, moral suasion school, and the counterhegemonic black cultural nationalist school (Washington, 2–11). No single generational shift or school, however, can claim one specific critical theorist; rather, numerous voices help to establish the ways in which African American critics interpret texts within a specific time period marked by various social and political aspirations.

Schools of thought. Baker's "generational shifts" began in the 1950s with the influential voices of Richard Wright, Arthur Davis, and Sterling Brown. The primary focus of this period of time was to write in a way that would bring about legislation supportive of social equality and black values. During the 1960s, the African American's political agenda shifted from integrationist ideals to the notion of black power. Advocates of black power—such as Stokely Carmichael, Larry Neal, and Amiri Baraka—believed that Negro art should be the primary force by which to foster the African American political agenda. Building on the idea of black power, the black aesthetic endeavored to be a means of "helping black people out of the polluted mainstream of Americanism" (Holmes, 37) as well as a way to encourage the African American artist to "'purify by fire' the old symbols, songs, myths, legends, and history that was the lost birthright of African peoples" (38). Larry Neal further asserts the idea of black art in his essay "The Black Arts Movement," stating that the movement's goal is not to write protest literature; rather, "it speaks directly to the Black people" (123) and is "radically opposed to any concept of the artist that alienates him from his community" (122). The black arts movement was essential to African American literary criticism as it glorified the tradition of African American literature and therefore assisted in the gradual acceptance of influential works into the mainstream literary canon. Thus, from both the black power movement and the appeal to the black aesthetic, the 1970s gradually allowed for the declaration that African American literature was truly literary, as many works were integrated into mainstream English classes and canonized within anthologies. During this time, blackness in literature was examined as purposeful rather than reactionary. African American authors constructed their own perception of their people, and now African American literature was autonomous and to be evaluated in the same way as its white counterpart.

In contrast, Washington's schools of thought begin in the 1920s—a time in which "Negroes" were trying to define more clearly their voice and purpose. Understandably, the primitivist school is perhaps the earliest attempt to define protest literature through cautious optimism and through the black voices of the Harlem Renaissance. Essentially, three main forces helped to shape African American criticism during the 1920s: The black middle class, who sought status and equality with whites; the Garvey movement, which tried to increase racial pride; and the primitivist literary school, which fostered social change through aesthetics and creativity (Washington, 47). In contrast to the naïveté of the primitivist school, the naturalistic protest school was influenced by the African's plight during the Great Depression and therefore sought a more realistic portrayal of the African American within literature. Consequently, many African American critics, particularly Richard Wright, interpreted African American literature from a Marxist perspective (Washington, 119). Furthermore, many critics were quick to dramatize the social issues of racial injustice and poverty, thus bringing disillusionment to the black movement, which became more evident after World War II in the existentialist school. Specifically, Ralph Ellison's *Invisible Man* depicted black America from the perspective of a "disillusioned, deracinated, and rootless individualism" (Washington, 191). Hence, black thought focused on the virtues of ALIENATION and disassociation from black ethnic culture (204). Contrasting sharply with the agenda of the existentialist school, the moral suasion school's focus rested on political reengagement through the protest for civil rights. Led by James Baldwin, the moral suasion school fought hard to bring about political change and integration into the literary mainstream. However, opponents of the moral suasion school feared that Baldwin sacrificed black culture for the sake of integration (273). From this idea, then, emerged the black cultural nationalist school. Black nationalist Amiri Baraka clearly defines the role of African Americans:

> The Black artist's role in America is to aid in the destruction of America as he knows it. His role is to report and reflect so precisely the nature of the society . . . that other men will be moved . . . if they are black men, [and] grow strong through this moving . . . ; and if they are white men, tremble, curse,

and go mad, because they will be drenched with the filth of their evil. (Washington, 281)

Thus, the black nationalist school upheld the idea of blackness within the African American people in stark contrast to the oppressive nature of the white majority. It was from this school that African American literature slowly incorporated itself into the mainstream canon. Clearly, African American literary criticism is a moldable, living criticism in that its agenda changes along with society's treatment of the minority.

Current criticism. Currently, one of the most influential theorists in regard to African American literary criticism is Henry Louis Gates Jr. In his critical works, Gates explores the relationship between African culture and Western culture and the role such cultures play in assessing literature. In contrast to Houston Baker, Gates asserts that both black and white literature are socially constructed rather than products of a cause-and-effect relationship. Moreover, Gates mainly tries to make note of the patterns of repetition and revision among texts by black authors. He writes: "Many black authors read and revise one another, address similar themes, and repeat the cultural and linguistic codes of a common symbolic geographic. For these reasons, we can think of them as forming literary traditions" (quoted in Bertens, 109). Specifically, in his most influential work, *The Signifying Monkey*, Gates refers to the trickster figure common to African American folktales in order to show how vernacular informs and becomes the foundation for formal black literature. Signifying, he maintains, is the process of "intertextual relations, . . . the troped revision, of repetitions and difference" (2). According to Gates, all black literature is intertextual (*see* INTERTEXTUAL CRITICISM; INTERTEXTUALITY) and related because most African Americans have encountered similar experiences that shape the ways in which they write. His view, then, reflects the influence of DECONSTRUCTION and poststructuralism in regard to applying literary theory to the reading of black texts. He is therefore a key figure in showing how African American literary criticism has branched out to include other types of CRITICISM.

Apart from the poststructuralist assertions of many contemporary critics, some question whether race is still a defining factor in determining the credibility of African American texts. Yet in spite of this debate, most African American theorists, writers, and critics assert, mainly from their own experiences, that it is "morally wrong to deny the authority of race" (Norrell, 289). Rather, contemporary critics more aptly believe that the study of race in regard to literature strengthens society and therefore is necessary for the preservation of not only African culture but American culture as well. Ralph Ellison writes, "Any viable theory of Negro American culture obligates us to fashion a more adequate theory of American culture as a whole" (quoted in Guerin, 256). Clearly, race does matter within the context of literary criticism.

African American criticism and the Bible. The issue of race has dominated the perspectives of the African American literary tradition. Additionally, not only does the issue dominate the secular interpretation of texts, but it also has provided and still provides African American critics with an interesting and extremely relevant way by which to interpret biblical texts. Basing one's INTERPRETATION on the idea that African Americans are an oppressed people group and under constant domination from the white majority, one can easily conclude that the BIBLE, through the words and actions of Jesus Christ, glorifies people groups of similar circumstances, such as the poor, widows, prostitutes, tax collectors, lepers, Samaritans, and others ostracized from the general community. Essentially, African Americans find it very easy to identify with those people who, like themselves, have had to fight for recognition from their oppressors; thus, the interpretation of biblical texts from an African American perspective is natural, expected, and necessary. James Cone, the father of BLACK THEOLOGY, defines the demand for this type of biblical interpretation as "a desperate need . . . [for] a theology whose sole purpose is to apply the freeing power of the gospel to black people under white oppression" (Cone, 31). Therefore, the African American literary critic has a duty to both race and faith to understand biblical texts from the perspective of the oppressed.

Many African American theologians have therefore applied their experience and perspectives on race to interpret biblical texts. Interpreting texts under the label of "black theology," theologians such as Howard Thurman, Emilie Townes, and most important, James Cone have insisted that African Americans, in order to fully understand the history and oppressive nature of the black experience, must interpret texts through ideas based on the suffering and redemption of Christ. As an expression of LIBERATION THEOLOGY, black theology's prominence can be attributed primarily to James Cone, who defines black theology as "a rational study of the being of God in the world in light of the existential situation of an oppressed community, relating the forces of liberation to the essence of the gospel, which is Jesus Christ" (19). Cone asserts that the black theology movement in the United States symbolizes Jesus as the black Messiah, the strong deliverer and liberator who "took upon himself the suffering of all oppressed people and transformed oppression to triumph through his resurrection" (Simmons, 3). Additionally, black theology affirms that God reveals himself in his blackness by liberating black humanity from the powers of white racism and oppression in America; it is therefore essential that African Americans see Jesus as black. Only then, states Cone, can the African American truly relate to a normally oppressive, predominantly white version of Christianity (Rhodes, 7). This being said, many African American critics have questioned whether there is indeed legitimate truth to be found in the Christian Bible since it was under the guise of Christianity that Africans were forced into slavery. Cone maintains that there is such a truth. Thus, Cone glorifies the black experience while condemning the oppression by the white majority. Specifically, Cone's ideals are immersed in the black experience of liberation, since "Jesus' work is essentially one of liberation" (Cone, 35); protest,

also known as the "political HERMENEUTICS of the gospel," by which Christianity becomes a religion of "protest against the suffering and affliction of man" (37); and slavery, as the black church was "born in slavery" and symbolizes a people "who were completely stripped of their African heritage as they were enslaved by the 'Christian' white man" (91).

Contrasting somewhat with Cone's ideas of black power and SCRIPTURE are the ideas of theologian DeOtis Roberts, who seeks liberation through reconciliation that "takes place between equals" (quoted in Rhodes, 13) rather than through the doctrine of black power. He maintains "it [liberation] cannot exist with a situation of White over Blacks" (13). Echoing the desire for this unity is the more contemporary perspective from black theologian Dwight N. Hopkins, who believes that if the black theological movement is to evolve, it must always be linked with the liberation of the poor and oppressed as well as with the black church, WOMANIST THEOLOGY, and a dialogue that will connect multiple VERSIONS of liberation theology. To foster social change through biblical interpretation, the African American literary critic applies methods like those used by African Americans in interpreting texts of a secular nature to advance their race ideologically, socially, and politically.

Bibliography. Abu Shardow Abarry, "Afrocentric Aesthetic in Selected Harlem Renaissance Poetry," in *Language and Literature in the African American Imagination* (ed. Carol Aisha Blackshire-Belay; Westport, CT: Greenwood, 1992), 133–46; Houston A. Baker Jr., "Toward a Critical Prospect for the Future," in *The Journey Back: Issues in Black Literature and Criticism* (Chicago: University of Chicago Press, 1980), 115–64 (excerpt repr. in *African American Literary Criticism, 1773 to 2000* [ed. Hazel Arnett Ervin; New York: Twayne, 1999], 192–97); Hans Bertens, *Literary Theory: The Basics* (London: Routledge, 2001); Carol Aisha Blackshire-Belay, "Afrocentricity and Literary Theory: The Maturing Imagination," in *Language and Literature in the African American Imagination* (ed. Carol Aisha Blackshire-Belay; Westport, CT: Greenwood, 1992), 3–7; James H. Cone, *Black Theology and Black Power* (New York: Seabury Press, 1969); W. E. B. Du Bois, "Criteria of Negro Art," in *African American Literary Criticism, 1773 to 2000* (ed. Hazel Arnett Ervin;

New York: Twayne, 1999), 39–43; Henry Louis Gates Jr., *The Signifying Monkey: A Theory of Afro-American Literary Criticism* (New York: Oxford University Press, 1988); Donald C. Goellnicht, "Black Criticism," in *Encyclopedia of Contemporary Literary Theory* (ed. Irena R. Makaryk; Toronto: University of Toronto Press, 1993), 5–10; Wilfred Guerin et al., *A Handbook of Critical Approaches to Literature* (4th ed.; New York: Oxford University Press, 1999), 256–60; Carolyn L. Holmes, "Reassessing African American Literature through an Afrocentric Paradigm," in *Language and Literature in the African American Imagination* (ed. Carol Aisha Blackshire-Belay; Westport, CT: Greenwood, 1992), 37–51; Langston Hughes, "The Negro Artist and the Racial Mountain," in *African American Literary Criticism, 1773 to 2000* (ed. Hazel Arnett Ervin; New York: Twayne, 1999), 44–48; Alain Locke, "Art or Propaganda?," in *African American Literary Criticism, 1773 to 2000* (ed. Hazel Arnett Ervin; New York: Twayne, 1999), 49–50; Alamin Mazrui, "African Languages in the African American Experience," in *Language and Literature in the African American Imagination* (ed. Carol Aisha Blackshire-Belay; Westport, CT: Greenwood, 1992), 75–90; Larry Neal, "The Black Arts Movement," in *African American Literary Criticism, 1773 to 2000* (ed. Hazel Arnett Ervin; New York: Twayne, 1999), 122–28; F. Burton Nelson, "Black Theology Revisited," *Christianity Today* 48, no. 3 (March 1, 2004), http://www.christianitytoday.com/ct/2004/march/37.77.html; Robert J. Norrell, "Race Does Matter," *Virginia Quarterly Review* 77, no. 2 (2001): 289; Anand Prahlad, "Guess Who's Coming to Dinner? Folklore, Folkloristics, and African American Literary Criticism," *African American Review* 33, no. 4 (1999): 565; Ron Rhodes, "Black Theology, Black Power, and the Black Experience," *Christian Research Journal* (1991), http://home.earthlink.net/~ronrhodes/BlackTheology.html; Anthony Simmons, "African Theology and Black Theology," *Black and Christian*, 2 parts (February–March/April 2004), http://blackandchristian.com/articles/2004.shtml; Robert E. Washington, *The Ideologies of African American Literature: From the Harlem Renaissance to the Black Nationalist Revolt* (Lanham, MD: Rowman & Littlefield, 2001); Sherley A. Williams, "The Blues Root of Contemporary Afro-American Poetry," in *African American Literary Criticism, 1773 to 2000* (ed. Hazel Arnett Ervin; New York: Twayne, 1999), 179–91.

AFRICAN LIBERATION THEOLOGY

Theological movements among African peoples guided by the central belief that it is God's will that people be free of all forms of oppression. *See* LIBERATION THEOLOGY.

AFRICENTRIC (AFROCENTRIC) THEOLOGY

A THEOLOGY (esp. among African American theologians) formulated by reference to African rather than Western resources and cultural CONTEXTs.

AGENDA

A word widely used by LITERARY and cultural CRITICs to describe a body of unconscious and often conscious theological, political, and historical opinions, preunderstandings, and (esp.) purposes that guide interpreters of literary, historical, and cultural objects (*see* SUBJECT/OBJECT). The claim is that one's agenda makes it impossible for one to approach an interpretable object with a disinterested objectivity. Every interpreter's work is always already conditioned or colored by his or her SOCIAL LOCATION and the expectations and rules set by that location. In BIBLICAL STUDIES, the INTERPRETATION of any biblical text will always be preceded by and conditioned by the interpreter's social location and the reason(s) for interpreting.

AGENT

A term introduced by Adele Berlin to describe a character type in biblical NARRATIVE. The agent is a functionary that the AUTHOR uses to fill out the narrative and serves the purpose of providing the necessary characters to populate a STORY. *See* CHARACTERIZATION.

Bibliography. Adele Berlin, *Poetics and Interpretation of Biblical Narrative* (Sheffield: Almond, 1983).

AGRAPHA

A Greek term meaning "unwritten" and used in BIBLICAL STUDIES to refer to "sayings attributed to Jesus but not found in the CANONICAL GOSPELS" (Soulen and Soulen, 2). *Agrapha* is also applied to the lost SAYINGS OF JESUS that circulated as part of the ORAL TRADITION in the early church. Since the evangelists (*see* GOSPEL) would have used only the sayings of Jesus that related directly to their theological purposes, many of Jesus's sayings were forgotten except where they were preserved in other sources. Possible *agrapha* can be found in the NT (Acts 20:35 and 1 Thess. 4:16–17), ancient manuscripts of the NT (e.g., Luke 10:16 in Codex Koridethi), the church fathers, the *Gospel of Thomas*, the Talmud (*'Abodah Zarah* 16b–17a; *Šabbat* 116a–b), and Islamic writings.

> Bibliography. Richard N. Soulen and R. Kendall Soulen, *Handbook of Biblical Criticism* (3rd ed.; Louisville: Westminster John Knox, 2001).

ALEATORY INTERTEXTUALITY

A term used in Michael Riffaterre's definition of INTERTEXTUALITY. According to Riffaterre, intertextuality is the relationship between readers and their recognition of a text's relationship to TEXTS that precede or follow it. *Aleatory intertextuality* refers to the way readers relate a text to other texts with which they are familiar, assuming features not present in the text under study. For example, a reader's understanding of Genesis will be heavily influenced by the reader's familiarity with other biblical texts as well as by extrabiblical texts. Aleatory intertextuality operates on the ASSUMPTION that all literature (any text, for that matter) is written and read on the shoulders of other texts.

> Bibliography. Michael Riffaterre, "Compulsory Reader-Response: The Intertextual Drive," in *Intertextuality: Theories and Practices* (ed. Michael Worton and Judith Still; Manchester, UK: Manchester University Press, 1990), 56–78; idem, *Text Production* (trans. Terese Lyons; New York: Columbia University Press, 1983).

ALEXANDRIAN TEXT

Within TEXTUAL CRITICISM, a group of NT manuscripts similar in textual properties and ideas, possibly originating from a common source in Alexandria, Egypt. As the biblical writings began to spread throughout the Mediterranean world, certain cities such as Rome, Alexandria, and Constantinople became what critics call "homes" of certain VERSIONS or families of texts and textual traditions. The Alexandrian text (also called the Egyptian text and the Neutral Text) may have originated in Alexandria because Alexandria was the center for CRITICISM of the Greek classics, and it is quite possible that the NT texts were examined through LITERARY and critical lenses. Consequently, the manuscripts in this family are characterized by stylistic VARIANT READINGS intended to correct perceived literary and grammatical imperfections of the NT writings. In text-critical terms, then, the Alexandrian text is an unreliable textual witness where the variants involve technicalities of grammar or where more sophisticated literary forms are substituted for more colloquial ones.

> Bibliography. J. Harold Greenlee, *Introduction to New Testament Textual Criticism* (Grand Rapids: Eerdmans, 1964; rev. ed., Peabody, MA: Hendrickson, 1995).

ALIENATION

Theologically, the separation of humans from God, other humans, and the self as a result of sin. Philosophically, Karl Marx used the term to refer to a historical condition in which humans suffer estrangement from nature, others, and the products of their labor. This condition is created by the advanced stage of interaction between the division of labor, private property, and the state in a capitalist society. At this stage, individuals experience the world as an alien force pitted against them. Such alienation can be overcome only by the abolition of economies based on the private ownership of property.

Alienation is also an important concept in existentialist philosophy, where it is considered to be the central condition of human existence. It is manifested in an individual's sense of helplessness and disenchantedness in an impersonal world in which there is no inherent MEANING.

> Bibliography. Susan R. Skand, "Alienation," in *A Dictionary of Cultural and Critical Theory* (ed. Michael Payne; Cambridge, MA: Blackwell, 1996), 22–23.

ALLEGORICAL SENSE OF SCRIPTURE

One of the four medieval "senses of Scripture" in which the biblical TEXTS are interpreted as having hidden, spiritual meanings outside the literal ones. *See* FOURFOLD SENSE OF SCRIPTURE.

ALLEGORY

An extended METAPHOR in which ACTIONS, objects (*see* SUBJECT/OBJECT), and/or persons in a

NARRATIVE correspond to or suggest MEANINGS outside the narrative (Harmon and Holman, 12). Allegory works through double SIGNIFICATION, in which the actions, persons, and objects represent ideas. Consequently, allegory takes an interest not only in the events, objects, persons, SETTINGS, and so forth but also in the ideas they are intended to suggest. Although the events, settings, persons, objects, and actions may be historical or fictitious, in true allegory they must suggest meanings independent of the STORY. For example, the story of Hosea's marriage in Hosea 2 is an allegory of God's relationship to Israel as a nation. Hosea is commanded by Yahweh to take a wife, who is then unfaithful. This becomes an allegory of the family. Yahweh as the husband speaks to Hosea as the son, accusing Israel as the wife of infidelity because she has left Yahweh and bestowed her favors on the pagan gods, her lovers. Other examples may be Isa. 5:1–6; Prov. 5:15–23; Eccles. 12:1–6; 1 Cor. 5:6–8; 9:8–10; Gal. 4:21–31; Mark 4:12–20; Matt. 13:36–43; 22:1–14. According to Soulen (Soulen and Soulen, 5), there are instances in the NT where allegorical elements are employed in PARABLES in order to adjust them to such things as the delay of the parousia or historical events (e.g., Matt. 22:11–13; 24:43–44; Mark 2:19b–20; 13:33–37).

Bibliography. William Harmon and C. Hugh Holman, *A Handbook to Literature* (8th ed.; Upper Saddle River, NJ: Prentice Hall, 1999); Richard N. Soulen and R. Kendall Soulen, *Handbook of Biblical Criticism* (3rd ed.; Louisville: Westminster John Knox, 2001).

ALLITERATION

The REPETITION of initial consonant or vowel sounds in either consecutive or closely related syllables. Proverbs 13:24 in Hebrew provides an example of alliteration: *ḥôśēk šibṭô śônēʾ běnô / wěʾōhăbô šiḥărô mûsār*, which is commonly translated (cf. KJV) as "Spare the rod and spoil the child" (Alter, 166). While the alliteration in the Hebrew TEXT is obvious and frequent, it is usually lost in TRANSLATION.

Bibliography. Robert Alter, *The Art of Biblical Poetry* (New York: Basic Books, 1985).

ALLUSION

An essential element in INTERTEXTUAL CRITICISM, allusion is a LITERARY DEVICE that makes reference to or attempts to conjure up in the memory of the reader a historical or LITERARY event, object (*see* SUBJECT/OBJECT), or character. A genuine allusion is indirect. It is effective to the extent that the AUTHOR is able to tap the knowledge and memory of the reader. In other words, literary allusion is successful only if the author and reader share a common body of knowledge. For example, when Herod in Mark's GOSPEL offers to give up to half his kingdom to Herodias's daughter if she will dance for him (Mark 6:23), the reader should recall Ahasuerus's similar offers to Esther (5:1–8). The response of the disciples when Jesus asks them to feed the crowds of 5,000 and 4,000 (Mark 6:37; 8:4) recalls the response of Elisha's servant in a similar situation, the feeding of a crowd of 400 (2 Kings 4:43). When such literary allusions occur, the reader is expected to interpret the passage in conversation with the referenced object, event, or person. In other words, recognition of allusions is often an essential factor in understanding the work.

ALREADY / NOT YET

The view held by some NT scholars that in the GOSPELS, Pauline epistles (*see* EPISTOLARY LITERATURE), and to some extent in the Johannine writings, Jesus and the authors taught that the kingdom or reign of God was "already" manifested in Jesus's life and ministry, but that it is "not yet" fully present and will not be until the parousia.

Bibliography. George E. Ladd, *A Theology of the New Testament* (Grand Rapids: Eerdmans, 1974).

ALTERITY

A term used by contemporary CRITICS to refer to the alternative or contending INTERPRETATIONS generated by TEXTS, thus creating impasses or APORIAS.

AMANUENSIS

A person who writes for another from dictation; a secretary or scribe. For many of his letters, the apostle Paul employed an amanuensis (e.g., Rom. 16:22; 1 Cor. 16:21; Gal. 6:11). Some scholars argue that the differences in STYLE, vocabulary, and THEOLOGY in the Pauline Letters of disputed authorship are due to differences in the writing styles and theological orientations of the amanuenses. *See* EPISTOLARY LITERATURE.

AMARNA TABLETS

A cache of 337 cuneiform tablets unearthed from 1887 to 1937 at Tell el-Amarna in Egypt, consisting mostly of diplomatic correspondence written in Akkadian, Hittite, and Hurrian during the early fourteenth century BCE. The tablets were written by Palestinian, Phoenician, and Syrian vassal kings and governors to Amenhotep III and Amenhotep IV when Amarna was Amenhotep's capital. The tablets are important generally in that they give scholars glimpses into the Mesopotamian culture of the period and particularly because of their mention of the 'Apiru ('Abiru), whom some scholars identify as the biblical Hebrews. Some of the TEXTS are available in English TRANSLATION in Pritchard's *Ancient Near Eastern Texts*. Another helpful resource is Moran's *Amarna Letters*.

Bibliography. W. L. Moran, *The Amarna Letters* (Baltimore: Johns Hopkins University Press, 1992); M. J. Mulder, "Israel to the Time of the Babylonian Captivity," in *The World of the Old Testament* (ed. A. S. van der Woude; Grand Rapids: Eerdmans, 1989), 2–76; J. B. Pritchard, *Ancient Near Eastern Texts* (3rd ed.; Princeton: Princeton University Press, 1969).

AMBIGUITY

In the strictest sense, the condition of a statement having more than one possible MEANING and the resultant uncertainty between the possibilities. Ambiguity may be caused by grammatical and/ or syntactical flaws and thus be unintentional. In LITERARY studies, however, *ambiguity* usually refers to the capacity of language to operate on levels beyond DENOTATION (Harmon and Holman, 16). Literary artists have long recognized that words and word groups may be used to suggest equally meaningful senses in the same CONTEXT, thus creating literary complexity. In *Seven Types of Ambiguity*, William Empson expands the concept to the point that it becomes almost synonymous with complexity. The seven types are (1) particulars of language that are effective in a number of ways at the same time; (2) alternative interpretations, which the reader eventually resolves into the author's intended meaning; (3) two apparently independent meanings invested in one word; (4) optional meanings that combine to elucidate a complex condition in the author's mind; (5) a SIMILE imperfectly referring to two disparate objects (*see* SUBJECT/OBJECT), a confusion revealing the author's discovery of ideas during the actual process of composition; (6) a statement so paradoxical or extraneous that readers must create their own interpretations; and (7) a statement so deeply contradictory that it actually reveals a basic rift in the author's psyche.

Although in NEW CRITICISM ambiguity became the fundamental characteristic of literary texts, in recent postmodern theories (*see* POSTMODERN CRITICISM) the SIGNIFICANCE of ambiguity has been extended to refer to the inherent multiplicity of all language rather than to the limited literary uses identified by Empson. All linguistic expressions (written or oral; literary or nonliterary) are ambiguous and thus defy any definitive INTERPRETATIONS. For readers of the biblical texts, such an ASSUMPTION precludes the finality of any doctrinal systems based on authoritative interpretations.

Bibliography. William Empson, *Seven Types of Ambiguity* (2nd ed.; London: Chatto & Windus, 1947); William Harmon and C. Hugh Holman, *A Handbook to Literature* (8th ed.; Upper Saddle River, NJ: Prentice Hall, 1999).

AMERICAN STANDARD VERSION (ASV)

A 1901 revision of the King James Version of the Bible (frequently called the Authorized Version, AV) by an interdenominational group of American scholars who intended the revision (to American Standard English) to be an American alternative to the REVISED VERSION. The most notable feature of the ASV is its faithfulness to the original languages, especially in SYNTAX and verb tenses. Although it was popular during the first half of the twentieth century, by midcentury, perhaps because of its rather outdated language, it fell into disuse. For more on the history of the ASV, see Freedman.

Bibliography. D. N. Freedman et al., eds., *Anchor Bible Dictionary* (New York: Doubleday, 1992), 6:835 (s.v. "Versions").

A MINORE AD MAJUS

A Latin phrase usually translated "from the lesser to the greater." According to Soulen and Soulen, "it is the Latin equivalent to *Qal wāḥōmer* (Heb.), the first of HILLEL's seven principal rules of interpretation: also translated 'from the easy to the difficult'" (6). When used in a statement with a PROTASIS and APODOSIS, it reads as "If such be true, . . . then how much more must it be true that . . ." (6). An example is Matt. 7:11: "If you then, who are evil, know how to give good gifts to your children, how much more will your Father in heaven give good things to those who ask him!" See also Matt. 10:25; Rom. 11:12; and Heb. 9:13–14.

Bibliography. Richard N. Soulen and R. Kendall Soulen, *Handbook of Biblical Criticism* (3rd ed.; Louisville: Westminster John Knox, 2001).

AMPLIFICATION

A figure of speech in which brief statements, apt to be overlooked or misinterpreted or undervalued, are emphasized by restating them with supplementary detail, by REPETITION, or by restating the SUBJECT or idea in completely different terms. Amplification may be seen in some BIBLICAL POETRY (e.g., Prov. 20:5) as well as in the apostle Paul's letters (e.g., Rom. 14:13–21; *see* EPISTOLARY LITERATURE) and the Gospel of John (e.g., 3:3–8).

ANACHRONISM

Assignment of something to a time when it did not exist or explanation of a biblical word or passage in terms of MEANINGs that developed after the original usage. While AUTHORs may use anachronism as a LITERARY DEVICE, especially for humorous effect, quite often TRANSLATIONS of TEXTs may contain anachronisms for theological reasons. Cotterell and Turner suggest that anachronism occurs

more often in more popular and devotional commentaries. For example, the modern sense of the Greek word *arrabōn* (engagement ring) is used to explain its meaning in 2 Cor. 1:22, where it should be translated either "pledge" or "first installment" (Cotterell and Turner, 133). In biblical EXEGESIS, explaining a word within a biblical passage in terms of the word's later senses is avoided.

Bibliography. Peter Cotterell and Max Turner, *Linguistics and Biblical Interpretation* (Downers Grove, IL: InterVarsity, 1989).

ANACOLUTHON

A failure to complete a sentence as the initial linguistic structure requires. Anacoluthon may be deliberate, in which case, as a LITERARY DEVICE, it may work to create a profound SENSE of cognitive dissonance or incoherence. It may also be accidental, such as when AUTHORs simply loses their chain of thought (e.g., Gal. 2:4–6).

ANAGOGE (ANAGOGY)

The mystical or spiritual MEANING derived from interpreting beyond the literal. The highest of the four senses of SCRIPTURE (*see* FOURFOLD SENSE OF SCRIPTURE), the others being the literal, allegorical, and moral. Not only is Jerusalem a literal city, but through anagogy, it is also God's heavenly city (Gal. 4:26), as Melchizedek is the prototype of Jesus's heavenly priesthood (Heb. 9:7). The differences between the four senses can be seen in the following comparison: Jerusalem as the literal city, morally as the believer, allegorically as the church, and anagogically as the city of God. Consequently, anagogy is a special form of allegorical interpretation in that allegory deals with a metaphor on the physical and earthly plane, while anagogy deals with a metaphor that is limited to the spiritual plane.

ANAGOGICAL SENSE OF SCRIPTURE. *See* ANAGOGE

ANALOGUE

Something similar to another thing. In LITERARY theory, an analogue has a dual SIGNIFICANCE. First, two versions of the same STORY may be analogues (e.g., the two creation accounts in Genesis or the flood accounts in Genesis and the Gilgamesh Epic). And second, an analogue is one of the two objects (*see* SUBJECT/OBJECT) compared in ANALOGY (e.g., both speaking in tongues and the musical instruments in 1 Cor. 14:6–9 are analogues).

ANALOGY

A comparison of two things similar in certain respects, but dissimilar enough that the more unfamiliar thing is clarified or explained in terms of the more familiar. Both SIMILE and METAPHOR as well as PARABLE and ALLEGORY are forms of analogy. Paul uses analogy extensively, as in 1 Cor. 15:18, where he employs the more familiar idea of sleep to describe death. See also 1 Cor. 14:6–8; Gal. 3:23–4:7.

ANALOGY OF FAITH

Based on an INTERPRETATION of Rom. 12:6—the teaching that the prophet should speak in accordance with what has previously been revealed in SCRIPTURE—the analogy of faith is a hermeneutical principle claiming that (1) doctrines should be formulated within the CONTEXT of the whole Bible, (2) difficult or vague passages of Scripture should be explicated in light of the clearer passages, and (3) the HEBREW BIBLE should be understood in light of the NT.

Bibliography. Walter C. Kaiser Jr. and Moisés Silva, *An Introduction to Biblical Hermeneutics* (Grand Rapids: Zondervan, 1994).

ANALOGY OF SCRIPTURE

The ASSUMPTION that because SCRIPTURE is a unified whole and inspired by God, a fuller understanding of any passage of Scripture is obtained by studying it in conjunction with other passages. More specifically, Bright (143) proposes that biblical passages embody some point of theological SIGNIFICANCE that connects them to the entire fabric of the BIBLE. Most often this connection is to be found in a biblical AUTHOR's making REFERENCE to antecedent passages of Scripture in one or more of three ways: (1) employing key terms that carry special theological MEANING (e.g., servant, circumcision, seed); (2) quoting directly from previous biblical authors; or (3) using ALLUSIONS to prior persons, events, objects (*see* SUBJECT/OBJECT), or places (e.g., the EXODUS, Sinai, crossing the Red Sea, or particularly, the OLD TESTAMENT COVENANTS). By referencing Scripture in such a manner, an author expects readers to allow the referenced material to inform their understanding of a passage (Kaiser and Silva, 195–96).

Bibliography. John Bright, *The Authority of the Old Testament* (Nashville: Abingdon, 1967); Walter C. Kaiser Jr. and Moisés Silva, *An Introduction to Biblical Hermeneutics* (Grand Rapids: Zondervan, 1994).

ANALYSIS

In LITERARY studies, a method that separates a TEXT into its parts or textual segments (e.g., paragraph, literary units such as parables, and larger units), which are then subjected to a meticulous and logical examination. The result should be a consistent, coherent, and complete account of the parts and their organization into a unified whole.

ANALYSIS, CONTENT. *See* CONTENT ANALYSIS

ANALYSIS, DISCOURSE. *See* DISCOURSE ANALYSIS

ANALYSIS, EXTRINSIC. *See* EXTRINSIC ANALYSIS

ANALYSIS, INTRINSIC. *See* INTRINSIC ANALYSIS

ANALYSIS, RHETORICAL. *See* RHETORICAL ANALYSIS

ANALYTICAL CRITICISM

A type of CRITICISM that assumes that the constituent parts of a literary work form an autonomous, unified whole and that the MEANING of the work is to be found in a rigorous, close ANALYSIS of the relationships among the various parts and between the parts and the whole. *See* NEW CRITICISM.

ANAPHORA

A type of REPETITION in which the same word or brief phrase is repeated at the beginning of two or more lines of POETRY. Anaphora is used extensively in BIBLICAL POETRY and is more than poetic embellishment. In Isa. 2:12–16, each line begins with "against all." Alter (64–66) suggests that the repetition in each successive line or VERSE invites the reader to see the material introduced by the repetition as part of a whole STRUCTURE as well as part of a development within the structure. For example, in Ps. 13, the development progresses from God's hiding his face to the psalmist's enemies' being exalted over him:

> How long, O LORD? Will you forget me
>   forever?
>   How long will you hide your face from me?
> How long must I bear pain in my soul,
>   and have sorrow in my heart all day long?
> How long shall my enemy be exalted over me?

Bibliography. Robert Alter, *The Art of Biblical Poetry* (New York: Basic Books, 1985).

ANASTASIS

A Greek word that means "resurrection" and refers to Jesus's being raised from the dead, as well as the resurrection of believers (Acts 2:31; 1 Pet. 1:3; 3:21; cf. 1 Cor. 15:12, 13, 21, 42; Rev. 20:5).

Bibliography. Donald K. McKim, *Westminster Dictionary of Theological Terms* (Louisville: Westminster John Knox, 1996).

ANCHOR BIBLE (AB)

A multivolume English TRANSLATION of the BIBLE published by Doubleday with extensive COMMENTARY provided by individual scholars (Jewish, Roman Catholic, and Protestant).

ANDROCENTRIC LANGUAGE

In most varieties of FEMINIST CRITICISM, the conventions or uses of language in male-centered cultures that legitimate and perpetuate the male values in those cultures as well as the PATRIARCHAL STRUCTURES that contribute to the oppression, MARGINALIZATION, and subordination of women. According to feminist critics, the language of the BIBLE, of scholarship, and of clerical proclamation perpetuate these oppressive structures.

ANDROCENTRISM

A key concept in FEMINIST CRITICISM referring to the male-centeredness of culture. Androcentrism takes *man* (the male) as the human PARADIGM while assigning less significance to women and women's experiences and contributions to culture. Within feminist criticism, theologies, and HERMENEUTICS, the fact that the BIBLE is written by men has crucial theological, political, and social ramifications. Not only is God rendered in male terms, but the Bible also serves to legitimate PATRIARCHAL STRUCTURES and the MARGINALIZATION of women. In other words, there is a mutually reinforcing connection between androcentric language and the marginalizing structures of PATRIARCHY. Such language and structures ultimately determine human (both men and women) perception of humanness and divinity. Consequently, the starting point of feminist hermeneutics is a HERMENEUTICS OF SUSPICION directed toward the biblical TEXTS, INTERPRETATIONS of the texts, and scholarship (all three viewed as equally male-centered) because either intentionally or unintentionally all three have been used to legitimate women's second-class status in all facets of society (Schüssler Fiorenza, xi–xiii).

Bibliography. Elisabeth Schüssler Fiorenza, *Bread Not Stone* (10th anniversary ed.; Boston: Beacon, 1995).

ANDROGYNY

A term derived from the Greek *anēr* (man) and *gynē* (woman) and technically referring to both male and female reproductive organs existing in a single organism (Carr, 29). In the 1960s and 1970s, however, those within FEMINIST CRITICISM adopted the term to describe the fusion of both masculine and feminine traits and virtues in humans. Feminist CRITICS, arguing for a distinction between sex and GENDER, claimed that sexist cultures create the categories of male and female and identify the traits that define the categories in such a way as to devalue the female one. This cultural move also results in a strict social system of dominance (male) and subordination (female). Feminist critics claimed that the introduction of androgyny into sexist cultures not only would encourage freedom to allow individuals to develop in accord with their own being but also would reveal that gender roles are social, cultural constructs rather than manifestations of natural givens.

By the 1980s, interest in androgyny began to wane. Not only did feminists fear that in androcentric (*see* ANDROCENTRISM) societies, androgyny would never be actualized, but also, influenced by the postmodern (*see* POSTMODERN CRITICISM) concept of DIFFERENCE, they felt that androgyny perpetuated the dominant/subordinate STRUCTURE and threatened the new tendency to explore and celebrate racial, cultural, and sexual differences. Thus fueled by the fear that androgyny would ultimately result in the perpetuation of an age-old problem, feminist critics jettisoned the concept.

Bibliography. Glynis Carr, "Androgyny," in *A Dictionary of Cultural and Critical Theory* (ed. Michael Payne; Cambridge, MA: Blackwell, 1996), 28–29.

ANECDOTE

A brief NARRATIVE detailing an interesting, unusual, or curious EPISODE, often biographical. The event usually concerns an incident in the life of a well-known person, may have a basis in TRUTH, though not necessarily dependent on that truth for its appeal, and is marked by IRONIC REVERSAL. While anecdote has some similarities to SHORT STORY, it differs from the latter in that it lacks a PLOT and is limited to a single episode. Though the short stories in the HEBREW BIBLE generally lack the humor usually associated with anecdote, some seem to correspond in other respects—single episode, well-known and interesting person, ironic reversal, and some historical basis. Possible anecdotes are stories in the book of Judges (esp. Samson, Ehud, Jael, and Abimelech).

Bibliography. J. A. Cuddon, *The Penguin Dictionary of Literary Terms and Literary Theory* (4th ed.; London: Penguin, 1998).

ANNALS

Yearly NARRATIVEs of historical events. These narrative accounts may have been written sometime after the events actually took place, giving rise to speculative dating, especially when the recorder tried to synchronize events from a variety of sources. In the case of the annals mentioned in the HEBREW BIBLE, the writer may have tried to synchronize sacred or ecclesiastical history and secular history. (Although annals of Israel and Judah are mentioned in the Hebrew Bible, there are none found in the biblical text nor are any extant.) The annals differed from CHRONICLES in that the latter were more concerned with broader aspects of history than with the mere recording of events.

Bibliography. William Harmon and C. Hugh Holman, *A Handbook to Literature* (8th ed.; Upper Saddle River, NJ: Prentice Hall, 1999).

ANNOTATED BIBLE

A BIBLE with explanatory notes to the text supplied by an editor. The notes may be historical, theological, or LITERARY and are designed to explain, translate, cite other sources, supply biographical or bibliographical information, or PARAPHRASE. The notes may appear in introductory sections and/or footnotes, but regardless of the nature of the annotations, they are the opinions of editors and may reflect their theological biases. A few of the better-known annotated Bibles are *The New Oxford Annotated Bible with Apocrypha, The HarperCollins Study Bible,* and *The Jerusalem / New Jerusalem Bible.*

Bibliography. Richard N. Soulen and R. Kendall Soulen, *Handbook of Biblical Criticism* (3rd ed.; Louisville: Westminster John Knox, 2001).

ANNUNCIATION STORY

Stories at the beginning of the GOSPELs of Matthew and Luke dealing with the events surrounding the birth of Jesus. These stories include LYRICAL DISCOURSE and angels' announcing things to humans about the birth of Jesus; they seem to have several possible purposes—to describe the uniqueness of Jesus's birth by placing it within the CONTEXT of supernatural occurrences, to validate the event of his birth, and to describe Jesus's birth as a fulfillment of OT messianic prophecies (Ryken, 36).

Bibliography. Leland Ryken, *Words of Life: A Literary Introduction to the New Testament* (Grand Rapids: Baker, 1987).

ANTAGONIST

In FICTION, the PLOT is sustained by a central CONFLICT, and the various characters are defined in terms of their involvement in this conflict. The antagonist is the character who is the enemy or rival of and in opposition to the main character (the PROTAGONIST). For example, in the Jacob SAGA (Gen. 29–31), Laban is the STORY's antagonist because the plot revolves around the conflict between Jacob and Laban.

ANTE CHRISTUM

Latin for "before Christ" (*see* BCE), referring to the time before the birth of Jesus.

ANTHOLOGY

A collection of writings, usually PROSE, POETRY, or both, generally by a variety of AUTHORS. Since it consists of works by different authors and in a variety of GENRES, the BIBLE may be considered an anthology.

ANTHROPOCENTRISM

A term derived from the Greek *anthrōpos* (human) and *kentron* (center) and referring to the ASSUMPTION that human autonomy and values constitute the central reality of the universe.

ANTHROPOLOGY. *See* CULTURAL ANTHROPOLOGY

ANTHROPOMORPHISM

Broadly, a term referring to a LITERARY DEVICE ascribing human characteristics to nonhuman objects, usually a god or an abstraction (*see* SUBJECT/OBJECT). For example, in mythologies the gods are often described as having human form and as manifesting human qualities. More specifically, in BIBLICAL STUDIES an anthropomorphism is the ascription of human characteristics to God, such as having hands, arms, fingers, or eyes (e.g., Ps. 18:15). At times, anthropomorphism may be confused with PERSONIFICATION. However, the former presents God as having human form or attributes; the latter describes a nonhuman object figuratively as possessing human form or attributes. To portray God as a loving father or jealous husband is anthropomorphism. To describe plants and animals as capable of speech (Job 12:7–8) is personification.

ANTHROPOPATHISM

The ascription to God of human emotions such as anger, grief, love, and pity (cf. Hosea 8:5).

ANTICIPATION

A term used in READER-RESPONSE CRITICISM to describe an effect of the TEXT on a reader. In the process of reading, a reader encounters textual segments in a linear fashion. Each segment contributes to the reader's creation of a THEME, an idea of what the text is about, which the reader holds in MEMORY. Based on what is held in memory, the reader anticipates what may come next. This anticipation may be satisfied or frustrated. If it is frustrated, the reader must then reevaluate what is in memory and modify the understanding or theme to this point. In this fashion, reading becomes a process of memory and anticipation. For example, when Jesus in Mark 4:11 tells his disciples "to you has been given the secret of the kingdom of God," the reader must necessarily wonder about the nature of this secret and when it was given to the disciples. Prior to this announcement, the reader cannot recall a time in the NARRATIVE when this secret was revealed to the disciples. Consequently, the reader must anticipate that Jesus will reveal it later in the narrative. One option is that when Jesus asks his disciples, "Do you not understand this parable? Then how will you understand all the parables?" (Mark 4:13), the reader must assume that the PARABLE of the sower is the secret. In subsequent reading, the reader anticipates that all the parables in Mark must be understood in terms of the sower parable. *See also* PROTENSION; RETENTION.

ANTIFOUNDATIONALISM

A philosophical view (esp. popular in POSTMOD-ERNISM/POSTMODERNITY) that denies the existence of universal standards of TRUTH underlying reality. According to this view, there are no such things as natural givens that humans may discover and then use as foundations to construct truth systems or epistemologies. All such givens or standards are human fabrications or cultural constructs. Consequently, all doctrinal systems founded on principles that the church has formulated from interpreting the BIBLE are exactly that—interpretive formulations—and not reflections of universal truths or standards.

ANTILEGOMENA

The books of the NT whose canonicity (*see* CANON; CANON, NEW TESTAMENT; CANONIZATION PROCESS) was in dispute for a time (Hebrews, Revelation, James, Jude, 2 Peter, 2–3 John).

ANTIPHRASIS

A type of IRONY usually involving the humorous use of a word or phrase to communicate the exact opposite of its denotative (*see* DENOTATION) SIG-NIFICANCE. Antiphrasis is common in colloquial or casual conversation, such as "I'm just doing great" for "I'm doing horribly" or "That was the right thing to say" instead of "That was the wrong thing to say." When Paul refers to his readers in 2 Cor. 11:19 as "being wise yourselves," he means just the opposite.

Bibliography. William Harmon and C. Hugh Holman, *A Handbook to Literature* (8th ed.; Upper Saddle River, NJ: Prentice Hall, 1999).

ANTIPROVERB

A term used by Robert Alter to describe two types of PROVERBs that problematize traditional WIS-DOM SAYINGS. In the first type, the first VERSET contains FIGURATIVE LANGUAGE and states the conventional, while the second verset turns con-

ventional expectation upside down. For example, in Eccles. 7:1, the first verset inscribes a traditional saying, but the second verset denies conventional wisdom: "A good name is better than precious ointment, and the day of death, than the day of birth." James L. Kugel, however, explains this proverb differently. Taking the proverb as a CHIASMUS in the HEBREW (*ṭôb šēm miššemen ṭôb*), Kugel argues that the first verset is certainly acceptable wisdom: a person's reputation is more valuable than possessions (Kugel, 10). The second verset, however, appears on the surface to contradict conventional wisdom, but because of its form—suggesting that if A is true, then B is also true—the second verset must stand as it is: "For the trouble with precious oil is that it is extremely fragile and spoils easily." Kugel continues,

> The value of a name is quite the opposite: intangible, it is thus protected from the physical decay of the world. Now the newborn child is like the precious oil in that he is entirely physical—no qualities, no character, in fact, *no name*, at least not for a while. As he grows he gains these less tangible attributes; then as he ages, his physical existence begins to decay. On the day of his death, all that will remain is intangible, the *šēm*; that day will be "better" in that on it the process of building the name (which only began at birth) will be complete. (Kugel, 10)

The second type and, according to Alter, the more common avoids figurative language altogether and point-for-point reverses traditional wisdom sayings. Examples are Eccles. 1:18: "For in much wisdom is much vexation, and those who increase knowledge increase sorrow"; and 7:3: "Sorrow is better than laughter, for by sadness of countenance the heart is made glad."

Bibliography. Robert Alter, *The Art of Biblical Poetry* (New York: Basic Books, 1985); James L. Kugel, *The Idea of Biblical Poetry: Parallelism and Its History* (Baltimore: Johns Hopkins University Press, 1981).

ANTI-SEMITISM

The hatred of or hostility to Jews. Throughout history, anti-Semitism has expressed itself in extermination, discrimination, and intolerance. Some biblical scholars suggest that underlying the GOS-PEL of John is a spirit of anti-Semitism.

ANTISTASIS

The occurrence of the same word in proximity but with a pronounced difference in MEANING (e.g., 1 Cor. 1:21: "For since, in the wisdom of God, the world did not know God through wisdom . . .").

ANTITHESIS

A FIGURE OF SPEECH in which contrasting words, clauses, sentences, and/or ideas are set against each other in similar grammatical STRUCTURES. Proverbs 10:1 is an example:

> A wise child makes a glad father,
> but a foolish child is a mother's grief.

Not only do the "wise child"/"foolish child" and "father"/"mother" contrast, but so do the ideas of gladness and grief. Antithesis is prevalent in BIBLICAL POETRY, especially in antithetic parallelism as seen in the above example.

Antithesis plays a prominent part in Jesus's SERMON ON THE MOUNT in Matthew's GOSPEL. Six times Jesus quotes from the TORAH (five times from the written Torah and once from the Oral Torah) using the quote as a THESIS and then countering with an antithesis. In Matt. 5:27, Jesus states the thesis ("You have heard that it was said, 'You shall not commit adultery'") and responds with the antithesis ("But I say to you that everyone who looks at a woman with lust has already committed adultery with her in his heart").

ANTITHETIC(AL) PARALLELISM. See BIBLICAL POETRY

ANTITYPE

In biblical typology, the counterpart of the TYPE; thus the antitype is the reality or idea that the type foreshadows. In the NT, Jesus is the antitype of, for example, Jonah, Melchizedek, and Solomon. *See* TYPE; TYPOLOGICAL INTERPRETATION.

ANTONOMASIA

A FIGURE OF SPEECH in which a proper name is applied to an idea. In Mark 10:3, Jesus's response to the PHARISEES' question on divorce is an example: "What did Moses command you?" Moses is substituted for the LAW. Another type of antonomasia is the paraphrastic substitution of an EPITHET for a proper name, as in "The Prince of Peace" for Christ (Harmon and Holman, 33).

> *Bibliography.* William Harmon and C. Hugh Holman, *A Handbook to Literature* (8th ed.; Upper Saddle River, NJ: Prentice Hall, 1999).

ANTONYM

A word that means the opposite of another word (e.g., "hot" is the antonym of "cold"). In BIBLICAL STUDIES, antonyms occur with regularity in antithetical parallelism (*see* ANTITHESIS) of BIBLICAL POETRY. For example, in "Crooked minds are an abomination to the LORD, but those of blameless ways are his delight" (Prov. 11:20), "crooked minds" is the antonym of "those of blameless ways," and "abomination" is the antonym of "delight."

ANXIETY OF INFLUENCE

A theory of literary influence developed by Harold Bloom to describe the impact of earlier writers on later ones. Unlike theories of INTERTEXTUALITY, which emphasize collaboration between earlier and later writers, Bloom's anxiety of influence focuses on literary contestation between an AUTHOR and predecessors. When a writer or reader first encounters the achievements of great writers of the past, the initial response may be that nothing more of substance can be said in the GENRE of the great writers. Later, however, the strong writer will engage in a complicated act of MISREADING, which allows the writer to reduce or disorder the predecessor's work in order to create a new space for creativity. According to Bloom, the strong writer will go through six stages or enact six defenses, which allow the strong writer to "transume" the predecessor's work and influence, to render the predecessor less intimidating (Endo, 507). *Clinamen* is the initial misreading, in which the writer disorders the predecessor's vision. *Tessera* involves the writer's attempts to piece this fragmented vision back together. In *kenosis*, the writer isolates him- or herself from the predecessor's position. *Daemonisation* refers to the writer's substituting the writer's own vision of the sublime for the predecessor's. *Askesis* describes the writer's attempt to purge the predecessor by limiting the predecessor's influence rather than simply denying it. Finally, *apophrades* is the stage in which the writer reintroduces the predecessor as him- or herself. Although Bloom did not extend his theory back beyond Milton, it is presently an inclusive model of analysis for literature dating to biblical times. For example, Trible has argued that the Song of Songs was written in conversation with Gen. 2–3 to challenge the conventional relationship between men and women, and it does so by using some of the familiar language in Genesis in a subversive manner.

Bibliography. Harold Bloom, *The Anxiety of Influence: A Theory of Poetry* (Oxford: Oxford University Press, 1973); Paul Endo, "Anxiety of Influence," in *Encyclopedia of Contemporary Literary Theory* (ed. Irena R. Makaryk; Toronto: University of Toronto Press, 1993); Michael Payne, ed., *A Dictionary of Cultural and Critical Theory* (Cambridge, MA: Blackwell, 1996); Phyllis Trible, *God and the Rhetoric of Sexuality* (Philadelphia: Fortress, 1978).

APHORISM

A concise, pithy expression taken to communicate a general or observable TRUTH. Examples abound in both the NT and HEBREW BIBLE: "Where your treasure is, there your heart will be also" (Luke 12:34); "The love of money is a root of all kinds of evils" (1 Tim. 6:10); "Bad company ruins good morals" (1 Cor. 15:33); "Train children in the right way, and when old, they will not stray" (Prov. 22:6). Vernon Robbins makes a distinction between aphorism and PROVERB, suggesting that the latter is general, popular wisdom unrelated to a specific person or occasion, while the former can be identified with a specific person and occasion or can be identified with a person's corpus of wisdom (37). Hence, according to Robbins, most of the sayings of Jesus are probably aphoristic. In form, however, the two are practically indistinguishable.

For an excellent discussion of the aphorisms of the NT, see Crossan.

Bibliography. John Dominic Crossan, *In Fragments: The Aphorisms of Jesus* (San Francisco: Harper & Row, 1983); Vernon Robbins, "Picking Up the Fragments," *Foundations and Facets Forum* 1, no. 2 (1985): 31–64.

APOCALYPSE

A literary GENRE in both the HEBREW BIBLE and the NT. Portions of Ezekiel, Isaiah, Zechariah, and Daniel are APOCALYPTIC as well as the book of Revelation and portions of the GOSPELs. Although apocalypse is not a modern literary genre, it was a common type of writing in JUDAISM during the middle HELLENISTIC period (second century BCE–second century CE). Second Esdras (= *4 Ezra*), *Ethiopic Enoch*, and the *Syriac Apocalypse of Baruch* are the purest representatives of this genre outside the BIBLE.

There is, however, scholarly debate over both the origin and extent of apocalypse. Some scholars like John Collins question whether pre-Danielic literature is apocalyptic or pre-apocalyptic. Collins offers the following definition of apocalypse:

> An apocalypse is a genre of revelatory literature with a narrative framework, in which a revelation is mediated by an otherworldly being to a human recipient. It also recognizes a common core of content: an apocalypse *envisages eschatological salvation and involves a supernatural world.* Finally, there is, on a rather general level, a common function: *an apocalypse is intended to interpret present, earthly circumstances in light of the supernatural world and of the future, and to influence both the understanding and the behavior of the audience by means of divine authority.* (Collins, 283)

For Collins, this definition encompasses the Jewish texts normally classified as apocalypses: Daniel, *1–2 Enoch*, *2–3 Baruch*, *4 Ezra*, and *Apocalypse of Abraham*; plus works of mixed genres: *Jubilees* and *Testament of Abraham*. With respect to Christian writings, the definition allows for Revelation, *Shepherd of Hermas*, *Apocalypse of Peter*, as well as *Apocalypse of Adam* and *2 Apocalypse of James*, with some variations. While Jewish apocalypticism, a worldview within which apocalypses were produced, "first emerges clearly in the Hellenistic age" (Collins, 284), it did spring from several influences that, according to Collins, included the Canaanite and Mesopotamian interest in a heavenly council, the Chaldean interest in dreams and their interpretations (e.g., Daniel), Akkadian prophecy (indeed, Kirk Grayson believes that the origin of apocalyptic literature had its beginning here ["Akkadian 'Apocalyptic' Literature," 282]), and the Persian apocalyptic tradition (although the relationship between Jewish and Persian apocalypticism is debated; Collins, 284–86).

The scope of apocalypse is cosmic, having characters moving with ease between heaven, earth, and hell. Conflict involves angels and immense human armies pitted against the powers of the Deity. This conflict and ultimate victory by the Deity is most commonly a result of a small group's persecution and vindication. After this minority experiences a time of extreme, hyperbolized suffering, the Deity will eventually rescue them, replacing this present age with a utopian one.

Apocalyptic cosmology is dualistic. Working within the universe are an evil and a good force, almost equally matched. In the end, however, the good force triumphs over the evil. The PERSONIFICATION of this evil force is typical of apocalypse.

Apocalypse is generally, but not always (e.g., the *Shepherd of Hermas*), eschatological (*see* ESCHATOLOGY): its focus is on the end of history, the final stages of human existence. However, a discrete distinction should be maintained between eschatology and apocalypse. Eschatology is concerned exclusively with the doctrine of the end of the age; *apocalypse* refers to a revelation and a particular type of writing that discloses that revelation. In addition, apocalypse could be used to communicate a body of knowledge that has nothing to do with end-time concerns. In other words, the symbolism (*see* SYMBOL) of apocalypse might be used without its eschatological character.

The mode of presentation is usually an ecstatic vision, dream, or supernatural journey experienced by the author, who is normally a great person from Israel's history. This vision is filled with images (usually very concrete in nature) that incarnate meaning through symbolism and ALLEGORY. For example, in Dan. 8 the visionary observes a male goat with one horn, which breaks off and is replaced by four other horns. This is followed by the appearance of a small horn growing out of one of the previous four. This small horn then overthrows the other horns. When the vision is explained in 8:19–26, the goat represents the Greek kingdom, and its horn is the first Greek king, Alexander the Great. The horns represent the four kingdoms into which Alexander's kingdom is divided, and the little horn is the fiercest king from among these four kingdoms.

Apocalyptic literature is extremely symbolic. In fact, the basic literary form in apocalypse is symbolism. Accordingly, throughout apocalypse the author uses metaphoric images and events to point to something else. Christ, for example, is represented as a lamb or a lion in the book of Revelation.

John Collins suggests that the function of apocalypticism is to address a variety of crises: "support in the face of persecution (Daniel), reassurance in the face of culture shock (the Book of the Watchers [*1 En.* 1–36]) or social powerlessness (the Similitudes of Enoch [*1 En.* 37–71]), reorientation in the face of humanity (*4 Ezra*)" (Collins, 287). By diverting attention away from the problems of the present to "the heavenly world and the eschatological future," apocalypticism offers a means by which to cope with present existence and make it meaningful (Collins, 287). Just as there are a variety of crises to which apocalypticism responds, there may also be a variety of theologies at the core, such as the differences between the legalism of Qumran and the wisdom traditions behind *4 Ezra* and *2 Baruch* (Collins, 287).

Bibliography. John J. Collins, "Early Jewish Apocalypticism," *Anchor Bible Dictionary* (New York: Doubleday, 1992), 1:282–88; A. Kirk Grayson, "Akkadian 'Apocalyptic' Literature," in *Anchor Bible Dictionary* (New York; Doubleday, 1992), 1:282; W. Randolph Tate, *Biblical Interpretation: An Integrated Approach* (Peabody, MA: Hendrickson, 1991).

APOCALYPSE, THE

A name for the book of Revelation, the last book in the NT.

APOCALYPSE, THE LITTLE

Mark 13, consisting of a description of the destruction of Jerusalem and a prediction of the parousia of the Son of Man.

APOCALYPTIC

A term in BIBLICAL CRITICISM designating a type of ancient literature that employs highly symbolic language, usually but not always to predict the destruction of the world or ultimate destiny. *See* APOCALYPSE.

APOCALYPTIC ESCHATOLOGY. *See* ESCHATOLOGY

APOCALYPTIC LITERATURE. *See* APOCALYPSE

APOCATASTASIS

The view, based on a variety of biblical passages (e.g., Isa. 65:17; 1 Cor. 15:24–28; 2 Pet. 3:13; Rev. 21:1, 7), that there will be a final universal restoration of things, perhaps including universal salvation.

APOCRYPHA

Originally meaning "hidden or secret things" but coming to mean "spurious," Apocrypha refers to the books or parts of books from the INTERTESTA-MENTAL PERIOD not regarded as inspired within Judaism and thus excluded from the HEBREW CANON. The early church, however, considered the Apocrypha, which is included in the LXX, as SCRIPTURE. When Jerome (ca. 400) prepared the VULGATE, he followed the Hebrew canon rather than the LXX and grouped together the books that are in the LXX but not in the Hebrew canon and labeled them Apocrypha (Soulen and Soulen, 10). Generally referred to as Deuterocanonical today, the Apocrypha include Tobit, Judith, the Wisdom of Solomon, Ecclesiasticus (= the Wis-

dom of Jesus, Son of Sirach; or simply, Sirach), Baruch, the Epistle of Jeremiah (the latter two are additions to the book of Jeremiah), the Prayer of Azariah, the Song of the Three Young Men, Susanna, Bel and the Dragon (these last three are additions to the book of Daniel), 1–2 Maccabees, 1–2 Esdras, and the Prayer of Manasseh. (*See* DEUTEROCANON / DEUTEROCANONICAL BOOKS.)

Bibliography. Richard N. Soulen and R. Kendall Soulen, *Handbook of Biblical Criticism* (3rd ed.; Louisville: Westminster John Knox, 2001); William Harmon and C. Hugh Holman, *A Handbook to Literature* (8th ed.; Upper Saddle River, NJ: Prentice Hall, 1999).

APOCRYPHA, NEW TESTAMENT

Noncanonical Christian writings from the second to sixth centuries in the form of GOSPEL, epistle, history (*Acts of . . .*), and APOCALYPSE, relating stories and teaching of and about Jesus and the early APOSTLES. These works have been discovered at different times both by accident and by professional archaeologists (a good number of them included in the NAG HAMMADI LIBRARY), and some (e.g., the *Gospel of the Ebionites*) have been reconstructed from the quotes of early church fathers. While these works are historically unreliable, they do provide insight into the varieties of Christianity in the early centuries of the church. The NT Apocrypha include the following (Soulen and Soulen, 11–12):

Gospels: *Gospel of Thomas, Arabic Gospel of the Infancy, Assumption of the Virgin, Gospel of Bartholomew, Book of the Resurrection of Christ by Bartholomew the Apostle, Gospel of Basilides, Gospel of the Hebrews, Protevangelium of James, Gospel of Marcion, Gospel of the Birth of Mary, Gospel of Philip, Gospel of Pseudo-Matthew, History of Joseph the Carpenter, Cerinthus, Gospel of the Ebionites, Armenian Gospel of the Infancy*

Epistles: *Epistle of Christ and Abgar, 3 Corinthians, Epistle to the Laodiceans, Epistle to the Apostles, Epistle of Lentulus, Apocryphal Epistle of Titus, Epistles of Paul and Seneca*

Histories: *Apostolic History of Pseudo-Abdias, Acts of Andrew and Matthias, Acts of Andrew, Acts of*

Andrew and Paul, Acts of Barnabas, Ascents of James, Acts of John, Acts of James the Great, Acts of John (by Prochorus), *Acts of Paul, Martyrdom of Matthew, Acts of Peter, Martyrdom of Paul, Acts of Peter and Andrew, Acts of Peter and Paul, Acts of Philip, Acts of Thaddaeus, Acts of Thomas, Martyrdom of Peter and Paul, Acts of Pilate*

Apocalypses: *1–2 Apocalypse of James, Apocalypse of Peter, Apocalypse of the Virgin, Apocalypse of Paul, Apocalypse of Thomas, Revelation of Stephen*

An excellent treatment of some of these texts can be found in two works by Ehrman. For an English translation of the Nag Hammadi Library, see Robinson.

Bibliography. Bart Ehrman, *Lost Christianities* (Oxford: Oxford University Press, 2002); idem, *Lost Scriptures* (Oxford: Oxford University Press, 2002); William Harmon and C. Hugh Holman, *A Handbook to Literature* (8th ed.; Upper Saddle River, NJ: Prentice Hall, 1999); James M. Robinson, ed., *The Nag Hammadi Library* (rev. ed.; San Francisco: HarperCollins, 1990); Richard N. Soulen and R. Kendall Soulen, *Handbook of Biblical Criticism* (3rd ed.; Louisville: Westminster John Knox, 2001).

APOCRYPHON

The singular of APOCRYPHA.

APODICTIC

A term for an argument that is subject to demonstration and proof. *See* APODICTIC LAW.

APODICTIC LAW

A term used in FORM CRITICISM of the HEBREW BIBLE for unconditional LAW (e.g., the Ten Commandments [*see* DECALOGUE]; Exod. 21:15–17; Deut. 27:15–26). Some scholars have argued that apodictic law was unique to Jewish religious law and unlike the CASUISTIC LAW of Canaan. Other scholars, however, have suggested that apodictic law is unique neither to Israel nor to religious law.

APODOSIS

The main clause or conclusion in a conditional sentence. In the sentence "If an unbeliever invites you to a meal and you are disposed to go, eat whatever is set before you without raising any question on the ground of conscience" (1 Cor. 10:27), the conditional portion beginning with "if" is the PROTASIS, which sets the conditions under which the conclusion (the apodosis) may be realized.

APOLOGY

A defense of opinions, position, or conduct. In the NT, use of the Greek word *apologia* is frequent (e.g., Acts 25:8, 16; 1 Cor. 9:3; Phil. 1:16). It is generally accepted that Acts is an apology of the early church in that Paul and other APOSTLES are innocent missionaries and not revolutionaries. Johnson argues that Luke-Acts is actually a THEODICY, an apology of God himself. A rather unusual apology can be found in 2 Cor. 10–13, in which Paul defends himself by calling attention to his weaknesses and failures rather than to his accomplishments (Soulen and Soulen, 12).

Bibliography. Luke T. Johnson, *The Writings of the New Testament: An Interpretation* (Philadelphia: Fortress, 1988); Richard N. Soulen and R. Kendall Soulen, *Handbook of Biblical Criticism* (3rd ed.; Louisville: Westminster John Knox, 2001).

APOPHRADES. *See* ANXIETY OF INFLUENCE

APOPHTHEGM (APOTHEGM)

Technically, an extremely terse, concise, and witty saying, similar to an APHORISM or PROVERB, but more pointed. It is preceded by a PRONOUNCEMENT STORY, a brief EPISODE or event that precipitates a SAYING OF JESUS. It originates in an ANECDOTE about a well-known person and climaxes in a significant statement or declaration. The episode or event exists for the saying and not vice versa. One example is the saying "I have come to call not the righteous but sinners" (Mark 2:16–17; Matt. 9:10–13; Luke 5:29–32). The NARRATIVE setting is a meal at which Jesus is eating with tax gatherers and sinners. No details, such as time and place, are given about the meal. Such matters are irrelevant since the saying is the focal point; the meal serves only as a point of anchorage. The story may be nothing more than a pretext for the saying.

In FORM CRITICISM, the definition of apophthegm has been debated. Martin Dibelius distinguishes sayings having no SETTING from sayings set within a definite CONTEXT. The latter type Dibelius defines as CHREIAe, and since he feels that these developed out of the church's search for sermonic illustrations, he gives them the name PARADIGM. For Rudolf Bultmann, however, apophthegms are sayings of Jesus that have been given brief contexts. They are not historical utterances of Jesus, but creations of the very early church, intended to demonstrate ideas or conceptions that had their genesis in the historical Jesus (Soulen and Soulen, 12). These sayings, Bultmann contends, fall within two categories: conflict and didactic (e.g., Mark 3:22–30; 12:13–17), and biographical (e.g., Luke 9:57–62).

Bibliography. Richard N. Soulen and R. Kendall Soulen, *Handbook of Biblical Criticism* (3rd ed.; Louisville: Westminster John Knox, 2001); W. Randolph Tate, *Biblical Interpretation: An Integrated Approach* (rev. ed.; Peabody, MA: Hendrickson, 1997).

APORIA

In the strictest sense, a point of philosophical or argumentative impasse or indecision. For example, in Luke 16:3, the unjust steward illustrates such a point: "What will I do, now that my master is taking the position away from me? I am not strong enough to dig, and I am ashamed to beg" (see also Phil. 1:21–26).

Aporia is the heart of the Socratic method because only at that point does the person come to realize that the discovery of ignorance is the beginning of meaningful search for knowledge. For Aristotle, aporia is the positing of two equally valid but contrary arguments, the consideration of which leads to defining the problem more clearly and concisely, from which a more appropriate solution may be developed.

In recent CRITICISM, the concept refers to the point where the TEXT undermines or deconstructs (*see* DECONSTRUCTION) its own rhetorical STRUCTURE, to those unresolved conflicts and places where the text seems to contradict its own INTENTION (Odell-Scott, 55). Since Martin Heidegger's definition of being as "being-in-the-world," meaning that the human being is constituted in language, *aporia* has also come to refer to the undecidability that occurs when readers (whose world is constituted in language) confront a LITERARY object (*see* SUBJECT/OBJECT). At this point epistemology (how I know) is in tension with HERMENEUTICS (how I interpret). Such a definition of aporia requires that there always remain gaps of INDETERMINACY between readers and texts. It also means that at the heart of critical studies must be the idea that MEANING is always incomplete or at least indeterminate. Rather than leading to meaning, INTERPRETATION leads to more interpretation. Thus, in contemporary critical studies, aporia represents the need to formulate new questions with respect to the entire field of textual interpretation.

Bibliography. David W. Odell-Scott, "Deconstruction," in *Handbook of Postmodern Biblical Interpretation* (ed. A. K. M. Adam; St. Louis: Chalice, 2000), 55–61; Mario J. Valdés, "Aporia," in *Encyclopedia of Contemporary Literary Theory* (ed. Irena R. Makaryk; Toronto: University of Toronto Press, 1993), 507.

APOSTLE

From Greek meaning "one who is sent" to act on the authority of another person and generally refers to the earliest followers of Jesus. The term also designates an early Christian missionary (such as Paul and Barnabas) or, in the Eastern Orthodox Church, the seventy disciples of Jesus.

APOSTLES, THE TWELVE

The original twelve men whom Jesus chose to be his followers and coworkers (see Matt. 10:1–4; Mark 3:13–19; Luke 6:12–16). While Mark and Matthew have the same list, Luke's list differs in that rather than including Thaddaeus, he lists Judas, son of James.

APOSTOLIC FATHERS

A title for those Christian authors of the first and second centuries whose works did not become part of the NT CANON but were valued and circulated in the early church. Some of the early manuscripts of the NT included some of these works as canonical. Included in this group of texts are *1–2 Clement* (ca. 95 and 150 respectively), *Barnabas* (second century), the seven EPISTLES of Ignatius (ca. 115), *Diognetus* (late second or early third century), *Shepherd of Hermas* (ca. 145), *Didache* (late first or early second century), *Martyrdom of Polycarp* (second century), and Polycarp, *To the Philippians* (ca. 150). *See* CANON, NEW TESTAMENT.

Bibliography. Bart D. Ehrman, *The New Testament: A Historical Introduction to the Early Christian Writings* (3rd ed.; Oxford: Oxford University Press, 2004); Richard N. Soulen and R. Kendall Soulen, *Handbook of Biblical Criticism* (3rd ed.; Louisville: Westminster John Knox, 2001).

APOSTOLICON

A LECTIONARY that contains lessons from the EPISTLES. In lectionaries, Scriptures did not occur in canonical sequence, but in arrangements for reading in church services. A lectionary of GOSPEL readings is called an EVANGELISTARION. Apostolicons provide manuscript witnesses to the text of the NT (*see* TEXTUAL CRITICISM).

APOSTROPHE

An address—usually exclamatory—to an object (*see* SUBJECT/OBJECT) or person. The object or person addressed is sometimes, but not always, absent. As if thinking out loud, the speaker is addressing someone or something present in thought only (Mickelsen, 142). Jesus's LAMENT over Jerusalem is an apostrophe: "Jerusalem, Jerusalem, the city that kills the prophets and stones those who are sent to it! How often have I desired to gather your children together as a hen gathers her brood under her wings, and you were not willing!" (Matt. 23:37). A combination of PERSONIFICATION and apostrophe occurs in the liturgical Ps. 24: "Lift up your heads, O gates! And be lifted up, O ancient doors! That the King of glory may come in" (v. 7). As the ark of the COVENANT is brought to the house prepared for it on Mount Zion, the gates are personified and called upon (apostrophe) to open. In verse 8, the personified gates respond with "Who is the King of glory?" This type of fine line between personification and apostrophe is commonplace. The two forms are distinct in two ways. First, personification always ascribes to an inanimate object some human trait, while apostrophe may refer to a human being; and second, apostrophe will normally involve an exclamatory address, which is not necessarily the case in personification.

Bibliography. Berkeley A. Mickelsen, *Interpreting the Bible* (Grand Rapids: Eerdmans, 1963).

APOTHEGM. *See* APOPHTHEGM

ARAMAIC

A Semitic language of which texts are known from the ninth century BCE. Aramaic was originally the language of the Aramaeans but was later used in southwest Asia as a commercial and governmental lingua franca and adopted by many non-Aramaean people after the BABYLONIAN EXILE. Not only was it probably the language of Jesus, but some passages or terms in the HEBREW BIBLE and the NT are in Aramaic (Ezra 4:8–6:18; 7:12–26; Dan. 2:4b–7:28; Mark 5:41; 7:34).

ARCHAEOLOGY, BIBLICAL

The study of ancient cultures or past phases of cultures through the scientific investigation of excavated remains such as implements, artifacts, monuments, and inscriptions. Through the examination of the remains of those cultures related to the Hebrews and Greeks, biblical archaeologists try to reconstruct the characteristics of those cultures to better understand the biblical TEXTS. The underlying ASSUMPTION of biblical archaeology is that a culture's values and SYMBOLIC WORLD are reflected in its artifacts. Consequently, the more artifacts available for examination, the more an accurate portrait of a culture can be constructed.

ARCHAEOLOGY OF KNOWLEDGE

A form of ANALYSIS introduced by Foucault concerned with transformations in the field of knowledge and the relationships between knowledge or systems of knowledge and structures of power. This approach to the history of thought examines the ways in which statements are grouped into a science, a theory, or a TEXT (by "text" Foucault means anything that can be interpreted, not just a written document). In this type of analysis, a fundamental ASSUMPTION is that sciences, theories, epistemologies, WORLDVIEWS, doctrinal systems, and so forth are human constructs rather than reflections of universal realities. The archaeology of knowledge tries to expose the discursive practices (*see* DISCOURSE) by which societies construct these various systems and posit them as natural givens. With respect to BIBLICAL STUDIES, this form of analysis examines the discursive practices underlying the social, religious, and ideological systems reflected in the biblical texts and, by exposing them as human constructs, challenges their authoritative status.

Bibliography. Michel Foucault, *The Archaeology of Knowledge* (trans. A. M. Sheridan Smith; New York: Pantheon, 1972).

ARCHETYPAL CRITICISM

A criticism that focuses on the LITERARY CONVENTIONS of literature that cannot otherwise be attributed to historical or traditional influences. Underpinning this approach is the assumption that ARCHETYPEs present in all LITERARY expressions constitute the basis for studying literature. Archetypal critics are interested in explaining why some literary works perennially appeal to readers while others seem to be relegated to the literary dustbin.

The two major factors in the formation of archetypal criticism have been CULTURAL ANTHROPOLOGY and the psychological theories of Carl Jung. Since both areas give a special place to the function of MYTH, this approach is often referred to as MYTH CRITICISM. For the cultural anthropologist, myths constitute a symbolic representation of a people's hopes, aspirations, fears, and values. They represent the most fundamental and deepest instincts of human existence. Consequently, they are communal and collective in that they bind a people together in terms of psychological and spiritual

expressions. Archetypal CRITICs also assume that myth, as an expression of shared human experience, is found everywhere in human society. Yet myths do take their own specific cultural shapes depending on the cultural environments. But similar THEMES and MOTIFS appear among myths of different cultures. In other words, certain IMAGES recur among the myths of people who are separated by time and place. These images, themes, and motifs seem to come from extremely different cultures but generate similar responses. Such images, themes, and motifs are called archetypes (*see* ARCHETYPE). Such common images include light, blood, water, various colors, the circle, serpent, garden, certain numbers, desert, heroes, and seasons of the year.

Jungian psychology is the second major influence on archetypal criticism. According to Jung, beneath the personal unconscious posited by Freud, there exists a primeval, collective unconscious that is the psychic inheritance of all humans. Rather than being born with a tabula rasa, every human being inherits a "racial memory" that consists of a collection of psychic predispositions. Just like the body, the human mind is invested with forms of behavior that Jung calls "myth-forming" structures, the manifestations of which are motifs, "primordial images," or archetypes. Again, these archetypes are not identical to ideas or certain patterns of thought; instead, they are dispositions dictating that humans in various times and places will respond similarly to similar stimuli. So Jung differs from cultural anthropologists in defining archetypes as "inherited forms" (i.e., structures of the psyche itself) rather than as social forms handed down through generations via social practices, such as sacred rites. Jung relates archetype to myth by claiming that myths are the means by which the unconscious archetypes are made manifest to the conscious mind. But how does this idea relate to literature? The true artist, according to Jung, is the person who is in such possession of the "primordial vision" as to have the ability to employ these archetypal primordial images to communicate the experiences of the unconscious to the conscious in the form of art.

Three of Jung's most interesting archetypes are related to his idea of individuation, by which he refers to a person's psychological maturing. A maturing person comes to recognize those things, both good and bad, that make him or her an individual. While such individuation is extremely difficult, it is essential if a person is to become a well-balanced human being. *Persona*, the first of the archetypes associated with individuation, mediates between a person's ego and the external world. It is the actor's mask, which a person presents to the world. In other words, it is a person's social face, a personality that may be and often is different from the true self. The second archetype, the *anima*, is what Jung calls a person's "soul-image." It is a person's spirit or life force. Since Jung describes this *anima* in female terms when it relates to the male psyche, it is safe to say that the "anima-image" is projected on women. So the *anima* is the image of the opposite sex that a man holds in both his personal and collective unconscious. In a woman, this image is the *animus*. So although the psychological characteristics of the opposite sex are unconscious, the human psyche is bisexual. The *anima* or *animus* reveals itself usually in the projections on someone else or in dreams. Jung also claims that due to the *anima*, individuals are usually attracted to members of the opposite sex who tend to manifest the characteristics of their own inner selves. The third archetype is the shadow, which is the darker, more sinister side of our unconscious. It consists of those less desirable aspects of a person's personality, which one tends to suppress. The most common expression of this archetype is the devil, representing the most "dangerous aspect of the unrecognized dark half of the personality." In literature this archetype is seen in Iago, Satan, Mephistopheles, and Kurtz. Throughout literature, we can find projections of these archetypes in such characters as the hero, heroine, and the villain.

Many critics who ascribe significant value to literature have made use and still make use of the insights of both cultural anthropologists and Jungian psychology, arguing that archetypal myths are foundational to all literature, including biblical literature.

The best known among these scholars is Northrop Frye. While making use of the insights of both, Frye divorced archetypes from both anthropology and Jungian psychology. According to Frye, CRITICISM should not concern itself with the sources of myths, archetypes, the primordial vision, or with the manner in which these are or were transmitted. Regardless of how or why archetypes are in literature, they are there. Accepting this fact, criticism should use it as only one part of a more comprehensive critical approach to interpreting literature.

One implication of Frye's focus is that it diminishes the importance of the author's originality and INTENTION. The relative value of a TEXT depends not on originality or intention but on the images and themes—archetypes—it shares with other texts. In fact, a piece of literature can communicate only if both the AUTHOR and audience already share a SYMBOLIC WORLD. Consequently, archetypal criticism has an intertextual (*see* INTERTEXTUAL CRITICISM; INTERTEXTUALITY) concern: a work of literature is shaped by other literature. It takes its shape by imitating other literature. Obviously, in its focus on the archetypal structures, archetypal criticism adumbrates STRUCTURALISM, and in its claim that the author does not control the meaning of a text, it also anticipates READER-RESPONSE CRITICISM.

Archetypal criticism still has wide use in approaches that focus on GENRE and the intertextuality of literature. Many critics who seek to explain recurrent images and literary phenomena that somehow escape satisfactory historical analysis also employ archetypal criticism.

Bibliography. Martin Day, *The Many Meanings of Myth* (Lanham, MD: University Press of America, 1984); Northrop Frye, *Anatomy of Criticism: Four Essays* (Princeton: Princeton University Press, 1957); Carl Jung, *Collected Works* (20 vols.; London: Routledge & Kegan Paul, 1953–79); Alvin A. Lee, "Archetypal Criticism," in *Encyclopedia of Contemporary Literary Theory* (ed. Irena R. Makaryk; Toronto: University of Toronto Press, 1993), 3–5; Carol S. Rapprecht, "Archetypal Theory and Criticism," in *The Johns Hopkins Guide to Literary Theory and Criticism* (ed. Michael Groden and Martin Kreiswirth; Baltimore: Johns Hopkins University Press, 1994), 36–40; Leland Ryken, *The Literature of the Bible* (Grand Rapids: Zondervan, 1974);

Philip Wheelwright, *The Burning Fountain: A Study in the Language of Symbolism* (Bloomington: Indiana University Press, 1968).

ARCHETYPE

A term in LITERARY CRITICISM borrowed from the psychological theory of Carl Jung, who claims that behind each human's unconscious is a COLLECTIVE UNCONSCIOUS made up of shared "primordial images" and expressed in such things as MYTHS, dreams, fantasies, and literature. Literary critics now use the term for images, PLOT patterns, character types, or other details that repeatedly occur in literature. For instance, the THEME "from rags to riches," the character of the sassy servant in COMEDY, and the SYMBOL of the gathering storm—these are familiar to most readers. Since archetypes are symbols or IMAGES shared by all, their potential for communication is vast. When we encounter an archetype in literature, we are immediately faced with a body of MEANING that the AUTHOR does not need to explain. Archetypes such as the autumn of the year, the valley, the fox, the snake, birth, a smoothly flowing stream, a lamb, a rose, musical harmony, and the vulture communicate meaning without EXPLANATION. Phrases such as "Israel has played the harlot" or "tell that fox Herod" employ archetypes. These phrases need no explanation because the archetype, which is the master image, immediately suggests and organizes the meaning (Ryken, 22).

The BIBLE is the great storehouse of master images for literature in the Western world. An appreciation of literature outside the Bible is enhanced by a familiarity with the archetypes within the Bible. The primary reason for archetypal studies, however, is that the biblical texts themselves are saturated with these master images. *See* ARCHETYPAL CRITICISM.

Bibliography. Leland Ryken, *The Literature of the Bible* (Grand Rapids: Zondervan, 1974).

ARETALOGY

A NARRATIVE of the miraculous deeds of a god or hero. In LITERARY studies, it refers to a collection of miracle stories with a propagandistic motive or a biography of a religious hero or a *theios anēr* (divine man). In either case, the purpose of the aretalogy may be to elicit conversion to a person's teaching by offering evidence of the person's ability to perform supernatural acts. Some critics suggest that the GOSPELs belong to this GENRE.

ARGUMENT

In literary studies, a brief statement of a work's PLOT or MEANING. The term is used in NEW CRITICISM to refer to the THESIS or THEME of a literary work. The thesis or theme can usually be stated in terms of what a LITERARY work claims about a particular SUBJECT. For example, if the subject of the book of Jonah is divine grace versus divine justice, the argument (theme, thesis) would be a brief statement of the claim that the book makes about divine grace versus divine justice.

ARGUMENTATIO

A technical term in RHETORICAL ANALYSIS referring to the central part of an ARGUMENT, which sets forth the various proofs of the proposition being argued. *See* RHETORICAL CRITICISM.

ARGUMENTATION

One of the four primary types of DISCOURSE, the other three being EXPOSITION, NARRATION, and DESCRIPTION. Argumentation attempts to establish the TRUTH or falsity of a proposition. Many of the apostle Paul's writings are in the form of argumentation. *See* RHETORICAL CRITICISM.

ARGUMENT FROM SILENCE

A case made for a particular proposition on the basis that there is no direct evidence to the contrary. So, for instance, it can be argued that because the BIBLE does not make specific REFERENCE to instrumental music in worship settings, only a cappella singing should be permitted.

ARRANGEMENT

One of the fivefold divisions of classical rhetoric, arrangement is the selection and ordering of the individual parts into a persuasive whole. Also, the practice of AUTHORS' selecting from a number of possible events to include in their stories and then placing these events in some order. The arrangement of events according to some idea or purpose constitutes the PLOT of a STORY. Consequently, arrangement of events is a function of the author's purpose. In the literary study of the HEBREW BIBLE and the GOSPELS, scholars assume that the authors present events according to theological purposes. For example, some scholars suggest that Mark's GOSPEL is arranged in such a way as to answer the question "Who is Jesus?" Others argue that Mark is arranged in such a way as to compare two conflicting Christologies (see CHRISTOLOGY). See also REDACTION CRITICISM; SELECTION AND ARRANGEMENT.

ASIAN / ASIAN AMERICAN CRITICISM

An interpretive approach that focuses on the varied points of view, history, and TRADITIONS of Asians and Asian Americans. Generally, biblical interpretation by Asians within their own cultural and social contexts. Like feminist criticism (which includes French, Quebec, Anglo-American criticisms, WOMANIST THEOLOGY/CRITICISM, MUJERISTA THEOLOGY/CRITICISM, and those doing deconstructive CRITICISM (see DECONSTRUCTION), INTERTEXTUAL CRITICISM, NARRATIVE CRITICISM, PSYCHOANALYTIC CRITICISM, and RHETORICAL CRITICISM), Asian biblical criticism is difficult to define because of the religious, cultural, and racial diversity of its practitioners. For example, Asians from different cultures work within the HISTORICAL-CRITICAL METHOD, CULTURAL CRITICISM, POSTCOLONIAL CRITICISM, FEMINIST CRITICISM, and LIBERATION THEOLOGY.

This form of CRITICISM, like other types of criticism relating to non-Western culture, became more visible following World War II. Modern use and study of Asian criticism first developed out of Indology, which "from its eighteenth-century origins, focused primarily upon historical and literary subjects" (Rice, 505). Some of the key critics are C. S. Song, B. M. Ahn, and C. Moon

(Soulen and Soulen, 71). Although a broad definition of Asian criticism may be possible, it is difficult to define further for two reasons. First, the term *Asian* is itself challenging to define. *Asian* can include everyone in Asia, specific culture groups, or a specific group within a specific location. Second, Asian criticism is difficult to define because Asians perform a variety of criticisms. For example, Joo-sam Yang of Korea is known for his use of historical-critical criticism (70). Similarly, Kwok Pui-Lan from Hong Kong is well known for her use of feminist criticism (73). R. S. Sugirtharajah clearly describes the problem: there is not yet "a distinctive Asian mode of reading" ("Introduction," 251). Despite the many problems with Asian criticism and the lack of a specific description, there are some commonalities that unite many critics under this term. Asian criticism focuses on cultural hermeneutics, liberation perspectives, postcolonial interpretation, and the *wissenschaftliche* approach.

First, Asian critics focus on cultural hermeneutics or a text "in the context of [its] own cultures and native religious traditions" (Soulen and Soulen, 71). One aspect of the culture and religious tradition is plurality. For example, in Asian criticism "the biblical story is seen as one among many references in the search for truth" (Sugirtharajah, "Asian Readers," 65). For instance, C. S. Song took the idea of Jesus's death and resurrection and merged it with a Chinese folktale (see FOLKLORE) to create a new story called *Tears of Lady Meng* (Sugirtharajah, "Asian Readers," 59). In the past, many Asian people were displeased by the focus on one text as the sole source of revelation to humankind. This cultural approach to reading texts is a counterattack against a popular method that has been found to be "very inadequate in the multi-religious context of Asia. It ignores the existence of other sacred scriptures by which Asian people have been continuously nourished and nurtured and on which Asian spirituality and religiosity have been largely dependent" (Lee, 37). One of the goals of Asian criticism is to use folktales along with the BIBLE and other sacred texts to show how humans are connected (Sugirtharajah, "Asian Readers," 61). Asia is a large continent, marked by an array of various religions. There are many Hindus, Muslims, Buddhists, Christians, and others found throughout the Asian continent (Soulen and Soulen, 72). Sugirtharajah comments on the benefits of including many religions: "We can see iconic relationships in all sacred texts as a single continuum addressing issues which affect humanity, such as life, death, life after death, neighborliness, good conduct, suffering, happiness" ("Introduction," 258). However, Archie Lee recognizes more than just the multiplicity of religions present in Asia, goes on to stress multiplicity in other areas as well, and asks: "How could the Asian realities of plurality and diversity in races, peoples, cultures, social institutions, religions, ideologies, etc., not have any bearing on the way the text is to be read?" (36). Lee is not alone in his stance on this issue; many Asian critics attest the importance of recognizing the diversity found throughout numerous aspects of life in Asia.

Next, Asian criticism assumes a liberation perspective. Possibly, liberation theology is popular in Asian criticism because it is contextual and stems from the cultural hermeneutical approach. Many scholars who use cultural hermeneutical criticism are also interested in liberation perspectives (Soulen and Soulen, 72). There are three main liberation perspectives that Asian critics commonly use: minjung theology, dalit theology, and feminist hermeneutics.

First, liberation perspectives became especially popular among Asian critics in the 1970s, with the surfacing of the minjung theology. Basically, this theology was the "voice of Korean Christians in their struggle for democracy and human rights" (Soulen and Soulen, 72). Today, liberation theology is especially appealing to Asian scholars because many parts of Asia are still developing. Many people throughout Asia live in poverty and are exploited by their government.

Like minjung theology, dalit theology also deals with the oppressed people in a society. This theology became popular during the 1980s, about ten years after the emergence of minjung theology, and was a manifestation of liberation theology peculiar to India. *Dalit* refers to the people at the bottom of the Indian caste system. D. Carr suggests that the situation of the people at the bottom of the caste system in India was similar to that of the "despised Galileans, the exploited poor, the physically handicapped who were deemed cursed, the hated tax gatherers and the stigmatized women sex workers" (Soulen and Soulen, 73). Carr believes that God favored the oppressed in the Bible and therefore also favors the oppressed today, such as those at the bottom of the caste system (73).

Third, many Asian critics use feminist hermeneutics (*see* FEMINIST CRITICISM). Just as cultural hermeneutics and liberation perspectives are related, feminist hermeneutics is also interconnected with liberation perspectives. In fact, "feminism is an extension of liberationism" because liberation theology focuses on the inequality in the social and political sphere, while feminism focuses on the inequality between genders (Soulen and Soulen, 73). Two Asian critics who use feminist criticism are Kwok Pui-Lan, "foremost Asian feminist theologian," and A. Gnanadason of India (73). However, there are many other Asian critics who also use feminist criticism when examining a piece of literature.

In addition to the cultural hermeneutical approach and liberation perspectives, many Asian critics use postcolonial criticism. This type of criticism has only recently become popular among Asian critics. In fact, Asian critics have acknowledged postcolonial criticism only within the last ten years. However, the base used for much of this criticism is "Abdel-Malik's 'Orientalism in crisis' [*sic*] (1963) and Edward Said's more widely read *Orientalism* (1978)" (Rice, 505). Both of these works have been around for over forty years, but Asian critics have just recently begun referring back to them. Among the postcolonial Asian critics are feminist critics Kwok Pui-Lan and P. Chia. Kwok Pui-Lan wrote the well-known "Woman, Dogs, and Crumbs" (1995), which is an example of this type of criticism. Furthermore, P. Chia uses postcolonial criticism in his reading of the biblical story of Nebuchadnezzar and Daniel (1997). According to Chia, "The renaming of Daniel and his friends . . . is an act of colonization by Nebuchadnezzar that is countered by Daniel's resistance to the royal food, an act of rejecting the king's claim of colonial power over life and death" (Kuan, 74).

Last, Asian criticism often includes the *wissenschaftliche* approach. This approach is most popular among Asian biblical scholars with connection to the West. Essentially, this method is a historical-critical approach to reading a text that was established in the early twentieth century and continues to be widely accepted among Asian critics today. Joo-sam Yang was one of the early supporters of this approach. In fact, he is known for his work to familiarize fellow Korean scholars with the *wissenschaftliche*, or historical-critical, method. In 1970, C.-H. Kim used the *wissenschaftliche* approach to distinguish the differences between several NT EPISTLES and Hellenistic letters. More recently, in 1990, S. Widyapra-nawa used the *wissenschaftliche* approach to analyze Isaiah (Kuan, 70). Asian critics are still using this approach today and will likely continue to do so in the future.

To look at Asian criticism's place in BIBLICAL HERMENEUTICS, it is first necessary to refer back to the previously mentioned emphasis many Asians place on the importance of plurality. This emphasis has a substantial influence on the way in which Asian critics read the Bible. Sugirtharajah states, "One of the distinctive marks of Asian biblical interpretation is its effort to make sense in a continent which is replete with diverse religious texts" (*Hermeneutics*, 256). Because of the importance of plurality in the Asian culture, most Asian critics do not read or view the Bible as the only sacred or important text. For example, Archie Lee declares, "Many of our fellow Asians would feel offended to be told to throw away our cultural and religious resources in order to accept the biblical text" (37). In the past, Asian critics integrated and compared their Asian texts with the biblical text. However, there has been a recent move to view the Bible as just another story, instead of the text with which everything else is compared. Today, Asian criticism "questions the place of privilege accorded to the Bible" (Sugirtharajah, "Asian Readers," 65). Most Asian critics take this approach; they are not interested in viewing the Bible as the most important text. Asian critic Archie Lee writes, "Despite the missionary effort of the church in the past four centuries in Asia only 2 percent of the total population have become Christians" (37). Noticeably, Asian criticism does not view the Bible as an incomparable or holy text; instead, this type of criticism views the Bible as an ordinary text. R. S. Sugirtharajah believes, "The creative use Asian interpreters make of their own cultural heritage . . . indicates their respect for and pride in their religious and cultural inheritance" ("Asian Readers," 64). Kwok Pui-Lan believes "cultural borrowing may be tantamount to hermeneutical vandalism" (Sugirtharajah, *Hermeneutics*, 257). For many Asians, it would be very difficult to accept the Bible as the sole source of revelation and reject their folktales and literary traditions.

Asian criticism not only "questions the place of privilege accorded to the Bible" but also "reopens the question of the limitations of the closed Christian canon" (Sugirtharajah, "Asian Readers," 65). Therefore, Asian critics not only claim that the Bible is not the most important text; they also maintain that more texts should accompany the texts presently found in the Bible. Hyun Kyung Chung states, "The authentic memories of God's people were not completed two thousand years ago, and they cannot be imprisoned within the Christian canon. The text of God's revelation was, is and will be written in our bodies and our peoples' everyday struggle for survival and liberation" (111). Sugirtharajah explains that many Asian critics believe the idea of "there [being] no salvation outside the canonical text . . . is comparable to the outdated Roman Catholic soteriology that held that there is no salvation outside the Church" (Sugirtharajah, "Asian Readers," 66). Asian critics believe that many paths can be taken to reach salvation.

Asian criticism has "initiated a discussion about a society we live and dream for" (Sugirtharajah,

"Asian Readers," 66). Therefore, application of this principle can lead to a dialogue about society's past, current state, and future. Also, Asian criticism has "given a public profile to a people who have been largely ignored or neglected by mainline biblical scholarship" (62). Some of these groups are women, children, and the poor. Asian criticism enables people to look at issues from different perspectives. Asian critics "take the whole Bible's narrative as their own story in the making, sharply challenging our professional distance and lighter satisfactions" (Wire, 123).

Bibliography. Philip P. Chia, "On Naming the Subject: Postcolonial Reading of Daniel 1," *Jian Dao* 7 (1997): 17–36; Hyun Kyung Chung, *Struggle to Be the Sun Again: Introducing Asian Women's Theology* (New York: Orbis Books, 1990); John Hayes, ed., *Dictionary of Biblical Interpretation* (2 vols.; Nashville: Abingdon, 1999); J. Kuan, "Asian Biblical Interpretation," in *Dictionary of Biblical Interpretation* (ed. John H. Hayes; Nashville: Abingdon, 1999), 1:70–77; A. C. C. Lee, "Biblical Interpretation in Asian Perspective," *Asia Journal of Theology* 7 (1993): 35–39; Kwok Pui-Lan, "Woman, Dogs, and Crumbs," in *Discovering the Bible in the Non-biblical World* (Maryknoll, NY: Orbis Books, 1995), 71–83; James Rice, "South Asian Studies," in *A Dictionary of Cultural and Critical Theory* (ed. Michael Payne; Cambridge, MA: Blackwell, 1996), 505–7; R. Kendall Soulen and Richard R. Soulen, *Handbook of Biblical Criticism* (3rd ed.; Louisville: Westminster John Knox, 2001); Rasiah S. Sugirtharajah, *Asian Biblical Hermeneutics and Postcolonialism: Contesting the Interpretations* (Maryknoll, NY: Orbis Books, 1998); idem, "The Bible and Its Asian Readers," *Biblical Interpretation* 1 (1993): 54–66; idem, "Introduction and Some Thoughts on Asian Biblical Interpretation," *Biblical Interpretation* 1 (1993): 251–63; Antoinette Wire, "Chinese Biblical Interpretation since Mid-century," *Biblical Interpretation* 4 (1996): 101–23.

ASKESIS. *See* ANXIETY OF INFLUENCE

ASSIMILATION

In TEXTUAL CRITICISM, a term for an error in textual transmission in which the original passage is replaced with one from another source. For example, in the MT, 1 Sam. 12:15 reads, "The hand of Yahweh will be against you and your fathers." But the LXX has "and your king" rather than "and your fathers." Given that "fathers" occurs in verses 6–8, it was most likely assimilated into verse 15 of the MT.

ASSONANCE

The occurrence of the same or similar vowel sounds in stressed syllables ending with different consonants. For example, "pretend" and "begin" demonstrate assonance. RHYME differs from assonance in that rhyme requires similarity in both consonants and vowels, such as in "ring" and "sling." Assonance does occur in the biblical texts, but is mostly lost in TRANSLATIONS. In Exod. 15:12–13, the verbs (*nāṭîtā, nāḥîtā, nēhalta*) involve rhyme and assonance, which are lost in translation (Alter, 53). A NT example is the HYMN in 1 Tim. 3:16, in which the first word in each line has the same final sound:

> *Ephanerōthē en sarki,*
> *Edikaiōthē en pneumati,*
> *Ōphthē angelois,*
> *Ekērychthē en ethnesin,*
> *Episteuthē en kosmō,*
> *Anelēmphthē en doxē.*

Bibliography. Robert Alter, *The Art of Biblical Poetry* (New York: Basic Books, 1985).

ASSUMPTION

Commonly, (1) something taken for granted; a notion presumed to be true. In LITERARY studies, CRITICS claim that writers and readers have an entire body of assumptions through which their experiences are filtered and that condition the way AUTHORS write and the way readers interpret. *See* PRESUPPOSITION. (2) In theological studies, *assumption* also refers to the physical or bodily ascent of a person to heaven (e.g., Enoch in Gen. 5:24, Elijah in 2 Kings 2:11, and Jesus in Luke 24:51 and Acts 1:9–10) (McKim, 19).

Bibliography. Donald K. McKim, *Westminster Dictionary of Theological Terms* (Louisville: Westminster John Knox, 1996).

ASYNDETON

In rhetorical studies, a term for a STYLE of expression that omits conjunctions or particles between words or sentences normally containing them. Asyndeton is frequent in both the GOSPELS of Mark and of John. If, as most scholars assume, Matthew used Mark as one of his sources, then he frequently "corrects" Mark by supplying conjunctives.

ATMOSPHERE

The MOOD or feeling pervading a literary work. The atmosphere is created by the AUTHOR's manipulation of SETTING, CHARACTERIZATION, STYLE, and PLOT and is partly responsible for creating the reader's expectations and attitudes toward the STORY. For example, in 2 Sam. 1, when David hears the news of Jonathan's death, the setting and style (esp. in terms of DIALOGUE) create an atmosphere of grief. The entire David SAGA in 1–2 Samuel creates and sustains an atmosphere of intrigue.

ATOMISTIC EXEGESIS

The practice of interpreting isolated biblical passages with no attention to their contexts. This type of EXEGESIS is typical of typological and allegorical interpretation as exemplified in premodern biblical interpretation among the early church fathers. For example, Irenaeus interprets Moses's stretching out his arms in a battle with the Amalekites in order to secure a victory from YAHWEH (Exod. 17:11–12) as representing Jesus's stretching out his hands on the cross in order to secure victory for humans.

Bibliography. Anthony Thiselton, *New Horizons in Hermeneutics* (Grand Rapids: Zondervan, 1992).

AUDIENCE-CENTERED INTERPRETATION

INTERPRETATION that examines the role of the reading audience in the formulation of MEANING. Audience-centered critics ask significant questions about the locus of meaning: Why do we value some texts above others? Why do we continue to read and value texts even if the originating circumstances are irretrievable? Is it really legitimate to talk about meaning apart from a consideration of what happens when we read? What does happen when we read? Why do we respond to certain texts in certain ways? In various ways and degrees, audience-centered theories of interpretation try to answer these and similar questions as they pertain to the dynamic interaction between TEXT and reader, an interaction with a resultant reader response.

Audience-centered critics constitute a multifarious group. Along a continuum between text and reader, these critics may be placed according to the relative role that each CRITIC ascribes to the text or reader in the determination of meaning. They range from those who find the source of meaning in DIALOGUE between the enabling structures of the text and the creative activities of the reader, to those who find it in the role of the INTERPRETIVE COMMUNITY, to those who find it in examination of the individual responses of readers. *See* READER-RESPONSE CRITICISM.

Bibliography. Donald Keesey, ed., *Contexts for Criticism* (3rd ed.; Mountain View, CA: Mayfield, 1998).

AUDIENCE-ORIENTED INTERPRETATION

A group of interpretive methods that locate the MEANING of a TEXT in its audience. These methods assume that although texts were written at particular times, they continue to exist long after their authors have died and the causes of writing have vanished. Audience-oriented critics care little about AUTHORs and their intentions mainly because they recognize that texts exist independently of authors and are valued independently of their originating circumstances. Central to this group of methods is the assumption that readers respond to texts before they examine their causes and originating circumstances. Meaning is the function of the readers' responses to the text, the interaction between the audience and the work. In other words, a text can mean absolutely nothing until some reader assigns meaning to it in response. The study of readers' multiple responses is the main business of the audience-oriented CRITIC. Since different readers react in significantly different ways to the same texts—some superficially, some profoundly, some discovering chaos, some unity—the context and activities of readers must be studied as at least one constitutive element of meaning. *See* READER-RESPONSE CRITICISM.

AURA

A term introduced by Walter Benjamin, a Marxist critic, to describe the subjective experience of a work of art and the formal features of the work and the circumstances of production and exhibition that contribute to the experience. Benjamin also employs the term to describe the value attributed to the work of art due to its rarity, its history, or the conditions of its exhibition (Ross, 509). Consequently, the experience generates responses based on such things as ritual, tradition, and religion, which in turn generate a certain authority ascribed to the work, resulting in its canonization. Benjamin thinks, however, that in the modern industrial world, such a work of art loses its aura, its authority, because the modern world vitiates the possibility of any communities in the traditional sense.

Bibliography. Trevor Ross, "Aura," in *Encyclopedia of Contemporary Literary Theory* (ed. Irena R. Makaryk; Toronto: University of Toronto Press, 1993), 508–9.

AUTHENTICITY. *See* CRITERIA OF AUTHENTICITY

AUTHOR

In traditional BIBLICAL HERMENEUTICS, the idea of "author" has been determined by the classical theory of TEXTUALITY, which has viewed the author as the creator of a language object (*see* SUBJECT/OBJECT) that expresses the author's ideas (Thiselton, 55–57). In other words, the TEXT exists because of and mediates the author's INTENTION. Authorial context and intention are inseparable from what the text means. A text linguistically communicates an author's intention, which the reader may recognize. With the advent of NEW CRITICISM, however, critics began to insist on the AUTONOMY of the literary object and to argue that texts should be interpreted independently of authorial intentions. Legitimate interpretations of texts were independent of REFERENCES to authors' intentions. Then in 1981, Ricoeur argued that the act of writing guarantees the autonomy of the text relative to the author's intention, and thus the MEANING of a text does not necessarily coincide with what the author

intended. Recently, several POSTMODERN critics have questioned the concept of "author." Roland Barthes proclaims the DEATH OF [the] AUTHOR and sees the text as a "network" of relations that cannot be reduced to a single meaning but that encourage a plurality of meaning. Michel Foucault defines the author as a function, a historical and discursive construct (*see* DISCOURSE; DISCOURSE ANALYSIS). Both Jacques Derrida and Stanley Fish remind readers of the necessity of realizing that when reading a text, they must assume that they are interpreting an object created by an intentional being. However, readers are under no obligation to such intention, primarily because recognizing intention with respect to texts does not entail that such intention is inscribed in the text or that it can ever be reconstructed by readers (Adam, 11–12). In contemporary biblical hermeneutics, therefore, the shift has been away from AUTHORIAL INTENTION (as well as biographical and historical matters) to the impact of texts on readers and the role that readers play in creating meaning.

Bibliography. A. K. M. Adam, ed., *Handbook of Post-modern Biblical Interpretation* (St. Louis: Chalice, 2000); Stephen Heath, "Author, Death of," in *A Dictionary of Cultural and Critical Theory* (ed. Michael Payne; Cambridge, MA: Blackwell, 1996), 38; Paul Ricoeur, *Hermeneutics and the Human Sciences* (Cambridge: Cambridge University Press, 1981); Anthony C. Thiselton, *New Horizons in Hermeneutics* (Grand Rapids: Zondervan, 1992).

AUTHOR-CENTERED INTERPRETATION

INTERPRETATION that looks for MEANING in terms of the social, political, cultural, and ideological matrix of the AUTHOR. Methods that center on the author assume that every literary TEXT is created by a communicating mind. The author seeks to communicate meaning to an audience. "Every utterance is an attempt to express something—an idea, a feeling, a set of facts—and is successful to the extent that it communicates what it set out to communicate. A poem, then, would be good if it achieved what its author intended" (Keesey, 15). In author-centered interpretation, the meaning of the text must be related to the mind that created it. If the author creates a text, then interpretation

For the Christian, this is where truth is found.

35

should concern itself with the relationship between the author and the text. The text is the effect, the author the cause.

Author-centered interpretation seeks to ascertain as much as possible about the mind and world of the author in order to determine what that mind communicates through the text. The better the interpreters understand the author's creative mind, the better they will understand the creation of that mind.

Getting into the author's mind, however, is not easy. This holds especially true for ancient authors. If there is anything known at all about an ancient author, it is usually minimal. When the interpreter has other writings by the same author, these are examined to determine as much as possible about the author. In a sense, the author-centered CRITIC seeks to create a profile of the author. In addition to examining other writings by the same author, author-centered critics also try to find out about the author's world. Their ASSUMPTION is that if an author is the product of his or her world, the author's literary creation will reflect that world. The elements within the author's social, political, religious, and intellectual milieu are constitutive of the author's intended meaning. Therefore, understanding the author's world makes for a fuller understanding of the text.

Another important assumption of author-centered interpretation is that history is periodic: history can be divided into periods having relatively unique presumptions, values, beliefs. This assumption permits the study of texts under headings such as "Renaissance," "Medieval," "Romantic," "Neoclassical," or "Elizabethan." The best-equipped interpreter is knowledgeable of the assumptions, values, and beliefs characteristic of each period. Consequently, author-centered interpretation has a historical focus. The historical focus supplies a check against overly anachronistic interpretations.

Bibliography. Donald Keesey, ed., *Contexts for Criticism* (3rd ed.; Mountain View, CA: Mayfield, 1998).

AUTHOR, DEATH OF. *See* DEATH OF AUTHOR

AUTHORIAL INTENTION. *See* INTENTION

AUTHORIZED VERSION. *See* KING JAMES VERSION

AUTOBIOGRAPHICAL LITERARY CRITICISM

Also known as personal criticism and, in the area of BIBLICAL CRITICISM, autobibliocriticism, it is "an autobiographical moment [that] is made central to the activity of criticism, thus both foregrounding the identity of the critic and reconceptualizing the nature of the criticism itself" (Baker, 3). Autobiographical criticism encourages critics to include their personal experiences in their readings of literary texts. Its method of persuasion is to call on other readers to "believe this, because it happened to me" (3). Although this form of criticism is increasing in use, autobiography itself is a fairly recent invention. It was not until the 1980s that theoretical studies of autobiography were done, which is due to the rise of FEMINIST CRITICISM and "to the textualized, disappearing self of poststructuralist persona" (Staley, "Autobiography," 14). In the 1960s, Roy Paschal, a key figure in the study of the GENRE of autobiography, did a study concluding that autobiography "involves the reconstruction of the movement of a life, or part of a life, in the actual circumstances in which it was lived and is an interplay, a collusion between past and present" (quoted in Staley, 14). This suggests that autobiography is more about experience in the present than in the past.

It was not long after autobiography became established as a genre that autobiographical criticism arose. In the early 1990s, Jane Tompkins in "Me and My Shadow" and Nancy K. Miller in *Getting Personal* pioneered this form of criticism. A few of the other critics in this genre are Nicole Jouve, Linda Kaufman, Diane Freedman, Olivia Frey, and Francis Murphy Zauhar. While these critics differ in many aspects, they agree on the key concepts of autobiographical criticism.

The first key concept is the focus on the critic's life, which must be considered in order to understand the diversity of interpretations that arises in this criticism. All critics have a different BACK-

GROUND that influences their perception of the TEXT. These identity markers include race, ethnicity, geography, class, religion, GENDER, age, education, physical characteristics, marital status, and employment status. Besides identity markers, the "plurality and multi-dimensionality of the self, the personal plurals, play a key role, as well as the notion of a fluid, shifting nature of the self" (Kitzberger, 6). One critic/reader will emphasize a certain aspect of the text while another will downplay that aspect. The resulting readings will differ greatly because of the critics' differing backgrounds. Thus, for autobiographical criticism to be taken seriously, it must entail an "outspoken involvement on the part of the critic with the subject matter" (Caws, 2). It requires personal self-exploration, self-reflection, and self-analysis.

Steven Mailloux, however, points out three main dangers due to the explicit self-reflective nature of autobiographical criticism. One danger is that it will consider the "self-critique as self-display," so that instead of readers noticing the critique, they will think of it as a way for the critic to boast about him- or herself (quoted in Anderson and Staley, 14). A second danger is that its writing style will undermine its persuasiveness, causing the effectiveness of the INTERPRETATION to decrease. The final problem is a question of consequences: how will writing in a way in which "anything goes" affect the legitimacy of the criticism? Considering these dangers allows the critics to ask themselves, "How [do] we take responsibility for our interpretations, and how [do] we make judgments about the value of various interpretations?" (Anderson and Staley, 15). The answers to these questions became a second key component in autobiographical criticism.

This key component is the implication of choosing one interpretation over other possible and legitimate ones. "Critical studies involve acknowledging that the process of interpretation is nothing but a string of choices and making explicit the ways in which these decisions were made" (Patte, 21). This includes "taking over responsibility for one's interpretations, one's knowledge about the meaning of that text and entering into dialogue with others who have chosen other interpretations" (Kitzberger, 5). It is essential that CRITICS take on the responsibility and ownership for their interpretations. By recognizing the positive role of the interpreter's personal voice, one can see that interpreters choose among equally legitimate and plausible interpretations (Patte, 22). The key responsibility of a person who is interpreting a text is for that individual to recognize, to be fully cognizant of, how he or she came to view their own understandings of the important aspects of the text over against how another interpreter has understood the important aspects of the same text. This internal dialogue should occur not only between two interpreters but also between two interpretations by the same critic. The openness to the personal voice in autobiographical criticism can cause an interpreter's critique to change with each rereading because of the new experiences brought to the table. Patte explains it by saying, "I can only read with my personal voice of the moment" (21). In other words, each time a critic/reader reads the text, their personal voice picks a different aspect to focus on. Consequently, the choice of one interpretation over another, whether between two critics or two interpretations by the same critic, is completely subjective and must be determined by the individual.

The third key aspect of autobiographical criticism deals with the personal voice of the critic/reader. The increased self-awareness of autobiographical critics leads to their most private disclosure, the personal voice. Autobiographical criticism is the most personal and intimate variant of the personal voice (Kitzberger, 5). The personal voice is characterized by a certain pattern of relationships with others and is explained by clarifying for whom the interpretation is performed. It involves acknowledging that the interpretations are as constructed, partial, and selective as the personal voice is tentative, changing, and fleeting. The personal voice contributes to the shape of the critic's interpretations and allows it to play a positive and constructive role in interpretation (Patte, 13, 15, 21). Therefore, the critic's personal voice is essential to autobiographical criticism. Expressing one's personal voice is not easy, however, because of the intimacy involved. "To write about how our personal lives, economic situations, and prejudices affect our interpretation . . . is to reveal the tenuousness and interested nature of our exegetical moves" (Anderson and Staley, 12).

In autobiographical criticism, not only is the critic's identity important, but so is "the question of identity in the interaction between AUTHOR and reader," which is usually referred to as the autobiographical pact. "The 'autobiographical pact' is thus a 'referential pact' [referring to the critic's real life] and the autobiographical genre a 'contractual genre' in which the identity of name between author, narrator and protagonist is guaranteed." The pact claims to be referential even though Kitzberger believes an awareness exists that, to a degree, everything that represents oneself is at the same time "fictional and constructed" (Kitzberger, 7). This realization that the critic is sharing his or her identity allows the reader to trust that what is written actually refers to the critic's real self. However, Mary Ann Caws looks at it from the perspective of there being "a certain intensity in the lending of oneself to the act of writing, but argues that this 'participation in the subject seen and written about doesn't necessarily require autobiographical self-representation'" (2). In other words, even though autobiographical critics write about aspects of their lives, readers cannot be certain that what is written really represents the critics. Thus the emphasis is placed on the "individual, contemporary reader-critic's responses to texts" (Staley, "Autobiography," 18). The critic's sharing his or her experiences results in the reader's acknowledging and responding to the critic's interpretation, which develops the mutual agreement of the critic and reader. In other words, referring to the relationship between readers and critics, Kitzberger (7–8) writes of readers, "You can more or less trust us that what we chose to reveal about ourselves in the course of our readings and critical interpretations refers to our real selves, even if they remain, as they have to, constructs. On the other hand, since autobiography 'is a mode of read-

ing as much as it is a type of writing,' we trust that a new type of reading and consequently a new type of criticism will be engendered by our readings."

Another issue in autobiographical criticism is the mode of interpretive expression. By "mode" is meant the form in which an interpretation is conveyed. According to Olivia Frey, traditional academic interpretations assume a predictable form, which she characterizes as adversarial. After reading every essay published in *PMLA* from 1975 to 1988 "as well as in a scattering of other journals and literary magazines, such as *Signs, Critical Inquiry, College English*, and the *New York Review of Books*," she found only two essays that did not employ the adversarial method of argumentation (47). In describing this method, Frey characterizes it as reflecting the critic's sarcasm and condescending attitude. The goal of this method is "to establish cognitive authority not only by demonstrating the value of one's own idea but also by demonstrating the weakness or error in the ideas of others. At the heart of the literary critical enterprise seems to be competition, not cooperation" (48). Further, according to Frey, most of the signals that young scholars receive from their profession "indicate that this is our business—to refute, repudiate, or attack" (48). Consequently, any criticism of texts that is driven by the adversarial method always "treats literature as problems to be solved, and critics will frequently go to great lengths to solve them, sometimes at the expense of knowledge and understanding" (60). In addition, "we direct all of our creative efforts toward protecting ourselves and defending our theories" (60). Within this framework, creative thinking suffers. To counter this adversarial method, Frey calls for a "relational ethic" in which essays about literature should be "personal, revelatory, nonadversarial. They are nonhierarchal and mixed-genre, often validating a variety of voices—the critic's, her students', other critics' voices" (58). Frey further argues that literary critical activity is and should be intensely personal, motivated by the desire to "connect with someone else in a meaningful way" (53). Literary criticism, which is reading and writing about literature, should be forms of creation and should be expressed in a variety of forms other than the philosophical, persuasive essay (e.g., by HYMN, POETRY, letter, journal, diary). This language of expression should be "accessible, concrete, and real" and absolutely one's personal voice.

But this paradigm shift from the adversarial to the relational mode of critical activity is difficult. Thus Jane Tompkins observes:

> The problem is that you can't talk about your private life in the course of doing your professional work. You have to pretend that epistemology, or whatever you're writing about, has nothing to do with your life, that it's more exalted, more important, because it (supposedly) *transcends* the merely personal. Well, I'm tired of the conventions that keep discussion of epistemology, or James Joyce, segregated from meditations on what is happening outside my window or inside my heart. The public-private dichotomy, which is to say, the public-private *hierarchy*, is a founding condition of female oppression [*sic*] I say to hell with it. The reason I feel embarrassed at my own attempts to speak personally in a professional context is that I have been conditioned to feel that way. That's all there is to it. (25)

Peter Carlton describes his multiple readings of Eliot's *Middlemarch*, the ever-changing self that he brings to the text, and the way the self changes after each subsequent reading. The personal self shapes the reading and the reading reshapes the personal self:

> Since I have reread the same copy of the novel every time, and since I keep writing myself into the novel in my copious underlinings and marginalia, each rereading is both a new self-inscription and a rereading of previously inscribed versions of myself, more or less continuous with the self I currently know myself to be. The process keeps becoming more emotionally charged. One whole set of comments reveals to me the time I read myself into Fred Vincy and my fiancée into Mary Garth, hoping to find in their happy marriage the prefiguring of our own; and as I reread the novel this time, on the far side of that relationship, the poignancy of identifying

with Dorothea identifying with Aunt Julia took on an extra intensity because of the marginal afterlife of this earlier self, now ten years old but made present again in the inscriptions he left behind. (239)

In examining the manner in which women readers have connected themselves to the things they read, Frances Murphy Zauhar claims to have found numerous instances of "works of literary criticism that incorporate readings of the literary text with articulations of the reader's self. By any definition, these readings are 'good,' 'close,' 'strong' *because* they are coupled inextricably with the reader's personal response" (115–16). This ability to relate the real and personal selves to the literary experience is at the heart of autobiographical literary criticism. According to Zauhar, "It is important to acknowledge that the personal functions [*sic*] in the work of all of these writers is *to create criticism*. These essays demonstrate that reading the self through the text, reading the text through the self, is significant. Such reading and writing enrich the reader, her own reading and that of the others who read her work." As Judith Fetterley figures this relationship, in the spirit of feeding, each writer offers and shares her "feast of words" (Zauhar, 116).

A final key aspect of autobiographical criticism has to do with STRUCTURE. Fernando Segovia argues that "structure should not be seen as residing in the text itself . . . but rather in the interchange between the text and reader, or that structure should not be approached as fixed and stable but rather as variable and dependent on readers" (28). The focus on a universal reader gave way to a concern for the real reader, which resulted in the understanding that real readers can be approached only in terms of "the manifold and highly complex dimensions of human identity" (30). Segovia claims that this realization allowed critics to recognize that an objective and impartial reader does not exist, so interpretation is always contextual and ideological (31). When readers interpret, these contextual and ideological factors are brought to the text, resulting in diverse reactions. In this way, a reader becomes "a text himself and the interpretation of any given text thus involves two texts, the target text and the interpreter as second text" (Voelz, 159). It is in the space between these two texts that meaning resides, a meaning that is always only virtual, because the reader structures the text based on the reader's own person.

In the last two decades, autobiographical criticism has found such a home in BIBLICAL STUDIES that there is hardly a distinction between autobiographical criticism and autobibliocriticism (the name that Staley gives to biblical autobiographical criticism). According to Staley, "autobiographical interests have found their way into biblical studies as scholars have begun to think and write about the social and ideological constraints that have formed them as real readers of the Bible" ("Autobiography," 14). According to Kitzberger, on November 19, 2000, the American Academy of Religion and Society of Biblical Literature's annual meeting took place in Nashville's Opryland Hotel "to bring real life back to Scripture and Scripture back to life, to experiment within the open space between text and self" (1). The members who attended the annual meeting in 2000 participated in and contributed to a revolution occurring on a much greater scale in the humanities and sciences. Focus shifted from an objective paradigm to an explicitly subjective paradigm, which continues to break new ground where the objective paradigm prevails. According to Kitzberger (5), "autobiographical biblical criticism implies the choice of one interpretation over other possible and legitimate ones. Taking over responsibility for one's interpretations, one's knowledge about the meaning of a text, and entering into dialogue with others who have chosen other interpretations[—all this] is thus a truly ethical practice." Literary critics have developed this technique to further their understanding of the Scriptures. A goal of autobibliocriticism is "to raise personal voices in biblical studies precisely so that we all might be more aware of how we can bring crucial understanding to bear upon the ordinariness of all our readings" (Staley, "What Is Critical?," 19). Furthermore, the acknowledgment of the personal voice in interpretations should not undermine in any way the authority the Scriptures

possess (Patte, 17). Instead, it should complement the study of the Bible and further people's understanding. Mark Brett sets forth five reasons for inserting the personal voice into biblical interpretation: (1) showing how one's life can be configured by a biblical narrative; (2) using one's life story to form a hypothesis about literary structure; (3) exploring the ways in which personal experience might lead us to formulate questions and methods of research; (4) describing how a change in political commitments provoked the rereading of a particular text; and (5) evaluating the norms expressed through biblical texts (117–18).

When these reasons are considered, the personal voice becomes a tool that allows critics to feel free to contemplate the relationship between the biblical text and personal experience. It also points the way to a self-reflective and contextualized biblical criticism (Anderson and Staley, 11, 16).

Since most biblical interpretation is about the primary text, readers inevitably reconstruct the text out of the materials of their own identities and interpretative traditions (Brett, 114). For example, Mikeal Parsons offers autobiographical reflections on Luke 15. In his essay, he focuses on the homecoming aspect of the Prodigal Son PARABLE as well as his own homecoming STORY. He tells of the time in his life when he was figuratively eating with the pigs and how he came out of this to reunite with his father after many years of bitterness. Below is an excerpt:

> I thought of my own life, how this wound of my father was . . . a part of his legacy to me. And, I realized how my own sense of inadequacy as a man had helped sign the death warrant on several significant relationships. I got a piece of myself back that day that made me a little more whole. The Prodigal Father and the Wandering Son wept and embraced each other. And rejoicing in that which was lost and was now found, they made their way, hand in hand, back home. (137)

Bibliography. Janice Anderson and Jeffery Staley, "Taking It Personally: Introduction," *Semeia* 72 (1995): 7–16; Steve Baker, "Flying, Stealing: Design's Improper Criticism," *Design Issues* 13 (Summer 1997): 1–9; Mark G. Brett, "Self-Criticism, Cretan Liars, and the Sly Redactors of Genesis," in *Autobiographical Biblical Criticism* (ed. Ingrid Rosa Kitzberger; Leiden: Deo Publishing, 2002), 114–32; Peter Carlton, "Rereading *Middlemarch*, Rereading Myself," in *The Intimate Critique: Autobiographical Literary Criticism* (ed. Diane P. Freedman, Olivia Frey, and Frances Murphy Zauhar; Durham: Duke University Press, 1993), 237–44; Mary Ann Caws, *Women of Bloomsbury: Virginia, Vanessa, and Carrington* (London: Routledge, 1990); Diane P. Freedman, Olivia Frey, and Frances Murphy Zauhar, eds. *The Intimate Critique: Autobiographical Literary Criticism* (Durham: Duke University Press, 1993); Olivia Frey, "Beyond Literary Darwinism: Women's Voices and Critical Discourse," in *The Intimate Critique: Autobiographical Literary Criticism* (ed. Diane P. Freedman, Olivia Frey, and Frances Murphy Zauhar; Durham: Duke University Press, 1993), 41–65; Nicole Jouve, *White Woman Speaks with Forked Tongue: Criticism as Autobiography* (London: Routledge, 1991); Linda S. Kaufman, "The Long Goodbye: Against Personal Testimony, or an Infant Grifter Grows Up," in *American Feminist Thought at Century's End* (ed. Linda S. Kaufman; Cambridge, MA: Blackwell, 1993), 258–77; Ingrid Rosa Kitzberger, "Pre-liminaries," in *Autobiographical Biblical Criticism* (Leiden: Deo Publishing, 2002), 1–11; Nancy K. Miller, *Getting Personal: Feminist Occasions and Other Autobiographical Acts* (London: Routledge, 1991); Ross Murfin and Supryia M. Ray, "Personal Criticism," in *The Bedford Glossary of Critical and Literary Terms* (New York: St. Martin's Press, 2003), 339; Mikeal C. Parsons, "Hand in Hand: Autobiographical Reflections on Luke 15," *Semeia* 72 (1995): 125–52; Daniel Patte, "The Guarded Personal Voice of a Male European American Biblical Scholar," in *Personal Voice in Biblical Interpretation* (ed. Ingrid Rosa Kitzberger; New York: Routledge, 1999), 12–24; Fernando F. Segovia, "My Personal Voice: The Making of a Postcolonial Critic," in *Personal Voice in Biblical Interpretation* (ed. Ingrid Rosa Kitzberger; New York: Routledge, 1999), 23–37; Jeffery L. Staley, "Autobiography," in *Handbook of Postmodern Biblical Interpretation* (ed. A. K. M. Adam; St. Louis: Chalice, 2000), 14–19; idem, "What Is Critical about Autobiographical Biblical Criticism?," in *Autobiographical Biblical Criticism* (ed. Ingrid Rosa Kitzberger; Leiden: Deo Publishing, 2002), 12–33; Jane Tompkins, "Me and My Shadow," in *The Intimate Critique: Autobiographical Literary Criticism* (ed. Diane P. Freedman, Olivia Frey, and Frances Murphy Zauhar; Durham: Duke University Press, 1993), 23–40; James W. Voelz, "A Self-Conscious Reader-Response Interpretation of Romans 13:1–7," in *Personal Voice in Biblical Interpretation* (ed. Ingrid Rosa Kitzberger; New York: Routledge, 1999), 156–69; Frances Murphy Zauhar, "Creative Voices: Women Reading and Women's Writing," in *The Intimate Critique: Autobiographical Literary Criticism* (ed. Diane P. Freedman, Olivia Frey, and Frances Murphy Zauhar; Durham: Duke University Press, 1993), 103–16.

AUTOBIOGRAPHICAL NOTES

Remarks commonly found near the beginning of the body in most of Paul's Letters where he describes his activities. Paul recollects his former ministry among the Corinthians in 1 Cor. 1:1–17, and in Phil. 1:12–26, he talks about an imprisonment (cf. Gal. 1:10–2:21 and 2 Cor. 1:8–2:12). These autobiographical notes are not unrelated miscellany but have meanings that are integrated into his arguments. They reinforce Paul's message to his addressees.

AUTOBIOGRAPHY

Technically, the term refers to a firsthand account or STORY of one's own life but may be extended to include memoirs, diaries, journals, and letters. A memoir is usually an organized NARRATIVE account intended for public consumption, but diaries, journals, and letters usually are not. Furthermore, an autobiography focuses on the introspective narrative of the AUTHOR's life, while memoirs, diaries, journals, and letters may include a focus on other persons. To see this distinction between autobiography and the other four, one need only read Augustine's *Confessions* (Harmon and Holman, 46).

In the HEBREW BIBLE, autobiography in the terms of the memoir includes the books of Ezra and Nehemiah and first-person accounts appearing in the PROPHETS and the PENTATEUCH. In the NT, autobiography as letters appears in Paul's writings. See Rigaux for a classification of these autobiographical elements (Soulen and Soulen, 15–16)

Bibliography. William Harmon and C. Hugh Holman, *A Handbook to Literature* (8th ed.; Upper Saddle River, NJ: Prentice Hall, 1999); Beda Rigaux, *Letters of St. Paul* (Chicago: Franciscan Herald Press, 1968); Richard N. Soulen and R. Kendall Soulen, *Handbook of Biblical Criticism* (3rd ed.; Louisville: Westminster John Knox, 2001).

AUTOGRAPH

The original copy of a TEXT, the one directly from an AUTHOR's hand. There are no extant biblical autographs. The earliest copies of the NT are fragments dating from about a hundred years after the originals, and full codexes of the HEBREW BIBLE are even later, although Qumran scrolls of individual OT books predate the NT period.

AUTONOMY OF THE TEXT

A central concept in NEW CRITICISM that, once the TEXT leaves the hand of the AUTHOR, it becomes public domain, independent of the author's INTENTION, world, and COMMENTARY. A text is an entity, a world to itself which must be read and comprehended in terms of the internal unity of all its various parts.

B

BABYLONIAN EXILE. *See* DIASPORA; EXILE, THE

BABYLONIAN TALMUD. *See* TALMUD

BACKGROUND

In literary studies, a term referring to the real-world CONTEXT within which an AUTHOR creates a TEXT. This background includes the author's philosophical, theological, political, educational, social, and literary contexts. While most modern literary critics deny that background studies are a substitute for the aesthetic experiencing of a text, such studies do make readers more informed. The value of background studies rests on the ASSUMPTION that authors do not create their works within cultural vacuums but are heavily influenced by the various conventions (*see* LITERARY CONVENTION) that constitute their SYMBOLIC WORLDS. Consequently, the most plausible understanding of a text is the one that takes into consideration an author's background. Recent critics within NEW HISTORICISM have introduced a renewed interest in background issues, assuming the HISTORICITY of texts, that in varying degrees they reflect the ideological structures (*see* IDEOLOGICAL CRITICISM; IDEOLOGY) of the author's world. Authors have no choice but to communicate within these structures.

BASE

A key concept in MARXIST CRITICISM first used by Karl Marx and Friedrich Engels to describe material foundation, "the forces and relations of labor" (Skand, 47) and production that determine a society's social consciousness and class structure (the superstructure). These forces and relations form the foundation on which rests a society's legal and political superstructure along with its corresponding social consciousness. In other words, one's material and social context determines one's social consciousness (Skand, 47–48). According to Marx and Engels, a society's superstructure and social consciousness (IDEOLOGY) develop from the base. However, they do not always simply reflect the base but may in fact work to produce change within it. So a society such as that of classical Greece may produce highly creative expressions of art while being underdeveloped economically. In Marxist criticism, critics assume that texts reflect the class ideology that is the result of the economic base. Consequently, critics who employ insights from Marxism often attempt to expose oppressive structures in a society that are reflected in the texts of that society.

Bibliography. Susan R. Skand, "Base and Superstructure," in *A Dictionary of Cultural and Critical Theory* (ed. Michael Payne; Cambridge, MA: Blackwell, 1996), 47–48.

BASE COMMUNITY

A term in LIBERATION THEOLOGY describing a community's commitment to practical ACTION. In liberation movements, not only are there professional theologians, priests, and pastoral ministers involved in the work of liberation, but also lay communities, who live out their faith in terms of liberating action. *See also* LIBERATION HERMENEUTICS.

BC

"Before Christ," a designation of the time before the birth of Jesus.

BCE

"Before the Common Era," a designation equivalent to BC, the time before Jesus Christ, but without the specific reference to Christ.

BEATITUDE

From the Latin *beatitudo*, most often translated "blessing," it may also translate the Latin *benedictio* (in Greek, *makarismos* and *eulogia* respectively). In recent TRANSLATIONS, the distinction between the two words is maintained by "happiness" and "blessing" (Soulen and Soulen, 27). *Beatitude* may refer to utterances intended to impart well-being, to honor God, or to pronounce something holy (27). In the BIBLE, beatitudes or blessings are uttered by God on objects (Gen. 1:22) and on humans (Gen. 9:1; Exod. 20:24; 2 Sam. 6:11–12), and by humans on humans (Gen. 9:26–27; 2 Sam. 6:18; Mark 10:16) and on God (Gen. 24:27; Ps. 28:6; Mark 6:41; Rom. 1:25; 2 Cor. 11:31; 1 Pet. 1:3–5). A collection of beatitudes in the NT is found in the SERMON ON THE MOUNT in Matthew and in the SERMON ON THE PLAIN in Luke.

Bibliography. Richard N. Soulen and R. Kendall Soulen, *Handbook of Biblical Criticism* (3rd ed.; Louisville: Westminster John Knox, 2001).

BENEDICTION

A part of the CLOSING in a NT letter (*see* EPISTOLARY LITERATURE) generally taking the form of "The grace of the Lord Jesus be with you." It varies little in Paul's Letters, but it has taken on a distinctly Christian perspective. Sometimes, however, Paul prefaces the benediction with a warning or exhortation (e.g., 1 Cor. 16:22; 1 Thess. 5:27; Gal. 6:17).

BENEDICTUS

The name of Zechariah's lyrical HYMN in Luke 1:68–79, taken from the first word in the Latin text: *Benedictus* (Blessed). It is an example of both a NATIVITY HYMN and a SEPTUAGINTISM.

BEN SIRA

Also called Wisdom of Jesus ben Sira, Sirach, and Ecclesiasticus, it is part of a body of Jewish writing referred to as WISDOM LITERATURE. Though the work is considered part of the OT APOCRYPHA according to the REFORMATION CANON (Protestant canon), it is recognized as part of the authoritative canon by the Catholic Church. According to

Hauer and Young, Ben Sira, like Ecclesiastes, is an old sage's "collected wisdom," an ANTHOLOGY of HYMNs, advice on conduct, existential reflections, essays, and APHORISMS, and is similar to Proverbs in both STYLE and WORLDVIEW (220).

Bibliography. Christian E. Hauer and William A. Young, *An Introduction to the Bible: A Journey into Three Worlds* (2nd ed.; Englewood Cliffs, NJ: Prentice Hall, 1990).

BIBLE

From the Greek term *biblia*, meaning "little books," the Bible is a collection of Jewish and Christian sacred writings with two main divisions—the HEBREW BIBLE and the NT. The Hebrew Bible is divided into three sections or collections—the TORAH, the PROPHETS, and the WRITINGS—all, except for a few segments, written in ancient Hebrew (*see* ARAMAIC).

This threefold division of the Hebrew Bible is not reflected in most English translations. The NT texts were written in a Greek dialect called KOINE (*koinē*, common), the dialect spoken in the Mediterranean world during the time of Jesus. The NT contains GOSPELS, EPISTLES, HISTORICAL NARRATIVES (Acts of the Apostles), and APOCALYPSE. During the third century BCE, the Hebrew Scriptures were translated into Greek (the SEPTUAGINT = LXX) and became the version used by Jews of the DIASPORA as well as by the early Christians. Some texts (the APOCRYPHA) that did not become part of the HEBREW BIBLE (*see* CANON; CANON, OLD TESTAMENT) were included in the LXX. These apocryphal books eventually became a part of the CATHOLIC CANON (*see* DEUTEROCANON / DEUTEROCANONICAL BOOKS) but were not included in the REFORMATION CANON. The most important and influential Latin version of the Bible is the VULGATE, translated by Jerome around 400 CE and used by the Western church in the Middle Ages.

BIBLE AS LITERATURE

An approach to the study of the BIBLE based on the ASSUMPTION that the TEXTS of the Bible are examples of ancient Hebrew and Greek literature. By "literature" is meant that the texts are LITERARY creations, texts of the IMAGINATION constructed on creative and imaginative language, which is adorned with artistic devices. The assumption is that the AUTHORS use language to create textual worlds that may or may not be similar to the real world of the authors and that the biblical texts in their final forms are works of tremendous literary power and aesthetic quality. Biblical authors examine THEMES that are common to great literature (God, the human condition, morality, human destiny) and employ devices associated with verbal art—PLOT, CHARACTERIZATION, ACTION, DIALOGUE, FIGURATIVE LANGUAGE, principles of CONTRAST, SETTING, language of indirection, STYLE, and POINT OF VIEW. With respect to INTERPRETATION, the Bible-as-literature approach assumes that the most appropriate methods for interpreting these texts are those that focus on their literary qualities, approaching them in essentially the same way we approach other literary documents.

BIBLE, ENGLISH TRANSLATIONS OF

After Jerome's TRANSLATION of the SEPTUAGINT and the NT into Latin (the VULGATE) in the late fourth century, only isolated scholars attempted new translations over the next thousand years (Harris, 28). In Anglo-Saxon England, the Venerable Bede translated part of the Vulgate into Old English, and during the tenth and eleventh centuries some biblical books along with the PSALMS were translated into English. It was not until 1384, however, that the entire BIBLE was translated into English by John Wycliffe, whose purpose was to make the Bible accessible to the laity, who were not literate in Latin. Because the English church feared the consequences of laypersons' interpreting the Bible, in 1408, the church prohibited future translations and condemned Wycliffe's translation.

Fueled by Johannes Gutenberg's invention of movable type (1455) and the Protestant Reformation (1517), other English translations began to appear. In 1525 William Tyndale produced an English translation of the NT directly from Greek manuscripts, but due to official church hostility

to the translation, he was unable to complete the translation of the OT; in 1536 he was condemned and burned at the stake. While condemning both Wycliffe's and Tyndale's translations, the church permitted circulation of the COVERDALE BIBLE (1535), a translation of the Vulgate and Luther's Bible by Tyndale's student, Myles Coverdale. In 1539 the GREAT BIBLE appeared, which was Coverdale's revision of MATTHEW'S BIBLE (1537), a version by Tyndale's student, John Rogers, writing under the pseudonym (see PSEUDONYMITY) of Thomas Matthew. Matthew's Bible was essentially Tyndale's translation with the addition of OT books untranslated by Tyndale (Sheeley and Nash, 20).

In terms of linguistic elegance and imagery, the KING JAMES VERSION of 1611 is unsurpassed (Harris, 29). King James I appointed fifty-four scholars to produce a version of the BISHOP'S BIBLE (published in 1568 in reaction to the heavily Calvinist Geneva Bible) as the official version for the Anglican Church. These scholars consulted the manuscripts then available, and after seven years of work produced the Authorized Version, or King James Version of the Bible. However, since it was produced by scholars who were immersed in the works of Edmund Spenser and William Shakespeare, the DICTION and vocabulary of the King James Version create difficulties for today's readers (Harris, 29).

Because scholars realize that language changes over time, they have edited and revised the King James Version (Harris, 29). The REVISED VERSION was published in England between 1881 and 1885, and a modified edition, the AMERICAN STANDARD VERSION, was published in 1901. The NASB appeared in 1971, intended to replace and update the American Standard Bible. The newer modern translation was sponsored by a California corporation, the Lockman Foundation. The translators worked under the rubric of VERBAL EQUIVALENCE, intending to follow the original languages in MEANING and word order. The NASB generally replicates the tenses and meanings of the verbs of the original languages and opts for traditional readings even where textual evidence suggests the case should be otherwise. The NASB was updated in 1995, when the more archaic words such as "thee" and "thou" were removed. Although the updated VERSION generally retains the original word order, the translators removed some of the IDIOMS in the original languages that were confusing in a word-for-word translation into English. The translators also used modern equivalents for some words and rearranged some of the more confusing sentences. In 1946 (NT) and 1952 (OT), the REVISED STANDARD VERSION appeared, for which scholars employed the latest work in biblical ARCHAEOLOGY and LINGUISTICS. Then, based on more recent studies in the biblical languages and history, the NEW REVISED STANDARD VERSION with the APOCRYPHA was published in 1991. The first edition of the ESV, a revision of the RSV, was published in September 2001. Although the translators recognize the differences in such things as grammar, syntax, and idiomatic phrases between the original languages and today's English, they do produce a literal translation in which they attempt to capture not only the wording of the original text but also the individual style of the biblical authors.

Today there is a wide selection of English translations that make use of the latest scholarship in linguistics, historical studies, and literary analysis. Among these are the NEW ENGLISH BIBLE, the REVISED ENGLISH BIBLE, the NEW AMERICAN BIBLE, and the NEW INTERNATIONAL VERSION. There are some versions, however, that scholars consider paraphrases or too doctrinally oriented to be as reliable as those listed above. These include the LIVING BIBLE, the GOOD NEWS BIBLE, and the NEW WORLD TRANSLATION.

The multivolume Anchor Bible and the SCHOLARS VERSION are intended as study aids, as evidenced in the extensive COMMENTARY and annotation. The translators of the Scholars Version have produced *The Complete Gospels*, which includes both canonical and noncanonical gospels of the first three centuries CE (Harris, 33).

Bibliography. Stephen Harris, *The New Testament: A Student's Introduction* (4th ed.; Boston: McGraw-Hill, 2002); Steven M. Sheeley and Robert N. Nash Jr., *The Bible in English Translation: An Essential Guide* (Nashville: Abingdon, 1997).

BIBLICAL CRITICISM

In brief, the rational study of the BIBLE; the attempt to use reason to understand the Bible. In terms of INTERPRETATION, biblical criticism is the application of bias-free, scientific methods to the study of the Bible. While this type of posture is an ancient one, biblical criticism as generally understood today is a modern phenomenon; until the latter part of the twentieth century, it was tantamount to historical criticism (*see* HISTORICAL-CRITICAL METHOD; Soulen and Soulen, 18–19).

At least from the time of Augustine to the end of the early Middle Ages (ca. 1000), most biblical criticism was synonymous with allegorical interpretation (*see* ALLEGORY). The SCRIPTURE had a fourfold sense (*see* FOURFOLD SENSE OF SCRIPTURE): literal (*see* LITERAL MEANING), allegorical, moral, and anagogical (*see* ANAGOGE). With the rise of Scholasticism in the High Middle Ages (ca. 1000–1300), the literal approach became predominant. Among the Scholastics, culminating in Thomas Aquinas, the expression of faith was given a reasoned, systematic basis (Klein, Blomberg, and Hubbard, 38).

In the late Middle Ages and the Renaissance of the fourteenth to sixteenth centuries, Scholasticism fell into disrepute under the pressure of the rationalism and historical consciousness of the humanists, such as Erasmus of Rotterdam. A renewed interest in studying the Bible in its original Hebrew and Greek resulted in early critical editions of the Bible (e.g., the 1516 edition of the Greek NT by Erasmus) and interest in critical study of ancient manuscripts. Such critical interest was not lost on the church Reformers. For example, Martin Luther argued for the historical study of the Bible (in its historical CONTEXT) and the application of standard rules of grammar.

As early as the High Middle Ages, the relationship between reason and faith was a primary concern for theologians (e.g., Abelard, Anselm, Thomas Aquinas). But in the seventeenth to eighteenth centuries (a period normally referred to as the "Age of Reason"), an intellectual movement called rationalism solved the problem of the relationship between the two by assuming that all issues, even those of faith, are subject to rational EXPLANATION and examination. Consequently, under the sway of rationalists such as Baruch Spinoza, a Jewish philosopher of the seventeenth century, the Bible itself became an object to be examined like any other book, using the scientific methods of historical investigation (42–43).

With the rise of the modern scientific study of history in the nineteenth century, key German scholars advocated approaching the Bible with the same scientific precision as applied in other areas of study. This emphasis meant that the events in the Bible should be explained in terms of natural laws and understood within its cultural specificity. Consequently, interests turned to such issues as origin, sources, date, place, and authorship. By the end of the nineteenth century, the DOCUMENTARY HYPOTHESIS was introduced to explain the origins of the HEBREW BIBLE, and the TWO-SOURCE HYPOTHESIS was introduced to explain the origins of the Synoptic Gospels. Harnack argued that the NT texts obscured the Jesus of history (*see* HISTORICAL JESUS, THE) and that biblical interpretation should try to uncover this hidden figure, thus beginning the QUEST FOR THE HISTORICAL JESUS. In the area of Middle East research, ancient manuscripts were discovered that transformed TEXTUAL CRITICISM. The discovery of manuscripts of other peoples by archaeologists also transformed the *RELIGIONSGESCHICHTLICHE SCHULE* by changing the focus of study to the understanding of Israel and its religion within the context of its neighboring cultures. This historical focus, then, had a profound impact on the study of the Bible. Behind the biblical texts lay a complex social and religious history, the study of which led to critical questions about the Bible's historical reliability and its authority as divine revelation. Biblical criticism was no longer concerned primarily with unearthing the MEANING of the texts but rather with the sources and history of the texts (Soulen and Soulen, 20).

In the early twentieth century, Hermann Gunkel, a German scholar of the Hebrew Bible, introduced FORM CRITICISM in his study of the PSALMS. The task of form criticism was the recovery of the brief oral compositions that were the basis for the written forms in the biblical texts and the *SITZ IM LEBEN* (life setting) for the oral forms. Later, form criticism would engage many NT scholars, such as Martin Dibelius and Rudolf Bultmann. TRADITION CRITICISM (1930s) extended form criticism by its focus on the way in which forms were modified over time within traditions. With the introduction of REDACTION CRITICISM (1950s), scholars offered a corrective to what many saw in form criticism as an unbalanced attention to sources and history. The redaction critics argued that although the writers of the biblical texts made use of traditional forms and sources, they were also interpreters of traditions and thus invested the texts with new meaning.

During the interwar period, biblical scholars of both the Hebrew Bible and the NT sought to reestablish the theological relevance of the Bible in a period of global crisis. The tragic events of World War I stimulated interest in the existentialism of figures such as Martin Heidegger and Søren Kierkegaard. Karl Barth sought an approach that would focus on theology while incorporating historical criticism, an approach that advocated a personal encounter with God through the Bible. For Barth, there was to be no critical gap between CRITICISM and theology. Rudolf Bultmann, also influenced by existentialist philosophy, applied form criticism to the Gospels in order to recover the original forms and SAYINGS OF JESUS before they were corrupted by the later Christian communities. While such an approach contributed to doubt about the historical reliability of the Gospels, the motivation behind it was to discover the Jesus of history behind the CHRIST OF THE CHURCH. Bultmann also determined to DEMYTHOLOGIZE the Bible by recovering the KERYGMA (the original message), covered over by the mythological WORLDVIEW of the early Christian church. Bultmann assumed that when so presented, the kerygma would speak existentially to the modern rational and scientific world. Bultmann's approach to the texts was an existential hermeneutic, meaning that the readers should approach the texts not with the expectation of receiving objective TRUTH, but with the expectation of encountering its own understanding of human existence and then allowing that experience to shed light on their own personal existential situation. In this fashion, people become more authentically human (Doty, 17–27).

It is also during this period that a theological movement referred to as neoorthodoxy developed from the work of Barth and Bultmann. According to Klein, Blomberg, and Hubbard, the movement rested on three propositions about the nature of God and truth. First, God is a "Thou," not an "It," which means that language cannot communicate knowledge of God. Consequently, knowledge of God must derive from a personal encounter, an experience so mysterious and subjective that it is beyond scientific or rational understanding. The second proposition speaks of God as so transcendent that only MYTH has the capacity to reveal God to humans. And third, truth, especially divine truth, is paradoxical. As a result, neoorthodox theologians dealt with the conflicting statements, events, stories, and chronology in the Bible as PARADOXes that defied rational explanation (48).

After World War II, several important developments occurred that significantly altered the landscape of biblical criticism. First, there was a renewed interest in BIBLICAL THEOLOGY, resulting in the BIBLICAL THEOLOGY MOVEMENT, a theological movement whose major concern was the theological message of the Bible. The movement argued for the unity of the Bible, God's revelation in history, the distinctive Hebrew nature of the Bible, and the uniqueness of the Bible within its environment.

In the post–World War II period students of Bultmann began to question his claim that knowledge about the historical Jesus was forever hidden beneath the cultural incrustations of the church. As a result of their challenge, the new QUEST FOR THE HISTORICAL JESUS was given birth. Also in this period (1950s and 1960s), a movement or theory of meaning known as the NEW HERMENEUTIC arose. The new hermeneutic was based on a new understanding of the essence of language. Rather than being a passive phenomenon (i.e., language as a set of descriptive labels used to name objects), language is active in the sense of being an event that creates movement. Each instance of speech (written or oral) is an event, a "speech act" that (see SPEECH ACT THEORY) creates truth in conversation with the hearer's experience. If this is true of texts, then they are not simply static entities from which meaning is extracted by some interpretive method but rather speech acts that interpret their readers. The biblical texts as speech acts, then, confront the individual readers with the WORD OF GOD at the moment of reading. In this sense, the biblical texts interpret their readers, not the other way around. Rather than simply submitting themselves to the analytical scrutiny of readers, the biblical texts interpret readers or at least force readers to scrutinize their own world by being drawn into the WORLD OF THE TEXT (Klein, Blomberg, and Hubbard, 49–51).

By 1970 biblical criticism had moved away from theological interests and opted for an ever-increasing number of literary methodologies. These methodologies tended to concentrate more on the world of the text and the world of the reader (see WORLD IN FRONT OF THE TEXT) than on the world that produced the text. Standing between critical methods concerned with the world of the author and those concerned with the reader are NARRATIVE CRITICISM, RHETORICAL CRITICISM, STRUCTURALISM, and LINGUISTICS. However, by the 1980s and 1990s, biblical criticism became the gathering ground for approaches that began to question or problematize an array of modern assumptions about meaning and understanding—REFERENCE, representation, objectivity, history, universals (Bible and Culture Collective, 13). Perhaps the bridge between the historically oriented methods and the newer methods was READER-RESPONSE CRITICISM, which trained the interpretive gaze away from the text to the response generated in the reader and the reader's role in the process of constructing meaning. With the advent of what we may classify as POSTMODERN methods (e.g., FEMINIST CRITICISM, DECONSTRUCTION, WOMANIST THEOLOGY/CRITICISM, gay/lesbian criticism [*see* QUEER THEORY], *MUJERISTA* THEOLOGY, POSTCOLONIALISM, IDEOLOGICAL CRITICISM, INTERTEXTUALITY, LIBERATION THEOLOGY), the modern assumption (in postmodern reckoning, a MYTH) of disinterested (*see* DISINTERESTEDNESS), objective, apolitical meaning was called into question. From the perspectives of these postmodern methods, texts mean what interpreters intend them to mean. In other words, interpretation is always interested, subjective, political, ideological. These methods have called for not only a rereading of texts but also a rereading of readings under the assumption that not only were the biblical texts written within structures of PATRIARCHY and in male METANARRATIVES, but they also have been interpreted within systems of power that authorize and foreground some strategies and groups while marginalizing and disenfranchising others. These more recent methods, then, call for an openness to include issues of race, GENDER, IDEOLOGY, and sexual preference as important parts of the PRAXIS of biblical criticism (14–15).

> *Bibliography.* Bible and Culture Collective, *The Postmodern Bible* (New Haven: Yale University Press, 1995); W. G. Doty, *Contemporary New Testament Interpretation* (Englewood Cliffs, NJ: Prentice Hall, 1972); Adolf von Harnack, *What Is Christianity?* (trans. Thomas Bailey Saunders; New York: Putnam, 1901); William Klein, Craig Blomberg, and Robert Hubbard, *Introduction to Biblical Interpretation* (Dallas: Word, 1993); Richard N. Soulen and R. Kendall Soulen, *Handbook of Biblical Criticism* (3rd ed.; Louisville: Westminster John Knox, 2001).

BIBLICAL HERMENEUTICS

Generally, the theory of the reception and understanding of TEXTS and the methods of INTERPRETATION, their premises and limitations. HERMENEUTICS has traditionally been concerned with the study of the locus of MEANING and the principles of interpretation. Biblical hermeneutics focuses on the locus of meaning and principles of biblical interpretation. Hermeneutics in the broad sense is dual-focused: EXEGESIS and interpretation. Exegesis is the process of examining a text in order to ascertain what its first readers would have understood it to mean. The varied set of activities that the reader performs on a text in order to make meaningful inferences is exegesis. Interpretation is the task of explaining or drawing out the implications of that understanding for contemporary readers and hearers. Thus, the transformation of these inferences into applications or SIGNIFICANCE for the interpreter's world is interpretation. If exegesis is combined with interpretation along with an examination of the interpreter's presuppositional REPERTOIRE, the result is hermeneutics. The terms *hermeneutics* and *interpretation*, however, are often used interchangeably to refer to the process of determining the meaning and significance of a text.

The common ground for all approaches to interpretation is meaning. In terms of methodology, however, there is considerable debate among scholars over the source of meaning. AUTHOR-CENTERED approaches assume that meaning is associated with the authors and/or their worlds. TEXT-CENTERED approaches locate meaning in one way or another within the text. AUDIENCE-CENTERED approaches define meaning in terms of the reader's activities and/or responses. While these three groups provide helpful categories for discussing hermeneutics, they often tend to overlap. For example, scholars who focus on the structures and WORLD OF THE TEXT quite often make use of historical information that may shed light on a particular passage or concept. Most READER-RESPONSE critics assume that readers respond to textual structures and clues, thus giving attention to TEXTUAL STRATEGIES (*see* CRITICAL METHODOLOGY).

In terms of philosophy, hermeneutics has always turned on the tension between whether the interpreter surrenders to the power of the text or whether the text must submit to the creative activities of the interpreter. Such questions as "Is meaning the result of the reader's activity?" and "Does the interpreter control language, or does language control the interpreter?" move hermeneutics into the realm of a philosophy of human understanding (Bowie, 243). Early key figures in this move were Martin Heidegger and Friedrich Schleiermacher, who both assumed that any object must be understood in terms of its parts, and vice versa. Human understanding of anything turns out to be an ongoing adjustment between these two poles. Interpretation always involves a basic circularity because it can never operate independently of a person's SOCIAL LOCATION. Such is the insistence of another key figure in hermeneutics, Hans-Georg Gadamer, who points out that the interpreter is always located squarely within traditions and language. The text is always separated from its origin and interpreted within a new context. Based on this ASSUMPTION, Gadamer sees interpretation as a DIALOGUE between two worlds, a FUSION OF HORIZONS, in which the interpreter is involved in a process of self-understanding. Interpreters can understand past texts only in terms of their own prejudices and not by some suspension of them. Due to the attention on human understanding, contemporary hermeneutics tends to focus on the activities of readers and on the IDEOLOGICAL contexts that prevent the possibility of readers' reconstructing an author's INTENTION or world. Central to most contemporary hermeneutics is the assumption that human reality is an interpreted one mediated through social location and language, an assumption that encourages a corollary: that texts cannot be reduced to a single, definitive meaning but are objects that perpetually generate different meanings through readers in a variety of ways.

Bibliography. Andrew Bowie, "Hermeneutics," in *A Dictionary of Cultural and Critical Theory* (ed. Michael Payne; Cambridge, MA: Blackwell, 1996), 241–44.

BIBLICAL INTERPRETATION. *See* BIBLICAL HERMENEUTICS

BIBLICAL POETRY

A literary GENRE of the BIBLE, found primarily in the OT, but with a few small occurrences in the NT.

For example, we find hymns (Luke 1:46–55; 1:68–79; 2:14; Phil. 2:6–11), confessional statements (1 Tim. 3:16; Eph. 4:4–6; Rom. 8:38–39; 10:9), and other poetic prose (1 Cor. 15:42–44). Each of the above examples shares what may be called a poetic pattern. To these may be added the SAYINGS OF JESUS and parts of the Apocalypse of John. Approximately one-third of the OT is POETRY, and all but seven OT books contain poetry. Hebrew poetry is structured on parallelism of thought and employs FIGURATIVE LANGUAGE. Although there are a number of schools of thought about Hebrew poetry (e.g., Michael P. O'Connor, Stephen Geller, and Terence Collins; see the bibliography below), perhaps the most popular school is that reflected in James Kugel and Robert Alter. Each line of poetry consists of what Robert Alter calls "VERSETS." Most commonly, each line consists of two versets but may contain three. The second verset is related in some way to the first. For example, in "Oh that my vexation were weighed, and all my calamity laid in the balances!" (Job 6:2), "vexation" and "calamity" are related as are "weighed" and "laid in the balances." Parallelism of thought generally consists of three main types: synonymy, antithesis, and synthesis. In synonymous parallelism, the second verset restates in a different way the thought of the first verset:

> He washes his garments in wine
> and his robe in the blood of grapes. (Gen. 49:11b)

Antithetical parallelism expresses in the second verset the same idea as in the first, but in a negative manner:

> A wise child makes a glad father,
> but a foolish child is a mother's grief. (Prov. 10:1)

In synthetic parallelism, the second verset complements the first by clarification or EXPLANATION:

> So I will send a fire on the wall of Gaza,
> fire that shall devour its strongholds. (Amos 1:7)

The consuming of the strongholds is the result of the fire on the walls. But there is also a movement from verset to verset. For example:

Wine is a mocker,
strong drink a brawler. (Prov. 20:1)

"Wine" has been intensified in the second verset with "strong drink," and "mocker" has been heightened to "brawler." Words spoken in mockery are not as strong as the physical actions of the "brawler." There has been a FOCUSING through INTENSIFICATION. Such focusing or intensification is quite common in the graded numbers that follow the pattern of x, x+1:

Once God has spoken;
twice have I heard this. (Ps. 62:11)

Another type of movement between versets occurs in Amos 8:10:

I will turn your feasts into mourning,
and all your songs into lamentation.

In this line, "all your songs" is a specific element within the larger event of "feasts," as is "lamentation" of "mourning." This type of focusing is what Alter calls focusing through SPECIFICATION. Most instances of antithetical and synthetic parallelism are actually variations on the previously mentioned types of focusing. Alter also identifies a third type of focusing—through CAUSE-AND-EFFECT MOVEMENT:

I call upon the LORD, who is worthy to be praised,
so I shall be saved from my enemies. (Ps. 18:3)

The relation between these two versets is obviously one of cause ("call") and effect ("saved"). On the one hand, the importance of at least an elementary acquaintance with the structures and dynamics of Hebrew verse cannot be overemphasized. This emphasis becomes at once justified when one recognizes how much of the Hebrew Bible (WISDOM LITERATURE, PROPHECY, PSALMS, and poetic sections within NARRATIVE books) is Hebrew VERSE.

John Gabel and Charles Wheeler identify two other types of parallelism: emblematic parallelism and climactic parallelism. Emblematic parallelism is a variety of synonymous parallelism. But here the thought is expressed both literally and metaphorically:

Like a gold ring in a pig's snout
is a beautiful woman without good sense.
(Prov. 11:22)

The first verset is the metaphorical half, while the second verset is literal.

Climactic parallelism piles up repetitive versets to a CLIMAX:

That day will be a day of wrath,
a day of distress and anguish,
a day of ruin and devastation,
a day of darkness and gloom,
a day of clouds and thick darkness,
a day of trumpet blast and battle cry
against the fortified cities and against the lofty
battlements. (Zeph. 1:15–16)

Bibliography. Robert Alter, *The Art of Biblical Poetry* (New York: Basic Books, 1985); Terence Collins, *Line-Forms in Hebrew Poetry: A Grammatical Approach to the Stylistic Study of the Hebrew Prophets* (Studia Pohl, Series maior 17; Rome: Pontifical Biblical Institute, 1978); John Gabel and Charles Wheeler, *The Bible as Literature: An Introduction* (New York: Oxford University Press, 1986); Stephen Geller, *Parallelism in Early Biblical Poetry* (Harvard Semitic Monographs 20; Missoula, MT: Scholars Press, 1979); James Kugel, *The Idea of Biblical Poetry: Parallelism and Its History* (Baltimore: Johns Hopkins University Press, 1998); Michael O'Connor, *Hebrew Verse Structure* (Winona Lake, IN: Eisenbrauns, 1980); David Petersen and Kent Harold Richards, *Interpreting Hebrew Poetry* (Minneapolis: Fortress, 1992).

BIBLICAL STUDIES

A term used to designate the academic discipline in which the texts of the BIBLE are critically examined by using a variety of critical methods (*see* CRITICAL METHODOLOGY). Generally the academic study of the Bible is part of the liberal arts in the humanities. Biblical studies as an academic discipline takes a descriptive approach by focusing on historical, LITERARY, comparative, and methodological issues; it demands the same intellectual rigor and professionalism as any other academic discipline.

Biblical studies does not constitute a monolithic field but consists of subgroups such as FEMINIST CRITICISM, STRUCTURAL EXEGESIS, REDACTION CRITICISM, to name only a few. While these subgroups often overlap, each has its own focus and set of questions. The proliferation of approaches within the field of biblical studies has created a playing field on which traditional assumptions of authority, MEANING, OBJECTIVE TRUTH, and REFERENCE are being challenged by issues such as plurality of meaning (or even the possibility of meaning), HISTORICITY, TEXTUALITY, INTERTEXTUALITY, and IDEOLOGY. *See* BIBLICAL CRITICISM.

BIBLICAL THEOLOGY

The systematic presentation of biblical THEMES and/or teachings so that they become normative in the present; a philosophical-systematic approach that examines the biblical TEXTS in terms of their social and cultural CONTEXT with the goal of translating their MEANINGs into modern contemporary categories. The primary ASSUMPTION of biblical theology is that it is possible to translate "what the texts meant" into "what the texts mean" and then to systematically present these timeless TRUTHS in theological categories. Biblical theology faces a central question: "How can an ANTHOLOGY of writings from the past be interpreted so that they become normative for the present?" The answer is supplied by a second major assumption: that the biblical texts inscribe theological truth that is historical/transhistorical in nature. *See* BIBLICAL THEOLOGY MOVEMENT.

BIBLICAL THEOLOGY MOVEMENT

A theological movement that flourished between 1945 and the mid-1960s. Its genesis was in a reactionary response to the prevalent analytical, historical, and form-critical (*see* FORM CRITICISM) emphases that characterized "liberal" theology. In contrast, the biblical theology movement sought

to articulate the theological nature of the BIBLE by emphasizing five key points (Childs, 13–60). First was the claim that the biblical texts and their INTERPRETATION require an approach that is not inherently philosophical and recognizes that biblical thought is dynamic, not lending itself very well to dogmatic systematizing. Second was the ASSUMPTION that biblical thought is HEBRAIC rather than Greek and that using the Greek categories of systematic theology is a perversion of that thought. Apparently, this assumption overlooked the fact that at least the NT was a product of HELLENISM or, at a minimum, of a Jewish culture highly influenced by the Greek. Third, the movement emphasized the unity of the Bible, which meant that the NT was to be read and understood in terms of the Hebrew thought of the OT. A consequence of this assumption was the necessity of claiming that the LITERARY forms of the NT were grounded in and reflected the forms of the OT. This allowed the movement to posit a definite link between the thought of the OT and that of the NT. Fourth, the Bible was in some way distinct from its cultural environment. If the Bible is the repository of theological TRUTH or thought that is somehow independent of its social, historical contexts, it is understandable that the movement generally downplayed the role of historical-critical EXEGESIS. Fifth, the Bible's distinctiveness derived from its nature as God's revelation. This revelation constituted salvation history (*see* HEILSGESCHICHTE), a concept unique to Hebrew thought.

Although the movement is not popular today among the majority of scholars, its approach is still used by many people. This may be due to the fact that the approach does focus on the biblical texts and their salvific threads without the "baggage" of problems raised by historical-critical studies or other more contemporary approaches (e.g., READER-RESPONSE CRITICISM, STRUCTURALISM, DECONSTRUCTION, and CULTURAL CRITICISM). *See* BIBLICAL THEOLOGY.

Bibliography. Brevard S. Childs, *Biblical Theology in Crisis* (Philadelphia: Westminster, 1970).

BIBLICISM

A noncritical and unquestioning loyalty to the BIBLE and one's time-honored understanding of it.

BIBLIOGRAPHY

Generally, a list of sources relevant to a topic, but the term may be used in a variety of ways. First it may apply to a list of printed material on a particular SUBJECT, a *subject bibliography*. The list may be exhaustive or contain only a selection of the most important sources on the subject. A more nuanced form of the subject bibliography may the list of works consulted by the author while working, or of recommended sources for further study. An *enumerative bibliography* lists the works of a particular author or country. A list of lists of sources on a subject is a *bibliography of bibliographies*. An *annotated bibliography* is one in which each item is accompanied by descriptive and/or critical comments.

In TEXTUAL CRITICISM, the term refers to all the processes involved in producing a book—the history of writing, printing, binding, illustrating, and publishing. In this SENSE, then, it refers to the bibliographical evidence that textual critics use to establish the value of various editions of a TEXT in terms of history, originality, authenticity, and so forth.

BIBLIOLOGY

From the Greek *biblion* (book) and *logos* (study), the term refers to the study of the Bible.

BIBLIOMANCY

From the Greek *biblion* (book) and *manteia* (divination), the practice of opening the Bible at random, reading the first verse one sees, and accepting its content as divine guidance or the solution to a problem. For example, a man practiced bibliomancy in seeking a solution to insomnia and was greeted by 1 Cor. 15:51 in the KJV: "Behold, I shew you a mystery, we shall not all sleep, but we shall all be changed." The conversion of Augustine of Hippo provides a historical example, as he recounts it:

I snatched it [Romans] up, opened it and in silence read the passage upon which my eyes first fell: Not in rioting and drunkenness, not in chambering and impurities, not in contention and envy, but put ye on the Lord Jesus Christ and make not provision for the flesh in its concupiscences. I had no wish to read further, and no need. For in that instant, with the very ending of the sentence, it was as though a light of utter confidence shone in all my heart, and all the darkness of uncertainty vanished away. Then leaving my finger in the place or marking it by some other sign, I closed the book and in complete calm told the whole thing to Alypius and he similarly told me what had been going on in himself, of which I knew nothing. He asked to see what I had read. I showed him, and he looked further than I had read. I had not known what followed. And this is what followed: "Now him that is weak in faith, take unto you." He applied this to himself and told me so. And he was confirmed by this message and with no troubled wavering gave himself to God's goodwill and purpose—a purpose indeed most suited to his character, for in these matters he had been immeasurably better than I. (1020)

Bibliography. Augustine, *Confessions*, in *The Norton Anthology of World Masterpieces* (trans. F. J. Sheed; ed. Sarah Lawall; 7th ed.; New York: Norton, 1999), 1:1004–32.

BICOLON. *See* COLON

BINARY OPPOSITION/OPPOSITES

A central idea in STRUCTURALISM that refers to mutual exclusion between two opposing ideas such as white/black, light/dark, masculine/feminine, spirit/flesh, or heaven/hell. The concept first appears in the work of Claude Lévi-Strauss on MYTH. According to Lévi-Strauss, binary oppositions occur in all myths and consequently constitute a fundamental structure of STORY. Extrapolating from the way he assumed binary oppositions operated in myths, Lévi-Strauss posited an analogous structure in the human mind, language, and thought. From this point onward, other structuralists assumed that binary oppositions formed the basis of all NARRATIVE and are inherent in the structure of language itself (Innes, 64). If this is the case, then the MEANINGS of TEXTS are inseparable from these basic structures.

Poststructuralists such as Jacques Derrida PROBLEMATIZE the idea of binary oppositions by pointing out that such binaries are almost always hierarchical in nature (Hall, 162). In other words, the first term in the binary is the privileged one. For example, the binary oppositions of light/dark and white/black illustrate the manner in which Western culture has assigned unequal significance to these colors, which has led to enculturated racist judgments. Light and white have assumed the value of goodness, purity, and intellectual and even spiritual superiority, while dark and black have been associated with evil, the sinister, and intellectual and spiritual depravity. Poststructuralists argue that such oppositions do not reflect natural givens but are social constructs and that literary and cultural analysis should begin by reading texts in ways that uncover such oppositions or the unconscious reliance on them.

Derrida also argues that the Western practice of giving more value to the first term actually disguises or masks the fact that the second term in the opposition is perhaps the most powerful or predominant one (Hall, 163). The prime example for Derrida is the tendency in the Western metaphysical tradition to privilege speech over writing. But perhaps the most influential result of Derrida's work derives from his claim that the first term can have no SIGNIFICANCE apart from the second. In other words, the meaning of any word or idea is relational in terms of its DIFFERENCE from other terms, including its binary opposite. So meaning is never present in a term—or in a text, for that matter (*see* ABSENCE)—but is rather somewhere in the relational difference to other terms. So meaning is always deferred (*see* DEFERRING), an undefinable function of an endless chain of SIGN relations, because signs simply refer to other signs, not to extralinguistic objects.

Bibliography. Donald Hall, *Literary and Cultural Theory: From Basic Principles to Advanced Applications* (Boston: Houghton Mifflin, 2001); Paul Innes, "Binary Oppositions," in *A Dictionary of Cultural and Critical Theory* (ed. Michael Payne; Cambridge, MA: Blackwell, 1996), 64–65.

BIOGRAPHICAL FALLACY

In LITERARY studies, the fallacy of interpreting a TEXT based on aspects of the AUTHOR's life. Many literary critics reject this approach for two reasons. First, there is no assurance that the self who writes is identical to the self who lives. Second, when a text leaves the hands of the author, it becomes an autonomous object with its own world, independent of the world or life of the author. Readers are to interpret and understand a text in terms of its STRUCTURE and the relationship between its parts and the whole of the text. Readers interpret texts, not authors. *See* AFFECTIVE FALLACY; INTENTIONAL FALLACY; NEW CRITICISM.

BISHOP'S BIBLE

Published in England in 1568 in response to the GENEVA BIBLE by those in the Church of England who were uneasy with the Calvinism of the Geneva Bible. Published under the direction of Archbishop of Canterbury Matthew Parker, the Bishop's Bible became the official version for the Church of England until the publication of the KING JAMES VERSION in 1611. *See* BIBLE, ENGLISH TRANSLATIONS OF.

Bibliography. Steven M. Sheeley and Robert N. Nash Jr., *The Bible in English Translation: An Essential Guide* (Nashville: Abingdon, 1997).

BLACK CRITICISM. *See* BLACK THEOLOGY; RACE, CLASS, AND GENDER CRITICISM

BLACK THEOLOGY

Theological movements in North America, South Africa, and black African states that focus on interpreting the BIBLE in light of the spiritual, social, political, and economic oppression of black people in order to effect their liberation from such oppression. While several black theology movements share similarities with each other and with Latin American LIBERATION THEOLOGY and WOMANIST THEOLOGY, each has its distinctive characteristics based on different SOCIAL LOCATIONS.

First, central to all strands of black theology is the belief that the interpretation of the biblical texts must rest on the black experience and struggle (Thiselton, 420). Consequently, they tend to privilege the same portions of the Bible (e.g., the exodus, social critique of the prophets, and Jesus's teaching on liberation). This focus on "liberation passages" is what James Cone calls the biblical-textual pole of black theology's hermeneutic (*Black Theology*, 50–53).

Second, each strand of black theology offers critical challenges to the interpretive FRAME-WORKS of the dominant interpretive traditions. By *dominant traditions*, black theologians refer to Euro-American interpretive traditions that define canons (literary, theological, political, etc.) in terms of Western values, traditions that have historically and consistently marginalized those traditions and peoples who have their identities formed through oppression and marginalization. Black theologians assume that these white, colonial, racist, and imperialist frameworks tend to legitimate and perpetuate the oppressive ideologies of the dominant traditions.

Third, black theologies employ a variety of critical resources to expose the ways in which interpretations within the dominant traditions encourage practices of domination and oppression.

Black theology in South Africa revolves around the issues of colonial history and especially the impact of apartheid. This wing of black theology has its genesis in the black consciousness movement in the late 1960s and the early 1970s and is highly reflective of the writings of James Cone. Central to Cone's hermeneutic is the dialectic between the poles of the Bible and black experience of oppression (Cone, *God of the Oppressed*, 8). It is through the grid of this experience of oppression that one comes to understand God as the great Liberator. Furthermore, John Mbiti suggests that such understanding is possible only to the extent that theologians are able to render hermeneutical PRAXIS in terms of the SYMBOLIC WORLD of South Africa.

The uniqueness of North American black theology is found in the tension between theological praxis and the history and memory of slav-ery. Perhaps it is in North American black theology that there is the tightest link between SCRIPTURE and experience. The two cannot be separated because the Bible is or has become God's word to the oppressed and disenfranchised. So the Bible has a natural relevance to the black consciousness or experience of oppression. Theology, according to Cone, must find ways to replace the oppressive influence of white thought with a hermeneutic that takes into account the fact that black experience cannot be separated from interpretive practices and that this black experience has been formed over the centuries by STORY, especially in the stories and songs of slaves. The implication is that a North American black theology must be formulated in terms of the unique black experience, an experience created not only in terms of skin color but also in terms of the way North American blacks have been defined by other people (namely, whites) and that definition's role in self-understanding. Consequently, the Jesus as defined by traditional white theologies has no relevance to the black experience or black theology. If Jesus is to have relevance, then he must be identified with the oppressed and thus as "nonwhite."

Black theology in the black African states is concerned with contextualizing the Bible in African cultures. Theologians argue that since these cultures do not constitute a monolithic entity, Scripture must be interpreted and proclaimed within the social ethos of the individual cultures. *See* FEMINIST CRITICISM; LIBERATION HERMENEUTICS; LIBERATION THEOLOGY.

Bibliography. James Cone, *A Black Theology of Liberation* (New York: Lippincott, 1970); idem, *God of the Oppressed* (London: SPCK, 1975); John S. Mbiti, *New Testament Eschatology in an African Background* (London: SPCK, 1971); Anthony Thiselton, *New Horizons in Hermeneutics* (Grand Rapids: Zondervan, 1992).

BLAND EFFECT. *See* ROUTINIZATION

BLESSING. *See* BEATITUDE

BOOK OF THE COVENANT, THE
Also known as the Covenant Code, a collection of LAWS in Exod. 20:19–23:33. The collection con-

tains customary or common law, with CASUISTIC LAW predominating, and seems to provide SPEC-IFICATION for a number of the Ten Commandments (*see* DECALOGUE). For example, 21:15 and 17 spell out the fate of those who do not honor their parents. The civil and juridical nature of this collection has analogues throughout the ancient Middle East (e.g., the Code of Hammurabi, Hittite laws, and Middle Assyrian laws).

The collection covers a variety of aspects of community life reflecting the period of the judges. In fact, the collection seems to presuppose an agrarian community of farmers with vineyards and olive orchards. Also, the collection reflects a time before the sanctuary at Jerusalem since the sacrifices were made in the open and in a variety of places. Below is a summary of the collection (van der Woude, 161–62):

20:22–26 MT	Prescriptions for public worship
21:12–36	Prescriptions for protecting the life of humans
21:37–22:16	Prescriptions for protecting property (22:1–17 NRSV)
22:17–19	Regulations governing sins of magic, sodomy, and idolatry (22:18–20)
22:20–26	Regulations protecting the socially defenseless (22:21–27)
22:27–30	Regulations governing gifts and prohibitions against eating certain meat (22:28–31)
23:1–19	Admonitions (not commandments) concerning a variety of areas—cultic regulations, sabbatical year, feasts, boiling a young goat in its mother's milk

Bibliography. A. S. van der Woude, ed., *The World of the Old Testament* (Grand Rapids: Eerdmans, 1989).

BRACKETING

A term introduced by the German philosopher Edmund Husserl and subsequently adopted and adapted in PHENOMENOLOGICAL CRITICISM. The term refers to a reductive process in which interpreters suspend judgment about the real world by placing brackets around their own PRESUPPOSITIONS about the real world as well as around presuppositions about the connection between the object and the perceiving SUBJECT (Loughlin, 511). Objects are thought to have an inherent MEANING apart from the way they are perceived: this type of reduction assumes that an object has its own essence independently of any or all particularities. Bracketing enables the perceiving subject to probe into the essence of objects but also allows for the suspension of all nonessential and metaphysical concerns of natural perception; thus one may identify the universal or essential structures of the human consciousness (512). Consequently, the ultimate goal of bracketing is the intuition of and reflection on the essential nature of objects present in consciousness and the universal structures of consciousness itself: the goal is to articulate "unprejudiced" statements of knowledge about meaning or knowledge inherent in objects.

The method of bracketing begins with eidetic reduction (*see* PHENOMENOLOGICAL CRITICISM), a systematic subtracting from or adding to the particularities of the object in the consciousness. Each particular is then examined to determine if its addition or subtraction transforms the object into something different from that held in consciousness. The particularities that do transform the object are therefore necessary to identify the essence of the object (Schmitt, 141). This same process is employed to identify the essential or universal structures of the human consciousness. Such a process allows Husserl and others to posit a distinction between the object as it is perceived and the object in its essence and then to bracket off the particulars of the object as perceived in order to focus on the object's essence.

Although there are other forms of reduction (e.g., psychological, phenomenological, philosophical), they, like eidetic reduction, aim at a method by which a subject is able to see beyond appearance or everyday perception to the essence of an object, its inherent meaning. The hope is that this process of reduction will produce a FRAMEWORK by which humans can have absolute and certain knowledge of objects, events, and experiences and of the essences of human mental actions. If such a reduction is possible, then it is equally possible for Husserl to speak of a collection of original human experiences, what he calls *Lebenswelt* (life-world; Loughlin, 512).

Phenomenological literary critics use the idea of bracketing, claiming that readers can suspend their own ideological (*see* IDEOLOGY) biases and presuppositions to arrive at the essence or meaning inherent in the TEXT. The method makes two important claims: First, through bracketing it is possible to focus all interpretive attention on the text as an intentional object and thus to explicate a text with no reference to personal preferences or outside categories such as historical and cultural contexts. Second, phenomenological critics view the text as an expression of a consciousness (an object of human intention) in which the inherent textual structures and their relationship to each other are reflections of the author's life-world. In this sense, literary interpretation is tantamount to reconstructing the INTENTION of the author through a detailed description of the text's essence. *See* PHENOMENOLOGICAL CRITICISM.

Bibliography. Michael Hammond, Jane Howarth, and Russell Keat, *Understanding Phenomenology* (8 vols.; Oxford: Blackwell, 1991); Marie H. Loughlin, "Bracketing," in *Encyclopedia of Contemporary Literary Theory* (ed. Irena R. Makaryk; Toronto: University of Toronto Press, 1993), 511–14; Richard Schmitt, "Phenomenology," in *The Encyclopedia of Philosophy* (ed. Paul Edwards; New York: Macmillan, 1963), 6:131–51.

BREECHES BIBLE

The colloquial name for the GENEVA BIBLE based on the use of "breeches" to translate *ḥăgōrōt* (NRSV, "loincloths") in Gen. 3:7.

BRICOLAGE

A term derived from French, referring to a do-it-yourself approach to a job by using available materials at hand. A *bricoleur* is the person doing the job. In LITERARY theory, *bricolage* was introduced by Claude Lévi-Strauss to designate an inexact, rough-and-ready theoretical or conceptual instrument in the absence of a more appropriate one (*Savage Mind*, 16–33). For example, Lévi-Strauss employs the BINARY OPPOSITION of nature/cul-

ture to distinguish between what is universal and independent of a system of cultural norms on the one hand, and what is culturally bound and dependent on the other hand. In his examination of prohibitions on incest, he finds that they appear to be both natural and cultural. He concludes that the system is inadequate but necessary and therefore that it is a case of bricolage.

Jacques Derrida adapts the term with reference to DISCOURSE in general and uses it to refer to the inevitable and necessary practice of grounding every concept in a "text of heritage" even if the heritage is incoherent or no longer adequate ("Structure, Sign," 247–65). If such is the case, then every discourse is a *bricoleur* (*Writing and Difference*, 285). According to Derrida, the idea of a speaker or author constructing a NARRATIVE or discourse independently of a system or a TEXT of heritage is a MYTH. No person can be the absolute genesis or engineer of a discourse, and the idea that such a person exists is based on the theological ASSUMPTION of a TRANSCENDENTAL SIGNIFIED. So every discourse is an instance of bricolage or, perhaps better, grounded in bricolage as a text of heritage. Ultimately, then, no discourse can be a universal one independent of CONTEXTS. On the one hand, such an assumption immediately grounds BIBLICAL CRITICISM in bricolage, in culturally constructed systems. On the other hand, such a view necessitates that the biblical authors themselves were *bricoleurs*. The latter observation argues for understanding biblical texts within their many contexts; at the same time it suggests that since even criticisms are created on bricolage, an unbridgeable divide is created between the texts and CRITICISM.

Bibliography. Jacques Derrida, "Structure, Sign, and Play in the Discourse of the Human Sciences," in *Structuralist Controversy: The Languages of Criticism and the Sciences of Man* (ed. Richard Macksey and Eugenio Donato; Baltimore: Johns Hopkins University Press, 1972), 247–65; idem, *Writing and Difference* (trans. Alan Bass; Chicago: University of Chicago Press, 1978); Claude Lévi-Strauss, *The Elementary Structures of Kinship* (trans. James Herle Bell, Richard von Sturmer, and Rodney Needham; London: Eyre & Spottiswoode, 1969); idem, *The Savage Mind* (Chicago: University of Chicago Press, 1970).

BYZANTINE TEXT

In TEXTUAL CRITICISM, a TEXT type, or family, that became dominant after the sixth century and that is most likely a combination of the three other text types prior to the sixth century—the ALEXANDRIAN TEXT, WESTERN TEXT, and CAESAREAN TEXT. Textual critics argue that the manuscripts of the NT seemed to divide into families of readings, which can be roughly grouped according to the major centers of Christianity: Alexandria, Rome, and Jerusalem. The Byzantine Text is also called the Koine (*koinē*, common) or Majority Text. The Byzantine Text type became the foundation for the TEXTUS RECEPTUS, which was the source for the KING JAMES VERSION. In terms of VARIANT READINGS, it is characterized by "clarifying the harmonizing INTERPOLATIONS and a general smoothing of DICTION" (Soulen and Soulen, 28).

Bibliography. Richard N. Soulen and R. Kendall Soulen, *Handbook of Biblical Criticism* (3rd ed.; Louisville: Westminster John Knox, 2001).

C

CAESAREAN TEXT

In TEXTUAL CRITICISM, a name for a family of manuscripts bearing similar textual characteristics that are identified geographically with Caesarea Maritima. Though it is the least distinctive of the major text types, some scholars claim that it is marked by a tendency to harmonize the ALEXANDRIAN TEXT and the WESTERN TEXT. Other scholars doubt its status as a text family distinct from the Alexandrian and Western text types.

CALLING STORY

A type of story in the GOSPELs, identified by Leland Ryken, in which Jesus calls individuals either to follow him (e.g., the disciples) or to respond to some directive or instruction (e.g., the wealthy man in Matt. 19:16–22). According to Ryken, because characters in any STORY carry MEANING beyond themselves and represent humans in general, readers of these stories are implicitly asked to identify with the characters. Consequently, readers may ascertain the characters' SIGNIFICANCE and their own identification with the characters by asking four questions: Whom does Jesus call? What are the circumstances of the call? What does Jesus ask of the character? What is the character's response, and is it the right one (36)? In this sense, CHARACTERIZATION is constitutive of meaning.

Bibliography. Leland Ryken, *Words of Life: A Literary Introduction to the New Testament* (Grand Rapids: Baker, 1987).

CANON

From the Greek *kanōn*, meaning "rod, ruler," it designates a list of writings that a religious community deems sacred, authoritative, and normative for belief and living. The term also refers to a body of beliefs or doctrine that constitutes a standard by which all statements of belief are judged to be acceptable or not. In BIBLICAL STUDIES, *canon* designates the Christian canon, which varies among the Protestant, Catholic, and Eastern Orthodox traditions.

More recently, literary critics have begun to challenge the idea of a literary canon by suggesting that cultures construct literary canons that reflect the IDEOLOGY of the dominant segment of a culture, thereby marginalizing or trivializing the literary works of those in other segments. For example, most literary canons (romantic, realist, etc.) in the Western world have relegated the work of women to the margins or have simply excluded them. This idea of canon formation and its relation to the dominant culture and ideology has virtually reshaped the landscape of critical theory since the latter half of the twentieth century. In the field of BIBLICAL CRITICISM, critics in a variety of areas are examining the biblical texts to determine ways in which the dominant patriarchal cultures (*see* PATRIARCHAL STRUCTURES; PATRIARCHY) have marginalized groups of persons, especially women, and the manner in which this marginalization is perpetuated in the study and proclamation of the BIBLE. See BIBLE; CANON, NEW TESTAMENT; CANON, OLD TESTAMENT.

CANON, CATHOLIC. *See* CATHOLIC CANON

CANON, HEBREW. *See* BIBLE; HEBREW BIBLE

CANON, LITERARY. *See* CANON

CANON, MURATORIAN. *See* MURATORIAN CANON

CANON, NEW TESTAMENT

The writings in the second division of the BIBLE that are accepted by the Christian church as authoritative guides for faith and conduct. The twenty-seven books are a mixture of GENRES— the four GOSPELs (Matthew, Mark, Luke, and John), HISTORICAL NARRATIVES (Acts of the Apostles), EPISTLES (twenty-one in number), and an APOCALYPSE (Revelation). The Epistles are commonly grouped as genuine Pauline (1 Thessalonians, 1–2 Corinthians, Galatians, Romans, Philippians, and Philemon), DEUTEROPAULINE (2 Thessalonians, Colossians, and Ephesians), PASTORALS (1–2 Timothy and Titus), and CATHOLIC (or General) EPISTLES (James, 1–2 Peter, 1–3 John, Jude, and Hebrews). *See* CANONIZATION PROCESS.

CANON, OLD TESTAMENT

The writings of the first and oldest portion of the BIBLE that are considered to be sacred writings by Jews and Christians alike (although the order of the TEXTS in the Christian OT is different from that of the HEBREW BIBLE). The OT canon has three divisions: the TORAH (law), also called the PENTATEUCH, consisting of the first five books of the OT; the PROPHETS, which may be divided into the Former Prophets and the Latter Prophets. The Former Prophets consist of the books of Joshua–2 Kings (excluding Ruth); the Latter Prophets are what scholars refer to as the "writing prophets." The Latter Prophets are subdivided into the Major Prophets (Isaiah–Ezekiel [Jews do not classify Daniel as a prophetic book], excluding Lamentations) based on length, not content; the Minor Prophets (Hosea–Malachi are sometimes called the SCROLL OF THE TWELVE). The third division consists of the remaining texts and is called the WRITINGS, a collection of various types of texts (HISTORICAL NARRATIVES, APOCALYPSE, PSALMS, WISDOM LITERATURE, LAMENT). The CATHOLIC CANON of the OT includes the APOCRYPHA, while the Protestant or REFORMATION CANON of the OT does not. *See* BIBLE; CANONIZATION PROCESS.

CANON, REFORMATION. *See* REFORMATION CANON

CANONICAL

An adjective applied to a book or books within the Christian CANON with its variations within the Protestant, Catholic, and Eastern Orthodox TRADITIONS. The adjective is also used of texts within literary canons that reflect the IDEOLOGY of the dominant segment of a culture (e.g., romantic, realist, etc.).

CANONICAL CRITICISM

A CRITICISM that looks for MEANING in the CANONICAL texts that were produced within and taken up into the life of the believing communities. The BIBLE contains the sacred writings for both Jewish and Christian communities. They are considered to be both divinely inspired and revelatory, and as such they are given a special status: they embody TRUTH in a unique way, a truth that is accessible to every generation of believers. Since the TEXTS of the Bible are given this special status, believing communities interpret them with a set of expectations that differ from the expectations believers might have for any other texts. Faith communities read the biblical texts as believers who subscribe to the faith presupposed by the texts. In other words, they read within the CONTEXT of faith, which enables them to overlook what historical critics might consider problems or inconsistencies within the texts (e.g., the differences in chronology, geography, and factual details in the SYNOPTIC GOSPELS).

Unlike SOURCE CRITICISM (looking for the sources and traditions behind a text), FORM CRITICISM (seeking to identify the various forms within a text with their life settings within the early communities), and REDACTION CRITICISM (finding meaning in the AUTHOR's editorial activities), canonical criticism moves beyond the final redaction of texts to the point in history when the texts were accepted as canonical by believing communities. As Terrance Keegan sees it, "What is most important is the text which is accepted by the Church as canonical. This canonically accepted text is the starting point of all biblical EXEGESIS. The text is what the Church has taken into its life and what remains with the Church to the present day" (30). Canonical criticism is more concerned with the text as accepted by the believing communities than with what lies behind the text. Meaning as truth depends on the community because the texts are read with different expectations and habits.

For canonical critics, the biblical texts are not merely sources for what lies behind the texts. Meaning in any final sense does not lie in the history behind the text or in the redactional activity of the author. The locus of meaning is the canonical text, which was produced within and taken up into the life of the believing communities. For instance, the emphasis within synoptic studies should be not on what happened within the life of Jesus but on the question of what the single text, say Matthew, means. A valid reading of a text takes into account not only the final form of the text but also the final form of the text as SCRIPTURE. Canonical critics also advocate reading within an expanded LITERARY context. Although Matthew should be read on its own terms in its canonical form, it should also be interpreted in light of the GOSPEL tradition, the NT, and the entire Bible. This means that a canonical reading assumes an internal unity and cohesiveness of the whole of the Scriptures.

The most notable works in the field of canonical criticism are those of James Sanders in *Canon and Community* and Brevard Childs in *Introduction to the Old Testament as Scripture* and *The New Testament as Canon*. In his treatment of the HEBREW BIBLE, Childs notes, for example, that the books of Ezra and Nehemiah do not cooperate well with the historical CRITIC who tries an accurate HISTORICAL RECONSTRUCTION of the period encompassed by the two books. Childs goes on to suggest that such attempts at historical reconstruction simply miss the point of INTERPRETATION. The focus should be on what the canonical texts have to say as Scripture: what do the texts of Ezra and Nehemiah say in their present individual ARRANGEMENTS, and why were these texts, as they are, taken into the believing community as inspired texts? Exegetical concern is not primarily centered on what lies behind the text but on the text itself.

Since the texts are universally relevant, detached from their historical SETTING and specific audience, a canonical reading is not interested in the author's intended meaning but rather in the way the texts speak to faith. Consequently, important within canonical criticism is the situation of the reader. Readers produce meaning within their present situations. This idea of reader-produced meaning, however, holds true only for members of the believing community.

While their concern is not primarily centered on what lies behind the text, canonical critics do have some interest in historical studies. Canonical critics perform historical studies, but they do not read the biblical texts historically (Keegan, 105). Rather, they study the historical CANONIZATION PROCESS. A text is composed, copied, recopied, transmitted to subsequent generations, and finally canonized. This process is significant for how the church in every generation should understand and interpret a text. Such interest in the canonical process results in two interrelated activities in canonical criticism: (1) the examination of the process by which the biblical texts in a final, stable form were accepted as canonical; and (2) based on this process, the development of a HERMENEUTICS for the interpretation of these texts within the church today.

The canonization process of the biblical canon was always in a state of flux. During this process, what might be termed an orthodox idea of what constituted a sacred piece of writing simply did not exist. The SADDUCEES, PHARISEES, and ESSENES all recognized and used varying collections of books. In the process of the canonization of the NT books, various Christian communities regarded different collections as authoritative.

In order for a book to be finally accepted into the canon, it needed to have a universal quality: it had to be able to speak to the changing situations within the life of the believing community in every age. Flexibility of application was a prerequisite for canonization. The needs of the community and the ability of a writing to speak to those needs resulted in its being selected while others, not able to do this, were rejected. After the canon stabilized, believing communities continued to adapt and reapply the canonized books to their needs.

At every stage of the canonical process, believing communities applied the writings to their own situations. This took place through adaptation, expansion, and interpretation. Believing communities sought to understand the writings through resignification. Modern hermeneuts should study the process of resignification throughout the canonical process in order to produce guidelines for the interpretive process today. To some extent, the interpretive processes extrapolated from the canonical process itself should be used as interpretive guides in today's interpretation and resignification of the biblical texts.

The believing communities adopted and adapted entire texts, not partial ones. Entire texts were resignified so as to speak in toto to the needs of the believing communities. Consequently, canonical criticism advocates a hermeneutic that considers the text as a unified whole. This focus does not mean that canonical critics are uninterested in historical-critical studies. Indeed, canonical critics employ source, form, and redaction criticism, albeit with an ulterior motive. They are interested in source criticism because it is important to ascertain the ways in which sources were resignified; they are interested in form criticism because knowing the *SITZ IM LEBEN* is helpful for understanding how a community shaped and used the form; and they are interested in redaction criticism to the extent that it offers insights into the manner in which writers in the communities reinterpreted and reapplied their sources.

Since the early believing communities resignified the texts, a plurality of meanings is suggested for the texts. Canonical critics do not advocate interpretive license; on the contrary, they insist that their hermeneutics derives from the interpretive activities observable in the stages of the canonical process. Multiple meanings are possible, but only insofar as they flow from the hermeneutics of resignification.

giving a new meaning to something

Bibliography. Brevard Childs, *Introduction to the Old Testament as Scripture* (Philadelphia: Fortress, 1979); idem, *The New Testament as Canon: An Introduction* (Philadelphia: Fortress, 1985); Terence Keegan, *Interpreting the Bible: A Popular Introduction to Biblical Hermeneutics* (New York: Paulist Press, 1985); James Sanders, *Canon and Community* (Philadelphia: Fortress, 1984).

CANONICAL GOSPELS

The four GOSPELS (Matthew, Mark, Luke, and John) found in the NT.

CANONIZATION PROCESS

The historical processes by which the ancient Jews and early Christians determined that certain writings were sacred and others were not. Three CANONS resulted from these processes: HEBREW BIBLE, CATHOLIC CANON, and REFORMATION CANON. The biblical canons did not emerge overnight but developed over a period of hundreds of years.

The Hebrew canon, or the OT portion of the BIBLE, developed out of the ORAL TRADITIONS of JUDAISM as stories passed down from generation to generation. Certain stories, especially those dealing with God's unique relationship to Israel, had special SIGNIFICANCE for a people who were often themselves in need of spiritual encouragement. These stories were later collected, set down in writing, and eventually divided into three categories: TORAH, PROPHETS, and WRITINGS.

The Torah (first five books of the Hebrew canon) developed out of the oldest oral stories of Israel. Although these stories were written down about 1000 BCE, it was not until probably during the period of the southern monarchy following the fall of Samaria in 722 BCE that these written collections were edited into their present form. They were generally accepted as the legal foundation of faith by 400 BCE (Sheeley and Nash, 13–14).

The prophetic division of the Hebrew canon is divided into the Former Prophets and the Latter Prophets. The Former Prophets include the books Joshua, Judges, 1–2 Samuel, and 1–2 Kings; the Latter Prophets consist of the Major Prophets (Isaiah, Jeremiah, and Ezekiel; Daniel is not considered prophetic) and the Minor Prophets (the remaining twelve prophetic books, generally called the SCROLL OF THE TWELVE). All these books were accepted as CANONICAL or sacred by 200 BCE. The Writings (WISDOM LITERATURE, HISTORICAL NARRATIVES, PSALMS), an eclectic category, were generally accepted as sacred by the time the Hebrew canon was closed in 90 CE.

Two factors seems to have played a decisive role in leading to the closing of the canon at the rabbinic academy in Yavneh in 90 CE. First, after the fall of Jerusalem in 70 CE, the religious leaders thought it urgent to take steps to preserve the Jewish faith. A primary step toward this preservation was to determine which books should constitute a fixed and authorized source for orthodox faith. Second, in the first century, the version of the Hebrew Bible used by the Christians was the Greek translation of the Hebrew Bible called the SEPTUAGINT, which included the APOCRYPHA, a collection of around fourteen books or portions of books not accepted as part of the Hebrew canon. Consequently, it is possible that the Christians' widespread use of the Apocrypha along with the Hebrew canon was a decisive factor in the rabbinic decision to close the canon in about 90 CE.

The formation of the NT followed a similar but shorter development. The process probably began with early collections of the SAYINGS OF JESUS. In Paul's writings (50–62 CE) Jesus's words are quoted as authoritative in matters of faith. Also during the period of postapostolic Christianity (ca. 70–140 CE), certain LETTERS of Paul and others ascribed to him were circulated. Clement of Rome (96) refers to Romans, 1 Corinthians, and Hebrews; Ignatius of Antioch (110) knew of Romans, 1 Corinthians, and Ephesians. More than likely, Paul's Letters circulated independently among churches in Asia Minor, Palestine, and Italy and only later were preserved in a collection. Although a collection of Paul's Letters existed much earlier, the range of the collection was fluid until the third century. As early as 150 CE, Polycarp of Smyrna knew of seven Letters of Paul. Irenaeus (180) quoted ten Letters ascribed to Paul along with 1–2 Timothy. After this time, Titus was often assumed to belong

to Paul along with 1–2 Timothy. Because of its uncertain authorship, the authenticity of Hebrews was debated until the fourth century. During this period, the CATHOLIC EPISTLES were also circulated. When the book of Revelation was employed by the Montanists in support of their ideas, its status was questioned in many churches, especially in Asia Minor and Rome.

The four GOSPELS were in use by the mid-second century, but there was no consensus about their exclusive use. Early church fathers such as Justin Martyr, Irenaeus of Lyons, Clement of Alexandria, and Tertullian used the four Gospels as SCRIPTURE and argued for a closed collection of these four.

By 250 CE, Origen of Alexandria had written commentaries, SERMONS, and treatises on the books in use by the Egyptian churches. Using these as sources, the historian Eusebius in 320 compiled a list of books consisting of the four Gospels, Paul's Letters (except Philemon), Hebrews, 1 John, Acts, and Revelation. Origen, however, had used writings as authoritative beyond the list compiled by Eusebius, suggesting that the canon was still rather fluid in the time of Origen. Among these other books were the *Acts of Pilate,* the *Didache,* the *Shepherd of Hermas,* and the writings of Ignatius. The MURATORIAN CANON, discovered in 1740 and most likely dating from the fourth century, includes twenty-four books—the four Gospels, Acts, thirteen Letters of Paul, Jude, 1–2 John, Wisdom of Solomon, Revelation, and the APOCALYPSE *of Peter.* So at least into the fourth century, the canon of the NT was not finalized (Puskas, 263–64).

On January 7, 367, Athanasius, bishop of Alexandria, sent an encyclical Easter letter to his churches in which he listed all twenty-seven (and no other) books of the NT as "canonized." Even after this letter, individual churches made use of different canons. Toward the end of the fourth century, however, Jerome translated the Hebrew Bible and the NT into Latin (the VULGATE). Following Athanasius's list, he included the seven Catholic Letters, Revelation, and Hebrews. The Vulgate became the official Bible for the Catholic Church.

During the Protestant Reformation, a number of theologians and humanists such as Erasmus, Cardinal Cajetan, and Martin Luther had misgivings about certain books or at least about their apostolic origins—Hebrews, James, 2 Peter, Jude, 2–3 John, and to some extent, Revelation. In his TRANSLATION, Luther placed some of these at the end and referred to them as "less esteemed" (Puskas, 264–65). As a response, the Catholic Church issued a decree at the Council of Trent (1546) that the books of the Vulgate were "sacred and canonical in their entirety, with all their parts," thus bestowing equal authority on all twenty-seven books of the NT. Since Jerome had used the LXX from which to translate the OT into Latin, the Vulgate contains the Apocrypha. At the same council, therefore, the church affirmed its canonical authority. The Apocrypha, however, has traditionally been rejected by the Reformation churches as noncanonical, though beneficial for devotional purposes (265). Consequently, the Hebrew canon is what Protestants refer to as the OT; the Catholic canon contains the Hebrew Bible, the NT, and the Apocrypha; the Reformation canon contains the Hebrew Bible and the NT.

Bibliography. Charles B. Puskas, *An Introduction to the New Testament* (Peabody, MA: Hendrickson, 1989); Steven M. Sheeley and Robert N. Nash Jr., *The Bible in English Translation: An Essential Guide* (Nashville: Abingdon, 1997).

CANTICLE

A poem or HYMN taken from the BIBLE (other than from the PSALMS) and used in church liturgy. Among these canticles are Exod. 15:1–18; Deut. 32:1–43; Luke 1:46–55, 68–79; 2:29–32.

CAPTATIO BENEVOLENTIAE

A LITERARY DEVICE by which an AUTHOR offers flattery by assuming that the reader will be familiar with a particular body of knowledge. An example of flattery and ASSUMPTION is found in Rom. 7:1: "Do you not know, brothers and sisters—for I am speaking to those who know the law—that the law is binding on a person only during that person's lifetime?" The same assumption underlies 1 Cor.

9:24: "Do you not know that in a race the runners all compete, but only one receives the prize?" (cf. Acts 24:2–3).

CAPTIVITY EPISTLES. *See* PRISON EPISTLES

CARICATURE

In art, a portrait that criticizes someone by distorting and amplifying that person's most outstanding features. *See* CHARACTERIZATION.

CARNIVAL. *See* CARNIVALESQUE

CARNIVALESQUE

A term popularized by the Russian LITERARY critic Mikhail Bakhtin to describe the spirit of carnival in literature. The carnivalesque is characterized by PLAY, PARODY, subversion of conventional authority, and exaggeration (*see* EXAGGERATION, COMIC). According to Bakhtin, late medieval and early Renaissance folk culture developed parallel to the official ecclesiastical and feudal culture and in opposition to it. Through such tools as humor, parody, and exaggeration, this culture subverts the official IDEOLOGY, thus offering a means of escaping the latter's repression. For Bakhtin, the carnivalesque developed its own rituals and LITERARY CONVENTIONS, which for some scholars revealed the formal conventions underlying all parodic DISCOURSE. In its literary expression, the carnivalesque challenges all order and the sacrosanct within the official ideology while resisting demands of CLOSURE. In the READER-RESPONSE CRITICISM of Wolfgang Iser, the carnivalization of RHETORIC refers to the claim that the STRUCTURE of a literary TEXT can be configured in a variety of ways and that complex texts have as a component of their INTENTION such a configurative variety.

The GOSPEL of Mark may be used as an example of the carnivalesque and the carnivalization of rhetoric. With respect to the former, scholars in SOCIAL-SCIENTIFIC CRITICISM argue that Mark challenges the existing social structures of purity and impurity, while literary critics argue that it challenges the Markan community's emphasis on a Christology of power, which is corrected by a Christology of suffering in the second half of the work. With respect to the latter, the devices of openness in Mark's Gospel (e.g., its PARATAXIS STYLE, truncated ending, INTERCALATION, extensive literary ALLUSION) generate a variety of CONFIGURATIONS.

Bibliography. Mikhail Bakhtin, *Rabelais and His World* (trans. Helene Iswalsky; Cambridge, MA: MIT Press, 1968); Wolfgang Iser, *Prospecting: From Reader Response to Literary Anthropology* (Baltimore: Johns Hopkins University Press, 1989).

CASUISTIC LAW

In FORM CRITICISM of the HEBREW BIBLE, a type of case law that usually begins with an expressed or implied condition (PROTASIS) followed by a consequence expressed in terms of a penalty (APODOSIS). Form critics have argued that casuistic law was typical of ancient Mesopotamian law. In Exodus, a long section (21:2–23:33) of casuistic law follows the APODICTIC Ten Commandments (20:1–17; *see* DECALOGUE).

CATACHRESIS

The misuse or misapplication of a word (e.g., "the foot of the bed"). It can also refer to a mixed figure, as when an object of one sense is expressed in terms of another one ("amazing grace, how *sweet* the *sound*").

CATALOG

Any listing of objects, traits, persons, and so forth. *See* CATALOG OF VICES/VIRTUES; CATALOG STRUCTURE.

CATALOG OF VICES/VIRTUES

A common LITERARY form in the paraenetic (*see* PARAENESIS) sections of Paul's Letters and to some extent found in other NT LETTERS. These catalogs seem to have their origin in both Jewish and HELLENISTIC traditions (although the form does not seem well developed in the HEBREW BIBLE). They vary in length and do not necessarily reflect the situation at any particular church (e.g., Rom.

1:29–31; 1 Cor. 5:10–11; 2 Cor. 6:6–7, 14; Gal. 5:19–23; Phil. 4:8). A catalog of vices may stand alone, as in Rom. 1:29–31, or it may be paired with a catalog of virtues, as in Gal. 5:19–23. William Doty suggests that the HOUSEHOLD CODES, which offer specific domestic duties, should be included in this type of paraenesis (58). As is evidenced in Wis. 14:22–31, HELLENISTIC JUDAISM made use of the form to condemn the lifestyle of the Gentiles. Burton Easton suggests that the lists were conventional by quoting from Onosander's (first century) description of the moral qualifications of a general and then comparing it to the requirements of bishops in 1 Tim. 3:2–7:

> I say that the general should be chosen as sober minded, self-controlled, temperate, frugal, hardy, intelligent, no lover of money, not too young or old, if he be the father of children, able to speak well, of good repute.

Attempts to identify these catalogs with particular ecclesiastical communities will probably result in frustration or at best be nothing more than speculation. More likely, the authors adapted these catalogs to describe general moral behavior and problems (e.g., 1 Cor. 5:10–11; Col. 3:12–14). The NT catalogs include Rom. 1:29–31; 1 Cor. 6:9–10; 2 Cor. 6:6–7; Gal. 5:19–23; Eph. 6:14–17; Phil. 4:8; James 3:17; 1 Pet. 4:3; 2 Pet. 1:5–8; Rev. 9:20–21.

Bibliography. William G. Doty, *Letters in Primitive Christianity* (Philadelphia: Fortress, 1973); Burton Scott Easton, "New Testament Ethical Lists," *JBL* 51 (1932): 1–12.

CATALOG STRUCTURE

A term used by Leland Ryken to describe a particular STRUCTURE of a Hebrew poem. A poem that lists the various aspects of a SUBJECT has a catalog structure (e.g., Ps. 139:1–6 catalogs the marks of God's omniscience).

Bibliography. Leland Ryken, *Words of Delight: A Literary Introduction to the Bible* (Grand Rapids: Baker, 1987).

CATHOLIC CANON

The texts that constitute the SCRIPTURES of the Catholic Church. The Catholic canon is identical to the REFORMATION CANON with the exception that the Catholic canon includes the APOCRYPHA, the collection of texts that was included in the SEPTUAGINT but not in the HEBREW (BIBLE) CANON. Since the LXX was used by the Jews in the DIASPORA and by the early Christians, the Apocrypha became part of the Christian Scriptures. During the Protestant Reformation, Martin Luther excluded the Apocrypha from his canon. For a comparative listing of the texts of the Reformation canon and the Catholic canon, *see* REFORMATION CANON.

CATHOLIC EPISTLES

A group of seven LETTERS in the NT addressed to a general audience rather than to specific churches. These include James, 1–2 Peter, 1–3 John, and Jude. Since these letters differ from each other in their LITERARY forms, the title "EPISTLE" is perhaps inadequate to describe them as a group. The documents 1–3 John are actually a SERMON, a warning letter, and a private note respectively. Apart from its brief salutation, James gives no evidence that it is a letter, but rather it seems to be a collection of PROVERBS, short commentaries, and moral exhortation. Second Peter and Jude are tractates denouncing unidentified heretics, and 1 Peter is a tract describing proper Christian behavior. All but Jude are ascribed to leaders of the Jerusalem church—Peter, James, and John—while Jude is ascribed to Jesus's brother. With the exception of 1 Peter, the Catholic Epistles were the last works to be accepted into the NT canon (*see* CANON, NEW TESTAMENT), not being mentioned for the most part in lists of CANONICAL books until the third century. As a group, these letters have the distinct quality of being products of a church that is in the process of becoming institutionalized, with its own episcopate and CANON.

CAUSE-AND-EFFECT MOVEMENT

A type of FOCUSING relationship between the two clauses of a single line of BIBLICAL POETRY, identified by Robert Alter. The first half of the line is related to the second half through cause and effect as in the following:

I call upon the LORD, who is worthy to be praised,
so I shall be saved from my enemies. (Ps. 18:3)

The relation between these two parts is one of cause ("call") and effect ("saved"). *See* BIBLICAL POETRY

Bibliography. Robert Alter, *The Art of Biblical Poetry* (New York: Basic Books, 1985).

CE

Abbreviation for "Common Era." It is synonymous with AD (abbreviation for Latin *anno Domini*, "in the year of the Lord"). Thus CE designates the years since the birth of Jesus without the religious overtones of AD but still recognizes this event as the major dividing point in the history of the Western world. Like BCE, since it is a religiously neutral term, Christians, Muslims, and Jews as well as others can use it.

CENTER

A concept within POSTMODERNISM designating the process by which society creates ideological foundations (*see* IDEOLOGY) or STRUCTURES that serve as ways of perceiving and defining reality and values. These centers exist only at the expense of ignoring or marginalizing other possibilities because society assumes that these centers or foundations are universal. Since held to be universally true, such centers become normative, occupying privileged positions, and are themselves immune to doubt. They are considered natural givens and thus unassailable. Such centers can be seen in the BINARY OPPOSITIONS on which Western culture has rested—male over female, nature over culture, spirit over flesh, reason over emotion. "The history of thought has produced a succession of 'centers,' or metaphors around which system, doctrine, and meaning have been organized" (Thiselton, 111). Poststructuralists such as Jacques Derrida, Michel Foucault, and Jacques Lacan have argued that these centers are not universal but constructs of social, economic, linguistic, and political perspectives. By rethinking these "natural givens," poststructuralist critics (*see* POSTMODERN CRITICISM) PROBLEMA-TIZE the centers and argue that they do not exist. Such givens as the existence of the self, essential human nature, and the primacy of SPEECH over writing are constructs arbitrarily and artificially created over time and stand in need of decentering. Such decentering will permit new possibilities and reveal the limitations of systems based on supposed centers.

In recent biblical scholarship, those centers or foundations and value systems from which the biblical writers proceed are examined as human constructs rather than natural givens. In other words, such social, political, and religious systems as honor/shame and purity/impurity are decentered and exposed as structured realities that have resulted in the MARGINALIZATION of other possibilities and groups. *See* DECONSTRUCTION; POSTMODERN CRITICISM; POSTMODERNISM/ POSTMODERNITY.

> *Bibliography.* Anthony Thiselton, *New Horizons in Hermeneutics* (Grand Rapids: Zondervan, 1992).

CEREMONIAL LAWS

Laws in the HEBREW BIBLE that relate to temple service, regulating sacrifice and purification, as opposed to civil and moral laws. Much of the material from Exod. 25 through Num. 10 (often called the PRIESTLY CODE) can be classified as ceremonial law.

CERTAINTY

With respect to the BIBLE, the idea that absolute and firm claims can be made about the MEANING of texts or the Bible's capacity to supply dependable, unambiguous knowledge and TRUTH. Even though there may be vague and obscure words and phrases in the biblical texts, their general meanings can be known with certainty.

Many contemporary critics, however, argue that since meaning is always mediated through an interpreter, who brings a matrix of perspectives to the act of INTERPRETATION, absolute certainty is impossible to achieve. Meaning is always perspec-

tival, formulated within CONTEXTS, and never from a point of absolute objectivity.

CEV. *See* CONTEMPORARY ENGLISH VERSION

CHABURAH

A religious gathering of friends within JUDAISM that flourished in the Second Temple period and into the Mishnaic and Talmudic periods (*see* MISHNAH; TALMUD). Separate from the synagogue functions but including fellow Jews, it always included a meal. It may be thought of as a type of social gathering (more like a dinner group than a small-group Bible study) to build and reinforce Jewish identity, especially in the DIASPORA. John 13:1–20 may be read as such a gathering of Jesus and his friends (disciples) for a common meal rather than as a Passover meal. At a minimum, Acts 2:46; 20:7; and 1 Cor. 11:17–22 provide evidence that the early Christians participated in such a meal.

CHARACTER, DYNAMIC. *See* DYNAMIC CHARACTER

CHARACTER, FLAT. *See* FLAT CHARACTER

CHARACTER, FULL-FLEDGED. *See* FULL-FLEDGED CHARACTER

CHARACTER, STATIC. *See* STATIC CHARACTER

CHARACTER, STEREOTYPE. *See* STEREO-TYPE CHARACTER

CHARACTER, STOCK. *See* STOCK CHARACTER

CHARACTERIZATION

In literature, the art of creating fictional characters who appear to be realistic. First, authors may create characters through EXPOSITION, which may occur in the introductory part of the work and/ or throughout the work. Second, characterization may be developed throughout the work through the ACTION of the character with little if any direct comment by the AUTHOR. In this case, the author expects the reader to discern the character's person by deducing traits from the action. Third, the reader is expected to construct a character by REFERENCE to that person's responses to actions and situations without comment by the author (Harmon and Holman, 89).

In literature, a range of characters appear: STATIC, DYNAMIC, ROUNDED, FLAT, STEREOTYPE, and STOCK characters plus CARICATURE. A flat character is one-dimensional, with a single dominant trait; the rounded character is more complex and fully developed. This rounded character is usually presented from more than one perspective; the person acts and reacts both to internal and external forces and thus is the one who carries the PLOT. The static character never changes, remaining the same because things only happen *to* the person, not within the person. The dynamic character is not only rounded but also one who changes over time. Usually the latter type is the PROTAGONIST of a STORY. If the author focuses on a single trait to the extreme, the character is not believable but a caricature. Stock characters are both flat and predictable. A stock character who is consistently predictable is a stereotype.

All three methods and all character types can be found in the BIBLE. Adele Berlin identifies three kinds of characters in HEBREW NARRATIVE: FULL-FLEDGED, TYPE, and AGENT—roughly equivalent to ROUNDED/DYNAMIC, flat/static, and stock/stereotype respectively. The full-fledged character is multidimensional and complex, manifesting a range of character traits. This character confronts the reader with psychological, emotional, and spiritual complexities. David's wife Michal is a full-fledged character. The author goes to great lengths in presenting her as a woman with her own emotions and opinions.

A single character trait distinguishes the *type*. Such a character is Laban. From the first time we meet him in Gen. 24, we are struck by his distinguishing trait of materialism. His materialistic motivation is sustained in his dealings with Jacob in Gen. 29.

The agent is nothing more than a functionary, which the author uses to fill out the NARRATIVE. This character is usually not developed at all but simply serves the purpose of providing the necessary characters for a story. Depending on the narrative and its purpose, however, a single character's role may change. A character who is full-fledged in one narrative may become an agent or a type in another.

The Hebrew Bible evidences a variety of characterization techniques. First is DESCRIPTION. HEBREW NARRATIVE is rather sparse in its descriptive details. Some descriptive details are present, but only in the service of the plot. For example, the information that Eglon in Judges is fat leads the reader to see Eglon as the calf fattened for the slaughter. Bathsheba's beauty partly anticipates David's actions. But beyond occasional general descriptions (e.g., the ruddiness of David, the height of Saul, the handsomeness of Absalom, the beauty of Sarah), Hebrew narrative gives precious little specific detail. Detailed physical description of characters is simply not present in Hebrew narrative. The reader must gain insight into character differently than one would in most modern novels. It therefore seems that Hebrew narrative is less interested in presenting the appearance of a character than in guiding the reader to discover what kind of a person the character is.

INTERIORIZATION occurs when the NARRATOR supplies the reader with windows into the mental or emotional state of a character. The reader views the action (or a portion of it) through the eyes of the character. The author can achieve this interiorization in two ways. First, the narrator may comment on a character's thought or opinion. We become privy to the thoughts of a character, but the thoughts are expressed in the words of the narrator: "So Noah knew that the waters had subsided from the earth" (Gen. 8:11b). Even God himself is not exempt: "God heard their groaning, and God remembered his COVENANT with Abraham, Isaac, and Jacob. God looked upon the Israelites, and God took notice of them" (Exod. 2:24–25). This type of interiorization is called *external interiorization*. Second, through *interior monologue* the narrator makes extensive use of direct quotes of a character's thoughts. "Then Moses was afraid and thought, 'Surely the thing is known'" (Exod. 2:14). Such windows into a character's thoughts enable the reader to make judgments about a character's emotion and motivation. These judgments in turn help the reader fill out the character, to know what kind of person the character is.

Direct DIALOGUE is the preferred method in Hebrew narrative for sustaining the action within the PLOT. Direct dialogue conveys the internal psychological and ideological dimensions of a character and is much more dramatic than exterior narration. The direct speech of Samson in Judg. 14–16 illustrates the point. After returning from Timnah, Samson says to his parents, "I saw a Philistine woman at Timnah; now get her for me as my wife" (14:2). Although he is discouraged from taking a foreign wife, especially since he is a Nazirite, Samson replies, "Get her for me, because she pleases me" (14:3b). The sharp, demanding tone of this speech reveals Samson's character as marked by a sense of immediate, thoughtless gratification. Even in his remarks to God, Samson exhibits this same tone of ingratitude: "By then he was very thirsty, and he called on the LORD, saying, 'You have granted this great victory by the hand of your servant. Am I now to die of thirst, and fall into the hands of the uncircumcised?" (15:18). Gratification and revenge mark Samson's character as seen through his direct dialogue. Nothing changes at his death, for even here revenge is his motivation: "Lord GOD, remember me and strengthen me only this once, O God, so that with this one act of revenge I may pay back the Philistines for my two eyes" (16:28).

Although in Hebrew narrative direct SPEECH and actions usually are combined, actions can be narrated without speech. These speechless accounts highlight character. They tend to serve as unannounced COMMENTARY on a character's speech. We already know from Laban's past record that he is adept at deception. Therefore, when we hear Jacob's proposal to Laban in Gen. 30:30–33 and Laban's response in 30:34, we suspect that we are in store for yet another ruse (30:35–36). But we also know that Jacob is perhaps Laban's

equal when it comes to ingenuity and originality in trickery. So we are not entirely surprised by Jacob's response to Laban's ploy and are entertained by his creativity (30:37–43). By placing characters in juxtaposition, an author highlights character traits, especially those traits that appear to be incongruent to a character's social status.

For instance, Adele Berlin describes how the author of 1 Sam. 18–20 successfully, yet subtly, contrasts character traits in Michal and Jonathan. The reader is struck with the incongruity. Jonathan displays characteristics usually identified as feminine, while Michal exhibits definite masculine traits. The relationship between Michal and David is marked by purely pragmatic considerations, and "the feelings of love and tenderness that David might have been expected to have for Michal are all reserved for Jonathan" (25). The story of Deborah and Barak is another example of character CONTRAST (Judg. 4–5). Deborah is decisive. She sizes up the situation and then without delay acts. She says to Barak, "The LORD, the God of Israel, commands you, 'Go, take position at Mount Tabor, bringing ten thousand from the tribe of Naphtali and the tribe of Zebulun'" (4:6). But Barak hesitates: "If you will go with me, I will go; but if you will not go with me, I will not go" (4:8). At once Deborah recognizes his hesitation, rebukes him, and then goes with him. Later, once again Barak does not move until Deborah commands him (4:14a). Without a doubt, each character's personality is heightened by contrast.

Bibliography. Robert Alter, *The Art of Biblical Narrative* (New York: Basic Books, 1981); Adele Berlin, *Poetics and Interpretation of Biblical Narrative* (Sheffield: Almond, 1983); William Harmon and C. Hugh Holman, *A Handbook to Literature* (8th ed.; Upper Saddle River, NJ: Prentice Hall, 1999); Meir Sternberg, *Poetics of Biblical Narrative* (Bloomington: Indiana University Press, 1985).

CHIASMUS

Derived from the Greek letter *chi* (X), chiasmus is a LITERARY DEVICE in which the words, poetic lines, or events are inversely repeated in order to shape EPISODES, SPEECHes, or entire cycles of stories. John F. Kennedy's famous line, "Ask not what your country can do for you; ask what you can do for your country," is an example (A = your country; B = you; B′ = you; A′ = your country). Sometimes the chiasmus will have an odd number of parts, as in Amos 5:4b–6a:

A Seek me and live;
    B but do not seek *Bethel*,
        C and do not enter into Gilgal
            D or cross over to Beersheba;
        C′ for *Gilgal* shall surely go into exile,
    B′ and *Bethel* shall come to nothing.
A′ *Seek* the LORD and *live*.

A more complex example is Num. 11:11–15:

A First question: Why has God mistreated Moses? "Why have you treated your servant so badly?"
    B Second question: What has Moses done to deserve an undue burden? "Why have I not found favor in your sight, that you lay the burden of all this people on me?"
        C Third question: Why should Moses carry these people as a nurse carries a baby? "Did I give birth to them, that you should say to me, 'Carry them in your bosom, as a nurse carries a suckling child,' to the land that you promised on oath to their ancestors?"
            D Fourth question: How can Moses supply food? "Where am I to get meat to give to all this people?"
            D′ Response to fourth question: "For they come weeping to me and say, 'Give us meat to eat!'"
        C′ Response to third question: "I am not able to carry all this people alone,"
    B′ Response to second question: "for they are too heavy for me."
A′ Response to first question: "If this is the way you are going to treat me, put me to death at once."

Bibliography. W. Randolph Tate, *Biblical Interpretation: An Integrated Approach* (rev. ed.; Peabody, MA: Hendrickson, 1997).

CHICAGO SCHOOL

A group of CRITICS from the University of Chicago who were active between the two World Wars and who were concerned with social issues and urban studies. They did, however, develop ASSUMPTIONS about the nature of literature and its CRITICISM. As LITERARY critics, they were neo-Aristotelian in their attention to literary POETICS (the principles governing the construction of texts) and GENRE considerations. They took as their starting point Aristotle's four causes and applied them to literary texts: the material cause (language), the efficient cause (the AUTHOR), the formal cause (genre), and the final cause (the effect on the reader). They argued that present criticism tended to focus only on one of the causes at the expense of the others. Consequently, LITERARY CRITICISM tended to become a hodgepodge of competing disciplines, often appearing to contradict each other. For these critics, literary criticism should concern itself with all four causes, with the text as an author's language construct according to certain analyzable structures, which produce effects of pleasure and instruction (insight experiences) in the reader. Nevertheless, they tended to account for MEANING in terms of the formal cause, the STRUCTURE and FORM of a literary work. In other words, they were concerned with what a writer does as an *author* and with how this structurally creative activity is distinct from the writer as a social, philosophical, psychological, or moral person. The latter concerns, according to the Chicago school, should be the domain of other disciplines such as psychology, theology, or sociology (Vince, 118). The literary CRITIC should focus on the traits of the text that characterize it as poiesis, something creatively made, and on the relationship between structure and effect. Thus, mimesis (imitation) becomes a central item in their system: a literary work imitates aspects of human life in such a way as to produce in the reader an insight into human existence. Logically, then, their attention was on PLOT and genre.

The Chicago critics, however, favored pluralism of methods because they recognized that methods are actually systems of questions and that what will be claimed about a text depends on the questions put to it. They assumed that there is no absolute system that will provide definitive results. While few critics follow the Chicago school today, such an openness to pluralism of methods has remained an essential part of literary criticism as seen in the variety of POSTMODERN theories, which challenge claims of critical elitism.

Bibliography. R. S. Crane, ed., *Critics and Criticism: Ancient and Modern* (Chicago: University of Chicago Press, 1952); Ronald W. Vince, "Neo-Aristotelian or Chicago School," in *Encyclopedia of Contemporary Literary Theory* (ed. Irena R. Makaryk; Toronto: University of Toronto Press, 1993), 116–19; René Wellek, *American Criticism, 1900–1950* (vol. 6 of *A History of Modern Criticism, 1750–1950*; New Haven: Yale University Press, 1986).

CHREIA

In FORM CRITICISM, a term adopted from Greek meaning "a need/want" and defined by Martin Dibelius in *From Tradition to Gospel* (London: James Clarke, 1971) as "a sharp pointed saying of general significance, originating in a definite person and arising out of a definite situation." According to Dibelius, a chreia is different from the APOPHTHEGM and the GNOME in its connection to a definite situation and person (Soulen and Soulen, 33). Dibelius claims that many of the sayings of Jesus were molded (esp. in Luke) to chreia by taking an uncontextualized saying and giving it a definite context (e.g., Luke 11:27–28; 19:39–40).

Bibliography. Richard N. Soulen and R. Kendall Soulen, *Handbook of Biblical Criticism* (3rd ed.; Louisville: Westminster John Knox, 2001).

CHRIST

From Greek, *christos*, meaning "anointed one" and similar in MEANING to the Hebrew *māšîaḥ* (messiah), "anointed one." Early Christians viewed Jesus as fulfilling the messianic expectations and thus applied the term to him. In Greek culture, however, *christos* did not carry messianic SIGNIFICANCE as in the Hebrew. Consequently, scholars point out that in time the Greek term became a proper name (e.g., Gal. 1:1, 3, 6; Heb. 9:11) in early Christianity while "Son of God" became a theological title (e.g., Mark 1:1).

CHRISTIAN

According to Acts 11:26, a term first used for the followers of Jesus in Antioch. The designation stuck and is used today for those who profess faith in Jesus as divine and attempt to follow his teachings.

CHRISTOCENTRISM

A term with both theological and hermeneutical SIGNIFICANCE. Theologically, it refers to the view that CHRIST and the Christ event are the central, pivotal point in theological systems and that all claims of the systems proceed from this centrality. Hermeneutically, the term designates at least three claims: (1) that Christ's person, his coming, and events in his life fulfill the rule of God begun in the HEBREW BIBLE; (2) that Christ is the center of the SCRIPTURE, the ANTITYPE for everything that happens in the Hebrew Bible; and (3) that the Hebrew Bible must be interpreted with a backward view in light of the Christ event: everything in the Hebrew Bible must be interpreted as prototypical of Christ even if the authors did not intend it to be christocentric.

Bibliography. James W. Voelz, *What Does This Mean? Principles of Biblical Interpretation in the Postmodern World* (St. Louis: Concordia, 1995).

CHRIST OF THE CHURCH

A theological figure created by the early church and quite distinct from the historical person. Some scholars of the NT argue that the figure of Christ we find in the NT is a theological INTERPRETATION of the actual figure of Jesus. Consequently, since this actual historical figure is obscured by the theological layers of the NT TEXTS, we have access only to the Christ of the church, or the Christ of faith. *See* HISTORICAL JESUS; QUEST FOR THE HISTORICAL JESUS.

CHRISTOLOGICAL HYMN

A GENRE of the NT consisting of lyrics written in parallelism. While there is a variety of HYMNS in the NT, the christological hymns focus exclusively on CHRIST. Some are characterized by formal, stylistic, and patterned ARRANGEMENT and FIGURATIVE LANGUAGE, while others are less stylized. Yet all contain clear christological THEMES. Consequently, they function as CREEDS and theological confessions. Most of these hymns were borrowed by the NT writers from liturgies of the early church, where the more rhythmic ones were sung in worship CONTEXTS. Furthermore, these christological hymns seem to be structured through a movement from Christ's exaltation to humiliation to exaltation again (Bailey and Vander Broek, 79). The best-known christological hymn is in Phil. 2:6–11. Other examples are Col. 1:15–20; John 1:1–18, and 1 Tim. 3:16. *See* CONFESSIONAL HYMN; HYMN; MEDITATIVE HYMN; SACRAMENTAL HYMN.

Bibliography. James L. Bailey and Lyle D. Vander Broek, *Literary Forms in the New Testament: A Handbook* (Louisville: Westminster John Knox, 1992).

CHRISTOLOGY

The theological INTERPRETATION and systemization of the person and work of Jesus. The interpretation of the divinity, preexistence, and creative role in the universe were developed over time and formalized in church councils. Though theologians may speak of a NT Christology, meaning a theological view of the person and work of Jesus based on the NT as a whole, they may also refer to more narrowly defined Christologies—Mark's Christology, the Christology of Luke-Acts, Pauline Christology, the Christology in Hebrews, and so forth. For brief definitions of some other Christologies, see Donald K. McKim, *Westminster Dictionary of Theological Terms* (Louisville: Westminster John Knox, 1996).

CHRISTOPHANY

A term referring to a manifestation of Christ, especially referring to the appearances of the resurrected Jesus in the NT (e.g., Matt. 28:9–10, 16–17; Mark 16:9–10, 12, 14–20; Luke 24:13–35; Acts 9:3–16). Scholars who hold a christocentric (*see* CHRISTOCENTRISM) view of the BIBLE may also assume that theophanies (*see* THEOPHANY) in the HEBREW BIBLE are christophanies.

CHRONICLE

A genre of historical writing that is distinct from historical narrative in that a chronicle usually lists events and persons without giving attention to cause and effect or SIGNIFICANCE. Consequently, 1–2 Chronicles in the HEBREW BIBLE is technically not of the chronicle genre. There are, however, references in the Hebrew Bible to chronicles as sources for historical narratives (e.g., 1 Kings 14:29).

CHRONICLER

One who writes a CHRONICLE. In BIBLICAL CRITICISM, the *Chronicler* refers to the AUTHOR or school of authors who produced the CHRONISTIC HISTORY in 1–2 Chronicles, Ezra, and Nehemiah.

CHRONISTIC HISTORY (CHRONICLER'S HISTORY)

Most scholars describe the books of 1–2 Chronicles, Ezra, and Nehemiah as constituting a history independent of the DEUTERONOMISTIC HISTORY. Yet many scholars today think that 1–2 Chronicles constitutes a work that is distinct from Ezra and Nehemiah, although these two works do take up Judah's history at the point where 2 Chronicles ends (cf. 2 Chron. 36:22 and Ezra 1:1).

The prophets of the exilic period (EXILE, 586–538 BCE) introduced the prospect of a return to the homeland in rather idealized imagery, along with a hope of a reestablished Davidic monarchy. When the former captives returned, however, they were faced with the depressing disparity between the ideal and reality. They returned to a land that had been devastated by Nebuchadnezzar's army, there was no enduring prospect of a restored Davidic dynasty, and the splendors of city and temple were a thing of the past. Into this reality stepped the Chronicler(s), who recognized that Judah was faced with a new course of history and from this new perspective began to rethink Judah's history. The past would thenceforth be interpreted not from the perspective of obedience to the TORAH but from the new perspective that saw Israel's destiny in terms of ethical and ritual purity. From the vantage point of the Chronicler, this destiny can be and is being realized in terms of redefining Israel as a people of the book rather than as a national autonomous state with a Davidic monarchy. In fact, rather than being led by kings, Judah will be governed by priests. It is probably for this reason that the Chronicler presents the kings in Judah's history as assuming both monarchical and priestly functions.

If the Deuteronomistic history and the Chronistic history are read comparatively, it becomes obvious that the books of Samuel and Kings are the primary INTERTEXTS. In other words, the Chronicler has used these texts as primary sources and, using other sources as well (ANNALS of Samuel the seer, annals of Nathan the prophet, the annals of Gad the seer, and the Solomonic and Hezekiah archives [1 Chron. 29:29–30; 2 Chron. 9:29; 32:32]), constructed a highly stylized account of Israel's past. The reason for such a rewriting of Israel's history is described very well by Stephen Harris: "The Chronicler's primary intent ... is to insist that the nation's principal mission is to worship Yahweh wholeheartedly and to demonstrate that the failure of later kings to honor the Jerusalem sanctuary led to the monarchy's collapse" (226). The reigns of David and Solomon are especially subjected to this purpose, which means that they are portrayed via omitting most of the unflattering events found in the Deuteronomistic account. For example, the Bathsheba and Uriah story and Solomon's corruption by his wives are carefully omitted. Rather than portraying David as a great warrior-king, the Chronicler presents us with a David who is a devout Yahwist (*see* J; YAHWEH), a priest-king whose primary concern is to establish the temple cult and prepare for the construction of the temple itself, a task that becomes the Chroni-

cler's primary focus in describing Solomon's reign. Even the story of Manasseh is recast to present him as repenting from his sins and becoming a zealous religious reformer.

The Chronistic history interpreted the nation's downfall as the direct result of the neglect of temple worship. To make this point, the Chronicler reinterpreted history by selectively using his sources. But the purpose of the Chronicler was not simply to indict the kings of the past, especially those following David and Solomon. He was looking to the future of the nation and trying to revive in his audience a zealous attitude toward the temple and its priestly services. We might conclude that the Chronistic history is a priestly account of Israel's past. Again, like the Deuteronomistic history, it is not an unbiased, disinterested account. By structuring Israel's and Judah's past in particular ways, both the Deuteronomist(s) and Chronicler(s) attempted to persuade their contemporary audiences to think and live in particular ways in the present. In order to understand their present conditions and to carve out a meaningful vision for the future, these authors reflected on the past. Only by standing squarely within the contemporary effects could these writers interpret the past in terms of cause. Thus, history in this sense is not simply a sequence of events but a perspectival interpretation and narrative of some of those events for the purpose of making sense of the present.

Bibliography. Stephen Harris, *Understanding the Bible* (6th ed.; Boston: McGraw-Hill, 2003); Christian E. Hauer and William Young, *An Introduction to the Bible: A Journey into Three Worlds* (Upper Saddle River, NJ: Prentice Hall, 1998), 199–200; Shemaryahu Talmon, "Ezra and Nehemiah," in *The Literary Guide to the Bible* (ed. Robert Alter and Frank Kermode; Cambridge, MA: Belknap Press of Harvard University Press, 1987), 357–64; idem, "1 and 2 Chronicles," in *The Literary Guide to the Bible* (ed. Robert Alter and Frank Kermode; Cambridge, MA: Belknap Press of Harvard University Press, 1987), 365–72.

CHRONOLOGY

The design of a work along a temporal axis. When events in a NARRATIVE are recounted in the order in which they actually occurred, the chronology is linear. When the temporal axis is interrupted by FLASHBACKS or begun IN MEDIAS RES, then the chronology may be complex. This means that the chronology of the actual events may differ from the sequence of their presentation within a narrative. For example, in Jon. 4:2a the reader discovers that Jonah has prayed to Yahweh, "O LORD! Is not this what I said while I was still in my own country? That is why I fled to Tarshish at the beginning." Here is the NARRATION of an event that occurred after God's initial commission in 1:2 and before Jonah's flight in 1:3. It is an account of a conversation that Jonah had with Yahweh several EPISODEs back. Another example is found in Matt. 14:1–12. In this EPISODE, Herod tells his servants how he believes that Jesus is the resurrected John the Baptist (1–2), and then the NARRATOR informs the readers that Herod had previously imprisoned John and subsequently put him to death (3–12). Consequently, the narrator reports a series of events that actually occurred earlier.

CIRCUMSTANTIAL SELECTIONS

A term used by Umberto Eco to designate the relationship between a term or phrase and external circumstances. Readers are expected to connect the term or phrase within a TEXT to circumstances in the "extraverbal environment." So while "aye" may mean a yes vote in a board meeting, it may signify obedience to an order within the CONTEXT of the Navy (Eco, 19). The reader must infer the appropriate SENSE from the circumstances suggested by the text. In this way, circumstantial selections limit the possible inferences a reader can make.

Bibliography. Umberto Eco, *The Role of the Reader: Explorations in the Semiotics of Texts* (Bloomington: Indiana University Press, 1984).

CLARITAS SCRIPTURAE

Latin meaning "clarity of Scripture," it refers to the belief that the BIBLE provides an unequivocal, certain ground for faith and practice. To some, *claritas scripturae* has meant that the Bible is clear in its MEANING to any believer irrespective of any training in EXEGESIS or HERMENEUTICS. To oth-

ers, the concept suggests that the meaning of the Scriptures is accessible to anyone who approaches it from a distinctly rational perspective. To the Reformers such as Martin Luther and John Calvin, however, the concept of the clarity of Scripture is not independent of hermeneutical concerns, though they still believed that the Scriptures were the repositories of meaning that could be accessed. This meaning, however, was always contextual and literal, historical, so that clarity (or perspicuity) did not void the necessary work of hermeneutics. For these Reformers, the literal or historical SENSE of Scripture provided the basis for faith and doctrine. When done well, exegesis and interpretation could provide a clear, sound, and confident foundation for faith and doctrine. This in no way undermined the idea that individual words and passages might be quite obscure. Nonetheless, the general truth of the Scriptures could be found and responded to (Thiselton, 179–86).

Bibliography. Anthony Thiselton, *New Horizons in Hermeneutics* (Grand Rapids: Zondervan, 1992).

CLARITY

In literary studies, the claim that TEXTs clearly reflect the INTENTIONs of their AUTHORs and that these intentions may be discerned by the texts' readers. This view has been seriously challenged by more contemporary LITERARY theorists (e.g., Roland Barthes, Jacques Derrida, Jean-François Lyotard). These theorists emphasize the HISTORICITY of language and texts as well as the TEXTUALITY of history. In other words, language, authors, and readers are all conditioned by a complex matrix of CONTEXTs. One's understanding, writing, and language can never be objectively disinterested but rather is always shaped by an IDEOLOGY or a matrix of ideologies. For example, Barthes points out that there is no innocent writing, reading, or language; each reflects a society's power structures and relations on many levels (e.g., religious, political, aesthetic), vitiating any neutral or objective position. Thus clarity, in the sense of objective writing or reading, is impossible. In TRANSLATION theory, *clarity* refers the attempt to remove ambiguities and awkward constructions in translation. Biblical scholars such as David Gunn, Robert Alter, and Stephen Prickett, however, argue against the blanket removal of ambiguities, pointing out that quite often the biblical authors employ deliberate AMBIGUITY, PARADOX, and indirectness as LITERARY DEVICES.

Bibliography. Robert Alter, *The Art of Biblical Narrative* (New York: Basic Books, 1981); Roland Barthes, *Critique and Truth* (Minneapolis: University of Minnesota Press, 1987); idem, *Mythologies* (London: Jonathan Cape, 1972); idem, *Writing Degree Zero* (London: Jonathan Cape, 1967); David Gunn, *The Fate of King Saul: An Interpretation of a Biblical Story* (JSOTSup 14; Sheffield: University of Sheffield Press, 1980); idem, *The Story of King David: Genre and Interpretation* (JSOTSup 6; Sheffield: University of Sheffield Press, 1978); Stephen Prickett, *Words and the Word: Language, Poetics, and Biblical Interpretation* (Cambridge: Cambridge University Press, 1986).

CLASS IDEOLOGY. *See* IDEOLOGY

CLICHÉ

Any expression that has lost its original LITERARY attraction or expressive value due to overuse. Most readers are familiar with such clichés as "A penny saved is a penny earned" or "This is just the tip of the iceberg." Even great expressions from literature may become clichés (e.g., "To be or not to be, that is the question"). Robert Alter has identified clichés within BIBLICAL POETRY, clichés that the poets have transformed into poetry. Such expressions as "All flesh is grass" (Isa. 40:6 KJV), "The grass withers, the flower fades" (Isa. 40:7), "Guard me as the apple of the eye; hide me in the shadow of your wings" (Ps. 17:8), and "The LORD is . . . my stronghold" (18:2) occur with regularity within Hebrew poetry and are probably clichés transformed by poetic invention (190–92).

Bibliography. Robert Alter, *The Art of Biblical Poetry* (New York: Basic Books, 1985).

CLIMACTIC PARALLELISM

A type of parallelism in BIBLICAL POETRY in which the second part of the line repeats a portion of the first part and then adds to it, yielding a climax.

The floods have lifted up, O LORD,
   the floods have lifted up their voice. (Ps. 93:3)

See BIBLICAL POETRY; SYNTHETIC PARALLELISM.

CLIMACTIC STRUCTURE

The movement within BIBLICAL POETRY in which there is an INTENSIFICATION from line to line, leading to a CLIMAX. For example, like a Shakespearean sonnet, Ps. 128 describes the nature of a happy home: the man who is faithful to God will be happy and eat the fruit of his labor, have a fruitful wife, and children like olive shoots. The poet then moves to the climax by making an ANALOGY between these images and Zion and her children.

Bibliography. Robert Alter, *The Art of Biblical Poetry* (New York: Basic Books, 1985).

CLIMAX

In a sequence of events or ideas, *climax* refers to both the rising order, or sequence, and the most important event or idea within the sequence. In NARRATIVE, climax is the point where the ACTION turns and brings about the most emotional response in the reader. Roberts and Jacobs define it as "the story's high point and may take the shape of a decision, an action, an affirmation or denial, or an illumination or realization. It is the logical conclusion of the preceding actions; no new major developments follow it. In most stories, the climax occurs at the end or close to it" (110). In modern NARRATIVE theory, a STORY may be described in terms of a five-part STRUCTURE: EXPOSITION, CONFLICT, crisis, CLIMAX, and resolution (DENOUEMENT). The book of Esther can be explained in terms of this structure, the climax being Esther's disclosure (*see* DISCLOSURE FORMULA) of her dilemma to the Persian king.

Bibliography. Edgar V. Roberts and Henry E. Jacobs, *Literature: An Introduction to Reading and Writing* (7th ed.; Upper Saddle River, NJ: Pearson Prentice Hall, 2004).

CLINAMEN. *See* ANXIETY OF INFLUENCE

CLOSED TEXTS

Texts that demand relatively few decisions on the part of the reader. We might better understand the idea of closed texts as opposed to OPEN TEXTS by relating it to the concept of didacticism: the idea that all authors intend for their texts to communicate something to readers. In other words, all texts can be seen as instances of teaching. Yet texts are DIDACTIC in different ways. It is a mistake to assume that a single method is the key to interpreting every kind of TEXT. If we place the biblical texts along a continuum (see figure below) from closed to open, left to right, the epistles would fall toward the closed end of the continuum while the GOSPELS would fall toward the open end.

We could illustrate the point by replacing the terms "closed" and "open" with "propositional" and "STORY" respectively. On the one hand, the EPISTLES in the NT fall toward the propositional pole because they do not communicate by using the devices and strategies usually associated with storytelling (e.g., PLOT, CHARACTERIZATION, SETTING, POINT OF VIEW, CONFLICT, COMPLICATION, and resolution/DENOUEMENT). The Gospels, on the other hand, fall toward the story pole of the continuum. The book of Proverbs fits toward the propositional pole, and we place the books of Esther and Jonah toward the story pole. Again, if we place all the biblical texts along this didactic continuum, we would find that as we move from left to right, more readerly activity is required in order to understand the text. However, all readerly activity is circumscribed by the textual constraints of GENRE conventions. To be a competent reader, one should have a sufficient knowledge of genre conventions, especially if the same text contains two or more genres. Another way to put it is that every text presupposes a reader who shares the LITERARY CONVENTIONS demanded by the text.

CLOSE READING

A process of reading in NEW CRITICISM that tries to account for every detail of a text, such as PLOT, SETTING, CHARACTERIZATION, FIGURATIVE LANGUAGE, ALLUSION, and POINT OF VIEW. New Critics and NARRATIVE critics (*see* NARRATIVE CRITICISM) alike assume that any detail of a text must be understood not only in its relationship to all the other parts but also in terms of its contribution to the entire STORY.

CLOSING

The ending of an EPISTLE, normally including a PEACE WISH, GREETINGS, a BENEDICTION, and sometimes an apostolic pronouncement. Often these are prefaced by a list of final instructions. The greetings occur between the peace wish and benediction. While these may be stock materials within the conclusion of the Pauline LETTERS, they are not simply meaningless formalities. In the peace wish, Paul returns to the major concern(s) of the letter. Note this return in 1 Thess. 5:23: "May the God of peace himself sanctify you entirely; and may your spirit and soul and body be kept sound and blameless at the coming of our Lord Jesus Christ." The coming of the Lord and the readiness of the saints are major concerns of the epistle. The peace wish in Gal. 6:16 ("As for those who will follow this rule—peace be upon them, and mercy, and upon the Israel of God") returns to Paul's concern with the bondage of circumcision versus freedom in Christ and true Israel. The benediction ("The grace of the Lord Jesus be with you") varies little in Paul's Letters, but it has taken on a distinctly Christian perspective. However, sometimes Paul prefaces the benediction with a warning or exhortation (see 1 Cor. 16:22; 1 Thess. 5:27; Gal. 6:17).

CLOSURE

A term describing a STORY with a PLOT that unfolds within NARRATIVE TIME and that brings the ACTION to a coherent and necessary conclusion (Thiselton, 571). In other words, the action in a story does not simply end but has a sense of conclusion and completeness as a result of the coherent plot. Examples in the HEBREW BIBLE are Esther, the Joseph NARRATIVE in Genesis, and Job. It can also be argued that BIBLICAL POETRY, while not possessing plot in the SENSE of narrative, has logical movement from beginning to end, resulting in closure. The GOSPELs also have conclusions that develop naturally from the plot. While the EPISTLES are not stories, most do have conclusions that follow from their main arguments.

Bibliography. Anthony Thiselton, *New Horizons in Hermeneutics* (Grand Rapids: Zondervan, 1992).

CODE

A system of SIGNs, including the rules governing the organization of those signs, from which all textual MEANING is derived. A code may be as simple as "rules of etiquette" or the grammar and syntax of a spoken language. For example, any particular sentence is meaningful only because it is based on a complex set of rules (a code) that governs the manner in which the words are combined. For the most part, individuals employ the code unconsciously. The term has slightly different senses in LINGUISTICS, SEMIOTICS, and STRUCTURALISM.

Ferdinand de Saussure first introduced the term with respect to his distinction between *LANGUE* and *parole*, where *langue* is the language system that governs the actual utterance, or *parole*. Before two persons may engage in communication, each must be familiar with the code.

In semiotics, a code is not limited to a language or communication system but can be any system of signs—DNA, rules of kinship, dress, marriage. In other words, signifying systems undergird all aspects of human life.

Structuralists extend the idea of code to LITERARY texts by claiming that a TEXT is an instance of *parole* that is based on a literary signifying system (*langue*). For example, NARRATIVE stories, while differing in specifics on the surface level (different SETTINGS, characters, events, CHRONOLOGY), on deeper levels reflect a similar if not identical STRUCTURE. So underlying every STORY is a system, a literary grammar. For example, Roland Barthes views a text as a composite of five different codes: the hermeneutic code (elements in the text organized into BINARY OPPOSITIONs), the code of "semes" (textual elements of meaning such as characters and events), symbolic code (levels of meaning beyond the literal gathered around persons, objects, settings, ideas), proairetic (plot) code, and cultural code (shared body of knowledge within a given culture). Since the role of the reader is to ascertain the manner in which these codes relate, and since readers vary, so does meaning. So Barthes's idea of code and the reader's task of decoding a multiple-coded text crosses over into READER-RESPONSE CRITICISM.

Bibliography. Roland Barthes, *S/Z / Roland Barthes* (trans. Richard Miller; Oxford: Blackwell, 1970); Terry Eagleton, *Literary Theory: An Introduction* (Minneapolis: University of Minnesota Press, 1983); Ferdinand de Saussure, *A Course in General Linguistics* (ed. Charles Bally and Albert Sechehaye; trans. Wade Baskin; New York: McGraw-Hill, 1959).

CODE, COVENANT. *See* COVENANT CODE

CODE, DEUTERONOMIC. *See* DEUTERONOMIC CODE

CODE, HOLINESS. *See* HOLINESS CODE

CODE, PRIESTLY. *See* PRIESTLY CODE

CODE, SEMIOTIC. *See* SEMIOTIC CODE

CODE, SOCIAL. *See* CODE

CODEX

An ancient book-form manuscript made by stacking sheets of PAPYRUS or VELLUM (animal skin) and binding them together. Used as early as the second century CE, the codex eventually replaced the scroll as the form of choice for biblical manuscripts. Dating from the fourth to the sixteenth centuries CE, more than twelve hundred biblical manuscripts exist in codex form.

CODICOLOGY

The study of the physical relationships between manuscripts with little or no attention to content.

COHERENCE

Strictly speaking, a principle of composition requiring that all the parts of any TEXT be structured such that they add up to a unified whole with internal consistency. In NEW CRITICISM, *coherence* refers to the internal unity of a text based on the LITERARY rather than the logical or linear relationship between the parts. AMBIGUITY, PARADOX, and even *in*coherence may contribute to the internal literary unity of a text. Consequently, literary coherence must be distinguished from *unilateral coherence* (Keesey, 79–81).

Coherence is also a term used by Hirsch as one of the four criteria in his concept of VERIFICATION, by which he tries to establish the most probable reading of a text with respect to an author's intended MEANING. Coherence requires the interpreter to establish the most probable CONTEXT by reconstructing the relevant aspects of the author's outlook. Ultimately, according to Hirsch, the best way to adjudicate between probable readings is to show that one context is more probable than the others.

In the QUEST FOR THE HISTORICAL JESUS, the criterion of coherence is also used as one way of judging deeds or SAYINGS OF JESUS as authentic (*see* CRITERIA OF AUTHENTICITY).

In POSTMODERNISM, however, the ASSUMPTION that literary texts constitute coherent, internally consistent unities has been challenged. Rather than the text being a coherent whole, perhaps the reader imposes a coherence on the text through the process of CONSISTENCY BUILDING. For example, when a scholar argues that a coherent Pauline theology can be found in terms of Paul's proclamation of Christ within the context of his APOCALYPTIC conception of history, the question must be raised whether such a coherent theology is Paul's or the scholar's.

Bibliography. E. D. Hirsch Jr., "Objective Interpretation," *PMLA* 75 (1960): 463, 470–79; William Harmon and C. Hugh Holman, *A Handbook to Literature* (8th ed.; Upper Saddle River, NJ: Prentice Hall, 1999); Donald Keesey, *Contexts for Criticism* (4th ed.; Boston: McGraw-Hill, 2003).

COHERENCE CRITERION. *See* CRITERIA OF AUTHENTICITY

COLLATION

In TEXTUAL CRITICISM, the term denoting the practice of comparing ancient manuscripts of a particular TEXT for the purpose of identifying differences and reconstructing the original text. Textual critics generally compare the manuscript with an existing and already-accepted form of the text (e.g., the TEXTUS RECEPTUS).

Bibliography. Richard N. Soulen and R. Kendall Soulen, *Handbook of Biblical Criticism* (3rd ed.; Louisville: Westminster John Knox, 2001).

COLLECTIVE UNCONSCIOUS

A concept in Jungian psychology and ARCHETYPAL CRITICISM for the inherited shared ideas perennially existing in the memory of a race. These ideas or ARCHETYPES are in the individual unconscious mind and as such are responsible for attitudes and responses on the unconscious level over which the individual has no control. Such shared ideas are prior to individual personalities and exist as shared SYMBOLS, dreams, and fantasies. In other words, all human beings share a symbolic content just as they share common instincts and physical features. *See* MYTH.

COLON

A term proposed by W. F. Albright to designate a single unit of Hebrew poetry with respect to the number of feet it contains. It is the same as Robert Alter's VERSET and the traditional term STICH. Albright also proposed the terms "bicolon" and "tricolon" to designate poetic lines consisting of two and three cola (pl. of colon) respectively, thus matching the traditional distich and tristich. For example, the following verse (in the Hebrew) contains a tricolon:

> For you will spread out to the right and to
> the left,
>   and your descendants will possess the
>   nations
>   and will settle the desolate towns. (Isa. 54:3)

In TEXTUAL CRITICISM, *colon* refers to a single clause line of nine to sixteen syllables. Some ancient manuscripts were composed colometrically: each line is a colon.

Bibliography. Marjo C. A. Korpel and Johannes C. de Moor, *The Structure of Classical Hebrew Poetry: Isaiah 40–55* (Old Testament Studies 41; Leiden: Brill, 1998); Richard N. Soulen and R. Kendall Soulen, *Handbook of Biblical Criticism* (3rd ed.; Louisville: Westminster John Knox, 2001).

COLONIALISM/COLONIALIZATION. *See* POSTCOLONIAL CRITICISM

COLOPHON

Technically, a publisher's statement, sometimes including a device or logo, placed at the end or on the title page of a book. The colophon may include information about the publisher, the title of the book, the printer, the author, or the date and place of publication. *Colophon* may also refer to any concluding device or statement such as "The End" or "Finis" (Harmon and Holman, 105). Although the first known example of colophon in the former sense comes from the fifteenth century, colophons of the latter type may be found in some biblical texts, such as Lev. 26:46, at the end of the HOLINESS CODE; Job 31:40b; and Rev. 22:18–19 (Soulen and Soulen, 36).

Bibliography. William Harmon and C. Hugh Holman, *A Handbook to Literature* (8th ed.; Upper Saddle River, NJ: Prentice Hall, 1999); Richard N. Soulen and R. Kendall Soulen, *Handbook of Biblical Criticism* (3rd ed.; Louisville: Westminster John Knox, 2001).

COMEDY

A name for a particular type of PLOT involving a "U-shaped" STORY that begins in prosperity, descends into despair or fall, and then returns upward to a happy ending when a series of obstacles are overcome. Read in this sense, the Gospel of John and the various CHRISTOLOGICAL HYMNS can be viewed as following the archetypal comic plot (*see* ARCHETYPE). In the Aristotelian TRADITION, TRAGEDY involves a plot that generates pity and fear in the audience toward the PROTAGONIST and involves the hero's movement from happiness

to misery due to undeserved misfortune. Comedy, in contrast, generates a sense of indignation in the audience and involves the protagonist's movement to a state of undeserved good fortune. Furthermore, though the comic character may be multidimensional, that comic figure never develops or changes over time but remains a prisoner of a single flaw: avarice, hypochondria, jealousy, a sense of revenge, and so forth. In this respect, the story of Samson may be read as a comedy. But according to John Dominic Crossan, comedy in the Bible may be examined in terms of the comic dimension of IRONY, PARODY, PARABLE, and PARADOX. For example, certain texts take a playful approach in questioning other texts or earlier traditions. Ruth challenges Ezra–Nehemiah's prohibition against mixed marriages, and certain of Jesus's teachings and parables subvert tradition or reverse accepted expectations, as with the six antitheses (*see* ANTITHESIS) in Matt. 5 and the parables of the good Samaritan, the rich man and Lazarus, and the PHARISEE and the tax collector.

Bibliography. John Dominic Crossan, *Raid on the Articulate: Comic Eschatology in Jesus and Borges* (New York: Harper & Row, 1976); Anthony C. Thiselton, *New Horizons in Hermeneutics* (Grand Rapids: Zondervan, 1992).

COMMANDMENTS, TEN. *See* DECALOGUE

COMMENTARY

One of the four modes of NARRATION (the other three being direct narration, dramatic narration, and DESCRIPTION). Commentary includes the narrator's details and BACKGROUND information in the STORY. Commentary enables the storyteller to clarify things that readers may need to know in order to make SENSE of the PLOT. In the biblical texts, dramatic narrative is by far the most prevalent. When commentary does occur, it is usually in terms of brief comments on a limited aspect of the story.

Commentary also refers to a book that discusses the BIBLE as a whole or individual books of the Bible. The discussion may be chapter by chapter and verse by verse. Critical commentaries discuss the LITERARY, social, historical, and linguistic aspects of a text. In most critical commentaries, each text will be preceded by a detailed introduction. For two excellent sources on available commentaries on the Bible, see Tremper Longman III, *Old Testament Commentary Survey*; and D. A. Carson, *New Testament Commentary Survey*. The value of these two surveys is that each entry is annotated, and each commentary is evaluated for strengths and weaknesses.

Bibliography. D. A. Carson, *New Testament Commentary Survey* (6th ed.; Grand Rapids: Baker Academic, 2007); Tremper Longman III, *Old Testament Commentary Survey* (4th ed.; Grand Rapids: Baker Academic, 2007).

COMMISSIONING STORY

A call STORY found both in the HEBREW BIBLE and the NT. Benjamin Hubbard has identified these in the Hebrew Bible with the characteristics of introduction, confrontation, reaction, commission, protest, reassurance, and conclusion (e.g., Gen. 12:1–4a; 17:1–14; Exod. 3:1–4:16; Josh. 1:1–11; Isa. 6; and Jer. 1:1–10). Based on this structure, Terence Mullins suggests that some stories in the GOSPELs and Acts fit the form of the commissioning story. Since the Gospel of Luke makes extensive use of the prophetic paradigm with respect to both Jesus and his followers, Mullins finds that the commissioning story occurs more frequently in Luke than the other Gospels. Examples are Luke 4:16–30; 7:16; 13:31–33; and Acts 3:22. While not all of the components may occur in a given story, the three necessary ones seem to be confrontation, commission, and reassurance.

Bibliography. James Bailey and Lyle Vander Broek, *Literary Forms in the New Testament: A Handbook* (Louisville: Westminster John Knox, 1992); Benjamin Hubbard, "Commissioning Stories in Luke-Acts: A Study of Their Antecedents, Form, and Content," *Semeia* 8 (1977): 103–26; Terence Mullins, "New Testament Commission Forms, Especially in Luke-Acts," *JBL* 95 (1976): 603–14.

COMMON BIBLE

A 1966 edition of the REVISED STANDARD VERSION of the Bible.

COMMUNITY OF READERS. *See* INTERPRETIVE COMMUNITY

COMPARATIVE LINGUISTICS. *See* LINGUISTICS

COMPARATIVE LITERATURE

Works contemporary with a TEXT under study. The ASSUMPTION underlying the practice of comparing one text to other texts of the same period is that the writings of any period usually reflect ideas and forces shaping the culture of that period. Literary works develop in conversation with other literature of the same period. So a knowledge of and a willingness to consult such literature in a comparative sense can greatly enhance a person's understanding of a particular text or a portion of it. According to Damrosch, Hebrew literature reveals a history of conscious generic adaptation, modification, and transformation, and these changes are significant for determining MEANING. Hence, studying texts such as the Gilgamesh Epic, RAS SHAMRA TEXTS, MARI TABLETS, AMARNA TABLETS, and EBLA TABLETS will enhance one's understanding of the HEBREW BIBLE. Similarly, studying texts such as the writings of Josephus, Philo of Alexandria, the DEAD SEA SCROLLS, RABBINIC LITERATURE, the Apostolic Fathers, the NAG HAMMADI LIBRARY, and the APOCRYPHA will enhance the study of the NT.

Bibliography. David Damrosch, *The Narrative Covenant: Transformations of Genre in the Growth of Biblical Literature* (San Francisco: Harper & Row, 1987).

COMPETENCE/PERFORMANCE

Terms introduced by Noam Chomsky, an American linguist. Competence defines the implicit knowledge that speakers have of their native language. Included in this competence are the creative ability to develop and understand novel utterances, the recognition of relationships between various parts of SPEECH, the ability to handle AMBIGUITY, and the ability to recognize grammatical mistakes. Chomsky argues that only a small portion of this competence is learned, while the rest is innately determined. For example, very young children master an extremely complex system of language as a SIGN system with little exposure to other data. This linguistic competence combines with other materials such as MEMORY and logic to determine linguistic performance in particular situations. LINGUISTICS focuses almost exclusively on competence rather than on performance. The distinction between competence and performance is roughly equivalent to Saussure's distinction between *LANGUE* and *PAROLE*. Competence has been extended by some literary theorists, especially in STRUCTURALISM and GENRE CRITICISM, to include LITERARY COMPETENCE, the mastery or understanding of the LITERARY CONVENTIONS that govern the formation and understanding of literary TEXTS. In the former sense of competence, most readers of the biblical texts have the linguistic competence to make sense of the words on the page; in other words, they are capable of understanding the text on the surface level of relationships between parts of a sentence, recognizing figurative expressions, and even dealing with ambiguity. In the latter sense of *literary* competence, however, understanding of the GENRE rules underlying a text may be a more formidable challenge. According to structuralists and genre critics, without an understanding of *how* a text means, the construction of MEANING is impossible.

COMPETENCE, LITERARY. *See* LITERARY COMPETENCE

COMPLETE GOSPELS

A work by the translators of the SCHOLARS VERSION of the Bible, which includes all the GOSPELS and gospel materials (CANONICAL and noncanonical) produced in the first three centuries CE.

Bibliography. Stephen L. Harris, *The New Testament: A Student's Introduction* (4th ed.; Boston: McGraw-Hill, 2002).

COMPLICATION

In the study of literature, a series of CONFLICTS between competing or opposing forces. It is often referred to as the "tying of the knot of the ACTION," while resolution/DENOUEMENT is the untying of the knot. Some theorists refer to complication as RISING ACTION. In other words, the complication gets the PLOT rolling by presenting the reader with the story's various conflicts. The point at which the complications pile up and the ACTION begins to turn (and fortune changes) is the crisis. The Joseph STORY in Gen. 37–47 serves as an excellent example of the complication in terms of conflict: it begins with Joseph's strained relationship with his brothers, their selling of Joseph, Joseph's conflicts in Potiphar's house, and his imprisonment. The action begins to turn when Joseph interprets the dreams of his fellow prisoners and eventually Pharaoh's dream. At this point in the story, Joseph's fortunes change, and so does the focus of the action: to a series of encounters with his family, with whom he is eventually reunited.

COMPOSITIONAL CRITICISM

The analysis of texts composed from preexisting sources, whether oral or written. Its focus is on the manner in which the sources were combined, the changes the compositor made to the sources, and the reasons for adding new material to the sources. Composition criticism should not be confused with REDACTION CRITICISM, however, for the former tends not to focus on the way that the different sources function within the work as a finished product, but rather on the stages of composition and the theological perspective and INTENTION of each source.

CONCLUSIO

Also *peroratio*, a technical term in classical RHETORIC for the short conclusion of an argument in DELIBERATIVE RHETORIC. The speaker recapitulates the argument, encourages the audience to hate the refuted arguments, and attempts to gain a favorable judgment from the audience. In recent RHETORICAL CRITICISM, classical rhetorical theory has been used to interpret biblical texts, especially the EPISTOLARY LITERATURE. George Kennedy has also applied classical rhetoric to the GOSPELS. Examples in Paul's Letters are Rom. 15:14–16:23; 1 Cor. 15:58; and Gal. 6:11–18.

Bibliography. George Kennedy, *New Testament Interpretation through Rhetorical Criticism* (Chapel Hill: University of North Carolina Press, 1984).

CONCORDANCE

A book with biblical words, listed in alphabetical order, accompanied by Scripture references indicating where these words occur in the BIBLE. There are different types of concordances, but the most useful to English-speaking readers lacking skills in the original languages are analytical concordances. These concordances allow the student to find the Hebrew or Greek word translated by the English word. Listed here are several noteworthy concordances:

Horst Bachmann and W. A. Slaby, eds., *Concordance to the Novum Testamentum Graece* (3rd ed.; Berlin: de Gruyter, 1987).

Abraham Even-Shoshan, ed., *A New Concordance of the Old Testament Using the Hebrew and Aramaic Text* (2nd ed.; Grand Rapids: Baker, 1990).

John R. Kohlenberger, Edward W. Goodrick, and James Swanson, *The Greek-English Concordance to the New Testament: With the New International Version* (Grand Rapids: Zondervan, 1997).

John R. Kohlenberger and James A. Swanson, *The Hebrew-English Concordance to the Old Testament: With the New International Version* (Grand Rapids: Zondervan, 1998).

Gerhard Lisowsky, ed., *Konkordanz zum Hebräischen Alten Testament / Concordance to the Hebrew Old Testament* (2nd ed.; Peabody, MA: Hendrickson, 2010).

William F. Moulton and Alfred S. Geden, *A Concordance to the Greek Testament according to the Text of Westcott and Hort, Tischendorf and the English Revisers* (Edinburgh: T&T Clark, 1897; repr. of 5th rev. ed., New York: T&T Clark, 1997).

James Strong, *The Exhaustive Concordance of the Bible* (New York: Methodist Book Concern, 1890; updated ed., Peabody, MA: Hendrickson, 2007).

George V. Wigram, *The New Englishman's Hebrew Concordance of the Old Testament* (Peabody, MA: Hendrickson, 1996).

Robert Young, *Analytical Concordance to the Bible* (Edinburgh: G. Adam Young, 1879; repr., Peabody, MA: Hendrickson, 1984).

An excellent source for concordances is David Bauer, *An Annotated Guide to Biblical Resources for Ministry* (Peabody, MA: Hendrickson, 2003).

CONCRETE UNIVERSAL

The idea that a work of art communicates a universal MEANING through the particular, concrete elements that constitute the work. In the Western literary TRADITION, the earliest formal expression is Aristotle's *Poetics,* where he argues that art is more similar to philosophy than to history because philosophy communicates how things should be while history depicts things as they actually are. Philosophy deals with the universal, history with the particular. Aristotle expresses the universality of art by his concept of mimesis (*see* MIMETIC CRITICISM), by which he means that there is a meaningful connection between art and human experience. The particular piece of art brings about an insight experience in the viewer or reader. Consequently, the concept of the concrete universal makes a work of art metaphorical in that the work always points beyond itself, its own particulars, to thing(s) universal. According to this view, then, such books as Ruth, Esther, Jonah, Ezekiel, the Gospels, and Revelation are DIDACTIC and thus mimetic in that they suggest some universal meaning through the particular structures that make up the texts.

The concept can be illustrated with the book of Jonah. If the reader focuses on Jonah's ACTIONS at the end of the account, one may assume that Jonah's problem is theological. In Jonah's judgment, Nineveh has perpetrated unspeakable atrocities on Jonah's people and deserves judgment. But Jonah knows that a single act of repentance can erase a lifetime of sins. Jonah's problem is that he does not want to live in a world where God's grace, rather than his justice, is extended to the Assyrians.

CONCRETIZATION

A term in READER-RESPONSE CRITICISM describing the reader's process of making sense of a TEXT. According to Roman Ingarden and Wolfgang Iser, a reader puts a text together by the process of MEANING ASSEMBLY. Through a series of interpretive decisions, the reader creates the literary work (the imaginative creation of the reader) out of the literary text (the imaginative creation of the author). In other words, MEANING is only virtually present in the text, and the reader must coherently configure an understanding of the text in the process of reading. A work of literature is a written CODE and must be decoded through the imaginatively creative act of a reader. Since different readers bring different presuppositions (due to background, competencies, expectations, purposes) to the text, different concretizations may result. Reader-response critics (*see* READER-RESPONSE CRITICISM) suggest that such is the case because in the dynamic process of reading, the reader decides how the gaps will be filled. A second reading of a text always produces a different impression from the first because of the reader's changed circumstances. Upon a second reading, earlier perspectives recede into the background and formerly insignificant segments receive a more prominent place. A second reading cannot possibly be identical to the first because, due to the reader's familiarity with the PLOT, one will make inferences about segments of the text that were not made at the first reading. The virtual text is concretized differently on each reading.

Concretization is also a type of FOCUSING in BIBLICAL POETRY, as identified by Alter. Within a line containing SYNTHETIC PARALLELISM, concretization occurs when there is a movement from a general term in the first verse to a more specific "instance of the general category in the second verse" (Alter, 19). Jeremiah 2:15 provides an example: "They have made his land a waste; his cities are in ruins, without inhabitant." The movement is one of concretization from "land" to "cities" in the land. The movement may also be one of heightening, along with specification, or concretization (Alter, 19).

Bibliography. Robert Alter, *The Art of Biblical Poetry* (New York: Basic Books, 1985).

CONFESSIONAL HYMN

According to Ralph Martin, a category of NT HYMN found in the EPISTOLARY LITERATURE but originating in the context of worship in the early church. Examples are 1 Tim. 6:11–16 and 2 Tim. 2:11–13. Similar to CHRISTOLOGICAL HYMNS, confessional hymns are likely derived from creeds and theological confessions focusing on the content of faith. Evidence of this creedal character can be seen in 2 Tim. 2:11, "The saying is sure," and in Eph. 5:14, "Therefore it says." Yet the distinction between christological hymns and confessional hymns is not clear since the former certainly contain confessional, theological material. *See* CHRISTOLOGICAL HYMN; HYMN; MEDITATIVE HYMN; SACRAMENTAL HYMN.

CONFESSIONAL STATEMENT

Formulaic statement or profession of belief; a compact summary of theological understanding and doctrine that was most likely used and recited within liturgical situations, such as baptism. Terms such as "confess" or "believe" suggest confessional statements. Also a rhythmic quality may indicate a confessional statement (but this is also a quality of a HYMN). The following passages typify the confessional statement.

Because if you confess with your lips that Jesus is Lord and believe in your heart that God raised him from the dead, you will be saved. (Rom. 10:9)

He was revealed in flesh,
vindicated in spirit,
seen by angels,
proclaimed among gentiles,
believed in throughout the world,
taken up in glory. (1 Tim. 3:16)

Bibliography. W. Randolph Tate, *Biblical Interpretation: An Integrated Approach* (rev. ed.; Peabody, MA: Hendrickson, 1997).

CONFESSIONAL THEOLOGY

Theological systems that take a confessional or creedal approach to interpreting the BIBLE and formulating church beliefs. In the true sense of the term, once a CREED or confession is formulated, an associated religious movement tends to interpret the Bible and to judge any theological statement by the creed. Consequently, the movement has a confessional theology.

CONFIGURATION

A term used by Paul Ricoeur to designate a reader's understanding of a TEXT. Although Ricoeur invests the term with a historical and social sense, meaning that the reader configures a meaning within a definite historical and social context, configuration is otherwise synonymous with CONCRETIZATION. Ricoeur and critics employing READER-RESPONSE CRITICISM generally do not use "reconfiguration," a term suggesting that the AUTHOR's intended MEANING can somehow be reconstructed by a later reader.

Bibliography. Paul Ricoeur, "The Narrative Function," *Semeia* 13 (1978): 177–202.

CONFLATE READING

A term in TEXTUAL CRITICISM denoting a deliberate scribal error in copying. When the scribe encountered two different versions of a TEXT, he would combine the two versions, thus producing a third reading different from the other two. For example, in some manuscripts, Luke 24:53 reads "praising God," while others read "blessing God." A third group of manuscripts, however, preserves both versions in "praising and blessing God." The latter group is probably the result of conflation.

CONFLATION. *See* CONFLATE READING

CONFLICT

In the study of literature, one of the five elements of PLOT (the other four being EXPOSITION, crisis, CLIMAX, and resolution/DENOUEMENT). Conflict serves to complicate the ACTION of the STORY. It is the heart of the plot, the raw material for the formation of plot. It may be internal or external. Internal conflict occurs when a character, usually the PROTAGONIST, struggles with him- or herself (e.g., conflicting motives, goals, loyalties). External conflict may be with other characters, society, TRADITION, destiny, or nature. Some theorists suggest that the sum total of conflict constitutes narrative COMPLICATION. Clearly, external conflict is at the heart of the plots in the Gospels and Acts, where Jesus and his followers are in conflict with tradition and other characters. The plots of stories such as those of David, Joseph, Moses, Abraham, Jacob, and Isaiah in the Hebrew Bible involve both internal and external conflict.

CONFLICT STORY

The most common or typical STORY in the GOSPELS, in which Jesus is pitted against a person or a group. These stories are responsible for furthering the ACTION of the Gospels. It is typical of these CONFLICTS that Jesus always gets the upper hand; as a consequence, the conflicts move the action of the Gospels to their inevitable conclusion, the trial and execution of Jesus. While both conflict stories and ENCOUNTER STORIES involve a meeting between Jesus and another person or group, encounter stories differ in that they do not normally involve conflict.

Bibliography. Leland Ryken, *Words of Life: A Literary Introduction to the New Testament* (Grand Rapids: Baker, 1987).

CONNOTATION

The emotional overtones, senses, and associations that words carry beyond their dictionary MEANING (*see* DENOTATION) within a particular linguistic community. While a person may assume a private connotative sense of a word, before that connotation can be understood, it must be shared with another person or group. For example, in Phil. 3:2, Paul writes, "Beware of the dogs, beware of the evil workers, beware of those who mutilate the flesh!" While Paul's audience would certainly know the dictionary meaning of "dogs," Paul has given the word a connotative value. The reader must decide between several possibilities (e.g., male prostitutes, Gentiles, Cynics), but the most likely reference in the Philippian CONTEXT is to Judaizers within the church who were promoting circumcision.

CONSISTENCY BUILDING

A term used by Wolfgang Iser for the reader's activities in reconciling the various POINTS OF VIEW and filling the gaps of INDETERMINACY in a TEXT in order to make SENSE of it. For a more complete discussion, see READER-RESPONSE CRITICISM.

CONSOLATION POETRY

A term used by Robert Alter to describe a characteristic of BIBLICAL POETRY in its portrayal of the transformation of history and nature into an eternal harmonious order. The images that the poets employ are those of "flourishing vineyards and fields, planting and building, shining light, liberation and regal dignity, splendid garb, marital reconciliation and sexual union, firm foundations and calm" (156). Examples are Amos 9:13–15 and Isa. 44:3–4. See MONITORY POETRY.

Bibliography. Robert Alter, *The Art of Biblical Poetry* (New York: Basic Books, 1985).

CONSTRUCTIVE PARALLELISM. *See* SYNTHETIC PARALLELISM

CONTEMPORARY ENGLISH VERSION

A TRANSLATION of the BIBLE produced by the American Bible Society in 1995. The goal of the translators was to create a translation that would be "user friendly." The translators were guided by the idea of DYNAMIC EQUIVALENCE, and they tried to make the language more palatable to modern readers by removing the natural RHYTHM of both the Hebrew and the Greek.

CONTENT. *See* FORM/CONTENT

CONTENT ANALYSIS

A tool that sociologists originally used to evaluate mass media. It functions on two ASSUMPTIONS:

(1) it is possible to distinguish between the objective (*see* OBJECTIVE KNOWLEDGE) verbal signs in a TEXT and the reading CONTEXT; and (2) the verbal content of a text can be objectively measured by different readers (Frith, 117). While content analysis has been discredited by cultural theorists who assume that the reading process is highly subjective (*see* SUBJECTIVE KNOWLEDGE), some biblical interpreters still assume that the objective verbal content of a text exerts definite controls on readers, thus guaranteeing standard readings.

Bibliography. Simon Frith, "Content Analysis," in *A Dictionary of Cultural and Critical Theory* (ed. Michael Payne; Cambridge, MA: Blackwell, 1996), 117.

CONTEXT

The materials and situations surrounding an object to be interpreted. In literary studies, *context* may refer to the materials and situations surrounding the writing or reading of a TEXT. These materials and situations are historical, cultural, geographical, ecclesiastical, ideological, and LITERARY. The ASSUMPTION of literary critics who emphasize context is that both AUTHORS and readers are influenced by these various contexts and that an awareness of them will result in a more informed understanding of the text. Communication of any kind is culturally grounded. Biblical authors communicated through their cultural filters, speaking to people within the same culture and to people who understood the communication within the same cultural patterns. Information about these cultural patterns may be internal (information found within the text) or external (information found outside the text). Although some texts virtually stand alone as far as BACKGROUND is concerned, these are exceptions. Most often the reader must use both internal and external information in an attempt to more plausibly understand the context of the work.

CONTEXT AS FRAME

In READER-RESPONSE CRITICISM, as well as most culturally oriented theories of INTERPRETATION, the ASSUMPTION that a reader's CONTEXT serves as the frame or grid through which one processes a TEXT. Accordingly, it is impossible for readers to step outside their contexts into some purely objective, PRESUPPOSITION-free vantage point from which to interpret texts. Readers always observe from inside their SOCIAL LOCATIONS. Hence, all interpretations are conditioned by the contexts of readers.

CONTEXT-SPECIFIC

In both literary theory and HERMENEUTICS, the idea that an author creates and a reader understands TEXTS from within particular circumstances. On the one hand, while contemporary literary theorists assume that it may be ultimately impossible to reconstruct the specific matrix of CONTEXTS within which a text was composed, most of these theorists recognize that the better the understanding of the context-specific conditions of the world in which the text was produced, the more informed is the INTERPRETATION. The attempts of HISTORICAL RECONSTRUCTION are not identical to the INTENTIONAL FALLACY, but rather they are a recognition that scholarly responsibility demands for interpreters to understand as much as they can about the WORLD OF THE TEXT. On the other hand, most theorists also recognize that the critic's RECONSTRUCTION of any context is influenced by his or her own matrix of contexts or SOCIAL LOCATION. In other words, a reader's IDEOLOGY shapes his or her understanding of the past and interpretation of the past.

CONTEXTUALIZATION

The assumption that theological systems and interpretive practices should develop out of and reflect the social and cultural world of the people in which the systems are produced. Put another way, theology should be formulated within and communicated to groups in terms of their particular existential situation. Black, liberation, and feminist critics and theologians try to counter the dominant INTERPRETIVE FRAMEWORKS, which they perceive as Western, bourgeois-capitalist, white, colonial, racist, imperialist, androcentric (see ANDROCEN-

TRISM), or patriarchal (see PATRIARCHY). These critics and theologians feel that because the traditional interpretive frameworks tend to perpetuate the ideologies (see IDEOLOGY) of the dominant TRADITIONS, they should be rejected (at least in part) and replaced by approaches that reflect the particular CONTEXT and experiences of those outside the dominant traditions. (See CULTURAL CRITICISM; FEMINIST CRITICISM; LIBERATION THEOLOGY; POSTCOLONIAL CRITICISM; RACE, CLASS, AND GENDER CRITICISM.)

CONTEXTUAL SELECTIONS

A term used by Umberto Eco to describe a particular relationship between words, sentences, and units of a TEXT in the text's linear development. Contextual selections are the "coded abstract possibilities of meeting a given term in connection with other terms belonging to the same semiotic system" (19). Thus, a term may have one connotative MEANING (see CONNOTATION) in one language system while having a different meaning within another. A well-known example is the use of the word *know* in a Hebrew CONTEXT to refer to sexual intercourse, while it has no such use in modern English. Also, in a Hebrew context, *dog* may refer to a Samaritan or a male prostitute, while in English it may refer connotatively to a homely person.

Bibliography. Umberto Eco, *The Role of the Reader: Explorations in the Semiotics of Texts* (Bloomington: Indiana University Press, 1984).

CONTEXTUAL THEOLOGY. See
CONTEXTUALIZATION

CONTRAST

An element of CHARACTERIZATION in STORY, and also a NARRATIVE pattern. The former works in biblical literature by placing characters in juxtaposition to highlight character traits, especially the traits that appear to be incongruent with a character's social status. The latter use of contrast as a narrative pattern involves arranging the material of an entire text or part of a text by associating or juxtaposing things that are dissimilar or opposite. Such juxtaposing may be done in block or point-by-point fashion. In block structure, one item is completely discussed before the other. In point-by-point, the contrast moves back and forth between the two things being contrasted. In the biblical texts, contrast is usually accomplished point-by-point. This is especially the case in BIBLICAL POETRY (e.g., the contrast between the righteous and the wicked in Ps. 1). For examples of contrast, *see* CHARACTERIZATION.

CONTROLLING PARADIGM

In HERMENEUTICS, the interpretive theory that governs a person's reading or examination of a TEXT. These theories determine a person's understanding of the text because they determine what kinds of questions will be put to the text. For example, POSTCOLONIAL CRITICISM asks quite different questions of a text or focuses the reader's attention on different aspects of the text than does NARRATIVE CRITICISM or FEMINIST CRITICISM. The idea of a controlling paradigm therefore carries with it that MEANING is a function of the reading PARADIGM employed by the reader. Additionally, a controlling paradigm may be a doctrinal or theological system. A Pentecostal reader certainly reads Acts 2 and 1 Cor. 12 differently from a non-Pentecostal. Ultimately, the idea of a controlling paradigm vitiates the possibility of an innocent, objective (*see* OBJECTIVE KNOWLEDGE) understanding of a text.

CONTROVERSY STORY. *See* CONFLICT STORY

CONVENTION. *See* LITERARY CONVENTION

CORONATION PSALMS. *See* PSALM(S)

CORPUS HERMETICUM

A collection of mystical and dualistic religio-philosophical treatises produced in Egypt between the mid-first century and the mid-third century, which the Neoplatonists assumed to have been written by Hermes Trismegistos (the Thrice Great), the Greek name for the Egyptian god Thoth (Fer-

guson, 250). A. D. Nock and A.-J. Festugière's standard edition of the Hermetic writings consists of eighteen tractates, a SPEECH by Hermes Trismegistus to Asclepius, and twenty-nine pieces from the writings of Stobaeus. Also belonging to the Hermetic writings are the Coptic Hermetica from Nag Hammadi CODEX VI, some LETTERS, and papyri (Soulen and Soulen, 76).

These texts have some similarities to some of the NT writings in their DUALISM of birth/death, light/darkness. According to Ferguson (250), "of most interest to NT scholars is Tractate I, the *Poimandres* (second century at the earliest, in which Logos and Creative Mind mediate between the transcendent God and the world and *Anthropos* descends through the seven planetary spheres to reveal God)." For an expanded discussion of their relationship to the NT texts, see Dodd.

Although the religious and philosophical focus of the tractates varies, they all have in common a syncretistic approach to religion in which its content is a revelation that is taught. Some of the texts promote gnostic teachings, while others are characterized by DUALISM and pantheism. They try to reconcile GNOSTICISM and Greek philosophy, yet there are also Jewish and Egyptian influences. Recent scholarship suggests that these writings reveal a CONTEXT in a pagan Gnosticism that had developed out of MYSTERY RELIGIONS, though in their concurrent form they are designed as "reading mysteries." In other words, as Helmut Koester explains, "these writings do not argue in a philosophical manner, as would be expected in writings from a philosophical school, nor in the form of the dialogue used solely as an instrument of literary STYLE. Rather, the dialogues mirror instruction . . . in the secrets of the mystery initiation and in which the one who is to be initiated learns the proper questions and answers" (389). As such, then, the writings were transformed from their liturgical settings to become didactic in nature. Some scholars are also reintroducing the possibility that there may have been a fully developed pagan gnostic mystery religion independent of and perhaps predating Christianity, especially in light of the discovery of the NAG HAMMADI LIBRARY.

Bibliography. C. H. Dodd, *The Interpretation of the Fourth Gospel* (Cambridge: Cambridge University Press, 1953); Everett Ferguson, *Backgrounds of Early Christianity* (Grand Rapids: Eerdmans, 1989); Helmut Koester, *History, Culture, and Religions of the Hellenistic Age* (vol. 1 of *Introduction to the New Testament*; New York: de Gruyter, 1987); A. D. Nock and A.-J. Festugière, *Corpus hermeticum* (4 vols.; Paris: Les Belles Lettres, 1945–54; 3rd ed., 1991); Richard N. Soulen and R. Kendall Soulen, *Handbook of Biblical Criticism* (3rd ed.; Louisville: Westminster John Knox, 2001).

CORRESPONDENCE

One of the four criteria set forth by E. D. Hirsch Jr. in his definition of VERIFICATION by which to establish a reading of a TEXT as a probable representation of the author's intended (*see* INTENTION) MEANING. The criterion of correspondence requires that the reading must account for every linguistic component of the text. If a reading ignores any of these components or does not adequately account for them, then the reading should be viewed as an improbable representation of the author's intended meaning. *See* COHERENCE; GENERIC APPROPRIATENESS; LEGITIMACY.

Bibliography. E. D. Hirsch Jr., "Objective Interpretation," *PMLA* 75 (1960): 463, 470–79.

COSMIC IRONY. *See* IRONY

COSMOGONIC IMAGERY

Images involving elements of creation stories. Robert Alter uses the term to refer to instances in BIBLICAL POETRY in which the poet enlists images drawn from ancient creation MYTHS, such as the cosmic elements and agents mentioned in Job 3 and Ps. 8.

Bibliography. Robert Alter, *The Art of Biblical Poetry* (New York: Basic Books, 1985).

COSMOGONIC MYTH

A creation MYTH. Although ancient Israel was monotheistic and thus tended to eschew myths involving the world of gods, its poets and PROPHETS made extensive critical use of the creation myths of those people around them. Among these cosmogonic myths are the Babylonian Creation Epic (*Enuma Elish*, referred to in Jer. 5:22; Job 26:10; 38:10–11; Hab. 3:10) and the Atrahasis Epic (*Atra-Ḥasīs*, extremely wise), which parallels the creation STORY in Gen. 2–9. The use of such names as Yam (sea), Tannin, Rahab, Leviathan, and Nahash (*nāḥāš*, serpent) suggests a familiarity with Canaanite and Babylonian creation myths (van der Woude, 116).

Bibliography. A. S. van der Woude, ed., *The World of the Old Testament* (Grand Rapids: Eerdmans, 1989).

COSMOGONIC VERSE

In BIBLICAL POETRY, verse that employs cosmic images of creation. Examples are in Pss. 82:5; 89:9, 12, 36–37 (Alter, 127).

Bibliography. Robert Alter, *The Art of Biblical Poetry* (New York: Basic Books, 1985).

COSMOLOGY

The study of the origin, evolution, and STRUCTURE of the universe, and the manner in which different cultures define reality in terms of their cosmologies. Understanding the cosmologies of ancient Near Eastern and Greek cultures may often provide a key to better understanding the biblical TEXTs.

COSMOS

From the Greek *kosmos*, meaning "world" or "universe."

COTEXT

In EXEGESIS, the concern with the relationship between words in sentences, paragraphs, and chapters as opposed to TEXT, which refers to the portion of a work immediately under study, and CONTEXT, which focuses on the historical and sociological SETTING of the text.

COUNCIL ON THE STUDY OF RELIGION, THE

A federation of professional societies in religion having as a common purpose to "strengthen and advance scholarship and teaching." The members of the group are the American Academy of Religion, American Society of Christian Ethics, American Society of Missiology, American Theological Library Association, Catholic Biblical Association, Catholic Theological Society of America, College Theology Society, Religious Education Association, Society of Biblical Literature, and Society for the Scientific Study of Religion.

COUNTERPOINT

A type of poetic RHYTHM in which the poet superimposes a different rhythm on the dominant rhythm, which has already been established. The SIGNIFICANCE of counterpoint, then, is to call attention to the line(s) with the alternate rhythm. In BIBLICAL POETRY, counterpoint occurs when the normal FOCUSING in the lines is interrupted by what Alter refers to as static semantic parallelism, in which there is no dynamic movement between the VERSETs of a line (e.g., movement by SPECIFICATION, FOCUSING, HEIGHTENING) in the midst of lines in which there is obvious movement. For example, in Ps. 8, of the ten lines (verses), the fifth is the only one in which the second verset does not in some way develop the first one. In other words, both versets are identical in conception:

> What are human beings that you are mindful
> of them,
>   mortals that you care for them?

Bibliography. Robert Alter, *The Art of Biblical Poetry* (New York: Basic Books, 1985).

COUPLING, LINGUISTIC

In BIBLICAL POETRY, the LITERARY CONVENTION of stating an idea twice with carefully controlled differences. For example, "Let the righteous strike me; let the faithful correct me" (Ps. 141:5). The second part of the line restates the first but with slight differences: "righteous" becomes "faithful" and "strike" becomes "correct."

COVENANT

A contract or treaty between two parties that articulates a relationship of reciprocal obligations and responsibilities. There are several covenants in the BIBLE (e.g., Noahic [Gen. 9:8–17], Abrahamic [Gen. 15:1–21], Mosaic [Exod. 20:1–24:8], and Davidic [2 Sam. 7; cf. 2 Chron. 13:5]), with varying degrees of obligations and responsibilities. In Exod. 19:5–6 is found the heart of the Sinai covenant: "Now therefore, if you obey my voice and keep my covenant, you shall be my treasured possession out of all the peoples. Indeed, the whole earth is mine, but you shall be for me a priestly kingdom and a holy nation. These are the words that you shall speak to the Israelites." According to Hauer and Young, "Unlike the earlier covenants, it is not an unconditional promise by God to the people. It is a conditional agreement, dependent on allegiance to the Lord and faithfulness to the covenant. The Sinai covenant introduces the way to fulfillment of the third element of the patriarchal promise: blessing" (90). The commandments associated with the Sinai Covenant became TORAH and collectively the most important texts in Israel's understanding of itself.

Bibliography. Christian E. Hauer and William A. Young, *An Introduction to the Bible: A Journey into Three Worlds* (4th ed.; Englewood Cliffs, NJ: Prentice Hall, 1998).

COVENANT CODE. *See* BOOK OF THE COVENANT, THE

COVENANT FORM

In FORM CRITICISM, a type of ancient Near Eastern treaty. In the middle of the twentieth century, scholars began to notice the similarities between the book of Deuteronomy and the Hittite suzerainty treaty of the fourteenth–thirteenth centuries BCE. The suzerainty treaty has seven parts:

1. A preamble identifying the suzerain and the vassal(s).
2. A historical PROLOGUE noting the suzerain's deeds of protection in the past.
3. General guidelines that the vassals are to follow in order for both the suzerain and vassals to recognize if the treaty is being honored.

4. Detailed obligations imposed on the vassals. These obligations are specific cases relating to the general guidelines.
5. Directions as to the deposit of the treaty and its future public reading; thus the descendants of the vassal are bound by the treaty.
6. A list of witnesses (usually the suzerain's gods).
7. CURSES that will result if the treaty is broken and blessings that will occur if the treaty obligations are followed.

The book of Deuteronomy generally follows this treaty form:

1. Preamble (1:1–5)
2. Historical prologue (1:6–4:49)
3. Stipulations (5–11)
4. Detailed obligations (12–26)
5. Curses and blessings (27–30)
6. Witnesses (4:26; 30:19; 31:28)
7. Provision for deposit and public reading (31–34)

Although Deuteronomy follows the treaty form, it contains some features that are not found in a suzerainty treaty. These include Yahweh's revelation in a cloud, smoke, and thunder and the ceremony of blood that seals the treaty. While the issue of dependence is still debated, it is safe to assume that the book of Deuteronomy and the suzerainty treaty belong to the same practice of making treaties.

How does a knowledge of the suzerainty treaty assist us in understanding the book of Deuteronomy? The suzerainty treaty focuses on relationships and loyalty. Consequently, the treaty between God and Israel should be understood as covenantal rather than contractual. This means that the relationship between the parties is primary: the actions are secondary and should flow out of the relationship rather than the other way around. This covenantal relationship sets the CONTEXT for all legal material in Deuteronomy. The legal material constitutes a way to show loyalty to the relationship. The treaty in Deuteronomy contains both vertical and horizontal guidelines. In the suzerainty treaty, a wrong committed by one vassal against another is actually a wrong perpetrated against the suzerain. In the Deuteronomic treaty, the first four guidelines (commandments) speak to the relationship between God and humans, while the final six speak to the relationships among humans. We might assume that the treaty partially defines loyalty to God in terms of the relationship between humans.

COVENANT LAWSUIT

Also known as the *rîb* pattern, or the prophetic lawsuit, a concept in FORM CRITICISM of the HEBREW BIBLE referring to a complaint that one member of a COVENANT registers against an offending member. In the Hebrew Bible, YAHWEH typically registers the complaint, often through the words of a prophet. The lawsuit or complaint generally follows a four-part pattern: (1) the offending party is summoned, (2) past blessings that have been bestowed on the offender are listed, (3) the offender is read the accusations, and (4) both heavenly and earthly witnesses to the COVENANT are called on (e.g., Isa. 1:2–9; Hosea 4:1–10; and Ps. 50).

Bibliography. Richard N. Soulen and R. Kendall Soulen, *Handbook of Biblical Criticism* (3rd ed.; Louisville: Westminster John Knox, 2001).

COVERDALE BIBLE

An English TRANSLATION of the Latin VULGATE and Martin Luther's German Bible by Myles Coverdale in 1535. Having received a royal license from Henry VIII and being the first complete Bible published in England, the Coverdale Bible was circulated throughout England.

CREED

A formal statement of faith usually constructed within the cultic life of a religious community. Examples in the HEBREW BIBLE are Deut. 26:1–11 and Josh. 24:1–13. Creeds or portions of them may also occur in prayers, HYMNS, or NARRATIVES in both the Hebrew Bible and the NT (e.g., Pss. 105; 136; 1 Tim. 3:16; Eph. 4:4–6). *See* CHRISTOLOGI-

CAL HYMN. While there are creedal affirmations embedded within the hymns and prayers in the NT, especially within the EPISTLES, there is also creedal material that focuses on the content of faith in less poetic or lyrical language.

Neufeld suggests that in Paul's writings, creedal material can be identified by four characteristics: (1) an introductory word such as "confess," (2) some grammatical device that suggests either quoted or indirect material, (3) the use of repetitive devices, and (4) the presence of an antithetical THEME. While each occurrence of the creedal material may not contain all of the above elements, it is usually easy to identify it as a creedal statement. Examples are Rom. 1:3–4; 10:9; 1 Cor. 8:6; 15:3–5; 1 Tim. 2:5.

Bibliography. Vernon Neufeld, *The Earliest Christian Confessions* (Grand Rapids: Eerdmans, 1963), 42–68.

CRITERIA OF AUTHENTICITY

Technically, the set of criteria, established within the various expressions of the QUEST FOR THE HISTORICAL JESUS, that are used to judge which sayings within the CANONICAL and extracanonical TEXTS can be attributed to Jesus. Although the criteria underwent various modifications from the original quest of the nineteenth century and the new QUEST FOR THE HISTORICAL JESUS in the 1950s, most scholars involved in the quest have relied on three criteria. The third quest for the historical Jesus, initiated in the 1980s, either significantly revised the first criterion or simply rejected it (Soulen and Soulen, 40). The three most referenced criteria are (1) the criterion of dissimilarity, (2) the criterion of multiple attestations, and (3) the criterion of coherence. There are, however, at least three other criteria that historians employ in determining if a saying is authentic: (1) memorable content and form, (2) language and environment, and (3) explanation. Below is a description of the most referenced ones first and then the three additional ones. While these six criteria are used by most or at least many historians, there is certainly no universal consensus among historians as to the relative value of each or the order of importance.

The criterion of dissimilarity (also called distinctiveness, contradiction, discontinuity, originality) requires that a saying must be dissimilar to both church teaching and JUDAISM to be among the authentic SAYINGS OF JESUS. According to Stephen Harris, "Luke's Gospel preserves some of Jesus's most distinctive teaching, containing numerous parables that defy conventional thought and overturn ordinary expectations. These include provocative stories involving an irresponsible and ungrateful son (Luke 15:11–32), a despised Samaritan who is a moral hero (10:25–37), a lazy and unjust judge (18:1–8), and a righteous Pharisee who is out-classed by a sinful tax collector (18:9–14a)" (259). In other words, if the Gospel writers present Jesus as saying things that are out of place in both Palestinian Judaism and early Christianity, then there exists a high degree of plausibility that the saying derived from Jesus himself (Powell, 47). Accordingly, if a SAYING or event presented in the Gospels may have been a source of embarrassment to the early church yet is still reported, then there is the likelihood that it is authentic. Because this criterion suggests that an important historical person such as Jesus could stand in a position of absolute historical discontinuity, most scholars count it as an unrealistic means of judging the authenticity of the sayings. Scholars have developed alternatives to this first criterion, such as "plausibility" (Soulen and Soulen, 40). Those sayings that best reflect a context of first-century Galilean Judaism but still suggest originality have a higher degree of plausibility as genuine sayings of Jesus. Also, those sayings that seem to conflict with the concerns of the early Christian sources have more plausibility.

The criterion of multiple attestation focuses on the reduplication of material. The sayings whose themes are repeated elsewhere in the same or similar FORM (e.g., PARABLE, BEATITUDE, CHREIA) in two or more independent sources carry a higher possibility of being authentic. So if "a saying appears in Mark, the Q document, and the *Gospel of Thomas*—all of which are presumed to be independent of one another—it is likely to be genuine" (Harris, 259). Mark Allan Powell points out, however, that "though most scholars make use of this important criterion, most do not think it essential for determining that an event is historical" (47). So just because a saying or event is mentioned only once does not vitiate the possibility of its being authentic.

The criterion of coherence requires that any saying must cohere in FORM and CONTENT with other material deemed authentic by other criteria. So, for example, any allegorizing or spiritualizing of material must be questioned because this generally does not cohere with the generally accepted form of Jesus's teaching. Based on this criterion, the BEATITUDES in Luke are probably more authentic than the more spiritualized ones in Matthew. Generally, then, if the material under question is consistent with material that has already been established as authentic, then it may be judged itself to be authentic. As Powell observes, the saying in *Gospel of Thomas* 8:2 ("Whoever is near me is near the fire; whoever is far from me, is far from the Father's domain") may be judged to be authentic because of its similarity or coherence to Mark 9:49; 12:34.

The criterion of memorable content or form turns on the claim that if a saying is expressed in content and form that is easy to remember, it is more likely authentic. Since Jesus's culture was predominantly oral, in which little was recorded, historians usually assume that short, pithy sayings would have been more easily remembered: examples include PROVERBS, beatitudes, and even parables since these brief stories are inherently easy to remember (Powell, 48). Things that add to the memorable character of sayings or stories would include humor, HYPERBOLE, and PARADOX (e.g., Mark 6:4; Matt. 5:5; 23:24; 7:3–5).

The criterion of language and environment works on the assumption that if material is to be authentic, it must be consistent with the language and environment of the time to which it is ascribed. If any material turns out be anachronistic, it cannot be authentic. In other words, a person could not possibly say something that the language or SOCIAL LOCATION would not allow. Since the CONTEXT for Jesus's activities was first-century

Palestinian Judaism generally and a peasant rural culture specifically, any material that would relate more to a Gentile urban setting than to the rural Palestinian one must be deemed anachronistic. Powell rightly points out that Jesus's remarks in Mark 10:11–12 ("Whoever divorces his wife and marries another commits adultery against her; and if she divorces her husband and marries another, she commits adultery") are probably not authentic because while Roman law allowed a woman to divorce her husband, Jewish law did not (49).

Many scholars also employ the criterion of explanation in determining the authenticity of material by examining the way in which the material helps explain "developments in the Jesus tradition" (49). If, for example, materials are set forth to explain Jesus as a first-century prophet, a Hellenistic philosopher, a social revolutionary, a Jewish wise man, or the embodiment of Sophia, they must be judged on the basis of their ability to account for the Jesus tradition that arose in the early church.

Bibliography. Stephen Harris, *The New Testament: A Student's Introduction* (4th ed.; Boston: McGraw-Hill, 2002); Mark Allan Powell, *Jesus as a Figure in History* (Louisville: Westminster John Knox, 1998); Richard N. Soulen and R. Kendall Soulen, *Handbook of Biblical Criticism* (3rd ed.; Louisville: Westminster John Knox, 2001).

CRITERION OF COHERENCE. *See* CRITERIA OF AUTHENTICITY

CRITIC

A person who interprets a work of art in order to judge its quality and value. In BIBLICAL STUDIES, a critic uses a particular type of CRITICISM in order to interpret a biblical TEXT.

CRITICAL APPARATUS

In Hebrew and Greek editions of the HEBREW BIBLE and the NT, an extensive set of footnotes listing VARIANT READINGS and the ancient sources (manuscripts, TRANSLATIONS, VERSIONS, commentaries [*see* COMMENTARY], quotations, lectionaries [*see* LECTIONARY], and church fathers) in which the variants occur. Most critical editions include only some of the variant readings, while a few others list every variant within a TEXT. Although modern translations do not have a critical apparatus, those that are committee translations are based on serious attention to the critical apparatuses of the critical editions. They offer footnotes that indicate the most crucial variants and include abbreviated information on the type of variant (addition, omission, etc.). *See* CRITICAL TEXT.

CRITICAL DISTANCE

The historical, ideological, and cultural differences between the world that produced a TEXT and the world of the reader (*see* WORLD BEHIND THE TEXT; WORLD IN FRONT OF THE TEXT). A lack of a sense of critical distance usually results in interpretive anachronisms. For example, if "the story of Cain and Abel (Gen. 4:1–26) is assimilated directly into the experience of struggle between the landed and landless, or the farmers and the shepherds" (Thiselton, 412), the critical distance between the STORY in the text and the interpreter is ignored.

Bibliography. Anthony C. Thiselton, *New Horizons in Hermeneutics* (Grand Rapids: Zondervan, 1992).

CRITICAL METHODOLOGY

In HERMENEUTICS, *critical methodology* refers to the interpretive approach a CRITIC uses to examine a TEXT. The interpretive approach influences the way in which a critic perceives and uses the data of the text. In other words, method colors the reader's understanding of the text and the way in which one makes SENSE of it. This is true because methods are anchored to a set of underlying PRESUPPOSITIONS that determine the questions to be put to the text. To interpret a text means to interpret it in one way and not another. An interesting taxonomy of methodology is supplied by Keesey as he groups critical methods into seven categories:

1. Historical criticism: Author as context
2. Formal criticism: Text as context
3. Reader-response criticism: Audience as context
4. Mimetic criticism: Reality as context
5. Intertextual criticism: Literature as context
6. Poststructural criticism: Language as context
7. Historical criticism II: Culture as context

Each critical methodology is placed under one of these categories (although there is some overlap between categories) based on the primary focus of the method. Understanding depends on the contextual focus of the method.

Bibliography. Donald Keesey, *Contexts for Criticism* (4th ed.; Boston: McGraw-Hill, 2003).

CRITICAL TEXT

A hypothetical RECONSTRUCTION by textual CRITICS of the NT and HEBREW BIBLE from extant ancient manuscripts and other sources. The critical text usually contains a CRITICAL APPARATUS, which lists alternate readings for those appearing in the critical text. Among the most popular critical texts are the Nestle-Aland *Novum Testamentum Graece* for the NT and the *Biblia Hebraica Stuttgartensia* for the Hebrew Bible (OT).

Bibliography. Eberhard and Erwin Nestle, Barbara and Kurt Aland, et al., eds. *Novum Testamentum Graece* (27th ed.; Stuttgart: Deutsche Bibelgesellschaft, 1993); Karl Ellinger, Wilhelm Rudolph, et al., eds., *Biblia Hebraica Stuttgartensia* (4th ed.; Stuttgart: Deutsche Bibelgesellschaft, 1997).

CRITICAL THEORY

A term first introduced by Max Horkheimer in 1932 to describe an approach that defines all knowledge (scientific, moral, aesthetic, political, etc.) as being rooted in social interests and is concerned with the place of emancipatory interests in social orders. Though *critical theory* has been used synonymously with CRITICAL METHODOLOGY, there is a fundamental difference between them. Critical methodology focuses primarily on the interests of HERMENEUTICS: INTERPRETATION, MEANING, and EXPLANATION of texts. Critical theory, however, examines the role that knowledge plays in the formation of social practices of class, GENDER, ETHNICITY, and race (*see* RACE, CLASS, AND GENDER CRITICISM). Critical methodology is interested in discovering meaning by interpreting the textual representations of social practices. Critical theory, however, examines the power structures of knowledge within a social order and, by offering alternative explanations of the social practices, seeks to produce an emancipatory knowledge within the SUBJECTS of a social order (Nielsen, 527). Thus, in its attempts to understand the formation of social practices, critical theory always aims at emancipation of the subject constructed by social practices. Under the rubric of critical theory in BIBLICAL STUDIES, we might include the methods whose motivation for interpreting texts is liberation (e.g., FEMINIST CRITICISM, LIBERATION THEOLOGY, POSTCOLONIAL CRITICISM, *MUJERISTA* CRITICISM, and CULTURAL CRITICISM).

Bibliography. Max Horkheimer, *Critical Theory: Selected Essays* (New York: Seabury, 1972); Gerd Nielsen, "Critical Theory," in *Encyclopedia of Contemporary Literary Theory* (ed. Irena R. Makaryk; Toronto: University of Toronto Press, 1993), 527–28.

CRITICISM

The analysis, study, and evaluation of works of art based on formal principles of evaluation. Criticism traditionally encompasses the artist, the work, the world, and the audience (Harmon and Holman, 124). Criticism concentrating on the artist is *expressive* (e.g., GENETIC CRITICISM); on the work as an autonomous object, *objective* (e.g., CANONICAL CRITICISM; NEW CRITICISM; REDACTION CRITICISM); on the world within which the work was produced, *mimetic* (e.g., FORM CRITICISM; GENETIC CRITICISM; SOURCE CRITICISM); and on the audience, *pragmatic* (e.g., READER-RESPONSE CRITICISM; RECEPTION THEORY; TRANSACTIVE CRITICISM). *See* BIBLICAL CRITICISM; CRITICAL METHODOLOGY.

Bibliography. William Harmon and C. Hugh Holman, *A Handbook to Literature* (8th ed.; Upper Saddle River, NJ: Prentice Hall, 1999).

CRITICISM, AFFECTIVE. *See* READER-RESPONSE CRITICISM

CRITICISM, ARCHETYPAL. *See* ARCHETYPAL CRITICISM

CRITICISM, ASIAN / ASIAN AMERICAN. *See* ASIAN / ASIAN AMERICAN CRITICISM

CRITICISM, AUTOBIOGRAPHICAL LITERARY. *See* AUTOBIOGRAPHICAL LITERARY CRITICISM

CRITICISM, BIBLICAL. *See* BIBLICAL CRITICISM

CRITICISM, BLACK. *See* BLACK THEOLOGY; RACE, CLASS, AND GENDER CRITICISM

CRITICISM, CANONICAL. *See* CANONICAL CRITICISM

CRITICISM, COMPOSITIONAL. *See* COMPOSITIONAL CRITICISM

CRITICISM, CULTURAL. *See* CULTURAL CRITICISM

CRITICISM, CULTURAL MATERIALIST. *See* CULTURAL MATERIALISM

CRITICISM, FEMINIST. *See* FEMINIST CRITICISM

CRITICISM, FORM. *See* FORM CRITICISM

CRITICISM, FORMAL. *See* FORMALISM

CRITICISM, GAY/LESBIAN. *See* QUEER THEORY

CRITICISM, GENETIC. *See* GENETIC CRITICISM

CRITICISM, GENRE. *See* GENRE CRITICISM

CRITICISM, HIGHER. *See* HIGHER CRITICISM

CRITICISM, HISTORICAL-CRITICAL. *See* HISTORICAL-CRITICAL METHOD

CRITICISM, IDEOLOGICAL. *See* IDEOLOGICAL CRITICISM

CRITICISM, INTERTEXTUAL. *See* INTERTEXTUAL CRITICISM

CRITICISM, LINGUISTIC. *See* LINGUISTIC CRITICISM

CRITICISM, LITERARY. *See* LITERARY CRITICISM

CRITICISM, LOWER. *See* HIGHER CRITICISM

CRITICISM, MARXIST. *See* MARXIST CRITICISM

CRITICISM, MIMETIC. *See* MIMETIC CRITICISM

CRITICISM, *MUJERISTA*. *See* MUJERISTA THEOLOGY/CRITICISM

CRITICISM, MYTH. *See* MYTH CRITICISM

CRITICISM, NARRATIVE. *See* NARRATIVE CRITICISM

CRITICISM, NEW. *See* NEW CRITICISM

CRITICISM, PHENOMENOLOGICAL. *See* PHENOMENOLOGICAL CRITICISM

CRITICISM, POSTCOLONIAL. *See* POSTCOLONIAL CRITICISM

CRITICISM, POSTMODERN. *See* POSTMODERN CRITICISM

CRITICISM, POSTSTRUCTURALIST. *See* POSTMODERN CRITICISM

CRITICISM, PRACTICAL. *See* PRACTICAL CRITICISM

CRITICISM, PSYCHOANALYTIC. *See* PSYCHOANALYTIC CRITICISM

CRITICISM, RACE, CLASS, AND GENDER. *See* RACE, CLASS, AND GENDER CRITICISM

CRITICISM, READER-ORIENTED. *See* READER-RESPONSE CRITICISM

CRITICISM, READER-RESPONSE. *See* READER-RESPONSE CRITICISM

CRITICISM, RECEPTION. *See* RECEPTION THEORY

CRITICISM, REDACTION. *See* REDACTION CRITICISM

CRITICISM, RHETORICAL. *See* RHETORICAL CRITICISM

CRITICISM, SOCIAL-SCIENTIFIC. *See* SOCIAL-SCIENTIFIC CRITICISM

CRITICISM, SOCIO-RHETORICAL. *See* SOCIO-RHETORICAL CRITICISM

CRITICISM, SOURCE. *See* SOURCE CRITICISM

CRITICISM, SUBJECTIVE. *See* READER-RESPONSE CRITICISM

CRITICISM, *TENDENZ*. *See* TENDENZ CRITICISM

CRITICISM, TEXTUAL. *See* TEXTUAL CRITICISM

CRITICISM, TRADITION. *See* TRADITION CRITICISM

CRITICISM, TRANSACTIVE. *See* TRANSACTIVE CRITICISM

CRITICISM, WOMANIST. *See* WOMANIST THEOLOGY/CRITICISM

CROSS ACROSTIC. *See* ACROSTIC

CROWD MOTIF

A structural device in the GOSPELS and Acts. In terms of NARRATIVE CRITICISM, the crowds that surround Jesus in the Gospels and the disciples in Acts constitute a character role. They serve not only as an audience for Jesus's teaching and healing but also as a POINT OF VIEW. In John's Gospel, the crowds are a distinct structural device in that they will always be divided in their response to Jesus's teaching into those who believe and those who do not.

CRYPTOGRAM

A type of written TEXT that employs SYMBOLS encoded in such a way as to permit one with access to the codes to decipher the MEANING hidden behind the symbols. In this sense, APOCALYPSE is cryptogrammatic because of its heavy use of SYMBOLISM. The original readers of an apocalyptic text, however, would probably have been more familiar with the conventional symbolism than are modern readers. The most serious hermeneutical problem arises when modern interpreters assume that an apocalyptic text is a cryptogram by which contemporary events can be used to interpret the symbols of the text.

CSR. *See* COUNCIL ON THE STUDY OF RELIGION, THE

CULTIC DECALOGUE. *See* DECALOGUE

CULTURAL ANTHROPOLOGY

Although it includes a variety of approaches and is related to other disciplines (e.g., ethnology, ARCHAEOLOGY, history, and sociology), cultural anthropology is the "comparative analysis of cultures with particular emphasis on such issues as social roles and religious systems" (Overholt, vii). The chief goal of cultural anthropology is to understand a culture in terms of its broad social CONTEXTS. Biblical anthropologists are concerned with understanding biblical TEXTS within the social organizations and structures and group dynamics that are natural for both AUTHORS and audiences. Since authors compose their texts within these structures and dynamics, cultural anthropologists argue that the most plausible understanding of an ancient text is the one that accounts for its social context. This means that anthropologists try to reconstruct the manner in which a group of persons thought, imagined, expressed feelings, and communicated conventionally. This last-named category—to understand how a group of persons communicated conventionally—requires that a group's SYMBOLIC WORLD be interpreted.

Cultural anthropology is based on the ASSUMPTION that individuals within a cultural group communicate with each other through a "pattern of meanings embodied in symbols, a system of inherited conceptions expressed in symbolic forms by means of which men communicate, perpetuate and develop their knowledge about and attitudes toward life" (Geertz, 89). This, however, is not only the basis of cultural anthropology but also its most difficult challenge. For one culture to understand another culture's symbolic world is not easy, and not all cultural anthropologists employ the same methods in the attempt. Nonetheless, all cultural anthropologists do try to employ theories or methods that they believe best account for material in a text. Thomas Overholt, however, has argued that the most useful approaches agree on three issues: anthropological studies must work with both agency and social structure, must assume that social life is naturally contradictory, and must remember that the results of anthropological study provide "one of several possible maps that can guide us in our attempts to understand society" (5).

According to Overholt, a basic reality of a culture is a type of "informal knowledge" that allows a culture to operate according to consistent patterns but that also allows an individual within that culture to operate according to options within a matrix of possible relationships, the latter of which he calls "modal states." Obviously, to understand an author best is to understand this field of informal knowledge within which the writer works, relates, and communicates. Cultural anthropology therefore must give attention to both the social structure and to the field of choices available to the individual within the STRUCTURE. With respect to the inherent contradictoriness of social life, Overholt suggests that a number of explanations are possible, but basic to each is the reality of the tension between "human action and social restraint" (8). For example, there may be tension between classes, an individual and an institution, ideologies, and the culture and social structure. For each of these contradictions, or fields of tension, cultures develop ways to cope or at least gloss over CONVENTIONS, rituals, ideologies. The most important of these are ideologies that establish structures of power for the elite in the culture and the institutionalization of these structures, which formalize patterns of expected behavior. Overholt's final idea—that anthropological theories serve as maps for understanding a culture and its texts rather than as mirrors reflecting the way the culture actually was—is an important disclaimer for the discipline of cultural anthropology and for biblical cultural anthropology. He writes: "When we turn to anthropology for assistance in interpreting biblical texts, our goal will not be to establish a normative pattern that mirrors Israelite society. Rather, we will employ ethnographic examples and anthropological theory to help us construct a 'map' of the social and religious situation reflected in particular texts" (10). It is one way to map an understanding of a text, not the only way. For an extended example of the way cultural anthropology is applied to the biblical text, see Overholt.

Bibliography. Clifford Geertz, *Thick Description: Toward an Interpretive Theory of Culture* (New York: Basic Books, 1973); Thomas W. Overholt, *Cultural Anthropology and the Old Testament* (Minneapolis: Fortress, 1996).

CULTURAL CRITICISM

A relatively new and influential interdisciplinary analysis of cultural institutions and TEXTS practiced since the mid-twentieth century, also known as cultural studies, cultural theory, and in BIBLICAL STUDIES, biblical cultural criticism. Although the term "cultural studies" was first used in the 1960s and had its beginning in Theodor Adorno and the Frankfurt school, the Centre for Contemporary Cultural Studies (at the University of Birmingham, UK, 1964–2002) has also been the major foundational institution responsible for the implementation of cultural criticism. However, "those origins, originally Marxist in orientation, have since been largely abandoned for theoretical positions more eclectic, interdisciplinary, and international in scope" (Soulen and Soulen, 23).

In CRITICISM, the term *culture* has a diverse and ambiguous MEANING. In the introduction to the *Dictionary of Cultural and Critical Theory*, Michael

Payne provides a comprehensive definition: "That complex whole which includes knowledge, belief, art, law, morals, custom, and other capabilities and habits acquired by man as a member of society" (1–2). Clearly culture includes all aspects of a particular society, such as agriculture, economics, politics, religion, TRADITION, education, and geography. All AUTHORS write out of their own particular culture. Conversely, all readers interpret texts out of their cultural frame of reference. In fact, with regard to the ability for objective human INTERPRETATION, cultural critics claim that "born into a language, culture, and race, class and gender politics, the subject is never fully autonomous" (3). Complicating the issue of interpretation is the fact that culture itself is dynamic, always changing. New beliefs, terms, traditions, and morals are integrated as a result of transitions in technology, experience, and education. Subcultures also provide an extended development of culture. Subcultures form as smaller sects of the whole system, developing additional practices and customs as a result of common interests or community interaction.

Alice Templeton defines cultural criticism by dividing it into three main categories. First, "cultural studies must be interdisciplinary (and sometimes antidisciplinary) in its tendency, making use of insights from anthropology, history, sociology, psychology, philosophy, and other fields" (19). Insights from the broad perspectives of different fields of study allow this criticism to deal more comprehensively with a particular text. The social sciences and humanities have adopted cultural studies as a valuable tool of inquiry. Specifically, the "cultural critic borrows from other disciplines in order to challenge the blindnesses of institutionalized literary study" (19). Second, cultural criticism makes no "distinction between high and low culture. . . . As opposed to traditional text-bound scholarship, cultural studies recognizes the simple fact that audiences make their own, sometimes subversive meanings out of literature, music, television, and commodities in general" (20). Literature can both express and challenge prominent ideals of a society. Third, cultural criticism is intimately related to politics and economics. Templeton states, "Cultural criticism fulfills its political role—to liberate us from destructive, restrictive systems of thought and action, to criticize [a culture] for the purpose of improving, and to avail ourselves and our students of 'really useful knowledge'" (20). Cultural criticism deals with the conflicts of race, class, and gender.

The *Dictionary of Cultural and Critical Theory* describes three main components of cultural criticism to which theorists subscribe or which they reject. "Human subjectivity and consciousness, ideology and hegemony, critique and polysemy provided then, as now, the key coordinates of cultural studies" (2). With regard to subjectivity and consciousness, a comparison can be made to the long-standing theories of psychologist Jean Piaget. Piaget defines learning as a process of assimilation and accommodation. Humans assimilate information through the senses into previously made schemas, whereas accommodation comes from the construction of new schemas. Learning is accommodation. Thus, personal human understanding stems from a person's preexisting schemas, and one cannot completely delete or construct them without exposure to new sensory experience. In terms of IDEOLOGY and HEGEMONY, "it is not the consciousness of men that determines their existence, but their social existence that determines their consciousness" (3). Oppressive structures, ruling-class authorities, and economics impact the existence of freedom and expression within a society. The culturally accepted norms, values, and morals will also influence the ideology of society. Critique and POLYSEMY demand that "any attempt to know (or theorize) the processes of society must begin with a radical criticism of the dominating forces of ideology in order to disengage consciousness from what keeps it politically unconscious" (3). Aspects of social awareness and influence must be analyzed in order to develop a wider understanding of political impact on thinking. Cultural criticism has several meaningful and practical aspects that can be applied to the interpretation of the BIBLE. First, in the analysis of a

text, cultural studies utilizes aspects of society such as the political scene, religious climate, and popular culture. Popular biblical EXEGESIS understands that authors' words cannot be separated from the context in which they were spoken. For example, the GOSPELS and EPISTLES were written to and within a particular historical context. Religious customs were also intimately involved in political and social structures. Hebrew and NT communities were bound by social ideals, and social existence determined status, worth, role, and consciousness in the religious community. Aspects of hegemony such as domination and enculturation are themes that permeate the HEBREW BIBLE, and the theme of social responsibility that cultural criticism proposes is consistent with the mind-set that the Bible is to apply to modern circumstances.

Biblical cultural criticism tries to "analyze the influence of the Bible on the Western tradition, ancient and modern, and especially its impact, whether as icon or commodity, on contemporary culture. It also seeks to illuminate how culture and sociohistorical location influence the interpretation of the Bible" (Soulen and Soulen, 42). Both the impact and interpretation of SCRIPTURE are influenced by tradition, culture, and geography. Cross-cultural biblical interpretation "refers to the conscious use of contemporary, culturally indigenous texts and concepts as hermeneutical keys in the interpretation of the Bible" (42). Cross-cultural interpretation is evident in the TRANSLATIONS and applications of the biblical texts, because the culture of the Bible is different from the one in which it is now read.

Several publications have showcased interpretations of biblical texts through the lens of cultural criticism. *Semeia* has devoted whole issues to biblical interpretation in light of expanded cultural contexts; thus in *Semeia* 78 (1997) Phyllis Bird, Katharine Doob Sakenfeld, and Sharon Ringe served as editors for a number of articles under the general topic of "Reading the Bible as Women: Perspectives from Africa, Asia, and Latin America." In this issue, Leticia A. Guardiola-Sáenz offers a cultural reading of Matt. 15:21–28, the story of the Canaanite woman (69–81), in which she examines the story's "socio-historical conditions of production." In the same issue, Madipoane J. Masenya examines Prov. 31:10–31 within the framework of the liberation of South African women (55–68). In *Semeia* 73 (1996) Musa W. Dube examines Matt. 15:21–28 from the perspective of Batswana women.

Traditional LITERARY CRITICISMS have tried to determine what the Bible meant to its original hearers or readers and what the text should mean to modern audiences. Cultural criticism deals with how narratives reflect underlying ideologies of race, class, and GENDER: specifically, how society, economics, and religious belief have interrelated throughout the centuries by influencing one another. Cultural interpretations of Scripture continue to develop and expand in a variety of cultures, and an appreciation of those who interpret in non-Western contexts is gaining ground in academic circles. Cultural criticism promises to supply new perspectives on the Bible, its interpreters, and interpretations—perspectives previously unavailable or forced to the margins of academia.

Bibliography. Phyllis Bird, Katharine Doob Sakenfeld, and Sharon Ringe, eds., "Reading the Bible as Women: Perspectives from Africa, Asia, and Latin America," *Semeia* 78 (1997): 11–165; Brian K. Blount, *Cultural Interpretation: Reorienting New Testament Criticism* (Minneapolis: Augsburg Fortress, 1995); Musa W. Dube, "Readings of Semoya: Batswana Women's Interpretations of Matt. 15:21–28," *Semeia* 73 (1996): 111–29; Leticia A. Guardiola-Sáenz, "Borderless Women and Borderless Texts: A Cultural Reading of Matthew 15:21–2," *Semeia* 78 (1997): 69–81; Madipoane J. Masenya, "Proverbs 31:10–31 in a South African Context: A Reading for the Liberation of African (Northern Sotho) Women," *Semeia* 78 (1997): 55–68; Michael Payne, ed., *A Dictionary of Cultural and Critical Theory* (Cambridge, MA: Blackwell, 1996); Richard N. Soulen and R. Kendall Soulen, *Handbook of Biblical Criticism* (3rd ed.; Louisville: Westminster John Knox, 2001); Alice Templeton, "Sociology and Literature: Theories for Cultural Criticism," *College Literature* 19 (June 1992): 19–30; Cheryl Wall, "Reviews of the Book *Borders, Boundaries, and Frames: Cultural Studies and Cultural Criticism,*" *African American Studies* 31 (Fall 1997): 508.

CULTURAL MATERIALISM

In the LITERARY sense, a type of CRITICISM that views a TEXT as both a cultural form and a formation, as both a product and a producer of culture. Cultural materialism has its roots in the traditional Marxist concept that economy determines all social and political changes within a society.

Ivo Kamps suggests that a spontaneous diversification of materialist criticism appeared in the 1970s due to its "fierce emphasis on economic determination" (4). Theories such as cultural materialism and NEW HISTORICISM emerged out of a tendency to shy away from the notion that economics determines *all* social and political changes without giving attention to other cultural facets of society (4–10). Similarly, Wilson asserts that a shift from a Marxist emphasis on economic class multiplied the growing numbers of materialist approaches (27). Thus, the concept(s) of cultural materialism developed from the avoidance of unequal attention toward and treatment of economic class in literature and the inclusion of other cultural systems (e.g., art, GENDER, race, and sexual orientation) as real material rather than mere reflections of the "economic BASE."

Recent study and practice in cultural materialism mirrors much of the work of Raymond Williams, who named and began developing this literary theory in *The Country and the City* (1974), *Marxism and Literature* (1977), and *Problems in Materialism and Culture* (1980). In these texts, Williams rejects and revises several principles of traditional Marxism.

> His quarrel with the orthodox [Marxist] position revolved around the model of the economic "base" which was held to determine the cultural "superstructure," a scheme that Williams felt had only reinforced the notion of literature and other cultural products as immaterial shadows, his own insistence being, to the contrary, that culture was fully *material*. (Baldick, 179)

Therefore, while traditional MARXIST CRITICISM separates "'culture' from material social life," Williams's cultural materialism regards "culture as a constitutive social process, creating specific and different 'ways of life'" (*Marxism and Literature*, 19). In cultural materialism, economics no longer serves as sole determinant of the cultural superstructure because no solely functioning economic base exists in society. Instead, economics serves as a form of culture, which also forms culture. Hence, in cultural materialism a literary work or text itself is itself a cultural form and formation. The main emphasis and object of study behind cultural materialism, then, underlies the ASSUMPTION that a literary work is like all other forms of culture: both a product of and a producer of culture.

Williams's shift away from traditional Marxist theory has resulted in debate within the circle of materialist critics. One scholar in particular, Terry Eagleton, has accused Williams of undermining the Marxist superstructure by imposing human and idealist notions of transcendent cultural forms. To Eagleton, forms of culture merely reflect the Marxist economic base as IDEOLOGY or ideologies (44–63). Although Eagleton represents one of many arguments in opposition to Williams's cultural materialism, the wide debate between critics from the materialist/Marxist circle could not suppress the minority view of cultural materialism. The movement as a literary theory and criticism grew into the subcircle of cultural materialist criticism, where it has become as complex and diverse as the theory from which it sprang.

Although defining cultural materialism is difficult due to the wide range of disagreement concerning its methods of application to a literary text, an adequate description of common principles is possible. Jonathan Dollimore and Alan Sinfield, two of today's leading critics in cultural materialism, name four elements that they think help define cultural materialism: (1) historical CONTEXT, (2) theoretical method, (3) political commitment, and (4) textual analysis. Though literary critics may disagree on how to apply these elements, the principles behind them hold cultural materialism together.

First, to understand what Dollimore and Sinfield mean by inquiry into a text's historical context, one needs to remember Williams's claim that a text, being a form of culture that also forms culture, deserves treatment beyond that granted to any other social practices and products. Thus, cultural materialism "refuses to privilege 'literature' in the way that literary criticism has done hitherto" (Dollimore and Sinfield, 4). Therefore, cultural materialists ignore literary texts' technical and aesthetic qualities. To cultural materialists, political pamphlets, religious tracts, medical records, houses, and other artifacts and objects of interpretation carry just as much political and social significance as so-called literary texts. In other words, no text deserves "literary" status. Indeed, inquiry into a text's historical context matters more than examining its formal, literary qualities. Specifically, what matters to the cultural materialist is a text's function in society throughout history, not just the history of its initial production but also the text's reproductions and interpretations throughout history. No text escapes its historical conditions of production. Texts, their interpretations, and their reproductions are embedded in history, having an interest in the politics, social structures, and institutions. "Historical context undermines the transcendent significance traditionally accorded to the literary text and allows us to recover its histories" (vii).

Second, the theoretical method involves the task of interpreting a text in relation to other texts or social issues and problems, especially in light of the particular text's conditions of production and reproduction. The theoretical method takes the study of a literary text out of the traditional field or study of literature to interpret the text in light of other social practices. The theoretical method of cultural materialism, then, entails interpreting a text in light of its historical, cultural, and political contexts rather than interpreting it from the traditional, formal POINT OF VIEW. "Theoretical method detaches the text from immanent criticism which seeks only to reproduce it in its own terms" (vii). And rather than reproduce a text in light of the critic's own terms, the CRITIC must try to interpret or reproduce a text on its own terms, which keep the particular text true to its history as a cultural product and to its conditions of production and reproduction. Further still, cultural materialists claim that no interpretation or reproduction gives the absolute, intended MEANING of the text. All interpretation is theory. And while remaining true to their theoretical method, cultural materialists demystify the norms of the absolutist claims of traditional, formal criticisms (*see* FORMALISM; NEW CRITICISM).

The third element concerns the critic's political commitment. A cultural materialist strongly believes that all social practices involve political partiality and biases. Wilson explains, "There is no 'cultural practice' that is not political, no area of cultural life that cannot be accounted for, explained, transformed by political discourse; it becomes *the* metalanguage" (Dollimore and Sinfield, 16). Indeed, cultural materialists do not exempt themselves from this principle that all texts function within the conditions of history as product and producer of political DISCOURSE. Most admit that they interpret through a cultural lens that places emphasis on the oppression of minority groups. Dollimore and Sinfield state in their political declaration:

> Cultural materialism does not pretend to political neutrality. It knows that no cultural practice is ever without political significance—not the production of *King Lear* at the Globe, or at the Barbican, or as a text in school, popular or learned edition, or in literary criticism, or in the present volume. Cultural materialism does not, like much established literary criticism, attempt to mystify its perspective as the natural, obvious or right interpretation of an allegedly given textual fact. On the contrary, it registers its commitment to the transformation of a social order which exploits people on the grounds of race, gender, and class. (viii)

The fourth element relates closely to the previous one. According to Wilson, textual analysis in cultural materialism "has become totally subordinate to politics" (19). Cultural materialism warns against superimposing a literary STRUCTURE on any text. So cultural materialists ignore analyzing a text on the basis of its thematic and technical qualities, as a formalist would do. Instead, they seek to find the political and social representations and ideas they believe all texts to contain. Finding contradictions and oppositions involving representations of power structures and oppressed minority groups falls under the cultural materialist's objective.

Nevertheless, as a whole, cultural materialists employ historical inquiry to examine the social conditions of a text's production and reproduction, a theoretical method that snatches the "literary" out of literary texts, a political commitment to expose oppression and unequal treatment based on society's norms, and a textual analysis dedicated to that commitment.

Although these elements of cultural materialism have been organized and separated here for the sake of clearer explanation, a cultural materialist would not do so in application. No step-by-step method dictates the cultural materialist's interpretation; rather, the combination of these principles guides the critic. In fact, cultural materialists warn against imposing any formal, technical structure on a literary text. Furthermore, the presentation here of the commonality in cultural materialism has swept past its diversity. Dollimore and Sinfield have recently worked on expanding and integrating cultural materialism into QUEER THEORY; others, such as Scott Wilson, integrate it with DECONSTRUCTION; and Kathleen McLuskie produces valid feminist cultural materialist arguments.

Even though it serves as an object of faith, the BIBLE contains political discourse, and to separate politics from the Bible—its production and reproduction—is to ignore its role in creating and legitimating political discourses. Oppression, wars, nations, and other political aspects play significant roles in both the HEBREW BIBLE and the NT. Like other texts, the Bible can never escape its historical contexts. It is molded by and in a particular social setting, and no text has influenced Western culture to the same extent as the Bible. In other words, no text has been more of a producer of culture than the Bible. Luke-Acts may have been written in the latter part of the first century CE to convince the Roman authorities that the Christian church presented no political threat to the empire. In order to do so, the AUTHOR selected and arranged his sources to present both Jesus and his followers as innocent of charges brought against them. In fact, the parallels between Jesus and Paul are so pronounced that they cannot be ignored. Consequently, Luke-Acts reflects cultural conditions and functions to create a particular church culture. As such, it is a political discourse with a political agenda (recall Wilson's claim that there is no cultural practice that is not political). The same may also be said for the disputed Pauline texts of Ephesians and Colossians as well as the PASTORAL EPISTLES, which seem to reflect a time in the Christian church when it was becoming an institution, with its own CREED and hierarchical structure that mirrored the social structure of the Roman Empire. Some scholars argue that in order for the church to survive, it had no choice but to adopt the Roman social structure. To do so, the later disciples of Paul consciously reinterpreted his thought, which made their interpretations political discourses. Furthermore, throughout history the church has interpreted these texts as if these hierarchical structures of the first century are universally binding on subsequent generations in cultures that differ significantly from the original. As a result, the church's interpretations carry political import. Such observations suggest that the Bible constitutes a ripe field for cultural materialism.

Bibliography. Chris Baldick, ed., Criticism and Literary Theory: 1890 to the Present (New York: Longman, 1996); Jonathan Dollimore and Alan Sinfield, eds., Political Shakespeare: New Essays in Cultural Materialism (Manchester, UK: Manchester University Press, 1985); Terry Eagleton, Criticism and Ideology: A Study in Marxist Literary Theory (London: New Left Books, 1976); Ivo Kamps, ed., Materialist Shakespeare: A History (London: Verso, 1995); Alan Sinfield, Faultlines: Cultural Materialism and the Politics of Dissident Reading (Oxford: Oxford University Press, 1992); Raymond Williams, The Country and the City (New York: Oxford University Press, 1973); idem, Marxism and Literature (Oxford: Oxford University Press, 1977); idem, Problems in Materialism and Culture (London: Verso, 1980); Scott Wilson, Cultural Materialism: Theory and Practice (Oxford: Blackwell, 1995).

CURSE

A pronouncement of harm or evil, usually in the name of God, on a person. See IMPRECATORY PSALMS.

CURSIVE. See MINUSCULE

CYCLIC STRUCTURE

A NARRATIVE pattern or STRUCTURE in which a sequence of events is encountered a number of times but successively couched in different terms. An example is the book of Revelation, in which the same repetitive movement in each section between the PROLOGUE and EPILOGUE is from the evil of fallen humanity and the misery generated by this evil onward to a final judgment of evil and glorification of the righteous.

CYNICISM

A philosophical school founded by Antisthenes, a student of Socrates. Its most noted figures, Diogenes (404–323 BCE) and Crates (d. ca. 270 BCE), taught that virtue is the ultimate goal of human existence, stressed rigorous self-control, and openly opposed conventional values such as money and political power (Harris, 44). The Cynics disdained traditional comforts and, traveling barefoot with only the barest of clothing, earned enough to keep alive by teaching and begging. This spirit of Cynicism can be seen in Jesus's instructions to his disciples to travel about Israel barefoot, teaching and living on handouts (Matt. 10; Luke 10:1–10).

Bibliography. Stephen Harris, The New Testament: A Student's Introduction (4th ed.; Boston: McGraw-Hill, 2002).

D

D

Designation for the DEUTERONOMIC CODE, which, according to the DOCUMENTARY HYPOTHESIS, was one of the sources from which the PENTATEUCH was compiled. It consists of the collection of laws in Deut. 12–26. *See* SOURCE CRITICISM.

DAEMONISATION. *See* ANXIETY OF INFLUENCE

DASEIN

A critical term employed by the German philosopher Martin Heidegger to refer to the mode of being a human, as opposed to a thing. In his rejection of defining human nature in metaphysical and religious terms, Heidegger uses *Dasein* to mean a mode of being that is thoroughly historical. He defines it as "being in-the-world" (lit., "being there") and as characterized by a sense of care and anxiety due to its orientation toward death. The term has had profound influence on several postmodern philosophers and critics, most notably Jacques Derrida and Michel Foucault, and has been instrumental in directing their focus on TEXTS, the self, DISCOURSES, TRUTH, history, and systems of knowledge as human constructs.

DAUGHTER TRANSLATION

Generally, a TRANSLATION of a translation. More specifically it refers to the translation of the SEPTUAGINT (LXX) into another language. Since the LXX is itself a translation of the HEBREW BIBLE into Greek, any translation of it into another language is a daughter translation.

DAVIDIC COVENANT

A COVENANT between God and David (2 Sam. 7:12–16) in which God promised salvation through the Davidic kingdom and the continuance of the Davidic dynasty.

DEAD SEA COMMUNITY. *See* DEAD SEA SCROLLS; ESSENES

DEAD SEA SCROLLS

A group of manuscripts in HEBREW, ARAMAIC, and KOINE GREEK discovered in 1947–56 in eleven different caves at QUMRAN along the northeast coast of the Dead Sea. The TEXTS date from the mid-second century BCE and the late first century CE, roughly just before and during the formative period of Christianity. Although there continues to be debate over origins, the majority of scholars attribute the texts to the ESSENES, a Jewish ascetic sect dating from about 140 BCE to 68 CE, when the Roman army destroyed it. Perhaps the major value of the texts for NT studies is the information they provide on Christian origins. The ideas, rituals, and terms suggest that many of the Christian liturgical and cultic practices have Palestinian rather than Hellenistic (*see* HELLENISM) roots. Such rites and ideas include a communal meal, water purification rites, and the belief that the Essene community formed the new Israel. Works such as the *War of the Sons of Light against the Sons of Darkness* and the MANUAL OF DISCIPLINE reveal a number of similarities between the Qumran community and early Christians (e.g., both groups felt that Israel had broken its COVENANT with YAHWEH, both regarded themselves as the new Israel, both advocated holding all things in common, and both evidence a cosmic DUALISM).

The manuscripts total more than 870 whole scrolls or fragments and can be divided into four groups. First, there are copies of texts of the

HEBREW BIBLE. Some of these are the oldest copies of the books available, dating to the second century BCE. The Isaiah[a] scroll (1QIsa[a]) is about nine hundred years older than any previous copy available. While it varies little from the MASORETIC TEXT of the HEBREW BIBLE, other manuscripts are significantly different from the MT. The Isaiah[b] scroll (1QIsa[b]), for example, has many variants. The second group contains manuscripts of APOCRYPHA and PSEUDEPIGRAPHA (e.g., Tobit, *1 Enoch*, *Jubilees*). The third group are Essene commentaries on some of the CANONICAL books, such as Habakkuk and Isaiah, employing interpretive methods similar to those of Matthew, methods that see or treat the prophetic books of the Hebrew Bible as predictions relating to one's own community. The fourth group consists of manuscripts produced particularly for the Essene community, including a *Manual of Discipline* (outlining the rules of community life), the *Damascus Document* (*Zadokite Fragments*, describing the new covenant with the "Land of Damascus"), the *War of the Sons of Light against the Sons of Darkness* (a battle plan for a final cosmic war), and the *Temple Scroll* (a description of the ideal temple).

For an accessible treatment of the DSS, consult García Martínez (1996), García Martínez with Tigchelaar (2000), and the other valuable works on the DSS listed below.

Bibliography. Martin Abegg Jr., Peter Flint, and Eugene Ulrich, *The Dead Sea Scrolls Bible* (San Francisco: HarperSanFrancisco, 1999); Frank M. Cross, *The Ancient Library of Qumran* (2nd ed.; Grand Rapids: Baker, 1980); Joseph Fitzmyer, *Responses to 101 Questions on the Dead Sea Scrolls* (New York: Paulist Press, 1992); Florentino García Martínez, *The Dead Sea Scrolls Translated: The Qumran Texts in English* (trans. Wilfred G. E. Watson; 2nd ed.; Leiden: Brill, 1996); Florentino García Martínez and Eibert J. C. Tigchelaar, eds., *The Dead Sea Scrolls Study Edition* (2 vols.; New York: Brill, 1997–98; repr., Grand Rapids: Eerdmans, 2000); Theodor H. Gaster, *The Dead Sea Scriptures in English Translation* (3rd ed.; Garden City, NY: Doubleday/Anchor, 1976); Timothy H. Lim et al., eds., *The Dead Sea Scrolls Electronic Reference Library* (3 CD-ROMs; New York: Oxford University Press, 1997); Hershel Shanks, *Understanding the Dead Sea Scrolls* (New York: Random House, 1992); Emanuel Tov, ed., *The Dead Sea Scrolls Electronic Library* (Noel B. Reynolds and Kristian Heal, producers; rev. ed.; CD-ROM; Provo, Utah: Brigham Young University, 2006); Géza Vermès, trans. and ed., *The Complete Dead Sea Scrolls in English* (rev. ed.; London: Penguin Books, 2004); idem, *An Introduction to the Complete Dead Sea Scrolls* (rev. ed.; Minneapolis: Fortress, 1999).

DEATH OF AUTHOR

In POSTMODERNISM, the rejection of the AUTHOR as the origin or determiner of MEANING. Definitions of *author* vary from a construct of language to a confluence of DISCOURSES.

DECALOGUE

Although the Greek term *deka logoi* (ten words) appears in the SEPTUAGINT at Exod. 34:28 and Deut. 10:4 (cf. Deut. 4:13, *deka rhēmata*), it usually refers to the Ethical Decalogue in its two versions (Exod. 20:1–17; Deut. 5:6–21). The commandments as we now have them are more than likely expansions of the originals due to theological development over the history of transmission. For example, the Sabbath commandment in Exodus is associated with God's resting on the Sabbath day after creating for six days. In Deuteronomy, however, the same commandment is associated with Israel's Egyptian captivity.

The term *decalogue* can also refer to two types of laws found in Exod. 34:10–28. One type deals with relationships between humans and God and between humans, while the other type deals only with relationships between humans.

DECENTER. *See* CENTER

DECODING/ENCODING

Terms used in STRUCTURALISM and SEMIOTICS to designate two poles of communication. Every utterance, written or oral, presupposes a CODE on which the utterance has communicatory possibility. For example, a composer creates a musical score based on a complex musical code. In other words, the composer encodes the musical text, which in turn must be decoded by a conductor, musician, and so forth. Complex utterances may be encoded from a number of overlapping or interlocking codes, and the reader, to more plausibly decode it, must be familiar with each one. For example, the book of Revelation in the NT involves the coding systems of the Greek language, LITERARY CONVENTIONS of apocalypse, the social context of the AUTHOR and audience, and the INTERTEXT of the HEBREW BIBLE.

DECONSTRUCT. *See* DECONSTRUCTION

DECONSTRUCTION

A school of thought in philosophy that originated in France in the late 1960s but gained momentum in the 1970s and early 1980s in the United States, where it has had its most significant impact. It has been associated with a group of literary scholars in the departments of COMPARATIVE LITERATURE and English at Yale University after Jacques Derrida delivered an annual seminar at Yale from 1977 to 1985.

Deconstruction is also one among many theoretical developments that have come to be known collectively as POSTMODERNISM. On the one hand, along with all the developments that define postmodernism, deconstruction has a basic suspicion of all traditional models of defining and understanding history, literature, subjectivity, and knowledge. On the other hand, with more conservative LITERARY theories, it shares a distinct (if rather different) interest in the INTERPRETATION of texts (Adamson, 30).

To understand the finer points of deconstruction requires at least brief mention of the more blunt edges of its historical philosophical predecessor. STRUCTURALISM as a linguistic approach to textual analysis began gaining critical attention and popularity in the 1950s and 1960s. In the early twentieth century, Ferdinand de Saussure, considered the father of modern LINGUISTICS, shifted the focus of linguistics with his *Course in General Linguistics*, in which he presents structural linguistics as resting on a few basic principles. First, language is a system of rules that govern its every aspect, which all speakers of a language know either consciously or unconsciously—these rules Saussure calls LANGUE. He recognizes that individual speak-ers evidence *langue* in their individual SPEECH, and this he terms PAROLE. According to Saussure, the task of the linguist, then, is to articulate the *langue* by analyzing *parole* (Bressler, 121).

From this point, Saussure begins an exhaustive investigation of the structures that compose language and of the differences in sound that denote differences in word MEANING, with the purpose of refuting the former linguistic ASSUMPTION of language's mimeticism (*see* MIMETIC CRITICISM) in favor of the idea that language is determined by its own internal rules (PHONOLOGY, SYNTAX, etc.) and, most important, in favor of the idea that the linguistic SIGN that makes up language is itself both arbitrary and conventional (122). This linguistic sign is composed of two parts: the signifier (the thing actually spoken or written) and the signified (the concept signaled by the signifier). Their relationship is what Saussure sees as arbitrary and conventional, making the linguistic sign one not of innate properties but rather defined by the differences that distinguish it from other signs. In so doing, he undermines the long-held belief that there is some natural link between the word and the thing it represents. This idea is subsequently borrowed by the French philosopher Jacques Derrida as one of the fundamental elements in the formulation of deconstruction.

Perhaps no other figure is more associated with deconstruction than Jacques Derrida, whose name has become almost synonymous with deconstruction. For Derrida, deconstruction is concerned with (1) exposing the problematic nature of all DISCOURSEs that are centered in any concept, such as TRUTH and origin; (2) challenging metaphysics by exposing its conceptual limits and its hidden and unexamined foundations (*see* FOUNDATIONALISM); and (3) showing how texts undermine themselves by contradicting these very foundations (Adamson, 25). Important texts by Derrida for understanding deconstruction are *Of Grammatology, Writing and Difference*, and *Margins of Philosophy*. Important texts by other scholars include Harold Bloom et al., *Deconstruction and Criticism*; Paul de Man, *Allegories of Reading: Figural*

Language in Rousseau, Nietzsche, Rilke, and Proust and *The Resistance to Theory*; J. Hillis Miller, *Fiction and Repetition: Seven English Novels*; and Jonathan Culler, *On Deconstruction: Theory and Criticism after Structuralism.*

Derrida agrees with Saussure that the linguistic sign is beset with uncertainty that is resolved only by the differences in the relationship between the signifier and the signified; however, unlike Saussure, Derrida maintains that this reasoning applies to the signified. A concept is known only by its differences from other concepts.

From this idea—that SIGNIFICATION is fraught with AMBIGUITY—Derrida asserts that the entire history of Western metaphysics is in error for its striving to find a TRANSCENDENTAL SIGNIFIED: an external point of REFERENCE on which a philosophy or concept rests (Bressler, 123–24). Points of reference that have been attempted include (but are not limited to) God, self, being, truth, reason, and world spirit. In each case, the supposed transcendental signified must operate as a unifying principle on which one's world is structured. Subsequently, other objects, concepts, or ideas achieve meaning only as they are filtered through the lens of the ultimate, unifying transcendental signified.

The key here is that the concept that is chosen to serve as this central concept is self-sufficient or self-originating, capable of being known independently of any other signifiers, and also known for its own intrinsic value, not for some extrinsic contrast it makes with another concept. This Western predilection for a center is what Derrida names LOGOCENTRISM—the belief that there is an ultimate reality or truth-center that can function as a basis for our thoughts and actions. Derrida maintains that the habit of logocentric thinking is one from which we will never be entirely free, as any attempt to decenter any transcendental signified is immediately forced to operate within the terminology of such a centering concept.

Derrida explains this kind of logocentric thinking as having its roots in the ideas of Aristotle, particularly his principle of noncontradiction, which states that an object cannot both have a given property and not have that same property (Bressler, 125). Derrida claims that this has led Western metaphysics to an either-or mentality, whose logic inevitably arrives at dualistic thinking, at the centering and decentering of the transcendental signified. Because the decentering of one signified becomes the centering of another, he proposes that the same Western metaphysics is based on a system of BINARY OPPOSITIONS, or thematic oppositions. This can be seen in FORMALISM, when two themes will be set in opposition to one another, and normally clustered in groupings of similar conceptual oppositions, in an attempt to extract meaning from a work by examining the tenuous unity afforded by the contrasting ideas. The underlying ASSUMPTION of Western philosophy that fuels this sort of CRITICISM is that in each binary opposition, one concept is superior and able to be defined by its opposite or inferior center. "Truth" is known by its difference from "deception," "happy" holds significance only when "sad" exists, and so too with male and female, rationality and irrationality, and so forth. It is this sort of hierarchical binary-ism that Derrida takes exception to as the basis of Western metaphysics.

Another key concept of Derrida is PHONOCENTRISM, the privileging of SPEECH over writing. He claims that the spoken word has long been given precedence over the written word because it has been assumed that there is a higher degree of fidelity to the author's original MEANING—and less opportunity for misunderstanding/MISREADING—with the work of listening than with reading. "Writing" (*écriture*) for Derrida is not the inscription of thought but the fundamental human activity, which precedes such inscription. In most Western hermeneutical thinking, individuals are able to write a text because they have previously "read the world"; put another way, the world of reality that we variously encode within our texts already exists as a metaphysical reality: it is a given. Derrida rejects this assumption by claiming that the world we are capable of knowing comes into being through the act of "writing." There is no world waiting to be read. Language is not rooted in a perceivable reality that precedes it; on the contrary, language itself sets the parameters of thought and therefore our world. If this is the case, we cannot be aware of the presence of that which is beyond our thoughts but only of its ABSENCE (Walhout, 36).

In Derrida's estimation, since all human activity takes place in time, such activity is historically bound. This does not mean that human activity is in toto historically or culturally determined. Human activity also determines and perpetually reshapes and redefines culture. Culture does not exist prior to individual acts of "writing." A priori assumptions about reality may exist, but these are themselves products of cultural "writings." This is the reason Derrida can assert that "writing" precedes speech. It is simply impossible to know something that exists prior to what is known.

According to Derrida, phonocentrism is due to an assumed honesty of presence over absence. To this thinking, Derrida gives the name "METAPHYS-ICS OF PRESENCE." It is the shakiness of this kind of thinking that Derrida seeks to expose, and in deconstructing it, he opens the door to a reading strategy that promises interpretations previously disallowed by the constraints of Western thought. Given Derrida's claim that writing precedes speech and that language is a special kind of writing in which we encode human consciousness, he can argue that the relationship between the components of any binary hierarchy is always unstable because it is grounded in language. Rather than simply reversing all binary oppositions, Derrida means to show the fragile basis on which these oppositions are established and then to invert their order, possibly to gain new insights into language, text, meaning, and life. He uses the term SUPPLÉ-MENT to refer to this unstable relationship between binary terms, to explain the preference of one over the other. Realizing that supplementation operates in all of Western metaphysics' binary operations and that his subsequently inverting the order of terms is also such an opposition, Derrida uses three concepts, one of which he coins.

The first two concepts are TRACE and mark. Each and every human action leaves a mark on culture, and each and every mark gives witness to its originating human action, an action that itself escapes complete specification. Therefore, the mark that our "writing" makes is also a trace of the indeterminate origin of the "writing." Since the genesis or origin of "writing" is always prior to any act of understanding, the trace becomes a witness to the indescribability of the source of writing.

If every human action has both a culturally specific mark and a trace of the moment of origination, then every human action has not only a determinate meaning but also an indeterminate meaning. More simply put, if every human action is shaped by culture while at the same time shaping the culture, then culture is constantly and infinitely undergoing modification and change while in a reciprocal fashion influencing the actions that change it. This complex of mutual influence gives rise to both continuity and discontinuity between the action and the culture. Therefore, interpretations of human actions (including literary ones) must focus on both the way in which the action is shaped by culture (i.e., the action's continuity with the culture) and the way in which an action is discontinuous with the culture.

Carrying Saussure's definition of the sign (meaning can never be absolute but must perpetually be deferred among the signifiers) to its logical conclusion, Derrida invents the neologism DIFFÉRANCE to describe the system of difference that defines the nature of language: difference and deferral. This word is a deliberate misspelling of the word *différence*, combining the two French words for "differing" and "DEFERRING." Using Saussure's definition of *sign*, Derrida says that a text derives meaning in its differences from other texts. But every text also evidences the trace of an indeterminate origination. Since this indeterminate quality itself creates change within the culture, meaning is always deferred. Interpretation itself becomes an activity laden with AMBIGUITY: it is a human AC-TION with a determinate and indeterminate meaning. Every reader, when approaching a text within a culture, is both influenced by and exerting influence on the culture. Since this is part of an infinite process of shaping and reshaping, interpretation is itself an endless, ever-changing process of creation. All meaning is bound by cultural context, but that context becomes boundless. Consequently, any act of signification is always immediately diverted from its intended destination due to the disseminal nature of all communicatory acts. As Derrida suggests, every act of signification is a purloined letter, never reaching its proper destination.

Positing the existence of a transcendental signified immediately establishes the binary opposition presence/absence, and Western metaphysics suggests that presence is somehow preferential to absence. However, if we reverse this hierarchy, no longer can we accord a transcendental signified any merit; there is no absolute or unifying standard from which all knowledge must logically proceed. Instead, all things are known by difference and absence, not by presence. Such a reversal of metaphysics' integral binary postulate has two results. First, all human knowledge is a result of absence (ideas are known only by their difference from other ideas). Second, closure becomes an impossibility: with the absence of a transcendental signified, all interpretations are legitimate (Bressler 129).

The search for a text's correct meaning or authorial INTENTION now becomes, in effect, insignificant or meaningless: since meaning is gained by differences in a context-related, ongoing process, all texts have multiple meanings and interpretations. As a result, meaning evolves as the reader interacts with a text, with both (reader and text) providing the social and cultural context for interpretation. Deconstructive critics have taken the premises of FORMALISM (textual unity by the inner tension created by opposing themes) and sought to illuminate how a text will belie such presupposed unity—turning in on itself to eliminate the possibility of concrete understanding by the slippery nature of the very elements (i.e., the signifier and signified of language) that coagulate supposedly to shore the meaning. The POSTMODERN claim that meaning cannot escape language in striving to represent reality, that words can only (and will always) refer to other words, has led these critics to a liter-

ary approach that stresses the ambiguity, multiplicity, and word slippage that pervade language and are inherent in any attempt to translate meaning via literature. As a result, postmodernists employ a critical technique that seeks to show exactly the terminus at which a text's apparent unity breaks down and that then deconstructs the components having led to such DISSONANCE—exposing the contradictions in a discourse to reveal how a text undermines its own ideological foundations. For the deconstructive critic, this technique, rather than being an intricate version of "destruction," offers a means for opening texts that formerly appeared closed or limited (in terms of the variety of readings gained by other critical methods) to new, and often limitless, angles of understanding. In many cases, these new readings assume a sense of playfulness, marked by their irreverence for LITERARY CONVENTION.

Paul de Man and others of the Yale school have adapted Derrida's views to a method of reading that challenges interpretive methods earlier viewed as normative. For de Man, with the death (or removal) of the subject who controls or establishes meaning, all discourse is groundless with respect to meaning, a groundlessness that guarantees misinterpretation. Consequently, all discourse is inherently ambiguous. Thus the correct or CANONICAL interpretation of any text can be supported only arbitrarily. With no grounding in intentionality, meaning, or truth, there is nothing to vitiate errors of reading, especially since error is the very condition of language. The result is an inevitable collapse of meaning (Adamson, 29). These deconstructive critics assume a reading strategy of radical doubt and seek to expose the contradictory nature of meaning that we derive from our readings.

By focusing attention on the marginal aspects of the text, deconstructive critics point out a text's contradictions of its own unexamined foundational assumption. Deconstructive CLOSE READINGS therefore demonstrate that a text will inevitably undermine its own position. Paul de Man, J. Hillis Miller, and others tend to focus on the rhetorical aspects of a text in trying to demonstrate how the text will always resist reduction to any stable meaning and how the text also resists the reader's attempts to make sense of its metaphorical language. The idea that a proper and stable meaning, addressed by one SUBJECT to another, ever arrives at its destination—that idea is no longer tenable (Adamson, 30).

Bressler, then, offers the following working definition of the guidelines, or steps, for a deconstructive reading of a text:

- Discover the binary oppositions that govern a text.
- Comment on the values, concepts, and ideas behind these oppositions.
- Reverse these present binary oppositions.
- Dismantle previously held worldviews.
- Accept the possibility of various perspectives or levels of meaning in a text on the basis of the new binary inversions.
- Allow meaning of the text to be undecidable. (131)

Obviously, with the inclusion of particular "tenets" in this list, certain deconstructivist presuppositions are in operation. One of these is the assumption that any text, necessarily having multiple interpretations, allows itself to be reread and consequently reinterpreted countless times. Ultimately, the meaning of any text is indeterminate since each reading possesses the likelihood of different interpretations. In attempting deconstruction, one must try to override inherited logocentrism as far as textual interpretation is concerned and to seek to expose similar binary oppositions at work in the text itself. By "objectively" viewing these operations, reversing them for added interpretive variety, and refusing to measure qualitatively either the textual binary hierarchies or the differing interpretations, the deconstructor displays the impossibility of ever finding a "correct" meaning and opens the text to a never-ending hermeneutic (*see* HERMENEUTICS). Criticism becomes not the search for definitive meaning but rather the pursuit of conversation with an ever-expanding interpretive entity.

A deconstructive reading of a text looks for inconsistencies in the way the text expresses its purpose and invariably deals with the way the text employs binary oppositions. Some of these oppositions regularly found in the Bible include God/Satan, light/darkness, Jew/Gentile, spirit/flesh, and man/woman. By showing how the text marginalizes (*see* MARGINALIZATION), for instance, women instead of men or literal language instead of figurative, the critic exposes the underlying discursive structures that reveal the ways in which a culture defines itself. For example, when the apostle Paul responds to some problems in the Corinthian church, he appeals to the second account of creation in Gen. 2–3 to make his case. In 1 Cor. 11, Paul argues that the "husband is the head of his wife"; that the man "is the image and reflection of God, but woman is the reflection of man"; and that the woman was created "for the sake of man." The author of 1 Timothy also subordinates the woman to the man: "Let a woman learn in silence with full submission. I permit no woman to teach or to have authority over a man; she is to keep silent. For Adam was formed first, then Eve; and Adam was not deceived, but the woman was deceived and became a transgressor" (2:11–14). In each of these cases, place of privilege is given to the first term of the binary opposition, man/woman. Man is created first and is the image of God: woman is created second and from the man. As David W. Odell-Scott observes,

> The identities of this oppositional pair are elaborated by their associations with other oppositional pairs, in which identifications are made with other concepts, which are also defined in dyadic sets:
>
> - Man-Woman
> - First-Second
> - God-World
> - Sacred-Profane
> - Soul-Body. (60)

In each case, the first term is invested with value while the second is divested of value. Because the man was created first, directly from the earth, he is closer to God, identified with God, and therefore more sacred than the woman, who was created second—from Adam, not directly from God—and is therefore of the world and profane. Since the soul is associated with God and the sacred, man is "identified with soul, and man's opposite, woman, is identified with body, which is the opposite of soul" (60–61).

The problem with this kind of investment and divestment, however, is that in order for the first term to be privileged, the second term must already always be present if the difference between the two is to be possible. In other words, the second term must be present in order for there to be a first term. Consequently, attempts to "identify an original, a first, a beginning, are self-contradictory by definition, because a first is first to a second, an original is an original to a copy, a beginning is a beginning of that which follows" (Odell-Scott, 61). The deconstructive reading thus PROBLEMATIZES the possibility of establishing an original anything, a basis for establishing any kind of discursive structure that is an original, given one.

Bibliography. Joseph Adamson, "Deconstruction," in *Encyclopedia of Contemporary Literary Theory* (ed. Irena R. Makaryk; Toronto: University of Toronto Press, 1993), 25–31; Harold Bloom et al., *Deconstruction and Criticism* (New York: Seabury, 1979); Charles E. Bressler, *Literary Criticism: An Introduction to Theory and Practice* (2nd ed.; Englewood Cliffs, NJ: Prentice Hall, 1994); Lawrence Cahoone, *From Modernism to Postmodernism: An Anthology* (Cambridge, MA: Blackwell, 1996); Jonathan Culler, *On Deconstruction: Theory and Criticism after Structuralism* (Ithaca, NY: Cornell University Press, 1982); Paul de Man, *Allegories of Reading: Figural Language in Rousseau, Nietzsche, Rilke, and Proust* (New Haven: Yale University Press, 1979); idem, *The Resistance to Theory* (Minneapolis: University of Minnesota Press, 1986); Jacques Derrida, *Margins of Philosophy* (trans. Alan Bass; Chicago: University of Chicago Press, 1982); idem, *Of Grammatology* (trans. Gayatri Chakravorty Spivak; Baltimore: Johns Hopkins University Press, 1977); idem, *Writing and Difference* (trans. Alan Bass; Chicago: University of Chicago Press, 1978); Donald Keesey, *Contexts for Criticism* (4th ed.; Boston: McGraw-Hill, 2003); Steven Lynn, *Texts and Contexts: Writing about Literature with Critical Theory* (New York: HarperCollins, 1994); J. Hillis Miller, *Fiction and Repetition: Seven English Novels* (Cambridge, MA: Harvard University Press, 1982); Stephen D. Moore, "Deconstructive Criticism: The Gospel of Mark," in *Mark and Method: New Approaches in Biblical Studies* (ed. Janice Capel Anderson and Stephen D. Moore; Minneapolis: Fortress, 1992), 110–45; David W. Odell-Scott, "Deconstruction," in *Handbook of Post-modern Biblical Interpretation* (ed. A. K. M. Adam; St. Louis: Chalice, 2000), 55–61; Ferdinand de Saussure, *Course in General Linguistics* (trans. Wade Baskin; ed. Perry Meisel and Haun Saussy; New York: Columbia University Press, 2011); Bonnie Klomp Stevens and Larry L. Stewart, *A Guide to Literary Criticism and Research* (3rd ed.; Fort Worth: Harcourt, 1996); Clarence Walhout, "Texts and Actions," in *The Responsibility of Hermeneutics* (ed. Roger Lundin et al.; Grand Rapids: Eerdmans, 1985), 31–77.

DECONSTRUCTIVE. *See* DECONSTRUCTION

DEEP STRUCTURES

Within STRUCTURALISM, basic underlying LITERARY CONVENTIONS, common to all languages, constituting one of the levels of MEANING in a TEXT. According to structuralists, a text has three MEANING EFFECT levels, which correlate to types of STRUCTURES. The first level is the STRUCTURES OF ENUNCIATION. These structures are determined by features such as the AUTHOR'S INTENTION, *SITZ IM LEBEN*, and audience. Second are the STRUCTURES OF CULTURE. Culture's structures consist of the specific CODES of a specific people at a specific time. The third level of meaning effect is determined by the text's deep structures that are universal in all human activity. On the level of any GENRE of literature, such as NARRATIVE, certain narrative and mythological structures are present. It is the goal of structuralism to uncover these deep structures that produce a meaning effect. The structuralists employ Lévi-Strauss's idea that MYTHS are attempts to deal with BINARY OPPOSITIONS inherent in human existence. These fundamental oppositions cannot be logically mediated. Some of these oppositions are love/hate, life/death, youth/old age, sin/righteousness. Myths attempt to mediate the oppositions by offering parallel oppositions that are proportional to the binary ones and capable of reconciliation. Structuralists seek to uncover these mythic structures and, by arranging them in paradigmatic order, discover the author's semantic universe (the fundamental system of convictions on which an AUTHOR operates).

DEFAMILIARIZATION. *See* FORMALISM

DEFENSE SPEECHES

Within RHETORICAL CRITICISM, some speeches (*see* SPEECH) in the NT (esp. in Acts) reflect the rhetorical patterns of speeches in the Greco-Roman TRADITION. In Greco-Roman JUDICIAL RHETORIC, there are two subtypes of speeches: accusation and defense. Paul's speeches in Acts 22–26 correspond to the defense speeches. Fred Veltman (251–53) has identified five components of the defense speech:

1. A NARRATIVE opening with a DESCRIPTION of the trial scene, charges, defendant.
2. The speech's introduction, in which the speech is defined as an APOLOGY.
3. The body of the speech, opening with a mention or refutation of the charges, treatment of the charges, rhetorical questions, and statement of innocence.
4. The conclusion of the speech, with term of address and claim of innocence (the speech may be interrupted).
5. A narrative CLOSING with description of trial scene and verdict.

Although the speeches in Acts 22–26 correspond to this framework, Veltman points out that since the speeches are usually interrupted before they are completed, their conclusions cannot be compared to the pattern.

Bibliography. Fred Veltman, "The Defense Speeches of Paul in Acts," in *Perspectives on Luke-Acts* (ed. C. H. Talbert; Edinburgh: T&T Clark, 1978), 243–56.

DEFERRING

A term that Jacques Derrida derives from his concept of *DIFFÉRANCE*. Using Saussure's definition of "SIGN," Derrida says that a word derives its MEANING from its differences from other words. But every word also evidences the TRACE of its similarly indeterminate origination. Since meaning is de-

rived from differences between words, all of which are indeterminate, meaning is always deferred.

DEICTIC

From Greek *deiktikos*, "showing, pointing out," in a DISCOURSE *deictic* identifies the function of a pronoun, adjective, adverb, or tense in pointing the reader to another element within the discourse rather than to some object outside the discourse. The deictic pointing is dependent on the speech situation. For example, in 2 Sam. 12:6, "*He* shall restore the lamb fourfold, because *he* did this thing, and because *he* had no pity," the deictic "he" refers to the man in Nathan's STORY, not to some person outside it. Also "*Here* am *I*" in Isa. 6:8 contains two deictics, "here" and "I," which point to a specific person and location in the NARRATIVE.

DELIBERATIVE RHETORIC

In RHETORICAL CRITICISM, a type of argument in a SPEECH. The deliberative speech attempts to persuade an audience to take some action in the future or dissuade them from it. In the Greco-Roman world, the setting of the deliberative speech was the public assembly or an occasion where the suitability of an ACTION was under deliberation. According to George Kennedy, the deliberative argument usually has the following form:

1. An introduction (PROEM/EXORDIUM) identifying the audience and the occasion
2. A narration (NARRATIO) and/or proposition (PROPOSITIO) giving background information and the primary point of the speech
3. The proof of the proposition
4. The conclusion (EPILOGUE), which summarizes the argument and appeals to the audience to accept the validity of the proof

The argument may also contain a refutation (REFUTATIO), in which the speaker anticipates and refutes any opposing views. An example of a deliberative argument can be seen in 1 Cor. 15:1–58. *See* EPIDEICTIC; JUDICIAL RHETORIC.

Bibliography. George Kennedy, *New Testament Interpretation through Rhetorical Criticism* (Chapel Hill: University of North Carolina Press, 1984).

DELIVERY

One of the fivefold divisions of classical RHETORIC, delivery is concerned with the rules for control of voice and the use of gesture. *See* RHETORICAL CRITICISM.

DEMYTHOLOGIZE/ DEMYTHOLOGIZATION

A term popularized by the German existentialist theologian Rudolf Bultmann, referring to the reINTERPRETATION of biblical myths into existential terms. According to Bultmann, a MYTH is an expression of something otherworldly in terms of this world. For example, the fall of Adam is a myth that deals with the subject of universal sin. Myths are not true scientifically or cosmologically but are true attempts to understand some human experiences or phenomena.

The term has been expanded within STRUCTURALISM and poststructuralism in the discussion of IDEOLOGY. Within CULTURAL CRITICISM, scholars argue that in all societies the things that are thought to be inherently natural givens are actually social constructs and given their natural status through usage. In other words, societies tend to mystify social constructs into the universal (e.g., absolute values, God, TRUTH, and the unified self). Critics in CULTURAL MATERIALISM seek to identify the manner in which MEANING is structured in a culture and then demythologize or demystify that STRUCTURE by revealing its cultural constructedness.

Roland Barthes goes further and identifies social myths with the use of language as a means of sustaining and maintaining a culture's ideological myths. For Barthes, however, these myths are structures of alienation and repression that enforce structures of power. The CRITIC must read the culture and its productions in such a way as to expose these structures of myth, with the purpose of encouraging multiple perspectives within the culture. To demythologize or "denaturalize" the structures diminishes their power.

Michel Foucault has also examined the connection between language and ideology in order to identify the roots of a society's structures of power as they are embedded in language. His assumption is that structures of power are always discursive and therefore difficult to demythologize. Nonetheless, the attempt must be made because all DISCOURSES are arbitrary cultural constructs.

Jacques Derrida also examines language usage and argumentation by critiquing important texts in the Western literary TRADITION. In doing so, he unearths their ASSUMPTIONS and underlying values and then exposes what he sees as ruptures, weaknesses, or points of self-contradiction, all of which suggest that natural givens assumed by the texts are actually nothing more than arbitrary constructs. The consequence is that these texts are then open to new interpretations.

Such critical READING AGAINST THE GRAIN of the biblical texts is at the heart of a host of postmodern approaches, such as DECONSTRUCTION; FEMINIST CRITICISM; POSTCOLONIAL CRITICISM; RACE, CLASS, GENDER CRITICISM; gay/lesbian criticism (*see* QUEER THEORY); and WOMANIST CRITICISM. Such biblical categories as race, gender, and sexuality have received an enormous amount of demythologization in the past few decades.

Bibliography. Roland Barthes, *A Barthes Reader* (ed. Susan Sontag; New York: Hill & Wang, 1982); Jacques Derrida, "Structure, Sign, and Play in the Discourse of the Human Sciences," in *The Structuralist Controversy: The Languages of Criticism and the Sciences of Man* (ed. Richard Mackey and Eugenio Donato; Baltimore: Johns Hopkins University Press, 1972), 247–72; Michel Foucault, *The Archaeology of Knowledge* (trans. A. M. Sheridan Smith; London: Routledge, 1972).

DENOTATION

The dictionary MEANING of a word apart from its emotional or figurative associations or CONNOTATIONS.

DENOUEMENT

Also called the resolution, denouement is the final element in the five-part STRUCTURE of a story's PLOT. The denouement (untying the knot) completes the story after the CLIMAX, the point after which the story's TENSION and COMPLICATIONS are settled. After the story's major CONFLICTS are concluded, the denouement ties up any loose ends and brings the plot to an end. The multiple conflicts in the Joseph story in Gen. 37–48 are not completely resolved until Joseph's final revelation to his brothers in Egypt.

DEPATRIARCHALIZATION

A key concept in FEMINIST CRITICISM referring to the varied means by which PATRIARCHAL STRUCTURES are rendered ineffectual. Elisabeth Schüssler Fiorenza defines PATRIARCHY as "a male pyramid of graded subordinations and exploitations [that] specifies women's oppression in terms of the class, race, country, or religion of the men to whom we 'belong'" (xiv). Employing this definition, women then examine patriarchy in terms of sexism, racism, and property-class relationships and indict all structures of patriarchy and its TEXTS (esp. those of biblical religion). Depatriarchalization, then, is the active pursuit of neutralizing the alienation and dehumanization caused by patriarchy through the assessment of TRADITIONS, texts, and communities that have legitimated and propagated such STRUCTURES.

Bibliography. Elisabeth Schüssler Fiorenza, *Bread Not Stone* (10th anniversary ed.; Boston: Beacon, 1995).

DEPRIVILEGING OF THE AUTHOR

The redirection in interpretive theories away from the AUTHOR and authorial INTENTION as the source of MEANING in historical-critical theories to a focus on the structures of the TEXT or the activities of readers as the locus of meaning.

DESCRIPTION

One of the four primary types of composition. Its purpose is to cause the reader to imagine or re-create the scenes and ACTION of the STORY. It may be physical (persons and places) or psychological (emotions). While description may stand alone, it is more commonly used in the service of one of the other three types of composition,

which are NARRATION, ARGUMENTATION, and EXPOSITION. Because excessive description may impede the story's action, most writers include the minimum necessary to keep the action moving. Biblical NARRATIVE, Hebrew in particular, is especially sparse in its descriptive details, which are included only in the service of the PLOT. *See* CHARACTERIZATION.

DEUTEROCANON / DEUTEROCANONICAL BOOKS

From the Greek for "second CANON," the Deuterocanon consists of the books in the SEPTUAGINT not included in the HEBREW BIBLE. Considered to be inspired and authoritative early in the history of the church, they were declared to be so for the Catholic Church by the Council of Trent (1545–63). The Deuterocanon is called the APOCRYPHA by Protestants. In TEXTUAL CRITICISM, the term has been expanded to include the passages in the BIBLE that may be later additions (e.g., Mark 16:9–20 and John 7:53–8:11).

DEUTEROGRAPH

From the Greek meaning "second writing," the term describes a TEXT or passage of text that is a retelling, rewriting, and/or reinterpretation of earlier material. First and Second Chronicles are a deuterograph of 1 Samuel–2 Kings. In rewriting an earlier text, the deuterograph does so on the basis of a different theological and historical BACKGROUND or may simply revise the STYLE of the earlier work. For example, the DECALOGUE in Deut. 5 is quite different from that in Exod. 20, and Ps. 53 is quite similar to Ps. 14 but adds a stronger note of judgment on the ungodly (v. 5b). Also compare Deut. 15:12–15 and Exod. 21:2; Pss. 40 and 70.

DEUTERO-ISAIAH

Literally, "Second Isaiah." On the basis of stylistic matters and historical REFERENCES, chapters 40–55 in Isaiah are usually ascribed to an AUTHOR living during the BABYLONIAN EXILE (586–538 BCE) of the Jews.

DEUTERONOMIC CODE

A major collection of law in Deuteronomy, delivered as part of Moses's SPEECH in chapters 12–26. According to 2 Kings 22, a book of the LAW was found in the temple during the reign of Josiah in the year 622 BCE. Biblical scholars think that this book or a part of it is the basis for the present book of Deuteronomy. In CONTENT, it appears to be a TEXT of legislative reform that reinterprets the LAW OF MOSES for a new time and new needs. The PROLOGUE (1–11) and EPILOGUE (27–34) provide a historical SETTING that was perhaps intended to create the impression that the code originated with Moses. The code is a compendium of laws governing doctrine and a wide area of everyday living. The regulations range from restricting sacrifices to Jerusalem (thus centralizing worship) to regulations against idolatry and foreign mourning customs, to regulations concerning the payment of tithes, clean and unclean animals, the income of priests and Levites, false PROPHECY, theft of land, warfare, protection of birds, treatment of slaves, charging of interest, and showing mercy (van der Woude, 163–64).

Bibliography. A. S. van der Woude, ed., *The World of the Old Testament* (Grand Rapids: Eerdmans, 1989).

DEUTERONOMIST

In SOURCE CRITICISM, the title given to the person(s) authoring and redacting the book of Deuteronomy and portions of the HEBREW BIBLE that echo the theology of Deuteronomy. These portions may be found in Genesis through 2 Kings. *See* DEUTERONOMISTIC HISTORY.

DEUTERONOMISTIC HISTORY

A term introduced by Martin Noth in 1943 to refer to the books of Deuteronomy–2 Kings, with the book of Deuteronomy establishing a theological grid or guideline for evaluating Israel's history, a guideline that is sustained throughout the history. Although modern scholars still debate the process by which the Deuteronomistic History reached its present form, many OT scholars feel that the final result is the product of layers of redaction by a DEUTERONOMISTIC SCHOOL over a long period of time, with each layer having perhaps its own unique theological purpose, and with the final DEUTERONOMIST interpreting Israel's history in terms of a hard-and-fast rule: Israel's fate at any time depends on its obedience or disobedience to the Mosaic LAW. In other words, Israel's history is evaluated by the sole principle that obedience to the Mosaic law brings prosperity and disobedience brings divine judgment, especially in terms of defeat in battle (cf. Deut. 28). It is through this lens that the Deuteronomistic History may be read. Consequently, this is history with an ideological AGENDA, not unbiased, objective (*see* OBJECTIVE KNOWLEDGE) history. Probably finally edited during the BABYLONIAN EXILE after 586 BCE, this history reflects back on events in Israel's history and interprets those events in terms of the Deuteronomistic principle. Many scholars believe that if we read these historians as if they intended to present a scientific, complete, and objective account of Israel's past, we will simply misread them. These historians selected and arranged their material as it was relevant to their theological thesis. The Deuteronomistic History was never intended simply to record a factual past but to evaluate the theological SIGNIFICANCE of that past. This is true whether the work is dealing with kings, wars, natural phenomena, or surrounding nations. Israel's moral character (defined in terms of loyalty to the Mosaic law) determined historical outcomes.

DEUTERONOMISTIC SCHOOL

A term developed to address the complexity of authorship of the DEUTERONOMISTIC HISTORY. Rather than being the product of a single AUTHOR/compiler, the history arrived at its present form in the hands of several redactors. The original compilation was the work of the Deuteronomistic Historian (Dtr). This work was later edited by a redactor who wanted to correlate it to the prophetic TRADITION (DtrP), and this edition was finally revised by a person (DtrN) who wanted to link Israel's history with obedience or disobedience to the LAW (Soulen and Soulen, 47).

Bibliography. Richard N. Soulen and R. Kendall Soulen, *Handbook of Biblical Criticism* (3rd ed.; Louisville: Westminster John Knox, 2001).

DEUTEROPAULINE EPISTLES

A term for the Epistles in the NT ascribed to Paul but whose Pauline authorship a number of scholars reject because of significant differences from the undisputed Pauline Epistles in LITERARY STYLE, vocabulary, and theology (*see* CANON, NEW TESTAMENT). These disputed Epistles fall into two groups: the PSEUDO-PAULINE (2 Thessalonians, Colossians, and Ephesians) and the PASTORAL EPISTLES (1–2 Timothy and Titus). The scholars who reject Pauline authorship of these books suggest that they are products of a church well on its way to becoming an institution. *See* EPISTOLARY LITERATURE.

DIACHRONIC

From the LINGUISTICS of Ferdinand de Saussure, *diachronic* (from the Greek for "through time") refers to the study of the changes and developments in a language over time. In STRUCTURALISM, diachronic analysis has been expanded to include the study of human artifacts in general, including LITERARY texts. For example, the analysis of the ways in which the LAW or TRADITIONs have been interpreted over time is a diachronic study. In READER-RESPONSE CRITICISM, *diachronic* may be used to refer to the reading process in that it takes place through time. When we consider that this diachronic process is affected both by textual and by reader-responsive considerations, we might assume that the reading process is not static but dynamic, open-ended, and always subject to modification, change, evaluation, and rereading. *See* SYNCHRONIC.

DIALECTICAL MATERIALISM

Karl Marx's adaptation of Hegel's dialectic to history, in which he defines history as a process of CONFLICT and resolution determined by the forces of material production, a process that moves toward a classless society. *See* MARXIST CRITICISM.

DIALECTICS OF DISCOURSE

The points of TENSION in the communication process, whether oral or written, that have important implications for understanding and MEANING. There are six significant dialectics. First, in oral DISCOURSE, the gap between the speaker's conceptualization and the SPEECH's meaning constitutes a dialectic. The oral message has at least two levels of meaning—the speaker's and the speech's. The two meanings may or may not be identical, for the speech's meaning may not objectively represent the speaker's conceptualization.

The second dialectic is between meaning and REFERENCE. The meaning of a SIGN (whether a single word or an entire DISCOURSE) is the object, event, or concept that the sign names in the real world, while the reference of a sign is concerned with the thing to which the sign refers. For example, the meaning of the word "snake" is a "scaly, legless reptile," while the reference may be to a particular person with a particular personality trait. In this SENSE, meaning is what a statement says; reference is that to which the statement is applied. A major problem in HERMENEUTICS is that the term "meaning" is also used in the same sense as "reference," especially in the case of written discourse; what a TEXT means is identified with what a text is about. Since a text's (i.e., a sign's) reference must be construed by a reader, there is the possibility of multiple INTERPRETATIONs. In other words, if a sign has multiple referents, there will be multiple interpretations because different readers (or the same reader at different readings) may assign different referents to the sign. The GOSPEL of Matthew includes individuals and places that existed and events that happened in first-century Palestine. The meaning of the text has its context in first-century Palestine. But to whom do the terms *Pharisee, disciple,* or *publican* refer? To what do the events and places refer?

The third dialectic concerns the reader in written discourse. A dialectic exists on the reader's part between understanding (the reader's conceptualization of the text) and subsequent EXPLANATION. The former is private, the latter is public. There is no guarantee that a reader's explanation adequately represents the reader's understanding. This dialectic is further complicated since different readers understand texts differently due to a wide range of elements within readers' worlds.

Fourth is the dialectic between the original languages and TRANSLATIONS. BIBLICAL HERMENEUTICS includes a special problem: the languages of the texts are not the same as those of modern readers. If readers use a translation, they are already working with an interpretation. It is impossible for a translation to have a one-to-one correspondence with the original. Therefore, any interpretation of a biblical text based on a translation is actually an interpretation of an interpretation: the interpretation based on a translation is an interpretation of the translator's explanation of the original.

Fifth, there is the dialectic between the LITERARY CONVENTIONS of the NATURAL LANGUAGE and the conventions of the LITERARY LANGUAGE of a text (Hebrew, Aramaic, and Greek in the BIBLE). In literary texts, a literary language is superimposed on the natural language, requiring readers to coordinate the conventions of the natural language and those of the literary language. A reader lacking any appreciable understanding of the dynamics of the LITERARY CONVENTIONS may make no distinction between what a text says and what it is about; thus the DIFFERENCE between the meaning and the reference is not perceived.

The sixth and perhaps the most significant dialectic is between the text and the work, a distinction made by Wolfgang Iser. When reading a text, a reader must take into account two factors: the text and the response to the text. The literary work is not synonymous with the text but is created in the act of reading. The work exists somewhere between the artistic pole (the text created by the AUTHOR) and the aesthetic pole (the realization accomplished by the reader). The text exists on paper; the work is born out of the interaction between the text and the reader. Since dispositions of readers vary and since a single reader's disposition may change between readings, the literary work can never be precisely pinpointed. Iser asserts that gaps of INDETERMINACY and the filling of these gaps are the central factor in literary communication. An author cannot possibly incorporate every detail from the real world into the text, for the text would become unmanageable. There are therefore gaps of silence within the text that readers are required to fill by drawing from their own knowledge. Such gaps, according to Iser, exist on different levels: SYNTAX, SEMANTICS, PRAGMATICS, NARRATIVE flow, CHARACTERIZATION, ACTION, and the role assigned to the reader. *See* READER-RESPONSE CRITICISM.

Bibliography. Wolfgang Iser, *The Act of Reading: A Theory of Aesthetic Response* (Baltimore: Johns Hopkins University Press, 1978).

DIALOGISM

A term introduced by Mikhail Bakhtin to name what he saw as a property of all speech, the fact that since DISCOURSE does not exist or occur in isolation but is always a part of a greater CONTEXT, it is never value-neutral or unintentional. Every word is always already built on the "scaffolding" of past usage. The consequence of dialogism, or double-voicing, is that the LITERARY use of language is not unique but always multivoiced due to the history of its own language.

Bakhtin also uses the term for literary TEXTS in which characters speak with their own voices, seemingly independent of the control of the AUTHOR. The consequence is that the text is characterized by "a plurality of independent and unmerged voices and consciousness, a genuine polyphony of fully valid voices" (*Problems*, 81). Examples in the BIBLE are such characters as Bathsheba, Michael, and Vashti. Bakhtin uses the term further to refer to a property of literary PROSE: when a speaker intends the listener to assume that words are spoken as if in quotation marks. Literary prose is built almost entirely on this type of dialogism: it always operates with two voices. A single-voiced word (such as scientific language) suppresses its scaffolding and any alternative POINT OF VIEW in order to give the impression that it is the only voice possible on a SUBJECT.

The dialogic word, however, consciously includes its scaffolding and other voices so that they are audible to the listener. Examples are IRONY and PARODY, both of which are double-voiced in that they state one thing but inscribe the opposite. Bakhtin further states that in order for a word to be dialogic, the double-voicing must be part of the INTENTION of the speaker. If the speaker or author agrees with the second voice, the utterance is "stylized." But if the speaker or author disagrees with the second voice, then the result is parody. When the speaker/author is in control of the second voice, the utterance is a passive double-voicing. When the second voice is in TENSION with the first voice to the extent that the second voice struggles against the attempts of the first voice at parody, escaping the control of the speaker/author, the result is active double-voicing. An example of the use of Bakhtin's theory of dialogism is Robert Polzin's work *Moses and the Deuteronomist*, in which he examines the voices (i.e., ideologies; *see* IDEOLOGY) of the NARRATOR and characters in Deuteronomy, Joshua, and Judges. Polzin discovers that the books differ in their understanding of divine purpose and speech on the one hand, and human response and INTERPRETATION on the other hand. Each book, then, responds to earlier ones, correcting their views on the nature of the relationship between the divine and the human. In these three texts, the ideologies of other texts are incorporated, thus setting up the possibility of double-voicing. The same may be said of the texts (Job, Ecclesiastes) in the WISDOM TRADITION that restate the traditional wisdom and then challenge it. Also, Gen. 1–3 seems to be in dialogue with Canaanite COSMOLOGY.

Bibliography. Mikhail Bakhtin, *The Dialogic Imagination* (ed. Michael Holquist; trans. Caryl Emerson and Michael Holquist; Austin: University of Texas Press, 1981); idem, *Problems of Dostoevsky's Poetics* (ed. and trans. Caryl Emerson; Minneapolis: University of Minnesota Press, 1984); Phyllis Margaret Paryas, "Double-Voicing/Dialogism," in *Encyclopedia of Contemporary Literary Theory* (ed. Irena R. Makaryk; Toronto: University of Toronto Press, 1993); Robert Polzin, *Moses and the Deuteronomist* (New York: Seabury, 1980).

DIALOGUE

In its broadest sense, a conversation between two people. It has, however, acquired more specialized MEANINGS. First, it is used to describe a TYPE of literary TEXT in which two characters discuss or debate a proposition, the most notable being Plato's *Dialogues*, in which Socrates debates his students on subjects ranging from justice to memory. Second, it is used in LITERARY texts to break up passages that would otherwise be wholly DESCRIPTION or EXPOSITION; it must be consistently appropriate to the characters to create a SENSE of naturalness. For its use in HEBREW NARRATIVE, *see* CHARACTERIZATION.

DIASPORA

From the Greek meaning "dispersion," *Diaspora* is roughly equivalent to the Hebrew *gôlâ*, meaning "exiles." The Diaspora, however, included Jews who voluntarily moved from their homeland for various reasons, such as better living and business opportunities. *Gôlâ* was used to refer to those who were forcibly moved from their homeland. The descendants of the latter became part of the Diaspora. The largest dispersions occurred when Assyrians deported Israelites from Samaria in 722 BCE and Babylonians deported Judahites from Jerusalem in 586 BCE. There were later dispersions during the Roman period. The LXX and TARGUMS (or targumim) were produced by the Diaspora, as was some of the literature of the HEBREW BIBLE (e.g., Job, Proverbs, and some of the psalms) and some PSEUDEPIGRAPHA and APOCRYPHA. Some scholars think that the synagogue also arose in the Diaspora. *See* EXILE.

DIATESSARON

A harmony of the four CANONICAL GOSPELS produced by Tatian, a Syrian Christian of the second century CE. The *Diatessaron*, now lost, combined Matthew, Mark, Luke, John, and some ORAL TRADITION into a unified NARRATIVE and was widely used in the church in the East for centuries.

DIATRIBE

A TYPE of argument in which a writer/orator creates a hypothetical inquirer or objectioner (a dialogue partner). The writer or orator then proceeds to answer the objections of this imaginary questioner. While the inquirer may be hypothetical, the issue at stake is not. An example is in Rom. 6. Here the inquirer asks, "What then are we to say? Should we continue in sin in order that grace may abound?" Paul then goes on to answer this challenge in verses 2–14. Apparently this inquirer is persistent, because another question is asked in verse 15: "What then? Should we sin because we are not under law but under grace?" The answer is recorded in 6:15c–7:6. This type of ARGUMENTATION continues with further rounds of question and answer in 7:7, 13 and 9:14, 19, 30. Another example is James 2:18–22, which begins with "But someone will say, 'You have faith and I have works.'" The AUTHOR then proceeds with an elaborate retort. The hypothetical opponent may even be a PERSONIFICATION, as in 1 Cor. 12:15–21 (the speakers are body parts) and Rom. 2:21–22 (the speaker is righteousness).

DICTION

The word choice of a writer or speaker. In literary studies, the rule of thumb is that the words should be appropriate to CHARACTERIZATION, SETTING, and SUBJECT. It may be formal, or high; neutral, or middle; or informal, or low. Formal diction is characterized by correct word order and elegance in the sense that the words are above those used in everyday SPEECH. Neutral diction is ordinary, everyday vocabulary that does not draw attention to itself like formal diction. Informal diction ranges from colloquial to slang.

Diction may also be classified as specific-general and concrete-abstract, according to its degree of explicitness.

DICTIONARIES/ENCYCLOPEDIAS

In BIBLICAL STUDIES, works that offer background information on a variety of words and topics. For example, the *Zondervan Pictorial Encyclopedia of the Bible* (ed. M. C. Tenney; 5 vols.; Grand Rapids: Zondervan, 1975) provides a fifteen-page discussion of the word "righteousness." The discussion is divided into topics such as "The meaning of the term linguistically," "Righteousness in the OT," "Righteousness in the NT," and "Righteousness in the modern world." Other useful dictionaries and encyclopedias include the one-volume *New Bible Dictionary* (ed. J. D. Douglas and N. Hillyer; 2nd ed.; Downers Grove, IL: InterVarsity, 1982) and the *Mercer Dictionary of the Bible* (ed. W. E. Mills; Macon, GA: Mercer University Press, 1990) and the following multivolume works: *The Interpreter's Dictionary of the Bible* (ed. G. A. Buttrick; 4 vols.; Nashville: Abingdon, 1962); *International Standard Bible Encyclopedia* (ed. G. W. Bromiley; rev. ed.; 4 vols.; Grand Rapids: Eerdmans, 1979–88); *Theological Dictionary of the New Testament* (ed. G. Kittel and G. Friedrich; trans. G. W. Bromiley; 10 vols.; Grand Rapids: Eerdmans, 1964–76).

Some later Bible dictionaries include *The Anchor Bible Dictionary* (ed. D. N. Freedman; 6 vols.; New York: Doubleday, 1992); *Baker's Evangelical Dictionary of Biblical Theology* (ed. W. A. Elwell; Grand Rapids: Baker, 1996); *Eerdmans Dictionary of the Bible* (ed. D. N. Freedman; Grand Rapids: Eerdmans, 2000); *Harper's Bible Dictionary* (ed. P. J. Achtemeier; San Francisco: Harper, 1996); *New International Dictionary of Old Testament Theology and Exegesis* (ed. W. A. VanGemeren; Grand Rapids: Zondervan, 1997); *New International Dictionary of the Bible* (ed. M. C. Tenney and J. D. Douglas; Grand Rapids: Zondervan, 1987); *The Interpreter's Dictionary of the Bible: Supplementary Volume* (ed. K. Crim; Nashville: Abingdon, 1976); *The New Bible Dictionary* (ed. I. H. Marshall et al.; 3rd ed.; Downers Grove, IL: InterVarsity, 1996); *The Oxford Guide to People and Places of the Bible* (ed. B. M. Metzger and M. D. Coogan; Oxford: Oxford University Press, 2001).

A number of dictionaries and encyclopedias of literary, critical, and cultural theory are also available. Listed here are some of the most useful: *The Penguin Dictionary of Critical Theory* (by D. Macey; London: Penguin, 2000); *The Penguin*

Dictionary of Literary Terms and Literary Theory (ed. J. A. Cuddon and C. E. Preston; 4th ed.; London: Penguin, 1998); *A Dictionary of Cultural and Critical Theory* (ed. M. D. Payne; Cambridge, MA: Blackwell, 1996); *Encyclopedia of Contemporary Literary Theory* (ed. I. R. Makaryk; Toronto: University of Toronto Press, 1993).

DICTIONARY MEANING

The denotative (*see* DENOTATION) sense of a word, its working definition in everyday usage, as opposed to a word's CONNOTATIONS.

DIDACHE

Also known as *The Teaching of the Twelve Apostles*, a second-century manual of church instruction. In 1875 P. Bryennios discovered a Greek copy from 1056 CE in the library of the Jerusalem Monastery of the Holy Sepulchre in Constantinople, modern Istanbul. Its major value lies in its information about the life and liturgical practices of the early Christian communities. We learn about the rituals of baptism, Eucharist, prayers, and fasting as well as about the role of prophets, APOSTLES, and teachers and their status in the communities.

Bart Ehrman (447–450) explains the organization of the text in its major divisions. The first six chapters consist of ethical exhortations arranged around two modes of living, the "Two Ways": the "Way of Life" and the "The Way of Death." The former is described in terms of things to be avoided (e.g., jealousy and anger) and things to pursue (reminiscent of the Stoic division of things into those to be pursued and those to be avoided). Christians should associate with people who are humble and righteous, should not show favoritism, and should minister to the needy by sharing goods. The "Way of Death" is constituted by the vices that we find in the LISTS OF VIRTUES AND VICES in the NT: lust, fornication, idolatry, arrogance, filthy speech, and so forth.

The second section of the *Didache* consists of a manual on church order. Christians are to baptize in cold running water if available, but may substitute warm standing water or, as a last resort, pour water over the head "in the name of the Father, Son, and Holy Spirit." Christians are also to fast on Wednesdays and Fridays rather than on Mondays and Thursdays as the "hypocrites" (nonbelievers) do. They should recite the Lord's Prayer three times a day and celebrate the Eucharist with the cup first and the bread second (an order that puzzles modern scholars).

The third section of the *Didache* gives instructions on the treatment of traveling apostles, prophets, and teachers who minister in the communities, while the final instructions concern the treatment of prophets who decide to settle permanently in one of the communities.

Bibliography. Bart Ehrman, *The New Testament: A Historical Introduction to the Early Christian Writings* (3rd ed.; New York: Oxford University Press, 2004).

DIDACTIC

Any work of literature that has instruction as its primary INTENTION. It might be argued that all TEXTS are didactic in that they can be seen as instances of teaching; they seek to communicate some message(s) to readers. So the primary distinction between didactic and nondidactic texts seems to depend on the AUTHOR's actual or ostensible purpose. If teaching is the primary function of the text, if the primary effect of the text is beyond itself, then the text is properly didactic. The major concern about the didacticism of texts is that if, as a primary purpose, it is taken too far, the intrinsic SIGNIFICANCE of art as art will be subverted. Although the texts of the BIBLE are artistic in the sense that they generate aesthetic pleasure and enjoyment, they do not exist solely for that purpose. These texts are religious and have as their primary function religious instruction. While LITERARY artistry permeates the biblical texts, the aims are distinctly didactic. Yet texts are didactic in different ways. The language of some texts is direct whereas that of others is indirect, demanding more participation from the reader. If we place the biblical texts along a continuum from closed to open, or didactic to nondidactic, where CLOSED TEXTS tend to involve fewer readerly decisions than open ones (*see* OPEN

TEXTS), texts such as the EPISTLES and PROVERBS would fall toward the closed end of the continuum, while Genesis and the GOSPELS would fall toward the open end. In other words, the didacticism of the Epistles and Proverbs is more obvious and direct; that of the Gospels and Genesis is indirect and less obvious.

DIEGESIS

A term in NARRATIVE studies that distinguishes between the voice of the NARRATOR and that of the characters (Hauch, 533). The narrator's voice narrates without EXPLANATION or judgment. The term originates in Plato's two narrative modes, mimesis and diegesis: the former consists of NARRATION of ACTION in the words of characters, and the latter represents action in the words of the poet. Diegesis therefore is the more authorially controlling mode, usually by way of report, COMMENTARY, and SUMMARY (Genette, 161–66). The distinction between the SENSE of immediacy of mimesis and the authorial distance of diegesis has generated recent discussions of narrative authority. Beginning in the nineteenth century, the distinction between mimesis and diegesis almost disappeared when novelists made extensive use of indirect SPEECH (reported speech). Within MODERNISM, the narrator's voice was suppressed to the point that the result was a sense of complete authorial control. In POSTMODERNISM, however, diegesis has been foregrounded with a focus on the process of narration itself. Consequently, the narrator's voice has actually lost its authoritative position, becoming instead a fictional and textual construct that is now subject to critical INTERPRETATION. In READER-RESPONSE CRITICISM, the narrator's voice constitutes only one POINT OF VIEW among many others within a TEXT; in POSTMODERN CRITICISM, the concept of INTERTEXTUALITY denies the presence of a single authoritative voice standing behind all other voices and ensuring a unified text. In Mark's GOSPEL, for example, the voice of the narrator heard in direct statements to the reader, DESCRIPTIONS, and summaries is not the controlling voice but one competing with the voices of the IMPLIED READER, PLOT, and characters. As a

textual construct, then, the narrator's voice (often identified with that of the AUTHOR) must be critically analyzed without special privileging.

Bibliography. Gérard Genette, *Narrative Discourse: An Essay in Method* (trans. Jane E. Lewin; Ithaca, NY: Cornell University Press, 1980); Linda Hauch, "Diegesis," in *Encyclopedia of Contemporary Literary Theory* (ed. Irena R. Makaryk; Toronto: University of Toronto Press, 1993), 533–34.

DIFFÉRANCE

A term coined by the French philosopher Jacques Derrida. It is a deliberate misspelling: *différance* combines the French words for "differing" and "DEFERRING." Using Saussure's definition of SIGN, Derrida says that a word derives MEANING in its differences from other words. But every word also evidences the TRACE of an indeterminate origination. Since this indeterminate quality creates change within the culture, MEANING is always deferred. INTERPRETATION itself becomes an activity laden with AMBIGUITY. It is a human ACTION with a determinate and indeterminate meaning. Every reader approaches a TEXT within a culture, both influenced by and exerting influence on the culture. Since this is an infinite process of shaping and reshaping, interpretation is an endless, ever-changing process, an infinite process of creation. All meaning is bound by cultural CONTEXT, but because of ambiguity this context becomes boundless.

DIFFERENCE

In critical studies, "difference" is used in at least three ways. First, in FEMINIST CRITICISM some essentialist feminists emphasize the difference between men and women while also working to ensure the social valuation of women. Such CRITICS focus on women's reproductive capacity, nurturance, cooperation, and emotion; they question the values traditionally associated with men. In analyzing TEXTS, these critics look for the distinct qualities of men's and women's perspectives on the world. In such readings, they look to isolate hints of alternative systems not established on hierarchy and competition but on mutual caring and concern. For example, Elisabeth Schüssler Fiorenza argues that the texts of the NT are products of KYRIARCHY, yet embedded within these texts are traces of alternative TRADITIONS, especially a divine WISDOM TRADITION.

Second, the term is used in STRUCTURALISM as a major property of words. A word has meaning only by its difference from other words. For example, the English word "cat" does not have any inherent meaning but has meaning only in its difference from bat, hat, rat, mat, dog, and so forth. In terms of BINARY OPPOSITIONS, *difference* refers to the relationship between the two terms of an opposition in which the first term is traditionally privileged, such as male/female, spirit/flesh, youth/old age. In DECONSTRUCTION, however, Jacques Derrida has argued that the second term is prior to the first because the first is defined in terms of difference to the second, which is the other. Thus the second term is always already there. Such use of the term calls into question the privileging of the male in the hierarchical system in the BIBLE.

And third, difference is a key idea in contextual theology. Liberation theologians (*see* LIBERATION THEOLOGY) assume that theological systems and INTERPRETIVE FRAMEWORKS reflect the social and cultural world in which the systems are produced and do not reflect the existential differences of other people. Consequently, theology should be formulated within and communicated to groups in terms of their particular existential situation. Black, liberation, and feminist critics and theologians try to counter the dominant interpretive frameworks, which they perceive as Western, bourgeois-capitalist, white, colonial, racist, imperialist, androcentric (*see* ANDROCENTRISM), or patriarchal (*see* PATRIARCHY). These critics and theologians believe that because the traditional interpretive frameworks tend to perpetuate the ideologies (*see* IDEOLOGY) of the dominant traditions, they should be rejected (at least in part) and replaced by frameworks that reflect the particular CONTEXT and different experiences of those outside the dominant traditions.

Bibliography. Elisabeth Schüssler Fiorenza, *Jesus, Miriam's Child, Sophia's Prophet: Critical Issues in Feminist Christology* (New York: Continuum, 1994).

DIFFERENTIATION

A term used by James Kugel to refer to a property of parallelism in BIBLICAL POETRY. Assuming a semantic parallelism between A and B in a line of poetry, Kugel argues that B asserts itself as different from A in a variety of ways, suggesting that A does not equal B but that A + B is a "single statement." By completing or complementing A, in other words, B ensures that the line itself is a unified whole. For example, "You brought a vine out of Egypt; you drove out the nations and planted it" (Ps. 80:8) implies a sequence of ACTION in which B does not simply repeat A. According to Kugel, differentiation may occur in a number of ways, including CHIASMUS, the movement from singular to plural, the switch from noun to pronoun, the change from one person to another, and prepositional alternation, to mention a few.

Bibliography. James Kugel, *The Idea of Biblical Poetry: Parallelism and Its History* (Baltimore: Johns Hopkins University Press, 1998).

DIFFERING. *See* DIFFÉRANCE

DIGRESSION

The insertion of material seemingly not closely related to the subject or other material of a work. If the digression is long and formal, it is called an excursus. While a digression may serve only to violate the unity of the PLOT, in some cases it is an intentional LITERARY DEVICE. Meir Sternberg argues that rather than being instances of sloppy patchwork, digressions constitute a literary device in Hebrew literature that creates a pause in the reading, a retardation. For example, the GENEALOGY in Gen. 22:20–24 is inserted into a personal STORY and seems out of place on the surface. The reader is forced to pause and ask about its appropriateness at this point in the story. A more extensive digression is Gen. 38 (the story of Tamar and Judah) in the larger Joseph NARRATIVE. Scholars have debated about the function of this digression for decades.

Bibliography. Meir Sternberg, *The Poetics of Biblical Narrative* (Bloomington: Indiana University Press, 1985).

DIPTYCH

Two tablets of wood, ivory, or metal hinged together and covered on the inside with wax, used in the Greco-Roman period to write on with a stylus.

DIRECT NARRATION. *See* NARRATION

DIRGE

A song of mourning associated with a funeral or sung to commemorate death and used in ancient mourning rites. According to Gerstenberger, the dirge consisted of an expression of wailing, a DESCRIPTION of a disaster, and a call for others to weep. The dirge usually opens with "How ... !" and employs the QINAH (*qînâ*, Hebrew for "dirge, lamentation"), a poetic meter with five stressed syllables per line. Some examples are David's LAMENTS over Saul and Jonathan (2 Sam. 1:19–27) and for Abner (2 Sam. 3:33–34). In Lamentations are dirges that lament the destruction of a city (chaps. 1–2, 4). PROPHETS also used the dirge in reference to Israel as a corpse (e.g., Amos 5:1–3; Isa. 14:3–21; Ezek. 19:1–14).

> *Bibliography.* E. S. Gerstenberger, "Psalms," in *Old Testament Form Criticism* (ed. J. H. Hayes; San Antonio, TX: Trinity University Press, 1977).

DIS-CLOSURE

A modern notion that a LITERARY text such as a novel or poem resists CLOSURE or completeness in the SENSE of a wrapping up or a DENOUEMENT. The notion of literary closure goes as far back in the Western literary TRADITION as Aristotle's *Poetics*, which claims that a work of art should be "whole" and "complete." As late as the 1960s, it was still popular to count textual resolution as the point where no further development was appropriate, and to reckon such resolution or closure as part of the STRUCTURE of the text. Such an ASSUMPTION was at the heart of the claim in NEW CRITICISM that a TEXT was a unified whole.

Later critics, however, questioned the idea of closure as a formal structure of the text by suggesting that texts, especially modern and POSTMODERN texts, are open-ended: they are characterized by dis-closure (lacking closure). Some, such as Stanley Fish and Wolfgang Iser, have argued that closure is the result of the reader's attempt to master the text. Consequently, closure is not a formal part of the text but the result of the reader's effort to understand the text through INTERPRETATION. CRITICS such as Jacques Derrida go so far as to argue that dis-closure must always be the result of interpretation because there is no MEANING outside language. A signifier points to other signifiers in an endless chain of signifying, making it impossible for the meaning of a text to be a fixed one. Consequently, meaning is always fluid due to the very nature of signification (*see* DEFERRING) and to the ever-changing SOCIAL LOCATION of readers. Any claim to closure is nothing more than an illusion, an assertion of the reader's expectation that the text is a unified, closed whole.

The concept of dis-closure, then, has profound implications for HERMENEUTICS. If a text as a linguistic product is open to infinity, then the claim that meaning is enclosed within the structures of the text and that a reader may somehow discover it is not valid. Dis-closure means that hermeneutics must redirect itself toward the text as an event and toward the act of interpretation as an experiencing of the text rather than as a means by which a reader solves the text by DECODING its structures to discover the enclosed meaning. It also means that hermeneutics must focus more on the activities of readers and their motivations. Dis-closure means that every reading is in some way a MISREADING.

> *Bibliography.* Stanley Fish, *Is There a Text in This Class?* (Cambridge, MA: Harvard University Press, 1980); Wolfgang Iser, *The Act of Reading* (Baltimore: Johns Hopkins University Press, 1978).

DISCLOSURE FORMULA

One of the formal features in the body of Pauline Letters. According to Doty, the disclosure formula provides a heading for paragraphs, briefly stating their content and introducing new material within the body of the letter. Examples are "I want you to know that ..." and "We do not want you to be unaware" (Rom. 1:13; 2 Cor. 1:8; 1 Thess. 2:1;

Phil. 1:12; Gal. 1:11). *See* JOY FORMULA; REQUEST FORMULA.

Bibliography. William Doty, *Letters in Primitive Christianity* (Philadelphia: Fortress, 1973).

DISCOURSE

In its least technical SENSE, a term meaning SPEECH or conversation, sometimes with a DIDACTIC goal. It is also a mode of expression, which in grammatical terms may be direct (i.e., a quotation) or indirect (i.e., a reference to speech):

Direct: "He said to her, 'Daughter, your faith has made you well; go in peace.'" (Luke 8:48)

Indirect: "She declared in the presence of all the people why she had touched him, and how she had been immediately healed." (Luke 8:47c)

Since the 1960s, however, the term has accumulated a number of uses in a variety of disciplines. In LINGUISTICS, *discourse* means language actually used by a speaker in contradistinction to the SIGN system underlying the speech. DISCOURSE ANALYSIS studies the structures of language units (usually texts) within their linguistic and sociocultural CONTEXTS. The followers of Mikhail Bakhtin focus discourse analysis on the study of actual utterances (including texts) within the contexts of their enunciation while relegating the sociocultural study of sign systems to the field of semiology (*see* SEMIOTICS). For the Bakhtin circle, an utterance must always be analyzed and understood in terms of its contexts: the social position of the speaker, who is a socially formed subject; the ideological horizon of the hearer; and the historical development of the words used in an utterance, which entails the ASSUMPTION that words can carry MEANINGS the same as, or similar to, those used in other discourses. Furthermore, discourses become systems that formulate and control reality by creating knowledge. These competing systems, discourses, actually create society. A society's objects of interest and value are created by discourse.

Within POSTMODERNISM, theorists such as Michel Foucault and Jacques Derrida have argued that the focus of discourse analysis should be on the relationship between knowledge and power in discourse. Discursive practices—which include institutional bases and controls, qualified members, accepted procedures of expression, the production of objects, and the determination of rules of legitimation—actually determine objects or contents of knowledge. In this sense, then, discourses are not value-neutral or objective but constitute the ideological vantage point from which all thought and knowledge are possible. Similarly, no utterance that is not part of a larger discourse is able to determine beforehand the object of knowledge. As a result, the speaking SUBJECT is already the spoken subject, the subject created by discourse; as such, the human subject can never stand outside the determining structures of discourse as an autonomous, self-contained subject and is therefore unable to examine or know anything beyond the play of discourse.

When BIBLICAL STUDIES is approached within the context of discourse analysis, each utterance or unit of text is understood to have been written within, and inalterably characterized by, the dominant discourse of the author's period. This is set against the fact that any text is read and interpreted within the sociocultural contexts of the reader. Such an approach simply vitiates any possibility of articulating a meaning that is not reflective of the discourse of the *reader*, with its practices of power, institutional bases, and legitimation.

Bibliography. Marie-Christine Leps, "Discourse," in *Encyclopedia of Contemporary Literary Theory* (ed. Irena R. Makaryk; Toronto: University of Toronto Press, 1993), 535–36; Christopher Norris, "Discourse," in *A Dictionary of Cultural and Critical Theory* (ed. Michael Payne; Cambridge, MA: Blackwell, 1996), 144–48.

DISCOURSE ANALYSIS

Also known as text linguistics, discourse analysis is a multidisciplinary approach to studying the syntactic structures of TEXTS within their linguistic, social, and cultural dimensions with the purpose of understanding how MEANING is produced. Gilbert L. Encinas (55) defines discourse analysis as "a specific direction focusing on the detailed study of language use in a social context"; Guy Cook (48) suggests that discourse analysis is a conversation between the author and the text. Whether DISCOURSE occurs in a conversation in a New York ghetto or in the form of poetry from the pen of Emily Dickinson, discourse defines one's world and constructs one's own personal identity. Discourse creates links between the emotional, physical, mental, and spiritual aspects of a person's character to formulate a conscious expression of the self to the world. Humanity judges a person on the basis of the person's own discourse.

In recent years discourse analysis has steadily moved away from the rhetorical and structural analysis of texts and other forms of communication toward the relationship between discourse, knowledge, and the structures of power and authority in all types of communication in everyday life, including written and oral, "high" and "popular." Discourse analysis has increasingly focused on written communication as it functions within its political, cultural, and institutional CONTEXTS. Regardless of the type of discourse being studied, however, all discourse analysts assume that structures of power profoundly shape the ways humans in society communicate, understand, and know.

Perhaps the scholar who has had the most significant influence on discourse analysis as it is presently practiced is Michel Foucault, whose work examines the relationship between power structures in discourse and the institutionalization of power and authority. Consequently, contemporary discourse analysis raises questions about the production and influence of the various units or parts within an IDEOLOGY at a specific historical time. In other words, discourse analysis examines the variety of LITERARY CONVENTIONS, rules, and social measures employed to legitimate discourses. By studying the relations between LITERARY, political, historical, scientific, theological, philosophical, and other texts, discourse analysts can intertextually see how discursive structures at a particular moment

are inscribed in and perhaps perpetuated through texts by a number of means. This allows the analyst to discover the types of texts, the discursive practices, the relations of power, the production of knowledge, and the relationship between them within a particular political, cultural, and socioeconomic context.

In BIBLICAL STUDIES, discourse analysis has taken many directions and may be classified broadly under the heading of semiology (*see* SEMIOTICS). It ranges from a focus on texts, NARRATIVE, and rhetorical structures to the role the reader plays in INTERPRETATION and the ethics involved in the act of interpretation. Probably the most helpful resource for ways in which discourse analysis or semiology has been used in biblical studies is Alfred M. Johnson's *Bibliography of Semiological and Structural Studies of Religion*. Also helpful is Stanley Porter and Jeffery T. Reed's *Discourse Analysis and the New Testament* and Walter Bodine's *Discourse Analysis of Biblical Literature*.

Bibliography. Walter Bodine, ed., *Discourse Analysis of Biblical Literature* (Atlanta: Society of Biblical Literature, 1995); Guy Cook, *Discourse and Literature* (Oxford: Oxford University Press, 1994); Teun A. van Dijk, ed., *Handbook of Discourse Analysis* (4 vols.; London: Academic Press, 1985); Gilbert Encinas, *Prison Argot* (Lanham, MD: University Press of America, 2001); Michael Groden and Martin Kreiswirth, eds., *The Johns Hopkins Guide to Literary Criticism* (Baltimore: Johns Hopkins University Press, 1993); Alfred M. Johnson, *A Bibliography of Semiological and Structural Studies of Religion* (Pittsburgh: Clifford E. Harbour Library, Pittsburgh Theological Seminary, 1979); Robert Longacre, *The Grammar of Discourse* (New York: Plenum, 1996); Diane Macdonell, *Theories of Discourse: An Introduction* (Oxford: Blackwell, 1986); Stanley Porter and Jeffery T. Reed, *Discourse Analysis and the New Testament* (Sheffield: Sheffield Academic Press, 1999).

DISCURSIVE. *See* DISCOURSE

DISINTERESTEDNESS

In LITERARY studies and HERMENEUTICS, the quality of doing EXEGESIS with objectivity, without any conflict of interest. It is based on the ASSUMPTION that an interpreter can bracket out all PREUNDERSTANDING and PRESUPPOSITIONS and do absolutely objective (*see* OBJECTIVE KNOWL-

EDGE) exegesis. Yet disinterestedness has met with severe CRITICISM by CRITICS who view readers as sociocultural constructs, not able under any circumstances to step outside their worlds and observe anything with disinterestedness.

DISPOSITIO

One of the five parts into which ancient rhetoricians divided their subjects, *dispositio* refers to the proper ARRANGEMENT of the material in DELIBERATIVE RHETORIC into a unified whole based on the SUBJECT, audience, and occasion of the argument. *See* RHETORICAL CRITICISM.

DISPUTATION

A form of PROPHETIC SPEECH in which the prophet argues with opponents—for example, in Mic. 2:6–11 and Isa. 28:23–29. Several disputations occur in Jeremiah between Yahweh and Israel.

Bibliography. Claus Westermann, *Basic Forms of Prophetic Speech* (Louisville: Westminster John Knox, 1991).

DISSEMINATION

A term adapted by Jacques Derrida to suggest that MEANING is always a function of language and is never positively rooted or final but constantly scattered, deferred. *See* DEFERRING; DIFFÉRANCE.

DISSONANCE

In poetry and music, a harsh, cacophonous sound that breaks the RHYTHM of the pattern (Harmon and Holman, 158). The term has been adopted in the study of the BIBLE AS LITERATURE to refer to the places in a TEXT that seem to disturb the STRUCTURE. For example, the Song of Deborah in Judg. 5 seems to disturb the surrounding PROSE account of Deborah and Barak. Phyllis Trible (161–62) has offered an excellent example of dissonance in Jon. 2:1–11 MT (1:17b–2:10 NRSV). In the prose account of Jonah in the belly of a large fish, the flow of the EPISODE is disrupted by a prayer in VERSE. Not only does the switch from prose to verse create dissonance; so do the differences between the details in the two accounts. Furthermore, as Trible points out, while the CONTEXT demands a complaint or LAMENT, the poem is actually a thanksgiving song, creating IRONY.

Bibliography. William Harmon and C. Hugh Holman, *A Handbook to Literature* (8th ed.; Upper Saddle River, NJ: Prentice Hall, 1999); Phyllis Trible, *Rhetorical Criticism: Context, Method, and the Book of Jonah* (Minneapolis: Fortress, 1994).

DISTANCE

In LITERARY studies, the level of detachment or dispassion with which a reader can view the CONTENT of a literary work. First, the term can refer to the level of disinterest an AUTHOR manifests toward the content of the author's own work. Second, it can designate the degree to which an interpreter of a literary work can bracket out PRESUPPOSITIONS and PREUNDERSTANDING that one may have about a work. And third, *distance* can designate the temporal, historical, and ideological separation between a TEXT, its world, and that of the reader/CRITIC. Recent critics argue that the distance between reader and text, between author and text, between interpreter and presuppositions, and between the temporal, historical, ideological FRAMEWORK and the reader can never be completely closed, with the implication that MEANING is always fluid and provisional. *See* DISINTERESTEDNESS.

DISTANCIATION

A term introduced into HERMENEUTICS by Paul Ricoeur (139) to refer to the state of a TEXT's being autonomous from the INTENTION of the AUTHOR. Since the reader is not present at the time of writing and the author is absent at the time of reading, the immediate dialogic relationship presumed by a speaker and a hearer is lost, and the text is freed from and understood apart from the author. It is no longer the representation of an author's mind but a summons to the reader to participate in creating MEANING. Texts are not repositories of facts from which to construct history; rather, they simply set in motion the activities of creating meaning. In this SENSE, distanciation redirects the focus of hermeneutics away from the WORLD BEHIND THE TEXT to the text itself and to the influence it has on contemporary readers (Thiselton, 56–57, 70–71). When the words of Jesus or any other person in the BIBLE are placed into written texts, distanciation is automatically in effect because the writer (as opposed to the speaker in oral DISCOURSE) is absent from the text. Some scholars (e.g., Kelber, 141–43) have argued, however, that texts such as Q and the LETTERS of Paul are characterized by orality and could or should be studied as oral discourse. Unlike the writers of the SYNOPTIC GOSPELS, these scholars are not interpreting TRADITIONs but are creating a space in which the words in the Epistles or in Q have the immediacy of presence. Consequently, in this oral space, distanciation breaks down. If these scholars are correct, then these texts are better understood in terms of a hermeneutic of orality or speaking (oral communication) than in terms of a hermeneutic of writing.

Bibliography. Werner H. Kelber, *The Oral and the Written Gospel: The Hermeneutics of Speaking and Writing in the Synoptic Tradition, Mark, Paul, and Q* (Philadelphia: Fortress, 1983); Paul Ricoeur, *Hermeneutics and the Human Sciences* (Cambridge: Cambridge University Press, 1981); Anthony Thiselton, *New Horizons in Hermeneutics* (Grand Rapids: Zondervan, 1992).

DITTOGRAPHY

In TEXTUAL CRITICISM, the erroneous duplication of a word or letter in the scribal copying of a text. Examples may be in 1 Thess. 2:7, *egenēthēmen nēpioi*, "We were infants," in which an *n* is duplicated—instead of *egenēthēmen ēpioi*, "We were gentle" (NRSV). Also, some manuscripts of Mark 12:27 read *ho theos theos*, where "God" is copied twice.

DOCUMENT

Any written or printed TEXT. The term does not define or refer to the LITERARY or aesthetic dimension of a text but only to the technical fact of its existence as inscribed text.

DOCUMENTARY HYPOTHESIS

In SOURCE CRITICISM, the theory that the TEXTs Genesis–Deuteronomy were composed from four different sources, TRADITIONs, or DOCUMENTs, which date from different periods of Israel's history.

The four documents are J (YAHWIST), E (ELOHIST), D (DEUTERONOMIST), and P (PRIESTLY CODE) and designated as JEDP. For a more detailed definition, *see* GRAF-WELLHAUSEN HYPOTHESIS; SOURCE CRITICISM.

DOGMATIC THEOLOGY

The theological study of the dogma, CREED, or beliefs of a religious community. Ideally, dogmatic theology is the relevant, timely application of the creeds that the religious community understands to be timeless, universal biblical TRUTHs. Consequently, BIBLICAL THEOLOGY (the extrapolation of these truths from the writings of the BIBLE) serves as the foundation for dogmatic theology. From this perspective, dogmatic theology may be perpetually adaptable to the community as the needs and social situation of the community change.

DOGMATICS

The systematic and organized study of Christian faith. *See* BIBLICAL THEOLOGY; DOGMATIC THEOLOGY.

DOMINICAL SAYING

A saying of Jesus. *See* SAYINGS OF JESUS.

DOOMSAYING POETRY. *See* MONITORY POETRY

DOUAY BIBLE

Also known as the Douay-Rheims Bible, an English translation of the VULGATE during the reign of Elizabeth I by English Catholics who fled to the Continent during her reign. Remaining as faithful as they could to the Vulgate in order not to introduce unacceptable ideas into the TEXT, these Catholic scholars produced an extremely literal text. They completed the NT at Rheims, France, in 1582 and the OT at Douay, France, in 1610. Subjected to several revisions, the Douay Bible remained the most used Bible for English Catholics for more than three centuries.

Bibliography. Steven M. Sheeley and Robert N. Nash Jr., *The Bible in English Translation: An Essential Guide* (Nashville: Abingdon, 1997).

DOUBLE-CONSCIOUSNESS

A key idea in BLACK THEOLOGY, Black criticism, and LIBERATION THEOLOGY that African Americans always experience a conflict between two identities—black and American. The conflict has its genesis in the compulsory exclusion of African Americans from mainstream society. The result of such double-consciousness is that African Americans are hindered from developing their own self-consciousness and identity because they are constrained to invent and evaluate their identities through the grid of the white dominant culture. *See* RACE, CLASS, AND GENDER CRITICISM.

Bibliography. W. E. B. Du Bois, *The Souls of Black Folk* (New York: New American Library, 1969).

DOUBLE ENTENDRE

From the obsolete French *double entendre* (now *double entente*), the intentional use of a word or phrase that is sufficiently ambiguous in the CONTEXT to suggest two possible MEANINGS, one usually socially acceptable and the other frivolous, bawdy, or suggesting some impropriety. Alter finds examples of double entendre in the Song of Songs:

> Awake, O north wind,
>   and come, O south wind!
> Blow upon my garden
>   that its fragrance may be wafted abroad.
> Let my beloved come to his garden,
>   and eat its choicest fruits.
> I come to my garden, my sister, my bride;
>   I gather my myrrh with my spice
>   I eat my honeycomb with my honey,
>   I drink my wine with my milk. (Song 4:16–5:1)

On one level, words such as garden, choicest fruits, myrrh, spice, honeycomb, honey, and wine carry their ordinary meaning associated with a literal garden with its produce (or with feasting), but on another level (esp. given the greater context) the words carry erotic sexual overtones and suggest lovemaking.

Bibliography. Robert Alter, *The Art of Biblical Poetry* (New York: Basic Books, 1985).

DOUBLE MEANING

A type of IRONY in which a word or phrase can have two different MEANINGS in the same CONTEXT. For example, in his DIALOGUE with Nicodemus (John 3), Jesus tells Nicodemus that a person must be "born from above" in order to see the kingdom of God. The word Jesus uses is *anōthen*, which can mean either "from above" or "again." Nicodemus understands the word in the latter SENSE, which prompts Jesus to offer further EXPLANATION.

DOUBLET

A parallel or second VERSION of the same event or NARRATIVE, both of them growing out of the ORAL TRADITIONS of the Hebrews or the early Christians. As oral traditions developed in various locations and times, the same event was narrated with different details and then combined into a single narrative as two separate events. Doublets are fairly common in the HEBREW BIBLE. For example, Gen. 12:10–13 and 20:1–18 are two accounts in different contexts in which Abraham attempts to pass Sarah off as his sister. Furthermore, in Gen. 26:6–11, Isaac attempts the same maneuver with Rebekah. An example in the NT may be the double feeding miracle in Mark 6:35–44 and 8:1–9.

DOUBLE TRADITION

A term denoting the passages, especially DIDACTIC material, from the SYNOPTIC GOSPELS, found in both Matthew and Luke but not in Mark. In some instances, the material is verbatim in the two Gospels. In SOURCE CRITICISM, scholars hypothesize that this material may have been drawn from an independent sayings source called Q (*see* Q).

DOUBLE-VOICING. *See* dialogism.

DOUBLING

A phenomenon in BIBLICAL POETRY in which words in the first part of a line of VERSE are repeated with a synonym. For example, in Ps. 141:5a ("Let the righteous strike me; let the faithful correct me"), "the righteous" and "the faithful" are synonymous, as are "strike" and "correct."

However, as Robert Alter (14) points out, more often than not the doubling is not static but dynamic, with a movement of MEANING between the two parts or VERSETS. In Ps. 88:11, such a movement is evident: "Is your steadfast love declared in the grave / or your faithfulness in Abaddon?" While the first term in each verset ("steadfast love" and "faithfulness") remains static, the move from "grave" to "Abaddon" (perdition) is one in which the concreteness of the grave develops into the consequences of death.

Bibliography. Robert Alter, *The Art of Biblical Poetry* (New York: Basic Books, 1985).

DOXOLOGY

Technically, a praise to God. In the EPISTOLARY LITERATURE of the NT, especially in Paul, a variety of LITURGICAL FRAGMENTS (e.g., BEATITUDE, HYMN, CREED, BENEDICTION, acclamation) appear, the doxology being one of them. Since the Letters were probably intended to be read aloud in churches, it would not be unusual for Paul to include these liturgical fragments in his correspondence. The doxology has a three-part STRUCTURE: (1) an initial REFERENCE to God, (2) ascription of glory (*doxa*) to God, and (3) a concluding "Amen" (Bailey and Vander Broek, 74). Examples are Rom. 11:36; 16:25–27; and 1 Tim. 6:16.

Bibliography. James L. Bailey and Lyle D. Vander Broek, *Literary Forms in the New Testament: A Handbook* (Louisville: Westminster John Knox, 1992).

DRAMATIC IRONY

The situation in a STORY in which a character is not privy to some knowledge or understanding that the audience has. Because the audience enjoys the position of knowing the secret, dramatic interest is created. For example, the reader of Job knows the reasons behind Job's troubles, but Job does not, nor does he ever find out. It can be argued that the entire PLOT of Mark's GOSPEL is built on dramatic irony. The reader is supposed to have insights that the DISCIPLES do not. For example, when the disciples do not understand Jesus's predictions about his passion, the reader is expected to have insight into its MEANING and SIGNIFICANCE. Indeed, in one instance the NARRATOR of Mark makes a direct appeal to the reader's privileged status: "Let the reader understand!" (13:14).

DRAMATIC NARRATION. *See* NARRATION

DRAMATIC STRUCTURE

The technical ARRANGEMENT of material in a drama in order to create dramatic CONFLICT. For example, a well-constructed TRAGEDY will have five interrelated parts: introduction or EXPOSITION, RISING ACTION or COMPLICATION, CLIMAX or crisis (the turning point of the drama), FALLING ACTION, and catastrophe or DENOUEMENT. The exposition sets the CONTEXT and TONE of the drama; the complication introduces the various CONFLICTS; the climax or crisis is the high point of the ACTION, when the TENSIONS of the conflicts are at their highest point; and the falling action contains the consequences of the conflicts, which then lead to the catastrophe, usually the death or exile of the main character. It could be argued that the Gospel of Mark mirrors this dramatic structure (Puskas, 128–29):

Exposition (1:1–13)
Complication (rising action; 1:14–8:26)
Crisis (8:27–29)
Falling action (8:30–15:47)
Denouement (16:1–8)

See PLOT.

Bibliography. Charles B. Puskas, *An Introduction to the New Testament* (Peabody, MA: Hendrickson, 1989); Edgar V. Roberts and Henry E. Jacobs, *Literature: An Introduction to Reading and Writing* (7th ed.; Upper Saddle River, NJ: Pearson Prentice Hall, 2004).

DRAMATIS PERSONAE

Characters in a STORY.

DUAL TORAH. *See* TORAH

DUALISM

Generally, any view that allows for the existence of two fundamentally antithetical principles, such as good and evil or flesh and spirit. In the Western philosophical tradition, dualism is generally attributed to Plato, who posits two realms of being—the metaphysical world of ideal forms or essences (e.g., courage, beauty, justice), which are then reflected in the objects, actions, and institutions of the physical world. The physical world is at best only a shadowy reflection of the more important world of ideal forms. When the writer of the Epistle to the Hebrews makes a distinction between the heavenly temple and the earthly one, he is working within Platonic dualism. His definition of faith in 11:1 ("Now faith is the assurance of things hoped for, the conviction of things not seen") also reflects his dependence on a dualistic WORLDVIEW.

Also in BIBLICAL STUDIES, *dualism* is used to describe one of the characteristics of an APOCALYPTIC worldview as reflected in the book of Revelation. In cosmic dualism, working within the universe are an evil and a good principle almost equally matched. "Postulating a dualistic two-dimensional universe composed of visible earth and invisible heaven, apocalyptists see human society profoundly influenced by unseen forces—angels and demons—operating in a celestial realm. Events on earth, such as persecution of the righteous, reflect the machinations of these heavenly beings" (Harris, 397). Ethical dualism divides humans into two types—those who live in darkness and those who walk in light. In other words, in APOCALYPSE, persons who are beyond redemption are willing victims of a world that is intrinsically evil, while those of the writer's community are ethically superior and will eventually be vindicated by God. Ethical dualism also assumes that evil is a principle that both balances and opposes good and operates in the world of humans through some sort of agency. In the postexilic period of Hebrew culture, this agency was Satan, Belial, or Azazel and enters the GOSPELS as Beelzebul. Perhaps the Jewish view of the PERSONIFICATION of evil derives from Zoroastrianism, to which the Jews were exposed during the BABYLONIAN EXILE, but it may have its beginnings in its own history, as suggested by Gen. 6:1–4. Cosmic dualism differs from ethical dualism in that the conflict between good and evil assumes cosmic dimensions.

Bibliography. Stephen L. Harris, *The New Testament: A Student's Introduction* (4th ed.; Boston: McGraw-Hill, 2002).

DURATION

In NARRATOLOGY, the way in which the NARRATIVE handles EPISODES. Episodes may be expanded, summarized, or elided. In Gen. 37:36, the author summarizes Joseph's being sold into slavery: "Meanwhile the Midianites had sold him in Egypt to Potiphar, one of Pharaoh's officials, the captain of the guard." The author offers no details of the transaction. Two summaries of episodes flank an expanded episode in Gen. 39:10–23. Preceding the seduction episode (vv. 11–20), the text reads, "Although she [Potiphar's wife] spoke to Joseph day after day, he would not consent to lie beside her or to be with her" (v. 10); after the seduction episode, the AUTHOR presents an equally brief account of Joseph's tenure in prison: "He remained there in prison. But the LORD was with Joseph and showed him steadfast love; he gave him favor in the sight of the chief jailer" (vv. 20b–21). The way in which God actually blesses Joseph in prison is described in great detail in 39:21–41:40.

The narrative is elided (*see* ELLIPSIS) when "the discourse time stops while the STORY time continues" (Powell, 38). The reader therefore must assume that although the NARRATOR does not report what happens, time does continue within the story. As Powell (38) points out, the narratives of the GOSPELS are frequently elided. An example is in Mark 1:32–35: between verses 32–34 and 35, the reader must assume that the story time continues although the narrator does not disclose what happened in the intervening hours.

Bibliography. Mark Allan Powell, *What Is Narrative Criticism?* (Minneapolis: Fortress, 1990).

DYAD

A term in SOCIAL-SCIENTIFIC CRITICISM for a group-oriented personality. According to Malina and Neyrey, persons of the first-century CE

Mediterranean culture would not have understood themselves in terms of modern Western individualism. Rather, the "basic, most elementary unit of social analysis is not the individual but the dyad, a person in relation with and connected to at least one other social unit, in particular, the family. . . . Group-oriented persons internalize and make their own what others say, do, and think about them because they believe it is necessary if they are to be human beings, to live out the expectations of others" (73). When modern readers bring their individually oriented expectations of personality with them to the reading of the TEXTS of the BIBLE, they will inevitably misunderstand the text insofar as first-century AUTHORS and readers would have thought in terms of "concern for public awards of respect and honor" (67).

Bibliography. Bruce J. Malina and Jerome H. Neyrey, "First-Century Personality: Dyadic, Not Individualistic," in *The Social World of Luke-Acts: Models for Interpretation* (ed. Jerome H. Neyrey; Peabody, MA: Hendrickson, 1991).

DYNAMIC CHARACTER

In literature, a multidimensional and complex character, who manifests a range of character traits and changes or develops over time. This character confronts the reader with psychological, emotional, and spiritual complexities. Both David and his wife Michal are dynamic characters. The author goes to great lengths in presenting both with their own emotions and opinions. In most literature, the dynamic character is the PROTAGONIST. *See* CHARACTERIZATION.

DYNAMIC EQUIVALENCE/ TRANSLATION

A method of translating texts in which the SENSE and spirit of the source language are captured in the idioms, grammar, and SYNTAX of the target language. Translators employing this method are not overly concerned with producing a word-for-word VERSION but rather try to reflect the flavor of the source language in the target. Two variations of dynamic equivalence can be seen. The first is the idiomatic approach, in which translators try to use phrases that capture the MEANING of the TEXT but are not word-for-word TRANSLATIONS. In these texts—such as the Jerusalem Bible, the New English Bible, and the Revised English Bible—idioms in the source text are translated into the nearest equivalent idioms in the target language. The second approach is the common language approach, in which translators employ linguistic analysis based on theories of meaning communication. These translations, such as TODAY'S ENGLISH VERSION and the CONTEMPORARY ENGLISH VERSION, reflect the translators' interest in communicating meaning rather than details such as LITERARY qualities. *See* TRANSLATION; TRANSLATION STUDIES.

Bibliography. Steven M. Sheeley and Robert N. Nash Jr., *The Bible in English Translation: An Essential Guide* (Nashville: Abingdon, 1997).

DYNAMIC INTERPLAY

The relationship between the two or three cola of a line of BIBLICAL POETRY. In most lines, in which the second and/or third part repeats the first part either positively or negatively, the repetition is not simply static or verbatim. Instead, the second and/or third cola develop the first colon by means of INTENSIFICATION, clarification, expansion, and so forth.

DYSPHEMISM

The opposite of EUPHEMISM. Whereas euphemism is the deliberate use of language to avoid offense, dysphemism is direct to the extreme, often with the INTENTION of shocking the hearer. For example, using "senior citizen" for "old person" is a euphemism, but describing an elderly person as an "old coot" is a dysphemism. In the NT, Paul's use of *skybalon* (excrement) in Phil. 3:8 may be a dysphemism. Also, the language in Ezek. 16 may be dysphemic.

E

An abbreviation for "ELOHIST." *See* GRAF-WELL-
HAUSEN HYPOTHESIS.

ÉCRITURE

A key concept in the DECONSTRUCTION of
Jacques Derrida, who claims that the spoken
word has long been given precedence over the
written word because it has been assumed that
there is a higher degree of fidelity to the AUTHOR's
original MEANING—and less opportunity for
misunderstanding/MISREADING—with the work
of listening than with reading. "Writing" (*écriture*)
for Derrida is not the inscription of thought but
the fundamental human activity that precedes such
inscription. In most Western hermeneutical thinking, individuals are able to write a TEXT because
they have previously "read the world"; put another
way, the world of reality that we variously encode
within our texts already exists as a metaphysical
reality. It is a given. Derrida rejects this ASSUMP-
TION by claiming that the world we are capable
of knowing comes into being through the act of
"writing." There is no world waiting to be read.
Language is not rooted in a perceivable reality that
precedes it; on the contrary, language itself sets the
parameters of thought and therefore our world. If
this is the case, we cannot be aware of the presence
of that which is beyond our thoughts but only of
its ABSENCE (Walhout, 36).

In Derrida's estimation, since all human activity takes place in time, such activity is historically
bound. This does not mean that human activity
is in toto historically or culturally determined.
Human activity also determines and perpetually
reshapes and redefines culture. Culture does not
exist prior to individual acts of "writing." A priori

assumptions about reality may exist, but these are
themselves products of cultural "writings." This
is the reason Derrida can assert that "writing"
precedes SPEECH. It is simply impossible to know
something that exists prior to what is known.

> Bibliography. Clarence Walhout, "Texts and Actions," in
> *The Responsibility of Hermeneutics* (ed. Roger Lundin et
> al.; Grand Rapids: Eerdmans, 1985), 31–77.

EBLA TABLETS

Texts discovered in 1974–76 in Tell Mardikh in
northern Syria by Italian archaeologists. The texts
use cuneiform script and are in Sumerian and in a
previously unknown language now called Eblaite.
Containing texts from a wide spectrum of society
(e.g., economic, historical, judicial, administrative,
and literary) and syllabaries, they provide valuable knowledge about the third-millennium BCE
ancient Near East (Soulen and Soulen, 51). A good
technical source is Gordon's *Eblaitica*.

> Bibliography. C. H. Gordon et al., eds., *Eblaitica: Essays on
> the Ebla Archives and Eblaite Language* (Winona Lake, IN:
> Eisenbrauns, 1987); Richard N. Soulen and R. Kendall
> Soulen, *Handbook of Biblical Criticism* (3rd ed.; Louisville:
> Westminster John Knox, 2001).

ECOCRITICISM / ECOLOGICAL
HERMENEUTICS

A form of INTERPRETATION whose focus is a
radical reposturing of the READER before the
texts with a view of the earth as subject rather
than object. ECOLOGICAL HERMENEUTICS has
its roots in ECOCRITICISM (sometimes referred
to as environmental CRITICISM, green studies, or
nature criticism), whose scope of influence has
included everything from environmentalists who
use it as a voice for their own conservationist and
political viewpoints to critiques of Romantic works

like Thoreau's *Walden*. Although this method has normally been applied to "nature texts," biblical scholars have begun examining ways in which biblical texts can be interpreted through the lens of ecocriticism.

"The term 'ecocriticism' first appears in William Rueckert's 1978 essay 'Literature and Ecology: An Experiment in Ecocriticism,' in which he uses ecological principles as a model for thinking about how literature functions" (Gorn, 10). Although Rueckert may have introduced the POSTMODERN world to the mode of ecocriticism now emerging as a valid literary critique, its roots are ancient, relating all the way back to biblical and Mayan texts. "Humankind's earliest stories are of earth's creation, of its transformation by gods or human ingenuity's 'second nature,' as Cicero first called it—tales that frame environmental ethics in varied ways" (Buell, 2–3). Most ancient creation accounts include humans' *and* nature's roles in the world. As authors began to recognize nature's importance to society in literature, ecocriticism's scope began to broaden. In Romantic literature, ecocritics focused on the reassertion of nature in writing and its affirmation of the intrinsic value of nature in texts (Gifford, 38). Ecocritics moved beyond a study of environmentalism or a love of nature to a "proto ecological knowledge and environmentalist commitment" to the study of the way nature shapes literary theory and imagination (Buell, 2).

As a CRITICAL METHOD, ecocriticism appeared in two distinct phases. In *The Future of Environmental Criticism*, Lawrence Buell details these two phases and the way they have affected readers' views on nature and the environment in a text:

> "First wave" environmental criticism concerns itself with conventional nature writing and conservation-oriented environmentalism, which traces its origins to the work of Emerson, Muir, and Thoreau. "Second wave" environmental criticism redefines the environment in terms of the seventeen Principles of Environmental Justice and increasingly concerns itself with "issues of environmental welfare and equity" and "critique of the demographic homogeneity of traditional environmental movements

and academic environmental studies." (quoted in Adamson and Slovic, 1)

As ecocriticism has grown in acceptance and popularity over the past thirty years, "Rueckert's original usage of the term ecocriticism is narrower than what the term has [now] come to embrace" (Gorn, 10). Cheryll Glotfelty defines ecocriticism as "the study of the relationship between literature and the environment" ("Introduction," xvii). Modern use of ecocriticism has expanded to include nature not only as SETTING or SYMBOL but also as a tangible and important part of understanding culture and society. "Ecocriticism is not just a means of analyzing nature in literature; it implies a move toward a more biocentric WORLDVIEW, an extension of ethics, a broadening of humans' conception of global community to include non-human life forms and the physical environment" (Estok, 2). Although its original focus was on "romantic poetry, wilderness NARRATIVE, and nature writing," ecocriticism has now turned toward a more general and cultural definition of nature as its own character in works, which shapes or is shaped by the society that dwells within it (Garrard, 4).

> While a concentration on this form of writing makes perfect sense as a starting point for a critical school that takes the natural environment and human relations to that environment as its special focus, we believe that one of ecocriticism's most important tasks at this time is expanding its boundaries beyond these topics to address a wider spectrum of texts. (Armbruster and Wallace, 2)

With the increase in concern over environmental issues since Rueckert's introduction of the term, ecocriticism has also changed the way the term is perceived and accepted as a critical method. In recent years, ecocriticism has been linked to the "green" movement and the media's unfailing coverage and critique of all natural phenomena and society's reactions to them. More than ever, readers are looking to texts to explain not only the changes in environment but also what the appropriate response is to these changes. Ecocriticism "testifies to the need to correct somehow against the MARGINALIZATION of environmental issues in most versions of critical theory" (Buell, 3). Almost in parallel to Romanticism's lofty elevation of the natural world, recent ecocritics seek to reinstate the role of nature in literature. It is in this expansion and rebirth of modern ecocriticism that Adamson and Slovic find the emergence of a third wave of ecocriticism, which accounts for a more collective human experience in nature, one that recognizes "ethnic and national particularities and yet transcends ethnic and national boundaries" (2). Ecocritics seek not only to identify works of literature that function as mirrors or models of nature or affirm its value but also to reconcile nature and culture in literature. By expanding the previously narrow perspective of nature in culture, ecocritics began to provide a means of understanding how inextricably connected the two terms are. Yet in this paradigm the subjectivity of ecocriticism emerges. Nature can be experienced only through human interaction and knowledge, and this relationship often leads to an anthropocentric view of humanity's supposed authority over nature. (Ecocritical study has generally discarded this view, however, because of a lack of modes of observation of nature other than through human experience.) Ecocritics are now less concerned with the amount of "nature" in a text or its support of certain Romantic inclinations toward nature and more concerned with how the text connects humanity and nature and the effects of this connection. "What constitutes ecocritical work is intentionally broad and open-ended inasmuch as ecocriticism quite literally takes the entire world as its subject" (Gorn, 10).

In the ecocritical study of biblical texts, an ecological hermeneutic recognizes the biases in both readers and the texts that have generated an understanding of nonhuman entities as objects, thus creating a sense of distance from these non-human entities, which are seen as other and alien. Such a hermeneutic tries to counter these biases by redefining earth and its nonhuman entities as subjects, as ends in themselves and not as means to human ends and objects for human research and analysis.

Consequently, an ecological biblical hermeneutic rests on two key ideas: empathy and diversity. By empathy, the biblical ecocritic means that humans identify with earth, listening to earth's voice while reading. *Diversity* refers to the great variety of voices and communities that form an interconnected web of being and an openness to those voices.

What eventually developed into ecological hermeneutics had its genesis in the Earth Bible Project and a work edited by Norman Habel, *Readings from the Perspective of Earth*. From the outset, the participants in the project had to frame a set of six aims, out of which they developed six guiding principles. The six aims can be summarized as follows (Habel and Trudinger, 1–2):

1. To acknowledge that readers are anthropocentric and patriarchal in their approach to biblical texts
2. To admit that readers are participating members of communities that have exploited and raped the earth to such an extent that the survival of some species and even the earth itself are threatened
3. To recognize that we humans also constitute a community of an endangered earth, especially as we read ancient texts
4. To recognize and accept the earth as a subject in the text to whom we should give ear and not only as an object to critically examine
5. To become activists in the sense that we respond to earth and communities where they have been subject to injustice and oppression as we read the texts
6. To formulate interpretive strategies that will retrieve those instances where the voices of earth and earth communities have been silenced

As stated above, out of these six aims, the project team developed six principles in conversation with ecologists (for a development and explanation of the principles, see Habel, "Guiding"). After some further refinements of the principles and in conversation with other critical approaches that had already wrestled with issues of injustice, AN-THROPOCENTRISM, PATRIARCHY, and imperialism (e.g., FEMINIST CRITICISM; POSTCOLONIAL CRITICISM), the Earth Bible team collapsed the six principles into three steps, which constitute a radical approach to reading and interpreting biblical texts: (1) HERMENEUTICS OF SUSPICION, (2) identification, and (3) retrieval.

The first step, a hermeneutic of suspicion, rests on an ASSUMPTION that both the text and past readings are inherently anthropocentric. In other words, the anthropocentric bias may reside in the text or interpretive tradition or both. Most often this ANTHROPOCENTRISM expresses itself in two ways. First, humans assume that they are of a natural order in which everything nonhuman is subject to human control, that humans form a community distinctly different from and superior to all other earth communities. Second, humans tend to think of earth and all of its nonhuman earth communities as objects to be exploited for human benefit and profit. They have no value as subjects in themselves.

The second step, identification, requires that readers in some way admit to their deep-rooted connections to earth and its nonhuman communities. In other words, readers should accept that they are part of the ecological web of being, not separate from or above it. With respect to reading, this step involves identifying instances in the text where the earth has suffered injustices and exploitations from humans or God. The critic exposes those instances in which the earth and its communities have suffered abuse and then finds the instances and ways that the earth and its communities have resisted such abuse and injustice. It is in this exposure that readers take up the cause of ecological justice.

In the third step, retrieval, the reader looks for instances in which nonhuman characters play significant roles in the story, roles that anthropocentric readings have ignored or suppressed. For example, texts may refer to nonhuman characters as mourning, praising, singing, or laughing. Traditionally, critics have simply explained such voices

as anthropomorphisms: the assigning of human characteristics to nonhuman entities. They are metaphorical (*see* METAPHOR). The retrieval of explicit and implicit voices of earth and nonhuman entities as integral characters in the text is the heart of the retrieval step. The reader will assume that these characters are more than mere literary embellishment or ornate scenery; rather, they are voices to be heard. To reconstruct these voices (which do not often correspond to the constructs of human language) may be a tricky task, but ecocritics claim that readers can exegete a text in such a way that earth and/or its nonhuman subjects become major voices, NARRATORS, or even interpreters of the text.

Melissa Tubbs Loya offers a good example of ecological hermeneutics at work in her treatment of Hosea 4:1–3. In this passage, Yahweh brings a covenant lawsuit against the inhabitants of the land for breaking the covenant. The land's people have committed crimes against the land, which prompts Yahweh to bring the lawsuit. However, as Loya points out, even though Yahweh does bring the lawsuit, he is not the executor of it. She says that when we recognize the earth's reaction to the people's sins and impact on the land ("The land mourns") and the subsequent description of the ecological effects, the earth becomes an agent of action, or better, the executor of the lawsuit (55–56). The earth's mourning is more than anthropomorphism; it has an effect on the earth. In Gen. 1:1–2:4a, the author lays out the order of God's creating activity; God creates in a particular order—the fish, birds, cattle, and wild animals. The order is repeated when God gives humans dominion over the earth. However, Hosea reverses the order, as if unmaking creation (60). In Hosea, we see the earth with an active role in responding to the sins of the people of the land, which threaten the order of creation.

The Bible not only provides a detailed creation account in Genesis, which authors like Buell have already recognized for its potential value in ecocritical study, but also provides a guide for humans' action and treatment of the natural world as created by God. Betsy S. Hilbert recognizes the ecocritical potential in the Bible, especially in the Torah. Hilbert focuses specifically on the book of Deuteronomy, which "centers on a sense of place" (29). As the fifth and final book of the Torah, Deuteronomy concludes the Israelites' journey out of Egypt, into the wilderness, and finally into Canaan, the promised land. "In the ensuing narrative, Moses will remind his people over and over that the price of their continuance in the promised land is social justice—justice not only among themselves but [also] for every occupant: human, animal, and the land" (29). The Mosaic law in Deuteronomy explains God's behavioral standards for the Israelites, addressing everything from sexuality to preservation of nature and the fair treatment of animals. The Israelites must follow these laws to remain in God's favor and in the land he has given them (the issue of taking another people's land by force is another matter). In Deuteronomy, culture and nature cannot be separated; without the given promised land, the Israelite culture would not exist. It is not only by the installation of Mosaic law that the landscape is made paramount but also through the framing of Deuteronomy with accounts of landscape and journey. Here ecocritics find an instinctive human connection to the land without claims of dominating ownership.

> Deuteronomy is suffused with the theme of connection to the landscape; it consistently expounds the idea that human beings, in their intricate connections to the earth and to one another, bear the responsibility of justice and righteousness as a condition of their continued survival in the places that give them nurture. (29)

Cheryll Glotfelty sounds a similar note in her reading of Gen. 1:26: "Then God said, 'Let us make humankind in our image, according to our likeness; and let them have dominion over the fish of the sea, and over the birds of the air, and over the cattle, and over all the wild animals of the earth, and over every creeping thing that creeps on the earth.'" Glotfelty labels this reading anthropocentric because it separates humans and nature and places

humans in dominion over nature, which creates an arrogance rather than humility toward nature. Ecocritics condemn anthropocentrism because it creates an environment in which humans abuse and discard nature because they have full control over it (38–39). There is no "wise acceptance of limitations and compliance with natural laws" (6).

Using Gen. 1:26 as his starting point, Greg Garrard finds that the common assumptions about the role of nature in the Bible are widely misunderstood. Humans are neither solely intelligent caretakers nor rulers of environment but are, instead, ruled by nature and its forces. Garrard explains that in biblical texts, nature is "God's tool of reward and punishment." This role of nature is clear in the ecological catastrophes of the OT, such as the flooding of the earth in Genesis and the plagues in Exodus. Nature is either the loving PROTAGONIST or the raging ANTAGONIST, controlling the action of the people involved. According to Garrard, this view seems most plausible because it does not place humans in a semisubmissive role to nature in which they must obey its laws or be punished, but neither does it give humans complete dominion over nature to control and manipulate it. Instead, nature and culture are connected and affected by each other, and this is the purest ecocritical premise.

Ecological biblical hermeneutics offers a way of reading the biblical texts that elevates earth and its nonhuman communities to active participants in the ongoing business of life; at the same time, it raises awareness of the intricate relationship between earth and humans. However, ecocritics have recognized the need to move from hermeneutics to what we may call activism. These critics have begun framing the discussion in ways that are inclusive of the great variety of theological communities, moving the discussion beyond the academy into communities of faith. A primary issue, then, is how to frame the hermeneutical construction in ways that do not alienate the voices of the communities of faith who do believe the Bible to be their guide to faith and behavior. As evidence that ecocritics are cognizant of this issue, Habel, Rhoads, and Santmire have edited a book (*Season of Creation*) in which they offer a plan for preaching on creation that reflects the ideas of ecological hermeneutics, a move from the academy to the local church.

Bibliography. Joni Adamson and Scott Slovic, "Guest Editor's Introduction: The Shoulders We Stand On; An Introduction to Ethnicity and Ecocriticism," *MELUS: Multi-Ethnic Literature of the U.S.* 34, no. 2 (2009): 5–209; Karla Armbruster and Kathleen R. Wallace, eds., *Beyond Nature Writing: Expanding the Boundaries of Ecocriticism* (Charlottesville: University of Virginia Press, 2001); Fiona Becket and Terry Gifford, eds., *Culture, Creativity and Environment: New Environmentalist Criticism* (Amsterdam: Rodphi, 2007); Lawrence Buell, *The Future of Environmental Criticism: Environmental Crisis and Literary Imagination* (Malden, MA: Blackwell, 2005); Simon C. Estok, "A Report Card on Ecocriticism," *AUMLA: Journal of Australasian Universities Modern Language Association* 96 (November 2001): 220–38; Greg Garrard, *Ecocriticism* (New York: Routledge, 2004); Cheryll Glotfelty, "Introduction: Literary Studies in an Age of Environmental Crisis," in *The Ecocriticism Reader: Landmarks in Literary Ecology* (ed. Cheryll Glotfelty and Harold Fromm; Athens: University of Georgia Press, 1996); idem, "The Strong Green Thread," in *Essays in Ecocriticism* (ed. Nirmal Selvamony and Rayson K. Alex; Chennai: OSLE-India; New Delhi: Sarup & Sons, 2007), 1–10; Heather Gorn, "Ecocriticism: The Intersection of Literature and the Environment," *Vegetarian Journal* 30, no. 2 (2011): 10–11; Norman C. Habel, "Guiding Ecojustice Principles," in *Readings from the Perspective of Earth* (ed. Norman C. Habel; Earth Bible 1; Sheffield: Sheffield Academic Press, 2000), 38–53; idem, "The Origins and Challenges of an Ecojustice Hermeneutic," in *Relating to the Text: Interdisciplinary and Form Critical Insights on the Bible* (ed. Timothy Sandoval and Carleen Mandolfo; London: T&T Clark, 2003), 141–59; idem, ed., *Readings from the Perspective of Earth* (Earth Bible 1; Sheffield: Sheffield Academic Press, 2000); Norman C. Habel, David M. Rhoads, and H. Paul Santmire, eds., *The Season of Creation: A Preaching Commentary* (Minneapolis: Fortress, 2011); Norman C. Habel and Peter Trudinger, eds., *Exploring Ecological Hermeneutics* (Atlanta: Society of Biblical Literature, 2008); Betsy S. Hilbert, "Beyond 'Thou Shalt Not': An Ecocritic Reads Deuteronomy," in *Beyond Nature Writing: Expanding the Boundaries of Ecocriticism* (ed. Karla Armbruster and Kathleen R. Wallace; Charlottesville: University of Virginia Press, 2001), 29–44; Melissa Tubbs Loya, "'Therefore the Earth Mourns': The Grievance of Earth in Hosea 4:1–3," in *Exploring Ecological Hermeneutics* (ed. Norman C. Habel and Peter Trudinger; Atlanta: Society of Biblical Literature, 2008), 53–62; William Rueckert, "Literature and Ecology: An Experiment in Ecocriticism," reprinted in *The Ecocriticism Reader: Landmarks in Literary Ecology* (ed. Cheryll Glotfelty and Harold Fromm; Athens: University of Georgia Press, 1996).

EIDETIC REDUCTION. *See* PHENOMENOLOGICAL CRITICISM

EISEGESIS

Reading MEANING into a TEXT. The opposite of EXEGESIS, which means reading meaning out of a text. Eisegesis may occur by reading a meaning derived from one text into another, usually earlier, text. It may also occur by investing a text with meaning by reading it through the grid of a theological system and thereby reading a theological idea into a text. Many postmodern scholars claim that all interpretation is eisegetical and, consequently, so is meaning. In other words, there is simply no guarantee that readers (professional or otherwise) can assume a posture of absolute objectivity, which would enable them to tease AUTHORIAL INTENTION out of a text. Readers invest texts with meaning and yet are apt to assume that the meaning derives in toto from the text itself.

EKKLĒSIA

A term used for "church" in the NT, derived from the Greek words for "call" and "out." Though Matthew is the only GOSPEL in which the term is found, it does occur throughout the NT (e.g., Matt. 18:17; Acts 5:11; 1 Cor. 4:17; Rev. 1:4, and many other places). It does, however, have meanings other than "church." For example, in Acts 19:32 and 41, the term means assemblage or meeting, and in Acts 7:38 it means "the congregation of the Israelites." It may also become more nuanced to refer to the church as the "totality of Christians living in one place" (e.g., Acts 5:11; 1 Cor. 4:17; Phil. 4:15), "house churches" (e.g., Rom. 16:5; 1 Cor. 16:19), "the church universal" (e.g., Matt. 16:18; Eph. 1:22), the "church of God" (e.g., 1 Cor. 1:2; 2 Cor. 1:1; Gal. 1:13; 1 Thess. 2:14), "church of Christ" (e.g., Rom. 16:16), or "church of the saints" (1 Cor. 14:33).

Bibliography. W. Bauer, F. W. Danker, W. F. Arndt, and F. W. Gingrich, *Greek-English Lexicon of the New Testament and*

Other Early Christian Literature (3rd ed.; Chicago: University of Chicago Press, 2000), 303–4.

EKKLESIA OF WO/MEN

A phrase introduced by Elisabeth Schüssler Fiorenza to name "both a radical democratic discursive and political formation, and the center and horizon of a critical feminist hermeneutics and rhetorics of liberation" (174). For her, the concept is at the heart of a critical FEMINIST HERMENEUTICS. It endorses practices of self-affirmation and solidarity and discusses challenges with a view toward enabling women to work toward total emancipation from sociopolitical, religious, and other oppressive situations inherent in what she calls KYRIARCHY, the structures in Western traditions that have precluded full citizenship and self-determination for women. In terms of the feminist tradition, it calls for the democratic equality of women and, in religious terms, for the "discipleship of equals" (179).

Bibliography. Elisabeth Schüssler Fiorenza, *Bread Not Stone* (10th anniversary ed.; Boston: Beacon, 1995).

ELABORATION. *See* AMPLIFICATION

ELEGY

In Latin and Greek literature, a type of meditation on subjects such as love, death, and war. Although the term assumed a number of MEANINGs through the centuries (e.g., the Elizabethan poets defined it as a love poem with a complaint theme; in the seventeenth century, the term was used for a love poem or a poem of LAMENT), it eventually came to mean a poem of mourning, especially over the death of a person. Possible examples of a biblical elegy are 2 Sam. 1:19–27 and Isa. 14:1–31.

ELLIPSIS

A rhetorical device in which one or more words are omitted, with the understanding that the reader will supply them. Unlike their modern use, ellipses were not marked in ancient texts. For example, in 2 Pet. 1:5–7, the passage begins with "For this very reason, you must make every effort to sup-

port your faith with goodness, and goodness with knowledge." The words "make every effort to support your" are stated only once and implied in the rest of the passage. Some scholars argue that in James 1:13b, "For God cannot be tempted by evil and he himself tempts no one," an ellipsis occurs at the end of the sentence and that the sentence should read, "for God cannot be tempted by evil and he himself tempts no one *with evil.*" Ellipsis is common in the parallelism of BIBLICAL POETRY, as in Ps. 68:21: "But God will shatter the heads of his enemies, the hairy crown of those who walk in their guilty ways."

ELOHIST

In classical SOURCE CRITICISM of the HEBREW BIBLE, one of the sources used in the composition of the PENTATEUCH. The Elohist favors the name Elohim (ʾĕlōhîm, as in Gen. 1:1) for God and associates the divine name Yahweh with a revelation to Moses. The hand of the Elohist is found primarily in the PATRIARCHAL NARRATIVES. The Elohist depicts divine revelation as occurring through indirect means, such as dreams (Gen. 20:3) or a divine messenger (21:17). The vocabulary of the Elohist is also distinctly different from that of the YAHWIST (e.g., the reference to Mount Horeb instead of Mount Sinai, and Amorites instead of Canaanites). The Elohist source may date to the ninth or eighth century BCE in northern Palestine. *See* GRAF-WELLHAUSEN HYPOTHESIS.

EMANCIPATORY PRAXIS

In FEMINIST CRITICISM, both a hermeneutical focus and a result. Within the CONTEXT of women's struggle to free themselves of all oppressive PATRIARCHAL STRUCTURES and models, a critical approach to evaluating biblical TEXTS, TRADITIONS, and INTERPRETATIONS must be formulated. According to Elisabeth Schüssler Fiorenza (58–63), the evaluative criteria for these texts, traditions, and interpretations must be the experiences of oppression and liberation. Such a critical approach will seek to uncover and reject traditions and theological systems that perpetuate oppression, violence, and ALIENATION while promoting traditions that encourage the emancipation of the oppressed. Consequently, only nonpatriarchal, nonsexist biblical traditions and interpretive paradigms will be accepted as possessing any authority. Such a critical hermeneutic of liberation should result in ongoing emancipatory practices.

Bibliography. Elisabeth Schüssler Fiorenza, *Bread Not Stone* (10th anniversary ed.; Boston: Beacon, 1995).

EMBELLISHED STORY

A basic STORY that the AUTHOR expands and places in a NARRATIVE CONTEXT. For example, the stories in John's GOSPEL begin with an EPISODE from Jesus's life, but within the narrative the author expands the event by transforming it from a simple episode to one that takes on spiritual SYMBOLISM (John 6:1–71). In this particular episode, the feeding story is expanded to a narrative on the eucharistic value of Jesus, onward to the nature of his message, and also to a DISCOURSE on belief and disbelief.

Bibliography. Leland Ryken, *Words of Life: A Literary Introduction to the New Testament* (Grand Rapids: Baker, 1987).

EMBLEMATIC PARALLELISM

According to Gabel and Wheeler, a type of synonymous parallelism "in which the thought is expressed half literally and half metaphorically" (39). An example is Job 14:1–2:

> A mortal, born of woman, few of days and full
> of trouble,
> comes up like a flower and withers, flees like a
> shadow and does not last.

The first line is a literal statement of the plight of the human, while the second line is a metaphorical expansion of the literal condition. *See* BIBLICAL POETRY.

Bibliography. John B. Gabel and Charles B. Wheeler, *The Bible as Literature: An Introduction* (New York: Oxford University Press, 1986).

EMOTIVE LANGUAGE. *See* REFERENTIAL LANGUAGE

ENACTMENT/REALIZATION

Two terms used by F. R. Leavis to describe a property of LITERARY LANGUAGE. In opposition to the static, naming quality of the ordinary, everyday use of language, literary language does not simply name or reflect some external object or state of existence but also performs, enacts, or incarnates the object or state of existence in its FORMS, figures, and RHYTHM; literary language also invites the reader to become involved in the act of realization. Seen from this perspective, the BIBLE AS LITERATURE does not simply tell its stories but also performs them before the reader, perhaps inviting participation.

Bibliography. John Casey, *The Language of Criticism* (London: Methuen, 1966).

ENCODING. *See* CODE; DECODING/ENCODING

ENCOMIUM

A praise of a living great person, character TYPE, abstract quality, or event in Greek literature. Although the Hebrews preserved stories about religious and political heroes (e.g., Samson, David, Deborah) that may serve as the LITERARY antecedents for the GOSPELs, the eulogistic accounts typical of encomium may also serve as antecedents. Leland Ryken claims that "the encomium is one of the most refreshing and artistic forms in the Bible" (293). According to Ryken (293), not only does encomium occur in the OT and the NT; its biblical examples have a number of common MOTIFS:

1. The introduction of the SUBJECT to receive praise
2. A description of the subject's distinguished ancestry
3. A listing of the subject's praiseworthy acts/qualities
4. A description of the subject's superior nature
5. A plea to the reader to emulate the subject

Ryken (294–311) suggests that Pss. 1; 15; 112; Prov. 3:13–20; and 31:10–31 are examples from the OT and that John 1:1–18; 1 Cor. 13; Col. 1:15–20; and Heb. 11 are NT examples.

Bibliography. Leland Ryken, *Words of Delight: A Literary Introduction to the Bible* (Grand Rapids: Baker, 1987).

ENCOUNTER STORY

A story in the GOSPELS in which Jesus encounters a single person or a group. The stories of Zacchaeus (Luke 19:1–10) and the rich young man (Matt. 19:16–30) are examples. Usually the person or group will react positively or negatively to the encounter's demand. The person or group also serves as a symbol or representative of people in general with similar problems or situations; this invites the reader to identify with the person(s). In other words, Jesus makes a claim or poses a response, to which the person(s) must react.

ENCULTURATION

In BIBLICAL STUDIES, the practice of adapting the INTERPRETATION and proclamation of the Bible to different cultural CONTEXTS.

ENCYCLOPEDIAS. *See* DICTIONARIES/ ENCYCLOPEDIAS

ENDOGAMY

A marriage within one's group, family, tribe, or class, thus preserving the wealth and status of the group and individuals in the group. In SOCIAL-SCIENTIFIC CRITICISM, the term is used to describe a characteristic of the social structure of ancient Israel's kinship system. Endogamous marriage was the norm and functioned to maintain the family lineage through the male.

ENGLISH REVISED VERSION. *See* REVISED VERSION

ENTHRONEMENT PSALMS

PSALMS that proclaim the Lord as King (e.g., Ps. 96). They may have been used in an annual enthronement festival in Israel at the beginning of a new agricultural year, in the autumn, when Yahweh was enthroned as king. Although there is no solid evidence of such a festival, some scholars have suggested that there was an annual Zion festival in association with the enthronement of the Davidic king, a festival in which these psalms were sung. Other possibilities are Pss. 20; 21; 45; 72; 89; 101; 110; 132.

ENVELOPE STRUCTURE

Also known as *Wiederaufnahme*, or (narrative) resumption. A LITERARY technique of repeating, at the end of a unit of TEXT, an idea or statement that begins the unit, thus suggesting that the materials between these literary bookends are thematically related. Examples may be found frequently in both the HEBREW BIBLE and the NT. In Amos 9:1–4, the idea of God's slaying with a sword is introduced in verse 1 and repeated in verse 4. In Mark 9:36, Jesus sets a child among his disciples and begins to teach them about discipleship. In 10:13, children are introduced again. *See* INCLUSIO.

EPANAPHORA. *See* ANAPHORA

EPIC

A long NARRATIVE poem whose PROTAGONIST is a famous hero, often with national significance. Epic may incorporate LEGEND, MYTH, history, and/or FOLKLORE. Other elements may include extraordinary deeds of heroism and courage, supernatural participants in the ACTION, an elevated STYLE, a broad SETTING, a statement of the THEME or purpose of the poem, the invocation of muses, and SPEECHes by the main characters. Some of the better-known epics are Homer's *Iliad* and *Odyssey*; the *Song of Roland*; *Beowulf*; Virgil's *Aeneid*; Dante's *Divine Comedy*; and Milton's *Paradise Lost*.

Since the book of Acts contains some of these elements—famous heroes, extraordinary deeds, supernatural figures, broad geographical sweep, and speeches by the main characters—some commentators such as Bonz have suggested that it is an early Christian epic. MacDonald examines the parallels between Homer's epics and the Gospel of Mark. Ryken has examined three books/stories as epic in terms of style, supernatural participants, cosmic sweep, and focus on conquest: the book of Revelation (*Words of Life*), the exodus, and the STORY of David (*Words of Delight*).

Bibliography. Marianne Palmer Bonz, *The Past as Legacy: Luke-Acts and Ancient Epic* (Minneapolis: Fortress, 2000); Dennis R. MacDonald, *The Homeric Epics and the Gospel of Mark* (New Haven: Yale University Press, 2000); Leland Ryken, *Words of Delight: A Literary Introduction to the Bible* (Grand Rapids: Baker, 1987); idem, *Words of Life: A Literary Introduction to the New Testament* (Grand Rapids: Baker, 1986).

EPICUREANISM

A Hellenistic philosophy deriving from the Greek philosopher Epicurus (341–270 BCE). Epicureanism advocated the higher pleasures of the mind along with an emphasis on friendship and contentment. Like Paul, Epicurus was a father figure to his followers: he founded communities of followers and instructed these communities through LETTERS. Unlike Paul, his birthday was celebrated annually, and his followers bestowed divine honors on him.

Epicurus sought to deliver his followers from what he perceived to be the darkness of religion. He accomplished this through his materialistic approach to the universe. If the soul itself is a type of physical object composed of atoms, it will die when the body dies. Therefore, since the soul does not survive the death of the body, there is no future life of bliss or punishment to worry about now. If there is no future life to be concerned about, we should live with our attention directed squarely toward this life, of which the highest good is tranquility, the absence of agitation.

Also basic to Epicureanism is the ideal of maximizing pleasure and minimizing pain. But Epicurus considered the pleasures of the mind most desirable and the pleasures of the stomach least desirable. He further classified all human desires as natural and unnatural. He divided natural desires into necessary and unnecessary (e.g., food and sex respectively). The necessary desires he further divided into things needed for life (food, shelter, clothing), for ease (a good bed), and for happiness (friendship, contemplation, knowledge). The last especially should lead to the tranquility of the soul.

In the wake of the devaluating effects of the universalization of HELLENISM, Epicurus succeeded in substituting a circle of close friends and associates to compensate for that loss. Within the circle of friends, one finds the greatest pleasure of the soul and a sense of community. This idea of friendship is basic, for the individual is a stranger in the world.

Some similarities between Epicurean and early Christian communities exist, but they are only superficial. Still, Epicureans and Christians were responding to the same loss precipitated by Hellenism: the devaluation of the individual. Characteristic of both was the founding of a community where all were equal—whether slave, free, woman, or man—and where the community was insulated and separated from the world and bound together by worship and reverence (e.g., the characteristics found in 1 Thess. 4:9–12). Gilbert Murray has suggested that the early Christian communities were patterned after the Epicurean communities, even down to the use of the title "friends" in John 15:15 and 3 John 15. *See* HELLENISTIC PHILOSOPHIES.

Bibliography. Gilbert Murray, *Five Stages of Greek Religion* (Garden City, NY: Doubleday, 1955).

EPIDEICTIC

In RHETORIC, one of the three major Greco-Roman categories of rhetorical STYLE, in which praise or blame is used to urge a person or persons to accept a particular point of view or a set of values in the present. *See* RHETORICAL CRITICISM.

EPIGRAM

A short, witty SAYING in VERSE or PROSE. Originally an inscription found on monuments or statues, the epigram later became a literary GENRE among the Greeks and Romans and popular among the seventeenth-century metaphysical poets in England and again in nineteenth-century England. Some authors, however, have used the epigram in prose FORM. For example, J. H. Cabell offers, "The optimist proclaims that we live in the best of all possible worlds; and the pessimist fears this is true." In the HEBREW BIBLE, we find both the MASHAL (*māšāl*) and the *melitzah* (*mĕlîṣâ*), which the NRSV translates "PROVERB" and "figure" respectively, but which the Jewish Study Bible translates "proverb" and "epigram." While the distinction between the proverb and the epigram is not always clear, the difference may lie in the wit, humor, and/or SATIRE usually associated with the epigram (e.g., epigram: "Like vinegar to the teeth, and smoke to the eyes, so are the lazy to their employers" [Prov. 10:26]; proverb: "If you are wise, you are wise for yourself; if you scoff, you alone will bear it" [9:12]).

Bibliography. J. A. Cuddon, *The Penguin Dictionary of Literary Terms and Literary Theory* (4th ed.; London: Penguin, 1998).

EPIGRAPH

An inscription on a surface such as marble, stone, a building, a statue, an ostracon (potsherd), or a coin. In some cases the only extant instances of an ancient language are epigraphic in nature.

EPIGRAPHY

The study and INTERPRETATION of EPIGRAPHS. The most recognized sources for inscriptions relevant to biblical study are James B. Pritchard, *Ancient Near Eastern Texts Relating to the Old Testament* (3rd ed.; Princeton: Princeton University Press, 1969), and William W. Hallo, *The Context of Scripture* (3 vols.; Leiden: Brill, 2003).

EPILOGUE

A concluding statement or remark of an actor to the audience. Although the epilogue was popular during the Age of Reason (seventeenth and eighteenth centuries), it is not common today. In BIBLICAL STUDIES, the term is sometimes used to refer to the conclusion of some TEXTS, such as John 21:24–25 and Rev. 22:8–21, where the author addresses the readers directly. *See* PROLOGUE.

EPINICION

Originally an ODE or song celebrating a victory in the Greek Olympics. The term, however, has been applied in BIBLICAL STUDIES to refer to a song commemorating a victory in battle. Examples are Judg. 5; 15:16; and Exod. 15:21.

Bibliography. Richard N. Soulen and R. Kendall Soulen, *Handbook of Biblical Criticism* (3rd ed.; Louisville: Westminster John Knox, 2001).

EPIPHANY

An appearance or manifestation of the divine to humans. The manifestation may take place through natural or physical events and objects or through supernatural events such as the possession by a god. The appearance of the Spirit in Acts 2, Paul's conversion in Acts 9, the call of Moses in Exod. 3, the call of Isaiah in Isa. 6, and the call of Ezekiel in Ezek. 1—all these are instances of epiphany.

EPIPHORA

A LITERARY DEVICE in which a word or group of words is repeated at the end of two or more consecutive lines in poetry or prose. Although most are lost in TRANSLATION, there are some examples, especially in the NT (e.g., the REPETITION of "Jews" and "law" in 1 Cor. 9:19–21 and "weak" in 1 Cor. 9:22). *See* ANAPHORA.

EPISODE

In a STORY, the NARRATION of an event as a single continuous ACTION. For example, in Mark's Gospel, the narration of the beheading of John the Baptist, the baptism of Jesus, and the cleansing of the temple are each episodes.

EPISODIC STRUCTURE

When the EPISODES in a STORY are not arranged according to any apparent logical sequence, it is said to have an episodic structure, which does not create narrative COMPLICATION. Some POSTMODERN literary CRITICS argue that all stories are episodic and place demands on the reader to make SENSE of the story by supplying logical connections between the episodes. For example, because Mark's Gospel places one episode within another (e.g., the story of Jairus's daughter and the hemorrhaging woman in Mark 5), the reader is expected to ask about their relationships. The same may be said about Mark's recording of two feeding miracles (Mark 6; 8).

EPISTEME

A Greek word used by Foucault to name the discursive practices (*see* DISCOURSE) and historical conditions that underlie theories of knowledge in any field of study (e.g., science, theology, politics). The consequence of such a notion is that epistemologies (i.e., theories of knowledge) are always historically conditioned human constructs rather than representations of natural givens or reflections of the way things are. So at any moment, the examination of a range of knowledge fields or systems will expose a set of discursive structures, or epistemes, on which all fields are constructed and which by their discursive nature ground all knowledge in history. Accordingly, an examination of the cosmologies (*see* COSMOLOGY) in the HEBREW BIBLE and NT should reveal their being locally, historically constructed, thus challenging their universality. Cosmology is a way of looking at the world based on the episteme of a particular time and place.

Bibliography. Michel Foucault, *The Archaeology of Knowledge* (trans. A. M. Sheridan Smith; New York: Pantheon, 1972).

EPISTLE. *See* EPISTOLARY LITERATURE

EPISTOLARY LITERATURE

In general, PROSE literature written in the FORM of a letter. The epistolary literature in the NT consists of twenty-one writings that display the formal features of a letter to varying degrees, along with letters embedded within other books. Since this literature was written primarily during the first century CE, it mirrors the formal features of Hellenistic epistolary writing. Letter writing in HELLENISM followed a stereotypical form:

Opening, or Prescript. This consists of three parts: the AUTHOR's name, the addressee's name, and a greeting. The greeting is often a wish for good health, a prayer-wish, and various other information that may be offered concerning the writer or addressee.

Body. Here the purpose of the letter is elaborated. It may be brief or long. The body proper is quite often prefaced with a prayer to the gods, an expression of thanksgiving, further mention of the author's circumstances, or some mention of a favorable remembrance of the addressee. These preliminary statements serve as a transition from the opening to the body and make explicit the relationship between the writer and the addressee. However, in many instances these transitional matters are omitted, and the writer moves directly to the body. Attached to the end of the body proper may also be a request for reciprocal communication, notification of a prospective visit, or a challenge to action.

Closing. The closing usually consists of a final greeting. It may also include a second wish for health for the addressee and/or other persons. A word of farewell (*errōsthe*) is usually placed at the end along with the date.

The letter expressed a relationship of friendship between two parties and was to have a certain "presence" about it, substituting for the actual PRESENCE of the writer. Thus a person would write to someone as if the addressee were present. The Hellenistic letter is extremely stereotyped. The salutation, final greeting, and prayer (or wish for health) appear in Hellenistic letters with almost predictable wording. David Aune (162), describing what he calls the private or documentary letter with its three-part STRUCTURE, observes that the basic structure of the letter varied only slightly over the centuries. Within the basic three-part structure, however, there was room for modifications. For example, within the prescript of the typical letter occur three elements: the superscription, the adscription, and the salutation. Each of these could be expanded, and epithets, titles, geographical references, a health wish, or a prayer might be added.

Aune goes on to describe two other categories of Greco-Roman letters; these he calls official letters and literary letters. Official letters were from government officials to someone often in a government position. They were very similar to the private letter. Literary letters were preserved and valued primarily for their artistic qualities. These letters fall into three categories. First, letters of recommendation were written by educated persons who had no intention of publishing them. These allowed an influential person to recommend a friend for a particular political or civil position. The framers of such letters made their recommendations on the basis of moral traits rather than on vocational ability. Second, letter-essays are properly treatises rather than formal letters because they use the standard epistolary structure in a limited fashion. While they may display the customary opening and closing, these letters are actually philosophical or ethical treatises (e.g., Quintilian's *Institutes* and Plutarch's O*n Tranquillity*). Epicurus, Diogenes Laertius, and even Plato and Aristotle used the letter as a means of philosophical instruction. Third, pseudepigraphical letters were fictional presentations of stories about great men of the past. Other fictional letters, which Aune terms imaginative letters, were written in the names of the past, often in an explicit attempt to capture the WORLDVIEW of people from the past (Aune, 165–69).

Although it seems that the personal letter was the norm in Hellenism, there were instances (Epicurus, Seneca) in which ethical questions were addressed in the form of the letter. These were actually treatises and not letters in the strict sense, and they were probably written with the intention of producing a highly LITERARY document. This observation has led some scholars to make a distinction between *letter* and *epistle* (e.g., Gabel and Wheeler; Fee and Stuart). This distinction is based on whether the audience is private or public; a letter is seen as being nonliterary and written for an individual or particular audience, whereas an epistle is regarded as literary and written for posterity or the public. Second Peter, 1 John, and James are cited as examples of the epistle. For instance, neither James nor 2 Peter has a final greeting or a specific addressee. Gabel and Wheeler (216) suggest that genuine letters differ from epistles in that epistles were intended for publication rather than for mailing. These scholars feel that the most

distinctive aspect of NT letters is their occasional nature. They were not written for posterity but were intended to address the particular and actual situations of the audience. As with their Greek and Roman counterparts, their basic purpose was to convey information between two people or audiences. They are not essays. For the most part, the NT Epistles (with the exceptions of Romans and Hebrews) are personal correspondences rather than systematic theology (Ryken, 90–91).

Most scholarship today, however, has reached what Doty calls a "balance." The letters of the NT fall somewhere between purely occasional responses to local situations and purely theological treatises intended to express Christian theological ideologies that extend beyond historical situations.

This observation brings us to a crucial point in our discussion of the NT epistolary literature. Since we find a variety among the "letters" in the NT, we might expect to find that some of the letters resemble the personal correspondence in Hellenism while others may be more similar to the formal treatise. For this reason it is best to distinguish between certain groups of letters in the NT and then discuss the literary particularities of each group in turn. Below is a listing of the five groups:

1. Undisputed Pauline Letters. These are usually accepted as authentically written by Paul around the middle of the first century: Romans, 1 Thessalonians, 1–2 Corinthians, Philemon, Galatians, and Philippians.
2. Disputed Pauline Letters. These letters fall into two subgroups: the Pastorals and what scholars refer to as the Pseudo-Pauline letters. The Pastorals, 1–2 Timothy and Titus, are within the Pauline tradition as far as IDEOLOGY is concerned, but more and more scholars believe that they were not written by Paul. The authors appear to speak to a situation in the way that they assumed Paul would have. The Pseudo-Pauline letters—2 Thessalonians, Colossians, and Ephesians—are usually ascribed to Paul but are so different in STYLE and theological

CONTENT that many scholars today reject any possibility of Pauline authorship.

3. Lukan letters. These are found in Acts 15:23–29 and 23:26–30.
4. Catholic Letters (also called General Epistles/Letters). These letters have the distinct quality of being products of a church that was in the process of becoming institutionalized, with its own episcopate and canon. They are 1–2 Peter, 1–3 John, James, and Jude (and some include Hebrews).
5. Seven letters of the book of Revelation. These are found in Rev. 2–3.

Undisputed Pauline Letters. Paul wrote as an APOSTLE to churches. This is somewhat different from writing as a private person to a friend, and we should expect his letters to exhibit characteristics different from strictly private, personal correspondence. This does not necessarily mean that Paul wrote formal theological treatises, but his writings do bear the stamp of apostolic proclamation. This gives his letters a public character. Yet whether he is preaching, exhorting, reprimanding, or teaching, he uses a modified and expanded epistolary FRAMEWORK. Following is the basic form of the Pauline letter:

I. Salutation (sender, addressee, greeting)
II. Thanksgiving (may be a blessing; sometimes with intercession)
III. Body (may include introductory formulas and statement of future plans)
IV. Paraenesis (ethical exhortation and instructions)
V. Closing (peace wish, greetings, benediction, writing process)

To understand how Paul adapted and expanded the form of the Hellenistic letter, we need to examine each of the parts of the genuine Pauline letter.

Salutation. The standard Greek salutation often contained the word *chairein* (greeting), followed by a formulaic wish for well-being. Paul changed the word to *charis* (grace) and expanded the salutation to include references to his apostleship and his fellow workers. He might also refer to the status of his addressees, as in 1 Corinthians:

> Paul, called to be an apostle of Christ Jesus by the will of God, and our brother Sosthenes,
>
> To the church of God that is in Corinth, to those who are sanctified in Christ Jesus, called to be saints, together with all those who in every place call on the name of our Lord Jesus Christ, both their Lord and ours:
>
> Grace to you and peace from God our Father and the Lord Jesus Christ. (1 Cor. 1:1–3)

Notice that Paul not only has substituted *charis* for *chairein* but also has added *eirēnē* (peace), which in its Hebrew equivalent, *šālôm*, was the traditional Jewish epistolary greeting. So Paul has expanded and modified the formulaic Hellenistic salutation to include both his Jewish and his Christian heritage. In the salutation of Romans, Paul's expansion includes a SUMMARY of his GOSPEL. Since Paul did not found the church at Rome and had not visited it, he probably felt the need to establish his authority to speak.

Thanksgiving. Most work done today on the Pauline thanksgivings is little more than commentary on the efforts of Paul Schubert. Schubert contends that the thanksgiving serves three functions: it terminates the salutation, gives the basic purpose of the letter, and may offer an outline of the primary topics in the body of the letter. Hellenistic letters frequently have thanksgivings in which the writer gives thanks to the gods or reports that mention is made of the addressee before the gods. With the exception of Galatians, Paul follows this tradition. In that letter, Paul is eager to move on to the problem and therefore contravenes the convention. But in 1 Thessalonians, Paul's thanksgiving section is so disproportionate to the rest of the letter (it consumes well over half the letter) that the letter seems convoluted. While Paul follows epistolary custom with the inclusion of a thanksgiving, he does inject modifications based on his religious perspective. For instance, the thanksgiving becomes the occasion to offer praise for the faithfulness of the addressees and to express a wish that this faithfulness will continue (Sanders, 352–62).

As indicated above, the Pauline thanksgiving tends to announce at least some of the major topics of the body. Consider the thanksgiving in 1 Corinthians:

> I give thanks to my God always for you because of the grace of God that has been given you in Christ Jesus, for in every way you have been enriched in him, in speech and knowledge of every kind—just as the testimony of Christ has been strengthened among you—so that you are not lacking in any spiritual gift as you wait for the revealing of our Lord Jesus Christ. He will also strengthen you to the end, so that you may be blameless on the day of our Lord Jesus Christ. God is faithful; by him you were called into the fellowship of his Son, Jesus Christ our Lord. (1 Cor. 1:4–9)

Here Paul refers to the charismatic gifts of speech and knowledge and to the "day of our Lord." Both of these subjects are primary concerns in the body of 1 Corinthians, where Paul puts the charismatic enthusiasm in perspective by emphasizing the eschatological nature of the day of the Lord.

Paul also seems to include in his thanksgivings liturgical elements, such as the note in the thanksgiving of 2 Corinthians: "Blessed be the God and Father of our Lord Jesus Christ" (2 Cor. 1:3). So, as James Robinson (132–49) has successfully demonstrated, though Paul follows the general epistolary form, he also adapts elements from his liturgical tradition to it, resulting in some essentially new patterns.

Body. The material within the bodies of the Pauline Letters is diverse. The controlling factor is a need or problem of the recipients. In 1 Corinthians, for example, Paul seems to be responding to questions. The reader would not necessarily expect any consistent form within this variegated Pauline landscape called the body of the letter. But this is only partially the case. Among the variety of topics in Paul's Letters is a recurring pattern of formal features, such as these:

1. *The request, or injunction formula.* The following is an example: "Now I appeal to you, brothers and sisters, by the name of our Lord Jesus Christ, that all of you be in agreement and that there be no division among you, but that you be united in the same mind and the same purpose" (1 Cor. 1:10). A verb occurs, followed by a direct address and the actual request. This request or appeal formula, however, also occurs in other places within the body of the letter, especially where new material is introduced.

2. *The disclosure formula.* Examples are "I want you to know that . . ." or "We do not want you to be unaware . . ." (Rom. 1:13; 2 Cor. 1:8; Phil. 1:12; Gal. 1:11; 1 Thess. 2:1). According to Doty, this formula (as well as the request formula) provides a heading "for the following paragraph(s) and states briefly its content, analogous to a newspaper headline and subtitle" (34). As with the request formula, the disclosure formula introduces new material within the body of the letter (e.g., Rom. 11:25; 1 Cor. 10:1; 11:3; 1 Thess. 4:13).

3. *The joy formula.* Expressions of joy ("I have indeed received much joy") were usually a result of some pleasing information that the apostle had received. An example is Paul's joy over Philemon's progress as a disciple (Doty, 35).

4. *Autobiographical notes.* Near the beginning of the body in most of his Letters, Paul remarks on his activities. He recollects his former ministry among the Corinthians in 1 Cor. 1:10–17; Phil. 1:12–26; he writes about his past experiences and hardships, including an imprisonment (cf. Gal. 1:10–2:21; 2 Cor. 1:8–2:12). These autobiographical notes are not unrelated miscellany but have great significance within his arguments. They reinforce Paul's demands on his addressees.

5. *The travelogue.* Toward the end of the body of the Letters (with the exception of Gala-

tians, in which he simply reproves his audience; Gal. 4:12–20), Paul alludes to a possible future visit by himself or an emissary (cf. Rom. 15:14–33; 1 Cor. 4:14–21; 2 Cor. 12:14–13:13; Phil. 2:19–24; 1 Thess. 2:17–3:13; Philem. 22). Roetzel (35) suggests that the function of the travelogue is to add immediacy to the message of the letter by promising an apostolic visit.

Paraenesis. Paul was especially adept at tailoring general ethical materials to specific situations. That Paul utilizes traditional materials from Jewish and Hellenistic sources should not obscure the fact that he did not intend to develop a new Christian moral system. As Roetzel observes, "These [paraeneses] act not as a rulebook for solving every problem; rather, they are examples or illustrations of how the gospel is to take effect. These ethical sections provide practical guidance, but they also convey information, make requests, and issue reminders" (36).

The paraenetic sections consist of three types of ethical materials. First, Paul combines various moral statements that have little inherent connection. For example, Rom. 12:9–13 encompasses the topics of love, hate, evil, good, brotherly affection, the bestowing of honor, zeal, spiritual aliveness, service, hope, patience, constancy in prayer, liberality in giving, and hospitality. Paul presents each topic in the form of a moral injunction. Most probably Paul received this material from an existing tradition.

The second type of material is found in LISTS OF VIRTUES AND VICES, where there is borrowing from both Jewish and Hellenistic traditions. The lists vary in length and do not necessarily reflect the situation at any particular church (e.g., Rom. 1:29–31; 1 Cor. 5:10–11; 2 Cor. 6:6–7, 14; Gal. 5:19–23; Phil. 4:8). A list of vices may stand alone, as in Rom. 1:29–31, or it may be paired with a list of virtues, as in Gal. 5:19–23. Doty suggests that rules for the household (*see* HOUSEHOLD CODES) that offer specific domestic duties (*Haustafeln*) should be included in this type of paraenesis (58).

Third, Paul employs what can be called homiletical exhortations centering on a particular topic. These are usually of a personal and pastoral nature. Most of 1 Cor. 5–15 is taken up with a series of homiletical exhortations on a variety of topics. Another example of this type of paraenesis is Paul's discussion of the resurrection in 1 Thess. 4:13–18.

Closing. The closing normally includes a peace wish, greetings, a BENEDICTION, and sometimes an apostolic pronouncement. Most often these are prefaced with a list of final instructions. The greetings occur between the peace wish and the benediction. Although these may be stock materials within the conclusion of the Pauline letter, they are not meaningless formalities. In the peace wish, Paul returns to the major concern(s) of the letter. An example of this occurs in 1 Thess. 5:23: "May the God of peace himself sanctify you entirely; and may your spirit and soul and body be kept sound and blameless at the coming of our Lord Jesus Christ." The coming of the Lord and the readiness of the saints are major concerns of the letter. The peace wish in Gal. 6:16, "As for those who will follow this rule—peace be upon them, and mercy, and upon the Israel of God," returns to Paul's concern with the bondage of circumcision versus freedom in Christ and the true Israel.

The benediction, typically "the grace of the Lord Jesus be with you," varies little in Paul's Letters, but it has taken on a distinctly Christian perspective. However, sometimes Paul prefaces the benediction with a warning or exhortation (see 1 Cor. 16:22; Gal. 6:17; 1 Thess. 5:27).

Disputed (Deutero-)Pauline Letters. The Pastorals are recognized by most scholars today as the products of a church well on its way to becoming an institution. The outlook of the Pastorals is advanced in their concern for the survival of the institution. In the undisputed Pauline Letters, the author is constantly on the offensive: both internal and external problems are confronted with an almost fever-pitched debate. Faith for Paul is defined as a trust in God, a belief in Jesus as the Messiah, yet faith in the Pastorals is a body of received truth to be defended. Furthermore, in the undisputed Pauline Letters, the parousia, or the coming of Jesus, is imminent, whereas in the Pastorals it becomes more distant.

Not only is the outlook in the Pastorals different from that in the undisputed letters; there also exist linguistic differences. Approximately 20 percent of the vocabulary in the Pastorals consists of hapax legomena (terms "being said once" in the NT; *see* HAPAX LEGOMENON), and about 30 percent of the vocabulary in the Pastorals is not found in the undisputed Letters. When we add to this the absence in the Pastorals of very key words of the undisputed Letters, we have the sense that we are now without a doubt in a world with highly different theological interests from those of the undisputed Letters. Along with the differences in outlook and vocabulary, we may also make reference to a difference in form: the Pastorals are almost entirely paraenetic.

Pseudo-Pauline Letters. Some of the same observations given above for the Pastorals pertaining to vocabulary and outlook can be applied also to the Pseudo-Paulines. Ephesians (which parallels about one-third of Colossians) is perhaps best viewed as a summary of Pauline theology. Second Thessalonians appears to offer a modification of Paul's eschatological thought.

PSEUDONYMITY was commonplace in antiquity. Although many scholars claim that pseudonymity was not considered an unethical practice in antiquity, such is not the case (for informative discussions of the ethical character of pseudonymity and its motives, see Metzger; Meade; Ehrman). Regardless of its ethical or unethical character, however, pseudonymity was a fact of life. Calvin Roetzel (93) proposes two primary characteristics of pseudonymous works: first, the writer purports to stand squarely within the TRADITION of his mentor (Paul, John, Peter, James) and thus serves as interpreter or defender of the theology associated with the historical figure; second, the writer appeals to the historical figure's name in order to add authority and credibility to the writer's own view. We might therefore suppose that since Paul's writings were among the earliest

within the church, they established a sort of model or CANON for succeeding letters.

Catholic Letters. The Catholic Letters, or General Epistles, have more of the character of a conscious literary production. Second and 3 John appear in traditional letter form, but 1 John has moved entirely away from the traditional letter toward the form of an essay on Christian love. James, Jude, and 2 Peter retain little of the letter form. For example, James retains the salutation, but this is followed by a list of moral admonitions and exhortation. It appears to be a moral tractate rather than a letter.

While 1–2 Peter and Jude employ epistolary conventions, they also move in the direction of the theological tractate. Doty (70) thinks that these letters are expressions of support for those who are experiencing persecution from those within and outside the church and that the letters are no longer concerned with formulating religious concepts but rather with reflection on already-accepted traditions.

Lukan Letters. The two letters of Luke (Acts 15:23b–29 and 23:26–30) more closely resemble the traditional Hellenistic letter than any of the above Letters. The first letter does not have the characteristic Pauline christianized greeting or farewell (only "greetings" and "farewell"). Neither does it have the thanksgiving or benediction.

The second letter is a correspondence from Claudius Lysias to the Roman governor, Felix, concerning Paul. It is obviously not a Christian letter but resembles other extant official Hellenistic letters. It has the expected Hellenistic introduction and body but not the usual conclusion.

Seven Letters of the Book of Revelation. It might be argued that Rev. 1–3 is actually one letter intended for seven churches. The opening itself certainly suggests such: "John, To the seven churches that are in Asia: Grace to you and peace" (1:4a). On the one hand, if seven individual letters were intended, why should there be a common salutation? On the other hand, after the author addresses each church in turn, he repeats a closing formula: "Let anyone who has an ear listen to what the Spirit is saying to the churches" (e.g., 2:11, 17). We might still argue that Revelation is itself a letter to the churches, especially in light of the closing benediction: "The grace of the Lord Jesus be with all the saints. Amen" (22:21). The number of churches addressed may simply be determined by the apocalyptic significance of the number seven, as reflected in the rest of the work.

Bibliography. David Aune, *The New Testament in Its Literary Environment* (Philadelphia: Westminster, 1989); William G. Doty, *Letters in Primitive Christianity* (Philadelphia: Fortress, 1973); Bart D. Ehrman, *The New Testament* (3rd ed.; Oxford: Oxford University Press, 2004); Gordon Fee and Douglas Stuart, *How to Read the Bible for All Its Worth* (3rd ed.; Grand Rapids: Zondervan, 2003); John Gabel and Charles Wheeler, *The Bible as Literature: An Introduction* (New York: Oxford University Press, 1986); David G. Meade, *Pseudonymity and Canon* (Grand Rapids: Eerdmans, 1986); Bruce M. Metzger, "Literary Forgeries and Canonical Pseudepigrapha," *JBL* 91 (1972): 3–24; James M. Robinson, "The Historicality of Biblical Language," in *The Old Testament and Christian Faith* (ed. Bernhard W. Anderson; New York: Harper & Row, 1963), 132–49; Calvin J. Roetzel, *The Letters of Paul: Conversations in Context* (Atlanta: John Knox, 1982); Leland Ryken, *Words of Life: A Literary Introduction to the New Testament* (Grand Rapids: Baker, 1986); Jack T. Sanders, "The Transition from Opening Epistolary Thanksgiving to Body in the Pauline Corpus," *JBL* 81 (1962): 352–62; Paul Schubert, *Form and Function of the Pauline Thanksgivings* (Berlin: Alfred Töpelmann, 1939).

EPITHALAMION

A HYMN or poem celebrating a wedding (e.g., Song 3:6–11; 6:13–7:5).

EPITHET

Technically, an adjective that describes an identifying characteristic or trait of an object, especially in an EPIC. For example, in Homer's epics are found epithets such as "blue-eyed Athena" and "swift-footed Achilles." In X. J. Kennedy's *Old Men Pitching Horseshoes* are "dirt-burnished iron" and "withered pitchers." In the HEBREW BIBLE, most of the epithets are relational, such as "Jael, the wife of Heber the Kenite," but some may also be nonrelational, such as "tent-dwelling women" and "a land flowing with milk and honey."

EQUALITY

A central focus in all expressions of FEMINIST CRITICISM, in which all aspects of women's experiences, values, opinions, and persons are considered equal in importance to those of men.

EQUIVOCALITY

In some expressions of READER-RESPONSE CRITICISM, the concept that a TEXT never communicates any final or complete MEANING. In other words, a text equivocates in terms of meaning. Wolfgang Iser denies the value of the idea in his understanding of gap-filling (*see* READER-RESPONSE CRITICISM). According to Iser, all LITERARY texts are riddled with gaps (informational, literary, lexical, etc.) that readers must fill. This presents a PARADOX for Iser. On the one hand, a reader can never simply freewheel through a text, for the text clues the reader in different ways as to the manner in which the gaps are to be resolved. On the other hand, the text formulates nothing but requires the reader's imagination to build up the pattern of the text—a pattern that varies according to the reader. Things become more complicated with Iser's claim that part of the INTENTION of the text is the very fact that no single projected meaning can exhaust the possibilities of a text. In other words, literary works are structured in such a way that they not only are capable of legitimating multiple readings but also actually encourage such multiplicity. This multiplicity, however, is not synonymous with equivocality. Iser never claims that a text has the capacity to legitimate any reading, only multiple ones, an idea that may be called PLURIVOCALITY.

Bibliography. Wolfgang Iser, *The Act of Reading: A Theory of Aesthetic Response* (Baltimore: Johns Hopkins University Press, 1978); idem, *The Implied Reader: Patterns of Communication in Prose Fiction from Bunyan to Beckett* (Baltimore: Johns Hopkins University Press, 1974).

ESCHATOLOGICAL PARABLE

A parable that deals with the end of time (e.g., Matt. 25:31–46). *See* PARABLE.

ESCHATOLOGY

From the Greek word for "last" (*eschatos*), the study of the momentous events associated with the end of time and human history and society as we know it. These events include the parousia, judgment, resurrection, the final CONFLICT, and so forth. In the study of the HEBREW BIBLE, *eschatology* refers to Israel's view of the future, in which God will fulfill his promises to Israel's ancestors, usher in the "day of the Lord," and inaugurate an age of peace and prosperity. Scholars have also distinguished between prophetic eschatology and apocalyptic eschatology (Soulen and Soulen, 55). The former refers to the future within history, as envisioned by the PROPHETS and expressed in both warnings and promises; the latter refers to a future that is discontinuous with present history, bringing a new world and new world order. In other words, the prophetic is a continuation of the present and is itself part of the course of history. In apocalyptic eschatology, the future is a decisive break with the present age, brought about by the direct intervention of God: history will actually terminate.

Bibliography. Stephen Harris, *The New Testament: A Student's Introduction* (4th ed.; Boston: McGraw-Hill, 2002); Richard N. Soulen and R. Kendall Soulen, *Handbook of Biblical Criticism* (3rd ed.; Louisville: Westminster John Knox, 2001).

ESCHATOLOGY, REALIZED

A view, introduced by C. H. Dodd in *The Parables of the Kingdom*, holding that in some texts of the NT (e.g., the Gospel of John) the ESCHATON is fulfilled in the person of Jesus and in the presence of the Spirit in the church. Scholars today assume that there were at least three views current in the early church: belief that the eschaton had not occurred but was immediate (Paul's eschatology); the realized eschatology of John; and the view that saw in Jesus's words and deeds the rule or kingdom of God in the present, though the complete fulfillment or consummation was in the distant future (Luke-Acts). The last view may be referred to as "proleptic eschatology." *See* ALREADY / NOT YET.

Bibliography. C. H. Dodd, *The Parables of the Kingdom* (London: Nisbet, 1935).

ESCHATON

The end of the age. *Eschaton* (from the Greek word for "last") refers to the actual events of the end time, while ESCHATOLOGY is the study of these events as they are expressed in the various texts of the Bible.

ESSENES

Although debate continues over their identity, most scholars agree that the Essenes were an ascetic Jewish sect dating from the mid-second century BCE. The distinguishing characteristic of this group was their strict observance of the LAW. When Jonathan, a Hasmonean, became high priest in 161 BCE, the leader (referred to as the Teacher of Righteousness) of the Essenes along with his followers left Jerusalem and settled near the Dead Sea. This settlement was a community of scribes (legal experts) who, along with the Zadokite high priest, waited for the end of the age. During this interim period, the scribes of the community spent time interpreting the SCRIPTURES, especially the PROPHETS, using a method called PESHER. According to this method of INTERPRETATION, the Essenes interpreted prophecies as being fulfilled in their own circumstances. The DEAD SEA SCROLLS produced by the QUMRAN community give evidence of a group that lived according to a strict order of discipline. Activity within the community included a common meal, water baptism, copying of texts, and strict observance of the Sabbath. New members faced a three-year probationary period. The initiate was required to follow the strict habits, rules, and regulations. Furthermore, the newcomer was forbidden to share any information with outsiders as to the practices and beliefs of the sect. The majority of the Essenes did not marry. They saw women as selfish and unstable. Women, they felt, would cause their sect to become weak. If a man was bound to a woman, he was a slave and would not be a productive part of the sect. This sounds remotely like the apostle Paul in 1 Cor. 7.

Much like the early Christians, the Essenes believed that they were living in the last days. They saw themselves as the righteous remnant of Israel. This is the main reason they withdrew into the wilderness of Judea—to prepare themselves for the coming events. They pictured their present world as coming to an end and wickedness being defeated; following this would be the inauguration of the kingdom of God. Consequently, their literature had a strong eschatological thrust.

One of the prominent features in Essene ESCHATOLOGY is a messianic hope (*see* MESSIANIC PROPHECIES). Hippolytus states that "all [Jewish] parties alike were looking for the Messiah" (Thompson, 998, citing Hippolytus, *Refutation of All Heresies* 9.25). This messianic hope is evident in the form of three figures foretold in the Prophets: the prophet like Moses (Deut. 18:15–22), the Davidic messiah, and a great priest of Aaron's lineage.

There are many similarities between Essene literature and the NT, but nowhere in the NT is this similarity so prominent as in the Gospel of John. For example, John writes, "In the beginning was the Word, and the Word was with God, and the Word was God. He was in the beginning with God. All things came into being through him, and without him not one thing came into being" (John 1:1–3). The *MANUAL OF DISCIPLINE*, part of the Qumran literature, states, "From the God of knowledge exists all that is and will be, . . . and by his knowledge everything has been brought into being. And everything that is, he established by his purpose; and apart from him, nothing is done" (1QS 3.15; 11.11; Brown, 186).

Other similarities between Essene writings and the Gospel of John include eschatological views, expectations regarding the messiah, and a strongly dualistic outlook (e.g., light vs. darkness, truth vs. error, death vs. life). Without question a study of the Qumran documents casts light on numerous NT terms and concepts.

Bibliography. Raymond E. Brown, "The Qumran Scrolls and the Johannine Gospel and Epistles," in *The Scrolls and the New Testament* (ed. Krister Stendahl; Westport, CT: Greenwood, 1975), 184–95; J. E. H. Thompson, "Essenes," *International Standard Bible Encyclopedia* (ed. G. W. Bromiley; rev. ed.; Grand Rapids: Eerdmans, 1979–88), 1:997–1005.

ESSENTIALISM

In philosophy, the assumption that objects have inherent qualities or essences existing beneath external particulars. For example, all humans may be said to participate in or share the essence of human nature or humanness. Among some feminist critics, essentialism designates a feminist nature unique to women, which is expressed in predilections such as motherhood and female bonding.

ETHNICITY

A group's self-awareness of its distinctiveness from other groups, when such distinctiveness is seen as superior to that of other groups, is called ethnocentricism. Although anthropologists define a group in terms of its customs (or the anthropologist's conception of those customs), customs alone never constitute a group's ethnicity, for several reasons. First, ethnicity is a group's self-awareness, which may not be fully incarnated into its customs. Second, a group's culture is fluid over time. Third, ethnicity is the product of more than visible customs; it also derives from such varied sources as foundational MYTHS, ORAL TRADITIONS, a strong sense of homeland, religious history, various taboos of dress and food, distinctive music and art, and not least, language. Consequently, cultural anthropologists' RECONSTRUCTIONS of ethnicity should always be accepted for what they are—critical constructs.

Bibliography. Thomas Greaves, "Ethnicity," in *A Dictionary of Cultural and Critical Theory* (ed. Michael Payne; Cambridge, MA: Blackwell, 1996), 182–83.

ETHNOCENTRISM. *See* ETHNICITY

ETHNOHERMENEUTICS

A hermeneutical method developed by Larry W. Caldwell that combines HERMENEUTICS and anthropology.

According to Caldwell, the hermeneutical task includes three horizons—the culture of the biblical TEXT, the culture of the interpreter, and the culture of the receptor (i.e., the persons for whom a text is being interpreted). For Caldwell and others, it seemed obvious that each of these horizons or CONTEXTS carries its own cultural particulars, which must be taken seriously in the process of INTERPRETATION, yet without making any single one of them normative.

Caldwell and others, however, recognized that *receptor* might refer, for example, to Paul's contemporary audiences, or it may refer to Paul's modern audiences. Furthermore, the NT writers interpreted the Hebrew Bible from within their own SOCIAL LOCATIONS or Christian WORLDVIEW, virtually ignoring its original contexts. Paul and others employed MIDRASH to interpret the Hebrew Bible, making it refer directly to their contexts. Caldwell and others then have suggested that modern interpreters are justified in employing the same practice to make the BIBLE relevant for today.

Bibliography. Larry W. Caldwell, "Doing Theology across Cultures: A New Methodology for an Old Task," *International Journal of Frontier Missions* 4 (1987): 3–7; idem, "Third Horizon Ethnohermeneutics: Reevaluating New Testament Hermeneutical Models for Intercultural Bible Interpreters Today," *American Journal of Theology* 1 (1987): 314–33.

ETHOS

One of Aristotle's rhetorical categories that provide the theoretical basis for examining persuasive DISCOURSE. Ethos is the ethical appeal to the audience or, more precisely, the emotions that a speaker or writer portrays to affect an audience. *See* RHETORICAL CRITICISM.

ETIOLOGICAL LEGEND. *See* LEGEND

ETIOLOGY (AETIOLOGY)

A STORY that explains the origins of a phenomenon. *Etiology* also refers to the study of such stories. The Tower of Babel NARRATIVE (Gen. 11:1–9) is an example, which may have been told to explain the source of the many, mutually unintelligible languages (McKim, 95). Genesis 6:1–4 may involve an etiology that originally explained the origin of

ancient heroes and later the origin of unusually tall people.

Bibliography. Donald K. McKim, *Westminster Dictionary of Theological Terms* (Louisville: Westminster John Knox, 1996).

ETYMOLOGY

According to Barr, scholarly etymology is the study of the CHRONOLOGY of changes within a language, the study of the cognate relationships and historical influences between languages, and the study of the sound relationships between languages or between developmental stages of the same language. In practice, etymology includes the examination of the historical development of MEANING forms, the identification of words from other languages, the reconstruction of linguistic forms in protolanguages, and the examination of words' constituent MORPHEMES.

Bibliography. James Barr, *Language and Meaning* (Leiden: Brill, 1974); Richard N. Soulen and R. Kendall Soulen, *Handbook of Biblical Criticism* (3rd ed.; Louisville: Westminster John Knox, 2001).

EUHEMERISM

The EXPLANATION of MYTHS as the extensions and exaggerations of human ACTIONS and ordinary events, and the INTERPRETATION of implausible or fanciful stories in practical terms. For example, the STORY of the transformation of Lot's wife into a pillar of salt may be read as an explanation of some unusual or curious salt formation.

Bibliography. William Harmon and C. Hugh Holman, *A Handbook to Literature* (8th ed.; Upper Saddle River, NJ: Prentice Hall, 1999).

EUPHEMISM

An intentional understatement in which an AUTHOR substitutes a less direct or less distasteful word or phrase for a more direct or shocking one. Modern translators of the BIBLE usually supply equivalent euphemisms for the target language. In Judg. 3:24, Eglon's guards hesitate to enter the king's chambers because they think that he "coventh his feet" (KJV). This Hebrew clause euphemistically refers to a bowel movement. The translators of the NIV and NRSV supply an equivalent euphemism with "He must be relieving himself." In Leviticus, the phrase "uncover the nakedness" (18:6, 7, 8, etc.) is a euphemism for sexual relations, including incest.

EVALUATIVE HERMENEUTICS

A "pastoral-theological" approach to interpreting the BIBLE advocated by Elisabeth Schüssler Fiorenza. The approach is based on the ASSUMPTION that if the biblical TEXTS are pastoral-theological responses to specific situations within their own communities, then there are some biblical texts that do not have SIGNIFICANCE for the modern community. Consequently, the historical and theological MEANING deriving from the doctrinal and historical approaches is inadequate. Texts must also be examined theologically by asking questions about such issues as the relevance of patriarchal language in the Bible and its subsequent use in religious communities, or the use of CURSEs in light of the destructive power of modern warfare. A critical theological approach will evaluate how traditional INTERPRETATIONS have functioned and are functioning in contemporary Christian communities.

Evaluative hermeneutics argues for a criterion that the pastoral-theological approach should be employed when evaluating texts or their interpretations. According to Schüssler Fiorenza, the criterion cannot derive from the Bible but must be developed out of contemporary Christian communities. Unlike the historical approaches, which evaluate texts according to their significance for their original communities, the pastoral-theological PARADIGM evaluates them in terms of the concerns and questions of today's communities. This criterion focuses on salvation or the critical evaluation and judgment of texts and TRADITIONS in terms of the extent to which they contribute to salvation. Salvation, however, is understood not only as the traditional salvation of the soul but also as the liberation of the human person from all forms of oppression (political, social, racial, class,

etc.). Consequently, biblical revelation can come only from texts and traditions that "transcend and criticize" the oppressive structures and practices of their own time.

Bibliography. Elisabeth Schüssler Fiorenza, *Bread Not Stone* (10th anniversary ed.; Boston: Beacon, 1995).

EVANGELISTARION (EVANGELISTARIUM, EVANGELISTARY)

A term relating to a large group of manuscripts of the NT called lectionaries (*see* LECTIONARY), in which SCRIPTUREs from the GOSPELs do not occur in ordinary sequence but in arrangements for reading in church services.

EXAGGERATION, COMIC

A type of SATIRE or HYPERBOLE with a humorous edge. An example is Matt. 23:24: "You blind guides! You strain at a gnat but swallow a camel!" In WISDOM LITERATURE, the device is common, as in Prov. 19:24, "The lazy person buries a hand in the dish, and will not even bring it back to the mouth," and Prov. 17:12, "Better to meet a she-bear robbed of its cubs than to confront a fool immersed in folly."

EXAMPLE STORY

Usually a PARABLE that calls for its audience to imitate the moral virtue of character described in the STORY (e.g., the parable of the good Samaritan in Luke 10:25–37). An example story is not allegorical but DIDACTIC: it teaches a lesson and calls for an appropriate response.

Bibliography. Leland Ryken, *Words of Life: A Literary Introduction to the New Testament* (Grand Rapids: Baker, 1987).

EXCURSUS. *See* DIGRESSION

EXEGESIS

The analysis and EXPLANATION of a TEXT. Exegesis is the process of examining a text to ascertain what its first readers would most likely have understood it to mean. *Exegesis* also refers to the varied set of activities that an interpreter performs on the text in order to make meaningful inferences about the text for the interpreter and the contemporary audience.

EXEGESIS, ATOMISTIC. *See* ATOMISTIC EXEGESIS

EXEGESIS, GRAMMATICO-HISTORICAL.
See GRAMMATICO-HISTORICAL EXEGESIS

EXEGESIS, INNER-BIBLICAL. *See* INNER-BIBLICAL EXEGESIS

EXEGESIS, STRUCTURAL. *See* STRUCTURALISM

EXEGESIS, THEOLOGICAL. *See* THEO-LOGICAL EXEGESIS

EXEGETE
The person who does EXEGESIS.

EXEGETICAL METHOD
The method or CRITICISM that an interpreter/scholar employs to interpret a TEXT. The methods/criticisms are covered in some detail throughout this handbook. With respect to MEANING, these methods fall into four broad categories: those that focus on the world that birthed the text, those that focus on the text itself, those that focus on the readers of the text, and those that combine two or all of these approaches. *See* CRITICAL METHODOLOGY.

EXILE, THE
In Jewish history, the deportation of the Judean king and leaders to Babylonia in 586 BCE. The term "exile" alone is frequently employed in contemporary CRITICISM (e.g., FEMINIST CRITICISM; POSTCOLONIAL CRITICISM; RACE, CLASS, AND GENDER CRITICISM) to describe the ALIENATION from one's own culture produced by the varied forms of MARGINALIZATION within patriarchal (*see* PATRIARCHY) and colonized cultures.

EXODUS
The escape of the Israelites from oppression in Egypt under the leadership of Moses, as recounted in the biblical book of the same name. Although the events of the exodus were recorded centuries after the event and there exists no extrabiblical data to confirm the account of the event, the date of the exodus has been placed between the fifteenth and thirteenth centuries BCE. In Israel's history, the exodus served as a symbol of God's deliverance and plays a prominent role in other books of the HEBREW BIBLE.

EXOGAMY
Marriage outside one's group, family, tribe, or class.

EXORDIUM
In a classical speech, the introduction, which is the first of five parts. The other four parts are the *PROPOSITIO, NARRATIO, PROBATIO,* and *PERORATIO*. Since the EPISTLES of the NT are essentially written DISCOURSES that serve as the personal PRESENCE of the writer to the audience, they closely follow the basic pattern of the classical speech (examples of the exordium are Gal. 1:6–10 and Heb. 1:1–4:16). *See* RHETORICAL CRITICISM.

EXPECTATION
An event, ACTION, or outcome anticipated by a reader based on the reader's CONFIGURATION of the segments of a TEXT. *See* CLOSURE; READER-RESPONSE CRITICISM.

EXPLANATION
The final step in EXEGESIS. Through one or more interpretive approaches, a reader configures an understanding of a TEXT and then transfers this understanding into an explanation. This explanation may include both a DESCRIPTION of the process that led to the understanding and a description of the understanding itself. Understanding, however, is not a verbal construct but an aesthetic, ideational object. So because the explanation is a verbal object, it can never be equivalent to the understanding.

In NEW CRITICISM, understanding has an experiential dimension that is not translatable into an explanation. The basis for this claim is that art (including LITERARY texts) does not necessarily describe life in terms that are immediately translatable into intellectual categories. In other words, an explanation that reduces the MEANING of a text into propositional statements or summaries cannot capture the emotional and experiential part of understanding. For example, to reduce the book of Job into a statement such as "The book of Job suggests that there is not a one-to-one correspondence between a person's social and financial status and that person's piety" captures neither the aesthetic quality of the work nor the emotional experience of the reader in the process of arriving at an understanding that permits such an explanation. For this reason, New Critics refer to any attempt to summarize a literary work as the HERESY OF PARAPHRASE.

EXPOSITION

In NARRATIVE CRITICISM and NARRATOLOGY, one of the five parts of a STORY; in the exposition the material establishes the SETTING and direction. Though the material of the exposition usually occurs at the beginning, it may also occur throughout the story. In BIBLICAL HERMENEUTICS, *exposition* refers to the stage of INTERPRETATION that follows EXEGESIS. In this SENSE, exegesis is the process by which the interpreter arrives at the MEANING the text would have had in its culture; then exposition establishes the relevance of that meaning to the interpreter's own time and situation.

EXPOSITION OF SCRIPTURE. *See* EXPOSITION

EXTRABIBLICAL SOURCES

Materials and TEXTS relevant for the study of the BIBLE but not found in the Bible. These sources include texts contemporary with the biblical texts, such as the RAS SHAMRA TEXTS, the MARI TABLETS, inscriptions from other cultures, HELLENISTIC PHILOSOPHIES, the DEAD SEA SCROLLS, historians, rabbinic literature (*see* RABBINIC HERMENEUTICS), and the APOSTOLIC FATHERS. A study of such sources often helps place a biblical text in a more reliable CONTEXT and may assist in clarifying an otherwise obscure text or practice.

EXTRACANONICAL

Texts that are outside the CANON. Yet since there are different canons for the Catholic, Orthodox, and Protestant TRADITIONS, the term "extracanonical" has a different MEANING for each tradition. *See* APOCRYPHA; APOCRYPHA, NEW TESTAMENT; PSEUDEPIGRAPHA/PSEUDEPIGRAPHY.

EXTRALINGUISTIC WORLD

In MIMETIC CRITICISM, the REAL WORLD outside the TEXT to which the text makes a connection. In other words, through the STRUCTURES of the text, a reader will make inferences about some aspect of human experience or about the real world outside the text, inferences based on the world as the reader experiences it.

EXTRATEXTUAL

In some interpretive approaches to the BIBLE, the idea that the MEANING of a TEXT or of a passage of text is external to the text itself. In other words, a text has REFERENTIAL MEANING that is beyond the text itself, somewhere in the REAL WORLD outside the text. *See* MIMETIC CRITICISM.

EXTRINSIC ANALYSIS

In BIBLICAL STUDIES, the investigation of the history of a TEXT's development and the use of historical sources (including the biblical texts) to examine the text's world. Consequently, the object of extrinsic analysis is not the study of the Bible itself for the purpose of understanding it. In the first instance, the HISTORICAL-CRITICAL METHOD is employed to reconstruct the historical development of the text. Included within the historical-critical method are TRADITION, FORM, SOURCE, and REDACTION CRITICISMS, each focusing on a different stage in the history of the text's development. Since TEXTUAL CRITICISM is concerned with the history of the text's transmission and CANONICAL CRITICISM focuses on the place and function of the text within faith communities, both are extrinsic analyses.

In the second instance, extrinsic analysis examines the world of the biblical texts through a number of empirical methods. Among these methods or disciplines are historical, sociological, archaeological, and anthropological methodologies, all of which assume that since the Bible is an artifact of a historical world, an understanding of that world leads to a more reliable understanding of the biblical texts. Historical critics see the value of extrinsic analysis as its ability to assist the present-day reader to understand what the biblical texts would have meant in their own time and CONTEXT. The focus is on a more reliable understanding of the world in which the texts were produced, rather than on the texts directly, although the texts are used as one of the many sources for such an examination. *See* INTRINSIC ANALYSIS.

FABLE

A short piece of literature in PROSE or VERSE usually involving nonhuman or inanimate objects to teach a moral. An example in the HEBREW BIBLE is the fable of the trees in Judg. 9:8–15.

FALLACY, AFFECTIVE. *See* AFFECTIVE FALLACY

FALLACY, BIOGRAPHICAL. *See* BIOGRAPHICAL FALLACY

FALLACY, GENETIC. *See* GENETIC FALLACY

FALLACY, INTENTIONAL. *See* INTENTIONAL FALLACY

FALLING ACTION

Technically, the part of a play that follows the crisis. In Aristotle's theory of TRAGEDY, COMPLICATION consists of the ACTION occurring in the STORY up to the point where the situation of the hero begins to change (RISING ACTION). The events from that point to the end constitute the falling action. Some scholars suggest that the GOSPELs may be read in such a way; for example, Peter's confession in Mark 8:27–30 serves as the crisis from which the PLOT inevitably moves to its resolution/DENOUEMENT in Jesus's death (the falling action).

FALSE CONSCIOUSNESS

A term in Elisabeth Schüssler Fiorenza's EVALUATIVE HERMENEUTICS designating the possibility that the ideologies (*see* IDEOLOGY) in biblical TEXTs and in the INTERPRETATIONS of texts contribute to the oppression of women and others rather than to their liberation. These false consciousnesses therefore demand a critical-pastoral evaluation on the part of the CRITIC.

False consciousness is also a term in MARXIST CRITICISM; Terry Eagleton defines it as "the complex structure of social perception which ensures that the situation in which one class has power over the others is seen as 'natural' or not seen at all" (5).

Bibliography. Terry Eagleton, *Marxism and Literary Criticism* (Berkeley: University of California Press, 1976).

FAMILY OF TEXTS. *See* ALEXANDRIAN TEXT; BYZANTINE TEXT; CAESAREAN TEXT; TEXTUAL CRITICISM; WESTERN TEXT

FEMINIST CONSCIOUSNESS

A concept within FEMINIST CRITICISM concerning the recognition of women's own unique experience as a way of understanding the biblical TEXTs. Two primary convictions function within feminist consciousness: equality and mutuality. The conviction of equality demands that women's interests and aims (including interpretive ones) are as valid as those of men. Any inequality in GENDER must be rejected out of hand. The conviction of mutuality demands that women (indeed all persons) be viewed as both autonomous and rational beings. Each person stands as an individual, but because all are primarily rational, there exists a universal bond between persons, a bond that transcends roles. Any INTERPRETATION that vitiates this feminist consciousness is to be rejected as having no binding authority.

Bibliography. Margaret A. Farley, "Feminist Consciousness and Scripture," in *Feminist Interpretation of the Bible* (ed. Letty M. Russell; Philadelphia: Westminster, 1985), 41–51.

FEMINIST CRITICISM

A multifaceted CRITICISM that tries to expose the PATRIARCHAL STRUCTURES (along with other oppressive elements) within TEXTs and the legitimizing and perpetuating of these structures in INTERPRETATIONS of texts. The term "feminist criticism" covers a variety of theoretical, ideological (*see* IDEOLOGY), and LITERARY interests; and feminism cannot be reduced to a single methodology or comprehensive definition. Yet feminist criticisms of all stripes do share the same basic concern. Their goal is to offer critique in a variety of areas where patriarchal structures are self-perpetuating and self-legitimating and thereby to transform society, especially in terms of social relations. While no two feminist approaches are identical, they all in one way or another focus on liberation. Borrowing from an array of disciplines and ideologies (e.g., Marxism, psychoanalysis, DECONSTRUCTION), feminist criticism has trained its critical gaze on a variety of areas, such as women's history, GENDER as a social construction, the representation of women in art, ANDROGYNY, the formation of CANONS, patriarchal language, the construction of a woman's epistemology, the nature of women's writing, the possibility of a uniquely female language, subjectivity, POSTCOLONIALISM and cultural imperialism, equality and mutuality, and FEMINIST CONSCIOUSNESS (Walker, 40).

Throughout history, MISOGYNY and the perception of women as inferior not only in strength but also in intelligence have promoted gender inequality and defined women as second-class citizens. Although women constitute the majority of the population in many cultures, it was only in 1900 that women were given the right to vote in a country: New Zealand. Not until the middle of the twentieth century did women in most first-world countries gain the right to vote. Nonetheless, as late as 1985, the World Conference on Women found that while women make up 50 percent of the world's population and contribute two-thirds of the world's working hours, they receive only one-tenth of its income and own less than 1 percent of the world's property. Although inequality has always been a fact of history, it was not until the twentieth century that feminism as a quest for gender equality became an international movement.

Feminism, however, has been around in the Western world since the late fourteenth and early fifteenth centuries, when Christine de Pisan (1363–ca. 1430) wrote books to counteract misogyny and promote appreciation for women's valuable contributions to society. In 1792 Mary Wollstonecraft published *A Vindication of the Rights of Women*. Marie-Jean de Caritat (Marquis de Condorcet) in the eighteenth century and John Stuart Mill in the nineteenth century argued for gender equality. In the early and mid-twentieth century, writers and poets in the West championed the rights of women. On the one hand, in her novels and essays, Virginia Woolf argued that equal opportunity in education and economic position was more important than the right to vote. She also proposed that women needed to achieve financial and psychological independence from men. In *A Room of One's Own* (1929), Woolf claims that since freedom is a prerequisite for creativity, women must work to secure freedom through financial independence. On the other hand, Simone de Beauvoir argued that women must achieve independence through action. In *The Second Sex* (1949), de Beauvoir challenged the "myth of femininity": the disempowering ASSUMPTION of the existence of a natural clinging female personality. She argued, rather, that women's subordination to men was due to a political and social structuring of society, and she complained that women had been too willing to accept the role of "the other."

In the 1960s, Betty Friedan published *The Feminine Mystique*, in which she claimed that American society had brainwashed women into preferring such traditional, culturally defined roles as wife and mother. Friedan was also one of the first women to challenge Freud's patriarchal view of women as failed men. In 1966, the National Organization for Women (NOW) called for a total restructuring of Western institutions that had been founded on the patriarchal MARGINALIZATION of women. In poetry since the 1960s, the emphasis has been on the equality and self-identity of women. Poets such as Sylvia Plath, Anne Sexton, Sonia Sanchez, and Adrienne Rich have examined the issues of the socialization of women; the search for female identity; traditionally inscribed roles for women; racism and identity; the relationship among gender, personality, and politics; and the disempowerment of women (Fiero).

In the mid-twentieth century in the United Kingdom and the United States, feminist criticism was informed by MARXIST CRITICISM, with its definition of culture as a social and historical construct, and was defined by contemporary economic and social relations. Since writing tends to inscribe and promote the dominant IDEOLOGY of the time, feminist critics worked to formulate a Marxist feminist criticism that would examine the relationship between culture, writing, capitalism, and PATRIARCHY. This meant that these feminist critics took the relationships between gender and class and culture seriously and were committed to demonstrating that gender was the product of historical and social specificity rather than the result of some natural order (Weedon, 41).

In terms of LITERARY studies, feminist critics of the poststructuralist (see POSTMODERN CRITICISM; POSTMODERNISM/POSTMODERNITY) bent are especially interested in deconstructing texts (esp. texts belonging to the LITERARY CANON) and thus revealing that the discursive structures (see DISCOURSE) of these texts both reflect and at least implicitly encourage power relations. Not only do these poststructuralist feminist critics examine texts from the literary canon for power relations; they also do deconstructive (see DECONSTRUCTION) reading of critical texts to demonstrate that critics operate from within discursive fields: they read from within locations and positions that tend to produce meanings affirming and perpetuating social values and constructs that are bound up with structures of power. Such readings are important for these feminist critics because they recognize that definitions of the feminine are created not only in literary texts but in critical ones as well (Weedon, 41–42).

French feminist criticism differs from the Anglo-American in that French feminist critics

have not rejected the idea of a fundamental and ineradicable DIFFERENCE between masculine and feminine. While some disagree, most of the French feminists assume that the difference between men and women is not located in individuals but in the very concept of man and woman. Based on this ASSUMPTION, they can then argue for a specifically feminine writing or language, a concept that other feminists reject as an essentialist (see ESSENTIALISM) concept (Gelfand, 44–46).

Among the individuals associated with biblical feminist criticism, which reflects the same variety of methodological emphases as feminist criticism at large, there is a common assumption and several underlying principles. The common assumption is that all the biblical texts were written in the contexts of patriarchal culture and have been subsequently translated and interpreted within patriarchal cultures. These patriarchal contexts have dehumanized and marginalized women, treating them as second-class citizens. Within these contexts, women's SIGNIFICANCE is a function of the degree to which their actions enhance the position of men. Women are treated as means to patriarchal ends rather than as ends within themselves. All feminist biblical interpretation in one way or another seeks to depatriarchalize not only the biblical texts but also theological TRADITIONs and systems that are based on patriarchal interpretations of the patriarchal texts.

There are three interpretive principles of feminist hermeneutics. First, all feminist critics attach extreme importance to the feminist consciousness (Farley, 41–51). Any interpretation that vitiates this feminist consciousness is to be rejected as having no binding authority. Second, all women are fully human and are to be valued as such. Any biblical passage or interpretation that devalues the humanity of women cannot be accepted as binding revelation. "Only nonsexist, nonandrocentric, nonoppressive traditions and interpretations can have the status of revelation" (Schüssler Fiorenza, 108). And third, because women have found that traditional interpretations of their identity regularly contradict their own identity consciousness and self-experience, the basic criterion for judging TRUTH is women's experience.

Katharine Doob Sakenfeld (56–64) lists three optional approaches to the biblical texts: (1) Feminist critics may use texts about women in order to offset the famous texts that have been traditionally used against women. (2) Feminists may refer to the Bible in general (as opposed to specific texts) in order to discover a theological perspective that in turn may be employed against patriarchy. (3) Feminists may look to biblical texts about women in order to identify the commonalities in the lives and stories of women living in patriarchal cultures, both modern and ancient. These are not exclusive options but rather broad categories within which critics may move back and forth.

Approaches within the first option may reinterpret texts that marginalize women, or they may bring to bear on these texts other texts that seem to portray women in a more positive light. For example, Gen. 2–3 may be reinterpreted in such a way that women and men are seen as equal. Mutual subjection can be claimed as the import of Eph. 5. Galatians 3:28 may be brought to bear on texts such as 1 Tim. 2:13–14 and 1 Cor. 14:34–35.

The second option contains approaches that attempt to extrapolate from the Bible in general a perspective that is in its essence Christian. Exactly what this central witness or perspective is varies from CRITIC to critic. One of the best-known approaches is that of Rosemary Radford Ruether. Ruether examines the entire biblical text and discovers a PROPHETIC PRINCIPLE (what we might call a "prophetic consciousness" or "prophetic impulse") that is present at different places and times within the biblical canon. According to Ruether (117), this prophetic principle rejects the attempt to elevate one social group above others by claiming that the dominant group somehow reflects the image of God. Every attempt to use the idea of God to justify social dominion and subordination is to be rejected. Ruether asserts that religion (along with sacred texts and interpretations of such texts) throughout history has sanctioned existing social orders that divide human beings into classes in

which the superior rules over the inferior. But this religious sanction of the existing social order is counteracted by an alternative principle—the prophetic principle. God periodically speaks through the prophetic person in order to criticize and condemn the society that, in the name of religion, perpetuates injustices on some social groups. Therefore, the prophetic principle criticizes both society's injustices and its religious justification of them (118). True religious and divine experience do not support such social injustice; instead, they expose structures that lead to injustices. The emphasis of feminist criticism in a very real sense parallels this prophetic principle because of the feminist critics' concentration on structures that perpetuate the marginalization of women.

However, the prophets in the biblical texts were limited in their perspective as to precisely who those oppressed persons were. They were, according to Ruether, unaware of the oppression of women and slaves. To put it another way, due to the limited view dictated by the prophets' social context, women and slaves were not included within the prophets' range of perception. The result is a limitation of the prophetic consciousness. Furthermore, after the initial prophetic renewal, because of its limited perspective, the renewed perspective may itself become the catalyst for subsequent social stratification (119). This recognition that the prophetic consciousness is tied to its social context means that the prophetic consciousness requires perpetual reinterpretation. This is actually the pattern that we see in the biblical texts themselves and in church history; for example, the initial messianic freedom of the Christian experience was deformed to marginalize Judaism, and the freedom-giving servanthood of Jesus is deformed when the language of servanthood is identified with human roles of power (120–21). Feminist critics such as Ruether correlate the feminist consciousness with this prophetic consciousness and call for the reinterpretation of texts and traditions within new contexts. At the same time, they take steps to guarantee that the fruits of feminist interpretation will always be a viable part of Christian communities.

Within Sakenfeld's third option, all texts (positive or negative) are viewed as speaking realistically to the condition of women as oppressed persons, yearning for freedom. The Bible can show women their true condition as oppressed persons but also as persons who have a different vision of heaven and earth and how to live within that new vision (33).

By observing how women of the past have been treated within ANDROCENTRISM, women today may identify with these women in their oppression and struggle for freedom. Elisabeth Schüssler Fiorenza argues that the Bible has been employed as a weapon against women's struggle for freedom. Accordingly, a feminist hermeneutic challenges the authority of the patriarchal texts and their use as a weapon against women's struggle. It also examines ways in which the Bible may be employed as a positive resource in women's struggle for freedom. To explain how this hermeneutic works, Schüssler Fiorenza has set forth five key elements within it.

First, feminist critics must assume a posture of suspicion (*see* HERMENEUTICS OF SUSPICION) rather than of acceptance of biblical authority. This task is twofold: (1) The critic must recognize any oppressive, sexist, or racist elements within the Bible and refuse to explain these elements away. (2) Honest attempts should be made to uncover any antipatriarchal undertones in the biblical texts, undertones that may be hidden within the ANDROCENTRIC LANGUAGE of the texts.

Second, critics must evaluate rather than correlate. This means that some texts and interpretations must be rejected if they perpetuate and legitimate PATRIARCHAL STRUCTURES.

Third, interpretation is inseparable from proclamation. Texts or traditions that perpetuate patriarchal oppressive structures should not be proclaimed as the "word of God" for people today. Before texts are translated with inclusive language, a careful selection process should be engaged. Texts that support patriarchal structures should not be allowed proclamational status. Only texts that affirm persons as equals should be allowed into the lectionary.

Fourth, texts that perpetuate and legitimate patriarchal structures of oppression should not be abandoned. Rather, these texts should become resources for remembering how women were oppressed and marginalized. Schüssler Fiorenza refers to this reclamation of suffering as a HERMENEUTICS OF REMEMBRANCE. While feminists may recognize these texts as reflecting reality, they do not equate this with accepting the validity of that reality. This hermeneutic of remembrance should allow critics to reconstruct the origin of the history of early Christianity from a feminist perspective. The biblical canon retains only scattered remnants of the early nonpatriarchal Christian community, but these remnants give evidence that patriarchal structures were not originally part of the Christian community.

Fifth, interpretation must include celebration and ritual. This actualizes the text into the present. Bible stories are retold from the perspective of the feminist imagination, especially the RECONSTRUCTION of those nonpatriarchal remnants. Included within this imaginative reconstruction are creative tools such as music, dance, drama, and literary creativity. As the church through history has ritualized parts of the biblical texts and traditions in order to celebrate "forefathers," so the present church should engage in the creative formulations of rituals that will celebrate our "foremothers."

Bibliography. Margaret A. Farley, "Feminist Consciousness and Scripture," in *Feminist Interpretation of the Bible* (ed. Letty M. Russell; Philadelphia: Westminster, 1985), 41–51; Gloria K. Fiero, *The Humanistic Tradition* (6th ed.; 6 vols.; Boston: McGraw-Hill, 2010); Elissa Gelfand, "Feminist Criticism, French," in *Encyclopedia of Contemporary Literary Theory* (ed. Irena R. Makaryk; Toronto: University of Toronto Press, 1993), 44–50; Rosemary Radford Ruether, "Feminist Interpretation: A Method of Correlation," in *Feminist Interpretation of the Bible* (ed. Letty M. Russell; Philadelphia: Westminster, 1985), 111–24; idem, *Sexism and God Talk: Toward a Feminist Theology* (Boston: Beacon, 1983); Katharine Doob Sakenfeld, *Faithfulness in Action: Loyalty in Biblical Perspective* (Philadelphia: Fortress, 1985); idem, "Feminist Uses of Biblical Materials," in *Feminist Interpretation of the Bible* (ed. Letty M. Russell; Philadelphia: Westminster, 1985), 55–64; Elisabeth Schüssler Fiorenza, "A Feminist Biblical Hermeneutics: Biblical Interpretation and Liberation Theology," in *The Challenge of Liberation Theology: A First-*

World Response (ed. Brian Mahan and L. Dale Richesin; Maryknoll, NY: Orbis Books, 1981), 91–112; Victoria Walker, "Lesbian and Black Feminists," in *Encyclopedia of Contemporary Literary Theory* (ed. Irena R. Makaryk; Toronto: University of Toronto Press, 1993), 40–41; Chris Weedon, "Feminist Materialists," in *Encyclopedia of Contemporary Literary Theory* (ed. Irena R. Makaryk; Toronto: University of Toronto Press, 1993), 41–42.

FEMINIST HERMENEUTICS. *See* FEMINIST CRITICISM

FICTION

Any type of writing (e.g., SHORT STORY, TRAGEDY, NARRATIVE POEM) based on the imagination rather than on history or factuality. Fiction can also apply to literature that pulls from history but is not written for a historical purpose (a modern example is the historical novels of James Michener). Within BIBLICAL STUDIES, there is an ongoing debate over the issue of history and fiction in the BIBLE. Most advocates of the BIBLE AS LITERATURE assume that the Bible contains fiction even though it does have historical value. Smaller narratives such as FABLES and PARABLES are obviously fiction in that they arise from the imagination rather than from historical fact. Some scholars also argue that longer TEXTS such as Jonah, Job, Esther, and Song of Songs are fictions. It can be argued that even HISTORICAL NARRATIVES such as Kings, Chronicles, and Samuel are fictional in that the SELECTION AND ARRANGEMENT of the events are controlled by the imaginative AGENDA of the writer rather than by a SENSE of historical objectivity.

FIGURATIVE LANGUAGE

Language that employs FIGURES OF SPEECH, such as METAPHOR, SYMBOL, and PERSONIFICATION. Figurative language differs from literal language in that the latter states or describes in objective fashion. For example, "My beloved is to me a bag of myrrh" (Song 1:13a) is a metaphor, whereas "My beloved smells good" is literal language.

FIGURE OF SPEECH

An expression that departs from the customary order, usage, and/or construction. Some LITERARY scholars make a distinction between RHETORICAL FIGURES and TROPES, saying that a figure departs from the traditional usage without significantly changing the MEANING of the words, while a trope produces significant changes to the meaning of the word or words. Such devices of sound as RHYTHM, RHYME, parallelism, REPETITION, and ASSONANCE are also rhetorical figures. Since APOSTROPHE does not normally radically change the meaning of a word, it is also a rhetorical figure. However, SYNECDOCHE is a trope. All of the figures of speech can be classified as either rhetorical figures or tropes but are usually grouped together under the heading of FIGURATIVE LANGUAGE.

FIVE SCROLLS, THE. *See* MEGILLAH

FIXED PAIRS

In BIBLICAL POETRY, synonymous or antithetical words that are regularly used in pairs within a single line (e.g., rich/poor, wise/foolish, love/despise, give ear / hear, voice/speech).

FLASHBACK

An element of ORDER in a NARRATIVE, POETRY, or drama, in which an EPISODE is inserted to reveal events that happened at an earlier time, possibly outside the NARRATIVE TIME of the STORY or poem. Examples are Gen. 26:15 and 1 Sam. 7:16–17.

FLAT CHARACTER

In literature, a usually minor character with one dominant trait who remains unchanged and static throughout the STORY (e.g., Laban in Gen. 24–29). *See* CHARACTERIZATION.

FLOATING LOGION. *See* LOGIA

FOCALIZATION

A term in NARRATIVE CRITICISM (esp. that of Mieke Bal) denoting the POINT OF VIEW within a NARRATIVE. A narrative or events in a narrative may be presented or focalized by the NARRATOR or a character. Bal focuses on how the point of view shifts (sometimes in very subtle ways) between narrator and characters and reflects on the hermeneutical implications of these shifts. Bal demonstrates that by focusing on whether the speaker is a man or a woman, God, or a major or minor character, one discerns SIGNIFICANCEs that might otherwise be overlooked (Jobling, 109). For example, in Judg. 19, a focus on the male speaker's point of view reveals that the women in his speech are objectified by the narrator, who even asks the male hearers to assume that the evil actions they propose to take against the men would actually be good when taken toward women.

Bibliography. Mieke Bal, *Death and Dissymmetry: The Politics of Coherence in the Book of Judges* (Chicago: University of Chicago Press, 1988); David Jobling, "Structuralist Criticism: The Text's World of Meaning," in *Judges and Method* (ed. Gale A. Yee; Minneapolis: Fortress, 1995), 21–118.

FOCUSING

According to Robert Alter, a parallelistic movement within a line of BIBLICAL POETRY achieved through INTENSIFICATION, SPECIFICATION, or CAUSE AND EFFECT. In Prov. 20:1, "Wine is a mocker, strong drink a brawler," "wine" has been intensified in the second VERSET with "strong drink," and "mocker" has been heightened to "brawler." Focusing through intensification is also common in graded numbers that follow the pattern of x, x + 1: "Once God has spoken; twice have I heard this" (Ps. 62:11) and "We will raise against them seven shepherds / and eight installed as rulers" (Mic. 5:5b).

Focusing through specification entails movement from the general to the more specific, as in "I will turn your feasts into mourning, and all your songs into lamentation" (Amos 8:10). In this line, "all your songs" is a specific element within the larger event of "feasts," as is "lamentation" of "mourning." Most instances of antithetical and SYNTHETIC PARALLELISM are variations on focusing through specification. Alter's last type of focusing, cause and effect, can be seen in Ps. 18:3: "I call upon the LORD, who is worthy to be praised,

so I shall be saved from my enemies." The effect of calling is salvation from enemies.

Bibliography. Robert Alter, *The Art of Biblical Poetry* (New York: Basic Books, 1985); W. Randolph Tate, *Biblical Interpretation: An Integrated Approach* (rev. ed.; Peabody, MA: Hendrickson, 1997).

FOIL

Within a STORY, a minor or secondary character designed to highlight qualities of a major character. A foil, however, may also be a character or an event that serves to emphasize or highlight an element in a story. In Gen. 13, the materialistic Lot is a foil to the faithful Abraham. In the story of David, Saul is the foil to David.

FOLKLORE

According to a definition by the Folklore Society of London in the latter part of the nineteenth century, "the comparison and identification of the survivals of archaic beliefs, customs, and traditions in modern ages." According to Alexander H. Krappe in *The Science of Folklore*, however, folklore is limited to "a study of the unrecorded traditions of the people as they appear in popular fiction, custom and belief, magic and ritual." Also included in folklore may be superstition, PROVERB, MYTH, STORY, RIDDLE, LEGEND, CURSE, BEATITUDE, and all kinds of customs of kinship, marriage, death, birth, initiation rites, medicine, and entertainment. Folklore may derive from literate cultures in both written and oral form, or from illiterate cultures in oral form. Among LITERARY scholars, it is a well-known fact that AUTHORS not only make use of folklore in their works but may also base an entire piece on a popular tale or legend. For example, Shakespeare's *Hamlet* is a retelling of an old folktale that may be rooted in religious ritual.

Biblical scholars in the field of folklore mostly agree that Hebrew folklore must be understood in a similar fashion. According to Susan Niditch, Hebrew folklore is rooted in the literature of the HEBREW BIBLE and must be understood not merely in terms of orality but also comprehensively in terms of literary TRADITION. "Repetitions in language and content reveal the thoughts and concerns that are at the conceptual heart of the tradition" (5). Niditch explains oral roots in biblical literature by pointing out its oral characteristics: its oral-style NARRATION, parallel pairs, "the lexical patterns of biblical prosody," economy of PLOT, typological characters, and other narrative patterns. However, it may ultimately be impossible to say whether Hebrew literature was originally composed orally and then later written down, or was composed on earlier oral forms. Nonetheless, argues Niditch, "there is much to be learned by treating the Bible as folklore" (7).

As already indicated, Niditch argues that Hebrew folklore should be defined and described in terms of "the traditional." This traditional is characterized by "symbols, words, syntax, elements of content, structures, and thoughts [that] recur in a profound economy of expression and density of emphasis" (9). She points out what seem to be traditional elements repeated from one STORY or NARRATIVE to another. For example, the similarities between the Joseph story (Gen. 41) and the story of Daniel (Dan. 2), between the accounts of two patriarchs' each claiming his own wife as a sister (Gen. 12:1–20; 20; and 26:1–18), between the rivalry of Joseph and his brothers and that of Cain and Abel, and the traditional manner in which the prophets "chastise a king or berate a faithless people; ways in which an author develops the success story of an unlikely hero; ways in which battles are described and enemies said to be subdued; situations that call for proverbs and certain patterns of SPEECH underlying the proverbs quoted" (10–12). Consequently, Hebrew folklore as a discipline includes the "analysis of context and form" and deals with questions of "defining, describing, and classifying the varieties of folklore" (12).

Niditch (22–31) presents an excellent description of the connections between folklore, as a study of the traditional, and other disciplines or critical fields such as STRUCTURALISM, history, sociology, anthropology, and WOMEN'S STUDIES. Structuralists uncover the DEEP STRUCTURES in narratives and point out the similar elements or unity among these narratives. Historians examine oral traditions as they may be embedded in writings to see how this material and use or treatment reflect the period in which the works were written. There is a natural connection between folklore and sociology in that both disciplines ask questions about the author's audience in terms of GENDER, status, age, social dynamics, and so forth. The anthropologist tries to understand cultures by examining their SYMBOLIC systems, family and group structures, and how these change over time. This interest in cultural systems and structures is intimately connected to examining the literary forms and their transmission over time in folklore. Finally, the interests of folklore and WOMEN'S STUDIES overlap in questions about the role of women as "creators of folklore," the role of gender in the choice and telling of a story, the manner in which a story reflects attitudes about sexuality, how a story perpetuates the dominant culture or reinforces the structures of PATRIARCHY, and the way stories or traditional material define expectations with respect to the roles of men and women.

Bibliography. Susan Niditch, *Folklore and the Hebrew Bible* (Minneapolis: Fortress, 1993); Alexander H. Krappe, *The Science of Folklore* (New York: Barnes & Noble, 1974).

FOREGROUNDING

The prominent highlighting of some element, often formal, in a particular piece of art. In VERSE, for example, a particular RHYTHM or RHYME scheme may be highlighted throughout the poem, or an alternative rhyme may be inserted in the middle of the dominant rhyme in order to highlight the alternative one.

In READER-RESPONSE CRITICISM, *foregrounding* refers to the reader's act of emphasizing or highlighting some things in the text while glossing over or ignoring others. For example, when readers elect to make certain passages in 1 Corinthians binding on a community (e.g., the hierarchical relationship between men and women, between husband and wife) while ignoring others (e.g., the relationship between slave owner and slave), they are engaged in foregrounding. Usually lying behind and guiding such a practice are certain ASSUMPTIONS about the nature of reality and/or a person's SOCIAL LOCATION.

FORESHADOWING

The ARRANGEMENT of events in a NARRATIVE so that later events are anticipated in earlier ones. Foreshadowing can be used on a small or large scale. An example of the former is Luke 4:16–30, in which Jesus says that a prophet is rejected in his own country, after which his townspeople reject him. Foreshadowing on a larger architectonic level is found in Luke-Acts, where the things that happen to Jesus serve as adumbrations of events in the life of the disciples and the church. Also in Luke-Acts the relationship between SPEECHes and narratives is one of anticipation and fulfillment: the content of the speeches foreshadows the events in the narratives that follow (Johnson, 204–10).

Bibliography. Luke T. Johnson, *The Writings of the New Testament: An Interpretation* (Philadelphia: Fortress, 1986).

FORM/CONTENT

In LITERARY studies, *form* refers to the TYPE of a TEXT or the GENRE to which a text belongs (e.g., SHORT STORY, GOSPEL, ROMANCE, EPISTLE, APOCALYPSE). FORM also refers to a text's shape or STRUCTURE, the way a text is put together in terms of PLOT, CHARACTERIZATION, SETTING, NARRATIVE sequence, and so forth. While scholars in NEW CRITICISM and NARRATIVE CRITICISM hold that a text's form is inseparable from its content, it is possible to separate them at least in terms of analysis. Thus, while a reader may isolate Mark's method of characterization, plot structure, and use of setting for investigation because these formal elements contribute to one's understanding of the text as a whole, they are part of the content. In other words, content consists of words formed into the structure of plot, setting, characterization, FIGURATIVE LANGUAGE, and so on. In the final analysis, these critics argue that form is content and content is form.

FORM CRITICISM

A CRITICISM that tries to identify the oral forms within the Hebrew and Christian TRADITIONS before they became sources for the written documents. This critical approach has its genesis in the work of Hermann Gunkel (1862–1932). *Form criticism* is a TRANSLATION of the German *Formgeschichte* (lit., "history of form") and is concerned to recover the history of development of LITERARY forms within the HEBREW BIBLE and the NT. Form criticism in NT studies began with Martin Dibelius (1883–1847), Ruldolf Bultmann (1884–1976), and Vincent Taylor (1887–1968). Bultmann's *History of the Synoptic Tradition* and Taylor's *Formation of the Gospel Tradition* still stand as seminal works in NT form criticism.

Form criticism proceeds on the premise that parts (e.g., miracle story, PRONOUNCEMENT STORY, SAYINGS) of the early Christian and Israelite traditions circulated as individual oral units, were finally collected, and eventually became sources for the composition of the biblical texts.

Substantial efforts have been made to identify the individual forms of the biblical texts. For example, the book of PSALMS has been subdivided into psalms of LAMENT, thanksgiving, coronation, and HYMN, among others. The prophetic books have also come under the scrutiny of form-critical studies: the prophetic address may be, among other things, judgment, exhortation, admonition, or promise. Gunkel posits two literary classifications, PROSE and poetry. Prose includes such forms as MYTH, LEGEND, HISTORICAL NARRATIVES, ROMANCE, folktale (*see* FOLKLORE), FABLE, and SAGA. Poetry includes lyric poetry, HYMN, WISDOM SAYING, PROPHETIC ORACLE, and thanksgiving. In the NT, much of the form-critical activity has centered on the SYNOPTIC GOSPELS. Some of the forms identified by Dibelius, Bultmann, and Taylor include PARADIGM, a brief account of an event that is designed to supply the context for a "pronouncement" of Jesus; miracle story, which Bultmann claims was designed for propaganda and apologetic purposes; legend, which Dibelius defines as religious narrative "of a saintly man in whose work and fate interest is taken" (Taylor, 104); and SAYINGS OF JESUS, which Bultmann divides into proverbial sayings, prophetic sayings, legal sayings, and parabolic sayings. Most of these general forms are further subdivided.

Form critics are concerned with the ways in which individual forms were utilized in the ancient culture of Israel and the life of the early church before the forms became fixed in writing. Underlying this concern is the ASSUMPTION that small units of folk memory are the means by which a people's tradition is preserved and passed on. Form criticism seeks to isolate these small units of tradition and then discover how these units were used within the community. Different literary forms originate in the various functions and institutions of a community and can be used to elucidate aspects of the community's life. For example, the psalms were produced in Israel within specific social contexts and in turn reflect social aspects of Israel's culture. The EPISTOLARY LITERATURE and GOSPELS in the NT contain units that reflect the faith and worship of the early church. As the individual stories were told and retold, they tended to be told within common settings, such as preaching, teaching, and worship. As a result, the pericopes (*see* PERICOPE) assumed discernible forms that fit the settings. For example, the forms within the Gospels received their shape within the Christian communities. Usage dictated form. This means that by the time the evangelists produced their Gospels, the individual pericopes were already molded into definite shapes. Perhaps recognizing that a single STORY could assume different shapes in different settings might account for some of the variations of the same story as told by the evangelists. In other words, differences in material may be due to the process of oral transmission.

Form criticism, however, goes further than correlating form with setting. It is also concerned with the history of the individual forms, the way in which the forms were transmitted and adapted (Tuckett, 101). This concern is sometimes called TRADITION CRITICISM. This means that form criticism tries to inquire as far back into the form as possible, even to the form's origin. Therefore, form criticism concerns itself with a process of development from origin to present context.

The concern with the origin and development of forms and traditions has led many scholars to assume that many of the Gospel stories (or at least details of the stories) did not originate in the life of Jesus but were "invented" by the church. Debate continues concerning the extent to which early Christians modified existing traditions about Jesus or created new ones.

Form criticism has successfully called attention to the range of forms utilized by biblical authors. With form criticism's insistence that the forms in the biblical texts are simply METAPHORS reflecting problems or events in the early Christian communities, attention was diverted away from the text itself. For Bultmann and his followers, what actually happened in the life of Jesus is not important; in fact, historical certitude is impossible to obtain. What becomes foremost therefore is the discovery of the faith of the early believing community and the traditions through which that faith was expressed. This position says that the controversy between Jesus and the Jewish authorities over the Sabbath really describes controversies between the early Christians and Jews. Form criticism concentrates on the stories and sayings as types of expressions rather than as historical events in the life of Jesus, a prophet, or a patriarch. Consequently, form criticism focuses on the ways in which ancient religious communities used and shaped forms. Thus, "form criticism allows the interpreter to understand and appreciate the role and significance of the faith and practices of the believing community in the formation of the traditions that the community would hold sacred and declare canonical" (Hayes and Holladay, 89).

Bibliography. Rudolph Bultmann, *The History of the Synoptic Tradition* (trans. J. Marsh; rev. ed.; San Francisco: Harper & Row, 1976); Martin Dibelius, *From Tradition to Gospel* (trans. Bertram Lee Woolf; New York: Scribner's, 1965); John Hayes and Carl Holladay, *Biblical Exegesis: A Beginner's Handbook* (Atlanta: John Knox, 1987); Vincent Taylor, *The Formation of the Gospel Tradition* (London: Macmillan, 1960); Christopher Tuckett, *Reading the New Testament: Methods of Interpretation* (Philadelphia: Fortress, 1987).

FORMALISM

A LITERARY approach to TEXTS that dates from the first part of the twentieth century and in which the Russian formalists sought to develop (1) a way of discussing literature that would be completely literary and (2) a way of analyzing literature that would be based solely on STRUCTURE. Russian formalism arose around 1914 and by 1930 had been suppressed. In Russia it had two centers of activity: St. Petersburg and Moscow. The group of scholars associated with St. Petersburg became known as Opojaz (Society for the Study of Poetic Language), and the group in Moscow became known as the Moscow Linguistic Circle. Roman Jakobson, one of the most noted members of the latter group, moved to Prague in 1920, before the formalist movement was fully suppressed. By 1926 a group called the Prague Linguistic Circle was solidified, with Roman Jakobson as one of its leading spokesmen. The Russian brand of formalism differed in some respects from the Czech brand, primarily in the latter's work in the theory of language. After discussing the Russian brand of formalism, this article will proceed with the modifications proposed by the Prague Linguistic Circle.

Russian Formalism. The elements of Russian formalism were formulated in reaction to trends in literary studies that the formalists perceived as essentially nonliterary. They felt that the study of literature had become subsumed by genetic studies (*see* GENETIC CRITICISM). According to the formalists, there had been an invasion on literary studies by nonliterary methods, such as historical, ideological, and psychological approaches. The formalists became convinced that the practice of literary studies in the second half of the nineteenth century, with its emphasis on evaluating and explaining literary works of art by using the methods of the natural sciences, was inappropriate for the study of literature.

One of the most common approaches to the study of literature had been biographical, a focus on the life of the AUTHOR. It was assumed that knowledge of the author's life could shed light on literary production. There must be a cause-and-effect relationship between the private life of the author and the author's literary work. The formalists rejected the ASSUMPTION that a literary work serves as a mirror reflecting the life and experiences of the author. These experiences rather become material that undergoes transformation under the pressure of LITERARY CONVENTIONS. The same can be said of ideological, psychological, and sociological approaches. The formalists argued that works of literature do not serve as sources for understanding the psychological and ideological FRAMEWORK of an author. They also argued that a literary work is independent of social causes and does not automatically reflect the society in which it was produced. To focus attention at these points is to disregard the very essence of literature and to ignore problems that are specifically literary.

Therefore, perceiving that literary study had no unique discipline, the formalists set about developing literary study into a discipline completely separate from the above disciplines. Their primary concern was to work out a way of discussing literature that would be completely literary and to find a way of analyzing literature that would be based solely on structure.

> The formalists also felt that before entering into such murky theoretical areas as the relationship between sound and meaning, they should first determine the facts of literature—how do poets actually use rhyme, rhythm, the tonal properties of vowels and consonants, and so on? To answer these questions, they had to seal off their subject from ethics, sociology, philosophy, psychology, and what have you until they attained a precise and detailed knowledge of what actually happens with literary works. (Lemon and Reis, xiv)

For the formalists, literature had its own justification and intrinsic value apart from its relationship to these other disciplines. The forerunners of the formalists, the symbolists, had already addressed the problem of the intrinsic value of literature. Their leading spokesman, Aleksandr Potebnja, taught that the unique value of literary art was its symbolism because "art is thinking in images." For the formalists, however, a study of symbolism and IMAGES would go beyond the work itself to epistemology and psychology (Jefferson and Robey, 19). In the process of wrestling with this problem of the intrinsic value of literature, deciding what constitutes literature, the formalists succeeded in producing a literary theory.

Defamiliarization. Although the symbolists had claimed that art explains the unfamiliar in terms of the familiar, formalists such as Victor Shklovsky and Boris Ejxenbaum claimed that the opposite was true, that art explains the familiar in terms of the unfamiliar (Erlich, 24–25). This observation has its roots in a fundamental concept in formalism—Shklovsky's idea of "defamiliarization." According to Shklovsky, our perception of things or concepts becomes automatic through habitual exposure or usage:

> Habitualization devours works, clothes, furniture, one's wife, and the fear of war. . . . And art exists that one may recover the sensation of life; it exists to make one feel things, to make the stone stony. The purpose of art is to impart the sensation of things as they are perceived and not as they are known. The technique of art is to make objects "unfamiliar," to make forms difficult, to increase the difficulty and length of perception because the process of perception is an aesthetic end in itself and must be prolonged. Art is a way of experiencing the artfulness of an object; the object is not important. (12)

Shklovsky claims that defamiliarization, "making it strange," can be accomplished in many ways. Such things as METAPHOR and SIMILE serve to transfer meaning through a semantic shift. Reading can also be impeded by imposing RHYTHM on ordinary speech. The poet's mode of presentation hinders communication, impedes reading, and results in prolonged attention to the text. This prolonged attention through the various means of the impeded form heightens one's perception and therefore one's aesthetic experience. The author need not "make it strange" by substituting the complex for the simple but may do just the opposite: substituting the profane, the colloquial, for the elaborate if the elaborate has become "automatized." For

example, Shklovsky describes Tolstoy's defamiliarization of the familiar act of flogging:

> In "Shame" Tolstoy "defamiliarizes" the idea of flogging in this way: "to strip people who have broken the law, to hurl them to the floor, and to rap on their bottoms with switches," and, after a few lines, "to lash about on the naked buttocks." Then he remarks: "Just why precisely this stupid, savage means of causing pain and not any other—why not prick the shoulders or any part of the body with needles, squeeze the hands or the feet in a vise, or anything like that?" (13)

In poetry, defamiliarization (the impeding of form) becomes synonymous with artistic creation. Poetic language is a difficult, roughened language. In ordinary language, what the formalists called "practical" language, words are pronounced and perceived automatically. This practical, everyday language is made strange in poetry through the presence of forms, sounds, vocabulary, RHYTHM, RHYME, IMAGE, parallelism, HYPERBOLE, REPETITION, and SYNTAX not usually found in everyday speech. All of these devices commit an organized violence on everyday language. Poetic language also violates the SEMANTICS of ordinary language by introducing secondary or archaic meanings of words, creating AMBIGUITY, itself a device that impedes progress. Such a broadening of the SEMANTIC RANGE of words in ordinary language means that communication fails. Thus what is literary is defined by the opposition between poetic language and ordinary language. This LITERARINESS, defined as what constitutes a work as literary, became the focus of formalist studies. For this reason Shklovsky could define art as device. As later formalists realized, however, LITERARY DEVICES themselves tend to become familiar and consequently automatized, themselves subject to undergoing defamiliarization. As Ann Jefferson points out, "This means that the habitual/made-strange opposition is now located within literature itself and is no longer coextensive with the distinction between literature and nonliterature. Literariness is a feature not just of form as impeded speech, but more important, of impeded form" (Jefferson and Robey, 21).

The formalists also applied their concept of defamiliarization to PROSE. Defamiliarization occurs in the opposition between what the formalists called *fabula* and *syuzhet*. *Fabula* refers to the chronological sequence of events as they actually occurred, while *syuzhet* refers to the ORDER and means of presentation of those events in the NARRATIVE. *Fabula* is the raw material consisting of the events in their causal-temporal relationships, while *syuzhet* is the manipulation of that raw material. The difference between the two is essentially that of STORY and PLOT. Perception is prolonged through a number of devices of retardation. These devices include transposition of material, temporal displacements, DIGRESSIONS, delayed exposition, and mixed NARRATION. The raw material of the fabula is not the focus of narrative art; the presentation of the material is. The fabula may have some grounding in reality, but realism is continually disrupted by the devices of the *syuzhet*. It is in this opposition between *fabula* and *syuzhet* that the literary quality of prose is to be found.

Boris Ejxenbaum writes that "the Formalists simultaneously freed themselves from the traditional correlation of 'form-content' and from the conception of form as an outer cover or as a vessel into which a liquid (the content) is poured. The facts testified that the specificity of art is expressed not in the elements that go to make up a work but in the special way they are used" (12). For example, events within a novel are arranged in a particular order, thus becoming part of the form. "Dissociated from this way of arrangement, they have ... no artistic effect whatsoever" (Wellek and Warren, 140). Form becomes inseparable from content. In fact, in narrative, the story (content) is only material for the formation of a plot. So the essence of literary studies is the analysis of the opposition between practical language and poetic language and the opposition between *fabula* and *syuzhet*, using the concept of defamiliarization as the focal point for the opposition. This brings us to an important development in formalism: the distinction between device and material.

Device and Material. Instead of employing the terms "form" and "content," a practice that suggests a dichotomy, the formalists later substituted the ideas of "device" and "material." Material is the source of literature, the "raw stuff" that can participate in a work, thereby taking on aesthetic quality as it is shaped by a set of devices unique to literature (Erlich, 188–89). Things such as ideas, the psychology of the author, biography, and the outside world as a whole are not content but the material on which the devices can operate. Form, then, is reinterpreted as the principle that integrates and controls the aesthetic application of the raw material. Ejxenbaum (16–17) suggests that a device exerts a unifying effect over a diversity of material while at the same time transforming it through SELECTION and reconstruction in a literary work. Obviously, content becomes subordinate to form. Literature comes into being by formally transforming materials, giving them an aesthetic quality that they do not have in nonliterary circumstances. In this method, devices that become overly familiar, or automatized, can become material for defamiliarization. In other words, devices (forms) that lose their ability to defamiliarize may stand in need of defamiliarization and thus become part of the work's material, just like other aspects of reality.

For all practical purposes, formalism gives no place to the author and the author's world. Krystyna Pomorska claims that this is necessary because of the procedure of formalist investigation.

> In order to know our subject intimately, we must make this subject the starting point of our study. Only then can we move outward and set up further relations. If we proceed in the opposite direction, from the environment toward the subject, we always run the risk of applying ready-made theories to something not suited to them. (276)

Literature has no grounding in authorial imagination or vision. Such things as authorial IDEOLOGY and psychology are only part of the possible materials to be acted on by the devices. Ideas function in literature like colors on a canvas in painting: they are not ends or causes but means to an end, an end that is absolutely artistic. The author is primarily a craftsman, and the work of literature develops according to its own laws. The author's primary function is to be familiar with literature, not necessarily with reality (Jefferson and Robey, 24–25). As devices lose their ability to defamiliarize over a period of time, newer devices will develop, or older, obscure devices will be resurrected. Therefore, developments in literature depend on the reworking of devices and not on the personal vision or circumstances of authors. Changes in literature are changes in devices. Biographical elements do not determine a literary work but may become part of the raw material for the work. LITERARY LANGUAGE (poetic and narrative) has its own set of rules, completely independent of the author's existence and personality. The author is a product of the work, not its source. Juri Tynjanov goes so far as to claim that "the structural function, that is, the interrelationship of elements within a work, changes the 'author's intention' into a catalyst but does nothing more" (74).

Since literature does not derive from nonliterary sources but from other literature, concerns of reality become meaningless in the production and critique of literary works. Mimetic concerns (*see* MIMETIC CRITICISM) are simply unimportant within the formalist's world. As indicated above, changes within literature come about because of a need to replace forms that have become automatized with ones that will function to renew our perception. mimesis, the communication of some meaning relevant to reality, is a by-product of the literary work. Reality is material available for a literary work, not its referent.

The formalists recognized that a literary work may communicate a sense of reality or refer to some external reality. This possibility, however, is only a side effect, something Shklovsky refers to as "motivation." Motivation is a term that describes the nature of a device in relationship to another device. Some devices are used solely for their ability to defamiliarize, while others are used to present a SENSE of realism. The latter includes such things as a work's ideology, emotional content,

and characters' psychology, which are employed as devices in order to make the work "more palatable, more appealing to the common sense of a Philistine reader" (Erlich, 77). Literary works are not true pictures of social reality, mirrors of life, or reproductions of reality. Literature may be used to tell us something about a society or a time period, but that is secondary. Simply put, literature is not an imitation of life in any aspect. If it were, then literature would be a function of social science, behavioral science, philosophy, or history. However, it has its own life, function, and justification. A writer's concern is not the representation of reality but the manipulation and deformation of language. In narrative, explanation of plot elements such as a character's behavior or ideas is not to be found with REFERENCE to some aspect of a social reality or psychological pattern but appears in the structure of the literary work. Everything that enters a work of literature is conditioned, deformed, and transformed by the structure of the work itself. Every element within the literary work becomes part of its aesthetic whole. Great works of literature may be conducive to TRUTH, offering insights into the human condition. Through the manipulation of language and the creation of even a fictitious world, the author may reveal truth. But this revelation is indirect, incidental, and secondary. Generally, mimetic concerns are irrelevant. Reality is subservient to the device. Reality becomes a component of the work, material on which the form works. The rose in poetry is not the one in nature. The relevance of literature is its aesthetic quality, which comes about by prolonging our perception of the literary work itself.

Even the emergence of new schools of literature is not based on social changes but rather on evolution within literature itself. As old forms lose their ability to defamiliarize, as types of literature become too familiar, new forms and types will evolve or old forms and types will be resurrected. What was once considered to be inferior may actually become heralded as creative. But the new forms and types evolve from literature and in conversation with earlier forms and types. Literary change therefore is not related to social interests but is a dialectic within literature itself.

The formalists refused to admit into their theory the subjective response of the reader simply because they viewed such response as unscientific. The reader is a passive spectator, who can do nothing but observe the "objective" features of the text. The formalists gave little importance to poetic IMAGERY and its ability to elicit sensory responses. The sensory images evoked by literature (esp. poetry) are highly subjective and individualistic, depending primarily on a reader's "idiosyncratic associations" (Erlich, 174). Since emotions and sensory perception are so subjective and the formalists were persistent in their objective, scientific analysis of literature, the reader was given little if any space. Literature for the formalists consisted neither of images nor of emotions but of words. Literature is the art of words. Art is device.

As mentioned above, within formalism (at least in its early stages), the language of literature was marked by its deformation of ordinary SPEECH. The language of literature performed "organized violence" on everyday speech. This violence was studied in terms of sound and vowel harmonies, rhyme, prose, rhythm, METER, and consonant clusters. Lev Jakubinskij explains this distinction:

> The phenomena of language ought to be classified according to the purpose for which the speaker uses his language resources in any given instance. If the speaker uses them for the purely practical purpose of communication, then we are dealing with the system of practical language (discursive thought), in which language resources (sounds, morphological segments, and so forth) have no autonomous value and are merely a means of communication. But it is possible to conceive of and, in fact, to find language systems in which the practical aim retreats to the background (it does not necessarily disappear altogether), and language resources acquire autonomous value. (9)

The language of literature is not distinguished from ordinary language by its imagery or symbolism but by its construction, a construction that is itself experienced. When words are removed from their use in ordinary speech and placed within a literary construct, their semantic range expands, and they are then perceived no longer against the background of ordinary speech but within the context of the literary construct. In a sense, then, ordinary speech is material for the language of literature. This means that there exists poetic and nonpoetic language as well as artistic and nonartistic prose, distinctions based solely on the very structure of language. For example, in his study of verse construction, Osip Brik (117–25) illustrates that sound is elevated from a subordinate role in everyday communication to a prominent one of autonomous value in poetic language. In ordinary speech, sound is not consciously perceived. In poetic language, however, the systematic use of sound patterns impresses itself on the reader. In poetic language, sound (which has become automatized in ordinary speech) is defamiliarized. A work of literature becomes a special, complex construction, created by the laws of the language of literature, which are not identical to the laws of ordinary speech.

The Prague Linguistic Circle. When Roman Jakobson moved from Russia, ultimately to become a member of the Prague Linguistic Circle in 1926, formalism was destined to undergo some significant changes. One such change developed when Russian formalism came into contact with Saussurian LINGUISTICS. This combination addressed a particular weakness of Russian formalism—the absence of a theory of language—and led to two important developments within formalism.

First, Yuri Tynjanov had already observed that not all elements within a literary work are equally functional. Some elements are foregrounded as dominant, while others are subordinated and deformed by the dominant ones. Ladislav Matejka defines this dominant element as "the focusing component which rules, determines, and transforms the remaining components. . . . The concept of the dominant and of fore-grounding was expanded so as to be relevant not only to the hierarchy in an individual work or art, viewed as a system, but also to higher structures viewed as a system of systems" (Matejka and Pomorska, 289). By the last statement, Matejka refers to Jakobson's expanded use of the dominant. Jakobson defined the dominant in terms of the whole work and the work's function. A piece of writing may have a multiplicity of functions—emotive, conative, referential, metalingual, phatic, or poetic. One of these functions will serve to unite the work. Jakobson therefore observes:

> From this point of view, a poetic work cannot be defined as a work fulfilling neither an exclusively aesthetic function nor an aesthetic function along with other functions; rather, a poetic work is defined as a verbal message whose aesthetic function is its dominant. . . . The definition of the aesthetic function as the dominant of a poetic work permits us to determine the hierarchy of diverse linguistic functions within the poetic work. (84)

A literary work, then, may have several functions, but the poetic function is its dominant one. This function will be identified primarily by the work's use of language as already defined by the formalists. Quite often a work's functions may overlap, but elements associated with the other functions are transformed by the dominant poetic function, meaning the aesthetic function.

Second, the Prague Linguistic Circle made room for discussing the MEANING of a literary work. This modification came about based on Saussure's concepts of SIGN, LANGUE, and PAROLE. Concerning linguistics, Saussure claims that a language consists of a series of "signs" involving relationships between signs and what the signs refer to. Every sign consists of a "signifier" and a "signified." The signifier is the "immediate object of perception"; the signified is "that which the perception evokes" (see Saussure). For example, the word *rose* is a sign signifying the concept of a species of flower. The signifier is the word-sound *rose*, and the signified is the mental image of the flower. We might say that the flower is denoted by the signifier *rose*. The signified may have not only a denotative (*see* DENOTATION) meaning but also a connotative one (*see* CONNOTATION). For example, the signifier *rose* may refer to both the real flower and a lovely person. Also according to Saussure, meaning depends on an underlying system of conventions and relationships, which he refers to as *langue*. *Parole* refers to the individual, meaningful act of speech that is based on *langue*, which is the subconscious system of literary conventions and relationships.

Formalists conceived of a literary work as a particular kind of sign understandable within a theory of signs. The result of this conception is that literary works carry literary meaning distinct from, but also related to, the REAL WORLD. As a sign or a system of signs, a literary work has meaning only as a product of a structure of DIFFERENCEs and relationships. Furthermore, every individual expression is produced by selecting items from the *langue* (system of codes) and then arranging and combining these items into a unique sequence. In literary works this combination is governed by the poetic, or the aesthetic, function. The referential function, meaning the denotative meaning, is subordinated to the poetic function. Consequently, the process of selection and combination produces associations and parallelisms in sets of words that are not present in everyday language. This does not result in an obliteration of meaning but in ambiguity. The "signified" is not to be found in the real-world referent but in the structure of the work, a work produced by recontextualizing signs from the *langue* into an aesthetic construction. Again, this recontextualizing of the signs does not obliterate their referential qualities; it simply produces new associations, expanding their semantic range, and thus it produces ambiguity and multiplicity of meaning.

Many of the issues currently being discussed in READER-RESPONSE CRITICISM and NARRATIVE CRITICISM have their roots in formalism: the issues of form and content, multiplicity of meaning, story and plot, literary devices that create ambiguity, multiperspectives, language of indirection. For example, if we read the story of Joseph in Gen. 37–47 from a formalist perspective, we observe the causal-temporal sequence of events (*fabula*) of the story and the actual order of the events (*syuzhet*) as they are presented in the text. We then ask such questions as these: What means (e.g., multiperspectives, displacement of time or events, digressions, summaries, unusual vocabulary) does the author employ in order to retard the action? Is there one THEME, MOTIF, or device that is dominant? How do we account for the placement of chapter 38? We also notice the instances of reported speech in this text and inquire as to the ways the reported speech differs from the original. In addition, we ask if we feel that the message of this narrative is clear or if there exists sufficient ambiguity (esp. in the CHARACTERIZATION of Joseph and his brothers) to give rise to multiple meanings. In a similar manner, we can make a case for ironic reversal as the "dominant" device in the book of Esther and recognize that INTERIOR MONOLOGUE serves to retard the NARRATIVE TIME in Jonah.

Bibliography. Osip Brik, "Contributions to the Study of Verse Language," in *Readings in Russian Poetics: Formalist and Structuralist Views* (ed. Ladislav Matejka and Krystyna Pomorska; Ann Arbor: Michigan Slavic Publications, 1978), 117–25; Boris Ejxenbaum, "The Theory of the Formal Method," in *Readings in Russian Poetics: Formalist and Structuralist Views* (ed. Ladislav Matejka and Krystyna Pomorska; Ann Arbor: Michigan Slavic Publications, 1978), 3–37; Victor Erlich, *Russian Formalism: History, Doctrine* (Paris: Mouton, 1980); Roman Jakobson, "The Dominant," in *Readings in Russian Poetics: Formalist and Structuralist Views* (ed. Ladislav Matejka and Krystyna Pomorska; Ann Arbor: Michigan Slavic Publications, 1978), 82–90; Lev Jakubinskij, "On Sounds in Verse Language," as quoted by Boris Ejxenbaum in "The Theory of the Formal Method," in *Readings in Russian Poetics: Formalist and Structuralist Views* (ed. Ladislav Matejka and Krystyna Pomorska; Ann Arbor: Michigan Slavic Publications, 1978), 3–37; Ann Jefferson and David Robey, eds., *Modern Literary Theory: A Comparative Introduction* (Totowa, NJ: Barnes & Noble, 1982); Lee T. Lemon and Marion J. Reis, trans., *Russian Formalist Criticism: Four Essays* (Lincoln: University of Nebraska Press, 1965); Krystyna Pomorska, "Russian Formalism in Retrospect," in *Readings in Russian Poetics: Formalist and Structuralist Views* (ed. Ladislav Matejka and Krystyna Pomorska; Ann Arbor: Michigan Slavic Publications, 1978), 273–80; Ferdinand de Saussure, *A Course in General Linguistics* (ed. Charles Bally and Albert Sechehaye; trans. Wade Baskin; New York: McGraw-Hill, 1959); Victor Shklovsky, "Art as Technique," in *Russian Formalist Criticism: Four Essays* (trans. Lee T. Lemon and Marion J. Reis; Lincoln: University of Nebraska Press, 1965), 3–57; Juri Tynjanov, "On Literary Evolution," in *Readings in Russian Poetics: Formalist and Structuralist Views* (ed. Ladislav Matejka and Krystyna Pomorska; Ann Arbor: Michigan Slavic Publications, 1978), 66–78; René Wellek, *Concepts of Criticism* (ed. Stephen G. Nichols Jr.; New Haven: Yale University Press, 1963); René Wellek and Austin Warren, *Theory of Literature* (New York: Harcourt Brace Jovanovich, 1977).

FORMAL PARALLELISM. *See* BIBLICAL POETRY

FORMAL SATIRE. *See* SATIRE

FORMER PROPHETS. *See* PROPHETS, THE

FORMGESCHICHTE. See FORM CRITICISM

FORMULA

In FORM CRITICISM, a short phrase or sentence used to introduce an ACTION or PERICOPE. Among the formulas are the emphatic ("Truly, I tell you"), the prophetic ("Thus says the LORD"), and the accusatory ("What is this you have done?" and variations). In the PROPHETS in the HEBREW BIBLE, the MESSENGER FORMULA is also common, such as "Whom shall I send?" In BIBLICAL POETRY, *formula* refers to an oft-repeated phrase used as one of the halves of a line of VERSE (e.g., "Hear, my child, your father's instruction," "Deliver me, O LORD," "I cry to you, O LORD," "Incline you ear to me," "Praise the LORD").

Bibliography. R. Culley, *Oral Formulaic Language in the Biblical Psalms* (Toronto: University of Toronto Press, 1967).

FOUNDATIONALISM

The philosophical ASSUMPTION that there exist underlying, inalterable universal TRUTHS or LAWS as the basis for all knowledge. For example, in the physical world, there are universal laws that govern its operation; in the area of morals, there exist universal laws by which all expressions of individual moral behavior can be judged as acceptable or not. During the Age of Reason (seventeenth and eighteenth centuries), Adam Smith even argued for universal economic laws. The search for such foundational laws of knowledge and judgment has been the focus of philosophy since René Descartes in the seventeenth century and possibly from the time of Plato. The majority of POSTMODERN philosophers resist foundationalism. Some are antifoundationalists, who deny that there are standards as a basis for truth; others nonfoundationalists, who argue that foundations are unnecessary, opting instead for philosophies such as Richard Rorty's neopragmatism. They assume that rational DISCOURSE is possible without subscribing to universals and also seek to replace epistemology with HERMENEUTICS.

FOUR DOCUMENT HYPOTHESIS

In the study of the SYNOPTIC GOSPELS, a hypothesis, first proposed by Streeter, that there existed two sources other than Mark and Q, which circulated about the same time as Mark and Q. These other sources have been labeled M, from which the material exclusive to Matthew derived; and L, from which the material unique to Luke originated. *See also* PROTO-LUKE; SOURCE CRITICISM; SYNOPTIC PROBLEM, THE; TWO-SOURCE HYPOTHESIS.

Bibliography. B. H. Streeter, *The Four Gospels* (London: Macmillan, 1924).

FOURFOLD SENSE OF SCRIPTURE

A designation for one of a variety of ways of classifying the MEANING in the SCRIPTURES and methods of their INTERPRETATION, first advanced by John Cassian (ca. 360–435) and extending at least until the Reformation. Although the Scriptures have both literal and spiritual meaning, the latter can be subdivided into the tropological (moral), the typological (allegorical), and the anagogical (eschatological). Consequently, any scriptural passage can be interpreted in all four senses (Soulen and Soulen, 65). The literal meaning derives from the historical and textual CONTEXT; the tropological meaning derives from the application of the TEXT to a current situation; the allegorical meaning is an extension of the literal to the theological (e.g., the christological); and the anagogical meaning speaks in some way to the eschatological consummation. So Jerusalem is a literal city, tropologically the human soul, allegorically the church, and anagogically the heavenly Jerusalem (Klein, Blomberg, and Hubbard, 38).

Bibliography. William W. Klein, Craig Blomberg, and Robert Hubbard Jr., *Introduction to Biblical Interpretation* (Dallas: Word, 1993); Richard N. Soulen and R. Kendall Soulen, *Handbook of Biblical Criticism* (3rd ed.; Louisville: Westminster John Knox, 2001).

FOUR-SOURCE HYPOTHESIS. *See* DOCUMENTARY HYPOTHESIS; GRAF-WELLHAUSEN HYPOTHESIS; SOURCE CRITICISM

FRAME STORY

A STORY that contains another story or a series of stories, as opposed to a FRAMEWORK STORY, which is a story contained within a frame story. Some of the best-known are Boccaccio's *Decameron*, Chaucer's *Canterbury Tales*, and the book of Job. In the book of Job, the frame story begins with an account of Job's family and character and his testing and subsequent loss of family, friends, and belongings. At the end of the story, Job's friends are humiliated and his fortunes restored. Encapsulated in this frame story is a series of framework stories in VERSE that consist of conversations between Job and his friends. Another famous example is the framework story of Judah and Tamar (Gen. 38) within the frame story of Joseph (Gen. 37; 39–45; 50). Also embedded in this story is the story of Jacob's last days, death, and burial.

The practice in the NT is usually called INTERCALATION and is essentially the same. For example, the Gospel of Mark is well known for its practice of framing one story with another one (e.g., 5:21–43; 6:7–30; 11:12–25).

FRAMEWORK

The conscious or unconscious CONTEXTS (social, political, ideological, methodological, etc.) through which a person or community understands reality or objects within that reality, including LITERARY ones. In contemporary literary studies, a primary ASSUMPTION is that it is impossible to interpret any object outside a framework. This idea can be found as early as Martin Heidegger's idea of forestructure (*Vorstruktur*). According to Heidegger, interpretation is always grounded in three things: something we have in advance, "a [be]fore-having"; something we see in advance, "a fore-sight"; and something we grasp in advance, or "a fore-conception."

> An interpretation is never a presuppositionless apprehending of something presented to us. If, when one is engaged in a particular concrete kind of interpretation, in the sense of exact textual interpretation, one likes to appeal to what "stands there," then one finds that what "stands there" in the first instance is nothing other than the obvious undiscussed assumption of the person who does the interpreting. (Heidegger, 191–92)

Any interpreter brings to the act of INTER-PRETATION a forestructure. This forestructure includes the interpreter's PREUNDERSTANDING, a vast array of PRESUPPOSITIONS, and the purpose of interpretation.

> *Bibliography.* Martin Heidegger, *Being and Time* (trans. John Macquarrie and Edward Robinson; New York: Harper & Row, 1962).

FRAMEWORK STORY. *See* FRAME STORY

FRAMING

A term introduced by Jonathan Culler to refer to the way readers contextualize TEXTs on the basis of the conventional systems of their communities. In Culler's reckoning, MEANING is not discovered within texts but is constructed as the reading of a text is filtered through the prior expectations, CODEs, horizons, and interpretive strategies of a community. So a reader "frames" his or her reading of a text within the limits that their community will allow, within the "modes of order which culture makes available" (Culler, ix). In agreement with most CRITICS within READER-RESPONSE CRITI-CISM, then, Culler claims that there are no definitive or final meanings of a text but rather understandings within infinite RECONTEXTUALIZATIONS.

> *Bibliography.* Jonathan Culler, *Framing the Sign: Criticism and Its Institutions* (Oxford: Blackwell, 1988).

FREQUENCY

In NARRATOLOGY, the relationship between an EPI-SODE and its NARRATION. An event may happen once in the STORY and be narrated once; it may happen once and be narrated more than once (that Joseph was sold to Midianites, taken to Egypt, and sold there is told three times: Gen. 37:28, 36; 39:1); it may happen more than once and be narrated more than once (Abraham's attempt to pass Sarah off as his sister: Gen. 12:10–20; 20:1–17); or it may happen more than once and be narrated only once.

FULL-FLEDGED CHARACTER

A multidimensional, complex character with a range of character traits. *See* CHARACTERIZATION.

FUSION OF HORIZONS

A term introduced by Hans-Georg Gadamer to refer to the meeting of two worlds, that of the TEXT and that of the reader, in the process of hermeneutical understanding. Because a text is alienated from its AUTHOR, when readers read and interpret a text, they do not re-create the author's INTENTION or original situation but filter the text through their own present. On the one hand, although a reader does engage a text, that reader confronts the horizon of the text, not that of the author. On the other hand, the reader understands the text within his or her own present. But the text is a product of the past, and therefore INTERPRETATION is a present engagement with the past, a fusion of the past and present. In this fusion of horizons, a reader's PREUNDERSTANDING allows him or her to interrogate the text, but that preunderstanding is also interrogated by the text. Out of this mutual interrogation comes understanding. Consequently, when readers study the Acts of the Apostles, for example, they study the text, not the author. But since Acts is a historical object, it has its own horizon with expectations of the reader. In turn, the reader comes to Acts with an independent set of expectations that allows Acts to speak to that reader in the present situation. It is easy to understand that the concept of fusion of horizons has had such a profound influence on most expressions of READER-RESPONSE CRITICISM because it places the role of the reader in a hermeneutically positive light.

> *Bibliography.* Hans-Georg Gadamer, *Truth and Method* (London: Sheed & Ward, 1975).

G

GAP-FILLING. *See* READER-RESPONSE CRITICISM

GAPS OF INDETERMINACY. *See* INDETERMINACY; READER-RESPONSE CRITICISM

GAY/LESBIAN CRITICISM. *See* QUEER THEORY

GEMARA

The "tradition" consisting of rabbinic comments on the MISHNAH, stories about the Mishnaic rabbis, discussion about rabbinic decisions relative to the Mishnah, and a store of other Hebrew stories added to the Mishnah. *See* MISHNAH; TALMUD.

GENDER

In some contemporary CRITICISM, especially FEMINIST CRITICISM, a designation for socially defined roles in terms of behavior and responsibility considered appropriate for a culture at any given time. Whereas the terms "man" and "woman" define human beings in terms of biological traits, "male" and "female" are purely social constructs relative to defined roles. In a PATRIARCHAL CULTURE, the socially constructed "female" is subordinate to that of "male." Criticism of gender has focused on three areas. First, in critique of the division of sexual identity engendered by BINARY OPPOSITIONS, CRITICS argue against a natural connection between gender and sex, suggesting that the categories of femininity and masculinity impose a singularity on identities that may be constructed in any number of ways. Second, attention has been given to studying cultural practices, the way in which the gender hierarchies and roles may be disrupted. And third, the relationship between gender, sexuality, and sexual orientation has been examined (Carter, 218). Critics challenge the no-

tions that gender is biologically determined and argue that sexuality is not a matter of nature but is the product of cultural processes. Sexuality or sexual orientation is thus not the result of birth but is culturally developed. Consequently, the Western claim that heterosexuality is the norm does not represent a natural biological given but a forced definition of normalcy.

Bibliography. Erica Carter, "Gender," in *A Dictionary of Cultural and Critical Theory* (ed. Michael Payne; Cambridge, MA: Blackwell, 1996), 217–18.

GENDER-INCLUSIVE LANGUAGE. *See* INCLUSIVE LANGUAGE

GENEALOGY

In BIBLICAL STUDIES, a LITERARY DEVICE that traces a person's or people's ancestry (e.g., Gen. 5; Num. 1; 1 Chron. 1:1–6:30). The two outstanding genealogies in the NT are in Matt. 1:1–17 and Luke 3:23–38. Matthew divides the genealogy of Jesus into three sets of fourteen each, tracing Jesus's lineage back to Abraham. His purpose suggests that the entire history of Israel led directly to Jesus, and given Matthew's doubling of the number seven, he may have intended to suggest that Israel's history was divinely superintended. Luke, however, traces Jesus's lineage to Adam.

In the Hebrew Bible are several genealogies beginning in Gen. 4; 5; 10; and 11, two before the flood (4; 5) and two after the flood (10; 11). Genesis 5 and 11 give accounts of the line from Adam to Noah, and from Noah to Abraham, with each genealogy consisting of ten links. The author traces the lineage of Ishmael in Gen. 25, of Esau in Gen. 36, and of Jacob in Gen. 46. First Chronicles records tribal genealogies with emphasis on the ancestries of famous persons such as David, Samuel, and Aaron.

Genealogy has also been introduced into the vocabulary of cultural and critical theory by Michel Foucault to designate the relationship between structures of power and knowledge. According to Foucault, traditional approaches to historical analysis have assumed that reality consists of stable forms and that history is a matter of continuity. Genealogy attempts to expose the contingencies, cracks, and discontinuities between historical events, and the DISCURSIVE nature of HISTORIOGRAPHY. What passes as objective, continuous history is actually discourses of power that always involve perspectivity. All knowledge, including historical and scientific knowledge, is perspectival and involves issues of power and control. Genealogy study applied to the BIBLE, then, proceeds on the assumption that all of the biblical texts were produced by individuals who consciously or unconsciously inscribed into the texts structures of power that result in the MARGINALIZATION of certain persons or groups.

Bibliography. Michel Foucault, "Nietzsche, Genealogy, History," in *Language, Counter-Memory, Practice* (ed. Donald F. Bouchard; Ithaca, NY: Cornell University Press, 1971), 139–64.

GENERAL EPISTLES. *See* CATHOLIC EPISTLES

GENERAL LETTERS. *See* CATHOLIC EPISTLES

GENERIC APPROPRIATENESS

One of the four criteria by which E. D. Hirsch Jr. argues that the reader may show that one reading of a TEXT is more probable than the others. According to Hirsch, "If the text follows the conventions of a scientific essay, for example, it is inappropriate to construe the kind of allusive meaning found in casual conversation." *See* VERIFICATION.

Bibliography. E. D. Hirsch Jr., "Objective Interpretation," *PMLA* 75 (1960): 463, 470–79.

GENETIC CRITICISM

Any type of CRITICISM that focuses on the AUTHOR as the source of MEANING or that grounds

the meaning of a TEXT in the mind of the author at the time of writing. Since the mind of the author is the source of meaning, the genetic CRITIC must examine any object that may have influenced that mind. When other documents by the same author are available, the task of the critic becomes easier. But even when these documents or other sources which might cast light on the author's life and mind are not available, genetic critics claim that they can still gain much information from studying the world and time of the author. Consequently, the political, social, intellectual, economic, religious, and scientific milieus of the author's world become areas of examination for understanding the life and times of the author.

In the nineteenth century, two interests converged to direct the study of LITERARY texts toward a focus on the biographical and historical: the author as an individual creative mind and the individual character of the age. This is why English and humanities departments in universities still offer even today courses on eighteenth-century English literature or Renaissance studies or the modern British novel. The circumstances of the text's composition and the ASSUMPTION that a text could be understood in terms of the life and times of the author became central to literary study in the nineteenth century. Since the author is the product of an age, an understanding of that age should assist in understanding the mind that produces a text. The most valid INTERPRETATION of a text, then, is the one that invokes the most probable CONTEXT relative to the author (Keesey, 11).

Publishers continue to offer works on the "world" of the BIBLE, background studies of both the HEBREW BIBLE and the NT, the world of the early church, the "mind" of Paul and others, and the literary, cultural, and religious environments of the Bible. The assumption behind these works is that a knowledge of the various contexts within which the biblical texts were written produces more plausible interpretations. The GOSPELS are better understood if studied in their first-century Greco-Roman and Judaic contexts. The works of the Hebrew Bible should be studied in the light of their Mesopotamian contexts. Although the reliability and extent of our historical knowledge are being challenged by many POSTMODERN theories, the sense that genetic criticism has a "scientific" nature continues to have a profound attraction in BIBLICAL STUDIES.

Bibliography. Donald Keesey, *Contexts for Criticism* (4th ed.; Boston: McGraw-Hill, 2003).

GENETIC FALLACY

In NEW CRITICISM, any claim that the MEANING of a TEXT is to be found in the originating circumstances of the text is mistaken. According to the New Critics, if an AUTHOR were somehow successful in INTENTION, then since the intention is identical with the text itself, there would be no need to appeal to the world behind the text for meaning. Issues of BIOGRAPHY, the psychological condition of the author, and any aspects of the text's genesis are irrelevant if meaning rests in the STRUCTURES of the text itself.

GENETIC STRUCTURALISM

A method of cultural analysis formulated by Lucien Goldman in the 1950s but remaining an important part of CULTURAL CRITICISM. Like STRUCTURALISM in general, Goldman focuses on the mental structures of literary works rather than their CONTENT, but he places those structures within their CONTEXT of historical and cultural processes. Any object such as a TEXT is always part of a greater whole, both historical and cultural. All art, including literature, is embedded in the life activities of people and constitutes a means of examining or responding to problems that surface in their societies. Consequently, any writer's or text's WORLDVIEW is always a part of a stage of history and will reflect the collective SUBJECT of the period. If applied to the study of biblical texts, genetic structuralism would examine the texts as parts and expressions of the collective worldview at a particular stage of Jewish or church history.

Bibliography. Lucien Goldman, *The Hidden God* (London: Routledge & Kegan Paul, 1964).

GENEVA BIBLE

Published in Geneva in 1560, a revision of the GREAT BIBLE and translated by William Whittingham from the original languages with strong Protestant leanings, especially in its marginal notes. The Geneva Bible was the first English TRANSLATION to employ VERSE numbering.

GENRE

A term for the grouping of LITERARY works according to shared FORM and literary technique. The term implies that works can be grouped together into a TYPE based on formal and technical similarities independent of AUTHOR, place or time of composition, and subject matter. The concept of genre, in other words, suggests that TEXTS can be identified or placed within a type based on LITERARY CONVENTIONS. For the HEBREW BIBLE, literary scholars generally have identified HISTORICAL NARRATIVES, POETRY, PROPHECY, and WISDOM LITERATURE as the main genres; and GOSPEL, EPISTLE, and APOCALYPSE for the NT. Most of these, however, may contain other more narrowly defined genres—such as PARABLE, FABLE, SHORT STORY, and SAGA—as subdivisions of narrative. Furthermore, the Gospels reflect characteristics of Hellenistic ROMANCE, HISTORIOGRAPHY, and BIOGRAPHY. In recent critical studies, the ideas of genre formation and conventions have been challenged as being too arbitrary and not a reflection of universal categories.

GENRE CRITICISM

A type of CRITICISM that focuses on a text's literary TYPE or kind as the source of its MEANING (*see* GENRE). Genre criticism is as old as Aristotle's *Poetics.*

The biblical texts are commonly categorized by genre as HISTORICAL NARRATIVES, PROPHECY, BIBLICAL POETRY, PSALMS, WISDOM LITERATURE, APOCALYPSE, epistle, and GOSPEL. Actually, genre criticism is part of a larger, more comprehensive critical approach that usually goes by the title of INTERTEXTUAL CRITICISM, which assumes that the CONTEXT for understanding a piece of literature is not such things as reality, history, or AUTHO-RIAL INTENTION but literature itself. Literature is best comprehended by reading it in the context of LITERARY CONVENTIONS, and unless readers know these conventions, they cannot fully appreciate literature.

The major ASSUMPTION of generic classification is that formal or technical characteristics exist among texts of the same kind irrespective of time, place, AUTHOR, or SUBJECT. A second assumption is that a text cannot be fully appreciated and understood if it is approached without some understanding of its genre. Since all literature (all art, for that matter) is conventional, it can only be rightly understood by individuals who are familiar with the conventions. For example, if the Gospel of Luke is read as a romantic COMEDY, it will simply be misread (although it does manifest some of the generic characteristics of Hellenistic ROMANCE, BIOGRAPHY, EPIC, and HISTORIOGRAPHY). Although a particular text may not conform absolutely to its genre FRAMEWORK and thus may be unique, if it did not conform to some degree—if it is completely unique—it would simply be unintelligible.

Genre critics generally assume that if readers know the genre of a text, they already know some things about it and will read it in a particular way because the knowledge of the genre creates a set of expectations with which the reader approaches the text. Critics such as E. D. Hirsch argue that the accuracy of readers' understanding depends on the accuracy of their identification of the genre. Plausible understanding will occur only to the extent that the reader operates under the same expectations as the author. If readers approach the book of Revelation with the same expectations that they have for the Song of Songs, they will misunderstand Revelation. Critics such as Hirsch can make such claims because they assume that different types of texts can be similarly categorized on the basis of shared literary conventions. Consequently, a text is more appropriately understood when the reader can recognize the manner in which these conventions are fulfilled or imaginatively adapted. Since literary conventions, like linguistic ones,

are arbitrary, it is the responsibility of LITERARY CRITICISM to teach these conventions because the text is available ultimately only to those who have mastered the appropriate conventions.

Within a single week, a person will read a short story, a poem, a tragic play, labels on food containers, a newspaper, a letter, a telephone directory, and a recipe. All of these forms communicate differently and represent different literary genres. When readers approach a text, they either consciously or unconsciously identify its genre. Even the casual reader knows that a poem must be read and interpreted differently from a recipe. There is an intimate relationship and interconnectedness between form and content. Literary criticism must concern itself not only with the content but also with the form of the text. Such concern entails understanding the conventions of the generic systems. This is true because different genres involve different CODES or conventions. In most cultures, unspoken rules govern what is worn and when it is worn. Rules of dress dictate that a person not wear a ski suit to a formal wedding. Also with a given society, rules or principles dictate family relationships. On the basis of these rules, persons within a particular social group will relate to other members of the group, making decisions such as whom they can or cannot marry.

In language, similarly, rules of grammatical construction and SYNTAX govern the way we group words or SYMBOLS. This ensures communication. Furthermore, rules govern or identify literary genres. Consequently, we read different genres with different expectations and interpret them differently. Knowing the genre of a text allows the reader to know what type of questions can sensibly be asked of the material.

Hirsch and others (esp. Northrop Frye) have argued that without at least minimally shared conventional frameworks, communication of any sort would be impossible. Consequently, they tend to define these genre conventions in terms of typologies and recurrent patterns. Yet other critics, such as Mikhail Bakhtin, Barbara Lewalski, Sandra Gilbert, and Susan Gubar, have challenged this definition of genre. Bakhtin sees genre as existing in everyday communicative acts such as shopping lists, telephone calls, and private letters. These conventional features are not universal givens or abstract systems but social constructs designed to mediate between the world and the text. So underlying their existence are the PRAGMATICS of performance and not abstract typological systems. Given this performance orientation of conventions, genre is perennially reborn. Rather than being grounded in universally shared forms, literature is grounded in specific social situations and ideological struggles (*see* IDEOLOGY).

According to Lewalski, Gilbert, and Gubar, conventional codes change over time and are irretrievably mixed with political, historical, and GENDER issues. Gubar claims that genres are the products of patriarchal social structures of power (*see* PATRIARCHY), forms invented to communicate male stories about the world. Genres are nothing more than social, historical, and political constructs. Like DECONSTRUCTION, with its emphasis on the indeterminacy of textual meaning, critics such as Lewalski, Gilbert, and Gubar have subjected the age-old concept of genre to the POSTMODERN critique of universal givens and have exposed the possible relationship between generic conventions in literature and issues such as the formation of gender and social structures of power.

Bibliography. Robert Alter, *The Art of Biblical Narrative* (New York: Basic Books, 1981); Mikhail Bakhtin, *The Dialogic Imagination: Four Essays* (ed. Michael Holquist; trans. Caryl Emerson and Michael Holquist; Austin: University of Texas Press, 1981); Alistair Fowler, *Kinds of Literature: An Introduction to the Theory of Genres and Modes* (Cambridge, MA: Harvard University Press, 1982); Sandra Gilbert and Susan Gubar, *The Mad Woman in the Attic: The Woman Writer and the Nineteenth-Century Literary Imagination* (New Haven: Yale University Press, 1979); John Hayes and Carl Holladay, *Biblical Exegesis: A Beginner's Handbook* (Atlanta: John Knox, 1987); E. D. Hirsh Jr., *Validity in Interpretation* (New Haven: Yale University Press, 1967).

GENTILE

A term used by Jews for anyone not Jewish by race. In the NT, *ta ethnē* (the nations) is used to refer to non-Jewish nations or people (e.g., Luke 7:5; John 11:48, 50–52) while *hellēn* refers to a Greek rather than a barbarian (e.g., Rom. 1:14) and to a Gentile who speaks Greek (e.g., Gal. 3:28). In the HEBREW BIBLE, *gōyīm* is used (e.g., Gen. 10:5).

GESCHICHTE

German for history as SIGNIFICANCE in contradistinction to history as fact (*HISTORIE*). In theological studies of the twentieth century, scholars recognized that some events may be verified as factual (e.g., Jesus's existence as a first-century Jew) and thus historical. This is history as fact. However, the church's claims that Jesus was the Christ, the Son of God, the eschatological judge are historically unverifiable and constitute history as significance (*Geschichte*). Such claims are faith statements originating from the historic significance of the Jesus of history.

Contemporary critics, however, have challenged the distinction between history as fact (*Historie*, historical) and history as significance (*Geschichte*, historic) by arguing that all history is perspectival. Perhaps a better understanding comes from the distinction between history (the sum of past events) and HISTORIOGRAPHY (the NARRATIVE arrangement of past events). Since the only access historians have to the past is through TEXTS, all historiography is ideological INTERPRETATIONS of ideological interpretations. ("Text" here refers to any object that must be interpreted, whether manuscripts, physical ruins, archaeological discoveries, or pieces of art.) In other words, we do not have objective access to the past but only to interpretations of that past. A number of biblical scholars today point to the differences between the DEUTERONOMISTIC HISTORY and the CHRONISTIC HISTORY in the HEBREW BIBLE, and to the differences between the GOSPELS in the NT, arguing that these texts were written with theological AGENDAS that guided the SELECTION AND ARRANGEMENT of materials and sources.

GESTALT

A term in Gestalt psychology referring to the property of a whole thing that is not derivable from its parts and is greater than the sum of its parts. In LITERARY analysis, the idea has been extended to refer to a work's organic unity in terms of the relationship between the various elements and their roles in producing an overall or total effect. New Critics (*see* NEW CRITICISM) have thus argued that the MEANING of a piece of literature is greater than the sum of its parts and that this meaning can never be reduced to something that is paraphrasable. Any element within a literary work has value only to the extent that it becomes configured in a particular way with respect to the other elements. For example, the element of stone may be quite neutral when occurring in isolation, but when it is used in the Jacob NARRATIVE (Gen. 27–35), it serves as a major MOTIF, as do water in the Moses SAGA (Exod. 2–Num. 36) and fire in the Samson STORY (Judg. 13–16).

GLOSS

In TEXTUAL CRITICISM, a brief EXPLANATION, definition, or TRANSLATION of a word placed above that word or in the margin of a manuscript. When scribes inadvertently copied the gloss into the TEXT of the manuscript, a VARIANT READING would be produced. For the types of variants that may be the result of glosses, *see* TEXTUAL CRITICISM.

GNOME / GNOMIC VERSE

Deriving from the Greek for "opinion," a short, pithy statement of a general TRUTH, an APHORISM, dating from about the sixth century BCE in the West, although earlier in Egyptian, Chinese, and Sanskrit. One of the best examples of gnomic verse is the book of Proverbs in the HEBREW BIBLE.

GNOSTICISM

In BIBLICAL STUDIES, a term for a religious movement in the early period of the church that came to be recognized as heretical during the second century. Whether Gnosticism began as an expression within the church or was a rival religion to Christianity from outside is not known for certain. What scholarship does know with relative certainty is that although there were nuanced expressions

of Gnosticism, a religious outlook we refer to as Gnosticism came to be seen as heretical during the period of the second-century church. References to what we call Gnosticism in biblical studies can be found in the PASTORALS, the Gospel of John, and the Epistles of John. Combined with the NAG HAMMADI LIBRARY, these texts allow scholars to identify at least some of the key points of Gnosticism. At the heart of Gnosticism is the liberation of the spirit from its enslavement in the world of matter. The spirit is the divine part of the person, with its origin in the transcendent realm of God, but in order for the entrapped spirit to return to that realm, it must be freed from the world of matter by a special knowledge (*gnōsis*) given by a "redeemer." Since this present world of matter is evil, it could not have been created by the gnostic god. It is the work of an inferior god, a demiurge, sometimes identified with the God of the HEBREW BIBLE. These aspects of Gnosticism threatened the early church's central doctrines, such as creation, salvation, and CHRISTOLOGY.

GOOD NEWS BIBLE (GNB, TEV)

A committee-produced DYNAMIC EQUIVALENCE TRANSLATION of the BIBLE published by the American Bible Society (NT in 1966, OT in 1976, APOCRYPHA in 1979) as the GOOD NEWS BIBLE (GNB) or Today's English Version (TEV). As a common-language version, the Good News Bible tries to convey the SENSE of the original language in the IDIOMS and STRUCTURES of the receptor language—in this case, English. The translation is marked by CLARITY, simplicity, and unambiguity and is based on the United Bible Society's *Greek New Testament* and Kittel's edition of the MASORETIC TEXT. It also includes line drawings that are timeless, intended to bridge the gap between the contemporary and biblical worlds.

Sheeley and Nash believe that the GNB successfully translates the IDIOMS of the Hebrew and Greek, but they criticize the translation on two points. First, it tends to oversimplify some complex passages. For example, they point out that the Song of Songs reads like a "simple love story" (Sheeley and Nash, 85) and does not capture the more erotic and passionate nature of the TEXT. Second, it is inconsistent in its use of GENDER-INCLUSIVE LANGUAGE. In both text and chapter headings, it often uses gender-exclusive language (85). Since living languages change over time, some of the language of this translation has already become outdated. *See also* DYNAMIC EQUIVALENCE/ TRANSLATION.

Bibliography. Steven M. Sheeley and Robert N. Nash Jr., *The Bible in English Translation: An Essential Guide* (Nashville: Abingdon, 1997).

GOSPEL

A TRANSLATION of the Greek *euangelion*, used in Mark's Gospel (1:1) to refer to the NARRATIVE of Jesus's life. Therefore, the term has come to designate any narrative concerning Jesus. In the NT, there are four GOSPELS—Matthew, Mark, Luke, and John. While only these four were eventually included in the NT, other gospels circulated between the second and sixth centuries CE. For a list of these, *see* APOCRYPHA, NEW TESTAMENT.

Scholars disagree over the generic classification of the CANONICAL GOSPELS. Some assume that the AUTHOR of Mark created a new GENRE by selecting and arranging (*see* SELECTION AND ARRANGEMENT) materials from oral sources and references from the HEBREW BIBLE. Other scholars choose to see the Gospels as BIOGRAPHY, HISTORIOGRAPHY, Hellenistic ROMANCE, or varying combinations of the three. Biographies in the Greco-Roman TRADITION were characterized by ANECDOTE and SAYINGS of the SUBJECT, an interest in the essence of the subject or the representation of the subject as an ideal TYPE, and a defense of the subject. Also included in ancient biographies were LEGEND, PANEGYRIC, ARETALOGY, AMPLIFICATION, and comparison. The CANONICAL GOSPELS have obvious affinities with such biography. The Gospels also reflect the influence of romance by incorporating items characteristic of it: the JOURNEY MOTIF (Luke 9:51–19:44), aretalogy (throughout the Gospels), dreams (Matt. 1:20–25; 2:13), visions (Luke 1:22; 24:23), courtrooms scenes (Matt.

26:57–67; Luke 22–23), the crowd motif (seen surrounding Jesus in all the Gospels), SPEECHES (Matt. 5–7), storms (14:22–23), narrow escapes (2:13–20), historical characters (Pilate, Herod the Great, Herod Archelaus, etc.), and divine direction (throughout the Gospels).

Although the Gospels are not strictly biographies, historiography, or romance, they are not entirely unique narratives. The Gospels may be unique in their christological emphasis, but they are not unique in their FORM of presentation. It seems that the writers capitalized on the modes of literary production current in their day. Indeed, some recent scholars have argued that the authors of the Gospels may have been quite familiar with the genres of EPIC and TRAGEDY and produced their texts in conscious dialogue with them. *See* FOUR DOCUMENT HYPOTHESIS; MARKAN PRIORITY.

Bibliography. Elizabeth Haight, *Essays on the Greek Romances* (Port Washington, NY: Kennikat, 1943); Helmut Koester, *Introduction to the New Testament* (New York: de Gruyter, 1982), vol. 1; Albin Lesky, *History of Greek Literature* (New York: Thomas Y. Crowell, 1966); Charles Talbert, *Literary Patterns, Theological Themes, and the Genre of Luke-Acts* (Society of Biblical Literature Monograph Series 20; Missoula, MT: Scholars Press, 1974).

GOSPEL OF SIGNS

A designation for the Gospel of John based the AUTHOR's use of *sēmeion* (SIGN) and the STRUCTURE of the material when the word occurs. The first twelve chapters are commonly referred to as the Book of Signs, with the remaining passion and resurrection accounts explained in various ways. This observation has led some scholars to hypothesize that the first twelve chapters were originally a separate document and/or derive from an independent source. Each passage containing a sign has the following structure: (1) a NARRATION of the sign; (2) Jesus's INTERPRETATION of the sign, which invests it with some enigmatic SIGNIFICANCE; (3) misunderstandings among the audience; and (4) an EXPLANATION, which gradually divides the observers into those who are "drawn by the Father" to make an act of faith and seek further revelation and those who (mis)understand the explanation literally.

The pattern is illustrated well by the miracle of the feeding of the five thousand in John 6. The chapter begins with the feeding of the five thousand as a sign. It weaves from miraculous bread (v. 26) to a new heavenly bread (vv. 27–34), onward to life-giving bread that is somehow Christ himself (vv. 35–51a), culminating with the challenge: "Very truly, I tell you, unless you eat the flesh of the Son of Man and drink his blood, you have no life in you" (v. 53). This produces a split among his audience, with some crying, "This is more than we can stomach!" (cf. v. 60). The believers are represented by Peter's confession, "We have come to believe and know that you are the Holy One of God" (v. 69).

John 1–12 presents seven signs: changing water into wine at Cana (2:1–11), healing the official's son (4:46–54), healing the paralytic (5:1–15), feeding the crowd (6:1–15), walking on the sea (6:16–21), healing the blind man (9), and raising Lazarus (11).

GOSPEL PARALLEL. *See* SYNOPSIS

GRAF-WELLHAUSEN HYPOTHESIS

A theoretical account of the development of the PENTATEUCH, developed by K. H. Graf and refined and popularized by Julius Wellhausen between 1866 and 1884. They argued that the Pentateuch was formed over a long period of time by combining and revising written sources, a process guided by changing theological perspectives. These documents were composed at different times by and for people with different concerns and purposes. Each source thus constitutes a layer within the HEXATEUCH, and each layer has its peculiar language, STYLE, and theological POINT OF VIEW (van der Woude, 188–90). In the mid-seventh century BCE, two documents—the J (YAHWIST) document from the mid-ninth century and the E (ELOHIST) document from the eighth century—were combined by a REDACTOR. A later redactor added the D (DEUTERONOMIC CODE) in the mid-sixth century,

and an even later redactor added the P (PRIESTLY CODE) about 400 BCE. A summary of the characteristics of each source follows.

J (Yahwist). The hand of the Yahwist is first detected in Gen. 2:4b, where the divine name Yahweh appears. The Yahwist's depiction of God is simple, personal, and highly anthropomorphic. God walks, talks, forms with his hands, and experiments. God differs sharply from the transcendent being in Gen. 1:1–2:4a. Sections coming from the hand of the Yahwist include Gen. 2:4b–4:26; 6:1–8; 11:1–9; 12:1–4a, 6–20.

E (Elohist). This source favors the name Elohim for God and associates the divine name Yahweh with a revelation to Moses. The hand of the Elohist is found primarily in the PATRIARCHAL NARRATIVES. The Elohist depicts divine revelation as occurring through indirect means, such as dreams (Gen. 20:3) or a divine messenger (21:17). The vocabulary of the Elohist is also distinctly different from that of the Yahwist (e.g., the reference to Mount Horeb instead of Mount Sinai). Elohistic passages include Gen. 20:1–8; 21:8–34; 22:1–19.

P (Priestly). The Priestly Document differs in many ways from the Yahwist and Elohist sources. The interests of the priestly writer include cultic and priestly stipulations, brief historical notations, the sacrificial system after Moses, minute details, and the calendarizing of events. The priestly writer's style is formulaic and repetitive. God is depicted as a transcendent being, creating and arranging through fiat. The primary concern of the priestly writer is God rather than human beings. The God of Gen. 1 could never be characterized in the anthropomorphic terms of Gen. 2–4. Included among the priestly portions are Gen. 1:1–2:4a; 5:1–27; 9:1–17; 11:10–27; 25:7–10.

There is no unanimity among scholars about the extent, origin, and dating of these three sources (J, E, P). Van der Woude explains:

> The classical theory detected the three sources through Joshua. Since Noth, there is a tendency to extend J, E, and P only to Deuteronomy. Eissfeldt and others find J and E from Genesis through Kings. In general there is greater certainty about the

P sections. Researchers emphasize, however, their heterogeneous character, stressing the fact that P contains material from various times and sources. As regards the distribution of the narrative material over the various sources, there is a measure of unanimity with respect to Genesis, but not to the other books. . . . Presently it is generally assumed that J was composed in southern Israel and E in northern Israel. . . . It is customary now to consider P postexilic, while acknowledging that it contains much old material. There have always been some voices, however, that consider P preexilic. Most scholars think that P was composed in Babylon, but some would locate him in Jerusalem. (189)

D *(Deuteronomist).* The bulk of Deuteronomy (chaps. 12–26) is the book of the LAW found in the temple during the reign of Josiah in the seventh century. The book has its own paraenetic style (*see* PARAENESIS) and vocabulary. Most scholars today, however, agree that Deuteronomy is the product of a complex process of compilation and contains much older material. Characteristic of Deuteronomy is the attention given to the Levites and the proclamation and interpretation of the laws in the book (van der Woude, 190). Some scholars today propose that Deuteronomy was composed in the courts of Hezekiah and Josiah, receiving its final form in the second half of the seventh century BCE, at the hands of a circle of writers who produced the DEUTERONOMISTIC HISTORY (Weinfeld).

The Documentary Hypothesis, however, is not without its critics. Perhaps the most damaging criticism comes from R. N. Whybray, who offers two major critiques. First, Whybray challenges one of the fundamental ASSUMPTIONs of the hypothesis, that the Pentateuch may be divided into sources or documents because the TEXTs as we have them are riddled with REPETITION and contradictions, while the original sources before being redacted (selectively merged) were nonrepetitious and noncontradictory. Whybray inquires into the validity of this assumption by asking why the writing practices of the Hebrew writers changed so drastically from the original sources to the redacted texts. Is it possible that the earlier sources did contain contradictions and repetitions, just as the texts of the Pentateuch do? If this is the case, then the reconstruction of the sources becomes extremely difficult. Second, Whybray offers an alternative explanation for the repetitions and different styles in the Pentateuch. Since other literary documents use a variety of names for God, why should scholars assume that this practice in the Pentateuch necessarily signals a different source? There may be other reasons for the change, such as LITERARY, didactic, theological, emphatic, or simply unconscious reasons.

Bibliography. Moshe Weinfeld, *Deuteronomy and the Deuteronomic School* (Oxford: Oxford University Press, 1972); R. N. Whybray, *The Making of the Pentateuch: A Methodological Study* (JSOTSup 53; Sheffield: JSOT Press, 1987); A. S. van der Woude, ed., *The World of the Old Testament* (Grand Rapids: Eerdmans, 1989).

GRAMMATICAL CONTEXT

The concern with the original thought world of the AUTHOR as it is expressed through the language of the TEXT. An author combines words and phrases to express ideas. These words and phrases carry MEANING simply because they are arranged into what we might call sense units. The importance of grammatical considerations is that they increase the probability of the reader's recognition of these sense units. Consequently, the grammatical context will include attention to PHONOLOGY (word sounds), MORPHOLOGY (word forms), LEXICOLOGY (word meanings), and SYNTAX (word relationships).

GRAMMATICO-HISTORICAL EXEGESIS

The practice of interpreting or explicating a TEXT or passage by a careful analysis of the original language of the text and the historical CONTEXT in which the text was written. Both the languages of the Bible and the historical and cultural contexts differ from those of modern readers. Although many contemporary scholars argue that modern readers can never totally divest themselves of their SOCIAL LOCATION—with all its attending preconceptions, interpretive AGENDAs, and so forth—

most biblical scholars do not deny the value of an understanding of the language and culture of the biblical texts to the extent that such an understanding is possible.

GRAMMATOLOGY

Technically, the study of writing, its deciphering, and its historical origins. Grammatologists seek to correct what they see as an unfair treatment that writing has traditionally received in LINGUISTICS. From the time of Plato to Saussure, writing has been viewed as an imposition on SPEECH, the natural form of language. Jacques Derrida in *Of Grammatology* PROBLEMATIZEs the place of privilege given to speech over writing and the ASSUMPTION that MEANING is immediately present in the spoken word by arguing that writing actually precedes speech. For a definition of Derrida's concept of writing, see ÉCRITURE.

Bibliography. Jacques Derrida, *Of Grammatology* (trans. Gayatri Chakravorty Spivak; Baltimore: Johns Hopkins University Press, 1977).

GREAT BIBLE

The first authorized English VERSION and a revision of MATTHEW'S BIBLE by Miles Coverdale and Richard Grafton. The purpose behind the TRANSLATION was to correct what Thomas Cranmer, Archbishop of Canterbury, saw as a heavy Protestant bias of the COVERDALE BIBLE and Matthew's Bible. It was first published in 1539.

GREATER INTERPOLATION, THE

A long section of Luke's Gospel (9:51–18:14), containing a mixture of material from Q and that found only in Luke (the material peculiar to Luke is designated L). In FORM it is a JOURNEY MOTIF, from Galilee to Jerusalem. In CONTENT, however, it is a collection of miscellaneous ANECDOTES, PARABLES, and SAYINGS (Harris, 182). The section contains some of the most familiar parables in the NT (the prodigal son, the dishonest steward, the lost coin, the lost sheep, Lazarus and the rich man, the importunate widow, and the good Samaritan). In this section, Luke devel-

ops some of his major THEMES—prayer, reversal of fortunes, forgiveness, and acceptance of the marginalized.

Bibliography. Stephen L. Harris, *The New Testament: A Student's Introduction* (4th ed.; Boston: McGraw-Hill, 2002).

GREEK. *See* GREEK, KOINE

GREEK, KOINE

The vernacular Greek of the NT. In the centuries after the death of Alexander the Great, significant changes occurred in the Attic dialect, the form of Greek in which Alexander was most likely schooled. During the HELLENIZATION process beginning in the last part of the fourth century BCE, the Attic dialect came into contact with Eastern languages and eventually became the lingua franca of the Mediterranean world.

In the NT are three levels of Koine (from *koinē*, "common"). First, texts such as Mark, Revelation, and the Epistles of John evidence a TYPE of marketplace Koine, characterized by a lack of coordinate and subordinate clauses. Second, the Pauline corpus is written in a conversational STYLE of Koine, probably the style of the generally educated person. And third, Luke-Acts and the Epistle to the Hebrews use what may be called a LITERARY Koine, the polished, poetic style of a person consciously writing for literary quality.

Although some of the NT texts may not fit neatly within these categories, the following placement may be helpful:

Literary Koine	Conversational Koine	Marketplace Koine
Luke-Acts	Matthew	Mark
Hebrews	1–2 Corinthians	John
	Romans	1–3 John
	Galatians	Revelation
	1–2 Thessalonians	
	Philemon	
	Philippians	
	Colossians	
	Ephesians	
	1–2 Timothy	
	Titus	
	James	
	1–2 Peter	
	Jude	

GREEK DUALISM

An ancient Greek COSMOLOGY that posits two realms of reality: the physical and the metaphysical. Best expressed in Plato's writings, the metaphysical world consists of ideal forms or essences (e.g., beauty, perfection, justice); the physical world consists of objects that to varying degrees reflect the ideal forms. This dualism found its way into later HELLENISTIC PHILOSOPHY, which in turn directly influenced the NT writers and the early church fathers. Writers such as Paul and the AUTHOR of the Epistle to the Hebrews assume this dualistic cosmology. Furthermore, such major church doctrines as original sin and the Trinity were formulated within Greek dualism. For example, when Paul explains the universality of sin in Rom. 5:12–21, he claims that its universality is the result of the sin of Adam. It may very well be that Paul is founding his assessment on the idea that a universal essence (human nature) was originally corrupted and, consequently, every manifestation of that nature (individual humans) is likewise corrupted. It also is possible that the Christian doctrine of the Trinity was developed within a dualistic cosmology since it speaks of one divine essence (*ousia*) with three individual manifestations (*prosōpa*) of the same essence. Otherwise it could be argued that tritheism (the belief in three individual gods) is the result.

GREETING

A part of the opening and closing of an epistle. In the opening, the greeting is often a wish for good health. In the closing, greetings occur between the PEACE WISH and BENEDICTION. *See* EPISTOLARY LITERATURE.

GRIESBACH HYPOTHESIS

A theory about the relationship between the SYNOPTIC GOSPELS, introduced by J. J. Griesbach in 1783 and periodically resurrected and reformulated, most recently by Farmer. Griesbach hypoth-

esized that Matthew was the first Gospel, that it was a source for Luke, and that Mark, a conflation (*see* CONFLATE READING) of Matthew and Luke, was the last of the three to be written (Hauer and Young, 251–52).

Bibliography. W. R. Farmer, *The Synoptic Problem* (New York: Macmillan, 1964); Christian E. Hauer and William A. Young, *An Introduction to the Bible: A Journey into Three Worlds* (2nd ed.; Englewood Cliffs, NJ: Prentice Hall, 1990).

GUTENBERG BIBLE

The first BIBLE produced with movable type, by Johannes Gutenberg in 1456 in Germany.

GYNOCRITICISM

A mode of FEMINIST CRITICISM introduced by Elaine Showalter that is concerned with all types of writings by women, all matters pertaining to their production and INTERPRETATION, and the recovery and reevaluation of works authored by women. Showalter also uses the term to refer to the study of works by women for the purpose of articulating a women's literary history and the question of how SIGNIFICANCE is produced in communities of dominated women. Showalter also seeks to expand literature to include such marginalized works as diaries and journals. One of Showalter's main goals is freedom from male/patriarchal theories of LITERARY analysis and CANON. Consequently, gynocriticism encourages the construction of a uniquely female FRAMEWORK for analyzing literary works by women, and new models that are based on female experience, without reliance on models and theories constructed by men.

Bibliography. Elaine Showalter, "American Gynocriticism," *American Literary History* 5, no. 1 (1993): 111–28; idem, "A Criticism of Our Own: Autonomy and Assimilation in Afro-American and Feminist Literary Theory," in *The Future of Literary Theory* (ed. Ralph Cohen; New York: Routledge, 1989), 347–69; idem, *A Literature of Their Own: British Women Novelists from Brontë to Lessing* (Princeton: Princeton University Press, 1977).

HAGGADAH

One of the two basic types of content (*see* FORM/ CONTENT) in the literature of RABBINIC JUDAISM. The haggadah content derives from INTERPRE- TATION of the nonlegal material in the HEBREW BIBLE. "Haggadah" is also the name for the NARRA- TIVE GENRE of the rabbinic literature. For a more detailed discussion of haggadah, *see* MIDRASH; MISHNAH.

HAGIOGRAPHA

The name, derived from Greek, for the third divi- sion of the HEBREW BIBLE (*see* WRITINGS, THE).

HALAKAH

One of the two types of content (*see* FORM/CON- TENT) in the literature of RABBINIC JUDAISM. It consists of the INTERPRETATION of the legal ma- terial of the HEBREW BIBLE to deduce specific rules for governing conduct. "Halakah" is also the name for the legal GENRE of the rabbinic literature. *See* MIDRASH; MISHNAH.

HALLEL

A name for the psalms from Pss. 104 to 150 (esp. Pss. 113–118) in which "hallelujah" occurs and that are sung during Jewish festivals.

HAMARTIA

In Greek, a bad judgment, an accident, a miscal- culation, a hereditary weakness, bad character, or even ignorance. In Aristotle's description of TRAG- EDY in *Poetics*, it is the miscalculation that the hero makes because of a bit of missing information. Ar- istotle does, however, seem to leave room for the miscalculation being due to an error in character. In the NT, however, the Greek term *hamartia* (and

its cognates) has the SENSE of "missing the mark" of what is required to be faithful to God (e.g., Rom. 6:23; Heb. 9:28).

HAPAX LEGOMENON

A word that occurs only once in either the NT or the HEBREW BIBLE. It may also refer to a word that occurs only in the writings of a single AUTHOR. The problem in translating these solitary words is that there is no other CONTEXT within the text to help determine its CONNOTATION. An example of a hapax legomenon in the NT is *anaideia*, trans- lated "persistence" by the NRSV in Luke 11:8. The translators apparently chose "persistence" because of the repetitious requesting in the immediate con- text (11:2–4) and because persistence is at the heart of the PARABLE of the widow and the judge in 18:1–8.

Solutions, however, are not always obvious. The problem with languages such as the Greek in the NT and the Hebrew in the HEBREW BIBLE is that although their earlier stages are fixed in time, the languages continue to evolve, a fact that fre- quently makes the retrieval of the meaning of a hapax legomenon difficult. In an active language, when there is uncertainty about the MEANING of a word or phrase, one may ask someone who speaks the language to clarify. As shown above, in the case of Greek and Hebrew, however, context is the starting point for retrieving the meaning. Since the Bible, especially the Hebrew Bible, regu- larly employs synonyms or antonyms in a single context, especially in HEBREW POETRY, the mean- ing of hapax legomenona (plural) may often be inferred. Etymology may also help in suggesting the meaning. A word whose form is similar to that of a hapax legomenon in Hebrew may occur in another Semitic language, whether ancient, such as Akkadian, or modern, such as Arabic, and therefore such a cognate may shed light on the meaning in Hebrew. The interpreter should be careful, however, about assuming that a given word means the same thing in Biblical Hebrew as it did or does in another Semitic language. Last, ancient VERSIONS may be helpful in determining the meaning of a hapax legomenon. So, for example, the Greek word in the SEPTUAGINT may still carry the sense of the Hebrew word or phrase in question because the word may have been known to those who translated the text, in this case, from Biblical Hebrew into Greek more than two millennia ago.

HAPLOGRAPHY

A manuscript copying error in which a section of the text being copied is accidentally omitted because the omitted section lies between identical or similar words or phrases. For example, at least one manuscript of Luke omits all of 10:32 because both v. 31 and v. 32 end with the word *antiparēlthen*. Having finished copying v. 31, the scribe's eye fell to the identical word ending in v. 32 and commenced copying v. 33, omitting all of v. 32. This is an example of HOMOEOTELEUTON, from the Greek meaning "similar ending." HOMOEOARCHTON, "similar beginning," is essentially the same type of omission but occurs because of similar beginnings of a portion of text.

HARMONY OF THE GOSPELS

A work that integrates the four GOSPELs in such a way as to tell a single, unified STORY. Since such a work necessarily must gloss over the more distinct differences between the four, this GENRE has fallen into disrepute and has been replaced by synopses (*see* SYNOPSIS) of the four Gospels. The earliest extant harmony is Tatian's *DIATESSARON*, from the second century CE.

HASIDIM

A Hebrew word meaning "faithful ones"; a group within JUDAISM during the HELLENISTIC PERIOD dedicated to traditional practices such as dietary laws. During the period of Antiochus Epiphanes (175–164 BCE), who tried to impose Greek culture and religious practices on the Jews, the Hasidim engaged in passive resistance. The majority of scholars today believe that the book of Daniel was written for a community of Hasidim. Most of the various parties within Judaism during the NT period descended from the Hasidim (Harris, 61).

Bibliography. Stephen L. Harris, *The New Testament: A Student's Introduction* (Boston: McGraw-Hill, 2002).

HASMONEANS. *See* MACCABEES

HEBRAIC

An adjective denoting anything concerning Hebrew culture, in particular as presented in the HEBREW BIBLE.

HEBRAISM

Specifically, in BIBLICAL STUDIES, a characteristic of the Hebrew language occurring in the LXX or the NT. It is possible that certain expressions are Hebraisms, such as "they feared a great fear" (Mark 4:41, lit. trans.), "sin a sin" (1 John 5:16 KJV), "they rejoiced with exceeding great joy" (Matt. 2:10 KJV), and "judge righteous judgment" (John 7:24 KJV)—all instances of the cognate-accusative construction (with verb and direct object from the same root). On a larger stylistic level, however, the influence of Hebrew may be seen in the instances in the NT where AUTHORs employ polysyndeton (the practice of conjoining words or ideas with the multiple use of "and" in close succession). Apparently the author of Mark's GOSPEL was especially influenced in this way (e.g., Mark 8).

Hebraism has also come to refer to an attitude or a defining characteristic of a way of thinking that subordinates everything to the ideal of obedient conduct, as opposed to a HELLENISM, which subsumes everything to the intellect (Harmon and Holman, 244).

Bibliography. William Harmon and C. Hugh Holman, *A Handbook to Literature* (8th ed.; Upper Saddle River, NJ: Prentice Hall, 2000); Richard N. Soulen and R. Kendall Soulen, *Handbook of Biblical Criticism* (3rd ed.; Louisville: Westminster John Knox, 2001).

HEBREW

(1) As a noun, an ancient language, also called Biblical Hebrew; the Semitic language of the ancient Hebrews in which most of the HEBREW BIBLE is written; (2) as an adjective, used in the Bible (primarily in the Pentateuch and 1 Samuel) to refer to an Israelite.

HEBREW BIBLE

A term frequently used as a synonym for the thirty-nine books of the Christian OT, referring to the texts that became authoritative for JUDAISM sometime around 100 CE. The books in the Hebrew Bible actually number twenty-four because the twelve Minor Prophets are counted as only one book (*see* SCROLL OF THE TWELVE), as are the two books of Samuel, the two of Kings, the two of Chronicles, and Ezra–Nehemiah. The language is HEBREW, with the exception of Dan. 2:4b–7:28; Ezra 4:8–6:18; 7:12–26; Jer. 10:11; and two words (*yĕgar śāhădûtāʾ*) in Gen. 31:47, which are written in Aramaic. The Hebrew Bible has three divisions: the TORAH (LAW), the NEVIʾIM (Former and Latter PROPHETS), and the KETUBIM (WRITINGS). Within Judaism, these books are referred to as the TANAK, an acronym constructed from the first letter of the name of each of the three divisions (T-N-K), similar to the English *radar* for R-D-R (radio detection and ranging).

Although among scholars the term sometimes replaces the term *Old Testament*, the two may not always refer to exactly the same thing. First, the order of the texts in the church's OT differs from that of the Hebrew Bible. Second, the OT CANON for the Catholic Church includes the APOCRYPHA (from LXX, the Greek version), a collection of texts whose canonicity was rejected by Judaism and later by the churches of the Reformation. *See* BIBLE.

HEBREW CANON. *See* BIBLE; HEBREW BIBLE

HEBREW FOLKLORE. *See* FOLKLORE

HEBREW NARRATIVE

Hebrew PROSE writing as opposed to BIBLICAL POETRY. Although Hebrew narrative is similar in many respects to NARRATIVE in general, it has some interesting and unique differences. Meir Sternberg has offered a compelling argument for one of the key characteristics of Hebrew narrative. According to Sternberg, the author of Hebrew narrative translated certain doctrinal views into LITERARY correlatives. The doctrinal view of the omniscience of God is reflected in the standard literary use of the OMNISCIENT NARRATOR (although there are exceptions, such as the books of Ezra and Nehemiah). Just as Yahweh knows all TRUTH but does not reveal its totality to humanity, so the omniscient narrator does not make the reader privy to all the truth of a NARRATIVE WORLD. Human beings stumble and grope their way through life, learning through trial and error, reflection, and retrial. In a similar fashion, readers make their way through a TEXT. The narrator tells the truth, but not the whole truth. As a result, the text contains "gaps of INDETERMINACY" (places in the narrative where some pertinent information is missing), which the reader must fill in. As the reader moves through the text, information is encountered that generates inferences. As the reader progresses, however, the text offers additional information (e.g., information concerning time, motive, cause, effect) that requires the reader to reread the text, adjusting the previous inferences. Another product of these intentional gaps is the raising of "narrative interest" via suspense, surprise, and curiosity. Other TRANSLATIONS of doctrinal views into literary correlatives include "the doctrine of free will into complex characterization, . . . human restrictedness into studies in ambiguity, omnipotence and providence into well-made plots, control of history into cyclical and analogical design imposed upon recalcitrant matter, and the demand to infer from past to present into ordeal by interpretation" (Sternberg, 157). For discussions of the mechanics of Hebrew narrative, see CHARACTERIZATION; INTRATEXTUAL DYNAMICS; PLOT; POINT OF VIEW; SETTING.

Bibliography. Meir Sternberg, *The Poetics of Biblical Narrative* (Bloomington: Indiana University Press, 1985).

HEBREW POETRY. *See* BIBLICAL POETRY

HEGEMONY

A term used especially by Marxist critics (*see* MARXIST CRITICISM) to refer to political dominion of a certain class within a society. It has, however, been defined more narrowly by Antonio Gramsci to refer to the ascendancy of a class and the process by which the ascendancy is accomplished. His ASSUMPTION is that economic and political ascendancy is preceded by cultural and especially intellectual dominion. The intellectuals in a class must first articulate a unified WORLDVIEW and then work to STRUCTURE the institutions to reflect that worldview.

> Bibliography. Antonio Gramsci, *Selections from the Prison Notebooks* (ed. and trans. Quintin Hoare and Geoffrey Nowell Smith; New York: International Publishers, 1971).

HEIGHTENING

A term used by Robert Alter as a characteristic of semantic parallelism in BIBLICAL POETRY. Heightening occurs in a poetic line when the movement from the first half of the line to the second half either focuses, concretizes, or further specifies the content of the first. For example, Prov. 3:10 is an example of heightening by SPECIFICATION: "Then your barns will be filled with plenty, / and your vats will be bursting with wine."

> Bibliography. Robert Alter, *The Art of Biblical Poetry* (New York: Basic Books, 1985).

HEILSGESCHICHTE

A German word variously translated as "SALVATION HISTORY," "redemptive history," or "sacred history" in OT theology and denoting a theological principle that governs INTERPRETATION of the Bible as an account of God's continuous salvific acts in history. The term may be applied to the theological history found in the DEUTERONOMISTIC HISTORY and in Luke-Acts.

HELLENISM

In philosophical and cultural studies, the Greek frame of mind, which subordinates everything in the human person to the intellect. It stands in contradistinction to HEBRAISM. *Hellenism* also refers to the culture that developed out of the interpenetration of Eastern and Greek cultures after the death of Alexander the Great in the late fourth century BCE. While the Greek culture dominated, there was a mixing of religious and philosophical influence. This process of interpenetration of cultures is usually referred to as hellenization, while the period of such cultural confluence, beginning with Alexander and continuing into the Roman imperial period, is referred to as the Hellenistic period. This does not mean that Hellenism ceased to be influential during the Roman imperial period. On the contrary, Hellenism continued to be effective throughout that period. By the first century BCE, a distinctively universal culture (an amalgamation of Greek and Oriental) had emerged under the umbrella of a single political entity: Rome. Because Christianity had its birth during the Roman imperial period, we might rightly expect it to exhibit Hellenistic traits. Christianity was the heir of a HELLENISTIC JUDAISM. For the most part, the earliest Christians were people whose lives and thoughts were partially formed and molded by Hellenism. The earliest Christians used the SEPTUAGINT (the Greek translation of the HEBREW BIBLE) as their BIBLE. This is significant when we recognize that religious and philosophical concepts are modified when writings are translated from one language to another.

Hellenism is characterized by syncretism (the mixture of WORLDVIEWS and ideologies), especially in the area of philosophy and religions, where there is an obvious mixture of Greek and Oriental elements. Even where local and territorial religious expressions remained the same in essence, these expressions in time appeared in Greek dress. The LXX is an example of this syncretism. Because language is the depository of a culture's symbols, when the texts of one culture are translated into the language (symbols) of another culture, the symbols of both cultures gain new meanings and lose old resonances. In other words, the LXX reflects the SYMBOLIC WORLDS of both Jew and Greek.

Moreover, the syncretistic tendency of hellenization resulted in a sort of universalization. When the local deities of the East came into contact with the Greek pantheon, some equating of these two pantheons was inevitable. This incipient universalization in turn led to the idea of the existence of a single divine power with multiple manifestations. Thus, when the highest god of another culture (e.g., the Canaanite god Baal ha Shemaim [lord of heaven]) was regularly identified with the highest god of Greek culture (e.g., the Greek deity Zeus), the result was to "reduce local allegiances in favor of more universal ones" (Johnson, 25). There is not a long stretch from equating the highest gods of different cultures to the assumption that these gods are nothing more than individual manifestations of a single supreme power (25). Thus, at least in some areas, this syncretism hastened the move toward monotheism.

But the sacrifice of local deities on the altar of universalism produced a view of the universe as being governed by chance and fate. This in turn resulted in a search for a more profound, individual religious experience, since the universalization of Hellenism presented a universe in which individuals had no control over their existence. A spirit of fatalism characterized the period. When the ideal of individual citizen participation in the community was frustrated by the decline of the city-state, the citizens lost their social identity. When the local deity became identical with similar gods of other people (i.e., when individual religious experience gave way to religious universalism or monotheism), people lost their religious identity, and their lives became meaningless, governed by chance and fate. Since human life was predestined by these powers, humans had little or no control over their existence. In the wake of such losses, a need for individual salvation became paramount. This attitude characterizes the Hellenistic period, especially during the period of Roman rule, when individual identity was expected to give way to the welfare of the state. As a result, both religious and philosophical expression in the Hellenistic period placed increased importance on the individual and the salvation of the individual from the control of a universe governed by chance and fate. It was

to this matter of individual salvation that all the philosophical and religious expressions spoke. *See* HELLENISTIC PHILOSOPHIES.

Bibliography. Luke T. Johnson, *The Writings of the New Testament: An Introduction* (Philadelphia: Fortress, 1986); W. Randolph Tate, *Biblical Interpretation: An Integrated Approach* (rev. ed.; Peabody, MA: Hendrickson, 1997).

HELLENISTIC JUDAISM

Although JUDAISM was a mixture of competing sects during the Hellenistic period, it was profoundly influenced by Greco-Roman culture. By the third century BCE, most Jews of the DIASPORA and many in Palestine spoke Greek. Eventually the Jews of the Diaspora used a Greek TRANSLATION of the HEBREW BIBLE, the SEPTUAGINT, later adopted by the Christians.

HELLENISTIC PERIOD. *See* HELLENISM; HELLENISTIC PHILOSOPHIES

HELLENISTIC PHILOSOPHIES

Philosophical schools or movements that became popular after the death of Alexander the Great (323 BCE). Before the HELLENISTIC PERIOD (323 BCE–200 CE), Greek philosophies were primarily concerned with creating a world in which there was some rational system of MEANING, a universe governed by some ontological reality, against which everything has its meaning and SIGNIFICANCE. But when the universal ideal of the Greek golden age failed, a sense of skepticism became prevalent. Therefore, Hellenistic philosophies (such as STOICISM, EPICUREANISM, and NEOPYTHAGOREANISM) contained an element of skepticism.

Hellenistic philosophical schools were both religious and philosophical. Members of such schools tended to live according to the teachings of their founding masters. The schools emphasized ethics, offered their members a WORLDVIEW, and suggested practical ways for adherents to conduct themselves in everyday living. In a world where individuals were on their own, many were looking for such guidance within a group of friends, who would supply a sense of community. The Hellenistic philosophies spoke to individuals and their place in the universe. Paul Tillich offers the following insight: "During this period when the skeptical mood permeated the ancient world, they wanted certainty above all; they demanded it in order to live. Their answer was that their great teachers, Plato, Aristotle, Zeno, Epicurus, Plotinus, were not merely thinkers or professors, but they were inspired men" (5). Stories about the founders of these philosophical communities resemble accounts Christians have related about their founder. For instance, Epicurus was called *sōtēr*, "savior," by his followers. Commenting on this, Tillich says: "What does this mean? He was called *sōtēr* because he did the greatest thing anyone could do for his followers: he liberated them from anxiety" (5). In one way or another the Hellenistic philosophies offered freedom from the anxiety of the age by giving the individual a pattern of living that afforded at least a measure of control. These philosophical schools constitute one of the immediate sources for a great deal of early Christian thought.

Stoicism. STOICISM was one of the most influential philosophical systems of the Hellenistic period. Founded in Athens by Zeno of Citium (332–260 BCE), Stoicism acquired its name from the painted porch (*stoa*) in the Agora, where Zeno taught. Stoicism was introduced to Rome (161 BCE) by Panaetius, who made Stoicism more practical. Seneca (ca. 4 BCE–65 CE), a contemporary of Paul, did much to popularize the ethical teachings of Stoicism by his writings.

Resting on a religious basis, Stoicism made a strong appeal to the Roman character. For the Stoic, the universe itself was God, and the ultimate substance of the universe was a "fiery breath" or "spirit," which was distributed throughout in varying degrees (Martin, 42). This spirit was considered to be alive and rational, and in its manifestation as reason (LOGOS), it introduced order into the world. By having reason, humanity possessed a particle of the divine breath, and the individual was capable of entering into communion with the supreme reason. *Logos* referred to the reasonable STRUCTURE indicated by a word, thus MEANING

the universal law of reality. The Logos was also the LAW that determined the movement of all reality. According to the Stoics, the Logos was in everything (cf. John's comment, "The true light, which enlightens everyone, was coming into the world" [John 1:9]). This idea of the Logos was one of Stoicism's major influences on early Christianity.

The fundamental tenet of Stoicism is that virtue is the only good, and vice is the only evil. The wise person is not mastered by pain or pleasure, wealth or poverty, or success or misfortune. Self-control or contentment (*enkrateia*) is the hallmark of the wise person (cf. Paul's comments in Phil. 4:11–12).

There are similarities between the teachings of the NT and those of Stoicism. This is especially true of the writings of Paul. Paul's JUDAISM was itself influenced by Hellenistic concepts and modes of expression. Paul adapts the religious views of the HEBREW BIBLE and PALESTINIAN JUDAISM along with the style and views of Hellenistic popular philosophy (Furnish, 46). Paul read a Greek Bible, which bore the impressions of the Hellenistic society; he wrote in Greek and labored among Gentile people.

Paul's ethical teaching is indebted to Hellenistic sources in a general way. Scholars have pointed out the numerous Pauline phrases, METAPHORS, and terms that were familiar in Stoicism. These include metaphors of life as warfare (2 Cor. 10:3; 1 Thess. 5:8) or as an athletic competition (1 Cor. 9:25); descriptions of God as "all in all" (1 Cor. 15:28) and as the one "from, through, and to whom" all things are (Rom. 11:36); the term "your duty" (Philem. 8); the concepts of "spending" and "being spent" for others (2 Cor. 12:15) and disregarding the external circumstances of one's life (2 Cor. 6:8–10; Phil. 4:11–12; Furnish, 46). Philippians 4:8 also contains clear Stoic influence. Paul commends two qualities in this verse that are not mentioned elsewhere in the NT: "pleasing" and "commendable." Other terms in this verse that have a significant place in Stoic ethics are "excellence" and "worthy of praise."

The moral teachings of Seneca exhibit many parallels to the teachings of Jesus in the Sermon on the Mount. Examples include Seneca's statements that "the mind, unless it is pure and holy, comprehends not God" and that "a man is a robber even before he stains his hands; for he is already armed to slay, and has the desire to spoil and to kill" (Lightfoot, 287–88). There are also echoes of the PARABLE of the sower, of the mustard seed, and of the forgiven debtor.

Other NT writings also reflect Stoic concepts, such as John's Gospel and his portrayal of the Logos. The metaphor that instructs the readers to "gird up the loins" of their minds (cf. 1 Pet. 1:13 KJV) also appears in Seneca's writings as an instruction to let the mind stand ready. Thus it is reasonable to assume that because the NT writers were so influenced by Stoicism, any reading and understanding of a TEXT is enhanced by a familiarity with Stoicism.

Epicureanism. Epicureanism advocated the higher pleasures of the mind along with an emphasis on friendship and contentment. Like Paul, Epicurus was a father figure to his followers; he founded communities of followers and instructed these communities through LETTERs. Unlike Paul, his birthday was celebrated annually, and his followers bestowed divine honors on him.

Epicurus (341–270 BCE) sought to deliver his followers from what he perceived to be the darkness of religion. He accomplished this through his materialistic approach to the universe. If the soul is a type of physical object composed of atoms, it will die when the body dies. Therefore, since the soul does not survive the death of the body, there is no future life of bliss or punishment to worry about now. This ABSENCE of any future life was intended to relieve the followers of any fear of punishment after death. If there is no future life to be concerned about, people should live with their attention directed squarely toward this life, of which the highest good is tranquility, the absence of agitation.

Amid the devaluing effects of the universalization of HELLENISM, Epicurus succeeded in creating a community or circle of close friends and associates, countering the loss of the sense of community so prevalent in Hellenism. Within this circle of friends, one could find the greatest pleasure of the soul. This idea of friendship is basic to Epicureanism, for the individual is a stranger in the world. Each person needs friends who offer shelter and give pleasure (see Lightfoot, 298–301).

Some similarities between Epicureanism and the early Christian communities exist, but they seem to be only superficial. Still, the Epicureans and Christians were responding to the same loss precipitated by Hellenism—the devaluation of the individual. The founding of a community where all are equal, whether slave, free, woman, or man, and where the community is insulated and separated from the world and bonded together by worship and reverence—all this is characteristic of both Epicureans and Christians. The following passage in 1 Thess. 4:9–12 illustrates this point:

> Now concerning love of the brothers and sisters, you do not need to have anyone write to you, for you yourselves have been taught by God to love one another; and indeed you do love all the brothers and sisters throughout Macedonia. But we urge you, beloved, to do so more and more, to aspire to live quietly, to mind your own affairs, and to work with your hands, as we directed you, so that you may behave properly toward outsiders and be dependent on no one.

Paul is describing a quiet, separated life of tranquility. Gilbert Murray (204–5) has suggested that the early Christian communities were patterned after the Epicurean communities, even down to the use of the title "friend" in John 15:15 and 3 John 15.

Neopythagoreanism. In the first century BC, there was a revival of the ideas of Pythagoras (ca. 569–475 BCE). The Neopythagoreans were interested in astrology and in the stellar space between God and the material world. This space was inhabited by intermediary demons, arranged in a descending order. The Neopythagoreans also conceived of the material world as evil since it is so far removed from a transcendent god. This negative view of the material world became one of the primary tenets of GNOSTICISM.

The best-known adherent of Neopythagorean-ism was Apollonius of Tyana (first century CE), who is known through his biographer, Philostratus, who portrays him as an itinerant teacher, traveling to the major cities of the Roman Empire. He was a wise man with miraculous powers to heal the sick. He rejected marriage (at least for himself), was able to see into the past and future, and taught a substitution of prayer and meditation for animal sacrifice. The following parallels exist between Philostratus's account of the life of Apollonius and that of Jesus (Ferguson, 306–7): (1) his miraculous birth; (2) the gathering of a circle of disciples; (3) itinerant teaching; (4) a collection of miracle stories (demon-possessed boy, lame man, blind man, paralytic); (5) disappearance of Apollonius at his trial; (6) the charge that Apollonius was a magician.

Conclusion. The writings of earliest Christianity primarily took shape within and were addressed to the Hellenistic world. Many scholars therefore argue that interpreters should give due weight to the positive influence of Hellenistic philosophical thought on the NT writings.

Bibliography. Everett Ferguson, *Backgrounds of Early Christianity* (Grand Rapids: Eerdmans, 1987); Victor P. Furnish, *Theology and Ethics of Paul* (Nashville: Abingdon, 1968); J. B. Lightfoot, *St. Paul's Epistle to the Philippians* (Grand Rapids: Zondervan, 1963; repr., Peabody, MA: Hendrickson, 1993); Ralph P. Martin, *New Testament Foundations* (2 vols.; Grand Rapids: Eerdmans, 1978); Gilbert Murray, *Five Stages of Greek Religion* (Garden City, NY: Doubleday, 1955); Paul Tillich, *A History of Christian Thought* (New York: Simon & Schuster, 1968).

HELLENISTIC ROMANCE. *See* ROMANCE

HELLENISTS

A term used in Acts 6:1 and 9:29, most likely referring to Greek-speaking Jews in the Christian community in Jerusalem.

HELLENIZATION. *See* HELLENISM; HELLENISTIC PHILOSOPHIES

HENDIADYS

A FIGURE OF SPEECH in which two parts of a single idea are connected by a coordinating conjunction for effect instead of placing the two in a lead-noun-and-modifier relationship. Mark makes great use of this practice (e.g., Mark 6:26), and in John 1:17 the phrase "full of grace and truth" may be a hendiadys for God's gracious truth.

HENDIATRIS

Found in both the HEBREW BIBLE and the NT, the use of three words to communicate one idea. Examples are in John 14:6, "I am the way, and the truth, and the life"; as well as in Matt. 7:7, "Ask, and it will be given you; search, and you will find; knock, and the door will be opened for you." A further sample is in the Hebrew Bible, in Dan. 3:7, with Nebuchadnezzar's instructions involving "all the peoples, nations, and languages."

HENOTHEISM

The belief in one superior God among many. There is some evidence in the HEBREW BIBLE that before embracing MONOTHEISM, the Hebrews were henotheists (e.g., Exod. 20:3; Deut. 5:7).

HERESY OF PARAPHRASE

A term introduced into NEW CRITICISM by Cleanth Brooks to describe the ASSUMPTION that the essence of a LITERARY work can be captured in a paraphrase. Since a TEXT is a complex integration of FORM and CONTENT and means what it means in terms of that integration, a paraphrase not only is incapable of capturing that meaning but also will usually distort it.

Bibliography. Cleanth Brooks, *The Well Wrought Urn: Studies in the Structure of Poetry* (New York: Harcourt, Brace, 1947).

HERMENEUTIC(AL) CIRCLE

The ASSUMPTION that a reader can understand a part of the TEXT only after the whole has been grasped and that the whole can be grasped only after each of the parts has been understood. Accordingly, as a reader progresses through a text, the reader will form a provisional SENSE of the whole, modifying it as the parts accumulate. But as the reader's ever-changing sense of the whole develops, this person will modify their understanding of the parts. Also included in the concept is the assumption that understanding is always partially a product of the reader's forestructure (*see* FRAMEWORK). As this forestructure changes over time, so will the reader's posture before the text and thus the reader's reconfiguration of the process.

HERMENEUTICAL METHOD

The CRITICAL METHODOLOGY that a CRITIC or reader employs to interpret a TEXT. *See* HERMENEUTICS.

HERMENEUTICAL PRINCIPLE

In HERMENEUTICS, the interpretive key or frame through which one understands a TEXT. For example, Luther understood Romans through the key "justification by faith." Robert Jewett, on the other hand, argues that the key to Romans is the equity between Jews and Gentiles in grace. In contemporary hermeneutical theory, scholars generally agree that all INTERPRETATION is situated in and therefore conditioned or guided by AGENDAS and previous ASSUMPTIONS. In most forms of FEMINIST CRITICISM, the key assumption is that the biblical texts were written within the structures of PATRIARCHY and reflect that viewpoint. Therefore, they must be read and interpreted from a posture of suspicion. In other words, there is no interpretation that begins without a hermeneutical principle.

Bibliography. Robert Jewett, *Christian Tolerance: Paul's Message to the Modern Church* (Philadelphia: Westminster, 1982).

HERMENEUTICAL QUESTION

The question as to whether and by what interpretive methods the biblical texts can communicate meaningfully to contemporary culture.

HERMENEUTICAL SPIRAL

A modification of what biblical scholars refer to as the HERMENEUTICAL CIRCLE: the relationship between understanding the parts in light of the whole and the whole in light of the parts. The hermeneutical spiral emphasizes the role that reader

PRESUPPOSITIONS play in understanding and the construction of MEANING (Osborne, 324–25). Readers confront TEXTS with biases and PREUNDERSTANDINGS that influence their CONFIGURATIONS of the text. In turn, these configurations may challenge preunderstandings. Consequently, the reader becomes not only the interpreter but also the interpreted. When a person's preunderstanding changes, so will one's next reading of the text. When this process continues over time, the result is a progressive, spiraling development of understanding.

Bibliography. Grant Osborne, *The Hermeneutical Spiral* (Downers Grove, IL: InterVarsity, 1991).

HERMENEUTICS

Generally, the study of the locus of MEANING and the principles of interpreting TEXTS. Traditionally, BIBLICAL HERMENEUTICS has been defined as bipolar, involving EXEGESIS and INTERPRETATION: exegesis is the process of examining a text to ascertain what its first readers would have understood it to mean; interpretation is the task of explaining or drawing out the implications of the understanding for contemporary readers and hearers.

In contemporary biblical studies, however, hermeneutics has expanded to include the idea of interpretive methodology employed by the interpreter along with the repertoire the interpreter brings to the text. The ASSUMPTION is that the time-honored HISTORICAL-CRITICAL METHOD of interpreting texts is too limited in that it short-circuits the process by excluding consideration of the role the reader and the reader's repertoire play in determining meaning. In present scholarship, there are three different categories of methods regarding the process and principles of interpretation: AUTHOR-CENTERED INTERPRETATION (with attention directed to the WORLD BEHIND THE TEXT), TEXT-CENTERED INTERPRETATION (with the focus on the WORLD OF THE TEXT), and READER-CENTERED INTERPRETATION (with a focus on the WORLD IN FRONT OF THE TEXT and reader activities). There has been a growing recognition not only that texts are written within historical, cultural, and ideological (*see* IDEOL-OGY) CONTEXTs but also that texts are interpreted within these contexts. Because the latter contexts include either conscious or unconscious assumptions, some being methodological or theoretical, current considerations of hermeneutics include the examination of interpretive theories. These theories occupy a considerable part of this manual. *See also entries under* INTERPRETATION.

HERMENEUTICS, BIBLICAL. *See* BIBLICAL HERMENEUTICS

HERMENEUTICS, EVALUATIVE. *See* EVALU-ATIVE HERMENEUTICS

HERMENEUTICS, FEMINIST. *See* FEMINIST CRITICISM

HERMENEUTICS, JEWISH. *See* RABBINIC HERMENEUTICS

HERMENEUTICS, LIBERATION. *See* LIBERA-TION HERMENEUTICS

HERMENEUTICS, MIDRASHIC. *See* MID-RASH; RABBINIC HERMENEUTICS

HERMENEUTICS, NARRATIVE. *See* NARRA-TIVE HERMENEUTICS

HERMENEUTICS, RABBINIC. *See* RABBINIC HERMENEUTICS

HERMENEUTICS OF CONSENT

A term in FEMINIST CRITICISM denoting the tendency in traditional BIBLICAL HERMENEUTICS to subscribe to MEANING derived from historical-critical-theological study and its application to contemporary culture. Feminist critics such as Elisabeth Schüssler Fiorenza call for an evaluation of TEXTs and their INTERPRETATIONs as they have functioned in the history of the church, which may lead to the conclusion that not all texts have theological significance for today's church.

> Feminist theology questions whether we can repeat the patriarchal biblical language for God today,

and political theology doubts that biblical texts that speak of God as an absolute monarch are still adequate. What is necessary for theological interpretation today, therefore, is not only an understanding of their historical-theological meaning but also a critical-theological evaluation of their functions in the history of the church and in the contemporary church. (Schüssler Fiorenza, 39)

Bibliography. Elisabeth Schüssler Fiorenza, *Bread Not Stone* (10th anniversary ed.; Boston: Beacon, 1995).

HERMENEUTICS OF REMEMBRANCE

Part of Elisabeth Schüssler Fiorenza's feminist hermeneutic. She argues that although TEXTs that have traditionally marginalized or have been used to perpetuate the MARGINALIZATION of women should no longer be counted as authoritative, they should become resources for remembering how women were oppressed and marginalized. While feminists may recognize these texts as reflecting reality, they should not equate this with acceptance of the validity of that reality. The hermeneutics of remembrance should allow CRITICs to reconstruct the origin and history of early Christianity from a feminist perspective. The biblical CANON retains only scattered remnants of the early nonpatriarchal Christian community, yet these remnants give evidence that PATRIARCHAL STRUCTURES were not originally part of it.

HERMENEUTICS OF SUSPICION

In FEMINIST CRITICISM, an interpretive approach based on the ASSUMPTION that the biblical TEXTs were written in androcentric language (*see* ANDROCENTRISM) and reflect PATRIARCHAL STRUCTURES. This assumption is supported by the claim that the biblical AUTHORs were men and that most biblical interpreters in the church and in academia have been and are men. Consequently, feminist CRITICs read these texts, TRADITIONs, and INTERPRETATIONs with suspicion in order to uncover suppressed traditions behind the androcentric language and patriarchal structures. Examples are maternal God-language in the HEBREW BIBLE, women apostles in the early church, and women leaders in the synagogue. Of equal importance is the exposure of patriarchal interests in the CANON-IZATION PROCESS, the treatment of women in both the HEBREW BIBLE and the NT (e.g., the way the PASTORAL EPISTLES develop a patriarchal model of leadership), the use of gender-exclusive language in TRANSLATIONS, and "linguistic sexism" in contemporary translations (Schüssler Fiorenza, 15–18).

Bibliography. Elisabeth Schüssler Fiorenza, *Bread Not Stone* (10th anniversary ed.; Boston: Beacon, 1995).

HERMETIC LITERATURE. *See* CORPUS HERMETICUM

HERSTORY

A term current in FEMINIST CRITICISM that calls attention to the ANDROCENTRISM of the writing of history. Although the word *history* does not, in fact, originate from the words *his* and *story*, feminists emphasize that the word "history" itself announces that his-story is told and interpreted from a male perspective at the expense of negating or ignoring the role of women in the past. Feminist CRITICS therefore try to resurrect women's subjugated role in the past by retelling the past from the perspective of women.

HETEROGLOSSIA

A term in the CRITICAL THEORY of Mikhail Bakhtin referring to the PRESENCE of more than one voice in a TEXT. *See* DIALOGISM.

HETEROTOPIA

A term in the work of POSTMODERN philosopher Michel Foucault to designate a universe or world without a center. The postmodern world is a collection of diverse societies, each with its own collection of standards, systems, and values.

HEXAEMERON

The six days of creation in Gen. 1.

HEXAPLA

A six-column edition of the OT by Origin of Alexandria (185–254 CE), preserved only in some fragments. The columns consist of the Hebrew, a TRANSLITERATION of the Hebrew into Greek, and four Greek versions, including the LXX. The adjective *Hexaplaric* denotes the versions of the LXX that have been influenced by the Hexapla.

HEXATEUCH

A term in the SOURCE CRITICISM of Julius Wellhausen for the first six books in the HEBREW BIBLE (Genesis–Joshua), which he assumed were based on the same LITERARY sources.

HIERARCHICALISM

The creation of levels of values, responsibilities, roles, and authority in societies. A key ASSUMPTION in FEMINIST CRITICISM is that in patriarchal societies (*see* PATRIARCHY), such levels are created by men to reflect and legitimate male power. In CULTURAL CRITICISM and LIBERATION THEOLOGY, the assumption is that these levels are established by the dominant culture.

HIERARCHICAL STRUCTURES

An important issue in FEMINIST CRITICISM, designating levels of institutionalized power that establish, reflect, and perpetuate the cultural values and norms of men in a society. *See* PATRIARCHY.

HIGH-CONTEXT SOCIETIES. *See* SOCIAL-SCIENTIFIC CRITICISM

HIGHER CRITICISM

A term, with roots in the late eighteenth century at the University of Göttingen, for the critical study of the BIBLE concerning dates of composition, authorship, and cultural and historical BACKGROUNDS. It was later expanded to include the LITERARY study of the Bible. Higher criticism is distinct from LOWER CRITICISM, a term now used only infrequently to refer to TEXTUAL CRITICISM.

HILLEL, SCHOOL OF

A school of PHARISAIC JUDAISM following the teachings of Rabbi Hillel, a first-century sage who held to a more flexible INTERPRETATION of the

TORAH. This school had a profound impact on the development of JUDAISM after the temple's destruction in 70 CE. The interpretive rules attributed to Hillel provided a means of adapting and applying the SCRIPTURES to new and novel situations. Seven rules are attributed to Hillel: (1) that which applies in a minor case will apply in a major case; (2) when the same words apply to two cases, the same considerations should apply to both; (3) if the same phrase appears in more than one passage, then a consideration found in one of them applies to all; (4) a principle can be formulated from two or more texts and then applied to other texts; (5) a general rule may be particularized in another verse, or a particular rule may be expanded into a general principle; (6) a problem or difficulty in one passage may be clarified by comparing it to another passage that has points of similarity; and (7) the SENSE of words or phrases may be understood by examining the immediate LITERARY and GRAMMATICAL CONTEXT.

HISTORICAL CONSCIOUSNESS

The awareness that TEXTS of the past were influenced by the cultural CONTEXT in which they were written and by the ideologies (*see* IDEOLOGY) of those who wrote them. Consequently, modern expectations of logic and cultural categories are not sufficient or appropriate for understanding the texts. This consciousness is especially important in studying the biblical texts because of the historical distance between them and the modern reader. For example, the SYNOPTIC GOSPELS, though covering some of the same events, were composed within different contexts by authors who had distinctly different agendas.

HISTORICAL-CRITICAL METHOD, THE

A foundationalist (*see* FOUNDATIONALISM) form of scholarship encompassing a group of CRITICAL METHODOLOGIES. The historical-critical method tries to interpret TEXTS in light of their *SITZ IM LEBEN* (life setting). In other words, it focuses on the "career of the text," the text's history and its originating circumstances (Hayes and Holladay,

46). This historical orientation seeks to gain as much knowledge as possible about the situations out of which the text arose and the historical, religious, and cultural situation described by the text. It asks questions such as these: By whom and for whom was the text written? What were the circumstances that gave it birth? Why was it preserved and transmitted? What sources were used? How will a knowledge of the social, political, and religious conditions that generated the text aid the interpreter in a better understanding of the text? The text is seen as a shell with many layers. If the layers were appropriately peeled away, the scholar could discover the core and its original setting. Perhaps underlying the approach is the assumption that the real MEANING resides in the text's originating circumstances and that subsequent development and recontextualization have distorted this meaning.

The three styles of CRITICISM associated with the historical-critical method are SOURCE CRITICISM, FORM CRITICISM, and REDACTION CRITICISM. Both source and form critics suppose that meaning rests in the original text and its setting in life. Since these primal texts have been distorted through the church's subsequent use of them, historical critics have sought to salvage the original texts in their originating settings.

Although source critics seek to uncover the sources on which the present texts rest, form critics desire to return to the oral phase of a particular LITERARY form. The ASSUMPTION is that the key to meaning lies in the original oral form, not in the final written form. The original form in its original sociological setting determines meaning. Original form and setting are constitutive of meaning.

In its interest with the final form of the text, redaction criticism is more akin to present-day LITERARY CRITICISM than are source and form criticisms. Redaction criticism is dependent on source and form criticism because of its stress on the identification of the theological purpose that guided the author in the selection and organization of the individual, isolated forms. To varying degrees, each of the methods associated with the historical-critical method stresses that the best approach to interpreting a text hinges on a RECONSTRUCTION of the text's historical milieu. The historical approach ultimately leads to the view that the text is an artifact that can and must be understood by using the scientific tools of anthropology, ARCHAEOLOGY, and LINGUISTICS, just as one would employ them for examining any artifact.

Bibliography. John H. Hayes and Carl R. Holladay, *Biblical Exegesis: A Beginner's Handbook* (Atlanta: John Knox, 1987); Richard N. Soulen and R. Kendall Soulen, *Handbook of Biblical Criticism* (3rd ed.; Louisville: Westminster John Knox, 2001).

HISTORICAL JESUS, QUEST OF THE. *See* QUEST FOR THE HISTORICAL JESUS, THE

HISTORICAL JESUS, THE

A term used to distinguish between the Jesus of history and the CHRIST OF THE CHURCH. In contemporary critical Jesus studies and the study of the GOSPELS, an important ASSUMPTION is that little can be known about the Jesus who actually existed as a historical person. Our main sources for information about Jesus are the four CANONICAL GOSPELS and the pseudepigraphical gospels, which were written decades after Jesus lived. Since these texts are not essentially biographical but are theological INTERPRETATIONS of Jesus, they communicate what scholars refer to as the Christ of the church, a theological figure quite distinct from the historical person. However, many scholars assume that this historical figure can be reconstructed to some extent by applying the tools of historical research. For an excellent introduction to this issue, see Mark Allen Powell. *See also* QUEST FOR THE HISTORICAL JESUS, THE.

Bibliography. Mark Allen Powell, *Jesus as a Figure in History: How Modern Historians View the Man from Galilee* (Louisville: Westminster John Knox, 1998).

HISTORICAL NARRATIVES

In the HEBREW BIBLE, the Former PROPHETS of Joshua–2 Kings and the writings of Ruth, Esther, Ezra, Nehemiah, and 1–2 Chronicles. Joshua, Judges, 1–2 Samuel, and 1–2 Kings constitute what many scholars refer to as the DEUTERONO-MISTIC HISTORY, while 1–2 Chronicles, Ezra, and Nehemiah form the CHRONISTIC HISTORY.

The first five books of the OT, the PENTATEUCH, also may be viewed as historical narratives. Likewise, NT scholars may refer to the Acts of the Apostles as early Christian history.

When we think of modern history, we generally assume that the historian records a dispassionate, unbiased, objective, and chronological account of events within a period of time. The historian is not an interpreter of events as much as a recorder of events. Even Aristotle assumed that drama and philosophy described the way things should be, while history presented things the way they were. We tend to think that a historical TEXT should record one-to-one correspondences between the events and its presentation of the events. In other words, historical writing is thought to be a representation, or slice, of the past.

This idea of history, however, is being strongly challenged today. Critics of history have recognized that there is a distinction between history (the events of the past) and HISTORIOGRAPHY (the writing about those events). A writer of history selects events to be included in the historical text and some to be excluded. This choice is governed by the writer's predetermined AGENDA. Is the historian trying to persuade the audience to accept a particular attitude toward the events or period? Is the historian guided by political, religious, or ideological (*see* IDEOLOGY) concerns? If so, then the linguistic result is anything but objective (*see* OBJECTIVE KNOWLEDGE; OBJECTIVE TRUTH). Two historians may well present different versions of the same period of time, depending on which events are included and excluded and how these events are weighted. In historiography, past events are placed within a NARRATIVE and become significant by virtue of being a part of that narrative.

The historical narratives in the Hebrew Bible do not re-present the past but present past events within narrative. The AUTHORS of the history books selected and arranged materials taken from a range of both oral and written sources. Some authors mention their written sources: "the Book of

Jashar" (Josh. 10:13; 2 Sam. 1:18), royal archives such as "the Book of the Acts of Solomon" (1 Kings 11:41), "the Book of the Annals of the Kings of Judah" (1 Kings 14:29), "the Book of the Annals of the Kings of Israel" (1 Kings 14:19; 2 Chron. 33:18), and "the Accounts of [Manasseh's] Prayer" and "of the Seers" (2 Chron. 33:18–19 LXX NETS).

Multiple VERSIONS of the same event (sometimes combined into a single report) also witness to the use of sources. Genesis begins with two different versions of creation; the Genesis account of the flood is a composite of two originally separate versions (evidence of this composition are the two different numbers of animals taken on board the ark [6:19–20 and 7:2–3] and the length of the flood [7:4–12 and 7:24]). There are two accounts of the march around Jericho (Joshua instructs the people to march around Jericho seven times [Josh. 6], whereas the priests are to circumscribe the city thirteen times [Josh. 6:4–8, 11–13]), two accounts of Samuel's installing Saul as king (1 Sam. 9:14–10:8 and 1 Sam. 10:17–27), and two accounts of David's making acquaintance with Saul (1 Sam. 16:14–23 and 1 Sam. 17:55–56).

The similarities between biblical texts and other nonbiblical texts also suggest that the authors utilized sources. There are similarities (and also differences) between the Genesis account of the creation and the flood and ancient Near Eastern accounts found in such works as the Gilgamesh Epic and *Enuma Elish*. Another example is the Akkadian LEGEND that Sargon I was rescued from a river after his mother had placed him there in a basket. He later became the founder of the dynasty of Akkad.

The point is that the authors of the historical narratives selected and arranged materials from their sources to produce texts with purpose. These books contain history but are not history in the modern sense. They may be described as theological history or, as Robert Alter suggests, "fictionalized history" or "historicized fiction." The authors were interested in communicating theological messages and not overly concerned about historical verisimilitude. To recount events by placing them end-to-end may be our idea of good historiography, but these authors shaped the presentation of events into stories that transcend the events. For this reason, most literary critics— such as Meir Sternberg and Robert Alter—argue that we should not confuse the presentation of events with the MEANING of the text. To put it simply, there is a large distinction between the STORY told by the narrative and the events themselves, and the SIGNIFICANCE of these texts is not to be found in the attempt to establish the historicity of the events recorded in the texts. By focusing on the task of establishing the historicity of these texts, the primary task of interpreting these texts on their own terms is short-circuited. For example, if we spend our time trying to reconcile the Genesis account of creation with modern scientific explanations of the origin and age of the earth, we will succeed only in neglecting the power of the story. These texts do not focus primarily on history but on story, and approaches that focus on history tend to misinterpret them.

Bibliography. Robert Alter, *The Art of Biblical Narrative* (New York: Basic Books, 1981); Meir Sternberg, *The Poetics of Biblical Narrative: Ideological Literature and the Drama of Reading* (Bloomington: Indiana University Press, 1987).

HISTORICAL RECONSTRUCTION

The re-creation of the circumstances surrounding an event. In HERMENEUTICS, the interest is in reconstructing the conditions surrounding a historical event or the writing of a TEXT. The ASSUMPTION is that one is in a better position to understand an AUTHOR's purpose when the conditions for the writing are known, because texts are most often generated in response to these conditions. For example, historically oriented hermeneutics assumes that the more the reader knows about Paul's Corinthian audience and the generative circumstances of the Corinthian correspondence, the more accurately one is able to configure a plausible understanding of the letters.

POSTMODERN critical theories, however, PROBLEMATIZE the idea of historical reconstruction by pointing out that the only access to past events or circumstances is textual. By "textual," postmodern critics mean any object that must be interpreted. In other words, we have access to the past only through some kind of text—a written or oral account or an artifact. We do not have direct, unmediated access to the past. In new historicism this dilemma is referred to as the textuality of history. Furthermore, any account or object of the past is always interpreted from within the SOCIAL LOCATION of the reader or historian, a position that is itself not a disinterested one but rather is conditioned by a matrix of assumptions, biases, purposes, and methodological and ideological controls. So what we may call a RECONSTRUCTION is actually a construction that will never re-present a thing from the past. The contraction will always be a creation of the historiographer under the influence of agenda.

HISTORICAL UNDERSTANDING

The knowledge of the past deriving from critical examination of its objects, persons, culture, and so forth. Although many modern scholars question the extent to which we can obtain a clear understanding of the past, most still feel that historical understanding is a valuable part of HERMENEUTICS. An integral part of hermeneutics has always been the attempt to understand a text within its cultural CONTEXT. *See* CRITICAL DISTANCE; HISTORICAL RECONSTRUCTION; NEW HISTORICISM.

HISTORICISM

The theory of historical investigation that assumes all human objects (physical, intellectual, artistic, etc.) to be products of particular cultures rather than expressions of transhistorical essences or universal forms. Consequently, any historical object will only reflect its cultural CONTEXT, and any INTERPRETATION of that object will be colored by the interpreter's cultural context. *See* NEW HISTORICISM.

HISTORICITY

A term, current in NEW HISTORICISM, used for the idea that all TEXTS are produced and interpreted within a complex of historical circumstances. Although *historicity*'s primary usage outside new

historicism is to refer to historical authenticity, according to new historicists, neither AUTHORS nor readers can step outside their SOCIAL LOCATION and assume an objective vantage point from which to write or read. Consequently, all texts and their INTERPRETATIONS are radically historical.

HISTORIE

A concept in the NARRATOLOGY of Gérard Genette, meaning the sequence in which the events in a STORY or NARRATIVE actually occurred as ascertained from the TEXT rather than the ORDER in which the events are presented. One need only think of FLASHBACK to see the distinction. For example, in Mark 6:17 the reader discovers that Herod has previously had John the Baptist arrested, bound, and imprisoned. So here is an earlier event recorded at a later time in the narrative. *See also* GESCHICHTE.

Bibliography. Gérard Genette, *Narrative Discourse: An Essay in Method* (trans. Jane E. Lewin; Ithaca, NY: Cornell University Press, 1980).

HISTORIOGRAPHY

The actual writing of history. In current scholarship, the distinction between the events of the past (history) and the NARRATIVE arrangement of those events (historiography) has received much attention. In NEW HISTORICISM, critics emphasize that the only access we have to the past is through TEXTS (defined as any artifact from the past), and since these texts are already one step removed from the events they describe or interpret, questions arise as to how certain we can be about our knowledge of the past. This skepticism about the reliability of historical knowledge is complicated by the ASSUMPTION that both writers of history and interpreters of these texts have AGENDAS and write within ideologies (*see* IDEOLOGY), both of which vitiate objectivity. These critics also point out that what we call "history" is actually historiography. For a discussion of historiography in the BIBLE, *see* HISTORICAL NARRATIVES.

HISTORY. *See* HISTORICAL NARRATIVES

HISTORY, CHRONISTIC. *See* CHRONISTIC HISTORY

HISTORY, DEUTERONOMISTIC. *See* DEUTERONOMISTIC HISTORY

HISTORY-OF-RELIGIONS SCHOOL. *See* *RELIGIONSGESCHICHTLICHE SCHULE*

HOLINESS CODE

A name for the hortatory material in Lev. 17–26 that prescribes moral behavior and sets standards of purity for priests and Levites.

HOMILY

In practical theological parlance, a DISCOURSE given to an audience for instruction and/or exhortation. In BIBLICAL STUDIES, however, *homily* refers to a GENRE found in both Judaism and the early church. David Aune suggests that while its origin in the Jewish synagogue SERMON is obscure, exegetical preaching had become customary by 70 CE both in Palestine and among the DIASPORA. Homilies were preached in the synagogue on Sabbaths and based on the TORAH reading of the day. These sermons evidence different traits as they developed over time. The proem homily begins with a quotation from the WRITINGS and then links it to the TEXT from the Torah for that day. This type probably appeared in the first two centuries CE and became popular in the Amoraic period (200–500 CE). What Aune (202) calls the *Yelammedenu* (Hebrew for "Let him teach us") type, which begins with "May our master teach us," followed by a legal question, developed at a later time.

With respect to the NT, Aune thinks that the homily is more difficult to define. Although preaching of the GOSPEL and moral exhortation were at the center of the life of the early church, NT scholars have found it difficult to describe an early Christian homily. In the NT itself, there is no single text that is actually an early Christian homily (197). However, some LETTERS may contain sermonic material or may actually be sermons framed as letters (e.g., Hebrews, James, 1 Peter).

James Bailey and Lyle Vander Broek, however, working from Lawrence Wills's study on the homily as a literary genre, argue that the material in Hebrews, 1 Peter, 1 Cor. 10:1–14, and 2 Cor. 6:17–7:1 consists of EXPOSITION and exhortation. The pattern includes a repetitive exposition of a theological TRUTH, an exhortation of hearers or readers, and in the case of Hebrews, the use of sophisticated rhetorical strategies. Along with the SPEECHES in Acts, these texts have a three-part structure: (1) theological and/or scriptural examples, as in Acts 13:16b–37; (2) a conclusion from the evidence, as in 13:38–39; and (3) an exhortation, as in 13:40–41 (Bailey and Vander Broek, 191). According to Bailey and Vander Broek, this structure reflects the elements of Greco-Roman DELIBERATIVE (or JUDICIAL) RHETORIC, suggesting that the early Christian sermons were formulated according to well-known rhetorical patterns and can thus be analyzed through RHETORICAL CRITICISM (191).

Bibliography. David Aune, *The New Testament in Its Literary Environment* (Philadelphia: Westminster, 1989); James L. Bailey and Lyle D. Vander Broek, *Literary Forms in the New Testament: A Handbook* (Louisville: Westminster John Knox, 1992).

HOMOEOARCHTON

A manuscript copying error of omission occurring when a manuscript has similar beginnings of two lines separated by another line. The copyist's eyes may fall on the second of the similar beginnings, thus omitting a line of text. *See* HAPLOGRAPHY.

HOMOEOTELEUTON

In RHETORICAL CRITICISM, homoeoteleuton is a LITERARY DEVICE in which a series of words have the same or similar endings, or two or more sequential words, clauses, or lines have the same or similar endings. An example is the Greek of 1 Tim. 3:16, although in most English TRANSLATIONS this literary device is not reproduced. *See* HAPLOGRAPHY.

HOMOLOGOUMENA

The NT texts that the church recognized as CANONICAL without dispute as opposed to those that were disputed (ANTILEGOMENA). For some time the list of accepted books of the NT varied. For example, Eusebius as late as 320 CE listed James, Jude, 2 Peter, and 2–3 John as disputed and Revelation as "spurious." About fifty years later Athanasius (367 CE) listed as "canonized" all the twenty-seven (and no other) books that now compose the NT.

HONOR-SHAME SOCIETY

According to Bruce Malina and Richard Rohrbaugh, the defining value STRUCTURE of first-century CE Mediterranean society. Honor was not only a person's status in a community but also the recognition of the same status for other members of the community. Consequently, the concept of honor dictated the manner in which a person communicated with others in the community: to superiors, inferiors, and equals (76).

Malina and Rohrbaugh point out that honor could be "ascribed or acquired." The former was a function of birth into an honorable family, while the latter resulted from some skill in the social game of challenge and riposte, a game played in every area of life. Since honor or sense of honor was the basis for marriage, business, habitat, and religious role, family honor had to be defended absolutely.

Shame was defined in two ways: negative and positive. Negative shame resulted from the public loss of honor. Positive shame referred to sensitivity about one's own honor or family honor. To lack such sensitivity was tantamount to being shameless. Therefore, people such as "prostitutes, innkeepers, actors" were looked on as having no shame. The sexual honor of women was especially important, according to Malina and Rohrbaugh. While the honor of men was "flexible," that of women was "absolute": when lost, it could not be regained and would destroy not only the woman's honor but that of the males in her paternal group as well (76–77).

Bibliography. Bruce J. Malina and Richard L. Rohrbaugh, *Social-Science Commentary on the Synoptic Gospels* (Minneapolis: Fortress, 1992).

HORIZON OF EXPECTATION

A term in the RECEPTION THEORY of Hans Robert Jauss, denoting the shared criteria (esp. ASSUMPTIONS) by which people of a particular generation interpret, value, and judge a LITERARY work and construct MEANING. Since this horizon of expectation changes over time, the judgments and INTERPRETATIONS of one generation do not establish those of another one. Consequently, neither judgment nor value is permanently fixed because the expectations change from period to period. Each period interprets and judges texts in the light of its own environment, knowledge, and experience. For this reason, Jauss argues that a literary TEXT does not stand by itself as a fixed entity but presents a different face to each generation. Therefore, literary meaning is never settled but always changing according to the expectations of the period.

Bibliography. Hans Robert Jauss, *The Aesthetic Experience and Literary Hermeneutics* (trans. Michael Shaw; Theory and History of Literature 3; Minneapolis: University of Minnesota Press, 1982); idem, *Toward an Aesthetic of Reception* (trans. Timothy Bahti; Theory and History of Literature 2; Minneapolis: University of Minnesota Press, 1982).

HORIZON OF MEANING

The CONTEXT within which a reader configures MEANING. This horizon usually involves the nature of the INTERPRETIVE COMMUNITY to which the reader belongs as well as the method of INTERPRETATION (*see* CRITICAL METHODOLOGY) either consciously or unconsciously employed. In other words, the community and methodological contexts of the reader determine the parameters of possible meaning. If these parameters change by changing contexts, so will the horizon of meaning.

HORIZON OF THE READER. *See* HORIZON OF EXPECTATION

HORIZON OF THE TEXT

The set of ASSUMPTIONS that underlie a TEXT and establish its POINT OF VIEW within its own historical circumstances.

HORIZON OF UNDERSTANDING. *See* HO-
RIZON OF MEANING

HOUSEHOLD CODES

Usually a part of the PARAENESIS in the EPISTO-
LARY LITERATURE of the NT, rules that outline
the relationships within the household—master/
slave, husband/wife, and father/children (e.g., Col.
3:18–4:1; Eph. 5:22–6:9; 1 Pet. 2:13–3:7). The
codes have their roots in Hellenistic culture and
establish a hierarchical (*see* HIERARCHICALISM)
and patriarchal family structure (*see* PATRIARCHAL
STRUCTURES; PATRIARCHY). Because the codes
do not occur in the undisputed Pauline Epistles,
some scholars feel that the adoption of the codes
in the later life of the church was a concession to
the social structure at large, perhaps as a way of
suggesting that the church was not a threat to the
social structure of the Roman Empire or simply as
a matter of survival.

According to Carolyn Osiek, the household
in the Hellenistic world served as a microcosm of
the state, and thus "maintenance of order in one is
integral to maintenance of order in the other. The
quality of harmony in the state is then intimately
dependent on the harmony of the family" (74).
Thus, in practical terms, in a patriarchal family, if
the family head could not govern his family, he
was not capable of governing in the civil realm. In
1 Tim. 3:4–5, we find that if a bishop or deacon
cannot govern his family, he is not fit to govern in
the church (74).

Osiek further claims that implicit in the household codes "is the assumption that good order
requires a hierarchical pattern of dominance and
submission not only with regard to children and
slaves, but also with regard to wives. . . . Women
. . . were always in some way under the protection
and dominance of male authority" (75). Thus, in
the world of HELLENISM, the realm of public ad-
ministration was viewed as the natural domain of
men, while the domestic realm was the domain of
women. Regardless of their cause and function in
the early church, the HERMENEUTICAL QUESTION
as to the household codes' legitimacy in today's
Christian communities is hotly debated among
scholars, especially those who see it as a patriarchal
tool to perpetuate the oppression and subordination of groups not only in the church but also in
society at large.

> *Bibliography.* Carolyn Osiek, *What Are They Saying about
> the Social Setting of the New Testament?* (New York: Paulist
> Press, 1984).

HOUSEHOLD RULES. *See* HOUSEHOLD CODES

HYBRIDITY

A term in POSTCOLONIAL CRITICISM for the general idea of occupying in-between spaces. For
example, in the cultural realm, hybridity signifies
being composed of many, being composite, such
as a Creole language or a culturally intermixed
people. The term is mostly used in the CONTEXT
of identity formation in postcolonial criticism.

HYBRID STORY

Stories in the NT that exhibit the characteristics of
two or more kinds of stories and can therefore be
analyzed in terms of either of them. For example,
the CALL STORY may also include some miraculous
element characteristic of the MIRACLE STORY, or
the RECOGNITION STORY may also be a miracle
story.

> *Bibliography.* Leland Ryken, *Words of Life: A Literary Intro-
> duction to the New Testament* (Grand Rapids: Baker, 1987).

HYMN

In the NT, material that is marked by a pronounced
and recognizable RHYTHM and found primarily
embedded within other LITERARY forms in the
EPISTOLARY LITERATURE (e.g., the Magnificat
in Luke 1:46–55; the BENEDICTUS in 1:68–79;
the Nunc Dimittis in 2:29–32; and the song of
the angels in 2:14). Although there is a variety of
hymns in the NT (NATIVITY, CHRISTOLOGICAL,
CONFESSIONAL, SACRAMENTAL, and MEDITA-
TIVE), they are all characterized by a language
that is highly structured, cadenced, compressed,
intense, and economical, with unusual grammatical features.

HYMN, CHRISTOLOGICAL. *See* CHRISTO-
LOGICAL HYMN

HYMN, CONFESSIONAL. *See* CONFESSIONAL
HYMN

HYMN, MEDITATIVE. *See* MEDITATIVE HYMN

HYMN, NATIVITY. *See* NATIVITY HYMN

HYMN, SACRAMENTAL. *See* SACRAMENTAL
HYMN

HYMN TO WISDOM

Job 28, which most scholars feel was a later addition from the WISDOM PSALMS. *See also* PSALM(S).

HYPERBOLE

A deliberate exaggeration for effect. An example
is 1 Kings 1:40: "And all the people went up after
him, playing flutes and rejoicing greatly, so that
the ground shook with the sound" (NIV). Another
well-known example is Yahweh's promise to Abraham that his descendants would be "as numerous
as the stars of heaven and as the sand that is on the
seashore" (Gen. 22:17). The NT also contains many
examples; for instance, "If your right eye causes you
to sin, tear it out and throw it away" (Matt. 5:29a).

HYPONOIA

Among the Jews of the DIASPORA, especially in
Alexandria, the deeper, spiritual MEANING of the
Jewish SCRIPTURES, derived primarily through
allegorical INTERPRETATION (*see* ALLEGORICAL
SENSE OF SCRIPTURE; ALLEGORY). The model of
allegorical interpretation was Philo of Alexandria
(20 BCE–50 CE), who solved what he saw as problems of contradiction, impropriety, or incongruity
in the Scripture by looking for ways to interpret
the passages spiritually. In other words, he looked
beyond the veneer of the TEXT to the hyponoia.

HYPOTAXIS

The arrangement of words, phrases, or clauses
in terms of coordinate and subordinate relationships. This STYLE of writing more clearly reflects
logical, causal, or temporal relationships than does
PARATAXIS, the arrangement of phrases and clauses
by using coordinating conjunctions. The writings
of Paul in the NT are characterized by hypotaxis,
and Mark's Gospel by parataxis.

I

ICON

Charles Sanders Peirce's theory of SEMIOTICS describes three types of signs: INDEX, SYMBOL, and ICON. An icon displays the same property as the object that it represents. An example is a pictorial road sign marking a deer crossing, which visually mirrors the thing it represents. Another example is the visual representation of a dish on a restaurant menu. Also, according to Peirce, an icon may be classified according to one of three categories: the IMAGE (e.g., a model ship for a ship), the diagram (e.g., similarity, as in "I plowed through the book"), or the METAPHOR (e.g., a blueprint for a house).

ICONOLOGY

A term used by Erwin Panofsky for his notion that a piece of art can have its total MEANING only when studied within its historical and cultural CONTEXT. Consequently, a work of art can be treated as a concrete historical document that contributes to the understanding of a particular period. In other words, any work of art is just one more means by which the gap between a past culture and the present is bridged. Certainly at the heart of SOURCE CRITICISM and FORM CRITICISM is an element of iconology. More recently, however, issues arising out of the relationship between iconology and ideas of class, GENDER, and race within ideological structures have been raised, the fear being that one's IDEOLOGY may, and probably does, dictate decisions about historical iconic SIGNIFICANCE.

Bibliography. Erwin Panofsky, *Renaissance and Renascences in Western Art* (New York: Harper & Row, 1960).

IDEAL READER

In the READER-RESPONSE CRITICISM of Wolfgang Iser, the imaginary person who should completely understand a TEXT as an AUTHOR intended it to be understood and who should thereby respond as the author expects. While historically conditioned REAL READERS will reflect their own SOCIAL LOCATIONS, the ideal reader would have CODES identical to those of the author. Since all readers are only real ones, there is, according to Iser, no possibility that they will exhaustively grasp the text's meaning. *See also* IMPLIED READER.

IDEOLECT

In LITERARY studies, the recognizable STYLE of an AUTHOR, a style that can be recognized throughout that writer's corpus of works. For example, Pauline scholars use the idea of ideolect as one component in their argument that the PASTORALS and PSEUDO-PAULINE epistles are pseudonymous (*see* PSEUDONYMITY). The argument rests on differences in style, atypical vocabulary, and theological differences from the EPISTLES judged to be authentically Pauline.

IDEOLOGICAL CRITICISM

An interpretive method that tries to uncover the IDEOLOGY of a TEXT and the ideological influences during the history of its INTERPRETATION. The term "ideology" is most widely associated with Marxist philosophy within the CONTEXT of others' oppression by the dominant political and social class. Although ideology has carried with it negative political and economic CONNOTATIONS, in "recent decades, the concept of ideology has been widely extended to encompass many other social structures marked by patterns of dominance and subordination, i.e., race, ethnicity, gender, religion, etc." (Soulen and Soulen, 84). To better understand the wide range of usage of the word, Elliot (252) has separated ideology into four simple concepts: (1) the epistemologically *negative*: ideology as a type of distorted, false thought (e.g., the "consciousness" of human subjects in capitalist society); (2) the socially *relative*: ideology as any set of opinions, beliefs, or attitudes (e.g., the "worldview" of a social group or class); (3) the *restricted*: "theoretical ideology" (a more-or-less conscious system of ideas); (4) the *expanded*: "practical ideology" (the more-or-less unconscious medium of habitual behavior). At the risk of oversimplification, we may say that the central focus of ideological criticism is to offer an approach to examining texts that asks readers to be aware of and account for their ideological FRAMEWORK, the awareness of which introduces an ethical component into the critical analysis of texts. There are, however, at least three areas to which ideological critics may direct their attention: (1) the ideological context in which an author produces a text, (2) the ideology reproduced within the text itself, and (3) the ideology of a text's readers or "customers." Ideological criticism asks questions such as these: What assumptions are being made about what is natural, just, and right? What (and whom) do these assumptions distort or obscure? What are the power relations (Soulen and Soulen, 84)?

An author's attitudes and thoughts on such issues as social class, economics, GENDER, and race are said to affect the way in which the author writes, not to mention the content of the writing. Thus the reader can better understand the text by trying to grasp the author's PRESUPPOSITIONS. Additionally, many hold to the notion that the text itself implies a certain ideology. Again, the astute reader looks for such things as the oppression of groups or the patriarchal dominance (*see* PATRIARCHY) of women. Finally, readers must be aware of their own ideological biases that they bring to the reading of a text.

Ideological criticism may include such diverse approaches as CULTURAL CRITICISM, DECONSTRUCTION, FEMINIST CRITICISM, MARXIST CRITICISM, PSYCHOANALYTIC CRITICISM, POSTCOLONIAL CRITICISM, and SOCIOECONOMIC CRITICISM. The reader should consult especially the descriptions of Marxist, feminist, and socioeco-

nomic criticisms in order to gain insight into the major concerns of ideological criticism. Although ideological criticism is varied in expression, the common thread running through all its expressions is the assumption that texts are not value-neutral but to different degrees reflect the relations and structures of race, gender, and class, which empower some persons and disenfranchise others. Ideological criticism demands that interpreters of texts not only read from a posture of suspicion but also critically examine the interpretive traditions within which they have learned to interpret. In other words, in ideological criticism, readers cannot divorce themselves from ethical issues that become inherent in the act of interpretation.

Bibliography. A. K. M. Adam, *What Is Post-modern Biblical Criticism?* (Minneapolis: Augsburg Fortress, 1995); George Aichele et al., *The Postmodern Bible* (New Haven: Yale University Press, 1995); Gregory Elliot, "Ideology," in *Dictionary of Cultural and Critical Theory* (ed. Michael Payne; Cambridge, MA: Blackwell, 1996), 252–57; Danna Nolan Fewell, "Reading the Bible Ideologically: Feminist Criticism," in *To Each Its Own Meaning* (ed. Steven L. McKenzie and Stephen R. Haynes; rev. ed.; Louisville: Westminster John Knox, 1999), 268–82; Richard N. Soulen and R. Kendall Soulen, *Handbook of Biblical Criticism* (3rd ed.; Louisville: Westminster John Knox, 2001); Clarence Walhout and Leland Ryken, eds., *Contemporary Literary Theory: A Christian Appraisal* (Grand Rapids: Eerdmans, 1991).

IDEOLOGICAL HORIZON

In IDEOLOGICAL CRITICISM, the CRITIC's description of the unspoken base—IDEOLOGY—that underlies a TEXT but never appears explicitly in the text. In discerning ideological horizon, then, a critic tries to unearth the silent ideology of a text by examining things assumed but not stated.

IDEOLOGICAL OVERCODING

A term in the READER-RESPONSE CRITICISM of Umberto Eco for the ideological perspective by which a reader confronts a TEXT and its counterpart, the ideological perspectives of the text. The ideological orientation of the reader is always present. It may be suppressed but not dismissed. An informed reader, however, is aware of the influence that the ideological orientation of the author has on INTERPRETATION. The ideological perspectives of a text are reflected in both textual STRUCTURE and language. The vocabulary of a text may be such that it seeks to persuade or dissuade a reader in specific areas. In this way, a text shapes and to a great extent seeks to determine a reader's response.

Bibliography. Umberto Eco, *The Role of the Reader: Explorations in the Semiotics of Texts* (Bloomington: Indiana University Press, 1984).

IDEOLOGICAL STATE APPARATUSES (ISAS)

A term introduced into IDEOLOGICAL CRITICISM by Louis Althusser to denote the structures—family, schools, mass media, and so forth—that function to perpetuate existing modes and relations of production by subjecting social classes to the dominant IDEOLOGY.

IDEOLOGY

The body of ideas on which a person's values, thoughts, judgments, and the like are based. An ideology may be political, economic, religious, or social. For a more detailed definition, *see* IDEOLOGICAL CRITICISM.

IDIOM

An expression, peculiar to a particular language, that cannot be translated word for word into another language and retain its meaning. The words of an idiom lose their customary MEANING when combined in the expression. For example, "to close one's bowels" in 1 John 3:17 KJV (alt.) means "to have no compassion"; the expression "to cover one's feet" in Judg. 3:24 KJV (alt.) refers to "relieving" oneself (NRSV), or going to the bathroom, both of which are idioms in English. The recognition of idioms is essential for understanding the SIGNIFICANCE of expressions that might otherwise be interpreted literally.

ILLOCUTIONARY ACT

An act that is itself performed by a speaker's utterance; a performative utterance (e.g., a command, promise, oath, warning). See LOCUTIONARY ACT.

ILLUMINATION

Theologically, the act of the Holy Spirit in granting to individuals the knowledge and grace of God through the proclamation of the GOSPEL. In some evangelical circles, the term refers to the work of the Holy Spirit in elucidating some passage of the BIBLE for a person while studying.

ILLUSTRATIVE STORY

A name sometimes used for a PARABLE that prescribes some type of behavior. The moral of the parable is contained in it rather than lying metaphorically outside it (Soulen and Soulen, 85). Examples are the parables of the good Samaritan (Luke 10:29–37) and the rich man and Lazarus (16:19–31). The distinction between an illustrative story and a "true" parable is most often ignored in contemporary parable studies.

Bibliography. Richard N. Soulen and R. Kendall Soulen, *Handbook of Biblical Criticism* (3rd ed.; Louisville: Westminster John Knox, 2001).

IMAGE

In literature, a representation of an object, event, or experience that can be grasped by the senses. Characteristics of the image are its tendency to present or suggest MEANING in terms of complexity rather than CLARITY; concreteness; and the appeal to the senses. An image may be literal or figurative. The literal image is one that suggests no change in the customary meaning of the words, while the figurative image introduces some twist on the literal meaning. Both types of images abound in the HEBREW BIBLE. An example of the figurative image is Ps. 1:1, "Happy are those who do not follow the advice of the wicked, or take the path that sinners tread, or sit in the seat of scoffers," where both "path" and "seat" refer to ways of conducting one's life. In verses 3 and 4 the images are also figurative: "They are like trees planted by streams of water, which yield their fruit in its season, and their leaves do not wither" and "The wicked are not so, but are like chaff that the wind drives away."

In Ps. 104:14 ("You cause the grass to grow for the cattle, and plants for people to use, to bring forth food from the earth"), the images "grass," "cattle," "plants," "people," and "earth" are all literal since they do not point to any figurative meaning beyond the actual concepts/objects.

IMAGERY

In LITERARY studies, the collection of IMAGES in a literary work. The pattern of imagery within a literary text may be central to understanding a text. Some scholars see this pattern as the best key to a text's MEANING, perhaps as important or more so than PLOT, SETTING, ACTION, or CHARACTERIZATION. Both the HEBREW BIBLE and the NT are replete with images: military (Eph. 6), agricultural (Ps. 72), birth (Job 3), anatomical (Prov. 7), cosmic (Job 37), mythological (Job 3; Rev. 12), and so forth.

IMAGINATION

In LITERARY studies, especially in READER-RESPONSE CRITICISM, an important component in the reading of TEXTS. Through a variety of LITERARY DEVICES and strategies, imaginative literatures create a role for the reader's imagination. For example, Wolfgang Iser goes so far as to claim that the MEANING of a text is found in the interaction between the "enabling structures" of the text and the "imaginative activities" of the reader. In BIBLICAL STUDIES, most types of reader-response criticism assume that the BIBLE contains imaginative texts, which engage the imagination of readers in order to configure meaning. *See* INDETERMINACY; READER-RESPONSE CRITICISM.

IMITATION

An Aristotelian LITERARY term from Greek (*mimēsis*) used in MIMETIC CRITICISM, referring to the relationship between a work of art and reality: art imitates life. Hence, the MEANING of a work is not to be found within it but, rather, in what the work suggests or teaches about some aspect of human experience.

IMMASCULATION

A term introduced by Judith Fetterley to refer to the possible effect on a female reader when reading an androcentric (*see* ANDROCENTRISM) or patriarchal (*see* PATRIARCHY) text. Fetterley claims that because the female is forced by such texts to read and identify as male, she identifies against herself:

> The cultural reality is not the emasculation of men by women but the *immasculation* of women by men. As readers and teachers and scholars, women are taught to think as men, to identify with a male point of view, and to accept as normal and legitimate a male system of values, one of whose central principles is misogyny. (xii)

Bibliography. Judith Fetterley, *The Resisting Reader: A Feminist Approach to American Fiction* (Bloomington: Indiana University Press, 1978).

IMPLIED AUTHOR

A LITERARY entity who is found only within or constructed from a TEXT. The implied author is not the same as the real author but is only a partial and incomplete reflection of the real author. For example, in the Gospel of Mark, the only AUTHOR whom readers encounter is the one whom they may be able to construct from the text alone. Even more revealing is the reading of several of Paul's EPISTLES. In 1 Corinthians, the reader encounters one entity, in Galatians, another entity. These two implied authors are not the same, because each text yields different information about the author. The text of Mark does not present the real flesh-and-blood Mark, nor does Galatians present the real-world Paul. When Paul authored 1 Corinthians, he donned one hat, but he wore yet a different one when authoring Galatians. Accordingly, it is possible for a real-world person to author several texts, each one having a different implied author. In a sense, the implied author is the composite of discernible ideologies (*see* IDEOLOGY) underlying a particular text. *See* NARRATIVE CRITICISM; READER-RESPONSE CRITICISM; RECEPTION THEORY.

IMPLIED READER

The entity defined by the TEXT. The IMPLIED AUTHOR may consciously or unconsciously construct a text in such a manner as to provide guidance to a reader. This means that a text contains unspoken ASSUMPTIONS about the reader. It is obvious that the implied author of Mark did not have a twentieth-century reader in mind. Even though the text provides directives for the reader by giving definition to the implied reader, that reader is not entirely defined by the text. For the implied reader, the implied author may assume a set of values, LITERARY COMPETENCE, and BACKGROUND. But there is simply no way to ensure that every reader will satisfy this assumption.

On the one hand, if we assume that the role of the implied reader may be completely defined, no single reader can perfectly and completely conform to the role the text provides for the implied reader. A reader may approach the text and perfectly conform to the role of the implied reader by consciously or unconsciously accepting the IDEOLOGY of the implied author inherent within the text, but there is no objective way to measure such conformity. On the other hand, to the degree that the reader fulfills the role of the implied reader provided by the text, the reader becomes captive to the text and its ideology. *See* IDEAL READER; NARRATIVE CRITICISM; READER-RESPONSE CRITICISM; RECEPTION THEORY.

There is yet a difficulty with the whole concept. If an IMPLIED AUTHOR is not the same as a real author but is a matrix or "composite of discernible ideologies," how can it "consciously" do anything?

IMPRECATION
A CURSE.

IMPRECATORY PSALMS
PSALMS in which the psalmist appeals to God to CURSE Israel's enemies or the enemies of God (e.g., Pss. 58; 68:21–23; 137:7–9).

INCLUSIO
A literary-rhetorical device by which textual material is framed by the same object or words at the beginning and end. Many biblical scholars argue that the framed textual material must be seen as a thematic unity. Examples include Ps. 1 (which

begins and ends with parallelism contrasting the righteous and the wicked) and Amos 1:3–5. The dual healings of a blind man in Mark 8:22–26 and 10:46–52 as well as the attention Jesus gives to children in Mark 9:36 and 10:13–16 have been suggested as inclusios for the textual material framed by them (Mark 8:27–10:45 and 9:37–10:12, respectively).

INCLUSIVE LANGUAGE
Language that is not GENDER-, race-, or ability-specific. Particularly feminist CRITICS (*see* FEMINIST CRITICISM) such as Elisabeth Schüssler Fiorenza have campaigned for inclusive language in TRANSLATIONS of the BIBLE, in commentaries (*see* COMMENTARY), lectionaries (*see* LECTIONARY), and in proclamations. According to such critics, since the Bible was written by men, it still functions in many religious CONTEXTS as a justification and legitimization of PATRIARCHY and the MARGINALIZATION of women and minorities. Furthermore, since language defines our SYMBOLIC WORLD, the language of patriarchy and ANDROCENTRISM defines that world in terms of male reality. Consequently, one important focus in Fiorenza's HERMENEUTICS OF SUSPICION is the recognition of the world-shaping role of androcentric and patriarchal language and the means of counteracting it.

Bibliography. Elisabeth Schüssler Fiorenza, *Bread Not Stone* (10th anniversary ed.; Boston: Beacon, 1995).

INCULTURATION. *See* ENCULTURATION

INDETERMINACY
The idea that the MEANING of a LITERARY work (or any work of art for that matter) is ultimately equivocal. Since humans are circumscribed by language, IDEOLOGY, and circumstances, all of which may change over time, so may the understanding of TEXTS.

Indeterminacy will always increase with the complexity and length of the text. *Indeterminacy* may also refer to elements in a text that produce gaps to be filled by the reader. *See* READER-RESPONSE CRITICISM; RECEPTION THEORY.

INDEX

In the SEMIOTICS of Charles Sanders Peirce, a type of SIGN (there are two other types: ICON and SYMBOL) that has a natural relationship to its object rather than a conventional one, as we might see in a METAPHOR. There are two types of indexes, one in which the relationship between signifier and signified is causality and the other in which the relationship is one of contiguity. An example of the first type is the relationship between a fever and illness, and of the second, between smoke and fire.

INDIFFERENCE. *See* ADIAPHORA

INDIVIDUAL LAMENT. *See* LAMENT

INFANCY GOSPELS

A collection of GOSPELS probably written after the NT Gospels and probably motivated by an interest in Jesus's childhood, a subject about which the CANONICAL GOSPELS say very little. According to Bart Ehrman, "After the New Testament gospels were written—and possibly earlier, although we have no hard evidence one way or the other—Christians began to tell stories about Jesus as a young boy. For the most part, the legendary character of these creative fictions is easily detected. We are fortunate that later authors collected some of them into written texts . . . which began to be produced by the first part of the second century at the latest" (191). An example is the infancy *Gospel of Thomas*, which dates from about 125 CE. Among other stories in this gospel, one presents Jesus as cursing a boy when he accidentally runs into Jesus. The boy subsequently dies, but Jesus later raises him from the dead.

> *Bibliography.* Ron Cameron, ed., *The Other Gospels: Noncanonical Gospel Texts* (Philadelphia: Westminster, 1982); Bart D. Ehrman, *The New Testament: A Historical Introduction to the Early Christian Writings* (2nd ed.; New York: Oxford University Press, 2000).

INFANCY STORY

The stories in Matt. 1–2 and Luke 1–2. These stories should be approached as part of the theological SIGNIFICANCE of the GOSPELS rather than as history in the modern sense of the word. As Bailey and Vander Broek point out, these stories have christological significance in that they introduce important THEMES that appear later in the Gospel NARRATIVES. For example, the similarities introduced in Matthew's infancy story between Jesus and Moses anticipate later material suggesting that Jesus is the new Moses. Furthermore, since the theological and christological purposes of the writers differ, the two accounts should not be collapsed into a harmonized account.

> *Bibliography.* James L. Bailey and Lyle D. Vander Broek, *Literary Forms in the New Testament: A Handbook* (Louisville: Westminster John Knox, 1992).

INFERENCES FROM COMMON FRAMES

A situation in life that is generally understood throughout a culture. AUTHORS assume that some information or knowledge pervades a culture. Possible frames of common cultural references include rules of etiquette, agricultural practices, religious traditions and practices, legal concerns, and literature. If an author either consciously or unconsciously refers to one of these frames of reference, it enables the informed reader to recollect an entire body of knowledge. The reader may then perform a correlation between the frame of reference and the elements of the TEXT. A single term may find its SIGNIFICANCE within a particular frame of reference. For example, when the NT authors use the term "circumcision," the entire historical and religious matrix of the practice of circumcision is immediately called to mind. Common frames of reference therefore may supply the CONTEXT, which limits the reader's INTERPRETATION.

> *Bibliography.* Umberto Eco, *The Role of the Reader: Explorations in the Semiotics of Texts* (Bloomington: Indiana University Press, 1984).

INFERENCES FROM INTERTEXTUAL FRAMES

The result of an amalgamation of the various LITERARY traditions with which a reader is familiar. When an AUTHOR alludes (*see* ALLUSION) to another TEXT or literary TRADITION, the reader is asked to make inferences based on a tradition outside the author's own. Through allusions to another tradition of text, the author asks the reader to "overcode" a secondary frame of REFERENCE on the primary one. When the author of 1 Pet. 2:21–25 makes reference to Isa. 53:5–12, the reader is expected to overcode the present frame of reference with inferences originating in the context of the Suffering Servant theme in Isaiah. The reader is, in a sense, guided in the process of filling in the gaps by the author's intertextual frame of reference.

Bibliography. Umberto Eco, *The Role of the Reader: Explorations in the Semiotics of Texts* (Bloomington: Indiana University Press, 1984).

IN-GROUP/OUT-GROUP

In SOCIAL-SCIENTIFIC CRITICISM, in-group members share the same values and interests and understand themselves as "we" as opposed to nonmembers (the out-group), who are usually viewed negatively as "they." Bruce Malina suggests that "a person's in-group generally consisted of one's household, extended family and friends. The boundaries of an in-group were fluid; in-groups could and did change, sometimes expanding and sometimes contracting" (88). Such an attitude is typical of the Johannine TEXTS (Gospel of John; 1–3 John), but can be found in the SYNOPTIC GOSPELS as well (e.g., Matt. 10:5–6).

Bibliography. Bruce J. Malina and Richard L. Rohrbaugh, *Social-Science Commentary on the Synoptic Gospels* (Minneapolis: Fortress, 1992).

IN MEDIAS RES

Literally meaning "in the midst of things," the technique of beginning a STORY in the middle of the ACTION and later supplying the information about the beginning. In other words, the EXPOSITION occurs within the story rather than at the beginning (e.g., Jon. 4:2a).

INNER-BIBLICAL EXEGESIS

A term introduced by Michael Fishbane, designating the practice of later Hebrew writers using earlier TEXTS, recontextualizing (*see* RECONTEXTU-

ALIZATION) and thus reinterpreting them. A later writer then uses prior texts as INTERTEXTS, drafting them into service in a different CONTEXT. For example, according to Fishbane, Isa. 45:18 recontextualizes IMAGERY from Gen. 1; and the Chronicler recontextualizes, by extension or SPECIFICATION, material from 1–2 Kings. The same practice is evident in the NT writers as well. For example, the two feeding miracles in Mark (6:30–44 and 8:1–13) recontextualize both an event in the life of Moses (Num. 11) and the life of Elisha (2 Kings 4:43). *See* ALLUSION; INTERTEXTUALITY.

Bibliography. Michael Fishbane *Biblical Interpretation in Ancient Israel* (Oxford: Clarendon, 1985).

INNER-BIBLICAL INTERPRETATION

A method of reading the biblical texts that seeks to identify a later author's knowledge, use, and appropriation of earlier biblical texts. According to Dozeman, inner-biblical (intrabiblical) interpretation looks for "the repetition of certain phrases or words from familiar biblical texts in order to provide further INTERPRETATION of a given theme" (208). Menn describes it as "the phenomenon of biblical texts that seem to clarify, rework, or allude to identifiable precursor texts" (58). Simply stated, inner-biblical interpretation is a method of examining two biblical passages to see if the AUTHOR of the second passage references the first passage. These passages must have a "marker, an identifiable element or pattern in one text belonging to another independent text" (Williamson, 734).

Identifying instances of inner-biblical interpretation is often complicated by the fact that the Bible has many parts that reference similar ideas, beliefs, and situations. Therefore, finding two separate passages referencing the same thing does not necessarily mean that the later AUTHOR had any knowledge or memory of the earlier passage. As Berger points out,

> The probability that one text alludes to another will generally depend on the distinctiveness and frequency of their common features. . . . An especially dense cluster of similarities might prove decisive even where each of them, taken individually, could

otherwise have been seen as coincidental: the larger the number of moderately suggestive parallels, the more compelling they become when considered together. (254)

So, while many passages of Scripture have similar themes and even situations, they must have an abundance of common points for them to have any inner-biblical interpretative significance.

Inner-biblical critics often describe the similarities found between two or more sections of the Bible as having a double-voice characteristic, in which one person may acquire the common speech of another person (Harris, 60). When one person has spent considerable time studying prior texts, it is likely that some of the first author's semantic and structural habits will find their way into the second author's text, and it is quite probable that the later author will use similar sentence structure and word choice. The second passage "represents not only the words of someone else but also the manipulative hand of the narrator who, for whatever thematic, ideological, lexical or literary reason, freely plays with the discourse of another" (61).

For the Hebrews, the process of writing, collecting, and revising texts occurred primarily during times of national catastrophe, expansion, and revival to ensure their relevance for future generations. Most frequently, the focus was on a text's specific GENRE. Thus legal codes, HISTORICAL NARRATIVES, liturgical POETRY, WISDOM LITERATURE, and prophetic oracles were all studied as separate entities (Menn, 60).

Inner-biblical interpretation of legal codes generally compares two instances of legal instruction in search of differences. For example, the inter-biblical critic will compare the law regarding the release of Hebrew slaves found in Deut. 15:12–18 and Exod. 21:2–6. The Exodus passage is much shorter than the one in Deuteronomy, probably because the later Deuteronomy passage expands on the ideas found in the Exodus passage. The first passage requires a Hebrew slave to be released after six years of service unless he wants to stay with his master. If the slave chooses to stay, the master must perform a ceremony ensuring that the slave has

been claimed for life. "The Deuteronomic Code extends the scope of the law to include female slaves as well as male slaves, provides for slaves to receive payment on release, and changes the location of the ceremony in which the slave announces his intention to stay with his master" (65). Therefore, the second passage contains much of the same information, but knowledge of its distinct differences from the original passage helps one understand the way laws changed over time as they adapted to new contexts or lifestyles. "As certain texts achieved prominent and revered status, they came to be studied and interpreted in light of each other as parts of a selected library of texts" (72).

To the casual reader, Prov. 1:8–19 and Gen. 37:12–36 seem to have little if anything in common. However, from an inner-biblical perspective, the passage in Proverbs may be a rereading or at least an appropriation of the Genesis passage. The Genesis passage recounts the story of Joseph's search for his brothers and their plot to sell him to the Ishmaelites. The two passages share a significant number of words and expressions. References to coming, blood, going into a pit, evil, bloodshed, paths, ill-gotten gain, and life appear in both Scripture portions in ways that are very similar (Harris, 63). Not only are many words and phrases similar, but the two passages also share images of consuming. Genesis 37:20 reads, "Come now, let us kill him and throw him into one of the pits; then we shall say that a wild animal has devoured him, and we shall see what will become of his dreams." The idea of being consumed also appears in Prov. 1:12, "Like Sheol let us swallow them alive and whole, like those who go down to the Pit." Both passages portray someone as being consumed by a pit—either a physical pit/cistern in the case of Joseph or the pit of hell against which the parents warn their children in Proverbs. The action of Joseph's brothers "actually initiates a series of events which result both in uncovering the brothers' deceitfulness and in bringing the family together again" (Harris, 66). The brothers' intent was to harm Joseph, but in an amazing reversal, Joseph now has the power of life and death over his brothers. Similarly, the parents in Prov. 1:8–19 warn their children against following those who do evil: "These men lie in wait for their own blood; they waylay only themselves!" (NIV). When the reader examines the Proverbs passage in light of Gen. 37, "it is as if the narrator/parent is appealing to the son's and reader's common knowledge of the lesson" (66). These two passages suggest that although Proverbs does not generally deal with specific historical facts, it still reflects an awareness of Israel's history (70).

The story in the book of Ruth and the story of Abigail in 1 Sam. 25 also offer interesting similarities. Both stories open with a reference to an unnamed man, followed shortly thereafter by the disclosure of both the man's name and his wife's name. "As these are the only two instances in the Bible where this formula appears, there arises the legitimate possibility of an intended connection" (Berger, 257). Ruth's journey into the fields in hope of finding favor in someone's eyes and being allowed to work is similar to that of David's servants in 1 Sam. 25, who are sent to the fields of Nabal in hope of gaining his favor. Boaz instructs his servants not to harm Ruth just as David instructs his men not to harm Nabal or his men. One of Boaz's servants speaks in favor of Ruth, and Boaz promises to provide for her; similarly, a servant in Nabal's house vouches for David's men, so Abigail provides them with food. Ruth declares her dedication to Naomi by using the same formulaic terminology as David's declaration to annihilate Nabal's household (Berger, 258). For the inner-biblical critic, these similarities suggest the possibility that the author of Ruth had the story of David and Abigail in mind. Berger suggests that the author of Ruth used a similar writing style to encourage a connection and comparison between the two couples (266).

For the inner-biblical critic, examining one text in relationship with other biblical texts offers some interesting insights into ways that later writers may have used earlier texts to enhance their own. However, some scholars have pointed out possible problems with this particular form of LITERARY CRITICISM. According to H. G. M. Williamson,

"It will never be possible finally to prove that a writer was consciously dependent on one source rather than another" (739). That is, it may never be possible to say with certainty that one writer is consciously referencing another text. Although there seem to be similarities between the story of Ruth and David's encounter with Abigail, the truth may be that the author of Ruth was so immersed in the historical and literary tradition as to unintentionally reference those traditions.

Critics may also perform inner-biblical analysis on the NT. These scholars are fully aware of the NT authors' practice of conjuring up passages in the Hebrew Bible, especially as they relate to Jesus. For example, in Mark's Gospel when Herod offers to give up to half his kingdom to Herodias's daughter if she will dance for him, the evangelist may have had in mind Ahasuerus's similar offers to Esther (Esther 5:1–8). In addition, the response of the disciples when Jesus asks them to feed the crowds of five thousand and four thousand (Mark 6:37; 8:4) recalls the response of Elisha's servant in a similar situation, the feeding of a crowd of one hundred (2 Kings 4:43).

Hence, inner-biblical criticism seems to be an extension of the literary device of ALLUSION, which may or may not be intentional. Furthermore, the claims and praxes of inner-biblical interpretation are similar to some of the claims of INTERTEXTUAL CRITICISM, especially the concepts of INTERTEXT, ALEATORY INTERTEXTUALITY, and obligatory intertextuality.

Bibliography. Yitzhak Berger, "Ruth and Inner-Biblical Allusion: The Case of 1 Samuel 25," *JBL* 128, no. 2 (2009): 253–72; Thomas B. Dozeman, "Inner-Biblical Interpretation of Yahweh's Gracious and Compassionate Character," *JBL* 108, no. 2 (1989): 207–23; Scott L. Harris, "'Figure' and 'Riddle': Prov. 1:8–19 and Inner-Biblical Interpretation," *Biblical Research* 41 (1996): 58–76; Esther Menn, "Inner-Biblical Exegesis in the Tanak," in *The Ancient Period* (vol. 1 of *A History of Biblical Interpretation*; ed. Alan J. Hauser and Duane F. Watson; Grand Rapids: Eerdmans, 2003), 55–79; H. G. M. Williamson, "Isaiah 62:4 and the Problem of Inner-Biblical Allusions," *JBL* 119, no. 4 (2000): 734–39.

INNER-TEXTUALITY. *See* INNER-BIBLICAL EXEGESIS

INTENDED READER

The hypothetical person for whom a TEXT is written. Some CRITICS in NARRATIVE CRITICISM and READER-RESPONSE CRITICISM assume that this reader can be reconstructed in whole or in part from the text. For example, Mark makes extensive explicit and implicit use of LITERARY ALLUSION to the HEBREW BIBLE in order to present Jesus as the divine servant of God who suffers innocently at the hands of the Jewish leaders and as the eschatological Son of Man who brings judgment. Mark never explains the allusions' SIGNIFICANCE. The implication is that the reader whom he has in mind has sufficient familiarity with the Hebrew Scriptures so as to need no EXPLANATION. We might assume that the intended reader therefore is Jewish. There is, however, a practice in Mark's NARRATIVE that vitiates such an ASSUMPTION.

No less than fifteen times the NARRATOR breaks frame in order to explain some point of Jewish religious custom or the MEANING of some word with which an Aramaic-speaking Jew in Mark's time would have certainly been familiar. We might conclude, then, that Mark's intended reader is a Gentile Christian familiar with the Hebrew Scriptures in Greek translation (LXX) but largely ignorant of Jewish religious practices and Aramaic terms.

INTENSIFICATION

A basic intralinear characteristic of BIBLICAL PO-ETRY where the force of an idea in the first part of a line is redoubled in the second part. Robert Alter argues that intensification is also a common *inter*linear practice.

Bibliography. Robert Alter, *The Art of Biblical Poetry* (New York: Basic Books, 1985).

INTENTION

In LITERARY studies, the purpose for which an AUTHOR writes, the idea(s) an author intends to communicate. Before the advent of NEW CRITI-CISM, MEANING was assumed to lie in the author's intention, which was formulated in terms of the social, political, cultural, and ideological matrix of the author. Without an immersion into the author's world and the occasion that prompted the text, one could not attain meaning with any acceptable degree of plausibility. The text was seen as a shell with many layers. If the layers were appropriately peeled away, the reader could discover the core and its original SETTING. This was the locus of meaning. The appropriate questions to ask were these: What circumstances prompted the author to write? What sources were used? What was the location? What was the history of the text's development?

INTENTIONAL FALLACY

An idea introduced into LITERARY discussion by W. K. Wimsatt Jr. and M. C. Beardsley for the AS-SUMPTION that the MEANING of a literary work is determined by the AUTHOR's expressed or ostensible purpose for producing the work. For these and other CRITICS working in NEW CRITICISM, the meaning of a literary work is inextricably bound up in its verbal STRUCTURE. When the text leaves the hands of the author, it becomes public domain in a sense, and the text itself is the arbiter of its own meaning independent of any appeal to the author's purpose or CONTEXT. Meaning is a function of the text, not the INTENTION of the author.

Bibliography. W. K. Wimsatt Jr. and M. C. Beardsley, *The Verbal Icon* (Lexington: University of Kentucky Press, 1954).

INTENTIONALITY. *See* INTENTION; INTEN-TIONAL FALLACY

INTERCALATION

The technique of sandwiching one STORY or block of material within another story or block. Since the relationship of the two is generally not explained, the reader is forced to ask questions about the SIGNIFICANCE of the arrangement. For example, in Mark 5:21–43, the account of Jesus's healing a woman with a hemorrhage interrupts the story of Jairus's daughter. The intercalation generates a number of questions: How do the faiths of Jairus and the woman complement each other? What is the relationship between the two types of healings? What is the connection between the twelve-year-old girl and the woman's twelve-year illness? Does the significance lie in the fact that the two recipients are female? Is there significance in the fact that Jairus, a chief of the synagogue, represents cultic purity, and the hemorrhaging woman represents traditional cultic impurity? Intercalation as a LITERARY DEVICE prompts such questions from the reader without supplying any definitive answer. Consequently, intercalation is a literary device that involves the reader in determining MEANING. *See* FRAME STORY.

INTERIOR MONOLOGUE

The technique of recording the thoughts of characters in a LITERARY work. It technically includes all forms of revelation in which the reader is given insight into the mind of a character. In Hebrew NARRATIVE, the reader is given extensive quotes of a character's thoughts: "Then Moses was afraid and thought, 'Surely the thing is known'" (Exod. 2:14). "Then Moses said, 'I must turn aside and look at this great sight, and see why the bush is not burned up'" (Exod. 3:3). These windows into a character's thoughts enable the reader to make judgments about a character's emotions and motivation. Such judgments in turn help the reader fill out the character, to know what kind of person this might be. See CHARACTERIZATION.

INTERIORIZATION

Two techniques by which a NARRATOR supplies the reader with windows into the mental or emotional state of a character. First, the narrator may comment on a character's thought or opinion so that the reader becomes privy to the thoughts of the character, but the thoughts are expressed in the words of the narrator: "So Noah knew that the waters had subsided from the earth" (Gen. 8:11b). Even God is not exempt: "God heard their groaning, and God remembered his covenant with Abraham, Isaac, and Jacob. God looked upon the Israelites, and God took notice of them" (Exod.

2:24–25). This type of interiorization is called external interiorization. When the narrator employs the use of direct quotes of a character's thoughts, the interiorization is internal. *See* INTERIOR MONOLOGUE.

INTERLINEAR PARALLELISM

Poetic parallelism that is sustained among successive lines of BIBLICAL POETRY. For example, in Isa. 45:12, the movement between lines is from a space to something within that space:

> I made the earth
> and created humankind upon it.
> It was my hands that stretched out the
>   heavens
> and I commanded all their host.

Bibliography. Robert Alter, *The Art of Biblical Poetry* (New York: Basic Books, 1985).

INTERNAL PARALLELISM

In BIBLICAL POETRY, a parallelism within a bicolon or tricolon (*see* COLON) of poetry.

INTERPOLATION

In TEXTUAL CRITICISM, material either intentionally or unintentionally inserted into a TEXT during scribal copying. An interpolation therefore changes the MEANING of the original text. One of the reasons why the more modern TRANSLATIONS are preferable to the KJV is that they are based on older manuscripts and contain fewer interpolations. In most modern translations, the interpolations are placed in footnotes.

INTERPRETANT

A term in SEMIOTICS for the response to a SIGN rather than for the person who gives the response, the interpreter.

INTERPRETATION

Traditionally, the task of explaining or drawing out the implications of understanding for contemporary readers and hearers. In recent scholarship, however, *interpretation* is used synonymously with

HERMENEUTICS and the various methods used to examine TEXTS.

INTERPRETATION, AUDIENCE-CENTERED. *See* AUDIENCE-CENTERED INTERPRETATION

INTERPRETATION, AUDIENCE-ORIENTED. *See* AUDIENCE-ORIENTED INTERPRETATION

INTERPRETATION, AUTHOR-CENTERED. *See* AUTHOR-CENTERED INTERPRETATION

INTERPRETATION, BIBLICAL. *See* BIBLICAL HERMENEUTICS

INTERPRETATION, POSTCRITICAL. *See* POSTCRITICAL / POSTCRITICAL INTERPRETATION

INTERPRETATION, PROVISIONALITY OF. *See* PROVISIONALITY OF INTERPRETATION

INTERPRETATION, READER-CENTERED. *See* READER-RESPONSE CRITICISM

INTERPRETATION, TEXT-CENTERED. *See* TEXT-CENTERED INTERPRETATION

INTERPRETATION, TYPOLOGICAL. *See* TYPOLOGICAL INTERPRETATION

INTERPRETIVE COMMUNITY

A term in the READER-RESPONSE CRITICISM of Stanley Fish for readers who share the same AS-SUMPTIONS and strategies of INTERPRETATION. An interpretation is correct to the degree that it conforms to the conventions and assumptions of the community. Fish argues that a reader's aesthetic and hermeneutical judgments are not individual but socially constructed. For the individual reader, these judgments along with the interpretive strategies guide understanding.

> *Bibliography.* Stanley Fish, *Is There a Text in This Class? The Authority of Interpretive Communities* (Cambridge, MA: Harvard University Press, 1980).

INTERPRETIVE CONVENTIONS

The practices and strategies that govern the way a reader or a community interprets TEXTS. *See* INTERPRETIVE COMMUNITY.

INTERPRETIVE FRAMEWORK

The matrix within which a person interprets a TEXT. The matrix includes methodological as well as ideological (*see* IDEOLOGY) ASSUMPTIONS and strategies.

When this matrix of assumptions (doctrinal, denominational, philosophical, theological, methodological) is taken as a whole at any one point in a reader's life, it constitutes the framework within which all texts are perceived and interpreted. The interpretive framework postures a reader before a text in a particular way and determines how one will ultimately configure understanding.

INTERSUBJECTIVITY

In PHENOMENOLOGICAL CRITICISM, the interactive communication between SUBJECTs. It refers to the shared experience between subjects on the basis of a common language. Accordingly, the only way two subjects can communicate in any meaningful fashion is to belong to a common world that is inscribed in language.

INTERTESTAMENTAL PERIOD

Traditionally, the historical period between the composition of the book of Malachi (first half of the fifth century BCE) and the destruction of Herod's temple in Jerusalem (70 CE). This period encompasses the Maccabean period (*see* MACCABEES), falling within the Hellenistic period (*see* HELLENISTIC JUDAISM). The books of the (OT) APOCRYPHA derive from this period.

INTERTEXT

A TEXT that serves as the basis for another text. For example, James Joyce's *Ulysses* is a retelling of Homer's *Odyssey,* and the intertext for Salman Rushdie's *Satanic Verses* is the Qur'an. With about 165 direct or indirect ALLUSIONs to it, Mark's intertext is the HEBREW BIBLE. *See* INTERTEXTUAL CRITICISM; INTERTEXTUALITY.

INTERTEXTUAL CRITICISM

An interpretive method based on the term "INTERTEXTUALITY," introduced by Julia Kristeva in 1969 in a critique of the modern ASSUMPTIONS that TEXTS contain MEANING and that by using objective (*see* OBJECTIVE KNOWLEDGE) methods, CRITICS can excavate that meaning. Kristeva used the term "text" in such a way as to include not only written texts but also anything that might be read, such as a person, ritual, or anything in culture that must be interpreted. Just as an individual is a composite of intersecting and contradictory signifying systems—a confluence of roles, personae, and DISCOURSES as opposed to an autonomous, independent self—so a text is a centerless convergence of various signifying systems, an intersection of other texts. It is a conjunction of other texts of which it is a rereading. So a text is a kind of patchwork constructed out of pieces of other texts, which are themselves constructed through the interweaving of other texts and discourses.

If a text is a centerless conflation of other texts and signifying systems and therefore without any determinate meaning, then INTERPRETATIONS of texts can never exhaust what may be said about texts. A single interpretation can never be the last word but will always be simply one possible way among an infinite number of ways to walk through the indeterminacy of the text's intertextuality. This means that any interpretation (or method of interpretation, for that matter) exists only at the expense of excluding other possibilities. To use the terminology of Umberto Eco, any interpretation results from a process of "blowing up" parts of the text while "narcoticizing" other parts. In other words, interpretation is a matter of tracing intertextual relations guided by ideological and methodological AGENDAS, personal interests, and affiliatory expectations (academic, theological, philosophical, etc.). The object of any textual analysis, then, is not necessarily meaning in terms of the relationship between the language of

the text and an EXTRATEXTUAL referent but SIGNIFICATION in the SENSE of unlimited semiosis: the relationship of SIGNS and texts to other signs and texts as indeterminate objects. Furthermore, if a text is an indeterminate network of other texts and signifying systems, an interpretation is not a matter of figuring out the text but rather simply a matter of stopping.

Although the concept of intertextuality is limited to the idea that texts are indeterminate networks of other texts and signifying systems, some CRITICS have extended the definition of intertextual criticism to mean something much broader. For example, Donald Keesey (265–77) sees intertextual criticism as having a twofold focus. First, he includes what other critics call GENRE CRITICISM under the umbrella of intertextual criticism. Accordingly, literary texts do not imitate life but other texts of the same TYPE. Authors do not mimetically transform reality but transform the conventions of the GENRE within which they are working. In writing the *Aeneid,* Virgil expected his readers to recognize that he was writing an EPIC that would look a lot like Homer's *Odyssey.* Although his epic is structurally similar to Homer's, it is an interpretive appropriation of the *Odyssey.* If Virgil's readers did not recognize this appropriation, they would be unable to grasp his purpose.

Since all texts are conventional, they can best be analyzed within the contexts of their linguistic and LITERARY CONVENTIONS. Though any single work may not conform exactly to the conventions of its genre, it would be unintelligible if it were absolutely unique. So when a reader analyzes a text by relating it to other texts of the same genre, the reader is practicing a type of intertextual criticism. A PARABLE, for example, is best read in light of all other parables ever written. Similarly, the best reading of the WISDOM LITERATURE in the HEBREW BIBLE reads it in the context of all other wisdom literature.

The last observation points to the second focus of intertextual criticism—the reciprocal nature of intertextuality. First, since texts are constructed networks of prior texts, the most plausible reading of any text is the one that recognizes an author's

INTERTEXTS and the manner in which these texts are interpretively appropriated. For example, a reading that takes into account Mark's appropriation of texts from the Hebrew Bible is an intertextual reading. Mark recontextualizes these texts, thereby giving them a new significance. For the intertextual critic, a reading that does not or cannot recognize such appropriation is impoverished. This idea of one author appropriating or alluding to other texts has become an important part of biblical intertextual criticism. The interest in the idea of intertexts is reflected in recent studies claiming that the authors of the SYNOPTIC GOSPELS used Greco-Roman epics as intertexts, such as Homer's *Iliad* and *Odyssey* and Virgil's *Aeneid* (see McDonald; Bonz). For interpretation, the significance of this aspect of intertextuality as the appropriation of former texts, however, extends beyond the simple concept of LITERARY ALLUSION. If the appropriated texts are themselves networks of appropriated texts, then the act of interpretation potentially extends indefinitely. There simply is no backward boundary for the interpretive process. Interpretation may end, but it is never finished. There is nothing final that one can ever say about the text.

The other end of intertextual reciprocity is its extension into the indefinite future. Not only does reading former texts inform the reading of later texts; the reversal is true as well. That is, reading later texts informs the reading of former texts. For example, one's reading of Pope's *Rape of the Lock* and Milton's *Paradise Lost* makes for a more plausible reading of Virgil's *Aeneid*, which in turn informs one's reading of Homer's *Odyssey*. If some modern critics are correct in their claim that the author of Luke-Acts constructed his work in conversation with Greco-Roman epic (esp. Virgil's *Aeneid*), then one's reading of Luke-Acts would be greatly enhanced by reading epics such as *The Rape of the Lock* and *Paradise Lost*, which were written centuries after Luke-Acts. Consequently, when a text is interpretively appropriated by other texts, when a text becomes an intertext for other texts, its literary signification extends beyond itself. The intertextual critic therefore is

also interested in examining how other texts have appropriated a given text and then using this information in a reexamination of the appropriated text. But texts that appropriate a particular text are in turn appropriated by other texts ad infinitum. Consequently, a text is really never completed but is always in the process of being written. In a sense it becomes an intersection of a multitude of writings. A text is always in an intertextual process of production, which includes both past and future texts.

So intertextual criticism—depending on the critic—may be concerned with the issue of genre and linguistic and literary conventions, but it will always be concerned with the reciprocity of intertextuality and INDETERMINACY, which it naturally inscribes. Michael Riffaterre sums up intertextuality by defining it as the relationship between readers and their recognition of a text's relationship to texts that precede or follow it. Riffaterre goes further and defines intertextuality in terms of ALEATORY INTERTEXTUALITY and obligatory intertextuality. In aleatory intertextuality, a reader handles a text in terms of the texts with which the reader is familiar but which are absent from the text at hand. Obligatory intertextuality refers to the core intertext presupposed by the text at hand.

Bibliography. Marianne P. Bonz, *The Past as Legacy: Luke-Acts and Ancient Epic* (Minneapolis: Fortress, 2000); Jonathan Culler, "Presupposition and Intertextuality," *Modern Language Notes* 91, no. 6 (1976): 1380–97; Danna Nolan Fewell, ed., *Reading between Texts: Intertextuality and the Hebrew Bible* (Louisville: Westminster John Knox, 1992); Sean Hand, "Missing You: Intertextuality, Transference, and the Language of Love," in *Intertextuality: Theories and Practices* (ed. Michael Worton and Judith Still; Manchester, UK: Manchester University Press, 1990), 79–91; Julia Kristeva, "The Bounded Text," in *Desire in Language: A Semiotic Approach to Literature and Art* (trans. Thomas Gora, Alice Jardine, and Leon S. Roudiez; New York: Columbia University Press, 1980), 36–63; Dennis R. McDonald, *The Homeric Epics and the Gospel of Mark* (New Haven: Yale University Press, 2000); Michael Riffaterre, "Compulsory Reader-Response: The Intertextual Drive," in *Intertextuality: Theories and Practices* (ed. Michael Worton and Judith Still; Manchester, UK: Manchester University Press, 1990), 56–78; idem, *Text Production* (trans. Terese

Lyons; New York: Columbia University Press, 1983); Patricia K. Tull, "Rhetorical Criticism and Intertextuality," in *To Each Its Own Meaning: An Introduction to Biblical Criticisms and Their Application* (ed. Steven L. McKenzie and Stephen R. Hayes; rev. ed.; Louisville: Westminster John Knox, 1999), 156–80.

INTERTEXTUALITY

A term introduced into LITERARY theory by Julia Kristeva for the idea that a TEXT makes sense only in terms of its interconnections with earlier uses and understanding. Because of the fluid contextuality of former uses of the text and the context in which a contemporary reader tries to understand the text, MEANING is never definitive but always provisional. The term has been extended to refer to the idea that texts are produced in conversation with prior texts and that prior texts are renewed or reconfigured as they are appropriated by later texts. For a fuller explanation of intertextuality, *see* INTERTEXTUAL CRITICISM.

INTERTEXTUALITY, ALEATORY. *See* ALEATORY INTERTEXTUALITY

INTERTEXTUALITY, OBLIGATORY. *See* INTERTEXTUAL CRITICISM

INTRALINGUISTIC

A term referring to the POSTMODERN ASSUMPTION that the MEANING of a TEXT derives from the interplay of SIGNS within a sign system rather than from an AUTHORIAL INTENTION.

INTRATEXTUAL DYNAMICS

A LITERARY term for the DIALOGUE between earlier and later texts in the HEBREW BIBLE. This dialogue is present at a variety of levels. First, there is the practice of recasting and reapplying earlier texts to later situations. This is especially true of the prophetic texts. Second, there are numerous instances of one AUTHOR consciously offering a critique or even a PARODY of an earlier TEXT or GENRE. For example, the author of Ecclesiastes seems to challenge the idea of linear, progressive history found in earlier works such as Genesis. This

same author also questions the conventional view of wisdom. LaSor states it well:

> In a word, he sought to use traditional tools of wisdom to refute and revise its traditional conclusions. Like Job, he protested the easy generalizations with which his fellow teachers taught their pupils to be successful. They had oversimplified life and its rules so as to mislead and frustrate their followers. Their observations seemed superficial and their counsel thin in a world beset by injustice, toil, and death. (589)

Finally, there is the common practice of ALLUSION, in which an author (perhaps sometimes unconsciously) frames a STORY or an EPISODE like one written earlier. For example, by constructing an ANALOGY between the stories of Ruth and Abraham, the author of Ruth portrays Ruth as a matriarch of the Davidic line. Thus Boaz says to Ruth: "All that you have done for your mother-in-law since the death of your husband has been fully told me, and how you *left your father and mother and your native land and came to a people that you did not know before*" (Ruth 2:11). Compare this with God's word to Abraham: "Go from your country and your kindred and *your father's house to the land that I will show you*" (Gen. 12:1). The regularity of allusions such as this is persuasive evidence that the writers were at home in texts written hundreds of years earlier. This is possible because the texts are all part of the same religious tradition, sharing common literary as well as WORLDVIEW elements.

Bibliography. William LaSor et al., *Old Testament Survey* (2nd ed.; Grand Rapids: Eerdmans, 1996).

INTRATEXTUAL WORLD

The linguistic world of a TEXT: the story world created by the language of the text, as opposed to the real world of the author.

INTRINSIC ANALYSIS

INTERPRETATION that focuses on the TEXT rather than on the environment that produced the text. It is primarily concerned with the FORM and CONTENT of the text. Thus LITERARY theories may be classified as either intrinsic analysis or EXTRINSIC ANALYSIS. NEW CRITICISM, RHETORICAL CRITICISM, and REDACTION CRITICISM are examples of intrinsic analysis. The line between intrinsic and extrinsic should not be drawn too clearly, however, since intrinsic analysis makes use of extrinsic concerns when such concerns shed light on the form and content of a text.

INTRUSIVE NARRATOR

A NARRATOR who interrupts a NARRATIVE to explain or interpret some aspect of the narrative. For example, the narrator in Mark interrupts in several places to explain Jewish customs (3:17; 5:41; 6:17–18; 7:3–4, 11, 19; 7:34; 13:14; etc.) and to address the reader directly (13:14, "Let the reader understand").

INVECTIVE

A type of vituperative SPEECH or argument characterized by verbal insults and abuse, especially characteristic of SATIRE but not limited to it. The short Epistle of Jude is an example of this TYPE of RHETORIC. Rather than presenting or challenging his opponents' arguments, Jude engages in ad hominem name-calling: "brute beasts" (v. 10 KJV), "perverters of God's grace" (cf. v. 4), "blemishes on love feasts" (v. 12).

> Bibliography. J. A. Cuddon, The Penguin Dictionary of Literary Terms and Literary Theory (4th ed.; London: Penguin, 1998).

INVENTION

One of the five parts of classical RHETORIC, invention is concerned with the discovery of material appropriate for the occasion and topic of the oration. In the classical world, the writer or speaker did not invent (create) the material out of imagination but looked for it in nature. See RHETORICAL CRITICISM.

INVERTED PARALLELISM. See CHIASMUS

IPSISSIMA VERBA

A loan term from Latin for "very words," which is used in the QUEST FOR THE HISTORICAL JESUS to designate words Jesus actually spoke as opposed to those that later TRADITION ascribed to him. Since the NT was written in Greek, but Jesus probably spoke Aramaic, it is difficult to know what Jesus's exact words were. See CRITERIA OF AUTHENTICITY.

IPSISSIMA VOX

Literally, Latin for "very voice" and used in the QUEST FOR THE HISTORICAL JESUS to designate the words or sayings that may communicate the sense of Jesus's words but not the exact form.

IRONIC REVERSAL

The reversal of expected outcomes or fortunes. The reversals of the fortunes of Haman, Mordecai, and the Jews in Esther are examples.

IRONY

Broadly, a FIGURE OF SPEECH that is a means of indirection; a method of establishing a distance between reality and appearance; the incongruity between words and their MEANINGS, actions and outcomes, or INTENTIONS and results. Traditionally, irony has been divided into four types: First is verbal irony, which depends on the interplay of words in order to communicate that where one thing is said, the opposite is meant. In this SENSE, DOUBLE ENTENDRE, EUPHEMISM, and HYPERBOLE are forms of verbal irony (Roberts and Jacobs, 354). Sometimes SARCASM is considered a type of verbal irony, but generally speaking, verbal irony is less caustic than sarcasm. When Paul tells his Corinthian audience that "we are fools for the sake of Christ, but you are wise in Christ" (1 Cor. 4:10), he is using verbal irony in that he means just the opposite of what he actually says.

Situational irony occurs when there is a gap between what a person expects and what actually happens. Such irony is often pessimistic because it emphasizes the fact that humans have little or no control over the forces that impact their lives.

A special type of situational irony is cosmic irony, which emphasizes the power of chance and fate. Also referred to as the irony of fate, cosmic irony posits a universe that is indifferent to the concerns of humans, who are themselves objects of blind chance, capricious accident, and perpetual misfortune. Both Ecclesiastes and Job have as their centers cosmic irony (Roberts and Jacobs, 355).

Dramatic irony occurs when a character in a STORY has no information about a situation or misjudges information while the readers (and sometimes other characters) have the information or understand the situation completely. In Judg. 3, Ehud informs the Moabite king, Eglon, that he has a word from God for him. The king supposes that the word has been received by oracle, but the reader knows that the word is really the double-edged "dagger" (KJV) concealed beneath Ehud's "clothing" (NIV). One of the most gripping instances of dramatic irony is in the book of Job. The reader overhears the conversation and bargain between God and "the adversary," but Job does not. If not given this insight, the reader might assume that Job is being unjustly punished rather than tested. Job's ignorance of the situation and the reader's privileged knowledge are both required for the irony.

Bibliography. Edgar V. Roberts and Henry E. Jacobs, *Literature: An Introduction to Reading and Writing* (7th ed.; Upper Saddle River, NJ: Prentice Hall, 2004).

J

J (YAHWIST)

One of the four hypothetical sources for the composition of the PENTATEUCH. Although the date and origin of the source is debated among scholars, many believe that the source originated during the tenth or ninth century BCE. It associates the well-being of Israel with the promise of Yahweh to Abraham that his people would become a great nation. *See* GRAF-WELLHAUSEN HYPOTHESIS; SOURCE CRITICISM.

JERUSALEM BIBLE / NEW JERUSALEM BIBLE (JB/NJB)

An English TRANSLATION of the BIBLE (1966) from the original languages with notes and introductions by the Roman Catholic Dominican Biblical School of Jerusalem. A qualification, however, should be added here that the JB is based extensively on the French *Bible de Jérusalem*, which was completed between "1948 and 1954 by the French Dominicans of L'École Biblique de Jerusalem in Israel" (Sheeley and Nash, 71). Further, according to Sheeley and Nash, while the original French VERSION contained several volumes of notes and commentary, these notes were reduced to a single volume in 1956, and this volume was later translated into English at Christ's College in Liverpool, England. Some scholars have concerns about the JB's dependence on the French version (71). In fact, the translators acknowledge in the foreword that "in the case of a few books the initial draft was made from the French and was then compared word for word with the Hebrew or Aramaic." A second English edition (New Jerusalem Bible [NJB], 1985) has less PARAPHRASE than the first edition and tends to use more GENDER-INCLUSIVE LANGUAGE. With extensive notes and introductions, it is more suitable as a study Bible than one for everyday use.

Bibliography. Steven M. Sheeley and Robert N. Nash Jr., *The Bible in English Translation: An Essential Guide* (Nashville: Abingdon, 1997).

JESUS, HISTORICAL. *See* HISTORICAL JESUS, THE

JESUS OF HISTORY, THE. *See* HISTORICAL JESUS, THE

JESUS SEMINAR

An association of NT scholars established in 1985 with Robert W. Funk as its leader. The task of the seminar is to examine all the SAYINGS attributed to Jesus within the CANON and outside it in order to determine their authenticity. For the criteria used to determine authenticity, see CRITERIA OF AUTHENTICITY. The findings of the seminar can be found in Funk and others. For an excellent introduction to the Jesus Seminar and its future plans, see Powell.

Bibliography. Robert W. Funk et al., *The Parables of Jesus, Red Letter Edition: A Report of the Jesus Seminar* (Sonoma, CA: Polebridge, 1988); Mark Allan Powell, *Jesus as a Figure in History: How Modern Historians View the Man from Galilee* (Louisville: Westminster John Knox, 1998).

JEWISH CHRISTIANITY

The Christianity of the earliest churches, whose membership was primarily Jewish. Both the book of Acts and Paul's Letters present a picture of the early church in which there developed a Jewish Christianity centered in Jerusalem and a developing Gentile mission. After the destruction of Jerusalem and the temple in 70 CE, Christianity gradually became predominantly Gentile.

JEWISH HERMENEUTICS. *See* RABBINIC HERMENEUTICS

JEWISH RECONSTRUCTIONISM

A systematic ideology for interpreting the CANON of Jewish Scriptures in a manner conducive to assimilation into a modern society. Reconstructionist Judaism, the most common form of Judaism practiced today (Posen), began when Rabbi Mordecai Kaplan founded the "proto-Reconstructionist organization" called the Society for the Jewish Renascence (later known as The Society for the Advancement of Judaism) in 1922 (Cedarbaum, 29). Kaplan's reconstructionist INTERPRETATION was the forerunner to literary READER-RESPONSE CRITICISM as well as several other subversive rereadings of established texts and ultimately changed the way that not only Jews but all people of faith approach the interpretation of Scripture.

Kaplan was writing in America at a time when many Jews were dissatisfied with their religion. Tension between Orthodox and Reform JUDAISM had brought about the hybrid sect of Conservative Judaism, which satisfied the ideals of neither (Eisen, 8). None of these formal doctrines solved the problem that American Jews were confronted with every day: how to live as members of a religious society that is called to be set apart while also engaging in the culture that they were a part of, a culture that offered all the benefits of modern life and differing morals. Speaking in 2004, at Stanford University's conference to mark the seventieth anniversary of Kaplan's original publication, Arnold Eisen explained that "for centuries, Jews had been kept apart from gentile society and culture by political and economic circumstances, and their religion had made ultimate sense of that apartness with a story of supernatural providence and revelation" (5). Kaplan found that the main barrier to the progression of Judaism was an outmoded idea of a personal, supernatural God found in Jewish Scripture and that Jews focused too much on the authority of the past and relied only on the traditions and the words of others. They should instead look at claims such as divine origin as symbols of the high worth of tradition. Kaplan argued that American Jews could still read, assess, and value Jewish laws and traditions while taking into account their own cultural situation as precedent for understanding. The overabundance of literature available on the work of Kaplan and its application to various disciplines ninety years after his publication attests to the impact that his ideas have had on the national conscience. Although the sociological implications of the foundation of Kaplan's Reconstructionism are apparent and interesting, his followers also represent a shift in the way Jews approach their holy texts, for the first time allowing a break with the authority of historical CONTEXT.

Little did Rabbi Mordecai Kaplan know that his ideas of religious reform would line up so neatly with the groundbreaking work of literary critics some fifty years later. In much the same way that Kaplan reacted to the overly strict structures of Orthodoxy and even Reform Judaism, the loose grouping of literary critics classified as reader-response critics found a path beyond the unbending structures of the formalists and the limiting context of historical critics. In general, these reviewers forsook the study of the historical or cultural context of the AUTHOR or the intended meaning to value only the words that exist and the affects that those words can create at this moment. Any relevant CRITICISM, they claimed, must be based on such pivotal facts (Keesey, 129). Rabbi Patti Haskell discusses how the Reconstructionist process is based on the "readdressing" and "reevaluation" of the text, pointing out that "the way a Reconstructionist community answers a particular question yesterday may differ from the way in which that very same community will answer the very same question tomorrow" (58). Kaplan himself wrote early on of a need to reinterpret Jewish law so that it reflects the conditions and spiritual needs of contemporary life. While it is impossible to show any direct connection or influence of Kaplan's theories on the later critics, the similarities are obvious. Reconstructionists are essentially reader-response critics who lack the literary vocabulary to describe themselves as such.

Further proof of the reader-response nature of Jewish Reconstructionism comes in the retrospective application of what Stanley Fish calls interpretive communities.

> Thus the act of recognizing literature is not constrained by something in the text, nor does it issue from an independent and arbitrary will; rather, it proceeds from a collective decision as to what will count as literature, a decision that will be in force only so long as a community of readers continues to abide by it. (11)

Fish goes on to claim that any stability in INTER-PRETATION of a text comes from the continued agreement of a certain reader community rather than because of the stability inherent in the text (15). In the same way, Reconstructionists find meaning in the LAW based not on what the text appears on the surface to say but only on how the meaning best applies to and is accepted by the larger American Jewish community.

In his article on the role of Jewish law in Reconstructionist decision making, Daniel Cedarbaum says that the law should not be viewed as a set of fixed rules that one chooses to disobey or regard. Rather, "we, as a community, must construct for ourselves a set of rules that are at once rooted in our tradition and consonant with the actual conditions and spiritual needs of modern life" (31). The rest of the article describes the need for a formal governing body to decide ultimate meaning in a fairly democratic manner.

In reality, the collective interpretations of several official bodies carry importance with the larger community of Reconstructionist Jews: the Federation of Reconstructionist Congregations and Havurot (FRCH) and the Reconstructionist Rabbinical Association (RRA). These groups work together and separately at events such as the Reform Central Conference of American Rabbis to issue formal resolutions on interpretive issues, such as patrilineal descent and intermarriage (Staub, 97). Such resolutions suggest that although the basics of Reconstructionism put the reader as the arbitrator of meaning, as does reader-response theory, in practice the larger interpretive community determines what is or is not an acceptable reading.

Burton Cohen describes his experience of finding a new meaning in the Akedah, the story of Abraham's binding Isaac. At the beginning of his analysis, Cohen admits that the passage has been interpreted several ways, but his purpose is to add his own interpretation by relating the text to his experience as a Jewish father (Cohen, 33). He is clearly setting up himself, the reader, as a new context for meaning. Cohen then shares his emotions at the birth of his son, summing it up with a connection to the Akedah with the phrase "it seems to me" (33). Again, the reader ultimately determines SIGNIFICANCE. The analysis includes a section titled "Levels of Interpretation," in which the author goes through previous explications, including FORMALISM ("takes the story literally") and historical interpretation ("attempts to determine what message was intended by the authors"; 34). Cohen subsumes these contexts under what the story says about him in his current circumstances. For him, Abraham represents the quintessential father, and all the other characters in the story are manifestations of different aspects of fatherhood. The tension of Abraham's decision to sacrifice his son in the STORY represents the tension that all fathers feel between control of a human life and a simultaneous understanding of how humans are incapable of determining the future (34). Cohen concludes his interpretation by relating how being Jewish provides "various entry points" into understanding life (34). Nearly every sentence in this analysis relates somehow to personal experience. TRADITION and CRITICAL METHODOLOGY give way to the shifting experiences of the individual or community as the starting point for interpretation. Thus, reconstructionism is truly rabbinic in nature and practice.

Bibliography. Daniel Goldman Cedarbaum, "The Role of Halakha in Reconstructionist Decision Making," *Reconstructionist* 65, no. 2 (2001): 29–38; Burton J. Cohen, "On Being a Jewish Father: A Reconstructionist Interpretation of the Akedah," *Reconstructionist* 53, no. 1 (1987): 33–34; Arnold Eisen, "Mordecai Kaplan's Judaism as a Civilization at 70: Setting the Stage for Reappraisal," *Jewish Social*

Studies 12, no. 2 (2006): 1–16; Stanley Fish, *Is There a Text in This Class? The Authority of Interpretive Communities* (Cambridge, MA: Harvard University Press, 1980); Patti Haskell, "Belonging, Behaving, Believing: Exploring Reconstructionist Process," *Reconstructionist* 72, no. 1 (2007): 58–61; Donald Keesey, *Contexts for Criticism* (4th ed.; Boston: McGraw-Hill, 2003); Francis J. Mootz III, "Belief and Interpretation: Meditations on Pelikan's 'Interpreting the Bible and the Constitution,'" *Journal of Law and Religion* 21, no. 2 (2005): 385–99; Felix Posen, "An Experiment Whose Time Is Yet to Come," *Center for Cultural Judaism*, Posen Foundation, http://www.culturaljudaism.org/ccj /articles/24; Jacob J. Staub, "A Reconstructionist View on Patrilineal Descent," *Judaism* 34, no. 1 (1985): 97–106.

JEWISH STUDY BIBLE, THE

A VERSION of the Hebrew Bible based on the Jewish Publication Society's *Tanakh* (JPS, 1985; NJPS, 1999; *see* TANAK) TRANSLATION of the MASORETIC TEXT, produced by biblical scholars and rabbis from Orthodox, Conservative, and Reform JUDAISM. It is designed to introduce students and laypersons to the Tanak through a number of features. Along with the Tanak translation, some of the more important features are (1) section and book introductions that offer background and structural information; (2) commentary alongside the biblical TEXT that offers INTERPRETATIONS of the text from a Jewish perspective; (3) a glossary of technical terms; (4) essays on the Judaic use and interpretation of the Tanak throughout history; and (5) a discussion of the use of the Tanak in the Synagogue.

Bibliography. *The Jewish Study Bible: Jewish Publication Society* Tanakh *Translation [1985, 1999]* (ed. Adèle Berlin and Marc Zvi Brettler; New York: Oxford University Press, 2004).

JOHANNINE DISCOURSE

The extended DIALOGUES and MONOLOGUES in the GOSPEL of John, which are characterized by Jesus's awareness of his divinity and mission. Most scholars assume that this revelatory DISCOURSE mirrors the confessional belief of the Johannine community. Although the SYNOPTIC GOSPELS contain some extended SPEECHES of Jesus, these differ from those in John in that the synoptic speeches are essentially small units or SAYINGS strung together. Jesus's speeches in John, however, are unified around concerns such as faith and the nature of "Christhood" (Bailey and Vander Broek, 172–73). Each of the discourses in John also manifests a similar formulaic STRUCTURE: a discourse about some event; Jesus's INTERPRETATION of the event, which invests it with some enigmatic SIGNIFICANCE; misunderstandings in the audience because of Jesus's use of ambiguity, double meaning, or IRONY; and further EXPLANATION, which gradually divides the observers into those "drawn by the Father" to make an act of faith and seek further revelation and those who understand the explanation only literally. For example, in Jesus's dialogue with Nicodemus (John 3), Jesus tells Nicodemus that a person must be "born from above" before he can see the kingdom of God. The word Jesus uses is *anōthen*, which can mean either "from above" or "again." Nicodemus understands the word in the latter SENSE, which prompts Jesus to offer further explanation. When Nicodemus asks Jesus another question about this spiritual birth, Jesus responds with an ironical question of his own about Nicodemus's inability to understand something that he, a teacher of Israel, should understand. For further explanation, *see* GOSPEL OF SIGNS.

Bibliography. James L. Bailey and Lyle D. Vander Broek, *Literary Form in the New Testament: A Handbook* (Louisville: Westminster John Knox, 1992).

JOURNEY MOTIF

An organizational pattern for a NARRATIVE in which the PROTAGONIST is involved in ACTION while traveling toward a destination. Much of the great literature of the Western TRADITION turns on this particular MOTIF (e.g., Homer's *Odyssey*, James Joyce's *Ulysses*, Chaucer's *Canterbury Tales*, and Welty's "A Worn Path"). In both the HEBREW BIBLE and the NT, the journey motif is used extensively. Examples are the SYNOPTIC GOSPELS (esp. Luke), Acts, Jonah, the PATRIARCHAL NARRATIVES, and Ruth. Sometimes the journey motif has theological SIGNIFICANCE, as in the book of Acts, where the journeying of the APOSTLES becomes symbolic of the Christian way and the journey of Paul, especially as a prisoner of Rome, mirrors Jesus's journey and perhaps that of other Christians.

JOY FORMULA

One of the recurring elements in the BODY of Paul's Letters, the expression of joy ("I have indeed received much joy") was usually a result of some pleasing information that the apostle had received. An example is Paul's joy over Philemon's Christian progress.

Bibliography. William G. Doty, *Letters in Primitive Christianity* (Philadelphia: Fortress, 1973).

JUDAIC

An adjective connoting that which pertains to JUDAISM or is characteristic of it.

JUDAISM

Generally, the religion and culture of the Jewish people. However, Judaism has been variously defined depending on the historical period. Judaism of the first century was anything but monolithic. There were numerous ideological threads running through it—messianism, apocalypticism, legalism, HELLENISM. Often these threads were intertwined. To complicate matters, Judaism existed in two general forms—PALESTINIAN JUDAISM and Judaism of the Greek DIASPORA, or HELLENISTIC JUDAISM.

By the time of the rise of Christianity, however, some characteristics had developed that define Judaism. During the Babylonian captivity, the Jews were forced to consider adopting a religious system that did not include the temple and sacrifice. Consequently, the religion moved toward observance of the ancient laws of purity as expressed in the PENTATEUCH and toward communal study of their sacred texts, a practice that led to the institution of the synagogue. Thus the most characteristic focus in Judaism was on keeping the law, especially by the time of the Hellenistic period.

The historical trek that eventually produced first-century Judaism, or what some call PHARISAIC JUDAISM, is long and complex. A RECON-STRUCTION of that history would begin with the EXILE, proceed to the Persian period (538–332 BCE), continue through the Greek period (332–167 BCE) and the Maccabean period (167–63 BCE), until finally it arrived at the Roman period (from 63 BCE). In its many expressions, Judaism passed on a variety of ideological and pedagogical traits to early Christianity and the NT. *See* ESSENES; HELLENISTIC JUDAISM; PALESTINIAN JUDAISM; PHARISAIC JUDAISM; PHARISEES; SADDUCEES.

JUDAISM, HELLENISTIC. *See* HELLENISTIC JUDAISM

JUDAISM, PHARISAIC. *See* PHARISAIC JUDAISM

JUDAISM, PALESTINIAN. *See* PALESTINIAN JUDAISM

JUDAISM, RABBINIC. *See* RABBINIC JUDAISM

JUDAIZERS

Christians in the early church who thought and taught that Jewish laws should be a necessary part of Christian belief and practice. Thus NT scholars think that after Paul had established churches in Asia Minor, some of them were later infiltrated by Judaizers (e.g., see Galatians; Acts 15:1–21).

JUDICIAL MODEL

One of two ways (the other is the PARTICIPATIONIST MODEL) that Paul conceptualized the relationship between salvation and Jesus's death. In this model, salvation is similar to a legal decision in which God, the lawmaker and judge, pronounces humans acquitted of their guilt (i.e., their sins). The basis for such an acquittal is Jesus's death as a payment for sins (Ehrman, 324–25).

Bibliography. Bart Ehrman, *The New Testament: A Historical Introduction to the Early Christian Writings* (2nd ed.; New York: Oxford University Press, 2000).

JUDICIAL RHETORIC

A type of ancient RHETORIC by which the speaker/writer attempted to persuade an audience to make a decision about something in the past. *See* DE-FENSE SPEECHES; RHETORICAL CRITICISM.

JUXTAPOSITION
The placing of two things back-to-back for rhetorical effect. For example, in 1 Cor. 13:9–10, Paul juxtaposes "partial," or incomplete, things (*ek merous*) and "that which is perfect" (*to teleion*) to make a case that some things, such as knowledge and prophecy, will become ineffectual when the perfect thing appears in the future.

KAL WAHOMER. *See* A MINORE AD MAJUS

KERYGMA

In the narrow SENSE, the CONTENT of the early message preached by the apostles, focusing on the salvific nature of Jesus's life, death, resurrection, and ascension. Since the early twentieth century in BIBLICAL CRITICISM, however, the term has taken on wider MEANING. Biblical criticism (in particular, REDACTION CRITICISM) made the case that the Gospels were more theological than historical and that to read them as the latter was to misread them. The BIBLICAL THEOLOGY MOVEMENT reacted by focusing on the kerygma as proclamation and on the response that it seemed to demand (e.g., Rudolf Bultmann and Karl Barth). Others, however, focused on recovering the earliest kerygma in the life of the church by finding elements of it within the writings of the NT. According to C. H. Dodd, the content of the kerygma is found in Acts 2:14–39; 3:13–26; 4:10–12; 5:30–32; 10:36–43; 13:17–41; and in Gal. 1:4–6; 3:1b; 4:6; 1 Thess. 1:10; 1 Cor. 15:1–7; Rom. 1:1–3; 2:16; 8:34; 10:8–9 (Soulen and Soulen, 94). The problem, however, is that from the time of the crucifixion of Jesus (ca. 30–33 CE) to the writing of Mark's Gospel (ca. 66–70 CE), the kerygma was oral proclamation. As Stephen Harris points out, "The oral kerygma began in Judea, Galilee, and adjoining regions where Aramaic was spoken. When Christian missionaries carried their message into Greek-speaking territories, important changes had to be made" (104). As the message found new audiences, not only was it necessary to translate it into Greek; it also had to be interpreted and explained within a variety of urban SETTINGS. In other words, the early Jewish Christians probably understood the kerygma in messianic terms: the Messiah had appeared in Jesus, and although he had been killed by his enemies, God had resurrected him and invested him with the agency of salvation. Jesus would eventually return "to restore the fortunes of Israel and usher in the full realization of the reign of God on earth. Those who signified their trusting confidence in the Messiah thereby established their citizenship in the messianic kingdom" (Hauer and Young, 286). As Christianity moved further into the Roman world, however, the kerygma was transformed into a message of individual salvation: deliverance "from a decaying world, from death, and from demonic powers" (286). The result was variations in FORM and CONTENT, probably accounting for some of the differences in the Gospels.

Bibliography. Stephen Harris, *The New Testament: A Student's Introduction* (4th ed.; Boston: McGraw-Hill, 2002); Christian E. Hauer and William A. Young, *An Introduction to the Bible: A Journey into Three Worlds* (2nd ed.; Englewood Cliffs, NJ: Prentice Hall, 1990); Richard N. Soulen and R. Kendall Soulen, *Handbook of Biblical Criticism* (3rd ed.; Louisville: Westminster John Knox, 2001).

KETUBIM

The Hebrew term (*kĕtûbîm*) for "Writings," denoting the third division of the HEBREW BIBLE. *See* HAGIOGRAPHA; WRITINGS, THE.

KING JAMES VERSION / NEW KING JAMES VERSION (KJV/NKJV)

The VERSION of the BIBLE produced from the available Greek and Hebrew manuscripts under the order of King James I of England in 1611. Although it was indebted to other prior TRANSLATIONS, it was most dependent on Tyndale's translation from 1525. Also known as the AUTHORIZED VERSION (AV), the King James Version was revised (NT in

1979, OT in 1983: NKJV) because of the discovery of older manuscripts in the nineteenth and twentieth centuries and the archaic nature of its Elizabethan English. The revision did replace the archaic words with modern synonyms and omitted cumbersome pronouns (e.g., "thee," "thou," "thine") and verb endings (e.g., "-est," "-eth"); yet the revisers did not employ the older Greek and Hebrew manuscripts discovered in the nineteenth and twentieth centuries.

KOINE

The (*koinē*, common) dialect of Greek arising from a combination of several dialects and spoken by most people in the Mediterranean Basin (as a lingua franca) in the HELLENISTIC PERIOD (of which the NT period was a part) and in which the books of the NT were written.

KOMPOSITIONSGESCHICHTE

A German word equivalent to REDACTION CRITICISM and meaning "composition history."

KOMPOSITIONSKRITIK. See COMPOSITIONAL CRITICISM

KYRIARCHY

A term introduced by Elisabeth Schüssler Fiorenza to replace the term PATRIARCHY. Meaning "the rule of master, lord, father, or emperor," *kyriarchy* more adequately and fully captures the multiple nature of the oppression that women have experienced on the societal, religious, familial, and political levels.

KYRIOS

A Greek term usually translated "Lord" but having no exact equivalent in English. It was used in the LXX to translate two Hebrew words for God, *YHWH* (a personal name for the deity; *see* YAHWEH) and *ădônay* (master). Like the two Hebrew words it translates, it suggests power and competency (Hawthorne, 959). Although the LXX regularly employs *kyrios* to translate *YHWH*, the early Christians, when quoting passages from the LXX that use *kyrios* to translate *YHWH*, assigned its meaning to Jesus (e.g., Rom. 10:13; Heb. 1:10; 1 Pet. 2:3; 3:15).

In some English TRANSLATIONs, the word "Lord" is written in small capital letters, "LORD" (e.g., Mark 5:19). *Kyrios* is also used in the NT in the sense of "master" (John 15:20), "Sir" (John 12:21), and "Lord," meaning the exalted Christ (Phil. 2:11).

Bibliography. G. F. Hawthorne, "Lord (Christ)," in *The Zondervan Pictorial Encyclopedia of the Bible* (ed. Merrill C. Tenney; Grand Rapids: Zondervan, 1977), 3:959–60.

L

L

The designation for the material unique to Luke. *See* FOUR DOCUMENT HYPOTHESIS.

LAMENT

Technically, a poem expressing intense communal or personal grief. In BIBLICAL STUDIES, the lament usually refers to a type of PSALM that makes up the largest category of psalms and that can be individual or communal. According to Leland Ryken (240–41), a lament consists of five parts, which may occur in any order and more than once in a single lament.

1. An invocation to God
2. The lament or complaint, which usually arises from a specific circumstance in the life of the poet or community
3. Petition
4. A statement of confidence in God
5. A praise to God

Compare Ps. 22 with the above structure.

The lament is also used by the PROPHETS as an announcement of judgment. There is a lament over Israel (e.g., Amos 5:1–3; Jer. 8:4–7) and a lament by Yahweh over his land (e.g., Jer. 2:31–37; 15:5–9).

Bibliography. Leland Ryken, *Words of Delight: A Literary Introduction to the Bible* (Grand Rapids: Baker, 1987).

LANGUAGE GAMES

A term in the LINGUISTICS of Ludwig Wittgenstein for his claim that all words acquire their MEANINGS within the CONTEXTS in which they are used. Within each context there exists a set of rules (language games) that govern usage. Consequently, in order to understand the meanings of words within any given context, a person must know the rules of the game. For example, in the context of a formal meeting, "aye" means a vote in the affirmative, while in a Navy context, it signifies obedience.

LANGUE

In the STRUCTURALISM of Ferdinand de Saussure, the underlying system of conventions and relationships: the complete set of linguistic elements and the rules or codes governing their combinations (grammar, SYNTAX, etc.) that make individual instances of SPEECH (both oral and written), which he calls PAROLE, possible and meaningful. People use *langue* when conceptualizing, as opposed to the individual utterance, or *parole*. For a more detailed discussion of *langue* and *parole*, see SEMIOTICS; STRUCTURALISM.

The American linguist Noam Chomsky has developed a similar distinction between the coded system (competence) and actual instances of speech (performance). According to Chomsky, competence is the implicit knowledge and mastery that speakers and hearers have of their native language. Such knowledge includes the relationships between sentences, the ability to resolve ambiguities, and mastery of the rules of grammar and syntax, all of which derive from a set of innate principles. When competence interacts with cognitive systems such as memory and logical reasoning, linguistic behavior in concrete situations is determined. Chomsky refers to the result as performance.

LASTERKATALOG

German for the list of vices found in the NT. *See* LIST OF VIRTUES AND VICES.

LATINISM

A word, phrase, or grammatical construction founded on a Latin form. In the NT, Latinisms from the Greek text are translated into English in several areas: in military terminology (e.g., "legion," "centurion"), in measurements (e.g., "liter," "mile"), in money (e.g., "denarius," "drachma," "quadrans"), in legal terms (e.g., "colony," "freedman").

Bibliography. Richard N. Soulen and R. Kendall Soulen, *Handbook of Biblical Criticism* (3rd ed.; Louisville: Westminster John Knox, 2001).

LATTER PROPHETS. *See* PROPHETS

LAW

Technically, the standards (moral, political, cultic, etc.) that are intended to govern the life of a people. In the HEBREW BIBLE, law is inseparable from the idea of COVENANT in that it establishes the standards for the maintenance of the relationship between Yahweh and Yahweh's people. In the Hebrew Bible are five units of law: DECALOGUE (Exod. 20:2–17; Deut. 5:6–21), BOOK OF THE COVENANT (Exod. 20:22–23:33), PRIESTLY CODE (Exod. 25:31; 34:29–Lev. 16), HOLINESS CODE (Lev. 17–26), and DEUTERONOMIC CODE (Deut. 12–26).

LAW, APODICTIC. *See* APODICTIC LAW

LAW, CASUISTIC. *See* CASUISTIC LAW

LAW, CEREMONIAL. *See* CEREMONIAL LAW

LAW, MOSAIC. *See* TORAH

LAW OF MOSES. *See* TORAH

LEAD WORDS

A form of REPETITION in which a word recurs within a unit of NARRATIVE and may function in a variety of ways, such as to carry emotional freight (in Gen. 22, the repetition of "your son, your only son"; "so the two of them walked on together"), to denote social position (in Gen. 4, the repetition of "ground" and "a fugitive and wanderer on the earth"), to convey reversal and IRONY (in Gen. 11, the repetition of "scattered abroad upon the face of the earth"), to express thematic interest (in Gen. 1, the repetition of "and it was so"), or to forge links between stories.

LECTIONARY

A book of selected scriptural passages arranged according to the calendar year or church year and used in private and public worship contexts. In JUDAISM, readings were from the PROPHETS and the LAW in the synagogue as early as the third century CE. In the church, the readings come from the GOSPELs and EPISTLES and began sometime between the fourth and seventh centuries. The lectionaries arranged for the calendar year were used for feast days, saints' days, and special occasions. Those arranged for the church year began at Easter and were used for Saturdays, Sundays, and the weekdays of the church year. The lectionaries are important manuscripts in TEXTUAL CRITICISM for deciding between VARIANT READINGS.

LEGAL SAYINGS. *See* SAYINGS OF JESUS

LEGEND

In contemporary use, a STORY or NARRATIVE, lying between MYTH and history, about a famous person or place. These stories generally grow in detail over time, and many are eventually written down or recited in song. In many cases, the stories that developed originally had nothing to do with the person or place. In the HEBREW BIBLE, many legends are etiologies (*see* ETIOLOGY) that explain the development of an institution. Legends may also develop around a sanctuary, a cultic object associated with the sanctuary, a national hero, a prophet, or a martyr. Scholars have identified many legends in the Hebrew Bible, as in these examples (van der Woude, 123–35): (1) Gen. 28:10–22, account of the origin of the sanctuary at Bethel; (2) 1 Sam. 5, account of the power associated with the ark of the covenant; (3) Exod. 2, account of Moses's birth (striking similarities exist between the birth account of Moses and those of Sargon I of Babylon and Cyrus of Persia); (4) 1 Kings 22, account of the encounter between Micaiah and Ahab; (5) account of the miraculous deliverance of Shadrach, Meshach, and Abednego in Dan. 3 and of Daniel in Dan. 6.

Bibliography. A. S. van der Woude, ed., *The World of the Old Testament* (Grand Rapids: Eerdmans, 1989).

LEGITIMACY

According to E. D. Hirsch Jr., one of the ways of verifying that a reading of a TEXT is the most probable one. Since Hirsch assumes that no reader can be absolutely certain of reconfiguring the author's MEANING, the reader's goal must be to show that a given reading is more probable than all the others. One of the four criteria by which this is accomplished is legitimacy, which establishes that "the reading must be permissible within the norms of the language in which the text was composed." The other three criteria in this process of VERIFICATION are CORRESPONDENCE, GENERIC APPROPRIATE-NESS, and COHERENCE.

Bibliography. E. D. Hirsch Jr., "Objective Interpretation," *PMLA* 75 (1960): 463, 470–79.

LEITMOTIF (LEITMOTIV)

Originally a term used to denote a musical THEME pervading an entire work, as employed extensively in the music of Berlioz and Wagner. The German AUTHOR Thomas Mann adopted the term and used it to denote a recurrent theme in a literary TEXT, a MEANING it has retained ever since. It has, however, also been used to refer to the favorite theme of an author across texts. In Mann's sense, the leitmotif is frequently used in the biblical texts. For example, the first eleven chapters of Genesis contain a theme that is traceable throughout the remainder of the Hebrew Bible: the separation between humankind and God. It is reflected at the level of the family, especially in the PATRIARCHAL NARRATIVES (Gen. 12–50) and the monarchical narratives (1 Sam.–2 Kings). The theme of blessing is emphasized in Gen. 27:1–45 by the twenty-one repetitions of the root for "to bless."

Although the leitmotif has been narrowed to denote the REPETITION of an object, IMAGE, or AC-

TION, such repetition is probably more accurately termed LEITWORT. Examples are the stones in the Jacob NARRATIVE, water in the Moses STORY, and fire in the Samson story.

LEITWORT

A LITERARY DEVICE in the HEBREW BIBLE in which an AUTHOR exploits the range of MEANING of a word root by repeating different forms of the root within a PERICOPE or across several units. This technique may provide thematic cohesion or thematic emphasis within a unit of TEXT (e.g., the twenty-one repetitions of the root for "to bless" in Gen. 27:1–45). The Hebrews, like other social groups, established social conventions to safeguard family cohesion. One of these conventions was the father's practice of passing on to the eldest son the family inheritance and paternal blessing. When Jacob steals Esau's blessing in Gen. 27, the established social convention has the opposite effect. Instead of safeguarding the family cohesion, it is actually the source of family division and separation. Through the repetitive use of the word "to bless," the author draws the reader's attention to the convention and its reverse effect. *See* LEITMOTIF.

LESSER INTERPOLATION

A section of Luke's GOSPEL (6:20–8:3) in which he interweaves material also found in Matthew (perhaps from Q) with material unique to his Gospel.

LETTER. *See* EPISTOLARY LITERATURE

LEVIRATE MARRIAGE

Described in Deut. 25:5–10, a TYPE of marriage in which a man marries his sister-in-law if her husband dies without offspring. The child born of this marriage is regarded as the child of the dead brother. For an interesting story in which the levirate marriage plays a central role, see Gen. 38.

LEXICOLOGY

A branch of LINGUISTICS that is concerned with word meanings. Often the plausible EXPLICATION of a passage of text may hinge on the MEANING

of a word that appears to be vague. When such a word is understood in a way in which it would have been understood within the culture of the AUTHOR, the entire passage may assume a different nature. In reference to word studies, Hayes and Holladay observe,

> We gradually broaden our understanding of the term, the passage itself and the other biblical writings in which it occurs. It is through this process of interrogation and analysis that we begin to increase our own understanding of the passage by actually re-entering and re-creating the thought-world of the author or text itself. (62)

Tools that may serve to clarify meanings of words are a CONCORDANCE, a DICTIONARY, an ENCYCLOPEDIA, and a LEXICON.

Bibliography. John H. Hayes and Carl R. Holladay, *Biblical Exegesis: A Beginner's Handbook* (Atlanta: John Knox, 1987).

LEXICON

In BIBLICAL STUDIES, a DICTIONARY of GREEK, HEBREW (ARAMAIC), or Latin words used in the BIBLE or church fathers. A useful lexicon provides the reader with ETYMOLOGIES, an identification and discussion of irregular grammatical forms, possible MEANINGS, and the usage of a word within a given CONTEXT. Below are separate listings for lexicons for the Greek NT and the Hebrew OT. *See also* CONCORDANCE.

Greek Lexicons

Walter Bauer, *Greek-English Lexicon of the New Testament and Other Early Christian Literature* (rev. and ed. Frederick W. Danker, William F. Arndt, and F. Wilbur Gingrich; 3rd ed.; Chicago: University of Chicago Press, 2000).

George Ricker Berry, *A Dictionary of New Testament Greek Synonyms* (Grand Rapids: Zondervan, 1979).

———, *A New Greek-English Lexicon to the New Testament* (Chicago: Wilcox & Follett, 1944).

Ethelbert W. Bullinger, *A Critical Lexicon and Concordance to the English and Greek New Testaments* (London: Samuel Bagster & Sons, 1969).

Henry George Liddell, Robert Scott, and Henry Stuart Jones, *A Greek-English Lexicon* (9th ed. with revised supplement; Oxford: Clarendon, 1996).

Johannes P. Louw, Eugene A. Nida, Rondal B. Smith, and Karen A. Munson, eds., *Greek-English Lexicon of the New Testament Based on Semantic Domains* (2nd ed.; New York: United Bible Societies, 1989).

William D. Mounce, *The Analytical Lexicon to the Greek New Testament* (Grand Rapids: Zondervan, 1993).

Wesley J. Perschbacher, ed., *The New Analytical Greek Lexicon* (Peabody, MA: Hendrickson, 1990).

Ceslas Spicq, *Theological Lexicon of the New Testament* (ed. and trans. James D. Ernest; Peabody, MA: Hendrickson, 1994).

Joseph Henry Thayer, *A Greek-English Lexicon of the New Testament* (Grand Rapids: Baker, 1977).

George V. Wigram, *The Analytical Greek Lexicon of the New Testament* (Peabody, MA: Hendrickson, 1983).

———, *The New Englishman's Greek Concordance and Lexicon* (rev. Jay P. Green Sr.; Peabody, MA: Hendrickson, 1982).

Hebrew Lexicons

Terry A. Armstrong, Douglas L. Busby, and Cyril F. Carr, *A Reader's Hebrew-English Lexicon of the Old Testament* (Grand Rapids: Zondervan, 1989).

Francis Brown, S. R. Driver, and C. A. Briggs, *A Hebrew and English Lexicon of the Old Testament* (Oxford: Clarendon, 1978).

Benjamin Davidson, *The Analytical Hebrew and Chaldee Lexicon* (Grand Rapids: Zondervan, 1972; repr., Peabody, MA: Hendrickson, 2002).

Bruce Einspahr, compiler, *Index to Brown, Driver, and Briggs Hebrew Lexicon* (Chicago: Moody, 1976).

H. W. F. Gesenius, *Gesenius' Hebrew-Chaldee Lexicon to the Old Testament* (Grand Rapids: Baker, 1979).

William L. Holladay, *A Concise Hebrew and Aramaic Lexicon of the Old Testament* (Grand Rapids: Eerdmans, 1988).

Ernst Jenni and Claus Westermann, *Theological Lexicon of the Old Testament* (Peabody, MA: Hendrickson, 1997).

Ludwig Koehler, Walter Baumgartner, and J. J. Stamm, *The Hebrew and Aramaic Lexicon of the Old Testament* (trans. and ed. under the supervision of M. E. J. Richardson; 5 vols.; Leiden: Brill, 1994–2000).

LIBERATION HERMENEUTICS

A group of interpretive approaches to TEXTS, TRADITIONS, and/or institutions that has as its purpose (1) the exposing of the means by which these texts, traditions, and institutions serve as instruments of power, oppression, domination, MARGINALIZATION, and/or manipulation; and (2) the liberation of those on whom the instruments of power operate. In BIBLICAL STUDIES, these approaches include Black criticism, CULTURAL CRITICISM, FEMINIST CRITICISM, gay/lesbian criticism (*see* QUEER THEORY), *MUJERISTA* CRITICISM, POSTCOLONIAL CRITICISM, and WOMANIST CRITICISM. Each of these criticisms assumes that in the Western biblical tradition, reading praxes have served to legitimate and perpetuate oppressive traditions and institutional structures. While all the above approaches seek to liberate both persons and texts, each has its own methodology and goals. So for a fuller development of liberation hermeneutics, *see* the individual listing for each and LIBERATION THEOLOGY.

LIBERATION THEOLOGY

The general term given to a variety of specialized theologies, such as feminist theology, gay/lesbian theology, African American theology, and Latin American theology. The most common form of liberation theology, however, is typically found in Latin America and the third-world countries. The purpose of such a theology is to bring to light the injustices that are endured by the masses and to dismantle the structures that create and allow such injustices to occur.

Liberation theology is a reading or INTERPRETATION of the BIBLE from the perspective of the poor/oppressed, who are concerned with their struggle for liberation. It then applies the message of the Bible to some of the contemporary problems in today's society (Hopfe and Woodward). Liberation theologians believe that the church was designed by God to bring liberation to all who are in need (Urban). It is a common misconception that "poor" refers only to the economically poor. There are many people in need of liberation: immigrants; the unemployed; the underemployed, as in the case of seasonal farmers as well as indigenous peoples who have been overrun by faster moving, more technologically advanced cultures; the elderly; and children. Typically, society blames individuals for their situations, citing reasons such as ignorance or laziness, or it believes that others are poor because they are guilty of some wickedness. An example of this attitude can be found in John 9. When Jesus and his disciples encounter a blind man, the disciples ask Jesus, "Who sinned, this man or his parents?" According to liberationists, all of these groups are "kept down," or oppressed, by social structures or mechanisms governed by materialism and a lust for power. The social structures or mechanisms that cause the oppression can be anything that creates separation between groups of people. They can be economic systems or political and social parties. Because of these structures, the rich get richer at the expense of the poor (Boff and Boff, *Introducing*).

The primary interest of liberation theology is to encourage and direct the church's activity toward providing assistance to the poor, with the hope that liberation of the individuals will be the end result. "Liberation theology was born when faith confronted the injustice done to the poor" (Boff and Boff, *Introducing*, 3), suggesting that it is the church's responsibility not only to recognize the need for liberation but to take steps to make it a reality. Some liberation theologians point to James 2:15–17 as a paradigm for liberation: "If a brother or sister is naked and lacks daily food, and one of you says to them, 'Go in peace; keep warm and eat your fill,' and yet you do not supply their bodily needs, what is the good of that? So faith by itself, if it has no works, is dead." Liberation theologians recognize that there is a danger in helping the poor and the oppressed, however, if it is forgotten that the purpose is not temporary relief but the eventual liberation and self-sufficiency of the individual. The danger arises when one follows what is called "naive voluntarism." This occurs when one sees only the superficial or immediate need rather than the long chain of causes of the need. By simply "fixing" the immediate need, one causes the oppressed to become even more trapped and dependent because they begin to rely on the assistance rather than learning to overcome their situation. Instead of the church's assuming the dominant role, in which it is above the oppressed poor, handing down assistance, the church should assume the responsibility to "suffer with" the poor in their struggle and to give the poor opportunities to help themselves (Boff and Boff, *Salvation*, 44).

Four assumptions. Liberation theologians hold not only that the Bible takes the side of the oppressed and the poor but also that God himself commands that it is the duty of every Christian to strive for the liberation of all oppressed people. They also insist that the poor in a way represent the "disfigured Son of God" because Jesus himself was the suffering and rejected Servant. These points are based on four ASSUMPTIONS. First, the *theological* assumption—God's motivation on behalf of the poor—says that "God feels impelled" to come to the aid of the oppressed (Boff and Boff, *Introducing*, 44). Exodus 3:7–9 is used to show that God comes to the assistance of the oppressed and abused. When the Israelites, who were enslaved by the Egyptians, called out to God to rescue them

(2:23–25), God responded by sending Moses, who would lead them out of Egypt and into the promised land. In a similar fashion, in Isa. 1:17 God is pleased by those who "learn to do good, seek justice, reprove the ruthless [oppressor], defend the orphan [fatherless], plead for the widow" (NASB).

The second assumption is the christological, which sees that Christ's mission was to break the bonds of the oppressed and give aid to those in need. Beginning in Luke 6:20–21, Jesus tells the disciples, "Blessed are you who are poor, for yours is the kingdom of God. Blessed are you who are hungry now, for you will be filled. Blessed are you who weep now, for you will laugh. Blessed are you when people hate you, and when they exclude you, revile you, and defame you." He then tells them that their reward will be great in heaven (6:23). Also in Luke, Jesus cures the sick, sets free those with infirmities and afflictions, raises the dead, and preaches the gospel to the poor (7:21–22). Jesus also tells the story of the good Samaritan (10:25–37), in which he commands his disciples to be like the Samaritan man who had compassion on the one who had fallen among the thieves and was in need. It is Gustavo Gutiérrez's opinion that Jesus was interested not only in liberating people spiritually but also in thereby setting people free from physical or tangible oppression: "Sin is evident in oppressive structures, in the exploitation of humans by humans, in the domination and slavery of peoples, races, and social classes. Sin appears therefore as the fundamental alienation, the root of a situation of injustice and exploitation" (Gutiérrez, 103). So Jesus was interested not only in forgiving sin but also in providing a reprieve from the injustices created by an imperfect world.

The third assumption is the *eschatological*, the belief that a person's eternal destiny will be determined by his or her attitude of acceptance or rejection of the poor. According to Matt. 25:31–46, on the great day when the Son of Man returns, all the nations will be gathered before him. And he will separate the nations, drawing near to him all those who fed the hungry, clothed the naked, gave drink to the thirsty, and visited the sick and imprisoned—while rejecting all those who did not do such things. They "will go away into eternal punishment, but the righteous into eternal life" (Matt. 25:46).

The fourth assumption is *social*, deriving from the apostles' belief that they and their followers should share everything so there might not be any poor among them (e.g., Acts 2; 4). It is clear that the apostles understood the importance of taking care of those in need and that it was the responsibility of those who were wealthy to provide for those less fortunate. Liberation theologians believe that the church has been motivated to provide assistance to the poor; but before the church can help the poor, it must first be in contact with them.

Levels of liberation theology. According to Boff and Boff (*Introducing*, 11–21), three different levels of liberation theology are performed by three different groups of people: the popular, the pastoral, and the professional. Even though they differ, they share the same goal of bringing liberation to the poor by means of "faith confronting oppression." At its base, liberation theology is a *popular* movement. It is on this level that liberation theology was created and is constantly being fed. It is the level of the common people, who meet together and discuss their fears, doubts, frustrations, and struggles. These meetings are called "base communities" and are usually in the form of a small Bible group or social gathering. Such base communities offer enlightenment to the cause of liberation because of their experiences. The people who make up these groups are the originators of liberation theology. They are the first theologians (Boff and Boff, *Introducing*, 15–17).

The "highest" level of liberation theology is the *professional* level. This group is made up of scholars, theologians, professors, and teachers. Their focus is on analyzing the method of liberation theology, discovering hermeneutical evidence in the Scriptures for the theology, and theorizing the causes of oppression and the steps necessary to end the oppression. Their main method of expressing liberation theology is confined to lectures, conferences, and scholarly works, including doctoral dissertations, master's theses, and critical analyses.

The third level is the *pastoral* level, which serves as a bridge between the popular and the professional classes. The job of those in this level is to listen to the problems at the popular level and then apply solutions that are discovered by the professional level. The pastoral level is composed of pastors, priests, bishops, and anyone else who is in a position of leadership over the popular class. They are the mediators, and their role is to see areas of need, judge what action is necessary to remedy the situation, and then to act accordingly on behalf of the popular class. In most situations, there is some integration or mixing of the groups. In Bible studies, there might be representatives of the popular class under the supervision of representatives of the pastoral level. And in other situations all three groups might be mixed, as in the case of a seminar or conference. Typically, the professional level will be speaking, with persons from both the pastoral and the popular levels attending. So, even though the groups are different, they are also irreversibly linked to one another. Without one, the others could not function properly.

Methods of commitment. Within liberation theology are three methods by which a person may make a commitment to the poor. The first method, referred to as "more or less restricted," means sporadic encounters with the poor by visits to base communities and meetings. A less sporadic approach involves some pastoral work on the weekends, which may include acting as an adviser to the popular movement. The second method consists of alternating periods of scholarly work (research, teaching, and writing) with periods of practical work or action that might include taking a position such as that of a pastor or Sunday school teacher in a church in a poor community. The third method is the most demanding: choosing to live permanently alongside the popular class. The specific method of interaction that is chosen is not as important as the imperative to have some understanding of the poor and their struggle (Boff and Boff, *Introducing*, 23–24).

Stages of liberation theology. There are also three basic stages of liberation theology. *Socioanalytical mediation* (seeing) asks the fundamental questions. At this stage, liberationists want to know why the oppressed are oppressed: they want to identify the causes of oppression (Boff and Boff, *Introducing*, 24). The second is *hermeneutic mediation* (judging). At this stage, theologians try to discern what God's plan for the poor is. They want to know what the Bible says about liberation. This is the stage at which the theology is constructed (32–37). The third stage is *practical mediation* (acting), where according to God's will, liberationists take courses of action designed to overcome oppression. Before making decisions, it is important to consider the consequences of the planned action (39–42).

Conclusion. Liberation theology has been called the "young theology" because it was born in the 1970s (Boff and Boff, *Introducing*, 78). It has, however, exerted a profound influence on the world. Liberation theology has influenced the theologies of the churches and the people who are associated with it. It is also responsible for creating waves of influence in third-world countries, so much so that liberation theology has become synonymous with Latin American theology. It has also been the cause of a theological wake-up call to more "advanced" societies of the first world. It has revealed contradictions between the Christian faith claimed by the first-world nations and the way they treat their poor. Consequently, other theologies, such as black and feminist, have developed according to their specific needs. Liberation theology has had a tremendous influence, mainly on the Catholic Church. An example is the "preferential option for the poor," defined by the Medellín conference in 1968 and ratified at Puebla in 1979, when the bishops reaffirmed "the need for conversion on the part of the whole church to a preferential option for the poor, an option aimed at their integral liberation" (Boff and Boff, *Introducing*, 76–77).

Bibliography. Gerald H. Anderson, ed., *Mission Trends* (New York: Paulist Press, 1979), vol. 4; Leonardo Boff and Clodovis Boff, *Introducing Liberation Theology* (New York: Orbis Books, 1989); idem, *Salvation and Liberation* (New York: Orbis Books, 1985); Gustavo Gutiérrez, *A Theology of Liberation* (New York: Orbis Books, 1988); Lewis M. Hopfe and Mark R. Woodward, *Religions of the World* (Upper Saddle River, NJ: Prentice Hall, 1998); Ronald H. Nash, ed., *Liberation Theology* (Grand Rapids: Baker, 1989); Schubert M. Ogden, *Faith and Freedom* (Nashville: Abingdon, 1979); Linwood Urban, *A Short History of Christian Thought* (New York: Oxford University Press, 1995); Theo Witvliet, *A Place in the Sun* (New York: Orbis Books, 1985).

LIMINALITY

A concept in anthropology for important "passages" in life that serve as MEANING thresholds (e.g., marriage, graduation, consecration, funeral) that have become ritualized and around which social meaning clusters. When one is in a state of liminality, one is in a state of suspension, between two stages of existence.

In LITERARY studies, the term is used for times when social conventions are suspended.

LINGUISTIC CRITICISM

A type of textual analysis that focuses on the relationships between language and the social world. Key figures in the field are Roger Fowler, Robert Hodge, Gunter Kress, Tony Trew, and Gareth Jones. A central tenet of linguistic criticism is that individuals do not have unmediated, objective (*see* OBJECTIVE KNOWLEDGE) access to their world because their belief systems and ideologies (*see* IDEOLOGY and IDEOLOGICAL CRITICISM) determine their conception of reality. In other words, a person's world is a social construct, and a primary element of that construct is language. Consequently, a thorough and systematic analysis of the language of TEXTS that a culture or subculture produces will reveal the processes and techniques by which a person of the culture or subculture perpetuates and legitimates or challenges aspects of that culture. Furthermore, linguistic CRITICS assume that social situations partially dictate language usage.

While any text may be subjected to linguistic criticism, critics generally limit their analysis to the literary CANON. However, while the texts of the canon have been and are given a special status among most types of LITERARY CRITICISM, linguistic critics hold that there is nothing intrinsic about these texts that gives them their privileged status. In addition, these critics argue that literary texts have MEANING only as it is ascribed to them by readers who have varying ideologies within their social contexts. Therefore, meaning varies and is never objective.

The practitioners of linguistic criticism are aware that other disciplines can contribute to the analysis of texts because nonlinguistic factors (i.e., things outside the text) influence linguistic choices. These critics thus make use of other disciplines such as philosophy, sociology, history, and psychology.

Bibliography. Roger Fowler, *Linguistic Criticism* (New York: Oxford University Press, 1986); idem, *Literature as Social Discourse: The Practice of Linguistic Criticism* (London: Batsford, 1981).

LINGUISTICS

The scientific study of language, generally divided into descriptive linguistics, which classifies the characteristics of language, and comparative linguistics, which focuses on the historical growth and development of language. The various branches of linguistics are ETYMOLOGY, SEMANTICS, MORPHOLOGY, LEXICOLOGY, PHONOLOGY, PRAGMATICS, and SYNTAX.

Literature is one of the linguistic expressions of a culture's SYMBOLIC WORLD, the maze of interrelated customs, ideologies (*see* IDEOLOGICAL CRITICISM; IDEOLOGY), religious expressions, and social relationships within which a people finds its identity, its self-understanding, and its ultimate reason for being. If a culture's literature is the linguistic expression of this world, or at least the linguistic attempt to interpret the symbolic world, then a study of that culture's linguistic expression—language in its many facets—should be an integral part of HERMENEUTICS.

LISIBLE

A term used by Roland Barthes for what he calls a "readerly" TEXT, which demands little if any interpretive effort on the part of the reader. According to Barthes, the lisible text is highly conventional and depends on the reader to recognize the conventions. The opposite of lisible is a "scriptible" or "writerly" text, one that is complex and requires interpretive analysis by the reader. Not only does the scriptible text insist on the activities of the reader in constructing MEANING; it also imposes its own internal "mechanics" on the reader as the SUBJECT of INTERPRETATION. Since Barthes claims that the scriptible text is a modern phenomenon, it is perhaps difficult to apply the concept to biblical texts. However, such a distinction might be made between biblical texts that are fairly closed, such as the Epistle of James, and the more open, complex ones, such as Job or the Gospel of Mark (esp. with its internal STRUCTURE of INTERCALATION, INTRUSIVE NARRATOR, and LITERARY ALLUSION).

Bibliography. Roland Barthes, *S/Z / Roland Barthes* (trans. Richard Miller; Oxford: Blackwell, 1975).

LIST OF CIRCUMSTANCES

Autobiographical notes in the LETTERS of Paul that reflect some details of his career. For example, in 2 Cor. 12:10 Paul offers a list: "Therefore I am content with weaknesses, insults, hardships, persecutions, and calamities for the sake of Christ; for whenever I am weak, then I am strong." Another such list is found in 2 Cor. 11:22–28.

LIST OF RULES OF BEHAVIOR

Lists in the EPISTOLARY LITERATURE that show concerns with articulating how Christians should live in the world on a day-to-day basis. These lists of relationships are not unique to the NT, but as part of the general Hellenistic cultural milieu (*see* HELLENISM), they became part also of the daily life of the church. Most of these lists occur in the later LETTERS of the church (e.g., Eph. 5:21–6:9; Col. 3:18–4:1; 1 Tim. 2:1–15; 5:1–21; Titus 2:1–10; 1 Pet. 2:13–3:7). Such lists may suggest a later period in the church when it was becoming institutionalized and adopting the social structures at large in Roman imperial culture.

LIST OF VIRTUES AND VICES

Part of the PARAENESIS of the EPISTOLARY LITERATURE in the NT, borrowed from both Jewish and Hellenistic (*see* HELLENISM) TRADITIONS. Although there are lists of vices in the HEBREW BIBLE (e.g., Jer. 7:9; Prov. 6:17–19), it was probably not a developed LITERARY form. In Hellenistic culture, however, lists of both vices and virtues were common and traditional in STOICISM. Quoting Easton, Bailey and Vander Broek point to the striking similarity between the ideal requirements from the Greek philosopher Onosander (first century CE) for a general and those for a bishop in 1 Tim. 3:2–7:

> I say that the general should be chosen as sober minded, self-controlled, temperate, frugal, hardy, intelligent, no lover of money, not too young or old, if he be the father of children, able to speak well, of good repute. (Easton, 10–11)

The lists vary in length and do not necessarily reflect the situation at any particular church (e.g., Rom. 1:29–31; 1 Cor. 5:10–11; 2 Cor. 6:6–7, 14; Gal. 5:19–23; Phil. 4:8; Titus 1:7–8; James 3:17; 1 Pet. 4:3; 2 Pet. 1:5–8). A list of vices may stand alone, as in Rom. 1:29–31, or it may be paired with a list of virtues, as in Gal. 5:19–23.

Bibliography. James L. Bailey and Lyle D. Vander Broek, *Literary Forms in the New Testament* (Louisville: Westminster John Knox, 1992); Burton Easton, "New Testament Ethical Lists," *JBL* 51 (1932): 1–12.

LITERAL MEANING

In the study of TEXTS, the MEANING of words in their primary, nonfigurative SENSE. Generally speaking, the literal INTERPRETATION of a text is the meaning that is derivable from the grammatical level or from the AUTHORIAL INTENTION determined within the author's historical CONTEXT. In the latter sense, the literal may involve the use of FIGURATIVE LANGUAGE if its use was part of the author's intention. In present-day BIBLICAL STUDIES, however, CRITICS emphasize the difficulty of determining the author's intention and of translating (*see* TRANSLATION; TRANSLATION STUDIES)

the grammatical level of a text from one language to another. Complicating matters is the recognition that meaning does not exist apart from the AUTHOR, TEXT, or reader. Consequently, "literal" may refer to the meaning that can be inferred from an examination of the text within the world of the author, meaning that is derived from the STRUCTURES and rhetorical strategies of the text, meaning that is configured from within the interpretive conventions of a community, or meaning as the result of a combination of the first three.

LITERARINESS

A term used in FORMALISM to name that which makes a TEXT a LITERARY one. In ordinary language, what the formalists called "practical" language, words are pronounced and perceived automatically. This practical, everyday language is made strange in poetry through the presence of FORMS, sounds, vocabulary, RHYTHM, RHYME, IMAGE, parallelism, HYPERBOLE, REPETITION, and SYNTAX not usually found in everyday SPEECH. All of these devices commit an organized violence on everyday language. Poetic language also violates the SEMANTICS of ordinary language by introducing secondary or archaic meanings of words, creating AMBIGUITY, itself a device that impedes progress. Such a poetic broadening of the SEMANTIC RANGE of words means that communication fails. This means that what is literary (i.e., literariness) is defined by the opposition between poetic language and ordinary language. This literariness, defined as what constitutes a work as a literary work, becomes the focus of formalists' studies. As later formalists realized, however, literary devices themselves tend to become familiar and consequently automatized, themselves subject to defamiliarization (*see* FORMALISM). Thus Ann Jefferson points out: "This means that the habitual/made-strange opposition is now located within literature itself and is no longer co-extensive with the distinction between literature and nonliterature. Literariness is a feature not just of form as impeded speech, but more important, of impeded form" (21). The formalists also applied their concepts of literariness and defamiliarization to PROSE.

Argument may be made that the texts of the BIBLE are literary. In the book of Esther, for example, reversal is the "dominant" device in the book, while INTERIOR MONOLOGUE in Jonah serves to retard NARRATIVE TIME. In the story of Joseph (Gen. 37–47), the writer employs multiperspectives, displacement of time or events, digressions, summaries, and unusual vocabulary to retard the ACTION and creates ambiguity by changing instances of reported SPEECH from the original and giving rise to multiple meanings by CHARACTERIZATION.

Bibliography. Victor Erlich, *Russian Formalism: History, Doctrine* (Paris: Mouton, 1980); Ann Jefferson, "Russian Formalism," in *Modern Literary Theory: A Comparative Introduction* (ed. Ann Jefferson and David Robey; Totowa, NJ: Barnes & Noble, 1982), 16–37; Victor Shklovsky, "Art as Technique," in *Russian Formalist Criticism: Four Essays* (trans. Lee T. Lemon and Marion J. Reis; Lincoln: University of Nebraska Press, 1965), 3–57.

LITERARY

When applied to TEXTS, a special use of language as creative and imaginative, language adorned with artistic devices that transform and intensify ordinary language or everyday SPEECH and requiring INTERPRETATION. A literary text employs an array of devices, such as REPETITION not found in ordinary language, METAPHOR, SYMBOL, and ALLUSION. It also exploits the AMBIGUITY inherent in language to play with multiple MEANINGS of words and phrases and the range of associations these meanings evoke. So this kind of language usage calls attention to itself, constantly reminding readers that they are dealing with language, a text, not with the REAL WORLD.

LITERARY ALLUSION. *See* ALLUSION

LITERARY CANON. *See* CANON

LITERARY COMPETENCE

A term within STRUCTURALISM for the essential skills needed to relate a TEXT to the language that lies behind the text. The idea includes a knowledge of cultural and LITERARY STRUCTURES and REFERENCES necessary for the plausible CONFIGURATION of MEANING. A corollary ASSUMPTION is that the more literary competence a reader of a text has, the more plausible the INTERPRETATION. For example, a reader unaware of the social defining structures of the HONOR-SHAME SOCIETY of JUDAISM or of the rhetorical structures and strategies characteristic of LETTER writing in HELLENISM is a less competent reader than a person familiar with such things.

LITERARY CONVENTION

A device, procedure, principle, or FORM that both AUTHOR and reader accept as a characteristically recurring element of a particular TYPE of TEXT. For example, although there are exceptions, a sonnet has fourteen lines, COMEDY generally has a STOCK CHARACTER, and FLASHBACK is a characteristic of short fiction. A literary convention of BIBLICAL POETRY is parallelism, while HEBREW NARRATIVE employs conventions of CHARACTERIZATION, PLOT, and SETTING that are found in most PROSE. In the NT, the book of Revelation makes use of conventions common to apocalypse in general, the GOSPELs use conventions associated with Hellenistic ROMANCE and BIOGRAPHY, and the epistles display complete awareness of the conventions associated with Greek letter writing. Ignorance of the literary conventions of a text often leads to misunderstanding and thus misinterpretation. In addition, to assume that a particular text is a certain kind of writing when it actually is not can have the same results. For example, to interpret the Song of Songs as an ALLEGORY of the relationship between Jesus and the church when it is actually a series of erotic love poems asks the text to communicate in a way it was never intended to do.

LITERARY CRITICISM

Criticism generally understood in three ways: (1) as SOURCE CRITICISM, (2) as an explication of a TEXT that attempts to understand the INTENTION and accomplishment of the AUTHOR by analyzing the compositional and structural elements of the text (*see* HISTORICAL-CRITICAL METHOD), and (3) as an approach that interprets the biblical texts as literature. The last approach is grounded in the ASSUMPTION that the biblical authors were imaginative, creative crafters of art, employing structural elements and LITERARY DEVICES usually associated with the POETICS of literature (i.e., the creation of literature) and GENRE.

Structural elements. Structural elements include the three basic components of literary texts: first, PLOT, with its five components of EXPOSITION, COMPLICATION/RISING ACTION, CLIMAX, crisis, and resolution/DENOUEMENT/FALLING ACTION; second, SETTING, the time, the place, and all the objects included in the time and place; and third, CHARACTERIZATION, the manner in which the various characters populating a text are portrayed either as ROUNDED, STATIC, DYNAMIC, FLAT, FULL-FLEDGED, or STEREOTYPICAL. Other elements of structure are STYLE, TONE, ATMOSPHERE, POINT OF VIEW, SYNTAX, and DICTION.

Literary devices. Literary devices at the disposal of authors are used to enhance the reading experience by engaging the reader in a variety of ways. Some of these devices will create informational gaps, or gaps of INDETERMINACY, that the reader must fill. For example, a METAPHOR asks the reader to make a comparison between two items (sometimes between two concrete items and sometimes between a concrete item and an abstract one). The author also creates a gap by alluding to another text, cultural object, or historical event or person (*see* ALLUSION). By introducing a prior text, object, event, or person into a new context, the author expects the reader to glean the SIGNIFICANCE of the ALLUSION. Other literary devices that authors regularly employ are SIMILE, MYTH, HYPERBOLE, SYMBOL, UNDERSTATEMENT, SYNECDOCHE, parallelism, and PERSONIFICATION. Rhetorical techniques usually fall under three general categories—ETHOS, PATHOS, and LOGOS. (*See* RHETORICAL CRITICISM for a discussion of these techniques.)

Genre. Another important issue within literary criticism is GENRE (*see* GENRE CRITICISM). Literary critics generally assume that while texts may share common literary devices (listed in the previous paragraph), different types of texts operate according to different LITERARY CONVENTIONS. For example, readers generally do not expect to find complex plot development within poetry. Literary critics also claim that readers do not approach different types of texts in the same manner because they do not have the same expectations for every text. The readers of the BIBLE do not approach a PROVERB with the same expectations as they would have for the book of Genesis. The literary CRITIC approaches the PENTATEUCH as theological history and the Proverbs as a collection of APHORISMS. In the HEBREW BIBLE, the genres include theological history (e.g., the Pentateuch, DEUTERONOMISTIC HISTORY, CHRONISTIC HISTORY), SHORT STORY (e.g., Ruth, Jonah, Esther), PROPHECY (e.g., Isaiah, Jeremiah, Amos), and POETRY (e.g., Psalms, Proverbs, Song of Songs). The latter genre, however, is complicated by the fact that there is poetry within most of the books of the Hebrew Bible, especially the prophetic books. Thus with the prophetic books, for example, the reader is faced with the responsibility of interfacing the genre conventions of both prophecy and poetry. The NT genres include GOSPEL, APOCALYPSE, and EPISTOLARY LITERATURE.

In addition to ASSUMPTIONS about STRUCTURE, devices, and genre, literary critics also assume that any single text is a unified whole, in which the parts must be understood in terms of the whole and the whole in terms of the parts. This assumption is based on the prior assumption that authors select and arrange (*see* SELECTION AND ARRANGEMENT) their materials according to a predetermined plan. Such a plan contributes to the possibility of the text's being a unified whole and therefore its being read as an autonomous literary object. This is not to say that a literary text is univalent (*see* UNIVALENCE), with a single determinant meaning. Indeed, the best pieces of literature are multivalent (*see* MULTIVALENCE): they have the capacity to generate and legitimate a number of plausible understandings. Another way to put it is that great literature may have more than one THEME and may encourage a number of inferences about those themes. Take the book of Jonah as an example. A reader might read the book of Jonah and see that God has done a supernatural thing in causing the great fish to swallow the prophet. From a modern scientific perspective, such a thing is impossible or at least improbable. Yet the reader might assume that this story teaches that natural laws and human possibilities do not bind God and that God will at times intervene in lives miraculously. This is a legitimate reading of Jonah. Reading the same book, another reader might notice that when Jonah decides to flee from God, he heads to Tarshish, which in ancient reckoning was a metaphor for paradise. This same reader might also notice that Jonah's trek to what he thinks is paradise is actually a descent into death, denoted by a series of downward movements: Jonah goes down to Joppa, down into the belly of the ship, down into the belly of the fish, and down to Sheol. While Jonah thinks his flight is to paradise, his flight from God is actually a flight into death. Again, this reading is both suggested and legitimated by the text itself. Finally, a third reader may focus on Jonah's actions at the end of the account. Jonah's problem seems to be theological. Nineveh had perpetrated unspeakable atrocities on Jonah's people and deserved judgment. But Jonah knows that a single act of repentance can erase a lifetime of sins. Jonah's problem is that he does not want to live in a world where God's grace is always poised to win out over justice. God is just, but God's grace is always superabundant. Did the author intend for readers to arrive at all these possibilities? It is impossible to know for certain. The point is that a text such as Jonah and the others that we have looked at depend on readers to make SENSE of them, and this sense-making may be pluralistic.

Bibliography. John Hayes and Carl R. Holladay, *Biblical Exegesis: A Beginner's Handbook* (Atlanta: John Knox, 1987); Richard N. Soulen and R. Kendall Soulen, *Handbook of Biblical Criticism* (3rd ed.; Louisville: Westminster John Knox, 2001).

LITERARY DEVICE

A strategy or apparatus employed by an AUTHOR to enhance the reading experience and to engage the reader in making inferences about MEANING. These literary devices may be rhetorical, as in issues of STRUCTURE and PLOT, or more direct, as in FIGURATIVE LANGUAGE (e.g., METAPHOR, SIMILE, PERSONIFICATION, SYNECDOCHE, ALLUSION).

LITERARY LANGUAGE

The CODES of GENRE employed in the production of a TEXT. The NATURAL LANGUAGES of the biblical texts—Hebrew, Aramaic, and Greek—are governed by grammatical, syntactical, and lexical codes. But literature also uses literary languages with their codes, which enable a reader to move beyond what the text says in its natural language to the meaning of the text. In other words, a literary text has a referential (*see* REFERENTIAL [QUALITY OF] LANGUAGE) and a mimetic (*see* MIMETIC QUALITY OF LANGUAGE) quality. The referential quality is the relationship between the language of the text and the world projected by that language. The mimetic quality is the relationship between the REAL WORLD and the WORLD OF THE TEXT. On the one hand, by means of the referential quality, an author is able to use language to create the world of the text. This world may or may not be similar to the real word of the AUTHOR (e.g., science fiction). In this textual world, words refer to objects, which may or may not be recognizable in the real world. The referential quality enables the world of the text to have a STORY line and PLOT. On the other hand, the mimetic quality enables the author to challenge the reader to discover some message or insight to which the textual world points.

LITERARY REPERTOIRE

The set of social norms underlying a text and the LITERARY and rhetorical strategies employed by an author to produce a literary work. The literary and rhetorical strategies include the creative maneuvers usually associated with a piece of literature (e.g., ALLUSION, PLOT, SETTING, FIGURA-

TIVE LANGUAGE, POINT OF VIEW). All this may be referred to as the repertoire of the text. The things the reader brings to the reading of the text (e.g., LITERARY COMPETENCE, PRESUPPOSITIONS, PREUNDERSTANDING, IDEOLOGY) may be called the "repertoire of the reader."

LITERATURE, APOCALYPTIC. *See* APOCALYPSE

LITERATURE, COMPARATIVE. *See* COMPARATIVE LITERATURE

LITERATURE, EPISTOLARY. *See* EPISTOLARY LITERATURE

LITERATURE, HERMETIC. *See* CORPUS *HERMETICUM*

LITERATURE, PROPHETIC. *See* PROPHECY

LITERATURE, RABBINIC. *See* RABBINIC LITERATURE

LITERATURE, WISDOM. *See* WISDOM LITERATURE

LITOTES. *See* MEIOSIS

LITURGICAL FRAGMENTS

Pieces of traditional worship elements found primarily in the Pauline Letters (both disputed and undisputed). These fragments include acclamations expressing praise (e.g., "Amen" [Phil. 4:20], "Maranatha" [1 Cor. 16:22, mg.]); grace benedictions at the end of the letter (Rom. 16:20; 2 Cor. 13:13); HYMNs (Eph. 5:14; Titus 3:4–7) and CREEDS (Rom. 8:34; Col. 1:26–27); blessings (2 Cor. 1:3–5); and DOXOLOGIES (Rom. 11:36; 1 Tim. 6:16). Also included in these fragments may be worship instructions (e.g., about tongues, prophecies, corporate prayer) or references to the order of worship (e.g., the greeting kiss, the treatment of unbelievers, the Lord's Supper) (Bailey and Vander Broek, 72–80).

Bibliography. James L. Bailey and Lyle D. Vander Broek, *Literary Form in the New Testament: A Handbook* (Louisville: Westminster John Knox, 1992).

LIVING BIBLE, THE (LB)

A PARAPHRASE of the BIBLE in English by Kenneth N. Taylor published in 1971. Basing it on the AMERICAN STANDARD VERSION, Taylor intended to produce a version of the Bible that would be more easily understandable to the average reader. He was guided by two principles: to use different words to state the authors' thoughts and to work from a "rigid evangelical position."

Although Taylor recognized that the inherent danger of paraphrase was that it could render in its DICTION something that the original author did not intend, he thought that the risk was justified by the goal of simplifying the "complex words of the Bible" and thereby making it easier for readers to "follow their Lord."

Some scholars express concerns about the Living Bible, not least of which is the concern about reading the Bible through a predetermined theological posture. The Living Bible also tends to make changes when passages seem to be in conflict. For example, 1 Sam. 17 recounts the story of David's killing Goliath while 2 Sam. 21:19 (paralleled in 1 Chron. 20:5) says that Elhanan son of Jaare-Oregim, not David, killed Goliath. The Living Bible solves the problem by changing the latter passage to read "the brother of Goliath the Gittite."

Bibliography. Steven M. Sheeley and Robert N. Nash Jr., *The Bible in English Translation: An Essential Guide* (Nashville: Abingdon, 1997).

LOANWORD

A word or phrase that passes more or less unchanged from one language to another language without being translated. A recent example is the Russian word *perestroika*, directly imported into English. A biblical example is the Aramaic independent clause *māranā' tā'*, "Our Lord, come!" (or possibly *māran 'ătā'*, "Our Lord has come") taken directly into the NT Greek (1 Cor. 16:22) as *Marana tha* and subsequently directly from the Greek text into English as "Maranatha" (KJV).

LOCALE

The geographical and scenic aspects of SETTING. In the biblical texts, the locale most often serves the purpose of creating a distinct ATMOSPHERE or serves a symbolic purpose (e.g., the pit and prison scenes in the Joseph NARRATIVE, the pastoral setting in Gen. 18:1–8, the mountain locale for Jesus's discourse in Matthew).

LOCUS CLASSICUS

A text usually cited as the PARADIGM of a principle or TYPE. For example, the soliloquy in the play *Hamlet* that contains the phrase "To be, or not to be" is the locus classicus for the whole concept of soliloquy. Romans 3:21–26 is the locus classicus for the apostle Paul's concept of justification.

LOCUTIONARY ACT

Also called an utterance act, a term in SPEECH ACT THEORY to designate the mere act of speech whether it makes sense or not. It is one of the four types of SPEECH ACTS, the others being the PROPOSITIONAL (an utterance that predicates one thing upon another), the ILLOCUTIONARY (an utterance that itself performs a function such as a demand or promise), and the PERLOCUTIONARY (an illocutionary statement that affects the state of mind and/or action of the addressee).

> Bibliography. Ross Murfin and Supryia M. Ray, *The Bedford Glossary of Critical and Literary Terms* (2nd ed.; Boston: Bedford / St. Martin's Press, 2003).

LOGIA

A word that is used to refer to the collection of SAYINGS OF JESUS found in Matthew and Luke but not in Mark. According to FORM CRITICISM, the reference is usually to the hypothetical Q source for the SYNOPTIC GOSPELS. Its singular form (*logion*) serves as a technical term for a saying of Jesus that is succinct. A special type of logion is the "floating" logion, which appears in more than one SETTING within the Gospel TRADITION (e.g., Matt. 19:30: "[The] first will be last, and the last will be first"; cf. 20:16).

LOGICAL POSITIVISM. *See* POSITIVISM

LOGION. See LOGIA

LOGOCENTRISM

A term introduced into DECONSTRUCTION by Jacques Derrida to refer to the belief, in the Western philosophical TRADITION from the time of Plato, that there is an ultimate reality or TRUTH center that can function as a basis for our thoughts and actions. In other words, it is the ASSUMPTION that certain truths exist apart from and prior to human understanding and language and that human language should simply conform to and reflect those truths. Derrida and other deconstructionists argue that those truths or systems of truths do not preexist language or human understanding but instead are human artificial and arbitrary constructs.

LOGOS

A term in Greek philosophy, especially STOICISM, for the universal principle of reason that orders and unifies the universe. According to the Stoics, since the Logos is the unifying principle, the universe is a rational one, in which each area has its own ordering laws that humans are capable of understanding. Consequently, in order to live a pleasant life, humans must live in conformity with Logos, accepting the things they cannot change while controlling their attitudes toward them. In the PROLOGUE to his GOSPEL, John (1:1–18) describes the Logos as preexistent and identifies Jesus as the physical, historical manifestation of the Logos.

LOW-CONTEXT SOCIETIES. *See* SOCIAL-SCIENTIFIC CRITICISM

LOWER CRITICISM. *See* HIGHER CRITICISM

LUKE'S GREAT OMISSION

A reference to material in Mark 6:45–8:26, the bulk of which is not present in Luke (Luke also omits most of Mark 9:41–10:12). The ABSENCE becomes an issue only under the ASSUMPTION that Luke used Mark as a primary source for his Gospel. Scholars have posited several explanations for the absence: Luke used an earlier version of

Mark (UR-MARKUS) that did not contain the material, Luke's COPY of Mark was damaged, or Mark is a RECENSION of Luke. It is also possible that Luke omitted the material to avoid repetitions (e.g., the second version of the feeding miracle). The best explanation, however, seems to be that Luke chose to use material parallel to that from Mark but from another source or other sources because the material fit better with his theological purpose.

LXX

Traditional designation for the SEPTUAGINT, the Greek TRANSLATION of the OT. *See also* APOCRYPHA; BIBLE.

LYRICAL DISCOURSE

In the NT, a type of DISCOURSE that is highly patterned (in terms of RHYTHM and sometimes RHYME) and compressed. Lyrical discourse is common in the NT EPISTLES in HYMNS, LITURGICAL FRAGMENTS, and CREEDS. The following is an example:

> Without any doubt, the mystery of our religion is great:
> He was revealed in flesh,
> vindicated in Spirit,
> seen by angels,
> proclaimed among Gentiles,
> believed in throughout the world,
> taken up in glory. (1 Tim. 3:16)

M

A designation for the material unique to Matthew's GOSPEL, with the exception of the INFANCY STORIES in chapters 1–2. *See* FOUR DOCUMENT HYPOTHESIS.

MAJOR PROPHETS

A name given to the TEXTS of Isaiah, Jeremiah, and Ezekiel, based on their length rather than on their CONTENT or SIGNIFICANCE. The other twelve writing PROPHETS are thus called the Minor Prophets due to the shorter lengths of their texts. These include Hosea, Joel, Amos, Obadiah, Jonah, Micah, Nahum, Habakkuk, Zephaniah, Haggai, Zechariah, and Malachi.

MANUAL OF DISCIPLINE

A manuscript from the DEAD SEA SCROLLS that gives the requirements governing life in the QUMRAN community. For NT studies, an interesting feature is the *Manual*'s division of humans into two mutually exclusive groups: the "children of light" and "the children of darkness." The former are guided by a "spirit of truth" and ruled by the "Prince of Light," while the latter are under the rule of the "Angel of Darkness." This same truth/error and light/darkness opposition is reflected in the Gospel of John, prompting some to hypothesize that John and/or his community was part of or influenced by the Qumran community.

MARCIONISM/MARCIONITES

An early gnostic Christian movement and group named after the second-century Christian Marcion, who claimed to have found the true Christian TRUTH in the writings of Paul. Marcion argued that Paul's revelation from Christ convinced him that

the Jewish LAW had no role in salvation and that Paul's writings reject the law completely in favor of the gospel of Jesus.

The Marcionites believed that the God of the Jews and the God of Jesus were two different beings. The former was a God of wrath and creator of the material world; the latter sent Jesus to save the world from the God of the Jews. Furthermore, Jesus was beyond the material world of the God of the Jews, having no real flesh-and-blood body. Consequently, Jesus only *seemed* to be human, a doctrine that would be held by other groups and would become known as Docetism (from the Greek *dokein*, "to seem").

The Marcionites also accepted only a shorter version of Luke's Gospel and ten LETTERS of Paul (not 1–2 Timothy and Titus). Where there appeared references in these letters to the God of the Jews, Marcion removed them, claiming that earlier heretics had inserted the REFERENCES.

MARGIN. *See* MARGINALIZATION

MARGINALIZATION

A term that, along with its derivatives, has taken on significant philosophical and theoretical MEANING since it appeared in the work of Jacques Derrida. Derrida employed the idea of the white margin of a page to develop the idea of supplementarity (*see* SUPPLÉMENT) and "the Other" in the Western philosophical tradition. On the page of a book, the TEXT is center, while the margin is a fixed space outside the text. Consequently, the page with its text and margin leads to the center/margin opposition, or interiority/exteriority opposition. The center or interior has no meaning unless there exists already an understanding of the margin or exterior.

In other words, no object can exist meaningfully without its other or margin or DIFFERENCE.

The origin of any idea cannot be conceived of apart from its derivative, what allows the center to be center, which means that the derivative already exists, calling into question the very idea of origin. Rather than now being understood as the traditional place of COMMENTARY, "the added later," the secondary, the margin must be understood as that which is necessary for thinking of a center, the primary. Derrida did not want to make the margin into a new center but simply to PROBLEMATIZE the idea of originality or center. Derrida then moved from thought to language, which for him is a "field of infinite substitutions" by which humans use SIGNS to name the center that never really exists. Since this center never exists, there is nothing present to arrest or ground this play of substitutions.

The ideas of infinite play, the meaning-constitutive role of the margin, the Other, and the relationship between centers and margins have been developed in different ways by other POSTMODERN critics. Michel Foucault and others, especially scholars in FEMINIST CRITICISM and CULTURAL CRITICISM, have examined the relationship between systems that operate on the ideas of centers and margins (specifically those that have to do with systems of knowledge) on the one hand, and the strategies of exclusion, race, class, GENDER, and colonialism on the other. The ASSUMPTION is that structures of power, domination, and marginalization are inherent in language as DISCOURSE. Language does not reflect structures of extralinguistic reality but creates its reality especially in terms of BINARY OPPOSITIONS in which the first term is the center, the standard, and the second is the margin, the SUPPLÉMENT: male/female, spirit/flesh, and so forth. Postmodern critics of the biblical texts are examining the structures of reality as they appear in the language of these texts to detect structures of marginalization. According to these critics, since language does not reflect reality but constructs it according to structures of power that will always exist at the expense of marginalizing or censoring

other possibilities, these texts, like any other texts, are examined through a HERMENEUTICS OF SUSPICION and a basic mistrust of totalizing systems (*see* TOTALIZATION).

Bibliography. Jacques Derrida, *Of Grammatology* (trans. Gayatri Chakravorty Spivak; Baltimore: Johns Hopkins University Press, 1977).

MARGINALIZE. *See* MARGINALIZATION

MARGINALITY. *See* MARGINALIZATION

MARI TABLETS

A cache of about twenty thousand clay tablets discovered between 1933 and 1955 in the excavated palace of Zimri-Lim (1730–1700 BCE) at the ancient city of Mari (Tell el-Hariri), located on the south bank of the Euphrates River on the border of Mesopotamia and Syria. Included in the cache are LETTERS, inventories, lists of workers, contracts, and official correspondence. Because the texts are roughly contemporary with the period of the biblical patriarchs and reveal a great deal of Amorite influence, they contain some writings that in many ways are similar to Hebrew PROPHECY (esp. the letters). The Mari tablets are important not only for the study of prophecy but also for a more complete understanding of the cultures that may have influenced early Hebrew culture. To date there is no English TRANSLATION of all the tablets, but a few are translated in *Ancient Near Eastern Texts*.

Bibliography. A. S. van der Woude, ed., *The World of the Old Testament* (Grand Rapids: Eerdmans, 1989); J. B. Pritchard, ed., *Ancient Near Eastern Texts Relating to the Old Testament* (3rd ed.; Princeton: Princeton University Press, 1969).

MARK. *See* DECONSTRUCTION; TRACE

MARKAN HYPOTHESIS. *See* MARKAN PRIORITY

MARKAN PRIORITY

The ASSUMPTION by the majority of NT scholars that the Gospel of Mark was composed first and served as a source and chronological framework for Matthew and Luke. *See* FOUR DOCUMENT HYPOTHESIS.

MARXISM. *See* MARXIST CRITICISM

MARXIST CRITICISM

An approach to literature holding that art often serves as an ideological mechanism, legitimating and perpetuating the system of social values, beliefs, and relationships by which one class exercises power over the others. The process by which this is accomplished is articulated in Marxism, of which Marxist criticism is a subset, and draws heavily from the concept of the SUPERSTRUCTURE. It is therefore necessary for gainful understanding of Marxist criticism that we begin with a cursory treatment of certain fundamental concepts of Marxist theory in general.

Marxism was originally postulated as a theory by Karl Marx and Friedrich Engels in the mid-1800s and is an attempt to understand scientifically the forces that direct the course of history. It inherits from materialism the presupposition "that physical matter is the only reality and that everything, including thought, feeling, mind, and will can be explained in terms of matter and physical phenomena" (Dictionary.com). In this view, individual human consciousness, cultural experience, and even society itself are products of discrete material processes and can be understood in scientific terms. In other words, Marxism is an attempt to scientifically discover and understand the dynamics of society and its history; thus it is a science of history.

For Marx and Engels, the underlying dynamic of social change was the struggle for dominance between economic classes. They observed that every alteration to the economic structure of a society was invariably accompanied by a corresponding change to its social order. This relationship led them to believe that the economic form, in which one class has power over the others, somehow determines the ways in which the social hierarchy develops.

In recent Western history, for example, this class struggle has taken the form of capitalism. In a capitalistic economy, the modes of production are controlled by a ruling class but operated by a working class. Marx and Engels call the ruling class the bourgeoisie, and the working class they call the proletariat. Because the modes of production—the way in which production is carried out and the structures that control it—are owned by the bourgeoisie, workers are dependent on them for survival. In other words, self-sufficiency is a result not so much of an individual's ability to procure material necessities as it is an individual's ability to enter into a relationship with those who control the distribution of material necessities.

However, for this system to work, there must exist a superfluity of labor: the number of workers must exceed the number of jobs. There must be a measure of unemployment. Because there are more workers than jobs, laborers are forced to compete with each other for employment. Competition for jobs, in turn, drives down job wages because those who have no work become willing to work for less in order to obtain employment. In this way, workers are not paid for the full value of their labor. In some of the less regulated forms of capitalism, this wage atrophy advances to the point where a harmony is struck between the minimum cost of survival and a worker's income, reducing the working force to what has been called "wage slaves." In the end, an artificial disparity is created between the market value of a product and the actual cost of production. This artificial disparity is called the surplus value of labor and is absorbed by the bourgeoisie as profit by mere virtue of the fact that they own the means of production and are able to leverage this economic ordering to their benefit. In order to survive, individual workers have no choice but to participate in this exploitive social structuring and are essentially powerless to remedy their situation.

Also important for an understanding of both Marxism and Marxist criticism is a familiarity with the Marxist concepts of life and consciousness. In Marxism, life determines consciousness. Marx and Engels rejected the notion that society and culture originate from the collective consciousness of individuals; instead they asserted that the social, cultural, and physical environment into which one is born determines, to a large degree, the development of the individual consciousness. In other words, do we make society, or does society make us? For Marx, the latter response is the most credible. Interestingly enough, this view of consciousness is similar to that held by postmodernists (*see* POSTMODERN CRITICISM; POSTMODERNISM/ POSTMODERNITY): the ideas, values, and social roles that make up who we are as persons are inseparably bound to the context in which we exist.

The ingenuity of Marxism is perhaps most readily apparent in the application of this conception of consciousness to the class-struggle view of history. If the social structure of a society is in some way determined by its economic structure, then consciousness ultimately derives from that economic structure also. This synthesis between the views of the economic basis of social structure and the development of consciousness results in a bipartite formulation of society according to which society is composed of two divisions: the BASE, which is the economic structure, and the superstructure. The superstructure, in this sense, is the collective social consciousness that develops in the CONTEXT of the economic base. It is much like an all-inclusive IDEOLOGY or WORLDVIEW and includes such things as religion, morality, aesthetics, philosophy, politics, and LAW.

However, because the superstructure—a perspective of reality—derives from an exploitive economic base, it is viewed as a FALSE CONSCIOUSNESS that functions to legitimate the existing social structures. In other words, it is "the complex structure of social perception which ensures that the situation in which one class has power over the others is seen as 'natural' or not seen at all" (Eagleton, *Marxism*, 5). Since the economic base, which is controlled by the dominant class, determines the form of the superstructure, the self-interested values of the dominant class are subsequently promulgated throughout the remainder of society.

In a letter to Joseph Bloch in 1890, Engels wrote:

> According to the materialist conception of history, the determining element in history is ultimately the production and reproduction in real life. More than this neither Marx nor I have ever asserted. If therefore somebody twists this into the statement that the economic element is the only determining one, he transforms it into a meaningless, abstract and absurd phrase. The economic situation is the basis, but the various elements of the superstructure—political forms of the class struggle and its consequences, constitutions established by the victorious class after a successful battle, etc.—forms of law—and then even the reflexes of all these actual struggles in the brains of the combatants: political, legal, and philosophical theories, religious ideas and their further development into systems of dogma—also exercise their influence upon the course of the historical struggles and in many cases preponderate in determining their form. (Quoted in Eagleton, *Marxism*, 9)

The base and superstructure exist in a relationship in which neither can be entirely isolated from the other, and changes within one will have recursive effects both on itself and in the other. Consciousness is not only an object within a particular environment; it is also an integral element in the total composition of that environment. However inextricably bound the two components are, it is ultimately the base that determines the nature of the superstructure, since it is the base that grants one class power over the other classes. The superstructure merely exists to obscure the fact that the exploited classes are the victims of exploitation.

Marxist criticism is an application of the theory of superstructure to art with the view that art, which is an element of the superstructure, exhibits in its very composition the ideology of the dominant class. Ideology, as it is used here, "is not in the first place a set of doctrines; it signifies the way men live out their roles in class-society, the values, ideas and images which tie them to their social functions and so prevent them from a true knowledge of society as a whole. In this sense . . . it shows a man making sense of his experience in ways that prohibit a true understanding of his society, ways that are consequently false" (Eagleton, *Marxism*, 17).

This relationship between literature and ideology is identified in two ways: vulgar criticism and what can be called sophisticated criticism. The former sort of criticism is called vulgar because it fails to probe much beyond the surface level of a LITERARY text. It examines the characters and social norms and how they relate to the modes of production within a work as unmediated attributes of the social base. This sort of criticism might identify an exploitive economic relationship between the PROTAGONIST and the ANTAGONIST or express a pervasive THEME within the PLOT as a direct result of the alienating forces in capitalism, but it will fail to be more perspicacious than that. It reduces a complex piece of literature to a mechanistic product of a particular economic situation. A sophisticated Marxist criticism, on the other hand, is more concerned with the complex relations uniting a work of literature to the ideology in which it originated. A nonsimplistic understanding of a work must not overlook the several elements of the base-and-superstructure model—an AUTHOR's class position and ideological forms and their relation to literary forms, spirituality and philosophy, techniques of literary production, aesthetic theory, and the economic base—that typify a period and how these elements converge to produce a literary specimen. A literary work, after all, is an elaborate concoction of values, images, and ideas specific to a time; it is a symphony written in the tonality of a culture's ideology and performed on the inescapable stage of history.

However, the Marxist is not interested in perpetuating an exploitive ideology within a society by merely acknowledging the weave of art and ideology. The Marxist wishes to expose the falsities and unnatural arrangements that endorse one class's power over the others. For the Marxist, all literature can be scrutinized for ideological ingredients, but good literature will typify the ideology of its period in such a way that it is experienced as both authentic and artificial: ideology becomes consciously visible rather than just unconsciously present. Good literature will communicate a sense of realism and faithfulness to the social experience while exposing and implicitly challenging the limitedness, inadequacy, and artificiality of the very real structures that have been imposed on it. In this way, it is able to generate a universal appeal and relevancy to all readers across time while being firmly rooted in its own context. Good literature is historically relevant by nature and socially beneficial in its perspicacious adherence to reality. In the end, a Marxist critique examines all aspects of a piece of literature—from FORM and STYLE to CHARACTERIZATION and PLOT, and even to the mode of production in which it was published—for social authenticity in order to expose the falseness of prevailing ideologies.

To what degree these critiques can be applied to the BIBLE is a matter of perspective. The Marxist approaches the Bible from a nontheistic point of view, seeing SCRIPTURE as any other text, albeit a text with perhaps more historically transparent qualities, but nevertheless subject to the same criticisms as all other texts. From a Marxist POINT OF VIEW, it would be difficult to construe the traditional ideas of inerrancy and infallibility as anything but pillars in the ideological mechanism sanctioning, by threat of damnation and promise of eternal reward, the structures that empower sacred authority. More devastating to an individual's hope of eschewing these social structures is the concept of original sin, whereby the lot of humanity is consigned to eternal punishment. The only escape, of course, is obsequious submission to the Almighty's authority, which he has, in his ever-merciful wisdom, seen fit to vest in the institution of the church.

However, as economic power shifted from the aristocracy to the bourgeoisie in the early Renaissance, the ideological influence of the church, which climaxed in heights of papal imperialism, dissipated into religion as a mode of production, inheriting certain vestigial traits and appropriating others in the service of new needs. Clerical authority was replaced with a right INTERPRETATION of the right texts and expressed in CREED. But the church was divested of its ability to exert political force on its adherents and was increasingly forced to rely on the efficacy of ideological illusion.

Terry Eagleton, a leading if not the foremost neo-Marxist critic, has applied these techniques to an interpretation of the biblical book of Jonah in his essay "J. L. Austin and the Book of Jonah." According to Eagleton, God sends Jonah to prophesy to Nineveh because God is really too maudlin to destroy the city himself and needs an excuse to spare the city in order to save face. Jonah sees right through God's self-deception and realizes that his own part in the narrative is only superficial. Consequently, Jonah is disturbed by what he judges to be God's manipulative motives, especially when Nineveh miraculously repents. Eagleton further concludes that the source of Jonah's despair is his recognition that as long as God is providentially guiding and directing everything, individual human action is meaningless. But then Jonah thinks that God may have put him up to this task just to make him question the meaningfulness of action. He realizes that he cannot even know if he knows whether action is meaningless or not. This realization plunges Jonah from existential despair into aimless subjectivism. The story ends with God's reproaching Jonah's despair and thus suggests, according to Eagleton, that despite the prophet's earlier assessment, the divine propensity to mercy is actually fickle and absurd.

Eagleton is painting Jonah's plight against the ideological backdrop of history. Jonah's relation to God, in this interpretation, is an ALLEGORY of the individual's relation to the Marxist conception of history. To what degree does human action matter if action is inseparable from history and that which is acted upon? And to what degree can we even know if human action matters? By raising these questions, Eagleton entices the reader to glimpse the individual's inescapable connection to history and the subjectivity (see SUBJECTIVE KNOWLEDGE) that results.

Such as it is, this interpretation is not a traditional Marxist reading of the book of Jonah, but then again Eagleton is not a traditional Marxist. What is important is the insight provided by the illumination of ideological elements: the conjunction of Jonah's well-founded reluctance, the

meaninglessness of his action, his subsequent despair, and God's ever-present and unpredictable "otherness" present a realistic image of social experience characteristic of false consciousness. Eagleton summarizes this dilemma: "The Book of Jonah leaves its protagonist caught in a transitional stage between false consciousness and some new, currently unnamable style of identity; and to this extent we have made little advance upon it" ("J. L. Austin," 181).

Much work has been done in narrowing the divide between Marxism and postmodernism, particularly in the work of Eagleton and Fredric Jameson; yet it seems that while the expanse between the theories is not so vast as it might at first appear, irreconcilability may be a foregone conclusion. Jameson seems more optimistic about the possibility of reconciliation and has been successful to an extent in synthesizing the two fields as well as many others, arguing that "whilst history is not a text, it is inaccessible to us except in textual terms" (Macey, 244); however, according to Eagleton, the attempt, while commendable, falls short of its anticipated goal. He states, "If Post-Modernism is right—if modernity is effectively over—then Marxism is most certainly superannuated along with it" (Eagleton, *Marxist Literary Theory*, 14). Nevertheless, Eagleton feels that the contradictions of modernity are yet within the scope of Marxism to resolve and reaffirm the theory. In the formulation of ideology, Marxism and Marxist criticism provide an invaluable conceptual tool for the monumental task of social reform, which, regardless of the state of modernity, can be applied to the benefit of humanity.

Bibliography. Terry Eagleton, "Introduction Part I," in *Marxist Literary Theory: A Reader* (ed. Terry Eagleton and Drew Milne; Cambridge, MA: Blackwell, 1996); idem, "J. L. Austin and the Book of Jonah," in *The Postmodern Bible Reader* (ed. David Jobling, Tina Pippin, and Ronald Schleifer; Malden, MA: Blackwell, 2001); idem, *Marxism and Literary Criticism* (Berkeley: University of California Press, 1976); Douglas Kellner, "Marxist Criticism," in *Encyclopedia of Contemporary Literary Theory: Approaches, Scholars, Terms* (ed. Irena R. Makaryk; Toronto: University of Toronto Press, 1993); David Macey, *The Penguin Dictionary of Critical Theory* (London: Penguin, 2000); "Ma-

terialism," in Dictionary.com (http://dictionary.reference
.com/search?q=materialism).

MASHAL

A Hebrew word (*māshāl*) naming an array of LITER-
ARY forms. In the PROPHETS, the term is generally
used in the SENSE of a song of mockery (Alter).
But it may also refer to a RIDDLE, DIRGE, or AL-
LEGORY. Biblical names for such forms are found
in Prov. 1:5–6.

> *Bibliography.* Robert Alter, *The Art of Biblical Poetry* (New
> York: Basic Books, 1985); Richard N. Soulen and R. Ken-
> dall Soulen, *A Handbook of Biblical Criticism* (3rd ed.; Lou-
> isville: Westminster John Knox, 2001).

MASORETIC TEXT (MT)

The standard text of the Hebrew OT with annotation and vowel pointings that guide punctuation
and pronunciation. While the Masoretic TRADI-
TION goes back to at least the sixth century CE, it
was not until the fourteenth century CE that the
Western and Eastern Masoretic traditions merged
to form the standard text that has served as the
basis for the *Biblia Hebraica*. For an excellent
discussion of the role of the MT in the TEXTUAL
CRITICISM of the HEBREW BIBLE, see Voelz, *What
Does This Mean?*

> *Bibliography.* Karl Ellinger, Wilhelm Rudolph, et al., eds.,
> *Biblia Hebraica Stuttgartensia* (5th ed.; Stuttgart: Deutsche
> Bibelgesellschaft, 1997); James W. Voelz, *What Does This
> Mean? Principles of Biblical Interpretation in the Post-modern
> World* (St. Louis: Concordia, 1995).

MASTER NARRATIVE. *See* METANARRATIVE

MATTHEW'S BIBLE

A 1537 TRANSLATION of TYNDALE'S NEW TES-
TAMENT along with the OT, which had not been
translated by the time of Tyndale's death (d. 1536).
John Rogers, a follower of Tyndale, translated the
books under the name of Thomas Matthew.

MATERIALISM, CULTURAL. *See* CULTURAL
MATERIALISM

MATERIALISM, DIALECTICAL. *See* DIALEC-
TICAL MATERIALISM

MEANING

In LITERARY studies, "meaning" may be defined
generally as a reader's understanding of a TEXT. The
central issue in these studies, however, is the most
plausible manner in which this understanding is
produced. There are a plethora of theories regarding meaning. A large portion of this handbook is
concerned with giving synopses of these theories.
Although the theories often overlap, they differ
significantly and may be grouped according to the
CONTEXT that they assume for the construction of
meaning. Keesey lists seven of these contexts and
then groups a number of theories accordingly. The
seven contexts are AUTHOR, text, audience, reality,
literature, language, and culture.

The theories that find meaning in terms of the
author's INTENTION, psychology, biography, culture (including the entire political, social, religious,
economic, and intellectual contexts), age, and so
forth fall into the first group. Included here are
FORM, GENETIC, HISTORICAL-CRITICAL, MARXIST,
PSYCHOANALYTIC, SOCIAL-SCIENTIFIC, SOURCE,
and TRADITION criticisms.

Theories that see the *text* as the central context
for meaning look primarily to the STRUCTURES,
rhetorical strategies, and LITERARY CONVEN-
TIONS of the text. Included in this second group
are ARCHETYPAL, COMPOSITION, FORMAL, GENRE,
MYTH, NARRATIVE, NEW, REDACTION, and RHE-
TORICAL criticisms, and STRUCTURALISM.

For the third group, which holds that the *audience* is the primary source for meaning, texts are
and have historically been valued independently
of the author and world that produced them. To
varying degrees, meaning is the function of the
activities and responses of readers. This group includes CANONICAL CRITICISM, READER-RESPONSE
CRITICISM, *TENDENZ* CRITICISM, TRANSACTIVE
CRITICISM, and RECEPTION THEORY.

Theories assuming that meaning is somehow
connected to *reality* or reflects reality vary in focus
because they define reality in different ways. In
other words, a Marxist defines reality differently
than did Aristotle, and they both understand reality differently than does a Freudian. Consequently,

the theories in this fourth group are extremely varied: IDEOLOGICAL CRITICISM, MARXIST CRITICISM, MIMETIC CRITICISM, and PSYCHOANALYTIC CRITICISM.

The fifth group understands meaning to have its source in a text's relationship to and interaction with other texts; thus the context for meaning is *literature*. For example, INTERTEXTUAL critics argue that the best way to understand a poem is to read a lot of poems. At the heart of this understanding is the ASSUMPTION that no text is entirely unique, but that each builds upon prior texts and conventions. Therefore, a person who has read the EPICS of Homer, Dante, and Virgil is better prepared to read Milton. But the reverse is also true: the person who has read Milton is better prepared to read Homer, Dante, and Virgil. The same is the case with all types of literature. Included here are ARCHETYPAL CRITICISM, GENRE CRITICISM, and INTERTEXTUAL CRITICISM.

The sixth group finds meaning to be inseparable from *language*. Although these theories differ in many respects, they all assume that the crucial issue for discussing meaning is the fact that humans are forced to talk about language through language. They also understand language as a system of SIGNS operating according to CODES, and they assert that there can be no meaning at all except within a system of signs. Some will claim that language is a transparent means of communication, while others will see language as inherently ambiguous, its signifiers pointing only to signifieds, which are themselves signifiers. Consequently, language does not have extralinguistic objects to which it points, with meaning already present in the objects; rather, language always points to more language. Included in this group are DECONSTRUCTION, POSTMODERN CRITICISM, and STRUCTURALISM.

The last group is perhaps the most varied and extensive. The context for meaning is *culture*, both that of the AUTHOR and that of the reader. Not only do authors reflect their SOCIAL LOCATIONS: so do readers. These theorists argue that the only access that we have to the past is text

("text" here meaning any object that claims to represent the past), itself an INTERPRETATION of some aspect of the past. Consequently, the degree to which we can have accurate and complete historical knowledge is questioned. Since texts are produced, read, and valued in all types of contexts, the possibility of objective writing or reading is also called into question. Listed here are only some of the theories: NEW HISTORICISM; CULTURAL MATERIALISM; CULTURAL, FEMINIST, gay/lesbian (*see* QUEER THEORY), RACE, CLASS, GENDER, and POSTCOLONIAL CRITICISMS; AND *MUJERISTA* AND WOMANIST theologies.

Other theories not mentioned here may fall into one or more of these categories, and those listed above may, in fact, fit only uncomfortably in one category. One thing is certain, however: the meaning of *meaning* is a fluid concept across disciplines. And it seems that if the trend continues, the term will only become more and more unsettled. Though not all of the theories in this handbook have been fully applied to the interpretation of biblical texts, most have been applied in some degree.

Bibliography. Donald Keesey, *Contexts for Criticism* (3rd ed.; Mountain View, CA: Mayfield, 1998).

MEANING, DICTIONARY. *See* DICTIONARY MEANING

MEANING, DOUBLE. *See* DOUBLE MEANING

MEANING, LITERAL. *See* LITERAL MEANING

MEANING, PLAIN. *See* LITERAL MEANING

MEANING, POLYVALENT. *See* POLYSEMY; POLYVALENCE

MEANING, REFERENTIAL. *See* REFERENTIAL MEANING

MEANING ASSEMBLY

A term introduced into READER-RESPONSE CRITICISM by Wolfgang Iser to denote the activities of readers as they encounter and respond to the various TEXTUAL STRATEGIES and LITERARY DEVICES of a LITERARY work, configuring an understanding and thus a MEANING.

MEANING EFFECT

A term in STRUCTURALISM, referring to the effect an individual TEXT has on readers. According to structuralists, a NARRATIVE text operates from a set of LITERARY CONVENTIONS that transcends cultures, literary TRADITIONS, time, and space. These conventions operate as DEEP STRUCTURES, producing upon readers a meaning effect. So the focus is not on *what* a text means but on *how* a text means in terms of its effect on its readers.

MEDITATIVE HYMN

A TYPE of HYMN identified by Ralph Martin in the Pauline and DEUTEROPAULINE EPISTLES, probably borrowed from the worship liturgies of the early church. Examples are Eph. 1:3–14; Rom. 8:31–39; and 1 Cor. 13.

> Bibliography. Ralph Martin, *Carmen Christi: Philippians 2:5–11 in Recent Interpretation and in the Setting of Early Christian Worship* (Grand Rapids: Eerdmans, 1983).

MEGILLAH

From the Hebrew for "scroll," the term refers to the book of Esther or to one of the Megilloth—the five scrolls of Esther, Song of Songs, Ruth, Lamentations, and Ecclesiastes.

MEIOSIS

A FIGURE OF SPEECH that understates for emphasis and may be used ironically. For example, a person may describe something that is spectacular as "rather good." A special form of meiosis is litotes, in which something is affirmed by stating the negative of its opposite. For example, in everyday SPEECH, a person might say "not bad" for "good." The AUTHOR of 1 Timothy uses litotes when he substitutes "must not be disrespectful" for "be respectful" (6:2), and Paul substitutes "I am not ashamed of the Gospel" for "I am proud of the Gospel" in Rom. 1:16a.

> Bibliography. J. A. Cuddon, *The Penguin Dictionary of Literary Terms and Literary Theory* (4th ed.; London: Penguin, 1998).

MEMORY

One of the five divisions of classical RHETORIC, memory is the preparation for delivery. *See also* PROTENSION; RETENTION.

MESOSTICH. *See* ACROSTIC

MESSAGE, THE

A PARAPHRASE of the NT first published in 1993 by Eugene Peterson, a Presbyterian pastor. Assuming that the NT was originally written in "the street language of the day, the idiom of the playground and the marketplace," Peterson rendered the Greek into English "not as a refined language that appeals to our aspirations after the best but a rough and earthy language that captures God's presence and action where we least expect it." As Sheeley and Nash (90–91) point out, however, since it is a paraphrase, Peterson tries to clarify ambiguous passages and applies idioms that sometimes result in improper embellishments and forced language. For example, Peterson renders Matt. 1:18 as "Before they came to the marriage bed, Joseph discovered she was pregnant. (It was by the Holy Spirit, but he didn't know that.)" Peterson completed a paraphrase of the OT in 2002.

> Bibliography. Steven M. Sheeley and Robert N. Nash Jr., *The Bible in English Translation: An Essential Guide* (Nashville: Abingdon, 1997).

MESSENGER FORMULA

One of the most common LITERARY forms used in the PROPHETS, in which Yahweh calls and sends the prophet with a message, as in Exod. 3:10, "So come, I will send you to Pharaoh"; and Isa. 6:8, "Whom shall I send, and who will go for us?" This LITERARY CONVENTION appears also in the Akkadian *Maqlu* text, as the supreme gods Anu and Antu assign a mission to a man: "Whom shall I send?" These examples suggest that the divine messenger and the messenger formula were well known in Mesopotamia. The Hebrew prophets usually prefaced this formula with another form designed to draw the recipient's attention to the message. This preface to the message was a designation of those for whom it was intended. Von Rad comments, "In the case of a divine threat, what was prefixed was a diatribe; in the case of a promise, an exhortation. These two, the messenger formula and prefixed clause, must both be present before we have the literary category of prophetic oracle" (43). As a rule, the prophets until the time of Jeremiah drew a clear distinction between the messenger formula and the DIATRIBE or exhortation that introduced it. The messenger formula was the word of God, while the prefaced form was an editorial addition by the prophet. The prefaced form had the purpose of leading up to and preparing the way for God's word and gave it its REFERENCE.

Bibliography. Gerhard von Rad, *Old Testament Theology* (trans. D. M. G. Stalker; New York: Harper & Row, 1962–65), vol. 2.

MESSIANIC PROPHECIES

Passages in the HEBREW BIBLE that predict a future messiah (e.g., Gen. 49:9–10; Isa. 7:14; 11:1–5; Jer. 23:4; Ezek. 17:22–23; Ps. 110). Christians see these passages as referring to Jesus.

MESSIANIC SECRET

A term introduced into the CRITICISM of the NT by William Wrede to designate what he saw as a conscious redactional activity of the AUTHOR of the GOSPEL of Mark, although the phenomenon also appears to a lesser degree in Matthew and Luke. Wrede observed that in Mark's Gospel, Jesus instructed his disciples (8:30; 9:9), those for whom he performed miracles (1:43–45; 5:43; 7:36; 8:26), and demons (1:25, 34; 3:12) not to reveal his identity. Furthermore, Jesus's PARABLES are designed to keep knowledge of Jesus's identity secret (4:1–13, 33–34). According to Wrede, the first half of Mark's Gospel is designed to present a CHRISTOLOGY of power, a perverted Christology to which Mark's community subscribed, while the second half presents a corrective Christology of the cross. Within this scheme, the messianic secret in the first half of Mark makes SENSE in that Mark (Jesus?) did not want Jesus's messiahship defined in terms of power but rather in terms of suffering.

Thus in the second half of Mark, the focus is on predictions of death and suffering and the teaching about the kingdom of God with little attention given to miracles.

Bibliography. William Wrede, *The Messianic Secret* (trans. J. C. G. Greig; Cambridge: James Clarke, 1971).

METACRITICISM

The study of CRITICISM, the examination of critical methodologies and their sets of criteria by which TEXTS are evaluated.

Issues involved in metacriticism may be grouped into two general categories: microlevels of study and macrolevels of study. At the microlevels, seven issues receive attention: the identity of the AUTHOR, the type of text, the CONTEXT of the original audience, the identity of the reader/interpreter, the reader/interpreter context, the INTERPRETATION, and the intended recipient(s) of interpretation. These seven issues developed out of the fact that (1) an author produces (2) a text (3) within a context for an audience, and (4) the text is read by a reader/interpreter (5) who stands within his or her own context and (6) offers an interpretation (7) for him- or herself or some audience.

The macrolevels have to do with methodologies (*see* CRITICAL METHODOLOGIES) employed in interpreting texts; these methods range from early allegorical approaches to historical to contemporary (e.g., STRUCTURALISM, READER-RESPONSE, DECONSTRUCTION, and POSTCOLONIAL).

METALANGUAGE

In simplest terms, a language about language. Metalanguages seek to stand above the objects that they examine in a disinterested, objective position. For example, since STRUCTURALISM, SEMIOTICS, and LINGUISTICS are critical systems whose focus is the examination of the ways in which a SIGN system (a LITERARY text, a NATURAL LANGUAGE, a NARRATIVE, a MYTH, a folktale [*see* FOLKLORE]) operates, they are metalanguages. Any critical theory, then, may be viewed as a metalanguage in that it employs a technical vocabulary in its critical analysis. The hermeneutical question that the idea of metalanguage raises is that of the location of MEANING. If a metalanguage establishes the categories and parameters within which a sign system is analyzed, do these categories and parameters not dictate a certain CONFIGURATION of meaning instead of finding that meaning in the text? In other words, a structuralist analysis would differ from a WOMANIST analysis, and both would differ from analyses within FORMALISM and NEW HISTORICISM. Thus in the SEMIOTICS of Roland Barthes, the metalanguage becomes a sign system itself which refers to another sign system, resulting in an infinite chain of metalanguages. This issue—about the relationships among a text, the metalanguage employed to examine the text, and the problem (or impossibility) that any CRITIC may face in stepping outside critical DISCOURSE—has become a crucial one in biblical hermeneutical discussion.

Bibliography. Roman Jakobson, *On Language* (Cambridge, MA: Harvard University Press, 1990); Susan Sontag, ed., *A Barthes Reader* (London: Fontana, 1982).

METANARRATIVE

A name for the thought systems that undergird a civilization. These systems may be political (Marxism, democracy), economic (free-market system), religious (Christianity), philosophical (that rational principles lead to human progress), and so forth. "Postmodern thinkers speak of these systems of legitimizing myths as 'narratives' (or 'metanarratives'). They contend that a narrative exercises a force apart from the argumentation and proof and, in fact, that it provides the principal means by which every community legitimates itself" (Grenz, 44). According to Jean-François Lyotard, all these life-defining systems are assumed to be universally valid by the Western world but have actually led to the oppression of a great part of the world by negating, demonizing, or marginalizing other possibilities. Lyotard's answer is that the POSTMODERN world needs to replace these metanarratives with "little narratives," local, limited systems that can serve as sufficient guides but are accepted only provisionally and not as universally

valid. Richard Rorty, for example, suggests that in the postmodern world, in which there has been a devaluing of universals, we should replace epistemology with HERMENEUTICS, which he defines as the ongoing conversation between local systems, discourses, or narratives. In postmodern forms of critical analysis of texts, critics assume that these metanarratives are in varying degrees reflected in texts, an ASSUMPTION that demands reading and CRITICISM which resist these metanarratives and their oppressive demands. For BIBLICAL STUDIES, this would mean that the social structures, institutions, systems of valuing, prescriptions for lifestyles, and the like which have their origins in the biblical texts and have been declared as universally valid need to be reconsidered as local, limited, and nonuniversal. *See* DECONSTRUCTION; FEMINIST CRITICISM; POSTMODERN CRITICISM; POSTMODERNISM/POSTMODERNITY.

Bibliography. Stanley J. Grenz, *A Primer on Post-modernism* (Grand Rapids: Eerdmans, 1996); Jean-François Lyotard, *The Postmodern Condition* (Minneapolis: University of Minnesota Press, 1984); Alan Malachowski, ed., *Reading Rorty* (Oxford: Blackwell, 1990); Richard Rorty, *Philosophy and the Mirror of Nature* (Princeton: Princeton University Press, 1979).

METAPHOR

In the most limited sense, a type of ANALOGY in which one object (or subject) is identified with another object (or subject) in such a way that the first has some of the qualities of the second. "Your eyes are doves" (Song 1:15c) is an example of a metaphor in its simplest form, where the tenor, "your eyes," is explained and developed by the vehicle, "doves." Such a view of metaphor is referred to as the "interaction" definition. However, not every metaphor has two subjects, and not all words in the analogy are used figuratively. It may have one subject, the tenor, conveyed by the vehicle. For example, Isa. 3:12 ("My people—children are their oppressors / and women rule over them") has as its subject the incompetence of Jerusalem's leaders, a subject communicated by the then-current social associations for women and children. It has only one subject, which is illuminated by the whole line.

David Sapir defines metaphor by using three related terms: "topic" (the subject), "continuous terms" (words that imply the topic), and "discontinuous terms" (modifiers of the continuous terms). Consider the following example: "They said to him, 'Thus says Hezekiah, This day is a day of distress, of rebuke, and of disgrace; children have come to the birth, and there is no strength to bring them forth'" (Isa. 37:3). Katheryn Pfisterer Darr argues that the topic of verse 3b is the inability of the powerless leaders of Jerusalem to deliver themselves or the city's inhabitants (a conclusion she reaches after considerable examination of CONTEXT). The continuous terms suggesting the topic are "children" and "strength," while the discontinuous terms are "birth" and "bring forth."

Bibliography. Katheryn Pfisterer Darr, *Isaiah's Vision and the Family of God* (Louisville: Westminster John Knox, 1994); J. D. Sapir, "The Anatomy of Metaphor," in *The Social Use of Metaphor: Essays on the Anthropology of Rhetoric* (ed. J. D. Sapir and J. C. Crocker; Philadelphia: University of Pennsylvania Press, 1977), 3–32.

METAPHYSICS OF PRESENCE

The ASSUMPTION that there is something transcendental in reality. TRUTH or knowledge objectively inheres in the STRUCTURE of things and is discovered by human reason, which is able to present it by way of the objective structures of language. Western metaphysics has assumed transparency as a property of language. As objects present themselves to the mind, humans are capable of making assertions about those objects. If that language is subsequently analyzed, humans can fully know that object because the logical structures of the universe (or object) are revealed in the assertions, which are themselves the MEANING of the object. Such an assumption, claim postmodernists, is tantamount to viewing language as denotative (*see* DENOTATION), as able to concisely represent the world. At the heart of this assumption is the related foundational assumption that there exists an objective world of realities independent of humans and our thoughts about it. Truth and meaning exist as TRANSCENDENTAL SIGNIFIEDS

before our discovery of them. In reaction, postmodernists claim that neither reality nor language is transcendental. All knowledge—and ultimately all truth—is socially conditioned. They reject the Enlightenment search for objective, universal truth in favor of a truth that is rooted in the communities in which humans participate. The idea that anyone can find a disinterested position outside the defining structures of SOCIAL LOCATION from which to objectively observe reality is rejected. Languages, as social constructs or conventions, map reality in a variety of ways, coloring and altering the way we experience reality. So languages do not represent or reconstruct the world: they construct the world. Languages are world-creating rather than world-describing systems. This means, then, that rather than an existing objective body of knowledge, truth, and even an objective world waiting to be discovered, there are only potential worlds and many truths. These worlds, each with its own truth, are SYMBOLIC WORLDs that we construct through languages. So postmodernists refuse to split language from reality; they assume that there is no direct access to the world that is unmediated by language. *See* DECONSTRUCTION; POSTMODERN CRITICISM; POSTMODERNISM/POSTMODERNITY.

METER

A term in poetry for the pattern of stressed and unstressed syllables. For example, a line in Coleridge's poem "Metrical Feet" illustrates an iambic pattern of weak, strong stress: "Iámbics márch from shórt to lóng." Yet the extent to which BIBLICAL POETRY lends itself to metrical analysis is a debated issue because of the uncertainty surrounding the vocalization of consonants in the original Hebrew: current vocalization is based on that of the Middle Ages. Some have argued that Hebrew meter is a matter of accent within cola (*see* COLON) and that the number of accents may be equal or unequal within the parallel lines. Others have opted for parallelism rather than phonetic meter as characterizing Hebrew poetry. Still others define the cola by the number of syllables, which range from four to thirteen (sometimes more), rather than by the weak and strong stresses. For an excellent overview of the various approaches to defining meter in Hebrew poetry, see both Stuart and Kugel.

Bibliography. James L. Kugel, *The Idea of Biblical Poetry: Parallelism and Its History* (Baltimore: John Hopkins University Press, 1998); Douglas K. Stuart, *Studies in Early Hebrew Meter* (Missoula, MT: Scholars Press, 1976).

METHOD, EXEGETICAL. *See* EXEGETICAL METHOD

METHOD, HERMENEUTICAL. *See* HERMENEUTICAL METHOD

METHOD, HISTORICAL-CRITICAL. *See* HISTORICAL-CRITICAL METHOD

METHODOLOGY. *See* CRITICAL METHODOLOGY

METONYMY

A FIGURE OF SPEECH in which one thing is substituted for another because of the close association between the two things. Common ones are "the Crown" for the monarchy, "the bench" for the judiciary, and "The pen is mightier than the sword." In the latter example, *pen* and *sword* are metonyms for the power of the written word and military power respectively. This type of substitution is common with most literary traditions. Paul states, "For it is we who are the circumcision" (Phil. 3:3). Most readers know that circumcision is the outward covenantal SIGN that identifies Israel as the chosen people of God. Paul enlists this concept in a new CONTEXT to suggest that Christians are now the people of God. Paul thus substitutes the metonym "circumcision" for "people of God." While walking with the two disciples on the road to Emmaus, Jesus instructs his two companions, "beginning with Moses and all the prophets" (Luke 24:27). *Moses* here is a metonym for the TORAH, the first five books of the HEBREW BIBLE.

MIDRASH

In both Hebrew and NT studies, a term that scholars currently apply in one or more of the following ways: (1) every INTERPRETATION and application of SCRIPTURE; (2) a specific literary GENRE; (3) an exegetical technique entailing the creative use of the HEBREW BIBLE; or (4) the underlying HERMENEUTICS of such a technique.

It is crucial to determine how scholars define their terms in order to understand their hypotheses and opinions. Most important, when asserting that NT writers used midrash, one must be clear in delineating the sense in which the term "midrash" is being defined.

Rabbinic midrash. The simplest definition of *midrash* is rabbinic interpretation of the Hebrew Bible. The Hebrew MEANING of the word conveys the idea of a directed search combined with the careful study of a biblical passage for the purpose of edification and instruction (Bloch, "Midrash," 30–31). There are basically two types of rabbinic midrash: HALAKAH and HAGGADAH. Halakah deals with interpreting the legal portions of the TORAH in an attempt to provide guidelines for obeying the law to the minutest detail. Haggadah, on the other hand, deals with the nonlegal portions of the Torah, such as stories, historical records, prophecies, and ethical teachings (Wright, 50). Some scholars designate midrash halakah as expositional midrash, and midrash haggadah as homiletic midrash (Porton, "Defining Midrash," 78).

"Formal" midrash arose during the period of the BABYLONIAN EXILE, during which time the Torah became a focal point in the lives of the Jews. The people had been swept from their homeland and their temple, so the Torah was the only remaining book on which they could hang their national identity. Public reading and COMMENTARY on the Torah were the authority that regulated their day-to-day life to the smallest detail. Since they viewed the Torah and its accompanying midrash as God's word, the Jews exalted them both as means by which they sought God's will (Wright, 49).

Initially, midrash was transmitted orally, and it is difficult to determine the date when the codification process began. The earliest written midrash dates from the fourth century CE and is composed of *Sifra* (on Leviticus), *Sifre Numbers*, and *Sifre Deuteronomy*. A second set, *Genesis Rabbah* and *Leviticus Rabbah*, dates from the fifth century CE. The MISHNAH was the codification of the traditional oral law and was written around 200 CE. Eventually, commentary called GEMARA was compiled on the Mishnah. These two works, the Babylonian Talmud (600 CE) and the earlier (ca. 400 CE) Palestinian Talmud, together form the TALMUD (Neusner, *What Is Midrash?*, 109). The primary difference between the Mishnah and midrash is their methodology. Midrash adheres closely to the Scripture and is a verse-by-verse exposition, while the Mishnah is a topical codification of the ORAL TRADITION (Russell, 38).

Because no rabbinic midrash in written form exists from the first century BCE, when the NT documents were being written, there are no concrete examples of the type of midrash done then. The characteristics of first-century (oral) midrash must be deduced from the characteristics of the later written forms (Wright, 46). No evidence, however, exists indicating that the methodology of midrash changed during this time period.

The Jews held a high view of SCRIPTURE, which for them consisted of the dual Torah, the written documents plus the oral tradition. The scribes and rabbis' interpretation of the written Torah, which the Hebrews believed was revealed to Moses at Sinai, became the Oral Torah. This exposition was vital because the Hebrews viewed the written Torah as God's revelation and therefore believed that it contained everything one needed to know in order to live properly (Porton, *Rabbinic Midrash*, 2).

Above all else, the purpose of rabbinic midrash was to provide practical relevance and application for day-to-day living. As a result of the elevated position of the Torah, even the smallest detail of the text became important. Thus the goal of midrash was to discover the spirit of the texts, thereby tease out the deeper meanings, and then apply those meanings practically (Bloch, "Midrash," 36). Therefore, the rabbis believed that any one particular TEXT could contain multiple meanings. The

starting point for the interpreter was the text itself and its PLAIN MEANING (*peshat* [*pĕšāṭ*]). Once this plain meaning was deduced and expounded or a difficulty in the plain meaning was resolved, the hidden, deeper meaning was sought (Wright, 64–65).

While the rabbis had a keen appreciation for the plain or LITERAL MEANING, their primary goal was to make the Torah's message relevant to a people far removed from the original text. Thus the focus shifts from interpreting to applying the text in ways that seem to differ considerably from what the text actually says (Neusner, *Description*, 34).

Midrash as exegetical method. When midrash refers to an exegetical method of interpreting the Hebrew Bible, this method may include rewriting a text within a new situation or explaining a text or portion of it within a new situation. Examples of the former are the CHRONICLER's rewriting the history in Samuel and Kings and TRANSLATION of the Hebrew Scriptures into Greek (SEPTUAGINT). In the Hebrew text of Exod. 24:10, we read that Moses and Aaron "saw the God of Israel." In the LXX's rendering of the same verse, however, it is paraphrased to read that Moses and Aaron "saw the place where the God of Israel stood." The change is probably an attempt by the translators to convey in Greek Israel's unspoken ASSUMPTION concerning the impossibility of seeing God and remaining alive (Neusner, *Invitation to Midrash*, 25). An example of explaining a text or portion of it within a new situation is the EXEGESIS of the Hebrew Bible texts at QUMRAN. Notice the prophetic application of the following interpretation of Num. 21:18.

But God remembered the Covenant with the forefathers, and He raised from Aaron men of discernment and from Israel men of wisdom, and He caused them to hear. And they dug the Well: the well which the princes dug, which the nobles of the people delved with the stave.

The *Well* is the Law, and those who dug it were the converts of Israel who went out of the land of Judah to sojourn in the land of Damascus. God called them all *princes* because they sought Him, and their renown was disputed by no man. The *Stave* is the Interpreter of the Law of whom Isaiah said, *He makes a tool for his Work* (Isa. liv, 16); and *the nobles of the people* are those who come to dig the *Well* with the staves with which the *Stave* ordained that they should walk in all the age of wickedness—and without them they shall find nothing—until he comes who shall teach righteousness at the end of days. (Vermès, 102–3)

Midrash as compositional unit. When midrash refers to the fruit of the method, to a compositional unit resulting from exegesis (e.g., the above exegesis of Num. 21:18) and two or more of the compositional units are collected, they are called MIDRASHIM. The collection and arrangement of these midrashim into a compilation may also be called midrash.

Underlying the midrashic exegesis of Scripture are two crucial PRESUPPOSITIONS: (1) the Scriptures were given by God and are consequently relevant for all subsequent generations, and (2) each part of the Scriptures (sentences, phrases, words, even single letters) has an autonomy independent of the whole. These two presuppositions then have an interesting corollary: since the Scriptures were given by an infinite God, a particular passage in part or in whole may have an infinite number of applications.

Other understandings of midrash. Modern scholars categorize midrash in various ways. Frequently these categories overlap and different terminology is used to describe the same event. For example, Richard Longenecker adopts the broad category of "Jewish exegesis," which he divides into literalist, midrashic, pesher, and allegorical. On the other hand, Jacob Neusner adopts the broad term "midrash" and divides it into three types: paraphrase, prophecy, and parable. Yet Longenecker's midrashic and Neusner's paraphrase refer to similar processes, as do their pesher/prophecy and allegorical/parable. Neusner does not discuss any category similar to Longenecker's literalist exegesis. Throughout his writings, Neusner describes the exegete's sole purpose as providing a new, contemporary, relevant meaning to the text irrespective of the text's original meaning.

Following Neusner's scheme, paraphrase is simply a rereading of a particular passage. This type of midrash is designed to amplify or clarify a passage in which the meaning is unclear. Clarification may be made by supplying a synonym, telling an illustrative STORY, giving a word-for-word explanation, or introducing another verse. In the first five verses of the Gospel of John, we find a rereading of the first few verses of Genesis. This is an example of midrash by paraphrase.

Prophecy as midrash identifies a contemporary event or situation with a scriptural passage. This original meaning or historical FRAME OF REFERENCE is not lost, but the reference does inform the present or the future. Thus we may find in Scripture (even historical sections) the meaning of what is happening now. As Neusner explains, "Midrash as prophecy treats the historical life of ancient Israel and the contemporary times of the exegete as essentially the same, reading the former as a prefiguring of the latter" (*What Is Midrash?*, 7).

In the NT, Matthew is known to engage in midrash as prophecy. For example, quoting from Isa. 7:14, he says, "All this took place to fulfill what had been spoken by the Lord through the prophet: 'Look, the virgin shall conceive and bear a son, and they shall name him Emmanuel'" (Matt. 1:22–23). Another example includes the interpretation of a historical reference from Hosea as applying to an event in the life of Jesus: "Then Joseph got up, took the child and his mother by night, and went to Egypt, and remained there until the death of Herod. This was to fulfill what had been spoken by the Lord through the prophet, 'Out of Egypt I have called my son'" (Matt. 2:14–15). Of particular note is that Hosea 11:1 is referring to the exodus of Israel as a nation (the son) from Egypt.

A special type of midrash as prophecy is called PESHER. This type of midrash assumes that what was written in the Scriptures was intended specifically for the contemporary situation. A given statement in Scripture has its SIGNIFICANCE in a contemporary event. In a classic example of a pesher interpretation, Peter interprets a prophecy of Joel in Acts 2:16–21 to refer to the events of PENTECOST ("This is that . . ." [KJV]).

Midrash as parable is similar to, if not identical with, allegorical interpretation. The more profound or authentic meaning of a statement or event is not the obvious historical or literal one. Scripture is interpreted in terms that the AUTHOR never intended. This is possible because of the presuppositions mentioned above. This real meaning of Scripture is hidden beneath the literal one and must speak in such a way as to offer guidance to everyday living. This last type is probably the most characteristic of RABBINIC HERMENEUTICS. While these three types of midrash differ somewhat in method and results, they share a common purpose: all midrash tries to interpret the Scriptures in order to make them authoritatively applicable and therefore binding upon the smallest everyday details of the life of a people.

Bibliography. Renée Bloch, "Methodological Note for the Study of Rabbinic Literature," in *Approaches to Ancient Judaism: Theory and Practice* (ed. William Scott Green; Missoula, MT: Scholars Press, 1978), 51–76; idem, "Midrash," in *Approaches to Ancient Judaism: Theory and Practice* (ed. William Scott Green; Missoula, MT: Scholars Press, 1978), 29–50; Jacob Neusner, *From Description to Conviction: Essays on the History and Theology of Judaism* (Atlanta: Scholars Press, 1987); idem, *Invitation to Midrash: A Teaching Book* (San Francisco: Harper & Row, 1989); idem, *What Is Midrash?* (Philadelphia: Fortress, 1987); Gary Porton, "Defining Midrash," in *The Study of Ancient Judaism* (ed. Jacob Neusner; Hoboken, NJ: Ktav, 1981), 55–92; idem, *Understanding Rabbinic Midrash: Text and Commentary* (Hoboken, NJ: Ktav, 1985); Géza Vermès, *Dead Sea Scrolls in English* (rev. ed.; Baltimore: Penguin, 1968); Addison Wright, *The Literary Genre Midrash* (Staten Island, NY: Alba House, 1967).

MIDRASHIC HERMENEUTICS. *See* MIDRASH; RABBINIC HERMENEUTICS

MIDRASHIM

Compositional units as the result of midrashic INTERPRETATION; the plural of MIDRASH.

MIMESIS. *See* MIMETIC CRITICISM

MIMETIC CRITICISM

A CRITICAL METHODOLOGY that finds the MEANING of a TEXT in the relationship between the text and reality. The notion that literature in some way imitates life has been a mainstay in Western thought from its earliest records. Almost any verbal representation seems to force some type of comparison with our experience. Any theory that assumes a correspondence between text and reality, inscribing that correspondence as the standard of LITERARY quality, is properly mimetic. The mimetic CRITIC, then, judges the worth of a literary text by its ability to represent or reflect some aspect of the world outside the text. Good literature, claims the mimetic critic, reveals some truth about the way humans experience nature. The text's relevance lies in its correspondence to some aspect of life as it is experienced or defined. In one way or another, all mimetic critics appeal to a shared human common sense or experience of the world and the text's imitation of that common sense or experience as the locus of meaning.

Although the English translation of the Greek word *mimēsis* is usually "imitation," mimetic critics admit that there are likely to be differences between the literary work and the world that it imitates. So the word "imitation" might be too strong, calling for a direct copy of reality. A modern example of the relationship between art object and reality is that even if the language or actions of an object may have negative effects on the audience, a mimetic critic in defense would state that the work nonetheless gives an accurate picture of reality. After all, people actually say and do such things, and the artist is simply representing the way things are. For the mimetic critic, truth through representation is the highest good.

Origins of the mimetic view. From the time of the ancient Greeks to the eighteenth century, the idea that literature was essentially mimetic was an unchallenged premise. Literature revealed truth about life (Keesey, 194). In his *Poetics*, Aristotle argued not only that the heart of TRAGEDY was its catharsis of pity and fear but also that tragedy produced in the viewer or reader an insight experience.

Such an experience was what the reader or viewer of the tragedy recognized as the truth that the text revealed about some aspect of the human condition, an insight into some universal aspect of a reality external to the text itself.

In the last two hundred years, however, critics have been reluctant to accept this literary theory. Modern thought has increasingly become dominated by an empirical view of reality, which assumes that the world apprehended by the senses is the real world and therefore tends to deny the existence of a reality composed of universals.

In his *Republic*, Plato objects to poetry (artistic representation) on the grounds that it always presents a false picture of the world. The world that is apprehended by the senses is an imperfect manifestation of true reality. For Plato, the real world is the world of immutable ideas, what he calls ideal forms, which can be apprehended only by the mind. For example, there is a perfect standard of a circle against which all physical circles we see and draw are measured. For everything we see, there is a perfect FORM or idea, which exists completely independently of that physical manifestation. He gives the example of a couch: The couch is constructed by the carpenter. The physical couch is nothing more than a physical imitation of the carpenter's TRANSLATION of the idea of a couch. When the painter paints a picture of the couch, this representation is actually an imitation of an imitation of the ideal form. So artistic representation, rather than directing the human mind toward the form, actually moves the mind in the opposite direction (Keesey, 195). In other words, the representation of an INTERPRETATION precludes a grasp of true reality. It prohibits rather than furthers knowledge.

One of the earliest critics of Plato's evaluation of art was his student Aristotle, to whom the concept of mimesis is attributed. He challenged Plato by redefining the sense in which art imitates reality. According to Aristotle, the material world, which we apprehend with our senses, is the real world, and true form is that which a thing most characteristically is. For example, the form of a man is best

represented by a vigorous male between the ages of 18 and 23, the stage toward which childhood develops and from which old age declines. Aristotle makes a division between form and appearance which has important implications for his concept of mimesis. First, it explains how it is possible for art to represent men as "better than they are" or things "as they ought to be." Second, it explains how the artist must look past the peculiarities to discover the form that underlies them. Aristotle's concept of mimesis may be best described by an example of an artist who studies many different models of a person or thing to "imitate" a form or ideal quality common in the different models. This is exactly the manner in which Aristotle developed his model for the ideal tragedy in his *Poetics*. He examined many tragedies and extracted their common elements. So while any tragedy may approach the ideal, perhaps none do so perfectly. After looking beyond the particulars of an object, the artist tries to reveal the ideal thing through artistic representation. This is why Aristotle can claim that art is more closely allied with philosophy than with history: like philosophy, art seeks the universal rather than the particular.

Difficulties faced by mimetic critics. One of the problems that mimetic critics face is the definition of "reality." There are different theories of reality, about the manner in which the world operates. During the latter half of the twentieth century, more and more critics argued that human reality is always constructed through the lenses of some thought system. For example, a Marxist definition of what constitutes reality differs significantly from that of the ancient Greeks. An existentialist's differs from that of a neopragmatist. If texts really mimic reality, they must do so according to the way reality is defined. These thought systems are fully developed theories about the way people live and why, providing a standard by which the value or accuracy of a text's representations can be judged. For example, a PSYCHOANALYTIC CRITICISM can read Sophocles or Shakespeare in Freudian or Lacanian terms. Since mimetic critics assume that all humans share some commonality of experience and sense of the world, the "truths" that writers of any period or culture communicate can be evaluated through the grid of psychoanalysis. In other words, truth about life is not limited by time and culture. The same may be said about a Marxist critic (*see* MARXIST CRITICISM); since Marxism claims that reality is structured in terms of the clash of classes, economic determinism, and the dialectic of history, a work of any period or culture may be analyzed and judged by the extent to which it reflects this structure. Since this structure is universal and a common experience of all humans, we should not be surprised when we find that Shakespeare's *Tempest* has inscribed these structures.

A second problem facing mimetic criticism is the increasingly empirical conception of reality. If reality is an infinite flux of ever-changing felt experience, a collection of raw, nonformal phenomena, then any formal pattern assigned to the text or to its INTERPRETATION cannot really imitate contingent reality as human experience. In other words, the idea of artistic design does not fit very well with an empirical view of reality.

The response of mimetic critics. Mimetic critics respond to the dilemma by claiming that the mimetic relationship between reality defined as the infinite flux of changing experience and a text is the complexity of both. Though the text may be formal in design and does not replicate reality, it does mirror it in the complexity of the design. The experience of reading a complex text is similar to our experience of life. We try to make sense of both by imposing an interpretive grid on them, a grid in terms of a system of thought.

Mimetic critics also respond that CHARACTERIZATION, SETTING, PLOT, and ACTION in literature seem to invite a comparison with life as we experience it outside the text. So, says the mimetic critic, if artistic representations invite comparison with nonartistic experience, literature does in important ways force us humans to ask important questions about life.

Mimetic criticism seems to correspond well to the way many readers and critics approach the biblical texts and to the way the BIBLE AS LIT-ERATURE courses in higher education handle the texts. When readers of the book of Job ask questions about the relationship between piety and divine blessing, they are assuming that Job suggests something theologically significant. When biblical scholars suggest that the Gospel of Mark is redefining the concept of messiahship, they are assuming that the Gospel employs literary strategies, FORM, and CONTENT to suggest something about the way we should view an aspect of life. Or when readers seek guidance in the Psalms or Proverbs, they are reading mimetically. NARRATIVE CRITICISM is also mimetic when it relates elements of plot, setting, action, and characterization to literary meaning.

Bibliography. Donald Keesey, *Contexts for Criticism* (4th ed.; Boston: McGraw-Hill, 2003).

MIMETIC QUALITY OF LANGUAGE

The relationship between the REAL WORLD and the WORLD OF THE TEXT. The mimetic quality enables the AUTHOR to challenge the reader to discover some TRUTH, message, or insight to which the textual world points.

MINOR PROPHETS. *See* MAJOR PROPHETS

MINUSCULE

In TEXTUAL CRITICISM, a manuscript written in lowercase cursive letters. This type of manuscript appeared around 800 CE and became the dominant style after the tenth century CE. Some minuscules have punctuation and spacing between words. The manuscripts are designated by Arabic numerals that do not begin with 0 (e.g., 1, 210) and are divided into families, the most important being families 1 and 13.

MIRACLE STORY. *See* ARETALOGY

MISHNAH

A collection of Pharisaic and rabbinic oral INTERPRETATIONS of the TORAH (mostly HALAKAH) edited and compiled by Rabbi Judah ha-Nasi about 200 CE. The Mishnah forms the basis for the

TALMUD. *See* MIDRASH; RABBINIC HERMENEU-TICS; TALMUD.

MISOGYNY

A term often used in FEMINIST CRITICISM for the hatred of women, especially hatred by men.

MISPRISION. *See* MISREADING

MISREADING

A term Harold Bloom introduced into LITERARY vocabulary for the reading of the relationship between TEXTS. Bloom assumed that every literary text is the product of a reading of other texts and that in order to deal with the ANXIETY OF INFLUENCE, AUTHORS will productively misread earlier texts, especially those deemed great ones within the LITERARY CANON. Misreading, then, should not be understood as misunderstanding but as a creative response to an awe-inspiring text. Consequently, a primary task of a reader is to determine the manner in which the text one is reading responds to its precursors. In this respect, one might argue that the Song of Songs is an intentional misreading of the account of creation in Gen. 2–3 or that Job and Ecclesiastes are deliberate misreadings of the WISDOM TRADITION as found in Proverbs. There is, however, a fine line between misreading as Bloom defines it and INTERTEXTUALITY.

Misreading also refers to a reading that makes a mistake in understanding or INTERPRETATION. The important issue for interpretation, however, is one of justification, meaning the criteria to which one may appeal to argue that a reading is a misreading. In POSTMODERN theories, since the understanding of any artifact of the past is configured within a CONTEXT foreign to the one within which the artifact was produced, any attempt to reconstruct the artifact's original SIGNIFICANCE is really a construction that makes SENSE within the interpreter's world. In this sense, then, every reading is actually a misreading.

Bibliography. Harold Bloom, *The Anxiety of Influence: A Theory of Poetry* (New York: Oxford University Press, 1984); idem, *A Map of Misreading* (New York: Oxford University Press, 1975).

MODEL

An earlier TEXT that is the verbal source of another text. The model does not necessarily or even usually serve as the thematic source of a later text. For example, NT scholars argue that the Gospel of Mark serves as both the verbal and the chronological source for Matthew and Luke without providing the thematic source for them. Within REDACTION CRITICISM, scholars argue that while Matthew and Luke both use Mark extensively, Matthew and Luke have their own distinctive thematic AGENDAS. The same argument may be made for the relationship between the undisputed Pauline EPISTLES and the disputed ones.

MODEL READER

In the READER-RESPONSE CRITICISM of Umberto Eco, the reader presupposed by the TEXT, who shares the CODES presupposed by the AUTHOR. According to Eco, some texts encourage the participation of the reader in making interpretive decisions based on a complex of codes (cultural, LITERARY, historical, etc.). A reader who is informed of the codes presupposed by the text is a more competent reader. Some texts, argues Eco, do not encourage a specific or determinate response from the reader, while others seek to produce a "precise response." Eco refers to the latter texts as CLOSED TEXTS, including Westerns, comic strips, and popular romances. In opposition to the closed texts are the OPEN TEXTS, which create a role for the reader to make decisions about MEANING (e.g., the open LETTER). Biblical texts that fall into the category of open are APOCALYPSE, GOSPEL, WISDOM LITERATURE, and some NARRATIVES, such as Genesis, Samuel, Kings, Ruth, Esther, and Jonah.

Bibliography. Umberto Eco, *The Role of the Reader: Explorations in the Semiotics of Texts* (Bloomington: Indiana University Press, 1984).

MODE OF PRODUCTION

A concept in Marxism claiming that social circumstances determine most of a person's life. In other words, the manner in which a person's material life is produced conditions every aspect of the person's life—political, intellectual, and so forth. The way people think and experience the world is determined by the way the economy is organized. Culture, then, and everything people might associate with it (education, religion, philosophy, the arts, literature) are defined by the economic BASE. Such determinism means that AUTHORs and readers are not totally free to create and interpret as they please, but do so within an economic FRAMEWORK. Thus, thinking and MEANING are subservient to economic conditions. Accordingly, readers within a capitalist culture will already be programmed to read the biblical texts a certain way, while readers in a third-world culture will be conditioned to read them in a significantly different manner. *See* MARXIST CRITICISM.

MODERNISM/MODERNITY

Specifically, a term used to refer to the artistic movements from about 1850 to 1950, a period when both economic and cultural life in the West were radically revolutionized. This period of the arts was marked by a rejection of the past, distrust of all forms of authority, the search for essences, and innovative experimentation—impressionism, abstract expressionism, cubism, nonobjective NARRATION, atonality, nonthematic structure, and DISSONANCE, to name a few.

Generally, however, modernism is a type of culture developed in Europe and North America during the last several centuries, beginning with the Renaissance (fifteenth century) at the earliest and with the Enlightenment (seventeenth century) at the latest, then coming to full fruition in the early twentieth century. While *modernity* is often used synonymously with *modernism*, it is actually the historical period during which the cultural expression of modernism developed. Although scholars may talk about modernism as if it were universally accepted and heralded as the apex of cultural expression, it was never without its critics in terms of the losses it precipitated, such as TRADITION, a sense of community, familiar forms of authority,

and religious grounding. Cultural historians mostly agree on the defining characteristics of modernism, which include (1) a profound trust in scientific knowledge to control nature and to unlock its secrets; (2) a premium on human freedom and rationality, which leads to social progress and a better material, political, and intellectual life; (3) the possibility of dispassionate, OBJECTIVE KNOWLEDGE of the world and history; (4) humanism; and (5) radical individuality. Some historians further include the ideas of a primarily secular culture, liberal democracy, and a free market. While there have been cultures throughout history with free markets, respect for the individual, trust in reason, and so forth, it seems that modernity differs in that all these characteristics appeared together.

Of all the above, however, perhaps most characteristic of modernism is its profound trust in scientific reason. Independent of tradition and all forms of authority, especially religious authority, reason becomes the means for judging morality, TRUTH, aesthetics, and political structures. Moderns identified separate spheres of knowledge, each demanding its own type of scientific investigation. For example, the truth of art and its method(s) of inquiry differ from that of economics or natural science or religion. The key idea here is that each area or discipline requires scientific investigation. In the case of the BIBLE, it is an artifact of the past, conditioned by that past, and must be studied scientifically from a radical historical posture apart from any theological biases or AGENDAS. With the advent of POSTMODERNISM, the ASSUMPTION that objective, scientific knowledge is possible has been challenged.

Bibliography. A. K. M. Adam, *What Is Post-modern Biblical Criticism?* (Minneapolis: Fortress, 1995); Lawrence Cahoone, ed., *From Modernism to Post-modernism: An Anthology* (Cambridge, MA: Blackwell, 1996); Michael Groden and Martin Kreiswirth, eds., *The Johns Hopkins Guide to Literary Theory and Criticism* (Baltimore: Johns Hopkins University Press, 1994).

MONITORY POETRY

According to Robert Alter, a type of BIBLICAL POETRY that is dominated "by images of wasteland, uprooting and burning, darkness, enslavement and humiliation, stripping of garments, divorce and sexual abandoning, earthquake and storm" (156). An example is Jer. 4:23–27.

Bibliography. Robert Alter, *The Art of Biblical Poetry* (New York: Basic Books, 1985).

MONITORY TALE

A term used by Robert Alter to describe the NAR- RATIVE movement or STORY line that occurs in many Hebrew poems. For an example, see Prov. 7, in which the "PLOT" moves from exhortation to the NARRATION of events that the NARRATOR recalls seeing, to the DENOUEMENT.

Bibliography. Robert Alter, *The Art of Biblical Poetry* (New York: Basic Books, 1985).

MONOGAMY

Marriage to only one spouse at a time. Monogamy seems to have developed as the norm for Christian marriage early in the life of the church (e.g., 1 Cor. 7:2–3; 1 Tim. 3:2).

MONOGRAPH

A scholarly TEXT on a limited topic.

MONOLOGISM

A term introduced by Mikhail Bakhtin to denote a work with a single, uninterrupted, consistent NARRATIVE voice that disallows DIALOGUE. For the most part, the book of Ezra is an example of monologism, in which any words uttered by individuals are reported or in the FORM of a SPEECH.

MONOLOGUE

A LITERARY CONVENTION in which a person speaks alone with or without an audience. However, it also has more-nuanced senses: (1) the presentation of what a person would say if one had an audience, although the person does not actually speak; (2) a soliloquy in which the thoughts of a person are represented when no audience is present; and (3) a solo address to an audience. Consequently, most prayers and LAMENTs are monologues. *See* INTERIOR MONOLOGUE.

Bibliography. J. A. Cuddon, *The Penguin Dictionary of Literary Terms and Literary Theory* (4th ed.; London: Penguin, 1998).

MONOSEMY

Having only a single MEANING. Any CRITICAL METHODOLOGY arguing that a TEXT can mean only what the AUTHOR originally intended is monosemic.

MOOD

One of the five analytical categories into which Gérard Genette divides NARRATIVE. Mood refers to the AUTHOR's attitude toward the SUBJECT of the TEXT, unlike TONE, which is the author's attitude toward the audience. Genette divides mood into distance and perspective. Distance is the relationship between the NARRATION and its own materials. Is the STORY told or represented, and is it in direct narration (in the third person; e.g., Nehemiah), in indirect narration (in the first person; e.g., 1 Chronicles), or in free direct SPEECH (direct quotes within a narrative; e.g., Exod. 2:14)? Perspective is what is usually referred to as POINT OF VIEW. The NARRATOR may be elevated above the characters, the characters above the narrator, or the narrator and characters may be evenhanded in their knowledge. The narrator may be omniscient and outside the ACTION of the story or a participant in the action. Narration may proceed from the author's perspective, from a character's perspective, or from the perspective of various characters.

Bibliography. Gérard Genette, *Narrative Discourse: An Essay in Method* (trans. Jane E. Lewin; Ithaca, NY: Cornell University Press, 1980).

MORPHEME

A minimal linguistic unit of MEANING. For example, the word "disrespectful" has three morphemes: "dis-," a prefix connoting "absence of"; the noun "respect"; and "-ful," a suffix that converts a noun into an adjective.

MORPHOLOGY

The study of word forms. The languages of the BIBLE are highly inflected languages, meaning that a word changes in FORM depending on tense, voice, mood, person, number, case, and gender. In KOINE (the Greek of the NT), word order is less significant than in English, which has fewer inflections. In English, the order is usually subject, verb, and direct object—with prepositional phrases, adverbial clauses, and relative clauses occurring according to rules of SYNTAX. In Greek, however, inflection is more crucial to meaning than word order. Hebrew and Aramaic, which have less inflection in their noun and adjective systems, are more word-order dependent, like English.

Word forms influence MEANING, and for this reason having the ability to recognize forms and their potential meanings is an essential part of INTERPRETATION. Readers may be able to ask a speaker of their own language what is meant by an unusual statement or word or word form; the writers of the biblical texts, however, are not available for questioning. Therefore, the best alternative is for readers to equip themselves with the knowledge or tools necessary for recognizing forms and their possible meanings. For example, in 1 Cor. 12:31, the word *zēloute* (strive) may be either an indicative or an imperative in form. How is the interpreter to decide? If the interpreter is not aware that there are two possibilities, there will be no choice except the one made by the translator. The point of the statement assumes a different meaning if it is translated as an indicative rather than as an imperative.

MOSAIC LAW. *See* TORAH

MOTIF

An element, such as an idea, character, or IMAGE, that serves as a unifying element of a STORY. For example, carpe diem, the maiden and the rescuer, color, light versus dark, from rags to riches, or a journey—any of these may serve as a motif for a story. *See* LEITMOTIF; *LEITWORT*.

MOTIF, CROWD. *See* CROWD MOTIF

MOTIF, JOURNEY. *See* JOURNEY MOTIF

MOTIF, QUEST. *See* QUEST MOTIF

MOTIF, RESCUE. *See* RESCUE MOTIF

MOTIF, TEST. *See* TEST MOTIF

MOTIF, TRAVEL. *See* TRAVEL MOTIF

MT

Abbreviation for MASORETIC TEXT.

MUJERISTA THEOLOGY/CRITICISM

A theology/criticism born out of a struggle of Latina women for freedom and acceptance in the world and to find a place where their beliefs and ideals are not merely included as part of the whole but are seriously considered and allowed to hold a place of respect equal to those of white and black women. Called the theology of grassroots Latinas, this theology has as its central focus the liberation of Hispanic women.

Historical background. The Latin American Conference on Theology from the Perspective of Women in Argentina met in 1985 in Buenos Aires from October 30 to November 3; there twenty-seven women from nine Latin American countries came together to set in motion the task of Latin American women's LIBERATION THEOLOGY. In 1986, this meeting was followed by the Intercontinental Women's Conference in Mexico. Both of these conferences recognized the contributions of women to the field of theology and marked the starting point of the serious development of *mujerista* theology. Some of the main players in the movement are Elsa Tamez, a Mexican Bible scholar and dean of the Latin American Biblical University in Costa Rica; Professor Maria Pilar Aquino; the Brazilian Ivone Gebara; and Cuban-American seminary professors Ada María Isasi-Díaz and Daisy Machado.

Hispanic women's theology. Mujerista theology is described by its founder and most vocal proponent, Ada María Isasi-Díaz, as "Hispanic women's theology . . . born of the intersection of feminism, Hispanic culture, and the struggle for liberation. It is a communal theology . . . and honors the distinctiveness of Hispanic culture" (Baker-Fletcher).

Through her experiences and struggles as a Cuban-American and female theologian, Isasi-Díaz desired to help form a dynamic theology taken from the voices and perspectives of Hispanic women in the United States; she wanted to bridge the gap between "the academic theological world and the Hispanic women's community" ("The Task," 89). For Isasi-Díaz and her colleague Yolanda Tarango (Mexican-American founder of Las Hermanas, a *mujerista* organization), the first and perhaps the most important step in developing a theology was to find a name (Isasi-Díaz, "*Mujerista* Theology's Method," 123–28). Isasi-Díaz and those working with her decided to turn to an integral part of Hispanic culture—its music—for inspiration in naming the "essence" of woman. In Spanish songs of all types, women are simply referred to as *mujer*. Thus, according to Isasi-Díaz, "those who make a preferential option for *mujeres* are *mujeristas*" ("The Task," 98). Officially organized in 1987, *mujerismo* as a movement establishes few theological parameters in deciding who can and cannot consider herself a *mujerista*; however, a *mujerista* must be a woman of Cuban, Mexican, or Puerto Rican descent who lives in the United States, and her primary motivation for interpreting the world and MEANING must be communal liberation (Floyd-Thomas and Gillman, 37–39; Isasi Díaz, "The Task," 99–100). What makes Hispanic women's theology different from any other theology, especially that of other women and of Hispanic men? Isasi-Díaz explains the "distinctness" of *mujerista* theology by discussing the Hispanic woman's need for liberation from various oppressors and oppressive lifestyles; the *mujerismo* definition of liberation as it encompasses certain ideas about solidarity and salvation; *mujerismo's* goals for theology; sources for theology; the way of doing theology as PRAXIS; and finally, some of *mujerismo's* unique theological beliefs.

The need for liberation. How are Hispanic women living in the United States in need of liberation? Are they not treated as equals, like all other individuals in our society? According to Isasi-Díaz, Hispanic women are not treated as equals in society and are in fact oppressed in a variety of ways. First of all, there exists a lack of respect in American society for Hispanic culture in general, rooted in the racist and ethnic prejudice prevalent in the United States today (*Mujerista Theology*, 17, 32). Hispanics are forced to give up many aspects of their culture in order to succeed in American society. Isasi-Díaz offers the example of her being able to transport only samples from her mother's garden in Cuba to the United States, just cuttings and pieces taken from the whole; she was unable to inherit the whole garden. She says, "That is what happens to the Hispanic culture in the United States. It is sacked and raped" (17).

Hispanic women experience oppression within their own culture as well, however, and are often marginalized and mistreated according to certain Latin norms. *Machismo* and other forms of male domination demean women's roles in the home as well as intellectually and sexually. Although Hispanic women's typical domains are within the domestic family SETTING, they are usually so overworked with daily tasks that it is not abnormal for many to suffer from sleep deprivation (Isasi-Díaz, "*Un poquito,*" 328). Outside the home, women are rarely taken seriously, both within and outside Hispanic circles. Hispanic women are seldom consulted in making decisions of policy or programs within the community, although they are often called on to do the work of implementing those decisions (Isasi-Díaz, "*Mujeristas*: A Name," 123; idem, "Praxis," 45). Not being allowed any other type of power or voice, many Hispanic women turn to using their sexuality for leverage. Barbara Strickland, a longtime missionary to Honduras and professor of Spanish and Hispanic studies in the United States, says, "Hispanic women are often forced to use their sexuality in order to live; it is their only playing card" (from interview with Strickland). *Mujeristas* say that the cause of women abusing their bodies sexually stems from their lack of understanding their bodies as being intrinsic to who they are; Hispanic culture denies women sexual desire or pleasure, and so the sexual act is rarely considered more than just a duty, a way to put food on the table, or a necessity for procreation (Isasi-Díaz, *Mujerista Theology*, 142–43).

Although *mujeristas* do admit to oppression within their own culture, they consider the greater American culture and society to be the main source of their oppression. In addition to American society's strangling of Hispanic cultural expression, American society uses oppressive language when referring to women and also robs them economically. Isasi-Díaz claims that the English word "woman" refers only to middle- and upper-class white women within traditional American society. When other groups want to be totally heard or visible, they must add adjectives to the word, such as "*poor* woman," "*African-American* woman," or "*Hispanic* woman." Furthermore, the term "feminist" always connotes "lesbian" or "bisexual," which is negative because such lifestyles deviate from the norm of the dominant and controlling society (Isasi-Díaz, *Mujerista Theology*, 20). In addition to inherent oppression within the English language, Hispanic women are economically oppressed by American society. Hispanic women are often the poorest members of American society and are almost always the ones responsible for supporting themselves and their children (Moody, 47).

Of all the various types of oppression they face, *mujeristas* are most vocal about the oppression they experience from other feminist organizations and also from the church and its TRADITIONS. Active feminist groups within the United States virtually ignore the plight of Hispanic women and refuse to acknowledge that Hispanic women have unique and individual needs that are unlike women of other ethnicities. Furthermore, such organizations refuse to admit that there is prejudice within their own circles. Even more than feminist prejudice, *mujeristas* feel very strongly about the oppressive structures of the church. Author on FEMINIST CRITICISM Linda Moody (50) writes in contempt for the Catholic Church's stubbornness in refusing to grant bona fide leadership positions to women. Others criticize the church for perpetuating what has become a church-sanctified sense of "holiness" in pain and struggle; this form of masochism is simply a way for the church's patriarchal society (*see* PATRIARCHY) to continue oppressing Hispanic women (Isasi-Díaz, "*Un poquito,*" 338). Isasi-Díaz further castigates the church for its claim to understand and possess OBJECTIVE TRUTH: "Most of the time, what is considered objectivity is the subjectivity of dominant groups who can impose their understandings on others and use those understandings as ideological tools for control over the poor and the oppressed" (*Mujerista Theology*, 37, 129). From Isasi-Díaz's point of view, objectivity is never attainable, and to claim it for one's INTERPRETATION is a falsehood and thus sin. *Mujerista* theologians strive to rise above such sin and admit to complete subjectivity, since their interpretations arise solely from the Hispanic woman's own CONTEXT and perspective.

The struggle. The Hispanic woman's daily experience of cultural, physical, intellectual, sexual, communicative, economic, organizational, and religious oppression is what *mujeristas* call *la lucha*, the struggle. *La lucha* includes not only a woman's physical fight for survival but also her cultural and spiritual fight. Out of the existence of that struggle comes the Hispanic woman's need for liberation. As a liberation theology, *mujerismo* defines liberation as an "expression of the aspiration of oppressed peoples and social classes" (Isasi-Díaz, "The Task," 89). Interestingly, however, the *mujerista* seems much more concerned with liberation for the oppressed Hispanic women living in the United States than with liberation for other oppressed groups. Within the female Hispanic community, liberation is not something that one individual can accomplish herself. Liberation is a communal process in which oppressed individuals work together to create a new reality that is different from the present oppressive one.

Liberation. The *mujerista* idea of liberation is intricately tied to what *mujeristas* consider solidarity and salvation. Isasi-Díaz suggests a new way for contemporary culture to look at the traditional Christian behavior of love; she calls it solidarity. By *solidarity* she means a sense of relation, support, and understanding primarily between members of communities of struggle but also between the oppressor and the oppressed. A Christian should always be concerned with loving the neighbor—that is the goal of Christianity. And who is our neighbor? Isasi-Díaz says that our neighbors are "the least of our sisters and brothers"; our neighbors are the poor and oppressed (*Mujerista Theology*, 88–89). Thus, in order to be in solidarity, oppressed people should always strive to care for one another and work together for the greater goal of liberation. Also, the oppressor should always strive not only to understand and empathize with the plight of the poor and oppressed but also to participate actively in helping them realize liberation (86): "There can be no salvation without liberation, though no single act of liberation can be totally identified with salvation in its fullness" (90). *Mujerista* theology is concerned with what Isasi-Díaz calls "the unfolding of the 'kindom' of God." The absence of the letter *g* from the word *kingdom* poignantly illustrates the *mujerista* belief that salvation and being part of the kingdom of God are achieved through a communal process of liberation—a necessary sense of kinship between God and the individual, and between the individual and others. Even though *mujeristas* usually recognize Christ as the Son of God and consider his death on the cross to be God's salvific act for humankind (although a few sources disagree with this view), they consider an individual's participation in the act of salvation as being a part of the active communal effort to transform the world from oppressive to liberating structures (90).

Within the framework of a liberation theology, *mujeristas* claim to have certain goals. Isasi-Díaz lists them as follows:

(1) to provide a platform for the voices of Latina grassroots women, (2) to develop a theological method that takes seriously the religious understandings and practices of Latinas as a source of theology, and (3) to challenge theological understandings, church teachings, and religious practices that oppress Latina women, that are not life-giving and therefore cannot be theologically correct.

Such are the sociological understandings, teachings, and practices that *mujeristas* consider to be oppressive and are trying to work against. As for a theological method, *mujerista* theology draws from a variety of sources and then uses those sources in unique ways to accomplish an active working theology referred to as praxis.

Source of theology. The primary source from which *mujeristas* draw their theology is the everyday life of average Hispanic women, known as *lo cotidiano*. A *mujerista* theologian is concerned about how the daily tasks of caring for a family, working at a job, dealing with various prejudices, and so forth affect the way Hispanic women view the world and go about finding their own truth. Why do Hispanic women pray? When do Hispanic women (who live in the United States) speak Spanish and when do they speak English, and what SIGNIFICANCE does that have? How do Hispanic women respond to different prejudices? A woman's daily experiences are considered to be the main source of her being—where she practices religion. How genuine a woman's faith may or may not be becomes much more obvious when she goes through her daily routine than when she attends mass or goes to confession. Isasi-Díaz states, "*Lo cotidiano* is the epistemological framework of our theological enterprise. It is a way of understanding theology, our attempt to explain how we understand the divine, what we know about the divine" (*Mujerista Theology*, 68, 71). She goes on to qualify the fact that although each woman's personal experience of life justifies her own sense of truth and religion, *mujeristas* cannot be said to adhere to total relativism or a lack of morality. "We do recognize and hold liberation to be the criterion or principle by which we judge what is right or wrong, good or bad, salvific or condemnatory" (69). Since *mujerista* theology seems to claim only liberation as a source of moral value, how do *mujeristas* hermeneutically approach the BIBLE, and what is its purpose?

"Bible stories become ours when we use them because we need to, and to make them be helpful in a given situation we change even central elements of the story itself, highlighting perhaps nonessential elements. It is not that the integrity of the text is not important; it is that the need to survive takes precedence" (Isasi-Díaz, *Mujerista Theology*, 152). *Mujerista* theology seeks to lift out of the Bible passages and concepts that serve to legitimate and perpetuate the fight for liberation. In many respects, the Bible does not speak directly to Hispanic women or even to women in general, when considering their need to free themselves from oppressive structures (125). Furthermore, many Hispanic women do not feel comfortable or prepared to interpret or decide what certain texts mean. Isasi-Díaz suggests that there is a need among Hispanic women for an increased familiarity with the Bible, primarily to ensure that a greater number of Hispanic women have a greater voice in BIBLICAL HERMENEUTICS (159). Isasi-Díaz further elaborates on her concern for Hispanic women who are currently comfortable in reading and deriving meaning from biblical texts (mostly evangelicals, charismatics, and Pentecostals), since many are being oppressed and forced into developing certain philosophies and ideas about certain texts because those guiding them in interpretation do not allow for deviance from "traditional views." According to *mujerista* theology, the Bible should be used as a source for theology only inasmuch as it adds to discussion and reflection on oppression and liberation (160–61).

Although certainly not considered a main source in the development of *mujerista* theology, the church—particularly the Roman Catholic Church—is a common element within the community of Hispanic women, and thus a legitimate source for theology. Most Hispanic women refer to themselves as Christian Catholics even if they do not attend church; as such, they apply at least some teachings of Catholicism to their faith. Even though many, if not most, aspects of Catholicism are oppressive in nature, according to *mujeristas*, the lived experience of Hispanic women reflects an intrinsic sense of church and religion that has become a defining part of their culture and that constitutes much of how Hispanic women view God, Jesus, prayer, and the Bible (Isasi-Díaz, "Mu-

jerista Theology's Method," 128). Nevertheless, the religious and theological views of most Hispanic women, while reflecting important Catholic beliefs, also reflect beliefs of other religions.

"We insist on the normative, graced, and even universal dimensions of the salvific manifestations of non-Christian religions." For a *mujerista*, theology relies on a diverse mixture of sources, which include not only pre-Reformation, Spanish European, and American Catholic religions but also African and Amerindian religions (Isasi-Díaz, *Mujerista Theology*, 74–75). For example, the common term "Our Lady of Regla" is a title for Mary that is identified with Yemaya, the Lucumi African religion's goddess of the sea (Moody, 79). The Cuban Santa Barbara is identified with Chango, the Yoruban god of thunder. The Mexican Lady of Guadalupe, while often identified with the mother of Jesus, is equally identified with Tonantzin, the Aztec goddess who was mother of all the gods (118). *Mujerista* leaders Isasi-Díaz and Tarango claim their theology to be Christian even as it draws from extra-Christian theological sources. According to them, *mujerista* theology can be considered a form of Christianity because most *mujeristas* identify themselves with Christianity. They maintain that it is not difficult for two or three traditions reflecting beliefs in different gods to be incorporated into a legitimate faith structure. "We take from each religious strand what is life-giving, what is important for the struggle of survival, and leave aside what is not relevant or harmful" (119). How do the sources of *lo cotidiano*, the Bible, Catholicism, and non-Christian religions work together to form an active, vibrant theology that helps define and liberate Hispanic women?

In *mujerista* theology, the most important part in deriving theological meaning from a variety of theological sources is the necessity of praxis. For *mujeristas*, *theology* is a verb: action is a primary component. Also, each individual woman is a theologian: theology is defined by the whole community rather than just by an academic elite (Isasi-Díaz, "The Task," 90). In doing theology, theologians gather in groups to discuss and reflect on their diverse views of life, their diverse experiences, and their diverse religious understandings in order to develop a communal theology with liberation at its core. In discussing their views, theologians should look for and discover the subversive and oppressive structures that they are forced to deal with every day. Through such reflection, the women as a group will begin to realize and create ways for each person to use her personal gifts so that greater liberation may be accomplished for the whole community. Some women may serve as artists, and others as musicians, writers, speakers, demonstrators, and more. Isasi-Díaz gives examples of what using personal gifts for doing theology is really about:

> Hispanic women protesting the lack of city services in the South Bronx, emptying a bag of trash on the desk of the city official who could order the garbage to be picked up more frequently in the area where the women live—that is doing Hispanic women's liberation theology [used in this context to refer to *mujerismo*]. A woman struggling in a meeting controlled by Hispanic men to pass a resolution that would ensure a certain percentage of women in each of the delegations to an important national meeting—that is doing Hispanic women's liberation theology. Four women testifying in front of a group of Roman Catholic bishops about the oppression of Hispanic women in church as well as in society, finishing their presentation by giving each of the bishops a stone and telling them, "We have asked for bread and you have given us a stone. Put these stones on your altars when you celebrate Eucharist and remember us Hispanic women, struggling for our liberation and the liberation of our people"—that is doing Hispanic women's liberation theology. ("The Task," 90–91)

Isasi-Díaz takes time to single out the gifts of women who possess certain skills and who lead their community in reflection. The first woman is comfortable in the area of EXEGESIS, social science, languages, ARCHAEOLOGY, or history. She will be the one to offer the ideas of her community to the theologians of her field in order to help them interpret reality from a *mujerista* perspective. She

is called the "theological technician." The second woman is in charge of making sure that the reflection of the community is gathered and recorded; she is called the "enabler." The third woman, who may or may not also be the enabler, gives a voice to her community by recording what the community is saying; she must accurately represent her fellow women and must be continuously accountable to them. She is called the "writer" (91–94). While affirming the importance of these individual roles, Isasi-Díaz emphasizes that the essence of *mujerista* theology is in communal reflection and action; no individual should be uplifted more than another. The community must experience all parts of life as a unit, for in community lies liberation, and in liberation lies salvation.

Praxis. This praxis that is called *mujerista* theology is used in the practical application of theological principles and SCRIPTURE in unique ways. One of the most written-about applications of praxis in *mujerista* theology is the *mujerista's* definition of God. God is seen as the God of the poor and oppressed, the God of life, and a relational God. In viewing God as the God of the poor and oppressed, *mujeristas* will not refer to God as *Dios todopoderoso,* "all-powerful God." While they do not deny that God is all-powerful, *mujeristas* simply do not consider that aspect of God's character to be important for them. Representing the voices of many Hispanic women, Isasi-Díaz questions, "If God is all-powerful, why am I oppressed, why do I not have enough money to send my children to school or to take my mother to the doctor?" ("Praxis," 47).

In an effort to reconcile their circumstances with their faith, *mujeristas* choose to focus on God as being all-merciful toward the poor and oppressed. God takes sides with the suffering (usually women and their children) and shows them mercy in big and small ways (Moody, 79). The notion of God as all-merciful is reflected in *mujerista* biblical exegesis also. God has mercy on those in need of liberation and often intervenes for them, sometimes using women to do it. Isasi-Díaz discusses the vital roles of Shiphrah and Puah in the exodus event. In Exod. 1:15–22, the midwives Shiphrah and Puah refuse to carry out the pharaoh's orders to kill the sons born to Hebrew women. "Without these women, the pharaoh might have been more successful in his attempt to check the Hebrew population. No liberation is possible without life; these women are indeed givers of life" ("*Mujerista* Theology's Method," 126–27). Shiphrah and Puah were vital to the exodus event in that they probably made it possible for Moses to survive as a baby and grow up to fulfill his role in God's intended liberation for the oppressed Hebrew people.

Parallel to the *mujerista* theological understanding of God as the God of the poor and oppressed is the understanding of God as the God of life. According to *mujeristas*, God cares first and foremost about our basic needs; God does not wish that anyone starve or perish due to a lack of basic food, water, shelter, and so forth. God is concerned with people's bodies, and a large part of God's concern, according to *mujeristas*, is for the physical and sexual abuse that Hispanic women suffer. Women need to become more aware of God's telling us that humans are both body and spirit. When either body or spirit suffers continuously, the other will bear the consequences (Isasi-Díaz, *Mujerista Theology*, 143). In bearing the burden of physical and sexual struggles, Hispanic women find help not in the Bible but from praying to God as their giver of life and also to Mary and the saints. "The Spirit of God and Mary are our only resources for resistance to poverty" (Moody, 79). *Mujeristas* believe that God accepts the fact that we can begin to focus on our spirituality only when all of our basic needs have been met.

Finally, *mujeristas* consider God to be a relational God: liberation occurs as humanity cries out to God and God hears. Together in relationship, God and humanity work toward liberation (79). Moody discusses how vital the story of Ruth is for *mujerista* theology. She says that the most important aspect of the STORY lies in the COVENANT between Ruth and Naomi because it provides a relational link between God and the two women. "These two women of differing cultural backgrounds make a commitment to each other to relate to one another just as God makes a relational commitment to humanity. The model [*mujerista*] offer is that Ruth and Naomi's relatedness in friendship across the boundary of difference *is* the embodiment of the covenanting God" (118). First, Ruth promises to accept Naomi's people as her people, altering the usual boundaries of familial and cultural allegiance. This has particular implications for the praxis of *mujerista* theology. Women should learn and understand each other's languages and cultures. Second, Ruth promises to hear the God of Naomi. This can be applied in women's efforts to read and hear each other's theologies about God; women need to engage in conversation. And third, the commitment of Ruth and Naomi is lifelong. Women should pledge their total selves to one another, their whole efforts. This effort should last until death (118).

Mujerista theology is one that includes feminist, liberationist, and Hispanic perspectives together in one active way of looking at life and Christianity. *Mujeristas* are deeply motivated by their desire for liberation from the numerous oppressive structures that are currently in place within their own and especially within American culture. They believe that solidarity is achieved through a sense of community and that communities achieve salvation through liberation. *Mujeristas* use everyday life, the Bible, Catholicism, and other religions as their sources for theology. Their theology is actively implemented by average Hispanic women who understand the importance of doing rather that just thinking or writing. Within their theological FRAMEWORK, *mujeristas* have interesting views and hermeneutical methods; their interpretations of the significance of the stories of Shiphrah and Puah and of Ruth and Naomi are particularly important for their theology. *Mujerista* theology is constantly in flux because the context of the women who do the theology is constantly changing. Perhaps out of this movement will come a more concrete method that speaks to the needs of Hispanic women while at the same time holding on to certain key constructs of Christianity. Even Isasi-Díaz states, "'This is the best I can do right now; this is the best way I can say it and do it right now.' I must pray that the next time around I will do it better, say it better. That is the spirit with which I write" (*Mujerista Theology*, 203).

Bibliography. Karen Baker-Fletcher, "An Irresistible Power Not Ourselves," *Encounter* 53 (Summer 1992): 270–89; Stacey M. Floyd-Thomas and Laura Gillman, "Facing the Medusa: Confronting the Ongoing Impossibility of Women's Studies," *Journal of International Women's Studies* 2 (May 2001): 35–52; Ada María Isasi-Díaz, *Mujerista Theology: A Theology for the Twenty-First Century* (Maryknoll, NY: Orbis Books, 1996); idem, "Mujerista Theology's Method: A Liberative Praxis, a Way of Life," in *Mestizo Christianity: Theology from the Latino Perspective* (ed. Arturo J. Bañuelas; Maryknoll, NY: Orbis Books, 1995), 123–28; idem, "Mujeristas: A Name of Our Own," in *Yearning to Breathe Free: Liberation Theologies in the U.S.* (ed. Mar Peter-Raoul et al.; Maryknoll, NY: Orbis Books, 1990), 44–55; idem, "Praxis: The Heart of Mujerista Theology," *Journal of Hispanic/Latino Theology* 1, no. 1 (November 1993): 44–55; idem, "The Task of Hispanic Women's Liberation Theology—*Mujeristas:* Who We Are and What We Are About," *Ministerial Formation* 62 (July 1993): 85–102; idem, "*Un poquito de justicia*—a Little Bit of Justice: A *Mujerista* Account of Justice," in *Hispanic/Latino Theology: Challenge and Promise* (ed. Ada María Isasi-Díaz and Fernando F. Segovia; Minneapolis: Augsburg Fortress, 1996), 326–40; Linda A. Moody, *Women Encounter God: Theology across the Boundaries of Difference* (Maryknoll, NY: Orbis Books, 1996).

MULTIVALENCE

A term current in LITERARY CRITICISM for the idea that TEXTS generate and legitimate multiple MEANINGS.

MURATORIAN CANON

A list of NT texts, traditionally dated to the late second or early third century CE but now thought by some scholars to be from the fourth century CE. It lists twenty-four texts: the four GOSPELS, Acts, thirteen LETTERS ascribed to Paul (excluding Hebrews), Jude, 1–2 John (but not 3 John), the Wisdom of Solomon, Revelation, and the *Apocalypse of Peter*. The Muratorian Canon demonstrates the fluidity of the NT CANON as late as the fourth century.

MUTUALITY

In FEMINIST CRITICISM, the conviction that women—indeed, all persons—should be viewed as both autonomous and rational beings. Each person stands as an individual, but because all are primarily rational, there exists a universal bond between persons, a bond that transcends roles.

MYSTERY RELIGIONS

A type of religion popular during the HELLENISTIC PERIOD. During this period, there was a loss of confidence in the established gods/goddesses, religions, and philosophies (*see* HELLENISM). Many people sought help to live meaningful lives within an impersonal world. The classical gods of Greece were impersonal and capricious, state religions were irrelevant to the immediate needs of the common person, and emperor worship was a political tool (Tenney, 117). The mystery religions functioned as one response to this loss of confidence.

The object of the mysteries was to secure salvation for people who were subject to moral and physical evil, dominated by destiny, and unable to free themselves from the corruption that beset the material side of nature (Barrett, 120). By participating in mystery rites and dramas of the cult, the adherents believed that they could share in the life of their deity. The mysteries allowed the worshipers to commune with their god or goddess and to enjoy a better life, confident of immortality. They offered emotional release for the participants through rituals, communal meals, pageantry, ecstatic ceremonies, festivals, and in some cases orgiastic rites (Bailey, 177).

Initiation usually involved purification of the initiate, the assembling of the initiates for a ceremonial procession, the procession of the initiates into the mystery's sacred precincts, and the encounter with the mystery's deity (61–62). Following the initiation, the initiate stood outside a fate-dominated world and was reborn into the cult's deity.

Purification was symbolized through animal sacrifice, application of water and/or blood, eating sacred meals, or a combination of these. Some of the mysteries included fasting; sacrifice; frenzied dancing; colorful processions; reenactments of the drama of their deity's wanderings, life, or entrance into immortality; orgiastic rites; and communal meals.

The deities of the mystery religions were originally fertility gods or goddesses of agriculture, and the rites that had initially secured crop and livestock productivity evolved into a personal religion. "In the myths of the mysteries, the deities are represented as wanderers whose journeys lead them from an existence of humanlike suffering to a transformed existence as celestial saviors" (Martin, 59). Some MYTHS were based on a wife (or mother) who grieves for her lost husband (or child), and after a period of suffering, the lost family member is restored to the seeker—usually from the dead—and begins a new life (Kee, 33). The STORY of the wanderings, sufferings, and homecoming of the god or goddess offered the possibility that one's own suffering and wandering might come to an end through a personal soteriological relationship under the deity's providential protection.

Although each mystery religion possessed its own rituals, SYMBOLISM, and INTERPRETATION of its rites, all of them shared several of the following characteristics:

> (1) a firm organization to which all members were subject; (2) membership through rites of initiation; (3) participation in regular meetings in which sacramental ceremonies were celebrated; (4) an obligation to observe moral and ascetic precepts; (5) the mutual support of all members; (6) obedience to the cult leader and the community of adherents; (7) the cultivation of secret traditions. (Koester, 198)

The mysteries became a primary institution in many hellenized cities prior to, during, and after the birth of Christianity.

When Paul and other NT writers penned their works, they employed many words, concepts, and categories current in the mysteries. Such concepts include divine instruction through dreams and visions, baptism, fasting, regeneration, rebirth, communion, heaven, hell, the conquest of evil, the savior-god as the mediator between deity and the individual, and the shedding of blood (many of these were also present in JUDAISM). In Rev. 12 is a REFERENCE to the woman and the dragon. Isis and Horus were also persecuted by a dragon named Typhon. The image in Rev. 12 depicts a woman attired in royal clothes, clothed with power, and giving birth to a child. Mithras was believed to have life-giving power: "You have rescued us, too, by shedding the blood that makes us immortal" (Rudolph, 236). The AUTHOR of Mark tells his readers that Jesus gave his blood for humanity's sins because he came "to give his life a ransom for many" (10:45). Mithras was the mediator between good and evil and also the representative of deity on earth. In his struggle with the bull, Mithras portrays the human struggle of those in pursuit of good; by slaying the bull for humanity's benefit, he brought life and victory over evil.

The mysteries also held that the initiate should strive for perfect unity and freedom from sensuality. Adherents were to show perfect loyalty to their god or goddess and companionship toward their comrades. They were to live a good life because they were giving the right service to the deity. The similarities between Mithraism and Christianity were so close that some of the early church fathers were amazed (Gilmore, 419). Yet, while some of the terminology and concepts were identical, the interpretations were often quite different. A case in point is the reinterpretation of the pivotal term in the mysteries: *mystery*. In the ordinary sense of the word, *mystery* refers to knowledge that is withheld. According to the author of Ephesians, a mystery is TRUTH revealed. In Eph. 1:9, there is a reference to the mystery, and in 3:6 it is defined. The mystery is that the Gentiles are also included in God's promises. Then the author goes on to say, "This grace was given to me . . . to make everyone see what is the plan of the mystery" (3:8–9). The mysteries sought to keep their rites secret from all but a select few. The writer of Ephesians took a term that was familiar to his audience and radically redefined it in order to declare the not-so-secret plan of God.

The writers of the NT could exercise no alternative but to express themselves in the ideological milieu of their times. To borrow terms and ideas from other religious, philosophical, or LITERARY traditions and then reapply, modify, or redefine them was probably the surest way that writers could make themselves both heard and understood. The reason for this is that such terms and concepts already carry with them a familiar range of meanings that the reader can then adjust when the terms and concepts are placed in a new CONTEXT.

Bibliography. Cyril Bailey, *Phases in the Religion of Ancient Rome* (Westport, CT: Greenwood, 1972); C. K. Barrett, *The New Testament Background: Selected Documents* (San Francisco: Harper & Row, 1987); George Gilmore, "Mithraism," in *The New Schaff-Herzog Encyclopedia of Religious Knowledge* (ed. Samuel M. Jackson; Grand Rapids: Baker, 1953), 7:419–23; Howard Clark Kee, *Understanding the New Testament* (4th ed.; Englewood Cliffs, NJ: Prentice Hall, 1983); Helmut Koester, *Introduction to the New Testament: History, Culture, and Religion in the Hellenistic Age* (New York: de Gruyter, 1982), vol. 1; Luther Martin, *Hellenistic Religions* (New York: Oxford University Press, 1987); Kurt Rudolph, "Mystery Religions," in *The Encyclopedia of Religions* (ed. Mircea Eliade; New York: Macmillan, 1987), 10:230–39; Merrill C. Tenney, *New Testament Times* (Grand Rapids: Eerdmans, 1975).

MYTH

In the traditional SENSE, a STORY that interprets natural events in terms of the supernatural, a nonliterary explanation of reality taken as TRUTH. According to Émile Durkheim, myth is a means by which a people legitimizes a secular IDEOLOGY by projecting social patterns onto the supernatural realm. Accordingly, each culture has its myths that share commonalities with the myths of other cultures in that they try to account for some of the deepest concerns of humans: creation, the MEANING of existence, divinity, death, and the SIGNIFICANCE of natural phenomena. It is no surprise, then, that in current studies, CRITICS see myths in two primary ways: (1) myths are the embodiments of a culture's deepest truths and concerns, and (2) myths serve artists as a means of giving FORM to their own personal perceptions. Artists either appropriate old myths, modify myths, or create their own. Myth plays a significant role in STRUCTURALISM.

MYTH CRITICISM

A criticism that examines the role and significance of the ARCHETYPE in a work of art. *See* ARCHETYPAL CRITICISM.

MYTHEME

A term introduced by Claude Lévi-Strauss in his structural theory of MYTH. Mytheme is a "set of items which share a single functional trait" (210). According to Lévi-Strauss, myths are based on fundamental BINARY OPPOSITIONS such as life/death, divine/human, and good/evil. However, the mythemes of a particular myth are culturally relative. In other words, while the surface details of a myth may be relative to the culture, the DEEP STRUCTURES of binary oppositions are transcultural. *See* ARCHETYPAL CRITICISM; STRUCTURALISM.

Bibliography. Claude Lévi-Strauss, *Structural Anthropology* (London: Basic Books, 1963).

NAB. *See* NEW AMERICAN BIBLE

NAG HAMMADI LIBRARY

A collection of thirteen textual fragments discovered in 1945 near the city of Nag Hammadi, Egypt. Although originally written in Greek, these TEXTS as we have them are composed of fifty-two treatises written in Coptic, an ancient Egyptian language. The text fragments date from the mid-fourth century CE, but the treatises themselves are from the second century CE. The texts include EPISTLES, GOSPELS, and APOCALYPSES used by gnostic (*see* GNOSTICISM) Christians from the second to fourth century CE. The Nag Hammadi texts were considered heretical by early orthodox Christianity. Although these texts improved the picture that scholars had of early Christian gnostics because these texts come out of gnostic communities, the picture is not complete. The reason for this incompleteness is that these texts do not set forth the gnostic system: a knowledge of the system seems to be taken for granted by the texts. Furthermore, the texts themselves are not entirely consistent in their worldview. Nonetheless, these texts do suggest that the Christian movement in the early centuries CE was anything but monolithic. For an accessible translation and commentary on the Nag Hammadi Library, see Robinson.

Bibliography. James M. Robinson, ed., *The Nag Hammadi Library in English* (4th rev. ed.; Leiden: Brill, 1996).

NARRATEE

The person to whom a NARRATOR addresses the DISCOURSE. This is not the same as the IMPLIED READER (the type of reader assumed by an AUTHOR) or the IDEAL READER (the type of reader who would understand everything the author/ narrator says and does). For example, the narratee of Luke-Acts is Theophilus.

NARRATIO

In ancient rhetoric, the facts presented in support of the thesis of a SPEECH. Because the NT EPISTLES for the most part are written discourses or SERMONS, scholars have found it possible to analyze the EPISTLES by REFERENCE to the basic pattern followed by these speeches. For an example of the *narratio*, see Gal. 1:11–2:14. The other elements of the pattern are EXORDIUM (introduction), *PROPOSITIO* (thesis or proposition), *PROBATIO* (argumentation), and *PERORATIO* (closing summary). *See* EPISTOLARY LITERATURE; RHETORICAL CRITICISM.

NARRATION

One of the four types of composition (the others being ARGUMENTATION, DESCRIPTION, and EXPOSITION). Narration presents the events of a STORY either chronologically or PLOT-structured, the AUTHOR arranging the events by design based on the effects the writer expects the NARRATIVE to have. For example, while the SYNOPTIC GOSPELS recount many of the same events, these events are not always presented in the same chronological order or in the same CONTEXT. Some of Matthew's material in the SERMON ON THE MOUNT is found in Luke's SERMON ON THE PLAIN, while some of it is found in a different context in Luke. When the Synoptics are compared with John's Gospel, we find that the cleansing of the temple scene in the Synoptics occurs toward the end of Jesus's ministry, but in John it happens toward the beginning of Jesus's ministry. In narration, authors select and arrange materials of the narrative on the basis of a predetermined plan or agenda. *See also* SELECTION AND ARRANGEMENT.

Narration may occur in four modes—direct narration, dramatic narration, DESCRIPTION, and COMMENTARY. In direct narration, the NARRATOR does nothing more than report events. According to Leland Ryken, biblical texts have just enough direct narration "to keep them moving." Direct narration serves "the function of lead-in and follow-up to the dramatized scenes" (44). Through commentary, narrators offer EXPLANATION, information, or BACKGROUND on the STORY. Commentary is so rare in biblical narratives that, according to Ryken, "when it appears, it tends to interpret only a specific detail in the story or only one aspect of the story's meaning" (44). Description, like commentary, is sparse in biblical narrative and can be found only in instances when a bit of information is necessary. This information, however, serves to move the reader to contemplate other matters relative to the story, especially CHARACTERIZATION. For example, we may know that David has a ruddy complexion, that Joseph was handsome, or what Esau wore, but beyond these elemental details, we are told little about the nature or appearances of characters. According the Ryken, therefore, dramatic narrative is the most prevalent mode of narration in biblical narratives. Dramatic narrative entails dramatizing "a scene as though it were in a play, quoting the speeches or dialogue of characters and noting the surrounding context" (43). Ryken goes on to suggest that the biblical writers' heavy dependence on dramatic narrative is "one of the best proofs that the Bible is a literary book" (45). This LITERARY impulse becomes clear when we consider that if the biblical writers had simply been interested in communicating information in propositional form, they would not have gone to the trouble to present their texts in dramatic mode, a mode that calls for readers to engage the texts in order not only to infer meaning but also to be engaged on an experiential level. In other words, the reader is expected to undergo an aesthetic experience.

Bibliography. William Harmon and C. Hugh Holman, *A Handbook to Literature* (8th ed.; Upper Saddle River, NJ:

Prentice Hall, 1999); Leland Ryken, *Words of Delight: A Literary Introduction to the Bible* (Grand Rapids: Baker, 1987).

NARRATIVE

A sequence of narrated events. *See* NARRATION; NARRATIVE CRITICISM.

NARRATIVE CRITICISM

A method of studying narratives, emphasizing not only traditional NARRATIVE elements such as PLOT, SETTING, and CHARACTERIZATION but also the role of the reader. Like READER-RESPONSE CRITICISM, narrative criticism assumes that the STORY does not exist autonomously within the TEXT but comes into being through the interaction between the text and the reader. Employing the concept of SIGN, narrative critics accept the narrative itself as the signifier, and the story, produced through the interaction between the narrative and reader, as the signified. The whole of narrative criticism may be seen as an analysis of the narrative CONTENT, with the CONTEXT of relationships between AUTHORs, texts, and readers.

In narrative criticism, the REAL WORLD is the actual world in which the author lived when the text was written. The real world refers to the author's world, with its patterns of behavior, social institutions, and ideological, economic, religious, and ethical structures. The STORY WORLD is the world found only in the text. Framed by the beginning and ending of the text, it is a creation of the author, who selects and arranges (*see* SELECTION AND ARRANGEMENT) events in a complex STRUCTURE. The arrangement of events and the characterization of individuals within the story do not correlate exactly with the historical CHRONOLOGY or with the real-world PERSONA. Events, characters, and places in the story world acquire their MEANING and SIGNIFICANCE from the world created by the author. For example, in the Gospel of Matthew, Jesus is defined and given significance only within the world of Matthew's text. The meaning of what Jesus says and does in Matthew must be ascertained from the story world of Matthew, not by recourse to the author's real world. The story world is not a mirror of the real world, with the author as the quicksilver behind the glass. Through artistic forms and strategies, the story world assumes its own reality, a reality that is capable of communicating its own TRUTH.

The real author is the flesh-and-blood person who at some point in history crafted the narrative text. The REAL READER is likewise some flesh-and-blood person who in time and space reads the text. Each of these persons exists apart from the text; the real author and real reader are not dependent on the text for existence.

Narrative critics have introduced the idea that there exists a LITERARY entity who is found only with the text. This entity is not the same as the real author but is only a partial and incomplete reflection of the real author. For example, when I read the Gospel of Mark, the only author I encounter is the one whom I may be able to construct from the text alone. Even more revealing is the reading of several Pauline EPISTLES. When I read 1 Corinthians, I encounter one entity; when I read Galatians, another one. These two IMPLIED AUTHORS are not the same because the texts yield different information about the implied authors. The text of Mark does not present the real flesh-and-blood Mark, nor does Galatians present the real-world Paul. When Paul authored 1 Corinthians, he donned one hat, but he wore yet a different one when authoring Galatians. Accordingly, it is possible for a real-world person to author several texts, each one having a different implied author. In a sense, the implied author is a composite of discernible ideologies (*see* IDEOLOGY) underlying a particular text.

The IMPLIED READER, like the implied author, is an entity defined by the text. The implied author may consciously or unconsciously construct the text in such a manner as to provide guidance to a reader. This means that a text contains unspoken ASSUMPTIONs about the reader. It is obvious that neither the implied author nor, for that matter, the real author of Mark's Gospel had a twentieth-century reader in mind while writing. Even though the text provides directives (*see* READER-RESPONSE CRITICISM) for the reader by giving definition to

the implied reader, the implied reader is not entirely defined by the text. The implied author may assume, on the part of the implied reader, a set of values, LITERARY COMPETENCE, and BACKGROUND. But there is no way to ensure that every reader will satisfy this assumption. Both the text and the reader are characterized by INDETERMINACY. On the one hand, even if we assume that the role of the implied reader may be completely defined, no single reader can perfectly and completely conform to the role the text provides for the implied reader. A reader may approach the text perfectly, intending to conform to the role of the implied reader by consciously or unconsciously accepting the ideology of the implied author inherent within the text, but there is no objective way to measure such conformity. On the other hand, to the degree that the reader fulfills the role of the implied reader provided for by the text, the reader becomes captive to the text and its ideology. The result is a new orientation for the reader, a reorientation that in turn produces a new person. The opposite of this may also occur. A reader may discover that the role demanded of the implied reader may be so foreign or ideologically unpleasing that the reader simply refuses to read, refuses to become the implied reader.

All narratives are told through the voice of a NARRATOR. For the narrative critic, therefore, the person and activity of the narrator occupy a place of special importance in the determination of meaning. A narrative may be told in the first or third person, and the narrator may be outside the ACTION or may be a character within the story. Further, a narrator may vary in degree of knowledge, from very limited knowledge to virtual omniscience.

The narrator should not be mistakenly identified with the implied author. The narrator is a fictive creation of the implied author and is dependent on the implied author for any characteristics and abilities that may be discernible from the text. The view of the narrator may or may not reflect the ideology of the implied author. This is true both of the third-person omniscient narrator and of the narrator who is also a character within the story.

The counterpart of the narrator is the NARRA-TEE. The narratee is the entity to whom the narrator tells the story and is distinct from the implied reader in a dramatic way. The narratee, on the one hand, receives the story as it unfolds moment by moment. The implied reader, on the other hand, reads what the narrator tells the narratee. The implied reader is an entity with a set of values and is able aesthetically to complete the work. The implied reader is implied by the text but is not totally defined by it. The narratee, however, is defined by the work. Like the narrator, the narratee may be a character within the story, but is usually a person who has no place within the story. The identity of the narratee will to a large degree determine the STYLE and complexity of the narrator's language. If the narratee is uninformed about the subject matter, the narrator may become very detailed, offering extensive EXPLANATION. For example, one narratee may have only limited competency in the subject matter of the narrative, while another one might be well versed in the subject.

The narrative critic does not identify the NAR-RATIVE WORLD with the real world. The real worlds of both author and reader alike are infinite, but observable and present, with all events apparently working together in an immediate system of inter-connectedness. The real world exists in time and space. The narrative world is limited, bounded. The only access to this narrative world is through the secondary medium of the text. The objects, persons, and events in the narrative may not correspond to anything in the real world. Narrative criticism rejects any necessary one-to-one correspondence between the real and narrative worlds. In order for the implied reader to reconstruct the narrative world, determinations as to relative importance of events must be made. The implied author highlights some events, subordinates others, and leaves gaps while moving from one narrative segment to another. The responsibility of bridging these gaps of INDETERMINACY belongs to the implied reader. The implied reader is expected to make inferences and judgments based on the author's narrative techniques.

According to the narrative critic, meaning is in the narrative world, not in the real world. The meaning of Mark's Gospel is not to be found in considering Mark an objective, historically accurate portrayal of the life and times of Jesus. What any character says or does in the narrative must find its significance within the world of the narrative, not within the real world in which the character purportedly lived. Even if we assume that Mark has achieved complete accuracy in relating events in Jesus's life, it certainly has not related all of the events. The implied author has shaped the story world by selecting some events and excluding others. This process of selectivity immediately excludes the possibility of the narrative world being a complete replica of the real one. All meaning therefore must be found in the narrative world, which is a construct of the text. Meaning must be a function of the relationships, experiences, and connections that the implied reader is called upon to create. Everything within the narrative world comes together to create the context and meaning.

Bibliography. W. Randolph Tate, *Biblical Interpretation: An Integrated Approach* (rev. ed.; Peabody, MA: Hendrickson, 1997).

NARRATIVE GAPS. *See* INDETERMINACY

NARRATIVE HERMENEUTICS

An interpretive program outlined by Walhout ("Narrative Hermeneutics") in conversation with the works of Nicholas Wolterstorff, Paul Ricoeur, Anthony Thiselton, Alvin Plantinga, Jürgen Moltmann, and Helmut Thielicke, among others. Walhout redefines the Aristotelian term *mimēsis* and places it within a FRAMEWORK of TEXT as object and instrument. Within this larger framework, he then discusses five levels of action an AUTHOR takes in constructing a fictional text; he argues that these actions are to be guides for a HERMENEU-TICS of fiction or narrative hermeneutics. Finally, Walhout suggests that narrative hermeneutics is incomplete without a consideration of the ethical dimension of INTERPRETATION.

First, Walhout points out that authors produce texts and readers read them within specific historical CONTEXTS. Consequently, hermeneutics should be concerned with the text as an ACTION taken by an author in historical time, just as all actions are. For this reason, readers need to consider things outside the text as well as things in it. So it seems that an integral part of narrative hermeneutics involves social and historical concerns not only about the world of the author but also about the world of the reader. Although the text does not change, the reader of the text does over time. Therefore, MEANING and hermeneutics are never finished.

Second, for Walhout, narrative hermeneutics involves a reconsideration of *mimēsis* not in the sense of a fictional text as a carbon copy of the actual world but in the sense that fiction serves as a means by which readers explore alternative possibilities relative to the actual world. In other words, fictional worlds are interpretations of the actual world. They "offer new ways of seeing and thinking about the world" (82). They assist readers in understanding their actual worlds because readers are able to compare the fictional world with the actual one. Such a definition of *mimēsis* does not require anything in the text to be real or true. Whether the characters in the fictional world are good or evil, noble or ignoble, readers still are asked to make comparisons with what they know of their actual world. Fiction, then, confronts readers with ways of looking at the world that they have perhaps not considered before. In this sense, says Walhout, fiction is itself heuristic and hermeneutical; otherwise it would hold no interest for readers.

Third, narrative hermeneutics views a text as both object and instrument. It is an object produced by an author and an object of analysis by readers. This idea of text as object is less important for Walhout than the text as instrument. Walhout argues that authors produce texts for reasons: the most important reason is what he refers to as authorial stance. Authorial stance is limited to the purpose(s) an author has in mind relative to readers and what the author claims about some aspect of the actual world. In fiction, these claims are generally implicit rather than explicit. It is part of the nature of fiction. So an author produces a text as an instrument to say something to readers about the actual world. Both the narrative strategies of the text and extratextual elements assist readers in finding the author's stance. This idea of stance as the claim that an author suggests to readers about the actual world is evidenced by the existence of different texts that tell the same story. For example, Sophocles's *Oedipus* is based on the same story as the *Oedipus* of Seneca. However, each author selects and arranges the events of the story in a different way. Why? Because each has a different stance, a different claim to make about the actual world. The same may be said of the SYNOPTIC GOSPELS. Each text is a STORY about the life, ministry, death, and resurrection of Jesus, containing similar and identical events. These events, however, are arranged (*see* SELECTION AND ARRANGEMENT) differently and with varying details, suggesting that really the authors are not telling the same story: they each have a particular authorial stance that makes a claim about the actual world.

Fourth, the task of getting at the authorial stance is described in five levels of actions that authors take in producing texts, actions that must then be mimicked by the reader. The following is a summary given by Walhout (89–90): (1) Through the deployment of language, the author forms a text. At this level we analyze the formal features of a text. (2) Through the descriptive references of the language, the author projects an imagined world. At this level we aim accurately to survey the details, structure, and scope of the fictional world. (3) Through the use of narrative strategies, the author establishes a point of view. At this level we compare the fictional world with the actual world, considering how the author interprets the actual world. (4) Through its anchorage in the actual world, the fictional world acquires a mimetic function. At this level we compare the fictional world with the actual world, inescapably employing the models we use in our understanding of the actual world. (5) Through its linguistic form, its projected world, its point of view, and its mimetic function, the text presents us with a model or paradigmatic way of viewing the world or some aspect of it. At this level we analyze the author's perspective on the events given in the text.

Last, for Walhout, narrative hermeneutics involves ethical concerns. Here Walhout introduces the concepts of teleology, ESCHATOLOGY, and utopia. In other words, readers interpret fictional texts not simply to acquire knowledge but to learn how they may live better lives in the actual world. Past texts are read in the present in order to better understand or make a better future. Thus narrative hermeneutics has a concern about the manner in which fiction imposes ethical reflection on readers. This reflection occurs on two levels: reflection on the NARRATIVE itself and reflection on the way authors and readers use texts. On the first level, readers are interested in the way characters face and react to conflict because it is an important part of human experience. According to Walhout, the identity of a character in narrative is not self-made but constructed in that figure's relations with others in the story. A character is strong or weak depending on the extent to which that figure is "immersed in the identities of others in a specific cultural situation" (123). Hence, one of the major draws of fiction is the resolution of conflict within and between characters. These situations in fiction provide the stuff for reflection on readers' situations and character. The second level of ethical concern recognizes that readers' interpretations of narratives are heavily influenced by their own ethical systems. In other words, readers analyze narratives in the light of their own systems: ethical, interpretive, theological, political, and so forth. Fiction affords all readers the opportunity to examine the implications of their own actions and beliefs.

Bibliography. Clarence Walhout, "Narrative Hermeneutics," in *The Promise of Hermeneutics* (ed. Roger Lundin et al.; Grand Rapids: Eerdmans, 1999), 65–132.

NARRATIVE POEM

A poem that presents occurrences or events in succession. Although most biblical poems are a mixture of STRUCTURES, an example of a predominately narrative poem is Ps. 73, in which the narrator recounts a series of doubts, which finally culminates in an acceptable resolution.

NARRATIVE TIME

In NARRATOLOGY, the time that unfolds within the events in a NARRATIVE. Put another way, narrative time is the time as it is employed within the narrative. As such, it is a function of PLOT. According to narratologists such as Seymour Chatman and Gérard Genette, a narrative consists of a RÉCIT, or telling of plot (the events presented in a particular ORDER and time), and a *HISTORIE* (the events as they would have actually happened in real sequential time). The former is narrative time. *See* NARRATOLOGY.

Bibliography. Seymour Chatman, *Story and Discourse: Narrative Structure in Fiction and Film* (Ithaca, NY: Cornell University Press, 1978); Gérard Genette, *Narrative Discourse: An Essay in Method* (trans. Jane E. Lewin; Ithaca, NY: Cornell University Press, 1980).

NARRATIVE VOICE

The person in which a STORY is narrated, first person or third person. *See* NARRATOR.

NARRATIVE WORLD

In NARRATIVE CRITICISM and NARRATOLOGY, the world found only in the TEXT, as opposed to the actual world in which the AUTHOR lives when writing a text. Framed by the beginning and ending of the text, it is a creation of an author who selects and arranges (*see* SELECTION AND ARRANGEMENT) events in a complex STRUCTURE. The arrangements of events and the CHARACTERIZATION of individuals within the story do not correlate exactly with historical CHRONOLOGY or with the real-world PERSONA. Events, characters, and places in the narrative world acquire their MEANING and SIGNIFICANCE from the world created by the author. For example, in the GOSPEL of Matthew, Jesus is defined and given significance only within the world of Matthew's text. The meaning of what Jesus says or does in Matthew must be ascertained from the narrative world of Matthew, not by recourse to the author's real world. The narrative world is not a mirror of the real world because, through artistic forms and strategies, the STORY WORLD assumes its own reality, a reality that is capable of communicating its own message.

NARRATOLOGY

The study or theory of NARRATIVE. Theories of narrative vary in terms of emphasis, but all assume that all narratives operate on a system of structures. STRUCTURALISM offers one theory, based especially on the MYTH theory of Claude Lévi-Strauss and his claim that underpinning all myths is a universal STRUCTURE.

A. J. Greimas, among others, has applied structuralist analysis beyond myth to narrative in general to delineate a universal grammar under the surface of all narratives. According to Greimas, every story involves up to six roles, which he refers to as ACTANTS. These actants are related along three different axes. A sender sends an object to a receiver, the object is carried to the receiver by the SUBJECT, and finally the subject may receive assistance from helpers and be frustrated by opponents. Every narrative can be examined as a series of sequences based on this actantial model.

Gérard Genette has also offered a detailed theory of narrative in *Narrative Discourse*. For Genette, there are three main elements in narrative: RÉCIT, the actual order of events as they are presented in the text (the PLOT); HISTORIE, the sequence in which those events actually occurred as ascertained from the TEXT (the STORY); and NARRATION, the actual act of narrating. Genette also treats in detail the relationship between NARRATOR, NARRATIVE VOICE, NARRATEE, and POINT OF VIEW. Thus Genette's analysis of narrative is based on the interaction of all the component parts on different levels, assuming that each component is dependent on all the others.

In BIBLICAL STUDIES, Robert Alter, Hans Frei, and Meir Sternberg are but three among many who offer ways of reading HEBREW NARRATIVES. Whether in terms of plot, CHARACTERIZATION, or other categories, they all assume that Hebrew narrative is structured DISCOURSE. The same may be said of NT scholars such as Frank Kermode; Stanley Kort; and David Rhoads and Donald Michie. For example, Kort analyzes the Gospel of Mark according to the narrative elements of character, plot, TONE, and ATMOSPHERE.

For detailed study of narratology, see Wallace Martin; Gerald Prince. *See also* NARRATIVE CRITICISM.

Bibliography. Robert Alter, *The Art of Biblical Narrative* (New York: Basic Books, 1981); Hans Frei, *The Eclipse of Biblical Narrative* (New Haven: Yale University Press, 1974); Gérard Genette, *Narrative Discourse: An Essay in Method* (Ithaca, NY: Cornell University Press, 1980); A. J. Greimas, "The Cognitive Dimension of Narrative Discourse," trans. Michael Rengstorf, *New Literary History* 7 (1976): 433–47; idem, "Narrative Grammar: Units and Levels," trans. Phillip Bodrock, *Modern Language Notes* 86 (1971): 793–807; Frank Kermode, *The Genesis of Secrecy: On the Interpretation of Narrative* (Cambridge, MA: Harvard University Press, 1979); Stanley Kort, *Story, Text, and Scripture: Literary Interests in Biblical Narrative* (University Park: Pennsylvania State University Press, 1988); Wallace Martin, *Recent Theories of Narrative* (Ithaca, NY: Cornell University Press, 1986); Gerald Prince, *A Grammar of Stories* (The Hague: Mouton, 1973); David Rhoads and Donald Michie, *Mark as Story* (Philadelphia: Fortress, 1982); Meir Sternberg, *The Poetics of Biblical Narrative: Ideological Literature and the Drama of Reading* (Bloomington: Indiana University Press, 1985).

NARRATOR

In literature, the person who tells the story. Although the narrator often seems to be the AUTHOR speaking directly, usually the narrator is actually the mask assumed by the author: the mask is the PERSONA with characteristics that separate that figure from the author. The narrator may be defined in terms of the POINT OF VIEW in the STORY. In this respect, the narrator may be first person or third person. The first-person narrator establishes a clearly defined relationship to the events in the story and may be intimately involved with the ACTION or only a minor participant. The third-person limited narrator may present the story from the point of view of a particular character, while the third-person omniscient narrator tells the story as if all the activities and thoughts of all characters are completely known to the narrator. A third type is the dramatic or objective narrator, through whom the events of the story are reported with no REFERENCE to the thoughts of any of the characters. For the most part, HEBREW NARRATIVE employs the third-person omniscient narrator, but it may use the first-person narrator, as in Nehemiah, and the dramatic and first-person, as in Ezra.

NARRATOR, OMNISCIENT. *See* NARRATOR

NARRATOR, UNINTRUSIVE. *See* UNINTRUSIVE NARRATOR

NARRATOR, UNRELIABLE. *See* UNRELIABLE NARRATOR

NASB. *See* NEW AMERICAN STANDARD BIBLE

NATIVITY HYMNS

The Magnificat in Luke 1:46–55 and the BENEDICTUS in Luke 1:68–79. The form of the Magnificat reflects a PSALM of praise in the HEBREW BIBLE and recalls the song of Hannah in 1 Sam. 2:1–10. Its CONTENT is a listing of God's dealings with Mary and Israel. The Benedictus also contains praise to God for fulfilling his promises to Israel, along with an address to the infant John the Baptist.

NATIVITY STORY

Accounts of events (esp. supernatural ones) surrounding the birth of Jesus, particularly those found in the early chapters of Matthew and Luke. Their primary purpose in each GOSPEL is to show that the prophecies of the messiah are fulfilled in Jesus.

Bibliography. Leland Ryken, *Words of Life: A Literary Introduction to the New Testament* (Grand Rapids: Baker, 1987).

NATURAL LANGUAGE

The everyday language spoken by a person or group and governed by grammatical, syntactical, and lexical CODES. The natural languages of the BIBLE are Hebrew, Greek, and Aramaic. *See* LITERARY LANGUAGE.

NEB. *See* NEW ENGLISH BIBLE

NEBI'IM. *See* PROPHETS, THE

NEOORTHODOXY. *See* BIBLICAL CRITICISM

NEUTRALITY

Generally, objectivity, impartiality, having no bias. This term is challenged especially in FEMINIST CRITICISM as characteristic of traditional academic scholarship. According to feminist critics, traditional historical-critical scholarship is inescapably bound in ANDROCENTRISM: it assumes that the experience of men is human experience, and consequently, the intellectual DISCOURSE and CRITICAL METHODOLOGY are all based on male perspectives and goals. Within structures of oppression and exploitation, neutrality is not possible.

The ASSUMPTION that readers (critical or otherwise) of TEXTS or any artifact can posture themselves within an objective FRAMEWORK of neutrality from which to interpret is rejected out of hand by POSTMODERN scholars. These scholars argue that readers of all stripes stand squarely within a matrix, an interlocking system of systems, that exercises a determining influence on INTERPRETATION. All interpretations tend to be institutional: they are grounded in systems (linguistic, religious, philosophical), and interpreters cannot escape this fact of grounding. Readers are never able to assume some system-free position that enables them to examine a text from a purely objective vantage point. Any reading that counts as competent is always the product of interpretive conventions defined by a group, usually an institution. It may be possible for interpreters to be ignorant of their own interpretive biases, failing to recognize that all interpretations and criticisms take place within and are governed by the institutional CONTEXT that sets the AGENDA for participation in the first place. This is another way of putting Heidegger's and Gadamer's HERMENEUTICAL CIRCLE, which claims that acts of understanding and interpretation take place within the context of interpretive horizons that dictate what constitutes acceptable or unacceptable responses. In other words, an interpretation is judged to be acceptable if it conforms to the relevant criteria that define the institution's orthodoxy. Simply put, the rejection of neutrality brings with it the assumption that language, DISCOURSE, and interpretation create what they claim only to represent.

Bibliography. W. Randolph Tate, *Reading Mark from the Outside: Eco and Iser Leave Their Marks* (San Francisco: Christian Universities Press, 1995).

NEVI'IM. *See* PROPHETS, THE

NEW AMERICAN BIBLE (NAB, NABRE)

A 1970 Catholic TRANSLATION of the BIBLE by the Catholic Biblical Association of America. Its translators followed the DYNAMIC EQUIVALENCE policy, but the revision of the NT in 1986 was based on a verbal approach in which both vocabulary and STRUCTURE followed the Greek. The NAB translators adopted GENDER-INCLUSIVE LANGUAGE. Then in 2011 a revised OT was published with this 1986 NT to make the New American Bible, Revised Edition (NABRE).

NEW AMERICAN STANDARD BIBLE (NASB)

A 1971 TRANSLATION intended to replace and update the AMERICAN STANDARD VERSION (ASV, 1901). The newer modern translation was sponsored by a California corporation, the Lockman Foundation. The translators worked under the rubric of VERBAL EQUIVALENCE, intending to follow the original languages in MEANING and word order. This translation generally replicates the tenses and meanings of the verbs of the original languages and opts for traditional readings even where textual evidence suggests the case should be otherwise. For example, it glosses over the problem of the ending of Mark's Gospel by placing the shorter ending (v. 20b NASB; in NRSV, between 16:8 and 9)—which does not appear in any other English version without alerts in brackets or margin—after

the longer ending (16:9–20) and denotes just the shorter ending as an addition. This suggests that the shorter ending is the only possible addition in the light of overwhelming evidence that the longer ending is *also* an addition not found in the older and more reliable manuscripts. Nevertheless, because of its word-for-word translation, the NASB has become a good study BIBLE.

The NASB was updated in 1995 with the more archaic words such as "thee" and "thou" replaced with their current equivalents. Although the updated VERSION generally retains the original word order, the translators removed some of the IDIOMS in the original languages that were confusing in a word-for-word translation into English. The translators also used modern equivalents for some words and rearranged some of the more confusing sentences.

Bibliography. Steven M. Sheeley and Robert N. Nash Jr., *The Bible in English Translation: An Essential Guide* (Nashville: Abingdon, 1997).

NEW COVENANT

Generally, a term used by the early Christians for their belief that Jesus at the Last Supper had established a new relationship with them with respect to their association with God. The term, however, has many meanings—for example, the effects that Jesus's death has on believers (Heb. 8:8–13; 10:16–17), the NT, and an expected renewal of the original COVENANT (Jer. 31:31–34). Stephen Harris points out that "the adjective *new*, not present in the earliest manuscripts [of Matt. 26:28 and Mark 14:24], was added later to emphasize the change in God's relationship with humankind. (Most modern English translations, including the NRSV, the NJB, and the REB omit the interpolated 'new' and use 'covenant' instead of 'testament')" (9). Yet the term "new covenant" does appear in two other accounts of the Last Supper (Luke 22:20; 1 Cor. 11:25).

Bibliography. Stephen Harris, *The New Testament: A Student's Introduction* (4th ed.; Boston: McGraw-Hill, 2002).

NEW CRITICISM

Sometimes called formal criticism (it developed out of formalism), a LITERARY CRITICISM that focuses on the relationship between a text's FORM and CONTENT.

Called New Criticism to distinguish it from historical and biographical kinds of writing that had dominated earlier literary studies, it became prominent in the late 1920s, flourished in the United States in the 1940s–60s, and dominated literary studies until the early 1970s. Even today many consider it the best and most reliable way to introduce students to the critical study of literature.

The name itself was not intentional but was adopted after the publication of John Crowe Ransom's *New Criticism* in 1941. "New Criticism" is a term descriptive of an amalgamation of LITER-ARY theories that, although ranging in detail and emphasis, share affinities that are still influential and significant for the study of literature today. However, it had its origins in the works of I. A. Richards and T. S. Eliot in England. The attractiveness of the approach is perhaps found in the fact that it is an INTRINSIC rather than an EXTRINSIC ANALYSIS. It immediately engages the student with the TEXT rather than with the historical, biographical, or psychoanalytic dimensions of the text and/or AUTHOR. In other words, New Criticism places the interpretive emphasis on the literary work as an independent, self-contained creation, to be studied in itself and not as part of a larger CONTEXT. It is sometimes referred to as FORMALISM due to its focus on the form of the work: the relationships between the various parts, such as PLOT, CHAR-ACTERIZATION, RHYME, POINT OF VIEW, IRONY, CONTRAST, and METAPHOR.

The New Critics' approach to interpreting a literary text proceeded from the ASSUMPTION that literature must be studied as literature. All extrinsic categories of evaluation, such as biographical, historical, and psychological, were incapable of providing access to a literary text because literature was regarded as an autonomous mode of expression, generating a TYPE of experience independent of other types of experience. This means that literary works are accessible only through literary means. Literature or the experience of literature

should not be judged by its mimetic correspondence to the world outside literature (*see* MIMETIC CRITICISM). The New Critics favored the concept of COHERENCE, which meant that a literary work should be judged and interpreted on the basis of its unity of parts, which formed a coherent whole. Based on this principle of coherence, the New Critics tried to link as inseparable the work's content and the literary and rhetorical devices through which the work produced MEANING. Simply put, although they may have gone about it with varying emphases, the New Critics considered it a primary task of CRITICISM to interpret literary works in their own right, without putting them in some contexts beyond that of literature (e.g., the author's biography, the historical setting, or the author's psychological makeup).

Beginnings: Richards. The work of Richards that gave birth to the New Criticism was *Principles of Literary Criticism*, published in 1925. This work, combined with his *Practical Criticism* and *The Meaning of Meaning* (coauthored by C. K. Ogden), constitutes Richards's theory of literature and literary criticism. In the latter work, Richards and Ogden argue for two distinct functions of language: referential and emotive. Language is referential when one uses words to refer to some aspect of objective reality, concrete or abstract. Scientific language is a good example of the referential function of language (*see* REFERENTIAL LANGUAGE). Language is used emotively when it functions to evoke feelings or attitudes solely through the associative properties of words. The purest example of the emotive function of language (*see* EMOTIVE LANGUAGE) is poetry. Poetic language is not directed toward any objective reality but rather functions to arouse feelings and attitudes. While other experiences may evoke feelings and attitudes, poetic experience arouses feelings and attitudes that are more intense, complex, and organized. (The New Critics often referred to literature as poetry, and thus their terminology of *poem* and *poetry* is frequently used in this article in order to retain the language of these critics. The terms *poem* and *poetry* need to be understood as defining literature more generally than *poem* or *poetry* does in common discourse.)

The primary purpose of literature is to communicate. According to Richards, however, an author who is overly conscious of this purpose will ultimately fail to communicate, because much that goes to produce a poem is unconscious (*Principles*, 29). An individual is a conglomeration of desires and impulses. These desires and impulses often conflict with each other. Some desires are disparate and even completely incompatible. Life, then, is spent in the attempt to conduct experiences in such a way that the greatest number of these desires and impulses are satisfied with the minimum amount of conflict. Such satisfaction demands an organization that is the "least wasteful of human possibilities." For Richards, the basis of morality for any society is attaining maximum satisfaction of conflicting desires through a coherent systematization. At this point Richards combines two observations: most of our desires and impulses are unconscious, and literature and the arts constitute the most successful means of reconciling conflicting desires, thereby producing the greatest satisfaction.

The artist is a person who is capable, at the moment of literary creation, of organizing a range of impulses and experiences into an ordered and coherent whole. These experiences, or at least such organized and coherent experiences, are rarely obtainable outside art. Richards posed a key question: Are these experiences of the artist reproducible in readers of literature? He responds that the creative moment of the artist can be reproduced in the reader through the medium of the text. This is possible because of the work's COHERENCE, its unified organization. If the poem is read in the right way, readers should expect to enjoy the same complex and coherent experience that was the author's at the moment of its creation. This suggests that the complexity and coherence of the creative moment is somehow reflected or captured in the text itself. Although Richards did not claim that the poem was the text, but rather the communicable experience, he did recognize that the text itself must

control the reader's experience in order to vitiate the possibility of different reader experiences. In this context, form becomes the primary means of producing uniform responses (*Principles*, 32).

Since the poem actually comes into being in the experience of reading, and a correct reading is (though extremely difficult) possible, criticism must concern itself with experiencing the work of literature through correct reading. The articulation of some suggestions for avoiding certain pitfalls that result in a bad reading was Richard's burden in *Practical Criticism*. In this work, Richards records the responses of several students to a number of poems. After giving the responses (which he calls "protocols"), he proceeds to describe what he views as deficiencies among the protocol writers. Accordingly, Richards feels they were in large measure avoidable mistakes due to inferior training (309). In writing, the total meaning is a combination of four types of meaning. Actually these types correspond to the tasks that language (esp. poetic language) performs simultaneously (180–234). These four tasks or functions are SENSE, feeling, TONE, and INTENTION. Sense is what the author actually says. Feeling refers to the author's attitude toward the things being said. Authors have feelings that color the way they say things. Tone describes the author's attitude toward the readers. Audience dictates the choice and arrangement of words. Richards believes that the author's attitude toward readers is reflected in the tone of the words in the text. Intention is the effect that the author seeks consciously or unconsciously to communicate. Purpose, says Richards, modifies and shapes SPEECH. Yet the type of text an author writes governs to a great extent the four functions. MISREADING can occur when one or more of the functions are overlooked or misrepresented. The solution to bad reading is good training and close attention to the text.

Richards's concern for the complexity and coherence of the artist's experience and the possibility of that experience being reproduced in the reader by careful reading is the immediate source for the two great pillars of New Criticism—complexity and coherence (or unity in variety)—and for the New Critics' preoccupation with such close scrutiny of texts apart from the author.

Expansion: Eliot. Whereas Richards was preoccupied with the effect that the text produced in the reader, T. S. Eliot, rejecting the notion that a poem is nothing more than a means of communicating the poet's experience to a reader, claimed that a literary text is the OBJECTIVE CORRELATIVE of feelings (*Sacred Wood*, 100). A literary text objectifies feelings indirectly by correlating them with things textually. If Eliot ever developed a formal literary theory, he never articulated it. This is probably due to the fact that his views were always in a state of development and therefore never constituted an organized whole. Nonetheless, his scattered observations that focused on the nature of the poetic text gave rise to two of the New Critics' tautologies: TEXTUAL AUTONOMY and TEXTUAL UNITY.

For Eliot, the text assumes a life all its own apart from author and reader. The meaning of a text transcends the conscious purpose of the author and its origins because an author may very well be dealing with areas of consciousness that are beyond verbal EXPLANATION. Consequently, a text may have meaning that the author never intended (*On Poetry*, 23). For Eliot, rather than being an expression of the author's personality, a literary text is an "escape from authorial personality" (*Selected Essays*, 10). In fact, Eliot thought that authors' statements about what they thought they were doing when writing should not be taken at face value. If authors are inspired, they may not wholly comprehend what they write, and they may even misinterpret it once the inspiration has left them (137). It is not necessary that a writer know what the text may come to mean when it leaves the writer's hands. This dimension of art simply escapes scientific research and explanation.

Obviously, a poet is the SUBJECT of a poetic experience that becomes translated into a poetic text. Yet the experience is not the text; therefore, the reading of the text becomes different, a new experience, even for the author. According to Eliot, a poet may give an honest account of his or her

own writing. It is the poet who has had the poetic experience, who is familiar with the circumstances and process of composition, and who knows what meaning one was trying to communicate. All of this information may be helpful to the reader of the text. Yet the meaning of the text is just as much what it means to the reader as what it means to the author. The author in time becomes just another reader of the text (*Use of Poetry*, 129–30). There is simply no way to guarantee that the poetic experience is successfully translated into the verbal SYMBOLS of the text. Through this TRANSLATION, the experience may not be recognizable even to the author. Furthermore, the poetic experience may be so complex a fusion of feelings that the poet may not be fully aware of what is being communicated. The conclusion of such observations therefore is that any attempt to analyze or explain a literary text by recourse to psychological or biographical research is for the most part useless and only results in distracting attention from the primary concern of interpretation: the text.

Not only is the literary text not a source for constructing the biography of the author; it also is neither a copy nor even necessarily a reflection of the author's world. The text constitutes its own reality, its own world apart from that of the author. According to Eliot, readers must make a distinction between what an author believes as an author and what the author believes as a person. This is true due to the fact that an author's private life becomes something different when it becomes poetry. At this point Eliot is quite close to the Russian formalists (*see* FORMALISM) with their definition of the author's real-life experiences or ideas as material on which LITERARY DEVICES work in order to transform them. On the one hand, the actual life of the author will serve as material; on the other hand, the author will abstract from real life in order to create the artistic world.

It is not necessary to the enjoyment of a literary text for a reader to believe in either the author's or the text's IDEOLOGY. It is essential, however, to suspend belief in favor of understanding the ideology of the text. But while Eliot warns against confusing factual information surrounding the author's era—current social conditions, ideology, language development—with the understanding of the text, he admits that such knowledge may serve a preparatory function for understanding a text. It is not the readers' goal to re-create the world of the author but to divest themselves of the confines of their world in order to attempt an "immediate" contact with the text (*On Poetry and Poets*, 130).

If the text is the "objective correlative" of the poetic experience and if such experience is not completely translatable into the text, then Eliot believes that the reader's experience of the text cannot be communicated in PARAPHRASE. In other words, the experience (meaning) of the text is partly emotional, and therefore the total meaning of the text cannot be explained in paraphrase. The understanding of a poem, for example, is the enjoyment of it in the right way and for the right reasons. Understanding does not equal explanation because the explanation is a verbal construction while understanding is not. Although discussion of literature is part of our experience of it, poetic experience is only partially translatable into explanation. In short, literature does not and should not serve the function of philosophy, theology, history, biography, or religion. It has its own function, an emotional one that cannot be described or defined intellectually. The creation of the artist transcends beliefs and philosophical systems; it is something that must be primarily experienced. Though it may speak to life, it does not necessarily describe life in terms that are immediately translatable into intellectual categories. Literature creates an illusion of life, but the worlds created by great authors such as Shakespeare, Homer, and Dante are experiential ones whose descriptions somehow defy intellectual formulation.

According to Eliot, the works of great authors constitute not just textual worlds but also unified ones. Readers, then, should approach a text with that expectation. What matters is the entire work. Every part of a literary text bears a relationship to the whole (*On Poetry*, 25). While Eliot emphasizes poetic inspiration, he argues for poetic organization also. Even such things as speeches within the text should not make a direct appeal to the reader but should further the ACTION (*Use of Poetry*, 146). They are not to be extracted from the whole in order to be scrutinized separately. In fact, this claim can be made for any part of a text. Eliot recognizes that an author, as creator of a world, also creates characters who conform to the logic of the text's world; they are not required to conform to the logic of the author's age or to that of the reader. Perhaps indifferent to the HERMENEUTICAL CIRCLE, Eliot assumes that this logic of the whole must be mastered by the reader before the SIGNIFICANCE of any single part may be apprehended. Eliot, however, does relate the logic of a text to our world by claiming that the logic of the text's world illuminates the actual world by giving us a new point of view from which to inspect it. The New Critics were fond of this tendency to relate art to everyday life. In addition to unity of action and logic, Eliot also seems to argue for a unity of form and content. "Unity" may not be the best term for Eliot's view, for he tends to make no distinction between the two. Form is not just an embellishment, something that mysteriously enhances the aesthetic quality of the content. The form (including conventional generic ones) is not constitutive of meaning, nor is content. Form is content, and content is form. Together they are constitutive of meaning.

For Eliot, the property of textual AMBIGUITY is related to the distinction between the poet's consciousness and the meaning of a text. The meaning of a text may be (and usually is) something that is greater than the author's conscious purpose. When the author's experience is transcribed, the transcription transcends the author's consciousness and the experience's origin. If we couple this observation with Eliot's claim that only a portion of a text's meaning can be communicated by paraphrase, it becomes possible for a text to mean different things to different readers. Furthermore, each of these meanings may differ from what the author intended to communicate. In other words, a text may be ambiguous because ordinary speech cannot communicate its total meaning. Consequently, there is simply no reason to assume that there exists a single right interpretation of the text as a whole (*Use of Poetry*, 126). While historical ALLUSIONS, grammatical peculiarities, social customs, dates, and so forth may deserve attention, these types of explanation certainly do not establish, much less exhaust, the meaning of a text. Eliot admits the possibility that the meaning of a text is what it means to different readers. This admission is possible if the meaning of a text is not necessarily what the author was consciously or unconsciously trying to communicate.

Reconciliation: Beardsley and Wimsatt. When Monroe Beardsley and William Wimsatt published their respective essays, "The Intentional Fallacy" and "The Affective Fallacy," the literary text as a VERBAL ICON became a well-entrenched commonplace within Anglo-American criticism. Wimsatt's starting point for his definition is Richards's idea that in the creative moment the poet holds competing and disparate impulses together in a kind of reconciled tension. Wimsatt transfers this idea of the reconciliation of opposites to the text itself. The essential and unique nature of poetry (literary art) resides in the reconciliation or harmonization of opposites. To explain this unique nature, Wimsatt employs the concept of METAPHOR because that concept becomes an actual metaphor for the concept of harmonizing opposites.

For Wimsatt, words within a culture have denotatative (*see* DENOTATION) and connotative (*see* CONNOTATION) meanings. In other words, concepts and associations are determined by a culture at the level of words. A text, then, is an objective organization of the meaning of words within a cultural matrix, and the form of such an objective organization is provided by the metaphor. A metaphor consists of two parts: TENOR and VEHICLE. For example, in the metaphor by Ezra Pound, "Your mind and you are our Sargasso Sea," the phrase, "your mind and you" is the tenor, and "our Sargasso Sea" is the vehicle. The compari-

son is one between two different classes of things. This comparison is more than an ANALOGY, for an analogy consists of the juxtaposing of two objects of the same class, such as claiming that a "certain traitor is like Judas" (Wimsatt and Beardsley, 150). In this analogy, both tenor and vehicle are men. The metaphor holds the similarities and differences between the tenor and vehicle in tension, a tension that produces a third object outside both. If this tension is relaxed in any way, the metaphor is destroyed. Both tenor and vehicle of a metaphor bring with them their ordinary meanings. Within the metaphorical association, they do not lose their meanings but rather retain and place them in a new mutual tension.

But how is a literary text a metaphor? First, a literary text is a composite of LITERARY CONVENTIONS and devices. Wimsatt argues that artists utilize such devices as ANTITHESIS, CONTRAST, REPETITION, ALLITERATION, PUN, METER, RHYME, and HOMOEOTELEUTON. When these devices or techniques are employed, the work assumes its own rhetorical STYLE. Style, however, is more than simple embellishment. When stylistic devices are placed within an ideational context, metaphoric tension is created. Consequently, Wimsatt (like most New Critics) is not interested primarily in individual devices but in the form of the whole rhetorical structure of the work. In other words, just as the metaphor, with its two parts, is one whole and conveys meaning as a whole, the literary work (composed of many parts) is one whole and conveys meaning as a whole (Wimsatt and Beardsley, 147).

The second part of the answer encompasses a list of dialectics: denotation/connotation, icon/reality, verbal object/referent, and coherence/correspondence. When referring to words, *denotation* describes the stated or dictionary meaning of a word, while *connotation* identifies the implied or suggested meaning. Within a metaphor, neither the denotation nor the connotation is obscured, adding to the metaphorical tension. In good literature, denotation and connotation are pushed together to such an extent that both are present in the "fullest meaning," creating the maximum of tension and ambiguity.

The structure of a metaphor consists of a "fusion" of verbal material and ideas, a fusion in which the sensory qualities of the verbal construct are not destroyed by the metaphoric abstraction. This is the peculiar nature of a metaphor. Wimsatt makes this claim for a literary text. In order to maintain this character of the text, the iconic property for language is important. By *iconic*, Wimsatt means a verbal sign that embodies and interprets the object it denotes. The most common example of the verbal icon is ONOMATOPOEIA. In a sense, all DISCOURSE incarnates an experience into sound. Yet since the discourse symbol is foreign to the experience it denotes, a disparity is created. Although this disparity goes unnoticed in ordinary discourse (the absence of the disparity is absolutely essential in scientific discourse), it is heightened in literary works between the verbal icon and its REFERENT. By claiming that the entire literary text is a verbal icon, a verbal object, Wimsatt necessarily emphasizes the disparity or ambiguity between the tenor (text as icon) and the vehicle (realities to which the text refers). It is this iconic property of the text more than anything else that accounts for the multiplicity of textual meaning. Since the meaning of the metaphor is inexhaustible, so is the meaning of the text (Wimsatt and Beardsley, 217).

The parts of a text fit together in such a way that their complex unity forms a coherent whole. On the one hand, this coherence is internal, a textual coherence independent of any necessary congruence with external reality. On the other hand, as a metaphoric construction, the text does necessarily correspond to reality in some manner. In the statement "Snow is white," the correspondence between the verbal object and the real state of affairs is factual. Since a literary text, however, is essentially a complex metaphorical object, it "generates an extra dimension of correspondence to reality, the symbolic or analogical." It is because of this symbolic dimension of correspondence (rather than congruence) that literary texts defy attempts at paraphrase. The text, as a metaphoric,

iconic, coherent rhetorical structure composed of a system of conventions and devices, stretches to the limit the referential relationship between text and reality. Again, the meaning that proceeds from the verbal icon cannot be put into logical terms. In other words, there is something in every text that simply cannot be expressed or captured in explanations.

What, then, is the function of literary criticism (see Wimsatt, 21–244)? It is to offer the wherewithal to point out what is needed for discerning what distinguishes every work as a literary one. For Wimsatt, three things are involved: explanation, DESCRIPTION, and explication. Explanation is the articulation of the elements within the text that have explicit meaning or at least the elements, especially obscure and disguised words, whose meaning can be clearly ascertained and stated. This level of activity is a lower but fundamental one. From this point, we move to the higher but still fundamental level of description. Here we are involved in describing the text's structure, shape, color, historical relations, and individual parts as well as their connections, meter, rhyme, and IMAGERY. This might be called the level of COMMENTARY. We are not addressing what the text says, only what it is structurally. At this level, the critic looks for relationships of the parts to the whole, but the critic may also need to go outside the text in order to bring to bear cultural, historical, and religious information on the description of some element within the text. During this process of describing the text's structure, however, the critic cannot avoid meanings that inhere within the structure that he/she is trying to describe. These meanings are implicit rather than explicit. So in a sense, there is no such thing as a pure description of structure. Apparently, there are two important aspects of this implicit meaning inherent in structure: the power of the text's pattern and the meaning of the total structure. During description, the critic should make explicit what is only implied through the pattern of the text. Second, since a text conveys meaning as a whole, the description of the implicit must be limited by the structure itself. In other words, what a reader believes may be implied by the text as a whole must be consistent with its structure and pattern. When the two activities of explanation and description are combined (i.e., the explicit and implicit) into offering a meaning, then we have performed the third activity: explication. The three together may be called by the generic term "interpretation."

In poetry, the connotative dimension of language takes precedence over the denotative. This fact is thrown into relief when we consider that the language of poetry is metaphor, PARADOX, and IRONY. In metaphor, two different classes of objects are juxtaposed; in paradox, two contradictory or conflicting elements are juxtaposed in the same statement; in irony, the attitudes are defined by qualification. The language of poetry therefore is one of indirection. It is the opposite of scientific language, which emphasizes the denotative dimension of words, allowing no room for ambiguity or secondary meanings beyond the dictionary meaning.

Further refinements: Brooks. What then is literature, and what does literature communicate? According to Cleanth Brooks, a literary text first is an experience or, perhaps better, a unification of experience (*Well Wrought Urn*, 194). Through paradox, irony, and metaphor, a literary text holds contradictory and conflicting elements of experience in a diversified unity. It does not choose one element over another; rather, it unifies them into a new pattern (195). The unity achieved by a literary text is not one in which there exists a cohering of propositions into a logical system. The unity is dramatic, in which a complex of attitudes are imaginatively related to each other. If the essence of literature is metaphor, irony, and paradox, then the logic of literature is not scientific or propositional but analogical ("The Quick and the Dead," 18). Second, literature communicates through its metaphorical and paradoxical nature. The metaphor—and hence literature—communicates ideas and assertions that are inexpressible in nonfigurative terms. What a text expresses can be expressed only through the text. In scientific discourse, ideally there would constantly be one meaning for one term. But in literary discourse, a word has potential meaning, a cluster of meanings. According to Brooks, this MULTIVALENCE is essential to literature because the artist seeks to present the total experience that is the text. Can this experience be communicated? Brooks says yes but warns that this communication is only partial. Through the use of imaginative understanding, the reader can share in the experience.

The above observation leads Brooks to warn against the "HERESY OF PARAPHRASE." The warning is based on his definition of literary unity. Paraphrases demand or assume logical coherence within the text where there may be only imaginative ones. A paraphrase abstracts a "central idea" from the poem and then tends to treat the essence of the text—metaphor, paradox, irony—as nothing more than decorative imagery, thus producing a dualism of form and content. The discussions of a literary text should never be substituted for the text but rather should lead us into the text. Thus what a literary text says can be said only by the whole text through its paradoxical structure, the hierarchy of attitudes. The elements within a text that are paraphrasable do not constitute the text's essence. The value of literature does not lie in the propositions that are capable of being abstracted from the text but in the relationships inherent in the text, relationships that are imaginative, analogical, and paradoxical rather than logical.

Like other New Critics, Brooks maintains the autonomy of the text. The text is not a window that the author opens into reality. Interpretive efforts must focus on the poem as an entity in its own right. Neither the author, the author's world, nor the reader's world is the nexus of the poem. Brooks, however, does recognize that historical considerations are important in an adjunctive role. He specifically refers to the responsibility of the critic or reader of literature to become acquainted with the author's language (*Well Wrought Urn*, 227). Since languages change over time, a study of history is advised in order to gain an understanding of how a language developed. Part of this historical study of language is a resulting history of literature. Every text is rooted in the language of a particular time, and this language is the vehicle of a society's ideas and the home of a society's SYMBOLIC WORLD. Thus a text, being rooted in the language of a particular period, will contain allusions to objects, ideas, and concepts that are a part of the language. This fact necessitates that the reader often must go outside the poem for certain crucial information. Yet the reader is neither asked nor expected to pass judgment on ethical, religious, or ideological issues. To do so would be tantamount to removing parts of the text from the total context, thereby distorting the total literary experience. Any part of a text is to be considered or judged not on the basis of the reader's acceptance or rejection of it on ideological grounds but in terms of its relationship to the total literary context, the analogical coherency of the whole. The text is an imaginative structure standing in its own right, and if a reader is to possess the text, the reader must do so on imaginative grounds.

Synthesis. From the foregoing discussion, we are in a position to offer a composite picture of New Criticism. First, a literary text is an organized, complex, and coherent whole in which any distinction between form and content is unacceptable. Form is content, and content is form. The text is composed of a variety of parts or elements. Action, character, THEMES, ideas, rhetorical devices, verbal stylistics, IMAGES, SETTINGS, scenes, EPISODES, repetitions, TONE, and ATMOSPHERE (the general feel that the reader gathers from the work) all combine to produce a unified effect. To isolate any part of a text for scrutiny apart from the whole is unacceptable. Individual parts are understandable and explainable only in terms of textual context. The parts form the whole, but the whole informs the parts.

Second, the unified effect is at least twofold: experiential and cognitive. The reader will experience an effect caused by the unity, and this experience is beyond description or explanation; it cannot be put into a propositional statement. This means that the understanding of a text is not identical with its explanation. Explanation is a verbal construct:

understanding is an experience. While understanding cannot be completely or satisfactorily put into words, the combined elements of a text point implicitly to a meaning that causes the reader to reflect on some aspect of reality. True literary texts, say the New Critics, do more than simply amuse readers; they also communicate a perspective that illuminates some aspect of human reality. Though New Critics demand that a text illuminate or correspond to some aspect of reality, this correspondence is not identical to reality; it is an analogical correspondence. The text is autonomous; it exists independently of author and reader. It creates its own world, which, while being internally coherent, does not necessarily cohere with the external reality of the author or reader. Since it may or may not cohere with the logic of external reality, readers should not try to explain a text's significance by demanding that it reflect the world in which it was produced or is read. As explained above, literary texts do illuminate reality, not by mirroring it but by analogically offering a different or new perspective from which to view reality. This perspective is synonymous with the text's theme or meaning and is what the story does with the main topic. For example, it could be argued that the topic of Mark's GOSPEL is the definition of discipleship. What Mark does with this topic is the meaning. The meaning of a good story is not stated by or implied through the organic unity of the various parts of the text. The meaning must be justified by the events in the story: the meaning must develop necessarily from the internal coherence of the story. All the parts have a bearing on the total meaning. If such a coherence is assumed up front, then the action, characterization, settings, tone, repetitions, style, and all the other aspects of the story must create a coherent unity through which the meaning is dramatically and consistently implied. The meaning is the thematic control, the unifying factor of the text, and all the textual elements must in some coherent and consistent fashion enhance and develop that meaning.

The above distinction between the experiential and the cognitive leads us to a third observation:

the more complex the text, the more ambiguous its meaning will be and, correspondingly, the more difficult to articulate. The complexity and metaphorical character of the text continually generate meaning possibilities. The metaphor's vehicle and tenor create a new object somewhere between the two, an object that continually escapes any definitive articulation. Similarly, the text as a metaphor (with coherence as vehicle and correspondence to reality as tenor) escapes any ultimate statement of meaning but perpetually generates meaningful discussion. As mentioned above, the key to interpreting a text is the discovery of the theme implicit in the structure of the text. Once the key is grasped, all parts of the text seem to fit into a pattern. From a New Critical perspective, readers will not make sense of a text unless they discover the theme. For the New Critic, the theme is incarnated within and thus discoverable from the text itself. It is what gives coherence to the text. In complex texts, however, the key is usually hard to come by, a fact that enhances a sense of ambiguity and generates differing and sometimes disparate interpretations. Complex texts do not easily yield their secrets. Indeed, it might be argued that a highly complicated text may lend itself to multiple relationships between the parts while maintaining internal coherence.

Finally (and this is perhaps a corollary to the first observation), since a literary text is a unity, any interpretation should reflect that unity. This interpretation will involve three things: explanation, description, and explication. These three activities are not sequential; rather they overlap. Explanation involves the statement of the things in the text that have explicit meaning. If outside information will enhance this activity, then such information should be welcomed. Description is the most detailed and time-consuming activity in New Criticism. Things such as images, rhetorical relationships between parts, use of devices, and ideas must be given attention. In short, the critic offers commentary on textual complexity, coherence, and unity. In the process, the critic should also comment on implicit as well as explicit meaning that inheres in the structure of the text. Such description of the implicit must be guarded by the total textual pattern. Explication is the combination of explanation and description in order to posit a meaning. Note that meaning here is *a* meaning and not *the* meaning. The complexity of the text—combined with that unparaphrasable dimension (whether described in terms of metaphor, irony, or tension between intention and extension) of the text and the reader's personal repertoire—prevents absolute closure by any single explication. Since New Criticism demands that any part of a text be understood in terms of its whole, an example of New Criticism applied to a biblical text would necessarily be extended.

Bibliography. Cleanth Brooks, "Literary Criticism: Poet, Poem, and Reader," in *Literary Criticism* (ed. Lionel Trilling; New York: Holt, Rinehart & Winston, 1970), 392–405; idem, "The Quick and the Dead: A Comment on Humanities Studies," in *The Humanities: An Appraisal* (ed. Julian Harris; Madison: University of Wisconsin Press, 1950), 1–21; idem, *The Well Wrought Urn* (New York: Reynal and Hitchcock, 1947); T. S. Eliot, *On Poetry and Poets* (New York: Farrar, Straus and Cudahy, 1957); idem, *The Sacred Wood: Essays on Poetry and Criticism* (1928; repr., London: Methuen, 1960); idem, *Selected Essays* (New York: Harcourt, Brace & World, 1960); idem, *The Use of Poetry and the Use of Criticism* (1933; repr., London: Faber & Faber, 1955); C. K. Ogden and I. A. Richards, *The Meaning of Meaning: A Study of the Influence of Language on Thought, with Supplementary Essays by B. Malinowski and F. C. Crookshank* (New York: Harcourt, Brace, 1923); John Crowe Ransom, *The New Criticism* (Norfolk, CT: New Directions, 1941); I. A. Richards, *Practical Criticism* (New York: Harcourt, Brace, 1952); idem, *Principles of Literary Criticism* (New York: Harcourt, Brace, 1925); W. K. Wimsatt Jr., *Hateful Contraries* (Lexington: University of Kentucky Press, 1965); W. K. Wimsatt Jr. and M. C. Beardsley, *The Verbal Icon* (Lexington: University of Kentucky Press, 1954).

NEW ENGLISH BIBLE (NEB)

Commissioned by the British churches, a committee TRANSLATION outside the AV tradition, with the NT appearing in 1961 and the OT and APOCRYPHA in 1970. The translation committee included scholars from the Church of England, the Church of Scotland, the Methodist, the Baptist, and the Congregationalist churches, Oxford and Cambridge University Presses, and a number of BIBLE societies. The target audience was three-fold: people who attend church only infrequently, people who are uncomfortable with the language of the KJV, and a younger audience, which prefers a more contemporary VERSION. Thus the English of the NEB is not archaic, colloquial, or overly stiff but has what the translators refer to as "sufficient dignity," offering "timeless English."

The translating committee developed its own Greek text by deciding to use the Greek manuscripts that they judged to reflect most closely the original words of the ancient writer for each passage under consideration. This decision, in the opinion of some scholars, resulted both in clarifying some passages and in some problems relative to INTERPRETATION. The translators also rearranged some verses, added phrases that certainly modified MEANING, and dropped others. For example, Gen. 26:18 occurs between verses 15 and 16; Matt. 9:34 is removed; and in Rom. 5:14 the phrase "by disobeying a direct command" is added in an attempt to explain Adam's sin. Non-British readers may also find the British IDIOMS confusing at best. Such words as "pannier" (Job 5:5), "batten" (Prov. 5:10), and "bedizened" (Rev. 18:16) would need clarification. *See also* REVISED ENGLISH BIBLE.

Bibliography. Steven M. Sheeley and Robert N. Nash Jr., *The Bible in English Translation: An Essential Guide* (Nashville: Abingdon, 1997).

NEW HERMENEUTIC, THE

A movement that gained notoriety especially after World War II and was based on the existentialism of Martin Heidegger and Rudolf Bultmann. The most notable representatives of the movement were Ernst Fuchs and Gerhard Ebeling. At the heart of the new hermeneutic was the issue of the relationships among language, understanding, and reality. The hermeneutical problem is that readers of the biblical TEXTS are separated by centuries from the cultures that produced the texts. In light of this separation, then, how are readers to arrive at understanding?

The representatives of the new hermeneutic also assumed, following Heidegger, that the problem is further complicated in that readers' understandings of the biblical texts are conditioned by their PREUNDERSTANDING, which they always bring to a text. In the new hermeneutic, this preunderstanding is the principle by which understanding of anything, including the biblical texts, is initiated.

The new hermeneutic was also based on a new understanding of the essence of language. Rather than being a passive phenomenon (language as a set of descriptive labels used to name objects), language is active in the sense of being an event that creates movement. Each instance of SPEECH (written or oral) is an event, a speech act (*see* SPEECH ACT THEORY), that creates TRUTH in conversation with the hearer's experience. If this is true of texts, then they are not simply static entities from which MEANING is extracted by some interpretive method but rather are speech acts that interpret their readers. The biblical texts as speech acts, then, confront the individual readers with the WORD OF GOD at the moment of reading. In this sense, the biblical texts interpret their readers, not the other way around. Rather than simply submitting themselves to the analytical scrutiny of the reader, the biblical texts interpret the reader or at least force the reader to scrutinize his/her own world by being drawn into the WORLD OF THE TEXT. Ernst Fuchs, for example, used the PARABLE of the laborers (Matt. 20:1–16) to illustrate this dialectic between reader and text. According to Fuchs, Jesus's audience identifies with those who have the good fortune of finding employment in hard times and with EXPECTATION that those who have worked the longest will receive a higher wage. This identification is possible because the readers are culturally conditioned to expect a fair reward for a full day's work and because the text itself encourages such an expectation. However, the audience (and the modern reader) is suddenly shocked by the parable's undermining of their preconceived notion of fairness. The audience and modern reader are faced with the new idea that grace always takes precedence over justice. The STORY of Jonah challenges its audience and readers in the same way on the same SUBJECT, and the story of

Job PROBLEMATIZES the preconceived idea that there is a cause-and-effect relationship between one's moral fiber and one's material well-being. Fuchs then argues that texts such as the parable of the laborers engage readers on a level that is deeper than an intellectual one. Texts confront readers in ways that force them to reevaluate their preunderstandings. *See* NARRATIVE HERMENEUTICS.

NEW HISTORICISM

A LITERARY CRITICISM that examines the social, economic, and political aspects of literature. New historicism as a type of critical textual analysis developed in the United States in the 1980s and was most succinctly defined by Stephen Greenblatt in 1982. Although it had its birth in Renaissance studies, its practice has spread to such fields as anthropology, art history, English, and BIBLICAL STUDIES. Catherine Gallagher suggests that both adherents and opponents of the theory would probably agree that new historicism views literary and nonliterary texts as "constituents of historical discourses that are both inside and outside of texts and that its practitioners generally posit no fixed hierarchy of cause and effect as they trace the connections among texts, discourses, power, and the constitution of subjectivity" (45).

Basic tenets. New historicism may have truly begun with the publication of Stephen Greenblatt's *Renaissance Self-Fashioning*. Because he wrote about Renaissance literature, much of the first criticisms using the theory focused on works from this period. Since then, however, it has spread to almost every other area of literary study. For the new historicist, history is seen in terms of power relations. "The order of things is not simply a given; it takes labour to produce, sustain, reproduce, and transmit the way things are" (Greenblatt, "Resonance and Wonder," 57). The new historicist term for this process by which the dominant culture maintains its position is HEGEMONY. There is always tension between constraint (hegemony) and mobility (change of power). Any text may be considered a power move in the game of cultural politics because it is an instrument that displays and enforces the doctrines of conduct, etiquette, and law. The goal of new historicists is to show what kind of cultural results the literature has caused and to seek out the marginalized voices.

The types of historical criticisms now at the center of critical discussion have not simply rejected the ahistorical critical approaches that developed with NEW CRITICISM but have been heavily influenced by MARXIST CRITICISM, DECONSTRUCTION, and POSTMODERN CRITICISM. These postmodern historical approaches make a basic distinction between history (the past) and HISTORIOGRAPHY (the writing about the past), rejecting the older historicists' claim that they reconstruct (*see* RECONSTRUCTION) the past by reading its artifacts. While new historicism cannot be classified as a single, unified critical approach (some critics refer to their work as sociological poetics, others as cultural studies, still others as CULTURAL CRITICISM), the critics who practice it do share some common concerns. These include the subjectivity of history, the historian's and the critic's situation in writing and reading, the relationship between historiography and FICTION, the relationship between DISCOURSE and IDEOLOGY, and the TEXTUALITY of the past.

First, all history is subjective. Those who are dominant in culture tend to write it, suppressing the minority voices and leaving a biased record of the events. Consequently, new historicism presupposes the "historicity" of texts and the "textuality of history." From this point onward, the critic will trace the "ideological filiations and effects of such documents and show how they support repressive regimes and social practices . . . and, more important, how literature can be used to undermine such repression" (Young, 87).

Second, the new historicists argue for a direct connection between a TEXT and its sociohistorical CONTEXT. A text of any kind is a product of social causes as well as a cause of social effects. They recognize that histories are not objective reconstructions of the past but are textual constructs of critics and historians within specific historical and LITERARY institutions; hence, literary texts do

296

not transcend their sociohistorical contexts to tap into some transcendent realm of mimetic TRUTH and knowledge. These critics are keenly aware that we cannot examine the past except through the lenses of the present. In fact, historians and literary critics alike cannot occupy some objective, transcendent position from which to examine the past. Nor can they find any natural, nonhistorical sources for their key, foundational ASSUMPTIONS. They can discover no natural givens, only their own historically constructed ideas, which have no essence, only a history. Both histories and ideas have genealogies constructed from the past. Historians, literary artists, CRITICS, and readers are all implicated in the act of writing and/or reading. Texts are written and interpreted within specific historical, sociopolitical, and literary institutions. The histories and INTERPRETATIONS of texts are as much constructs by historically constructed subjects as are the past objects to be examined. This dilemma is complicated by the fact that since the original contexts of past events and texts cannot be fully reconstructed, historians and critics must construct interpretive contexts.

New historicists such as Jerome McGann have suggested an approach that goes beyond New Criticism's ahistorical focus on the text, beyond geneticism's focus on the AUTHOR and the circumstances of a text's composition (*see* GENETIC CRITICISM), to a text's larger context of socializations. Starting with the material conditions and mode of publication, McGann encourages critics to go further and trace the entire history of the text's reception. McGann argues for this inclusive approach because he feels that present readers and critics respond not only to the text but also to its historical development and reception. In other words, readers respond not only to the text but also to its historical interpretive constructs as well.

Third, new historicism tends to blur the line between historiography and fiction, viewing the former as the NARRATIVE arrangement of past events. Since historians must supply the contexts for most past events and objects as well as include particular events while excluding others, an account of the past is always a misrepresentation, an interpretive object. A text's context is itself a construct of the historian or critic. In other words, the historian or critic constructs a context and then assumes that it is a representation of the circumstances of the text's composition. From this perspective, then, the contextual communities (e.g., Matthean community, Essene community, Johannine community, or Priestly community) that scholars employ to say something meaningful about biblical texts are fictional creations by the scholars themselves. Consequently, scholars and other readers of the biblical texts tend to substitute fictional constructs for objective realities. Through a fundamental epistemological sleight of hand, historians, critics, and readers of all sorts fail to make a distinction between the actual past and their (re)presentations of the past. In other words, there is a fundamental misconception that their constructions are reconstructions. The new historicists, recognizing this basic epistemological blind spot, argue that the literary products of historians and scholars are just as fictive as texts that profess to be such.

The new historicists do not claim that the fictiveness of historiography implies that there is no past or that historians should not write about it. They simply mean to point out that history is discursive and thus imposes SIGNIFICANCE upon the past. Furthermore, they point out that because history is DISCOURSE, there is no way outside appeal to the discourse itself to demonstrate that the past event has the meaning that the discourse has invested it with. Since discourse is a meaning-making activity, histories, interpretations, and readings are the imaginative creations of historians, critics, and readers. For example, the historical Jesus is the creation of critical discourses, and there is simply no way to guarantee that the portrait drawn by critical scholarship is an accurate representation of the actual first-century figure. What we take for historical truth is in reality historiography's or scholarship's discursive creation.

The last observation leads to the fourth concern of new historicism: the relationship between discourse and IDEOLOGY. Historical and critical discourses are not created within some pristine context of Cartesian cleanliness but are soundly rooted in ideologies. Rather than being objective, reflecting the way things were, accounts of the past reflect a particular present ideological perspective and are attempts to legitimize the present. In fact, Michel Foucault has argued that a discourse actually defines both its object of study and what constitutes knowledge about that object. A discourse is what an institution defines as Truth, and this definition is an agreed-upon set of operational practices that themselves are beyond question or scrutiny and circumscribe the knowledge presented by the historian or critic. Since historians and critics are located within ideologies (socioeconomic, political, theological), historical and critical analyses of the past or of texts are not value-free. Such an ASSUMPTION vitiates the possibility of objective historical narratives and, into the practice of historiography and CRITICISM, introduces the issue of ethical practice. This ethical dimension of new historicism is further emphasized by the view that both historical and literary texts display and enforce existing rules of conduct, etiquette, and laws. Human beings produce objects that are constructed by and are reflective of existing ideologies. Literary objects and their interpreters do not transcend the historical moment but are inevitably part of a complex ideological grounding. If this claim holds merit, the new historicists argue, then there is a correspondence between aesthetic conventions, on the one hand, and the political and socioeconomic forces, on the other. This correspondence, in turn, suggests that other voices in society have been silenced or marginalized (*see* MARGINALIZATION) by the dominant ideological voices. What past historians and critics have assumed to be natural givens (e.g., GENDER, race, and sexuality) are in reality social and historical constructs. To put it simply, both historical and literary texts are implicated in ideological AGENDAS. It is clear, then, that new historicism is deconstructive in that it has been quite effective in challenging foundationalist and essentialist claims, deconstructing ideologies, and demonstrating that almost everything humans consider to be universal, natural, or timeless is actually historically contingent and socially constructed. With respect to literary texts, such a claim PROBLEMATIZES the assumption that great literature transcends the circumstances of its production and thus suggests that all texts are tied to those circumstances. Hence, critics need to examine not only a text's productive circumstances but its historical consequences as well.

The fifth concern of new historicists is the textuality of the past. By "textuality," new historicists mean that the past no longer exists, and the only access we have to it is through its textual remains. "Textual" here may mean both written and material objects. So the historian accesses the past through reading and interpreting its textual remains. The historian's object of study is not the past but rather the texts about the past and the interpretive history of those texts. The historian reads all objects and traces of the past as texts to be interpreted. Put another way, any past culture is an ensemble of texts that are themselves already once removed from the events they try to represent. The historian who then reads these texts is twice removed from the past. Thus, the referent of historians' work is not the past but rather their textually constructed contexts. The language used by historians in examining the past does not function referentially as if through a mirror to reflect the past. Language creates the past rather than reflects it. Language constitutes reality. As Derrida claims, there is nothing outside the text. The textuality of the past is unavoidable.

So the new historicists view the whole of reality as "text" that calls for analysis. But while the world as linguistically constructed is readable, any reading of it is always a MISREADING because of the ideological situatedness of the reader. There can be no undistorted historical representation or reading.

Strategies. With these assumptions come certain strategies that many new historicists utilize when dealing with a specific piece of literature. In order to access the SIGNIFICANCE of a text, the critic must find a way to acknowledge the many diverse voices that make up the culture's collective consciousness at the given historical moment the text was written. There are some typical questions the new historicist asks in order to distinguish these voices: What are the relations of power? How is this power operating, and what might be a threat to it? What cultural/historical events could shed light on the text? New historicists believe that asking these questions will help them to restore literary works to their "multiple historical contexts" (Carroll, 52). The critic must also identify the author's assumptions and the critic's own personal ideologies, both of which alter the text. Last, the new historicist tries to highlight social rules and CODES in the literary work so that other readers can recognize them. Although these assumptions and strategies are usually agreed upon, it is important to remember that "the new historicist . . . is under no nominal compulsion to achieve consistency" (Gallagher, 54). New historicists do not form a single, unified school, nor do they all share the same theoretical program.

From the Enlightenment in the seventeenth and eighteenth centuries to well into the twentieth century, historical criticism has been dominant in the study of biblical texts. Since the 1970s, however, biblical scholars have taken a more austere, critical posture before the biblical texts by assuming that the biblical narratives reflect not only on the texts but also on earlier historiographies (Carroll, 54). This reevaluation of biblical texts has left room for new historicists to question other elements of previous interpretations. Two aspects that unify new historicists in biblical interpretation are a rejection of traditional approaches and "a fundamental questioning of the kind of historiography represented both by the writings in the Bible and by those contemporary biblical historians whose books may be regarded as the continuation of the biblical narratives by other means" (55). New historicists believe that focus is needed on the subjectivity of history and on the marginalized voices that have been left out by the utopian religious viewpoints of the biblical writers. For instance, historicists studying the Pauline Letters have con-

structed ideas of what the communities were like that received them (Corinthians, Ephesians, etc.). New historicists claim that it is impossible to know what those cultures were like because they can be accessed only through secondhand "historicity." New historicists also claim that the accounts of ancient Israel's history have silenced other cultures that may have actually been more dominant, such as Palestinian culture. Ultimately, many new historicists want repressed texts that are discovered to be included in the CANON, a goal that would be seriously opposed by many Christians.

Bibliography. A. K. M. Adam, ed., *Handbook of Post-modern Biblical Interpretation* (St. Louis: Chalice, 2000); Robert P. Carroll, "Poststructuralist Approaches: New Historicism and Post-modernism," in *The Cambridge Companion to Biblical Interpretation* (ed. John Barton; London: Cambridge University Press, 1998), 50–66; Michel Foucault, *The Order of Things: An Archaeology of the Human Sciences* (New York: Vintage, 1973); Catharine Gallagher, "Marxism and New Historicism," in *New Historicism and Cultural Materialism* (ed. Ryan Kiernan; London: Arnold, 1996), 45–54; Stephen J. Greenblatt, *Renaissance Self-Fashioning: From More to Shakespeare* (Chicago: University of Chicago Press, 1980); idem, "Resonance and Wonder," in *New Historicism and Cultural Materialism* (ed. Ryan Kiernan; London: Arnold, 1996), 55–60; Donald Keesey, *Contexts for Criticism* (3rd ed.; Mountain View, CA: Mayfield, 1998); Jerome McGann, *The Beauty of Inflections: Literary Investigations in Historical Method and Theory* (Oxford: Clarendon, 1985); Victor Shea, "New Historicism," in *Encyclopedia of Contemporary Theory* (ed. Irena R. Makaryk; Toronto: University of Toronto Press, 1993), 124–30; Richard N. Soulen and R. Kendall Soulen, *Handbook to Biblical Criticism* (3rd ed.; Louisville: Westminster John Knox, 2001); R. V. Young, *At War with the Word* (Wilmington, DE: ISI [Intercollegiate Studies Institute] Books, 1999).

NEW INTERNATIONAL VERSION (NIV)

A TRANSLATION of the Bible based on DYNAMIC EQUIVALENCE, completed in 1978 (and updated in 1984 and 2011) by some one hundred scholars from several evangelical denominations (mostly from the United States). According to the preface of the version, the guiding principle for the translators was "their commitment to the authority and infallibility of the Bible as God's Word in written form." The translators also wanted to produce a version that would address some of what they saw as incorrect or misleading translations found in the RSV. This concern can be seen in the translators' attempt to harmonize some passages in the HEBREW BIBLE with the NT (esp. for passages in the PROPHETS).

NEW JERUSALEM BIBLE. *See* JERUSALEM BIBLE

NEW KING JAMES VERSION. *See* KING JAMES VERSION

NEW QUEST FOR THE HISTORICAL JESUS, THE. *See* QUEST FOR THE HISTORICAL JESUS, THE

NEW REVISED STANDARD VERSION (NRSV)

A revision of the RSV completed in 1989. The translators of this Bible version were guided by a number of concerns: (1) to remain loyal to the original languages, (2) to maintain the LITERARY tradition of the KJV, (3) to modify the language to reflect idiomatic changes in English since the publication of the RSV, (4) to use GENDER-INCLUSIVE LANGUAGE wherever the texts warranted such usage, and (5) to produce a TEXT that is scholarly but readable.

NEW TESTAMENT. *See* BIBLE; CANON

NEW TESTAMENT CANON. *See* BIBLE; CANON; CANON, NEW TESTAMENT

NEW WORLD TRANSLATION

A 1961 TRANSLATION of the Bible by the Jehovah's Witnesses, for their own use.

NONINTRUSIVE NARRATOR. *See* UNINTRUSIVE NARRATOR

NOVELLA

Originally, a SHORT STORY such as those in Boccaccio's *Decameron*. The GENRE developed especially in Germany in the early nineteenth century according to the guidelines that it could be only a few pages or a few hundred pages; it should focus on a single event, CONFLICT, or situation; its PLOT should be suspenseful; and it should have a surprising conclusion.

The contemporary understanding of the novella, however, is a long short story or a short novel. Examples are Tolstoy's *Death of Ivan Ilyich*, Hemingway's *Old Man and the Sea*, and Conrad's *Heart of Darkness*.

In BIBLICAL STUDIES, some of the biblical texts have been described as novellas. The tale of Joseph in Genesis and the story of Jonah are two examples. Both plots turn on conflict and are suspenseful, the ending of each is surprising, and each focuses on a single event. For example, the conflict in Jonah is both external (God/Jonah, Assyrians/Jonah) and internal (Jonah's sense of justice / God's sense of grace), its plot is suspenseful (Jonah's flight, the storm, the encounter with the whale), the ending offers a surprise (God's decision to destroy the Assyrians is changed by their repentance; Jonah's reaction), and it focus on a single THEME (the relationship between God's justice and God's mercy).

NOVELETTE

A work of FICTION that is a long SHORT STORY. *See* NOVELLA.

NT

Abbreviation for *New Testament. See* BIBLE; CANON.

OBJECT. *See* SUBJECT/OBJECT

OBJECTIFICATION

In HERMENEUTICS, the idea that the AUTHOR's experience is somehow incarnated within the TEXT. Objectification is based on the ASSUMPTION that it is possible for an author to inscripturate an ideational object, which can then be successfully extracted by a reader. Objectification is based on the romantic theory that all humans share a common inner life, which allows them to understand, and be understood by, one another. The most pronounced version of objectification may be seen in the theories of Friedrich Schleiermacher and Wilhelm Dilthey.

Bibliography. Wilhelm Dilthey, "Development of Hermeneutics," in Dilthey, *Selected Writings* (ed. H. P. Rickman; Cambridge: Cambridge University Press, 1976), 149–64; Friedrich Schleiermacher, *Hermeneutics: The Handwritten Manuscripts* (ed. H. Kimmerle; Missoula, MT: Scholars Press, 1977).

OBJECTIVE CORRELATIVE

A term redefined by T. S. Eliot for a situation or a series of ACTIONS or objects in a TEXT that can arouse an emotional reaction but that does not state the emotion explicitly. The idea has to do with Eliot's EXPECTATION of unity or balance between FORM and CONTENT. If the emotion overwhelms the words or if the words overwhelm the emotion, unity is not achieved. *See* NEW CRITICISM.

OBJECTIVE KNOWLEDGE

Dispassionate and certain knowledge of the world and history, especially as characterized in the Enlightenment and MODERNISM, but challenged, if not rejected, by CRITICS within POSTMODERNISM, who believe that all knowledge is socially conditioned and biased, always a matter of INTERPRETATION, and often used as an instrument of power.

OBJECTIVE TRUTH

Truth that inheres in the structures of reality in a variety of domains: art, economics, politics, religion, nature, and so forth. According to some CRITICS of culture, the belief in objective truth as existing independently of methods by which humans seek to access it is a characteristic of the seventeenth- and eighteenth-century Enlightenment inherited by MODERNISM. As with the idea of OBJECTIVE KNOWLEDGE, POSTMODERNS generally argue that TRUTH is a social construct, thus opting for the idea of local truths.

OBJECTIVITY. *See* OBJECTIVE KNOWLEDGE; OBJECTIVE TRUTH

OBJECT OF CONSCIOUSNESS

Also referred to as the original intentional object, in HERMENEUTICS, the mental formulation of a TEXT. The object is not synonymous with the text and is not the same as AUTHORIAL INTENTION. The text is the concrete LITERARY product of the author's object of consciousness, an ideational object. For every literary text, there must be an originating moment when the AUTHOR conceives of the literary object and perceives it to be a certain way. On the one hand, since perception takes place through time, the object of consciousness undergoes a perpetual redefinition from moment to moment. On the other hand, this object (regardless of the author's literary purpose) receives concrete expression at a particular time in the form of an inscription (i.e., the text). Hence many literary scholars argue that there is no way to guarantee a one-to-one correspondence between the ever-changing object of consciousness and the permanent linguistic representation of it. They further claim that it is futile to argue for such a correspondence because there is no way to demonstrate objectively the TRUTH of such a relationship. It is impossible to enter the consciousness of another, especially when that consciousness is unavailable for questioning. Therefore, since it is the product of the author's individual consciousness, authorial MEANING is unobtainable. The conclusion to the matter, then, is that readers interpret texts but do not interpret authors.

OBLIGATORY INTERTEXTUALITY. *See* INTERTEXTUAL CRITICISM

OCCASIONAL LETTERS

A term referring to the nature of most of the LETTERS in the NT, especially those of Paul. The description assumes that although Paul employed LITERARY and rhetorical strategies current in letter writing at the time, his letters were occasioned by specific problems in specific congregations at specific times in the life of the infant church. Consequently, scholars point out that since Paul addressed problems and questions within the social structures of a time centuries removed from modern church life, his solutions (e.g., on slavery, family structure, the role of women in the church) must be carefully and critically examined before applying them universally.

ODE

From the Greek for "song," a lyric poem on a single THEME in exalted and elaborate language and complicated in FORM. Most readers are familiar with modern odes such as Keats's "Ode on a Grecian Urn" or Shelley's "Ode to the West Wind." According to Soulen and Soulen (123), however, odes or references to odes occur in both the NT and the HEBREW BIBLE, especially in the Psalms. For example, Ps. 139 employs exalted language and is on the single theme of the majesty of God, viewed in terms of God's omniscience, omnipresence, om-

nificence, and holiness. Soulen and Soulen (123) also suggest that in the LXX, thirty-six of the Psalms are classified as odes (e.g., LXX: 4; 17; 29; 38; 44; 47 [NRSV: 4; 18; 30; 39; 45; 48]). In the NT, the term (noun or the related verb) is used once in Rev. 5:9; twice each in Col. 3:16; Eph. 5:19; and Rev. 14:3; and thrice in Rev. 15:3.

> *Bibliography.* Richard N. Soulen and R. Kendall Soulen, *Handbook of Biblical Criticism* (3rd ed.; Louisville: Westminster John Knox Press, 2001).

OLD COVENANT

A TRANSLATION of the Greek *diathēkē* (COVENANT), rendered as *testamentum* in the VULGATE and subsequently used by Christians to refer to the OT. In another SENSE, however, the term within Christianity refers to the covenant that God made with Israel and serves as a foundation for the NEW COVENANT in Jesus (e.g., 2 Cor. 3:14; Heb. 8:6–13).

OLD TESTAMENT

A term long used by Christians to designate the thirty-nine books of the Hebrew SCRIPTURES as distinct from the books of the NEW TESTAMENT. Many scholars have argued that the term "Old Testament" should be limited to use on occasions when a Christian perspective on the canon is addressed. Yet even in Christianity, there is a difference between the Protestant or REFORMATION CANON of the Old Testament and the CATHOLIC CANON. The Catholic Old Testament includes additional works called the DEUTEROCANONICAL BOOKS that are not in the Reformation Canon. Protestants refer to these additional books as the APOCRYPHA.

OMNISCIENT NARRATOR. *See* NARRATOR

OMNISCIENT POINT OF VIEW. *See* NARRATOR

ONOMASTICA

Lists of names or vocabulary that serve as aids to MEANING. Some biblical texts may have used onomastica (e.g., animals in Job 38–39).

ONOMATOPOEIA

A FIGURE OF SPEECH in which the MEANING of a word or word cluster is reflected in the sound. Many slang words are onomatopoeic (e.g., "pop," "zap," "woof"). In TRANSLATION, the force of the figure is usually lost, as in the NRSV's rendering of Isa. 5:24, "The tongue of fire devours the stubble." The translation does not capture the hissing and crackling sound in the Hebrew as the fire burns dry wood. The description of the earthquake in Isa. 24:19–20 is also difficult to capture in translations, but Schökel gives an interesting attempt: "The earth shivers and staggers, stumbles and tumbles, quivers and quavers and quakes, jars and jerks and jolts" (Alter and Kermode, 182).

> *Bibliography.* Robert Alter and Frank Kermode, eds., *The Literary Guide to the Bible* (Cambridge, MA: Belknap, 1987).

OPEN-ENDEDNESS

In POSTMODERN literary theory, the idea that some TEXTS do not end with a DENOUEMENT that neatly ties up all the loose ends and thus lack CLOSURE. Some biblical texts are open-ended; for example, if the Gospel of Mark ends at 16:8, then it does not bring things to closure. Second Kings may also be seen as open-ended, as may Acts.

OPENNESS. *See* OPEN TEXTS

OPEN TEXTS

According to some contemporary LITERARY theorists, a characteristic of all literary TEXTS. Umberto Eco argues that due to the nature of language, every literary text is open to an unlimited number of readings. Any text succeeds aesthetically insofar as it generates openness and AMBIGUITY. This is especially the case with poetic texts that, through the poetic use of language, frustrate the normal REFERENTIAL QUALITY OF LANGUAGE. In other words, by OVERCODING the CODE of the NATURAL LANGUAGE with literary ones, the literary text vitiates the possibility of a univocal DECODING. The literary text becomes self-referential, drawing attention to its POETICS.

As such, the text does not point to some ontological reality beyond itself but demands that the reader approach it as the originator of a field of possible decoding activities. Because literary texts demand the cooperation of the reader in formulating MEANING, Eco can make the claim that all literary texts are subject to a multiplicity of meanings. No single reading can actualize all the possible readings that the text is capable of admitting.

Wolfgang Iser (165–69, 171–72), a German literary CRITIC, accounts for the openness of texts with his concept of gaps of INDETERMINACY on several levels: SYNTAX, SEMANTICS, PRAGMATICS, CHARACTERIZATION, ACTION, and NARRATIVE flow. He also argues that there are gaps between competing POINTS OF VIEW, literary gaps, poetic gaps, even grammatical gaps in a text, which the reader tries to fill. Obviously, the theories of both Eco and Iser place an emphasis on the activities of readers in filling these gaps. The Gospel of Mark, when read with openness in mind, reveals several kinds of gaps that the reader must fill. These include gaps between the perspectives of the NARRATOR, PLOT, IMPLIED READER, and characters, gaps created by ALLUSION to other texts, and gaps created by INTERCALATION, to name a few.

> *Bibliography.* Umberto Eco, *The Limits of Interpretation* (Bloomington: Indiana University Press, 1990); idem, *The Open Work* (Cambridge, MA: Harvard University Press, 1989); idem, *The Role of the Reader: Explorations in the Semiotics of Texts* (Bloomington: Indiana University Press, 1984); Wolfgang Iser, *The Act of Reading: A Theory of Aesthetic Response* (Baltimore: Johns Hopkins University Press, 1978).

ORACLE

Generally any communication of a deity to a human. Although there may have originally been a difference in the Bible between a priestly and a PROPHETIC ORACLE, recent scholarship tends to think that the distinction may be superficial because both PROPHET and priest were closely associated with the Israelite cult and thus with Israel's whole system of religious beliefs and ritual.

ORALITY

A criterion for determining the authenticity of Jesus's words. When trying to determine if a SAYING in the GOSPELs is actually from Jesus, scholars seek to determine whether the saying has the quality of orality. In other words, since Jesus's teaching was entirely oral and transmitted orally for some time before it was written down, then to be remembered and passed on by word of mouth, Jesus's sayings would probably be brief, catchy, and quotable. Examples are "The Sabbath was made for humankind, and not humankind for the Sabbath" (Mark 2:27) and "Prophets are not without honor, except in their hometown, and among their own kin, and in their own house" (Mark 6:4; cf. Matt. 13:15; *Gospel of Thomas* 33).

ORAL TORAH. *See* TORAH

ORAL TRADITION

Technically, any information passed from one generation to another by word of mouth. In the study of the biblical texts, oral tradition relates to both the HEBREW BIBLE and the NT because, before being recorded, much of the material was passed on orally for varying periods of time. Such material in the Hebrew Bible as the stories of the patriarchs, Moses, Aaron, and the exodus circulated as oral tradition long before they became the basis of the written forms we find in the PENTATEUCH. In NT studies, scholars assume that the SAYINGS OF JESUS were originally oral and orally transmitted by his followers for some decades before becoming the basis for the GOSPELs. Many NT scholars also argue that oral tradition lies behind the STORY of the church in Acts. *See* FORM CRITICISM.

ORDER

In NARRATOLOGY, the time order of the STORY. It may operate by ANTICIPATION, FLASHBACK, or discordances between story and PLOT. Both flashback and anticipation are found in the story of Micaiah in 1 Kings 22; Micaiah, in flashback, anticipates in 22:17 the defeat of Ahab's army and Ahab's death, which actually happens in 22:29–38.

ORGANIC UNITY

The ASSUMPTION, especially in most types of FORMALISM (NEW CRITICISM, NARRATIVE CRITICISM, and some versions of READER-RESPONSE CRITICISM), that a TEXT is a unified LITERARY object in which all the parts fit together and must be understood in terms of the whole and the whole in terms of its parts. Thus the MEANING of a literary text derives strictly from its FORM and CONTENT rather than from extratextual considerations.

ORIGINAL LANGUAGE

The language in which a TEXT was first written. The original languages of the HEBREW BIBLE were HEBREW and ARAMAIC, while KOINE Greek was the original language of the NT (though some argue that Matthew was originally written in Aramaic).

OT. *See* OLD TESTAMENT

OVERCODING. *See* IDEOLOGICAL OVERCODING; RHETORICAL OVERCODING

OXYMORON

A FIGURE OF SPEECH that juxtaposes incongruous or contradictory words or objects for effect, such as "an honest thief" or Romeo's "O loving hate." Given the early church's understanding of Jesus as the Christ, God's anointed Messiah, Paul in 1 Cor. 1:23 probably intended that the phrase "Christ crucified" be oxymoronic, as may be the beloved's description of her emotion in Song 5:2: "I slept, but my heart was awake."

P

P (PRIESTLY DOCUMENT)

According to the GRAF-WELLHAUSEN HYPOTHESIS, the last of four sources used for the formation of the PENTATEUCH. Two of the sources—J (Yahwist) and E (Elohist)—were combined in the late seventh or early sixth century BCE, and JE was combined with the D (Deuteronomic) source during the EXILE. The P (Priestly) material was then collected and added in Babylon or Jerusalem between about 458 and 444 BCE. The source is called Priestly due to its concern with legal and cultic issues.

PALEOGRAPHY

The study of the history and development of ancient TEXTS, here with a focus in TEXTUAL CRITICISM on the dating and DECODING of biblical manuscripts. Its scope extends from the DEAD SEA SCROLLS (second century BCE) to the fifteenth century CE and the invention of the printing press.

PALESTINIAN JUDAISM

Traditionally, the designation for the brand of JUDAISM in postexilic Palestine in contradistinction to the Judaism of the DIASPORA or HELLENISTIC JUDAISM. While scholars have assumed that the process of hellenization was less influential on the Judaism within Palestine than on that in the Diaspora, Martin Hengel has offered an extensive argument that by the mid-third century BCE, Judaism in Palestine had become thoroughly Hellenistic. He suggests that we should distinguish between the Greek-speaking Judaism of the Diaspora and the Aramaic/Hebrew-speaking Judaism of Palestine and Babylonia.

When scholars speak of Palestinian Judaism, however, they usually have in mind the major sects that developed in Palestine before and during the Hellenistic period until the destruction of the Jewish temple in 70 CE. These include the PHARISEES, SADDUCEES, ESSENES, and SAMARITANS.

Bibliography. Martin Hengel, *Jews, Greeks, and Barbarians* (Philadelphia: Fortress, 1980); idem, *Judaism and Hellenism* (2 vols.; Philadelphia: Fortress, 1974).

PALESTINIAN TALMUD. *See* TALMUD

PALIMPSEST

In TEXTUAL CRITICISM, a term for a manuscript whose original writing was removed by scraping so that another TEXT could be written on top of it, due to the scarcity of writing materials. This was especially the case with texts written on VELLUM. The original text, however, is often recoverable by photographic means, such as using infrared light, because it was not completely scraped off. The recovered text may be as much as seven centuries older than the one written over it. Currently there exist about fifty palimpsests of the NT whose original writing dates to earlier than the eleventh century CE.

PANEGYRIC

A poem or SPEECH praising an individual or group for an achievement. Paul's praise of Epaphroditus in Phil. 2:25–30 may be an example. *See* ENCOMIUM.

PAPYRUS

A writing material developed from the papyrus plant, a reed that grew plentifully in the delta of the Nile River but little elsewhere. The pithy center of the plant was cut into thin strips, which were laid side by side, the process being repeated for a second layer, which was then glued crosswise over the first. The sheets were then beaten and dried. Writing was done on the side of the sheet where the strips ran horizontally. In some rare cases, however, the side with the vertical strips was also used for writing (Rev. 5:1). When written on both sides, the papyrus is known as an opisthograph. Most, if not all, of the originals of the NT were written on papyrus.

Bibliography. J. Harold Greenlee, *Introduction to New Testament Textual Criticism* (Grand Rapids: Eerdmans, 1964; rev. ed., Peabody, MA: Hendrickson, 1995); Bruce M. Metzger, *The Text of the New Testament* (3rd ed.; Oxford: Oxford University Press, 1992).

PAPYRUS MANUSCRIPTS

The earliest extant manuscripts of the NT, numbering over 120 and ranging from small fragments with a few verses to manuscripts of entire books (e.g., Luke, John, parts of the Pauline EPISTLES, CATHOLIC EPISTLES). The extant NT papyri date from the second to the eighth centuries CE.

PARABLE

An extended METAPHOR generally employing familiar situations, persons, or events to illustrate or illuminate an unfamiliar or unrecognized TRUTH. "Parable" is derived from the Greek *parabolē*, which the LXX uses to translate the Hebrew MASHAL (*māshāl*, a PROVERB, RIDDLE, ALLEGORY, or taunt song; Bailey and Vander Broek, 106). In the Hebrew Bible, the parable is in the form of moral stories and allegories (e.g., Judg. 9:7–15; 2 Sam. 12:1–7; Ezek. 17:1–10). Judges 9:7–15 actually reads more like a FABLE; it also sounds like a parable in that the story illustrates a particular point. In 2 Sam. 12:1–7 Nathan uses a story about a rich man who steals a poor man's only lamb, which he loves more than anything else. Nathan uses the story to condemn David's affair with Bathsheba. This story (parable) is quite similar in structure (narrative and application) to the parables of Jesus. Ezekiel 17:1–10 is the allegorical narrative of two eagles and a vine, followed by an explanation in 17:11–24. Other possible parables are Ezek. 15:1–5; 21:8–17; 23:1–21; Jer. 24:1–10.

In the early twentieth century, Adolf Jülicher divided the parables of Jesus into four types: SIMILITUDE, STORY, EXAMPLE STORY, and allegory. A similitude has a customary sense about it in that it draws attention to some commonly recurrent event, such as the growth of the mustard seed, the leavening of bread, or the properties of salt. In this TYPE of parable, the reader must ascertain the relationship between the event and the more abstract issue being illuminated.

The parable as story is a PERICOPE with beginning, middle, and end. It will usually revolve around one or two characters engaged in some ACTION and will be marked by a brevity of detail. The action will move swiftly to a conclusion, inviting the reader to make a single comparison between the culminating action and the point of the story. Examples of such parables are the parables of the two sons, the friend at midnight, and the lost sheep.

Jülicher's third parable type is the example story. In this type, the central character exhibits exemplary behavior. The central point is to "look at this person and act likewise." One of the most familiar example stories is the parable of the good Samaritan. His moral behavior is exemplary and should thus be emulated.

The final type is the parable as allegory. Actually, this type is nothing more than a series of metaphors, which means that this parable (unlike the others) necessarily has a number of comparative points. Examples of this type are the parables of the tares, the net, and the sower.

In more recent scholarship, the above classifications have been challenged. C. H. Dodd makes a distinction between the parabolic saying (a FIGURE OF SPEECH that is closer to a proverb), the similitude, and the parable proper. When the parabolic saying (e.g., Matt. 5:14b, "A city built on a hill cannot be hid") is developed in a short narrative, it is called a similitude, which describes a universal situation. The parable proper, however, is a longer narrative, inviting a comparison to something outside itself (e.g., the parable of the workers in Matt. 20:2–15 compares the workers in the story to the kingdom of heaven). Recent scholarship has also focused on the characteristics of parable. A parable (1) is a brief narrative using an economy of words (probably reflecting its origin in the ORAL TRADITION); (2) employs everyday, vivid imagery; (3) follows a simple PLOT; (4) creates contrasts; and (5) employs metaphor (Dodd, 108–10).

A parable initially offers the hearer a typical or familiar view of some part of reality and then shocks the hearer with an alternative view. Parables demand response, choice between the conventionally inadequate and the radically new (e.g., the parables of the workers, the good Samaritan, and the unjust steward). In this sense, the parables are not allegories because they attempt not to describe the conventional world in cryptic language but to reveal a new vision of the world (111).

By the time the parables were recorded in the GOSPELS, however, their original SETTINGS had been lost. Therefore, the idea that a parable focuses on a single comparison must be qualified. Most parables told by Jesus concerned the kingdom of God, which itself is presented as a parable (Conzelmann and Lindemann, 78). Although parables do offer a comparison, the comparison is told in terms of IMAGERY, necessitating a consideration of multiple IMAGES and THEMES.

When readers encounter a parable in the Gospels, they need to ask not only what Jesus's point is but also what LITERARY function the parable has for the evangelist. For instance, in Mark's version of the parable of the sower (4:3–8) and Matthew's parable of the tares (13:24–30), each original parable is given an allegorical INTERPRETATION by the evangelist. The original settings of these parables cannot be discovered and indeed are irrelevant to their interpretation as they now stand in their present CONTEXTS. Furthermore, in Mark's Gospel the parables function almost exclusively to separate the insiders from the outsiders. Mark accomplishes this by reversing the parable's purpose. The parable is supposed to make some point more easily understood, but the parables in Mark become a means by which information is clothed in mystery, as far as the disciples and those outside are concerned. The disciples, who should understand the parables, are the very ones who do not. The astute reader of Mark's Gospel soon recognizes that the disciples consistently do not understand the parables and that those who think themselves to be insiders may actually be outsiders. This understanding of Mark's use of the parables at once causes modern readers to examine their own status within the circle of Christ.

Bibliography. James L. Bailey and Lyle D. Vander Broek, *Literary Forms in the New Testament: A Handbook* (Louisville: Westminster John Knox, 1992); Hans Conzelmann and Andreas Lindemann, *Interpreting the New Testament* (trans. Siegfried S. Schatzmann; Peabody, MA: Hendrickson, 1988); C. H. Dodd, *The Parables of the Kingdom* (London: Nisbet, 1935); Charles W. Hedrick, *Many Things in Parables: Jesus and His Modern Critics* (Louisville: Westminster John Knox, 2004); idem, *Parables as Poetic Fictions: The Creative Voice of Jesus* (Peabody, MA: Hendrickson, 1994); Adolf Jülicher, *Die Gleichnisreden Jesu* (2 vols.; Tübingen: Mohr, 1899–1910); Leland Ryken, *How to Read the Bible as Literature* (Grand Rapids: Zondervan, 1984).

PARABOLIC SAYINGS. *See* PARABLE

PARADIGM

A term that Martin Dibelius introduced into FORM CRITICISM to denote a brief NARRATIVE that sets the stage for a Jesus SAYING. The narrative exists for the saying rather than the saying for the narrative (e.g., Mark 2:1–12, the healing of the paralytic, with the saying in vv. 5 and 8–11; Mark 14:3–7, the anointing in Bethany, with the saying in vv. 6–7). *See* SAYING(s); STORY.

In recent LITERARY studies, the term has come to refer to interpretive methods (*see* CRITICAL METHODOLOGY) and their ideological FRAMEWORKS, the idea being that all interpretive methods are based on a system of PRESUPPOSITIONS, values, and social structures and are therefore never totally objective.

PARADIGMATIC AXIS. *See* SYNTAGMATIC/ PARADIGMATIC AXIS

PARADOX

A contradictory statement or state of affairs, which may or may not be reconciled. Particular paradoxes are brief, pithy statements that approach OXYMORON, while general paradoxes are complex conceptions that may be at the heart of understandings of reality. For example, at the center of the Christian faith is the paradox that humans will gain life through death. Also at the heart of the book of Jonah is the paradox pertaining to God as being both just and merciful. Some of the BEATITUDES in Matt. 5 are particular paradoxes. Paradoxes are also found in Paul's EPISTLES (e.g., 2 Cor. 4:8–11; Phil. 3:7; 1 Cor. 7:22).

New Critics (*see* NEW CRITICISM) argue that more than anything else, a poem is an experience or, perhaps better, a unification of experience. Through paradox, IRONY, and METAPHOR, a poem holds contradictory and conflicting elements of experience in a diversified unity. Cleanth Brooks even goes so far as to claim that the language of poetry is paradox.

Paradox is also at the heart of DECONSTRUCTION. If language is inherently ambiguous and self-referential, including the language of texts, then MEANING is ultimately indefinite and never completely recoverable because any EXPLANATION of meaning is presented in terms of an ambiguous language. Consequently, meaning is always provisional.

> *Bibliography.* Cleanth Brooks, *The Well Wrought Urn* (New York: Reynal and Hitchcock, 1947).

PARAENESIS

Sections of general moral exhortation in the epistles. For a detailed discussion of paraenesis, *see* EPISTOLARY LITERATURE.

PARALEIPSIS (PARALEPSIS, PARALIPSIS)

A FIGURE OF SPEECH by which an AUTHOR highlights an item or issue by ignoring it or by pretending to say nothing about it, actually proceeding to comment (often in some detail) on the subject. An example of the latter is Paul's comments to the Thessalonians in 1 Thess. 4:9–12.

PARALLELISM. *See* BIBLICAL POETRY

PARALLELISM, ANTITHETICAL. *See* BIBLICAL POETRY

PARALLELISM, CLIMACTIC. *See* CLIMACTIC PARALLELISM

PARALLELISM, CONSTRUCTIVE. *See* SYNTHETIC PARALLELISM

PARALLELISM, DYNAMIC. *See* DYNAMIC INTERPLAY

PARALLELISM, EMBLEMATIC. *See* EMBLEMATIC PARALLELISM

PARALLELISM, FORMAL. *See* BIBLICAL POETRY

PARALLELISM, INTERLINEAR. *See* INTERLINEAR PARALLELISM

PARALLELISM, INTERNAL. *See* INTERNAL PARALLELISM

PARALLELISM, INVERTED. *See* CHIASMUS

PARALLELISM, POETIC. *See* BIBLICAL POETRY

PARALLELISM, SEMANTIC. *See* BIBLICAL POETRY

PARALLELISM, STAIRSTEP. *See* STAIRSTEP PARALLELISM

PARALLELISM, SYNONYMOUS. *See* BIBLICAL POETRY

PARALLELISM, SYNTACTIC. *See* SYNTACTIC PARALLELISM

PARALLELISM, SYNTHETIC. *See* SYNTHETIC PARALLELISM

PARAPHRASE

In BIBLICAL STUDIES, a TRANSLATION of a TEXT that tries to capture the SENSE of the original text, opting for CLARITY rather than for fidelity to its linguistic structures and vocabulary. The extent to which a paraphrase translation involves interpretive bias is a point of perennial debate. Two well-known paraphrases are THE LIVING BIBLE and The Message (*see* MESSAGE, THE).

In NEW CRITICISM, *paraphrase* refers to the attempt to capture the essence of a LITERARY work in EXPLANATION. Since a text is a complex integration of FORM and CONTENT and means what it means in terms of that integration, a paraphrase not only is incapable of capturing that MEANING but will usually distort it (*see* HERESY OF PARAPHRASE).

PARATACTIC STYLE. *See* PARATAXIS

PARATAXIS

Writing or SPEECH that uses coordination rather than subordination between clauses. The coordination may be without the use of conjunctions or with conjunctions, especially with "and." The relationship between clauses and phrases in a sentence is left for the reader to determine. Parataxis is usually associated with unsophisticated speech or writing, is common in Semitic texts, and is central to the style in Mark's GOSPEL. Mark's lack of relative pronouns and subordinating conjunctions to join clauses strikes the modern reader as elementary and unsophisticated. He consistently employs the paratactic style, in which clauses are joined with "and." This paratactic style gives to the Gospel a certain regular cadence, a sense of rapid movement. Mark also frequently (over forty times) uses the word *euthys* (immediately), which, when combined with his paratactic style and his frequent use of the historical present, heightens his rapid pace into a sense of urgency. Undoubtedly, such a SENSE is communicated to the reader, perhaps without the reader's recognition of it.

Asyndetic parataxis occurs when the AUTHOR or speaker connects words, phrases, or sentences without any coordinating or subordinating connective (Soulen and Soulen, 135). Again, the reader must infer the syntagmatic relationship between the elements. Psalm 33:16 is an example: "A king is not saved by his great army; a warrior is not delivered by his great strength." The relationship between the two sentences may be "Just as a king is not saved by his great army, so a warrior is not delivered by his great strength."

Bibliography. Richard N. Soulen and R. Kendall Soulen, *Handbook of Biblical Criticism* (3rd ed.; Louisville: Westminster John Knox, 2002).

PARCHMENT. *See* VELLUM

PARODY

A type of SATIRE in which a writer imitates another writer's STYLE or work, usually intended as a CRITICISM. In literature, parody is similar to the caricature in art, poking fun at or ridiculing a person, style, or work. Leland Ryken (*Words of Life*, 111) argues that the PROLOGUE to John's GOSPEL parodies the *Hymn to Zeus* ("the universal Word, that flows through all, and the light celestial. . . . One Word—whose voice alas! The wicked spurn") by employing similar vocabulary to describe Jesus. Ryken also suggests that the antihero type in such Hebrew heroes as Gideon, Moses, and Joshua parodies the conventional hero, who relies on "his own abilities, wins victory through heroic action and is rewarded with fame and a political kingdom" (*Words of Delight*, 116).

Bibliography. Leland Ryken, *Words of Delight: A Literary Introduction to the Bible* (Grand Rapids: Baker, 1987); idem, *Words of Life: A Literary Introduction to the New Testament* (Grand Rapids: Baker, 1987).

PAROLE. See LANGUE; STRUCTURALISM

PARONOMASIA

A PUN or a wordplay with words that have different MEANINGS but similar or identical sounds. The punning is usually lost in TRANSLATIONS from the Hebrew and Greek. Paul puns in 2 Cor. 4:8 ("perplexed [*aporoumenoi*], but not driven to despair [*exaporoumenoi*]"). Paronomasia is also commonplace in the HEBREW BIBLE (e.g., Amos 8:1–2 where *qayiṣ*, "summer fruit," is used with *qēṣ*, "end").

PARTICIPATIONIST MODEL

One of two ways (the other way being the JUDICIAL MODEL) Paul conceptualizes the relationship between salvation of humans and Jesus's death (e.g., Rom. 5–6). In this model, human salvation from sin as a cosmic enslaving force comes from participating in Jesus's death through the act of baptism (Ehrman, 325–27).

Bibliography. Bart Ehrman, *The New Testament: A Historical Introduction to the Early Christian Writings* (2nd ed.; New York: Oxford University Press, 2000).

PASSION NARRATIVES

In the GOSPELS, the NARRATIVES of Jesus's suffering and death (Mark 14–15; Matt. 26–27; Luke 22–23; John 18–19). Most scholars agree that Mark's STORY was the earliest and was probably used as Matthew's and Luke's source. Although the narratives do have a sense of historical reality, they have been molded to reflect the theological concerns of the writers. A comparison of the three SYNOPTIC GOSPELS illustrates the point. Although Matthew and Luke generally follow the CHRONOLOGY of Mark's narrative, they both add and delete some details. For example, Matthew and Luke delete any REFERENCE to the temple's curtain being torn in half. Matthew adds the link between Judas Iscariot and a passage in Jeremiah, the dream of Pilate's wife, an earthquake that results in a resurrection of corpses, the confession by the centurion's men of the divinity of Jesus, the PHARISEES' persuading Pilate to provide soldiers to guard Jesus's tomb, and the SADDUCEES' bribing the soldiers to report that Jesus's disciples had removed his body (Harris, 172). While Mark's and Matthew's narratives record the Roman centurion as proclaiming that Jesus is the Son of God, Luke's centurion proclaims that Jesus is an innocent man. Mark's THEME of Jesus as the SUFFERING SERVANT and of Jesus's ironic fulfillment of Hebrew SCRIPTURE, Matthew's theme of Jesus as the fulfillment of PROPHECY, and Luke's theme of Jesus as the innocent Savior—all dictate their SELECTION AND ARRANGEMENT of source material. This selection and arrangement, based on theological concerns, has convinced many scholars that theological concerns were primary for the evangelists rather than historical facts. LITERARY critics argue further that the passion narratives should be interpreted in terms of the entire Gospels and understood as reflecting and focusing on major themes.

Bibliography. Stephen L. Harris, *The New Testament: A Student's Introduction* (4th ed.; Boston: McGraw-Hill, 2002).

PASTORAL EPISTLES

In the NT, the epistles of 1–2 Timothy and Titus. The title derives from the pastoral advice that the AUTHOR gives to his addressees Timothy and Titus. Many scholars argue that the Pastoral Epistles are PSEUDEPIGRAPHA due to their CONTENT and FORM. For a more detailed discussion of the Pastoral Epistles, *see* EPISTOLARY LITERATURE.

PATERNALISM

Particularly a concern in FEMINIST CRITICISM, a term for an approach to dealing with people in a manner that a father deals with children, especially in terms of subordination and power. Most, if not all, feminist critics argue that paternalism is the way that men in society at large and leaders in the church in particular relate to women.

PATHOS

One of the three kinds of appeals in Aristotle's theory of RHETORIC. Pathos is the appeal to the audience's emotions. In literature, "pathos" also refers to that quality of the work that generates emotions in the reader, such as pity, sorrow, and tenderness. *See* RHETORICAL CRITICISM.

PATRIARCHAL CULTURE. *See* PATRIARCHAL STRUCTURES; PATRIARCHY

PATRIARCHAL NARRATIVES

Sometimes referred to as the patriarchal legends and ancestral narratives, the stories of Israel's early patriarchs in Gen. 12–50. The focus of the NARRATIVES is the threefold promise of land, progeny, and blessing that God makes to Abraham. In a variety of ways, the promise is placed in jeopardy (esp. in terms of family conflicts) as the narrative moves from Abraham (12–25) to Isaac and Jacob (25–36) and to Joseph (37–50).

PATRIARCHAL PERIOD

In the HEBREW BIBLE, the period of the patriarchs: Abraham, Isaac, Jacob, and Joseph (Gen. 12–50).

PATRIARCHAL STRUCTURES

In FEMINIST CRITICISM, a matrix of social, economic, GENDER, aesthetic, political, and historical arrangements of authority and power within PATRIARCHAL CULTURES that define, authorize, legitimate, and perpetuate the value systems of men while marginalizing women (as well as other powerless groups).

PATRIARCHY

A term current in critical theory for male domination of women. This domination subordinates and oppresses women in all areas of culture: politics, economics, religion, sex, and so forth. Feminist critics argue that PATRIARCHAL STRUCTURES in cultures both legitimate and perpetuate such treatment and that in most Western cultures, many of these patriarchal structures have their origin in the BIBLE. The biblical TEXTS have been and are still used to justify the male domination of women in society. *See* FEMINIST CRITICISM.

PATRI-KYRIARCHY

Elisabeth Schüssler Fiorenza's combination of PATRIARCHY and KYRIARCHY, suggesting that patriarchy is a function of kyriarchy. As she puts it, "I understand patriarchy as a structure of kyriarchy, as a social and discursive system that interstructures GENDER, race, class, and colonialist oppressions and has as its focal point women at the bottom of the sociopolitical and religious pyramid" (211).

Bibliography. Elisabeth Schüssler Fiorenza, *Bread Not Stone* (10th anniversary ed.; Boston: Beacon, 1995).

PATTERNED RHETORICAL PROSE. *See* PATTERNED WRITING

PATTERNED WRITING

A type of writing that calls attention to its conscious structuring and artistic skill. Poetry in the HEBREW BIBLE is such writing, and the EPISTLES

in the NT also contain it. An example is found in 1 Cor. 15:42–44:

> What is sown is perishable,
> What is raised is imperishable.
> It is sown in dishonor,
> It is raised in glory.
> It is sown in weakness,
> It is raised in power.
> It is sown a physical body,
> It is raised a spiritual body.

In the NT, patterned writing may be referred to as patterned rhetorical prose. Examples are in Eph. 4 and Rom. 8:

> There is one body
> and one Spirit,
> just as you were called
> to the one hope
> of your calling,
> one Lord,
> one faith,
> one baptism,
> one God and Father of all,
> who is above all
> and through all
> and in all. (Eph. 4:4–6)

> For I am convinced that neither death,
> nor life,
> nor angels,
> nor rulers,
> nor things present,
> nor things to come,
> nor powers,
> nor height,
> nor depth,
> nor anything else in all creation,
> will be able to separate us
> from the love of God
> in Christ Jesus our Lord. (Rom. 8:38–39)

Bibliography. W. Randolph Tate, *Biblical Interpretation: An Integrated Approach* (rev. ed.; Peabody, MA: Hendrickson, 1997).

PEACE WISH

A formal part of the CLOSING in a Pauline epistle. In the peace wish, Paul returns to the major concern(s) of the letter. For example, the peace wish in Gal. 6:16, "As for those who will follow this rule—peace be upon them, and mercy, and upon the Israel of God," returns to Paul's concern with the bondage of circumcision versus freedom in Christ and with the nature of the true Israel. *See* EPISTOLARY LITERATURE.

PENITENTIAL PSALMS

A group of PSALMS (6; 32; 38; 51; 102; 130; 143) in which the speaker confesses sin and seeks a means of forgiveness, which usually comes about by God's grace.

PENTATEUCH

While technically referring to the case (*teuchos*) that contained the scrolls, Pentateuch (Greek for "five scrolls") is used to name the first five books in the HEBREW BIBLE. Also called the LAW and TORAH, it contains numerous collections of laws that eventually defined later expressions of JUDAISM. It also contains formative events (the exodus, the Passover, the occupation of Palestine) around which Jewish IDENTITY was formulated. For issues of authorship and dating, *see* GRAF-WELLHAUSEN HYPOTHESIS; SOURCE CRITICISM.

PERFORMANCE CRITICISM

An interpretive approach that looks for clues within texts as well as within the texts' contemporary culture that might shed light on the manner in which the texts were performed. Consider the following example:

> An anxious man—wiping the sweat from his brow—presses through a crowd of people, eager to hear the teacher's upcoming speech. A nearby woman hushes a whimpering child while a few children retire from playfully chasing each other on the slopes. The sun is at its zenith as the teacher sits down on a rock situated higher on the slope than all of the other people. He raises an arm and begins to speak: "Blessed are the poor in spirit, for theirs is the kingdom of heaven." His inflection remains placid, rising only time to time for potent and poignant remarks. He smirks coyly as he says, "Do not even the tax collectors do the same?" He

> finally concludes the speech somberly comparing the one who does not heed his words to a house that is damaged by natural disaster. He says, "It fell—and great was its fall." (author's rendering)

Though it is difficult or even impossible to determine with certainty and precision, Jesus's famous discourse in Matt. 5–7 and Luke 7 may have happened in a manner similar to that described above.

A nonbiblical example comes from the High Middle Ages in the *chansons de geste* (songs of deeds), a type of literature directed primarily to noble audiences. Although the origins of such stories are obscure, many historians suppose that the clergy in monasteries along the great pilgrimage routes encouraged poets to versify legends to entertain the pilgrims when they stayed overnight at the monasteries. These poems eventually spread all over France. The poets who composed the songs were called *trouvéres* in northern France and *troubadours* in the south. The poems were passed on by *jongleurs* (entertainers), who would perform the poems in the great hall on special occasions. The performance would include all kinds of gestures, dramatizations, and chant and was usually accompanied by a musical instrument. Although the details are lost to modern audiences in the mere reading of the poems, we can imaginatively reconstruct the performance. We can picture the great stone hall of the castle, the fire blazing and crackling in the huge hearth, the smoky torches lighting the hall, the members of the noble family in their furred coats and robes, the courtiers fawning over the family, the nervous dogs, the uproarious laughter of the crowd, and the *jongleur* performing his drama, alternating between characters, breaking at times for refreshment and a few juggling (derived from *jongleur*) tricks.

Performance criticism arose out of the desire to understand aspects of a TEXT that are embedded in the performance event, because written texts were often spoken or performed before and after their recording, especially in ancient societies. For example, it is difficult or even impossible to reconstruct with certainty the full CONTEXT, the scene, and nuances of Jesus's DISCOURSE in Matt.

5–7 and Luke 7. It is also difficult to capture all the potential nuances present in such a speech—the gestures, emphasis, body language, possible tongue-in-cheek statements, a change of pace, a pause, raising or lowering of the voice, and sly references. In other words, the readers are far removed from the original performance event and can only imagine the performance of the text. Because of their separation from the text's performance, readers are not privy to information that would enhance their understanding and experience of the text. From bards' recounting legendary tales of national history to the Elizabethan plays, texts and performances are often intertwined. Hence, texts need to be studied in light of the "theatrical conditions" in which they are written, and performance criticism attempts to do just that (McGee, 133). For example, some scholars have tried to create performable texts by experimenting "with a special typography and layout where type size and page design attempt to present analogs for the eye of what the ear would have heard" (Franklin, 8).

Performance critics assume that ancient storytellers, like modern ones, had at their disposal ready-mades, a stock of ideas, phrases, and words that were part of the common knowledge of an audience. Such knowledge allowed the storyteller to evoke certain memories and associations in the mind of the audience. The extent to which modern critics can recapture the immediacy, spontaneity, and contextual dynamics through studying texts is a major concern of performance critics. Although these critics recognize how difficult it is to tease such indicators out of a written text, they also realize that they may be somewhat recoverable. Such things as repetition, hints of orality, the differences between versions of the same story, and the choice of one word over another—all may be due not to different sources or traditions but to the teller's wish to say something a little differently, perhaps with tongue in cheek, in order to elicit a particular response from the audience, especially if the audience is familiar with the story or with another version. Such subtle changes may have elicited differing audience reactions.

Performance critics assume that the meaning of a text, especially the text of a PLAY, is fully realized in the performance event (McGee, 133). Moreover, performance critics assume that a play is written for the purpose of being performed. The MEANING of a text springs to life on stage through the actors' words and ACTIONS, and the performance adds a visual element for the audience to aid in text INTERPRETATION. Therefore, the theatrical condition of a text's performance is helpful to the understanding of a text. Accordingly, historical research of a text and its respective theatrical conditions is essential to a more accurate performance, which also generates a more plausible interpretation. The performance event is the "site of interpretation, including the dynamics of performance, the influence of place and circumstance, and the experience of an audience" (Rhoads). In other words, when compared with merely reading a written text, the performance of a text adds another dimension of meaning. Giles and Doen examine the way in which performance criticism broadens the scope of understanding when applied to the BIBLE. This interpretive approach assumes that certain biblical passages are actually textual versions of previously oral compositions, which were originally recited or performed before live audiences. Some examples of these biblical passages include the songs inserted into OT narratives, the Hebrew Psalter, the prophetic writings, numerous lines that appear to be songs in the NT, and even the whole Gospel of Mark. Such material, read aloud in a public context, takes on elements of performance, and scholarly analysis of such performance dynamics provides additional insight into the meaning of the text. This critical approach, then, can be applied to the original performance event or to oral readings of both sacred and secular written texts (one need only imagine the performance of the Song of Songs). Ultimately, the performance critic seeks to restore the performance aspect of a text (Loubser).

The earliest forms of performance criticism originate with ancient thinkers such as Plato. For example, in *Ion* (ca. 390 BCE) Socrates tells Ion that a muse delivers a meaning to the performer, and the performer then delivers that meaning to the audience (McGee, 133). This interplay of meaning between original source and the reception of meaning in an audience is crucial to performance theory. Plato further comments on the potency of such interplay. In his *Republic* Plato claims that dramatic poets foster emotion over reason and that they ought to be banned from the ideal republic (133). Such a statement suggests that the performance event may convey the meaning of a text more potently to an audience than just the text itself.

While the initial ideas of performance criticism seem to have formed among ancient thinkers such as Plato and even Aristotle, modern performance criticism seems to have originated with William Poel. In his 1881 production of *Hamlet*, Poel incorporated Elizabethan dress, a bare Elizabethan stage, and an Elizabethan rhythm in line delivery in an attempt to capture the original performance event as much as possible (McGee, 133). Poel's work initiated the need to study texts—including their historical context—in order to understand their original IDIOMS and then potentially to convert those idioms into their modern equivalents. Another figure, Bernard Beckerman, utilizes historical research to determine the taste of an audience, behavior at a theater, actors and acting styles, and even conventions governing speech on the stage in Shakespeare's works (135).

Numerous figures, however, have derogated the performance and its role in text interpretation. For example, Charles Lamb says that Shakespeare's *King Lear* is impossible to portray on stage because of its complex profundities, which are better left to a reader's imagination (McGee, 134). Despite such difficulties, performance theory has a major influence on editing the text of plays. Harley Granville Barker suggests that when considering a disputed passage in a play, one needs to exhaust all of its performance possibilities before making a decision on an edit. Moreover, edits of Shakespeare's plays reveal "how strong an impact performance criticism has made: 19th-century texts were overwhelmed by scholarly annotation . . . and employ

annotations to direct attention to performances, past and possible" (137). Thus, performance criticism has heightened scholarly awareness of how past performances can help show the meaning of the text.

Performance criticism can be applied in numerous ways to accomplish different ends. When applied linguistically, for example, it raises the possibility that the text of Q—a theoretical text that the SYNOPTIC GOSPELS use as a source—may have been not an actual text constructed by the wealthy or the poor but an ORAL TRADITION memorized through performance (Horsley, *Oral Performance*, 80). Richard Horsley uses Luke's record of the Sermon on the Mount as an example of a memorized performance to show that memorization is more common and is embedded into the text of ancient societies. Each of Luke's BEATITUDES replicates a series of stresses that are rhythmically easier to memorize, using a pattern of "cradling" and "lifting" (79–81). Horsley examines the nuances of KOINE Greek to suggest that synoptic authors may have been using an oral tradition in their works rather than an actual Q document. Based on historical criticism, Horsley suggests that people in the first century did not have easy access to written texts and therefore were more likely to memorize discourses or texts by using such methods. Thus, the performance critic isolates parts of biblical language to comment on the RHETORIC of the Greek text and its capacity to be memorized easily by an audience. Though replicating the sound of ancient Koine Greek seems nearly impossible, listening to any consistent replication of a dead language is beneficial for hearing recurring patterns (Daitz, 411–12). Thus, when applied to a biblical text, performance criticism suggests that the Q source may not have existed as a written text and that the Sermon on the Mount follows linguistic conventions that make it easy for an audience to memorize it.

Another valuable insight that performance criticism lends to biblical scholarship is the performance test. For example, some Markan scholars have difficulty understanding Jesus's words to his disciples about the poor widow in Mark 12. Some interpret Jesus's statement about her as a criticism "for contributing to a corrupt temple that is doomed to destruction" (Rhoads, 34). However, Rhoads suggests that Jesus's line—"Truly I tell you, this poor widow has put in more than all those who are contributing to the treasury. For all of them have contributed out of their abundance; but she out of her poverty has put in everything she had, all she had to live on" (Mark 12:43–44)—cannot be performed to convey such a meaning. Additionally, Rhoads asks, "How could one convey the Jesus cry of abandonment on the cross (from Ps. 22:1) so as to express hopefulness?" (34). He concludes that a text has a range of possible meanings and possible performances, and evaluating potential performances to a modern and an imaginary ancient audience may be one way to "test the limits of legitimate interpretations" (34).

Performance criticism coupled with historical criticism of Mark has led scholars such as Richard Horsley to believe that the whole text of Mark and even other works of antiquity were originally oral tradition and meant to be performed; they were "inscribed upon the memory as much as on papyri" (Horsley, *Jesus in Context*, 89). Such communication characterizes ancient societies, and texts were more likely to be performed than read silently, as is modern practice (91). In ancient societies, scrolls were costly, and though some persons appeared to be literate, many were not. The interplay of power between the literate and illiterate and its relationship to auditory performance is a new development in biblical scholarship, and this element of ancient society is quickly becoming the topic of performance criticism applied to the Bible.

Performance criticism has numerous appealing features, especially in the field of BIBLICAL STUDIES. For starters, it attends to the original context of the performance event, where the meaning of a spoken "text" is clearest. Such an approach seems to be beneficial for the scholars who seek authorial intent, given that performance criticism attempts to get closer to the personal agent. Additionally,

modern human experience seems to favor performance criticism in some cases. For example, in text messages, emails, and other social media where inflection is lost, meaning is often confused, especially if a statement is meant to be sarcastic or humorous. In such cases, the performance event conveys meaning better than the text alone. The performance event is the site and origin of meaning, in this case, with the written text being once removed. Whether or not they can be successful, performance critics feel that the attempt to isolate the performance event brings readers closer to the experience of earlier readers and thus closer to an understanding that more accurately approximates the authorial intention.

Although performance criticism in biblical interpretation may be hampered by historical distance, performance critics feel that the approach provides more insight into the culture of ancient societies and the nuances of a "performance-based" society. A method that started as an attempt to capture original Elizabethan performance has prompted biblical scholars to investigate the nature of their written texts and their capacity to be performed to the original audience.

Bibliography. S. G. Daitz, "Further Notes on the Pronunciation of Ancient Greek," *Classical World* 95 (2002): 411–12; Mark Edwards, *Sound, Sense, and Rhythm: Listening to Greek and Latin Poetry* (Princeton: Princeton University Press, 2002); Wayne Franklin, "Beginnings to 1700," in *The Norton Anthology of American Literature*, vol. A (ed. Wayne Franklin, Philip F. Gura, and Arnold Krupat; New York: Norton, 2011); Terry Giles and William Doan, *Twice Used Songs: Performance Criticism of the Songs of Ancient Israel* (Peabody, MA: Hendrickson, 2008); Richard Horsley, *Hearing the Whole Story: The Politics of Plot in Mark's Gospel* (Louisville: Westminster John Knox, 2001); idem, *Jesus in Context: Power, People, and Performance* (Minneapolis: Fortress, 2008); idem, *Oral Performance, Popular Tradition, and Hidden Transcript in Q* (Atlanta: Society of Biblical Literature, 2006); Bobby Loubser, "How Do You Report Something That Was Said with a Smile?—Can We Overcome the Loss of Meaning When Oral-Manuscript Texts of the Bible Are Represented in Modern Printed Media?," *Scriptura* 87 (2004): 296–314; C. E. McGee, "Performance Criticism," in *Encyclopedia of Contemporary Literary Theory: Approaches, Scholars, Terms* (ed. Irena R. Makaryk; Toronto: University of Toronto Press, 1993); David Rhoads, "Performance Criticism: An Emerging

Methodology in Biblical Studies," paper presented to the Society of Biblical Literature, http://www.sbl-site.org/assets/pdfs/Rhoads_Performance.pdf.

PERFORMATIVE LANGUAGE

In SPEECH ACT THEORY, instances of language that effect what they say. For example, persuasive utterances or oaths (ILLOCUTIONARY ACTS) and ceremonial rites such as marriage and the Eucharist (PERLOCUTIONARY ACTS) involve performance.

PERICOPE

In BIBLICAL STUDIES, a self-contained unit of SCRIPTURE (e.g., Mark 3:1–6).

PERIPETEIA

A rhetorical term used by Aristotle in the *Poetics* for the sudden reversal of the tragic hero's fortunes. The term has been used in LITERARY CRITICISM to refer to any sudden or unexpected reversal of events (e.g., 2 Sam. 12:1–15; Judg. 9:50–57; Esther 6–7; Luke 12:13–21).

PERLOCUTIONARY ACT

An utterance that has its MEANING in its effect, such as persuading, soothing, condemning, or commanding. Ceremonial rites such as marriage— "I declare you husband and wife"—and the Eucharist also qualify as perlocutionary acts. *See* ILLOCUTIONARY ACT; LOCUTIONARY ACT; SPEECH ACT THEORY.

PERORATIO. See CONCLUSIO; DELIBERATIVE RHETORIC

PERSONA

From the Latin for "mask," referring to the NARRATOR or speaker in a STORY or poem. In the LITERARY analysis of a piece of literature, it is important to understand the mask donned by the AUTHOR for the purpose of telling the story because it has a direct impact on the POINT OF VIEW from which the reader perceives the ACTION. For example, the persona of the narrator in Ezra is a priest, while that of the narrator in Nehemiah is a former cupbearer to the Persian king and a participant in the ACTION of the NARRATIVE.

PERSONIFICATION

A literary device in which an inanimate object or a group of persons assumes the properties of a single human being. Examples include the personification of wisdom, evil, death, and the nation of Israel: "Wisdom cries out in the street; in the squares she raises her voice" (Prov. 1:20); "Abaddon and Death say, 'We have heard a rumor of it with our ears'" (Job 28:22); "When Israel [here referring to the nation, not the patriarch, though wordplay is most likely present] was a child, I loved him" (Hosea 11:1a). In each of these examples, a concept (wisdom, destruction, death) or a nation (Israel) assumes some property of a human being.

PERSPECTIVISM

The ASSUMPTION that one's perspective (theological, political, LITERARY, etc.) conditions one's knowledge or even determines it. In literary studies, perspectivism refers to the SOCIAL LOCATION from which a person interprets. In this view, OBJECTIVE KNOWLEDGE is impossible because no one can step beyond one's own matrix of CONTEXTs to perceive anything without ideological biases. Having some perspective beforehand, a perceiver brings to the process of INTERPRETATION an entire "forestructure" (*Vorstruktur*, Heidegger's term; *see* FRAMEWORK) that colors every object of investigation. In NEW CRITICISM, perspectivism refers to the "process of getting to know the object from different points of view, which may be defined and criticized in their turn" (Wellek and Warren, 48).

Bibliography. René Wellek and Austin Warren, *Theory of Literature* (3rd ed.; New York: Harcourt, 1977).

PESHER

A Hebrew term (*pēšer*) for COMMENTARY and used to some extent among the writers of the DEAD SEA SCROLLS. It is also a TYPE of MIDRASH performed on the nonlegal sections of the HEBREW BIBLE by the sect at QUMRAN. Typically, the commentaries quote a passage and then interpret it in such a way that an event or idea has its fulfillment or MEAN-ING in the contemporary Qumran community. For example, the "righteous" in Hab. 1:4 becomes the "Teacher of Righteousness," the founder of the community. The ASSUMPTION seems to have been that what was written in SCRIPTURE was intended specifically for the contemporary situation. A given statement in Scripture has its SIGNIFICANCE in a contemporary event. In a classic example of pesher, Peter interprets a prophecy of Joel in Acts 2:16–21 to refer to the events of Pentecost. Matthew also employs pesher in interpreting the prophecies of the Hebrew Bible as applying specifically to his community (e.g., 1:22–23; 2:13–15).

Bibliography. Bart D. Ehrman, The New Testament: A Historical Introduction to the Early Christian Writings (3rd ed.; New York: Oxford University Press, 2004); Stephen L. Harris, The New Testament: A Student's Introduction (4th ed.; Boston: McGraw-Hill, 2002); Richard N. Soulen and R. Kendall Soulen, Handbook of Biblical Criticism (3rd ed.; Louisville: Westminster John Knox, 2002).

PESHITTA

Dating from the late fourth century CE, the BIBLE of the Syrian church, written in Syriac, a dialect of Aramaic that became the theological language of the non-Greek-speaking early Eastern church. In some of the earlier manuscripts, 2 Peter, 2–3 John, Jude, and Revelation are omitted because the Syrian church did not hold these to be CANONICAL.

PHALLOCENTRISM

In recent LITERARY theory, a system of power relations promoting and perpetuating PATRIARCHY. The term has its origin in the psychoanalytic theory of Ernest Jones and was popularized by Jacques Lacan as a SYMBOL of the emergence of a person into the realm of the symbolic. In recent FEMINIST CRITICISM the term is used synonymously with patriarchy as a system of GENDER-specific power structures that empower men. In the hands of Jacques Derrida, the term comes to include all METANARRATIVES of the Western literary, scientific, religious, philosophical, and historical TRADITIONS. Consequently, phallocentrism refers to DISCOURSES that privilege, promote, and legiti-

mate social structures empowering men. Biblical feminist critics approach the biblical texts with suspicion of their being phallocentric both in nature and as a source for historically promoting patriarchy.

Bibliography. J. A. Cuddon, The Penguin Dictionary of Literary Terms and Literary Theory (4th ed.; London: Penguin, 1998).

PHALLOGOCENTRISM

Jacques Derrida's conflation of PHALLOCENTRISM and LOGOCENTRISM to denote the tendency in the Western philosophical tradition to assume that the logos, or spoken word, is the locus of MEANING. The term has been used within FEMINIST CRITICISM to evaluate PATRIARCHY.

Bibliography. Donna Haraway, "A Manifesto for Cyborgs," in From Modernism to Post-modernism: An Anthology (ed. Lawrence Cahoone; 2nd ed.; Malden, MA: Blackwell, 2003), 464–81.

PHARISAIC JUDAISM

The type of JUDAISM associated with the PHARISEES between the Maccabean Wars of the second century BCE and the fall of Jerusalem in 70 CE. After this period, Pharisaic Judaism became RABBINIC JUDAISM. The term "Pharisee" itself is an Aramaic word that means "separated one" and probably reflects the Pharisees' strict pursuit of cultic purity.

The Pharisees seem to have appealed to, and filled their ranks with, the middle levels of society—artisans, farmers, merchants, and so forth. They were not part of the priesthood but were governed by a group of legal scholars, who adapted the TORAH to new and novel situations both within Palestine and among those of the DIASPORA. They engaged in a kind of free INTERPRETATION of the Torah (see MIDRASH) in which both legal and nonlegal portions of the Torah were adapted to new and different circumstances and times.

The Pharisees also held the view that there existed a dual Torah (see TORAH), one written and one oral, both of which Yahweh gave to Moses at Mount Sinai. The Oral Torah (see TORAH) consisted of teachings that the great Pharisee leaders had given, interpretations of the written Torah (*see* GEMARA; MISHNAH). Over a long period of time, these interpretations multiplied because of the Pharisees' flexibility in adapting the Torah to changing times and circumstances (Hauer and Young, 219–20). This free adaptation of the Torah in order to create a means by which the average Jew could live a pious life of ritual purity became the major characteristic of Pharisaic Judaism. It was also characterized by a tolerance of civil authority if the authorities would allow the practice of Jewish law, rejection of armed revolt, and belief in a messianic age.

Bibliography. Christian Hauer and William Young, *An Introduction to the Bible: A Journey into Three Worlds* (4th ed.; Upper Saddle River, NJ: Prentice Hall, 1998).

PHARISEES

A Jewish sect that was instrumental in giving JUDAISM its distinctive character and definition until the fall of Jerusalem in 70 CE. After this time, Judaism was primarily RABBINIC JUDAISM. The religious program of the Pharisees was supported by two primary underpinnings—the WRITTEN TORAH and the ORAL TORAH. The Pharisees believed that the written Torah stood in constant need of INTERPRETATION and application to new and changing circumstances. They believed that God had given Moses both the written and the Oral Torahs, the latter being the interpretation and explanation of the former. The Oral Torah became as authoritative for the Pharisees as the written Torah. The interpretive applications that the Pharisees gave to the written Torah were as binding as the written Torah itself. Because of this openness to the interpretation of the TORAH, the Pharisees were susceptible to doctrines that were unacceptable to the SADDUCEES (e.g., bodily resurrection, final judgment, and rewards and punishment after death).

Not usually recognized by the casual readers of the NT is the great amount of doctrinal agreement between the Pharisees and Jesus and the early Christians. A substantial amount of Jesus's ethical teaching is paralleled in the rabbinic writings. Even where there is disagreement, the MEANING of Jesus's teaching or that of the early church must be understood in comparison with Pharisaic teaching. For example, the practice of summarizing the Torah by the use of a few principles (Matt. 22:36–40) would become a rabbinic practice. Separation from the world meant to the Pharisees that the pious individual must avoid contact with people who neglected the Torah (both written and oral); but for Jesus and the early Christians, separation from the world was a matter of attitude. When Jesus reinterprets the Torah in Matthew's SERMON ON THE MOUNT, he offers six antitheses (*see* ANTITHESIS; Matt. 5), whose premises are drawn from the written and Oral Torahs. Another example where a comparison with rabbinic material is crucial for interpreting a remark by Jesus occurs in Matt. 18:20: "For where two or three are gathered in my name, I am there among them." This is a reapplication of a rabbinic teaching claiming that where two or three are together studying the Torah, God is with them (Mishnah, *Pirqe 'Abot* 3.2). Jesus also rejected the Pharisees' practice of giving priority to the ORAL TRADITION over the written Torah. He agreed with the Pharisees' desire to make the Torah applicable, but he disagreed with aspects of their methodology.

Bibliography. W. Randolph Tate, *Biblical Interpretation: An Integrated Approach* (rev. ed.; Peabody, MA: Hendrickson, 1997).

PHENOMENOLOGY. *See* PHENOMENOLOGICAL CRITICISM

PHENOMENOLOGICAL CRITICISM

A theory of reading that finds MEANING in the reader's perception of the TEXT. Put another way, rather than a text's being the container holding meaning that is waiting to be discovered by the reader, meaning comes into being during the reader's encounter with the structures of the text. Consequently, meaning is always only virtual. Phenomenology can refer to many fields and disciplines, from psychology to philosophy to literary theory. Typically, however, phenomenology refers to the philosophy of experience, in which the ultimate source of meaning is found in the experiences of human beings.

Phenomenology. The term *phenomenon* itself was originally coined by Johann Heinrich Lambert in the eighteenth century and was used to refer to the illusory nature of human existence. Generally, however, *phenomenon* is understood as the distinction drawn by Immanuel Kant (1724–1804) between the appearance of reality to the human consciousness—appearances as "phenomena"—and reality in itself, as "noumena" (Lauer, 1–2). Kant argued that genuine knowledge of experience was available through describing the structures of human existence. Georg W. F. Hegel (1770–1831) argued against Kant, claiming that phenomena and noumena should not be split as sharply as he had posited. Instead, Hegel proposed that phenomena were stages of knowledge progressing from consciousness to absolute knowledge; human beings arrive at true knowledge by examining the way experiences appear to their minds (Stace, 339–42). These two thinkers built the philosophical foundation for the German philosopher Edmund Husserl (1859–1938), who developed phenomenology as a CRITICAL THEORY. Husserl first introduced the term "phenomenology" to designate the method by which he tried to analyze the human consciousness as experienced independently of PRESUPPOSITIONS. He proposed that consciousness is a unified intentional act. By "intentional," Husserl was not referring to a deliberate act but rather meant that consciousness is always directed toward an object and is always conscious of something (Abrams, 220). In order for readers to be free of prior conceptions, Husserl conjectured that they must suspend all presuppositions of how human experience takes place and avoid the question (known as BRACKETING) of whether what is being perceived is reality outside one's consciousness (220). In other words, Husserl believed that one should focus on what is being presented to the consciousness itself without analyzing the root or STRUCTURE of the object or experience. Through this pure description, Husserl believed certain knowledge could be gained.

In the years following Husserl's hypothesis, several of his contemporaries challenged and revised his ideas of phenomenology. Max Scheler focused the theory on ethical and religious studies, turning the thrust of his studies toward essences and their role in phenomenology. Martin Heidegger, considered by many to be the father of existentialist phenomenology, concentrated on the things themselves and studied how a person interacts with language to understand experiences. For Heidegger, the LITERARY CRITICISM of phenomenology was a means of discovering one's relationship to language and how, through notions of language, one could arrive at authentic experience through societal roles (Detweiler, 37). Jean-Paul Sartre, the French existentialist, agreed in part with Husserl's theory and adapted Heidegger's work to the philosophy of consciousness; yet he felt that Husserl's claim for direct knowledge acquired through conscious meanings was too narrow. While he agreed that human beings experience reality through consciousness, he argued that they are pure and free from specialized conscious meanings for interpretation. Maurice Merleau-Ponty also contributed significantly to phenomenology. He argued that perception was central to finding meaning and denied that intentionality was always conscious and self-sufficient (Detweiler, 35). Instead he claimed that humans had an active, involved role in the pursuit and understanding of knowledge. Like Heidegger, Merleau-Ponty focused extensively on the task of language in the process of understanding. He believed that cognition was a symbolic act that tried to embody an original experience in the conscious language. "For Merleau-Ponty, (phenomenological) literary criticism means examining the literary artist's *parole* (his personal language style, composed of emotional and conceptual aspects) to elicit its meaning not as an end in itself but as an example of the phenomenology of perception" (Detweiler, 36). Through the philosophical groundwork of these men (as well as others including Gadamer, Ricoeur, and Poulet), the way was paved for phenomenology to emerge as a literary criticism, a critical theory under the umbrella of READER-RESPONSE CRITICISM.

Phenomenological Criticism. Two key figures in phenomenological criticism are Roman Ingarden and Wolfgang Iser. Ingarden, a Polish theorist, is considered the first to adopt phenomenology as a means of understanding a literary work. In 1931 he wrote *The Literary Work of Art*, in which he attempted to address the question "What are the essential properties, the invariant logical conditions of that being which the literary work of art uniquely possesses?" (1). In this study, Ingarden asserts that the literary work is the product of the artist's life-world and can be understood as a "fictive universe" (Detweiler, 32). Ingarden believed that a literary work is stratified, containing four layers for understanding: the first layer is that of word sounds, sentences, and sentence RHYTHMS; the second is the layer of meaning units, which are intentional or fictive objects that emerge from the sentence structures; the third layer is the schematized aspects, structures that organize the emerging fictive objects into characters and events to form the character of the work; and the fourth layer is the represented objectivities, or the perspective through which the fictive world is recognized and described (33). Ingarden then argued that the various layers contain places of INDETERMINACY, or gaps in the text, which readers must fill in for themselves. The reader must read actively, "filling out" any indeterminate aspects of the text, and in so doing concretizes the work (Abrams, 220). With this idea, Ingarden is clearly advocating a type of reader-response theory in which the reader cooperates in constructing meaning. He declares that there is nothing outside the text and that the text must guide the reader into individual truth. "He ruled out of bounds any consideration of the role of the AUTHOR, of the value of the work, of the environment to which it referred, and of the attributes, experiences, and psychic states of the reader" (Jackson, 139). In his later work *The Cognition of the Literary Work of Art*, Ingarden tried to explain the processes that lead to cognition of literary works and what the results of this cognition would be (xv). He also clarified and deepened his thoughts on the strata and reiterated the role of the reader in the meaning of the text. Although his theories did not immediately win support in the academic world, by the 1970s his early work in phenomenological criticism was the key catalyst for later development of the theory for reader-response criticism as a whole.

Iser, a German writer and teacher, was the foremost respondent to the work of Ingarden. Iser contended that Ingarden had too narrowly defined the relationship between the reader and the text. He claimed that Ingarden proposed "a one-way incline from text to reader and not . . . a two-way relationship," leaving the forms the text could take too unpredictable and possibly irreconcilable (173). Iser emphasizes the temporal process of reading, in which the reader is continuously adjusting his/her perceptions and expectations of the text and filling in the indeterminate gaps in the work (Vander Weele, 137). In this way, he agrees with Ingarden's notion that the reader is also in some ways the constructor of the text and that the text, reader, and social context must interact to develop meaning and understanding. "The reader's existing consciousness will have to make certain internal adjustments in order to receive and process the alien viewpoints which the text presents as reading takes place. This situation produces the possibility that the reader's own worldview may be modified as a result of internalizing, negotiating, and realizing the partially indeterminate elements of the text" (Selden, 114). In short, Iser believes that the reader is guided by the text but constantly reinterprets and constructs it, with the text having no reality apart from the reading of it (Vander Weele, 138).

The Geneva school, a group of critics (including notables such as Albert Beguin, Jean Rousset, and George Poulet) most of whom taught at the University of Geneva, regarded each work of literature as a fictional world embodying the author's consciousness (Abrams, 220). In their view, the *cogito*, or formations of consciousness of the author, pervaded the literary work, serving as a type of biographical projection into characters, PLOT, SETTING, IMAGERY, and STYLE (220). Like Husserl, the Geneva school believed that readers should bracket their presuppositions and EXPECTATIONS in order to fully arrive at meaning and interaction with the author and the author's consciousness. In other words, true meaning can be found only outside presuppositions and in interaction with the author's words in one's consciousness alone. Again, this is a reader-response theory, although perhaps to a lesser extent, in which the reader is in some way responsible for the construction of meaning. Gaston Bachelard, Ricoeur, Jacques Derrida, Hans-Georg Gadamer, J. Hillis Miller, and Robert Magnolia also greatly contributed to contemporary phenomenological criticism.

Paul Ricoeur is probably the key figure in phenomenological HERMENEUTICS. While others have written extensively on the subject, he seems to be the foremost scholar in the discipline. In *Essays on Biblical Interpretation*, Ricoeur attempts to develop a hermeneutical phenomenology of biblical interpretation that takes seriously the metaphorical and symbolic language of the Bible while examining the relationship between the issue of biblical truth and its method of reception. Ricoeur focuses most extensively on how a reader relates to SYMBOLS and language; he believes that the modern reader has been desensitized to symbolic language. Not only do readers dismiss much of the symbolic language they encounter; they are also afraid to get behind the symbolism of SCRIPTURE because they are unsure of what they will find and what it will disprove. He claims that, due to the writings of Nietzsche, Freud, and Marx (among others), the modern reader must subject all interpretations of biblical text to a HERMENEUTICS OF SUSPICION. In *The Symbolism of Evil*, Ricoeur proposes how this can take place. He asserts that humans have two "naïvetés," the second of which allows them to interpret and find religious belief. Lewis S. Mudge describes Ricoeur's proposal:

An early program for his attempt to do this appears in the final chapter of *The Symbolism of Evil*. Ricoeur there proposes a philosophical analysis of symbolic and metaphoric language intended to help us reach a "second naïveté" before such texts. The latter phrase,

which Ricoeur has made famous, suggests that the "first naïveté," an unquestioned dwelling in a world of symbol, which presumably came naturally to men and women in one-possibility cultures to which the symbols in question were indigenous, is no longer possible for us. But we may approximate that state—of course with a difference. For the second immediacy that we seek and the second naïveté that we await are no longer accessible to us anywhere else than in a hermeneutics; we can believe only by interpreting. It is the "modern" mode of belief in symbols, an expression of the distress of modernity and a remedy for that distress. (Mudge, vi)

In other words, Christian belief cannot be based on a book or event but instead must be based on the interpretation of both. Like Husserl and Iser, Ricoeur believes that there is nothing behind the text. Once a reader begins to read and interpret, there is no longer a tie to the original culture, author, meaning, and so forth. Ricoeur writes:

Not the intention of the author, which is supposed to be hidden behind the text; not the historical situation common to the author and his original readers; not the expectations or feelings of these original readers; not even their understanding of themselves as historical and cultural phenomena. What has to be appropriated is the meaning of the text itself, conceived in a dynamic way as the direction of thought opened up by the text. (xvi)

While others have written on how phenomenology should be applied to biblical studies, the method is itself summed up in Ricoeur's work. Hermeneutics should no longer be viewed as research or investigation but rather as a dialogue with the text. Ricoeur believes that through this process, living testimony is developed and the biblical text may actually transform the reader.

Bibliography. M. H. Abrams, *A Glossary of Literary Terms* (7th ed.; Fort Worth: Harcourt Brace, 1999); Robert Detweiler, *Story, Sign, and Self* (Philadelphia: Fortress, 1978); Edmund Husserl, *Ideas: A General Introduction to Pure Phenomenology* (trans. W. R. Boyce Gibson; New York: Allen & Unwin, 1969); Roman Ingarden, *The Cognition of the Literary Work of Art* (trans. Ruth Ann Crowley and Kenneth R. Olson; Evanston, IL: Northwestern University Press, 1973); idem, *The Literary Work of Art* (trans. George G. Grabowicz; Evanston, IL: Northwestern University Press, 1974); Wolfgang Iser, *The Act of Reading: A Theory of Aesthetic Response* (Baltimore: Johns Hopkins University Press, 1980); J. R. Jackson, *Historical Criticism and the Meaning of Texts* (London: Routledge, 1989); Quentin Lauer, *The Triumph of Subjectivity* (New York: Fordham University Press, 1978); A. Scott Moreau, "Phenomenology of Religion," in *Evangelical Dictionary of Theology* (ed. Walter Elwell; Grand Rapids: Baker Academic, 2000), 915–19; Lewis S. Mudge, introduction to Paul Ricoeur's *Essays on Biblical Interpretation* (Philadelphia: Fortress Press, 1980), http://www.religion-online .org/showchapter.asp?title=1941&C=1770; George Poulet, "Phenomenology of Reading," *New Literary History* 2 (1970): 123–62; Paul Ricoeur, *Essays on Biblical Interpretation* (Philadelphia: Fortress, 1980), http://www.religion-on line.org/showbook.asp?title=1941; idem, *Interpretation Theory: Discourse and the Surplus of Meaning* (Fort Worth: Texas Christian University Press, 1976); Raman Selden, *A Reader's Guide to Contemporary Literary Theory* (Lexington: University Press of Kentucky, 1985); W. T. Stace, *The Philosophy of Hegel* (Mineola, NY: Dover, 1955); Michael Vander Weele, "Reader-Response Theories," in *Contemporary Literary Theory: A Christian Appraisal* (ed. Clarence Walhout and Leland Ryken; Grand Rapids: Eerdmans, 1991), 125–48.

PHILOLOGY

In its broadest sense, the scientific study of language and literature. In its narrower sense, however, *philology* refers to the study of the historical and comparative development of languages, and the term LINGUISTICS is reserved for the scientific study of language, investigating the manner in which a language functions as a system of CODES. Central to philology is the recognition of similarities between the vocabulary of some natural languages (e.g., the German *Mutter* and the English *mother*) that suggest a common origin in an earlier language. Philologists track linguistic changes over time through an etymological study of surviving TEXTS and then codify the conventions that govern the languages. Although philology still has some use in BIBLICAL STUDIES in the form of word studies (e.g., word-study books and some DICTIONARIES and LEXICONS), modern linguistics has largely replaced the DIACHRONIC (the study of the historical evolution of a language through time and the recording of its changes) approach

associated with philology with the study of the SYNCHRONIC (the study of a language at a given stage of its evolution with attention given to the conventions that define it as a language) nature of language.

PHONEME

From the Greek for "speech sound," a basic unit of sound in a language. For example, in English, the letters *t* and *d* mark distinct phonemes (as in *tog* and *dog*) while *c* and *k* may mark separate phonemes (as in *cite* and *kite*) or the same (as in *cake*).

PHONOCENTRISM

According to Jacques Derrida, phonocentrism is a subcategory of LOGOCENTRISM, the latter being a term by which he designates any form of thought founded on notions of TRUTH. Phonocentrism is the privileging of SPEECH over writing, so that speech is considered closer to the truth than is writing. Derrida viewed language itself as a kind of writing that is no closer to the truth than any other type of expression. He developed this view of language in order to challenge the ASSUMPTION in the Western philosophical tradition that philosophy is a special kind of writing that is immune to ideological bias. As a type of writing, then, philosophy can make no more legitimate claim to truth than any other type of writing. *See* DECONSTRUCTION; POSTMODERN CRITICISM.

PHONOLOGY

The study of word sounds. *Phonology* also refers to the actual realization of sounds and sound patterns in speech. A knowledge of phonology can be useful in composing literary devices. In the study of the BIBLE, word sounds can best be appreciated when pronounced in the original languages (Hebrew, Aramaic, and Greek). As in most languages, the biblical writers used a range of sound combinations for a variety of purposes. Experienced writers employ word sounds for emphasis, for aesthetic and lyric expression, for IRONY, or for didactic purposes. With stylistic devices, AUTHORS call the reader's attention to some aspect of their message. The writers of BIBLICAL POETRY used word sounds extensively for a variety of purposes. *See* ALLITERATION; ASSONANCE; ONOMATOPOEIA; PARONOMASIA.

PLAIN MEANING. *See* LITERAL MEANING

PLATONISM

The philosophy of the Greek philosopher Plato (b. ca. 427 BCE), which has had a profound influence on the Western philosophical tradition. Plato posited two realms of reality, the physical and the metaphysical: the metaphysical consists of ideal forms, and individual manifestations of those forms are in the physical realm. For example, every individual triangle (different in shape and size, material, etc.) is a reflection of that preexistent, ideal form, triangleness. According to Plato, the metaphysical realm may be accessed only through reason. The distinction between the material, physical world and the metaphysical realm may be understood as that between an object and its essence, which makes an object what it is. Platonism had a profound influence on later philosophical schools such as EPICUREANISM and STOICISM, which in turn were the most immediate philosophical context for the writers of the NT. Nonetheless, the dualistic WORLDVIEW of Platonism did directly influence not only Paul's thought but also that of the AUTHOR of the Epistle to the Hebrews. Both writers assume a world of ideal forms, which is only vaguely reflected in the physical world. For example, when the author of Hebrews describes the earthly and heavenly sanctuaries in chapter 9, the heavenly "tent" is a "perfect" one, "not made with hands, that is, not of this creation" (9:11). In Heb. 11:1, faith is described in Platonic terms: "Now faith is the assurance of things hoped for, the conviction of things not seen."

When the early church fathers wanted to articulate the doctrine of the Trinity and original sin, they did so within a Platonic worldview. With respect to the former, there exists one divine essence but three individual manifestations of it. With respect to original sin, the church could claim that all humans were born sinners because when Adam sinned, the ideal form, human nature, was corrupted, and since each individual human partakes of that essence, each is born corrupted (see Rom. 5).

PLAY

Among some POSTMODERN theorists (e.g., Jacques Derrida, Roland Barthes) and postmodern biblical scholars (e.g., John Dominic Crossan, David Clines), that which is the result of the DEATHS OF THE AUTHOR and of the idea of a TEXT as the location of stable MEANING. According to Derrida, the text is anything but a definitive object; it is rather an infinite thing that is constantly being produced by readers. In a sense, the text becomes a musical score, which the reader plays over and over again, and in turn the reader is played by the text. Consequently, the idea of play replaces the idea of a fixed meaning having been determined by the author. Texts do not communicate TRUTH but constitute a process of interpretive play that is infinite. "Texts do not convey messages; they are simply processes which cannot stop; in which *anyone* is invited to participate. They are cut off from authors, from situations, and from the extralinguistic world, to constitute an infinite open system of endless signification" (Thiselton, 99). For an application of the idea of play to biblical texts, see works by John Dominic Crossan. For a more detailed treatment of play, see its treatment under READER-RESPONSE CRITICISM.

Bibliography. John Dominic Crossan, *The Dark Interval: Towards a Theology of Story* (Niles, IL: Argus Communications, 1975); idem, *Finding Is the First ACT: Trove Folktales and Jesus' Treasure Parable* (Missoula, MT: Scholars Press; Philadelphia: Fortress, 1979); idem, *In Parables: The Challenge of the Historical Jesus* (New York: Harper & Row, 1973); Anthony C. Thiselton, *New Horizons in Hermeneutics* (Grand Rapids: Zondervan, 1992).

PLEONASM

A redundant REPETITION of an expression or words—for example, the use of "in this day and age" instead of simply "today." While pleonasm may be intentional, it most often occurs unconsciously. Mark contains a number of pleonasms (e.g., 1:28, 35; 2:25; 3:26; 9:2; 15:26).

PLOT

The plan for a STORY, consisting of characters involved in a series of ACTIONS and their responses to CONFLICT. Aristotle describes plot as action having a beginning, middle, and end. Some type of conflict occurs at the beginning of the NARRATIVE, is complicated in various ways through the middle, and is finally resolved at the end. The basic plot therefore has a three-part structure: conflict, COMPLICATION, and resolution (DENOUEMENT). In the Joseph narrative, the conflict arises between Joseph and his brothers when the brothers perceive that their father, Jacob, loves Joseph more than them (Gen. 37:1–4). This conflict is complicated by Joseph's dreams, by the brothers' plot to kill Joseph, and by the brothers' selling Joseph into slavery. There is no resolution until Joseph's final revelation to his brothers in Egypt. The Joseph narrative, however, actually has multiple conflicts (Joseph/brothers, Jacob/sons, Joseph's dreams / the final fulfillment of the dreams). Each of these conflicts is complicated throughout the story and is finally resolved at the end.

In the tragic plot, the PROTAGONIST makes a miscalculation due to a bit of missing information. At some point in the action, the protagonist discovers this missing information, a discovery that propels the protagonist into a state of misery. The Jephthah story offers a good example. Jephthah promises to offer as a burnt offering to God the first thing coming out of his house if God will grant victory. Due to the layout of the common home (it would have a type of fenced yard around it where the animals were kept), Jephthah assumed that he would be greeted by a servant. It was a perfectly logical ASSUMPTION. Little did he know that he would be greeted by his only child, a daughter. The discovery of the missing information propels Jephthah from a state of happiness to a state of misery ("When he saw her, he tore his clothes and said, 'Alas, my daughter! You have brought me very low; you have become the cause of great trouble

to me. For I have opened my mouth to the LORD, and I cannot take back my vow'" [Judg. 11:35]).

PLURALISM

The claim that TEXTs encourage and legitimate more than one MEANING. Pluralism in this SENSE also rests on the ASSUMPTION that meaning is not only a function of the TEXTUAL STRATEGIES but also a function the interpretive method through which the text is read. Meaning is therefore relative to the CRITICAL METHODOLOGY and purpose that guide reading. Pluralism vitiates the idea that meaning is located in the text; it is instead always the product of a methodological FRAMEWORK. A formalist reading would differ from a feminist one, and both would differ from an archetypal one.

PLURIVALENCE

The idea that, based on the varieties of SOCIAL LOCATIONS, historical circumstances, and interpretive communities (see INTERPRETIVE COMMUNITY) of different readers, a plurality of understanding and therefore MEANING is at the heart of INTERPRETATION. Readers configure and legitimate interpretations from within methodological, ideological, and cultural CONTEXTs. Since these contexts vary, interpretive pluralism is a given among POSTMODERN CRITICs such as Paul de Man, Geoffrey Hartman, Jacques Derrida, and J. Hillis Miller.

PLURIVOCALITY

A term in READER-RESPONSE CRITICISM for the idea that a TEXT can generate and legitimate a number of meanings but not just any MEANING. Plurivocality is between UNIVOCALITY (the idea that a text can have only a single meaning, the one intended by the AUTHOR) and EQUIVOCALITY (the claim that a text can never be pinned down and therefore equivocates with respect to meaning). Plurivocality locates meaning between the enabling STRUCTUREs of the text and the creative activities of the reader, including the activities that derive from the interpretive method the reader is employing.

POETIC FRAGMENTS

Brief passages in the epistles that were most probably used in early Christian worship SETTINGS. These passages are characterized by parallelism, unusual grammatical construction, and/or formulaic language (Ryken, 109). Examples may be 2 Tim. 2:11–13; Heb. 1:3; 1 Pet. 1:18–21; 2:21–25; and Titus 3:5–7. Quite often the poetic qualities are lost in TRANSLATION. *See also* HYMN.

Bibliography. Leland Ryken, *Words of Life: A Literary Introduction to the New Testament* (Grand Rapids: Baker, 1987).

POETIC LICENSE

The freedom allowed to, and taken by, the poet to use language and employ devices for effect, often ignoring fact. This usage includes all types of FIGURATIVE LANGUAGE, unusual SYNTAX, RHYME, and RHYTHM. Poetic license allows the poet to distill experiences both real and perceived into concrete IMAGES that have both informational and aesthetic value. For an example, compare the PROSE and poetic accounts of the death of Sisera in Judg. 4:17–22 and 5:24–31.

POETICS

A term for the theorizing about LITERARY construction. The term may refer to theories about how POETRY or NARRATIVE is constructed. Thus, CRITICS may refer to the poetics of FICTION, the poetics of PROSE, or the poetics of the sonnet. Poetics differs from HERMENEUTICS in that the former relates to literary construction while the latter relates to the INTERPRETATION of the literary construction. For an example, see Sternberg.

Bibliography. Meir Sternberg, *The Poetics of Biblical Narrative* (Bloomington: Indiana University Press, 1987).

POETRY

A variable GENRE that is characterized primarily by the use of rhythmical language. While a poem may be extremely short or relatively lengthy, poetry's essential quality is conciseness and economy of expression. A poem is a single work, while the poet is one who writes poetry. The LITERARY DEVICES that the poet most frequently employs are SIMILE, METAPHOR, MYTH, ARCHETYPE, and SYMBOL. For a detailed discussion of Hebrew poetry, *see* BIBLICAL POETRY.

POETRY, BIBLICAL. *See* BIBLICAL POETRY

POETRY, CONSOLATION. *See* CONSOLATION POETRY

POETRY, DOOMSAYING. *See* MONITORY POETRY

POETRY, HEBREW. *See* BIBLICAL POETRY

POETRY, MONITORY. *See* MONITORY POETRY

POETRY, NARRATIVE. *See* NARRATIVE POETRY

POETRY, PROPHETIC. *See* PROPHETIC POETRY

POETRY, WISDOM. *See* WISDOM POETRY

POINT OF VIEW

The voice of a LITERARY work; the position from which the details of a work are related. There are two basic types of point of view—first person and third person—each with variations. In the first-person point of view, an "I" relates the events, thoughts, observations, and conclusions. The NARRATOR may speak in an authorial voice, but usually as a character in the STORY (the book of Nehemiah combines these two). This first-person narrator may be a major character, a minor character, or simply a reporter for others in the story.

The third-person point of view employs the third-person pronouns. This point of view may be limited, omniscient, or dramatic. The limited point of view presents the story through the eyes of a single character. The omniscient point of view has access to all the ACTIONS, words, and thoughts of all the characters in the story (most NARRATIVES in the NT and HEBREW BIBLE employ this type of point of view). The dramatic point of view (also called the objective point of view) simply reports the actions and SPEECHES of the characters with neither COMMENTARY on nor revelations of the thoughts of the characters. AUTHORS make use of point of view to assist readers in making reasonable inferences about the story. *See* CHARACTERIZATION.

POLITICAL CONTEXTUALISM

A branch of postmodern criticism as found in the writings of Michel Foucault, who PROBLEMATIZES history as written by the modern SUBJECT. Foucault tries to disjoin authority from authorship (as relates to individual power or deriving from knowledge) and disperse it into an impersonal and collective INTERTEXTUALITY, where the INTERTEXT is conceived as a function of the discursive formations and conformations of institutions and ideologies, as in Foucault (Felperin, 28–31). In Foucault's writings, historical DISCOURSE functions both as a regime, implicated in relations of power, and as an object, being subject to its own regime of discursive operations (Baross, 160). Foucault denies the possibility of traditional forms of history such as progress or dominant WORLDVIEW. He seeks to understand history within cultural discourse in order to discover the rules that arise from the specific CONFIGURATIONS of discourses. Foucault is particularly interested in rules and practices of exclusion that control the writing community, believing that these rules of discourse have shaped most theories and are barriers to ever writing anything objective, particularly about history.

In relation to LITERARY CRITICISM, Foucault is a radical textualist in believing that nothing precedes discourse and nothing escapes it. Writing activates a complex historical archive, or historical/experience-based understanding, that effectively delimits the signifier. When producing or analyzing a TEXT, Foucault finds it necessary to situate it within a historical or archival network. The CRITIC must conjure up the archive in order to discover the unconscious intertext, which is the CONTEXT of discourse.

In "Nietzsche, Genealogy, and History," Foucault seeks to analyze the discursive rules of formation, exclusion, and transformation and the resulting discontinuities as they relate to specific disciplines. This analysis resembles DECONSTRUCTION in its negative program. It employs discontinuity as a "methodological wedge" showing one aspect of negative operation to destroy the unifying view forced on history, which forms history into a teleological force moving forward. In his study of texts, he is primarily interested in identifying and demonstrating how the use of knowledge is an instrument of institutional advancement, self-legitimization, and self-perpetuation.

Bibliography. Zsuzsa Baross, "Post-structuralism," in *Encyclopedia of Contemporary Literary Theory: Approaches, Scholars, Terms* (ed. Irena R. Makaryk; Toronto: University of Toronto Press, 1993), 158–63; Howard Felperin, *Beyond Deconstruction: The Uses and Abuses of Literary Theory* (Oxford: Clarendon, 1985); Michel Foucault, "Nietzsche, Genealogy, and History," in *Language, Counter-memory, Practice: Selected Interviews and Other Writings* (ed. Donald Bouchard; trans. Donald Bouchard and Sherry Simon; Ithaca, NY: Cornell University Press, 1977), 139–64.

POLYANDRY

The practice of having more than one husband at one time, an arrangement typically rejected by PATRIARCHAL CULTURE.

POLYCOITY

A type of POLYGAMY in which the man in a society where endogamous marriage (*see* ENDOGAMY) functions to perpetuate the lineage through the father's line may add concubines or handmaids, who have a lower status than the man's primary wife. According to Naomi Steinberg, in ancient Jewish culture, the practice of adding a concubine to the household was not dependent on economics. Rather, the concubine either provided "sexual enjoyment" for the man who already had an offspring, or if the man did not have an offspring, the concubine could be used as a means to produce an offspring (e.g., Abraham, Sarah, and Hagar in Gen. 16). Such an arrangement, however, was considered monogamous (*see* MONOGAMY) rather than polygamous (*see* POLYGAMY), and the offspring was a legitimate heir to the father and the primary wife. Steinberg argues that the fate of Abimelech in Judges is the result of his being the son of a secondary wife, not the primary one.

Bibliography. Naomi Steinberg, "Social-Scientific Criticism: Judges 9 and Issues of Kinship," in *Judges and Method:*

New Approaches in Biblical Studies (ed. Gale A. Yee; Minneapolis: Fortress, 1995), 45–64.

POLYGAMY

The practice of being married to more than one person at the same time. Since POLYANDRY is rare, polygamy is often regarded as synonymous with POLYGYNY. In ancient cultures such as that of Israel, polygamy served as a way to continue the patrilineal custom of ENDOGAMY as well as a way to perpetuate the family through reproduction.

POLYGLOT

From the Greek for "many tongues," a designation for a BIBLE with the TEXT in a number of languages in parallel columns. The best known is the Complutensian Polyglot (1521–22). Known by the city in which they were produced, others are Antwerp (1569–72), London (1654–57), and Paris (1629–45).

POLYGYNY

A type of POLYGAMY in which a man has more than one wife at a time, each with equal status. The wives may dwell in separate residences or under the same roof with the husband.

POLYPTOTON

A rhetorical device in which two words having the same root occur in proximity. A well-known example is in Shakespeare's *Troilus and Cressida*:

> The Greeks are strong, and skillful to their strength,
> Fierce to their skill, and to their fierceness valiant.

The device occurs in both the HEBREW BIBLE and the NT, though often lost in TRANSLATION. For example, in Matt. 2:10 and Josh. 10:10, 20, the NRSV does not capture the REPETITION of words from the same root as does the KJV:

Matt. 2:10 NRSV: "When they saw that the star had stopped, they were overwhelmed with joy."
Matt. 2:10 KJV: "When they saw the star, they rejoiced with exceeding great joy."

Josh. 10:10, 20 NRSV: "who inflicted a great slaughter on them" ... "inflicting a very great slaughter on them."
Josh. 10:10, 20 KJV: "slew them with a great slaughter" ... "slaying them with a great slaughter."

Bibliography. J. A. Cuddon, *The Penguin Dictionary of Literary Terms and Literary Theory* (4th ed.; London: Penguin, 1998).

POLYSEMY

Multiplicity of MEANINGS. In contemporary LITERARY theory, there is much debate about the inherent nature of literary TEXTS to generate and legitimate multiple meanings or understandings. Multiple readings depend not only on the nature of language (esp. literary uses of language) but also on the SOCIAL LOCATION of the reader. Since different readers bring different repertoires to a text, they produce different understandings.

POLYVALENCE

A word borrowed from chemistry and presently used in LITERARY theory to refer to the PLAY of language in literary TEXTS, giving them multiple MEANINGS. *See* POLYSEMY.

POLYVALENT MEANING. *See* POLYSEMY; POLYVALENCE

POLYTHEISM

The belief in the existence of many gods. *See* HENOTHEISM.

POPULAR THEOLOGY

A term in LIBERATION THEOLOGY for the type of theology done by laypersons, the poor, and the marginalized (*see* MARGINALIZATION) in conversation with others in base or grassroots communities, as opposed to the theology produced by scholars or trained theologians.

POSITIVISM

Although dating as back as far as the Enlightenment (seventeenth and eighteenth centuries), a term usually associated with Auguste Comte in the nineteenth century. It refers to the philosophical claim that knowledge through DESCRIPTION rather than through metaphysical speculation and EXPLANATION should be the goal of philosophy. In the twentieth century, positivism developed into logical positivism, especially in the hands of Ludwig Wittgenstein, who argued that scientific and mathematical methods should be employed to logically clarify human thought. In the field of literary studies, positivism has encouraged the scientific and historical study of literature. This has been especially true with the HISTORICAL-CRITICAL METHOD.

POSTAPOSTOLIC AGE

The period of church history after the death of Jesus's original disciples.

POST-CHRISTIAN ERA

A term used to refer to the idea that by the late twentieth century, Christianity's influence in the West had waned to the point that it no longer constituted a relevant WORLDVIEW for MODERNISM or POSTMODERNISM.

POSTCOLONIAL FEMINIST CRITICISM

A relatively new theory in the field of LITERARY CRITICISM that first emerged in the 1970s as a liberation movement that would simultaneously confront imperialism and PATRIARCHY. Using the principles of justice and empowerment, founders of this movement sought to accomplish three main goals: (1) to promote an awareness of the marginalized identity of postcolonial women; (2) to create influential strategies of resistance and empowerment; and (3) to decolonize and depatriarchalize (*see* DEPATRIARCHALIZATION) Western literature through literary criticism.

Postcolonial women are characterized by multiple forms of MARGINALIZATION. First of all, as subjects of colonization, they are marginalized because of their nationality and race. The colonial powers, including the English, French, Portuguese, and Germans, treated their subjects as inferior, backward, and pagan savages. They believed that they

had been sent by God to rescue the natives from their primitive existence, and they accomplished this mission by stripping away every expression of native culture. The colonized were forced to abandon their TRADITIONS, religious practices, and social structures in favor of the Western ideals of their oppressors (Dube, "Post-coloniality," 100–101).

One of the greatest cultural changes that the colonizers imposed was a patriarchal structuring of society. Before this shift, many tribes exalted the role of women in the community. Among the Igbo in Nigeria, for example, women participated in crop production and earned prestigious titles. The prominence of the female figure was further demonstrated in the tribe's worship of a female deity. Upon the arrival of the colonizers, however, women were taken from their public positions and forced into the submissive role of housewives. Their religion was also patriarchalized as the Christian God, a male, was made to replace their native goddess (110–12).

Western feminisms are of no real assistance in challenging the patriarchal oppression of postcolonial women: they operate under the same mentality as that of the colonizers. They try to bring all third-world women under a Western paradigm and fail to acknowledge cultural distinctives. Postcolonial women are lumped into a single, homogeneous category, thus further solidifying their oppression rather than liberating them (Mohanty, 53–55).

Since postcolonial movements recognize only the oppression of imperialism, and feminist movements see only the oppression of patriarchy, it became necessary to establish a separate movement that would meet the unique needs of the doubly marginalized postcolonial woman. In forming this movement, proponents aimed to influence every possible social institution and bring freedom from the negative influence of imperialism and patriarchy. They began by implementing broad principles that would gradually exert influence in every social institution, including politics, education, and religion. These principles include the empowerment of women through resistance and liberation, political solidarity based on attitudes of endurance and overcoming, legitimization and embracing of indigenous cultural worldviews, and recognition of the diversity of women's experiences (Boehmer, 225–27).

A primary location for implementing these principles is in the field of literature. Postcolonial feminist writers emphasize the unique identity of third-world women in several ways. First of all, they express a sense of autonomy and self-liberation through works of autobiography. In Ellen Kuzwayo's *Call Me Woman*, for example, the AUTHOR shares her own life struggle of rising above racial marginalization and an abusive marital relationship to obtain a prestigious position in her community. She then uses this position to empower other women to experience the same liberation.

Novels such as *Our Sister Killjoy*, by Ama Ata Aidoo, also challenge the idea of the powerless, defeated third-world woman. In Aidoo's work, a young black female chooses to face the white world with an attitude of self-confidence and assurance, despite her marginalization. Aidoo creatively emphasizes the cultural background of the African woman by incorporating elements of African tribal tradition into the novel, making it resemble a polyphonic African oral performance.

A final strategy of postcolonial feminist writers is to analyze and PROBLEMATIZE literary works of the Western world. A text of primary interest is the BIBLE, which for years was used by colonizers to force native tribes into subjugation. The Bible was also instrumental in enforcing PATRIARCHAL STRUCTURES on the colonized. In light of these facts, postcolonial feminists seek to decolonize and depatriarchalize biblical texts. When studying problematic passages, readers must ask four main questions: (1) Does the text accept or reject the imperialism of its day? (2) Does the text encourage or discourage travel to distant and uninhabited lands? (3) Does the text accept or condemn cultural and religious differences? (4) Does the text use gender and divine representations to create relationships of subjugation and domination? (Dube, *Post-colonial Feminist Interpretation*, 200–201).

This model of reading has been called "Rahab's Reading Prism" because the STORY of Rahab is an excellent representation of the double marginalization of race and gender.

Within a period of just a few decades, this movement has produced global awareness of oppression and has effectively implemented strategies of resistance and empowerment for postcolonial women everywhere.

Bibliography. Ama Ata Aidoo, *Our Sister Killjoy; or, Reflections from a Black-Eyed Squint* (London: Longman, 1977); Elleke Boehmer, *Colonial and Postcolonial Literature* (Oxford: Oxford University Press, 1995); Musa Dube, *Post-colonial Feminist Interpretation of the Bible* (St. Louis: Chalice, 2000); idem, "Post-coloniality, Feminist Spaces, and Religion," in *Post-colonialism, Feminism, and Religious Discourse* (ed. Laura Donaldson and Kwok Pui-Lan; New York: Routledge, 2002), 100–22; Ellen Kuzwayo, *Call Me Woman* (San Francisco: Spinsters Ink, 1985); Chandra Mohanty, "Under Western Eyes: Feminist Scholarship and Colonial Discourses," in *Third World Women and the Politics of Feminism* (ed. Chandra Mohanty, Ann Russo, and Lourdes Torres; Indianapolis: Indiana University Press, 1991), 51–80; Sara Suleri, "Woman Skin Deep: Feminism and the Post-colonial Condition," *Critical Inquiry* 18 (1992): 756–69.

POSTCOLONIALISM / POSTCOLONIAL CRITICISM

A CRITICAL THEORY that focuses on the relationship between literature, LITERARY CANON, and imperialism. Postcolonialism, like other forms of IDEOLOGICAL CRITICISM, came in the wake of the third-world struggles for independence from colonialist powers (Bhabha, 2385–90). It was also influenced by the American civil-rights movements of the 1950s and 1960s, when literary critics started to address their own ASSUMPTIONS and cultural (as well as racial, GENDER, etc.) biases (Hall, *Literary and Cultural Theory*, 266). Some of the key figures in this rapidly developing field are Chinua Achebe, Homi Bhabha, Frantz Fanon, Edward Said, and Gayatri Spivak. Diversity is emphasized: each brings his or her own emphasis to the DISCOURSES.

Assumptions. These discourses center on several basic assumptions before branching out into the rich multiplicity inherent in this theory. Steven Moore asserts that postcolonialism is not only a method of INTERPRETATION; it is also a critical sensibility. This sensibility is attuned to the historical reality of imperialism: the domination of third-world peoples by the West. The dominating culture wrote the literature and decided what literature was canonized. This literature, even the very language that was used, affected society by propagating the differentiation and subsequent oppression of the colonized (Hall, 268–69).

Tasks. These basic assumptions dictate to postcolonialists their main tasks, the first and most prominent of these being what Alfred J. Lopez calls "a reckoning with the colonial past" (*Posts and Pasts,* 7). This entails critiquing the Western assumptions of what literature has been canonized as well as reinterpreting the texts with an awareness of their imperialist assumptions. The second task consists of a call for due attention and focus to be given to the literature produced by the marginalized people (*see* MARGINALIZATION). Postcolonialists' third task is to discuss postcolonial diasporas, pannationalism, and nationalism (Sagar, 424). This includes discourses on the production of culture and the complexity of identity—the inherent hybridity of both the colonists and the subjugated people. Postcolonialists employ many theoretical approaches, most often psychoanalysis and DECONSTRUCTION, and are commonly influenced by MARXIST and FEMINIST CRITICISM.

Focuses. Within this basic FRAMEWORK, however, there is a wide variety of facets and focuses among theorists, as the discourse spans many continents and cultures. This MULTIVALENCE of approaches is mandated by the emphasis on cultural diversity inherent in the critical school.

History of development. One of the founders of postcolonialist thought is Edward Said, from Palestine. Said is concerned with the duty of the CRITIC in the face of the Eurocentrism and cultural elitism of literary scholarship. He argues that the task of the critic is "oppositional criticism" against domi-

nation, for the goal of "noncoercive knowledge in the interests of human freedom" (Habib, 480). Said is acutely aware of the complexities of his own identity as a Palestinian, educated and living in the West, offering us an example of the identity issues that are central to the postcolonialist discourse. Said's most significant contribution to the field, however, is his book *Orientalism,* in which he examines Western images of the "Orient"—both in the academic disciplines, such as anthropology, and in popular representation in movies, literature, and so forth (Aichele, "Edward W. Said," 1988). Said states that these representations of the oriental "Other" (he specifies stereotypes of Islam but is referring more generally to all third-world cultures) are projections of the West, having little to do with the actual nature of the people represented. These constructions foster biases and justify Western domination of third-world cultures (Habib, 481).

This theme of imperialist representations of other cultures is common among postcolonialist theorists. Gerald Vizenor directs similar attention to the portrayal of Native Americans in the academic world and popular culture. This portrayal "proved" the Native Americans' natural inferiority and helped to justify the IDEOLOGY of "manifest destiny": an ideology of spreading over the continent and subjugating the Native Americans (Garane, "Gerald Vizenor," 1075). Vizenor calls for a "post-Indian" view, rejecting the American broad generalizations and condescending portrayals of Native American culture and history.

Chinua Achebe, from Nigeria, also deals with Western portrayals of other cultures, but his focus is on the Western representation of Africa, specifically in Joseph Conrad's canonized novel *Heart of Darkness,* where Africans are pictured as subhuman savages (Aichele, "Chinua Achebe," 1781). Even as Conrad's book is critical of imperialism, it reinforces racism by its construction of Africans. Achebe criticizes the academic community for its critical reception of this work while largely ignoring its racism.

Complaints. One of the main complaints that postcolonialists level against Western representations of other cultures is that they are too general, that they lump cultures of vast diversity and complexity into one monolithic group. Cultures are notoriously hard to define and categorize in the wake of colonization and global cultural upheaval. Homi Bhabha, from India, has written some of the definitive postcolonial work on the complexities of identity. He argues that no national culture is homogeneous: all are characterized by "hybridity." This fluid, multivalent (*see* MULTIVALENCE) state of identity is produced by the interaction of the cultures of the colonizer and the colonized. Each affects the other, synthesizing people into a hybrid that mixes both cultures (Bhabha, 2385–90).

Cultural imperialism is another of the main subjects of discussion among postcolonialists. A residual phenomenon arising in the wake of colonialism, this term encompasses the effects of colonization in language, culture, religion, and economic and political structures. Within this CONTEXT, Frantz Fanon explores the use of language to continue to dominate a people group after colonialism, specifically with regard to his home country, Martinique. Fanon notices the superior status attributed to French over Creole, which is seen as a degenerative local language (Garane, 190). He says that this acculturation dehumanizes the locals, forcing them to forget their own culture and history. Fanon called this the "whitening" of his race.

Other critics who explore the connection between language and cultural imperialism are Ngugi Wa Thiong'o, Tababn Lo Liyong, and Henry Owuor-Anyumba (2093–94; representing Kenya and Uganda) in "On the Abolition of the English Department." This essay explores the effect that literary education has in propagating cultural imperialism through the choice of texts for study and the presentation and INTERPRETATION of those texts. The essay suggests dismantling Anglocentric literature departments in African universities, refocusing them on African languages, literature, and ORAL TRADITION.

One of the most unsettling writers in postcolonial theory is Gayatri Spivak, from India. Her controversial essay "Can the Subaltern Speak?" levels CRITICISM at postcolonialist efforts at emancipating cultures. Spivak claims that postcolonialists can easily be condescending to the people to whom they are claiming to give a voice. They do this in the very notion that third-world cultures must lead the fight against cultural imperialism, assigning them value only as far as they follow Western scripts (Spivak, 2201–3). Theorists can also do this by romanticizing the oppressed, essentializing them, and thus replicating the colonists they criticize. Spivak pragmatically advocates "strategic ESSENTIALISM," however, making essentialist claims when necessary to achieve a political goal (2203–4). By *essentialism*, Spivak means a radical reduction of a people to an essence, a sameness that glosses over any distinctive differences within the group. An example is the notion of the "noble savage."

Spivak's pragmatic application of her theories to real-life political (in her case, feminist) goals is characteristic of many of the postcolonial theorists. It seems to be common among these critics to have a social view of art as the basis for their ideas, seeing art as propagating social values. They often go beyond recommending academic measures (such as Achebe's call for writing from the perspective of the oppressed and Ngugi's call for the abolition of the English department) to advocate practical political steps. Frantz Fanon was involved in the Algerian war of independence and advocates the use of force in liberation efforts. Homi Bhabha asserts that theory should be accompanied by political activism, not separated from it. Edward Said relates his criticism to real-world politics and is strategically involved with the Palestinian situation—both raising Western awareness of their plight and being directly a part of the Palestinian National Authority. Literary and social commentary is often accompanied by social action in the field of postcolonialism.

Conclusions. The critical theory of postcolonialism clearly has deep SIGNIFICANCE in how we view literature and society, and its value has been extended to other disciplines, such as the field of BIBLICAL STUDIES. Interpretive theory in the field of biblical studies has traditionally been strongly centralized, with Western interpretations of SCRIPTURE dominating to the exclusion of other voices. Fernando Segovia (125) asserts that postcolonialism has "particular importance and relevance for BIBLICAL CRITICISM" as it calls for more diverse theories from the margins. This is vital to avoid spiritual imperialism, as R. S. Sugirtharajah (45) explains in his essay concerning "white men bearing gifts." It has been argued that Western Christian missions have historically been an arm of Western imperialism. Since the early colonialism of the fifteenth century, the West has viewed itself as not only the political CENTER but also the religious center. Segovia (128) states that the West's view has been that those "culturally subordinated to the center must be brought into religious submission as well."

Postcolonialists focus on what Sugirtharajah (5) calls "discourse[s] of resistance": critical theories from indigenous peoples. These third-world theorists use "their own cultural resources to illuminate biblical narratives," offering valuable insights into the discourses on biblical interpretation (7). Postcolonialists also focus on the reality of ancient imperialism (Assyrian, Roman, etc.) throughout the biblical narratives and discuss how this reality colored the writing of texts.

However, postcolonial thought also extends beyond the texts themselves to modern readings and interpretations of the texts. The West's imperialist heritage colors our WORLDVIEW, causing us to see reality in terms of BINARY OPPOSITES. This seeing of people in terms of "us/them" or "center/margins" extends to our religion. For example, categorizing people as "believers/pagans" can be interpreted as being the product of this imperialist mentality, which sees humanity in terms of "the West / everyone else" (Segovia, 126). Postcolonial theory also analyzes the readers of the texts in how they position themselves in regard to this binary opposition, comparing it with how marginalized people position themselves.

Liberation readings are a popular ideological interpretive stance in biblical studies. There are many examples of these readings from people outside the center, such as Native American and African American readings, as well as a host of readings from people groups all over the world (e.g., the contemporary Jewish reading of Exodus).

Liberation theology has often focused on the biblical narrative of the Israelites' EXODUS from Egypt. Usually the marginalized or oppressed group relates itself to the Israelites in their achievement of freedom from bondage in Egypt and their resulting autonomy. Contemporary Jewish theologians often relate the formation of the modern state of Israel to this account, comparing the Diaspora to Egypt, and the Palestinians to the ancient Canaanites, who have to be driven out of the promised land (Aichele et al., *Postmodern Bible*, 292). This is the prominent reading of the text, but dissident voices of Jewish and Christian Palestinian theologians argue that the modern state of Israel, with its economic and political oppression of a people and expropriation and occupation of a land, is more directly related to Egypt in the biblical narrative. The Palestinians, then, would ironically be related to the ancient Israelites in this marginalized reading. This has profound ramifications for the theology regarding Israel and is an example of the rich possibilities of decentralizing our biblical interpretations.

Postcolonialism, with its critical sensibility to the effects of imperialism on texts and interpretations and to complex identity issues, offers a relevant critical theory to be applied to biblical studies. This focus on diversity has the potential of informing our literary vision, our theology, and even the way we live our lives—a pragmatic approach that postcolonial theorists would certainly approve of.

Bibliography. A. K. M. Adam, ed., *Handbook of Post-modern Biblical Interpretation* (St. Louis: Chalice, 2000); George Aichele, "Chinua Achebe," in *The Norton Anthology of Theory and Criticism* (ed. Vincent B. Leitch; New York: Norton, 2001), 1781–83; idem, "Edward W. Said," in *The Norton Anthology of Theory and Criticism* (ed. Vincent B. Leitch; New York: Norton, 2001), 1986–90; George

Aichele et al., *The Postmodern Bible* (New Haven: Yale University Press, 1995); Homi K. Bhabha, "The Commitment to Theory," in *The Norton Anthology of Theory and Criticism* (ed. Vincent B. Leitch; New York: Norton, 2001), 2385–90; Jeanne Garane, "Fanon, Frantz," in *A Dictionary of Cultural and Critical Theory* (ed. Michael Payne; Cambridge, MA: Blackwell, 1996), 190; idem, "Gerald Vizenor," in *The Norton Anthology of Theory and Criticism* (ed. Vincent B. Leitch; New York: Norton, 2001), 1075–77; M. A. R. Habib, "Said, Edward William," in *A Dictionary of Cultural and Critical Theory* (ed. Michael Payne; Cambridge, MA: Blackwell, 1996), 479–81; Donald E. Hall, *Literary and Cultural Theory* (Boston: Houghton Mifflin, 2001); Alfred J. Lopez, "Ngugi Wa Thiong'o, Taban Lo Liyong, Henry Owuor-Anyumba," in *The Norton Anthology of Theory and Criticism* (ed. Vincent B. Leitch; New York: Norton, 2001), 2089–92; idem, "Post-colonial Studies and Race and Ethnicity Studies," in *The Norton Anthology of Theory and Criticism* (ed. Vincent B. Leitch; New York: Norton, 2001), 25–26; idem, *Posts and Pasts: A Theory of Post-colonialism* (New York: State University of New York Press, 2001); Aparajita Sagar, "Post-colonial Studies," in *A Dictionary of Cultural and Critical Theory* (ed. Michael Payne; Cambridge, MA: Blackwell, 1996), 423–28; Edward W. Said, *Orientalism* (New York: Pantheon Books, 1978); Fernando Segovia, *Decolonizing Biblical Studies: A View from the Margins* (Maryknoll, NY: Orbis Books, 2000); Gayatri Chakravorty Spivak, "Can the Subaltern Speak?," in *The Norton Anthology of Theory and Criticism* (ed. Vincent B. Leitch; New York: Norton, 2001), 2197–2208; R. S. Sugirtharajah, *The Bible and the Third World: Precolonial, Colonial, and Post-colonial Encounters* (Cambridge: Cambridge University Press, 2001); Ngugi Wa Thiong'o, Tababn Lo Liyong, and Henry Owuor-Anyumba, "On the Abolition of the English Department," in *The Norton Anthology of Theory and Criticism* (ed. Vincent B. Leitch; New York: Norton, 2001), 2377–97.

POSTCRITICAL / POSTCRITICAL INTERPRETATION

A mode of understanding that results from a critical assessment of a belief or system of belief, subsequent doubts from the assessment, and finally a reassessment, which may produce new MEANINGS. When applied to biblical INTERPRETATION, "postcritical" designates a contemporary interpretive approach (or posture) that underscores the possibility of a relationship with God in the process of interpretation and the inability of most modern critical methods (*see* CRITICAL METHODOLOGY) to generate such a relationship.

POSTCRITICAL NAÏVETÉ. *See* SECOND NAÏVETÉ

POSTMODERN. *See* POSTMODERN CRITICISM; POSTMODERNISM/POSTMODERNITY

POSTMODERN CRITICISM

An umbrella term for a group of CRITICISMS that began to appear in the late 1960s and early 1970s and emphasize the unavoidable CONTEXTS and other barriers that influence both the writing and the reading of TEXTS. POSTMODERNISM as a cultural phenomenon denies and PROBLEMATIZES the existence of absolute TRUTH and the ability of humans to know truth or to have objective historical knowledge. It emphasizes the context-bound world in which all people and texts exist, criticizing totalizing systems (*see* TOTALIZATION) that claim to exist in the realm of the objectively disinterested. Postmodernism relates specifically to LITERARY CRITICISM in that the barriers to understanding truly are the barriers inherent within language. Additionally, postmodern criticism seeks to identify the underlying ASSUMPTIONS inscribed in all writings in order to dispense with the concept of objectivity. By identifying the inescapable contexts and linguistic barriers, postmodern criticisms "deconstruct" texts in order to aid readers in admitting to and identifying their own contextual understanding and discovering new ways of reading texts.

As postmodern criticism developed throughout the 1970s and into the present, two major schools developed: (1) DECONSTRUCTION, which includes such figures as Jacques Derrida (its founder), Roland Barthes, and the Yale school, with such figures as Geoffrey Hartman, Harold Bloom, Paul de Man, and J. Hillis Miller; and (2) POLITICAL CONTEXTUALISM, as represented by Michel Foucault, Jean François Lyotard, Richard Rorty, and Terry Eagleton. Foucault seeks to strip the author of any authority and replace it with a collective power that he defines as the product of institutional and ideological discourses, within which individual authors operate and are defined (Felperin, 28–31). Most, if not all, types of postmodern criticisms, however, are indebted to Ferdinand de Saussure, Friedrich Nietzsche, and Martin Heidegger. First, Saussure defined the SIGN in terms of its dual nature of signifier and signified, with the relationship between the two being arbitrary: there is no logical or necessary correspondence between the signifier (e.g., the word sound "cat") and the signified (the concept of a cat). Saussure further argued that a sign has meaning not in and of itself but only in its difference from all other signs. For example, *green* has meaning only in the fact that it is not red, yellow, purple, and so forth. Postmodern critics expanded these two ideas into a theory of language claiming that meaning is never present in a text but always absent. In other words, a text means only in the sense of its difference from other texts. In one way or another, postmodern criticisms such as DECONSTRUCTION, READER-RESPONSE, INTERTEXTUAL, AUTOBIOGRAPHICAL, and PHENOMENOLOGICAL proceed from the ASSUMPTION that meaning is not present in the text but that the reader invests the text with meaning.

Second, Nietzsche argued that all language is tropic (has a metaphorical character) and that absolute TRUTH does not exist but is actually a system of METAPHORS that people have forgotten to be so. Consequently, postmodern critics have used the ideas of Nietzsche to argue that Truth (with a capital T) does not exist. Instead, there are only local systems of truths that are culturally constructed. Furthermore, these systems do not reflect the way things actually are but rather reflect the manner in which individual cultures have defined their realities. Naturally, then, these systems come to be viewed as representing the natural structure of things and are therefore considered to be universal. Postmodern critics tend to view all systems (ideological, literary, scientific, etc.) as metadiscourses that exist only at the expense of excluding other possibilities and groups. Postmodern criticisms—such as IDEOLOGICAL, MUJERISTA, FEMINIST, ASIAN / ASIAN AMERICAN, CULTURAL, LIBERATION, MARXIST, POSTCOLONIAL, QUEER THEORY, gay/lesbian, RACE-CLASS-GENDER, and WOMANIST—assume that texts produced within the dominant thought system conceal other voices that are nonetheless recoverable. Hence, these critics try to discern the suppressed voices struggling for articulation within the dominant discourse and bring them to light.

Third, Martin Heidegger supplied the groundwork for the postmodern interest in contexts. According to Heidegger, being must be understood in terms of being-in-the-world. In other words, what it means to be human is inextricably linked to Dasein, a "being there," being historical creatures. There exists no ontological being (a human essence or nature) in which all humans participate. Everything humans are and everything they think, decide, interpret is from within what Heidegger calls a *Vorstruktur,* "forestructure," which consists of a "[be]fore-having, fore-sight, and fore-conception" (191). Postmodern critics have adopted Heidegger's emphasis on context by arguing that all human activities—including systems construction, artistic production, writing, and interpreting—are performed within an entire matrix of contexts, usually referred to as SOCIAL LOCATION. In addition to the critics in the areas listed above, other critics argue for INTERPRETATION within social locations (e.g., PSYCHOANALYTIC, NEW HISTORICISM, TRANSACTIVE , SOCIAL SCIENTIFIC, CULTURAL MATERIALISM, AFRICAN AMERICAN, and RECEPTION THEORY).

Bibliography. Joseph Adamson, "Deconstruction," in *Encyclopedia of Contemporary Literary Theory: Approaches, Scholars, Terms* (ed. Irena R. Makaryk; Toronto: University of Toronto Press, 1993), 25–31; Zsuzsa Baross, "Post-structuralism," in *Encyclopedia of Contemporary Literary Theory: Approaches, Scholars, Terms* (ed. Irena R. Makaryk; Toronto: University of Toronto Press, 1993), 158–63; Lawrence Cahoone, ed., *From Modernism to Post-modernism* (Oxford: Blackwell, 1996); Robert Ellrodt, "Literary History and the Search for Certainty," *New Literary History* 27, no. 3 (1996): 529–43; Howard Felperin, *Beyond Deconstruction: The Uses and Abuses of Literary Theory* (Oxford: Clarendon, 1985); Michel Foucault, "Nietzsche, Genealogy, and History," in *Language, Counter-memory, Practice: Selected Interviews and Other Writings* (ed. Donald Bouchard; trans. Donald Bouchard and Sherry Simon; Ithaca, NY: Cornell University Press, 1977), 139–64; Suzanne Gearhart, "The Taming of Michel Foucault: New Historicism, Psychoanalysis, and the Subversion of Power," *New Literary History* 28, no. 3 (1997): 457–80; Martin Heidegger, *Being and Time* (trans. John Macquarrie and Edward Robinson; New York: Harper & Row, 1992); Linda Hutcheon, *A Poetics of Postmodernism: History, Theory, Fiction* (New York: Routledge, 1988); Donald Keesey, *Contexts for Criticism* (2nd ed.; Mountain View, CA: Mayfield, 1987); Vincent Leitch, *Deconstructive Criticisms: An Advanced Introduction* (New York: Columbia University Press, 1983); Stephen Miller, "The Future of Disinterest and Foucault's Regime of Truth," *Partisan Review* 64, no. 1 (1997): 28–36; Christopher Norris, *The Deconstructive Turn: Essays in the Rhetoric of Philosophy* (New York: Methuen, 1983); William Ray, *Literary Meaning: From Phenomenology to Deconstruction* (Oxford: Blackwell, 1984).

POSTMODERNISM/POSTMODERNITY

A multidisciplinary critique or reaction to a series of foundational ASSUMPTIONS of MODERNISM (*see* FOUNDATIONALISM). *Postmodernity* refers to a period of cultural history from around 1965 to the present; postmodernism refers to the cultural expression characteristic of the period. Although postmodernism is only the latest in a history of critiques, it is the most sustained and widespread one. Though it may have begun in the 1930s, it began to gain momentum in the 1960s, especially in the field of architecture. From there the critique spread to other areas, such as philosophy, literary theory, and CRITICISM. While it is not monolithic, postmodernism does seem to focus its attention on rejecting or problematizing (*see* PROBLEMATIZE) what its proponents see as obsolete or ill-founded philosophical assumptions, principles, values, and ideas that are the modern residue of the eighteenth-century Enlightenment. As the name implies, postmodernism involves a movement beyond modernism, and it is against this backdrop of the assumptions of modernism that the diverse interests of postmodernism assume any semblance of a unified philosophical movement. The most notable of postmodernism's critiques concern the nature of TRUTH and knowledge, the nature of language, the autonomous self, the unity and harmony of nature, the nature of MEANING and REFERENCE, human reason, human progress, and totalizing systems.

According to Linda Hutcheon, postmodernism "challenges all forms of totalizing thought that do not acknowledge their role in the very constitution of their objects of study and in the reduction of the heterogeneous and problematic to the homogeneous and transcendental" (98). According to postmodernists, no human activity or thought occurs that is not grounded in historical, social, and political CONTEXTs. There is no meaning that is not controlled by or filtered through the totalizing METANARRATIVEs, systems by which we create reality, legitimate claims, and solve contradictions. These metanarratives (theological, philosophical, political, etc.) reduce the contingencies and complexities of reality to a meaningful, manageable, and defining STRUCTURE, thereby providing a FRAMEWORK of living as well as a set of social norms that lays claim to a universal validity. Concepts such as moral behavior and GENDER are always defined in terms of the dominant metanarrative. But when a system becomes dominant, it does so through a reduction of the complexity of realty. As it foregrounds some possibilities, it necessarily backgrounds or excludes others. According to Wolfgang Iser, "Each meaningful reduction of contingency results in a division of the world into possibilities that fade from the dominant to the neutralized and negated" (71). This exclusion creates marginality (*see* MARGINALIZATION) and ALIENATION. Whatever the system cannot incorporate becomes ex-centric, threatening, or abnormal, creating BINARY OPPOSITES, the first term of which is always privileged: white/black, male/female, self/Other, spirit/body, objectivity/subjectivity, West/East, rational/irrational, and so forth. Postmodernists reject the claim that these oppositions represent the way things naturally are, and they themselves claim that the oppositions are illusionary human constructs that try to unify and order human experience in terms of power and control. They are based on hierarchies that are assumed to be natural. In addition, postmodernists claim that there are no natural, given NARRATIVEs that reflect the way things are, but only those that humans construct. While postmodernists may see these systems as useful fictions, means by which humans manage the world, they reject them as reflecting any natural or given order in the nature of things. They assume the existence of a plethora of systems in the world, but rather than existing as universal givens, they are all created human fictions. These systems are different stories or LANGUAGE GAMES that humans construct to explain their experience of the world. Once constructed, these different metanarratives filter all subsequent experience and determine what we see when we look at the world. They determine our ideas of truth, meaning, history, and knowledge.

Postmodernists also argue that Western philosophy since the time of Plato has reflected a META-PHYSICS OF PRESENCE, at the heart of which is the foundational assumption that there exists an objective world of realities independent of humans and our thoughts about it. Truth and meaning exist as TRANSCENDENTAL SIGNIFIEDS prior to our discovery of them, objectively inhering in the structure of things, just waiting for human reason to discover the objective world of realities and then present it by way of the objective structures of language.

Western metaphysics has also assumed transparency as a property of language. As objects present themselves to the mind, humans are capable of making objective assertions about those objects. If that language is subsequently analyzed, humans can fully know that object because the logical structures of the universe (or object) are revealed in the assertions, which are themselves the meaning of the object. Such an assumption, claim postmodernists, is tantamount to viewing language as denotative (*see* DENOTATION), to affirming that language can objectively represent the world.

In reaction, postmodernists claim that neither reality nor language is transcendental. All knowledge—ultimately all truth—is socially conditioned. They reject the Enlightenment search for objective, universal truth in favor of a truth that is rooted in the communities in which humans participate. They reject the idea that anyone can find a disinterested position outside the defining structures of SOCIAL LOCATION, a position from which to objectively observe reality. Languages

are social constructs, social conventions that map reality in a variety of ways, coloring and altering the way we experience reality. So languages do not represent or reconstruct the world: they construct the world. Languages are world-creating rather than world-describing systems. This means, then, that rather than an already-existing objective body of knowledge or truth, or even an objective world waiting to be discovered, there are only potential worlds and many truths. These worlds, each with its own truth, are SYMBOLIC WORLDS that we construct through languages. So postmodernists refuse to split language from reality: they assume that there is no direct access to the world that is unmediated by language.

But postmodernists such as Derrida and Foucault take the issue of language further. If language actually constitutes what it represents, no DISCOURSE can be value-neutral (including science, philosophy, HISTORIOGRAPHY, LITERARY CRITICISM). What emerges in any act of knowing is only the perspective of the person interpreting. If every act of knowing is constituted by the knowing self within a particular discourse, there exists the possibility that INTERPRETATIONS of reality are assertions of power to gain mastery over nature rather than attempts to gain knowledge.

Bibliography. Linda Hutcheon, *A Poetics of Postmodernism: History, Theory, Fiction* (New York: Routledge, 1988); Wolfgang Iser, *The Act of Reading: A Theory of Aesthetic Response* (Baltimore: Johns Hopkins University Press, 1978).

POSTSTRUCTURALISM. *See*
POSTMODERNISM/POSTMODERNITY

POSTSTRUCTURALIST CRITICISM. *See*
POSTMODERN CRITICISM

PRACTICAL CRITICISM

A CRITICAL METHODOLOGY developed by I. A. Richards in the 1920s, focusing on close and detailed analysis of works of literature in isolation from other concerns such as the BACKGROUND, psychology, and INTENTION of the AUTHOR. For a more detailed discussion of Richard's method, *see* NEW CRITICISM.

PRAGMATICS

Theologically, a term for the study of the practical application of doctrine and theology in everyday life. The term, however, also has a specific MEANING in LINGUISTICS: the study of the circumstances surrounding individual linguistic expressions and their effects on interlocutors. As such, it is a part of EXEGESIS and the counterpart to SEMANTICS, the study of the language of a text. According to Peter Cotterell and Max Turner, semantics and pragmatics should be divided more conveniently into the categories of TEXT, COTEXT and CONTEXT. *Text* refers to the actual words of the text; *cotext* is concerned with the relationships between words in sentences, paragraphs, and chapters; and *context* focuses on the historical and sociological SETTING of the text. The first two areas are the concern of semantics, while the last is the domain of pragmatics. Cotterell and Turner base these definitions on the distinction between "sentence" and "utterance." A sentence, as a particular combination of particular words, may occur repeatedly, while an utterance (which is the same sentence within a unique context) can never occur more than once. Therefore, exegesis must be concerned with the explication of utterances, not sentences. This means that pragmatics must be an integral part of exegesis. When we begin to explore any text, we confront utterances instead of contextless sentences. When Paul wrote to the church at Corinth, he wrote within a particular context, a RECONSTRUCTION of which yields a more informed reading of the text.

Bibliography. Peter Cotterell and Max Turner, *Linguistics and Biblical Interpretation* (Downers Grove, IL: InterVarsity, 1989).

PRAISE PSALMS. *See* PSALM(S)

PRAXIS

A term used by Aristotle in his *Poetics* to denote ACTION as the central element in TRAGEDY. It has been adopted by LITERARY critics to refer to the "practice" of doing CRITICISM. In LIBERATION THEOLOGY, the term refers to the role that action

and reflection play in addressing oppression and transforming social order.

PRÉCIS

A SUMMARY or abstract of a TEXT, retaining the order of the events in the text.

PRECRITICAL

A designation of approaches to biblical INTERPRETATION that do not employ formal CRITICAL METHODOLOGY. Although the early church fathers did employ a variety of interpretive approaches (e.g., allegorical, gnostic), precritical interpretation was characterized by adherence to a creed as the framework for interpreting the biblical texts and by a sense that interpretation must take place within a community of faith and with definite didactic purposes. These emphases began to change with the rise of Cartesian rationalism in the seventeenth century and to some extent before that in the Renaissance of the fifteenth and sixteenth centuries. With the rise of critical interpretations, the individual becomes a rationally self-sufficient entity and thus capable of interpreting a TEXT from an objective, rational vantage point.

PRE-PAULINE

In critical studies of the biblical texts, the ideas, doctrines, HYMNS, CREEDS, and liturgical material (*see* LITURGICAL FRAGMENTS) current in the church before Paul's use of them in his writings.

PRESCRIPT

The formal elements in an epistle's beginning. These usually include the sender, addressee(s), brief greeting, and sometimes a prayer or wish for health (e.g., 1 Thess. 1:1–3). *See* EPISTOLARY LITERATURE.

PRESENCE

In literary studies, the idea that MEANING is somehow present in the language and STRUCTURES of a TEXT. In philosophical discussion, the ASSUMPTION in the Western metaphysical TRADITION that meaning is present in SPEECH and is immediately accessible to the human mind because the structures of language are inherently capable of representing the structures of reality. POSTMODERN thinkers such as Michel Foucault and Jacques Derrida have challenged this assumption by problematizing (*see* PROBLEMATIZE) the distinction between the autonomous thinking SUBJECT (e.g., the reader) and the object of investigation (e.g., text), as well as the transparency of language and its ability to represent reality. Derrida and others deny that meaning is present in the structure of reality and precedes language. Rather, meaning is absent and *created by* language. With respect to literary texts, then, meaning is not present in the structures of the text but is always virtual, somewhere between the activities of readers and the text. *See also* READER-RESPONSE CRITICISM.

PRESUPPOSITION

An a priori ASSUMPTION that underlies a person's thoughts and views of reality and through which every experience is filtered. Presuppositions are not generally subjected to examination or EXEGESIS, but they profoundly affect exegesis and INTERPRETATION. Once a reader realizes that he/she holds a certain presupposition, then it may become a belief that is open to examination and modification. Nevertheless, the presupposition that becomes a belief still exerts a powerful control on interpretation. When these presuppositions and beliefs are taken as a whole at any one point, one has the FRAMEWORK within which all texts are perceived and interpreted. This INTERPRETIVE FRAMEWORK consists of presuppositions, beliefs, and attitudes that are ethical, doctrinal, denominational, philosophical, theological, and methodological. They are not consciously categorized but exist in an ever-changing process of interrelatedness.

PRE-TEXTS

A term for previous texts that an AUTHOR either consciously or unconsciously incorporates into his or her own TEXT (Thiselton, 504). For example, Mark's "desolating sacrilege" (13:14) is taken from Dan. 12:11, and Mark's two feeding stories have pre-texts in Num. 11:13, 22; Exod. 16:24–25; and 2 Kings 4:43. Mark's reference in 6:34c to the crowd as being "like sheep without a shepherd" has parallels in 1 Kings 22:17; 2 Chron. 18:16; Isa. 13:14; Jer. 50:6; Ezek. 34:12; and Zech. 10:2. The idea of the pre-text or INTERTEXT is an integral part of INTERTEXTUAL CRITICISM.

Bibliography. Anthony Thiselton, *New Horizons in Hermeneutics* (Grand Rapids: Zondervan, 1992).

PREUNDERSTANDING

The horizon of understanding within which and from which all things are intelligible to a person. Every reader approaches a TEXT under the guidance of a perspective. Any text is read, perceived, and interpreted within a preexistent structure of reality. Since reality is infinite, no person can reach outside the realm of time and space to give an objective account of reality. Readers are always being affected by their present horizons of understanding (*see* HORIZON OF MEANING).

PRIESTLY CODE

A collection of cultic laws running from Exod. 25 to Num. 10. These laws include regulations for the sanctuary and sacrifices, definitions of clean and unclean, and rules for observing the Day of Atonement.

PRIESTLY DOCUMENT. *See* GRAF-WELLHAUSEN HYPOTHESIS; P; SOURCE CRITICISM

PRIESTLY NARRATIVE. *See* GRAF-WELLHAUSEN HYPOTHESIS; P; SOURCE CRITICISM

PRIESTLY WRITER. *See* GRAF-WELLHAUSEN HYPOTHESIS; P; SOURCE CRITICISM

PRIMEVAL PERIOD

The period in Gen. 1–11 before the appearance of the patriarchs, who begin with Abraham.

PRIMITIVE CHRISTIANITY

The earliest period of Christianity, predating the institutionalization of the church, which occurred perhaps as early as the latter part of the first century or the early second century. This primitive time was before the church developed an episcopate, CREED, or CANON, the development of which, according to some NT scholars, can be seen in the PASTORALS, Ephesians, and Colossians. During this period, the earliest Christians expected the imminent return of Jesus. When this return was delayed, the church compensated by moving toward institutionalization.

PRISON EPISTLES

The EPISTLES (Ephesians, Colossians, Philippians, and Philemon) attributed to Paul while he was imprisoned in Rome.

PROBATIO

In RHETORICAL CRITICISM, the argument of a SPEECH, in which the orator seeks to establish his/her case and to persuade the audience to accept it.

PROBLEMATIZE

A term current in most POSTMODERN theories, describing the various ways in which time-honored ASSUMPTIONS (e.g., the autonomous self, the AUTONOMY OF THE TEXT, OBJECTIVE TRUTH and MEANING, race, GENDER, sexuality, identity, REFERENCE, SUBJECT/OBJECT, historical knowledge, the objectivity of philosophy) are being challenged.

PRODUCTIVE TEXTS

A category of TEXTS in the READER-RESPONSE CRITICISM of Umberto Eco that he labels LITERARY. By *literary* or *productive*, Eco means texts that, through a variety of devices and strategies, create a role for the reader in producing meaning. Opposed to these kinds of texts are transmissive texts, which simply communicate or transmit MEANING or information. The productive text requires the cooperation of the reader in making interpretive choices, but the reader must be familiar with the CODES presupposed by the text in order to generate or produce a plausible reading. Arguably, the GOSPELS, the WISDOM LITERATURE of Job and Ecclesiastes, the book of Revelation,

and certain HEBREW NARRATIVES are productive texts. A text such as Philemon would be a transmissive one.

Bibliography. Umberto Eco, *The Role of the Reader: Explorations in the Semiotics of Texts* (Bloomington: Indiana University Press, 1984).

PROEM

Also referred to as the EXORDIUM, a preface, preamble, or introduction. In classical rhetorical SPEECH, the proem served to elicit the audience's interest and trust. Most of the epistles (esp. those of Paul) employed the proem for the same purpose.

Proem is also a type of Jewish homily that appeared in the first two centuries CE and was delivered in the synagogue on Sabbaths. It begins with a quotation from the WRITINGS and then links it to the TEXT from the TORAH for the day.

PROLEPSIS

In NARRATIVE, a FORESHADOWING, the NARRATION of an event before its chronological order in the world of the narrative. For example, in 1 Kings 22:17, the prophet Micaiah narrates an event which actually happens much later in the narrative (22:29–38).

PROLOGUE

The OPENING section of a work, an introduction that is actually a part of the TEXT (e.g., John 1:1–18).

PRONOUNCEMENT STORY/SAYINGS

A brief STORY that serves as a CONTEXT for a SAYING OF JESUS (Bailey and Vander Broek, 114). Generally, the story climaxes with the saying, which is intended to illustrate or explain the story (e.g., Mark 2:15–17; 3:22–27; 10:17–22). Bailey and Vander Broek (115–16) offer Vernon Robbins's summary of classifications of pronouncement stories as proposed by Robert Tannehill:

1. *Correction stories*, which end with the main character correcting one or more individuals (e.g., Mark 1:35–38; 9:33–37);

2. *Commendation stories*, which end with the main character commending one or more individuals (e.g., Matt. 13:51–52; Luke 10:17–20);

3. *Objection stories*, in which an objection calls forth the response from the main character (e.g., Mark 2:15–17; Matt. 3:13–15);

4. *Quest stories*, in which a secondary person's success or failure in a quest of something important to human well-being has prominence alongside the main character's response (e.g., Mark 10:17–22; 12:28–34);

5. *Inquiry stories*, which end with a response by the main character to an inquiry (Mark 7:17–23; Luke 3:10–14); and

6. *Description stories*, which end with a description of the situation by the main character (e.g., Luke 14:15–24).

Bibliography. James L. Bailey and Lyle D. Vander Broek, *Literary Forms in the New Testament: A Handbook* (Louisville: Westminster John Knox, 1992); Robert Tannehill "Introduction: The Pronouncement Story and Its Types," *Semeia* 20 (1981): 1–13.

PROEMIUM. *See* EXORDIUM; PROEM

PROOF TEXT

A scriptural verse or verses cited as proof of a theological or doctrinal position. The practice of proof-texting generally ignores the historical, LITERARY, and semantic CONTEXTs of the verse and forces it to support a contemporary position that could never have been intended or been understood.

PROPHECY

An oral or written utterance of a prophet. Although prophetic utterances occasionally were predictions, this aspect seems to have had only secondary import and was probably a late development in prophecy. Early in the development of Hebrew prophecy, ecstatic trances were common (e.g., 1 Sam. 10:6). However, among later prophets, this ecstatic element seems to have disappeared and was replaced by what is now referred to as classical prophecy, in which the SPEECH of the prophet is recast in BIBLICAL POETRY. This change may sug-

gest that the prophetic utterances were deemed important enough to eventually become a literary GENRE alongside other ones such as HEBREW NARRATIVE and WISDOM LITERATURE.

Generally, the material within a specific prophetic book of the HEBREW BIBLE is not necessarily in chronological order but is a collection of material. Chronology played a role only when the collectors knew the history of the material. This material was initially preserved together in larger or smaller collections and only at a later time became the groundwork for the prophetic books. Collectors had a wide variety of material at their disposal. Primarily ORACLES, other SAYINGS, larger prophetic compositions, and short narratives about EPISODEs in the life of the prophet were collected. In many cases, the utterances were not preserved in their original form but are in the form of free summaries or abstracts.

The principles that guided the collectors vary. The most dominating factor was similarity in subject matter. Antithetical ideas such as righteousness and unrighteousness or judgment and salvation also governed the association of passages. Passages consisting of the same STRUCTURE often occur in a series, such as the woe oracle (*see* PROPHETIC ORACLE) and the SERMON beginning with "hear." Catchwords were also used in grouping different passages.

As a rule, the collectors did their work after the death of the prophet whose teachings and utterances they recorded. They frequently recorded in writing, but smaller collections may have circulated in oral form. The main INTENTION was to preserve the prophecies for posterity and to adapt them for practical use.

REDACTIONAL work began where the collectors left off. Our present prophetic books are not identical with the original collections, for these have undergone changes and transformations of different kinds. There are numerous examples of additions, enlargements, and comments, showing that the texts were subjected to alterations in accordance with the tastes and needs of later times. The texts remained fluid for many centuries.

The REDACTORS of the prophetic books developed the prophets' original words in order to bring out their SIGNIFICANCE for a later age. This accounts for the presence of unfulfilled prophecies. For example, in the eighth century BCE Micah's prediction of the fall of Jerusalem, which appears to conflict with the prophecies of Isaiah that the city would be protected by God, was regarded as unfulfilled as late as Jeremiah's time (Jer. 26:17–19). Yet Micah's prophecies were preserved. Clements comments that "very significantly an important aspect of the redactional work on the prophetic books was to adapt and reinterpret prophecies in the light of later historical circumstances" (53). This indicates that the TRUTH of prophecy was seen to be a larger truth than could be contained within a simple prediction-fulfillment formula. Hosea, whose message was originally directed to the northern kingdom, is an example. Sometime later, slight editing—the insertion of the name "Judah" at several places—gave Hosea's message a new significance to the southern kingdom. Von Rad offers the following explanation:

> It was never presumed that the prophet's oracles were addressed to one set of people and one only, and were thereafter to be wrapped up in their rolls and deposited among the records. There must have been people who never forgot that a prophet's teaching always remained relevant for a coming day and generation, and who themselves played their part in making it appear relevant—in many cases their work can be clearly seen in the various secondary additions which they made. (43)

Several LITERARY forms are present in the prophetic texts, and as with other texts, the message of these books or singular oracles within them is inseparable from the FORM. Probably the most common form used to convey the prophetic message was the MESSENGER FORMULA.

The Hebrew prophets usually prefaced this formula with another form designed to draw the recipient's attention to the message. This preface to the message was a designation of those for whom it was intended. Von Rad comments: "In the case

of a divine threat, what was prefixed was a DIATRIBE; in the case of a promise, an exhortation. These two, the messenger formula and prefixed clause, must both be present before we have the literary category of prophetic oracle" (37). As a rule, the prophets (until the time of Jeremiah) drew a clear distinction between the messenger formula and the diatribe or exhortation that introduced it. The messenger formula was the WORD OF GOD, while the prefaced form was an editorial addition by the prophet. This prefaced form had the purpose of leading up to and preparing the way for God's word and gave it its REFERENCE.

But the messenger formula is only one among many forms in the prophetic texts. There was no hesitation in using multiple forms to clothe the messages. These are the exhortation to repent, reproach, woe and SATIRE, LAMENT, HYMNS, prayer, judicial debating, and ritual utterance. There are the short message and extended sermon, historical retrospect, PARABLE, ALLEGORY, SIMILE, and WISDOM SAYING.

By choosing a particular form, these prophets intended to attract attention. For example, when a prophet drafted into service a time-hallowed sacral form, his purpose was to shock the audience. In Isa. 40–55, the AUTHOR drew from the priestly oracle of weal and, by reshaping it into something more sweeping, made it the form of his preaching. Other messages were clothed in the form favored by wisdom teachers (Amos 3:3–8) or popular songs (Isa. 5:1–7). A vivid example of the way a prophet would take a well-known form or a LITERARY DEVICE and change it almost beyond recognition is the DIRGE. The later prophets actually turned it upside down and parodied it (Amos 5:1; Isa. 23:1–12; Ezek. 19:1–14; 27:2–11; Isa. 14:4–11).

The prophets thus attired their prophetic messages and oracles in nonprophetic, secular garb. However, the reverse is also true: the prophets sometimes also tailored their messages to the forms. Ezekiel derives a number of subjects from FOLKLORE and songs (cf. Ezek. 14:12–23; 16:1–43; 17:1–10; 19:1–14; 21:13–23; 23:1–27; 26:19–21;

28:1–10; 31:1–18; 32:17–32). Isaiah utilizes the types of the love song (5:1–7) and the wisdom instruction (28:23–29).

All of this means that INTERPRETATION must address the texts of the prophets with their multiple forms. While the predominantly poetic texts of the prophets differ from narrative texts (there is in prophetic works very little narrative or STORY WORLD in the strict sense), they are replete with forms constitutive of meaning.

Although there is no prophetic genre in the NT, there is abundant evidence of the presence of prophecy and prophets in the early church. (Some, however, would argue that the Apocalypse of John is prophetic, even though it is not technically an example of the prophetic genre.) John the Baptist and Jesus are referred to as prophets (e.g., Luke 1:76; Matt. 21:26), prophecy was one of the gifts of the Spirit (1 Cor. 14), and there are warnings against false prophets (e.g., Rev. 2:20). Although Paul describes the essence of prophecy as exhortation, the frequency, role, and essence of early Christian prophecy continue to be debated among NT scholars. For an overview of this debate, see Y. Gitay.

Bibliography. R. E. Clements, *Prophecy and Tradition* (Atlanta: John Knox, 1975); Y. Gitay, ed., *Prophecy and Prophets: The Diversity of Contemporary Issues in Scholarship* (Atlanta: Scholars Press, 1997); Gerhard von Rad, *Old Testament Theology* (2 vols.; New York: Harper & Row, 1965); W. Randolph Tate, *Biblical Interpretation: An Integrated Approach* (rev. ed.; Peabody, MA: Hendrickson, 1997).

PROPHET. *See* PROPHECY

PROPHETIC ESCHATOLOGY. *See* ESCHATOLOGY

PROPHETIC LAWSUIT. *See* COVENANT LAWSUIT

PROPHETIC LITERATURE. *See* PROPHECY

PROPHETIC ORACLE

A SAYING in which a PROPHET proclaims a message from God, often prefaced by the formula "Thus says the LORD" or "Hear the word of the LORD." The saying had many forms: ORACLE of repentance (Jer. 3:12), oracle of deliverance (Isa. 1:26), oracle of judgment (Isa. 1:24–26), oracle of woe (Hab. 2:6–8), or even wisdom oracle (Jer. 17:5–11). At times some of these types are combined.

Bibliography. Christian Hauer and William Young, *An Introduction to the Bible: A Journey into Three Worlds* (4th ed.; Upper Saddle River, NJ: Prentice Hall, 1998).

PROPHETIC POETRY

The preferred medium of the PROPHETS before the EXILE, which began in 586 BCE. According to Robert Alter, the poetry of the prophets differs substantially from that of other poetic books (e.g., Song of Songs, Proverbs, Psalms, and Job) in its "vocative character." Because the prophets addressed their messages to real audiences rather than imagined ones, the element of persuasion was stronger. "Since poetry is our best human model of intricately rich communication, not only solemn, weighty, and forceful but also densely woven with complex internal connections, meanings, and implications, it makes sense that divine speech should be represented as poetry" (141).

According to Alter (141), prophetic poetry has reproof as its primary purpose, which is accomplished in three ways: direct accusation, SATIRE, and monitory evocation of impending danger. The first involves name-calling, in which the audience is reminded of consequences of past actions. Satire (along with SARCASM and IRONY) attacks unacceptable "practices, attitudes, institutions, and paraphernalia." Moral depravity is the target of monitory evocation.

Bibliography. Robert Alter, *The Art of Biblical Poetry* (New York: Basic Books, 1985).

PROPHETIC PRINCIPLE

In the FEMINIST CRITICISM of Rosemary Radford Ruether, a prophetic consciousness or prophetic impulse that is present at different places and times within the biblical CANON. According to Ruether, this prophetic principle rejects the attempt to elevate one social group above others, claiming that the former group somehow reflects the image of God (*Sexism and God Talk*, 23). Every attempt to use the idea of God to justify social dominion and subordination is to be rejected. Ruether asserts that religion (along with sacred TEXTS and INTERPRETATIONS of such texts) throughout history has sanctioned existing social orders, which divide human beings into classes in which the superior rules over the inferior. But this religious sanction of the existing social order is counteracted by an alternative principle: the prophetic principle. God periodically speaks through the prophetic person in order to criticize and condemn the society that, in the name of religion, perpetuates injustices on some social groups. Therefore, the prophetic principle criticizes both society's injustices and its religious justification of them ("Feminist Interpretation," 118).

Bibliography. Rosemary Radford Ruether, "Feminist Interpretation: A Method of Correlation," in *Feminist Interpretation of the Bible* (ed. Letty M. Russell; Philadelphia: Westminster, 1985), 111–24; idem, *Sexism and God Talk: Toward a Feminist Theology* (Boston: Beacon, 1983).

PROPHETIC PROSE

Portions of the PROPHETS that are in PROSE rather than in PROPHETIC POETRY. These passages occur in Jeremiah, Ezekiel, and some of the later Minor Prophets (*see* SCROLL OF THE TWELVE). Robert Alter suggests that while we do not know why there may have been a partial shift from prophetic poetry to prophetic prose after the EXILE, from 586 BCE, some prophetic forms may have actually lent themselves to prose (e.g., the oracular vision, in which the prophet explains an image in an expository manner).

Bibliography. Robert Alter, *The Art of Biblical Poetry* (New York: Basic Books, 1985).

PROPHETIC SAYING. *See* SAYINGS OF JESUS

PROPHETIC SPEECH

According to Claus Westermann, one of the three major kinds of SPEECH in the prophetic books, the other two being accounts and utterances directed to God from humans. The prophetic speech, however, is "the major component of most prophetic books, i.e., the words of God delivered by a messenger of God" (90). According to Westermann, the prophetic speech formed the core of the eighth- and seventh-century BCE prophetic books. During the EXILE, the prayer (utterances directed to God by humans) is combined with the prophetic speech.

The addressee of the prophetic speech may be an individual, a group, or a nation, and the speech almost always includes an announcement of either judgment or salvation. When these speeches were collected and arranged by later REDACTORS, they seem to have been arranged according to the following pattern: judgment speeches to the prophet's own nation; judgment speeches to foreign nations; salvation speeches to the prophet's own nation; accounts (such as historical epilogues set at the end of the book; e.g., Jer. 52; Westermann, 95). While the judgment speeches are usually grouped together, the salvation speeches may occur as a group or may be attached to the end of the collection of judgment speeches (e.g., Isa. 2:1–4; 9:1–6; Amos 9:8b–15).

Bibliography. Claus Westermann, *Basic Forms of Prophetic Speech* (Louisville: Westminster John Knox, 1991).

PROPHETS, THE

The second division of the HEBREW BIBLE (NEVI'IM), consisting of the Former Prophets (Joshua, Judges, 1–2 Samuel, 1–2 Kings) and the Latter Prophets, which are divided into the MAJOR PROPHETS (Isaiah, Jeremiah, and Ezekiel) and the twelve Minor Prophets (SCROLL OF THE TWELVE: Hosea, Joel, Amos, Obadiah, Jonah, Micah, Nahum, Habakkuk, Zephaniah, Haggai, Zechariah, and Malachi). *See* EXILE.

PROPHETS, FORMER. *See* PROPHETS, THE

PROPHETS, LATTER. *See* PROPHETS, THE

PROPHETS, MAJOR. *See* PROPHETS, THE

PROPHETS, MINOR. *See* PROPHETS, THE

PROPOSITIO

The central part of a SPEECH in classical RHETORIC, presenting the aim of the argument. It may outline the various points of the argument. For example, in 1 Cor. 15:12–20, Paul states the point to be challenged (v. 12), the foolishness of rejecting the resurrection of Jesus (vv. 13–19), and, finally, the thesis of the argument (v. 20).

PROPOSITIONAL ACT

An utterance in SPEECH ACT THEORY that predicates something upon another thing. An utterance that says something about something else. *See* LO-CUTIONARY ACT.

PROPOSITIONAL TRUTH

TRUTH that can be stated in terms of a single sentence—for example, "God cannot be tempted by evil" or "The message of Jonah is that God's sense of grace will always take precedence over his sense of justice." Propositional truth is usually the result of collapsing an understanding of a TEXT into a single statement. In other words, it is the end product of EXEGESIS. Some·critics (e.g., NEW CRITICISM) argue that a text is not reducible to a PARAPHRASE or to a proposition because its MEANING is a mixture of FORM and CONTENT as well as the experience of the reader. Though the text may suggest something about life or generate reflection on life, it will always produce a residue of SIGNIFICANCE that simply cannot be put into words.

PROSE

Technically, all forms of writing that have no regular pattern of RHYTHM. Yet prose is stylized, employing a range of LITERARY DEVICES and rhetorical strategies. The line between biblical prose and POETRY is sometimes blurred, but biblical prose is generally found in HISTORICAL NARRATIVES (e.g., Genesis, Exodus, Kings) and stories (e.g., Ruth, Esther), although the distinction between history and STORY is a forced one with respect to biblical literature. They both exhibit the things that we expect in prose: PLOT, STRUCTURE, CONFLICT, crisis, COMPLICATION, CLIMAX, and resolution. However, some of the prophetic texts in the HE-BREW BIBLE are written in prose, as is the EPISTO-LARY LITERATURE in the NT. For a more detailed discussion of the characteristics of Hebrew prose, *see* HEBREW NARRATIVE.

PROSODY

The study of the POETICS of versification, the mechanics of poetry, including METER, RHYTHM, RHYME, and STANZA. For a description of Hebrew prosody, *see* BIBLICAL POETRY.

PROSOPOPOEIA

A species of PERSONIFICATION in which the personified object is capable of SPEECH. An example is found in Prov. 1:20–23:

> Wisdom cries out in the street;
>> in the squares she raises her voice.
> At the busiest corner she cries out;
>> at the entrance of the city gates she speaks:
> "How long, O simple ones, will you love
>> being simple?"

PROTAGONIST

The main character in a STORY. The protagonist is the character around whom the ACTION revolves. In some cases, the protagonist is dynamic and thus changes or develops over time (e.g., Joseph, Ruth); in other instances the protagonist does not change and therefore is static (e.g., Samson).

PROTASIS

The subordinate clause in a conditional sentence. Genesis 4:24 states, "If Cain is avenged sevenfold, truly Lamech [is avenged] seventy-sevenfold." In the sentence "If a thief is found breaking in, and is beaten to death, no bloodguilt is incurred; but if it happens after sunrise, bloodguilt is incurred" (Exod. 22:2–3), there are two protases, each beginning with "if." Following each protasis is the APODOSIS, the conclusion of the conditional. CA-SUISTIC LAW is usually stated in terms of protasis and apodosis.

PROTENSION

An important term in the READER-RESPONSE CRITICISM of Wolfgang Iser, referring to the expectations generated in the reader of a TEXT as he/she progresses through the text. On encountering the various textual units or segments, the reader begins to formulate an idea (THEME) as to the MEANING of the text, based on what is held in memory (RETENTION). The reader will then form certain expectations, which may or may not be fulfilled. If the protension is frustrated, the reader is forced to retrace his or her steps, modifying the idea (theme) and thus the content of memory (retention). This memory or retention Iser calls horizon (*see* HORIZON OF EXPECTATION), against which every succeeding segment is read. This horizon always arouses expectations of things to come, such as how a problem will be resolved.

In Mark 4:3–9, Jesus introduces the kingdom of God by the PARABLE of the sower. When his disciples do not understand the parable (v. 10), Jesus offers an INTERPRETATION (vv. 11–12), followed by a cluster of SAYINGS (vv. 21–25), the parable of the growing seed (vv. 26–29), and the parable of the mustard seed (vv. 30–32). In doing so, Jesus is constituting a new culture (similar acts can be found in Hippocrates, Antiphon, Seneca, and Quintilian), in which Jesus is the teacher, the seeds are Jesus's message, and the soils are the different hearers. Although they should understand, the disciples do not grasp that Jesus is establishing a new culture, an alternative society in CONFLICT with both Greek and Jewish ones. At this point, the PLOT involves the reader in a process of retention and protension, with two important concerns: (1) the nature of this new culture and (2) the problem of the insider's inability to understand the nature of the new culture. The first issue forces the reader to recall or reread the NARRATIVE to this point with eyes open to clues as to the nature of the new culture and to read the narrative subsequent to the parable section with expectations of clues that will offer insight into the nature of the kingdom. The second issue forces the reader to look for instances of insight on the part of the disciples or other characters within the narrative; thus the reader is forced to ask what distinguishes an insider from an outsider.

Bibliography. Wolfgang Iser, *The Act of Reading: A Theory of Aesthetic Response* (Baltimore: Johns Hopkins University Press, 1978).

PROTEVANGELIUM

From the Greek meaning "first GOSPEL," the term refers to God's statement to the serpent in Gen. 3:15: "I will put enmity between you and the woman, and between your offspring and hers; he will strike your head, and you will strike his heel." As early as the second century CE, the TEXT was interpreted typologically as the first prediction of Christ's ultimate victory over evil.

The *Protevangelium of James*, however, is an apocryphal infancy narrative, which presents an account of Jesus's birth and events before his birth but focuses primarily on legendary accounts of events in the life of Mary, the mother of Jesus.

Bibliography. Donald K. McKim, *Westminster Dictionary of Theological Terms* (Louisville: Westminster John Knox, 1996).

PROTO-LUKE

A hypothetical document introduced by B. H. Streeter, which consisted of Q (a hypothetical sayings source used by both Matthew and Luke) and L (the material unique to Luke's GOSPEL, but not including Luke 1–2). Streeter intended that this independent source would explain the verbal differences between Matthew and Luke. *See also* FOUR DOCUMENT HYPOTHESIS; SOURCE CRITICISM; SYNOPTIC PROBLEM, THE; TWO-SOURCE HYPOTHESIS.

Bibliography. B. H. Streeter, *The Four Gospels* (London: Macmillan, 1924).

PROTO-LXX. *See* SEPTUAGINT

PROVERB

A short, pithy SAYING that communicates a general or accepted TRUTH. In FORM and CONTENT, it is similar to the APHORISM. The proverb is ubiquitous and has existed since antiquity in virtually every culture. Examples abound: "Send a fool to close the shutters, and he'll close them all over the town" (Yiddish). "If vinegar is free, it is sweeter than honey" (Serbian). "Visits always give pleasure—if not the arrival, the departure" (Portuguese). Because proverbs relate to common experiences within a cultural CONTEXT, their complete SIGNIFICANCE will often be lost when they become part of a collection. For example, one person may claim that it is true that "out of sight, one is out of mind," while another will believe that "absence makes the heart grow fonder."

The largest sustained collection of proverbs in the BIBLE is the book of Proverbs. As a collection, the social context of individual proverbs has been lost. However, regardless of its loose organization, multiple perspectives, assumed SETTINGS, and types, the book of Proverbs does have a discernible coherence. Raymond Van Leeuwen (257–58) gives the following structure:

I. Title, Introduction, and Basic Principle (1:1–7)
II. Parental Instructions on Wisdom and Folly (1:8–9:18)
III. Solomonic Collection of Sayings (10:1–22:16)
IV. Sayings of the Wise (Admonitions) (22:17–24:22)
V. Further Sayings of the Wise (24:23–34)
VI. Second Solomonic Collection of Sayings (25:1–29:27)
VII. Sayings of Agur and Numerical Sayings (30:1–33)
VIII. Sayings of King Lemuel (31:1–9)
IX. Heroic Hymn to the Valiant Woman (31:10–31)

The proverbs in the GOSPELs are probably best described as aphorisms—terse, succinct statements easily remembered. The NT proverb is quite similar to the Hebrew WISDOM SAYING. Examples are easy to find:

> For those who want to save their life will lose it. (Mark 8:35)

> No one tears a patch from a new garment and sews it on an old garment. (Luke 5:36)

> Many who are first will be last, and the last will be first. (Matt. 19:30)

A proverb is open-ended. It demands contemplation because it is filled with universal applicability or speaks of a universal principle or truth. To ensure a broad range of MEANING, frequently a proverb uses FIGURATIVE LANGUAGE such as METAPHOR, HYPERBOLE, or SIMILE.

The legal sayings are those that have a juridical ring to them. They usually have to do with an area of ministry or ecclesiastical order:

> Laborers deserve their food. (Matt. 10:10b)

> If anyone will not welcome you or listen to your words, shake off the dust from your feet as you leave that house or town. (Matt. 10:14)

> Truly I tell you, whatever you bind on earth will be bound in heaven, and whatever you loose on earth will be loosed in heaven. (Matt. 18:18)

The PROPHETIC SAYINGS are usually salvific or judgmental:

> The women will be grinding meal together; one will be taken and one will be left. (Matt. 24:41)

Bibliography. Raymond Van Leeuwen, "Proverbs," in *A Complete Literary Guide to the Bible* (ed. Leland Ryken and Tremper Longman III; Grand Rapids: Zondervan, 1993), 256–67.

PROVISIONALITY OF INTERPRETATION

In contemporary LITERARY CRITICISM, the ASSUMPTION that since it is impossible to reconstruct the INTENTION of the AUTHOR, an INTERPRETATION is always provisional. This provisionality is further supported by factors such as the HISTORICITY of texts; the CONTEXT, purpose, and IDEOLOGY of the interpreter; the metaphorical nature of language; the level of the interpreter's LITERARY COMPETENCE; and the pressures of the INTERPRETIVE COMMUNITY on the reader. This provisionality does not preclude understanding, even critical understanding, but it does mean that an interpretation is always open for further modification.

PROVISION STORY

A name given by Antoinette Wire to the stories in the GOSPELs that describe Jesus's response to a need. What makes these stories different from the MIRACLE STORY is that there is no prior request for help. Examples are the two feeding miracles in Mark 6:30–44; 8:1–10; John 6:1–14. Most often, however, the evangelists have invested these miracles with SYMBOLIC SIGNIFICANCE (e.g., Luke 5:1–11). In fact, the two feeding miracles in Mark may symbolize the inclusion of both Jews and Gentiles into the people of God (Bailey and Vander Broek, 138).

Bibliography. James L. Bailey and Lyle D. Vander Broek, *Literary Forms in the New Testament: A Handbook* (Louisville: Westminster John Knox, 1992); Antoinette Wire, "The Structure of the Gospel Miracle Stories and Their Tellers," *Semeia* 11 (1978): 83–113.

PSALM(S)

A name (*Psalmoi* in Greek) for the collection of songs in the LXX. The equivalent in Hebrew is *mizmôr*, designating a "song sung to instrumental accompaniment" (as in the title for Ps. 4). Traditionally, the Psalms have been divided into five books: Pss. 1–41; 42–72; 73–89; 90–106; and 107–50, with each book ending with a DOXOLOGY: 41:13; 72:18–20; 89:52; 106:48; and 150, which is the concluding doxology for the entire collection.

In his FORM CRITICISM, Hermann Gunkel set the standard by which the Psalms have been studied, and his LITERARY categories for the Psalms are still used by contemporary scholars. The following is a summary of his six categories as they have been modified by later scholars, according to LaSor, Hubbard, and Bush.

Hymn. Also known as the psalm of praise, the HYMN typically has three components: a call to worship, a description of God's acts or attributes, and a conclusion, which calls for further praise or obedience (e.g., Ps. 105). Yet several subcategories that seem to be associated with special events

have been identified: victory songs recalling the song of Miriam (e.g., Ps. 68), processional hymns describing the feelings and expectations of the worshipers on their way to the temple (e.g., Ps. 84), Zion songs praising Yahweh for his PRESENCE in Zion (e.g., Ps. 76), and ENTHRONEMENT psalms celebrating Yahweh's reign over the nations (e.g., Ps. 93).

Complaints of the people. These are prayers offered by the congregation of Israel in times of invasion (e.g., Pss. 60; 79–80), oppression (e.g., Ps. 58), threat of attack (e.g., Ps. 88), and natural disasters such as plague or drought or famine (e.g., Ps. 126). Characteristic of the complaints of the people are (1) an appeal to Yahweh for help (74:1), (2) a description of the people's suffering (vv. 4–11), (3) a confession of trust in God based on God's past deeds (v. 12), (4) a plea for rescue and punishment of the people's enemies (vv. 19–23), (5) an appeal to Yahweh's reputation or a reminder of Yahweh's commitment to the COVENANT (v. 18), and (6) a promise that the people will celebrate publicly Yahweh's rescue of them (v. 13).

Complaints of the individual. More psalms fall into this group than any other, and they have virtually the same characteristics as the complaints of the people (e.g., Ps. 22).

Thanksgiving songs of the individual. Similar to the complaints of the individual, these psalms seem to have been used as a response to deliverance after the complaint. Components of this type are (1) a pronouncement of praise (116:1), (2) a summary of actions (vv. 1–2), (3) a recollection of the problem that generated the cry for help (v. 3), (4) a report of both the appeal and the answer (v. 4), (5) a proclamation of a vow of praise (v. 14), and (6) a praise (v. 19c).

Royal psalms. These constitute a small group of psalms that in some respect refer to the king. Although these do not form an independent literary GENRE of psalms, their contents do suggest a number of life settings (*see SITZ IM LEBEN*): weddings (e.g., Ps. 45), coronations (e.g., Pss. 2; 72; 110), and prayers offered before or after a battle (e.g.,

Pss. 20; 89). The early church read these psalms as predictions of the messiah and thus saw them as descriptions of Jesus.

Wisdom psalms. These few psalms are unique in that they, like WISDOM LITERATURE in general, offer instructions for living a wise and sensible life. According to present scholarship, these psalms fit the genre of WISDOM LITERATURE in that (1) they make use of techniques usually associated with the genre, such as the PROVERB, the ACROSTIC, and other FIGURES OF SPEECH drawn from nature; (2) they are obviously didactic; and (3) they are thematically commensurate with Wisdom literature (e.g., godly speech, the acceptable use of wealth, obedience, and the contrast between righteousness and wickedness). Examples are Pss. 1; 37; 49; 73; 127; and 128.

Bibliography. Hermann Gunkel, *The Psalms: A Form-Critical Introduction* (trans. T. M. Horner; Philadelphia: Fortress, 1968; repr., 1994); William S. LaSor, David A. Hubbard, and Fredrick W. Bush, *Old Testament Survey* (2nd ed.; Grand Rapids: Eerdmans, 1996).

PSALM, CORONATION. *See* PSALM(S)

PSALM, ENTHRONEMENT. *See* ENTHRONEMENT PSALM

PSALM, IMPRECATORY. *See* IMPRECATORY PSALM

PSALM, PENITENTIAL. *See* PENITENTIAL PSALM

PSALM, PRAISE. *See* PSALM(S)

PSALM, ROYAL. *See* PSALM(S)

PSALM, THANKSGIVING. *See* PSALM(S)

PSALM, WISDOM. *See* WISDOM PSALMS

PSALTER

From the Greek *psaltērion,* "stringed instrument," a stringed instrument used in ancient Jewish worship (e.g., Pss. 6; 54; 55; 61). "Psalter" is also a name for the book of PSALMS, especially as relates to its use in Christian liturgy.

PSEUDEPIGRAPHA/PSEUDEPIGRAPHY

Ancient Jewish and Hellenistic Jewish TEXTS and early Christian texts that are not included in the HEBREW CANON, the APOCRYPHA, or the NT canon and are falsely ascribed to famous individuals, probably in attempts to invest the texts with the authority carried by the names. While different TRADITIONS disagree on the contents of the Pseudepigrapha, the texts or fragments that may be included in an exhaustive list number more than a hundred. The texts range from APOCALYPSE to ETIOLOGY, from ORACLE to vision and LETTER. A partial list in English TRANSLATION has been edited and published by J. H. Charlesworth. For a complete list of Pseudepigrapha related to the OT and the NT, see Alexander (§§8.3.4; 8.3.13).

Bibliography. Patrick H. Alexander et al., eds., *The SBL Handbook of Style: For Ancient Near Eastern, Biblical, and Early Christian Studies* (Peabody, MA: Hendrickson, 1999); James H. Charlesworth, ed., *The Old Testament Pseudepigrapha* (2 vols.; New York: Doubleday, 1983–85).

PSEUDONYMITY

The practice of falsely ascribing authorship to a work, usually in the name of a famous person of the past. The practice may have had a number of motives: to honor a notable person of the past, to invest the work with the authority and recognition of the name, or to realize a profit (Ehrman, 373–75). Scholars have identified pseudonymity in the HEBREW BIBLE (e.g., Daniel), the APOCRYPHA (e.g., Wisdom of Solomon), and the NT (e.g., the PASTORALS, Ephesians, 1–2 Peter, and Colossians).

Bibliography. Bart D. Ehrman, *The New Testament: A Historical Introduction to the Early Christian Writings* (3rd ed.; Oxford: Oxford University Press, 2004).

PSEUDO-PAULINE EPISTLES

The three EPISTLES (Ephesians, Colossians, and 2 Thessalonians) that claim Pauline authorship but are denied such by some scholars on the basis of differences from the undisputed Pauline Epistles in STYLE, vocabulary, and theology. *See* EPISTOLARY LITERATURE.

PSYCHOANALYTIC CRITICISM

A method of textual analysis based on the clinical and interpretive science of psychoanalysis. For centuries various psychological considerations have been employed to evaluate culture and literature. Aristotle's description of TRAGEDY as a series of incidents arousing "pity and fear wherewith it effects a catharsis of such emotions" (Arp and Johnson, 1304) demonstrates his consideration of the emotive quality of literature. Furthermore, Aristotle's definition of the tragic hero as one who is flawed, commits a HAMARTIA due to a bit of missing information, and subsequently has a personal revelation—this description reflects the considerations of a person's psychology according to the foundational writings of LITERARY critics (Arp and Johnson, 1304–6). Much later, the philosophy and literature of the Elizabethan period also reflected the centrality of psychology to literature, as the idea that humors controlled human reason, emotion, and behavior was central to Elizabethan thinking (Tillyard, 67–79).

Freud. While psychological considerations have been central to literary understanding for centuries, psychoanalysis did not develop as a critical theory until the late nineteenth and early twentieth centuries, when Sigmund Freud (1856–1939) formulated his method of psychoanalysis as a clinical treatment for psychological disorders (Guerin et al., 121). His "discovery" of the realm of the unconscious, his theories of the effect of the unconscious on human behavior, and his analytic methods for the study and treatment of repressed unconscious drives—all these became the foundation of psychoanalytic theory. Freud believed that his psychoanalytic approach need not be reserved for clinical psychology but that it could be applied to all fields, especially the field of literature (Aichele et al., 188). Thus, he applied his approaches to literature and used literature as a means for analyzing an AUTHOR's psyche and the psyche in general. As others studied Freud's methods, they built on and modified his theories. Thus from Freud's psychoanalytic theories, several other theories and methods have evolved

and coexisted within the psychoanalytic critical field. While classical psychoanalytic criticism is based on the theories of Freud, other forms of psychoanalytic criticism have evolved with roots in archetypal theory (*see* ARCHETYPAL CRITICISM), ego psychology, object-relations theory, structural theory (*see* STRUCTURALISM), and feminist theory (*see* FEMINIST CRITICISM).

Classical psychoanalytic criticism is indebted to the psychoanalytic theories of Freud, who developed a theory of the evolution and makeup of the human mind. The foundation of his theory is the concept of the unconscious, which manifests itself in human behavior, speech, and images. The meaning of these manifestations, however, is unavailable to the conscious mind because of what Freud calls repression, the mind's way of censoring this material from consciousness. The content of the unconscious derives from deep-seated sexual drives, which strive to enter the conscious mind. Due to repression, however, any expression of these drives must be in disguised forms, such as dreams, parapraxes, jokes, and accidental gestures.

Over his career, Freud developed three descriptions of the unconscious. First, as described above, the dynamic description posits a conflict between unconscious drives and repression, which attempts to keep the drives from manifesting themselves. Out of this conflict emerge what Freud called compromise formations, which satisfy both the unconscious drives and the forces of repression revealed in IMAGES, ACTIONS, and SPEECH. The economic description of the unconscious identifies a quantity of instinctual energy associated with certain mental content, body parts, and objects. In a mentally healthy person, this energy will be distributed in definite quantities. Crucial to this description are Freud's concepts of displacement and condensation. Displacement is the attributing of the value usually assigned to one object to another, and condensation refers to one idea representing a group of associated effects. The third description of the makeup of the human mind is the topographical. Freud first divided the mind into the conscious (the perceptions of the outside world through the senses), the preconscious (associated with memory, to which we have access through language), and the unconscious (the realm of that which is barred from the preconscious and conscious). Later, in 1923, Freud divided the mind into the id (the seat of instinctual drives), the ego (that which mediates between the SUBJECT and external reality), and the superego (internalized parental and social taboos, the conscience).

Another concept central to Freud's analysis is the idea of sexuality. In Freud's definition, sexuality is not simply the traditional idea of genital sexuality; rather, it is anything that is not biologically or functionally necessary but is simply desired. He says that in their development, children pass through five psychosexual stages—oral, anal, phallic, latent, genital—during which their sexual energy is concentrated in an erogenous zone. The oral stage (0–18 months) focuses on sucking, biting, and chewing. It is during this phase that children's sexual pleasure is primarily from their mother, but they eventually begin to separate sexual pleasure from nutrition. The anal stage (18–36 months) is the phase during which children try to cope with a desire for control through elimination (Macey, 208–9). During the phallic stage (3–6 years) the genitals are the erogenous zone, and male children cope with incestuous feelings toward their mothers, females toward their fathers. The latent stage (6–puberty) is a stage of dormant sexual feelings, and the genital stage (puberty onward) brings a maturation of sexual interests as the focus turns to others (Hollenhorst). The concept of psychosexual stages is important to Freudian psychoanalysis: Freud believed that unresolved conflicts during one of the stages of sexual development would likely result in a fixation on one of the stages. This fixation, he believed, would be buried in the unconscious and carried on into adulthood, affecting a person's actions (Guerin et al., 129).

Probably the most interesting and controversial feature of Freud's theory of sexuality is that of the phallic stage. He suggests that during the phallic stage, boys experience the Oedipus complex, and girls the Electra complex. The Oedipus complex is a young boy's unconscious rivalry with his father for the affection and attention of his mother. During this time, a boy deals with incestuous feelings toward his mother but finds his father to be in the way (Guerin et al., 130). He at first despises his father and fears punishment (castration anxiety) but later identifies with his father—competing for his mother's desire—and his superego begins to develop. This identification with the father and the development of the superego are essential to a young boy's healthfully passing through the phallic stage. Young girls, on the other hand, experience the Electra complex, during which they discover that they do not have a penis and develop penis envy. Girls do not identify with a parent at this time and thus do not develop a superego. A woman's lack of superego, then, implies that she is dependent on a man for moral direction since she does not possess the ability to make moral decisions (Hollenhorst). This theory of GENDER development is a radical one that is rejected by most as ridiculous today; however, it did influence and perpetuate traditional definitions of gender in PATRIARCHY.

Freud believed that any fixations or childhood complications would be carried into adulthood in the unconscious, that all repressed contents within the unconscious were, at their base cause, a result of sexual desires, and that these contents inherently seek to rise to the surface, into consciousness. Yet he suggests that because of the strength of the ego and the superego, if our underlying unconscious desires do make it to the surfaces of our consciousness, they usually do so through accident or disguise (Camden, 163).

According to Freudian theory, in literature a writer may unknowingly bring to the surface pieces of the unconscious through SYMBOL, CHARACTERIZATION, PLOT, situations, colors, and so forth (Camden, 163). Freud theorized that unconscious energy was redirected by the ego through defense mechanisms: repression, regression, reaction formation, projection, rationalizations, displacement, and/or sublimation. He thought, however, that sublimation was the best redirection of anxiety or energy. In sublimation people do something socially expressible with their energy instead of something less acceptable (Hollenhorst). Literature is one such socially acceptable venue for sublimation. Furthermore, through literature, authors may carry out other defense mechanisms. They could, for example, regress to a stage of childhood through their characters or project their personality onto their characters. Because Freudian psychoanalysis was popular for a time, it was traditionally employed to analyze an author, and even today some critics continue to apply Freudian theory to author INTERPRETATION. A psychoanalytic critic of the classical tradition looks at character, symbol, METAPHOR, plot, and so forth in search of a "Freudian slip" and reads between the lines to construct something of the author's unconscious drives. A critic searches the text for hints of a fixation within a certain stage or perhaps an instance of projection, rationalization, or displacement. Such a critic may also study the life of the author in search of situations or clues that point toward a possible repression of desire or toward a fixation.

Later applications of psychoanalytical criticism. Earlier literary critics who employed psychological theory to analyze literature focused on the psychoanalysis of the author by assuming that a piece of literature expressed the unconscious of the author through a pattern of figures (unconscious figures called imagos) representing latent memories and conceptions of parents. Consequently, by interpreting the images, one could get at the psyche of the author. In addition, these critics assumed that in good Freudian style an author actually diverted the libido (an original sexual instinct) into a socially acceptable object: the creatively produced text. Later psychoanalytic critics such as Lionel Trilling and Norman Holland (*see* TRANSACTIVE CRITICISM), however, tended to move from the analysis of the author to the analysis of readers.

Rather than follow Freud's focus on the relationship between the individual's psyche and his/her cultural environment, Carl Jung developed a theory of universal symbols, or ARCHETYPES, with the resulting archetypal criticism. According to Jung, each individual consciousness participates

in or belongs to a "COLLECTIVE UNCONSCIOUS," which is expressed in a series of universal symbols or archetypes. His rationale for the idea of the collective unconscious was the appearance of similar archetypes or images in MYTHS and LEGENDS around the world. Rather than literary texts (or any other form of art, for that matter) being the result of a person's neurosis, literature for Jung was the result of an artistic thrust from the collective unconscious, channeled through the individual with that person's unique creative stamp. Thus a piece of literature carries with it a universal message or MEANING since it springs from the collective unconscious, with its universal mythic structures.

From Jung's conception of the collective unconscious with its universal mythic structures, it is not a long journey to Jacques Lacan's idea that the unconscious is structured like a language (his theory is often referred to as "structural psychoanalysis"). With this idea, the focus of psychoanalytic theory changed from the psyche of the author, character(s), or audience to the text's own psychic linguistic structure, placing language as the central object of psychoanalysis. For Lacan, language itself both structures and mediates human experience and understanding in the world. Rather than being the prelinguistic location of instincts, the unconscious for Lacan is the effect of a person's introduction to the linguistic order. A person, then, is born into a language (in Saussure's sense of *LANGUE* and *PAROLE*) that has imbedded in it a set of social requirements. This set of requirements Lacan calls a symbolic order, which turns on what Lacan calls three "orders" of human experience: the imaginary, symbolic, and real. Human development moves from the imaginary through the symbolic to the real. The infant in a state of helplessness and dependency experiences an imaginary sense of mastery and unity in body. According to Lacan, the child mistakes this state of unity with his or her own reflection in a mirror, assuming that this reflection is the means through which to interact with the outside world. The child then moves from this imaginary order to the symbolic by demanding that desires and impulses be mediated through the process of SIGNIFICATION. In other words, desire and impulse are repressed by this thrust toward signification, producing a distinction or split between conscious and unconscious knowledge. Furthermore, existing beyond the imaginary and symbolic order (a SIGN system) is the real, which both demands and refuses a reduction to representation. The real, then, exists as a PARADOX in that, while located beyond signification, it can be accessed only through the signifiers of language. Consequently, because the unconscious is structured like a language, its operations are tropic and can be described in terms of rhetorical TROPES. In its operation, the unconscious (a stock of signifiers, images, and memories) might mistake one signifier for another, substitute one for another, or create links between signifiers. This process of choice and substitution destroys any sense of unity and is never ending.

Lacan's idea of the human subject's being structured by language, on the one hand, and of the human subject's being always but never fully structured, on the other hand, has been adopted by POSTMODERN critics such as Jacques Derrida in his deconstructive (*see* DECONSTRUCTION) reading of texts and by psychoanalytic critics such as Roland Barthes, who problematize the distinction between author and reader and between author and critic because all are structured by language and, in a sense, at its mercy.

In BIBLICAL STUDIES, contemporary critics have applied Freudian, Jungian, post-Freudian, post-Jungian, and Lacanian psychoanalytic theory not only to biblical authors, texts, and characters but also to readers' responses, critical interpretations, and pastoral proclamations. Wayne Rollins defines biblical psychoanalytic criticism in the following broad areas:

> The goal of a psychological-critical approach is to examine texts, their origination, authorship, modes of expression, their construction, transmission, translation, reading, interpretation, their transposition into kindred and alien art forms, and the history of their personal and cultural effect, as expressions of the structure, processes, and habits of the human psyche, both in individual and collective manifestations, past and present. (77–78)

Perhaps the most accessible recent work on biblical psychoanalytic criticism is Andrew Kille's *Psychological Biblical Criticism.*

Bibliography. George Aichele et al., *The Postmodern Bible* (New Haven: Yale University Press, 1995); Thomas Arp and Greg Johnson, *Perrine's Literature: Sound, Structure, and Sense* (8th ed.; Boston: Heimle & Heimle, 2002); Vera J. Camden, "Psychoanalytic Theory," in *Encyclopedia of Contemporary Literary Theory: Approaches, Scholars, Terms* (ed. Irena R. Makaryk; Toronto: University of Toronto Press, 1993), 163–70; Wilfred Guerin et al., eds., *A Handbook of Critical Approaches to Literature* (4th ed.; New York: HarperCollins, 1999); Donald Hall, *Literary and Cultural Theory: From Basic Principles to Advanced Applications* (Boston: Houghton Mifflin, 2001); April Hollenhorst, "Introduction to Psychology" (lecture, Indian Hills Community College, Ottumwa, IA; Winter 2000); Andrew Kille, *Psychological Biblical Criticism* (Minneapolis: Fortress, 2001); David Macey, "Freud, Sigmund," in *A Dictionary of Cultural and Critical Theory* (ed. Michael Payne; Cambridge, MA: Blackwell, 1996), 207–10; W. G. Rollins, *Soul and Psyche: The Bible in Psychological Perspective* (Minneapolis: Fortress, 1999); Anthony Storor and Anthony Stevens, *Freud and Jung: A Dual Introduction* (New York: Barnes & Noble, 1998); E. M. W. Tillyard, *The Elizabethan World Picture* (London: Chatto & Windus, 1948; repr., New York: Vintage Books, 1959).

PSYCHOLOGICAL RECONSTRUCTION

In BIBLICAL STUDIES, a term referring to the attempt to reconstruct the thoughts of a person in the past or the way a person in the past thought. Normally, the RECONSTRUCTION has been the result of modern personality theories and the behavioral sciences. *See* PSYCHOANALYTIC CRITICISM.

PUBLIC MINISTRY STORY

A type of EPISODE in the ministry of Jesus that has to do with his identity (e.g., Mark 6:1–6a; 11:1–10; 11:15–18). According to David Aune, some of these stories include mythic elements (making them what he calls recognition oracles). Examples are the temptation STORY in the desert in Mark 1:12–13 and Matt. 4:1–11 (Jesus's encounter with evil in the person of "Satan"), Jesus's baptism in Mark 1:9–11 (the splitting of the heavens and the voice from heaven), and the story of the transfiguration in Mark 9:2–9 (the appearances of

Elijah and Moses and the heavenly voice). Bailey and Vander Broek suggest that these stories were given shape by the early Christian community in terms of their postresurrection confessions and experiences.

Bibliography. David Aune, *Prophecy in Early Christianity and the Ancient Mediterranean World* (Grand Rapids: Eerdmans, 1983); James Bailey and Lyle Vander Broek, *Literary Forms in the New Testament: A Handbook* (Louisville: Westminster John Knox, 1992).

PUN

A FIGURE OF SPEECH involving a PLAY on words. *See* PARONOMASIA.

PUNCH LINE

In what Robert Alter refers to as "the Poetry of Wit," the poetic line in which the second VERSET "clinches the point" introduced in the first verset.

In this type of poetic parallelism, the two versets stand in sharp incongruity to each other. For example, Prov. 11:22 reads, "A gold ring in a pig's snout / is a beautiful woman without good sense." See also Prov. 26:1; 25:14; 21:1. In each of these riddling parallelisms, the second verset serves as the punch line.

Bibliography. Robert Alter, *The Art of Biblical Poetry* (New York: Basic Books, 1985).

PUNCH WORD

In antithetical parallelism, the last word in the poetic line (*see* BIBLICAL POETRY). For example, in "Cheating scales are an abomination to the LORD, / an honest weight, his pleasure" (Prov. 11:1, trans. of MT), "his pleasure" (a single word in Hebrew) is the punch word.

Bibliography. Robert Alter, *The Art of Biblical Poetry* (New York: Basic Books, 1985).

Q

Q

A hypothetical source (probably derived from the German *Quelle*, "source") document, which NT scholars think was used by the AUTHORS of Matthew and Luke. The ASSUMPTION is that where Matthew and Luke agree against Mark (primarily in the SAYINGS OF JESUS), they had access to a sayings source that Mark did not use. Not only do these parts of Matthew and Luke often agree word for word; the writers also insert this material into a context different from the Markan NARRATIVE. While the bulk of the material consists of sayings of Jesus, two narratives are included: the narrative of Jesus's temptations (Matt. 4:1–11; Luke 4:1–13) and the healing of the centurion's servant (Matt. 8:5–10; Luke 7:1–10). Furthermore, unless Q was a written document, the strong agreement between Matthew and Luke is difficult to explain. It is possible, however, that because of some differences between Matthew and Luke, they each may have had a different version of the source. Of the two GOSPELS, scholars think that Luke has preserved the more accurate sequence of the material in Q. Consequently, scholars have attempted to reconstruct the document on the basis of Matthew and Luke but particularly from Luke. For proposed RECONSTRUCTIONS of Q based on Luke and for a summary of the development of Q scholarship, see Soulen and Soulen.

Bibliography. Richard N. Soulen and R. Kendall Soulen, *Handbook of Biblical Criticism* (3rd ed.; Louisville: Westminster John Knox, 2001).

QINAH

From Hebrew (*qînâ*) and usually translated "LAMENT," the 3+2 poetic RHYTHM that is prevalent in the book of Lamentations. Although this METER is debated by biblical scholars, some think that this type of irregular rhythm reflects the pronounced grief expressed in the lament. Like other poetic conventions, however, the *qinah* form is usually lost in TRANSLATION.

QOHELET

Hebrew for "the Preacher" (KJV, NASB) or "the Teacher" (NIV, NRSV, TNIV); the Hebrew name of the book of Ecclesiastes and its NARRATOR.

QUEER THEORY

A relatively recent critical theory characterized by denying that categories of identity, sexuality, and even expressions are innately anything: masculine, feminine, homosexual, or heterosexual. The theory accounts for the misnomer of identity by claiming that social structures are patriarchal (*see* PATRIARCHY) and heterosexual and that language reflects this structuring.

Origins. The development of queer theory can be traced to the prominent gay-rights movement of the late 1960s and early 1970s. There had been evidence of same-sex desires as early as the ancient Greeks and through later covert movements. The gay-rights movement brought the idea of same-sex desire into the foreground of thought. Throughout this movement, language has played an enormous part, as it has been the necessitating explanation for different opinions and ideas. Shortly after the gay-rights activists became well known, the use of the word "lesbian," referring to women, developed. Before this time "gay" could refer to both men and women. This seemed to "obscure" the unique problems faced by same-sex-desiring women who were doubly oppressed because of their GENDER and sexuality. In the early 1980s, another important development was the use of the term "queer." This term links the interests and problems of sexual nonconformists (both men and women). For LITERARY theorists, this change in language has presented quite a different idea altogether. Identity-based gay/lesbian criticism assumes that identities such as same-sex-desiring individuals exist already and are what define the representations of this idea (Hedges). On the other hand, queer theorists assume that the representations of the ideas concerning sexual identities already exist and that these preexisting representations frustrate sexual identities. Queer theorists see identity as being something that is "free-floating" and not subjugated to any set type of sexual identity (Gauntlett, 2). The idea of a free-floating gender is indebted to poststructuralism: reality reflects language, but this language is slippery; thus meaning is virtual, free-floating, and continually playing.

Early critics. The work of Michel Foucault, an early poststructuralist, focused on the "examination of the concepts and codes by which societies operate" (Jagose, 14). He trained his critical lens on the definitions and exclusions of races, genders, and mental conditions by which a society excludes some people and defines itself by others. Between 1946 and 1950, he discovered his own homosexuality and began to apply the discovery to his study of how people act and react to one another. After 1953, he began to study society's responses to the "different," primarily working with those who were mentally handicapped. In *The History of Sexuality*, a primary source for queer theory, Foucault examines structures of power and knowledge that both define and sustain sexual DISCOURSE, which in turn embodies the power structures that control everyday pleasure. According to Foucault, a discourse is any ACTION or TEXT that generates and legitimates power. He further defines EPISTEME as a system of discourses that creates unconscious rules in a variety of areas, including language. For example, a society's legal CODE defines social relationships in almost every area of life such as family, employment, even sexuality. The latter is not "natural" but coded by law. In other words, sexuality is a function of power.

Judith Butler expands on Foucault's idea of the PLAY of discourse by involving power in the study of BINARY OPPOSITIONS. She is primarily known as a "theorist of power, gender, sexuality, and identity" (Gauntlett, 1). Butler has written a variety of books discussing these issues, among them *Bodies That Matter* and perhaps her best-known and most influential book, *Gender Trouble*. The latter is credited with introducing queer theory to the world. Butler argues that gender is continually in flux and thus there is no such thing as a set gender. She has also argued against feminism, claiming that it has made a fundamental mistake "by trying to assert that 'women' were a group with common characteristics and interests" (Gauntlett, 2). This sets humans up into two very clear categories—men and women—that do not allow for a person to form her own individual identity. Feminism has, in essence, done the exact opposite of its original desire and has shut that choice down. According to Butler, gender is not a "distinction of physical difference, but . . . an artificial construct created for the purposes of oppression within a patriarchal society" (*Gender Trouble*, 5).

This artificial construction is better understood through Butler's use of binaries. She does not deny the biological differences between females and males; however, a difference between sex and gender does exist. Sex is intractable—male or female—while gender is a social construct and consequently fluid. Social constructs are similar to language in that they are always playing, moving, changing to accommodate those in power. Butler draws a sharp distinction between intractable sex and fluid gender: "The presumption of a binary gender system implicitly retains the belief in a mimetic relation of gender to sex whereby gender mirrors sex or is otherwise restricted by it" (*Gender Trouble*, 6). When gender is realized as a social construct, it becomes a free-floating artifice. Therefore, "man" or "masculine" can easily refer to a female sexed body. This socially constructed binary gender system reflects an oversexed semiology. In this system, masculine and feminine relationships cannot be defined in the signifying economy in which masculinity is a closed circle between the signified and signifier (11). In other words, the binary gender construct not only utilizes masculinity as a signifier; masculinity also is what is being signified.

For example, Athena is the Greek goddess of both wisdom and war. The myth utilizes masculine signifiers—reason and violence—to reflect a masculine version of the signified woman. Men cannot judge the case of women because they are both the judge and the party (Butler, *Gender Trouble*, 11). In this binary system, woman becomes the unintelligible sign because she is defined through masculine language. "Intelligible" genders cohere and continue the institutions of sex, gender, sexual practices, and desire (17). That is, woman becomes intelligible by remaining within the masculine semiotic system. Western ontology holds a thoroughly masculine HEGEMONY of mind over body, as in Plato, Descartes, Husserl, and Sartre (12). As a result, femininity cannot *be* because it is a mere negation of masculinity (18). The queer experience is a free-floating Cheshire grin: smiles, happiness, pleasures, and desires without a lasting substance (24). Butler further claims the complete INTERTEXTUALITY of gender signifiers, which never point to any stable signified: "There is no gender identity behind the expressions of gender; that identity is performatively constituted by the very 'expressions' that are said to be its results" (25). In other words, gender is stable only when woman is made intelligible by the word "pink"—a word that performs the act of identifying one's gender.

Just as "pink" is a performative use of language, so is the phrase "to queer." Queer theory takes Foucault's discourse, enlarged by Butler's DECONSTRUCTION of binaries, to form an operational definition of itself: to queer is "contra-, non-, or antistraight that doesn't identify people so much as forms of communication" (Dilley, 458). Thus queer theory approaches literature as a form of communication in which the CONFLICT between homosexuality and heterosexuality is figurative for the knowledge/power/pleasure regime—that which orders desires, behaviors, and social institutions (Butler, *Gender Trouble*, 4). To queer a text is

not to make it gay but "to perform a catachrestic operation on terms that have accrued a sedimentation of connotative range by directing them towards new meanings" (Lockhurst, 333). For instance, Jankowski places virgins as portrayed by Shakespeare in a queer space. Virgins are queer in this case because they do not participate in sexual acts at all, or if they do, it is only with women; therefore, they challenge the patriarchal and heterosexual system with their nonheterosexual actions (Jankowski, 230–32). This method of reading may seem to draw suspicion in its lacking justification. Sedgewick asserts that sexuality depends on the history of power relationships. Therefore, where men and women differ in power, access is the location where sexuality and gender also differ (*Between Men*, 2). As a result, the queering of Shakespearean virgins is a valid reading because the virgins in their sexual rebellion shake the traditional power foundations. Discursive language shares a bed with binaries such as male and female. These terms are manipulatively loaded, performing the action of making something right and another thing wrong. Discursive language is not often explicit. Sedgewick uses the term "closetedness" to mark this performative SPEECH ACT of silence, which gains significance by its surrounding discourse (*Epistemology*, 3). It is these closeted discourses with which queer theory occupies itself. The closet may be a dark recess of Shakespeare, an untidy drawer in the BIBLE, or a wide-open wardrobe in pop culture.

Gay/lesbian studies. The broad field of gay/lesbian studies looks mostly at definitions of normal versus deviant behavior regarding heterosexuality and homosexuality. The gay/lesbian literary theory examines sexual images in literature. Mary Klages gives five ways that this examination can occur. First of all, the reader looks for authors who were homosexual but hid it all their lives. For instance, a person might look at Shakespeare's life and literature and try to prove that he was a homosexual. Second, the reader can look at the themes that occur in writings by gay authors. Third, one can research all the writings by both gay and straight authors to see what they say about heterosexuality and homosexuality. Fourth, literature can be examined as to what it says regarding sexuality as a socially constructed principle. And last, gay/lesbian theorists examine how literature as a whole affects the sexual opinions of our culture.

So gay/lesbian studies look at normal behaviors in contrast to deviant ones. Queer theory does the same thing but in a broader sense. It claims that all sexual behaviors and identities are merely social constructs, established neither by biology nor universal moral standards. Queer theory looks at all kinds of sexual deviancy as defined by culture and does not simply concentrate on the limited categories of heterosexuality and homosexuality. It also considers sadomasochists, transsexuals, cross-dressers, pedophiles, and those expressing any number of other sexual behaviors and/or identities that differ from the social norm, which is generally considered to be heterosexuality.

According to Max H. Kirsh, the main task of queer theory is to place beliefs about sex, gender, and sexuality into their proper place, to "dissemble" them. Yet Kirsch is not merely interested in the principle but also in the action it compels people to take. He calls for persons to engage in what is called "queering culture." Novels need to be reread with the characters reconstructed, historical accounts need to be deconstructed and reconstructed, and labels should be ignored because they are limiting and used as power moves by the dominant culture. Furthermore, according to Robert McRuer, queering culture means that all boundaries should be crossed and revised. "Our profession has become increasingly concerned with the problem of boundaries. . . . These boundaries can be crossed, confused, consolidated, and collapsed; they can also be revised, reconceived, redesigned, or replaced" (124).

Application to biblical studies. A classic case in which many people think that the Bible condemns homosexuality is the STORY of Sodom and Gomorrah. The inhabitants of Sodom are destroyed by fire from God for their sinfulness. When divine messengers come to warn Lot to get out of the city, the men of the city riot for the messengers to be brought out so that they can have sex with

them. Therefore, it is often assumed that the sin of Sodom is homosexuality. McNeil (37–41), however, points out that homosexual behavior is not the same thing as the condition of homosexuality. The Bible does not address the homosexual condition but only homosexual acts and may actually be condemning engaging in sexual behavior that is contrary to one's condition. Thus, for a heterosexual person, homosexual behavior would be a sin, and for a homosexual person, heterosexual behavior would be wrong.

How, then, might the story of Sodom be reexamined from the perspective of queer theory? First, the word used to denote sexual activity here in Gen. 19:4–11 is *yāda'*, usually translated as "to know." It is used only a few times to imply sexual intercourse. But even if it implies sexual intercourse here, the real problem with the men of Sodom is their inhospitality. Whether they were men or women is insignificant. Although Sodom is called sinful throughout the HEBREW BIBLE and the NT, it is never actually called homosexual. And in Luke 10:10–13, Sodom is related to inhospitality. Jesus tells the disciples to shake the dust off their feet if anyone rejects them, instructions that seem to indicate inhospitality. Then he says that the sin of those who reject his disciples will be greater than that of Sodom (McNeil, 37–46).

McNeil also examines two words in 1 Cor. 6:9 used for homosexuality. The first one is *malakoi* and refers to morally weak behavior, often sexual behavior. But it does not need to be homosexual behavior. The other word is *arsenokoitai*, which means excessive sexual behavior and may translate to "male prostitution" when connected with men. According to McNeil, since culture plays a major role in how words are translated, modern TRANSLATIONS have variously translated it as "effeminate," "given to unnatural vices," "liers with mankind," and "homosexuals." Consequently, McNeil (50–53) argues that the NT may not really condemn homosexuality.

Another example of applying queer theory to the Bible comes from Lori Rowlett. She interprets the story of Samson and Delilah in Judg. 16 as having undertones of sadomasochism. Sadomasochism is a sexual role-playing game that involves two persons, a "femme dominatrix" and a "butch bottom." They can be of either sex. The femme dominatrix exerts power and may inflict pain on the butch bottom, and they both derive sexual pleasure out of this game. Because sadomasochism is defined as abnormal sexual practice in the dominant culture, it can be classified as queer.

The common interpretation of Judg. 16 is that Samson is the fallen man of God and Delilah is the evil temptress. Yet in the story, Delilah never actually needs to tempt Samson. She simply asks him what she wants, the secret of his strength, and he answers her. He lies several times in order to keep the game interesting. She is exerting power over him as the femme dominatrix and ties him up, a classic activity in sadomasochism. This relationship can be extended throughout the whole book of Judges to describe God's relationship with Israel. God continues to call a hero to free Israel and then lets them fall into captivity again. Why would an all-powerful God allow this violence to continue if God was not into some kind of power game such as sadomasochism? (Rowlett).

Bibliography. Richard Burt, Unspeakable Shakespeares: Queer Theory and American Kiddie Culture (New York: St. Martin's Press, 1998); Judith Butler, Bodies That Matter: On the Discursive Limits of Sex (New York: Routledge, 1993); idem, Feminists Theorize the Political (New York: Routledge, 1992); idem, Gender Trouble: Feminism and the Subversion of Identity (New York: Routledge, 1990); Patrick Dilley, "Queer Theory: Under Construction," International Journal of Qualitative Studies in Education 12, no. 5 (1999): 457–73; Michel Foucault, The History of Sexuality (New York: Pantheon Books, 1978); David Gauntlett, summary of Gender Trouble by Judith Butler (http://www.theory.org.uk/ctr-butl.htm); Warren Hedges, "Queer Theory Explained" (1997) (http://gamaputra.wordpress.com/2007/10/07/queer-theory-explained/); Annamarie Jagose, "An Extract from Queer Theory," Australian Humanities Review 4 (December 1996–February 1997): 13–14; Theodora Jankowski, "Pure Resistance: Queer(y)ing Virginity in William Shakespeare's Measure for Measure and Margaret Cavendish's The Convent of Pleasure," Shakespeare Studies 26 (1988): 218–56; Max H. Kirsch, Queer Theory and Social Change (London: Routledge, 2000); Mary Klages, "Queer Theory," University of Colorado at Boulder (October 29, 1997); Eric Lockhurst, "Queer Theory and Oscar Wilde: Review Essay," Journal of Gender Studies 4, no. 3 (1995): 333–40; John McNeil, The Church and the Homosexual (Boston: Beacon, 1993); Robert McRuer, The Queer Renaissance (New York: New York University Press, 1997); Lori Rowlett, "Violent Femmes and S/M: Queering Samson and Delilah," in Queer Commentary and the Hebrew Bible (ed. Ken Stone; Cleveland: Pilgrim Press, 2001), 106–15; Eve Kosofsky Sedgwick, Between Men: English Literature and Male Homosocial Desire (New York: Columbia University Press, 1985); idem, Epistemology of the Closet (Berkeley: University of California Press, 1990); Ken Stone, "Queer Commentary and Biblical Interpretation: An Introduction," in Queer Commentary and the Hebrew Bible (ed. Ken Stone; Cleveland: Pilgrim Press, 2001), 11–34.

QUELLE. *See* Q

QUEST FOR THE HISTORICAL JESUS, THE

The attempt to discover the JESUS OF HISTORY as opposed to the CHRIST OF THE CHURCH. The quest is usually identified with the English title of Albert Schweitzer's book *Quest of the Historical Jesus* (1906), in which he surveys the history of biographies of Jesus written in the nineteenth century. The quest has its genesis in the critical ASSUMPTION that the GOSPEL writers as well as Paul produced theological portraits of Jesus, INTERPRETATIONS of the theological significance of Jesus. This is tantamount to saying that the early authors of Jesus's life were less biographers than theologians, and therefore their accounts make it difficult for readers to find the Jesus of history behind the Christ of faith in the early Christian TEXTS. In attempts to reveal this Jesus of history, scholars as early as Hermann Samuel Reimarus (1694–1768) have offered various historical explanations of Jesus. Reimarus argued that Jesus was a Jewish revolutionary who was unsuccessful in overthrowing Roman rule. David Friedrich Strauss (1808–74) distinguished between the Jesus of history and the Christ of faith by arguing that the Gospels had christological AGENDAS and portrayed Jesus in mythological terms. Johannes Weiss (1863–1914) stated that a RECONSTRUCTION of the historical Jesus must take into account the first-century CE environment. Albert Schweitzer

(1875–1965) employed FORM CRITICISM in order to uncover the FORMS of the ORAL TRADITION before they were incorporated into the Gospels. According to Schweitzer, the historical Jesus was an eschatological apocalyptist who saw it as his mission to usher in the kingdom of God, which would then overthrow the present evil world order. This Jesus of history was rejected by the church, and in his place the church developed the Christ of faith (Harris, 256–57). Rudolf Bultmann (1884–1976), by analyzing the forms in the SYNOPTIC GOSPELS, argued that for the most part they have their origin in the life of the early church rather than in the life of Jesus. Bultmann therefore rejected the idea that the historical Jesus is recoverable from behind the mythological and theological portrayals in the Gospels. Furthermore, since Jesus was essentially Jewish and preached a form of JUDAISM whereas the Christianity as we have it in the Gospels is a Hellenistic (see HELLENISM) religion, the Jesus of history has little, if any, import for Christian faith.

In 1953 some scholars began to rethink the relationship between the historical Jesus and the Christ of faith. Ernst Käsemann urged scholars not to separate Christian faith from the historical Jesus. In response, a great number of scholars tried to reconstruct the life and teachings of the historical Jesus. This renewed interest became known as the "new quest for the historical Jesus," and the scholars involved (e.g., Joachim Jeremias, James M. Robinson, and Günther Bornkamm) focused on the continuity between the historical Jesus and the Christ of faith. To that end, the scholars of the new quest developed criteria for establishing the authenticity of the SAYINGS that the church had attributed to Jesus (see CRITERIA OF AUTHENTICITY).

By the 1980s the interest in the historical issue seemed to explode, and since that time, a plethora of works have appeared. N. T. Wright coined the term "the third quest" to refer to a view of Jesus as an eschatological apocalyptist (Schweitzer's view) presented in Mark's Gospel as reliable. Wright then categorized the various descriptions of Jesus according to this view or those that view Mark as essentially a LITERARY creation, with its ESCHATOLOGY the same as that of the early church. For the most part, current scholarship in the quest has opted for the tools of modern HISTORIOGRAPHY and sociology and makes use of both CANONICAL and noncanonical sources for reconstructions of the historical Jesus (Soulen and Soulen, 155). See JESUS SEMINAR.

Bibliography. Bart D. Ehrman, *The New Testament: A Historical Introduction to the Early Christian Writings* (3rd ed.; New York: Oxford University Press, 2004); Stephen Harris, *The New Testament: A Student's Introduction* (4th ed.; Boston: McGraw-Hill, 2002); Christian E. Hauer and William A. Young, *An Introduction to the Bible: A Journey into Three Worlds* (4th ed.; Upper Saddle River, NJ: Prentice Hall, 1998); Mark Allan Powell, *Jesus as a Figure in History: How Modern Historians View the Man from Galilee* (Louisville: Westminster John Knox, 1998); Richard N. Soulen and R. Kendall Soulen, *Handbook of Biblical Criticism* (3rd ed.; Louisville: Westminster John Knox, 2001).

QUEST MOTIF

A type of PLOT structure or organizing STRUCTURE in which the ACTION moves toward a goal, similar to the JOURNEY MOTIF, in which the action moves toward a destination. According to Leland Ryken, the miracles in the GOSPELs have an underlying quest motif evidenced by the fact that Jesus performs actions and speaks in order to produce a specific response from people. In a similar fashion, the Acts of the Apostles is organized around the quest motif to "conquer the world with the Christian Gospel" (79).

Bibliography. Leland Ryken, *Words of Life: A Literary Introduction to the New Testament* (Grand Rapids: Baker, 1987).

QUMRAN

A site near the northwest shore of the Dead Sea where the DEAD SEA SCROLLS were discovered in 1947–56. Scholars believe that the ruins at the site are those of a community of ESSENES dating from about 150 BCE to about 70 CE, when it was destroyed by the Romans. Although this majority view is represented by Magness, the Essene hypothesis is not universally held (e.g., Hirschfeld).

Bibliography. Jodi Magness, *The Archaeology of Qumran and the Dead Sea Scrolls* (Grand Rapids: Eerdmans, 2002); Yizhar Hirschfeld, *Qumran in Context* (Peabody, MA: Hendrickson, 2004).

R

RABBINIC HERMENEUTICS

The hermeneutics of MIDRASH with its purpose of comprehension, explication, and application of SCRIPTURE as Scripture. *Midrash* is a Hebrew word for "INTERPRETATION" and derives from *dāraš*, meaning "to study" or "to investigate." At the heart of midrashic interpretation is the view that TORAH perpetually speaks to and should be applied to life and all of its circumstances. This ASSUMPTION encompasses not only HALAKAH (legal texts) but HAGGADAH (all other texts) as well. Gerald Bruns quotes Joseph Heinemann to make the point: "While the rabbinic creators of the Aggadah looked back to Scripture to uncover the full latent meaning of the Bible and its wording, at the same time they looked forward into the present and future. They sought to give direction to their own generation, to resolve their religious problems, to answer their questions, and to guide them out of their spiritual complexities" (Bruns, 105). In this respect, then, rabbinic hermeneutics differs from many modern hermeneutical approaches, which focus on the history of the TEXT and its MEANING as a function of that history or at least as a function of an author's INTENTION as it is somehow inscribed in the LITERARY and rhetorical structures of the text. Midrashic hermeneutics always examines a text in light of the community's present situations because these differ in significant ways from the situations of the original audience and writer. In other words, midrashic hermeneutics is CONTEXT(s) bound, but the contexts are always changing. Consequently, so is interpretation. "The midrashic collections that come down to us figure interpretation as something social and dialogical. . . . Torah speaks to a public, communal situation, not to a solitary, single-minded, private reader" (Bruns, 107).

Also, according to Bruns, midrashic interpretive practice does not seek the propositional, the reduction of a theological issue to a valid statement that fits into a preestablished THEOLOGICAL FRAMEWORK. It is rather the space where disputes are allowed and expected, a space where there is always room for another interpretation. Again, the reason for such ACCOMMODATION of plurality and open-endedness is that midrashic interpretation assumes that the Scriptures have a perennial relevance to new and novel situations. But there also seems to be another reason for the accommodation:

> You must picture the text not as a formal object (so many fixed letters) but as an open canon whose boundaries are shaped and reshaped by the give-and-take of midrashic argument. This means studying not just an original text but also midrash itself, for the words of the Sages constitute Torah, make it what it is, and above all open it to the present and future. The words of the wise are not added to the text; they are the text as well, linking its words to form not an integrated, hierarchical system but an ongoing tradition, a structure of mutual belonging. (Bruns, 116)

After the BABYLONIAN EXILE, there developed an oral supplement to the Jewish Scriptures that eventually was viewed as having the same authority as the Scriptures themselves. By the first century CE, rabbis had developed several understandings of meaning: *pĕšāṭ*, literal, plain meaning of a text; *remez*, concealed, "hinted" meaning of a text; *dĕraš*, allegorical meaning; and *sôd*, mystical meaning. The principles that served as the INTERPRETIVE FRAMEWORK for understanding, explicating, and applying Scripture are known as *middôt*, a set of seven rules that traditionally go back to Rabbi Hillel, a contemporary of Jesus. A detailed EXPLANA-TION of these rules can be found in Mulder. Below is a summary and example of each rule offered by Walter C. Kaiser Jr.:

1. Inferences from the lighter to the heavier: what is true for the less important or less significant is also true for that of greater SIG-NIFICANCE. Therefore, a regulation placed on a festival day would also pertain to the Sabbath, since it is of greater significance than any of the others.

2. ANALOGY of expressions: difficult or ambiguous texts are explained by making inferences from similar expressions found in other texts. For example, when Lev. 16:29 says that Jews should "afflict [their] souls" (KJV) on the day of atonement, since the affliction is left undefined, it may be assumed that the Jews should not eat food because the same requirement is made in Deut. 8:3, where hunger is mentioned.

3. The movement from the specific to the general: a general principle or application is formulated from a single text and applied generally to similar texts. In Deut. 19, the case of the accidental killing of a man working in the woods (v. 5) would be applied to any accidental death occurring where two men work together in a public place.

4. Application by analogy with two provisions: this rule is the same as rule 3 with the exception that two verses are used to form the general principle. So the rule that a slave whose eye or tooth was destroyed could go free in Exod. 21:26–27 could be applied to the loss of any body part.

5. Inferences from a general principle to a specific case or example: this rule was applied by moving from the general to the specific or from the specific to the general. Exodus 22:9 requires that when a man lends an ox, ass, sheep, garment, "or any other thing" and the thing is lost, the person responsible must repay in double. Since the ox, sheep, and garment are examples only, the conclusion is that "any other thing" refers to anything that is lost and must be doubly restored.

6. Explanation from another passage: If, for example, the Passover were to fall on a Sabbath day, should the lamb be sacrificed? When presented with the question, Rabbi Hillel responded that since Num. 28:10 requires that daily sacrifices are to be offered on the Sabbath also, then by analogy, so should the sacrifice of the Passover when it falls on the Sabbath.

7. Application of self-evident inferences from the context: A passage of Scripture should always be understood in terms of its context and not in isolation. Thus, in Exod. 16:29, prohibiting a person from going outside the house on the Sabbath day applies only to the specific historical act of gathering manna on the Sabbath in the wilderness.

In the second century CE, Rabbi Ishmael ben Elisha expanded the rules to thirteen, and Rabbi Eliezer ben Jose expanded them further to thirty-two.

Bibliography. Gerald L. Bruns, *Hermeneutics Ancient and Modern* (New Haven: Yale University Press, 1992); Walter C. Kaiser Jr. and Moisés Silva, *An Introduction to Biblical Hermeneutics: The Search for Meaning* (Grand Rapids: Zondervan, 1994); Martin Jan Mulder, ed., *Mikra: Text, Translation, Reading, and Interpretation of the Hebrew Bible in Ancient Judaism and Early Christianity* (Philadelphia: Fortress, 1988; repr., Peabody, MA: Hendrickson, 2004).

RABBINIC JUDAISM

The JUDAISM that developed in the TRADITION of the PHARISEES—whose central activity was to expand the written SCRIPTURE in ORAL TRADI-TION in order to make it relevant to new and novel situations—after 70 CE, finally culminating in the written form of the TALMUD. *See* MISHNAH; RABBINIC HERMENEUTICS; TALMUD.

RABBINIC LITERATURE

The literature of RABBINIC JUDAISM not included in the HEBREW BIBLE. Existing in oral form for centuries, it began to be written down about 200 CE. This literature is the result of an interpretive method usually called MIDRASH and falls into two interpretive categories: HALAKAH and HAGGADAH. Halakah (the way) midrash is the INTERPRETATION of the legal portions of the TORAH and delineates the principles that were to guide the people in the ways they were to live their lives. Haggadah midrash, although it may examine any portion of the TANAK, generally interprets the nonlegal sections and is more devotional in nature than is halakah. The largest body of midrash is actually a haggadic collection called *Midrash Rabbah*, which covers every TEXT in the Tanak (Hauer and Young, 223).

These two categories have resulted in two major groups of literature—TALMUD and TARGUM. First, the Talmud is actually the written version of the ORAL TRADITION, which around 200 CE probably contained what we call the MISHNAH. It contained both halakah and haggadah but was dominated by halakah. Later material including rabbinic commentary on the Mishnah and other lore (a collection called the GEMARA) was added to form the Talmud, which exists in two editions—Babylonian and Palestinian—the former becoming the authoritative one for JUDAISM. The addition of the *Gemara* to the Mishnah dates from about 500 CE.

Second, targums (or targumim) are rabbinic TRANSLATIONS of the Hebrew Bible into Aramaic by synagogue leaders after Aramaic became the language of Israel. These translations were also interpretive and, as such, were expansive (Hauer and Young, 223).

Bibliography. Herbert Danby, *The Mishnah* (Oxford: Clarendon, 1933); Christian E. Hauer and William A. Young, *An Introduction to the Bible: A Journey into Three Worlds* (2nd ed.; Englewood Cliffs, NJ: Prentice Hall, 1990).

RACE, CLASS, AND GENDER CRITICISM

A conglomeration of criticisms (differing in several respects) that examine the role of race, class, and GENDER in the reading of TEXTS; the role of texts as instruments of power, domination, or social manipulation; and the manner in which literature is used to create socially constructed ideas and prejudices. Race, class, and gender criticism also examines the nuances in literature that shape the way the culture views race, class, and gender. Within POSTMODERNISM, none of these ideas are assumed to be universal or natural givens; rather, all are changing, depending on the CONTEXT of the reader. Since critics in these areas try to identify the PRESENCE of structures of oppression in texts, they engage the texts as interested readers "more attentive to the interests and methodologies of literary critics generally" (Soulen and Soulen, 114–15).

Origins. Various writers have addressed issues of race, class, and gender as far back as the nineteenth century. In 1864, Henry James published a critical work that argued for the inferiority of Americans, saying that American literature would never reach the greatness of British literature (Richards, 43). He attacked American females, exemplified by Harriet Beecher Stowe, for using feminine sentimentalism in their works (49). As a disinterested reader, James also attacked Stowe because her judgment of class divisions in her "humanitarian narrative [was] less pleasing" (53).

Gender criticism. Gender criticism gained a large following in the 1970s with the emergence of feminism in America. The women's liberation movement brought to the forefront the realization that females are oppressed in PATRIARCHAL CULTURES. It "describes women as an oppressed class, exploited as sex-objects, breeders, domestic slaves and cheap labor" (Mace, 403). Social feminism is a broad philosophy and believes that working in the community to encourage responsiveness to women's interests will increase the role of women in society (356–57). Radical feminism believes that the only way to change and end the oppression of women is to attack men and PATRIARCHY rather than attack the social structures that support males. FEMINIST CRITICISM defines patriarchal society as male dominated, with the primary institution being the family. The institution of the family supports the male dominance and female subjugation in society (291–92).

Gender criticism has gone through several changes over the years, especially in feminist literature. "In its earliest U.S. incarnation, feminist literary criticism either took on men's fantasies about women . . . or else explored the achievements of women writers" (Poovey, 415). By the late 1970s, the concept of gender had assumed a more technical place in literature. Critics began looking at the use of gender modifiers in the language of a text. They looked at the way in which labeling something feminine created a SENSE of DIFFERENCE apart from the normal masculinity (416). In more recent literature, the distinction between sex and gender has become a major issue, thus opening the door for gender criticism.

Class criticism. Class criticism is perhaps best understood as a type of sociocriticism. With respect to texts, it "seeks to penetrate beneath their surface-function to expose their role as instruments of power, domination, or social manipulation" (Thiselton, 379). Class criticism examines the ways in which literature deals with the poor versus the wealthy. It also compares the ways in which classes are portrayed in literature with the ways in which the classes work in society.

Race criticism. Race criticism is as varied as feminist criticism. Though race used to be viewed as a biological classification, it is now considered a social construct (Goellnicht, 5). It has become increasingly important because of the growing interest in African American influence on American culture and the development of African American writing (Harmon and Holman, 124). For some critics, African American criticism (*see* BLACK THEOLOGY) is the study of African American literature; for others, it includes literature from Africa and the Caribbean. The fundamental assumption behind African American criticism is that race is an essential element of literary analysis (Goellnicht, 5). It seeks to disprove the assumption that "traditional, canonical American literature is free of, uninformed and unshaped by the four-hundred-year-old presence of, first, Africans and then African-Americans in the United States" (Morrison, 5). African American critics acknowledge

that there is a lack of uniformity in black writing (Cooke, 42) except in the expression of "social and practical freedom" (Morrison, 7).

Race criticism has been misconstrued as something that only serves to shift the focus of reading. However, rather than "altering one hierarchy in order to institute another," it actually tries to evaluate how race and ethnicity affect the reader and the literature itself. Toni Morrison says that a parallel can be drawn between race criticism and gender criticism. Since the creation of the two criticisms, the amount of both racist and sexist readings has decreased, and awareness has increased (7–8).

Application to biblical studies. James Cone and Juan Luis Segundo are two important race critics in the area of BIBLICAL HERMENEUTICS in North America. Cone says that there are two aspects of BLACK THEOLOGY: the BIBLE and black culture. According to Anthony Thiselton (420), Segundo largely proceeds along the line of Cone's theory that "black theologians must work in such a way as to destroy the corruptive influence of white thought by guiding a theology on the sources and norm that are appropriate to the black community." They believe that the theologian is simply another observer of the text and, like anyone else, interprets it through his/her own context (421).

Fernando Belo and Michel Clévenot are two noted examples of critics employing class criticism in hermeneutics. Belo says that Marxism equips the reader with the tools necessary to distinguish the manner in which a text takes part in social formation; he believes that the Bible is saturated with a dualist mind-set when it comes to the social order, seen in the dualist codes, or sets of rules, that it imparts to the reader. One CODE, seen primarily in the OT, clearly defines the roles that separate the various groups in the Bible. The second code, found in Deuteronomy, calls for social justice. He points out that both of these codes are interwoven into the NT as well (Thiselton, 427).

Clévenot's approach works along the same basis as Belo's. He utilizes the historical method to determine which sociopolitical theories were applied when the text was created (Thiselton, 428). While there were two sociopolitical systems at work in the Bible, they were actually utilized by two different groups. The "elitist priestly caste" used one system, and Jesus used the other. The system that Jesus used was something of an egalitarian, equality-based system, while the priestly class used more of a monopoly-based system (427–28). Clévenot believes that by comparing the two systems, the reader can discover the Christlike system that should be employed in current society.

Johanna W. H. van Wijk-Bos traces the representations of women in the church back before the Protestant Reformation. She points out that with the advent of the Reformation, all visually aesthetic modes of art were forbidden. Before this time, women were portrayed in many artworks, suggesting the place and function they had in the GOSPEL. When art was removed from the church, women's roles in the biblical stories were removed as well. The primary focus became the role that men had in the stories, often forgetting that women took part in the stories as well. This defacing of women from art contributed to the masculinization of the church (Wijk-Bos, 94–95).

Gender critics argue that although the biblical texts may be expressed in masculine forms, they are not calling for a hierarchical explanation of gender. What God says in the Bible is meant for all human beings, not just for men. "The Bible speaks authoritatively in that *God* addresses us through this text at the deepest level of our questioning" (Wijk-Bos, 45). According to gender critics, the world need not be male dominated but should be opened to the possibility for new modes of gender relations (46).

Elisabeth Schüssler Fiorenza examines the patriarchal bias of translators and the early interpreters of the biblical texts. She says that the bias of these men caused the great majority of the traditions concerning women and their contribution to early Christianity to be lost. The women had no voice in the public arena, so their ways and their traditions were quickly forgotten in the patriarchal society (Thiselton, 431–32). When there is no manner in which to express the knowledge and traditions of women, the dominating male ideas become the only frame of reference, leading to the assumption that men have always dominated society.

While race, class, and gender criticism covers a wide range of topics, its focus is always on oppression and domination as socially constructed and as not part of the natural structure of things. It seeks to expose these structures in texts, society, and interpretations and to uncover the underlying assumptions that both create and are created by these structures.

Bibliography. Michael G. Cooke, *Afro-American Literature in the Twentieth Century: The Achievement of Intimacy* (New Haven: Yale University Press, 1984); Donald C. Goellnicht, "Black Criticism," in *Encyclopedia of Contemporary Literary Theory: Approaches, Scholars, Terms* (ed. Irena R. Makaryk; Toronto: University of Toronto Press, 1993), 5–11; William Harmon and C. Hugh Holman, *A Handbook to Literature* (7th ed.; Upper Saddle River, NJ: Prentice Hall, 1996); William Klein, Craig Blomberg, and Robert Hubbard Jr., *Introduction to Biblical Interpretation* (Dallas: Word, 1993); David Mace, *The Penguin Dictionary of Critical Theory* (London: Penguin, 2000); Toni Morrison, *Playing in the Dark: Whiteness and the Literary Imagination* (Cambridge, MA: Harvard University Press, 1992); Mary Poovey, "Recent Studies of Gender," *Modern Philology* 88 (May 1991): 415–20; Christine Richards, "Gender, Race, and the 'Art' in Fiction: Henry James's Criticism and Harriet Beecher Stowe," *Literature and History* 9, no. 1 (April 2000): 43–55; Tom Skinner, *How Black Is the Gospel?* (New York: Lippincott, 1970); Richard N. Soulen and R. Kendall Soulen, *Handbook of Biblical Criticism* (3rd ed.; Louisville: Westminster John Knox, 2001); Anthony C. Thiselton, *New Horizons in Hermeneutics: The Theory and Practice of Transforming Biblical Reading* (Grand Rapids: Zondervan, 1992); Johanna W. H. van Wijk-Bos, *Reformed and Feminist: A Challenge to the Church* (Louisville: Westminster John Knox, 1991).

RAS SHAMRA TEXTS

A cache of TEXTS, dating from 1400 to 1180 BCE, discovered in 1929 among the ruins of the temple and palace in the ancient city of Ugarit (modern Ras Shamra). Since there are apparent similarities between the Ugaritic poetic texts and older HEBREW POETRY found among texts in the BIBLE, the Ras Shamra texts have become an important source for a better understanding of the HEBREW

BIBLE. They are also valuable sources for a better knowledge of the culture of Canaan and the Canaanitic pantheon and the myths associated with the gods. For an English TRANSLATION of some of these texts, see de Moor.

Bibliography. Richard N. Soulen and R. Kendall Soulen, *Handbook of Biblical Criticism* (3rd ed.; Louisville: Westminster John Knox, 2001); J. C. de Moor, *An Anthology of Religious Texts from Ugarit* (Leiden: Brill, 1987).

RATIONALISM

A philosophical term generally used in the SENSE that the most reliable source of TRUTH and knowledge is reason, rational thought. Rationalism became one of the hallmarks of both scientific and philosophical thought in the Enlightenment of the seventeenth and eighteenth centuries CE with philosophers such as René Descartes and Immanuel Kant. Most POSTMODERN critics and philosophers argue that rationalism, understood as an overwhelming confidence in the power of science and reason to solve human problems and to provide for the increased welfare of humans, became the centerpiece of MODERNISM. Rationalism can also be understood as the belief that there exists a rational order in reality, an order that rational human beings can discover. Some rationalists, however, claim that while there may not be an inherent order in reality, reason can be used to impose order on reality.

READER-CENTERED INTERPRETATION.
See READER-RESPONSE CRITICISM

READER COMPETENCY. *See* LITERARY
COMPETENCE

READERLY TEXT. *See* LISIBLE

READER-ORIENTED CRITICISM. *See*
READER-RESPONSE CRITICISM

READER-RESPONSE CRITICISM

Any type of LITERARY CRITICISM that, in some fashion, identifies the reader as the source of MEANING. Although many scholars see the origin of reader-response criticism in this century,

and particularly as recently as the late 1960s and early 1970s, David Jeffrey looks to the fourteenth-century British scholar and theologian John Wycliffe as the founding father (287). Wycliffe proposed that only through an active response of the reader could a TEXT be brought into being and that the biblical text was not between the covers of a book but in Christ himself. Therefore, only through a reader's active and voluntary commitment to read SCRIPTURE, which is Christ, does the text become complete.

Although this form of literary criticism has been around in one SENSE or another over the centuries, there does appear to be some justification for tracing the modern roots of reader-response criticism to the late 1960s. The renewed interest in reader-response criticism came as a strong reaction against the scientific objectivity of STRUCTURALISM and NEW CRITICISM. For the New Critics, literary criticism was to be built on the scientific model, and they appealed to objectivity to determine what could be found in the text. From start to finish, meaning was a textual meaning somehow inscribed in the text's inseparable FORM and CONTENT. Based on the role that individual emotional response, personal experience, attitudes, values, and beliefs play in the interpretive process, however, reader-response critics believe that objectivity is a MYTH.

The theories that claim the reader as the interpretive CONTEXT go by various names: TRANSACTIVE CRITICISM, SPEECH ACT THEORY, subjective criticism, affective criticism, and reader-response criticism, the latter being the most popular and perhaps the most descriptive. Generally, New Critics (*see* NEW CRITICISM) claim that the literary text constitutes the objective standard of meaning. Through a CLOSE READING of the text as a static, autonomous literary object, the reader can extricate a meaning that is somehow incarnated within the text. Reader-response critics, however, have challenged the New Critics' claim of TEXTUAL AUTONOMY. Modern reader-response critics are asking if it is even legitimate to talk about meaning apart from a consideration of what happens when we read. What does happen when we read?

Why do we respond to literary texts the way we do? Is meaning in the mind of the AUTHOR, the text, the mind of the reader, or somewhere among these? For the reader-response critic, meaning originates completely or partly within the mind of the reader. The important words here are "completely or partly," for the critics who fall within the reader-response mode of INTERPRETATION constitute a multifarious group. Along a continuum between text and reader, reader-response critics may be placed according to the relative role that each critic ascribes to the text in the determination of meaning.

Another way to broach the subject of reader-response criticism and at the same time maintain a sense of continuity and variety is to divide the continuum into three shorter segments, each of which represents an attitude toward the relationship between the text and reader. These segments could be labeled as reader-controlled reading, text-reader dialogue, and text-controlled reading. The first segment would contain the critical theories that assign the reader the primary role in creating meaning; the second segment, the theories that claim an evenhandedness between the text and reader; and the third segment, the theories that give the text a slight edge in formulating meaning.

Theorists of the reader-response mode are in varying degrees concerned with developing a consistent theory that will govern the study of readers' responses and the relationship between response and literary meaning. Further, all reader-response critics assume that the "literary work" comes into existence only through an interaction between text and reader. They differ, however, in the relative importance they assign to the two components of interaction: text and reader. Those who remain closely tied to the text, ascribing to it a major role in the text-reader encounter, tend to impose limitations on the reading process by postulating a reader who is presupposed by the text, an IMPLIED READER. The starting point for these theorists, then, is the text itself. At the other end of the range are the affective critics, who insist that the reader's individual psyche or INTERPRETIVE COMMUNITY in some way controls the response to the text. The theory therefore must begin with the actual readers and work back to the text. Between these two poles at varying intervals are situated other theorists.

Four assumptions. James Resseguie (308) identifies four critical ASSUMPTIONS of reader-response criticism. First, the reader is an active participant in the creation of meaning. This claim primarily refers to the way in which a reader must use imagination to fill in the gaps of INDETERMINACY that exist in all literature. Even the most thorough and descriptive piece of writing is not complete until it is in some way reconstructed in the mind's eye of the reader. On the one hand, for instance, a writer describing a woman may make a strong appeal to the reader's senses. The author may describe the color of the woman's hair and eyes, her disposition, the texture of her skin, her alluring fragrance. It is not until the reader constructs a mental image of the woman, however, that the text comes to life and thus becomes meaningful. On the other hand, an author may offer almost no information about a character, place, or event. In such a case, the reader is forced to create the character, place, or event virtually from scratch. For example, if an author casually refers to "a man on a bench," the reader must decide the type of bench (bench of justice, park bench, a church pew), the appearance of the man (old, young, middle-aged), and perhaps even the purpose of the reference to begin with. The reader-response critic maintains that the reader's active interaction with the text is inherent in all reading and that there is no completed meaning until this activity occurs.

The second assumption concerns the relationship between the text and the reader. The text presupposes a certain kind of reader, usually referred to as the implied reader. This reader is one who is aware of certain social and cultural conventions and has a presupposed level of LITERARY COMPETENCE (Resseguie, 308).

The third assumption regards the common ground shared by the text and the reader. The reader shares the SYMBOLIC WORLD presupposed by the text. In order for the reader to make sense of the text, there must be shared concepts, knowledge of cultural situations, and emotional responses (308–9).

The fourth assumption is that communication involves conveying something new. The premise is that if there is nothing new to convey, communication would be unnecessary. So the author places the familiar in a new context, making the familiar appear unfamiliar to the reader, a process known as defamiliarization (308–9; *see* FORMALISM). There are two structural components of the text that have influence over the reader's reactions: (1) a repertoire of literary patterns, THEMES, and ALLUSIONS that draws the reader's attention to familiar contexts; and (2) literary strategies that place the familiar within unfamiliar contexts. Through this experience of defamiliarization, the reader is challenged to engage the text, to identify the familiar and the unfamiliar, and in this way to make sense of the text. Thus, the reader becomes involved in the process of reading in a way that reader-response critics see as both creative and re-creative. This dual process combines the rest of the assumptions to produce something unique.

So reader-response criticism partially focuses on the readerly activities that are responsible for producing literary communication. It is concerned with questions of what the reader does to the text, what the text does to the reader, the purpose of reading, and for what purpose a text engages the reader. As the critic answers these questions, a literary work (i.e., the reader's nonfigurative understanding) can to some degree be analyzed, categorized, and judged for plausibility. Ultimately, however, meaning is to be found in individual interpretations.

Middle ground: Wolfgang Iser. As already indicated, reader-response theorists to varying degrees fall away from the text as the controlling factor for determining meaning. What follows is a description of Wolfgang Iser's phenomenological approach, which lies at the middle point of the reader-response continuum.

Iser stakes his theory of interpretation on the dialogic nature of words, a characteristic necessitating that in any act of verbal communication,

a listener must interpret the speaker's words in order to comprehend them. Intentions are never automatically transferred from speaker to listener; instead, the listener ascribes most intentions to an utterance. Thus the activity of interpretation. But an utterance may contain implications never intended by the speaker. In every SPEECH ACT is a dimension of the unspoken that is as important to understanding or communication as what is actually verbalized. In other words, any utterance (esp. a literary one) carries possibilities beyond the control of the speaker's INTENTION. The verbalization of this unspoken dimension of the utterance is the context for meaning multiplicity. Such is also the case for literary acts of communication. Literary meaning, for Iser, comes into being through a communication process involving two poles: the artistic, the enabling structures of the text; and the aesthetic, the reader and the individual imagination. In the reading process, the reader actualizes a potential effect represented by the text. The text consists of a set of instructions that the reader must carry out, thus implying that the meaning, for Iser, must be assembled by the reader. Meaning is a productive, creative process set in motion by the text but involving the imagination and perception of a reader. Iser refers to this process of MEANING ASSEMBLY as "re-creative dialectics." It is clear that for Iser, then, meaning is not some treasure buried in the text that can be excavated through interpretation. If a buried meaning can be "lifted out of the text, the work is then used up." If interpretation is the task of digging up that meaning, then CRITICISM becomes self-defeating. Once the meaning has been extracted, we are left with nothing but an empty shell and no aesthetically good reason to continue. The interpreter has fallen prey to the literary equivalent of Nietzsche's will to power. If, on the other hand, meaning is seen as a product of interaction between the enabling structures of a text and a reader's acts of comprehension, meaning must be something other than what is found on the printed pages of the text.

The last observation brings us to an important point in Iser's reckoning: that the critic's main concern should be the effect of the text rather than its meaning. But why may we assume that the reader is a partner in a communication process? For Iser, the answer is supplied by the very nature of dyadic interaction (*see* DYAD). In any speech act, what is said can never totally translate what is meant. There is always an unspoken residue of indeterminacies that need to be resolved. In the literary text, these indeterminacies are in the form of gaps, blanks, and vacancies that must be filled by the reader (*Act of Reading*, 54).

At this point we reach a PARADOX: on the one hand, a reader can never simply freewheel through a text, for the text clues the reader in different ways as to the manner in which the indeterminacies are to be resolved. On the other hand, the text formulates nothing but requires the reader's imagination to build up the pattern of the text—a pattern that varies according to the reader (Iser, *Prospecting*, 17). The waters become muddier when we consider Iser's claim that part of the intention of the text is the very fact that no single projected meaning can exhaust the possibilities of a text. In other words, literary works are structured in such a way that they not only are capable of legitimating multiple readings but also encourage such multiplicity. This multiplicity is not synonymous with EQUIVOCALITY. Iser never claims that a text has the capacity to legitimate *any* reading. For example, after reading the Gospel of Mark, I claim to have discovered that the primary focus of the teaching of Mark's Jesus is the mating practices of young polar bears in the months of January and February. Such a reading would and should be laughed off the stage. Multiplicity is better understood as PLURIVOCALITY. Literary texts will generate and legitimate a plurality of readings, but not any or every reading.

According to Iser, reading is pleasurable only when it is active and creative. If the text is overdetermined for the reader, boredom sets in; if the text is extremely underdetermined, the reader will be overtaxed and will retreat from the field of play. The latter observation brings us to another key idea in Iser's theory: PLAY, an idea that needs some devel-opment before ending our introductory remarks and moving on to a systematic description of the dialogic activity between reader and text.

Play. Authors intentionally use texts as the playground for games involving the reader. Texts are intentional acts that aim at producing, in dialogue with a reader, an object that did not exist previously. In other words, rather than a text's being a representation of something already existing in the real world, it is a system of signals that engages the reader in a playful game of imaginatively and creatively producing something new and previously nonexistent. While this new creation is not predetermined by the text or contained intact within it, it is generated by the reader's interaction with the text. This interaction between text and reader moves toward a result, the imaging and interpretation of a world adumbrated but not identified by the text. This unidentified but adumbrated world may assume many shapes and thus is the context of play. For Iser, two facts ensure that the game is a never-ending one: (1) a series of differences and (2) the very nature of texts as playgrounds to resist final resolution. According to Iser, there exist in relationship to a text three levels of difference that allow the games to begin:

1. Extratextual:
   a. between the author and the world in which one intervenes;
   b. between the text and an extratextual world as well as between the text and other texts.
2. Intratextual:
   a. between the items selected from extratextual systems;
   b. between semantic enclosures built up in the text.
3. Between text and reader:
   a. between the reader's natural attitudes (now bracketed off) and those the reader is called upon to assume;
   b. between what is denoted by the world created by the text and what this DENO-TATION—now serving as a guiding ana-

logue—is meant to adumbrate. (Iser, *Prospecting*, 252)

When claims are made that these differences are bridged or removed, play ceases. Usually (or at least traditionally) the game ends with the discovery of meaning. To say, however, that a text means something also means that the reader has made a decision (or better, a series of decisions). But a final decision about the articulation of meaning is made at a cost. Since the game brings into being constantly shifting and interacting positions, the text resists any attempt at finality or CLOSURE. In other words, the text both encourages and resists the removal of difference. Any one decision is made at the expense of countless other possible decisions. Hence, while meaning is the result of play, it is the very nature of the game to allow an endless variety of reenactments (Iser, *Prospecting*, 252). On the one hand, this is not tantamount to saying that any reading of a text is tentative. A reading of a text is always subject to adjustment as the reader changes over time, but the reading may remain essentially legitimate. On the other hand, this is a claim that readers never exhaust the MEANING EFFECTS of a text.

The more deeply readers are lured into playing the game, the more they are "played by the text" (258). This is tantamount to claiming that a text must provide a role for the reader: the role of the reader is one of the text's structured parts. Texts therefore stage the play for their readers. This fact requires that we no longer view the role of the reader as one of spectator passively watching the pageant unfold from the text. Rather, the reader is asked to participate in a stage performance. In this respect, therefore, the language of a literary text is the language of mise-en-scène. This requirement of participation, then, produces two results: (1) the reader acts out the play of the text in a unique way, and (2) meaning becomes a transformative experience. Through this playful game instituted by the text, the reader undergoes a series of effects that ultimately produce an individual, unique aesthetic object. This object is actually what Iser calls the

literary work, which is identical neither to the literary text nor to the individual disposition of the reader. "The convergence of text and reader brings the literary work into existence" (Iser, *Implied Reader*, 275).

Attaining Meaning. Meaning is the result of a dialogue between a reader and a text. This dialogue is dependent on a pair of structures: structures of effect and structures of response. Although readers certainly bring their own individual SYMBOLIC WORLDS to the text, responses are not entirely arbitrary because the structures of response as well as the structures of effect are textually determined. Since these structures are interactive, we will discuss them in their dialogic relationships and not try to discuss them separately.

Every age has its own dominant thought system, which reduces the contingencies and complexities of reality to a meaningful and manageable structure. What any one epoch considers to be reality is not reality in its totality but instead an order imposed on reality. Every system imposes an order on contingent reality, thereby providing a FRAMEWORK for living as well as for a set of social norms that lay claim to universal validity. But when a system becomes dominant, it does so through a reduction of the complexity of reality. While it foregrounds some possibilities, it necessarily backgrounds or excludes others. The negated or neutralized possibilities are not eliminated but only deactivated, waiting to be reactivated. Literature is the means of resurrection. Literature tries to bring to light the possibilities neutralized or excluded by the dominant system. Thus literature interferes with the existing ordering of reality, drawing attention to its deficiencies. The result of such interference brings to light the system's inability to deal with the multifarious nature of reality. Once literature attacks the system at its seams, so to speak, a rearrangement of the meaningful structures of the system is called for. The excluded possibilities are the focus of literary works (Iser, *Act of Reading*, 71–78). For example, when John Bunyan wrote *The Pilgrim's Progress*, the theological subsystem was a type of Calvinism. Since the very heart of Bunyan's system was the concept of predestination, in which God and God alone chooses and knows who are predestined to eternal life, the individual was faced with a sense of uncertainty. How was one to gain any indication of one's own eternal destiny? The answer was that one should look to the outside; external matters such as success in vocation, frugality, and faithfulness in matters of liturgy became indicators of one's election. By FOREGROUNDING the answer in terms of external indicators, *The Pilgrim's Progress* activated the possibility of finding indicators of certainty within one's self. It called for a rearrangement of the structures of meaning within Calvinism. But how does a literary text accomplish the work of a gadfly?

What Iser calls the REPERTOIRE of a text consists of schemata and strategies. The schemata consist of social norms and LITERARY ALLUSIONS; the strategies consist of NARRATIVE techniques (esp. perspectives) and gaps of INDETERMINACY.

The negated or neutralized possibilities of the dominant thought system constitute the focal point of a literary text. At the same time, however, in order to establish this focal point, the text must implicitly incorporate the framework of the contemporary system. The text accomplishes this by "explicitly shading in the areas all around the system" (Iser, *Act of Reading*, 73). On the one hand, when a text incorporates elements of the current thought system, these elements are recorded in such a way that the familiar elements lose their validity. On the other hand, the text does not formulate an alternative validity but presents the elements in such a way that readers must discover or construct the intentions of recoding. Thus the readers are called upon to be partners in constructing meaning. Now, if the readers are contemporary with the text, they are provided with the possibility of a fresh look at the system that they have to this point accepted without question. If the readers, however, are no longer involved in the thought system of the text, they are able to reconstruct the framework from the text, to experience the system's deficiencies, and to discover the alternative answers implicit in the text. So the historical distance

between a text and later generations of readers does not vitiate a text's power. The contemporary reader is confronted with defamiliarized norms, necessitating a reassessment of the possibilities negated by such norms. The result is the construction of meaning. Later readers experience a reality that is now theirs and are able to transcend their own world, or *SITZ IM LEBEN*, resulting in a reassessment or broadening of their reality (78–79).

The schemata of the text also consist of past literary elements and entire traditions that are intertwined with the social and cultural norms. "If the function of the incorporated norms is to bring out the deficiencies of a prevailing system, the function of literary allusions is to assist in producing an answer to the problems set by these deficiencies" (Iser, *Act of Reading*, 79). These literary allusions offer the reader past answers to the problems presented by the social norms, but answers that are no longer valid. So what is the value of the allusions? Since the allusions are now stripped of their original context, the reader should assume that their function is more than simple reproduction, that they serve as guides or points of orientation for discovering a new meaning. Since the literary elements are depragmatized by a new context, the original or old context recedes into the background but does not disappear. The old context serves as a backdrop that throws the now-implied significance into relief. It is only against the background of the old context that the reader is able to construct new possibilities and their significance.

The repertoire of the text (schemata and strategies) constitutes the context for the dialogue between the text and the reader. The repertoire provides the reader with the wherewithal to produce an answer to the questions raised in the text. But before we move to TEXTUAL STRATEGIES, it is necessary to examine more thoroughly the relationship between the schemata and the role of the reader.

The social norms incorporated within a text originate in a historical thought system, while the literary allusions have their origin in past reactions to problems. Since the norms and allusions are not equivalent, a problem for the reader arises when they are joined together. The fact that they are joined suggests that they are related in some fashion. So the reader is called upon to look for a system of equivalences between norms and allusions even if their marriage is designed to highlight differences. The reader is called upon to create a system of equivalences between the two systems, but since a text always refers to something beyond itself, the reader is also called upon to create a system of equivalences between the work and the real world. The role of the schemata is to organize the reader's reaction to the problem implied within the text. But the schemata's structure must be realized through reading. The degree to which the structures of meaning are optimized will depend on the reader's awareness of these structures and the degree to which the reader is willing to open up to an unfamiliar and sometimes threatening experience. But according to Iser, "The meaning must inevitably be pragmatic, in that it can never cover all the semantic possibilities of the text" (*Act of Reading*, 85). This is tantamount to saying that the schemata present a range of organizational possibilities and these can be realized in a number of ways. It is here that the reader's own individual disposition and background come into play. Meaning originates, then, from the interplay between the reader's own decisions and the attitude that the text provokes in the reader toward the problems that the text implies. Nevertheless, the organizational structure of the schemata guards against any reader's indiscriminate meaning assembly by providing the context for meaning assembly.

For Iser, the most determinate guide relating to the schemata is negativity, which is actually a basic form of what he calls gaps of INDETERMINACY. For Iser, negativity is "the basic regulator of the human condition" (*Prospecting*, 142). Human beings are incapable of knowing how they experience one another. Because of this basic knowledge gap, we create our own conceptions of how others experience us and then substitute these conceptions for reality. Indeed, we even base our actions and reactions to others on our projections. We create an imaginary picture and base all our communication on this FICTION. But projections are not reality. Consequently, we spend our lives bridging a fundamental double gap by formulating imaginary projections based on imaginary perceptions.

Negativity is responsible for stimulating the processes of imagination that can bridge the knowledge gap. When applied to the text and reader, negativity must be understood as negation. When a text incorporates familiar social norms and literary allusions, it does so in order to negate them, to cancel them out. These negated norms and allusions, however, remain in the background and serve to stimulate the reader to assume a posture or attitude toward the text. In other words, when the norms are negated, the reader is expected to look for the positive elsewhere than in what is negated. The alternatives to the negated norms and literary conventions are only implicit in the text, and the reader must discover what they are. This is where the concept of negativity is important, for there is, Iser assumes, a hidden motive behind the many negations and deformations within the text. This motive is negativity, and it can be discovered only by the constitutive activity of the reader in recognizing that something is being withheld that must be discovered (Iser, *Act of Reading*, 214).

The meaning of the text is never that which is manifest but exactly that which is latent. But that which is stated serves as the primary context for what is unstated. So the reader is engaged in a constant switch between what is manifest or present and what is unstated or absent. It might be said that the reader must always distinguish between what a text says and what it might actually be about. And that "aboutness" is never explicit but will always come into being through the protracted attempts of the reader to initiate and engage in the play of the text. Such an engagement should not strike readers as an unfamiliar process, for it is exactly this process that ensures everyday instances of communication. What is spoken or manifest is always accompanied by the unspoken or latent. In other words, ABSENCE is always alongside PRESENCE.

The spoken is always impregnated with associations that cannot be dispensed with, and every object to which the spoken refers is one that has already been described in countless ways, so that whatever is said about it can only be a selection from possibilities, thus defining itself by what it excludes. (Iser, *Prospecting*, 102)

So when we as readers are lured into the text through negativity, we are engaged in a drama that mirrors the drama of life itself. More complex texts tend to make more ambiguous the signposts pointing the reader toward the hidden motive, thus dismantling any specific frame of REFERENCE from which the reader is to view the negations. When this occurs, the play of the text manifests itself in a multiplicity of possibilities.

While the repertoire of the text consists of the social norms and literary allusions that produce negativity, it also includes textual strategies. On the one hand, the schemata create the context within which the reader must actualize a system of equivalences between the norms and allusions and between the text and the real world. On the other hand, the textual strategies function to organize the readers' ACTUALIZATION, yet without making them feel as if they are being led by the nose. The strategies govern not only the structures of the text but also the acts of comprehension triggered in the reader. Put another way, it is the function of the strategies to carry the schemata (the primary code of the text) to the reader and to guide the reader's creation of the aesthetic object (the secondary code) by providing the meeting place for the schemata and the individual reader's own social and cultural code.

The textual strategies include the devices normally associated with the conventions of GENRE. For Iser, however, the emphasis falls on the unmanifested dimension of the text, what we may call seams or what he refers to as gaps. Literary texts offer readers only enough information to keep them "oriented and interested." Inferences that are to be drawn from the information are left up to the imagination of the reader. There result empty spaces or gaps within the text that must be filled by the reader.

The gap functions as a kind of pivot on which the whole text-reader relationship revolves. Hence, the structured blanks of the text stimulate the process of ideation to be performed by the reader on terms set by the text. (Iser, *Act of Reading*, 86)

The manner in which these gaps are filled is inseparable from Iser's treatment of textual perspectives.

Points of view. There are generally four perspectives (POINTS OF VIEW) in a literary work, especially the novel: the perspectives of the NARRATOR, of the characters, of the PLOT, and of the implied reader. The point of their convergence is the meaning of the text. This point of convergence is not provided by the text but must be supplied by the reader. In other words, the convergence of the perspectives must emerge from a vantage point beyond the four perspectives but prestructured by the text. The REAL READER, then, is a mediator between the various perspectives, including that of the implied reader. This mediating activity is created by gaps between the perspectives, gaps that Iser refers to as blanks. Between perspectives there is a "suspension of connectability," an empty space that must be filled by the reader (*Prospecting*, 9).

These blanks function to impede textual consistency or COHERENCE. While they are actually empty spaces, they do stimulate the reader's involvement; indeed they are responsible for the very dialogue between reader and text. The blanks between the perspectives also serve as the referential field for the reader's attention in any one moment of the reading process. When two or more perspectives must be related by the reader, it is the blank that makes such a relation possible.

The perspectives have the function of stimulating the production of the aesthetic object. Consequently, the aesthetic object is never congruent with a single perspective. The aesthetic object is produced through the CONSISTENCY-BUILDING activities of the reader. Since all the perspectives are interactive and this interaction is continuous throughout the work, the reader is called upon to mediate between the shifting perspectives in order to produce a consistent viewpoint. As the reader is confronted with the shifting and interacting perspectives, he/she is faced with the task of making them consistent. When we consider that this task is carried out during the time flow or the temporal axis of reading, the real reader's role is actually that of a wandering viewpoint. As the reader's attention shifts in the time flow of reading from one perspective to another, it is incapable of embracing all the perspectives at once. The perspective with which the reader is involved at any one moment is the "THEME." But this theme is set in relief by the previous perspectives with which the reader has been concerned. The previous segments constitute what Iser calls the "horizon" (*Act of Reading*, 97).

These complementary concepts of theme and horizon point up a strategic element in literary texts pertaining to the wandering viewpoint: the relationship between EXPECTATION and MEMORY, or PROTENSION and RETENTION. Every segment of perspective (theme) is viewed within the context of a horizon; but in the time flow of reading, a theme is immediately transformed into the background, thus becoming part of the horizon from which the next theme will be viewed. Therefore, while the horizon influences the theme, the theme will also modify the horizon. The horizon always arouses expectations of things to come (e.g., how a problem will be resolved), while the theme will either satisfy expectations or frustrate them. In addition, each new theme not only answers or frustrates expectations but also gives rise to new ones. In most literary texts, the theme serves to modify the expectations of the horizon or even to frustrate them. As a result, the theme has a retroactive influence on the horizon because the reader must go back and reconsider the previous segments and their relationship. So reading becomes an interplay between protension and retention. It is through this process of protension and retention that the wandering viewpoint continually seeks to relate the perspectives.

As we observed above, it is the function of the strategies to carry the schemata (the primary code of the text) to the reader and to guide the reader's creation of the aesthetic object (the secondary code) by providing the meeting place for the sche-mata and the individual reader's own social and cultural code. In narrative texts, the perspectives may be arranged in four different ways: counterbalance, opposition, echelon, and serial (the following is an overview of Iser's discussion of the four different arrangements; *Act of Reading*, 100–103).

In the *counterbalance* arrangement, the perspectives are arranged in a definite hierarchy. The hero's perspective is the principal one since it incarnates the norms that are desirable; the perspectives of the minor characters are subordinate since they violate the norms of the hero in varying degrees. In other words, by continually confirming the norms of the hero over against the shortcomings of the other characters, the plot perspective points up the deficiencies of the system represented by the minor characters. As Iser points out, counterbalancing of perspectives is favored by devotional and propagandist literature: rather than being concerned with producing an aesthetic object, their primary purpose is to offer an alternative to correct the deficiencies of the prevailing thought system.

The *oppositional* arrangement of perspectives tries to set norms against one another "by showing up the deficiencies of each norm when viewed from the standpoint of the others" (Iser, *Act of Reading*, 101). When such an arrangement is viewed within the context of theme and horizon, the norms represented by each perspective become the theme, while the negated ones forming the horizon become the context against which the thematic segment is judged. What is produced is a process of reciprocal negation. Readers find themselves in the position in which they must remove the conflicting norms from their pragmatic position within the thought system, thus discovering their functions within that very system. Consequently, if the readers are able to view the functions of the norms within the system, they ultimately discover exactly what impact the norms have on them in real life.

In the *echelon* arrangement of perspectives, the plot perspective is such that all characters are leveled out so that they all tend to point up the deficiencies of the thought system or systems under consideration. If no perspective is predominant, the readers find themselves in a predicament: they are unable to find reliable guidelines by which to produce a consistent viewpoint. When we say that all perspectives are leveled out, we include the perspective of the narrator, who not only refuses any guidelines but even contradicts readers' earlier evaluations. So, if the perspectives refuse the readers any guidelines in producing an attitude toward the system of norms, that is, in producing a consistent viewpoint toward the system of norms, the readers must themselves adopt a posture springing from their own dispositions.

Within the *serial* arrangement of perspectives, there is certainly no hierarchy. The reading process is drastically arrested or impeded by the fact that perspectives are not internally inconsistent but change from section to section, often from sentence to sentence. The process of alternating theme and horizon is so complex that the reader is constantly modifying or abandoning connections that were made earlier. In other words, the reciprocal process of theme and horizon that functions as the referential field for the wandering viewpoint becomes so vague that it becomes virtually impossible for the reader to make meaningful projections that result in any consistent viewpoint. Since the text refuses to provide the conditions under which reality can be perceived, the reader is forced to produce those conditions. Yet, while the text refuses to produce those conditions, the serial arrangement of perspectives does in one sense create the conditions under which the readers ideate their own reality. Obviously, such an arrangement of perspectives increases the possibility of actualizing multiple aesthetic objects.

Since the shifting perspectives challenge the reader to produce a consistent viewpoint (i.e., create the aesthetic object), consistency building is a configurative, productive activity. The wandering viewpoint travels through the text of interconnecting perspectives, making connections that will (at least for the reader) result in a mediated, consistent meaning. In other words, the wandering viewpoint seeks patterns of consistency. Now, since readers differ in terms of memory, mental capacity, train-

ing, and interest, patterns of connections may be realized to varying degrees. Hence, the intersubjective structure of the text is capable of generating a multiplicity of subjective actualizations (Iser, *Act of Reading*, 118).

Iser, however, is careful to guarantee a modest degree of determinacy created by the gaps of IN-DETERMINACY. He does this by redescribing the concept of horizon, calling it a *vacancy*, and thus transforming the horizon into a type of controlling or governing gap (a "determining indeterminant"). While the blanks are the empty spaces, the missing links between perspectives, the vacancies develop when a segment fades from relevance, thus forming the background for the next theme. Each new thematic segment must be approached against this background of the vacancy.

Balance in Iser. What Iser actually wants to ensure is a dialogic balance between the text and the reader, a free play producing an aesthetic object that is a product of both the governing structures of the text and the creative imagination of the reader. The aesthetic object is not a well-defined kernel of meaning that the author has placed into a text in some manner. Neither is the aesthetic object the result of the free play of the reader's imagination. In terms that recall Gadamer's definition of meaning, the aesthetic object is given birth when the horizons of the reader and the text converge (and perhaps sometimes clash). Until that convergence takes place, the meaning of the text (if indeed we should even be referring to the meaning of the text!) is only virtually present. It is not that the reader activates the meaning structures of the text to formulate meaning. Nor is it that the text simply activates the creative activities of the reader. The aesthetic object comes into being through the mutual interaction of the text's structures and the reader's imaginative activities. Without either, there simply is no aesthetic object produced. When either pole of this dialogue is absent, communication between a piece of literature and a human mind is impossible. Where, on the one hand, the text makes no strategic provision for the free play of the creative human imagination or, on the other hand, the reader is not willing to allow the imagination to play the text and to be played by the text, the game of literary communication never gets off the ground.

Bibliography. Wolfgang Iser, *The Act of Reading: A Theory of Aesthetic Response* (Baltimore: Johns Hopkins University Press, 1978); idem, *The Implied Reader: Patterns of Communication in Prose Fiction from Bunyan to Beckett* (Baltimore: Johns Hopkins University Press, 1974); idem, *Prospecting: From Reader Response to Literary Anthropology* (Baltimore: Johns Hopkins University Press, 1989); idem, "The Reading Process: A Phenomenological Approach," in *Reader-Response Criticism: From Formalism to Post-structuralism* (ed. Jane Tompkins; Baltimore: Johns Hopkins University Press, 1980), 50–59; David Jeffrey, "John Wyclif and the Hermeneutics of Reader Response," *Interpretation* 39 (1985): 272–87; James Resseguie, "Reader-Response Criticism and the Synoptic Gospels," *Journal of the American Academy of Religion* 52 (1984): 307–24.

READING, CLOSE. *See* CLOSE READING

READING, CONFLATE. *See* CONFLATE READING

READING, SYMPTOMATIC. *See* SYMPTOMATIC READING

READING AGAINST THE GRAIN

A concept in the READER-RESPONSE CRITICISM of Judith Fetterley, relating to her discussion of "the resisting reader," articulated in her book by the same title. According to Fetterley, since the Western LITERARY CANON is characterized by ANDROCENTRISM and MISOGYNY, as is the professional academy that interprets the CANON, readers (both men and women) have been conditioned to read and interpret TEXTS from this androcentric and misogynist perspective. By resisting, or reading against the grain, a person can approach these texts in a self-consciously critical posture. As she puts it, "The first act of the feminist critic must be to become a resisting rather than assenting reader and, by this refusal to assent, to begin the process of exorcising the male mind that has been implanted in us. The consequence of this exorcism is the capacity for what Adrienne Rich describes as revision—the act of looking back, of

seeing with fresh eyes, of entering an old text from a new critical direction" (xxii).

Bibliography. Judith Fetterley, *The Resisting Reader: A Feminist Approach to American Fiction* (Bloomington: Indiana University Press, 1978).

READING SITUATION

A concept in the LITERARY theory of Roland Barthes, referring to the role played by the reader in the determination of MEANING. According to Barthes, there is really little, if anything, in the TEXT or the AUTHOR's world that reveals the text's meaning. Hermeneutics should be concerned primarily with the reading situation because "this situation as it changes, composes the work and does not discover it" (72).

Bibliography. Roland Barthes, *Criticism and Truth* (Minneapolis: University of Minnesota Press, 1987).

REAL/ACTUAL READER

Terms introduced into literary theory by Wolfgang Iser as part of his READER-RESPONSE CRITICISM. The real reader is the flesh-and-blood person who in time and space reads the TEXT. This reader is conditioned by a range of variables: social, economic, political, ecclesiastical, doctrinal, methodological, and philosophical. This real reader may have been the original readers, readers during the Protestant Reformation, or those in an introductory literature class last week. *See* IMPLIED AUTHOR; IMPLIED READER; READER-RESPONSE CRITICISM; REAL AUTHOR.

REALIZATION. *See* ENACTMENT

REALIZED ESCHATOLOGY

A term introduced into NT studies for the view that the passages in the NT that deal with the ESCHATON should be understood as being realized in the life and ministry of Jesus rather than as having a future reference. The term is also used to describe the type of ESCHATOLOGY that some scholars find in John's GOSPEL: the view that things normally associated with the eschaton, such as divine judgment and eternal life, have been realized by Jesus's spiritual presence in the midst of his followers. In other words, the Gospel of John seems to advocate a type of eschatology in which the first coming of Jesus ensures that believers have new life in the present (e.g., 5:21–26; 11:25–27) as well as judgment (e.g., 3:18; 9:39; 12:31). When Jesus breathes on his disciples and says that they have received his Spirit (20:22–23), the eschaton has already been realized. See also Luke T. Johnson's reading of Luke (*Writings of the New Testament*, 197–238).

Bibliography. Stephen Harris, *The New Testament: A Student's Introduction* (4th ed.; Boston: McGraw-Hill, 2002); Luke T. Johnson, *The Writings of the New Testament: An Interpretation* (Philadelphia: Fortress, 1986).

REAL WORLD

In NARRATIVE CRITICISM, the actual world in which an AUTHOR lived when the TEXT was written. The real world refers to the author's world, with its patterns of behavior, social institutions, and ideological, economic, religious, and ethical structures. It differs from the STORY WORLD, which is the world found only in the text. This latter world, framed by the beginning and ending of the text, is a creation of an author who selects and arranges (*see* SELECTION AND ARRANGEMENT) events in a complex STRUCTURE.

RECEIVED TEXT. *See* TEXTUS RECEPTUS

RECENSION

Technically, in TEXTUAL CRITICISM, a critical revision of a TEXT. The term also refers to any manuscript family. Since all manuscripts of the BIBLE were hand-copied before the introduction of printing in the West, an important task in textual criticism is the comparison and explanation of the differences between manuscripts of the same text.

RECEPTION THEORY

A LITERARY theory that examines the manner in which readers interpret a literary work in light of the changes and effects of history. Hans Robert Jauss is the principal architect of reception theory, which he refers to as the aesthetics of reception, best outlined in a lecture he delivered at the University of Constance in 1967: "What Is and for What Purpose Does One Study Literary History?" His main idea is that in order to get a new reading of a TEXT, readers must be able to step outside their own historical PRAXIS and view the work without any preconceived notions. Jauss believes this to be virtually impossible because of the aesthetic receptions that cause a reader to come to a certain HORIZON OF EXPECTATION. According to Jauss, the traditional focus on historical objectivism must be replaced by an approach to literature that prioritizes an "aesthetics of reception and impact." Jauss's reception theory is an attempt to bridge the gap generated in literary theory by the differences between MARXIST CRITICISM and FORMALISM (*Toward an Aesthetic*, 63). Marxism dealt effectively with history, while formalism tended to neglect the importance of history in literary studies. Neither, however, dealt sufficiently with the influence of history on the reader. For Jauss, the AUTHOR, work, and reader form a fundamental triangle in the literary process, and he felt that neither Marxism nor formalism gave enough import to the reader and the manner in which the reader is influenced by history. For Jauss, the reader (the public) is more than "a chain of mere reactions"; the reader is a formative part of history, and the literary work has no historical life without the active participation of its audiences ("Literary History," 164). Jauss assumes further that the relationship between the work and the public has aesthetic as well as historical implications. The former lies in the first reading of the literary work, when the reader judges the aesthetic value of the work by comparing it to previously read texts. The latter, historical implication lies in the observation that the understandings of the first readers will be inscribed in the receptions of future generations.

According to Jauss, history is nothing more than opinion. For example, if history (or better, HISTORIOGRAPHY) is objective, all of the GOSPELS should be exactly the same. The fact that the Gospels are not the same but rather have irreconcilable differences does not mean that one or more of the texts is wrong. Jauss views history as a perspective of a certain group or individual. Thus history is in no way objective but is shaped by the perspective of the writer.

Jauss offers seven theses in his response to the issue of the manner in which literary history may be methodologically grounded and rewritten in new ways for each different reading public ("Literary History," 165). The first thesis deals with the problem of objectivity in reading a literary work: the historicity of literature does not depend on organizing literary facts but on the readers' prior experience of the literary work. As a reader engages a text, preconceived ideas are present in either the reader's conscious or unconscious. These presuppositions may originate from a number of sources: past text, status, economics, and so forth (166). In other words, certain receptions of past reading experiences are triggered with each new reading. These past experiences in turn influence any literary work a public reads. A literary work does not exist objectively by itself, offering to every reader in every period the same view. A work is more like an orchestration that strikes each reader differently. The historical contexts of both work and reader create a horizon of expectation. The horizon is what the reader believes will happen based on the reader's own horizon or historical background. Hence, the possibility of comprehending and representing a literary work in its unique historicity depends on the objectification of the horizon of expectation.

Jauss's second thesis is concerned with the manner in which one's HORIZON OF EXPECTATION is continually evolving. A reader's understanding of a text depends on the reader's horizon of expectation, which builds on all previous works and experiences. So what a reader expects a text to do will change as the reader reads other texts and accumulates more life experiences. This even applies to the rereading of a text. When certain understandings are established in the first reading, a later reading allows for new questions to be raised and old lingering questions to be answered. For example, a person studying the Gospel of Mark with little critical background reading may sense a certain

uneasiness with the manner in which the disciples are portrayed. If this same reader then reads a book or books that point out the literary role that the imperceptiveness of the disciples plays, not only will old questions be answered, but also new ones will be generated, only to be answered upon further critical reading.

The third thesis deals with the manner in which the horizon of expectation affects many different *audiences* over an extended period of time. Since readers and the conditions within which readers engage a text change, the text will have different effects at any historical moment. A work that is intended for a specific society at a specific time will not mean the same to that society twenty years later. Jauss calls this phenomenon the horizontal change. But the opposite can also happen. An author may write a work not intended for a particular audience but having a significant influence on a later society. Obviously, numerous texts in the HEBREW BIBLE had a formative impact on the writers of the NT.

The fourth thesis concerns the RECONSTRUCTION of the horizon of expectation and the production of a literary work. Reconstructing the horizon of expectation of the author and contemporary audience enables the contemporary reader to discover how the work should be viewed and understood (Jauss, "Literary History," 171). It points out the hermeneutic difference between the past and the current understanding of the text. Discovering how a work would have been viewed enables it to reach beyond its own contemporary audience. Hans-Georg Gadamer, however, differed with Jauss on this point. Gadamer believed that a work can no longer stand within its original horizon because the original historical horizon will always be consumed within the horizon of the present. But Jauss argues that a reader who is not part of the author's original audience must learn what the horizon of expectation might have been for the original audience by considering the reading and writing style of the period and the social, environmental, geographical, religious, and political contexts.

The fifth thesis focuses on the *evolution* of the text's HORIZON OF EXPECTATION. As new texts pose questions, the questions generated by old texts are answered. After a reader's theories and expectations have been upset, many questions may arise that the text has not answered. As a reader engages other texts, however, these original questions may be answered and new meaning found in the first text. Thus a text can be read hundreds of times with new meaning always evolving. Literary evolution is the principle in "which the new work arises against the background of preceding or competing works, reaches the high point of a literary period as successful form, is quickly reproduced and thereby increasingly automatized, until finally when the next form has broken through the former, vegetates on a used-up genre" (Jauss, *Question and Answer*, 49).

In his sixth thesis, Jauss argues that works *change* diachronically (*see* DIACHRONIC). Not only does a text change over time for a particular reader; it also takes on new meaning with each generation. One generation passes down its understanding of the text, with the next generation beginning where the preceding one ended. Thus a text's meaning is always evolving across time: diachronically. This means that as meaning perpetually evolves by building on itself, meaning is never settled or replicated.

In his seventh thesis, Jauss further develops his idea that *social influences* modify interpretations. Every social influence (from government programs to job pressures) has an impact on INTERPRETATION. While general ASSUMPTIONS may be made dependent on the major factors in a reader's life, the plethora of influencing factors precludes any predictability of the way a reader will interpret a text at any given moment.

It is obvious that Jauss based his theory on the triangle of interpretation, the points of which represent the three major constituents of interpretation: author, text, and reader. The author has his or her own interpretation of the text, the text holds the possibility of any number of interpretations, and the audience may create any number of interpretations. For Jauss, since each point of the triangle plays a significant part in the interpretive process, none of the points should be neglected or prioritized in any act of interpretation.

Bibliography. Hans Robert Jauss, *The Aesthetic Experience and Literary Hermeneutics* (trans. Michael Shaw; Theory and History of Literature 3; Minneapolis: University of Minnesota Press, 1982); idem, "Literary History as a Challenge to Literary Theory," in *Critical Theory since 1965* (ed. Hazard Adams and Leroy Searle; Tallahassee: University of Florida Press, 1986), 164–83; idem, *Question and Answer: Forms of Dialogic Understanding* (Minneapolis: University of Minnesota Press, 1989); idem, *Toward an Aesthetic of Reception* (trans. Timothy Bahti; Theory and History of Literature 2; Minneapolis: University of Minnesota Press, 1982).

RÉCIT

A term in the NARRATOLOGY of Gérard Genette, designating one of the three main elements in NARRATIVE. Récit is the order of events as they are presented in the TEXT. It is roughly equivalent to PLOT. Thus the CHRONOLOGY of the actual events within a STORY (*HISTORIE*) may differ from the sequence of their presentation (récit). FLASHBACK demonstrates the difference between the two. For example, in Jon. 4:2a we discover that Jonah prays to Yahweh. Here is the NARRATION of an event that occurred after God's initial commission in 1:2 and before Jonah's flight in 1:3. It is an account of a conversation that Jonah had with Yahweh several EPISODES back.

RECOGNITION STORY

A STORY in the GOSPELS in which a person discovers Jesus's identity. According to Leland Ryken (37), the focus is on the "moment of recognition." Two elements go into identifying a story as a recognition story: the circumstances surrounding the recognition and the nature of the character's recognition. These stories not only work to explain who Jesus is; they also further the PLOT by creating a variety of perspectives from which the reader may view Jesus. In Mark, some of the recognitions are valid (e.g., those of the characters [6:2–3; 8:28], NARRATOR [1:1], and God [1:11; 9:7]), and some are invalid (e.g., those of Jesus's opponents [2:6–8, 15–16; 3:22–28; 15:6–11]). The reader is forced to reconcile these various identifications into a plausible portrait.

Bibliography. Leland Ryken, *Words of Life: A Literary Introduction to the New Testament* (Grand Rapids: Baker, 1987).

RECONSTRUCTION

In HERMENEUTICS, the process by which an interpreter of a TEXT tries to create an understanding that objectifies the author's INTENTION. Most scholars, however, recognize that reconstruction is a creative and continuous process and thus always open to revision and modification. The interpreter must try to reach behind the text itself and reconstruct the reason for the text in the first place and also to get at the author's thought processes. In this sense, then, INTERPRETATION in terms of reconstruction becomes a process that reverses the process of the AUTHOR's composition. Yet the reservation that many critics have toward the concept focuses on the extent to which interpreters can divest themselves of their SOCIAL LOCATION in order to create a plausible reconstruction.

RECONTEXTUALIZATION

In HERMENEUTICS, the act of applying an INTERPRETATION of a past TEXT to a new situation. This process itself has a long history in biblical interpretation, stretching back to Jewish midrashic TRADITION (*see* MIDRASH; RABBINIC HERMENEUTICS), in which both HAGGADAH and HALAKAH were reinterpreted in new and novel situations. The writers of both the HEBREW BIBLE and the NT also recontextualized earlier texts. For example, Phyllis Trible has argued that the AUTHOR of the Song of Songs recontextualized the creation account in Gen. 2–3 by a process of reversal. The author of Mark's GOSPEL refers directly or indirectly to the HEBREW BIBLE some 160 times. Paul recontextualizes the idea of circumcision and the EXODUS and in the process changes their MEANING.

Recontextualization also refers to a community's use of an inherited text within a CONTEXT quite different from the text's original one. Some scholars believe that this practice is nothing more than an application of the text's original meaning to a new situation. Other scholars, however, believe that meaning is the result of the context in which the inherited text is interpreted, and since contexts change, so does meaning.

Bibliography. Phyllis Trible, *God and the Rhetoric of Sexuality* (Philadelphia: Fortress, 1978).

RECUPERATION

A term in a variety of CRITICISMS, including the STRUCTURALISM of Jonathan Culler and the poststructuralism of Roland Barthes and Jacques Derrida, that refers to the means of appropriating a TEXT (esp. a LITERARY text) in terms of the STRUCTUREs that make it comprehensible. Culler describes five CODES that are at work in a reader's process of recuperating or appropriating a text. First is the social code (or text) that defines reality for the reader. The second is also a social code but differs from the first one as a set of ASSUMPTIONS that a group holds but are open for modification or revision. The third code is the reader's LITERARY COMPETENCE in terms of the ability to recognize LITERARY CONVENTIONS associated with different GENRES. Fourth is the code established by the text itself in terms of values that may differ from those of other texts. And the fifth code is the intertextual one (*see* INTERTEXTUALITY), meaning that the reader appropriates a text in terms of its relationship to other texts that are in some way related to it.

If the above codes are understood as texts (in the sense that they provide the FRAMEWORKS for reading), then recuperation is the process through which one text (the literary one) is "effaced" by another one. Derrida, then, can refer to the recuperative text (i.e., the code through which a literary text is read) as erasing the material text (the literary one). However, this process of erasure or effacement is, according to Derrida, the precondition of SIGNIFICATION. In other words, signification in this sense results in the "closure of the text."

The recuperative texts (codes) are the lens through which any literary text is recuperated and signifies. The latter idea is reminiscent of Louis

Althusser's idea of IDEOLOGY. If ideology is the social, economic, political, theological, or other means of knowing the world or any object in it, then the recuperation of a text does mean that the material text is effaced or at least rewritten in terms that the ideology of the reader will allow. Nothing takes place outside ideology. In this respect, then, the "real" meaning of the text is never accessible, is always beyond reach, and the coded, textualized recuperation is substituted for the "real" meaning. Every literary text will be rewritten from within a preexisting labyrinth of texts and codes. Since any CRITICAL METHODOLOGY is a recuperative "text," every critical reading is a recuperation and thus an effacement or erasure of the literary text. This idea, then, precludes any hope of recovering an original intentional meaning, a historical RECONSTRUC-TION, or an original audience understanding.

Bibliography. Louis Althusser, "Ideology and Ideological State Apparatuses: Notes toward an Investigation," in *Lenin and Philosophy, and Other Essays* (trans. Ben Brewster; London: New Left Books, 1971), 121–73; Jonathan Culler, *Structuralist Poetics: Structuralism, Linguistics, and the Study of Literature* (London: Routledge & Kegan Paul, 1975); Jacques Derrida, "White Mythology," in *Margins of Philosophy* (trans. Alan Bass; Chicago: University of Chicago Press, 1982).

REDACTION

The process of splicing and editing older, shorter sources (usually written) into larger TEXTS. The process is guided by the REDACTOR's literary purpose. In NT studies, the AUTHORS of the GOSPELS are considered redactors. *See* REDACTION CRITICISM.

REDACTION CRITICISM

A movement toward a more concentrated focus on the TEXT as a whole. In contrast to FORM CRITI-CISM, redaction criticism emphasizes the unity of the text, the manner in which the smaller units are arranged to form a single unified whole. Although Günther Bornkamm and Hans Conzelmann were doing redaction criticism earlier, Willi Marxsen is credited with being the first (in 1956) to use the German term REDAKTIONSGESCHICHTE, "his-

tory of redaction," in studies of the Gospels, as in the subtitle of his *Mark the Evangelist.* That book, Bornkamm's coauthored *Tradition and Interpretation in Matthew* (offering his 1948 essay "The Stilling of the Storm in Matthew"), and Conzelmann's *Theology of St. Luke* (German, 1954) are three of the earliest and best examples of the method applied.

The roots of redaction criticism, however, probably go back to the work of earlier scholars. Hermann Reimarus (1694–1768) was the first to offer evidence that the GOSPELS were not written strictly from a historical perspective: they had a theological character about them. David Friedrich Strauss (1808–74) expanded Reimarus's idea by claiming that the Gospels were creative MYTH, based on religious concepts derived from experiences within JUDAISM or HELLENISM. Strauss also introduced the idea of the Markan hypothesis, which claims that Mark was the first Gospel and that since it is closer to the actual events, it provides the best source for establishing the truth for the life and teachings of Jesus (*see* MARKAN PRIORITY). But perhaps the work of Günther Bornkamm with his claim that the AUTHOR of Matthew interpreted and modified previous TRA-DITION, revealing himself as an author with his own theological and evangelistic purpose, set the table for applying redaction criticism to the whole of the BIBLE.

The basic ASSUMPTION underlying redaction criticism is that the authors were guided in their adaptation, modification, and SELECTION AND ARRANGEMENT of their sources by theological purposes. The theological purpose of an author can be discovered by examining how that writer uses sources. Writers selected, arranged, and altered their sources and traditions according to their own theological purposes or those of their community. This means that SOURCE CRITICISM and form criticism are PRESUPPOSITIONS for redaction criticism. Redaction criticism focuses on the author's use and alteration of the traditions rather than on the *SITZ IM LEBEN* of the traditions themselves. Sources and individual units of tradition must be available before an interpreter can determine to what extent and in what ways an author has adapted and reapplied the sources and traditions. It follows that redaction criticism focuses on four concerns: (1) the selection of traditional material and source; (2) the adaptation and modification of the material; (3) the arrangement of the material; and (4) the extent of the author's own theological contribution to the text.

When a text's sources are available to the interpreter, conclusions about the author's theological purposes reflected in the obvious modifications, selections, and arrangement are relatively simple to make. For example, if MARKAN PRIORITY is assumed when studying Luke, we can easily observe the ways in which Luke modifies his source. If the EXEGETE cannot detect any sources underlying a text, it becomes impossible to demonstrate any redactional activity. So what happens if the interpreter has no available underlying sources or when there is evidence that the author has simply incorporated a unit of tradition without any modification? The Gospel of Mark is a case in point. What are Mark's sources? The answer lies in the more modern approach of redaction critics to view a text as an entity within itself. This approach supposes that a final REDACTOR has produced a final VERSION of a text, and the text itself supplies the primary evidence for discovering the author's theological purpose. The interpreter must examine in detail the way in which each individual part of a text relates to the other parts and thus the way in which the text as a whole presents its message. This observation obviously vitiates any attempt to harmonize texts that make use of the same or similar traditions. The Gospels should not become only sources for constructing a homogenized gospel story (Hayes and Holladay, 105). Each Gospel is a biased (*see* TENDENZ; TENDENZ CRITICISM) NARRATIVE that has its own message to communicate. In the Hebrew Bible, both the CHRONICLER and the author of Samuel–Kings have their own messages, and any attempts to harmonize these two accounts of the same period stand in opposition to redaction criticism.

Redaction criticism makes it possible to speak of the theology of Mark, the theology of Luke, or the theology of Matthew. But while redaction criticism had its official beginning in the study of the SYNOPTIC GOSPELS, it has also been applied to portions of the Hebrew Bible, especially to the texts in which there is obvious use of previous traditions. For example, the Chronicler recasts certain stories and traditions found in Samuel–Kings. A case in point is the Chronicler's reinterpretation of the David material in a much more idealized fashion. A similar recasting of stories can be seen within Deuteronomy and even with smaller units such as 1 Sam. 8–12, in which two different viewpoints of the monarchy are juxtaposed.

Bibliography. Günther Bornkamm, Gerhard Barth, and Heinz Joachim Held, *Tradition and Interpretation in Matthew* (trans. Percy Scott; Philadelphia: Westminster, 1963); Hans Conzelmann, *The Theology of St. Luke* (trans. Geoffrey Buswell; New York: Harper, 1961); John Hayes and Carl Holladay, *Biblical Exegesis: A Beginner's Handbook* (Atlanta: John Knox, 1987); Willi Marxsen, *Mark the Evangelist* (trans. James Boyce et al.; Nashville: Abingdon, 1969); W. Randolph Tate, *Biblical Interpretation: An Integrated Approach* (rev. ed.; Peabody, MA: Hendrickson, 1997).

REDACTOR

One who compiles, selects, arranges, and edits both oral and written sources into a new LITERARY document. *See* REDACTION CRITICISM.

REDAKTIONSGESCHICHTE

German for "history of redaction" and equivalent to REDACTION CRITICISM or COMPOSITION CRITICISM.

REDEMPTIVE HISTORY. *See*

HEILSGESCHICHTE

REFERENCE

The act of denoting (*see* DENOTATION) an object, idea, or state of affairs within a particular context. A referent is the object, idea, or state of affairs that is denoted. Generally, when persons refer to things in everyday life, the MEANING is clear. For example, if one person points to a telephone and asks to use it, there arises no misunderstanding. Problems arise, however, in written DISCOURSE. Discussions of reference sometimes make a distinction between reference and SENSE: "sense" is what an utterance or sentence states; "reference" is that about which the utterance or sentence is stated. At this semantic level problems arise due to the fact that there is not a one-to-one correspondence between sense and reference.

REFERENTIAL (QUALITY OF) LANGUAGE

In LITERARY theory, language that intends to denote (*see* DENOTATION) something. Usually this type of language seeks to be extremely precise, such as the language of philosophy and science. Referential language is distinct from emotive language, which seeks to communicate or arouse emotional reactions toward the object or SUBJECT. The referential quality of language is the relationship between the language of the TEXT and the world projected by that language. This must not be confused with the MIMETIC QUALITY OF LANGUAGE, which is the relationship between the REAL WORLD and the WORLD OF THE TEXT.

REFERENTIAL MEANING

The extralinguistic object, situation, or idea to which an item in a TEXT may refer. According to many biblical scholars, this REFERENCE places constraints on what readers may infer about textual items. In other words, part of doing HERMENEUTICS is the responsible assessment of the extralinguistic situations to which items in a text refer because these limit the range of possible interpretive options available to the reader. For example, John's description of the Laodicean church in Rev. 3:15–16—"You are neither cold nor hot. I wish that you were either cold or hot. So because you are lukewarm, and neither cold nor hot, I am about to spit you out of my mouth"—should be understood according to its extralinguistic reference. According to Rudwick and Green, the church is being compared with the strengths and weakness of the city. Hierapolis was located within sight of Laodicea and was well known for its hot calcium salt waters, which were prized for their healing properties. Also close to Laodicea was the city of Colossae, famous for its cold, refreshing stream. As the city of Laodicea outgrew its water supply, it was forced to pipe water in from a long distance through stone pipes. When the water arrived, it was warm and contained a sludgy deposit, making it almost undrinkable. While the hot water of Hierapolis healed and the cold water of Colossae refreshed, the Laodicean church brought neither spiritual healing nor refreshment. Like the water supply, the works of the Laodicean church were fit only to be spit out. The reference, however, may also be to the three types of baths typical in a Roman bathhouse—the frigadarium, the caldarium, and the tepidarium. The first was the cold bath, the second the hot, and the third the lukewarm bath used as a transition between the first two and not intended to be a place of refreshment. These possible historical references place parameters around what the reader may infer about the meaning of this passage in the book of Revelation.

Bibliography. M. J. S. Rudwick and E. M. B. Green, "The Laodicean Lukewarmness," *Expository Times* 69 (1957–58): 176–78.

REFLEXIVITY

The act of referring to oneself. Reflexivity, however, has become one of the concepts that most clearly distinguishes MODERNISM from POSTMODERNISM. While modernism may be characterized by reflection, postmodernism is marked by reflexivity (Thiselton, 119). In postmodern theory, *reflexivity* refers to the theorist's awareness that his or her theory or method is itself a culturally constructed artifact and that it is positioned within the flux of time and history. In other words, it refers to the awareness that LITERARY and cultural theories are not disinterested METALANGUAGES that stand above the fray of human interests and subjectivity.

Bibliography. Linda A. Hutcheon, *Poetics of Postmodernism: History, Theory, Fiction* (London: Routledge, 1988);

Anthony Thiselton, *New Horizons in Hermeneutics* (Grand Rapids: Zondervan, 1992).

REFORMATION CANON

Also known as the Protestant canon; this CANON, developed during the Protestant Reformation, rejected the APOCRYPHA, which was included in the CATHOLIC CANON of SCRIPTURE. The Reformation canon includes the thirty-nine books of the HEBREW BIBLE (but in an order different from the Hebrew Bible) plus the twenty-seven books of the NT. The following list illustrates the different orders and groupings between the Roman Catholic canon and the Reformation canon of the OT. The texts belonging the Apocrypha are in italics.

Catholic Canon	Reformation Canon
Pentateuch	**Pentateuch**
Genesis	Genesis
Exodus	Exodus
Leviticus	Leviticus
Numbers	Numbers
Deuteronomy	Deuteronomy
History	**History**
Joshua	Joshua
Judges	Judges
Ruth	Ruth
1–2 Samuel	1–2 Samuel
1–2 Kings	1–2 Kings
1–2 Chronicles/1–2 Paralipomenon	1–2 Chronicles
Ezra and Nehemiah	Ezra and Nehemiah
Tobit	
Judith	
Esther (*with additions*)	Esther
1–2 Maccabees	
Poetry and Wisdom	**Poetry and Wisdom**
Job	Job
Psalms	Psalms
Proverbs	Proverbs
Ecclesiastes	Ecclesiastes
Song of Songs/Canticle of Canticles	Song of Songs
Wisdom of Solomon	
Ecclesiasticus/Wisdom of Jesus Son of Sirach/Ben Sira/Sirach	
Prophets	**Prophets**
Isaiah	Isaiah
Jeremiah	Jeremiah

Catholic Canon	Reformation Canon
Lamentations	Lamentations
Baruch	
Ezekiel	Ezekiel
Daniel (*with additions*)	Daniel
Hosea/Osee	Hosea
Joel	Joel
Amos	Amos
Obadiah/Abdia	Obadiah
Jonah	Jonah
Micah/Michea	Micah
Nahum	Nahum
Habakkuk/Habacuc	Habakkuk
Zephaniah/Sophonia	Zephaniah
Haggai/Aggai	Haggai
Zechariah	Zechariah
Malachi	Malachi

REFRAIN

A word, phrase, or line repeated at intervals in a poem and especially at the end of a STANZA. An example is the line "O LORD, our Sovereign, how majestic is your name in all the earth!" which occurs at the beginning and end of Ps. 8.

REFUTATIO

In classical RHETORIC, the part of the ARGUMENTATIO in which the arguments of the opponent are refuted. *See* RHETORICAL CRITICISM.

REIFICATION

A term in MARXIST CRITICISM, especially in that of Georg Lukács, for the economic process through which social relations between humans are transformed in capitalism into relations between objects or things. These relations are then described in scientific and mathematical terms. According to Lukács, there are two components to the phenomenon of reification: the objective and the subjective (*see* OBJECTIVE KNOWLEDGE; SUBJECTIVE KNOWLEDGE). Objective reification is the process by which human relations come to be viewed as real things, natural givens, thus concealing the HISTORICITY, the historical construction of the relations. But reification also has a subjective impact on the individual worker's consciousness and on that of humanity as a whole. Lukács explains this by claiming that both the production process and the world present themselves to individuals as fragmented. Reification also fosters the human ASSUMPTION that the world is fundamentally this way and therefore unchangeable. Thus, most literature is written and read by persons whose reified consciousness cannot grasp the world as it really is because the consciousnesses of these persons are fragmented. The literature and its INTERPRETATIONS of modern capitalistic cultures therefore will tend to reinforce reification.

Bibliography. Georg Lukács, *History and Class Consciousness: Studies in Marxist Dialectics* (London: Merlin, 1971); idem, *The Meaning of Contemporary Realism* (London: Merlin, 1963).

RELEVANCE THEORY AND BIBLICAL INTERPRETATION

A communication theory that explains how language communicates meaning, even or especially across language barriers, by means of certain universals. Relevance theory developed out of progress in the cognitive sciences over the past thirty to forty years. During the early stages of cognitive studies, cognitive scientists believed that MEANING is not fully transferable and that no universals exist across languages. Since that time, however, scientists have found that the cognitive functions of the human brain regarding the processing of language are universals rather than particulars.

Relevance theory was developed by Dan Sperber and Deidre Wilson in 1986. Sperber, a French researcher turned cognitive scientist with the Centre National de la Recherche Scientifique in Paris, collaborated with Wilson, who was a British linguist, philosopher, and reader in linguistics at University College London. They wrote *Relevance: Communication and Cognition*, the first work to introduce relevance theory and explain its worth in cognitive science as a central factor in human communication. Revised and updated in 1995, the book asserts that relevance theory is "a general theory of cognition and communication that provides a model for understanding how texts and CONTEXTS, authors and readers, collaborate in the communication of meaning" (253). Although usually classified as a contextualist theory, relevance theory belongs to a theoretical branch of pragmatic LINGUISTICS. Since its inception, relevance theory has gained notoriety and has become useful for the fields of PRAGMATICS, linguistics, and cognitive psychology.

Relevance theory examines how implication in language contributes to what is explicitly said. According to Sperber and Wilson, the goal of relevance theory is "to derive rich and precise nondemonstrative inferences about the communicator's informative intent" (254). Relevance is the potential property of an input to any perceptual or cognitive process to yield positive cognitive effects, also called contextual effects. Theorists evaluate input and deem these effects positive, or relevant, only when they increase rather than decrease the accuracy of information the brain takes in about the world around it. This theory, concerned with how language is processed, applies to both oral and written communication.

Katalin Egri Ku-Mesu, former senior lecturer at the Institute of English and American Studies at Kossuth University, Hungary, says that "relevance itself is defined in terms of contextual effect and processing effort" (44). Contextual effects are the results of new information interacting with a CONTEXT of already-existing ASSUMPTIONS, and this new information produces one of three types of effects: (1) new information may strengthen an existing assumption, (2) new information may contradict and eliminate an existing assumption, or (3) new information may yield a contextual implication (i.e., new material arising only from the combination of the information and the assumption; Ku-Mesu, 44). Ku-Mesu reduces relevance theory to the following expression: "The greater the effort required to derive contextual effects is, the lower the relevance will be. At the same time, the greater the contextual effects are, the greater the relevance will be" (44).

Relevance theory works within the domain of ostensive-inferential communication, that is, with the speaker's intention to communicate and the hearer's responsibility to infer that intention. Utterance INTERPRETATION, the inferring of intention, requires the detection and processing of a speaker or writer's explicatures and implicatures. The explicature is the explicit meaning revealed in the words and is considered textual information. Conversely, the implicature, or contextual information, is any implied meaning, which can be weak or strong. Communication is successful only when both parties cooperate, in the sense that the speaker believes that his or her utterance is relevant, and the hearer infers that the speaker intends to communicate. Communication is unsuccessful when input does not make a positive change in the hearer's cognitive environment. Gene Green points out that since "relevance theory postulates that humans process information in a way that seeks to balance processing effort with benefits received," processing stops "when the benefit is found. . . . When no benefit is found, . . . communication fails" (82).

According to Robyn Carston, there are two principles of relevance. The first, or cognitive, principle is that "human cognition is geared towards the maximization of relevance" (379). This means that the human brain tends toward gaining as many cognitive effects as it can for as little processing effort as possible. The second, or communicative, principle states that "every act of ostensive communication communicates a presumption of its own optimal relevance" (379). Ostensive communications, or utterances, come with an intended degree of relevance for their given contexts. At the heart of relevance theory, therefore, is the communicatory relationship between the intention of the text and the reader's response to it. Intention and application are not mutually exclusive, and they are balanced through use of relevance theory's unique concept of inference. As Carston explains, inference is the taking into account of the speaker's competence and preferences (15). Inference, then, promotes the interaction of the text and the reader. Relevance theory contends that it is possible to successfully unite intention and response for the overall effect of meaningful communication.

Tim Meadowcroft acknowledges that relevance theory "has had little interaction with biblical studies" (627). He observes that "the application of [relevance theory] explicitly to biblical interpretation is yet in its infancy and is attracting . . . interest . . . in Bible translation circles. . . . [It] is helpful in its recognition of both intention and contextual response in the process of communication" (625).

In the process of reading Scripture, there is always a tension between the intent of the biblical text (and its author) and the response of the reader. By redefining the position of the reader with respect to the text, relevance theory purports to balance and mediate between two incorrect approaches to Scripture interpretation. The first incorrect approach reads the biblical text subjectively, only in terms of what it means to oneself. The second incorrect approach views the text objectively, as being entirely outside of, and disconnected from, oneself (as opposed to engaging with it in order to make meaningful application). Both approaches represent undesirable extremes. Relevance theorists, however, suggest that these categories do not have to be mutually exclusive. Instead, their theory "challenges any hermeneutical approach that either denies the possibility of communicative intent or denies the importance of non-literal implication" (625). It does this by "appreciat[ing] the role of the reader in interpretation without surrendering respect both for the text and for the possibility of agency and intentionality that comes with an emphasis on the author" (614).

Green explains that "the books of the Bible are true human-to-human communication, and as such, the interpreter, whether ancient or modern, must attend to the recovery of both the explicatures and implicatures in order to understand the message intended by the biblical author" (84). The goal for both ancient and contemporary readers is the same: to find out what the biblical authors intended to communicate. Ancient and original readers accomplish this task by paying attention to the textual (ostensive) and contextual (inferential) information "drawn from [readers'] common cognitive environment" (84). Contemporary readers perform the task by "draw[ing] the relevant contextual material from both discourse and our fragmentary knowledge of the ancients' common cognitive environment" (84). Green points out that exegetical commentaries perform this task for contemporary readers because they operate from within the principles of relevance theory to discover authorial intention "against the background of the ancient languages and cultures, including the intersection of each biblical book with other biblical literature" (85).

Ernst-August Gutt examines Matt. 9:14–15 in light of relevance principles. In verse 14, John the Baptist's disciples ask, "Why do we and the Pharisees fast often, but your [Jesus's] disciples do not fast?" Jesus answers in a METAPHOR, which Gutt examines in terms of relevance theory. In Jesus's metaphor of the bridegroom and the wedding, the most highly accessible referents in the context are Jesus and his disciples, respectively. The resemblances between the actual people and the metaphor are accessible from Jesus's utterance and from the contextual assumptions, or implications, in the metaphor. As a result, when the reader applies the metaphor to Jesus and his disciples, Jesus is a cause of joy for his disciples: when he is with them, they cannot be sad, nor can they fast. When he is taken away, the disciples will be sad and will fast. Gutt explains that it "is clear from the inferential chains [that] . . . what Jesus is . . . saying is that for his disciples, his personal presence or absence determines whether or when they fast" (2).

Regarding implications, or contextual assumptions, Gutt credits John's disciples with "ask[ing] about [fasting that was] certainly . . . prescribed by the laws and traditions of Judaism. That time of fasting was fixed by law or tradition, not by feelings of sadness" (2). Therefore, Gutt concludes that in opposition to the Judaic background out of which John's disciples were operating, Jesus's response, instead of being a clear-cut answer, implies through context that fasting is not so much a religious duty as it is an expression of the disciples' feelings about Jesus, determined by their personal relationship with him. Gutt further points out that "by his an-swer Jesus is effectively disputing the recognized authority of the Judaistic regulations about fasting, and by implication putting himself above the ordinances of Judaism" (3). This view is consistent with other Scriptures proclaiming Jesus as the divinely authorized Messiah, who is establishing a new order outranking the old order of the law.

Most relevance theorists feel that the method provides a balanced approach to biblical interpretation. For example, Karen Jobes points out that relevance theory "seems compatible with Christian beliefs" because of "its emphasis on the speaker's or author's intention to communicate" (782). Relevance theorists assume that the text is a legitimate authority, an assumption congruent with what many Christians believe.

Additionally, relevance theory is rooted in an understanding of cognitive processes that are not language or culture specific, leading to an assumption that biblical interpretation and translation for any passage of the Bible always involves at least two languages. Relevance theory also explores the role that context plays in meaning, and Jobes comments that "previous models of language acknowledged but did not explicate [context's role]" (782). Relevance theory's emphasis on context considers attention to events and traditions an integral part of interpretation.

Bibliography. Robyn Carston, "Relevance Theory," in *Routledge Companion to the Philosophy of Language* (London: Linguistics, University College London, 2011); idem, *Thoughts and Utterances* (Oxford: Blackwell, 2002); Gene L. Green, "Relevance Theory and Theological Interpretation: Thoughts on Metarepresentation," *Journal of Theological Interpretation* 4, no. 1 (2010): 75–90; Ernst-August Gutt, "Matthew 9:4–17 in the Light of Relevance Theory," *Notes on Translation* 113 (1986): 13–20; Karen H. Jobes, "Relevance Theory and the Translation of Scripture," *Journal of the Evangelical Theological Society* 50, no. 4 (2007): 773–97; Katalin Egri Ku-Mesu, "Whose Relevance? Interpretation of Texts by a Hybrid Audience," *Edinburgh Working Papers in Applied Linguistics* 8 (1997): 44–53; Tim Meadowcroft, "Relevance as a Mediating Category in the Reading of Biblical Texts: Venturing beyond the Hermeneutical Circle," *Journal of the Evangelical Theological Society* 45.4 (2002): 611–27; Dan Sperber and Deidre Wilson, *Relevance: Communication and Cognition* (2nd ed.; Oxford: Blackwell, 1995).

RELIGIONSGESCHICHTE

A German term commonly translated as "the history of religions," referring to the historical study of the origins and growth of religions and their relationships to each other.

RELIGIONSGESCHICHTLICHE SCHULE

German for "history-of-religions school," the name for a group of German Protestant scholars in the late nineteenth and early twentieth centuries who studied and interpreted the writings and history of ancient Israel and early Christianity within the CONTEXT of the religions of the ancient Near East (Soulen and Soulen, 161). This group argued for the consistent application of historical research to the study of ancient Israelite religion and early Christianity. In other words, the approach of this group of scholars included the examination of these religions and their TEXTS in a comparative relationship to other religions of the period and in light of the archaeological and iconographical findings from the cultures surrounding both Israel and early Christianity. The ASSUMPTION underlying this approach was that Israel was strongly influenced by Mesopotamian, Syrian, and Egyptian cultures and that Christianity was influenced by Greek and Roman cultures (esp. the MYSTERY RELIGIONS).

This approach clashed with the apologetic Protestant liberalism of the late nineteenth century and later, in the 1930s, saw a new reaction in the more theological response to its strict historical focus in the BIBLICAL THEOLOGY MOVEMENT (Klein, Blomberg, and Hubbard, 49).

Bibliography. William Klein, Craig Blomberg, and Robert Hubbard Jr., *Introduction to Biblical Interpretation* (Dallas: Word, 1993); Richard N. Soulen and R. Kendall Soulen, *Handbook of Biblical Criticism* (3rd ed.; Louisville: Westminster John Knox, 2001).

REPERTOIRE

In LITERARY studies, a term relating to both reader and TEXT. With respect to the text, *repertoire* refers to the TEXTUAL STRATEGIES, LITERARY DEVICES, structural elements, and grammatical elements that make up the text itself and confront the reader in the process of INTERPRETATION. With respect to the reader, *repertoire* refers to the things that the reader brings to the reading of the text. This matrix of objects includes ASSUMPTIONS (political, methodological, religious, literary, ideological, etc.) as well as the level of the reader's LITERARY COMPETENCE. In READER-RESPONSE CRITICISM, MEANING is the result of a DIALOGUE between the repertoire of the text and the repertoire of the reader. *See* LITERARY REPERTOIRE.

REPETITION

An integral element in almost all POETRY and much PROSE that may take the FORM of repeated sounds, words, phrases, syllables, and even ideas. Thus REFRAIN, ASSONANCE, RHYME, ANAPHORA, and ALLITERATION are all forms of repetition.

REPETITION OF SEQUENCES

A REPETITION of an activity, usually three times or three times plus a fourth, with an INTENSIFICATION from one to the next occurrence. Examples include Balaam's three failures to give directions to the ass (Num. 22:22–30) and the catastrophes in Job (1:13–19).

REQUEST FORMULA

A type of injunction occurring regularly in Paul's LETTERS—for example, "Now I appeal to you, brothers and sisters, by the name of our Lord Jesus Christ, that all of you be in agreement and that there be no divisions among you, but that you be united in the same mind and the same purpose" (1 Cor. 1:10). A verb occurs, followed by a direct address and the request. This request or appeal formula, however, occurs in other places within the body of the letter, especially where new material is introduced. *See* EPISTOLARY LITERATURE.

RESCUE MOTIF

An ARCHETYPE serving as a means of structuring a STORY: a person is placed in a dangerous and helpless situation through the ACTIONS of a villain, only to be rescued by someone after sufficient

COMPLICATIONS. Examples are the rescue of Peter from prison in Acts 12 and the rescue of Paul and Silas from prison in Acts 16.

RESCUE STORY

According to James Bailey and Lyle Vander Broek, a TYPE of STORY in the GOSPELS in which Jesus's followers are in a situation from which Jesus must rescue them (e.g., Mark 4:35–41). This type of story can also be found in Acts, where different characters find themselves imprisoned and must be rescued by supernatural means. *See* RESCUE MOTIF.

Bibliography. James Bailey and Lyle Vander Broek, *Literary Forms in the New Testament* (Louisville: Westminster John Knox, 1992).

RESISTING READER, THE. *See* READING AGAINST THE GRAIN

RESOLUTION. *See* DENOUEMENT

RESURRECTION STORY

Stories in the GOSPELS serving as the legitimation of the early Christian foundational claim that Jesus died, was bodily resurrected, and appeared to his followers, as foretold by the Jewish SCRIPTURES (e.g., 1 Cor. 15:4–5). All four of the CANONICAL GOSPELS include a resurrection account, yet with varying details. Mark's account describes three women as they approach the tomb and find it open with a "young man" sitting inside on the right side. Matthew describes two women who come to the tomb, which is guarded by soldiers, to find that an earthquake has occurred and that an "angel" has descended from heaven and rolled the stone from the tomb and is sitting on it. As the women leave to take the angel's message to the DISCIPLES, Jesus meets them and repeats the angel's message to them. Matthew then adds the accounts of the Jewish elders' bribing the guards to broadcast that the disciples had stolen the body during the night and Jesus's instructions to his disciples in Galilee. Luke's account differs even more in that an uncertain number of women find not one being at the tomb but "two men," who give them a message that is significantly different from that of the young man in Mark and the angel in Matthew. Luke then adds an account of Peter's return to the tomb, Jesus's appearance to two disciples on the road to Emmaus, Jesus's appearance to the other disciples, and the ascension. Finally, John's account records that only Mary Magdalene comes to the tomb. After she reports to the disciples what she has found, Peter and another disciple visit the tomb. John's Gospel then reports Jesus's appearance to Mary and to his disciples, the unbelief of Thomas, and Jesus's appearance to seven disciples.

Various reasons have been offered to account for the differences in the four accounts. For example, Matthew and Luke used Mark's account but edited on the basis of their unique theological purposes; each evangelist had different VERSIONS of the same traditional STORY; the stories were the creation of the early Christian community, and as they circulated orally in a variety of places, they took on different details; and the four evangelists felt free to fashion the stories they received to fit their purposes and audiences.

RETENTION

In the READER-RESPONSE CRITICISM of Wolfgang Iser, the information that the reader holds in MEMORY at any one time in the reading process. For Iser, the perspective with which the reader is involved at any one moment is the THEME. But this theme is set in relief by the previous perspectives with which the reader has been concerned. The previous parts of the TEXT constitute what Iser calls the horizon, which is made up of the theme formulated by the reading up to this point. These complementary concepts of theme and horizon point up a strategic element in LITERARY texts pertaining to the relationship between EXPECTATION and memory (retention). Every previous part of the text is viewed within the CONTEXT of a horizon, but in the time flow of reading, an existing theme is immediately transferred into the BACKGROUND, thus becoming part of the horizon (memory) from which the next part of the text will be appropriated. *See* PROTENSION.

REVERSAL

A TYPE of IRONY in which there occurs a change of fortune for the PROTAGONIST or ANTAGONIST in a STORY (e.g., Job; Haman and Mordecai in the book of Esther).

REVISED ENGLISH BIBLE (REB)

A 1989 revision of the NEW ENGLISH BIBLE by a multidenominational group of British scholars. The translators opted for an easy style of English that would be suitable for liturgical use and readily accessible to the average reader.

REVISED STANDARD VERSION (RSV)

A revision of the AMERICAN STANDARD VERSION (1901). The translators retained much of the elevated language of the KJV so that it would be suitable for liturgical use. The translators also brought the language closer to the originals because of the availability of much older manuscripts that were not available to the translators of the KJV. The NT appeared in 1946, the OT in 1952, and an expanded edition with the APOCRYPHA in 1957, with the additions of 3 and 4 Maccabees and Ps. 151 in 1977. A Catholic edition of the entire RSV BIBLE with the Apocrypha appeared in 1966. *See also* NEW REVISED STANDARD VERSION.

Bibliography. Steven M. Sheeley and Robert N. Nash Jr., *The Bible in English Translation: An Essential Guide* (Nashville: Abingdon, 1997).

REVISED VERSION (RV)

A revision of the KING JAMES VERSION of the Bible begun in 1871 by both British and American translators. The NT appeared in 1881 and the OT in 1885. The APOCRYPHA was also published in 1898 along with the whole BIBLE. The revision was made because of new manuscript evidence in the original languages of the BIBLE.

RE-VISIONING

A concept in FEMINIST CRITICISM for the historical and cultural re-presenting of the past, especially of women, with the vision of creating HER-STORY, or a woman's history. The ASSUMPTION underlying this attempt is that history (his-story) has always been constructed and reconstructed from a male perspective, guided by male values and interests. As such, most history is patriarchal (*see* PATRIARCHY), in which the values, views, interests, products, and visions of women have been marginalized (*see* MARGINALIZATION), suppressed, and deemed unimportant.

RHETORIC

The art of composition for the purpose of persuading. Therefore, rhetoric implies that there are guidelines or rules of FORM and STRUCTURE for effective composition. Rhetoric is also an academic discipline that dates at least to the Sophists of the fifth century BCE. Modern scholars have employed classical rhetoric to analyze both the HEBREW BIBLE and the NT (e.g., Phyllis Trible and George Kennedy). In a more POSTMODERN vein, some scholars argue that all SPEECH is rhetorical and therefore to some degree propagandistic. Hence, TRUTH is always a linguistic construction.

Bibliography. George A. Kennedy, *Classical Rhetoric and Its Christian and Secular Tradition from Ancient to Modern Times* (Chapel Hill: University of North Carolina Press, 1983); idem, *New Testament Interpretation through Rhetorical Criticism* (Chapel Hill: University of North Carolina Press, 1984); Phyllis Trible, *Rhetorical Criticism: Context, Method, and the Book of Jonah* (Minneapolis: Fortress, 1994).

RHETORICAL ANALYSIS

The study of the rhetorical STRUCTURES of a TEXT, focusing only on the strategies of construction. The best-known attempt to define the rhetorical principles underlying the TEXTs of the HEBREW BIBLE is that by Nils W. Lund. Also important is the work by Jack Lundborn on Jeremiah. Now NT scholars assume that the NT texts can be analyzed by examining them in terms of classical Greek RHETORIC. George Kennedy has worked with the GOSPELs, while David Aune and others have applied rhetorical analysis to the EPISTOLARY LITERATURE. For the various types of classical rhetoric and its components, *see* RHETORICAL CRITICISM.

Bibliography. David Aune, "Romans as a Logos Protreptikos," in *The Romans Debate* (ed. Karl P. Donfried; rev.

and exp. ed.; Peabody, MA: Hendrickson, 1991), 278–96; Nils W. Lund, *Chiasm in the New Testament: A Study in Formgeschichte* (Chapel Hill: University of North Carolina Press, 1942; repr., 1992); George Kennedy, *New Testament Interpretation through Rhetorical Criticism* (Chapel Hill: University of North Carolina Press, 1984); Jack Lundbom, *Jeremiah: A Study in Ancient Hebrew Rhetoric* (Society of Biblical Literature Dissertation Series 18. Missoula, MT: Scholars Press, 1975).

RHETORIC, DELIBERATIVE. *See* DELIBERATIVE RHETORIC

RHETORIC, EPIDEICTIC. *See* EPIDEICTIC

RHETORIC, JUDICIAL. *See* JUDICIAL RHETORIC

RHETORICAL CRITICISM

Generally a LITERARY CRITICISM that focuses on the communication between an AUTHOR and a reader by analyzing the strategies an author employs in a work to influence a reader's view or shape a reader's response. Rhetorical criticism is not a single, well-delineated methodology but a collection of critical approaches to interpreting TEXTS. They all, however, share two ASSUMPTIONS: language is adequate, if imperfect, to communicate human INTENTIONS; and a communicative act includes an intentional use of language, a response, and a RHETORICAL SITUATION.

John Gerber traces the beginning of contemporary rhetorical criticism to the interest in communication skills in the late 1940s, along with the growing interest in communication as an intentional act between persons. This interest developed into a critical method that, while preserving the concerns of NEW CRITICISM for the literary work, focused in addition on the sender/author and receiver/audience. Given that the ancient emphasis of RHETORIC was on persuasion, it is not surprising that rhetorical criticism focuses on the interactions between the author, the text, and the audience. Hence, rhetorical criticism is interested in the product, the process, and the effect of literary communication. It looks on the text as an artistic object (also the concern of New Criticism) but also as a structured object of communication. So rhetorical criticism is interested not only in what the text is but also in what it does.

According to David Goodwin, modern rhetorical criticism is of three types: traditional (neo-Aristotelian), transitional, and contemporary. Neo-Aristotelian criticism is the most popular and most widely applied method of rhetorical criticism. The focus of this traditional approach is on intentionally persuasive DISCOURSE, both written and oral. Neo-Aristotelian critics also are concerned with the effect that the person of the communicator and the communicator's time have on the shaping of the discourse. Generally, they depend on classical models for their interpretive principles, especially those of Aristotle. Their analysis includes traditional GENRES such as public addresses, and they examine the communicator's strategies, SELECTION AND ARRANGEMENT of materials, and the structure of the argument. They also assume that Aristotle's rhetorical categories provide the most reliable theoretical basis for examining persuasive discourse. These categories include the three kinds of appeals (LOGOS, ETHOS, and PATHOS), two types of proofs (artistic and inartistic), and the fivefold division of rhetoric (INVENTION, ARRANGEMENT, STYLE, MEMORY, and DELIVERY).

Neo-Aristotelian rhetorical criticism divides the examination of a discourse into three parts: the rhetorical unit, the rhetorical situation, and the arrangement of materials. The determination of the rhetorical unit involves establishing the boundaries of the discourse: the distinct start and finish. With regard to the rhetorical situation, critics assume that a particular discourse exists because of some specific condition or situation. It is the task of the critic to determine these conditions and situations. The critic must determine how the materials are arranged to form a unified whole and to produce persuasion. The rhetorical strategies are present in the discourse because the speaker/author chooses between options available. Persuasion therefore is no accident but by design. The traditionalist focuses on this design.

The transitional type of rhetorical criticism faults the traditional approach's almost exclusive interest in the speaker/author and the original audience's response. The transitionalists offer a transactional model in which the function of CRITICISM is to examine the transactions between the rhetorical situation, the rhetorical strategies, and the rhetorical effects. Although they are more interested in the manner in which a discourse functions, with the traditionalists they do assume that criticism should focus on discourse that is self-consciously persuasive.

Contemporary rhetorical critics do not constitute a monolithic group. Some, such as Wayne Booth and Mark Klyn, assume that a single, systematic rhetorical method is possible. They define rhetorical criticism as the examination of the product (discourse), the process (speaker/author intention), and the effect (audience response) of communicative activity. A particular text is not necessarily rhetorical by intention but because the critic approaches a text as a communicative event.

Other contemporary rhetorical critics advocate a pluralistic approach and share a handful of key assumptions about reality and the nature of language. First is the POSTMODERN assumption that reality is not a natural given but a social and linguistic construct that is always fluid. Second is another postmodern claim, that all discourse itself is a nonobjective entity, thoroughly conditioned by sociopolitical forces. The third assumption is that the CRITIC, not the theory, is central to criticism. Thus critical theories should always be in a state of evolution by reflecting the activities of the critic rather than in a state of stasis, dictating method to the critic. In this view, methodology is always fluid, depending on and adapting to the insights of critics. And fourth, since changing reality perennially escapes definition, there should be no definitive method that dictates the interpretive domain of the critic.

On the one hand, there is no single method that can be called rhetorical criticism. Yet on the other hand, all rhetorical critics assume that reality in some fashion is a social phenomenon and that there is a mutually informing relationship between language and human activity. Thus most assume a rhetorical stance, borrowing from a variety of theories and methodologies that can assist in analyzing the relationships between intentions and motivations of speakers/authors, discursive structures, and audience responses. Perhaps underlying this stance is the assumption that a responsible examination of words in their linguistic patterns and formulations will reveal something about the speaker's/author's thought and intention.

Bibliography. Wayne Booth, *The Rhetoric of Fiction* (Chicago: University of Chicago Press, 1961); idem, *The Rhetoric Of Irony* (Chicago: University of Chicago Press, 1974); John Gerber, "Literature—Our Untamable Discipline," *College English* 28 (1967): 354; David Goodwin, "Rhetorical Criticism," in *Encyclopedia of Contemporary Literary Theory* (ed. Irena R. Makaryk; Toronto: University of Toronto Press, 1993), 174–78; Mark Klyn, "Towards a Pluralistic Rhetorical Criticism," in *Essays on Rhetorical Criticism* (ed. Thomas R. Nilsen; New York: Random House, 1968).

RHETORICAL FIGURE

A creative use and arrangement of words (REPETITION, CHIASMUS, ASSONANCE, RHYME, RHYTHM, etc.) to achieve emphasis or impression without changing the MEANING of the words as METAPHOR, SIMILE, and SYNECDOCHE do. For example, Amos 5:4b–6a arranges the material as a chiasmus without changing the meanings of the words.

RHETORICAL OVERCODING

Also called stylistic coding; in the LITERARY THEORY of Umberto Eco, one of the seven textual encyclopedic restraints that a TEXT imposes on a reader. According to this restraint, when a reader approaches the LITERARY DEVICES of a text, some LITERARY COMPETENCE is expected. FIGURES OF SPEECH and rhetorical devices require that readers avoid naively applying LITERAL interpretations to these devices and figurative constructions. Though figures of speech may lend themselves to POLYSEMY, they also limit denotative interpretations (*see* DENOTATION). Included in Eco's overcoding is the idea of GENRE. Conventions of genre set parameters within which INTERPRETATION must take place.

Bibliography. Umberto Eco, *The Role of the Reader: Explorations in the Semiotics of Texts* (Bloomington: Indiana University Press, 1984).

RHETORICAL QUESTION

A question for which an answer is not expected or for which the answer is self-evident. Quite often the rhetorical question is intended to appeal to the emotions of the audience. Another TYPE of rhetorical question is one for which the answer is immediately supplied. Each of these types is demonstrated in Jer. 2:5–6 and 8:5–7.

RHETORICAL SITUATION

A concept within RHETORICAL CRITICISM that turns on the ASSUMPTION that a particular discourse exists because of some specific condition or situation. It is the task of the CRITIC to determine these conditions and situations. The critic must determine how the materials are arranged (*see* SELECTION AND ARRANGEMENT) to form a unified whole and to produce persuasion.

RHYME

In its most general form, the REPETITION of concluding syllables in different words at the end of lines of POETRY. While rhyme has a long history, it is only in the last millennium that it has come to be a fixed part of the POETICS of VERSE. Greek and Roman verse were not rhymed, nor was the earliest extant verse in English, *Beowulf.* Although past critics have argued that BIBLICAL POETRY rhymes, James Kugel points out that among these critics

> the idea of biblical rhyme appeared among the Jews at a time when they used rhyme in their own poems; Christian commentators took up this theme when rhyme became established as a respectable feature of their (vernacular) poetry. What rhymes was always defined by the conventions of the theorists' own poetry, conventions that, as we have seen, changed from time to time and place to place. (250)

Several problems arise with respect to identifying rhyme in biblical poetry. First, almost any Hebrew text can be made to rhyme, depending on where the lines are divided. Petersen and Richards observe that "it is not always obvious where a colon begins and ends, since few ancient Hebrew manuscripts have set out Hebrew poetry in the lineation of our modern critical texts or translations" (23). Second, there are no extant ancient accounts of the workings of Hebrew poetry. And third, since there are no original texts, we cannot be certain about how poems were constructed, even in something as simple or basic as STANZA formation or the existence of stanzas, for that matter. Therefore most modern scholars focus on parallelism, METER, and/or RHYME.

Bibliography. James L. Kugel, *The Idea of Biblical Poetry: Parallelism and Its History* (Baltimore: Johns Hopkins University Press, 1981); David L. Petersen and Kent Harold Richards, *Interpreting Hebrew Poetry* (Minneapolis: Fortress, 1992).

RHYTHM

In PROSE or VERSE, movement communicated by the repeated pattern of stressed and unstressed syllables and by the duration of the syllables. In verse, the rhythm is metrical and therefore usually regular. In free verse, however, METER is not used. The presence of meter and therefore rhythm in BIBLICAL POETRY is still a debated issue. Although a chain of commentators have identified rhythm in Hebrew poetry with the presence of meter (from Philo, Josephus, Origen, and Jerome to modern critics), the present debate generally rejects any metrical structure similar to that in Greco-Roman or English verse (e.g., regular feet and meter such as iambic pentameter) and centers on the number of syllables or number of stressed words as defining rhythm in Hebrew poetry. Thus scholars such as Robert Alter, James Kugel, Michael O'Connor, and Terence Collins argue that rhythm in Hebrew poetry can be defined not in terms of meter but rather in terms of rhythmic patterns. The rhythmic pattern may be found in the number of accented words or number of syllables in each COLON or bicolon or tricolon line of verse. For example, according to Petersen and Richards, in Isa. 5:1, the first bicolon has a 3 + 3 pattern of accented words while there are actually seven syllables in the first part and six syllables in the second part of the bicolon. Hence, Petersen and Richards suggest that in Hebrew verse there is variation within regularity, a mark of POETRY in general. They go on to suggest that, since Hebrew verse is dominated by bicolon and tricolon grouping, it should not be a surprise that the dominant rhythmic pattern of accented words in Hebrew verse is 2 + 2 and 3 + 3.

Bibliography. David L. Petersen and Kent Harold Richards, *Interpreting Hebrew Poetry* (Minneapolis: Fortress, 1992).

RÎB PATTERN. *See* COVENANT LAWSUIT

RIDDLE

An ancient literary FORM that usually consists of a puzzling question. In the HEBREW BIBLE, the only clear riddle is the one spoken by Samson in Judg. 14:14. However, James Williams argues that the Hebrew word *ḥîdâ* (sometimes translated "dark sayings") may have been used on occasion to refer to a riddle. For example, in Num. 12:8 Yahweh says that he will speak to Moses "mouth to mouth . . . and not in dark speeches" (KJV). Williams also points out that in two PSALMS (49:4; 78:2), *ḥîdâ* is associated with the PARABLE or the PROVERB. He further suggests that the "dark saying" may have been an early form of folk literature (*see* FOLKLORE) and in the WISDOM LITERATURE may have been embedded within a proverb as the first half of it. An example is Prov. 11:22: "As a jewel of gold in a swine's snout / so is a fair woman which is without discretion." The riddle occurs in the first line, "[What is as amazing or incongruous as] a gold ring in a swine's snout?" (Williams, 272), and the answer is the second line. Williams also offers Prov. 6:27–28 (KJV) as an excellent example:

> Can a man take fire in his bosom,
> and his clothes not be burned?
> Can one go upon hot coals,
> and his feet not be burned?

According to Williams, the questions presuppose a prior question, "Who is it that?" with the answer supplied in 6:29 (KJV): "he that goeth in to his neighbour's wife."

Bibliography. James Williams, "Proverbs and Ecclesiastes," in *The Literary Guide to the Bible* (ed. Robert Alter and Frank Kermode; Cambridge, MA: Belknap, 1987), 263–82.

RISING ACTION

In a play, the COMPLICATION and development of CONFLICT before the crisis or CLIMAX. Although the term *rising action* is not normally part of the vocabulary used to describe the STRUCTURE of stories, complication and conflict are inherently part of a STORY's PLOT. For example, all the complications and types of conflicts in Mark's GOSPEL may be seen as constituting the rising action before the crisis of Jesus's arrest. From that point through his crucifixion, the events may be described as constituting the FALLING ACTION.

ROMANCE

A term used to describe a variety of works of FICTION, from the medieval works such as *The Song of Roland* to *The Faerie Queene* to Hawthorne's *The Scarlet Letter* and Faulkner's *Absalom, Absalom!* Northrop Frye defines romance as a GENRE that employs characters with powers greater than those of the normal human being but less than those of the gods. In popular usage, however, *romance* describes works of fiction that include exaggerated characters, heroic events and feats, passionate love, faraway and exotic places, and supernatural phenomena. Scholars have also used *romance* to describe a type of fiction popular within HELLENISM, the time during which the documents of the NT were written. Thus some scholars have pointed out the similarities between the GOSPELs, especially Luke-Acts, and the Hellenistic romance. Elizabeth Haight has identified parallels between the Gospels/Acts and the Hellenistic romance. When the parallels are placed side by side, there is an obvious similarity between the two. See the table below for a few of these parallels.

Parallels between Hellenistic Romance and the Gospels and Acts

Romance	Gospels/Acts
Travel motif	Luke 9:51–19:44; Acts 19:21–21:16
Aretalogy	Numerous in Gospels and Acts
Prevention of suicide	Acts 16:25–34
Dreams	Matt. 1:20–25; 2:13; 27:19
Visions	Luke 1:22; 24:23; Acts 9:10, 12
Courtroom scenes	Luke 22–23; Acts 22–26
Letters	Acts 15:23–29; 23:26–30
Crowd motif	In all Gospels and Acts
Speeches	Acts 2:14–36; 7:1–53; 17:22–31
Storms	Matt. 14:22–33; Acts 27:13–26
Shipwreck	Acts 27:27–44
Narrow escapes	Matt. 2:13–20; Acts 12:1–18
Ethnography	John 4:1–27; Acts 8:26–27; 14:11–13
Origin and birth of hero	Matt. 1–2; Luke 1–3
Historical characters	Pilate, Festus, Herod the Great, Felix
Divine direction	Throughout Gospels and Acts

Bibliography. Elizabeth Haight, *Essays on the Greek Romances* (Port Washington, NY: Kennikat, 1943).

ROUNDED CHARACTER

A multidimensional and complex character in a STORY, manifesting a range of character traits. This character confronts the reader with psychological, emotional, and spiritual complexities. David's wife Michal is a rounded character. The AUTHOR goes to great lengths in presenting her as a woman with her own emotions and opinions.

ROUTINIZATION

A term employed by Anthony Thiselton for the result of interpreting a TEXT within the perspectives of a reader or community, without due attention to the WORLD OF THE TEXT. INTERPRETATION becomes bland or routine when readers approach a text to extricate from it what they have already determined to say or to affirm something they already believe. Such reading is especially common within creedal communities, where interpretation serves to legitimate and perpetuate the CREED. Another way to put it is that routinization results from an overdependence on the HORIZON OF THE READER and an inadequate attention to the HORIZON OF THE TEXT. Where there is little interaction between these two horizons, bland and routine interpretations result, and the creative dimension of the text is short-circuited. Thiselton also suggests that routinization occurs when the INTERPRETIVE COMMUNITY elevates its conventional interpretive practices to the level of natural norms, when the community so habitually functions under certain reading or interpretive practices that it begins to assume that those practices are universal. Within such practices, the text becomes a pretext for saying something that the community already believes.

Bibliography. Anthony Thiselton, *New Horizons in Hermeneutics* (Grand Rapids: Zondervan, 1992).

ROYAL PSALMS. *See* PSALM(S)

RV. *See* REVISED VERSION

RULES OF CO-REFERENCE

According to Umberto Eco, one of the constraints that the TEXT places on a reader. Since words within any language can have multiple MEANINGS (think of the various meanings of the word "lot"), the meaning of a word at any point within the text must be determined by what Eco calls rules of coreference. Initially, the reader makes SENSE of terms based on cotextual relations: the relationships that a word has with the other words within a sentence. As reading progresses, terms that remain ambiguous will be clarified through other textual clues.

Bibliography. Umberto Eco, *The Role of the Reader: Explorations in the Semiotics of Texts* (Bloomington: Indiana University Press, 1984).

RUNNING COMMENTARY

A rabbinic practice employed by Paul whereby he alternates between quoting SCRIPTURE and commenting on it. For example, in Gal. 3, Paul quotes Gen. 15:6; 12:3; Deut. 27:26; Lev. 18:5; and Deut. 21:23, with interspersed COMMENTARY.

S

SACHEXEGESE

A German word current in theological studies in the early twentieth century, meaning "subject exegesis," designating the claim that the BIBLE must be interpreted on its own theological terms. In other words, theologians such as Karl Barth, Rudolf Bultmann, and Emil Brunner argued that while historical-critical examination of the Bible is an integral part of EXEGESIS, it is external to the concerns of the Bible itself. Since the Bible is a thoroughly theological book, INTERPRETATION should employ theological concerns to complete historical and critical concerns. If the central concern of the Bible is God, then it should also be the central concern of interpretation.

Bibliography. Richard N. Soulen and R. Kendall Soulen, *Handbook of Biblical Criticism* (3rd ed.; Louisville: Westminster John Knox, 2001).

SACHKRITIK

German for "subject criticism," practiced by Rudolf Bultmann, in which he assumed that there may be and usually is a distinction between what a TEXT says and what it means. *Sachkritik* incorporates SACHEXEGESE but goes further in its claim that the subject matter of a text must be the CANON, against which the exegete judges the extent to which the CONTENT of the text actually articulates the SUBJECT. Underlying this claim is the ASSUMPTION that there is no assurance that the AUTHOR of a text always expresses the subject matter adequately or clearly.

SACRAMENTAL HYMN

A type of HYMN (generally focusing on salvation and/or grace) found in the Pauline corpus of letters (including the DEUTEROPAULINE and PASTORAL EPISTLES) borrowed from the liturgies of the early church. Examples are Eph. 5:14 and Titus 3:4–7.

SACRED HISTORY

History as it is recorded in the BIBLE and interpreted from the Bible, with the ASSUMPTION that God actively works within history at large. *See also* HEILSGESCHICHTE.

SADDUCEES

The priestly party within JUDAISM and most closely associated with the temple. They were more open to hellenization and Roman rule than the other parties within Judaism. Acceptance of Roman rule ensured their power and influence. However, after the destruction of the temple and Jerusalem in 70 CE, resulting in the loss of their seat of authority, the Sadducees never again exerted any influence on Judaism.

The Sadducees accepted as authoritative only the written law of Moses and rejected as nonauthoritative the PROPHETS, the WRITINGS, and the ORAL TORAH. Therefore, when Jesus responded to the Sadducees' questions concerning the resurrection (Matt. 22:23–33), he answered them by appealing to a passage in the PENTATEUCH (Exod. 3:6). The Sadducees' acceptance only of the Pentateuch as authoritative explains why Jesus did not quote a passage from a TEXT that would have more clearly dealt with the resurrection, such as Dan. 12:1–3 (see Ferguson, 486). *See also* PHARISEES.

Bibliography. Everett Ferguson, *Backgrounds of Early Christianity* (2nd ed.; Grand Rapids: Eerdmans, 1993).

SAGA

From the Old Norse, meaning "narrative, saying" (cognate to German *sagen*, "to say"); strictly speaking, saga is a medieval Scandinavian NARRATIVE about a hero, a family, or the exploits of warriors and kings. These were not written down until the twelfth century CE. In BIBLICAL STUDIES, however, A. S. van der Woude has identified four types of sagas, defined as narratives that serve to "teach or explain something, such as a name or the origin of a custom or institution" (120). Consequently, according to van der Woude, the biblical saga is an ETIOLOGY or ETYMOLOGY. First, the nature saga explains how a place received its name. For example, Gen. 19 explains, in terms of the cities of Sodom and Gomorrah, why the area to the immediate east of the Dead Sea became so desolate. The tribal and national saga explains the relationship between or the origins of various peoples or the existence of certain customs. Genesis 25:19–26 explains the relationship between Edom and Israel through the STORY of Rebecca's giving birth to twin sons, who in turn became the founders of two nations. According to van der Woude, other tribal and national sagas are the explanation of the unusual tattooing practices of the Kenites. Genesis 19:30–38 explains the origin of the Moabites and the Ammonites. The name saga explains the origin of a person's name or that of a place. Van der Woude observes that about eighty name sagas have been identified in Genesis alone. Examples are the origin of the well of Esek (Gen. 26:20) and the origin of the place called Ramath-lehi (Judg. 15:9–19). According to van der Woude, the OT contains no hero sagas such as those found in the *Iliad* and the Gilgamesh Epic. The most plausible explanation for this lack is that Israel attributed all of its great victories to God.

Bibliography. A. S. van der Woude, ed., *The World of the Old Testament* (Grand Rapids: Eerdmans, 1982).

SALVATION HISTORY. *See* HEILSGESCHICHTE

SAMARITAN PENTATEUCH

A version of the first five books of the HEBREW BIBLE that became the authoritative SCRIPTURES of the SAMARITANS. Although the origin of the Samaritans is still debated, scholars do know that they claimed to be the faithful remnant of Israel. For an introduction to the Samaritan Pentateuch, see Anderson and Giles; and Parvis.

Bibliography. Robert Anderson and Terry Giles, *Tradition Kept* (Peabody, MA: Hendrickson, 2005); J. D. Parvis, *The Samaritan Pentateuch and the Origin of the Samaritan Sect* (Harvard Semitic Monographs 2; Cambridge, MA: Harvard University Press, 1968).

SARCASM

A TYPE of IRONY in the form of a caustic, acrimonious expression directed toward a person or group. In 1 Cor. 4:10, Paul means for his statement to be an accusation when he says to his audience, "We [the apostles] are fools for the sake of Christ, but you are wise in Christ."

SATIRE

A literary GENRE in which the speaker censures and ridicules social follies and vices. As such, satire is an expression of protest in the form of social COMMENTARY that seeks to refine what it mocks. Typical topics for derision are hypocrisy, greed, pride, manners, and materialism. Entire works can be satirical, or satire may be embedded within larger works. For example, the entire book of Jonah may be read as a satire that attacks the elitism of Jews who viewed God as Israel's God only, thus rejecting the universality of God and God's mercy. Also, Amos's reference to the women of Jerusalem as "[fat] cows of Bashan" is a satirical statement (4:1 [cf. Latin Vulgate]). For an excellent treatment of satire in the Bible, see Ryken, 329–40.

Bibliography. Leland Ryken, *Words of Delight: A Literary Introduction to the Bible* (Grand Rapids: Baker, 1987).

SAVIOR

A term applied to Jesus, especially by Luke, to designate his universal appeal. In the HELLENISTIC PERIOD, the term was commonly used of human rulers, gods, and demigods. The Roman emperor was heralded as savior, as were philosophers, because they brought a form of salvation, healing, and health to their subjects and followers. Luke presents Jesus as the Savior of humanity from the consequences of sin (e.g., Luke 2:11; Acts 13:23).

SAYING(S)

A LITERARY term in FORM CRITICISM designating a curt, memorable form of SPEECH, which is most often rhythmic. These sayings include APHORISM, BEATITUDE, ORACLE, CURSE, INVECTIVE, and exhortation. The saying may be legal, as found in Exodus, Leviticus, and Deuteronomy; PROPHETIC ORACLES, as in Isaiah and Jeremiah; or WISDOM SAYINGS, as in Proverbs. In the NT, numerous types of sayings are attributed to Jesus, and the Epistle of James is actually a collection of sayings, as is the *Gospel of Thomas*. See also SAYINGS OF JESUS.

SAYING, DOMINICAL. See DOMINICAL SAYING

SAYING, LEGAL. See SAYINGS OF JESUS

SAYING, PARABOLIC. See PARABLE

SAYING, PRONOUNCEMENT. See PRONOUNCEMENT STORY/SAYINGS

SAYING, PROPHETIC. See SAYINGS OF JESUS

SAYING, WISDOM. See WISDOM SAYINGS

SAYINGS OF JESUS

Succinct SAYINGS attributed to Jesus, especially in the GOSPELs. Most scholars are convinced that many sayings of Jesus were collected quite early in the life of the church and were later circulated. One of these hypothetical collections is referred to as Q (probably from *Quelle*, German for "source"). Most scholars believe that it was a source for the evangelists. In particular, Matthew and Luke are believed to have drawn on Q for their respective "sermons" of Jesus, each one providing his own CONTEXT for the various sayings. We may classify these sayings into the APOPHTHEGM, PROVERB, legal saying, and prophetic saying.

The apophthegm, or PRONOUNCEMENT STORY, is a brief EPISODE or event that precipitates a saying of Jesus. It originated in an ANECDOTE about a well-known person. The anecdote climaxes in a significant statement or declaration. The episode or event exists for the saying and not vice versa. One example is the saying "I have come to call not the righteous but sinners" (Mark 2:17; Matt. 9:10–13; Luke 5:29–32). The SETTING for the NARRATIVE is a meal at which Jesus is eating with tax gatherers and other sinners. No details, such as time and place, are given about the meal. Such matters were irrelevant, since the saying was the focal point; the meal served only as a point of anchorage.

The proverb in the Gospels is probably best described as APHORISM: a terse, succinct statement easily remembered. The proverb is quite similar to the WISDOM SAYING of the OT. Examples are "For those who want to save their life will lose it" (Mark 8:35) and "No one tears a piece from a new garment and sews it on an old garment" (Luke 5:36).

A proverb is open-ended. It demands contemplation because it is filled with universal applicability or speaks of a universal principle of TRUTH. Frequently a proverb uses FIGURATIVE LANGUAGE such as METAPHOR, HYPERBOLE, or SIMILE to ensure a broad range of MEANING.

The legal sayings have a juridical ring to them. They usually have to do with an area of ministry or ecclesiastical order: "Laborers deserve their food" (Matt. 10:10b). "If anyone will not welcome you or listen to your words, shake off the dust from your feet as you leave that house or town" (Matt. 10:14).

The prophetic sayings are usually salvific or judgmental: "Two women will be grinding meal together; one will be taken and one will be left" (Matt. 24:41). "The days are coming when you will long to see one of the days of the Son of Man, and you will not see it. They will say to you, 'Look there!' or 'Look here!' Do not go, do not set off in pursuit. For as the lightning flashes and lights up the sky from one side to the other, so will the Son of Man be in his day" (Luke 17:22–24).

Bibliography. W. Randolph Tate, *Biblical Interpretation: An Integrated Approach* (rev. ed.; Peabody, MA: Hendrickson, 1997).

SAYINGS SOURCE. *See* Q

SCHOLARS VERSION (SV)

An annotated multivolume English TRANSLATION of the BIBLE, known as the Five Gospels. Published by the JESUS SEMINAR, this VERSION includes the four CANONICAL GOSPELS and the *Gospel of Thomas*. The primary goal of the seminar was to produce a version of these five gospels that would reflect which SAYINGS of Jesus were authentic and which were not.

> The model of the red letter edition suggested that the Seminar should adopt one of two options in its votes; either Jesus said it or he did not say it. A vote recognizing the words as authentic would entail printing the items in red; a vote recognizing the words as inauthentic meant that they would be left in regular black print.... Academics do not like simple choices. The Seminar adopted four categories as a compromise with those who wanted more. In addition to red, we permitted a pink vote for those who wanted to hedge: a pink vote represented reservations either about the degree of certainty or about modifications the saying or parable had suffered in the course of its transmission and recording. And for those who wanted to avoid a flat negative vote, we allowed a gray vote (gray being a weak form of black). The Seminar employed colored beads dropped into voting boxes in order to permit all members to vote in secret. Beads and boxes turned out to be a fortunate choice for both Fellows and an interested public. (Miller, 36)

The Seminar left 82 percent of the words of Jesus either gray or black, with most of the remaining words in pink and a slim minority in red. The rationale for placing none of the words in John's Gospel in red was that "Jesus did not make claims for himself; the early Christian community allowed its own triumphant faith to explode in confessions that were retrospectively attributed to Jesus, its authority figure. The climax of that trajectory came with the Gospel of John. In John, Jesus does little other than make claims for himself. For that reason alone, scholars regard the Fourth Gospel as alien to the real Jesus, the carpenter from Nazareth" (33).

Bibliography. Robert J. Miller, ed., *The Complete Gospels: The Scholars Version* (3rd ed.; Salem, OR: Polebridge, 1995).

SCRIPTIBLE TEXT. *See* LISIBLE

SCRIPTURE

A writing or collection of writings that a people regard as a sacred and therefore authoritative guide for conduct, faith, and living. For Christians, the OT and NT are considered Scripture in their entirety, as well as any part thereof.

SCROLL OF THE TWELVE

A designation for the Minor Prophets, which, because of their relative brevity, were often contained on a single scroll. There seems to be no pattern that accounts for the arrangement of the TEXTs.

SECOND NAÏVETÉ

A term introduced into HERMENEUTICS by Paul Ricoeur to designate a faith that has moved from "a blind experience, still embedded in the matrix of emotion, fear, anguish" (7), through a critical, interpretive stage to become a rational faith.

Bibliography. Paul Ricoeur, *The Symbolism of Evil* (Boston: Beacon, 1969).

SELECTION AND ARRANGEMENT

In REDACTION CRITICISM, a concept for the claim that an AUTHOR selects materials from a variety of sources, oral and written, and then arranges those materials according to a theological AGENDA. When an author's sources are known, it is relatively simple to examine the manner in which the author has arranged them and, from that arrangement, work backward to the theological agenda. Selection and arrangement are at the heart of the redactional study of the GOSPELs and Acts in the NT and the HISTORICAL NARRATIVES in the HEBREW BIBLE.

This principle is also applied to a critical study of HISTORIOGRAPHY by examining the role that IDEOLOGY plays in the historian's work. Among the practitioners of NEW HISTORICISM, there is general agreement that, to some degree, all historiography is simply the NARRATIVE arrangement of historical events, an arrangement that is the result of the selection and arrangement of events, persons, institutions, and so forth, guided by ideology. *See* ARRANGEMENT.

SELF-ACTUALIZATION

A term in FEMINIST CRITICISM for the fulfillment of a person's potential and the autonomy by which it is realized. Women are called upon to assume total responsibility for their lives by making their own free decisions.

SEMANTIC DEVELOPMENT

A term used by Robert Alter to describe the relationship between the two or three parts of a line in BIBLICAL POETRY. According to Alter, the development between the parts of a line may be SPECIFICATION (movement from the general to the more specific), cause and effect (usually the second and/or third parts are the effects of the first), or INTENSIFICATION (movement in which the action becomes more intense).

> *Bibliography.* Robert Alter, *The Art of Biblical Poetry* (New York: Basic Books, 1985).

SEMANTIC DOMAIN

The hierarchical synonymous relationship between words, moving from the generic to the particular. For example, plant-perennial-flower-rose. As a component in INTERPRETATION, it governs the degree of specificity or generality a reader may assign to a word used by an AUTHOR. For example, in Acts 2:38, the interpreter must determine to what extent Peter's words reflect a limited baptismal formula (or a baptismal formula at all) or whether Peter is stating an established doctrine of regeneration through baptism.

SEMANTIC FIELD

A group of signifieds with common or overlapping MEANING (e.g., clock, watch, timepiece).

SEMANTIC MOVEMENT. *See* SEMANTIC DEVELOPMENT

SEMANTIC PARALLELISM. *See* BIBLICAL POETRY

SEMANTIC RANGE

The possible MEANINGS a word might have with respect to a variety of CONTEXTS. For example, the word "rose" has a wide range of meanings in such contexts as love, nature, literature, and religion. Not only does each context create a number of possibilities; context also creates boundaries that limit what a reader may legitimately infer about the word's meaning.

SEMANTICS

A branch of LINGUISTICS that deals with word MEANINGS, changes in meanings, the relationship between words and objects, and the relationship between words and behavior. Cotterell and Turner suggest that semantics should be divided into the categories of TEXT and COTEXT. Text refers to the study of the actual words of the text, while cotext is concerned with the relationship between words in sentences, paragraphs, and chapters.

> *Bibliography.* Peter Cotterell and Max Turner, *Linguistics and Biblical Interpretation* (Downers Grove, IL: InterVarsity, 1989).

SEMASIOLOGY

Equivalent to SEMANTICS, the study of the origin of words, the reasons for changes in MEANING of the words in a society's vocabulary, and the relationship between a society and the development and changes in vocabulary.

> *Bibliography.* Richard N. Soulen and R. Kendall Soulen, *Handbook of Biblical Criticism* (3rd ed.; Louisville: Westminster John Knox, 2001).

SEMIOSIS

Generally, the human ability to create and understand SIGNS. Aristotle understood semiosis as both the formation of signs and the act of interpreting these signs. According to Charles Peirce, semiosis consists of a mental process that includes the sign (an IMAGE, a word), the object referred to by the word (concrete or abstract), and the MEANING created by the conjoining of the sign and the object. For example, d-o-g is a verbal sign that connects the animal (the object) to the meaning "dog" (the actual animal that barks and chases cats). Peirce also introduced the idea of INTERPRETANT to the process of semiosis. The interpretant is a person's individual INTERPRETATION of the sign. "A sign addresses somebody, that is, creates in the mind of that person an equivalent sign, or perhaps a more developed sign. The sign which it creates I call the interpretant of the first sign" (Peirce, 228).

Contemporary semioticians make a distinction between unilateral semiosis and bilateral semiosis. The former refers to a the process by which a SUBJECT in isolation receives signals, while the latter refers to the processing of signals by subjects participating in the surrounding environment. Thus, bilateral semiosis refers to the system of communication for a particular species. Semiosis, then, may be defined simply as the mind's ability to transform sensory impressions into experiences in terms of images both concrete and abstract.

> *Bibliography.* Umberto Eco, *A Theory of Semiotics* (Bloomington: Indiana University Press, 1976); Charles W. Morris, *Foundations of the Theory of Signs* (Chicago: University of Chicago Press, 1938); Charles S. Peirce, *Collected Papers of Charles Sanders Peirce* (ed. Charles Hartshorne and Paul Weiss; 8 vols.; Cambridge, MA: Harvard University Press, 1931–58); Thomas Sebeok, *The Sign and Its Masters* (Austin: University of Texas Press, 1979).

SEMIOTIC CODE

A set of cultural rules that govern the way a person in that culture perceives the world. This set of rules also guides a person's reading of the TEXT. The semiotic code will determine what material in the text will be selected as significant as well as the way in which the selected material is arranged. Texts communicate MEANING through CODES, and readers must be familiar with the codes in order to successfully decode them. The code is the underlying network or system that governs the AUTHOR's choices of linguistic expressions through which he/she intends to convey a message. It is also a fact that a text can operate on a number of semiotic

codes that create the possibility of understanding a text on a variety of levels. For example, the book of Revelation in the NT certainly involves the semiotic code of KOINE Greek. A misconception about the nature of the code at this level will result in misinterpretation. But the book of Revelation also operates on the semiotic code of the GENRE of apocalypse, providing an additional level of encoding on the part of the author and decoding on the part of the reader (*see* DECODING/ENCODING).

SEMIOTICS

The science of SIGNs in general and the theory of linguistic sign systems in particular. The term *semiotics* was coined by Charles Sanders Peirce to designate the study of signs, systems of signs, and the MEANING derived from both. Although structuralists, psychoanalysts, anthropologists, and LITERARY critics popularized the use of semiotics after 1950, the core concepts had already been developed and articulated by Peirce and Ferdinand de Saussure, who is usually considered the founder of modern LINGUISTICS.

Origins of semiotics. Peirce divided his study into SEMANTICS (the ways in which signs represent and have meaning), SYNTAX (organization of signs), and pragmatic logic (the relationship between INTERPRETATION of the signs and CONTEXT). Peirce identified three types of signs according to how they represent objects: the ICON, SYMBOL, and INDEX. The icon represents by means of resemblance (e.g., sound effects and portraits). Symbols can represent only on the basis of cultural agreement (e.g., we agree to use the sign "tree" to represent a plant with a trunk, branches, and foliage). This agreement allows people of the same culture to communicate. Indexes operate on the principle of cause and effect (e.g., from smoke we can infer fire as the cause).

Saussure referred to this field of study as "semiology" and focused on a TEXT's signifying system and the conventional CODES needed to read and understand it. He argued that there is a range of sign systems beyond language and made the distinction between *LANGUE* (the conventional system of codes that makes communication possible) and PAROLE (individual utterances based on the conventional system). He also introduced the concepts of the signifier and signified and the arbitrary relationship between the two. It is on these two concepts that much of modern semiotic theory rests. According to Saussure, a language is made up of a series of "signs" and involves relationships between signs and what the signs refer to. Every sign consists of a signifier and a signified. The signifier is the "immediate object of perception," while the signified is "that which the perception evokes." For example, the word *rose* is a sign signifying the concept or mental representation of a rose. The signifier is the word sound *rose*, and the signified is the conception of a flower. Yet the signified may have not only a denotative meaning (*see* DENOTATION) but also a connotative one (*see* CONNOTATION). For example, the signifier *rose* may refer both to a real-world flower and to a person who is as lovely as a rose. Now, if a text (e.g., a NARRATIVE one) is itself a sign, it may also have both denotative and connotative meanings. On the denotative level, we would expect to find manifestations of AUTHORIAL INTENTION. On the connotative level, however, there exists a subconscious system of conventions and convictions that precede authorial intention, which becomes the focus of STRUCTURALISM.

Also important is Saussure's concept of PHONEME, the smallest unit of SPEECH. According to Saussure, phonemes stand in two types of relationships to each other: DIACHRONIC and SYNCHRONIC. In its diachronic sense, a phoneme has a horizontal relationship with others. For example, in any utterance or narrative, the phonemes have well-defined positions with respect to verb, subject, object, and so forth. In other words, the phoneme has meaning only in relationship to its place in the STRUCTURE. But a phoneme has synchronic or vertical value in terms of its relationship with the entire sign system (e.g., a language). In its diachronic relationship, then, a phoneme has meaning only in terms of position, while in its synchronic relationship it has meaning only in its difference from all the other phonemes. Thus the phoneme

red has no inherent meaning, but meaning only in its difference from *blue, green, up, down,* and so forth. Furthermore, the relationship between a phoneme and its referent or between a signifier and its signified is arbitrary.

Eco's use of semiotics in criticism. Umberto Eco, a more recent literary CRITIC, has based part of his literary theory of openness on Peirce's concept of unlimited semiosis. This complex concept involves the relationships between signs, codes, INTERPRETANTS, denotation and connotation, meaning as encyclopedic, and extracoding. Put simply, a sign is something that stands for something else. "There is a sign every time a human group decides to use and to recognize something as a vehicle of something else" (Eco, *Theory of Semiotics*, 17). A sign is bipolar, having an expression pole and a content pole. The expression plane or pole is actually a syntactical system (an "s-code") with rules that govern the ways in which words and expressions are put together. For example, the rules of syntax allow a speaker of the English language to make sense of the expression "Some cats are black," in which something is predicated upon something else. However, the expression is only one-half of the sign; it is what Eco calls the "sign-vehicle." When I read the expression "cat," I must assign to this sign-vehicle some CONTENT. Hence, this content is not of necessity the four-legged furry creature we may chance to see crossing our path on a particular day. The content of the vehicle "cat" is completely cultural and determined by language.

All cultures come into existence and are sustained through language. A culture is defined by the way its members speak, think, and explain the SIGNIFICANCE of thinking through thoughts. Therefore, a culture cannot exist outside language. Indeed, outside language there is no meaning, no reality. For every sign-vehicle, expression unit, there corresponds a cultural unit with content that is culturally determined. In other words, to determine the meaning of an expression, recourse should not be made to some ontological reality or referent outside the cultural content provided by language. Eco prefers to call this bipolar sign a "sign-function":

> A sign-function is realized when two functives (expression and content) enter into a mutual correlation; the same functive can also enter into another correlation, thus becoming a different functive and therefore giving rise to a new sign-function. (*Theory of Semiotics*, 49)

The correlation between these two planes is provided by a code. In other words, a code determines the way in which a society assigns to an expression a certain content, a content that is itself a cultural unit. Now the expression unit is itself governed by what Eco calls a subcode (s-code): a syntactical system (s-code) governs the contextual relationships of the expression plane. Similarly, the content plane is governed by another s-code, a system of semantics. Thus a code actually correlates the two s-codes and also defines the ways in which sign-functions may amalgamate with other sign-functions to form a text. Again, since codes set up a cultural world, their existence is independent of ontology. In other words, the cultural code does not correlate an expression unit with an object, but with a cultural content that can be analyzed as a set of cultural properties expressed in language. At this point, therefore, it becomes evident that a sign-function is ruled by at least one code and two s-codes. In fact, in literary texts, other codes associated with GENRE and literary strategies also control the sign-function.

Denotation, connotation, and interpretant. This brings us to the concepts of denotation, connotation, and interpretant. Faithful to his program of restricting the definition of meaning to cultural content, Eco defines denotation and connotation as follows:

> (a) a denotation is a cultural unit or semantic property of a given sememe [single unit of meaning] which is at the same time a culturally recognized property of its possible referents;
>
> (b) a connotation is a cultural unit or semantic property of a given sememe conveyed by its denotation and not necessarily corresponding to a cultur-

ally recognized property of the possible referent. (*Theory of Semiotics*, 86)

Actually, denotation and connotation become components within the rather broad, inclusive concept of interpretant. According to Eco, a sign-function is always understood by means of other sign-functions. This series of sign-functions that circumscribe a sign-function and constitute a continuous progression is the interpretant of the sign-function. An interpretant includes denotation and connotation. However, the concept includes even complex discourses. The interpretant is, then, a chain of sign-functions in which each one within the chain may have its own interpretant. What we have here is Eco's brand of "unlimited semiosis," a delimiting term for meaning. Each sign-function has an expression unit and a content unit, which then becomes the expression unit of another sign-function, ad infinitum. The chart below is one that Eco uses to explain the concept of unlimited semiosis:

| Expression | Content |
| Expression | Content |

This process continues in such a fashion that each sign-function becomes an expression unit of another sign-function in an infinite regression of unlimited semiosis. "Intepretants are testable and describable correspondents associated by public agreement to another sign" (Eco, *Role of the Reader*, 198). This guarantees that, in a sense, meaning is always deferred back through a chain of signs and that communication (whether oral, written, scientific, or literary) is always a matter of language and not a matter of ontological reality.

Obviously Eco rejects the notion that signs have dictionary-type meanings, according to which language is a system of words, each having a concise definition. Each sign is "composed by a finite set of semantic universals, that cannot be further analyzed" (*Limits of Interpretation*, 143). Indeed, Eco's definition of sign and interpretant demands an encyclopedia model in which every sign within a language conveys meaning via a chain of signs (the sign's interpretant; *Theory of Semiotics*, 84–86). For example, a lexeme such as *man* generates a possible infinite chain of associations, every piece of content that a culture has assigned to *man*. The encyclopedia of *man* would include biological, physical, psychological, historical, and traditional information along with grammatical rules that govern the ways (e.g., literary) in which *man* can be used and understood in various contexts. Clearly, such an encyclopedia is potentially infinite (*Limits of Interpretation*, 240). When the lexeme *man* becomes part of an expression with a context, when it becomes part of an utterance, the addressee is required to choose a portion of the encyclopedia while ignoring other portions. The context of an utterance requires the addressee to perform an abduction: the addressee chooses one interpretant chain from the encyclopedia, which consists of an infinite labyrinth of meaning units and connections. The encyclopedia is similar to a labyrinth of interlocking labyrinths.

A sign, however, is not only something that stands for something else but also something that requires interpretation. This requirement further complicates unlimited semiosis. On the one hand, the sender of an utterance or text (esp. literary ones) may superimpose certain codes on the code of the natural language. Such codes include ideological (*see* IDEOLOGY), rhetorical (*see* RHETORIC; RHETORICAL CRITICISM), GENRE, and LITERARY codes. Therefore, an utterance or text is an interlocking system of codes, the code of the natural language being overcoded by them.

On the other hand, in the process of interpreting (decoding) an utterance or a text, addressees may consciously or unconsciously apply aberrant codes, codes other than those assumed by the sender. In addition, an addressee, due to various types of incompetence, may be incapable of recognizing one or more codes employed by the sender and thus undercode an utterance or text by simply passing over certain portions. Consequently, addressees may accept or reject the sender's code and introduce their own, the result possibly being that every reading runs the risk of being a MISREADING.

The practice of studying language as a system of codes, laws, and relationships has had a profound influence on structuralist approaches to studying literature. The notions of the arbitrary relations between signifier and signified, that signs can have meaning only in their differences from other signs, and of unlimited semiosis paved the way for most poststructuralist and deconstructive theories of texts and how they communicate. *See* DECONSTRUCTION; POSTMODERN CRITICISM; POSTMODERNISM/POSTMODERNITY; STRUCTURALISM.

Bibliography. Umberto Eco, *The Limits of Interpretation* (Bloomington: Indiana University Press, 1990); idem, *The Role of the Reader: Explorations in the Semiotics of Texts* (Bloomington: Indiana University Press, 1984); idem, *A Theory of Semiotics* (Bloomington: Indiana University Press, 1979); Charles S. Peirce, *Collected Papers of Charles Sanders Peirce* (ed. Charles Hartshorne and Paul Weiss; 8 vols.; Cambridge, MA: Harvard University Press, 1931–58); Ferdinand de Saussure, *A Course in General Linguistics* (ed. Charles Bally and Albert Sechehaye; trans. Wade Baskin; New York: McGraw-Hill, 1959).

SEMITISM

A word, phrase, or other idiomatic construction in the Greek NT or the LXX that derives from a Semitic language, typically Hebrew or Aramaic. A word derived from Hebrew is referred to as a HEBRAISM, while one derived from Aramaic is called an Aramaism.

SENSE

A term not only for what is said but also for the MEANING of what is said. When associated with meaning, *sense* is normally used to refer to what is said about a REFERENT. In this respect, *sense* refers to the message that a TEXT (a sentence, paragraph, or an entire book) conveys through its various linguistic, rhetorical, and literary structures. For example, Rom. 9:30–10:12 is about righteousness (righteousness is the referent), but the sense of the passage is what Paul says about righteousness through a contrast between the righteousness of the Jews and that of the Gentiles (a righteousness derived solely from faith in the Christ).

SENSES OF SCRIPTURE. *See* FOURFOLD SENSE OF SCRIPTURE

SENSUS COMMUNIS

Literally meaning "common sense," a term for practical wisdom or judgment in INTERPRETATION. The term is sometimes used in opposition to interpretation based on scientific methods and can refer to a kind of judgment that knows what is important "within a practical and intersubjective frame of reference" (Thiselton, 321). In POSTMODERN thought, however, *sensus communis* is not a true given, a metaphysical reality, but a prejudgment or taste held in common within a community. A thing is plain only as it is held in common within a community. Thus, what is common sense or practically known is such only as an agreed-upon appraisal within a community.

Bibliography. Anthony Thiselton, *New Horizons in Hermeneutics* (Grand Rapids: Zondervan, 1992).

SENSUS PLENIOR

A term introduced in the 1920s by A. Fernandez and applied by Roman Catholic theologians in the mid-twentieth century to designate a "deeper meaning" of SCRIPTURE, intended by God but not necessarily by the AUTHOR (Soulen and Soulen, 171). This MEANING could be found in the progressive development of understanding of revelation. *Sensus plenior* does not preclude the literal, historical meaning of Scripture but makes room for theological INTERPRETATION. Although the term fell into disuse in the latter part of the twentieth century, the concepts of INTERTEXTUALITY, READER-RESPONSE CRITICISM, CANONICAL CRITICISM, and other contemporary interpretive approaches that recognize the role of the reader or community in interpretation have inadvertently taken up the concept.

Bibliography. Richard N. Soulen and R. Kendall Soulen, *Handbook of Biblical Criticism* (3rd ed.; Louisville: Westminster John Knox, 2001).

SEPTUAGINT

Originally, a Greek TRANSLATION of the TORAH under Ptolemy II in Alexandria, Egypt, in about 250 BCE. It was expanded over time by adding historical, prophetic, and other books, including the APOCRYPHA. The LXX became the biblical text for Greek-speaking (i.e., Hellenistic) Jews in the Greco-Roman world and later for Christians. When the NT writers quote from the OT, they generally do so from the LXX. As a result, the LXX lost favor with the Jews. In OT studies, the Lucianic RECENSION (Lucian of Antioch d. 312 CE) or "Proto-Septuagint" is used. Earlier recensions of the Greek TEXT are the "Proto-Lucian" (second to first century BCE) and the Kaige (first century CE). For an introduction to the LXX, see Jobes and Silva.

Bibliography. Richard N. Soulen and R. Kendall Soulen, *Handbook of Biblical Criticism* (3rd ed.; Louisville: Westminster John Knox, 2001); Karen Jobes and Moisés Silva, *Invitation to the Septuagint* (Grand Rapids: Baker, 2000).

SEPTUAGINTISM

A word or phrase that a NT writer borrows from the SEPTUAGINT. Most of the Hebraic style of the NT derives from the LXX. Whether a Septuagintism was conscious or not is hard to determine. Nonetheless, the SPEECHES in Acts 2:15–39 and 3:12–26 seem to be constructed according to the LXX style of Greek. Expressions such as "lifted up his voice" and "give ear" in Acts 2:14 (ASV) and Matthew's use of *parthenos* in 1:23 (a quote from Isa. 7:14) are other instances of Septuagintisms.

SERIAL MONOGAMY

A form of MONOGAMY in which a man may have only one wife at a time. For example, in ancient Hebrew culture, a man could divorce a barren woman to marry another woman.

SERMON

An early Christian text that has a didactic and/or hortatory character. According to David Aune, the terms *sermon* and *homily* "are not really labels for a literary genre, since NT scholarship has not yet been able to define what a sermon is" (197). Nonetheless, scholars have identified some letters as sermonic—Hebrews, James, 1 Peter, *1–2 Clement*, 1 John, and *Barnabas*. The letters in the NT that may be classified as sermons are probably indebted to the Jewish synagogue sermons, which, according to Aune, were common by 70 CE. These sermons were based on the "Torah reading of the day" (Aune, 202). Aune points out that the sermons may have had a variety of openings.

> One type begins with the formula "May our master teach us" followed by a halakhic question. Another type that probably reflects actual oral sermons is the "proem" homily of which about 2,000 are preserved. Proem homilies began with a quotation from a "remote" text from the WRITINGS. The object was to link the first text with the first verse of the Torah reading for the day, i.e., to resolve the tension between two seemingly unrelated passages by showing how they were complementary. (202)

James Bailey and Lyle Vander Broek (191), using the work of Lawrence Wills, argue that sermonic compositions in both early Christian and Jewish literature had "an emphasis upon theological and scriptural 'exampla' and upon exhortation." As examples, they refer to the sermons in Acts, all with a three-part structure. First, the sermon will have used "theological or scriptural" examples; second, it will present a conclusion drawn from the evidence of the examples; and third, it will offer an exhortation following from the first two parts. Accordingly, the sermons in Acts 13:16b–41; 2:14–40; 3:12–26; 20:17–35 follow this pattern. According to Wills, 1 Cor. 10:1–14; 2 Cor. 6:14–7:1; 1 Pet. 1–2; *1 Clement* 4.1–13.1a; 37.2–4 are all examples of early Christian sermons. *See* HOMILY.

Bibliography. David Aune, *The New Testament in Its Literary Environment* (Philadelphia: Westminster, 1987); James Bailey and Lyle Vander Broek, *Literary Forms in the New Testament* (Louisville: Westminster John Knox, 1992); Lawrence Wills, "The Form of the Sermon in Hellenistic Judaism and Early Christianity," *Harvard Theological Review* 77 (1984): 277–99.

SERMON ON THE MOUNT

The name traditionally assigned to the material in Matt. 5:1–7:27, the first of five major DISCOURSES in Matthew's GOSPEL. Many scholars believe that Matthew selected and arranged (*see* SELECTION AND ARRANGEMENT) material from his various sources into five major divisions, each containing NARRATIVE material and a discourse. Scholars also argue for the possibility that by arranging his material into five major sections along with a PROLOGUE and EPILOGUE, Matthew may have been presenting Jesus as the new Moses and his VERSION of the Gospel as the new TORAH. The Sermon on the Mount consists of the BEATITUDES (5:1–12), PARABLES (5:13–16), ANTITHESES in which Jesus reinterprets the Torah (5:17–48), and miscellaneous teachings (6:1–7:27).

SERMON ON THE PLAIN

The traditional name for the material in Luke 6:20–49, a shorter VERSION of Matthew's SERMON ON THE MOUNT. The Sermon on the Plain introduces a longer section of material in Luke, generally referred to as the LESSER INTERPOLATION (6:20–8:3), in which Luke combines material from Mark, Q, and L. The Sermon on the Plain begins with an abbreviated version of the BEATITUDES, which seem to be much more humanized or materialized when compared with those in Matthew's GOSPEL. For example, whereas Matthew refers to persons who hunger after righteousness, Luke's version refers directly to those who experience physical hunger. In Matthew, the poor are those "poor in spirit," while in Luke the poor are the penniless and impoverished. Following the Beatitudes is a truncated list of woes, which reflect one of Luke's major THEMES: the reversal of status between the rich and the poor. The sermon then offers a number of brief instructions on loving one's enemies, judging a tree by its fruit, building with or without a foundation, and a warning against judging others (6:27–49).

SERVANT SONGS

A series of four songs in Isa. 42:1–9; 49:1–7; 50:4–9; and 52:13–53:12. In Jewish TRADITION, the Servant in these songs is a PERSONIFICATION of the nation of Israel. Some OT scholars, however, variously believe the Servant to be an individual or the Prophet. Some Christians see in these songs the figure of the suffering of Jesus.

SETTING

One of the main components of NARRATIVE, providing the physical BACKGROUND for the ACTION in the narrative. The setting includes the time and physical CONTEXT accompanying the objects in that context, along with the occupations and living conditions (religious, social, political, intellectual) of the characters. The setting of an event is usually crucial for interpreting a narrative unit. For example, the narrative of David's encounter with Bathsheba takes place in the capital city of Jerusalem, a place where the king would not normally be during time of war. The Matthean account of Jesus's DISCOURSE on the LAW takes place on a mountain. This setting is not incidental when the reader discovers that Matthew is identifying Jesus, who interprets the TORAH, with Moses, who received Torah on Mount Sinai. It is also significant that the two feedings of multitudes in Mark occur in Jewish and Gentile territories respectively.

Biblical narrative usually exhibits a special relationship between the action, the characters involved in the action, and the setting (Ryken, 54–62). The setting in Hebrew narrative serves an aesthetic purpose, creating a distinct atmosphere (Sternberg, 44–56). The setting may accomplish this through symbolic SIGNIFICANCE, such as the pit and prison scenes in the Joseph narrative and the pastoral scene in Gen. 18:1–8. In the latter example, Abraham spots three travelers while he is sitting at the entrance of his tent in the heat of the day. In accordance with proper Mediterranean hospitality, Abraham goes out of his way to persuade the strangers to visit.

Bibliography. Leland Ryken, *Words of Delight: A Literary Introduction to the Bible* (Grand Rapids: Baker, 1987); Meir Sternberg, *The Poetics of Biblical Narrative* (Bloomington: Indiana University Press, 1985).

SETTING IN LIFE. *See* SITZ IM LEBEN

SEXISM

A term, dating from the early 1970s, used to designate the ASSUMPTION that the female is in some ways inferior to the male. It also refers to discrimination based on the PRESUPPOSITIONs about the universally defined nature of GENDER. Any objects, IMAGES, and productions that treat women as sex objects for the gratification of men are sexist. *See* FEMINIST CRITICISM; RACE, CLASS, AND GENDER CRITICISM.

SHAME/DISHONOR. *See* HONOR-SHAME SOCIETY

SHORT STORY

Although difficult to classify, the short story may be defined as a short NARRATIVE of FICTION in PROSE. It is also characterized by the presence of PLOT, CHARACTERIZATION, and SETTING. The short story will encourage thought with respect to a SUBJECT and THEME, making it more than a simple record of an ACTION or event. Given the above definition, the *Decameron* of Boccaccio, the *Canterbury Tales* of Chaucer, the medieval *Lais* of Marie de France, and the stories of Hawthorne, Poe, Irving, and Fitzgerald are short stories. In the Bible, Jonah, Esther, Ruth, and the Joseph narrative, to name a few, may be read as short stories.

SIGN

In the simplest SENSE, something that substitutes for or represents something else. For example, in the context of driving an automobile, a green light signifies "go." Animate and inanimate objects may serve as signs, and for any one sign, there may be several INTERPRETATIONS. Every sign is semiotic: it signifies or means within a system involving both sender and receiver (the green light is the sender, the driver of the automobile the receiver). In literature, the sender is the AUTHOR, NARRATOR, or character, and the receiver is the reader.

According to Charles Sanders Peirce, there are three types of signs—ICON, INDEX, and SYMBOL—to which Luis Prieto added a fourth, signal. The relationship between the *index* and what it signifies is natural; for example, a fever is the index for an illness. It has no communicative INTENTION. The relationship between a *signal* and what it signifies is conventional and arbitrary: it must be understood within a system. An example of a signal is a white flag, signifying "truce." An *icon* resembles the thing that it signifies. For example, a drawing of a car signifies the car. The relationship between the icon and what it signifies may be natural or conventional. The symbol is usually conventional and arbitrary, such as white robes for purity or black hats for bad guys. In this respect, words are symbols that stand in for what they signify (Whiteside-St. Leger Lucas, 624).

Ferdinand de Saussure described the sign as binary: the signifier (the thing heard or read) and the signified (the concept). For example, the acoustic sound *dog* signifies the four-legged, furry animal who is "man's best friend" and likes to chase cats. According to Saussure, the signified consists of two parts: the denotative (concept) and the connotative (that which is signified within a particular context; *see* CONNOTATION; DENOTATION). Furthermore, the relationship between the signifier and signified is completely arbitrary. So there is, for example, no necessary or logical relationship between the acoustic sound *trē* and a tree or the concept of tree. Finally, Saussure claimed that signs can signify only because of their differences from all other signs (Macey, 352).

Since Saussure, however, linguists have tended to define a sign as triadic rather than as binary. A sign has a signifier, signified, and REFERENT, although different linguists and semioticians have different names for the parts. For example, I. A. Richards used *symbol, thought,* and *referent*; Gottlob Frege used *sign, sense,* and *nominatum*; and Charles Morris used *sign vehicle, designatum,* and *denotatum.* They all, however, correspond to the same triad of signifier, signified, and referent, where referent is the actual object or state of affairs signified within a particular CONTEXT.

More recently, Jacques Derrida has rejected the sign with respect to context and system. According to Derrida, a sign is always split and is never completely present because it has meaning only in its DIFFERENCE from other signs. The meaning of a sign is always deferred and thus never completely determinate. The consequence is that a sign leaves a mark, which then serves as a TRACE of its SIGNIFICANCE. Since there exist only gaps between these traces, readers of texts, for example, may construe the significance as they desire.

Bibliography. Andrew Edgar and Peter Sedgwick, eds., *Cultural Theory: The Key Concepts* (New York: Routledge, 2002); Anna Whiteside-St. Leger Lucas, "Sign," in *Encyclopedia of Contemporary Literary Theory* (ed. Irena R. Makaryk; Toronto: University of Toronto Press, 1993), 623–27; David Macey, *The Penguin Dictionary of Critical Theory* (London: Penguin, 2000).

SIGNIFICANCE

According to E. D. Hirsch, "a relationship between meaning and a person, or a conception, or a situation, or indeed anything imaginable" (8). Significance, then, is the application to some situation of the understanding derived from a TEXT. Most often, when biblical scholars refer to significance, they are talking about the way INTERPRETATION relates to a contemporary audience. Consequently, significance extends beyond the MEANING a text may have had for the AUTHOR and original audience.

Bibliography. E. D. Hirsch, *Validity in Interpretation* (New Haven: Yale University Press, 1973).

SIGNIFICATION

In the LINGUISTICS of Ferdinand de Saussure, the relationship between the signifier and signified, a relationship that is arbitrary. Since a SIGN has no MEANING apart from its DIFFERENCE from other signs, signification occurs only within this ABSENCE.

SIGNIFIED. *See* SIGN

SIGNIFIER. *See* SIGN

SIGNIFYING PRACTICE

A term in the theory of Julia Kristeva for the idea that language is a socially communicable DISCOURSE. According to Kristeva, there are two modes of signifying practice: the semiotic and the symbolic. The semiotic mode consists of psychic and sex drives (mental and physical desires), while the symbolic consists of positions and judgments (rules of syntax and grammar that allow for people to make judgments and to assume a position on a subject). These two modes can be combined in a variety of ways, each combination constituting an identity.

Bibliography. Julia Kristeva, *Revolution in Poetic Language* (trans. Margaret Waller; New York: Columbia University Press, 1984).

SIGNS SOURCE

In NT studies, a hypothetical source for the "signs," which are thematic in the Gospel of John. *See* GOSPEL OF SIGNS.

SIMILE

A comparison of two objects, ACTIONS, or ideas by using words such as "like" and "as." The MEANING of a simile is the comparison itself. In most instances, the two objects of the simile are familiar within the experiences of the audience. Some property of the second half of the simile serves to illuminate an aspect of the first half. When Job says, "A mortal . . . comes up like a flower and withers" (14:1–2a), he is comparing the brevity of a person's earthly existence to the brevity of a flower's existence. The AUTHOR is obviously not concerned with other properties of the flower, such as color, fragrance, or shape. The comparison is direct and clear within the CONTEXT. When the suitor in the Song of Songs (4:1) says that his beloved's "hair is like a flock of goats moving down the slopes of Mount Gilead," he is not hinting that she should wash her hair. Apparently there is something about the scene of a flock of goats descending a mountain that recalls the TEXTURE or flowing smoothness of his beloved's hair. The reader obviously should not try to burden the comparison with other elements, such as the smell of a flock of goats or the height of the mountain. When a simile occurs, the reader should question why the author employs the particular simile at this place and how the simile elucidates the concept being presented.

SIMILITUDE

One of Adolf Jülicher's types of PARABLE, in which the parable draws attention to some commonly recurrent event, such as the growth of the mustard seed, the leavening of bread, or the properties of salt. In this type of parable, the reader must ascertain the relationship between the event and the more abstract issue being illuminated.

SITZ IM LEBEN

German for "setting in life," a term in FORM CRITICISM for the sociological SETTING in Israel or the early church in which certain LITERARY and rhetorical forms were developed and used. These forms include LEGEND, PARABLE, PSALM, SAYING, and so forth. In REDACTION CRITICISM of the NT, the term has come to refer to the LITERARY setting of the forms within the NT texts, especially the GOSPELS. In other words, the NT AUTHORS removed the forms from their original sociological settings and recontextualized (*see* RECONTEXTUALIZATION) them within the TEXTS.

SOCIAL CODE. *See* CODE

SOCIAL CONSTRUCTION

A designation for the ASSUMPTION that human reality is a social construct rather than an external fact. Groups of persons create thought systems that explain and impose an order on their myriad contingent experiences. These thought systems become major ideologies (*see* IDEOLOGY). Each culture or society understands itself and assesses everything within these constructions. For a discussion of this concept, see Berger and Luckmann.

Bibliography. Peter Berger and Thomas Luckmann, *The Social Construction of Reality* (London: Penguin, 1971).

SOCIAL FORMATION

A term, especially in contemporary MARXIST CRITICISM, to designate a certain kind of society (e.g., feudal, capitalist, bourgeois). According to Louis Althusser, these societies are determined by their economic substructure. Within this concept, Althusser has tried to develop a model for the relationship between society and literature. In order to do so, he divides social formation into four levels: economic, political, ideological, and theoretical. These four levels are related to each other in a hierarchical STRUCTURE in which the economic level is the determining one. For example, in modern capitalist societies, the economic level determines that the political level is dominant. Within this definition, Althusser makes room for the evaluation of writers without basing that evaluation on how closely or naturally they reflect their societies. They may actually have a relative autonomy in their societies, not reflecting their societies' ideologies (*see* IDEOLOGY), but are nonetheless related to their societies economically in the ways in which they produce.

Bibliography. Louis Althusser, *For Marx* (trans. Ben Brewster; London: New Left Books, 1977).

SOCIAL LOCATION

The CONTEXTS (ideological, cultural, LITERARY, religious, etc.) within which individuals understand, make judgments, value, and think. Contemporary literary and cultural theorists assume that both AUTHORs and readers perform their respective tasks within their social locations, never quite able to step outside them to perform objective actions.

SOCIAL-SCIENTIFIC CRITICISM

An interpretive method that seeks to understand TEXTS within the matrix of their social, cultural, historical, and LITERARY contexts. Social-scientific criticism is a series of questions about broad and specific details concerning social and cultural MEANINGS. The process of social-scientific criticism is concerned with the questions of How? Why? What? Where? When? and Is? These questions are asked of the text in order to understand the social institutions, the cultural values, and the norms of a particular era. Social-scientific criticism of the Bible is a part of the exegetical (*see* EXEGESIS) task that analyzes the social and cultural dimensions of a text and its environment. It is an adjunct to BIBLICAL STUDIES in that it seeks to clarify the differences between historical conditions, social

institutions, and cultural writings proper to the biblical accounts and those proper to the modern interpreter, thereby providing a clearer comprehension for the reading and use of the BIBLE and biblical history. It also complements other forms of CRITICISM by asking additional questions relative to societies that other methods do not ask. Social-scientific criticism's contribution to biblical studies is its focus on historical conditions, social institutions, and cultural writings.

Social-scientific criticism studies the text as within the social and cultural settings in which the text was produced. Its aim is to determine meanings both explicit and implicit in the text. Social-scientific critics assume that the meanings of a text are made possible and shaped by the social and cultural systems of the AUTHORs and intended audiences. They try to determine the patterns and CODES of social behavior, such as purity codes, honor-and-shame codes (*see* HONOR-SHAME SOCIETY), familial and friendship relations, and patron-client codes during the time of the text's production.

Since the modern reader is so far removed from the world that produced the text, meaning cannot be completely determined within the historical, geographical, and cultural milieu without consideration of social aspects. For example, the birth of Jesus is examined within the matrix of the social, economic, political, and cultural contexts. The ASSUMPTION is that environment shapes attitudes, expectations, values, and beliefs. The knowledge gained from social-scientific criticism fills in the gaps and provides a more reliable understanding of the texts.

The beginning point for social-scientific criticism is outside the text. When researching the social history of early Christianity, for example, one must question the social level of the first Christians, the church-sect typology, and the perspectives of sociology in order to understand the relations between early Christian beliefs and social situations. The social scientist will seek to understand the general cultural and historical features of the author's place in history and the modes of engagement with others in the audience. Bruce Malina, a prominent social scientist, suggests that the relevant question to ask about interpreting a text from a social-science perspective is, "Who says what to whom about what, in what setting and for what purpose?" (22).

Social-scientific criticism articulates three components involved in interpretation: interpreters, the object to be interpreted, and the method of INTERPRETATION. It also assumes that all knowledge is socially conditioned (Elliot, 36). This applies equally to interpreters, authors, and the group under investigation. The method itself should include a means of distinguishing and clarifying differences between the SOCIAL LOCATION of the interpreter, the author, and the object to be interpreted. Social location includes factors such as GENDER, age, class, roles, education, occupation, political and religious associations, language and cultural traditions, and location in place and time (Malina, 37–38).

Malina identifies two types of societies: low-context and high-context. Low-context societies produce detailed texts giving as much information as possible; high-context societies produce sketchy and mysterious information. He classifies authors of the Bible and other writings of the Mediterranean peoples as high-context communicators. The purpose of social-scientific criticism, according to Malina, is to fill in the gaps of high-context documents. The problem for modern readers is that the Bible is a culturally conditioned book, written in a different place and time, in a different social location. Only the original author and original hearer knew the totality of the conditions. The modern reader must be sensitive to the cultural diversity between Mediterranean cultures and Western culture (Malina, 25–27).

Social-scientific critics often begin with observations in the present and work backward to reconstruct a facsimile of an ancient culture. Social scientists look to modern Mediterranean cultures and, using models that they assume have remained relatively unchanged for centuries, attempt to make competent observations about the social data and dynamics of ancient Mediterranean cultures. In other words, the daily human values and social structures of contemporary Mediterranean cultures supply social scientists with examples resembling ancient biblical societies.

Social-scientific criticism is not a method that creates or manufactures new data; it is a way to view and understand all the data that is available. It serves a "heuristic" function and aids in the discovery and expansion of ideas (Elliot, 15). The important requirement for the social-scientific critic is to determine the means by which the differences between the social location of the interpreter and that of ancient authors can be decided. The method takes "into account what a text meant in its own historical, social, and literary context as well as what it means today" (Osiek, 2). The social context and structure of early biblical texts must be examined in every possible way to gain insights into the complete social description and analysis of the HEBREW BIBLE and the NT. The social-scientific method builds on the HISTORICAL-CRITICAL METHOD for new and inventive ways of gathering data in the process of INTERPRETATION.

To begin to understand religious acts, one must understand or have knowledge of ancient social structures and institutions. So social-scientific criticism raises questions about social structures and social circumstances. It focuses on issues of self-identity, social organization, kinship systems, patrilineal descent, economic implications of marriage (both ENDOGAMOUS and EXOGAMOUS), family, lineage, customs, economics, and political structures. By raising and examining such issues, the social-scientific critic hopes to diminish the tendency of modern readers to project the structures of their own social locations (individualism, progress, freedom, time, mobility, class structure, etc.) into the systems of both Israelite and formative Christian cultures (Yee, 45).

The social-scientific study of the NT consists of four approaches: the social description, the social history, the sociology of knowledge, and the use of models from the social sciences. The *social description* evaluates information gathered from NT literature and ARCHAEOLOGY, such as art, coins, inscriptions, and so forth. It seeks information concerning the NT SETTING, which includes travel, occupations, housing, money, economics, markets, clothes, food, and so on. Following are questions asked by scientists employing the social description model: How did the people dress? What did a synagogue look like? The *social-history* approach tries to determine the answers to questions concerning the social developments and movements of the early Christians within the Greco-Roman world. *Sociology of knowledge* provides insight into particular cultural groups, discovering how groups organize and interpret experiences within society. Sociology tries to reconstruct a group's WORLDVIEW.

Models from the *social sciences* involve the study of a number of similar cultures in order to create a grid or model that allows anthropologists to map the "dynamics of a culture and to describe certain phenomena that occur in many cultures" (Rhoads, 141). These models examine issues such as rituals, kinship relations, purity-pollution taboos, and economic systems. The ASSUMPTION of those who practice this approach is that the grid or model allows for a more objective examination of a culture with less ethnocentrism. In other words, the grid allows anthropologists to use a framework that differs from their own cultural context. An example, according to Rhoads (142), is that if social scientists study the characteristics common to cultures that believe in demon possession, they will be in a better position to examine the belief in demon possession in first-century Israel and early Christianity.

On the one hand, the BIBLE was produced by individual members of faith communities, and thus it reflects the historical perspective and cultural patterns of those communities. On the other hand, modern readers tend to interpret the Bible in terms of their own historical perspective and cultural patterns. Bridging the gap introduced by these two truisms is the domain of social-scientific criticism. It tries to do so by providing methods that explain what a text meant in its original historical and social contexts. By applying the constructs provided by sociologists and social anthropologists, social-science critics employ cross-cultural models of human interaction and methods of analyzing data regarding social organizations, politics, structures of authority, and social institutions. For example, social scientists have found that the Greco-Roman world was characterized by an intractable hierarchical structure that guarded and maintained a stable social order. The family was the microcosm of this structure, with its tripartite relational organization founded on a pattern of dominance and subordination: parent/child, husband/wife, and master/servant. Since the state was the structural macrocosm of the family, and the state's existence depended on this family pattern, any deviation from the structure on the level of the family would have been viewed as a threat to the state's well-being. After experimenting with a new egalitarian structure, the church realized that such an experiment threatened its existence. It thus adopted the pattern of dominance and subordination as its internal structure at both ecclesiastical and family levels. Based on such an insight from social-scientific criticism, the interpretation and application of passages such as Eph. 5:21–6:9; Col. 3:18–4:1; and 1 Pet. 2:13–3:8 take on new significance.

Social-scientific critics have identified several concerns with the method. They acknowledge that the method is still in its developmental stage and see it as falling short in several areas, such as in the lack of a unified and concise vocabulary, the indiscriminate use of models and methods, an indistinct sense of direction for how and when to use the method, and a lack of understanding regarding the PRESUPPOSITIONS underlying the social-science models. Some scholars are reluctant to use the method on biblical texts because there is insufficient data to serve as a basis for sociological analysis (Brown and Meier, 14).

Bibliography. Raymond E. Brown and John P. Meier, *Antioch and Rome: New Testament Cradles of Catholic Christianity* (New York: Paulist Press, 1983); John Elliot, *What Is Social-Scientific Criticism?* (Minneapolis: Fortress, 1993);

Philip F. Esler, *The First Christians in Their Social World: Social-Scientific Approaches to New Testament Interpretation* (New York: Routledge, 1994); idem, ed., *Modeling Early Christianity: Social-Scientific Studies of the New Testament in Its Context* (New York: Routledge, 1995); Bengt Holmberg, *Sociology and the New Testament: An Appraisal* (Minneapolis: Fortress, 1990); Diana Kendall, ed., *Race, Class, and Gender in a Diverse Society* (Boston: Allyn & Bacon, 1997); Bruce J. Malina, *The Social World of Jesus and the Gospels* (New York: Routledge, 1996); David A. May, *Social-Scientific Criticism of the New Testament: A Bibliography* (4 vols.; Macon, GA: Mercer University Press, 1991); Carolyn Osiek, *What Are They Saying about the Social Setting of the New Testament?* (New York: Paulist Press, 1984); David Rhoads, "Social Criticism: Crossing Boundaries," in *Mark and Method: New Approaches in Biblical Studies* (ed. Janice Capel Anderson and Stephen D. Moore; Minneapolis: Fortress, 1982), 135–61; Richard Rohrbaugh, ed., *The Social Sciences and New Testament Interpretation* (Peabody, MA: Hendrickson, 1996); Gale A. Yee, ed., *Judges and Method: New Approaches in Biblical Studies* (Minneapolis: Fortress, 1995).

SOCIOECONOMIC CRITICISM

This type of criticism examines the manner in which literature (and art in general) reinforces race, gender, and economic divisions in a society. It also tries to uncover the ways in which interpretations of literature inscribe, justify, and perpetuate those divisions. Fernando Segovia argues that socioeconomic class has had a profound influence on interpretation: "There was an interpretation of the poor-oppressed and an interpretation of the bourgeois-oppressor" (286). Socioeconomic criticism also encompasses LIBERATION THEOLOGY, "the interpretation of biblical and related texts from a self-conscious perspective and program of social transformation" (283).

Bibliography. Fernando F. Segovia, "Reading the Bible Ideologically: Socioeconomic Criticism," in *To Each Its Own Meaning* (ed. Steven L. McKenzie and Stephen R. Hayes; rev. ed.; Louisville: Westminster John Knox, 1999), 283–306.

SOCIO-RHETORICAL CRITICISM

A term introduced by Vernon Robbins in his book *Jesus the Teacher*, which subsequently developed into an interpretive method currently defined by Robbins as "a textually-based method that uses

programmatic strategies to invite social, cultural, historical, psychological, aesthetic, ideological and theological information into a context of minute exegetical activity" ("Criticism," 165). Since that time, other names associated to varying degrees with the approach are Michael A. K. Halliday, Clarise J. Martin, Clifford Geertz, David Aune, Burton Mack, Ched Myers, Brandon Scott, Bruce Malina, Jerome Neyrey, David Rhoads, Robert Tannehill, Donald Michie, and Richard Rohrbaugh, to mention only a few.

One of the hallmarks of the approach is that it is interdisciplinary, pulling together praxes from a number of areas. When performed according to prescription, socio-rhetorical criticism involves an extremely detailed analysis of texts through the grids of multiple disciplines—LITERARY CRITICISM, RHETORICAL CRITICISM, SOCIAL-SCIENTIFIC CRITICISM, CULTURAL ANTHROPOLOGY, PSYCHOANALYTIC CRITICISM, and HISTORICAL-CRITICAL METHOD. As Robbins puts it, "Socio-rhetorical critics . . . approach a text much like an anthropologist 'reads' a village and its culture" (165). For the socio-rhetorical critic, the focus of INTERPRETATION is the TEXT as a cultural, social, ideological, historical, and theological DISCOURSE, and the data from these various areas have an intertextual relation with respect to the textual SIGNS (166). The socio-rhetorical critic, then, understands the term "rhetorical" as referring to the text as a literary object, a STORY that must be read, and takes the term "socio-" as referring to the text as a cultural artifact that must be opened "to the past, present, and future" (Robbins, *Jesus the Teacher*, xxiii). From this posture, Robbins (xxiii) has articulated a fourfold framework within which socio-rhetorical criticism works: (1) rhetorical-literary aspects of the text; (2) the INTERTEXTUALITY of the text; (3) the social and cultural dynamics operating in the text; and (4) IDEOLOGY. After further observing that socio-rhetorical criticism presupposes that a text (at least a literary one) is the result of the social function of language, Robbins argues that "the task of interpretation is so large that no single person can achieve the insights necessary for interpreting all the aspects of a text. The task requires efforts by teams on various fronts who are willing to bring their insights and information together" (xxiv). As a result of this observation, then, Robbins restates the fourfold framework of the CRITICISM based on the various textures of the text.

Textures of text. By "texture" Robbins means that a text is composed of a labyrinth of SIGNIFICATION and communication: the signs of the text conjure up cognitive, social, emotive, and material meanings (*Jesus the Teacher*, xxvii). A corollary to this last claim is that readers of texts will focus on one texture at the expense of the others, suggesting that MEANING is the function of the reader's background, AGENDA, and activities as much as the result of the signs themselves. In other words, unless the reader invests the signs with significance, the text means nothing. The idea of texture, then, leads to the fourfold description (Robbins, "Criticism") that more appropriately accounts for the interpreter and INTERPRETIVE COMMUNITY's ideological involvement in the interpretive enterprise. The fourfold focus—or "arenas of interests," as Robbins calls them—is (1) inner-texture, (2) intertexture, (3) social and cultural texture, and (4) ideological texture. In a later publication, *Exploring the Texture of Texts*, Robbins adds a fifth texture: sacred texture.

Inner-texture. Inner-texture focuses on the features of the text's language, including such things as word patterns (e.g., REPETITION of words and the sequencing of terms); the beginning, middle, and end of a unit; form of argument; voices; mode of NARRATION; literary and rhetorical devices; and the mixing of SPEECH and NARRATIVE (Robbins, *Exploring*, 3–7). Inner-texture is the entry level of analyzing the argumentation of the text. Robbins identifies six types of inner-texture: (1) repetitive, in which a word or phrase occurs multiple times in a single unit; (2) progressive, in terms of the sequencing of words or phrases in a unit, such as the alternation of words (e.g., the language of kingship in Mark 15:1–16:8) and WORD CHAINS; (3) narrational, which encompasses the various voices in the text (narratorial voice, reported speech, written texts, characters' voices); (4) opening-middle-closing, in which the nature of the STRUCTURE of the unit is examined, often becoming extremely complicated (the opening, middle, or closing may itself have an opening, middle, and closing, and each may be of a different type); (5) argumentative, which examines the nature of the argument of the text, especially in terms of both modern and ancient rhetorical theory (the argument may be logical or qualitative, employing a variety of rhetorical strategies); and (6) sensory-aesthetic, which is concerned with the ways in which the language of the text evokes the senses, emotion, and thought patterns of readers (issues of GENRE on the level of text and subtexts become important in this texture) (Robbins, *Exploring*, 8–30). Obviously, concerns of inner-texture involve an extremely detailed and systematic examination of the language and structure of the text.

Inner-texture is also concerned with the "extrinsic" dimension of interpretation. Every act of interpretation carries with it a "subtext"—or perhaps better, a matrix of subtexts—that the interpreter brings to the act of reading. An interpreter works within a discipline such as anthropology or psychology and also within another CRITICAL METHODOLOGY as well as within a variety of blind spots.

> It also investigates the boundaries interpreters set that limit subtexts to "Jewish" modes of thinking rather than opening them to "Hellenistic-Roman" modes of thinking; theological modes rather than social, cultural, psychological and religious modes; formal literary modes rather than argumentative, interactive, rhetorical modes; and modes of the mind alone rather than modes that include both body and mind. (Robbins, "Criticism," 172)

Intertexture. Intertexture examines the manner in which material outside the text is interpreted and presented within the text itself. Two important questions guide this type of analysis: "From where has this passage adopted its language? With what texts does this text stand in dialogue?" (Robbins, "Criticism," 179). Robbins describes five dimensions of intertexture analysis: analysis

413

of REFERENCE, recitation, recontextualization, reconfiguration, and echo ("Criticism," 179–85; Robbins, *Exploring*, 40–50). The interest here is not simply on the manner in which intertexture works within the text but on the manner in which interpreters work with intertexture.

The first dimension of intertexture is reference to persons, objects, places, TRADITIONS, and texts. In other words, analysis of reference is concerned about things with which the text is in dialogue, about ways in which interpreters decide what traditions and texts are referenced, and about the significance that those determinations have. The importance of such determinations is addressed below.

The second dimension is recitation, such as the manner in which a speech is reported: exact language, modified language, or language altogether different from the original. Recitation also deals with how EPISODES or events differ from one reporting to another, whether the account is summarized, expanded, or just what episode or event is referenced. Robbins argues that the uncertainty of references leaves the interpreter a certain amount of freedom to determine the reference, a determination that may be ideologically motivated. Hence, this interpretive determination may foreground (*see* FOREGROUNDING) one possibility while negating others.

Recontextualization is the third dimension of intertexture and refers to the practice of placing narratives, speeches, and other elements into new contexts without announcing the fact. For example, Robbins refers to R. E. Brown's *Birth of the Messiah*, in which he points out a significant number of recontextualized speeches from the LXX in Luke 1:26–56.

The fourth dimension, reconfiguration, is perhaps the most difficult but certainly a crucial one with respect to both the text and the interpreter. Robbins argues that AUTHORS reconfigure not only texts but also well-known traditions. As an example, one might point out that in the Magnificat, Luke reconfigures the Israelite tradition (MOTIF) of the barren woman who conceives a child at an advanced age. However, Robbins argues, the case is not that simple. Given both the Judaic and Hellenistic milieus of Luke's GOSPEL, there configuration may have multiple sources, including stories of virgins in the LXX and Greco-Roman stories of women impregnated by gods ("Criticism," 180). Robbins raises the issue here of interpretive purity or canonical boundaries in light of the fact that interpreters have traditionally simply ignored the two latter possibilities. The socio-rhetorical critic will argue, however, that Luke's reconfiguration is actually multiple or at least "multi-cultural" (180).

The final dimension is intertextual echo, which goes beyond recontextualization and reconfiguration to include soundings from tradition and culture. Given that the NT texts were written within a Mediterranean culture that was multifaceted, socio-rhetorical critics demand that all cultural traditions be brought to bear on the analysis of texts. On the one hand, for example, scholars certainly have compared the Magnificat with the praise HYMNS in the PSALMS. On the other hand, however, Robbins asks about the frequency with which scholars are willing to compare the Magnificat with hymns of praise in Roman-Hellenistic literature as well as other Mediterranean literature. This interpretive blind spot suggests to Robbins that interpreters have interpretive CANONS with clearly drawn boundaries ("Criticism," 181). For a more detailed description of intertexture (oral-scribal, cultural, social, and historical), see Robbins, *Exploring*, 40–70.

Social and cultural texture. A third texture important to socio-rhetorical criticism is social and cultural texture, which involves theories of both anthropology and sociology. The primary focus here is on "the social and culture nature of the text" (Robbins, *Exploring*, 71). Not only is the text an artifact of a particular culture and SOCIAL LOCATION; it is also a response to that culture and social location, both inscribing and evoking a particular world in its language. Robbins delineates the parameters of this texture in terms of "specific social topics, common social and cultural topics, and final cultural categories" (71).

Specific social topics may vary from text to text or even within the same culture, depending on the interests and concerns of the author. In other words, texts may respond to the culture in a variety of ways. Using Bryan Wilson's typology of sects, Robbins examines the seven different cultures that a religious text may create through its language, with each cultural world revealed through the rhetoric of the text. Below is Robbins's summary of the seven types:

1. The *conversionist* response views the world as corrupt because all people are corrupt: if people can be changed, then the world will be changed.
2. The *revolutionist* response assumes that only the destruction of the world—more specifically, of the social order—will suffice to save people.
3. The *introversionist* response sees the world as irredeemably evil and presupposes that salvation can be attained only by the fullest possible withdrawal from it.
4. The *gnostic* (*manipulationist*) response seeks only a transformed set of relationships—a transformed method of coping with evil—since salvation is possible in the world if people learn the right means, improved techniques, to deal with their problems.
5. The *thaumaturgical* response focuses on the concern of individual people to receive special dispensations for relief from present and specific ills.
6. The *reformist* response assumes that people may create an environment of salvation in the world by using supernaturally given insights to change the present social organization into a system that functions toward good ends.
7. The *utopian* response presupposes that people must take an active and constructive role in replacing the entire present social system with a new social organization in which evil is absent. ("Criticism," 185–86)

Common social and cultural topics are those that persons in a particular culture are familiar

with either consciously or unconsciously (Robbins would say "instinctively"). So persons in a culture assimilate different codes, patterns of thought, and value systems. When an interpreter can access these topics, the extent of interpretive anachronism is diminished. In first-century Mediterranean texts, the interpreter will be faced with social structures of HONOR/SHAME, clean/unclean, purity/impurity, codes of argumentation, systems of legality, economic exchange systems based on a variety of subsystems (e.g., agriculture, business), and hierarchical social structure.

The third group of topics is composed of final cultural categories, "those topics that most decisively identify one's cultural location" (Robbins, *Exploring*, 86). These topics separate the members of a culture into groups, and this separation can be detected in the rhetoric of the text. Sociologists generally divide a culture into dominant culture, subculture, contraculture, counterculture, and liminal culture. The socio-rhetorical critic examines the rhetoric of the text to determine the individual groups in the text, their dynamics, and the relationship between the dominant culture and the others. The ASSUMPTION at work here is that the subculture, contraculture, counterculture, and liminal culture all define themselves with respect to being controlled by the dominant culture or being embedded in it.

The rhetoric of the dominant culture inscribes values, standards, and ideas that those within the culture assume to be binding and natural on persons within an extended geographical area. A subculture emulates the rhetoric of the dominant culture but claims to execute the standards, values, and ideas more perfectly than the dominant culture itself. Counterculture "rejects explicit and mutable characteristics of the dominant or subculture rhetoric to which it responds" (Robbins, *Exploring*, 87). Here sociologists would include consciously heretical groups, displaying a rhetoric that presents not only an alternative culture but also a better one via its own ideology (e.g., the rhetoric of Jesus, esp. in Mark). Contraculture rhetoric is a "group culture rhetoric that is deeply embedded in another form of culture to which it is a reaction formation" (Robbins, "Criticism," 190). The values of this culture are simply the inversion of those to which it is reacting. Liminal culture rhetoric is the rhetoric of MARGINALITY, often found among people who are between two cultural identities or who are in transition from one culture to another (*see* LIMINALITY). The rhetoric of liminality is characterized by lack of coherence and consistency, is disjunctive, and reveals no definable identity. Robbins suggests that the rhetoric of the Gospel of Mark is liminal with respect to the identity of Jesus in that there is ultimately no definitive identity [of Jesus] by anyone in the narrative. So Jesus exists for this author and audience on the edges of culture.

Ideological texture. Examination of the ideological texture is based on the assumption that every text inscribes, consciously or unconsciously, an IDEOLOGY. An ideology is the body of ideas on which a culture's values, thoughts, judgments, and so forth are based. An ideology may be political, economic, religious, or social. Within IDEOLOGICAL CRITICISM, ideology may refer to three contexts:

(1) the ideological context in which an author produces a text, (2) the ideology reproduced within the text itself, and (3) the ideology of a text's readers or "customers." It asks questions such as, What assumptions are being made about what is natural, just, and right? What (and whom) do these assumptions distort or obscure? What are the power relations? (Soulen and Soulen, 84)

Socio-rhetorical criticism examines all three ideological contexts but tends to focus on the first two. By examining the artifacts (including textual ones), scholars can partially reconstruct the ideology of a culture.

Much of the work of anthropologists and sociologists focuses on this RECONSTRUCTION. To reconstruct the ideology represented by the text or, perhaps better, to reconstruct the ideology underlying the text, socio-rhetorical critics must analyze the language (rhetorical structures). Robbins suggests that certain questions should be asked: "What and whose self-interests are being negotiated in this text? If the dominant voices in the text persuade people to act according to their premises, who will gain and who will lose? What will be gained and what will be lost? . . . Whose ideology is being advanced, for whose benefit?" ("Criticism," 194–95). From the perspective of the socio-rhetorical critic, then, every text is ideologically (political, theological, etc.) based, a fact ensuring that every text is to at least some degree propagandistic. If we therefore assume that early Christianity had its politics or ideological positions, then we may also assume that its texts are ideological. For example, Robbins examines the voices and dialogues in the Magnificat in an attempt to uncover the ideologies at work in the narrative:

Who, we must ask, is benefiting by having Mary speak as she does in the Magnificat? Who is benefiting by having Mary speak out about raising the lowly up to power and driving the powerful away empty-handed? Whose ideology is being advanced, for whose benefit, by Mary's dialogue with the angel and Elizabeth and by the argumentation in the Magnificat? (194–95)

He goes on then to make a case that both "social and political" benefits are at the heart of Luke-Acts and that this case can be made by examining the rhetoric.

In *Exploring the Texture of Texts*, Robbins expands his comments about the social, cultural, and ideological locations of the interpreter and their influence on the interpretive process (see above in the sections on intertexture and on social and cultural texture) and applies them to this level of ideological texture. To their work on texts, interpreters bring ideologies that frame all their thoughts, assumptions, and actions. They work within a variety of communities, including professional ones, which define the focus of interests and the limits of examination: HISTORICAL-CRITICAL METHOD, SOCIAL-SCIENTIFIC CRITICISM, POSTMODERN CRITICISM, NEW HISTORICISM, POSTCOLONIAL CRITICISM, and so forth. Thus recognition and examination of these ideologies have gained increasing interest and attention in socio-rhetorical criticism.

Sacred texture. By the "sacred texture" of texts, Robbins means not only what the text says about the divine but also the ways in which readers explore the sacred nature of texts. The problem that Robbins sees with the latter is that a focus only on the sacred nature of the text results in "a disembodiment of their sacred texture from the realities of living in the world" (*Exploring*, 130). He therefore recommends that since the sacred texture is embedded within the other four textures, a more plausible understanding and a THICK DESCRIPTION of the text develop as the interpreter allows the sacred nature to emerge from a detailed examination of the first four textures. Elements that make up the sacred texture include rhetoric, narration, ACTION, and the underlying ideology in the text. This underlying ideology is located in the text's references to deity, holy persons, spirit beings, divine history, human redemption, human commitment, religious community, and ethics (120–30). Again, these elements emerge from a multitextured analysis of the text.

At the center of socio-rhetorical criticism is the recognition that written and oral communicative acts and their interpretations are social acts in which authors, speakers, and readers all stand squarely within meaning-making ideologies and communities. Consequently, texts and their interpreters constitute a multicontextual matrix of signification with multiple boundaries. Socio-rhetorical criticism responds to this complex labyrinth by drawing from a variety of interpretive approaches in order to configure readings that account for the greatest number of meanings and meaning effects that may not be configured by more narrowly circumscribed methods.

Bibliography. Raymond E. Brown, *The Birth of the Messiah: A Commentary on the Infancy Narratives in Matthew and Luke* (Garden City, NY: Doubleday, 1977); Vernon K. Robbins, *Exploring the Texture of Texts: A Guide to Socio-Rhetorical Interpretation* (Harrisburg, PA: Trinity Press International, 1996); idem, *Jesus the Teacher: A Socio-Rhetorical Interpretation of Mark* (Minneapolis: Fortress,

1992); idem, "Socio-Rhetorical Criticism," in *The New Literary Criticism and the New Testament* (ed. Edgar V. McKnight and Elizabeth Struthers Malbon; Valley Forge, PA: Trinity Press International, 1994), 164–209; Richard N. Soulen and R. Kendall Soulen, *Handbook of Biblical Criticism* (3rd ed.; Louisville: Westminster John Knox, 2001).

SOUND-PLAY

A type of wordplay (see PARONOMASIA) in which sounds are repeated, adding a stylistic dimension to a TEXT, an effect usually lost in TRANSLATION. ALLITERATION is a type of sound-play. Robert Alter offers examples from the third chapter of Job that can be heard only in the original Hebrew: "Let the day perish in which I was born, and the night that said, 'A man-child is conceived'" (3:3). In a loose TRANSLITERATION showing the stressed syllables, the line sounds as *yóvad yom iváled bó / vehaláylah 'amár hórah gáver.* Alter (77–78) also points out the sound-play in 3:22–23 in which the words *qéve* (grave) and *géver* ([young/strong] man) occur close together (KJV).

Bibliography. Robert Alter, *The Art of Biblical Poetry* (New York: Basic Books, 1985).

SOURCE CRITICISM

One component in the HISTORICAL-CRITICAL METHOD, source criticism is the study of biblical TEXTS in terms of the sources used in their composition. The goal is not simply to isolate and study the sources as documents in their own right but also to examine the manner in which biblical AUTHORS adapt earlier documents to their own unique purposes.

Source criticism has enjoyed a long and venerable career in both HEBREW BIBLE and NT studies. Source-critical studies of the Hebrew Bible have focused on the PENTATEUCH but more recently have included other parts of the Hebrew Bible. For centuries, the Mosaic authorship of the Pentateuch was generally accepted without much question. Gradually, however, scholars began to doubt whether everything in the Pentateuch could be from the hand of Moses. Under the influence of seventeenth-century rationalism and because of passages that could not have been from Moses (e.g., the account of Moses's death [Deut. 34:5–8], familiarity with the monarchy [Gen. 36:31–39], and the phrase "until this day," which suggests that the passages containing it were written after the time of Moses [Gen. 35:4 LXX; Deut. 34:5–6]), many scholars further questioned Mosaic authorship of the Pentateuch. Based on these passages and other discoveries—such as historical inaccuracies, repetitions, and divergent writing styles—these scholars concluded that the Pentateuch was the product of an extended process of compilation.

Pentateuchal studies. In the second half of the nineteenth century, Julius Wellhausen and Abraham Kuenen popularized the view that the Pentateuch and, more broadly, the HEXATEUCH are made up of four sources. Both Wellhausen and Kuenen detected a close relationship between the Pentateuch and the book of Joshua. They therefore spoke of the four-source hypothesis as relating to the Hexateuch. Later followers of Wellhausen claimed that the sources of the Hexateuch also formed the basis of the books through Kings. All subsequent source-critical scholarship is deeply indebted to Wellhausen, and many scholars today feel that the four-source theory is still the best explanation for the composition of the Pentateuch. For a concise and informative discussion of the challenges and alternatives to Wellhausen, see van der Woude, 166–205.

Scholars did not begin with the ASSUMPTION that these texts necessarily adopted and adapted earlier TRADITIONs and documents; rather, in reading the texts closely, they discovered what they assumed to be evidence of different sources within the texts, particularly within the Pentateuch. These different sources were evidenced by parallel accounts of the same event, combined accounts of the event, different LITERARY terminology, different literary structures within an account or between accounts, different theological viewpoints, and a variety of recurring MOTIFs. Habel suggests that the examination of texts through the grid of source criticism should focus on three categories of issues: literary STYLE, terminology, and perspective, or POINT OF VIEW. Under each of these categories,

Habel has identified subcategories. Under issues of literary style are writing techniques, structural arrangement, and use of language. Under the issues of terminology are recurring terms, names, key expressions, and clusters of words. And under the issue of perspective are central thrust and vantage point.

In source criticism of the OT, the DOCUMENTARY HYPOTHESIS (or four-source hypothesis) is straightforward. The four sources (*see* D; E; J; P) or documents were composed at different times and for different purposes. Each source thus constitutes a layer within the Hexateuch, and each layer has its peculiar language, style, and theological viewpoint (van der Woude, 188–90). For a detailed description of these four sources, *see* GRAF-WELLHAUSEN HYPOTHESIS.

New Testament studies. Although source criticism has been applied to all the writings of the NT, its primary focus there has been on the SYNOPTIC GOSPELS. This focus is twofold: a concern for the relationship between two or more texts that suggests some kind of dependence, and the discovery of sources within a single text.

The nineteenth century witnessed a tremendous concern to uncover the history behind the Gospels. A great deal of energy was expended especially in the attempt to reconstruct the life of Jesus. For this reason, the Gospels were treated as sources for reconstructing history. If one Gospel was earlier than the others, then that one should be historically more reliable, for it would have been closer to the actual events. In the first quarter of the twentieth century, B. H. Streeter proposed a solution to the relationship between the Synoptic Gospels that became popular in the English-speaking world (*see* FOUR DOCUMENT HYPOTHESIS). His explanation was a refinement of H. J. Holtzmann's (1832–1910) TWO-SOURCE HYPOTHESIS. This solution remains dominant in source-critical studies today. Simply put, this hypothesis claims that Mark was the first Gospel and was a source for both Matthew and Luke. It also claims that Matthew and Luke made use of another, no longer extant source, which has come to be known as Q (probably from German *Quelle*, "source").

Recent scholarship has challenged the AS-SUMPTION that the Gospels can serve as sources for reconstructing the life of Jesus. Scholars today generally recognize not only that the Gospels are separated from the events they describe by at least a generation (Mark was composed ca. 70 CE, and Matthew and Luke between 80 and 90 CE) but also that the Gospels are theologically rather than historically motivated. Also, the two-source hypothesis has met with significant CRITICISM. One older hypothesis (the GRIESBACH HYPOTHESIS) claims that Matthew and Luke were written before Mark, and Mark borrowed from them, especially where Matthew and Luke agree.

Source criticism is also concerned with identifying lost sources within the text. When they encounter a portion of a text thought to be uncharacteristic of the author's style, vocabulary, or IDEOLOGY, source critics usually suspect that the author has drawn from a source. An example of this is John 21, where the vocabulary differs significantly from that found in the rest of the Gospel (*ischyein* rather than *dynasthai*, and *exetazein* instead of *erōtan*). In Rom. 3:25–26 (TEV), we encounter the idea that God has "overlooked" past sins (NRSV: "divine forbearance"). This seems to contradict (not only in vocabulary but also in concept) what Paul has already claimed in Rom. 1–2, that God punishes all sin (Tuckett, 85). Some suspect Paul's use of a source here.

Source critics assume that an author's usual or normal vocabulary, style, and ideology can be discovered. But can scholars sufficiently define an author's normal vocabulary, style, and ideology and then use that definition as a CANON by which to determine whether a passage is or is not the work of that author? Most source critics think so.

Bibliography. Norman Habel, *Literary Criticism of the Old Testament* (Philadelphia: Fortress, 1971); Christopher Tuckett, *Reading the New Testament: Methods of Interpretation* (Philadelphia: Fortress, 1987); Moshe Weinfeld, *Deuteronomy and the Deuteronomic School* (Oxford: Oxford University Press, 1972); A. S. van der Woude, ed., *The World of the Old Testament* (Grand Rapids: Eerdmans, 1989).

SPECIFICATION

In Robert Alter's theory of BIBLICAL POETRY, a type of poetic FOCUSING in which the second VERSET of a line of POETRY makes more specific the first verset. An example can be seen in Amos 8:10:

> I will turn your feasts into mourning,
>   and all your songs into lamentation.

In this line, "all your songs" is a specific element within the larger event of "feasts," as is "lamentation" within "mourning."

Bibliography. Robert Alter, *The Art of Biblical Poetry* (New York: Basic Books, 1985).

SPEECH

A rhetorical device common in Hellenistic HISTORIOGRAPHY (*see* HELLENISM) and employed especially by the AUTHOR of Acts. Greek historians such as Herodotus and Thucydides employed speeches in their histories to explain how and why people behave as they do in particular situations. Speeches generally constitute from 20 to 35 percent of the texts. Evidence from Thucydides, Herodotus, and others suggests that these historians used speeches to display their rhetorical skills and to present what characters would have appropriately spoken on any particular occasion. For the most part, historians did not record speeches but rather composed them according to the appropriateness for the speaker, audience, and occasion.

In the book of Acts are thirty-two speeches, making up about 25 percent of the book. According to David Aune, "Eight speeches should be attributed to Peter, eleven to Paul, and one each to Stephen, James, and James with the elders. Six are attributed to non-Christians: Gamaliel, Demetrius, the town clerk in Ephesus, Tertullus, and Festus. In addition are two prayers, two letters, and about sixteen short dialogue sections" (125). An important question is whether Luke records actual speeches, composes approximations of actual speeches, or invents them wholesale. If Luke follows the conventions of Hellenistic historians, then he would most likely have invented the speeches that were appropriate to his characters, audience, and occasions.

On the one hand, it is impossible to prove or disprove that Luke recorded actual speeches. One the other hand, as Aune points out, "Luke probably faced the same problem as Thucydides, or any historian of recent events: . . . speeches were not usually transcribed and published" (125). Luke was separated from the events about which he wrote by at least a generation and most likely did not have access to written speeches. Consequently, he seems to have searched for sources, both oral and written, and then composed his speeches following the Hellenistic practice of writing them to reflect appropriateness for his characters and situations.

The speeches in the early chapters of Acts are evangelistic speeches, while those in chapters 22–26 are DEFENSE SPEECHES. According to Eduard Schweizer, the evangelistic speeches have a definite form: direct address, call for attention, a misunderstanding, quotation from SCRIPTURE, reference to Jesus, scriptural proof, declaration of salvation, and a call to repentance (e.g., 2:14–21; 3:12–26; 4:8–12; 5:29–39; 10:34–43; 13:16–41).

Furthermore, NT scholars have examined the speeches in Acts by looking at the ways in which they conform to Greco-Roman rhetorical LITERARY CONVENTIONS. For example, Paul's speech in Acts 13:16–41 has the form of EXORDIUM (13:16b), NARRATION (13:17–25), PROPOSITIO (13:16b), proof (13:27–37), and EPILOGUE (13:38–41). The speeches' similarities in FORM and their rhetorical structures suggest that Luke followed the Hellenistic convention of composing speeches to fit the purpose of the text. For a more detailed discussion of the various speeches in Acts, see Aune.

Bibliography. David Aune, The New Testament in Its Literary Environment (Philadelphia: Westminster, 1989); James Bailey and Lyle Vander Broek, Literary Forms in the New Testament: A Handbook (Louisville: Westminster John Knox, 1992); Eduard Schweizer, "Concerning the Speeches in Act," in Studies in Luke-Acts (ed. L. E. Keck and J. L. Martyn; Nashville: Abingdon, 1966), 208–16.

SPEECH, DEFENSE. See DEFENSE SPEECH

SPEECH, PROPHETIC. See PROPHETIC SPEECH

SPEECH ACTS. See SPEECH ACT THEORY

SPEECH ACT THEORY

A "natural language philosophy concerned with the actual use of everyday language rather than with the truth or falsity of a restricted set of invented sentences" (Malmkjaer, 508). A major task of the theory is to show how speakers can succeed in what they do regardless of the various ways in which linguistic MEANING underdetermines use. Speech act theory was developed between 1939 and 1959 and first introduced by John L. Austin, an Oxford philosopher, when he presented the theory in his twelve William James Lectures at Harvard University in 1955. Austin and John R. Searle are the two main figures associated with speech act theory. Searle worked out corresponding rules for speech acts less rigidly tied to set scripts and ceremonial circumstances—everyday speech events such as promising, requesting, and stating, ordering—while Austin articulated appropriate conditions for such ritualized performatives as marrying and christening (Magnusson, 194). Many other theorists, however, have contributed to the speech act theory, creating a wide variety of uses. These theorists include Richard Ohman, Mary Louise Pratt, Stanley Fish, Keir Elam, and H. Paul Grice (Magnusson, 193). "The reason why many nonphilosophers found speech-act theory so appealing was their feeling that here at last was a 'natural language philosophy' concerned with the actual use of everyday language rather than with the truth or falsity of a restricted set of invented sentences" (Malmkjaer, 508). There are many different kinds of speech acts, including utterances, performatives, propositional utterances, illocutionary utterances, and perlocutionary utterances.

Utterance. The first type of speech act is utterance. To utter is simply to speak a word or string of words, basically to say a word for the sake of saying a word. John R. Searle says that utterances have NO INTENTION of communication or meaning. If someone were to speak a word with no particular meaning, that would be considered an utterance. A good example of this is a reflex. Someone who puts a hand on a hot pan or gets pinched may say "Ow!" or "Ouch!" This speech act is an utterance. There is no meaning, or intended meaning, in making this statement. Even though Searle implies that an utterance has no meaning except to utter, John L. Austin says, "Every utterance is in fact a speech act." "Consider the utterance 'Fire.' This may function as the speech act of warning, and if it does, it is expandable into the explicit form 'I warn you that there is a fire.' By this argument, every apparently constative utterance is expandable into the speech-act 'statement,' since utterance can be prefaced by 'I state that.'" Austin is saying that all linguistic behavior can be considered a speech action and that every utterance has a particular "force." All that one needs to do is classify these forces (Malmkjaer, 508).

Performative. The second kind of speech act is the performative, or locutionary. Austin describes this kind of speech act as "declarative sentences which do not describe, and in the case of which it makes no sense to ask whether they are true or false, namely those used in the making of speech acts" (Malmkjaer, 508). Austin also says of the performative speech act, "Speakers do not state facts; instead, given appropriate circumstances, speakers actually perform conventional actions with their words" (Magnusson, 193). A performative or locutionary speech act accomplishes something through the words being spoken. An action does not result from these words, nor is something described. Instead, it is the feeling and emotion that lead to the words being spoken that are the main purpose for this speech act. For example, the confession of one's own faith is a performative act. There is no actual physical movement that can show this, but it is through the promise within those words that the action is found. Anthony Thiselton describes this kind of speech act as "self-involvement" (223–30). According to Briggs, "The speaker 'standing behind' the words [gives] a pledge *and* personal backing that he or she is prepared to undertake commitments and responsibilities that are entailed in extralinguistic terms by the proposition which is

asserted" (133). When Isaac blessed his son Jacob, his utterance is a performative or locutionary act: "May God give you of heaven's dew and of earth's richness—an abundance of grain and new wine. May nations serve you and peoples bow down to you. Be lord over your brothers, and may the sons of your mother bow down to you. May those who curse you be cursed and those who bless you be blessed" (Gen. 27:28–29 NIV). Isaac is not only uttering words: the act of blessing is also implicit in the words.

Propositional utterances. Third, propositional utterances constitute another type of speech act. A propositional utterance refers to or describes a real or imaginary object. Austin uses the term "constatives" "for sentences which describe. Only constatives are true or false" (Malmkjaer, 508). Therefore, this type of speech act defines things that are real or imaginary, things that can be described through words. These words themselves hold no meaning; rather, it is the object they describe that holds the meaning. In Exod. 26:1, instructions are given: "Moreover you shall make the tabernacle with ten curtains of fine twisted linen, and blue, purple, and crimson yarns; you shall make them with cherubim skillfully worked into them." The rest of this chapter describes in detail how the tabernacle should be built and what should be placed inside. Here it is not the word *tabernacle* that holds meaning but rather the description of the tabernacle. Further examples may include the ark that Noah built, heaven and hell, pagan idols, the fruit of the Spirit, and the ark of the covenant.

Illocutionary utterances. Illocutionary utterances make up a fourth type of the speech act. Whereas a propositional utterance describes an object, an illocutionary utterance is spoken with the intention of making contact with a listener. Illocutionary utterances are sentences that usually contain a propositional utterance, but it is their intention that is of most importance. Georg Meggle describes the illocutionary utterance as having "two possible functions—or as speech act theoreticians would like to put it, two possible illocutionary forces—'to order' and 'to inform'" (211). Illocutions, then, are spoken with the intention to create some kind of contact with the person to whom the requests or comments are directed. "Strong illocutions create social reality which is thus sustained above and beyond the power of the individual to make arbitrary declarations about the world around him or her" (Briggs, 133). So it is an illocutionary utterance that portrays to the listener the object, place, or person being described. Something more than just an object, an illocution contains meaning in the thing being described.

Briggs (2) suggests that the "kingdom of God" is an illocutionary act. Even though the parable of the kingdom of God is a propositional utterance in that it describes a real or imaginary object, it is spoken with the intention of making contact with the listener. Matt. 13:24–26 says, "The kingdom of heaven may be compared to someone who sowed good seed in his field; but while everybody was asleep, an enemy came and sowed weeds among the wheat, and then went away. So when the plants came up and bore grain, then the weeds appeared as well." Here this STORY of the kingdom of heaven is a propositional utterance because it is describing a "real or imaginary object"; however, it is also an illocutionary utterance because of its intention to persuade the listener.

Perlocutionary utterance. Last are perlocutionary utterances. The perlocutionary speech act attempts to effect change in the actions of the listener. This type of speech act is also an utterance because it includes a proposition but with the intention to interact with the receiver. Austin lists the perlocutionary utterance as a class of "deed performed in word" (Magnusson, 194). A perlocution is not the action itself but the words used to initiate that action. Austin goes on to refer to this type of speech act as a "'behavitive' to our social behavior" (Magnusson, 194). The perlocutionary utterance does not merely utter a word, and it goes beyond simply making contact with the receiver. Instead, it tries to change the actions of the receiver. For example, if someone asks a friend for a glass of water, the person is not just trying to make small talk to describe something. The intention is to have the friend take

the action communicated by the utterance. For example, Matt. 9:6–7 says, "'But so that you may know that the Son of Man has authority on earth to forgive sins'—he then said to the paralytic—'Stand up, take your bed and go to your home.' And he stood up and went to his home." Jesus is not speaking for the sake of hearing himself, nor is he describing an object. He is speaking solely with the intention of making a change in the action of the man listening to him. Another example of perlocution is Mark 16:15 (NIV): "Go into all the world and preach the good news to all creation." Jesus's words communicate the actions he expects in the lives of the disciples.

Therefore, utterances, performatives, propositional utterances, illocutionary utterances, and perlocutionary utterances are all forms of speech act. It is through these that people speak, perform actions through words, describe objects, make contact with other persons, and create a change in the actions of others. It is possible to apply all of these types of speech act to biblical interpretation. In "Words in Actions" Richard S. Briggs "introduces his readers to the important issues of understanding texts as well as to some of the important role players in this field. He gives attention to the philosophy of language and indicates that speech act theory is not a comprehensive solution to hermeneutical problems, is not a comprehensive philosophy of language, and is not a variety of antifoundationalism" (Briggs, 132). Briggs suggests that even though speech act theory can be used for biblical interpretation, it may not be the best source to fully understand the message and meaning.

Bibliography. Richard S. Briggs, *Words in Action: Speech Act Theory and Biblical Interpretation; Toward a Hermeneutic of Self-Involvement* (New York: T&T Clark, 2001); Lynne Magnusson, "Speech Act Theory," in *Encyclopedia of Contemporary Literary Theory* (ed. Irena R. Makaryk; Toronto: University of Toronto Press, 1993), 193–99; Kristin Malmkjaer, "Speech Acts," in *A Dictionary of Cultural and Critical Theory* (ed. Michael Payne; Cambridge, MA: Blackwell, 1996), 507–9; Georg Meggle, "To Hell with Speech Act Theory," in *Dialogue: An Interdisciplinary Approach* (ed. Mercelo Dascal; Philadelphia: Benjamins, 1985), 205–11; Anne Reboul, "Conversational Implications: Nonce or Generalized," in *Foundations of Speech*

Act Theory: Philosophical and Linguistic Perspectives (ed. Savas L. Tsohatzidis; London: Routledge, 1996), 322–34; Barry Smith, "Towards a History of Speech Act Theory," in *Speech Acts, Meanings, and Intentions: Critical Approaches to the Philosophy of John R. Searle* (Berlin: de Gruyter, 1990), 29–61; Anthony C. Thiselton, "Communicative Action and Promise in Interdisciplinary, Biblical, and Theological Hermeneutics," in *The Promise of Hermeneutics* (ed. Roger Lundin, Clarence Walhout, and Anthony C. Thiselton; Grand Rapids: Eerdmans, 1999), 133–239.

STAIRSTEP PARALLELISM

A type of parallelism in the POETRY of the NT in which the last key word in a line is repeated as the key word at the beginning of the next line (Ryken 101). An example is John 1:3b–5 (emphasis added):

> What has come into being in him was *life*,
>   and the *life* was the *light* of all people.
> The *light* shines in the *darkness*,
>   and the *darkness* did not overcome it.

Bibliography. Leland Ryken, *Words of Life: A Literary Introduction to the New Testament* (Grand Rapids: Baker, 1987).

STANZA

In POETRY, a group of lines determined by the number of feet in each line and by the rhyming scheme. Since we have no original texts of the HEBREW BIBLE or NT, the existence and nature of the stanzas in BIBLICAL POETRY are uncertain. Nevertheless, some scholars try to read biblical poetry in terms of stanzas. *See* RHYME; RHYTHM; STROPHE.

STATIC CHARACTER

A character who is presented with a single dominant trait, a one-dimensional character. A single character trait distinguishes the static character. Such is Laban; from the first time we meet him in Gen. 24, we are struck by his distinguishing trait of materialism. His materialistic motivation is sustained in his dealings with Jacob in Gen. 29. *See* CHARACTERIZATION.

STEREOTYPE CHARACTER

In a STORY, a TYPE of character that is nothing more than a functionary, whom the AUTHOR uses to fill out the NARRATIVE. This character is usually not characterized at all but simply serves the purpose of providing the characters necessary for a story. *See* CHARACTERIZATION.

STICH

A line of POETRY. For example, a distich is a couplet or two lines of similar form, a tristich is a STANZA with three lines, and a hemistich is a half-line.

STOCK CHARACTER

A recurrent TYPE of character in literature, such as the sassy servant in commedia dell'arte. Other recurrent characters in literature are the nagging wife, the absentminded professor, the hypochondriac, and the duped husband. The stock character is the same as the STEREOTYPE CHARACTER. *See* CHARACTERIZATION.

STOCK SITUATION

A recurrent situation in literature, such as mistaken identity, a love triangle, and a journey. *See* ARCHETYPE; TYPE SCENE.

STOICISM. *See* HELLENISTIC PHILOSOPHIES

STORY

A sequential account of events and ACTIONS, the basis for all NARRATIVE and dramatic literature. Story is the sum total of everything that happens in a TEXT, whether the text be a novel, drama, SHORT STORY, EPIC, PARABLE, or any other FORM of narrative. For example, it is fairly simple to recount the events and actions in the book of Jonah, to describe what the book says. It is a different matter, however, to move from a DESCRIPTION of the events to an EXPLANATION of what the text means or suggestions about the character of God or the relationship between repentance and judgment. Once the latter becomes the focus, we have moved from story to PLOT, the manner in which the events and actions of the story are related in terms of causality in order to communicate an idea, persuade to action, or illuminate character.

STORY, ADMIRATION. *See* ADMIRATION STORY

STORY, CALLING. *See* CALLING STORY

STORY, COMMISSIONING. *See* COMMISSIONING STORY

STORY, CONFLICT. *See* CONFLICT STORY

STORY, CONTROVERSY. *See* CONTROVERSY STORY

STORY, EMBELLISHED. *See* EMBELLISHED STORY

STORY, ENCOUNTER. *See* ENCOUNTER STORY

STORY, EXAMPLE. *See* EXAMPLE STORY

STORY, FRAME. *See* FRAME STORY

STORY, FRAMEWORK. *See* FRAME STORY

STORY, HYBRID. *See* HYBRID STORY

STORY, ILLUSTRATIVE. *See* ILLUSTRATIVE STORY

STORY, INFANCY. *See* INFANCY STORY

STORY, MIRACLE. *See* ARETALOGY

STORY, NATIVITY. *See* NATIVITY STORY

STORY, PRONOUNCEMENT. *See* PRONOUNCEMENT STORY

STORY, PROVISION. *See* PROVISION STORY

STORY, PUBLIC MINISTRY. *See* PUBLIC MINISTRY STORY

STORY, RECOGNITION. *See* RECOGNITION STORY

STORY, RESCUE. *See* RESCUE STORY

STORY, RESURRECTION. *See* RESURRECTION STORY

STORY, SHORT. *See* SHORT STORY

STORY, WITNESS. *See* WITNESS STORY

STORY WORLD

The world found only in a TEXT. Framed by the beginning and ending of the text, it is a creation of an AUTHOR, who selects and arranges events (*see* SELECTION AND ARRANGEMENT) in a complex STRUCTURE. The arrangement of events and the CHARACTERIZATION of individuals within the STORY do not correlate exactly with the historical CHRONOLOGY or with persons of the REAL WORLD. Events, characters, and places in the story acquire their MEANING and SIGNIFICANCE from the world created by the author. For example, in the GOSPEL of Matthew, Jesus is defined and given significance only with the world of Matthew's text. The meaning of what Jesus says or does in Matthew must be ascertained from the story world of Matthew, not by recourse to the author's real world. The story world is not a mirror of the real world, with the author as the quicksilver behind the glass. Through artistic forms and strategies, the story world assumes its own reality, a reality capable of communicating its own TRUTHS.

This is something similar to a painter's capturing only a moment of a landscape in memory and then later presenting that moment on canvas through the media of line, perspective, vanishing point, color, tone, geometrical shapes, and so on. The painting is not the material reality of the landscape but an INTERPRETATION. The painting assumes its own identity. A similar case exists for a NARRATIVE. An author structures a story world in the text. This story world is not synonymous with the real world of either the author or the reader. The story world is the locus of meaning. For example, in the story of Jephthah (Judg. 11), we find that Jephthah has been exiled from his people because his mother was a prostitute. But because of his reputation as an able fighter, the men of Gilead seek his help when they find themselves in trouble with the Ammonites. Through some negotiation, Jephthah agrees to become Gilead's leader. After some interesting diplomacy, Jephthah requests help from Yahweh, vowing to sacrifice the first thing that comes out the door of his house if Yahweh will ensure victory. As we might expect, Jephthah is victorious, but upon his return home, the first to greet him from the door of his house is his daughter. Jephthah does fulfill his vow after his daughter bewails her virginity for two months. Basically, this is what is said in the story. But as interesting as the narrative is, what lesson or moral is the author offering the reader through the story? What application does the author expect from the reader? What insight about God, life, or humanity does the author suggest by the narrative? Perhaps in combination with the story of Samson (who himself has taken a vow and broken it), the story world is offering some instruction on the appropriateness or inappropriateness of making vows.

STROPHE

In contemporary usage, a synonym for STANZA and applied to a unit paragraph in free VERSE. For example, Isa. 48 may be divided into seven strophes, each beginning with a new introduction (e.g., "Hear this, O house of Jacob" [v. 1], "The former things I declared long ago" [v. 3], "You have heard" [v. 6], "Listen to me, O Jacob" [v. 12]). However, David Petersen and Kent Harold Richards question the value of reading biblical poetry in terms of strophes: "If stanza is determined only by 'feel,' it is doubtful that the interpreter gains much precision by using the term or its equivalent" (60). Still, they do recognize that because readers "segment poems into sense units as they read," it might be concluded that textual "elements signal these sense units to the reader" (60).

Bibliography. David Petersen and Kent Harold Richards, *Interpreting Hebrew Poetry* (Minneapolis: Fortress, 1992).

STRUCTURALISM

A method of textual analysis that focuses on the ways in which TEXTS mean rather than on what they mean. Within the field of LITERARY CRITICISM, there are many theorists who try to offer new methods for discovering the MEANING of a text. Structuralism, however, does not offer a "new way of interpreting literary works" (Culler, 302).

Rather, structuralists "attempt to understand how it is that works do have meaning" at all (303).

Origins. The development of structuralism resulted largely from a reaction to the existentialist foundations of liberal humanism, which dominated the philosophical world in the early 1900s (Clarke, 7, 24–29). According to the humanist ideal, TRUTH and reality were certain and accessible to humans through rational inquiry. Reality was fully expressed and depicted through language, and humans had the ability and power to freely use this language to express themselves. LITERARY texts, then, originated with a human AUTHOR, who determined the precise meaning of the words and works, which adequately reflected and followed from a personal experience.

The structuralist model challenges these ASSUMPTIONS, advocating that there are underlying STRUCTURES unconsciously produced by the mind, which sorts through units and structures them according to certain rules. Reality is entirely dependent on the structure of human language because it is through language that humans think and communicate. Thus, the reality and order that exist in the world are merely perceived and wholly a human-language construction. Meaning does not originate from an ideal truth or from human experience, existence, or essence. Rather, meaning results from the various operational systems and structures that dictate the world. It is dependent on the system of language and is independent of human INTENTION. Accordingly, a text does not originate with an AUTHOR, for the author does nothing more than simply work within a preexisting structural system, which allows one to produce a specific text. Any text that is produced has actually already been written and is merely a reformulation and combination of prefabricated elements. Issues such as the author's identity and purpose, original audience, and originating circumstances are bracketed out as areas of concern. Structuralism is not concerned with *what* a text means, but with *how* a text means. Therefore, only the final form of the text is of interest to structuralists. For the structuralist, all human social activity is nothing more than various manifestations of underlying systems of abstract rules or LITERARY CONVENTIONS that govern the way humans order their existence into meaningful structures. These systems of rules exist on a subconscious level. For example, when I formulate a sentence, I do not consciously recite beforehand the syntactical and grammatical rules that underlie my sentence, just as I do not consult a COMMENTARY on dress codes before I attend a funeral. At a fundamental level, the underlying linguistic and cultural codes of these systems are universal, having already been appropriated. In all areas of social activity, then, DEEP STRUCTURES can be found common to all human societies, regardless of other culturally identifying specifics. Within structuralism, all human activity is essentially a form of communication. Furthermore, a communication is possible precisely because people adhere to basic rules. Language is a form of communication and is therefore governed by a subconscious set of rules or conventions.

Structuralism in linguistics. The beginnings of structuralism are to be found in the model of LINGUISTICS proposed by Swiss linguist Ferdinand de Saussure (Guerin et al., 332; see also Patte, 1). Foundational to Saussure's linguistic theory is the idea that a system can be reduced to certain structural features (Guerin et al., 335). Communication is one such system that occurs through language, which consists of LANGUE ("language," referring to the entire underlying system) and PAROLE (a specific application of *langue* in which a word functions as a SIGN). This sign connects a signifier, or sound construction, with a signified concept or IMAGE of a particular item.

In Saussure's thought, if all human activities are governed by basic systems of subconscious rules, and if all these activities are actually forms of communication, then we may assume that literature is a form of communication and thus governed by a set of basic conventions or rules. Since deep structures are common to all languages, we can assume that, as a form of communication, there are likewise common deep structures within literature in general and the GENRE of narrative specifically. Since

parole is an instance of individual speech, based on the underlying enabling system of *langue*, a narrative text is a specific manifestation based on the enabling system of narrative. This means that the limited set of conventions of narrative transcends cultures, literary TRADITIONS, time, and space. All narrative traditions share the same basic conventions. It is the explicit task and goal of structuralism to uncover these deep structures within individual narratives, which produce what is referred to as a MEANING EFFECT on readers. Since all narratives communicate through a shared system of conventions, interest in individual textual meaning is replaced by an interest in the effect an individual text has on readers. These deep structures operate at levels of writing and reading alike. Not only have authors of narrative texts internalized these deep structures; competent readers have also internalized them. This is the only means possible for understanding a narrative text.

Meaning effects. According to structuralists, a text actually has three meaning effect levels, which correlate to types of structures. The first level is the STRUCTURES OF ENUNCIATION. These structures are determined by features such as AUTHORIAL INTENTION, authorial *SITZ IM LEBEN*, and audience (the concerns of the HISTORICAL-CRITICAL METHOD). Second are STRUCTURES OF CULTURE (Patte, 25). Culture's structures consist of the specific codes of a specific people at a specific time. Their level of meaning effect is determined by the text's deep structures, which are universal in all human activity. On the level of any genre of literature such as narrative, certain narrative and mythological structures are present. For more conservative structuralists, these three meaning-effect levels combine with their accompanying structures to produce a composite meaning effect. Thus texts have the potential for a plurality of meaning.

Sign. The second of Saussure's concepts that structuralism builds on is that of the dual character of the sign. Concerning linguistics, Saussure claimed that a language was composed of a series of signs involving relationships between signs and what the signs refer to. Every sign consists of a signifier and a signified. The signifier is the "immediate object of perception" while the signified is "that which the perception evokes." The meaning of the word *dog* is not naturally inherent in the word itself, nor is meaning naturally inherent in the IMAGE of a dog. Rather, meaning is found in the underlying way in which the word and the image are connected. Meaning is found by examining the structures of the language. Since there is no natural connection between the signifier and the signified, it is possible to separate the signifier from the signified and to change the relationship between the two (Pettit, 6–7). So even here within Saussure's model of linguistics, it becomes evident that meaning is potentially ambiguous and/or multiple. This brings us to a crucial point for structuralism. The signified may have not only a denotative (*see* DENOTATION) meaning but also a connotative one (*see* CONNOTATION). For example, the signifier *rose* may refer both to a flower of the REAL WORLD and to a person who is as lovely as a rose. Now if a text (e.g., a narrative one) is itself a sign, it may also have both denotative and connotative meanings. It is on the denotative level that we would expect to find manifestations of authorial intention. On the connotative level, however, there exists a subconscious system of conventions and convictions that precede authorial intention. Actually, it is more accurate to speak of a plurality of levels of connotative meaning. Deep within the text are three levels that structuralists try to excavate: narrative structures common to all narratives but manifested culturally at the surface level; universal mythical structures; and an author's semantic universe (*see* SEMANTIC DOMAIN), a system of convictions that underlies the author's work. The bottom level can be reached only by analyzing the narrative and mythical structures. So, along with examining endemic narrative structures, structuralists go even deeper in an effort to identify the presence of mythical structures. Narrative may contain mythical elements even though it is not mythical in general; thus a narrative may contain mythical elements even though the narrative (unlike a pure myth) is a conscious logical argument.

Therefore, according to biblical scholars who apply structuralism to the interpretation of the Bible, the Bible can be analyzed according to mythical structures.

Further development. Perhaps the most influential figure in the formation of the structuralist theory is the French anthropologist Claude Lévi-Strauss, who used Saussure's foundational principles to uncover certain cultural systems that structure human life and concluded that it is this structured "symbolic order" of the world that gives definition and meaning to reality (Clarke, 4). Lévi-Strauss hypothesized that the process whereby humans learn to operate within their particular culture requires that they conform to certain laws or "codes." Although these codes seem to be so "deep" and "imbedded" that they almost "evade a conscious arrangement" by those who operate according to them (Guerin et al., 335), Lévi-Strauss believed they were made more intelligible by examining the native MYTHS of a particular culture. Though different cultures perpetuate different myths, they all have striking similarities that connect them as one, because in them are revealed certain paradigms and structures of the human mind that are universal and culturally and temporally transcendent. In his analysis of the myths, Lévi-Strauss adopted a method based on the ASSUMPTION that the structure of myths is similar to the structure of language. Myths, like language, consist of units that are fitted together according to rules, and unit relationships depend on the differences between the units (Guerin et al., 336; McKnight, 93).

Structuralists have employed Lévi-Strauss's idea that myths are attempts to deal with "BINARY OPPOSITIONS" inherent in human existence. These fundamental oppositions cannot be logically mediated. Some of these oppositions are love/hate, life/death, youth/old age, sin/righteousness. Myths try to mediate the oppositions by offering parallel oppositions that are proportional to the binary ones and capable of reconciliation. Structuralists seek to uncover these mythic structures and, by arranging them in paradigmatic order, discover the author's semantic universe (the fundamental system of convictions on which the author operated).

Implications for biblical hermeneutics. Structuralists are less interested in analyzing the text's CONTENT, production, or how it is received. Their greater interest is in the text's structures that hold it together. This focus has implications for BIBLICAL HERMENEUTICS that sets the structuralist's approach in contrast to that of traditional EXEGESIS. Since SCRIPTURE was written by human authors, it was produced within the FRAMEWORK and confines of human language, just as any piece of literature (Blancy, 87). Since structuralism erases the author, "exegesis no longer aims at what [the writer] meant" (Patte, 14). This focus is different from that of traditional exegesis in that it does not demand a singular meaning of a biblical text. Although the structural analyst may likely affirm that the author of the biblical text did intend to communicate a single meaning, uncovering this meaning is not the structuralist's goal in exegesis (Patte, 15). Rather, biblical texts are examined to determine *how* the possible meaning(s) of a text are produced (Pettit, 66). The author's intentions are of no concern: the structures that underlie a text are unconsciously produced because they are impressed on the author as he/she communicates.

Thus, a second feature of biblical structural exegesis is that exegetes affirm a plurality of meanings in regard to the various structures. Any specific structure of a text is merely a reflection of the potentialities of the text and can "never exhaust" its potential (Patte, 22).

A third distinguishing feature of biblical structural exegesis is that it adopts a SYNCHRONIC, rather than DIACHRONIC, approach to interpretation. Thus, linear history is not relevant, and events are understood not in their chronological significance. Rather, the structure of an event is analyzed in comparison with the structures of other events, observing contrasts and correlations, regardless of whether the events are sequentially connected (Patte, 16).

Biblical structural exegesis is most widely applied to interpretation of narrative texts (Patte, 35).

Based on Propp's method of interpreting folktales, A. J. Greimas developed a structure for narrative interpretation that included six elements, which may be illustrated by examining the PARABLE of the good Samaritan in Luke 10:30–35 (Greenwood, 63–69; Patte, 54). The general framework for the narrative is provided by three successive sequences: a man leaves Jerusalem; the man is robbed; the priest, Levite, and Samaritan pass by. Each sequence is composed of three narrative SYNTAGMS: contract, disjunction/conjunction, and performance. First, a contract is established, as illustrated when the Samaritan sees the man and feels compelled to help him. Second, steps are taken to fulfill that contract when the Samaritan begins to move toward the man. Third, the contract is carried out when the Samaritan bandages the man's wounds and takes him to the inn. Also, the parable may be analyzed by examining the CANONICAL narrative functions or verbs that describe the actions taken by the Samaritan and the spheres of action in which the characters of the parable take part. These ACTANTs include a *sender*, who specifies the *object* (health) that will be given as a *helper* (donkey, innkeeper, money) to a *receiver* (wounded man) by a *subject* (Samaritan) after the wounded man encounters an *opponent* (robbers). For a closer look at this model, see Patte, 37–51.

Other biblical texts have also been analyzed to uncover mythical structures that mediate between perceived "contradictions" of a culture (Greenwood, 110). In such a text, two or more opposing positions are given and are restated in a way that reconciles them (for an in-depth look at and analysis of the mythical structures of Gal. 1:1–10, see Patte, 59–75). When the structure of this new position is examined, it is bombarded by another opposing position, which is reconciled, met with yet another opposition, and so on (Greenwood, 111).

Structuralism's aim at recognizing the structures of a text is valuable in that structures organize parts of a text into meaningful systems and reveal ways in which the human mind works. On the one hand, structuralism's characteristic erasing of the author, original audience, and intended meaning may be somewhat troubling to more conservative scholars or readers. On the other hand, structuralism appropriately applied to both the biblical and the extrabiblical literary texts does provide an interpretative approach that is quite compatible with other approaches (e.g., READER-RESPONSE CRITICISM; NEW CRITICISM; TRANSACTIVE CRITICISM) that problematize authorial intention.

Bibliography. Alain Blancy, "Structuralism and Hermeneutics," in *Structural and Biblical Hermeneutics* (trans. and ed. Alfred M. Johnson; Pittsburgh: Pickwick, 1979), 75–104; Simon Clarke, *The Foundations of Structuralism* (Totowa, NJ: Barnes & Noble, 1981); Jonathan Culler, "Structuralism and Literature," in *Contexts for Criticism* (ed. Donald Keesey; 3rd ed.; Mountain View, CA: Mayfield, 1998), 302–11; Michel Foucault, *The Archaeology of Knowledge* (trans. A. M. Sheridan Smith; New York: Harper Colophon, 1972); David C. Greenwood, *Structuralism and the Biblical Text* (Berlin: Mouton, 1985); Wilfred Guerin et al., *A Handbook of Critical Approaches to Literature* (4th ed.; New York: Oxford University Press, 1999); Claude Lévi-Strauss, *Structural Anthropology* (London: Basic Books, 1963); Edgar V. McKnight, *Meanings in Texts* (Philadelphia: Fortress, 1970); Daniel Patte, *What Is Structural Exegesis?* (Philadelphia: Fortress, 1976); Philip Pettit, *The Concept of Structuralism* (Berkeley: University of California Press, 1977); Ferdinand de Saussure, *A Course in General Linguistics* (ed. Charles Bally and Albert Sechehaye; trans. Wade Baskin; New York: McGraw-Hill, 1959).

STRUCTURAL EXEGESIS. *See* STRUCTURALISM

STRUCTURAL LINGUISTICS

A field of study in LINGUISTICS associated with Ferdinand de Saussure. Considered the father of modern linguistics, Saussure shifted the focus of linguistics in the early twentieth century with his *Course in General Linguistics*, in which he presents structural linguistics as resting on a few basic principles. First, language is a system of rules that govern its every aspect, which all speakers of a language know either consciously or unconsciously. These rules Saussure calls *LANGUE*. He recognizes that individual speakers evidence *langue* in their individual SPEECH, and this he terms *PAROLE*. According to Saussure, the task of the linguist, then, is to articulate the *langue* by analyzing *parole*. From this point, Saussure begins an exhaustive investigation of the STRUCTURES that compose language and of the differences in sound, which denote differences in word MEANING, in order to refute the former linguistic ASSUMPTION of language's mimeticism, the idea that language is determined by its own internal rules (PHONOLOGY, SYNTAX, etc.) and, most important, in order to assert that the linguistic SIGN that makes up language is itself both arbitrary and conventional. This linguistic sign is composed of two parts: the signifier (the spoken or written word sound) and the signified (the concept signaled by the signifier). Their relationship is what Saussure sees as arbitrary and conventional, so that the significance of the linguistic sign lies not in its innate properties but in the differences that distinguish it from other signs. In so doing, he undermined the long-held belief that there is some natural link between the word and the thing it represents. This idea was subsequently borrowed by the French philosopher Jacques Derrida as one of the fundamental elements in the formulation of DECONSTRUCTION.

Bibliography. Ferdinand de Saussure, *A Course in General Linguistics* (ed. Charles Bally and Albert Sechehaye; trans. Wade Baskin; New York: McGraw-Hill, 1959).

STRUCTURE

In NARRATIVE, the PLOT or the FRAMEWORK into which all the IMAGES/ideas and events/ACTIONS work to convey MEANING. The structure consists of EPISODES that occur in a particular arrangement that leads to a resolution (*see* DENOUEMENT). The five components of structure in narrative are EXPOSITION, COMPLICATION (a variety of CONFLICT), crisis, CLIMAX, and resolution. For example, the Joseph narrative in Gen. 37–45 begins with conflict between Joseph and his brothers when the brothers perceive that their father, Jacob, loves Joseph more than them (37:1–4). This conflict is complicated by Joseph's dreams, by the brothers' plot to kill Joseph, and by the brothers' selling Joseph into slavery. There is no resolution until Joseph's final revelation to his brothers in Egypt.

According to Leland Ryken, there is a variety of structures in POETRY. Structure may be primarily descriptive (e.g., a description of character, scene, idea). An expository structure presents a series of ideas, while a narrative structure presents a series of events or actions. A dramatic structure consists of an address from one person to another. When a poem presents an idea in a variety of ways, the structure is repetitive; if the poem moves logically from one idea to another, it has a logical structure. A catalog structure lists different aspects of the same idea. Finally, a poem may have a psychological structure when it moves from one topic to another with no organizing principle outside the mind of the poet. *See also* STRUCTURALISM.

Structure may also be understood sociologically since societies are identified by a matrix of structures: political, religious, ideological, and cultural. These systems of structures may define a society as hierarchical, egalitarian, LOW CONTEXT, HIGH CONTEXT, HONOR/SHAME, and so forth. So, in referring to the structures of PATRIARCHY, structures of power, structures of ANDROCENTRISM, or racial structures, a person is speaking of the ways in which societies are structured in terms of human relations. *See* SOCIAL-SCIENTIFIC CRITICISM.

Bibliography. Leland Ryken, *Words of Delight: A Literary Introduction to the Bible* (Grand Rapids: Baker, 1987).

STRUCTURE, CLIMACTIC. *See* CLIMACTIC STRUCTURE

STRUCTURE, CYCLIC. *See* CYCLIC STRUCTURE

STRUCTURE, DEEP. *See* DEEP STRUCTURE

STRUCTURE, DRAMATIC. *See* DRAMATIC STRUCTURE

STRUCTURE, ENVELOPE. *See* ENVELOPE STRUCTURE

STRUCTURE, EPISODIC. *See* EPISODIC STRUCTURE

STRUCTURE, HIERARCHICAL. *See* HIERARCHICAL STRUCTURES

STRUCTURE, PATRIARCHAL. *See* PATRIARCHAL STRUCTURE

STRUCTURE, SURFACE. *See* STRUCTURALISM

STRUCTURES OF CULTURE

In STRUCTURALISM, the second of the three levels of MEANING EFFECT of a TEXT. Structures of culture consist of the specific CODES of a specific people at a specific time.

STRUCTURES OF ENUNCIATION

In STRUCTURALISM, the first of three levels of MEANING EFFECT of a TEXT. Structures of enunciation are determined by features such as AUTHORIAL INTENTION, authorial *SITZ IM LEBEN*, and audience (the concerns of the HISTORICAL-CRITICAL METHOD).

STYLE

One of the five divisions of classical rhetoric, style is the characteristic manner in which an AUTHOR expresses him- or herself. Style includes DICTION, the use of FIGURES OF SPEECH, LITERARY DEVICES, TEXTUAL STRATEGIES, and sentence and paragraph construction. An author may characteristically employ loose or periodic sentences; formal, neutral, or informal diction; complex or simple sentences; and so forth. To talk about an author's style, readers must examine all aspects of language. Thus it is possible for scholars to speak of a Pauline, Markan, Lukan, or Johannine style. For example, Mark employs a paratactic style (*see* PARATAXIS), and Paul uses a vernacular style.

SUBJECT

In LITERARY CRITICISM, the topic of a piece of literature. In other words, that which a work is about. For example, the book of Job may examine the subject of the ineffability of God or the relationship between a person's piety and prosperity. Generally, literary critics assume that a work will make claims about the subject. This claim is referred to as the THEME of the work.

SUBJECTIVE CRITICISM

A CRITICAL THEORY developed in the classroom and primarily for the classroom by David Bleich in *Readings and Feelings* and *Double Perspective*. Bleich developed subjective criticism from his response to a conglomeration of many different theories and ideas from several fields and focused his efforts on validating the ASSUMPTION that literary TRUTH is not an objective fact independent of the reader's influence.

According to Bleich, the importance of the individual's subjective response to literature is nothing new. He says that the basis for the subjective theory of criticism dates as far back as Aristotle's views on the emotionally motivated cathartic influence of TRAGEDY on an audience. Bleich cites Sigmund Freud, Samuel Johnson, and Samuel Coleridge as having provided insight into the subjective nature of literary understanding. "In general, a great many time-honored insights and intuitions about the key role of literary response in human culture were tied together by the new understanding of literary experience as a species of overall psychological functioning" (Bleich, *Subjective Criticism*, 110). This mention of psychological function is especially important to the study of subjective criticism because much of Bleich's study on the nature of literary INTERPRETATION is taken directly from Freud's study on the interpretation of dreams; in *Subjective Criticism*, Bleich even performs a subjective analysis on several different Freud responses.

Regarding more recent critics, Bleich has formulated his theories from the different ways in which he agrees and, more often, disagrees with the work of such reader-response critics (*see* READER-RESPONSE CRITICISM) as I. A. Richards, Simon Lesser, and most important, Norman N. Holland (*see* TRANSACTIVE CRITICISM), none of whom bring their views closely enough into focus on readers to satisfy the methodology recommended by Bleich's theory.

As a school of thought, subjective criticism does not claim to mandate a way in which a text can be read most accurately; rather, it recognizes the powerful influence that each reader's personal

AGENDA will have on their understanding of the TEXT. This understanding does not claim to produce an objective MEANING for the text but is the response of one reader. A fundamental assumption for Bleich is that the sense of a text is never fixed. In other words, there are multiple possible meanings to every literary text, probably as many meanings as there are readers. The meaning of the text is determined by the history and skills of the person who reads it. Each reader brings certain things to the text that color their view of that text. According to what Bleich calls "the subjective paradigm," meaning is not contained in the text, or put another way, the text is not the bottle that houses the powerful genie of objective meaning; the text does not even exist as an object without some SUBJECT's viewing, interpreting, and creating a subjective perception of the text, and this subjective perception itself can be explored only retroactively through the eyes of a still subjective observer. The reader's responses to his or her own responses are subjective. Bleich says that "no work even exists unless someone is reading it, that no matter when a text is studied it has to be conceived as a function of some reader's mind, and that, inversely, it cannot be described 'without reference to the . . . reader'" (*Subjective Criticism*, 109).

Subjective criticism does not try to provide a final reading of any given text, or even the best current one. It rather, according to Anthony Thiselton (529), "operates largely with socio-political and educational concerns." Thus, the point is not to produce the final reading of the text, which can then be printed in some scholarly journal and shelved, never to be reexplored, but to create a reading of the text that the members of a specific community can discuss and test for functionality as a useful reading to inform the group of one reader's reasons for responding in a given way. This "navigation" of a response is not the discovery of some preexistent fact that is just being brought to light; rather, "all interpretations are interpretive and may be understood as the construction of *new* knowledge" (Bleich, *Subjective Criticism*, 213, emphasis added). Thus Bleich discards the traditional idea of the classroom's being a venue for disseminating independent facts in the form of discovered knowledge, transferring facts from one informed individual to other less informed individuals.

Bleich's theory abandons the currently favored ideal that each text should be analyzed with the intention of determining some transcendent meaning; instead, he aims at teaching students to produce clearly subjective responses that are nonetheless viable as productive topics for corporate study. Important to this theory is that a community of readers, according to Bleich, is not the academic community at large but the immediate members of a specific classroom, where readers can share their subjective responses with their peers (Thiselton, 532). "As a rule, the classroom and the academy are not only separate communities, but [also] separate institutions with different memberships, purposes, and histories" (Bleich, *Double Perspective*, 3). According to Bleich, a classroom is "any place where two or more people gather for the conscious purpose of developing new knowledge" (*Subjective Criticism*, 134). Subjective criticism is applied to the community of the classroom, and it is here that group navigation occurs and knowledge is constructed.

Bleich recommends that the subjective study of literature be taught in four stages, each of which can take anywhere from one semester to a year or longer. The assumption seems to be that some continuity of class membership will occur in the manner similar to the way that (foreign-)language students often find themselves together as a group for the whole course of their study. According to Bleich, each stage should be as long as possible, but the length of any stage is not as important as its position in the chronology of study; the steps should be taken one at a time, in proper order. The steps include (1) "Thoughts and Feelings," where the students are taught to explore feelings and how they differ from thoughts; (2) "Feelings and Literature," where students are taught to recognize that each time they read a piece of literature, their feelings are inextricably connected to

their responses to that piece; (3) "Deciding on Literary Importance," where students are taught to recognize the connection between the way they emotionally perceive a piece and the way they utilize their intellects for its judgment; and (4) "Interpretation as a Communal Act," where students are taught the importance of sharing their responses with others and discussing the interpretations of those people (Bleich, *Readings and Feelings*, 5).

This final stage is central to the thinking of subjective criticism: "Interpretation as a Communal Act" is viewed as the ultimate purpose of subjective criticism. Accordingly, "truth is not a state of affairs in the real world, but simply the product of one's current linguistic responses; it has no permanence but is constantly re-created in the face of new motivations" (Ray, 79). However, not all responses are created equal, and it is the communal aspect of interpretation that determines which responses are more useful to help construct the type of understanding sought by the class. As Bleich puts it, "Negotiability . . . is consciously variable according to what knowledge a community needs. . . . Determining the negotiability of response statements is part of the communal definition of its purposes" (*Subjective Criticism*, 189). This negotiability can be determined only through the group study of responses to literature:

> The assumption of the subjective paradigm is that collective similarity of response can be determined only by each individual's announcement of his response and subsequent communally motivated negotiative comparison. This assumption is validated by the ordinary fact that when each person says what he sees, each statement will be substantially different. The response must therefore be the starting point for the study of aesthetic experience. (*Subjective Criticism*, 98)

Bleich posits that when an individual reads a work of literature and remembers the way that he or she responds to that work but does not share that response with someone else, that response has all of the usefulness of a dream that is never discussed: none. For all practical purposes, the literary construct or dream remains nonexistent. For a text to exist, it must be perceived, and for a response to exist, it must be navigated. This group navigation "could throw light on our motives and strategies for reading" (Keesey, 137).

According to Bleich's research, these responses tend to come in three forms: (1) reader-oriented responses, (2) reality-oriented responses, and (3) experience-oriented responses. He claims that the third type of response is more useful for classroom use than the others because it does not try to explain the position of the reader or relate the response to real life but simply reports the responses that the reader perceives having had while interacting with the text (Bleich, *Subjective Criticism*, 170). Therefore, the primary application of subjective criticism is teaching students how to produce an experience-oriented response that can be navigated by the class in such a way that productive illumination will be achieved and shared by all.

As with most theories, subjective criticism is unable to provide a complete sense of how literature should be regarded; in this case, part of that inability stems from the psychological nature of the theoretical aspects of subjective criticism. The actual theory deals almost exclusively with the psychology of the reader, which is inevitable since, without the reader, there is no text about which to theorize. It is only in the practical aspects of the theory that literature is immediately addressed. One of the strengths of Bleich's theory, however, is his recognition that nothing can provide the final word in literary interpretation. Certain readings may be better than others, but none can claim to have objectively "finished" with the text. Bleich recognizes that there is a valid place for a close reading of each text and also states that understanding an AUTHOR can in some ways help provide an understanding of his or her work. However, his view of the usefulness of authorial INTENTION is hazy, and he hints that the purpose of learning about the author is more closely related to understanding the reader's purpose in reading than it is to actually discovering any kind of authorial intention: "When the knowledge sought concerns

the real, but permanently unavailable, historical author, awareness of one's motivated conception of the author is a necessity" (Bleich, *Subjective Criticism*, 263). Intextualism (*see* INTERTEXTUAL CRITICISM; INTERTEXTUALITY) is also legitimated by subjective criticism because each text that any given subject encounters will necessarily provide that reader with a greater framework on which to hang their understanding of all subsequent readings.

Critics have, however, pointed out several weaknesses in Bleich's theory, the majority of which are paradoxically synonymous with its strengths. Subjective criticism is strong because it recognizes the importance of the individual readings. It is weak because it fails to recognize that some readings are actually wrong. Subjective criticism is strong because it demands a reevaluation of the traditional literary CANON. It is weak because it provides no template with which to determine what works will be brought into the new CANON and which will not or even to state whether there will be a new canon. Thiselton lists these and other complaints in the final paragraph of his chapter on Bleich:

> In practice Bleich's *literary* theory is bound up with a familiar *socio-political agenda. Egalitarian social politics dictate the de-privileging of the author, the de-privileging of academic interpreters, and even the de-privileging of a literary or theological canon of "classics,"* in order to make the whole mixed community co-authors of texts: everyone constructs and no construction is "better" than another *because theory would already prejudice an answer in favor of the elite.* Once again, socio-pragmatic theory disintegrates into the anarchy in which *the most militant pressure-group actually carries the day about what satisfies their pragmatic criteria of "right" reading.* (Thiselton, 535, italics original)

It seems that in a theory where absolutes are abandoned and no one is wrong, only those who are violently vocal with their opinions are heard, leading to the clichéd "might makes right" mentality.

Subjective criticism may supply insights into BIBLICAL INTERPRETATION. Bleich's insistence that understanding comes from a communal navigation of the text provides insight into the nature of biblical interpretation, insight that has been largely ignored since the Reformation. "In the era after the Reformation itself a more scholastic Protestant rationalism arguably began to lose sight of the fundamentally corporate nature of interpretation, to which persons of all kinds could contribute" (Thiselton, 533). Many heresies have come about as a result of the singular subjective response of men and women who have not presented their responses to the Scriptures to the church at large for navigation but rather have gathered impressionable people, who became enamored of an untested idea. Although Bleich is not a biblical scholar, it is safe to assume that he would agree with the suggestion that biblical interpretation should not occur in a vacuum but through the group navigation of individual responses. Thiselton cites Mark Labberton as having noticed the "coherence of such a general reader-orientated approach with the theological principal that reading biblical texts is an activity of the whole community" (Thiselton, 532). He specifically responds to the mind-set that only those who have had extensive biblical/literary training are capable of properly understanding a text and supports his understanding biblically by pointing out Paul's emphasis in Gal. 3:28 on the equality of all believers. Although Labberton is comfortable with Bleich's emphasis on nonprofessional readers, "he is uncomfortable with the accompanying shift of primacy from texts to readers, and seeks some intermediate position" (533). Depending on their views of biblical inspiration, many Christians may elect to follow Labberton away from Bleich into the more traditional forms of criticism.

Bibliography. David Bleich, *The Double Perspective: Language, Literacy, and Social Regulations* (New York: Oxford University Press, 1988); idem, *Readings and Feelings: An Introduction to Subjective Criticism* (Urbana, IL: National Council of Teachers of English, 1975); idem, *Subjective Criticism* (Baltimore: Johns Hopkins University Press, 1978); Donald Keesey, *Contexts for Criticism* (4th ed.; Boston: McGraw-Hill, 2003); William Ray, *Literary Meaning: From Phenomenology to Deconstruction* (Oxford: Blackwell, 1984); Anthony C. Thiselton, *New Horizons in Hermeneutics* (Grand Rapids: Zondervan, 1992).

SUBJECTIVE KNOWLEDGE

Based on the belief that TRUTH, reality, and the knowledge of both truth and reality are not directly accessible to humans but are mediated in a variety of ways. With the advent of the Enlightenment of the seventeenth and eighteenth centuries, both scientific and philosophical thinkers assumed that truth and knowledge existed independently of the human SUBJECT. They also assumed that CLARITY was a property of language rather than a quality of the mind that persons imposed on reality. As objects presented themselves to the mind, humans were capable of making assertions about those objects. If language is subsequently analyzed, humans could fully know that object. This was possible because the logical structures of the universe (or object) are revealed in the assertions that are themselves the MEANING of the object. So readers can comprehend a LITERARY object through the analysis of the language, a language that is the actual meaning of the object. Such an ASSUMPTION views language as denotative (*see* DENOTATION), claiming that language can concisely represent an ideational object. Language, it is assumed, has a precise quality of representation about it, which ensures that it itself can be precisely analyzed. At the heart of this view of the power of language is the belief that an objective world of realities exists independent of humans and their thoughts about it. Correlatively, then, a TEXT and its meaning exist independently of humans and their thoughts about them. In other words, truth, meaning, or knowledge exists prior to the text itself and certainly before the reading of a text. Recent CRITICISM, however, claims that objects, including texts, are always perceived within some FRAMEWORK, some system of coordinates; as Ihab Hassan puts it, "In another system of coordinates the same events are not the same" (55). There is always a complicity between the observer and the observed, between the system of measurement and the one performing the measurement. So in this SENSE all knowledge and truth is subjective because humans cannot escape this fact of grounding. People are never able to assume some position free of system that enables them to look at a text from a purely objective vantage point. Any knowledge is a product of INTERPRETIVE CONVENTIONS defined by a group or institution and thus is never objective. Knowledge of a text is not a reconstruction of the AUTHORIAL INTENTION or of the textual meaning but a subjective construction, a creation rather than a re-creation out of the reading framework of reader.

Bibliography. Ihab Hassan, *The Postmodern Turn: Essays in Postmodern Theory and Culture* (Columbus: Ohio State University Press, 1987).

SUBJECTIVITY. *See* SUBJECTIVE KNOWLEDGE; TRUTH

SUBJECT/OBJECT

Since the time of Descartes, the subject is the autonomous, thinking self, which is capable of examining and understanding the physical world (an object) independently of any form of STRUCTURE. From the time of Martin Heidegger, however, and especially in recent scholarship, there has developed a reaction against this privileging of the human self. The recent tendency is to view the subject or self as a product of structure, a cultural construct incapable of assessing or understanding its world objectively or apart from an entire matrix of structures: methodological, ideological, religious, and so forth. Thus AUTHORS cannot step outside their worlds or SOCIAL LOCATIONS to create a TEXT (an object) that is free of their cultural structures or pressures. In this view, similarly, readers are incapable of stepping outside their social locations to examine a text from an objective vantage point. Any analysis of an object (LITERARY or otherwise) will bear the stamp of the subject's SOCIAL LOCATION.

SUBJECT OF ENUNCIATION/ ENUNCIATING

In LINGUISTICS, terms introduced by Émile Benveniste, "whose work has exerted a profound influence on developments in poststructuralist thought" (Norris, 525), that denote two differ-

ent concepts of the self or the pronoun "I." In the sentence "I, Paul, write this greeting with my own hand" (1 Cor. 16:21), two different kinds of "I" can be identified. First, the self-designation denoted by the pronoun is the subject of enunciation, the person who actually utters the sentence. Second, the subject of enunciating is the sum total of the being who utters the sentence, an entity not accessible to the reader. According to Roland Barthes, these concepts suggest that as the speaker (the "I") is a linguistic construct, so the AUTHOR is nothing more than an instance of writing. Writing, language, according to Barthes, does not recognize a person but a subject who has no substance outside the instance of enunciation. In recent literary theory, the "I" has become an ideological construct.

Bibliography. Christopher Norris, "Subject of the Enunciation (also Subject of the Enounced)," in *A Dictionary of Cultural and Critical Theory* (ed. Michael Payne; Oxford: Blackwell, 1996), 524–25.

SUB-PAULINE

The epistles in the NT that are ascribed to Paul but that some scholars question as authentically Pauline. These epistles include 2 Thessalonians, Ephesians, Colossians, 1–2 Timothy, and Titus. *See* DEUTEROPAULINE; EPISTOLARY LITERATURE; PASTORAL EPISTLES.

SUI IPSIUS INTERPRES

A rule of HERMENEUTICS, dating from the Reformation, holding that SCRIPTURE "is itself its own interpreter," or interprets itself. Later Protestant theologians claimed that since some portions of Scripture are clearer than others, the clearer portions should be employed to understand the more difficult ones (*see* ANALOGY OF SCRIPTURE).

SUMMARY

In the study of literature, a rarely used SYNOPSIS of a TEXT or portion of it. In BIBLICAL STUDIES, however, "summary" refers to the statements in a GOSPEL in which the NARRATOR condenses the ACTION of a period of time (e.g., "Then he went about among the villages teaching" [Mark 6:6b]). Other instances include Mark 6:13; Matt. 9:35; 11:1; Luke 7:1; 17:11.

SUPERSCRIPTION

Any type of heading written before a TEXT. In the HEBREW BIBLE, some of the PSALMS have superscriptions (or titles), such as "A Maskil of Asaph" (Ps. 74), "A Song. A Psalm of Asaph" (83), "To the leader. Of David. A Psalm. A Song" (68), "A Song. A Psalm of David" (108), and "To the leader: with stringed instruments. A Psalm of Asaph. A Song" (76).

SUPERSTUCTURE. *See* BASE

SUPPLÉMENT

A French word that can mean "substitute" or "addition." It has been used by Jacques Derrida to describe the unstable relationship between structuralist BINARY OPPOSITIONs. Derrida denies that these oppositions (e.g., speech/writing, nature/culture, truth/fiction) are related in such a fashion that the first term has priority over the second and that the second is derivative from the first. According to Derrida, there is no priority in these oppositions but only DIFFERENCE. This means that SPEECH, nature, and TRUTH have no MEANING apart from writing, culture, and FICTION; hence, the second term is not a *supplément* but must already always be present before the first term has meaning. From this perspective, then, what the Western philosophical TRADITION has always considered natural givens are themselves as much cultural constructs and derivative as their opposites. Derrida's concept of the *supplément* PROBLEMATIZEs the idea of truth, nature, the self, and other concepts as entities that exist apart from culture and language.

Bibliography. Jacques Derrida, *Of Grammatology* (trans. Gayatri Chakravorty Spivak; Baltimore: Johns Hopkins University Press, 1977); Vincent B. Leitch, *Deconstructive Criticism: An Advanced Reader* (New York: Columbia University Press, 1983).

SURFACE STRUCTURES. *See* STRUCTURALISM

SUSPENSION OF DISBELIEF

The withholding of questions about the TRUTH, HISTORICITY, VERISIMILITUDE, and probability of a LITERARY work. Such a suspension allows the reader to accept the WORLD OF THE TEXT created by the AUTHOR. Suspension of disbelief is an essential component in reading the BIBLE AS LITERATURE because underlying the BIBLE-as-literature approach is the ASSUMPTION that the biblical texts are works of the IMAGINATION, with imaginative worlds. For example, if Jonah is a work of the imagination, the reader is expected to accept Jonah's world of sea monsters, rapidly growing bushes, and bush-eating worms without asking questions about their actual historical probability. Rather, the reader is expected to ask questions about the MEANING of the text as it might be ascertained from the STORY.

SUZERAINTY TREATY. *See* COVENANT FORM

SYMBOLIC WORLD

The infinite maze of interrelated customs, ideologies (*see* IDEOLOGY), religious expressions, and social relationships within which a people finds its identity, its self-understanding, and its ultimate reason for being. If a culture's literature is the linguistic expression of this symbolic world, or at least the linguistic attempt to interpret the symbolic world, a study of that culture's linguistic expression—language in its many facets—should be an integral part of HERMENEUTICS. Also within this CONTEXT might be included the more formal LITERARY structures (e.g., GENRE, poetic and NARRATIVE devices).

SYMBOL/SYMBOLIC

A concrete object, known as the VEHICLE in a METAPHOR, that is displaced and used independently of its metaphorical CONTEXT while retaining its metaphorical MEANING or SIGNIFICANCE. A symbol can be any animate or inanimate object that stands for something else. For example, scales are symbolic of justice; a dove, of peace; a rose, of beauty; and a lily, of purity. Most Christians are familiar with the way in which objects such as the cross and the blood of the Christ have become symbols in Christian soteriology. In the BIBLE, objects (e.g., sheep, goat, lamb, lion, certain numbers, a race, or a fight) often stand alone to symbolize a more abstract idea or person.

Symbol is also one of the three types of SIGNS in the SEMIOTICS of Charles Sanders Peirce. According to Peirce, the relationship between the sign and SIGNIFICATION is both arbitrary and conventional in that the relationship is created through habitual association between the symbol and its object/concept. So in some circumstances, black is a symbol of evil, as in "He has a black heart" or in the black hat in the early Western movie GENRE.

SYMPLOCE

A FIGURE OF SPEECH that combines ANAPHORA and EPIPHORA; a word or phrase is repeated at the beginning of successive clauses and the same or another word or phrase is repeated at the end of the clauses (e.g., Ps. 67).

SYMPTOMATIC READING

A model for reading TEXTS (including LITERARY ones), developed by Marxist critic Louis Althusser and employed in English by Terry Eagleton, in which the unconscious IDEOLOGY of the text is exposed and analyzed.

Bibliography. Terry Eagleton, *Criticism and Ideology: A Study in Marxist Literary Theory* (London: New Left Books, 1976).

SYNAESTHESIA. *See* SYNESTHESIA

SYNCHRONIC/SYNCHRONY

In LINGUISTICS, the study of a linguistic system at a particular time apart from the history of its development. The same approach may be taken toward a TEXT (e.g., NEW CRITICISM), focusing on the text and its STRUCTURE apart from its history or its production. *See* DIACHRONIC.

SYNECDOCHE

The practice of using a part to refer to a whole or vice versa. When John says that "God so loved the world" (3:16), his REFERENCE is not to the created world as a whole but only to human beings. In this synecdoche, the whole stands for the part. An example of the reverse is Matt. 10:38: "Whoever does not take up the cross and follow me is not worthy of me." "Cross" here stands in for a whole range of self-sacrificial acts.

SYNESTHESIA (SYNAESTHESIA)

A LITERARY DEVICE in which there is the mixing of senses—for example, hearing a color or tasting a sound. Literature is replete with synesthesia: "a cold stare," "a soft voice," and "Amazing grace, how sweet the sound" are well-known examples. In the BIBLE, examples are "Your voice is sweet" (Song 2:14c), "His speech is most sweet" (Song 5:16a).

SYNONYMOUS PARALLELISM. *See* BIBLICAL POETRY

SYNOPSIS

A critical TEXT that presents the four CANONICAL GOSPELS in parallel columns in order to highlight the points of agreement and disagreement between them. A few of the better-known synopses are Kurt Aland, *Synopsis Quattuor Evangeliorum* (15th, rev. ed.; Stuttgart: Deutsche Bibelgesellschaft, 1996; repr. with corrections, 2005); idem, *Synopsis of the Four Gospels: Greek-English Edition of the Synopsis Quattuor Evangeliorum with the Text of the Revised Standard Version* (3rd ed.; New York: United Bible Societies, 1982); Albert Huck, *Synopse der drei ersten Evangelien* (13th ed.; Tübingen: Mohr, 1981); and James M. Robinson et al., *The Critical Edition of Q: Including the Gospels of Matthew and Luke, Mark and Thomas* (Minneapolis: Fortress, 2000).

SYNOPTIC GOSPELS

The GOSPELs of Matthew, Mark, and Luke. Because of their outward similarities, J. J. Griesbach, who is credited with being the first to apply the term to the first three Gospels, understood them to be "seeing together" (*see* SYNOPSIS).

SYNOPTIC PARALLEL

A passage in Matthew, Mark, or Luke that is also found in one or both of the other two SYNOPTIC GOSPELS.

SYNOPTIC PROBLEM, THE

The problem of explaining the extensive agreement in both CONTENT and ORDER between the SYNOPTIC GOSPELS: Matthew, Mark, and Luke. The problem raises questions about the relationships among the three Gospels in terms of copying, sources, order, and so forth. Many solutions to the problem have been put forth, the most notable ones being the Augustinian hypothesis, that the order of the four was Matthew, Mark, Luke, John with each one making use of its predecessor; the GRIESBACH HYPOTHESIS, that Mark used and abridged both Matthew and Luke; the TWO-SOURCE HYPOTHESIS, that both Matthew and Luke made use of an early sayings source (Q) and an early VERSION of Mark (UR-MARKUS); and the FOUR DOCUMENT HYPOTHESIS, an extension of the two-source hypothesis that posits a third source, M, for the material unique to Matthew, and a fourth, L, for the material unique to Luke.

SYNTACTIC PARALLELISM

A practice in BIBLICAL POETRY in which the semantic parallelism is accompanied by a parallel of word order: the word order in the first half of a poetic line is mirrored in the second half. An example is Prov. 24:19: "Do not fret because of evildoers. Do not envy the wicked."

Bibliography. Robert Alter, *The Art of Biblical Poetry* (New York: Basic Books, 1985).

SYNTAGM

A term introduced by Ferdinand de Saussure for a combination of words (e.g., "by the Nile," "with first-ripe fig," or "the life of leisure"). Normally, the words are combined according to linguistic rules and thus have distinctive MEANING.

SYNTAGMATIC/PARADIGMATIC AXIS

Two related concepts in the STRUCTURALISM of Ferdinand de Saussure, the first concerned with the combination of words and the second with the substitution of words. The syntagmatic axis refers to the horizontal relationship between the words in a sequence. In a sentence, for example, each word has a linear relationship with the words before and after it. The paradigmatic axis refers to the vertical relationship between the words in a sequence and other ones that might have been used but were not. For example, in the sentence "The batter drove the ball to the wall," a variety of words could have been substituted for "batter," "drove," "ball," or "wall," such as "hitter," "hit," "fence," and so on.

Bibliography. Jonathan Culler, *Structuralist Poetics* (London: Routledge & Kegan Paul, 1989).

SYNTAX

The arrangement of words in a sentence, governed by rules. It is a subdivision of DICTION, which also includes word choice. Poetic syntax may differ significantly from PROSE syntax because the rules governing the two are different. For example, the poet may arrange the words in a sentence on the basis of METER, RHYME, RHYTHM, CHIASM, and/or parallelism.

SYNTHETIC PARALLELISM

A type of parallelism in BIBLICAL POETRY in which the second half of a line of POETRY complements the first half by clarifying or explaining it:

> So I will send a fire on the wall of Gaza,
> fire that shall devour its strongholds. (Amos 1:7)

The consuming of the fortresses is the result of the fire upon the walls.

Bibliography. Robert Alter, *The Art of Biblical Poetry* (New York: Basic Books, 1985).

T

TALE

Any short and simple NARRATIVE, either true or fictional, distinguished from the SHORT STORY by the latter's formal STRUCTURE. In BIBLICAL STUDIES, "tale" is a TRANSLATION of Martin Dibelius's "NO-VELLE" in FORM CRITICISM. He identified nine tales in Mark (1:40–45; 4:35–41; 5:1–20; 5:21–43; 6:35–44; 6:45–52; 7:32–37; 8:22–26; and 9:14–29).

Bibliography. Martin Dibelius, *From Tradition to Gospel* (London: Ivor Nicholson & Watson, 1934; repr., Cambridge: James Clarke, 1971).

TALMUD

The combination of the MISHNAH and the GEMARA. There are two Talmuds: the Palestinian (Yerushalmi), from the fifth century CE, and the Babylonian (Bavli), from the sixth century CE. The latter is considered authoritative for JUDAISM.

TANAK

The traditional Hebrew designation for the HE-BREW BIBLE. It is an acrostic formed from the first letters of the Hebrew Bible's three parts, TORAH, NEVI'IM, and KETUBIM, with an "a" between each of these letters.

TARGUM

A term meaning "TRANSLATION" or "INTERPRETA-TION"; it normally refers to Aramaic translations of the OT. The targums (or targumim) have their origin in the synagogue, where the Hebrew TEXT was followed by an Aramaic reading for Jews who no longer spoke Hebrew. Since the translations were often accompanied by interpretive additions, the targums are not only a translation of the Hebrew text but a PARAPHRASE as well.

TELESTICH. *See* ACROSTIC

TEMPLE SCROLL. *See* DEAD SEA SCROLLS

TEN COMMANDMENTS. *See* DECALOGUE

TENDENZ

The POINT OF VIEW or purpose that dominates a TEXT.

TENDENZ CRITICISM

The analysis of a TEXT that tries to uncover AU-THORIAL INTENTION. F. C. Baur (1792–1860) assumed that the intention of the AUTHOR could be determined by an examination of the biased manner in which the writer structures the material of the text. For example, he argued that the author of the Acts of the Apostles shaped his material in such a way as to play down the theological differences between Peter and Paul, thus painting a portrait of a unified church (Soulen and Soulen, 187).

Bibliography. Richard N. Soulen and R. Kendall Soulen, *Handbook of Biblical Criticism* (3rd ed.; Louisville: Westminster John Knox, 2001).

TENOR/VEHICLE

Two terms introduced by I. A. Richards to describe the nature of METAPHOR. He defined tenor as the general idea or thought of the metaphor, whereas vehicle is the concrete IMAGE in which the idea is embodied. For example, in "I compare you, my love, to a mare among Pharaoh's chariots" (Song 1:9), the general idea or tenor is the beauty of the woman, while the concrete image or vehicle is the "mare among Pharaoh's chariots."

TENSION

A term devised by Allen Tate to describe the way in which a TEXT, especially a poem, has MEANING. He derives the term by removing the prefixes of *extension* (the literal meaning of a text) and *intention* (the metaphorical meaning of a text). The play between these two forces in a text constitutes meaning. However, the term has also been used by some critics to refer to the result of the various types of CONFLICT and COMPLICATION inherent in a LITERARY text.

TERNARY LINES

A unit of POETRY having three clauses. Though BIBLICAL POETRY is characterized by units of two clauses, there are some ternary lines. An example is Song 2:5: "Sustain me with raisins, / refresh me with apples; / for I am faint with love."

> Bibliography. James L. Kugel, *The Idea of Biblical Poetry: Parallelism and Its History* (Baltimore: Johns Hopkins University Press, 1981).

TESTAMENT. *See* COVENANT

TESSERA. *See* ANXIETY OF INFLUENCE

TEST MOTIF

In a NARRATIVE, the focus on some person or idea that is put to the test. Examples are the PARABLE of the good Samaritan (Luke 10:25–37), the EPISODE of the rich man (Mark 10:17–31), the question about paying taxes (12:13–17), and the question about the first commandment (12:28–34).

> Bibliography. Leland Ryken, *Words of Life: A Literary Introduction to the New Testament* (Grand Rapids: Baker, 1987).

TETRAGRAMMATON

The four Hebrew consonants that designate the name of the Hebrew God: *YHWH* (e.g., Exod. 3:15). *See* YAHWEH.

TETRATEUCH

While technically referring to the case (*teuchos*) that contained the scrolls, Tetrateuch (Greek for "four scrolls") is used to name the first four books of the HEBREW BIBLE (Genesis, Exodus, Leviticus, and Numbers), which, according to some scholars, derive from the same three sources: J, E, and P. *See* PENTATEUCH.

TEXT

Traditionally, a designation for a piece of writing such as a SERMON, STORY, or chemistry book. Under the influence of such POSTMODERN thinkers as Roland Barthes and Jacques Derrida, however, text has taken on a much broader usage. Text in the latter sense is to be understood as any system of SIGNIFICATION or means of examining any object. The IDEOLOGY or thought system through which people understand their worlds or through which they examine any object is a text; hence comes Derrida's famous dictum "There is nothing outside the text." So a text may be an oral report, an ancient artifact, or a modern CRITICAL METHODOLOGY or literary theory.

TEXT, BYZANTINE. *See* BYZANTINE TEXT

TEXT, CAESAREAN. *See* CAESAREAN TEXT

TEXT, READERLY. *See* LISIBLE

TEXT, RECEIVED. *See* TEXTUS RECEPTUS

TEXT, SCRIPTIBLE. *See* LISIBLE

TEXT, WRITERLY. *See* LISIBLE

TEXT-CENTERED INTERPRETATION

Interpretation that focuses on the TEXT and its STRUCTURE as the source of MEANING. The backbone of text-centered interpretation is its spotlight on artistic strategies, literary forms, and textual coherence as these relate to TEXTUAL AUTONOMY. Text-centered interpretation has been given several names, such as NEW CRITICISM and objective criticism. The latter designation springs from a basic ASSUMPTION of text-centered interpretation—that the text is autonomous, having a life of its own apart from the AUTHOR or reader. This assumption suggests that the standard by which we can rightly judge any interpretation of the text is the text itself. This second assumption then leads to at least a corollary: the text must be viewed spatially, as a whole. Because of this concept of wholeness, text-centered critics are dedicated to demonstrating how the parts of the text cohere in order to produce the whole. Understanding the whole, however, conditions our understanding of the individual parts. Since many text-centered theories share a focus on the formal aspects of a text, the designation FORMAL CRITICISM has become appropriate.

Bibliography. Donald Keesey, ed., *Contexts for Criticism* (3rd ed.; Mountain View, CA: Mayfield, 1998).

TEXT FRAGMENT

An incomplete or fragmentary TEXT in the BIBLE that derives from an earlier complete text (now lost). As an example from the NT, scholars argue that 2 Corinthians is actually a composite of at least two fragments of other letters. Various text fragments have been identified in the Hebrew Bible (e.g., two flood stories in Gen. 7 and 8, two accounts of creation in Gen. 1 and 2, and two accounts of the initial relationship between David and Saul in Gen. 16 and 17).

Bibliography. Richard N. Soulen and R. Kendall Soulen, *Handbook of Biblical Criticism* (3rd ed.; Louisville: Westminster John Knox, 2001).

TEXTS, CLOSED. *See* CLOSED TEXTS

TEXTS, FAMILY OF. *See* ALEXANDRIAN TEXT; BYZANTINE TEXT; CAESAREAN TEXT; TEXTUAL CRITICISM; WESTERN TEXT

TEXTS, OPEN. *See* OPEN TEXTS

TEXTS, PRODUCTIVE. *See* PRODUCTIVE TEXTS

TEXTS, RAS SHAMRA. *See* RAS SHAMRA TEXTS

TEXTS, TRANSMISSIVE. *See* PRODUCTIVE TEXTS

TEXTS, UGARITIC. *See* RAS SHAMRA TEXTS

TEXTUAL AUTONOMY

A primary ASSUMPTION of NEW CRITICISM that once a TEXT leaves the hands of its AUTHOR, it becomes public domain. In other words, the study and understanding of a text is independent of the author and his or her world and such attending interests as the author's biography, INTENTION, time, culture, and so forth. The focus of INTERPRETATION should be the text's STRUCTURE and the relationship between its parts.

TEXTUAL CONSTRAINTS

A concept in the LITERARY theory of Umberto Eco that allows for certain textual controls on the reader. While Eco is quite aware that literary TEXTS are open, lending themselves to a multiplicity of INTERPRETATIONS, he is also aware that this openness of the text does not mean that the text will allow any interpretation whatsoever. The text dictates (at least for the competent reader) the limits of interpretative creativity. For definitions of these textual controls, *see* CIRCUMSTANTIAL SELECTIONS; CONTEXTUAL SELECTIONS; DICTIONARY MEANING; IDEOLOGICAL OVERCODING; INFERENCES FROM COMMON FRAMES; INFERENCES FROM INTERTEXTUAL FRAMES; RHETORICAL OVERCODING; and RULES OF CO-REFERENCE.

Bibliography. Umberto Eco, *The Role of the Reader: Explorations in the Semiotics of Texts* (Bloomington: Indiana University Press, 1984).

TEXTUAL CRITICISM

A CRITICISM whose primary task is to compare the many biblical manuscripts and manuscript families in order to produce a Greek or HEBREW VERSION that most closely approximates the original. Its aim is threefold: (1) to determine the transmission process of a TEXT and the reason it exists in variant forms; (2) to determine the original wording if possible; and (3) to produce a reliable Greek or Hebrew text.

None of the AUTOGRAPHs of the biblical texts survive, only copies of copies, the earliest for the HEBREW BIBLE dating from the seventh century BCE (if one includes some short fragments of text) and, for the NT, from the second century CE. Since the available copies were handwritten by scribes and because there exists a gap between the originals and the earliest copies, textual critics cannot assume with complete certainty that they have recovered the original wording of the biblical texts.

Since the thousands of manuscripts (from complete texts to fragments) exist in various TRANSLATIONS (Greek, Latin, Syriac, Coptic) and in quotations in other kinds of texts, there are four broad categories of variants: (1) between manuscripts in the original languages; (2) between manuscripts in early translations; (3) between ancient manuscripts in the original languages and early translations; and (4) between quotations in early Jewish and Christian writings. But variants may also be intentional or unintentional. Intentional variants appear when scribes changed the wording of the text. The wording could be changed in order to correct a perceived spelling or grammatical error. Scribes also made changes in SYNTAX, rearranging the word order and sentence and paragraph STRUCTURE. Additions, omissions, changes, transpositions, and glosses were made in order to improve the text. Scribes also introduced theological and doctrinal changes to make the text conform to a more orthodox position. Substitutions were sometimes made to remove what might seem to a scribe to be offensive material. Regardless of the type of intentional changes made, textual critics usually assume that the INTENTION of the scribes was to improve the text.

Unintentional variants are usually those resulting from sight or hearing. Copying errors occurred when the scribe would look at the manuscript and then attempt to copy from it. For example, the scribe might skip a word or line, write a word or line twice, misspell a word, reverse the order of letters within a word, or confuse the order of words within a sentence. When a number of scribes were making copies while listening to a reader of a manuscript, errors of hearing were possible. A scribe might not hear the word or group of sentences correctly or might not write correctly what he did hear. Sometimes scribes would make notes or glosses in the margins of texts, and then years later these might be taken as part of the texts and incorporated into new manuscripts by copyists.

However, many OT textual critics doubt the "errors of hearing" problem.

With all the possible variants, how do textual critics determine the most plausible version? Generally, critics rely on two types of evidence: internal and external. As the term suggests, internal evidence arises from within the text itself. Since textual critics are familiar with the process by which ancient texts were composed, copied, preserved, and transmitted, they have identified the types of variants and the reasons they occur. Consequently, in trying to establish the most plausible version, textual critics simply work backward from the variants toward the original. First, on the ASSUMPTION that scribes tended to correct or smooth out difficulties, textual critics claim that when one is choosing between variants, the more difficult reading is to be preferred. Second, because scribes tended to expand texts rather than delete elements from them, the shorter reading is probably closer to the original. Third, since copyists tended to harmonize different versions of the same text, versions that seem to be harmonistic are rejected in favor of a more dissonant one. Fourth, when variant readings seem not to conform to an author's STYLE, TONE, or vocabulary within the same document or in other texts, textual critics generally reject these as inauthentic.

External evidence includes considerations outside the text, such as the date and nature of the manuscripts, the geographical locations of the manuscripts, and the relationship between families of texts. As the biblical writings began to spread throughout the Mediterranean world, certain cities became what critics call "homes" of versions of texts and textual traditions. In other words, in places such as Rome, Alexandria, and Constantinople, certain definable textual traditions arose. Textual critics have assigned the various NT and LXX versions to families or RECENSIONS based on their similarities and identification with geographical areas. Furthermore, textual critics have discovered that some families of texts tend to expand the material when compared with other groups. So if the critic is weighing the external evidence between a version where one group of manuscript witnesses reveals an expansionist tendency while another one does not, the textual critic will generally choose the latter reading. A second external piece of evidence is the date of the manuscript witnesses. Generally, the critic will assume that the earlier version is more likely to be authentic. A third point of external evidence is that manuscript witnesses are weighed rather than counted. For example, it is possible for one reading to be found in a number of fifth-century witnesses but another reading in a single tenth-century witness that better satisfies the components of internal evidence. Therefore, the textual critic would choose the single tenth-century witness as the more authentic one.

Critical editions of the NT and the Hebrew Bible are in the original languages and contain a CRITICAL APPARATUS, an extensive set of footnotes that list variants and the ancient sources (manuscripts, translations, versions, commentaries, quotations) in which the variants occur. Some critical editions include only some of the variants; others list every variant within a text. Although modern translations do not have a critical apparatus, those that are committee translations are based on serious attention to the apparatus of the critical editions. They sometimes offer footnotes that indicate the most crucial variants and include abbreviated information on the type of variant (addition, omission, etc.).

Once the critic has accumulated both internal and external evidence, the critic makes a decision as to which reading best approximates the original. Since no originals are extant, textual criticism depends on the available evidence and the informed judgment of the critic. For an excellent introduction to textual criticism, see Voelz.

Bibliography. J. Harold Greenlee, *Introduction to New Testament Textual Criticism* (Grand Rapids: Eerdmans, 1964; rev. ed., Peabody, MA: Hendrickson, 1995); John H. Hayes and Carl R. Holladay, *Biblical Exegesis: A Beginner's Handbook* (Atlanta: John Knox, 1987); Ralph W. Klein, *Textual Criticism of the Old Testament* (Philadelphia: Fortress, 1974); Charles B. Puskas, *An Introduction to the New Testament* (Peabody, MA: Hendrickson, 1989); Emanuel Tov, *Textual Criticism of the Hebrew Bible* (Minneapolis: Fortress, 1992); James W. Voelz, *What Does This Mean? Principles of Biblical Interpretation in the Post-modern World* (St. Louis: Concordia, 1995).

TEXTUAL FAMILY

In TEXTUAL CRITICISM, a grouping of the various NT and Greek VERSIONS of the HEBREW BIBLE, or of RECENSIONS, on the basis of similarities and identification with a geographical area.

TEXTUALITY

Traditionally, a term for the written nature of TEXTs relative to their construction as linguistic objects. In STRUCTURALISM and POSTMODERN studies, however, *textuality* has come to signify two important ideas. First, it refers to the nature of language to produce a multiplicity of possible SIGNIFICATIONS, rather than to its nature to refer to a world or object outside language. The multiple significations are activated in the process of reading itself. Second, *textuality* designates the textual nature of all systems, events, and objects. In other words, historical events, institutional ideologies (*see* IDEOLOGY) and STRUCTURES, CRITICAL METHODOLOGY, and so forth are systems of SIGNs that need to be deciphered and interpreted just like a LITERARY document. In addition, all these objects are interpreted with reference to their matrix of CONTEXTs, which are themselves systems that must be interpreted or read. But textuality also encompasses the contexts of the reader, CRITIC, historian, and so forth: a reader's INTERPRETATION of any object is contingent on the reader's own SOCIAL LOCATION (Jones, 642). This social location is a text from which one reads and that can itself be read by others. The concept therefore extends interpretive contexts indefinitely, eroding any possibility of interpretive CLOSURE.

Bibliography. Manina Jones, "Textuality," in *Encyclopedia of Contemporary Literary Theory* (ed. Irena R. Makaryk; Toronto: University of Toronto Press, 1993), 641–42.

TEXTUAL PLAY. *See* PLAY

TEXTUAL STRATEGIES

One of the elements or processes in the READER-RESPONSE CRITICISM of Wolfgang Iser that make up the REPERTOIRE of the TEXT (*see also* LITERARY REPERTOIRE). While the repertoire of the text consists of the social norms and LITERARY ALLUSIONS, it also includes textual strategies, which function to organize the readers' ACTUALIZATION without making them feel as if they are being led by the nose. The strategies govern not only the STRUCTURES of the text but also the acts of comprehension triggered in the reader. Put another way, it is the function of the strategies to carry the primary CODE of the text to the reader and to guide the reader's creation of the aesthetic object (the second code).

The textual strategies include the devices normally associated with the LITERARY CONVENTIONS of GENRE. For Iser, however, the emphasis falls on the unmanifested dimension of the text, what we may call seams and what he refers to as gaps of INDETERMINACY. Literary texts offer readers only enough information to keep them "oriented and interested." Inferences that are to be drawn from the information are left up to the IMAGINATION of the reader. Within the text empty spaces or gaps result, which must be filled by the reader.

Bibliography. Wolfgang Iser, *The Act of Reading: A Theory of Aesthetic Response* (Baltimore: Johns Hopkins University Press, 1978).

TEXTUAL UNITY

An important ASSUMPTION in NEW CRITICISM, that all the parts of a LITERARY work exist in such a close relationship that each part must be understood in terms of all the other parts and in terms of the whole, and the whole in terms of the parts.

TEXTUAL WORLD

In literature, the imaginative world that is structured within the TEXT, a world that may or may not resemble the REAL WORLD out of which the text originated. This concept is especially important in NARRATIVE CRITICISM, which focuses on the STORY WORLD as it is structured in the text itself, rather than on the historical, cultural, ideological world within which the AUTHOR lived. In this respect, therefore, texts such as a GOSPEL, the book of

Revelation, or Genesis should be read as imaginative works, giving attention to the worlds depicted in the text. It is in the examination of the textual world that MEANING is to be found, not in the world of the author or in AUTHORIAL INTENTION.

TEXTURE

In LITERARY studies, the surface qualities of a TEXT as opposed to its STRUCTURE (a study of structure will focus on such things as PLOT, SETTING, CHARACTERIZATION, POINT OF VIEW, and CONFLICT). Therefore, *texture* refers to a text's DICTION, IMAGERY, and sensuous qualities. In POETRY, texture includes RHYME, RHYTHM, and METER.

TEXTUS RECEPTUS

Latin for "received text." In NT studies, it refers to the Greek NT used from the sixteenth to nineteenth century as the basis for TRANSLATIONS, including the KING JAMES VERSION. It was published in 1550 by Robert Stephanus and was virtually a reproduction of the TEXT produced by Erasmus in 1535. In OT studies, the Textus Receptus refers to the second rabbinic BIBLE of Jacob ben Chaim, published in 1524–25.

Bibliography. Richard N. Soulen and R. Kendall Soulen, *Handbook of Biblical Criticism* (3rd ed.; Louisville: Westminster John Knox, 2001).

THANKSGIVING. *See* EPISTOLARY LITERATURE

THANKSGIVING PSALM. *See* PSALM(S)

THEME

Generally, in LITERARY studies, the topic or SUBJECT of a work (e.g., justice, revenge, forgiveness). However, literary works may have more than one theme. Luke's Gospel, for example, may have themes of innocence, reversal of fortune, prayer, divine guidance, and Jesus as Savior. "Theme" also may refer to a reader's statement of a THESIS relative to the work's subject. For example, if a reader determines that Jonah's primary subject is the relationship between God's justice and his grace, the theme becomes the claim that the reader perceives Jonah to be making about that relationship.

In the READER-RESPONSE CRITICISM of Wolfgang Iser, a theme is the perspective that a reader has at any one moment in the reading process. According to Iser, every textual segment is viewed within the CONTEXT of a horizon; but in the time flow of reading, a theme is immediately transformed into the BACKGROUND, thus becoming part of the horizon from which the next segment will be viewed. Therefore, while the horizon influences the theme, the theme will also modify the horizon. The horizon always arouses EXPECTATIONS (*see* HORIZON OF EXPECTATION) of things to come (e.g., how a problem will be resolved), and the theme will either satisfy the expectations or frustrate them. In addition, each new theme not only answers or frustrates expectations but also gives rise to new ones. As a result, the theme has a retroactive influence on the horizon because the reader must go back and reconsider the previous segments and their relationships. So reading becomes an interplay between MEMORY and expectation.

Bibliography. Wolfgang Iser, *The Act of Reading: A Theory of Aesthetic Response* (Baltimore: Johns Hopkins University Press, 1978); idem, "The Reading Process: A Phenomenological Approach," in *Reader-Response Criticism: From Formalism to Post-structuralism* (ed. Jane Tompkins; Baltimore: Johns Hopkins University Press, 1980), 50–69.

THEODICY

In religious studies, a defense of the ACTIONS of God. At least one scholar, Luke T. Johnson, suggests that Luke-Acts is a theodicy. His argument is based on Luke's remarks to his NARRATEE in Luke 1:4: "So that you may know the truth concerning the things about which you have been instructed." Johnson translates, "So that you may have certainty . . . ," and then details the manner in which Luke STRUCTURES his account of the events in both the history of Israel and the early church to show that God has not failed to fulfill his promises to Israel but is fulfilling them in the church.

Bibliography. Luke T. Johnson, *The Writings of the New Testament: An Interpretation* (Philadelphia: Fortress, 1988).

THEOLOGIA CRUCIS / THEOLOGIA GLORIAE

In NT studies, especially in the study of Mark's GOSPEL, the notion that in some early communities, some Christians developed a CHRISTOLOGY of power based on Jesus's acts of power, which became a *theologia gloriae* (theology of glory). Theodore Weeden and others even viewed Jesus as a *theios anēr* (divine man), essentially defined by his ability to perform miracles. Both messiahship and discipleship were defined in terms of the glory associated with Jesus as miracle worker. Some NT critics think that this is the type of THEOLOGY presented in the first half of Mark's Gospel, a view that is then corrected in the last half by a *theologia crucis* (theology of the cross). This view is based on the high concentration of miracles and exorcisms in the first half and a preponderance of teaching (including the passion and death of Jesus) in the second half. In the second half of Mark's Gospel, the essence of messiahship and discipleship is defined in terms of suffering and death. In other words, Jesus's claims about his mission and person must have SIGNIFICANCE only in light of his death.

Bibliography. Theodore Weeden, "The Heresy That Necessitated Mark's Gospel," in *The Interpretation of Mark* (ed. William Telford; Philadelphia: Fortress, 1985), 89–104; idem, *Mark: Traditions in Conflict* (Philadelphia: Fortress, 1971).

THEOLOGICAL EXEGESIS

A description of any method that has as its purpose the articulation of the theological SIGNIFICANCE of the biblical texts as opposed to methods that have historical, social, or LITERARY concerns. In reality, however, theological exegesis is rarely done independently of historical and literary issues.

THEOLOGICAL FRAMEWORK

In one SENSE, a theological thought system that serves as a grid through which experience is filtered and reality understood. In another sense, a *theological framework* may refer more narrowly to the theological grid through which a TEXT is interpreted.

THEOLOGICAL INTERPRETATION OF THE BIBLE

An approach to biblical interpretation holding the core belief that God is the focal point of Scripture and that Scripture exists to propagate the knowledge of God throughout history. Thus "theology" is central to the biblical texts; it is not merely a contributive element. In the first several centuries after Christ, Jews and Christians interpreted the OT as a means of knowing God: Jews saw the OT through the lens of continuing rabbinic tradition, and Christians saw it through the lens of Christ and the writings that would become the NT. For both groups, however, Scripture was a united body of literature that mediated divine TRUTH for the community of faith (Soulen and Soulen, 193).

In 1787, J. P. Gabler gave a speech in which he posited that the Bible contained a theology of its own, one that should not be influenced by church dogma. This ideological move was the beginning of what would become a "ditch" between critical biblical scholarship and theology. Originally meant to protect biblical studies from dogmatic TRADITION, this ditch eventually left God in the background, opposite the scholarly side of the ditch (Vanhoozer, "Theological Interpretation?," 20). The new approaches of historicism claimed that in order to let the TEXT speak for itself, one had to "let go of God" (Soulen and Soulen, 193). Sandy-Wunsch observes that these new critical methods of biblical study resulted from a combination of many social and political forces. Further, even critics as unorthodox as Reimarus and Lessing aimed to *reform* religion rather than to destroy it (554–56). The unity of Scripture as the witness to God's grand redemptive drama was challenged, and scholars often tried to uncover the various ancient religious beliefs in the canon without looking for contemporary application. In this period of historicism (from the late 1700s to mid-1900s), theologians such as F. C. Baur, D. F. Strauss, Albert Schweitzer, Rudolf Bultmann, Ernst Käsemann, and Karl Barth sought to reconstruct the traditional understanding of the Bible's message in different ways, often relying heavily on a variety of historical-critical approaches. Even scholars like these, many of whom were not orthodox, still tried to uncover the deep theological/philosophical truth communicated in Scripture (Boers, 556–58).

Today many scholars view Scripture as a witness to God's divine activity of redemption in the world. The ugly ditch that formed several hundred years ago between theology and BIBLICAL CRITICISM seems to be narrowing. Current biblical scholars utilize critical methods of scholarship to better understand God as the central figure of the Bible. Scholars such as Gerald O'Collins, Daniel Kendall, Charles Scalise, Francis Watson, Christopher Weitz, and Stephen Fowl are among them (Green, "Modernity," 308–9). And some scholars, like Michael Gorman, hope that the gap between EXEGESIS and theology will continue to close.

As stated, theological interpretation holds that the central figure of Scripture is God; thus the central purpose of Scripture is to communicate information about God to the world. The foremost concern is the "knowledge of and communion with God" (Soulen and Soulen, 192). Kendall Soulen summarizes the method's focus as "true knowledge of God and faithful orientation to the world" ("Believer," 177). God was prior to both the religious communities and the biblical texts. Thus the writers' purposes were theological: their writings are *"confessions"* of the knowledge of God and his word (Vanhoozer, "Theological Interpretation?," 22). If the biblical writings are documents that attest to God's activity in human history, and the writers penned them because of that activity, then the purpose of reading Scripture should be to better understand God's nature and his dealings with humanity. Vanhoozer proposes a "Theodramatic" approach to Scripture, in which one views the biblical text as the script of the great drama of redemption ("Theological Method," 894–97). Humanity was separated from God, and God acted to redeem them. Scripture is the documentation of that divine drama, and it exists to reveal the character of God.

Therefore, theological interpreters affirm that the Bible cannot be ignored as *Scripture* (i.e., sacred texts whose purpose is to reveal God). An interpretation of the text that does not account for theology is perhaps one that falls short, for the text is foremost a theological text (Vanhoozer, "Exegesis," 52–53). Theological interpreters claim that in traditional historical criticism, this consideration for theology was lost. Scholars disregarded the text as "testimonies" that act as a "medium of divine witness to the present" (Soulen, "Believer," 180). But even those who try to leave God out of the interpretive equation still approach the text with theological presuppositions (Vanhoozer, "Exegesis," 54–55). A stance that ignores theology in Scripture is one that makes a great theological presupposition: that God does not exist and can therefore be excluded from consideration. The nature of the texts, however, does not allow for completely excluding theology from them. Proponents of theological interpretation do not agree that such exclusion allows the text to speak for itself; rather, ignoring theology in Scripture is sometimes nothing more than "illusory neutrality" (Soulen and Soulen, 186). Vanhoozer observes, "If exegesis without presuppositions is impossible, and if some of these presuppositions concern the nature and activity of God, then it would appear to go without saying that biblical interpretation is always/already theological" ("Theological Interpretation?," 21). If biblical interpretation is inherently theological (for the text is so saturated that theology cannot be ignored), then it is up to interpreters to make sure that their approach "corresponds to the communicative intent of the text. Otherwise interpreters will describe not the theology of the text but their own agendas and ideologies" (Vanhoozer, "Exegesis," 63). A theological reading of Scripture is the only type of reading that can do justice to the texts; it is necessary to make sense of the text's claims.

So then, theological interpreters approach Scripture by this mantra: "God speaks in and through the biblical texts" ("Theological Interpretation?," 22). Scripture is not merely historical: it is "divine revelation" by which members of the believing community can reflect and learn (Green, "Rethinking," 162). Although this approach might seem narrow, it does not shortchange critical scholarship. Rather, it embraces a number of critical approaches. Vanhoozer allows for a certain amount of play in the boundaries of what is considered theological interpretation. Within the approach exists a diversity of interpretations, and this diversity is not enough to necessitate the exclusion of those who differ. Green holds that the Bible is an encounter with "the God who stands behind and is mediated in Scripture" ("Rethinking," 162). The aim of reading must be to experience transformation through God's word. Proponents of theological interpretation, similar to early Jews and Christians, believe that Scripture and the world enlighten each other, that Scripture is unified in its intent, and that Scripture is the basis for the church's deciding "conduct and creed" (Soulen, "Believer," 178).

These claims lead to a final characteristic of theological interpretation: the interpretation of Scripture is a decidedly (though not exclusively) *ecclesial* duty. The main field of operation for theological interpretation is the church, and Scripture is a sacred source that the church uses to establish community norms. Knowledge of how to interpret the Bible, then, is very important for the church. Because of its ecclesial center, the goal of theological interpretation is ultimately *personal* encounter with God and thus transformation. Becoming immersed in the world of the text, receiving its message, and thereby joining in the grand story of redemption leads a person to experience change. Theological interpretation seeks to move from text to truth to application in daily life; it seeks to make theology "practical" in a way that helps people experience God's "divine intent" for their lives (Vanhoozer, "Theological Method," 832–42). This divine intent of transformative renewal is a key theological idea in the biblical text. So, as Vanhoozer says, "Theological method succeeds when it equips the church to speak truly, live justly, and act in ways that befit her spouse—and when it equips individuals to think and live in right relation to the triune God" (897). Furthermore, the message of right relation with God should be extended to all denominations and cultures. Inherently, then, theological interpretation is "ecumenical" and "multicultural" (Gorman, 118). Gorman says that theological interpretation must retain its missional focus in order to be truly "ecclesial," for "nothing is more fundamental to theological interpretation than its connection to the *missio dei*" (128).

The accounts of the resurrection of Jesus, their connection to God's character, and the application to the community of faith illustrate theological interpretive method. The resurrection of Jesus is recorded as a historical event by the Gospel writers in the NT (see Matt. 28:1–15; Mark 16; Luke 24:1–12; John 20:1–18). The literary structures of their accounts are formed in such a way as to culminate in Jesus's resurrection. The book of Acts records the disciples' responses to Jesus's resurrection: they hold firmly to the fact that Jesus was raised, and they proclaim the fact both to fellow Jews and to pagans (see Acts 1:22; 3:15; 4:2; 17:18–33; 23:6; 24:15; 26:23). Beyond these historically oriented NT books, the Letters of Paul and Peter give insight into the Messiah-followers' views of Jesus's resurrection. Paul thought that Jesus was proved to be the long-awaited Messiah by his resurrection (Rom. 1:4). In addition, Paul saw Jesus's resurrection as a guarantee of what those who believed in him could expect in the future (1 Cor. 15:12–13, 16, 20–22; Col. 1:18). Peter believed that Jesus's resurrection inspired new believers with revivified hope and faith (1 Pet. 1:3, 21).

The NT authors who address Jesus's resurrection obviously give it great importance. When examined in the historical context of the Jewish expectation of the Messiah of God to come and redeem Israel, this importance makes sense. Jews in the first century (and before) were expecting God to restore the national state of Israel (as attested in OT prophecies and in intertestamental literature) and usher in a glorious "age to come," in which God would bring his people back to him, and he would rule them eternally. All injustices would be set straight, and resurrection from the dead would accompany the initiation of this "age to come." So, when Jesus's disciples and other Jews saw the man who accepted the title of Messiah (and performed the miracles to back it up) come back to life, they

understood that it was the beginning of the end. God had inaugurated the age to come, and he was beginning to restore his chosen people.

This act of God suggests that he was fulfilling his prior promises to restore the nation of Israel and to bless all the people of the world through Israel (see Gen. 26:4; Acts 26:23). Furthermore, God's plan of a good future in which all things would be made new and restored had now begun to enter the realm of his people's experience. Jesus's resurrection was a guarantee that these promised good things were beginning to come.

This speaks of God's faithful and good character, but what about its implications for people two thousand years later? Followers of Christ can have hope, just as Peter did, that God will make good on his promise to bring about such a great and glorious end as he started in Jesus. Furthermore, since the resurrection of the Messiah initiates the age in which all things are made new, followers can experience that newness in partial ways already. As Paul said to believers in Rome, "If the Spirit of him who raised Jesus from the dead dwells in you, he who raised Christ from the dead will give life to your mortal bodies also through his Spirit that dwells in you" (Rom. 8:11). Thus, believers can explain to others that God has initiated the age to come by way of the Messiah, whom he raised from the dead, and they can seek to cultivate an atmosphere in their communities of faith that reflects the radical hope of that belief.

The main focuses of the above interpretation are God and his activity in the world and in human affairs. Scripture is approached as texts that communicate God's truth, and the texts are examined as a unified whole. Theology is not ignored, for the claims of the NT writers express their conviction of God's good character (as they perceive it), as a result of what he has done; the interpretation reflects such conviction. It is a revelation of God first and foremost, a revelation set in the context of a grand, divine drama. Ultimately, the interpretation takes the "communicative intent" of the biblical texts and asks what implications such intent has for the contemporary community of faith. It then tries to apply those discerned implications appropriately in the ecclesial setting.

Bibliography. Hendrikus Boers, "Theology, New Testament," in *Dictionary of Biblical Interpretation* (ed. John H. Hayes; Nashville: Abingdon, 1999), 2:556–61; Michael J. Gorman, "A 'Seamless Garment' Approach to Biblical Interpretation?," *Journal of Theological Interpretation* 1, no. 1 (2007): 117–28; Joel B. Green, "Modernity, History and the Interpretation of the Bible," *Scottish Journal of Theology* 54, no. 3 (2001): 308–29; idem, "Rethinking 'History' for Theological Interpretation," *Journal of Theological Interpretation* 5, no. 2 (2011): 159–73; J. T. K. Lim, "Theological Hermeneutics: A Reading Strategy," *Asia Journal of Theology* 15, no. 1 (2001): 2–13; J. Sandy-Wunsch, "Theology, Biblical (to 1800)," in *Dictionary of Biblical Interpretation* (ed. John H. Hayes; Nashville: Abingdon, 1999), 2:553–56; R. Kendall Soulen, "The Believer and the Historian and Historical Investigation," *Interpretation* 57, no. 2 (April 2003): 174–86; Richard N. Soulen and R. Kendall Soulen, *Handbook of Biblical Criticism* (3rd ed.; Louisville: Westminster John Knox, 2001); Kevin J. Vanhoozer, "Exegesis and Hermeneutics," in *New Dictionary of Biblical Theology* (ed. T. Desmond Alexander and Brian S. Rosner; Downers Grove, IL: InterVarsity, 2000), 52–63; idem, "Theological Method," in *Global Dictionary of Theology* (ed. William A. Dyrness and Veli-Matti Kärkkäinen; Downers Grove, IL: InterVarsity, 2008), 889–98; idem, "What Is Theological Interpretation of the Bible?," in *Dictionary for Theological Interpretation of the Bible* (ed. Kevin J. Vanhoozer; Grand Rapids: Baker Academic, 2005), 21–25; Charles M. Wood, "The Task of Theological Hermeneutics," *Perkins Journal* 33 (1980): 1–8.

THEOLOGY

Literally, "speech about God," but usually understood as the systematic study of divine revelation. Normally implied in the term is the scientific, methodological, academic study of sacred TEXTs. In this sense, we may speak of doing theology. *Theology,* however, may also refer to the result of such study and designate the belief system of a person or group.

THEOLOGY, BIBLICAL. *See* BIBLICAL THEOLOGY

THEOLOGY, BLACK. *See* BLACK THEOLOGY

THEOLOGY, CONFESSIONAL. *See* CONFESSIONAL THEOLOGY

THEOLOGY, CONTEXTUAL. *See* CONTEXTUALIZATION

THEOLOGY, DOGMATIC. *See* DOGMATIC THEOLOGY

THEOLOGY, LIBERATION. *See* LIBERATION THEOLOGY

THEOLOGY, *MUJERISTA*. *See* MUJERISTA THEOLOGY

THEOLOGY OF GLORY. *See* THEOLOGIA CRUCIS / THEOLOGIA GLORIAE

THEOLOGY OF LIBERATION. *See* LIBERATION THEOLOGY

THEOLOGY OF THE CROSS. *See* THEOLOGIA CRUCIS / THEOLOGIA GLORIAE

THEOLOGY, POPULAR. *See* POPULAR THEOLOGY

THEOLOGY, WOMANIST. *See* WOMANIST THEOLOGY

THEOPHANY

Any manifestation of divinity. Generally, the mode of manifestation is natural (e.g., auditory and sight). Theophany occurs in both the HEBREW BIBLE and the NT. In the former, such events as the call of Moses (Exod. 3), the call of PROPHETs (e.g., Ezek. 1; Isa. 6), and the appearance of Yahweh at Sinai (Exod. 19–20) are all theophanies. In the NT, such events as Jesus's baptism (Mark 1:9–11), the transfiguration (9:2–13), and the conversion of Paul (Acts 9:4–16) are manifestations of the divine.

THESIS

In LITERARY studies, a statement of the MEANING of a TEXT. The thesis is based on the SUBJECT of the literary work. For example, if a reader determines that the subject of Job is the relationship between moral character and material prosperity, the thesis may be something like this: "The book of Job argues that a person's moral character is independent of material prosperity." *Thesis* is also used for Jesus's quotations from the TORAH in Matthew's SERMON ON THE MOUNT. The thesis is followed by Jesus's reinterpretation, the ANTITHESIS.

THICK DESCRIPTION

A concept coined by the British philosopher Gilbert Ryle in 1966 and popularized by Clifford Geertz in anthropology to designate the practice of making meaningful and stratified layers of inferences based on discoveries in the field. For example, a STORY that an anthropologist encounters may have complex conceptual STRUCTURES superimposed on layers of deeper structures. The anthropologist is faced with the task of analyzing and explaining the story in ever-thickening descriptions. *See* CULTURAL ANTHROPOLOGY.

Bibliography. Thomas W. Overholt, *Cultural Anthropology and the Old Testament* (Minneapolis: Fortress, 1996).

THIRD QUEST, THE. *See* QUEST FOR THE HISTORICAL JESUS, THE

THIRD-WORLD THEOLOGIES

Theologies emerging out of Latin America, Africa, and Asia, usually with an emphasis on liberation. *See* LIBERATION HERMENEUTICS; LIBERATION THEOLOGY.

THOUGHT RHYMES

According to some scholars of the HEBREW BIBLE, a characteristic of BIBLICAL POETRY in which the two or three parts of a line of POETRY RHYME conceptually rather than phonologically (*see* PHONOLOGY). For example, in "He washes his garments in wine / and his robe in the blood of grapes" (Gen. 49:11b), "garments" and "robe" are synonymous, as are "wine" and "blood of grapes." For a more complete discussion of this feature, *see* BIBLICAL POETRY.

TIME HORIZON

The FRAMEWORK within which a reader understands a TEXT. A reader actualizes the text by mak-

ing SENSE of it as a communicatory artifact within a matrix of CONTEXTs (ideological, communal, methodological, etc.). It is only within this time horizon that a reader can formulate a meaningful understanding of the text. However, texts also have their time horizon, the contexts within which an AUTHOR communicates (Thiselton, 64–65). This textual time horizon places restraints on what a reader may plausibly say about texts, especially those more CLOSED TEXTS. For example, the Epistles of Paul are more plausibly understood when the *SITZ IM LEBEN* of each is explored, simply because these epistles are strongly shaped by their historical SETTINGS.

Bibliography. Anthony C. Thiselton, *New Horizons in Hermeneutics* (Grand Rapids: Zondervan, 1992).

TODAY'S ENGLISH VERSION. *See* GOOD NEWS BIBLE

TOKEN. *See* TYPE

TONE

The AUTHOR's attitude toward the audience implied in the work. The tone may be formal, informal, ironic, serious, or playful.

TOPOS

In classical RHETORIC, a commonplace term, idea, structural pattern, or argument. The itinerant Hellenistic Cynic and Stoic preachers developed standardized responses to frequently asked questions on certain topics. Most often the topic concerned vice and virtue. These topoi (plural) could be strung together with no apparent controlling principle or arranged by the use of some *LEITWORT*. David Bradley has identified two topoi in Paul's Letters: Rom. 13 and 1 Thess. 4:9–5:11.

Bibliography. David Bradley, "The Topos as a Form in the Pauline Paraenesis," *JBL* 72 (1953): 238–46.

TORAH

Generally understood as the PENTATEUCH, the first five books of the HEBREW BIBLE: Genesis, Exodus, Leviticus, Numbers, and Deuteronomy. It may, however, signify the whole Hebrew Bible or, according to Jewish tradition, the entirety of God's revelation to Moses: the Hebrew Bible and the ORAL TORAH (MISHNAH and GEMARA). *See* LAW.

TOTALIZATION

In recent critical studies, any practice of examining and explaining reality or any object (including TEXTS) through an ideological system (*see* IDEOLOGY) that purports to account fully for reality. POSTMODERN critics (e.g., Jacques Derrida, Michel Foucault, and Edward Said), however, argue that these systems exist only by negating other possibilities and can offer unified and complete readings of texts only by eliding their diversity. For these postmoderns, the practice of assessing such things as texts with the ASSUMPTION that they have some inherent unity is nothing more than the exercise of the will to power and results in an imposed unity.

Bibliography. Linda Hutcheon, *A Poetics of Postmodernism: History, Theory, Fiction* (New York: Routledge, 1988).

TRACE

In the DECONSTRUCTION theory of Jacques Derrida, a term that almost defies definition because he applies it in a variety of ways. Perhaps the best attempt at definition is to consider it in tandem with another term used by Derrida: "mark." According to Derrida, each and every human ACTION leaves a mark on culture, and each and every mark gives witness to its originating human action, an action that itself escapes complete specification. Therefore, writing's mark leaves a trace of the indeterminate origin of the writing. The mark that our writing makes is also a trace of the indeterminate origin of the writing. Since the genesis or origin of writing is always prior to any act of understanding, the trace becomes a witness to the indescribability of the source of writing.

If every human action has both a culturally specific mark and a trace of the moment of origination, then every human action has not only a determinate MEANING but also an indeterminate meaning. More simply put, if every human action is shaped by culture while at the same time shaping the culture, the culture is constantly and infi-

nitely undergoing modification and change while in a reciprocal fashion influencing the actions that change it. This complex of mutual influence gives rise to both continuity and discontinuity between the action and the culture. Therefore, INTERPRETATIONS of human actions (including LITERARY ones) must focus on both the way in which the action is shaped by culture (i.e., the action's continuity with the culture) and the way in which an action is discontinuous with the culture.

Bibliography. Clarence Walhout, "Texts and Actions," in *The Responsibility of Hermeneutics* (ed. Roger Lundin et al.; Grand Rapids: Eerdmans, 1985), 31–77.

TRADITION

Generally, a collection of beliefs transmitted from generation to generation. The term can also refer to a body of conventional beliefs and practices that define a group in the present (Harmon and Holman, 521). So scholars may seek to delineate the elements of the Hellenistic tradition, Hebrew tradition, classical tradition, Reformed tradition, Pauline tradition, or Catholic tradition. In FORM CRITICISM, the focus on the ORAL TRADITION that underlies written sources. *See also* TRADITION CRITICISM.

Bibliography. William Harmon and C. Hugh Holman, *A Handbook to Literature* (8th ed.; Upper Saddle River, NJ: Prentice Hall, 1999).

TRADITION CRITICISM

Also referred to as tradition history, history of traditions, and traditio-historical criticism, the study of the history of both Hebrew and Christian ORAL TRADITIONS and their transmission (Soulen and Soulen, 198). It presupposes that many biblical TEXTS have a "prehistory," that they are based on and/or incorporate historical traditions and that these traditions are accessible. These traditions include STORY, CREED, POETRY, APHORISM, HYMN, confession, and so forth. Tradition criticism is a method of analyzing biblical literature in terms of TRADITION and its growth and development. These traditions circulated among and within communities in what critics call the "oral period," a period in which the stories and other forms were preserved and circulated, eventually developing into traditions that were then passed on from generation to generation (Hayes and Holladay, 93). Tradition criticism focuses on the nature of the traditions and the manner in which the communities over time used and adapted them. The discipline operates on the ASSUMPTION, introduced by Hermann Gunkel (1862–1932), that ancient communities produced texts through a lengthy transmission process rather than a single AUTHOR creating them. These traditions were handed down over a long period of oral transmission before later authors set them down in writing or incorporated them into other written documents. The traditions grow out of and reflect the SYMBOLIC WORLD of the communities that produce the traditions and thus also reflect their prejudices and values. Hence, tradition critics assume that by studying the genesis, transmission, and RECONTEXTUALIZATION of the traditions, scholars can discover much about the way in which these communities defined themselves in terms of faith and self-understanding.

Gunkel was persuaded that scholars could systematically reconstruct the manner in which different communities defined their faith and religious practices. First, it is possible to discover the original CONTEXT of the stories. Second, the scholar should be able to reconstruct the various stages through which the stories developed. Since the different stages of a tradition may have developed at different locations and in different ways within texts, the scholar may conclude that these stages reflect different periods and theological viewpoints (Hayes and Holladay, 92). Third, from this RECONSTRUCTION, it should be possible to discover the earliest form of each story. Fourth, on the basis of the first three steps, it should then be possible to trace the process through which the stories were combined into longer NARRATIVES. And fifth, since it is rarely possible to tease out reliable historical information from these stories or the process of transmission and development, the final goal is to say something meaningful about the faith and religious practices that defined these ancient com-

munities. Some scholars go a step further and use the knowledge gained through tradition criticism to understand the biblical texts as we now have them. The assumption here is that by examining the manner in which an author has recontextualized a tradition or a portion of it, the EXEGETE is in a better position to understand the text under examination. In other words, an author's recontextualization of traditional material is constitutive of meaning. For example, Pss. 105 and 106 both incorporate the traditional story of Israel's sojourn in the wilderness. But whereas Ps. 105 "translates" the story in a way that emphasizes the faithfulness of Yahweh to the people, Ps. 106 employs the story to stress the unfaithfulness of the people toward Yahweh. Furthermore, the author of Isa. 40–55 uses the tradition to describe as a new EXODUS the return from EXILE, and Hosea uses the tradition to describe the condition of Israel as a return to Egypt (Hayes and Holladay, 96).

As these examples illustrate, Israel recycled and dialogued with its traditions and in the process continually (re)developed its self-understanding. Individuals and communities receive the traditions but later reinterpret them in light of new situations and conditions and, in turn, transmit the reinterpreted tradition to successors (Hayes and Holladay, 98). So the tradition is always in a state of further development. Through a study of such recontextualizations, the biblical exegete can reach a more plausible understanding not only of the text but also of the development and use of the traditions. Although tradition criticism offers assistance in the former, its primary focus is the latter: it is concerned primarily with the manner in which the Hebrew and Christian communities participated in the process of transmission. Thus tradition criticism remains a historically focused discipline.

Bibliography. Hermann Gunkel, *The Legends of Genesis: The Biblical Saga and History* (trans. W. H. Carruth; New York: Schocken Books, 1964); John H. Hayes and Carl R. Holladay, *Biblical Exegesis: A Beginner's Handbook* (Atlanta: John Knox, 1987); Richard N. Soulen and R. Kendall Soulen, *Handbook of Biblical Criticism* (3rd ed.; Louisville: Westminster John Knox, 2001).

TRADITIONSGESCHICHTE. See TRADITION
CRITICISM

TRAGEDY

A literary GENRE that has its roots in the religious
rituals of ancient Greece but could be identified
by specific LITERARY CONVENTIONS by the time
of Aristotle. Although the genre expanded over
several decades from Aristotle's time through
the period of the Roman Empire, its chief FORM
remained the one found in Aristotle's *Poetics*, in
which he describes the various components of
tragedy (see below). Since tragedy would have
been well known and widely performed during
the first century CE, the question naturally arises as
to the similarities between the texts of the NT and
the genre of tragedy. Some NT scholars have argued
that the GOSPELS, while not specifically tragedies,
share enough particulars with the genre that they
can be read through the grid of the tragic genre.
This argument is further supported by the claim
that since tragedy was widespread, the AUTHORS
of the Gospels would have been quite familiar with
the conventions of tragedy and thus borrowed
freely from them.

Charles B. Puskas compares the Gospel of Mark
to Aristotle's description of tragedy in the *Poetics*.
First, Aristotle defines the tragic PLOT in terms of
COMPLICATION and DENOUEMENT. Some mod-
ern scholars use the terms "RISING ACTION" and
"FALLING ACTION" respectively. The complication
includes all the ACTIONS and instances of CON-
FLICT, which eventually produce a crisis: the point
in the action where the tragic hero begins to move
from a state of happiness to a state of misery or the
point at which the hero's fortune begins to change.
Then the denouement consists of the material that
follows the crisis. In Mark, the complication consists of the material up to 8:26. In the complication,
Jesus tries to proclaim his mission and purpose but
is prevented by the misunderstandings of those
around him. The crisis occurs at 8:27–30, with Peter's confession of Jesus as Messiah and Jesus's first
prediction of his death. From this point onward,
the denouement unfolds in Jesus's preparation of

the disciples for his death and the opposition from
religious leaders, which finally results in his death.

According to Aristotle, the tragic hero must
have nobility of character, suffer undeserved misfortune, commit a HAMARTIA (an error in judgment), and have a tragic flaw. Mark portrays Jesus
as having a high sense of morality and an unwaver-
ing sense of fulfilling his purpose. If he has a tragic
flaw, it might be his passive acceptance of violence
and his refusal to attempt any escape from his fate.
This act of turning a moral quality into a liability
may, in fact, be Jesus's hamartia. In the plot, Jesus
does suffer undeserved misfortune and moves
from a state of happiness to a state of misery. So,
if one reads from an Aristotelian perspective, Jesus
may be viewed as a tragic hero, even though Mark
may not have consciously intended to present him
as such.

Finally, according to Aristotle, a tragedy must
arouse both pity and fear in the audience and produce an insight experience for the audience. Pity
results from viewing undeserved misfortune, while
fear derives from the recognition that if such a fate
could befall a character of the status of the hero, it
certainly could befall the audience. The insight experience results from the combination of the form
and CONTENT, which work together to suggest an
insight into some aspect of the human condition.
It is not difficult to argue that Mark's Jesus and text
satisfy both of these conditions.

Bibliography. Gilbert G. Bilezikian, *The Liberated Gospel: A Comparison of the Gospel of Mark and Greek Tragedy* (Grand Rapids: Baker, 1977); Ernest W. Burch, "Tragic Action in the Second Gospel," *Journal of Religion* 11 (1931): 346–58; Charles Puskas, *An Introduction to the New Testament* (Peabody, MA: Hendrickson, 1989); Jerry H. Stone, "The Gospel of Mark and *Oedipus the King*: Two Tragic Visions," *Soundings* 67 (1984): 55–69.

TRAGIC FLAW. *See* TRAGEDY

TRANSACTIVE CRITICISM

A PSYCHOANALYTIC CRITICISM developed by Norman Holland based on Sigmund Freud's psychoanalysis. Before a synopsis of Holland's LITERARY
theory can be offered here, an excursion into the

rudiments of Freud's psychoanalytic theory is in order. Admittedly the following discussion of the theory is extremely simplified, but without such a simplification, the average reader will not be able to follow Holland's arguments.

Freudian psychoanalytic theory. All human beings have, at an unconscious level, fantasies that constitute a basis for experiencing life. These fantasies, primarily unconscious in adulthood, are formed in the early stages of childhood but constitute the determining source of how we think and respond to the world in adulthood. Desires, wishes, decisions, and so forth in adulthood are nothing more than transformations of infantile fantasies that were formed in the early stages of childhood.

It is commonplace in Freud's psychoanalytical theory that a child develops according to stages that are correlated to parts of the body or members of the family that provide the child with the most gratification or anxiety at that particular stage. A person's characteristic fantasies can be traced to one or more of these developmental stages. In fact, the development of fantasies is more appropriately explained as cumulative.

The following discussion of the developmental stages is based on Norman Holland, *Dynamics*, 34–62. In order to explain his transactive theory of reading, Holland confines his discussion to five stages: oral, anal, urethral, phallic, and oedipal. Since the urethral phase is actually a variation of the anal, the following discussion is limited to the remaining four.

The oral stage of development is the earliest. At this stage, the infant's life focuses on what goes in and comes out of the mouth. In the earliest phase of this stage, the infant does not distinguish between his or her ego and the outside source from which gratification of desires derives. In the first phase (passive) of the oral stage, then, the child senses no division between the world "out there" and the world "in here." Consequently, the infant must trust outside realities to satisfy desires. This passive phase is important in developing abilities to wait and to do nothing. After about six months, however, the child develops the ability to put things into the mouth, spit things out, and bite. This second phase of the oral stage is known as the sadistic phase. The child becomes able to perceive that there is an ego "out there" apart from one's own. By putting things into the mouth, the child seeks to make things a part of the self, ensuring they will always be there and thus can never be outside to cause harm. In literature, images having to do with the mouth, taking things in, or spitting them out are common. Also themes or language that tends toward either/or is common in images springing from oral fantasies. In the oral stage, therefore, "the child associates his or her mouth chiefly with a sense of dependency, of receiving things through the mouth. . . . In the second (sadistic) oral stage, the child thinks of mouths as a threat. He may imagine himself devouring or being devoured, being sucked dry, or getting rid of things by eating them" (Holland, *Dynamics*, 38).

The second stage of development is the anal stage. Apparently, the child experiences pleasure in the two conflicting acts of elimination and retention of excrement. During this stage, demands begin to be placed on the infant. The child is taught to do and not do certain things, initially centering on the demands of toilet training. Holding on to or giving up part of the body becomes an extremely important issue for the child, and lifelong patterns of giving or retaining are formed at this stage. The child learns the difference between things disgusting and things clean, things precious or valuable and things indifferent, and between messiness and neatness. In adulthood, the desire to retain things is transformed into habits of collecting things that are worthwhile, such as money, stamps, coins, and the like. Literature that transforms anal fantasies may be marked by images of dirt and being devoured by the unclean or disgusting. Images of disgusting smells and their opposites, such as a sweet fragrance and clean air, are also common. Other anal fantasies include attention to detail, timeliness, meticulous observance of laws and rituals, control either by oneself or by someone else, and forcing things out of other people or being forced to give up something.

In the phallic stage, the child learns that a source of pleasure is the genitals. The child also discovers that parents hold rather crucial attitudes toward these body parts. Given the child's two-part discovery—pleasure and the adult taboos associated with those body parts—we may understand the pleasure and guilt that suddenly descend on the child. At this stage the child becomes aware of personal autonomy, and the definition of such autonomy revolves around the phallus as a precious object. Closely associated with this SENSE of autonomy is the fear of castration, the loss of one's autonomous self. At this stage the child also begins to think magically: the thought and word are given status equal to the corresponding ACTION. Thus the child fears the prospect of being punished for thoughts as well as for actions. The child fantasizes about thinking things into being, often substituting the power to create mentally for the adult power to create sexually. Fantasies ("primal scene fantasies") associated with what adults do in their bedroom become important for the child. The child may imagine that the sexual act is a violent struggle followed by a "death-like sleep" (Holland, *Dynamics*, 45). The father's phallus is a weapon, and his mother's body a type of trap that engulfs. Literary images associated with this stage are those of prying into things and of the mind or body's entering dark, fearful places. Plots that focus on assertive action and distinguish clearly between the sexes are drawing on phallic fantasies. Any IMAGE dealing with peeping, spying, watching, vague or mysterious sounds in the dark, nakedness, objects appearing and disappearing, or fights and struggles have their source in the phallic stage.

The oedipal stage shapes the ways in which a child will develop relationships in adulthood. The ways a child relates to family members are mirrored in the way the child will respond to others in adulthood. The male child tends to think of his mother in two disparate ways: either as pure, perfect, and unattainable or as a slut, giving herself to everyone. The male child longs to become his father and have his mother; the female child longs to become her mother and have her father. This original incest fantasy may translate itself into several variations: brother/sister, uncle/niece, or taboos of race. Such fantasies give birth to tremendous guilt, which may then be expressed in such literary concepts as original sin, various kinds of debts, and fantasies of rescue.

In psychoanalytical terms, fantasies rooted in these early stages of childhood are defended against and controlled by the unconscious operations of the ego when it receives a signal of danger from reality. Following is a catalog of common defenses, with a brief definition for each: (1) repression, disallowing a thought or feeling from entering consciousness; (2) denial, refusing to perceive something in reality that we do not want to see; (3) displacement, attributing the value usually assigned to one object to another; (4) reversal, attributing the value or aim that is usually assigned to one object to an opposite object; (5) undoing, the annulment of an object, impulse, or event through some ritual action; (6) projection, suppressing an internal perception in order to distort it and then allowing it to enter one's consciousness as an external perception; (7) introjection, the management of an impulse perceived to be external by internalizing the impulse; (8) regression, the displacement of an object, event, or aim from the dangerous present to a safer time in the past; (9) splitting, the decomposing of one thing into several parts; (10) symbolization, substituting one thing for another on the grounds of physical or psychic similarity; (11) sublimation, transforming a taboo impulse or idea into one more socially acceptable; (12) rationalization, intellectually justifying something that is clearly illogical.

Identity theme. According to Holland, every individual has an "identity theme," an "initial organizing configuration" through which every experience is filtered and organized. The essence of this view of identity is that we can see one theme or style permeating all aspects of an individual's life. In that sense, we have an unchanging self; nevertheless, reality and one's own inner drives demand that the self reach out to new experiences. It then grows by adding these experiences as new variations to its unchanging central THEME. An "identity theme" is determined by past events, and then paradoxically it is the only basis for future growth and therefore freedom. It is the foundation for every personal and human synthesis of new experience, be it falling in love or simply reading a book (Holland, *5 Readers*, 61).

Every time a person faces a new experience, the experience will be interpreted in a way that correlates with the person's identity theme. The process through which a person manages and creates internal reality is governed by this identity theme. Not the same as, but part of, the identity theme is an individual's characteristic structure of adaptations and defenses. Holland defines an adaptation as "the progressive, constructive, and maturational mastery of inner drives and outer reality," and defense as the "mechanism put into action automatically and unconsciously at a signal of danger from within or without" (*5 Readers*, 115). On the one hand, all individuals filter experiences through the identity theme by employing characteristic adaptations and defenses. The experiences are then re-created in such a way that they satisfy one or more infantile fantasies. Once the experiences have been re-created in this manner, they are then transformed into more sophisticated adult expressions (artistic, religious, moral, etc.). If, on the other hand, a person cannot filter an experience through the adaptive and defensive structures of their identity theme, the experience will simply be ignored.

Application to literary criticism. With respect to literary criticism, an AUTHOR produces an object that satisfies fantasies and defenses.

> Creative writing [is] like any other act "in character," the selection of a vocation or avocation, wearing clothes, one's manner of speaking or walking, falling in love, getting a symptom, suicide—any human's act satisfies for him some combination of pleasure—giving and defensive needs, inner inertia and outer pressures to change, personal demands and society's stringencies. (Holland, *Poems*, 57)

A literary work has its birth in the psychological processes of an author. The act of creation fulfills for the author all or usually parts of the author's cluster of unconscious fantasies. In a characteristic mode of adaptations and defenses, an author responds to the pressures of inner and outer realities. Once these pressures have been filtered through the author's characteristic adaptations and defenses, the author can then re-create the infantile fantasies that bring the greatest pleasure. The author then proceeds to transform those fantasies into intellectual, aesthetic, or moral correlatives that finally find concrete expression in the STRUCTURE of a TEXT. In other words, in the process of creating a text, the author transforms an infantile fantasy into an intellectual correlative that we usually call the central MEANING or point of the work. For the author, the formal structure (the interrelationships of all the parts that create a unified whole) constitutes the literary transformation of the author's characteristic defensive structure. In a sense, the text will (at least for the author at the time of creation) reflect the author's own identity theme.

With respect to the act of reading, Holland recognizes that fantasies and defensive structures do not reside in texts: they reside in the minds of individuals. To read a text is to experience an outside reality, and like all other experiences of such reality, it must be re-created according to the identity theme of the one who experiences the reality. Texts contain only black marks on white paper, and they mean nothing until a reader invests them with life by re-creating from them a reality according to the reader's characteristic identity theme. In fact, texts do not contain patterns, themes, and so forth; a reader creates these from the raw material of the text.

To explain this process of re-creation according to one's identity theme, Holland offers four fundamental principles that describe overlapping processes involved in the act of reading (*Poems*, 76–98; *5 Readers*, 113–23). The first principle is that STYLE creates itself. Moving through a text linearly, the reader tries to create a literary experience that will reflect the reader's own identity theme. The reader will respond positively to the elements within the text that act, at least from the reader's perception, in ways that the reader would characteristically expect them to. If the elements of the text do not match the reader's expectations, they are usually ignored.

The second principle is the most complicated: defense must match defense. A reader can respond positively only if he or she can re-create from the elements of the text all or part of the characteristic structure of defenses and adaptations. In other words, the reader must be able to re-create from the text the structure through which real anxiety is defended against.

Once the reader has re-created this defensive structure totally or partially from the raw material of the text, this structure then serves as a filter through which the text must pass. As this material is filtered through the defensive structure, the reader then freely shapes the material in such a way as to project into the work a pleasure-giving fantasy characteristic of the identity theme. This projection of the fantasy into the work is the third principle: fantasy projects fantasies.

The fourth principle—character transforms characteristically—leads the reader to make sense of the text. The fantasy content that the reader has re-created from the material of the text and then projected back into the text is transformed into an intellectual point or central meaning. Just as in real life, the reader transforms an infantile fantasy into a more socially and intellectually acceptable form. This transformation of infantile fantasies is the origin of the literary experience. In this process of transformation, a reader seeks a COHERENCE to the re-created work. Holland sees the two agents of meaning and form as essential to the transformation of infantile fantasies into intellectual significance. In seeking meaning, the reader replaces infantile qualities of fantasies with more adult and sophisticated intellectual or aesthetic concerns. The cluster of drives and desires that make up the core fantasy is transformed through ANALOGY and SYMBOL into more acceptable representatives. For example, intellectually the reader may replace the various phallic emblems of manhood with activities commonly associated with manliness, such as fighting or hunting. This transformation closely resembles the defenses of symbolization and sublimation. The second agent, form, is the process by which the reader manages the fantasy material that the defensive structure has allowed through. A reader will impose a particular order on the material; perceive certain textual relationships; omit some elements and juxtapose other elements; establish a sense of TONE and RHYTHM; and translate recurring images, forms, and incidents into themes and finally into a central meaning. However, none of the associations, transformations, themes, or meaning are in the text just waiting to be extrapolated; they are the reader's re-creation of the literary work according to the reader's own identity theme, which happens as the material of the text is filtered through the reader's characteristic structure of adaptation and defense.

Holland does recognize two important things. First, not all readings are equally valuable:

> Recognizing the reader's creative role in the literary transaction readjusts many traditional ideas, but it does not imply that all readings of a poem have equal merit. True, all readers take over parts of a poem and assign them roles in their psychic economy, but any given reader may neglect part of the text, assign idiosyncratic meanings, and be inconsistent or arbitrary. Obviously, it is not true that anything anyone says about literature is as good as what anyone else says. One can judge a reading by a variety of objective criteria: completeness, unity, accuracy, directness, and so on. (*5 Readers Reading*, 148)

A greater part of a given community of readers will be able to share the pleasure of an individual reading if the reading itself satisfies the given principles of coherence, completeness, standards of logic, and universality. But the final word is that one person will be able to share the pleasure of another person's reading only to the extent that the reading matches the former's own identity theme and system of defenses.

Second, Holland also recognizes that the raw material through which an individual re-creates a literary work consists of more than just the text.

CRITICAL METHODOLOGY, pressures from interpretive communities (*see* INTERPRETIVE COMMUNITY), critical skills, knowledge of literature, and other INTERPRETATIONS all serve as raw material that will be filtered through the reader's structures of adaptation and defenses.

The implication of this transactive criticism is that there is no communication model that can be constructed where the text is the central component. Literature is not communication, interpretation is not extrapolating meaning latent in the text, and reading is not a process of DECODING. Interpretation is the psychological process of a reader's re-creating a literary work according to the reader's own identity theme. Texts are not inherently coherent, logical, or complex; these things are functions of the individual reader's psychological reconstruction of the raw material that the text provides. Further, elements within a text do not symbolize things in reality, nor do textual elements exhibit patterns or interrelations. Readers create SYMBOLS, interrelations, and patterns in their own minds. In brief, readers make texts into literary works.

Purpose of criticism. What then is the purpose of CRITICISM? In Holland's scheme, the only constant is a person's identity theme. The study of the identity theme seems to replace the study of the text. This, however, is not exactly true. As Holland tries to demonstrate in *5 Readers*, an individual's identity theme can be discovered from the way the individual responds to the text. This (again illustrated in *5 Readers*) can be done even for one's own identity theme. Once the identity theme is discovered, the CRITIC can then work back from the identity theme in order to understand the different components of the response. If this sounds circular, that is because it is circular. Holland apparently has displaced (PUN intended) the infamous HERMENEUTICAL CIRCLE. No longer is it the dilemma of textual parts or whole, but one between the reader and critic. On the one hand, criticism is no longer capable of objectively evaluating an author's work or that of another interpreter. When a critic reads a literary text or another's interpreta-

tion of the text, the result is (if Holland's theory is applied consistently) nothing more than a variation of the critic's identity theme. In other words, criticism is capable of finally representing only the critic's own self-replication. On the other hand, if author, reader, and critic are capable of agreeing totally or partially, then we can assume that the re-creations of reader and critic have incarnated an identity theme similar to the author's. To the degree that this happens within an interpretive community, we may claim that an interpretation is true. In fact, in *The Brain of Robert Frost*, Holland seems to entertain the possibility of a measure of objectivity within a greater subjectivity. When creating a text, an author employs a variety of techniques, some of which are "CANONS" characteristic of the author's age and shared by other authors. These canons include systems of RHYME, choice of words, dramatic time, use of IRONY, framing of sentences, and other literary conventions. An author also makes use of fewer personal skills, which Holland calls CODES, such as grammar, SYNTAX, rules of phonetics, and vocabulary. When engaging a text, a reader may share some of these canons and codes and thus share an area of commonality with the author. The same might certainly be true for the literary critic. Holland then assumes that this model of reading and writing literature "provides for both the author's unique expression of self and the reader's. It allows for both author and reader's individuality and their sharing of semantic codes, taught techniques, interpretive communities, or, in general, the features of reading shared by many readers" (*Brain of Robert Frost*, 138).

Bibliography. Norman Holland, *The Brain of Robert Frost: A Cognitive Approach to Literature* (New York: Routledge, 1980); idem, *The Dynamics of Literary Response* (New York: Oxford University Press, 1968); idem, *5 Readers Reading* (New Haven: Yale University Press, 1975); idem, *Poems in Persons* (New York: Norton, 1973).

TRANSCENDENTAL SIGNIFIED

An external point of REFERENCE on which a philosophy or concept rests. Reacting to Ferdinand de Saussure's STRUCTURAL LINGUISTICS, Jacques

Derrida argues that a concept is known only by its differences from other concepts, suggesting that all acts of SIGNIFICATION are inherently ambiguous. From this idea—that signification is fraught with ambiguity—Derrida asserts that the entire history of Western metaphysics is in error for its striving to find a transcendental signified. External points that have been attempted include (but are not limited to) God, self, being, TRUTH, reason, and world spirit. In each case, the supposed transcendental signified must operate as a unifying principle on which one's world is structured. Subsequently, other objects, concepts, or ideas achieve MEANING only as they are filtered through the lens of the ultimate, unifying transcendental signified. The key here is that whichever concept is chosen to serve as this central concept, it is self-sufficient or self-originating, capable of being known independently of any other signifiers and also known for its own intrinsic value, not for some extrinsic contrast it makes with another concept.

Bibliography. George Aichele et al., *The Postmodern Bible* (New Haven: Yale University Press, 1995); Jacques Derrida, "Of Grammatology," in *Critical Theory since 1965* (ed. Hazard Adams and Leroy Searle; Tallahassee: Florida State University Press, 1986), 94–119.

TRANSLATION

The rendering of a TEXT from one language to another. Translations can be grouped into three categories: (1) literal or verbal translations of the source language, in which the SYNTAX, IDIOMS, and grammar of the target language are virtually ignored (e.g., NASB, KJV, NAB, NKJV); (2) dynamic equivalent translations (*see* DYNAMIC EQUIVALENCE/TRANSLATION), in which the SENSE and spirit of the source language is captured in the idioms, grammar, and syntax of the target language (e.g., NEB, JB, REB); and (3) free translations or paraphrases, in which the sense and spirit of the source language are transferred to the target language in a process that considerably alters the idioms, STYLE, STRUCTURE, syntax, and grammar of the source language (e.g., TLB, The Message). For an excellent discussion of the various translations

of the biblical texts into English, see Sheeley and Nash.

Bibliography. Steven M. Sheeley and Robert N. Nash Jr., *The Bible in English Translation: An Essential Guide* (Nashville: Abingdon, 1977).

TRANSLATION STUDIES

Since the 1970s, a discipline, distinct from traditional TRANSLATION of a TEXT from one language to another, that examines the LITERARY and cultural history of translation practices, emphasizing the role of the translator's IDEOLOGY in the PRAXIS of translation. Translation studies as a discipline is closely linked to cultural studies in its focus on the transfer and influence of ideologies between source and target texts.

According to Susan Bassnett, current translation studies evolved as reactions against "(i) the marginalization of translation in literary studies; (ii) the decontextualized approach of much work on translation within linguistics" ("Translation Studies," 540).

Behind these reactions is the recognition that translation affects cultural change and influences the construction of LITERARY CANONS. So in the 1970s, the focus in translation studies moved away from a debate over the nature of equivalence to a focus on the culture of the target text.

First, polysystem theory trained its attention on the reception of the translated text by the culture of the target text. Since this branch of translation studies also takes a historical view, not only does it examine the influence of the translated text on the target culture; it also examines the history of translation theories and praxes. For an introduction to this focus, see both Holmes and Lefevere.

Second, translation studies joins forces with cultural studies with its interest in the ideological implications of translating an object from one culture into the CODES of another. In other words, some scholars (e.g., Bassnett, Lambert, and Lefevere) examine the role that the translators' politics play not only in the manner of translation but also in the question of which texts are translated. These scholars recognize that the praxes of translation are not disinterested.

Rather, translation both reflects the culture in which it is practiced and shapes the culture of the target text. Furthermore, in the process the source culture itself may be shaped. For this reason, these critics argue that the SOCIAL LOCATION of the translator should be an integral object of critical examination. For further reading on this focus, see Bassnett, *Translation Studies*, and Hermans.

Third, other scholars identify more with POST-COLONIAL CRITICISM by examining the role of the translator's ideology in the perpetuation of the oppressive structures of a dominant culture. If a text contains oppressive structures, the practice of DYNAMIC EQUIVALENCE simply translates and transfers those structures into the linguistic equivalents of the target text. For further information, consult Smith and Yilibuw.

Fourth, GENDER studies have played an important role in the development of translation studies. Using feminist studies, these scholars examine the ways in which structures of PATRIARCHY are transferred from the source to the target text. These scholars systematically reject the bipolarity between the source and target texts in particular and between the languages in general. For an excellent introduction to this focus, see Simon.

Bibliography. Susan Bassnett, *Translation Studies* (3rd ed.; London: Routledge, 2002); idem, "Translation Studies," in *A Dictionary of Cultural and Critical Theory* (ed. Michael Payne; Cambridge, MA: Blackwell, 1996), 540–42; Susan Bassnett and André Lefevere, *Translation, History, and Culture* (London: Pinter, 1990); Theo Hermans, ed., *The Manipulation of Literature* (London: Croom Helm, 1985); James Holmes, ed., *The Nature of Translation: Essays on the Theory and Practice of Literary Translation* (The Hague: Mouton, 1970); André Lefevere, *Translation, Rewriting, and the Manipulation of Literary Fame* (London: Routledge, 1992); Sherry Simon, *Gender in Translation: Cultural Identity and the Politics of Transmission* (London: Routledge, 1996); Abraham Smith, "The Productive Role of English Bible Translators," *Semeia* 76 (1996): 55–68; Delores Yilibuw, "Tampering with Bible Translation in Yap," *Semeia* 76 (1996): 21–38.

TRANSLITERATION
A character-by-character rendering of a word from one writing system into another.

TRANSMISSIVE TEXTS. *See* PRODUCTIVE TEXTS

TRAVEL MOTIF
In the Hellenistic ROMANCE, a common structural device in which the hero and/or followers travel to various places. Examples of the travel motif are found in Luke 9:51–19:44; Acts 19:21–21:16; and Acts 27:1–28:16. *See* JOURNEY MOTIF.

TRAVELOGUE
The promise of a visit in Paul's LETTERS toward the end of the body of the letter. The promised visit may be by Paul or an emissary (cf. Rom. 15:22–33; 1 Cor. 4:17–21; 2 Cor. 12:14–13:13; Phil. 2:19–24; 1 Thess. 2:17–3:13; Philem. 22). Roetzel suggests that the function of the travelogue is to add force to the message of the letter by promising an apostolic visit. *See* EPISTOLARY LITERATURE.

Bibliography. Calvin Roetzel, *The Letters of Paul: Conversations in Context* (Atlanta: John Knox, 1982).

TREATY FORM. *See* COVENANT FORM

TRIADIC LINE
A single line of POETRY with three VERSETS. While lines of BIBLICAL POETRY usually have two parts, there are many with three. An example is Prov. 8:34: "Happy is the one who listens to me, / watching daily at my gates, / waiting beside my doors."

TRICOLON. *See* COLON

TRIPLE TRADITION
In GOSPEL studies, the material common to the SYNOPTIC GOSPELS.

TROPE
Traditionally, any FIGURE OF SPEECH that changes the SENSE of a word away from the literal. In this sense, such figures as METAPHOR, SIMILE, IRONY, PARADOX, and SYMBOL are all tropes (Harmon and Holman, 528).

In the theories of some POSTMODERN scholars, there is the claim that all language is tropological, thus producing the idea of the rhetoricity of language in general. This claim becomes significant with the recognition that humans have access to the world only as it is mediated through language. Scholars such as Jacques Derrida, J. Hillis Miller, Harold Bloom, and Paul de Man have challenged the view that tropes are only linguistic decorations on a language that is otherwise transparent. These CRITICS argue that language itself is tropological and thus inherently ambiguous and unstable. Tropes continually subvert MEANING by producing an ambiguity as to whether the meaning is figural or literal. Both de Man and Derrida examine philosophical texts that purport to employ a language free of tropes; they demonstrate that language cannot be reduced to a set of CODES because of its innate tropological nature. In other words, no linguistic expression can escape trope (Harvey, 648–49). Even texts that have traditionally been viewed as free of the figural, such as philosophical and scientific texts, are unavoidably tropic. Obviously, these postmodern critics are collapsing the distinction between LITERARY and ordinary forms of DISCOURSE.

Bibliography. William Harmon and C. Hugh Holman, *A Handbook to Literature* (8th ed.; Upper Saddle River, NJ: Prentice Hall, 1999); Elizabeth Harvey, "Trope," in *Encyclopedia of Contemporary Literary Theory* (ed. Irena R. Makaryk; Toronto: University of Toronto Press, 1993), 647–49.

TROPOLOGICAL SENSE OF SCRIPTURE

One of the four traditional senses of SCRIPTURE, the figural MEANING of a TEXT. The figural meaning focused on the spiritual or moral SIGNIFICANCE of the text. *See* FOURFOLD SENSE OF SCRIPTURE.

TRUE ACROSTIC. *See* ACROSTIC

TRUTH

In the Western philosophical TRADITION from the time of Plato, the body of CONTENT, LAWS, and knowledge existing in the STRUCTURE of the universe in diverse areas (e.g., morality, politics, economics) independently of humans but accessible to humans through thought. Truth, then, is universal and open to discovery. Beginning with philosophers such as Nietzsche and Heidegger, however, the existence of OBJECTIVE TRUTH was problematized (*see* PROBLEMATIZE). This problematizing of truth, threatening the belief that truth exists independently of human activity, has recently been further advanced by POSTMODERN thinkers (e.g., Derrida, Hartman, de Man, Rorty, Lyotard). According to these thinkers, human beings create systems by which they try to understand the world and experience and then substitute these systems for truth.

Earlier interpretive methods such as NEW CRITICISM, MIMETIC CRITICISM, and NARRATOLOGY were founded on the ASSUMPTION that LITERARY texts communicate truth or that an interpreter using the right tools can find the true MEANING of the TEXT, if not that of the AUTHOR. More recent literary theories (e.g., READER-RESPONSE CRITICISM, DECONSTRUCTION, and CULTURAL CRITICISM), however, reject the idea that readers can reduce the structures of a text to its truth or to AUTHORIAL INTENTION. These theories argue that the SOCIAL LOCATION of the reader plays an undeniable role in the construction of meaning. In fact, the idea that any reading can be a RECONSTRUCTION or a re-cognition of the author's intention or the text's truth is impossible. Meaning or truth deriving from reading a text is the understanding, the construction of the reader based on the reader's REPERTOIRE. In this SENSE, then, meaning or interpretive truth is simply the reader's understanding.

TWO-SOURCE HYPOTHESIS

An explanation of the relationship between the SYNOPTIC GOSPELS, proposed by H. J. Holtzmann (1832–1910), which claims that Mark was the first Gospel and served as a source for both Matthew and Luke. It also claims that Matthew and Luke made use of another source, no longer extant, which has come to be known as Q (probably from German *Quelle*, "source"). Burton H. Streeter (1874–1937) expanded this idea into his FOUR DOCUMENT HYPOTHESIS, which is still popular. *See also* PROTO-LUKE; SOURCE CRITICISM; SYNOPTIC PROBLEM, THE.

TYNDALE'S NEW TESTAMENT

A TRANSLATION of the NT into English by William Tyndale in 1525; the translation was directly from Greek yet influenced by Luther's German translation.

TYPE

A literary GENRE or a kind of character in literature. Adele Berlin defines the type character as a person in whom a single trait is predominant. Such a type in Genesis is Laban. From the time we first meet him in Gen. 24, we are struck by his distinguishing trait: materialism. His materialistic motivation is sustained in his dealings with Jacob in Gen. 29.

Type is also a term in the SEMIOTICS of Charles Peirce; it is equivalent to the term *LANGUE* in the linguistics of Saussure. In other words, *type* refers to the abstract conventional STRUCTURE of a SIGN system, which makes any act of SPEECH possible. *Token*, on the other hand, refers to an individual concrete act of communication on a given occasion and is synonymous with Saussure's *PAROLE* (an individual utterance based on an underlying linguistic system).

Bibliography. Adele Berlin, *Poetics and Interpretation of Biblical Narrative* (Sheffield: Almond, 1983).

TYPE SCENE

A LITERARY DEVICE that is similar to a THEME but, according to George W. Savran, is the REPETITION of "conventions of speech and behavior in analogous situations, such as betrothal scenes (Gen. 24:10–61; 29:1–20; Exod. 2:15b–21) and annunciation stories (Gen. 18:1–15; Judg. 13; 1 Sam. 1; 2 Kings 4:8–37)" (7). To this list may be added the trial in the wilderness, the revival of the dead child, and the hero's journey from his homeland to a foreign country.

Each of these type scenes has its own basic literary STRUCTURE. The betrothal scene serves as a helpful illustration. In the betrothal scene, a prospective bridegroom or his representative journeys to a foreign land, where he encounters a young woman at a well. Either the man or the woman draws water from the well. After this initial meeting, the woman

(or women) hurries home to share the news of the stranger's arrival. A betrothal is then finalized, often after the stranger has shared a meal with the woman's family. This is the pattern followed in the servant's search for a wife for Isaac in Gen. 24.

The betrothal scene—and all others as well—may be innovatively refashioned, depending on the AUTHOR's purpose. For instance, in the Jacob NARRATIVE, the hero first meets shepherds at the well (Gen. 29:1–8), and only later does Rachel approach the well (29:9). Not only does Jacob draw the water; he must also remove an obstacle (a stone) from the mouth of the well. This obstacle adumbrates the obstacle (fourteen years of labor) that he must overcome before he is given Rachel as his wife.

In the Samson STORY, the hero journeys to a foreign country, leading the reader to expect a betrothal scene. But neither drawing of water from the well nor a meal of hospitality follows. This foreshadows Samson's characteristic penchant for disregarding accepted protocol.

An interesting NT application of this type scene occurs in the Gospel of John (4:1–42). Jesus travels from Judea to Sychar in Samaria. While Jesus is resting at Jacob's well, a woman comes to draw water. A conversation ensues, and the woman subsequently runs into the town and announces what the stranger at the well has told her. This prompts the whole town's EXODUS to the well, which finally results in the conversion of many of the Samaritans. Because of John the Baptist's remark in John 3:29 ("He who has the bride is the bridegroom. The friend of the bridegroom, who stands and hears him, rejoices greatly at the bridegroom's voice"), the reader must inquire about John's purpose in using this type scene, especially since there is no mention of a hospitality meal.

Bibliography. George W. Savran, *Telling and Retelling: Quotation in Biblical Narrative* (Bloomington: Indiana University Press, 1988).

TYPOLOGICAL INTERPRETATION

The practice of reading certain persons, events, objects, and places in the HEBREW BIBLE as

SYMBOLS or TYPES of persons, events, objects, or places in the NT. For example, Jonah and Solomon become types of Jesus, as does the Suffering Servant in Isaiah (esp. in Isa. 53). Paul sees Christian baptism as being prefigured in the Exodus (1 Cor. 10:1–6), and Adam as a type of Jesus (Rom. 5:14). The author of the Epistle to the Hebrews uses Melchizedek as a type of Jesus the high priest (Heb. 7).

ÜBERLIEFERUNGSGESCHICHTE

German for "history of transmission." *See* TRADITION CRITICISM.

UGARITIC TEXTS. *See* RAS SHAMRA TEXTS

UNCIAL

Uppercase characters used in some Greek and Latin manuscripts of the biblical TEXTS from the third to the tenth centuries CE. The term has also come to designate the group of texts in this period that were written in uncial on parchment or VELLUM. Since some of the PAPYRUS texts were also in uncial, these texts are designated by the material on which they were written (e.g., $\mathfrak{P}^{52}$).

UNDERSTATEMENT. *See* EUPHEMISM

UNINTRUSIVE NARRATOR

A term in NARRATIVE CRITICISM for a NARRATOR who generally does not offer COMMENTARY on the STORY as the PLOT develops. While the biblical narrators are generally unintrusive, there are instances in which they "break frame," so to speak, and address the reader directly, offering commentary for explanation or clarification (e.g., Mark 13:14; John 20:31).

UNIVALENCE

A term used to designate the claim that a TEXT has a single MEANING.

UNIVOCALITY

The ASSUMPTION that a TEXT has only one possible MEANING, the one intended by the AUTHOR. *See* EQUIVOCALITY; INTENTION; PLURIVOCALITY.

UNRELIABLE NARRATOR

A NARRATOR whose account of events or handling of information is faulty due to personal bias, limited knowledge, or personal involvement in the events narrated. An unreliable narrator does not necessarily lie or intentionally misrepresent material. Generally, biblical scholars accept the biblical narrators as reliable. They may know more than they tell (e.g., John), but what they do tell is reliable in terms of the STORY WORLD that they construct. In other words, the reader is expected to believe what the narrator presents.

UR-MARKUS

A term introduced by H. J. Holtzmann (1863) for a hypothetical written or oral source that was the basis for the GOSPEL of Mark. Scholars have based their claims on the presence of DOUBLETS (e.g., the two feedings) and collections of SAYINGS (e.g., 4:21–25 and 9:42–50), both of which may reflect Mark's use of a source.

URTEXT

The original VERSION of a TEXT. The term designates a lost original text but one that may be reconstructed through TEXTUAL CRITICISM.

VARIANT READING
A variation in wording (characters, words, sentences) between different manuscripts of the same TEXT. *See* TEXTUAL CRITICISM.

VEHICLE. *See* METAPHOR; TENOR/VEHICLE

VELLUM
Originally, calfskin used for writing material, as distinct from PARCHMENT, which is the skin of a sheep or a goat processed for writing. In recent word usage, however, this distinction is rarely observed, and "vellum" and "parchment" are used synonymously to refer to any animal skin used as a writing material. TEXTs on vellum date from the second century BCE but became widespread around the fourth century CE.

VERBAL EQUIVALENCE/TRANSLATION
A VERSION of the BIBLE in which the translators have sought to reproduce the words of the ancient texts in equivalent words in a target language. Some verbal translations have not only reproduced the equivalent words but also tried to retain the word order of the ancient TEXT. The NASB is a case in point. Furthermore, translators disagree over whether "each occurrence of the ancient word [should] be translated into the same English word" (Sheeley and Nash, 26). Although differing in many respects as to the extent to which the translators applied verbal equivalence, some of the better-known verbal translations are the KING JAMES VERSION, REVISED STANDARD VERSION, NEW AMERICAN STANDARD BIBLE (along with the updated version), NEW AMERICAN BIBLE, NEW KING JAMES VERSION, NEW JERUSALEM BIBLE, and the NEW REVISED STANDARD VERSION.

Bibliography. Steven M. Sheeley and Robert N. Nash Jr., *The Bible in English Translation: An Essential Guide* (Nashville: Abingdon, 1997).

VERBAL ICON
A term in the NEW CRITICISM of W. K. Wimsatt referring to a verbal SIGN that embodies and interprets the object it denotes. According to Wimsatt, the STRUCTURE of a METAPHOR consists of a "fusion" of verbal material and ideas, a fusion in which the sensory qualities of the verbal construct are not destroyed by the metaphoric abstraction. This is the peculiar nature of a metaphor. Wimsatt makes this claim for a literary TEXT. In order to maintain this character of the text, the iconic property for language is important. The most common example of the verbal icon is ONOMATOPOEIA. In a sense, all DISCOURSE incarnates an experience into sound. The important point is that since the discourse SYMBOL is foreign to the experience it denotes, a disparity is created. Although this disparity goes unnoticed in ordinary discourse (the absence of the disparity is absolutely essential in scientific discourse), it is heightened in LITERARY works in the distinction between the verbal icon and its REFERENT. By claiming that the entire literary text is a verbal icon, a verbal object, Wimsatt necessarily emphasizes the disparity or AMBIGUITY between the TENOR (text as icon) and the VEHICLE (realities to which the text refers). It is this iconic property of the text, more than anything else, that accounts for textual POLYSEMY. As the meaning of the metaphor is inexhaustible, so is the meaning of the text.

Bibliography. W. K. Wimsatt Jr. and M. C. Beardsley, *The Verbal Icon* (Lexington: University of Kentucky Press, 1954).

VERBAL OBJECT/REFERENT

In the NEW CRITICISM of W. K. Wimsatt, a dialectic between a literary TEXT and MEANING, at the heart of LITERARY studies. According to Wimsatt, the parts of a text fit together in such a way that their complex unity forms a coherent whole. On the one hand, this COHERENCE is internal, a textual coherence independent of any necessary congruence to external reality. On the other hand, as a metaphoric construction, the text does necessarily correspond in some manner to reality. In the statement "Snow is white," the correspondence between the verbal object and the real state of affairs is factual. Since a literary text, however, is essentially a complex metaphorical object, it "generates an extra dimension of correspondence to reality, the symbolic or analogical" (Wimsatt and Beardsley, 241). It is because of this symbolic dimension of correspondence (rather than congruence) that literary texts defy attempts at PARAPHRASE. The text, as a metaphoric, iconic, coherent rhetorical STRUCTURE composed of a system of LITERARY CONVENTIONS and devices, stretches to the limit its referential relationship to reality. Again, the meaning that proceeds from the VERBAL ICON cannot be put into logical terms. In other words, there is something in every text that simply cannot be expressed or captured in explanations.

Bibliography. W. K. Wimsatt Jr. and M. C. Beardsley, *The Verbal Icon* (Lexington: University of Kentucky Press, 1954).

VERIFICATION

According to E. D. Hirsch Jr., a process by which interpreters try to construe an author's MEANING while at the same time remembering that although they construe verbal meaning within their own subjectivity, they must attempt not to impose their PRESUPPOSITIONS on the AUTHOR. Since interpreters can never be absolutely certain that they have construed the author's meaning accurately, their goal must be to create a reading that is more probable than any other reading. Thus, for Hirsch, verification is "a process of establishing relative probabilities."

According to Hirsch, this process includes four criteria. First is LEGITIMACY, creating the reading that is most permissible within the norms of the LANGUE of the author. Second is CORRESPONDENCE, the reading that accounts for all of the linguistic components of the text. Third, GENERIC APPROPRIATENESS demands that the reading take into account the GENRE of the text, with all its inherent LITERARY CONVENTIONS. And fourth, the CRITERION OF COHERENCE requires the interpreter to establish the most probable CONTEXT by reconstructing the relevant aspects of the author's outlook. Ultimately, according to Hirsch, the best way to adjudicate between probable readings is to show that one context is more probable than the others.

Bibliography. E. D. Hirsch Jr., "Objective Interpretation," *PMLA* 75 (1960): 463, 470–79.

VERISIMILITUDE

The appearance of TRUTH or reality. In LITERARY studies, the extent to which a TEXT creates the appearance of truth. The term applies even to works of fantasy with respect to probability and necessity within the WORLD OF THE TEXT. Thus, such works as *Gulliver's Travels* or Voltaire's *Candide* or Rushdie's *Midnight's Children* will appear credible if the reader is willing to suspend disbelief (*see* SUSPENSION OF DISBELIEF) and accept the premise and world of the text. Readers who do not accept the NT writers' world of angels, evil spirits, and miracles or the world of talking animals, floating axheads, and parting waters in the HEBREW BIBLE are willing to accept the verisimilitude of the works based on the organic STRUCTURE of the texts themselves.

VERSE

A term for (1) a lyrical line of poetry, (2) a STANZA, or (3) POETRY. All three meanings are appropriate for BIBLICAL POETRY even though, in general, lines of Hebrew poetry do not RHYME in the conventional SENSE of the word. Some scholars suggest that there is rhyme in Hebrew poetry that may be referred to as thought rhyme. So these scholars do divide Hebrew poetry into stanzas, and most scholars use "verse" as a designation of Hebrew poetry.

VERSE, COSMOGONIC. *See* COSMOGONIC VERSE

VERSE, GNOMIC. *See* GNOME / GNOMIC VERSE

VERSET

A term employed by Robert Alter in his study of BIBLICAL POETRY, a verset is a single component of a line of poetry. In general, a line of Hebrew poetry contains two or three versets. For example, Prov. 9:1 is a single line containing two versets: "Wisdom has built her house, / she has hewn her seven pillars."

Bibliography. Robert Alter, *The Art of Biblical Poetry* (New York: Basic Books, 1985).

VERSION

In common parlance with respect to TRANSLATION, any translation of a TEXT based on an earlier translation in the same language; for example, the Revised Standard Version is a translation that makes use of the King James Version. In the field of TEXTUAL CRITICISM, the term is used for a translation of the BIBLE from the Greek of the NT or the Hebrew of the HEBREW BIBLE into another language (such as the LXX, in Greek). Generally, "version" designates early translations of the Hebrew Bible or NT into Latin, Syriac, Coptic, Ethiopic, and so forth.

VOICE

In NARRATIVE CRITICISM or NARRATOLOGY, the manner in which a TEXT is narrated. A NARRATOR may recount the ACTION as it actually unfolds, before it happens, or after the fact. The narrator may be absent from the NARRATIVE or inside the narrative in the first person, as the principal character in the narrative, or as a combination of these. In LITERARY works generally, voice is the POINT OF VIEW, provided by the speaker who does the narrating. It is the manner in which the reality of the STORY becomes or seems to become authentic. In other words, it is the angle from which things are reported and judged. For the most part, the voice in the texts of the HEBREW BIBLE is a third-person, omniscient narrator, while that of the GOSPELS is third-person, limited narrator. Portions of Ezra and Nehemiah have a first-person voice, as do the LETTERS in the NT. In the book of Revelation, the narrator is a person involved in the action itself.

VOLKSSPRUCH

In FORM CRITICISM of the HEBREW BIBLE, SAYINGS deriving from the lower class of society. Examples are 1 Sam. 10:11, Ezek. 18:2, and 1 Kings 20:11. Distinct from *Volksspruch* is *Kunstspruch*, sayings that grew out of the WISDOM TRADITION (e.g., Proverbs).

Bibliography. Richard N. Soulen and R. Kendall Soulen, *Handbook of Biblical Criticism* (3rd ed.; Louisville: Westminster John Knox, 2001).

VULGATE

A Latin TRANSLATION of the BIBLE, attributed to Jerome and translated between 382 and 405 CE. Pope Damascus commissioned the translation in the year 382, intending to make it the definitive translation of the Bible for the church and thereby curb the production of what the church considered inferior (Old) Latin VERSIONS. After circulating independently until the middle of the sixth century, Jerome's translations were finally bound together. Actually, while the translations of the HEBREW BIBLE, GOSPELS, and Tobit and Judith in the APOCRYPHA may be attributed to Jerome, the rest of the texts are earlier translations.

Bibliography. Stephen Harris, *The New Testament: A Student's Introduction* (4th ed.; Boston: McGraw-Hill, 2002).

WE-SECTIONS

Sections of the book of Acts in which the narrator employs the first-person plural rather than the third-person employed in the rest of the TEXT (Acts 16:10–17; 20:5–15; 21:1–18; 27:1–28:16). According to David Aune, several explanations have been proposed for the switch to the first-person plural. One idea is that the AUTHOR was trying to emphasize his own participation in the events. A second proposal is that the author used his own travel diary or that of someone else. A third explanation is that the author employed the first-person passages as "a stylistic device to dramatize the narrative" (Aune, 123). Although Aune cites precedents in Greek HISTORIOGRAPHY for the switch between third and first person, he concludes that "the occurrence of the 'we' passages in Acts constitutes an implicit claim that the author is not an armchair historian, but one who had personally visited the regions he describes (cf. Polybius 12.27.1–6; 12.28.6; 20.12.8; Lucian, *History*, 47)" (124).

Bibliography. David E. Aune, *The New Testament in Its Literary Environment* (Philadelphia: Westminster, 1987).

WESTERN TEXT

In TEXTUAL CRITICISM, the designation of a group of NT manuscripts sharing similar characteristics. This group is referred to as "Western" because the manuscripts in this group may be roughly located geographically around Rome, one of the major cultural centers in early Christianity. These manuscripts tend to add details to the TEXT or to give alternative accounts of stories. They also tend to correct perceived grammatical problems and have longer, more detailed readings. For example, Western witnesses typically have the longer version of the Lord's Prayer and the longer ending of Mark.

Bibliography. James W. Voelz, *What Does This Mean? Principles of Biblical Interpretation in the Post-modern World* (St. Louis: Concordia, 1995).

WISDOM LITERATURE

Broadly speaking, literature that focuses on the practical search for a life of happiness by living in accordance with rules governing the natural and social order. In BIBLICAL STUDIES, Wisdom literature includes Job, Proverbs, and Ecclesiastes in the HEBREW BIBLE, plus Ecclesiasticus (= Sirach) and the Wisdom of Solomon in the LXX.

James L. Crenshaw divides these TEXTS into four types of Wisdom literature, deriving from within three CONTEXTS. The four types are juridical, natural, practical, and theological, and the three derivative contexts are the clan, the court, and the school. Primarily through the use of the PROVERB, the clan taught people, especially children, how to live well in terms of work, the type of person to avoid or seek out, and basic morality. Court wisdom grew out of the search for wise counsel by kings and was also directed toward the secular education of a small group. School wisdom seems to have taken place within the context of the house or school, where the education was "dogmatico-religious, and a dialogico-admonitory method" was employed. The book of Ecclesiastes is an example of the latter type. For more detailed discussion of Wisdom literature, see Hayes; Murphy.

Bibliography. James L. Crenshaw, *Old Testament Wisdom: An Introduction* (Atlanta: John Knox, 1981); John H. Hayes, ed., *Old Testament Form Criticism* (San Antonio; Trinity University Press, 1974); Roland E. Murphy, *The Tree of Life: An Exploration of Biblical Wisdom Literature* (Garden City, NY: Doubleday, 1990).

WISDOM POETRY

Hebrew POETRY found in the WISDOM LITERA-TURE—in particular, Job and Proverbs. Robert Alter (186) feels that the poetry in these two books was composed by the "ancient Israelite intelligentsia," whereas the poetry in the prophetic books derived from the "spiritual-intellectual elite," and the poetry of the PSALMS reflects the cultic contexts of the priestly circles. *See* BIBLICAL POETRY.

Bibliography. Robert Alter, *The Art of Biblical Poetry* (New York: Basic Books, 1985).

WISDOM PSALMS

Psalms in the HEBREW BIBLE that have the same literary STYLE as, or reflect THEMES similar to, WISDOM LITERATURE in general. Walter C. Kaiser Jr. (99) gives seven features of the Wisdom Psalm: (1) alphabetic acrostics (successive verses begin with successive letters of the Hebrew alphabet); (2) numerical sayings ("Once God has spoken; twice have I heard this" [Ps. 62:11]); (3) "blessed" sayings; (4) "better" sayings ("Better is a little that the righteous person has than the abundance of many wicked" [Ps. 37:16]); (5) comparisons and admonitions; (6) addresses of father to son; (7) the use of proverbs, similes, rhetorical questions, and phrases such as "Listen to me" (Ps. 34:11). The psalms usually classified as having a wisdom style are 1; 19:7–14; 32; 34; 37; 49; 78; 111; 112; 119; 127; 128; and 133.

Bibliography. Walter C. Kaiser Jr. and Moisés Silva, *An Introduction to Biblical Hermeneutics: The Search for Meaning* (Grand Rapids: Zondervan, 1994).

WISDOM SAYINGS

Short, memorable, didactic statements generally found in WISDOM LITERATURE, giving advice for living well or describing common situations (e.g., Prov. 14:31, "Those who oppress the poor insult their Maker, but those who are kind to the needy honor him"). Wisdom sayings also occur in the NT: "A little yeast leavens the whole batch of dough" (Gal. 5:9). "Bad company ruins good morals" (1 Cor. 15:33). "Making the most of the time, because the days are evil" (Eph. 5:16).

WISDOM TRADITION. *See* WISDOM LITERATURE

WITNESS STORY

A story in which Jesus or someone else testifies about Jesus's identity or his actions. Although there are similarities between the witness story and the RECOGNITION STORY, the focus is on proclamation about Jesus rather than the moment of recognition. According to Leland Ryken, witness stories normally have three ingredients: the witness, the testimony, and the proof or evidence of the testimony.

Bibliography. Leland Ryken, *Words of Life: A Literary Introduction to the New Testament* (Grand Rapids: Baker, 1987).

WOE ORACLE. *See* PROPHETIC ORACLE

WOMANIST THEOLOGY/CRITICISM

A black women's LIBERATION THEOLOGY that "is a critique of all human domination in light of black women's experience, a faith praxis that unmasks whatever threatens the well-being of the poorest woman of color" (Moody, 82). Alice Walker, seeking an alternative word for organizing people's thinking about black women's "self-definitions, relationships, activities, and history, and their meaning for the black experience" (Gilkes, 10), coined the term "womanist" in 1982. According to Moody, Walker's definition of a womanist is fourfold: (1) a womanist is a black feminist, or one of color, acting grown up, being responsible and in charge; (2) a womanist is a woman who loves other women, sexually and/or nonsexually; (3) a womanist must have a love for "music, life, dance, and the Spirit—committed to 'the folk' without sacrificing one's own self"; and (4) "a womanist is to feminist as purple to lavender." This ANALOGY conveys the idea that womanists have their own unique style, value, and commitments while still having some relationship to white feminists (Moody, 83).

Origins of womanist theology. Womanist theology developed out of two painful realities: black male theology tended to make the experience of black women invisible, and FEMINIST THEOLOGY ignored the realities of the lives of black women

469

(Moody, 81). Because black women have felt the need to define new ways of being in the world, they have found it necessary to proclaim who they are as women and black in a world and society that does not place much value on either (Hayes, 28). To do so, black women, the mothers or bearers of African American culture, have chosen to speak for themselves because no one else is able or willing to do so. They have gone back to their spiritual roots in Africa and the United States (31).

Special interests of womanist theology. While womanist theology cannot be reduced to a set of characteristics, Diana Hayes identifies several interests. First, "mothering" is a critical way of being among womanists in the United States because they have passed down their heritage through their children. Second, womanists also view themselves as teachers and acknowledge that "if you educate a man, you educate an individual. If you educate a woman, you educate a nation." This statement is not intended as a denigration of men but is rather a positive posture toward both women and men. Third, womanists are not concerned about the "hereafter" but rather the "here and now." For example, womanists see the importance not only of feeding the hungry but also of teaching the hungry to feed themselves (Hayes, 48–53). Furthermore, according to Karen Baker-Fletcher, womanists tend to have a love and respect for nature, wear attire that has to do with a "freedom of choice, freedom of movement, and respect for self and others," and tend to dress in vibrant, deep, and passionate colors that reflect how they feel or want to feel in their spirits: creative and full of life (Baker-Fletcher, 69, 104–5).

Womanist theologians are trying to define themselves and their experiences—to embrace and love their culture, TRADITIONS, people, and people's struggles (Hayes, 49–50). In light of this definition, womanist theology understands itself to be a liberation theology centered on the experience of black women in the United States, and it has evolved into the mirror image of black masculinity: "strong, rebellious, surviving, resisting, and heroic" (Anderson, 112). Although womanist theology is centered on the experience of black women in the United States, it also "places itself in solidarity with all women who suffer oppression: it takes the courageous position of opposing racism, sexism, classism, and homophobia" (Moody, 83). It also insists on the "interconnectedness of the human race," which includes relatedness to African American men or to women of other racial and ethnic backgrounds (82). In addition, womanist theology tries to establish itself as a legitimate discipline within the academy while at the same time communicating in the language of "the folk," the poor African Americans (83).

Principles of womanist theology. With respect to HERMENEUTICS, Delores Williams gives the following four principles of womanist methodology: (1) It is intentionally multidialogical, practicing itself in community with others beyond the African American women's community. (2) It is informed by liturgical intent. It will be both accountable and challenging to the black church. (3) It is informed by a didactic intent, offering new ethical, spiritual, and moral insights to church and society. (4) It is committed to reason and black women's experience as related in their imagery and metaphoric statements (Moody, 85).

There is a twofold source for black women's understanding of God. The first is God's revelation directly to them, and the second is God's revelation as witnessed in the Bible when read and heard in the CONTEXT of their experience (Moody, 89). From a womanist perspective, God is spirit and historically has been seen as a "deliverer" who lifts one "out of the miry bog" (Baker-Fletcher, 110, 112). However, womanists relate mostly to God in Jesus, because he identifies with "the least," and they feel that black women in US society most appropriately represent "the least" (Moody, 103).

The Bible has been a significant source of spiritual, ethical, and political empowerment for black women, who have used social-service clubs, educational systems, and advocacy organizations as bases for social activism. This focus is especially evident in the works of some distinguished African American women activists of the twentieth century, such as Mary McLeod Bethune, Nannie Helen Burroughs, and Marian Wright Edelman (Sanders, 126–27). The central hermeneutical principle for womanist theology is that "the Bible must be read and interpreted in the light of black women's own experience of oppression and God's revelation within that context" (Moody, 90).

Women of the Bible. According to womanists, there are four black women in the Bible who should receive special attention: Hagar (Gen. 16:1–15; 21:8–20), Zipporah (Exod. 2:21–22; 4:24–26; Num. 12:1), the queen of Sheba (1 Kings 10:1–13; 2 Chron. 9:1–9), and Candace, queen of the Ethiopians (Acts 8:27; Sanders, 131). Of these four women, the most written about is Hagar, the slave of Sarah and Abraham and mother of Ishmael. Hagar is considered passive—barely a participant in her own STORY. Womanists feel that the story is not about Hagar or even Sarah but rather about Abraham (Hayes, 6). In this biblical story, Hagar stands in as a surrogate mother for Sarah, "who in her impatience and unfaithfulness, lost sight of who she was in relation to the sovereign Word of God, and so doing, lost sight of reality itself" (7). The liberation in Hagar's story was not given by God; rather, it was found in human initiative. So a connection between the trials of black women of the past and Hagar is drawn: "As Hagar learned how to survive and acquire an appropriate quality of life for herself and her son, so also did the African slaves, accommodating the Bible to the urgent necessities of their lives" (57). From a womanist perspective, this story is one of conflict, women betraying women, and mothers conspiring against mothers. "Theirs is a story of social rivalry" (8). Womanists view both Hagar and Sarah as victims of a societal system that privileged men and valued women only in terms of their relationship to those men—as daughter, wife, mother, and sister, unable to stand alone and with no identity to claim for themselves (7).

Black women also look to other females in the Bible, such as Phoebe, Priscilla, and Mary—coworkers with Paul—and interpret the experiences of these women in ways that reflect womanists'

interests. Womanist theologians notice that the ultimate allegiance of these women was to God, not to men (Townes, 33). Black women also take pride in the mothers of the Bible who became their role models for motherhood, such as the mothers of Isaac, Moses, Samson, and others. These mothers provide black women with a view of women as being "more than bodily receptacles through which great men were born" (33).

Womanist theology hermeneutic. Delores Williams devised a hermeneutic based on a view of "a God who liberates (the God of the enslaved Hebrews) and a God who does not liberate (the God of the non-Hebrew slave, Hagar)." Her hermeneutic is intended first to help theologians "to discover the subjective aspects of their own experience that they share with biblical events and characters." Second, it is intended to help theologians understand the ways that "contemporary Hagars," the most marginalized of black women, are excluded from the liberation MOTIF of black (male) liberation theology (Moody, 80). The bottom line seems to be that womanist theology "aims at reassuring the humanity of black women by disclosing forms of false and illusionary consciousness among black women and in the black community" (Anderson, 111).

While womanist theology is an expression of black women and their past, not all black women are womanists. But at the same time, "the potential is embedded in all Black women's experience" (Gilkes, 186). The womanist feels that it is necessary "to ground Black women's analysis in multiple voices"—in order to have the diversity, richness, and power of black women's ideas as part of a "longstanding African-American women's intellectual community" (Hayes, 4). A womanist, then, is a black feminist who is "audacious, willful, and serious; loves and prefers women, but also may love men; is committed to the survival and wholeness of an entire people; and is universalist, capable, all-loving, and deep" (Moody, 85).

Bibliography. Victor Anderson, *Beyond Ontological Blackness: An Essay on African American Religious and Cultural Criticism* (New York: Continuum, 1995); Karen Baker-

Fletcher, *Sisters of Dust, Sisters of Spirit: Womanist Wordings on God and Creation* (Minneapolis: Fortress, 1998); Kelly Brown Douglas, *Sexuality and the Black Church* (Maryknoll, NY: Orbis Books, 1999); Cheryl Townsend Gilkes, *If It Wasn't for the Women: Black Women's Experience and Womanist Culture in Church and Community* (Maryknoll, NY: Orbis Books, 2001); Diana Hayes, *Hagar's Daughters: Womanist Ways of Being in the World* (New York: Paulist Press, 1995); Linda A. Moody, *Women Encounter God: Theology across the Boundaries of Difference* (Maryknoll, NY: Orbis Books, 1996); Cheryl J. Sanders, ed., *Living the Intersection: Womanism and Afrocentrism in Theology* (Minneapolis: Fortress); Emilie M. Townes, *In a Blaze of Glory: Womanist Spirituality as Social Witness* (Nashville: Abingdon, 1995).

WOMAN'S BIBLE, THE

Produced by Elizabeth Cady Stanton and a Revising Committee in 1895–98 (2 vols.), a COMMENTARY on passages of the REVISED VERSION of 1888 that concern women in some way. The intent of the commentary was to counter many current INTERPRETATIONS that marginalized (*see* MARGINALIZATION) or negated women.

WOMEN'S REALITY

A term in FEMINIST THEOLOGY for the ways that women experience and perceive reality.

WOMEN'S STUDIES

Often used synonymously with FEMINIST CRITICISM but more generally a title for women's scholarship, including university departments, professional organizations, professional publications, academic presses, and so forth that promote the scholarship of women. Catherine Stimpson names three major goals of women's studies: "teaching the subject of women properly; ending sex discrimination in education at all levels, from prekindergarten to postdoctoral study; and integrating feminist activism with feminist thought" (Stimpson, 12–13).

Although there were lone voices before the twentieth century (e.g., Mary Wollstonecraft and Margaret Fuller), it was not until the 1960s in the United States and Britain that women's studies developed as a voice to be reckoned with. It was given

impetus by the black civil-rights movement and the women's liberation movement in the 1960s and by the rise of DECONSTRUCTION and POSTMODERNISM in the late 1960s and early 1970s.

Although the work in early women's studies focused on the critique of the ways in which women were represented in patriarchal cultures and how the oppression resulting from domination was internalized by women, by the 1980s the movement had become a major force in redefining and revising disciplines, critical theories, and pedagogical methods. Quoting Gilbert and Gubar, Glyns Carr (571) outlines four stages through which women's studies moved toward this redefinition. First is the *critique* of the "absence of women as subjects and objects of inquiry, as well as understanding andro-centric epistemologies that pose exclusive male subjects and points of view as universal and distribute sexist biases throughout the disciplinary field." The second stage is *recovery*, a "refocusing of women's historical experience and their agency as producers of culture" that seeks "to understand women's experience and cultural production on their own terms." The third stage, *reconceptualization*, focuses on "paradigms, theories, and methods. New categories of analysis are furnished and old theories are revised." The final stage, *reassessment*, consists of "the nonsexist reintegration of men and women, as both subjects and objects of inquiry." At this stage, women's studies focuses on "gender relations and uses both revised androcentric theories and new gynocentric ones to develop explanations that are truly universal."

In the 1980s and 1990s, women's studies expanded to include RACE, CLASS, AND GENDER CRITICISM; Native American women's studies; Asian American studies (*see* ASIAN / ASIAN AMERICAN CRITICISM); WOMANIST THEOLOGY; and *MUJERISTA* CRITICISM. With the boundaries of women's studies expanding to include the above groups, several results of the broader movement can be observed. First, women's studies has ensured the permanent distinction between sex and GENDER. Second, the movement has guaranteed that gender is an appropriate FRAMEWORK for the academic analysis of culture and its structures. Third, women's studies has raised the awareness of a number of inequities in cultures (e.g., the oppression of women at almost every level of society, the gender inequity in public life, the MARGIN-ALIZATION of women and their contributions in the history of art). And fourth, the movement has raised the awareness that women and their work should be treated with the same seriousness as men and their work.

Bibliography. Glyns Carr, "Women's Studies," in *A Dictionary of Cultural and Critical Theory* (ed. Michael Payne; Cambridge, MA: Blackwell, 1996), 568–73; Catherine Stimpson, *Women's Studies in the United States* (New York: Ford Foundation, 1986).

WORD OF GOD

In its simplest terms, the revelation of God. There are, however, a variety of MEANINGS assigned to this term. First is the ASSUMPTION that the Word of God is the same as the BIBLE.

A second position concerning the relationship between the word of God and the Bible depends on the identification of God's word and God's saving activities throughout history, culminating in the Christ event. These activities are recorded in the Bible, and God speaks through these activities. The Bible therefore is a record of God's redemptive activities and the human responses to them. Accordingly, the Bible is not God's word but gives access to it. God speaks to humanity through the Bible, but the Bible itself is not God's word.

Third, there is the position that Jesus is God's ultimate revelation, the living Word of God. The Bible is the essential historical witness to this supreme revelation of God in Jesus, but it is not itself God's revelation. The Bible constitutes the access to God's supreme revelation or word in Jesus.

A fourth position claims that the Bible becomes the Word of God in proclamation. As the Bible is proclaimed, it is assumed, the Spirit of God uses it to produce a faith response. A faith hearing results in a movement toward conformity to a distinctive Christian lifestyle (as defined by the particular community of faith in its INTERPRETATION of the Bible).

Each of these positions affects how an individual community interprets the Bible. If people assume that the Bible is synonymous with the Word of God, their interpretive approach may be characterized by a sense of literalism along with the deification of the Bible. If they believe that the Bible is a record of God's word to humans in history, they will probably fall squarely within the historical-critical camp. If the Bible is the primary access to God's supreme revelation in Jesus Christ, the interpretive method will concentrate on the NT and the passages in the HEBREW BIBLE that are perceived to pertain to Jesus as the Messiah. If the Bible becomes the Word of God in proclamation, then the INTERPRETIVE COMMUNITY must define a proper pedagogy for such proclamation. Since an interpretive community cannot accept just any proclamation, there must be a proclamational CANON.

WORD CHAINS

A LITERARY technique that links concepts together, usually in some causal manner, to produce a climactic effect. Romans 5:3–5 is an example:

> And not only that, but we also boast in our sufferings, knowing that suffering produces endurance, and endurance produces character, and character produces hope, and hope does not disappoint us, because God's love has been poured into our hearts through the Holy Spirit that has been given to us.

A similar chain is found in 2 Pet. 1:5–7:

> For this very reason, you must make every effort to support your faith with goodness, and goodness with knowledge, and knowledge with self-control, and self-control with endurance, and endurance with godliness, and godliness with mutual affection, and mutual affection with love.

WORDPLAY. *See* PARONOMASIA

WORLD BEHIND THE TEXT

The historical, ideological world in which a TEXT is produced. Because a text is the result of an ACTION performed by an AUTHOR and as such is conditioned by the conventional CODES that affect anything produced in that particular culture, a study of the world behind the text is an integral part of INTERPRETATION. In biblical HERMENEUTICS, the attention to the world behind the text includes a study of BACKGROUND: grammatical, LITERARY, cultural, ideological, historical, and so forth.

WORLD IN FRONT OF THE TEXT

The world or CONTEXT of the reader. In AUDIENCE-CENTERED INTERPRETATION, there is the ASSUMPTION that an unread TEXT carries no MEANING because it can mean nothing until there is a mutual engagement between reader and text. Meaning involves a process of SIGNIFICATION in the act of reading. The reader must make key decisions about what the text says.

Just as the author brings one WORLDVIEW and understanding of reality to a text, allowing the text to mirror at least some elements of that worldview and reality, so the reader brings to the text another worldview and conception of reality. Texts must be read and made sense of within the reader's complex and multifaceted world. In other words, readers understand another person's DISCOURSE only by relating it to what they already know and by putting questions to the text from within their own world. As they read a text, they infer meaning, and that meaning is in some measure determined by their understanding of their own world. The interpreter's world intrudes into the process of actualizing meaning.

WORLD OF THE READER. *See* WORLD IN FRONT OF THE TEXT

WORLD OF THE TEXT

The world created within the text by its language. This world may or may not be similar to the real world of the AUTHOR. In this world of the text, words refer to objects that may or may not be recognizable in the real world. The world of the text has a story line and plot, and objects, events, and persons within the text must be interpreted in terms of their relationship to the world of the text rather than solely in terms of their connection to the real world of the author. *See* NARRATIVE CRITICISM; NEW CRITICISM.

WORLDVIEW

A term generally used to refer to a person's or group's philosophy of life or ideology. In literary studies in general, a common assumption is that both writers and readers do their work (i.e., write and interpret) under the undeniable influence of a worldview.

WRITERLY TEXT. *See* LISIBLE

WRITING. *See* ÉCRITURE

WRITINGS, THE

The third division of texts constituting the HEBREW BIBLE, also called the KETUBIM (*kĕtûbîm*). The texts are an anthology of poetry, narrative, historiography, and apocalypse and include Psalms, Job, Proverbs, Ruth, Song of Songs, Ecclesiastes, Lamentations, Esther, Daniel, Ezra, Nehemiah, and 1–2 Chronicles.

WRITTEN TORAH. *See* TORAH

WYCLIFFE BIBLE

An English version of the BIBLE begun by John Wycliffe and completed by his followers after his death in 1384, out of the conviction that the Bible should be available and accessible to the laity. This first complete translation of the Bible into English was from the Latin VULGATE. The church condemned the Wycliffe Bible in 1408.

Y

YAHWEH

The probable pronunciation of the Hebrew name for God that, in the Hebrew text, consists of four consonants, *YHWH*, also called the TETRAGRAMMATON. In most modern translations of the BIBLE, the name's last three letters are rendered in small capitals as "LORD" (e.g., Gen. 15:1). When the Tetragrammaton appears in combination with the Hebrew title Adonai (*'ădōnāy*), "Lord," it is rendered in the NRSV with small capitals as GOD (e.g., Gen. 15:2; but see Ps. 8:1, where the NRSV renders it "O LORD, our Sovereign"). The NIV renders this combination as "Sovereign LORD" (e.g., Hab. 3:19).

YAHWIST. *See* GRAF-WELLHAUSEN HYPOTHESIS; J; SOURCE CRITICISM

YHWH. *See* TETRAGRAMMATON; YAHWEH

Z

ZADOKITE DOCUMENT. *See* DEAD SEA SCROLLS

Selected Bibliography

CRITICAL THEORY: GENERAL

Abelove, H., M. A. Barale, and D. M. Halperin, eds. *The Lesbian and Gay Studies Reader*. New York: Routledge, 1993.

Abrams, M. H. "The Deconstructive Angel." Pages 265–76 in *Modern Criticism and Theory: A Reader*. Edited by D. Lodge and N. Wood. 2nd ed. New York: Longman, 2000.

Achebe, C. "Colonialist Criticism." Pages 57–61 in *The Post-colonial Studies Reader*. Edited by B. Ashcroft et al. New York: Routledge, 1995.

Adam, I., and H. Tiffin. *Past the Last Post: Theorizing Post-colonialism and Post-modernism*. Hemel Hempstead, UK: Harvester Wheatsheaf, 1993.

Adamson, J., and S. Slovic. "Guest Editor's Introduction: The Shoulders We Stand On: An Introduction to Ethnicity and Ecocriticism." *MELUS: Multi-Ethnic Literature of the U.S.* 34, no. 2 (2009): 5–209.

Adorno, T. W. *Aesthetic Theory*. London: Routledge, 1984.

———. *Negative Dialectics*. Translated by E. B. Ashton. New York: Continuum, 1973.

Ahmad, A. "The Politics of Literary Post-coloniality." *Race and Class* 36, no. 3 (1995): 1–20.

Althusser, L. "Ideology and Ideological State Apparatuses: Notes toward an Investigation." Pages 121–73 in *Lenin and Philosophy, and Other Essays*. Translated by B. Brewster. London: New Left Books, 1971.

Altick, R. D. *The Art of Literary Research*. Rev. ed. New York: Norton, 1975.

Appiah, K. A. "Is the Post- in Post-modernism the Post- in Post-colonial?" *Critical Inquiry* 17, no. 2 (1991): 336–57.

Appleby, J., H. Lynn, and M. Jacob. *Telling the Truth about History*. New York: Norton, 1994.

Aristotle. *The Metaphysics*. Translated by H. Lawson-Tancred. Harmondsworth, UK: Penguin, 1998.

Armbruster, K., and K. R. Wallace, eds. *Beyond Nature Writing: Expanding the Boundaries of Ecocriticism*. Charlottesville: University of Virginia Press, 2001.

Armstrong, I., ed. *New Feminist Discourses: Critical Essays on Theories and Texts*. New York: Routledge, 1992.

Ashcroft, B. *Key Concepts in Post-colonial Studies*. New York: Routledge, 1998.

Ashcroft, B., G. Griffiths, and H. Tiffin. *The Empire Writes Back: Theory and Practice in Post-colonial Literatures*. New York: Routledge, 1989.

———, eds. *The Post-colonial Studies Reader*. New York: Routledge, 1995.

Atkins, G. D. *Reading Deconstruction: Deconstructive Reading*. Lexington: University of Kentucky Press, 1983.

Attridge, D., G. Bennington, and R. Young, eds. *Poststructuralism and the Question of History*. Cambridge: Cambridge University Press, 1987.

Austin, J. L. *How to Do Things with Words*. 2nd ed. Oxford: Clarendon, 1962.

Badcock, C. R. *Lévi-Strauss: Structuralism and Sociological Theory*. London: Hutchinson, 1975.

Bakhtin, M. *The Dialogic Imagination*. Edited by M. Holquist. Translated by C. Emerson and M. Holquist. Austin: University of Texas Press, 1984.

———. *Speech Genres and Other Late Essays*. Edited by C. Emerson and M. Holquist. Translated by V. McGee. Austin: University of Texas Press, 1986.

Baldick, C. *Criticism and Literary Theory, 1890 to the Present*. New York: Longman, 1996.

Bann, S., and J. E. Bowlt. *Russian Formalism: A Collection of Articles and Texts in Translation*. Edinburgh: Scottish Academic Press, 1973.

Barker, M. *Comics: Ideology, Power, and the Critics*. Manchester, UK: Manchester University Press, 1989.

Barr, M. S. *Alien to Femininity: Speculative Fiction and Feminist Theory*. New York: Greenwood, 1987.

Barrett, M. *Women's Oppression Today: Problems in Marxist Feminist Analysis*. London: New Left Books, 1980.

Barthes, R. *Critical Essays.* Translated by R. Howard. Evanston, IL: Northwestern University Press, 1976.

———. *Criticism and Truth.* Minneapolis: University of Minnesota Press, 1987.

———. *Empire of Signs.* Translated by R. Howard. London: Jonathan Cape, 1983.

———. "From Work to Text." Pages 73–81 in *Textual Strategies: Perspectives in Post-structuralist Criticism.* Edited by J. V. Harari. Ithaca, NY: Cornell University Press, 1979.

———. "Introduction to the Structural Analysis of Narratives." Pages 79–124 in *Image, Music, Text: Roland Barthes.* Translated by S. Heath. New York: Hill & Wang, 1977.

———. *The Pleasure of the Text.* Translated by R. Miller. London: Jonathan Cape, 1976.

———. *S/Z / Roland Barthes.* Translated by Richard Miller. London: Jonathan Cape, 1975.

Bassnett, S. *Feminist Experiences: The Women's Movement in Four Cultures.* London: Allen & Unwin, 1986.

Bauman, Z. *Intimations of Postmodernity.* London: Routledge, 1992.

———. *Postmodernity and Its Discontents.* New York: New York University Press, 1997.

Baxandal, L., and S. Morawski. *Marx and Engels on Literature and Art.* St. Louis: Telos, 1973.

Becket, F., and T. Gifford, eds. *Culture, Creativity and Environment: New Environmentalist Criticism.* Amsterdam: Rodopi, 2007.

Bell, D. S. *The End of Ideology.* Glencoe, IL: Free Press, 1960.

Bennett, T., et al., eds. *Culture, Ideology, and Social Process.* London: Batsford, 1981.

Bernard-Donals, M. F. *Mikhail Bakhtin: Between Phenomenology and Marxism.* Cambridge: Cambridge University Press, 1994.

Bernauer, J. W. *Michel Foucault's Force of Flight: Towards an Ethics for Thought.* Atlantic Highlands, NJ: Humanities, 1990.

Bertens, H. *The Idea of the Post-modern: A History.* London: Routledge, 1995.

Bertens, H., and D. Fokkema, eds. *International Postmodernism: Theory and Literary Practice.* Amsterdam: John Benjamins, 1997.

Bhabha, H. K. *Nation and Narration.* London: Routledge, 1990.

———. "Postcolonial Criticism." Pages 437–65 in *Redrawing the Boundaries.* Edited by S. Greenblatt and G. Gunn. New York: Modern Language Association of America, 1992.

Black, E. *Rhetorical Criticism: A Study in Method.* Madison: University of Wisconsin Press, 1978.

Bloom, H. *The Anxiety of Influence.* London: Oxford University Press, 1973.

———. *Deconstruction and Criticism.* New York: Seabury, 1979.

———. *A Map of Misreading.* New York: Oxford University Press, 1975.

Boehmer, E. *Colonial and Postcolonial Literature.* Oxford: Oxford University Press, 1995.

Booth, W. C. *The Rhetoric of Fiction.* Harmondsworth, UK: Penguin, 1991.

Bornkamm, G., G. Barth, and H. J. Held. *Tradition and Interpretation in Matthew.* Translated by P. Scott. Philadelphia: Westminster, 1963.

Bourdieu, P. *The Rules of Art: Genesis and Structure of the Literary Field.* Cambridge: Polity, 1996.

Bowie, A. *From Romanticism to Critical Theory: The Philosophy of German Literary Theory.* New York: Routledge, 1997.

Bowie, M. *Freud, Proust, and Lacan: Theory as Fiction.* Cambridge: Cambridge University Press, 1987.

Boyne, R., and A. Rattansi. *Postmodernism and Society.* London: Macmillan, 1990.

Brannigan, J. *New Historicism and Cultural Materialism.* London: Macmillan, 1998.

Brennan, T., ed. *Between Feminism and Psychoanalysis.* New York: Routledge, 1990.

Brock, B. L., and L. R. Scott, eds. *Methods of Rhetorical Criticism: A Twentieth-Century Perspective.* 3rd ed. Detroit: Wayne State University Press, 1989.

Bronner, S. E., and D. M. Kellner, eds. *Critical Theory and Society: A Reader.* London: Routledge, 1989.

Brooks, C. *The Hero with a Thousand Faces.* Rev. ed. Princeton: Princeton University Press, 1968.

———. *Understanding Poetry.* 3rd ed. New York: Holt, Rinehart, & Winston, 1960.

———. *The Well Wrought Urn: Studies in the Structure of Poetry.* 2nd ed. London: Dennis Dobson, 1968.

Brooks, C., and R. P. Warren, eds. *Understanding Fiction.* 2nd ed. Englewood Cliffs, NJ: Prentice Hall, 1959.

Bruns, G. L. *Hermeneutics Ancient and Modern.* New Haven: Yale University Press, 1992.

Buell, L. *The Future of Environmental Criticism: Environmental Crisis and Literary Imagination.* Malden, MA: Blackwell, 2005.

Burke, K. *Language as Symbolic Action*. Berkeley: University of California Press, 1966.

Burke, S. *The Death and Return of the Author: Criticism and Subjectivity in Barthes, Foucault and Derrida*. Edinburgh: Edinburgh University Press, 1992.

Butler, J. *Bodies That Matter: On the Discursive Limits of "Sex."* New York: Routledge, 1993.

———. *Gender Trouble: Feminism and the Subversion of Identity*. London: Routledge, 1990.

Carmichael, S., and C. V. Hamilton. *Black Power: The Politics of Liberation in America*. Harmondsworth, UK: Penguin, 1969.

Carston, R. "Relevance Theory." In *Routledge Companion to Philosophy of Language*. Edited by G. Russell and D. G. Fara. Routledge Philosophy Companions. New York: Routledge, 2011.

———. *Thoughts and Utterances*. Oxford: Blackwell, 2002.

Castle, T. *The Apparitional Lesbian: Female Homosexuality and Modern Culture*. New York: Columbia University Press, 1993.

Caughie, J., ed. *Theories of Authorship*. London: Routledge & Kegan Paul, 1981.

Chadwick, W. *Women, Art, and Society*. London: Thames & Hudson, 1990.

Charbonnier, G. *Conversations with Claude Lévi-Strauss*. Translated by John and Doreen Weightman. London: Cape, 1969.

Chatman, S. *Coming to Terms: The Rhetoric of Narrative in Fiction and Film*. Ithaca, NY: Cornell University Press, 1990.

Childs, P., and P. Williams. *An Introduction to Postcolonial Theory*. London: Prentice Hall, 1997.

Chodorov, N. J. *The Reproduction of Mothering: Psychoanalysis and the Sociology of Gender*. Berkeley: University of California Press, 1978.

Chomsky, N. *Aspects of the Theory of Syntax*. Cambridge, MA: MIT Press, 1965.

———. *Language and Politics*. Montreal: Black Rose Books, 1978.

———. *Studies on Semantics and Generative Grammar*. The Hague: Mouton, 1972.

———. *Syntactic Structures*. The Hague: Mouton, 1957.

———. *Topics in the Theory of Generative Grammar*. The Hague: Mouton, 1966.

Christian, B. *Black Feminist Criticism: Perspectives on Black Women Writers*. New York: Pergamon, 1985.

Cirlot, J. E. *A Dictionary of Symbols*. Translated by Jack Sage. New York: Philosophical Library, 1962.

———, ed. *Psychoanalysis and Literary Process*. Cambridge, MA: Winthrop, 1970.

Cixous, H. "Sorties." Pages 63–132 in *Modern Criticism and Theory: A Reader*. Edited by D. Lodge and N. Wood. 2nd ed. Harlow: Longman, 2000.

Clark, S. H. *Paul Ricoeur*. London: Routledge, 1990.

Clarke, C. "Living the Texts Out: Lesbians and the Uses of Black Women's Traditions." Pages 214–27 in *Theorizing Black Feminisms: The Visionary Pragmatism of Black Women*. Edited by A. Busia and S. James. New York: Routledge, 1993.

Coetzee, J. M. *White Writing: On the Culture of Letters in South Africa*. New Haven: Yale University Press, 1988.

Collier, P., and H. Geyer-Ryan, eds. *Literary Theory Today*. Cambridge: Polity, 1990.

Collins, P. H. *Black Feminist Thought: Knowledge, Consciousness, and the Politics of Empowerment*. 2nd ed. New York: Routledge, 2000.

Connor, S. *Postmodernist Culture: An Introduction to Theories of the Contemporary*. 2nd ed. Cambridge, MA: Blackwell, 1997.

Coote, A., and B. Campbell. *Sweet Freedom: The Struggle for Women's Liberation*. London: Picador, 1982.

Coward, R. *Patriarchal Precedents: Sexuality and Social Relations*. London: Routledge & Kegan Paul, 1983.

Culler, J. *On Deconstruction: Thought and Criticism after Structuralism*. London: Routledge & Kegan Paul, 1983.

———. "Presupposition and Intertextuality." *Modern Language Notes* 91 (1976): 1380–96.

———. *Structuralist Poetics: Structuralism, Linguistics, and the Study of Literature*. London: Routledge & Kegan Paul, 1975.

Daiches, D. *Critical Approaches to Literature*. Englewood Cliffs, NJ: Prentice Hall, 1956.

Daly, M. *The Church and the Second Sex*. Boston: Beacon, 1968.

———. *Gyn/Ecology: The Metaethics of Radical Feminism, with a New Intergalactic Introduction by the Author*. London: Women's Press, 1991.

———. *Pure Lust: Elemental Feminist Philosophy*. London: Women's Press, 1984.

Davidson, D. *Inquiries into Truth and Interpretation*. Oxford: Clarendon, 1984.

Davis, R. C., ed. *Lacan and Narration: The Psychoanalytic Difference in Narrative Theory*. Baltimore: Johns Hopkins University Press, 1983.

Davis, R. C., and R. Schleifer, eds. *Contemporary Literary Criticism: Literary and Cultural Studies*. 2nd ed. New York: Longman, 1989.

Day, G. *Re-reading Leavis: Culture and Literary Criticism.* Houndmills, UK: Macmillan Education, 1996.

De Beauvoir, S. *The Second Sex.* Translated by H. M. Parshley. Harmondsworth, UK: Penguin, 1984.

De Laurentis, T. "Queer Theory—Lesbian and Gay Sexualities: An Introduction." *Differences: A Journal of Feminist Cultural Studies* 3, no. 2 (1991): iii–xviii.

Denham, R. *Northrop Frye and Critical Method.* University Park: Pennsylvania State University Press, 1978.

Derrida, J. *Dissemination.* Translated by B. Johnson. London: Athlone, 1981.

———. *Margins of Philosophy.* Translated by A. Bass. Brighton, UK: Athlone, 1981.

———. *Of Grammatology.* Translated by G. C. Spivak. Baltimore: Johns Hopkins University Press, 1977.

———. *Positions.* Translated by A. Bass. London: Athlone, 1972.

———. *Writing and Difference.* Translated by A. Bass. London: Routledge & Kegan Paul, 1978.

Dirlik, A. "The Post-colonial Aura: Third World Criticism in the Age of Global Capitalism." *Critical Inquiry* 20 (1994): 328–56.

Dollimore, J., and A. Sinfield, eds. *Political Shakespeare: New Essays in Cultural Materialism.* Manchester, UK: Manchester University Press, 1985.

Doty, A., ed. *Making Things Perfectly Queer: Interpreting Mass Culture.* Minneapolis: University of Minnesota Press, 1997.

Du Bois, W. E. B. *The Souls of Black Folk.* Harmondsworth, UK: Penguin, 1989.

During, S. *Foucault and Literature: Towards a Genealogy of Writing.* London: Routledge, 1992.

Eagleton, M., ed. *Feminist Literary Theory: A Reader.* Oxford: Blackwell, 1986.

Eagleton, T. *Against the Grain: Selected Essays.* London: Verso, 1986.

———. *Criticism and Ideology.* London: New Left Books, 1976.

———. *The Function of Criticism: From the Spectator to Post-structuralism.* London: Verso, 1984.

———. *Ideology: An Introduction.* London: Verso, 1991.

———. *The Ideology of the Aesthetic.* Oxford: Blackwell, 1999.

———. *Literary Theory: An Introduction.* Oxford: Blackwell, 1983.

———. *Marxism and Literary Criticism.* London: Methuen, 1976.

———. *A Theory of Semiotics.* Bloomington: Indiana University Press, 1979.

Eikhenbaum, B. M. "Introduction to the Formal Method." Pages 8–16 in *Literary Theory: An Anthology.* Edited by J. Rivkin and M. Ryan. Oxford: Blackwell, 1998.

Einstein, H. *Contemporary Feminist Thought.* London: Unwin, 1984.

Eliot, G. *Althusser: The Detour of Theory.* London: Verso, 1987.

Eliot, T. S. *The Sacred Wood: Essays on Poetry and Criticism.* London: Methuen, 1920.

Ellis, J. M. *The Theory of Literary Criticism: A Logical Analysis.* Berkeley: University of California Press, 1974.

Empson, W. *Seven Types of Ambiguity.* Harmondsworth, UK: Penguin, 1995.

———. *The Structure of Complex Words.* London: Chatto & Windus, 1951.

Erlich, V. *Russian Formalism: History, Doctrine.* Paris: Mouton, 1965.

Felman, S., ed. *Literature and Psychoanalysis: The Question of Reading; Otherwise.* Baltimore: Johns Hopkins University Press, 1982.

Fiedler, L. *An End to Innocence: Essays on Culture and Politics.* Boston: Beacon, 1955.

Fish, S. *Is There a Text in This Class? The Authority of Interpretive Communities.* Cambridge, MA: Harvard University Press, 1980.

———. *Professional Correctness: Literary Studies and Political Change.* Oxford: Clarendon, 1995.

———. *Surprised by Sin: The Reader in "Paradise Lost."* New York: St. Martin's Press, 1967.

Flynn, E., and P. P. Schweickart. *Gender and Reading: Essays on Readers, Texts, and Contexts.* Baltimore: Johns Hopkins University Press, 1986.

Foss, Sonja K. *Rhetorical Criticism: Exploration and Practice.* Prospect Heights, IL: Waveland, 1989.

Foucault, Michel. *The Archaeology of Knowledge.* Translated by A. M. Sheridan Smith. New York: Pantheon Books, 1972.

———. *Ethics: Subjectivity and Truth.* Vol. 1 of *The Essential Works.* Edited by Paul Rabinow. London: Allen Lane, 1997.

———. *Madness and Civilization: A History of Insanity in the Age of Reason.* Translated by R. Howard. London: Tavistock, 1967.

———. "Nietzsche, Genealogy, History." Pages 139–64 in *Language, Counter-Memory, Practice.* Edited by D. F. Bouchard. Oxford: Blackwell, 1977.

———. *The Order of Things: An Archaeology of the Human Science.* London: Tavistock, 1970.

———. *Power-Knowledge: Selected Interviews and Other Writings, 1972–1977.* Edited by Colin Gordon. New York: Pantheon, 1980.

Fowler, A. *Kinds of Literature: An Introduction to the Theory of Genres and Modes.* Oxford: Clarendon, 1982.

Fowler, R., ed. *Essays on Style and Language: Linguistic and Critical Approaches to Literary Style.* London: Routledge & Kegan Paul, 1970.

———, ed. *Linguistic Criticism.* Oxford: Oxford University Press, 1986.

———, ed. *Literature as Social Discourse: The Practice of Linguistic Criticism.* London: Batsford, 1981.

Frank, M. *The Subject and the Text: Essays on Literary Theory and Philosophy.* Edited with an introduction by A. Bowie. Translated by H. Atkins. Cambridge: Cambridge University Press, 1997.

Freud, S. "Beyond the Pleasure Principle." Pages 1–64 in vol. 18 of *The Standard Edition of the Complete Psychological Works of Sigmund Freud.* Edited and translated by J. Strachey. London: Hogarth Press and Institute of Psycho-Analysis, 1974.

———. *Civilization and Its Discontents.* Pages 59–146 in vol. 21 of *The Standard Edition of the Complete Psychological Works of Sigmund Freud.* Edited and translated by J. Strachey. London: Hogarth Press and Institute of Psycho-Analysis, 1974.

———. "Creative Writers and Day-Dreaming." Pages 141–54 in vol. 9 of *The Standard Edition of the Complete Psychological Works of Sigmund Freud.* Edited and translated by J. Strachey. London: Hogarth Press and Institute of Psycho-Analysis, 1974.

———. "The Ego and the Id." Pages 1–66 in vol. 19 of *The Standard Edition of the Complete Psychological Works of Sigmund Freud.* Edited and translated by J. Strachey. London: Hogarth Press and Institute of Psycho-Analysis, 1974.

———. *The Interpretation of Dreams.* Vols. 4–5 of *The Standard Edition of the Complete Psychological Works of Sigmund Freud.* Edited and translated by J. Strachey. London: Hogarth Press and Institute of Psycho-Analysis, 1974.

———. *New Introductory Lectures on Psychoanalysis.* Pages 1–182 in vol. 22 of *The Standard Edition of the Complete Psychological Works of Sigmund Freud.* Edited and translated by J. Strachey. London: Hogarth Press and Institute of Psycho-Analysis, 1974.

———. "An Outline of Psychoanalysis." Pages 139–208 in vol. 23 of *The Standard Edition of the Complete Psychological Works of Sigmund Freud.* Edited and translated by J. Strachey. London: Hogarth Press and Institute of Psycho-Analysis, 1974.

———. *Three Essays on the Theory of Sexuality.* Pages 1–246 in vol. 7 of *The Standard Edition of the Complete Psychological Works of Sigmund Freud.* Edited and translated by J. Strachey. London: Hogarth Press and Institute of Psycho-Analysis, 1974.

———. "The Uncanny." Pages 217–52 in vol. 17 of *The Standard Edition of the Complete Psychological Works of Sigmund Freud.* Edited and translated by J. Strachey. London: Hogarth Press and Institute of Psycho-Analysis, 1974.

———. "The Unconscious." Pages 159–216 in vol. 11 of *The Standard Edition of the Complete Psychological Works of Sigmund Freud.* Edited and translated by J. Strachey. London: Hogarth Press and Institute of Psycho-Analysis, 1974.

Freund, E. *The Return of the Reader: Reader-Response Criticism.* London: Methuen, 1987.

Friedan, B. *The Feminine Mystique.* New York: Norton, 1963.

Friedman, A. B. *Myth, Symbolic Modes, and Ideology: A Discursive Bibliography.* Claremont, CA: Claremont Graduate School, 1976.

Frye, N. *Anatomy of Criticism: Four Essays.* Princeton: Princeton University Press, 1957.

———. *The Critical Path: An Essay on the Social Context of Literary Criticism.* Indianapolis: Indiana University Press, 1971.

———. *The Great Code: The Bible and Literature.* London: Routledge & Kegan Paul, 1982.

———. *Stubborn Structure: Essays on Criticism and Society.* London: Methuen, 1970.

Fuss, D., ed. *Inside/Out: Lesbian Theories, Gay Theories.* New York: Routledge, 1991.

Gadamer, H.-G. *Truth and Method.* Translated and revised by J. Weinsheimer and D. G. Marshall. New York: Continuum, 1998.

Gallagher, C., and S. Greenblatt. *Practicing New Historicism.* Chicago: University of Chicago Press, 2000.

Gallop, J. *Feminism and Psychoanalysis: The Daughter's Seduction.* London: Macmillan, 1982.

Gandhi, L. *Postcolonial Theory: A Critical Introduction.* New York: Columbia University Press, 1998.

Gardiner, M. *The Dialogics of Critique: M. M. Bakhtin and the Theory of Ideology.* London: Routledge, 1992.

Garrard, G. *Ecocriticism.* New York: Routledge, 2004.

Garvin, P. L., ed. *A Prague School Reader on Esthetics, Literary Structure, and Style.* Washington, DC: Georgetown University Press, 1964.

Gasché, R. *The Wild Card of Reading: On Paul de Man.* Cambridge, MA: Harvard University Press, 1998.

Gates, H. L., Jr., ed. *Race, Writing, and Difference.* Chicago: University of Chicago Press, 1988.

———. *The Signifying Monkey: A Theory of African-American Literary Criticism.* Oxford: Oxford University Press, 1988.

Gay, P., et al. *Doing Cultural Studies: The Story of the Sony Walkman.* London: Sage, 1997.

Geertz, C. J. *The Interpretation of Cultures: Selected Essays.* New York: Basic Books, 1973.

Genette, G. *Figures of Literary Discourse.* Translated by A. Sheridan with introduction by M. R. Logan. New York: Columbia University Press, 1982.

———. *Narrative Discourse: An Essay in Method.* Translated by J. E. Lewin. Ithaca, NY: Cornell University Press, 1980.

———. *Narrative Discourse Revisited.* Translated by J. E. Lewin. Ithaca, NY: Cornell University Press, 1988.

———. *Paratexts: Thresholds of Interpretation.* Translated by J. Lewin. Cambridge: Cambridge University Press, 1987.

Gentzler, E. *Contemporary Translation Theories.* Translation Studies. London: Routledge, 1990.

Geuss, R. *The Idea of a Critical Theory: Habermas and the Frankfurt School.* Cambridge: Cambridge University Press, 1981.

Gilbert, S. M., and S. Gubar. *The Female Imagination and the Modernist Aesthetic.* New York: Gordon & Breech, 1986.

Gilroy, P. *The Black Atlantic: Modernity and Double Consciousness.* Cambridge, MA: Harvard University Press, 1993.

Glotfelty, C. "Introduction: Literary Studies in an Age of Environmental Crisis." In *The Ecocriticism Reader: Landmarks in Literary Ecology.* Edited by C. Glotfelty and H. Fromm. Athens: University of Georgia Press, 1996.

———. "The Strong Green Thread." Pages 1–10 in *Essays in Ecocriticism.* Edited by N. Selvamony and R. K. Alex. Chennai: OSLE-India; New Delhi: Sarup & Sons, 2007.

Goldberg, J., ed. *Queering the Renaissance.* Durham, NC: Duke University Press, 1994.

Gorn, H. "Ecocriticism: The Intersection of Literature and the Environment." *Vegetarian Journal* 30, no. 2 (2011): 10–11.

Graham, P., ed. *The New Wave: Critical Landmarks.* London: Secker & Warburg in association with the British Film Institute, 1968.

Gramsci, A. *Selections from Cultural Writings.* Edited by D. Forgacs and G. Nowell-Smith. Translated by W. Boelhower. London: Lawrence & Wishart, 1985.

———. *Selections from Political Writings.* Edited and translated by Q. Hoare. London: Lawrence & Wishart, 1978.

Green, G., and C. Khan, eds. *Making a Difference: Feminist Literary Criticism.* London: Methuen, 1985.

Green, M. "Raymond Williams and Cultural Studies." *Working Papers in Cultural Studies* 6 (1974): 41–48.

Greenblatt, S. *The Forms of Power and the Power of Forms in the Renaissance.* Norman: University of Oklahoma, 1982.

———. *Renaissance Self-Fashioning: From More to Shakespeare.* Chicago: University of Chicago Press, 1980.

———. *Shakespearean Negotiations: The Circulation of Social Energy in Renaissance England.* London: Clarendon, 1988.

Greimas, A. J. *On Meaning: Selected Writings in Semiotic Theory.* Translated by P. Perron and F. Collins. Minneapolis: Minnesota University Press, 1978.

———. *Structural Semantics.* Lincoln: Nebraska University Press, 1983.

Grossberg, L., N. Cary, and P. A. Treichler, eds. *Cultural Studies.* New York: Routledge, 1992.

Grosz, E. *Jacques Lacan: A Feminist Introduction.* London: Routledge, 1990.

Habermas, J. "Modernity versus Post-modernity." Translated by S. Ben-Habi. *New German Critique* 22 (1981): 3–14.

———. *Moral Consciousness and Communicative Action.* Translated by C. Lenhardt and S. W. Nicholsen. Cambridge: Polity, 1990.

———. *The New Conservatism: Cultural Criticism and the Historians' Debate.* Cambridge, MA: MIT Press, 1989.

———. *Postmetaphysical Thinking: Philosophical Essays.* Translated by W. M. Hohengarten. Cambridge, MA: MIT Press, 1992.

———. *Theory and Practice.* Boston: Beacon, 1971.

Hall, S. *Critical Dialogues in Cultural Studies.* London: Routledge, 1996.

———. "Cultural Studies and the Centre: Some Problematics and Problems." Pages 15–47 in *Working Papers in Cultural Studies, 1972–1979*. Edited by Stuart Hall et al. Birmingham: University of Birmingham Press, 1980. Repr., London: Routledge, 2002.

Hamilton, P. *Historicism*. New York: Routledge, 1996.

Handy, W. J. *Kant and the Southern New Critics*. Austin: University of Texas Press, 1963.

Harari, J. V., ed. *Textual Strategies: Perspectives in Post-structuralist Criticism*. London: Methuen, 1980.

Harland, R. *Superstructuralism: The Philosophy of Structuralism and Post-structuralism*. New York: Methuen, 1987.

Harris, Z. S. *Methods in Structural Linguistics*. Chicago: University of Chicago Press, 1951.

Hartmann, G. *Beyond Formalism*. New Haven: Yale University Press, 1970.

———, ed. *Deconstruction and Criticism*. London: Routledge, 1979.

Harvey, D. *The Condition of Postmodernity: An Enquiry into the Origins of Cultural Change*. Oxford: Blackwell, 1989.

Haslett, M. *Marxist Literary and Cultural Theory*. New York: St. Martin's Press, 1999.

Hassan, I. "Post-modernism: A Practical Bibliography." Pages 39–59 in *Paracriticisms: Seven Speculations of the Times*. Urbana: University of Illinois Press, 1975.

———. *The Postmodern Turn: Essays in Postmodern Theory Culture*. Columbus: Ohio State University Press, 1987.

Hawkes, T. *Structuralism and Semiotics*. London: Methuen, 1977.

Hawthorn, J. *A Concise Glossary of Contemporary Literary Terms*. 3rd ed. New York: Oxford University Press, 1998.

Heidegger, M. *The Basic Problems of Phenomenology*. Translated with introduction and lexicon by A. Hofstadter. Bloomington: Indiana University Press, 1982.

———. *Poetry, Language, Thought*. Translated by A. Hofstadter. New York: Harper & Row, 1975.

Held, D. *Introduction to Critical Theory: Hokheimer to Habermas*. London: Hutchinson, 1980.

Hobson, M. *Jacques Derrida: Opening Lines*. London: Routledge, 1998.

Hodder, I. *Theory and Practice in Archaeology*. London: Routledge, 1990.

Hoffman, F. J. *Freudianism and the Literary Mind*. 2nd ed. Baton Rouge: Louisiana State University Press, 1957.

Holland, N. *The Dynamics of Literary Response*. New York: Oxford University Press, 1968.

Holquist, M. *Dialogism: Bakhtin and His World*. London: Routledge, 1990.

Holtzmann, H., and M. S. James. *Yearning: Race, Gender, and Cultural Politics*. Boston: South End Press, 1990.

Holub, R. C. *Crossing Borders: Reception Theory, Post-structuralism, Deconstruction*. Madison: University of Wisconsin Press, 1992.

Hooks, B. *Black Looks: Race and Representation*. Boston: South End Press, 1992.

Horowitz, D. *Betty Friedan and the Making of the Feminine Mystique: The American Left, the Cold War, and Modern Feminism*. Amherst: University of Massachusetts Press, 1998.

Howe, S. *Afrocentrism*. London: Verso, 1998.

Humm, M. *Practicing Feminist Criticism: An Introduction*. New York: Prentice Hall, 1995.

Hutcheon, L. *A Poetics of Postmodernism: History, Theory, Fiction*. London: Routledge, 1988.

———. *The Politics of Postmodernism*. New York: Routledge, 1989.

———. "The Post Always Rings Twice: The Postmodern and Postcolonial." *Material History Review* 41 (1994): 205–38.

Hyman, S. E. *The Armed Vision: A Study of the Methods of Literary Criticism*. Rev. ed. New York: Random House, 1955.

Inglis, F. *Cultural Studies*. Oxford: Blackwell, 1993.

Ingold, T., ed. *Key Debates in Anthropology*. London: Routledge, 1996.

Innis, R. E., ed. *Semiotics: An Introductory Reader*. London: Hutchinson, 1986.

Irigaray, L. *Culture of Difference*. New York: Routledge, 1992.

———. *An Ethics of Sexual Difference*. London: Athlone, 1993.

———. *Sexes and Genealogies*. Translated by G. C. Gill. New York: Columbia University Press, 1993.

———. *Speculum of the Other Woman*. Ithaca: Cornell University Press, 1985.

———. *Speech Is Never Neutral*. London: Athlone, 1989.

———. *This Sex Which Is Not One*. Ithaca, NY: Cornell University Press, 1985.

Iser, W. *The Act of Reading*. Baltimore: Johns Hopkins University Press, 1978.

———. *The Fictive and the Imaginary: Charting Literary Anthropology*. Translated by D. H. Wilson and W. Iser. Baltimore: Johns Hopkins University Press, 1991.

—————. *The Implied Reader: Patterns in Communications in Prose Fiction from Bunyan to Beckett.* Baltimore: Johns Hopkins University Press, 1974.

Jackson, S., et al., eds. *Women's Studies: A Reader.* Hemel Hempstead, UK: Harvester Wheatsheaf, 1993.

Jagose, A. *Queer Theory: An Introduction.* New York: New York University Press, 1997.

Jakobson, R. *Selected Writings III: Poetry of Grammar and Grammar of Poetry.* The Hague: Mouton, 1981.

James, H. *Theory of Fiction.* Edited by J. E. Miller Jr. Lincoln: University of Nebraska Press, 1972.

Jameson, F. *The Political Unconscious: Narrative as a Socially Symbolic Act.* London: Methuen, 1981.

—————. *The Prison-House of Language: A Critical Account of Structuralism and Russian Formalism.* Princeton: Princeton University Press, 1972.

—————. *Situations of Theory.* Vol. 1 of *The Ideologies of Theory: Essays, 1971–1986.* Minneapolis: University of Minnesota Press, 1988.

—————. *Syntax of History.* Vol. 2 of *The Ideologies of Theory: Essays, 1971–1986.* Minneapolis: University of Minnesota Press, 1988.

Jarvis, S. *Adorno: A Critical Introduction.* Cambridge: Polity, 1998.

Jefferson, A., and D. Robey, eds. *Modern Literary Theory: A Comparative Introduction.* 2nd ed. London: Batsford, 1986.

Jencks, C. *What Is Post-modernism?* London: Academy Editions, 1996.

Johnson, B. *The Critical Difference.* Baltimore: Johns Hopkins University Press, 1980.

Johnson, C. *System and Writing in the Philosophy of Jacques Derrida.* Cambridge: Cambridge University Press, 1993.

Johnson, L. *The Cultural Critics: From Matthew Arnold to Raymond Williams.* London: Routledge & Kegan Paul, 1979.

Jung, C. G. *The Archetypes and the Collective Unconscious.* Vol. 9, part 1 of *Collected Works.* Translated by R. F. C. Hull. 2nd ed. Princeton: Princeton University Press, 1968.

—————. *The Collected Works of C. G. Jung.* 18 vols. London: Routledge & Kegan Paul, 1953–78.

—————. *Man and His Symbols.* Garden City, NY: Doubleday, 1964.

Keesey, D. *Contexts for Criticism.* 4th ed. Boston: McGraw-Hill, 2003.

King, U. *Women and Spirituality: Voices of Protest and Promise.* Basingstoke, UK: Macmillan, 1989.

Kirk, G. S. *Myth: Its Meaning and Functions in Ancient and Other Cultures.* Berkeley: University of California Press, 1970.

Kockelman, J. J., ed. *Phenomenology: The Philosophy of Edmund Husserl and Its Interpretation.* Garden City, NY: Doubleday, 1967.

Kofman, S. *Freud and Fiction.* Translated by S. Wykes. Cambridge: Polity, 1991.

Kristeva, J. *Language: The Unknown.* Translated by A. M. Menke. Hemel Hempstead, UK: Harvester Wheatsheaf, 1989.

—————. *Powers of Horror.* Translated by L. S. Roudiez. New York: Columbia University Press, 1982.

—————. *Revolution in Poetic Language.* Translated by L. S. Roudiez. New York: Columbia University Press, 1984.

Kuhn, T. S. *The Structure of Scientific Revolutions.* Chicago: University of Chicago Press, 1962.

Ku-Mesu, K. E. "Whose Relevance? Interpretation of Texts by a Hybrid Audience." *Edinburgh Working Papers in Applied Linguistics* 8 (1997): 44–53.

Lacan, J. *The Four Fundamental Concepts of Psychoanalysis.* Translated by A. Sheridan with a new introduction by D. Macey. Harmondsworth, UK: Penguin, 1994.

Larrain, J. *The Concept of Ideology.* London: Hutchinson, 1979.

Lavers, A. *Roland Barthes: Structuralism and After.* London: Methuen, 1982.

Leavis, F. R. *Valuation in Criticism and Other Essays.* Edited by G. Singh. Cambridge: Cambridge University Press, 1986.

Lee, Kyung-Won. "Is the Glass Half-Empty or Half-Full? Rethinking the Problems of Postcolonial Revisionism." *Cultural Critique* 36, no. 2 (1997): 89–117.

Lentricchia, F. *After the New Criticism.* Chicago: University of Chicago Press, 1980.

LeVay, S. *Queer Science: The Use and Abuse of Research into Homosexuality.* Cambridge, MA: MIT Press, 1996.

Lévi-Strauss, C. *The Raw and the Cooked.* Translated by J. Weightman and D. Weightman. London: Jonathan Cape, 1970.

—————. *Structural Anthropology.* Translated by C. Jacobson, B. G. Schoepf, and M. Layton. 2 vols. New York: Basic Books, 1963–76.

—————. "The Structural Study of Myth." *Journal of American Folklore* 68, no. 270 (1955): 428–44.

Lipking, L. I., and A. W. Litz, eds. *Modern Literary Criticism, 1900–1970.* New York: Random House, 1955.

Llewelyn, J. *Beyond Metaphysics? The Hermeneutic Circle in Contemporary Continental Philosophy.* Atlantic Heights, NJ: Humanities, 1985.

Loades, A. *Feminist Theology: A Reader.* London: SPCK, 1990.

Lodge, D., ed. *After Bakhtin: Essays on Fiction and Criticism.* London: Routledge, 1990.

———, ed. *Modern Criticism and Theory: A Reader.* London: Longman, 1988.

———. *20th Century Literary Criticism.* London: Longman, 1972.

Lodge, D., and N. Wood, eds. *Modern Criticism and Theory: A Reader.* 2nd ed. New York: Pearson, 2000.

Loomba, A. *Colonialism/Postcolonialism.* London: Routledge, 1998.

Lukács, G. *History and Class Consciousness: Studies on Marxist Dialectics.* Translated by R. Livingstone. London: Merlin, 1971.

Lyotard, J.-F. *The Postmodern Condition: A Report on Knowledge.* Minneapolis: University of Minnesota Press, 1984.

Macherey, P. *The Object of Literature.* Translated by D. Macey. Cambridge: Cambridge University Press, 1995.

———. *A Theory of Literary Production.* London: Routledge, 1978.

Man, Paul de. *Aesthetic Ideology.* Minneapolis: University of Minnesota Press, 1996.

———. *Blindness and Insight: Essays in the Rhetoric of Contemporary Criticism.* 2nd ed. London: Methuen, 1983.

———. *The Resistance to Theory.* Minneapolis: University of Minnesota Press, 1986.

Mandel, E. *Marxist Economic Theory.* London: Merlin, 1972.

Marcuse, H. *Negations: Essays in Critical Theory.* Translated by J. J. Shapiro. Harmondsworth, UK: Penguin, 1972.

Marks, E., and I. de Courtivron. *New French Feminisms.* Brighton, UK: Harvester, 1979.

Martin, W. *Recent Theories of Narrative.* Ithaca, NY: Cornell University Press, 1986.

Marx, K. *A Contribution to the Critique of Political Economy.* Moscow: Progress, 1970.

———. *The Poverty of Philosophy.* New York: International, 1963.

McCarthy, T. *The Critical Theory of Jürgen Habermas.* Cambridge: Polity, 1984.

McGee, C. E. "Performance Criticism." Pages 133–39 in *Encyclopedia of Contemporary Literary Theory: Approaches, Scholars, Terms.* Edited by I. R. Makaryk. Toronto: University of Toronto Press, 1993.

McGowan, J. *Postmodernism and Its Critics.* Ithaca, NY: Cornell University Press, 1991.

McLeod, J. *Beginning Postcolonialism.* Manchester, UK: Manchester University Press, 2000.

Merrell, F. *Sign, Intertexuality, World.* Bloomington: Indiana University Press, 1992.

Meszaros, I. *Marx's Theory of Alienation.* London: Merlin, 1971.

Mills, S., et al. *Feminist Readings / Feminists Reading.* Hemel Hempstead, UK: Harvester Wheatsheaf, 1989.

Milner, A. *Contemporary Cultural Theory.* London: UCL Press, 1994.

Mirza, H. S., ed. *Black British Feminism: A Reader.* London: Routledge, 1997.

Mishra, V., and B. Hodge. "What Is Post(-)colonialism?" *Textual Practice* 5, no. 3 (1991): 399–415.

Mitchell, J. *Psychoanalysis and Feminism.* London: Allen Lane, 1974.

———. *Women—the Longest Revolution: Essays in Feminism, Literature, and Psychoanalysis.* London: Virago, 1984.

Moi, T. *French Feminist Thought: A Reader.* Oxford: Blackwell, 1987.

———. *The Kristeva Reader.* Oxford: Blackwell, 1986.

———. *Sexual/Textual Politics: Feminist Literary Theory.* London: Methuen, 1985.

Mongia, P., ed. *Contemporary Postcolonial Theory: A Reader.* London: Arnold, 1996.

Moore-Gilbert, B. *Postcolonial Theory: Contexts, Practices, Politics.* London: Verso, 1997.

Moore-Gilbert, B., G. Stanton, and W. Maley, eds. *Postcolonial Criticism.* New York: Routledge, 1997.

Morris, W. *Toward a New Historicism.* Princeton: Princeton University Press, 1972.

Morrison, C. C. *Freud and the Critic: The Early Use of Depth Psychology in Literary Criticism.* Chapel Hill: University of North Carolina Press, 1968.

Myrsiades, K., and J. McGuire, eds. *Order and Partialities: Theory, Pedagogy, and the "Postcolonial."* Albany: State University of New York Press, 1995.

Neumann, E. *The Great Mother: An Analysis of the Archetype.* Translated by Ralph Manheim. Princeton: Princeton University Press, 1963.

Nicholson, L., ed. *Feminism/Postmodernism.* New York: Routledge, 1990.

Norris, C. *Deconstruction: Theory and Practice.* Rev. ed. London: Routledge, 1986.

―――. *William Empson and the Philosophy of Literary Criticism*. London: Athlone, 1978.

Oakley, A. *Sex, Gender, and Society*. London: Temple Smith, 1972.

Ogden, C. K., and I. A. Richards. *The Meaning of Meaning: A Study of the Influence of Language on Thought; With Supplementary Essays by B. Malinowski and F. C. Crookshank*. New York: Harcourt, Brace & World, 1923.

Ogden, S. *Faith and Freedom: Toward a Theology of Liberation*. Belfast, ON: Christian Journals, 1979.

Ohmann, R. M., ed. *The Making of Myth*. New York: Putnam, 1962.

Parker, R., and G. Pollock. *Framing Feminism: Art and the Women's Movement, 1970–1985*. London: Pandora Books, 1987.

Peck, J., and M. Coyle. *Practical Criticism*. London: Macmillan, 1995.

Pettit, P. *The Concept of Structuralism: A Critical Analysis*. Dublin: Gill & Macmillan, 1975.

Poletta, G. T., ed. *Issues in Contemporary Literary Criticism*. Boston: Little, Brown, 1973.

Portoghesi, P. *Postmodern: The Architecture of the Postindustrial Society*. New York: Rizzoli, 1983.

Poster, M. *The Mode of Information: Poststructuralism and Social Context*. Chicago: University of Chicago Press, 1990.

Prince, G. *A Grammar of Stories*. The Hague: Mouton, 1973.

Propp, V. *Morphology of the Folktale*. Translated by L. Scott. Bloomington: Indiana University Press, 1958.

Putman, H. *Representation and Reality*. Cambridge, MA: Harvard University Press, 1988.

Radway, J. A. *Reading the Romance: Women, Patriarchy, and Popular Literature*. Chapel Hill: University of North Carolina Press, 1984.

Ransom, J. C. *The New Criticism*. New York: New Directions, 1941.

Rattansi, A. "Post-colonialism and Its Discontents." *Economy and Society* 26, no. 4 (1997): 480–500.

Ray, W. *Literary Meaning: From Phenomenology to Deconstruction*. New York: Blackwell, 1984.

Readings, B. *Introducing Lyotard: Art Politics*. London: Routledge, 1991.

Rice, P., and P. Waugh. *Modern Literary Theory: A Reader*. London: Edward Arnold, 1989.

Richards, I. A. *Practical Criticism: A Study of Literary Judgement*. London: Routledge & Kegan Paul, 1929.

―――. *Principles of Literary Criticism*. London: Routledge & Kegan Paul, 1924.

Richter, D. H. *Fable's End: Completeness and Closure in Rhetorical Fiction*. Chicago: University of Chicago Press, 1947.

Ricoeur, P. *The Conflict of Interpretations: Essays in Hermeneutics*. Edited by D. Ihde. Evanston, IL: Northwestern University Press, 1969.

―――. *Freud and Philosophy: An Essay on Interpretation*. Translated by D. Savage. New Haven: Yale University Press, 1970.

―――. *The Rule of Metaphor: Multi-disciplinary Studies in the Creation of Meaning*. Translated by R. Czerny with K. McLaughlin and J. Costella. London: Routledge, 1978.

―――. *Time and Narrative*. Translated by K. McLaughlin, D. Pellauer, and K. Blamey. 3 vols. Chicago: University of Chicago Press, 1984–88.

Rivkin, J., and M. Ryan, eds. *Literary Theory: An Anthology*. Oxford: Blackwell, 1998.

Robinson, V., and D. Richardson, eds. *Introducing Women's Studies*. 2nd ed. London: Macmillan, 1997.

Rorty, R., ed. *Essays on Heidegger and Others*. Vol. 2 of *Philosophical Papers*. Cambridge: Cambridge University Press, 1991.

―――. *The Linguistic Turn: Recent Essays in Philosophical Method*. Chicago: University of Chicago Press, 1967.

―――. *Objectivity, Relativism, and Truth*. Vol. 1 of *Philosophical Papers*. Cambridge: Cambridge University Press, 1991.

―――. *Philosophy and the Mirror of Nature*. Princeton: Princeton University Press, 1979; Oxford: Blackwell, 1980.

Rowbotham, S. *Women's Consciousness, Man's World*. Harmondsworth, UK: Penguin, 1973.

Ruitenbeek, H. M., ed. *Psychoanalysis and Literature*. New York: Dutton, 1964.

Ruthven, K. K. *Feminist Studies: An Introduction*. Cambridge: Cambridge University Press, 1990.

Ryan, M. *Marxism and Deconstruction: A Critical Articulation*. Baltimore: Johns Hopkins University Press, 1982.

―――, ed. *New Historicism and Cultural Materialism: A Reader*. New York: Oxford University Press, 1996.

Said, E. W. *Beginnings: Intentions and Method*. London: Granta Books, 1997.

―――. *Culture and Imperialism*. New York: Alfred Knopf, 1992.

————. *Orientalism*. London: Routledge & Kegan Paul, 1978.

————. *The Politics of Dispossession*. London: Vintage, 1994.

————. *The World, the Text, and the Critic*. New Haven: Yale University Press, 1983.

San Juan, E. *Beyond Postcolonial Theory*. New York: St. Martin's Press, 1998.

Saussure, F. de. *Course in General Linguistics*. Translated by W. Baskin with an introduction by J. Culler. London: Fontana Collins, 1974.

Sayers, J. *Biological Politics: Feminist and Anti-feminist Perspectives*. London: Tavistock, 1982.

Schiffrin, D. *Approaches to Discourse*. Oxford: Blackwell, 1993.

Schleifer, R. *A. J. Greimas: Linguistics, Semiotics, and Discourse Theory*. London: Croom Helm, 1987.

Schneir, M. *The Vintage Book of Feminism*. London: Vintage, 1995.

————. *The Vintage Book of Historical Feminism*. London: Vintage, 1996.

Scholes, R. *Structuralism in Literature: An Introduction*. New Haven: Yale University Press, 1974.

Scholes, R., and R. Kellogg. *The Nature of Narrative*. London: Oxford University Press, 1966.

Schrift, A. D. *Nietzsche's French Legacy: A Genealogy of Poststructuralism*. New York: Routledge, 1995.

Scott, B. K. *The Gender of Modernism: A Critical Anthology*. Bloomington: Indiana University Press, 1990.

Scott, W., ed. *Five Approaches of Literary Criticism*. New York: Macmillan, 1962.

Searle, J. R. *The Construction of Social Reality*. New York: Free Press, 1995.

————. *Expression and Meaning: Essays in the Theory of Speech Acts*. Cambridge: Cambridge University Press, 1979.

————. *Speech Acts: An Essay in the Philosophy of Language*. Cambridge: Cambridge University Press, 1969.

Sebeok, T. *An Introduction to Semiotics*. London: Pinter, 1994.

Sedgwick, E. K., ed. *Novel Gazing: Queer Readings in Fiction*. Durham, NC: Duke University Press, 1997.

Segal, L. *Is the Future Female? Troubled Thoughts on Contemporary Feminism*. London: Virago, 1987.

Segal, R. *The Black Diaspora*. London: Faber & Faber, 1995.

Seidman, S., ed. *Queer Theory/Sociology*. Oxford: Blackwell, 1996.

Selden, R. *A Reader's Guide to Contemporary Literary Theory*. Lexington: University of Kentucky Press, 1989.

Sheridan, A. *Michel Foucault: The Will to Truth*. London: Tavistock, 1980.

Shipley, J. T., ed. *Dictionary of World Literature: Criticism, Forms, Techniques*. New York: Philosophical Library, 1942.

Showalter, E. *The New Feminist Criticism: Essays on Women, Literature, and Theory*. New York: Pantheon, 1985.

Silverman, K. *The Subject of Semiotics*. Oxford: Oxford University Press, 1983.

Sim, S., ed. *The Routledge Critical Dictionary of Postmodern Thought*. New York: Routledge, 1999.

Simon, S. *Gender in Translation: Cultural Identity and the Politics of Transmission*. Translation Studies. New York: Routledge, 1996.

Sinfield, A. *Cultural Politics—Queer Reading*. London: Routledge, 1994.

————. *Faultlines: Cultural Materialism and the Politics of Dissident Reading*. Oxford: Oxford University Press, 1992.

Sontag, S. *Against Interpretation*. London: Vintage, 1994.

Spender, D. *Man-Made Language*. London: Routledge, 1980.

Sperber, D., and D. Wilson. *Relevance: Communication and Cognition*. 2nd ed. Oxford: Blackwell, 1995.

Spitzer, L. *Linguistics and Literary History: Essays in Stylistics*. New York: Russell & Russell, 1962.

Spivak, G. C. *In Other Worlds: Essays in Cultural Politics*. New York: Methuen, 1987.

————. *The Post-colonial Critic: Interviews, Strategies, Dialogues*. Edited by S. Harasym. New York: Routledge, 1990.

Steiner, G. *After Babel: Aspects of Language and Translation*. Rev. ed. Oxford: Oxford University Press, 1992.

Stevick, P. *The Chapter in Fiction: Theories of Narrative Division*. Syracuse, NY: Syracuse University Press, 1970.

Stoller, R. J. *Sex and Gender*. New York: Science House, 1968.

Storey, J., ed. *Cultural Theory and Popular Culture: A Reader*. London: Routledge, 1997.

Sturrock, J., ed. *Structuralism and Since: From Lévi-Strauss to Derrida*. Oxford: Oxford University Press, 1979.

Tate, A. *Collected Essays*. Denver: Swallow, 1958.

Thorpe, J., ed. *Principles of Textual Criticism.* San Marino, CA: Huntington Library, 1972.

———. *Relations of Literary Study: Essays on Interdisciplinary Study.* New York: Modern Language Association, 1967.

Todorov, T. *The Fantastic: A Structural Approach to a Literary Genre.* Translated by R. Howard. Cleveland: Case Western Reserve University Press, 1982.

———. *Mikhail Bakhtin: The Dialogical Principle.* Translated by W. Godzich, Minneapolis: University of Minnesota Press, 1984.

———. *The Poetics of Prose.* Translated by R. Howard. Ithaca, NY: Cornell University Press, 1977.

———. *Theories of the Symbol.* Translated by C. Porter. Ithaca, NY: Cornell University Press, 1982.

Tompkins, J. P., ed. *Reader-Response Criticism: From Formalism to Post-structuralism.* Baltimore: Johns Hopkins University Press, 1980.

Treichler, P., ed. *Cultural Studies.* London: Routledge, 1992.

Trivedi, H., and M. Mukherjee, eds. *Interrogating Postcolonialism: Theory, Text, and Context.* Shimla, India: Indian Institute of Advanced Study, 1996.

Ulanov, A. B. *The Feminine in Jungian Psychology and in Christian Theology.* Evanston, IL: Northwestern University Press, 1971.

Vachek, J., ed. *A Prague School Reader in Linguistics.* Bloomington: Indiana University Press, 1964.

Vattimo, G. *The End of Modernity: Nihilism and Hermeneutics in Post-modern Culture.* Translated by J. R. Snyder. Cambridge: Polity, 1988.

Veeser, H. A., ed. *The New Historicism.* New York: Routledge, 1989.

———, ed. *The New Historicism Reader.* New York: Routledge, 1994.

Vice, S., ed. *Psychoanalytic Criticism: A Reader.* Cambridge: Polity, 1996.

———, ed. *Psychoanalytic Criticism: Theory and Practice.* London: Methuen, 1984.

Vickers, B. *In Defense of Rhetoric.* New York: Oxford University Press, 1988.

Walby, S. *Patriarchy at Work.* Cambridge: Polity, 1986.

———. *Theorizing Patriarchy.* Oxford: Blackwell, 1990.

Walker, A. *In Search of Our Mothers' Gardens: Womanist Prose.* New York: Harcourt Brace Jovanovich, 1983.

Walter, N. *The New Feminism.* London: Little, Brown, 1998.

Warhol, R. R., and D. P. Herndl, eds. *Feminisms: An Anthology of Literary Theory and Criticism.* New Brunswick, NJ: Rutgers University Press, 1991.

Watney, S. "The Banality of Gender." *Oxford Literary Review* 18 (1986): 12–21.

Webster, R. *Studying Literary Theory.* London: Arnold, 1990.

Wellek, R. *Concepts of Criticism.* New Haven: Yale University Press, 1963.

Wellek, R., and A. Warren. *Theory of Literature.* Harmondsworth, UK: Penguin, 1966.

Wetherill, P. M. *The Literary Text: An Examination of Critical Methods.* Berkeley: University of California Press, 1974.

White, H. V. *The Content of the Form: Narrative Discourse and Historical Representation.* Baltimore: Johns Hopkins University Press, 1987.

———. *Tropics of Discourse: Essays in Cultural Criticism.* Baltimore: Johns Hopkins University Press, 1978.

Williams, L. R. *Critical Desire: Psychoanalysis and the Literary Subject.* London: Arnold, 1995.

Williams, P., and L. Chrisman, eds. *Colonial Discourse and Post-colonial Theory: A Reader.* New York: Columbia University Press, 1994.

Williams, R. *Marxism and Literature.* Oxford: Oxford University Press, 1977.

Wimsatt, W. K., Jr., ed. *Explication as Criticism: Selected Papers from the English Institute, 1941–1952.* New York: Columbia University Press, 1963.

———. *The Verbal Icon: Studies in the Meaning of Poetry, with Two Preliminary Essays Written in Collaboration with Monroe C. Beardsley.* London: Methuen, 1970.

Wimsatt, W. K., Jr., and C. Brooks. *Literary Criticism: A Short History.* New York: Knopf, 1957.

Winnicott, D. W. *Playing and Reality.* Harmondsworth, UK: Penguin, 1980.

Woods, T. *Beginning Postmodernism.* Manchester, UK: Manchester University Press, 1999.

Worton, M., and J. Still, eds. *Intertextuality: Theories and Practices.* Manchester, UK: Manchester University Press, 1990.

Wright, E. *Feminism and Psychoanalysis: A Critical Dictionary.* Oxford: Blackwell, 1992.

———. *Psychoanalytic Criticism: Theory in Practice.* London: Methuen, 1984.

Wright, P. *On Living in an Old Country: The National Past in Contemporary Britain.* London: Verso, 1985.

Young, R. J. C. *Postcolonialism: An Historical Introduction.* Oxford: Blackwell, 2000.

CRITICAL THEORY: BIBLICAL

Achtemeier, E. "The Impossible Possibility: Evaluating the Feminist Approach to Bible and Theology." *Interpretation* 42 (1988): 45–57.

Aichele, G., and G. A. Phillips, eds. *Intertextuality and the Bible. Semeia* 69–70 (1995).

Aichele, G., and T. Pippin, eds. *Fantasy and the Bible. Semeia* 60 (1992).

Aland, K., and B. Aland. *The Text of the New Testament: An Introduction to the Critical Editions and to the Theory and Practice of Modern Textual Criticism.* Translated by E. F. Rhodes. Grand Rapids: Eerdmans, 1989.

Altizer, T. J. J. *Deconstruction and Theology.* Chico, CA: Scholars Press, 1980.

Amihai, M., et al. *Narrative Research on the Hebrew Bible. Semeia* 46 (1989).

Anderson, B. W. "Biblical Theology and Sociological Interpretation." *Theology Today* 42 (1985): 292–306.

Anderson, J. C. "Mapping Feminist Biblical Criticism: The American Scene, 1983–1990." *Critical Review of Books in Religion* (1991): 21–44.

Anderson, J. C., and S. D. Moore. *Mark and Method: New Approaches in Biblical Studies.* Minneapolis: Fortress, 1992.

Anderson, V. *Beyond Ontological Blackness: An Essay on African-American Religious and Cultural Criticism.* New York: Continuum, 1995.

Armour, E. T. *Deconstruction, Feminist Theology, and the Problem of Difference: Subverting the Race/Gender Divide.* Chicago: University of Chicago Press, 1999.

Bach, A., ed. *The Pleasure of Her Text: Feminist Readings of Biblical and Historical Texts.* Philadelphia: Trinity Press International, 1990.

———. *Women, Seduction, and Betrayal in Biblical Narrative.* Cambridge: Cambridge University Press, 1997.

Bailey, R. C., and T. Pippin, eds. *Race, Class, and the Politics of Biblical Translation. Semeia* 76 (1998).

Bal, M., ed. *Anti-covenant: Counter-Reading Women's Lives in the Hebrew Bible.* Sheffield: Almond, 1989.

———. *Death and Dissymmetry: The Politics of Coherence in the Book of Judges.* Chicago: University of Chicago Press, 1988.

———. *Lethal Love: Feminist Literary Readings of Biblical Love Stories.* Bloomington: Indiana University Press, 1987.

Barbour, R. S. *Tradition-Historical Criticism of the Gospels.* London: SPCK, 1972.

Bar-Efrat, S. *Narrative Art in the Bible.* Sheffield: Sheffield Academic Press, 1989.

Barnstone, W. *The Poetics of Translation: History, Theory, Practice.* New Haven: Yale University Press, 1993.

Barr, J. *Holy Scripture: Canon, Authority, Criticism.* Philadelphia: Westminster, 1983.

———. "The Literal, the Allegorical, and Modern Biblical Scholarship." *Journal for the Study of the Old Testament* 44 (1989): 3–17.

———. *Old and New in Interpretation.* New York: Harper, 1966. 2nd ed., London: SCM, 1982.

Barthes, R., et al. *Structural Analysis and Biblical Exegesis.* Pittsburgh: Pickwick, 1974.

Barton, J. "Classifying Biblical Criticism." *Journal for the Study of the Old Testament* 9 (1984): 19–35.

———. *The Nature of Biblical Criticism.* Louisville: Westminster John Knox, 2007.

———. *Reading the Old Testament: Method in Biblical Study.* Philadelphia: Westminster, 1984.

Bathstone, D. *From Conquest to Struggle: Jesus of Nazareth in Latin America.* Albany: State University of New York Press, 1984.

Beck, B. *Reading the New Testament Today: An Introduction to New Testament Criticism.* Cambridge: Lutterworth, 1992.

Belo, F. A. *Materialist Reading of the Gospel of Mark.* Maryknoll, NY: Orbis Books, 1981.

Berlin, A. "On the Bible as Literature." *Prooftexts* 2 (1982): 323–27.

———. *Poetics and Interpretation of Biblical Narrative.* Sheffield: Almond, 1983.

Bible and Culture Collective. *The Postmodern Bible.* New Haven: Yale University Press, 1995.

Bird, P. A. *The Bible as the Church's Book.* Philadelphia: Westminster, 1982.

———. *Missing Persons and Mistaken Identities: Women and Gender in Ancient Israel.* Overtures to Biblical Theology. Minneapolis: Fortress, 1997.

Bird, P. A., et al., eds. *Reading the Bible as Women: Perspectives from Africa, Asia, and Latin America. Semeia* 78 (1998).

Black, F. C., R. Boer, and E. Runions, eds. *The Labour of Reading: Desire, Alienation, and Biblical Interpretation.* Atlanta: Scholars Press, 1999.

Boff, L., and C. Boff. *Introducing Liberation Theology.* London: Burns & Oates; Maryknoll, NY: Orbis Books, 1987.

Boyarin, D. *Intertextuality and the Reading of Midrash.* Bloomington: Indiana University Press, 1990.

———. *A Radical Jew: Paul and the Politics of Identity.* Berkeley: University of California Press, 1994.

Brenner, A. *Ruth and Esther: A Feminist Companion to the Bible.* Sheffield: Sheffield Academic Press, 1999.

Brenner, A., and F. van Dijk-Hemmes. *On Gendering Texts: Female and Male Voices in the Hebrew Bible.* Biblical Interpretation Series 1. Leiden: Brill, 1993.

Brett, M. *Biblical Criticism in Crisis?* Cambridge: Cambridge University Press, 1991.

Brodie, T. L. *The Crucial Bridge: The Elijah–Elisha Narrative as an Interpretive Synthesis of Genesis–Kings and a Literary Model for the Gospels.* Collegeville, MN: Liturgical Press, 2000.

Brown, R. E. *The Critical Meaning of the Bible.* Ramsey, NJ: Paulist Press, 1981.

Brown, R. M. *Unexpected News: Reading the Bible with Third World Eyes.* Philadelphia: Westminster, 1984.

Buchmann, C., and C. Spiegel, eds. *Out of the Garden: Women Writers on the Bible.* New York: Fawcett Columbine, 1994.

Bultmann, R., and K. Dundsin. *Form Criticism: Two Essays on New Testament Research.* New York: Harper Torchbooks, 1962.

Burnett, F. W. "Postmodern Biblical Exegesis: The Eve of Historical Criticism." *Semeia* 51 (1990): 51–80.

Caird, G. B. *The Language and Imagery of the Bible.* London: Duckworth; Philadelphia: Westminster, 1980.

Calvert-Koyzis, N., and H. E. Weir, eds. *Strangely Familiar: Protofeminist Interpretations of Patriarchal Biblical Texts.* Atlanta: Society of Biblical Literature, 2009.

Camp, C. V., and C. R. Fontaine, eds. *Women, War, and Metaphor: Language and Society in the Study of the Hebrew Bible. Semeia* 61 (1993).

Cannon, K. G., and E. Schüssler Fiorenza, eds. *Interpretation for Liberation. Semeia* 47 (1989).

Caputo, J. D. *Radical Hermeneutics: Repetition, Deconstruction, and the Hermeneutic Project.* Bloomington: Indiana University Press, 1987.

Carson, D. A., ed. *Biblical Interpretation and the Church.* Exeter, UK: Paternoster, 1984.

Cartwright, M. G. "Ideology and the Interpretation of the Bible in the African-American Christian Tradition." *Modern Theology* 9, no. 2 (1993): 141–58.

Castelli, E. *Imitating Paul: A Discourse of Power.* Louisville: Westminster John Knox, 1991.

Cedarbaum, D. G. "The Role of Halakha in Reconstructionist Decision Making." *Reconstructionist* 65, no. 2 (2001): 29–38.

Childs, B. S. *Introduction to the Old Testament as Scripture.* Philadelphia: Fortress, 1979.

———. *The New Testament as Canon: An Introduction.* Philadelphia: Fortress, 1985.

Chopp, R. S. *The Power to Speak: Feminism, Language, God.* New York: Crossroad, 1989.

Christ, C. P., and J. Plaskow. *Womanspirit Rising: A Feminist Reader in Religion.* San Francisco: Harper & Row, 1979.

Clements, R., ed. *The World of Ancient Israel: Sociological, Anthropological, and Political Perspectives.* Cambridge: Cambridge University Press, 1989.

Clevenot, M. *Materialist Approaches to the Bible.* Maryknoll, NY: Orbis Books, 1985.

Clines, D. J. A. *Interested Parties: The Ideology of Writers and Readers of the Hebrew Bible.* Journal for the Study of the Old Testament: Supplement Series 205. Sheffield: Sheffield Academic Press, 1995.

Clines, D. J. A., et al., eds. *Art and Meaning: Rhetoric in Biblical Literature.* Sheffield: JSOT Press, 1982.

Coats, G. W. "Tradition Criticism, OT." Pages 912–14 in *The Interpreter's Dictionary of the Bible: Supplementary Volume.* Edited by K. Crim. Nashville: Abingdon, 1976.

Cobb, J. B., Jr. *Process Theology as Political Theology.* Louisville: Westminster John Knox, 1982.

Coggins, R. J., and J. L. Houlden, eds. *A Dictionary of Biblical Interpretation.* Philadelphia: Trinity Press International, 1990.

Cohen, B. J. "On Being a Jewish Father: A Reconstructionist Interpretation of the Akedah." *Reconstructionist* 53, no. 1 (1987): 33–34.

Collins, A. Y., ed. *Feminist Perspectives on Biblical Scholarship.* Chico, CA: Scholars Press, 1985.

Collins, T. "Decoding the Psalms: A Structural Approach to the Psalter." *Journal for the Study of the Old Testament* 37 (1987): 41–60.

Cone, J. H. *A Black Theology of Liberation.* Philadelphia: Lippincott, 1970.

Coote, R. B., and M. P. Coote. *Power, Politics, and the Making of the Bible: An Introduction.* Minneapolis: Fortress, 1990.

Cross, F. M. *Canaanite Myth and Hebrew Epic.* Cambridge, MA: Harvard University Press, 1973.

Crossan, J. D. *Cliffs of Fall: Paradox and Polyvalence in the Parables of Jesus.* New York: Seabury, 1980.

———. *The Dark Interval: Towards a Theology of Story.* Niles, IL: Argus Communications, 1975. Repr., Sonoma, CA: Polebridge, 1991.

Crotwell, H. *Women and the Word: Sermons.* Philadelphia: Fortress, 1977.

Culley, R. *Studies in the Structure of Hebrew Narrative.* Semeia Supplements. Philadelphia: Fortress, 1976.

Culpeper, R. A. *Anatomy of the Fourth Gospel: A Study in Literary Design.* Philadelphia: Fortress, 1983.

Damrosch, D. *The Narrative Covenant: Transformations of Genre in the Growth of Biblical Literature.* San Francisco: Harper & Row, 1987.

Darr, J. *On Character Building: The Reader and the Rhetoric of Characterization.* Louisville: Westminster John Knox, 1992.

Day, P., ed. *Gender and Difference in Ancient Israel.* Minneapolis: Augsburg, 1989.

Demson, D. E. *Hans Frei and Karl Barth: Different Ways of Reading Scripture.* Grand Rapids: Eerdmans, 1997.

Detweiler, R., ed. *Derrida and Biblical Studies. Semeia* 23 (1982).

———, ed. *Reader Response Approaches to Biblical and Secular Texts. Semeia* 31 (1985).

Dibelius, M. *From Tradition to Gospel.* 2nd ed. Cambridge: James Clarke, 1971.

Donaldson, L., ed. *Postcolonialism and Scriptural Reading. Semeia* 75 (1998).

Doty, W. G. "The Concept of Genre in Literary Analysis." Pages 413–48 in vol. 2 of *Society of Biblical Literature 1972 Proceedings.* Edited by L. C. McGaughy. Missoula, MT: Society of Biblical Literature, 1972.

Dozeman, T. B. "Inner-Biblical Interpretation of Yahweh's Gracious and Compassionate Character." *Journal of Biblical Literature* 108, no. 2 (1989): 207–23.

Draisma, S., ed. *Intertextuality in Biblical Writings: Essays in Honor of Bas van Iersel.* Kampen, NL: Hok, 1989.

Eisen, A. "Mordecai Kaplan's Judaism as a Civilization at 70: Setting the Stage for Reappraisal." *Jewish Social Studies* 12, no. 2 (2006): 1–16.

Epp, E. J. *Perspectives on New Testament Textual Criticism: Collected Essays, 1962–2004.* Atlanta: Society of Biblical Literature, 2008.

Epp, E. J., and G. Fee, eds. *New Testament Textual Criticism: Its Significance for Exegesis.* New York: Oxford University Press, 1981.

Epp, E. J., and G. W. MacRae, eds. *The New Testament and Its Modern Interpreters.* Atlanta: Scholars Press, 1989.

Eslinger, L. M. "Inner-Biblical Exegesis and Inner-Biblical Allusion: The Question of Category." *Vetus Testamentum* 42 (1992): 47–58.

———. *Kingship of God in Crisis: A Close Reading of 1 Samuel 1–12.* Sheffield: Almond, 1985.

Estok, S. C. "A Report Card on Ecocriticism." *AUMLA: Journal of Australasian Universities Modern Language Association* 96 (2001): 220–38.

Exum, J. C. *Fragmented Women: Feminist (Sub)Versions of Biblical Narratives.* Valley Forge, PA: Trinity Press International, 1993.

———. "Murder They Wrote: Ideology and the Manipulation of Female Presence in Biblical Narrative." Pages 45–67 in *The Pleasure of Her Text.* Edited by A. Bach. Philadelphia: Trinity Press International. 1990.

———. *Tragedy and Biblical Narrative: Arrows of the Almighty.* Cambridge: Cambridge University Press, 1992.

Exum, J. C., J. W. H. Bos, and A. Y. Collins, eds. *Reasoning with the Foxes: Female Wit in a World of Male Power. Semeia* 42 (1988).

Exum, J. C., and S. Moore, eds. *Biblical Studies / Cultural Studies: The Third Sheffield Colloquium.* Journal for the Study of the Old Testament: Supplement Series 266. Gender, Culture, Theory 7. Sheffield: Sheffield Academic Press, 1998.

Fee, G. *New Testament Exegesis: A Handbook for Students and Pastors.* 3rd ed. Philadelphia: Westminster, 2002.

Felder, C. H., ed. *Stony the Road We Trod: African American Biblical Interpretation.* Minneapolis: Augsburg, 1991.

Fewell, D. N. "Feminist Reading of the Hebrew Bible: Affirmation, Resistance, and Transformation." *Journal for the Study of the Old Testament* 39 (1987): 77–87.

———, ed. *Reading between Texts: Intertextuality and the Hebrew Bible.* Louisville: Westminster John Knox, 1992.

Fewell, D. N., and D. M. Gunn. *Gender, Power, and Promise: The Subject of the Bible's First Story.* Nashville: Abingdon, 1993.

Fortna, R. T. "Redaction Criticism, NT." Pages 733–35 in *The Interpreter's Dictionary of the Bible: Supplementary Volume.* Edited by K. Crim. Nashville: Abingdon, 1976.

Fowl, S. E. *Engaging Scripture: A Model for Theological Interpretation.* Oxford: Blackwell, 1998.

———. "The Ethics of Interpretation; or, What's Left after the Elimination of Meaning." Pages 379–98 in *The Bible in Three Dimensions.* Edited by D. J. A. Clines et al. Sheffield: JSOT Press, 1990.

Fowler, R. M. *Let the Reader Understand: Reader-Response Criticism and the Gospel of Mark.* Minneapolis: Fortress, 1991.

———. "Who Is 'the Reader' in Reader Response Criticism?" *Semeia* 31 (1985): 5–23.

Fox, M. V. *Character and Ideology in the Book of Esther.* Columbia: University of South Carolina Press, 1991.

Freyne, S. *Galilee, Jesus, and the Gospels: Literary Approaches and Historical Investigation.* Philadelphia: Fortress, 1988.

Funk, R. W., ed. *Literary Critical Studies of Biblical Texts. Semeia* 8 (1977).

———. *The Poetics of Biblical Narrative.* Sonoma, CA: Polebridge, 1988.

Gager, J. G. *Kingdom and Community: The Social World of Early Christianity.* Englewood Cliffs, NJ: Prentice Hall, 1975.

Gallagher, S. V., ed. *Postcolonial Literature and the Biblical Call for Justice.* Jackson: University of Mississippi Press, 1994.

Giles, T., and W. J. Doan. *Twice Used Songs: Performance Criticism of the Songs of Ancient Israel.* Peabody, MA: Hendrickson, 2008.

Goldberg, M. *Theology and Narrative: A Critical Introduction.* Nashville: Abingdon, 1982.

Goldingay, J. *Approaches to Old Testament Interpretation.* Updated ed. Leicester, UK: Apollos, 1990.

Gonzalez, J. L., and C. G. Gonzalez. *Liberation Preaching: The Pulpit and the Oppressed.* Nashville: Abingdon, 1980.

Good, E. M. *Irony in the Old Testament.* 2nd ed. Sheffield: Almond, 1981.

Gottwald, N. K. *The Hebrew Bible: A Socio-Literary Introduction.* Philadelphia: Fortress, 1985.

Gottwald, N. K., and R. A. Horsley, eds. *The Bible and Liberation: Political and Social Hermeneutics.* Maryknoll, NY: Orbis Books, 1993.

Gottwald, N. K., and A. C. Wire, eds. *The Bible and Liberation.* Rev. ed. Maryknoll, NY: Orbis Books, 1983.

Grant, P. *Reading the New Testament.* Grand Rapids: Eerdmans; London: Macmillan, 1989.

Grant, R. M., with D. Tracy. *A Short History of the Interpretation of the Bible.* 2nd ed. Philadelphia: Fortress, 1984.

Green, G., ed. *Scriptural Authority and Narrative Interpretation.* Philadelphia: Fortress, 1987.

Greene, G. L. "Relevance Theory and Theological Interpretation: Thoughts on Metarepresentation." *Journal of Theological Interpretation* 4, no. 1 (2010): 75–90.

Greenstein, E. L. "Biblical Narratology." *Prooftexts* 1 (1981): 201–8.

———. "Deconstruction and Biblical Narrative." *Prooftexts* 9 (1989): 43–71.

———. *Essays on Biblical Method and Translation.* Atlanta: Scholars Press, 1989.

———. "Theory and Argument in Biblical Criticism." *Hebrew Annual Review* 10 (1986): 77–93.

Greenwood, D. C. "Poststructuralism and Biblical Studies." Pages 263–88 in vol. 3 of *Gospel Perspectives.* Edited by R. T. France and D. Wenham. Sheffield: JSOT Press, 1983.

———. *Structuralism and the Biblical Text.* Berlin: Mouton, 1985.

Gros Louis, K., et al. *Literary Interpretations of Biblical Narratives.* 2 vols. Nashville: Abingdon, 1974–82.

Gudorf, C. E. "Liberation Theology's Use of Scripture." *Interpretation* 41 (1987): 5–18.

Gunkel, H. *The Legends of Genesis: The Biblical Saga and History.* New York: Schocken, 1964.

Gunn, D. M. "New Directions in the Study of Biblical Hebrew Narrative." *Journal for the Study of the Old Testament* 39 (1987): 65–75.

Gunn, D. M., and D. N. Fewell. *Narrative in the Hebrew Bible.* Oxford: Oxford University Press, 1993.

Gutiérrez, G. *A Theology of Liberation.* Maryknoll, NY: Orbis Books, 1973; London: SCM, 1984.

Gutt, E.-A. "Matthew 9:4–17 in the Light of Relevance Theory." *Notes on Translation* 113 (1986): 13–20.

Habel, N. C. *The Land Is Mine: Six Biblical Land Ideologies.* Overtures to Biblical Theology. Minneapolis: Fortress, 1995.

———. "The Origins and Challenges of an Ecojustice Hermeneutic." Pages 141–59 in *Relating to the Text: Interdisciplinary and Form-Critical Insights on the Bible.* Edited by T. Sandoval and C. Mandolfo. Journal for the Study of the Old Testament: Supplement Series 384. London: T&T Clark, 2003.

———, ed. *Readings from the Perspective of Earth.* Sheffield: Sheffield Academic Press, 2000.

Habel, N. C., D. Rhoads, and H. P. Santmire, eds. *The Season of Creation: A Preaching Commentary.* Minneapolis: Fortress, 2011.

Habel, N. C., and P. Trudinger, eds. *Exploring Ecological Hermeneutics.* Atlanta: Society of Biblical Literature, 2008.

Hampson, D. *Theology and Feminism.* Cambridge, MA: Blackwell, 1990.

Handelman, S. *The Slayers of Moses: The Emergence of Rabbinic Interpretation in Modern Literary Theory.* Albany: State University of New York Press, 1982.

Haskell, P. "Belonging, Behaving, Believing: Exploring Reconstructionist Process." *Reconstructionist* 72, no. 1 (2007): 58–61.

Hayes, J. H., ed. *Dictionary of Biblical Interpretation.* 2 vols. Nashville: Abingdon, 1999.

———. *Old Testament Form Criticism.* San Antonio: Trinity University Press, 1974.

Hayes, J. H., and C. R. Holladay. *Biblical Exegesis: A Beginner's Handbook.* Atlanta: John Knox, 1987.

Haynes, S., and S. McKenzie. *To Each Its Own Meaning: An Introduction to Biblical Criticisms and Their Application.* Rev. ed. Louisville: Westminster John Knox, 1999.

Hebel, U. J. *Intertextuality, Allusion, and Quotation: An International Bibliography of Critical Studies.* New York: Greenwood, 1989.

Henderson, I. *Myth in the New Testament.* London: SCM; Chicago: Regnery, 1952.

Herzog, F. "Liberation Hermeneutic as Ideology Critique?" *Interpretation* 28 (1974): 387–403.

Hilbert, B. S. "Beyond 'Thou Shalt Not': An Ecocritic Reads Deuteronomy." Pages 29–44 in *Beyond Nature Writing: Expanding the Boundaries of Ecocriticism.* Edited by K. Armbruster and K. R. Wallace. Charlottesville: University of Virginia Press, 2001.

Holmberg, G. *Sociology and the New Testament: An Appraisal.* Minneapolis: Fortress, 1990.

Horrell, D. G. *The Bible and the Environment: Towards a Critical Ecological Biblical Theology.* Sheffield: Equinox, 2010.

Horsley, R. *Jesus in Context: Power, People, and Performance.* Minneapolis: Fortress, 2008.

———. *Oral Performance, Popular Tradition, and Hidden Transcript in Q.* Atlanta: Society of Biblical Literature, 2006.

———. *Sociology and the Jesus Movement.* Philadelphia: Fortress, 1989.

Humphreys, W. L. *The Tragic Vision and the Hebrew Tradition.* Philadelphia: Fortress, 1985.

Jackson, J. J., et al. *Rhetorical Criticism.* Pittsburgh: Pickwick, 1974.

Jasper, D. *The New Testament and the Literary Imagination.* London: Macmillan; Atlantic Highlands, NJ: Humanities, 1987.

Jeppesen K., and B. Otzen, eds. *The Productions of Time: Tradition in Old Testament Scholarship.* Sheffield: Almond, 1984.

Jobes, K. H. "Relevance Theory and the Translation of Scripture." *Journal of the Evangelical Theological Society* 50, no. 4 (2007): 773–97.

Jobling, D. *The Sense of Biblical Narrative.* 2 vols. Sheffield: JSOT Press, 1978–86.

Jobling, D., P. L. Day, and G. T. Sheppard. *The Bible and the Politics of Exegesis.* Cleveland: Pilgrim, 1991.

Jobling, D., and S. D. Moore, eds. *Poststructuralism as Exegesis. Semeia* 54 (1991).

Jobling, D., and T. Pippin, eds. *Ideological Criticism of Biblical Texts. Semeia* 59 (1993).

Kaiser, O., and W. G. Kümmel. *Exegetical Method: A Student's Handbook.* New York: Seabury, 1981.

Kaiser, W. C. *Toward an Exegetical Theology: Biblical Exegesis for Preaching and Teaching.* Grand Rapids: Baker, 1981.

Kee, H. C. *Knowing the Truth: A Sociological Approach to New Testament Interpretation.* Philadelphia: Fortress, 1989.

Kelle, B. E., and F. R. Ames, eds. *Writing and Reading War: Rhetoric, Gender, and Ethics in Biblical and Modern Contexts.* Atlanta: Society of Biblical Literature, 2008.

Keller, C. *Apocalypse Now and Then: A Feminist Guide to the End of the World.* Boston: Beacon, 1996.

Kennedy, G. A. *New Testament Interpretation through Rhetorical Criticism.* Chapel Hill: University of North Carolina Press, 1984.

Kirk, J. A. *Liberation Theology.* London: Marshall; Atlanta: John Knox, 1979.

Klein, R. W. *Textual Criticism of the Old Testament: From the Septuagint to Qumran.* Philadelphia: Fortress, 1974.

Koch, K. *Growth of the Biblical Tradition.* New York: Macmillan, 1975.

Kort, W. *Story, Text, and Scripture.* University Park: Pennsylvania State University Press, 1988.

———. *Take, Read: Scripture, Textuality, and Cultural Practice.* University Park: Pennsylvania State University Press, 1996.

Krentz, E. *The Historical-Critical Method.* Philadelphia: Fortress, 1975.

Kuan, J. "Asian Biblical Interpretation." Page 70 in vol. 1 of *Dictionary of Biblical Interpretation.* Edited by J. H. Hayes. Nashville: Abingdon, 1999.

Kugel, J. L. "On the Bible and Literary Criticism," with response by A. Berlin. *Prooftexts* 1 (1981): 217–36; 2 (1982): 323–32.

Kümmel, W. G. *The New Testament: The History of the Investigation of Its Problems*. Translated by M. Gilmour and H. C. Kee. Nashville: Abingdon, 1972.

Küng, H., and J. Moltmann, eds. *Conflicting Ways of Interpreting the Bible*. Concilium 138. Edinburgh: T&T Clark; New York: Seabury, 1980.

Laffey, A. L. *Introduction to the Old Testament: A Feminist Approach*. Philadelphia: Fortress, 1988.

Leach, E. R. *Genesis as Myth and Other Essays*. London: Jonathan Cape, 1969.

Leach, E. R., and D. A. Aycock. *Structuralist Interpretations of Biblical Myth*. Cambridge: Cambridge University Press, 1983.

Lemcio, E. E. "The Gospels and Canonical Criticism." *Biblical Theology Bulletin* 11 (1981): 114–22.

Lerner, G. *The Creation of Patriarchy*. Oxford: Oxford University Press, 1986.

Lines, D. J. A. "Notes for an Old Testament Hermeneutic." *Theology, News and Notes* 21 (1975): 8–10.

Linnemann, E. *Historical Criticism of the Bible*. Grand Rapids: Baker, 1990.

Lohfink, G. *The Bible: Now I Get It! A Form Criticism Handbook*. Garden City, NY: Doubleday, 1979.

Long, T. G. *Preaching and the Literary Forms of the Bible*. Philadelphia: Fortress, 1989.

Longenecker, R. N. *Biblical Exegesis in the Apostolic Period*. Grand Rapids: Eerdmans, 1975.

Loubser, B. "How Do You Report Something That Was Said with a Smile?—Can We Overcome the Loss of Meaning When Oral-Manuscript Texts of the Bible Are Represented in Modern Printed Media?" *Scriptura* 87 (2004): 296–314.

Mack, B. L. *Rhetoric and the New Testament*. Guides to Biblical Scholarship. Minneapolis: Fortress, 1990.

Mackey, L. "Slouching toward Bethlehem: Deconstructive Strategies in Theology." *Anglican Theological Review* 65 (1983): 255–72.

Maguire, D. "The Feminization of God and Ethics." *Christianity and Crisis* 42, no. 4 (1982): 63–66.

Mahan, B., and L. D. Richesin, eds. *The Challenge of Liberation Theology: A First-World Response*. Maryknoll, NY: Orbis Books, 1981.

Maier, G. *The End of the Historical-Critical Method*. St. Louis: Concordia, 1977.

Malbon, E. S., et al., eds. *The New Literary Criticism and the New Testament*. Sheffield: Sheffield University Press, 1994.

Malherbe, A. *Social Aspects of Early Christianity*. 2nd ed. Philadelphia: Fortress, 1983.

Malina, B. *Christian Origins and Cultural Anthropology: Practical Models for Biblical Interpretation*. Atlanta: John Knox, 1986.

———. *The New Testament World: Insights from Cultural Anthropology*. Atlanta: John Knox, 1981.

Marshall, I. H., ed. *New Testament Interpretation: Essays on Principles and Methods*. Grand Rapids: Eerdmans, 1978.

Marxsen, W. *Mark the Evangelist: Studies on the Redaction History of the Gospel*. Translated by J. Boyce et al. Nashville: Abingdon, 1964.

Mayes, A. D. H. *The Story of Israel between Settlement and Exile: A Redactional Study of the Deuteronomistic History*. London: SCM, 1983.

McCarter, P. K., Jr. *Textual Criticism: Recovering the Text of the Hebrew Bible*. Philadelphia: Fortress, 1986.

McConnell, F., ed. *The Bible and the Narrative Tradition*. Oxford: Oxford University Press, 1986.

McFague, S. *Metaphorical Theology: Models of God in Religious Language*. Fortress, 1982.

McKnight, E. V. *The Bible and the Reader*. Philadelphia: Fortress, 1985.

———. *Meaning in Texts*. Philadelphia: Fortress, 1985.

———. *Postmodern Use of the Bible: The Emergence of Reader-Oriented Criticism*. Nashville: Abingdon, 1988.

———, ed. *Reader Perspectives on the New Testament*. *Semeia* 48 (1989).

———. *What Is Form Criticism?* Philadelphia: Fortress, 1969.

Meadowcroft, T. "Relevance as a Mediating Category in the Reading of Biblical Texts: Venturing beyond the Hermeneutical Circle." *Journal of the Evangelical Theological Society* 45, no. 4 (2002): 611–27.

Meeks, W. *The First Urban Christians: The Social World of the Apostle Paul*. New Haven: Yale University Press, 1983.

Menn, E. "Inner-Biblical Exegesis in the Tanak." Pages 55–79 in *The Ancient Period*. Vol. 1 of *A History of Biblical Interpretation*. Edited by A. J. Hauser and D. F. Watson. Grand Rapids: Eerdmans, 2003.

Meyer, B. J. F., and G. E. Rice. "The Interaction of Reader Strategies and the Organization of Text." *Text* 2 (1982): 155–92.

Meyers, C. L. *Discovering Eve: Ancient Israelite Women in Context*. New York: Oxford University Press, 1988.

Mills, K. *Justifying Language: Paul and Contemporary Literary Theory*. New York: St. Martin's Press, 1995.

Miranda, J. *Being and the Messiah*. Maryknoll, NY: Orbis Books, 1977.

———. *Communism in the Bible.* Maryknoll, NY: Orbis Books, 1982.

———. *Marx and the Bible.* Maryknoll, NY: Orbis Books, 1974; London: SCM, 1977.

Miscall, P. D. *The Workings of Old Testament Narrative.* Philadelphia: Fortress, 1983.

Moi, T. *Sexual Textual Politics: Feminist Literary Theory.* New York: Routledge, 1994.

Mollenkott, V. R. *The Divine Feminine: The Biblical Imagery of God as Female.* New York: Crossroad, 1987.

———. *Women, Men, and the Bible.* Nashville: Abingdon, 1977.

Moore, S. D., ed. "Biblical Studies and the New Historicism." *Biblical Interpretation* 5 (1997): 289–99.

———. *Literary Criticism and the Gospels.* New Haven: Yale University Press, 1989.

———. *Poststructuralism and the New Testament: Derrida and Foucault at the Foot of the Cross.* Minneapolis: Fortress, 1994.

Morgan, R., with J. Barton. *Biblical Interpretation.* Oxford: Oxford University Press, 1988.

Mosala, I. J. *Biblical Hermeneutics and Black Theology in South Africa.* Grand Rapids: Eerdmans, 1989.

Neufeld, D. *Reconceiving Texts as Speech Acts: An Analysis of I John.* Leiden: Brill, 1994.

Neuhaus, R. J., ed. *Biblical Interpretation in Crisis.* Grand Rapids: Eerdmans, 1989.

Neusner, J. *Invitation to Midrash: A Teaching Book.* San Francisco: Harper & Row, 1989.

———. *Midrash in Context: Exegesis in Formative Judaism.* Philadelphia: Fortress, 1983.

———. *What Is Midrash?* Philadelphia: Fortress, 1987.

Newsom, C. A., and S. H. Ringe, eds. *The Women's Bible Commentary.* Louisville: Westminster John Knox, 1992.

Neyrey, J., ed. *The Social World of Luke-Acts: Models of Interpretation.* Peabody, MA: Hendrickson, 1991.

Nida, E. A., and C. R. Taber. *The Theory and Practice of Translation.* Leiden: Brill, 1982.

Noth, M. *The Deuteronomistic History.* Journal for the Study of the Old Testament: Supplement Series 15. Sheffield: JSOT Press, 1981.

Osiek, C. "The New Handmaid: The Bible and the Social Sciences." *Theological Studies* 50 (1989): 260–78.

———. *What Are They Saying about the Social Setting of the New Testament?* New York: Paulist Press, 1984.

Ostriker, A. S. *The Nakedness of the Fathers: Biblical Visions and Revisions.* New Brunswick, NJ: Rutgers University Press, 1994.

Pardes, I. *Countertraditions in the Bible: A Feminist Approach.* Cambridge, MA: Harvard University Press, 1992.

Patrick, D., and A. Scult. *Rhetoric and Biblical Interpretation.* Sheffield: Almond, 1990.

Patte, D. *The Religious Dimensions of Biblical Texts: Greimas's Structural Semiotics and Biblical Exegesis.* Semeia Studies 19. Atlanta: Scholars Press, 1990.

———. *Structural Exegesis: From Theory to Practice.* Philadelphia: Fortress, 1978.

———. *What Is Structural Exegesis?* Philadelphia: Fortress, 1976.

Pelias, R. J. *Performance Studies: The Interpretation of Aesthetic Texts.* New York: St. Martin's Press, 1992. 2nd ed., Dubuque, IA: Kendall/Hunt, 2007.

Penchansky, D. *The Betrayal of God: Ideological Conflict in Job.* Literary Currents in Biblical Interpretation. Louisville: Westminster John Knox, 1990.

Perrin, N. *What Is Redaction Criticism?* Philadelphia: Fortress, 1969.

Petersen, N. *Literary Criticism for New Testament Critics.* Philadelphia: Fortress, 1978.

Phillips, G. A., ed. *Poststructural Criticism and the Bible.* Semeia 51 (1990).

Phillips, G. A., and D. N. Fewell, eds. *The Bible and Ethics of Reading.* Semeia 77 (1998).

Pippin, T. *Apocalyptic Bodies: The Biblical End of the World in Text and Image.* New York: Routledge, 1999.

———. "Ideology, Ideological Criticism, and the Bible." *Currents in Research: Biblical Studies* 4 (1996): 51–78.

Pixley, G., and L. Boff. *The Bible, the Church, and the Poor.* Maryknoll, NY: Orbis Books, 1989.

Polzin, R. M. *Biblical Structuralism: Method and Subjectivity in the Study of Ancient Texts.* Philadelphia: Fortress, 1977.

———. *Moses and the Deuteronomist: A Literary Study of the Deuteronomic History.* New York: Seabury, 1980.

Porter, S. E. "Reader-Response Criticism and New Testament Study: A Response to A. C. Thiselton's *New Horizons in Hermeneutics.*" *Journal of Literature and Theology* 8 (1994): 94–102.

———. "Why Hasn't Reader-Response Criticism Caught On in New Testament Studies?" *Literature and Theology* 4 (1990): 278–92.

Powell, M. A. *What Is Narrative Criticism?* Minneapolis: Fortress, 1990.

Poythress, V. S. "Structuralism and Biblical Studies." *Journal of the Evangelical Theological Society* 21 (1978): 221–37.

Preminger, A., and E. L. Greenstein, eds. *The Hebrew Bible in Literary Criticism.* New York: Ungar, 1986.

Rashkow, I. N. *The Phallacy of Genesis: A Feminist-Psychoanalytic Approach.* Louisville: Westminster John Knox, 1993.

Rast, W. E. *Tradition History and the Old Testament.* Philadelphia: Fortress, 1972.

Resseguie, J. "Reader-Response Criticism and the Synoptic Gospels." *Journal of the American Academy of Religion* 52 (1984): 307–24.

Rhoads, D. "Performance Criticism: An Emerging Methodology in Biblical Studies." Paper presented at the annual meeting of the Society of Biblical Literature. New Orleans, November 21, 2009.

Richardson, M. *Black Women and Religion: A Bibliography.* Boston: G. K. Hall, 1980.

Richter, P. J. "Recent Sociological Approaches to the Study of the New Testament." *Religion* 14 (1984): 77–90.

Ringe, S. *Jesus and the Jubilee: Images in Ethics and Christology.* Philadelphia: Fortress, 1985.

Robertson, D. *The Old Testament and the Literary Critic.* Philadelphia: Fortress, 1977.

Rosenberg, J., ed. "Biblical Narrative." Pages 31–82 in *Back to the Sources: Reading the Classic Jewish Texts.* Edited by B. W. Holtz. New York: Touchstone, 1984.

———. *King and Kin: Political Allegory in the Hebrew Bible.* Bloomington: Indiana University Press, 1986.

———. *Religion and Sexism.* New York: Simon & Schuster, 1974.

———, ed. *Sexism and God Talk: Toward a Feminist Theology.* Boston: Beacon, 1983.

Ruether, R. R., and E. McLaughlin. *Women of Spirit.* New York: Simon & Schuster, 1979.

Russell, L. M., ed. *Feminist Interpretation of the Bible.* Philadelphia: Westminster, 1985.

———. *Growth in Partnership.* Philadelphia: Westminster, 1981.

———. *Imitators of God: A Study Book on Ephesians.* New York: Mission Education and Cultivation Program Department for the Women's Division, General Board of Global Ministries, United Methodist Church, 1984.

———, ed. *The Liberating Word: A Guide to Nonsexist Interpretation of the Bible.* Philadelphia: Westminster, 1976.

Ryken, L., ed. *The New Testament in Literary Criticism.* New York: Ungar, 1984.

Sackenfeld, K. D. *Faithfulness in Action: Loyalty in Biblical Perspective.* Philadelphia: Fortress, 1985.

Sanders, J. A. *Canon and Community: A Guide to Canonical Criticism.* Philadelphia: Fortress, 1984.

———. *From Sacred Story to Sacred Text.* Philadelphia: Fortress, 1987.

———. *Torah and Canon.* Philadelphia: Fortress, 1974.

Schüssler Fiorenza, E. *Bread Not Stone: Introduction to a Feminist Interpretation of Scripture.* Boston: Beacon, 1985.

———. *But She Said: Feminist Practices of Biblical Interpretation.* Boston: Beacon, 1992.

———. *In Memory of Her: A Feminist Theological Reconstruction of Christian Origins.* New York: Crossroad, 1983.

———. *Rhetoric and Ethic: The Politics of Biblical Studies.* Minneapolis: Fortress, 1999.

———, ed. *Searching the Scriptures: A Feminist Introduction.* New York: Crossroad, 1993.

———. "Toward a Feminist Biblical Hermeneutics: Biblical Interpretation and Liberation Theology." Pages 91–112 in *The Challenge of Liberation Theology: A First-World Response.* Edited by B. Mahan and L. D. Richesin. Maryknoll, NY: Orbis Books, 1981.

Schwartz, R., ed. *The Book and the Text: The Bible and Literary Theory.* Oxford: Blackwell, 1990.

Segovia, F. F., and M. A. Tolbert, eds. *Social Location and Biblical Interpretation in the United States.* Vol. 1 of *Reading from This Place.* Minneapolis: Fortress, 1995.

Segundo, J. L. *The Liberation of Theology.* Maryknoll, NY: Orbis Books, 1976.

Silva, M. *God, Language, and Scripture: Reading the Bible in the Light of General Linguistics.* Grand Rapids: Zondervan, 1990.

Snell-Hornby, M. *Translation Studies: An Integrated Approach.* Amsterdam: John Benjamins, 1988.

Sonnet, J. *The Book within the Book: Writing in Deuteronomy.* Biblical Interpretation Series 14. Leiden: Brill, 1997.

Soulen, R. N., and R. K. Soulen. *Handbook of Biblical Criticism.* 3rd ed. Louisville: Westminster John Knox, 2001.

Stanton, E. C., and the Revising Committee. *The Woman's Bible.* 2 vols. New York: European Publishing, 1895–98.

Staub, J. J. "A Reconstructionist View on Patrilineal Descent." *Judaism* 34, no. 1 (1985): 97–106.

Steiner, G. *After Babel: Aspects of Language and Translation.* Oxford: Oxford University Press, 1975.

Stroup, G. W. "Between Echo and Narcissus: The Role of the Bible in Feminist Theology." *Interpretation* 42 (1988): 19–32.

Stuart, D. *Old Testament Exegesis: A Primer for Students and Pastors.* Philadelphia: Westminster, 1984.

Stuart, E., et al. *Religion Is a Queer Thing: A Guide to the Christian Faith for Lesbian, Gay, Bisexual, and Transgendered People.* Cleveland: Pilgrim, 1997.

Sugirtharajah, R. S., ed. *The Postcolonial Bible.* Sheffield: Sheffield Academic Press, 1998.

———, ed. *Voices from the Margin: Interpreting the Bible in the Third World.* Maryknoll, NY: Orbis Books, 1991.

Suleiman, S. R., and I. Crosman, eds. *The Reader in the Text: Essays on Audience and Interpretation.* Princeton: Princeton University Press, 1980.

Sullivan, R. R. *Political Hermeneutics: The Early Thinking of Hans-Georg Gadamer.* University Park: Pennsylvania State University Press, 1989.

Taber, C. R. "Translation as Interpretation." *Interpretation* 32 (1978): 130–43.

Taylor, V. *The Formation of the Gospel Tradition.* 2nd ed. London: Macmillan, 1935.

Tolbert, M. A., ed. *The Bible and Feminist Hermeneutics. Semeia* 28 (1983).

Trible, P. *God and the Rhetoric of Sexuality.* Philadelphia: Fortress, 1978.

———. *Texts of Terror.* Philadelphia: Fortress, 1984.

Tucker, G. *Form Criticism of the Old Testament.* Philadelphia: Fortress, 1971.

Tuckett, C. *Reading the New Testament: Methods of Interpretation.* Philadelphia: Fortress, 1987.

Vanhoozer, K. J., ed. *Dictionary for Theological Interpretation of the Bible.* Grand Rapids: Baker Academic, 2005.

———, ed. *Theological Interpretation of the New Testament: A Book-by-Book Survey.* Grand Rapids: Baker Academic, 2008.

———, ed. *Theological Interpretation of the Old Testament: A Book-by-Book Survey.* Grand Rapids: Baker Academic, 2008.

———. "What Is Theological Interpretation of the Bible?" Pages 21–25 in *Dictionary for Theological Interpretation of the Bible.* Edited by K. J. Vanhoozer. Grand Rapids: Baker Academic, 2005.

Vaux, R. de *The Bible and the Ancient Near East.* Garden City, NY: Doubleday, 1971.

Via, D. *Kerygma and Comedy in the New Testament: A Structuralist Approach to Hermeneutics.* Philadelphia: Fortress, 1975.

Wachtel, K., and M. W. Holmes, eds. *The Textual History of the Greek New Testament: Changing Views in Contemporary Research.* Atlanta: Society of Biblical Literature, 2011.

Wahlberg, R. C. *Jesus according to a Woman.* New York: Paulist Press, 1975.

———. *Jesus and the Freed Woman.* New York: Paulist Press, 1978.

Walhout, C., and L. Ryken, eds. *Contemporary Literary Theory: A Christian Appraisal.* Grand Rapids: Eerdmans, 1991.

Warner, M., ed. *The Bible as Rhetoric.* London: Routledge, 1990.

Weems, R. *Just a Sister Away: A Womanist Vision of Women's Relationships in the Bible.* San Diego, CA: LuraMedia, 1988.

Weingreen, J. *Introduction to the Critical Study of the Text of the Hebrew Bible.* New York: Oxford University Press, 1982.

Wharton, J. A. "Redaction Criticism, OT." Pages 729–32 in *The Interpreter's Dictionary of the Bible: Supplementary Volume.* Edited by K. Crim. Nashville: Abingdon, 1976.

White, H. C. *Narration and Discourse in the Book of Genesis.* Cambridge: Cambridge University Press, 1991.

———, ed. *Speech Act Theory and Biblical Criticism. Semeia* 41 (1987).

Wilder, A. *The Bible and the Literary Critic.* Minneapolis: Augsburg Fortress, 1991.

Wilson, R. R. *Sociological Approaches to the Old Testament.* Philadelphia: Fortress, 1984.

Yee, G., ed. *Judges and Method: New Approaches in Biblical Studies.* Minneapolis: Fortress, 1995.

Yoder, P. *From Word to Life: A Guide to the Art of Biblical Study.* Scottdale, PA: Herald, 1982.

HERMENEUTICS

Achtemeier, P. J. *An Introduction to the New Hermeneutic.* Philadelphia: Westminster, 1969.

Aland, K., and B. Aland. *The Text of the New Testament: An Introduction to the Critical Editions and to the Theory and Practice of Modern Textual Criticism.* Grand Rapids: Eerdmans, 1987.

Althaus-Reid, M. "The Hermeneutics of Transgression." Pages 251–72 in *Liberation Theologies on Shifting Grounds: A Clash of Socio-Economic and Cultural*

Paradigms. Edited by G. de Schrijver. Leuven: Leuven University Press, 1998.

Bartholomew, C., C. S. Evans, M. Healy, and M. Rae, eds. *"Behind" the Text: History and Biblical Interpretation.* Scripture and Hermeneutics Series 4. Grand Rapids: Zondervan, 2003.

Bartholomew, C., C. Greene, and K. Möller, eds. *After Pentecost: Language and Biblical Interpretation.* Scripture and Hermeneutics Series 2. Grand Rapids: Zondervan, 2001.

————, eds. *Renewing Biblical Interpretation.* Scripture and Hermeneutics Series 1. Grand Rapids: Zondervan, 2000.

Bartholomew, C., S. Hahn, R. Parry, C. Seitz, and A. Wolters, eds. *Canon and Biblical Interpretation.* Scripture and Hermeneutics Series 7. Grand Rapids: Zondervan, 2006.

Bartholomew, C., M. Healy, K. Möller, and R. Parry, eds. *Out of Egypt: Biblical Theology and Biblical Interpretation.* Scripture and Hermeneutics Series 5. Grand Rapids: Zondervan, 2006.

Bauer, D. R., and R. A. Traina. *Inductive Bible Study: A Comprehensive Guide to the Practice of Hermeneutics.* Grand Rapids: Baker Academic, 2011.

Berger, Y. "Ruth and Inner-Biblical Allusion: The Case of 1 Samuel 25." *Journal of Biblical Literature* 128, no. 2 (2009): 253–72.

Bernstein, R. J. *Beyond Objectivism and Relativism: Science, Hermeneutics, and Praxis.* Philadelphia: University of Pennsylvania Press, 1983.

Black, D. A., and D. S. Dockery, eds. *New Testament Criticism and Interpretation.* Grand Rapids: Zondervan, 1991.

Black, F., ed. *The Recycled Bible: Autobiography, Culture, and the Space Between.* Atlanta: Society of Biblical Literature, 2006.

Bleicher, J. *Contemporary Hermeneutics: Hermeneutics as Method, Philosophy, and Critique.* Boston: Routledge & Kegan Paul, 1980.

Blomberg, C. L., and J. F. Markley. *A Handbook of New Testament Exegesis.* Grand Rapids: Baker Academic, 2010.

Boer, R., ed. *Bakhtin and Genre Theory in Biblical Studies.* Atlanta: Society of Biblical Literature, 2007.

Boers, H. "Theology, New Testament." Pages 556–62 in vol. 2 of *Dictionary of Biblical Interpretation.* Edited by J. H. Hayes. Nashville: Abingdon, 1999.

Boff, C. "Hermeneutics: Constitution of Theological Pertinency." Pages 9–35 in *Voices from the Margin: Interpreting the Bible in the Third World.* Edited by R. S. Sugirtharajah. London: SPCK, 1991.

Botta, A. F., and P. R. Andiñach. *The Bible and the Hermeneutics of Liberation.* Atlanta: Society of Biblical Literature, 2009.

Braaten, C. E. *History and Hermeneutics.* Philadelphia: Westminster, 1966; London: Lutterworth, 1968.

Bray, G. L. *Biblical Interpretation: Past and Present.* Downers Grove, IL: IVP Academic, 2000.

Bruns, G. L. *Hermeneutics Ancient and Modern.* New Haven: Yale University Press, 1992.

Cady, L. E. "Hermeneutics and Tradition." *Harvard Theological Review* 79 (1986): 439–63.

Caputo, J. D. *Radical Hermeneutics: Repetition, Deconstruction, and the Hermeneutic Project.* Bloomington: Indiana University Press, 1987.

Carson, D. A. *Biblical Interpretation and the Church.* Nashville: Nelson, 1984.

Carson, D. A., and J. D. Woodbridge, eds. *Hermeneutics, Authority, and Canon.* Grand Rapids: Zondervan, 1986.

————, eds. *Scripture and Truth.* Grand Rapids: Zondervan, 1983.

Cavalcanti, T. "Social Location and Biblical Interpretation: Tropical Reading." Pages 201–18 in *Social Location and Biblical Interpretation in Global Perspective.* Vol. 2 of *Reading from This Place,* edited by F. F. Segovia and M. A. Tolbert. Minneapolis: Fortress, 1995.

Clines, D. J. A. "Deconstructing the Book of Job." Pages 65–80 in *The Bible as Rhetoric: Studies in Biblical Persuasion and Credibility.* Edited by M. Warner. London: Routledge, 1990.

Collins, A. Y., ed. *Feminist Perspectives on Biblical Scholarship.* Chico, CA: Scholars Press, 1985.

Cottrell, P., and M. Turner. *Linguistics and Biblical Interpretation.* Downers Grove, IL: InterVarsity, 1989.

Croatto, J. S. *Biblical Hermeneutics.* Maryknoll, NY: Orbis Books, 1987.

Crossan, J. D. *The Dark Interval: Towards a Theology of Story.* Niles, IL: Argus Communications, 1975.

————, ed. *Paul Ricoeur on Biblical Hermeneutics. Semeia* 4 (1975).

Croy, N. C. *Prima Scriptura: An Introduction to New Testament Interpretation.* Grand Rapids: Baker Academic, 2011.

De Groot, C., and M. A. Taylor, eds. *Recovering Nineteenth-Century Women Interpreters of the Bible.* Atlanta: Society of Biblical Literature, 2007.

Deppe, D. B. *All Roads Lead to the Text: Eight Methods of Inquiry into the Bible.* Grand Rapids: Eerdmans, 2011.

Dilthey, W. "The Rise of Hermeneutics." Translated by F. Jameson. *New Literary History* 3 (1972): 229–44.

Dockery, D. S. *Biblical Interpretation Then and Now: Contemporary Hermeneutics in the Light of the Early Church.* Grand Rapids: Baker, 1992.

Duvall, J. S., and J. D. Hays. *Grasping God's Word: A Hands-On Approach to Reading, Interpreting, and Applying the Bible.* 2nd ed. Grand Rapids: Zondervan, 2005.

Dyck, E., ed. *The Act of Bible Reading.* Downers Grove, IL: InterVarsity, 1996.

Efird, J. M. *How to Interpret the Bible.* Atlanta: John Knox, 1984.

Epp, E. J., and G. W. MacRae, eds. *The New Testament and Its Modern Interpreters.* Atlanta: Scholars Press, 1989.

Erikson, M. J. *Evangelical Interpretation: Perspectives on Hermeneutical Issues.* Grand Rapids: Baker, 1993.

Farmer, R. L. *Beyond the Impasse: The Promise of a Process Hermeneutic.* Macon, GA: Mercer University Press, 1997.

Fee, G. D. *New Testament Exegesis: A Handbook for Students and Pastors.* 3rd ed. Louisville: Westminster John Knox, 2002.

Fee, G. D., and D. Stuart. *How to Read the Bible for All Its Worth.* 3rd ed. Grand Rapids: Zondervan, 2003.

Ferguson, D. S. *Biblical Hermeneutics: An Introduction.* Atlanta: John Knox, 1986; London: SCM, 1987.

Fishbane, M. *Biblical Interpretation in Ancient Israel.* New York: Oxford University Press, 1986.

———. *Garments of Torah: Essays in Biblical Hermeneutics.* Bloomington: Indiana University Press, 1989.

Fowl, S. E. *Engaging Scripture: A Model for Theological Interpretation.* New York: Blackwell, 1998.

Frame, J. M. "The Spirit and the Scriptures." Pages 213–35 in *Hermeneutics, Authority, and Canon.* Edited by D. A. Carson and J. D. Woodbridge. Grand Rapids: Zondervan, 1986.

Frei, H. *The Eclipse of Biblical Narrative: A Study in Eighteenth- and Nineteenth-Century Hermeneutics.* New Haven: Yale University Press, 1974.

Froehlich, K. *Biblical Interpretation in the Early Church.* Philadelphia: Fortress, 1985.

Funk, R. W. *Language, Hermeneutic, and Word of God.* New York: Harper, 1966.

Gadamer, H. *Philosophical Hermeneutics.* Edited and translated by D. E. Linge. Berkeley: University of California Press, 1976.

———. *Truth and Method.* Translated by G. Broden and J. Cumming. 2nd ed. New York: Crossroad, 1982.

Georgi, D. *The City in the Valley: Biblical Interpretation and Urban Theology.* Atlanta: Society of Biblical Literature, 2005.

Gerber, K. G., and W. Swartley, eds. *Perspectives on Feminist Hermeneutics.* Elkhart, IN: Institute of Mennonite Studies, 1987.

Goldingay, J. "The Hermeneutics of Liberation Theology." *Horizons in Biblical Theology* 4, no. 2 (1982): 133–61.

———. *Key Questions about Biblical Interpretation: Old Testament Answers.* Grand Rapids: Baker Academic, 2011.

Goldsworthy, G. *Gospel-Centered Hermeneutics: Foundations and Principles of Evangelical Biblical Interpretation.* Downers Grove, IL: IVP Academic, 2010.

Gooder, P. *Searching for Meaning: An Introduction to Interpreting the New Testament.* Louisville: Westminster John Knox, 2008.

Gorman, M. J. *Elements of Biblical Exegesis: A Basic Guide for Students and Ministers.* Revised and expanded ed. Grand Rapids: Baker Academic, 2008.

Gottwald, N. K. *The Bible and Liberation: Political and Social Hermeneutics.* Maryknoll, NY: Orbis Books, 1983.

———. *The Hebrew Bible: A Brief Socio-Literary Introduction.* Edited by R. J. Kruger-Gaudino. Abridged ed. Minneapolis: Fortress, 2009.

———. "Sociological Method in the Study of Ancient Israel." Pages 142–53 in *The Bible and Liberation: Political and Social Hermeneutics.* Edited by N. K. Gottwald. Maryknoll, NY: Orbis Books, 1983.

Grant, P. *Reading the New Testament.* London: Macmillan, 1989.

Grant, R. M., and D. Tracy. *A Short History of the Interpretation of the Bible.* 2nd ed. Philadelphia: Fortress, 1984.

Green, J. B. "Modernity, History and the Interpretation of the Bible." *Scottish Journal of Theology* 54, no. 3 (2001): 308–29.

———. *Practicing Theological Interpretation: Engaging Biblical Texts for Faith and Formation.* Grand Rapids: Baker Academic, 2012.

———. "Rethinking 'History' for Theological Interpretation." *Journal of Theological Interpretation* 5, no. 2 (2011): 159–73.

Gruenler, R. G. *Meaning and Understanding: The Philosophical Framework for Biblical Interpretation.* Foundation of Contemporary Interpretation 2. Grand Rapids: Academie Books, 1991.

Harris, S. L. "'Figure' and 'Riddle': Prov 1:8–19 and Inner-Biblical Interpretation." *Biblical Research* 41 (1996): 58–76.

Hayes, J. H., ed. *Dictionary of Biblical Interpretation*. 2 vols. Nashville: Abingdon, 1999.

Hayes, J. H., and C. R. Holladay. *Biblical Exegesis: A Beginner's Handbook*. 3rd ed. Louisville: Westminster John Knox, 2007.

Haynes, S. R., and S. L. McKenzie, eds. *To Each Its Own Meaning: An Introduction to Biblical Criticisms and Their Application*. Revised and expanded ed. Louisville: Westminster John Knox, 1999.

Helmer, C., ed. *Biblical Interpretation: History, Context, and Reality*. Atlanta: Society of Biblical Literature, 2005.

———, ed. *The Multivalence of Biblical Texts and Theological Meanings*. Atlanta: Society of Biblical Literature, 2006.

Henn, T. R. *Talking the Talk*. Cambridge: Lutterworth, 2008.

Hirsch, E. D. *Validity in Interpretation*. New Haven: Yale University Press, 1967.

Holter, K., and L. C. Jonker, eds. *Global Hermeneutics? Reflections and Consequences*. Atlanta: Society of Biblical Literature, 2010.

Howard, R. J. *Three Faces of Hermeneutics*. Los Angeles: University of California Press, 1982.

Johnson, E. E. *Expository Hermeneutics*. Grand Rapids: Zondervan, 1990.

Jones, G. V. *The Art and Truth of the Parables: A Study in Their Literary Form and Modern Interpretation*. London: SPCK, 1964.

Juhl, P. D. *Interpretation*. Princeton: Princeton University Press, 1980.

Kaiser, O., and W. G. Kümmel. *Exegetical Method: A Student's Handbook*. Rev. ed. New York: Seabury, 1981.

Kaiser, W. C. *Toward an Exegetical Theology: Biblical Principles for Preaching and Teaching*. Grand Rapids: Baker, 1981.

Kaiser, W. C., and M. Silva. *An Introduction to Biblical Hermeneutics: The Search for Meaning*. 2nd ed. Grand Rapids: Zondervan, 2007.

Kermode, F. *The Genesis of Secrecy: On the Interpretation of Narrative*. Cambridge, MA: Harvard University Press, 1979.

Klein, W. W., C. L. Blomberg, and R. L. Hubbard Jr. *Introduction to Biblical Interpretation*. Dallas: Word, 1993.

Klemm, D., ed. *Hermeneutical Inquiry*. 2 vols. Atlanta: Scholars Press, 1986.

Kogler, H. H. *The Power of Dialogue: Critical Hermeneutics after Gadamer and Foucault*. Cambridge, MA: MIT Press, 1996.

Kugel, J. L., and R. A. Greer. *Early Biblical Interpretation*. Philadelphia: Westminster, 1986.

Kuhn, K. A. *The Heart of Biblical Narrative: Rediscovering Biblical Appeal to the Emotions*. Minneapolis: Fortress, 2008.

Küng, H., and J. Moltmann, eds. *Conflicting Ways of Interpreting the Bible*. Concilium 138. Edinburgh: T&T Clark; New York: Seabury, 1980.

Larkin, W. J., Jr. *Culture and Biblical Hermeneutics: Interpreting and Applying the Authoritative Word in a Relativistic Age*. Grand Rapids: Baker, 1988.

LeMon, J. M., and K. H. Richards, eds. *Method Matters: Essays on the Interpretation of the Hebrew Bible in Honor of David L. Petersen*. Atlanta: Society of Biblical Literature, 2009.

Lim, J. T. K. "Theological Hermeneutics: A Reading Strategy." *Asia Journal of Theology* 15, no. 1 (2001): 2–13.

Longman, T., III. *Literary Approaches to Biblical Interpretation*. Foundations for Contemporary Interpretation 3. Grand Rapids: Zondervan, 1987.

Love, S. *Jesus and Marginal Women: The Gospel of Matthew in Social-Scientific Perspective*. Cambridge: Clarke, 2010.

Loya, M. T. "'Therefore the Earth Mourns': The Grievance of Earth in Hosea 4:1–3." Pages 53–62 in *Exploring Ecological Hermeneutics*. Edited by N. Habel and P. Trudinger. Atlanta: Society of Biblical Literature, 2008.

Lundin, R. *The Culture of Interpretation: Christian Faith and the Postmodern World*. Grand Rapids: Eerdmans, 1993.

———, ed. *Disciplining Hermeneutics: Interpretation in Christian Perspective*. Grand Rapids: Eerdmans, 1997.

Lundin, R., A. C. Thiselton, and C. Walhout. *The Responsibility of Hermeneutics*. Grand Rapids: Eerdmans; Exeter, UK: Paternoster, 1985.

Marrow, S. B. *Basic Tools of Biblical Exegesis*. Rome: Biblical Institute Press, 1978.

McGowan, A. B., and K. H. Richards, eds. *Method and Meaning: Essays on New Testament Interpretation in Honor of Harold W. Attridge*. Atlanta: Society of Biblical Literature, 2011.

McKim, D. K., ed. *A Guide to Contemporary Hermeneutics.* Grand Rapids: Eerdmans, 1986.

McKnight, E. V. *Meaning in Texts: The Historical Shaping of a Narrative Hermeneutics.* Philadelphia: Fortress, 1978.

———. *Postmodern Use of the Bible.* Nashville: Abingdon, 1988.

McKnight, S. *The Blue Parakeet: Rethinking How You Read the Bible.* Grand Rapids: Zondervan, 2008.

Mickelsen, A. B. *Interpreting the Bible.* Grand Rapids: Eerdmans, 1963.

Moore, S. D. *The Bible in Theory: Critical and Postcritical Essays.* Atlanta: Society of Biblical Literature, 2010.

———. "Negative Hermeneutics, Insubstantial Texts: Stanley Fish and the Biblical Interpreter." *Journal of the American Academy of Religion* 54 (1986): 707–19.

Mootz, F. J., III. "Belief and Interpretation: Meditations on Pelikan's 'Interpreting the Bible and the Constitution.'" *Journal of Law & Religion* 21, no. 2 (2005): 385–99.

Morgan, R., and J. Barton. *Biblical Interpretation.* New York: Oxford University Press, 1988.

Mosala, I. J. *Biblical Hermeneutics and Black Theology in South Africa.* Grand Rapids: Eerdmans, 1989.

Mueller-Vollimer, K., ed. *The Hermeneutics Reader.* New York: Crossroad, 1985; Oxford: Blackwell, 1986.

Najman, H., and J. H. Newman, eds. *The Idea of Biblical Interpretation: Essays in Honor of James L. Kugel.* Atlanta: Society of Biblical Literature, 2009.

Neill, S. *The Interpretation of the New Testament, 1861–1986.* 2nd ed. Oxford: Oxford University Press, 1988.

Noble, P. R. "Hermeneutics and Postmodernism: Can We Have a Radical Reader-Response Theory? Part I." *Religious Studies* 30 (1984): 319–36.

Olthuis, J., et al. *A Hermeneutics of Ultimacy: Peril or Promise.* New York: University Press of America, 1987.

Osborn, G. R. *The Hermeneutical Spiral: A Comprehensive Introduction to Biblical Interpretation.* Downers Grove, IL: InterVarsity, 1991.

———. "Hermeneutics and Women in the Church." *Journal of the Evangelical Theological Society* 20, no. 4 (1977): 337–52.

Palmer, R. E. *Hermeneutics: Interpretation Theory in Schleiermacher, Dilthey, Heidegger, and Gadamer.* Evanston, IL: Northwestern University Press, 1969.

Poland, L. M. *Literary Criticism and Biblical Hermeneutics.* Chico, CA: Scholars Press, 1985.

Porter, S. E., and J. C. Robinson. *Hermeneutics: An Introduction to Interpretive Theory.* Grand Rapids: Eerdmans, 2011.

Posen, F. "An Experiment Whose Time Is Yet to Come." *Jewish Chronicle,* June 1, 2001. The Center for Cultural Judaism. http://www.culturaljudaism.org/ccj/articles/24.

Poythress, V. S. *Science and Hermeneutics: Implications of Scientific Method for Biblical Interpretation.* Foundations for Contemporary Interpretation 6. Grand Rapids: Academie Books, 1988.

Pregeant, R. *Encounter with the New Testament: An Interdisciplinary Approach.* Minneapolis: Fortress, 2009.

Prickett, S. *Words and the Word: Language, Poetics, and Biblical Interpretation.* Cambridge: Cambridge University Press, 1986.

Ramm, B. *Hermeneutics.* Grand Rapids: Baker, 1961.

———. *Protestant Biblical Interpretation.* 3rd ed. Grand Rapids: Baker, 1970.

Reventlow, H. G. *From Late Antiquity to the End of the Middle Ages.* Translated by J. O. Duke. Vol. 2 of *History of Biblical Interpretation.* Atlanta: Society of Biblical Literature, 2010.

———. *From the Old Testament to Origen.* Translated by L. G. Perdue. Vol. 1 of *History of Biblical Interpretation.* Atlanta: Society of Biblical Literature, 2009.

Ricoeur, P. "Biblical Hermeneutics: The Metaphorical Process." *Semeia* 4 (1975): 75–106.

———. *The Conflict of Interpretations: Essays in Hermeneutics.* Evanston, IL: Northwestern University Press, 1974.

———. *Essays on Biblical Interpretation.* Philadelphia: Fortress, 1980; London: SPCK, 1981.

———. "Toward a Hermeneutic of the Idea of Revelation." Pages 73–118 in *Essays on Biblical Interpretation.* Edited by L. S. Mudge. Philadelphia: Fortress, 1980.

Robinson, J. M., and J. B. Cobb, eds. *The New Hermeneutic.* New York and London: Harper, 1964.

Rogers, J. B., and D. K. McKim. *The Authority and Interpretation of the Bible.* New York: Harper & Row, 1979.

Rogerson, J., C. Rowland, and B. Lindars. *The Study and Use of the Bible.* Grand Rapids: Eerdmans, 1988.

Rosen, S. *Hermeneutics as Politics.* New York: Oxford University Press, 1987.

Rowland, C., and M. Corner. *Liberating Exegesis.* London: SPCK; Louisville: Westminster John Knox, 1990.

Sandy-Wunsch, J. "Theology, Biblical (to 1800)." Pages 553–56 in vol. 2 of *Dictionary of Biblical Interpretation*. Edited by J. H. Hayes. Nashville: Abingdon, 1999.

Schleiermacher, F. D. E. *Hermeneutics and Criticism, and Other Writings*. Edited by A. Bowie. Cambridge: Cambridge University Press, 1808.

———. *Hermeneutics: The Handwritten Manuscripts*. Edited by H. Kimmerle. Missoula, MT: Scholars Press, 1977.

Schneiders, S. M. "Feminist Ideology Criticism and Biblical Hermeneutics." *Biblical Theology Bulletin* 19 (1989): 3–10.

Schüssler Fiorenza, E. *Democratizing Biblical Studies: Toward an Emancipatory Educational Space*. Louisville: Westminster John Knox, 2009.

———. "The Ethics of Biblical Interpretation." *Journal of Biblical Literature* 107 (1988): 3–17.

Segundo, J. L. *Liberation of Theology*. Maryknoll, NY: Orbis Books, 1976; Dublin: Gill & Macmillan, 1977.

Seitz, C. R. *Prophecy and Hermeneutics: Toward a New Introduction to the Prophets*. Grand Rapids: Baker Academic, 2007.

Silverman, H. J., ed. *Gadamer and Hermeneutics*. New York: Routledge, 1991.

Soulen, R. K. "The Believer and the Historian: Theological Interpretation and Historical Investigation." *Interpretation* 57, no. 2 (2003): 174–86.

Soulen, R. N. *Sacred Scripture: A Short History of Interpretation*. Louisville: Westminster John Knox, 2010.

Stacey, D. *Interpreting the Bible*. London: Sheldon, 1976.

Stein, R. H. *A Basic Guide to Interpreting the Bible: Playing by the Rules*. 2nd ed. Grand Rapids: Baker Academic, 2011.

Stone, K. "The Hermeneutics of Abomination: On Gay Men, Canaanites, and Biblical Interpretation." *Biblical Theology Bulletin* 27 (1997): 36–41.

Stuart, D. *Old Testament Exegesis: A Primer for Students and Pastors*. Philadelphia: Westminster, 1980.

Sugirtharajah, R. S. *Asian Biblical Hermeneutics and Postcolonialism: Contesting the Interpretations*. Maryknoll, NY: Orbis Books, 1998.

Sullivan, R. R. *Political Hermeneutics: The Early Thinking of Hans-Georg Gadamer*. University Park: Pennsylvania State University Press, 1989.

Tate, W. R. *Biblical Interpretation: An Integrated Approach*. Rev. ed. Peabody, MA: Hendrickson, 1996.

Terry, M. S. *Biblical Hermeneutics: A Treatise on the Interpretation of the Old and New Testaments*. Grand Rapids: Zondervan, 1974.

Thatcher, T., and S. D. Moore, eds. *Anatomies of Narrative Criticism: The Past, Present, and Futures of the Fourth Gospel as Literature*. Atlanta: Society of Biblical Literature, 2008.

Thiselton, A. C. "Authority and Hermeneutics: Some Proposals for a New Agenda." Pages 107–41 in *A Pathway into the Holy Scripture*. Edited by P. E. Satterthwaite and D. F. Wright. Grand Rapids: Eerdmans, 1994.

———. *Interpreting God and the Postmodern Self: On Meaning, Manipulation, and Promise*. Grand Rapids: Eerdmans, 1995.

———. *New Horizons in Hermeneutics: The Theory and Practice of Transforming Biblical Reading*. Grand Rapids: Zondervan, 1992.

———. *The Two Horizons: New Testament Hermeneutics and Philosophical Description, with Special Reference to Heidegger, Bultmann, Gadamer, and Wittgenstein*. Grand Rapids: Eerdmans, 1980.

———. "Understanding God's Word Today." Pages 90–122 in vol. 1 of *Obeying Christ in a Changing World*. Edited by John Stott. 3 vols. London: Collins, 1977.

———. "The Use of Philosophical Categories in New Testament Hermeneutics." *Churchman* 87 (1973): 87–100.

Thiselton, A. C., R. Ludin, and C. Walhout. *The Responsibility of Hermeneutics*. Grand Rapids: Eerdmans, 1985.

Thoma, C., and M. Wyschogrod, eds. *Understanding Scripture*. Mahwah, NJ: Paulist Press, 1987.

Thompson, J. B. *Critical Hermeneutics*. Cambridge: Cambridge University Press, 1981.

Tolbert, M. A. *Perspectives on the Parables: An Approach to Multiple Interpretations*. Philadelphia: Fortress, 1979.

Treier, D. J. *Introducing Theological Interpretation of Scripture: Recovering a Christian Practice*. Grand Rapids: Baker Academic, 2008.

Trible, P. "Depatriarchalizing in Biblical Interpretation." *Journal of the American Academy of Religion* 41 (1973): 30–48.

Vanhoozer, K. J. "Exegesis and Hermeneutics." Pages 52–63 in *New Dictionary of Biblical Theology: Exploring the Unity and Diversity of Scripture*. Edited by T. D. Alexander and B. S. Rosner. Downers Grove, IL: InterVarsity, 2000.

———. *Is There a Meaning in This Text? The Bible, the Reader, and the Morality of Literary Knowledge*. Grand Rapids: Zondervan, 1998.

———. "Theological Method." Pages 889–98 in *Global Dictionary of Theology: A Resource for the Worldwide Church*. Edited by W. A. Dyrness and V-M. Kärkkäinen. Downers Grove, IL: IVP Academic, 2008.

Van Til, C. *The New Hermeneutic*. Nutley, NJ: P&R, 1977.

Vattimo, G. *Beyond Interpretation: The Meaning of Hermeneutics for Philosophy*. Translated by D. Webb. Cambridge: Polity, 1997.

———. *The End of Modernity: Nihilism and Hermeneutics in Post-modern Culture*. Translated by J. R. Snyder. Baltimore: Johns Hopkins University Press, 1985.

———. "Hermeneutics as *Koinē*." Translated by P. Caravetta. *Theory, Culture and Society* 5 (1988): 2–3.

Wachtel, K., and M. W. Holmes, eds. *The Textual History of the Greek New Testament: Changing Views in Contemporary Research*. Atlanta: Society of Biblical Literature, 2011.

Wachterhauser, B. R., ed. *Hermeneutics and Modern Philosophy*. Albany: State University of New York Press, 1986.

Wadsworth, M., ed. *Ways of Reading the Bible*. Brighton, UK: Harvester; Totowa, NJ: Barnes & Noble, 1981.

Weinsheimer, J. *Gadamer's Hermeneutics: A Reading of "Truth and Method."* New Haven: Yale University Press, 1985.

———. *Philosophical Hermeneutics and Literary Theory*. New Haven: Yale University Press, 1991.

West, G. O. *Biblical Hermeneutics of Liberation: Modes of Reading the Bible in the South African Context*. 2nd ed. Maryknoll, NY: Orbis Books, 1995.

———, ed. *Reading Otherwise: Socially Engaged Biblical Scholars Reading with Their Local Communities*. Atlanta: Society of Biblical Literature, 2007.

Westermann, C., ed. *Essays on Old Testament Hermeneutics*. Richmond: John Knox, 1963. = *Essays on Old Testament Interpretation*. London: SCM, 1963.

THE BIBLE AS LITERATURE

Alter, R. *The Art of Biblical Narrative*. New York: Basic Books, 1981.

———. *The Art of Biblical Poetry*. New York: Basic Books, 1985.

———. *The World of Biblical Literature*. New York: Basic Books, 1991.

Alter, R., and F. Kermode, eds. *The Literary Guide to the Bible*. Cambridge, MA: Harvard University Press, 1987.

Bailey, J. L., and L. D. Vander Broek, eds. *Literary Forms in the New Testament: A Handbook*. Louisville: Westminster John Knox, 1992.

Bar-Efrat, S. *Narrative Art in the Bible*. Translated by D. Shefer-Vanson. Journal for the Study of the Old Testament: Supplement Series 70. Sheffield: Almond, 1989.

Barr, J. "Reading the Bible as Literature." *Bulletin of the John Rylands University Library of Manchester* 56 (1973): 10–33.

Barton, J. "Reading the Bible as Literature." *Literature and Theology* 1 (1987): 135–53.

Berlin, A. *The Dynamics of Biblical Parallelism*. Bloomington: Indiana University Press, 1985.

———. *Poetics and Interpretation of Biblical Narrative*. Sheffield: Almond, 1983.

Brenner, A. *The Israelite Woman: Social Role and Literary Type in Biblical Narrative*. Sheffield: JSOT Press, 1985.

Brichto, H. C. *Toward a Grammar of Biblical Poetics*. New York: Oxford University Press, 1992.

Caird, G. B. *The Language and Imagery of the Bible*. London: Duckworth, 1980.

Clines, D. J. A., et al. *Art and Meaning*. Sheffield: Almond, 1982.

Cohn, R. L. *The Shape of Sacred Space: Four Biblical Studies*. Chico, CA: Scholars Press, 1981.

Culley, R. *Themes and Variations: A Study of Action in Biblical Narrative*. Atlanta: Scholars Press, 1992.

Damrosch, D. *The Narrative Covenant: Transformations of Genre in the Growth of Biblical Literature*. San Francisco: Harper & Row, 1987.

Eskenazi, T. C. *In an Age of Prose: A Literary Approach to Ezra–Nehemiah*. Society of Biblical Literature Monograph Series 36. Atlanta: Scholars Press, 1988.

Exum, J. C. *Tragedy and Biblical Narrative*. Cambridge: Cambridge University Press, 1992.

———, ed. *Tragedy and Comedy in the Bible*. Semeia 32 (1984).

Falk, M. *Love Lyrics from the Bible*. Sheffield: Almond, 1976.

———. *The Song of Songs: A New Translation and Interpretation*. San Francisco: HarperCollins, 1990. Rev. ed. of *Love Lyrics from the Bible*, 1982.

Fewell, D., and D. Gunn. *Compromising Redemption: Relating Characters in the Book of Ruth*. Louisville: Westminster John Knox, 1990.

Fisch, H. *Poetry with a Purpose: Biblical Poetics and Interpretation*. Bloomington: Indiana University Press, 1988.

Fishbane, M. *Text and Texture: Close Readings of Selected Biblical Texts.* New York: Schocken, 1979.

Fokkelman, J. P. *Narrative Art in Genesis.* Assen, NL: Van Gorcum, 1975.

Frye, N. *The Great Code: The Bible and Literature.* New York: Harcourt Brace Jovanovich, 1982.

———. *Words with Power: Being a Second Study of "The Bible and Literature."* New York: Harcourt Brace Jovanovich, 1990.

Funk, R. W. *The Poetics of Biblical Narrative.* Sonoma, CA: Polebridge, 1988.

Gabel, J., and C. Wheeler. *The Bible as Literature: An Introduction.* New York: Oxford University Press, 1986.

Good, E. M. *Irony in the Old Testament.* Rev. ed. Sheffield: Almond, 1981.

Gottcent, J. *The Bible: A Literary Study.* Boston: Thayne, 1986.

Gunn, D. M. *The Fate of King Saul: An Interpretation of a Biblical Story.* Sheffield: Sheffield University Press, 1980.

Gunn, D. M., and D. N. Fewell. *Narrative in the Hebrew Bible.* New York: Oxford University Press, 1993.

Habel, N. C. "The Narrative Art of Job: Applying the Principles of Robert Alter." *Journal for the Study of the Old Testament* 27 (1983): 101–11.

Henn, T. R. *The Bible as Literature.* New York: Oxford University Press, 1970.

Inch, M. A., and C. H. Bullock. *The Literature and Meaning of Scripture.* Grand Rapids: Baker, 1984.

Innes, K. *The Bible as Literature.* London: Jonathan Cape, 1930.

Jobling, D. *The Sense of Biblical Narrative.* Sheffield: JSOT Press, 1978.

Kingsbury, J. D. *Matthew as Story.* Philadelphia: Fortress, 1986.

Kort, W. A. *Story, Text, and Scripture: Literary Interests in Biblical Narrative.* University Park: Pennsylvania State University Press, 1987.

Kugel, J. *The Idea of Biblical Poetry: Parallelism and Its History.* New Haven: Yale University Press, 1981.

———. "On the Bible as Literature." *Prooftexts* 2 (1982): 328–32.

Letagen, B., and W. Vorster. *Text and Reality: Aspects of Reference in Biblical Texts.* Philadelphia: Fortress, 1985.

Licht, J. *Storytelling in the Bible.* Jerusalem: Magnes, 1978.

Longman, T., III. *Literary Approaches to Biblical Interpretation.* Foundations for Contemporary Interpretation 3. Grand Rapids: Zondervan, 1987.

Louis, K. G., with J. Ackerman and T. S. Warshaw. *Literary Interpretations of Biblical Narratives.* Nashville: Abingdon, 1974.

Magonet, J. *Form and Meaning: Studies in the Literary Techniques in the Book of Jonah.* Rev. ed. Sheffield: Almond, 1983.

O'Connor, M. *Hebrew Verse Structure.* Winona Lake, IN: Eisenbrauns, 1980.

Patterson, R. D., and M. E. Travers. "Nahum: Poet Laureate of the Minor Prophets." *Journal of the Evangelical Theological Society* 33 (1990): 437–44.

Peterson, D. L., and K. H. Richards. *Interpreting Hebrew Poetry.* Minneapolis: Fortress, 1992.

Polzin, R. *Deuteronomy, Joshua, Judges.* Part 1 of *Moses and the Deuteronomist: A Literary Study of the Deuteronomic History.* New York: Seabury, 1980.

Preminger, A., and E. L. Greenstein, eds. *The Hebrew Bible in Literary Criticism.* New York: Ungar, 1986.

Reid, M. E., ed. *The Bible Read as Literature.* Cleveland: Howard Allen, 1959.

Rhoads, D., and D. Michie. *Mark as Story: An Introduction to the Narrative of a Gospel.* Philadelphia: Fortress, 1982.

Robertson, D. "Literature, the Bible as." Pages 547–51 in *The Interpreter's Dictionary of the Bible: Supplementary Volume.* Edited by K. Crim. Nashville: Abingdon, 1976.

Ryken, L. *How to Read the Bible as Literature.* Grand Rapids: Zondervan, 1984.

———. *The Literature of the Bible.* Grand Rapids: Baker, 1987.

Sands, P. C. *Literary Genius of the New Testament.* New York: Oxford University Press, 1932.

Savran, G. W. *Telling and Retelling: Quotation in Biblical Narrative.* Bloomington: Indiana University Press, 1988.

Schwartz, R. *The Book and the Text: The Bible and Literary Theory.* Cambridge, MA: Blackwell, 1990.

Shuler, P. I. *A Genre for the Gospels: The Biographical Character of Matthew.* Philadelphia: Fortress, 1982.

Sider, J. W. "Nurturing Our Nurse: Literary Scholars and Biblical Exegesis." *Christianity and Literature* 32, no. 1 (1982): 15–21.

Sternberg, M. *The Poetics of Biblical Narrative: Ideological Literature and the Drama of Reading.* Bloomington: Indiana University Press, 1985.

Talbert, C. *Literary Patterns, Theological Themes, and the Genre of Luke-Acts.* Society of Biblical Literature Monograph Series 20. Missoula, MT: Scholars Press, 1974.

Tannehill, R. C. *The Gospel according to Luke.* Vol. 1 of *The Narrative Unity of Luke-Acts: A Literary Interpretation.* Philadelphia: Fortress, 1986.

Thompson, L. *Introducing Biblical Literature: A More Fantastic Country.* Englewood Cliffs, NJ: Prentice Hall, 1975.

Watson, E. G. E. *Classical Hebrew Poetry.* Sheffield: JSOT Press, 1984.

Williams, J. G. *Those Who Ponder Proverbs: Aphoristic Thinking and Biblical Literature.* Sheffield: Almond, 1981.

GENERAL BIBLICAL STUDIES: HEBREW BIBLE

Aharoni, Y. *The Archaeology of the Land of Israel.* Translated by A. F. Rainey. Philadelphia: Westminster, 1982.

———. *The Land of the Bible.* Rev. ed. Philadelphia: Westminster, 1979.

Baly, D. *Basic Biblical Geography.* Minneapolis: Fortress, 1987.

Barstad, H. M. *A Brief Guide to the Hebrew Bible.* Louisville: Westminster John Knox, 2010.

Barton, J. *Reading the Old Testament.* Philadelphia: Westminster, 1984.

Ben-Tor, A. *The Archaeology of Ancient Israel.* Translated by R. Greenberg. New Haven: Yale University Press, 1992.

Blenkinsopp, J. *A History of Prophecy in Israel.* Rev. ed. Louisville: Westminster John Knox, 1996.

Bright, J. *A History of Israel.* 3rd ed. Philadelphia: Westminster, 1981.

Bruce, F. F. *New Testament History.* Garden City, NY: Doubleday, 1972.

Clements, R. E. *A Century of Old Testament Study.* Cambridge: Lutterworth, 1992.

Coote, R., and D. Ord. *The Bible's First History.* Philadelphia: Fortress, 1988.

Crenshaw, J. L. *The Old Testament Wisdom: An Introduction.* Atlanta: John Knox, 1981.

Green, W. H. *General Introduction to the Old Testament: The Canon.* New York: Scribner's, 1888.

Halpern, B. *The First Historians: The Hebrew Bible and History.* San Francisco: Harper & Row, 1988.

Hartman, L. *Prophecy Interpreted: The Formation of Some Jewish Apocalyptic Texts and of the Eschatological Discourse.* Lund, Sweden: Gleerup, 1966.

Hasel, G. F. "Major Recent Issues in Old Testament Theology, 1978–1983." *Journal for the Study of the Old Testament* 31 (1985): 31–53.

———. *Old Testament Theology: Basic Issues in the Current Debate.* Grand Rapids: Eerdmans, 1975.

Hayes, J. H. *Introduction to Old Testament Study.* London: SCM, 1982.

Jacobsen, T. *The Treasures of Darkness: A History of Mesopotamian Religion.* New Haven: Yale University Press, 1976.

Kaiser, O. *Introduction to the Old Testament.* Minneapolis: Augsburg, 1980.

Kaiser, W. C., Jr. *Toward Rediscovering the Old Testament.* Grand Rapids: Zondervan, 1987.

Knapp, A. B. *The History and Culture of Ancient Western Asia and Egypt.* Chicago: Dorsey, 1988.

LaSor, W. S., D. A. Hubbard, and F. W. Bush. *Old Testament Survey: The Message, Form, and Background of the Old Testament.* Grand Rapids: Eerdmans, 1982.

Leiman, S. Z. *The Canonization of Hebrew Scripture: The Talmudic and Midrashic Evidence.* Hamden, CT: Archon Books, 1976.

Matthews, V. H., and D. C. Benjamin. *Old Testament Parallels: Laws and Stories from the Ancient Near East.* 3rd ed. Mahwah, NJ: Paulist Press, 2006.

Merrill, E. H. *Kingdom of Priests: A History of Old Testament Israel.* Grand Rapids: Baker, 1987.

Miller, J. M., and J. H. Hayes. *A History of Ancient Israel and Judah.* Philadelphia: Westminster, 1986.

Morenz, S. *Egyptian Religion.* Translated by A. E. Keep. Ithaca, NY: Cornell University Press, 1973.

North, M. *The History of Israel.* Revised and translated by P. Ackroyd. New York: Harper & Row, 1960.

Pixley, J. *Biblical History: A People's History.* Minneapolis: Fortress, 1992.

Ramsey, G. W. *The Quest for the Historical Israel.* Atlanta: John Knox, 1981.

Rendtorff, R. *The Old Testament: An Introduction.* Philadelphia: Fortress, 1985.

Ringgren, H. *Religions of the Ancient Near East.* Translated by J. Sturdy. Philadelphia: Westminster, 1973.

Rosenberg, J. *King and Kin: Political Allegory in the Hebrew Bible.* Bloomington: Indiana University Press, 1986.

Ryle, H. E. *The Canon of the Old Testament: An Essay on the Gradual Growth and Formulation of the Hebrew Canon of Scripture.* New York: Macmillan, 1892.

Sasson, J. M., et al., eds. *Civilizations of the Ancient Near East.* 4 vols. New York: Charles Scribner's Sons, 1995.

Sawyer, J. F. A. *Prophecy and the Prophets for the Old Testament.* New York: Oxford University Press, 1987.

Shafer, B. E., ed. *Religion in Ancient Egypt.* Ithaca, NY: Cornell University Press, 1991.

Shanks, H., ed. *Ancient Israel: A Short History from Abraham to the Roman Destruction of the Temple.* Englewood Cliffs, NJ: Prentice Hall, 1988.

Shanks, H., and D. P. Cole. *Archaeology and the Bible: The Best of BAR.* Washington, DC: Biblical Archaeology Society, 1990.

Shields, M. E. *Circumcising the Prostitute: The Rhetorics of Intertextuality, Metaphor, and Gender in Jeremiah 3:1–4:4.* Ann Arbor: University of Michigan, 1996.

Schmidt, W. H. *Old Testament Introduction.* London: SCM, 1984.

Soggin, J. A. *Introduction to the Old Testament: From Its Origins to the Closing of the Alexandrian Canon.* Philadelphia: Westminster, 1980.

Sundberg, A. C. *The Old Testament of the Early Church.* Harvard Theological Studies 20. Cambridge, MA: Harvard University Press, 1964.

Walton, J. *Ancient Israelite Literature in Its Cultural Context.* Grand Rapids: Zondervan, 1989.

Weems, R. J. *Battered Love: Marriage, Sex, and Violence in the Hebrew Prophets.* Overtures to Biblical Theology. Minneapolis: Augsburg Fortress, 1995.

Whybray, R. N. *The Making of the Pentateuch.* Sheffield: JSOT Press, 1987.

Wiseman, D. J., ed. *Peoples of Old Testament Times.* Oxford: Clarendon, 1973.

Wood, L. *A Survey of Israel's History.* Rev. ed. Grand Rapids: Zondervan, 1986.

Woude, A. S. van der. *The World of the Old Testament.* Grand Rapids: Eerdmans, 1989.

Yamauchi, E. *Persia and the Bible.* Grand Rapids: Baker, 1990.

———. *The Stones and the Scriptures: An Introduction to Biblical Archaeology.* Philadelphia: Lippincott. Repr., Grand Rapids: Baker, 1981.

GENERAL BIBLICAL STUDIES: NEW TESTAMENT

Allison, D. *The Jesus Tradition in Q.* Harrisburg, PA: Trinity Press International, 1997.

Baez-Camargo, G. *Archaeological Commentary on the Bible.* Garden City, NY: Doubleday, 1984.

Barrett, C. K., ed. *The New Testament Background: Selected Documents.* 2nd ed. New York: Harper & Row, 1989.

Blaiklock, E. M. *The Archaeology of the New Testament.* Grand Rapids: Zondervan, 1974.

Bruce, F. F. *The Canon of Scripture.* Downers Grove, IL: InterVarsity, 1988.

———. *New Testament History.* Garden City, NY: Doubleday-Galilee, 1980.

Burridge, R. *What Are the Gospels? A Comparison with Greco-Roman Biography.* Cambridge: Cambridge University Press, 1992.

Cartlidge, D. R., and D. L. Dungan, eds. *Documents for the Study of the Gospels.* 2nd ed. Philadelphia: Fortress, 1994.

Charlesworth, J. H., ed. *The Old Testament Pseudepigrapha.* 2 vols. Garden City, NY: Doubleday, 1983–85.

Cohen, S. J. D. *From the Maccabees to the Mishnah.* Library of Early Christianity. Philadelphia: Westminster, 1987.

Crossan, J. D. *The Historical Jesus: The Life of a Mediterranean Peasant.* San Francisco: Harper & Row, 1992.

Dunn, J. *Unity and Diversity in the New Testament: An Inquiry into the Character of Earliest Christianity.* 2nd ed. London: SCM, 1990.

Farmer, W. R., and D. M. Farkasfalvy. *The Formation of the New Testament Canon.* New York: Paulist Press, 1983.

Ferguson, E. *Backgrounds of Early Christianity.* Grand Rapids: Eerdmans, 1993.

Filson, F. *A New Testament History.* Philadelphia: Westminster, 1964.

Finegan, J. *The Archaeology of the New Testament.* Rev. ed. Princeton: Princeton University Press, 1992.

Frederickson, P. *From Jesus to the Christ: The Origins of the New Testament Images of Christ.* New Haven: Yale University Press, 1990.

Freedman, R. *Who Wrote the Bible?* Englewood Cliffs, NJ: Prentice Hall, 1988.

Funk, R. W., et al. *The Five Gospels: The Search for the Authentic Words of Jesus.* Santa Rosa, CA: Polebridge, 1993.

Gamble, H. Y. *The New Testament Canon: Its Making and Meaning.* Philadelphia: Fortress, 1985.

Goppelt, L. *Typos: The Typological Interpretation of the Old Testament in the New.* Translated by D. H. Madvig. Grand Rapids: Eerdmans, 1982.

———. *The Variety and Unity of the Apostolic Witness to Christ.* Vol. 2 of *Theology of the New Testament.* Edited by J. Roloff. Translated by J. E. Alsup. Grand Rapids: Eerdmans, 1982.

Guthrie, D. *New Testament Introduction*. 3rd ed. Downers Grove, IL: InterVarsity, 1990.

Hasel, G. F. *New Testament Theology: Basic Issues in the Current Debate*. Grand Rapids: Eerdmans, 1978.

Hengel, M. *Jews, Greeks, and Barbarians: Aspects of the Hellenization of Judaism in the Pre-Christian Period*. Translated by J. Bowden. Philadelphia: Fortress, 1980.

Holmberg, B. *Sociology and the New Testament: An Appraisal*. Minneapolis: Fortress, 1990.

Horsley, R. *Hearing the Whole Story: The Politics of Plot in Mark's Gospel*. Louisville: Westminster John Knox, 2001.

Hultgren, A. J. *The Rise of Normative Christianity*. Minneapolis: Fortress, 1994.

Jeremias, J. *Jerusalem in the Time of Jesus: An Investigation into Economic and Social Conditions during the New Testament Period*. Translated by F. H. and C. H. Cave from the 3rd German ed. Philadelphia: Fortress, 1969. Repr., London: SCM, 1991.

Jewett, R. *A Chronology of Paul's Life*. Philadelphia: Fortress, 1979.

Johnson, L. T. *The Real Jesus: The Misguided Quest for the Historical Jesus and the Truth of the Traditional Gospels*. San Francisco: HarperSanFrancisco, 1996.

Koester, H. *History, Culture, and Religion of the Hellenistic Age*. Philadelphia: Fortress, 1982.

———. *Introduction to the New Testament*. 2 vols. Philadelphia: Fortress, 1982.

MacMullen, R. *Paganism in the Roman Empire*. New Haven: Yale University Press, 1981.

———. *Roman Social Relations, 50 B.C. to A.D. 200*. New Haven: Yale University Press, 1976.

Malherbe, A. *Social Aspects of Early Christianity*. Philadelphia: Fortress, 1983.

Malina, B. J., and R. L. Rohrbaugh. *Social Science Commentary on the Synoptic Gospels*. 2nd ed. Minneapolis: Fortress, 2002.

McDonald, L. M. *The Formation of the Christian Biblical Canon*. Nashville: Abingdon, 1988.

McKnight, S. *Interpreting the Synoptic Gospels*. Grand Rapids: Baker, 1988.

McRay, J. *Archaeology and the New Testament*. Grand Rapids: Baker, 1991.

Meade, D. G. *Pseudonymity and Canon: An Investigation into the Relationship of Authorship and Authority in Jewish and Earliest Christian Tradition*. Grand Rapids: Eerdmans, 1986.

Meeks, W. *The First Urban Christians: The Social World of the Apostle Paul*. New Haven: Yale University Press, 1983.

———. *The Moral World of the First Christians*. Philadelphia: Westminster, 1986.

Meier, J. P., ed. *The Ancient Mysteries: A Sourcebook*. San Francisco: Harper & Row, 1987.

———. *A Marginal Jew: Rethinking the Historical Jesus*. 4 vols. New York: Doubleday, 1991–2009.

Mitchell, S. *The Gospel according to Jesus*. San Francisco: Harper & Row, 1991.

Moule, C. F. D. *The Birth of the New Testament*. 3rd rev. ed. San Francisco: Harper & Row, 1982.

Neusner, J. *The Rabbinic Traditions about the Pharisees before 70*. 3 vols. Leiden: Brill, 1971.

Niswonger, R. L. *New Testament History*. Grand Rapids: Zondervan, 1988.

Riches, J. K. *A Century of New Testament Study*. Cambridge: Lutterworth, 1992.

Roetzel, C. J. *The Letters of Paul: Conversations in Context*. Atlanta: John Knox, 1982.

Rostovtzeff, M. *Social and Economic History of the Roman Empire*. 2nd rev. ed. 2 vols. New York: Oxford University Press, 1957.

Safrai, S., and M. Stern, eds. *The Jewish People in the First Century*. Compendia rerum Iudaicarum ad Novum Testamentum. 2 vols. Philadelphia: Fortress, 1974–76.

Sanders, E. P. *Jesus and Judaism*. Philadelphia: Fortress, 1985.

Sanders, E. P., and M. Davies. *Studying the Synoptic Gospels*. Philadelphia: Trinity Press International. 1989.

Schiffman, L. H. *Reclaiming the Dead Sea Scrolls: The History of Judaism, the Background of Christianity, the Lost Library of Qumran*. Philadelphia: Jewish Publication Society, 1994.

Smallwood, M. *The Jews under Roman Rule*. Leiden: Brill, 1970.

Stambaugh, J. E., and D. L. Balch. *The New Testament in Its Social Environment*. Library of Early Christianity. Philadelphia: Westminster, 1986.

Stein, R. H. *Studying the Synoptic Gospels: Origin and Interpretation*. 2nd ed. Grand Rapids: Baker Academic, 2001.

Stephens, W. H. *The New Testament World in Pictures*. Nashville: Broadman, 1987.

Talbert, C. *What Is a Gospel? The Genre of the Canonical Gospels*. Philadelphia: Fortress, 1977.

Trucan, R. *The Cults of the Roman Empire.* Oxford: Blackwell, 1996.

Vermès, G. *The Dead Sea Scrolls in English.* 4th ed. New York: Viking Penguin, 1993.

————. *Jesus the Jew: A Historian's Reading of the Gospels.* Philadelphia: Fortress, 1981.

Wilson, A. N. *Jesus: A Life.* New York: Norton, 1992.

Winter, M. T. *The Gospel according to Mary: A New Testament for Women.* New York: Crossroad, 1993.

Author Index

Eco, Umberto 74, 86, 206, 207, 210, 211, 217, 264, 285, 303, 339, 391, 392, 394, 400, 401, 402, 403, 441
Edgar, Andrew 75, 128, 221, 407, 417, 429
Edwards, Mark 57, 315
Ehrman, Bart D. 24, 26, 119, 147, 148, 210, 226, 310, 317, 348, 359
Einspahr, Bruce 234
Eisen, Arnold 223, 224
Ejxenbaum, Boris 167, 168, 172
Elam, Keir 420
Eliot, T. S. 39, 286, 288, 289, 290, 294, 301
Elliot, John 410, 411
Ellrodt, Robert 334
Empson, William 13
Encinas, Gilbert L. 124
Engels, Frederick 43, 248, 249
Ernest, James D. 233
Esler, Philip F. 412
Estok, Simon C. 132, 136
Even-Shoshan, Abraham 82

Fanon, Frantz 329, 331, 333
Farley, Margaret A. 156, 158, 160
Farmer, W. R. 185
Faulkner, Robert 393
Felperin, Howard 326, 333, 334
Ferguson, Everett 87, 88, 193, 395
Festugière, A. J. 87, 88
Fetterley, Judith 39, 208, 375
Fewell, Danna Nolan 206, 218
Fiero, Gloria 158, 160
Fish, Stanley 35, 122, 216, 224, 225, 420
Flint, Peter 104
Floyd-Thomas, Stacey M. 268, 274
Foucault, Michel 26, 27, 35, 66, 103, 112, 123, 124, 142, 176, 196, 247, 298, 299, 326, 333, 334, 335, 336, 338, 355, 356, 358, 429, 451
Fowler, Alistair 179
Fowler, Roger 237, 238
Franklin, Wayne 313, 315
Freedman, D. N. 14, 36, 41, 118
Freedman, Diane P. 14, 36, 41, 118
Frege, Gottlob 407
Frei, Hans 283
Frey, Olivia 36, 38, 41
Friedan, Betty 157
Friedrich, G. 43, 50, 118, 248, 301, 334, 358, 380
Frith, Simon 85
Fromm, Harold 136
Frye, Northrop 28, 178, 393
Fuchs, Ernst 295, 296

Fuller, Margaret 472
Funk, Robert W. 222
Furnish, Victor P. 191, 193

Gabel, John 51, 138, 143, 148
Gadamer, Hans-Georg 50, 174, 284, 319, 321, 374, 377
Gallagher, Catherine 296, 299
Garane, Jeanne 330, 331, 333
García Martínez, F. 104
Garrard, Greg 132, 135, 136
Gaster, Theodor H. 104
Gearhart, Suzanne 334
Gebara, Ivone 267
Geertz, Clifford 96, 97, 412, 450
Gelfand, Elissa 158, 160
Genette, Gérard 120, 200, 266, 282, 283, 378
Gerber, John 390, 391
Gerstenberger, E. S. 122
Gesenius, J. W. F. 234
Gifford, Terry 132, 136
Gilbert, Sandra 124, 140, 178, 179, 192, 193, 450, 453, 472
Giles, Terry 313, 315, 396
Gilkes, Cheryl Townsend 469, 471, 472
Gilmore, George 275, 276
Gingrich, F. 136, 233
Gitay, Y. 342
Glotfelty, Cheryll 132, 135, 136
Gnanadason, A. 31
Goldman, Lucien 177, 224
Goodrick, Edward W. 82
Goodwin, David 390, 391
Gordon, C. H. 131, 148
Gorman, Michael, J. 446, 448, 449
Gorn, Heather 132, 133, 136
Grabowicz, George G. 322
Grafton, Richard 184
Gramsci, Antonio 189
Grayson, A. Kirk 22
Greaves, Thomas 150
Green, Gene L. 136
Green, Joel B. 136
Green, William Scott 136
Greenblatt, Stephen 296, 299
Greenlee, J. Harold 11, 306, 443
Greenwood, David C. 9, 10, 150, 276, 428, 429
Greimas, A. J. 2, 283, 428
Grenz, Stanely J. 256
Grice, H. Paul 420
Griesbach, J. J. 185, 437
Groden, Michael 28, 124, 265
Guardiola-Sáenz, Leticia A. 98

Scripture Index

2:15 83
2:31–37 230
3:12 342
4:23–27 266
5:22 88
7:9 239
8:4–7 230
8:5–7 392
10:11 188
15:5–9 230
17:5–11 342
23:4 255
24:1–10 306
26:17–19 341
31:31–34 285
50:6 338
52 343

Lamentations

1–2 122
4 122

Ezekiel

1 449
14:12–23 341
15:1–5 306
16 130
16:1–43 341
17:1–10 306, 341
17:11–24 306
17:22–23 255
18:2 469
19:1–14 122, 341
21:8–17 306
21:13–23 341
23:1–21 306
23:1–27 341
26:19–21 341
27:2–11 341
28:1–10 342
31:1–18 342
32:17–32 342
34:12 338

Daniel

1 33
2 163
2:4b–7:28 26, 188
3 232
3:7 193

6 232
8 22
8:19–26 22
12:1–3 395
12:11 338

Hosea

2 12
4:1–3 134, 136
4:1–10 90
8:5 18
11:1 260
11:1a 316

Amos

1:3–5 209
1:7 50, 438
3:3–8 341
4:1 396
5:1 341
5:1–3 122, 230
5:4b–6a 70, 391
8:1–2 309
8:10 51, 162
9:1 139
9:1–4 139
9:4 139
9:8b–15 343
9:13–15 85

Jonah

1:2 74, 378
1:3 74, 378
1:17b–2:10 125
2:1–11 125
4:2a 74, 211, 378

Micah

2:6–11 125
5:5b 162

Nahum

1:2–10 2

Habakkuk

1:4 317
2:6–8 342
3:10 88
3:19 475

Zephaniah

1:15–16 51

Zechariah

10:2 338

**OLD TESTAMENT
APOCRYPHA/
DEUTEROCANONICAL
BOOKS**

Wisdom of Solomon

14:22–31 65

NEW TESTAMENT

Matthew

1–2 74, 210, 246, 394
1:1–17 175
1:18 254
1:20–25 181, 394
1:22–23 260, 317
1:23 404
2:10 187, 327
2:13 181, 394
2:13–15 317
2:13–20 181, 394
2:14–15 260
3 104
3–12 74
3:13–15 340
4:1–11 352, 354
5 79, 308, 318
5–7 181, 312
5:1–12 405
5:1–7:27 405
5:5 92
5:13–16 405
5:14b 306
5:17–48 405
5:27 20
5:29a 204
6:1–7:27 405
7:3–5 92
7:7 193
7:11 14
8:5–10 354
9:6–7 422
9:10–13 24, 397
9:14–15 386